Literature for Composition

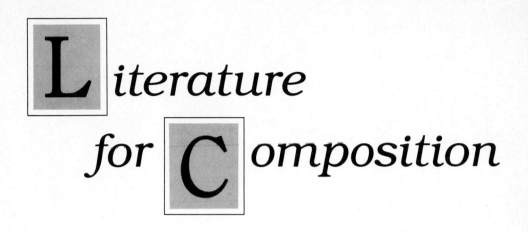

Literature for Composition

Essays, Fiction, Poetry, and Drama

SECOND EDITION

Edited by

SYLVAN BARNET
Tufts University

MORTON BERMAN
Boston University

WILLIAM BURTO
University of Lowell

Scott, Foresman/Little, Brown College Division

SCOTT, FORESMAN AND COMPANY

Glenview, Illinois □ Boston □ London

Library of Congress Cataloging-in-Publication Data

Literature for composition.

Includes index.
 1. College readers. 2. Literature—Collections.
I. Barnet, Sylvan. II. Berman, Morton. III. Burto,
William.
PE1122.L556 1987   808'.0427   87-23319
ISBN 0-673-39706-8

 5 6 7 8 9 10 — KPF — 93 92 91 90 89

Printed in the United States of America

Photo Credit

Photograph of Greek theater of Epidaurus on the Peloponnesus east of Nauplia. (Photograph: Frederick Ayer, Photo Researchers, Inc.)

Text Credits

Edward Albee, *The Sandbox*. Reprinted by permission of William Morris Agency on behalf of the author. Copyright © 1960 by Edward Albee.

Sherwood Anderson, "The Egg" and "I Want to Know Why" from *The Triumph of the Egg*. Reprinted by permission of Harold Ober Associates Incorporated. Copyright 1921 by B. W. Huebsch, Inc. Copyright renewed 1948 by Eleanor C. Anderson.

Maya Angelou, "Graduation" from *I Know Why the Caged Bird Sings* by Maya Angelou. Copyright © 1969 by Maya Angelou. Reprinted by permission of Random House, Inc.

Margaret Atwood, "Siren Song" from *Selected Poems* by Margaret Atwood. Copyright 1976 by Margaret Atwood. Reprinted by permission of Margaret Atwood and Oxford University Press Canada.

W. H. Auden, "The Unknown Citizen" and "Musée des Beaux Arts." Copyright 1940 and renewed 1968 by W. H. Auden. Reprinted from *W. H. Auden: Collected Poems*, edited by Edward Mendelson, by permission of Random House, Inc., and Faber and Faber, Ltd.

Toni Cade Bambara, "The Lesson" from *Gorilla, My Love* by Toni Cade Bambara. Copyright © 1972 by Toni Cade Bambara. Reprinted by permission of Random House, Inc.

Kristine Batey, "Lot's Wife." Reprinted with permission from *Jam To-Day #6*. Copyright © 1978 by Jam To-Day.

Bruno Bettelheim, "The Three Little Pigs" from *The Uses of Enchantment: The Meaning and Importance of Fairy Tales*, by Bruno Bettelheim. Copyright © 1976 by Bruno Bettelheim. Reprinted by permission of Alfred A. Knopf, Inc.

Elizabeth Bowen, "The Demon Lover." Copyright 1946 and renewed 1974 by Elizabeth Bowen. Reprinted from *Collected Stories* by Elizabeth Bowen. Reprinted by permission of Alfred A. Knopf, Inc.

Ray Bradbury, "October 2026: The Million-Year Picnic" from *The Martian Chronicles*,

(continued on page 785)

Preface

This book is based on the assumption that students in a composition course should encounter—if not at the start, then certainly by the midpoint—first-rate writing. By this we mean not simply competent prose but the powerful reports of experience that have been recorded by acknowledged masters of the language. We assume that the study of the best writing yields pleasure and insight into life, and that it also yields a sense of what the best words in the best places can do.

Helen Vendler, in her presidential address (1980) to the Modern Language Association, eloquently stated the case for teaching literature in introductory composition courses. Her address is available in *PMLA* 96 (1981) 344–350, but we summarize part of it and quote a few passages here. Vendler, addressing an audience of teachers, begins by quoting Wordsworth:

I choose as my text Wordsworth's vow at the end of *The Prelude*:

> What we have loved,
> Others will love, and we will teach them how.

She goes on to argue that "just as spoken language is absorbed by the ear, so written language has to be learned from the pages of writers—from writers who wrote for the love of the art. Our composition classes, on the whole, neglect this elementary truth." Later in her talk she says:

The divorce of composition from the reading of powerful imaginative writing is our greatest barrier to creating an American public who understand what we love. . . . If we could awaken in our beginning students, in their first year, the response that they can all feel to the human story told in compelling ways, we would begin to form a general public who approve of what we are and what we do. After all, in their first course in music they hear wonderful scores; in their first course in art they see wonderful paintings—and their minds should receive equal stimulus from us. That is the first step in teaching people how to love what we have loved.

Vendler then goes on to point out that the secondary schools teach little great literature, thus depriving students of familiarity with the enduring legends which both challenge and comfort human beings. It is especially important, then, for instructors to introduce into the required composition course great writing, since most students will never again encounter it in the classroom.

> Our students come to us from secondary school having read no works of litera-
> ture in foreign languages and scarcely any works of literature in their own lan-
> guage. . . .
>
> Every adult needs to be able to think of Job, or Orpheus, or Circe, or Ruth,
> or Lear, or Jesus, or the Golden Calf, or the Holy Grail, or Antigone in order to
> refer private experience to some identifying frame of solacing reflection. . . .
>
> It is not within our power to reform the primary and secondary schools,
> even if we have a sense of how that reform might begin. We do have it within our
> power, I believe, to reform ourselves, to make it our own first task to give,
> especially to our beginning students, that rich web of associations, lodged in the
> tales of majority and minority culture alike, by which they could begin to under-
> stand themselves as individuals and as social beings.

Toward the end of her talk she says:

> We owe it to ourselves to show our students, when they first meet us, what we
> are; we owe their dormant appetites, thwarted for so long in their previous
> schooling, that deep sustenance that will make them realize that they, too, having
> been taught, love what we love.

Literature for Composition, Second Edition, is in large part an anthology of literature, but it is more: It also offers instruction in writing. Part I (Getting Started) begins with two chapters on writing about intellectual prose; in accord with our assumption about the value of first-rate writing, the first chapter includes George Orwell's "Shooting an Elephant." The second chapter of Part I examines the development of a student's essay on "Shooting an Elephant," from preliminary notes to the final version. The third chapter is chiefly a small collection of distinguished essays. In our introduction to these essays we try to talk both about the essay as a literary form and (briefly) about qualities in the writing of students. In this chapter most of the "Suggestions for Writing," appended to the essays, call for paragraphs rather than for essays, or for personal rather than for analytical essays.

In the fourth chapter of Getting Started, we discuss at some length the writing of analytical essays about literature; in the fifth, we discuss writing a comparison. We realize that the chief aim of the course is not to turn students into literary critics but to help them develop skill in writing (partly by letting them hear how those who love language use it). The five chapters of Part I will enable them to develop some of the skills that all writers need. By "all writers" we mean all of us—the social worker writing up a case report, the member of a committee summarizing a meeting, the applicant for a job.

After these five preliminary chapters comes Part II, which forms the heart of the book, A Thematic Anthology of essays, stories, poems, and plays grouped around six themes. All of the selections are followed by questions or suggestions for writing, or both. The aim of such questions and suggestions is to assist students in examining their responses, reflecting on them, and perhaps modifying or expanding them, partly aided by the act of writing.

The next three chapters, constituting Part III, Reading and Writing about Literature, offer advice on writing about stories, poems, and plays. (Writing about essays has been discussed at some length in the first two chapters.) These chapters provide a critical vocabulary, not to enable readers to use jargon but to help them think about and respond to literature. Some instructors may wish to assign one or another chapter when studying particular works; other instructors may simply suggest that the students read the relevant passages—for instance, about point of view in fiction, or about the persona in lyric poetry—when preparing essays on a given topic.

The book concludes with three appendices, one on the research paper, one on manuscript form, and one containing a glossary of terms. The material on manuscript form may seem to be yet another discussion of writing, and some readers may wonder why it is put toward the back of the book. But manuscript form is chiefly a matter of editing rather than of writing or revising. It is, so to speak, the final packaging of a product that develops during a complicated process, a process that begins with reading, and finding a topic, a thesis, and a voice (Chapters 1 and 2), not with worrying about the width of margins or the form of footnotes. The last thing that one does in writing an essay, and therefore the last thing in our book, is to set it forth in a physical form fit for human consumption.

And now a few words about the literature in this book. We have, as we mentioned, arranged it by themes. Writers write about something. Of course they write essays or stories or poems or plays, but these are *about* something, for instance about love, which comes in many varieties. We arranged the works thematically so that we can give, if not responses to the whole of life, at least a spectrum of responses to large parts of it. Our thematic groups are Strange Worlds; Innocence and Experience; Love and Hate; American Dreams and Nightmares; The Individual and Society; and Men, Women, God, and Gods. By grouping the works according to themes, and by beginning each group with essays that help to set the reader to thinking about the theme, we hope to call attention not only to resemblances but to important differences, even between superficially similar works such as, say, two sonnets by Shakespeare. Obviously one work is not "right" and another "wrong." There is, after all, no one correct view of, say, love or happiness. We trust that these multiple views are welcome, though we uneasily recall the Ballyhough railway station, which has two clocks that differ by six minutes. When an irritated traveler asked an attendant what was the use of having two clocks that didn't tell the same time, the attendant replied, "And what would we be wanting with two clocks if they told the same time?"

But works of literature are not clocks; we hope that each work will be valued for itself and will also be valued for the light it throws on other works of literature, and on life. Behind this hope, of course, is the assumption that good writing—the accurate report of powerful thinking and feeling—is an interpretation of life, and that it is therefore educative. We cannot do better than to quote Coleridge on this point:

The heart should have fed upon truth, as insects on a leaf, till it be tinged with the color and shows its food in every minutest fiber.

A Note on the Second Edition

Instructors familiar with the first edition will notice several changes in this edition: (1) The first two chapters of this book (which in the first edition formed a single chapter) include much new material about summarizing, outlining, and making preliminary jottings; (2) three new thematic chapters have been added: "Strange Worlds," "American Dreams and Nightmares," and "The Individual and Society"; (3) the appendix on the research paper explains the new MLA style; (4) the glossary of terms.

Acknowledgments

In preparing the first edition of *Literature for Composition* we were indebted to Judith Stanford, Donald A. Daiker, Clayton Hudnall, Michael Johnson, Charles Moran, Linda Robertson, Robert Schwegler, Marcia Stubbs, and Beverly Swan. In preparing the second edition we have profited greatly from suggestions made by Jim Streeter, Kathleen Shine Cain, Bertha Norman Booker, Margaret Blayney, Dorothy Trusock, Billie Varnum, Mickey Wadia, L. D. Galford, William Shelley, Leonard W. Engel, Bruce A. Reid, Raymond L. Thomas, Gary Zacharias, James R. Payne, Bill Kelly, Susan D. Tilka, JoAnna S. Mink, John P. Boots, Robin W. Bryant, Janice Slaughter, John O'Connor, Don K. Pierstorff, Bill Elliott, Patricia G. Morgan, Jim Schwartz, William Epperson, Diana Cardenas, Walter B. Connolly, Kathleen McWilliams, Kay Fortson, Joyce A. Ingram, Linda Cravens, Louis H. Pratt, Leesther Thomas, William McAndrew, Nancy Morris, Marie Foster, Donna Friedman, Sandra H. Harris, and Kathy J. Wright.

Finally we want to thank Joe Opiela, Janice Friedman, Nan Upin, Carolyn Potts, and Amy Johnson at the publisher who have greatly eased our work.

Contents

PART II   *A Thematic Anthology*

9 *American Dreams and Nightmares*   436

PART III   *Reading and Writing about Literature*

Literature for Composition

PART
I

Getting Started

Reading 1 and Summarizing

Skimming and Reading

"Some books are to be tasted, others to be swallowed, and some few to be chewed and digested." Francis Bacon wrote these words almost four hundred years ago, and they are still true: Not all books are to be read in the same way. We daily see advertisements for courses in speed reading; one ad claimed that President Kennedy took such a course and learned to read a couple hundred pages an hour. Probably that's about the right speed for most of the stuff that crossed his desk. But despite what the advertisements said, he wasn't reading; he was skimming. The art of skimming is essential if we are to survive the daily deluge of paper loosed upon us, and most of us have developed the art satisfactorily: We get through junk mail in a matter of seconds, the newspaper and *Time* or *Newsweek* in a matter of minutes. That is, we skim, perhaps taking in only the captions, and then, when an item catches our interest, we begin to mix skimming with reading. If the item holds our interest, we stop skimming and really read. Sometimes we even go back and read the opening paragraphs that we had skimmed.

Skimming has its place in academic life too. In doing a research paper you will probably skim many pages to find the material that is relevant and that will require close reading. Even if you know at the outset that an article or book is important, you may skim it first, so you can then read it more easily a second time (really a first time) and take notes on it. Skimming may reveal, for instance, that each chapter ends with a summary, so even before you begin to read closely you will know that you do not have to take very general notes when you go through each page later.

But inevitably, and especially in a composition course, much of the assigned reading must be read slowly and with all of your powers of attention. In the best writing, every word counts. Consider this passage from Thoreau's *Walden*. Thoreau moved to Walden Pond in 1845 not to escape from life but, in his words,

to live deliberately, to front only the essential facts of life, and see if I could not

3

learn what it had to teach, and not, when I came to die, discover that I had not lived.

Notice that even this single sentence reveals Thoreau's powerful handling of words. There is parallelism in "to live" and "to front"; there is alliteration (repetition of an initial consonant) in "live," "life," and "learn" (the linking in sound suggests also a linking in fact, i.e., living should be learning), and again in "discover" and "die." If you **paraphrase** this sentence (put it into other words) you will see how much of the power of the sentence depends on Thoreau's exact words in Thoreau's order.

Tone

Only by reading closely can we hear in the mind's ear the writer's tone— whether it is ironic or earnestly straightforward, indignant or genial. Perhaps you have heard the line from Owen Wister's novel, *The Virginian:* "When you call me that, smile." Words spoken with a smile mean something different from the same words forced through clenched teeth. But while speakers can communicate by body language and by gestures, by facial expressions and by changes in tone of voice, writers have only words in ink on paper. As a writer, you are learning control of tone as you learn to take pains in your choice of words, in the way you arrange sentences, and even in the punctuation marks you may find yourself changing in your final draft. These skills will pay off doubly if you apply them to your reading, by putting yourself in the place of the writer whose work you are reading. As a reader, you must make some effort to "hear" the writer's tone as part of the meaning the words communicate. Skimming is not adequate to that task. Your teachers expect you to think carefully about the works in this book. And to think carefully about them means, first of all, to read them carefully, listening for the sound of the speaking voice, so that you can perceive the **persona**—the personality or character the author presents in the essay.

Listen to George Orwell at the start of "Shooting an Elephant" (page 6):

> In Moulmein, in Lower Burma, I was hated by large numbers of people—the only time in my life that I have been important enough for this to happen to me. I was sub-divisional police officer of the town, and in an aimless, petty kind of way anti-European feeling was very bitter. No one had the guts to raise a riot, but if a European woman went through the bazaars alone somebody would probably spit betel juice over her dress.

The first part of the sentence—"In Moulmein, in Lower Burma, I was hated by large numbers of people"—immediately gains our attention, but not with a blare of trumpets. The speaker seems midway in the sentence to realize that he may seem conceited by his simple statement of a fact and so he modestly adds that this was "the only time in my life that I have been important enough for this to happen to me." His language is that of an ordinary person conversing with friends. Instead of saying, "No one had the courage to raise a riot," he says colloquially, "No one had the guts to raise a riot." Compared to Thoreau's passage this passage seems artless, but in fact Orwell is artfully creating the image that he is a thoroughly ordinary fellow chatting quietly with a friend.

Reading with an Eye toward Writing

Thinking about the Title

"It is thinking," the philosopher John Locke wrote, that "makes what we read ours. We are of the ruminating kind, and it is not enough to cram ourselves with a great load of collections; unless we chew them over again they will not give us strength and nourishment." Reading a work begins with reading and at least briefly thinking about the title. If we pick up an essay called "Do-It-Yourself Brain Surgery," we ought to know at once that we can prepare to be amused. Such a title must be ironic; it simply cannot be taken straight by a thoughtful reader.

The title of the work you are writing about is the place to start, but it may convey very little: E. M. Forster's "My Wood" (page 49) does not prepare us for Forster's meditation on acquisitiveness. George Orwell's "Shooting an Elephant" (page 6) deliberately misleads us, for this title suggests some sort of hunting tale—though if we know that Orwell is fundamentally a social critic we suspect he is not really going to give us a yarn about an Englishman's pleasure in shooting big game. A related point: In your years in college you will become familiar with many writers, and this familiarity will assist you in reading other works by them, for you will approach the new work with some sense of the writer's subject and methods. You should, of course, be prepared to change your initial frame of mind if the work requires you to do so. Even the most straightforward and serious writer may write a good-natured spoof or an occasional work that is otherwise atypical.

Identifying the Topic and the Thesis

If the writer's **thesis** or point is not stated or implied in the title, it ought to become increasingly evident as you work your way into the essay. This thesis is an argument, and a point or argument implies an *attitude* toward a **topic.** In reading, then, try to identify the topic (the topic of "Do-It-Yourself Brain Surgery" is not really brain surgery but do-it-yourself books) and the attitude (amused contempt for such books). Even an essay that is largely narrative, recounting a personal experience or a bit of history, will usually include an attitude toward the event being narrated, and it is that attitude—the interpretation of the event—rather than the event itself that is usually the richest part of the essay. "Shooting an Elephant" does in fact recount an episode in which Orwell shot an elephant, but the essay is really about *why* he shot the elephant, and what the experience revealed. His analysis of the episode brought him, he says, to an understanding of "the real nature of imperialism—the real motives for which despotic governments act."

The thesis may not be evident when you first read an essay, but if you reread it, and outline it paragraph by paragraph, you will almost surely perceive the writer's point.

Outlining and Summarizing Your Reading

Read with a pencil in hand, jotting brief comments and queries in the margins and underlining key expressions and sentences that strike you as especially important—for instance, topic sentences or sentences that summarize. But beware of underlining so much material that you make the text unreadable.

For an especially complex or detailed essay, you probably will find it helpful to jot down a sentence summarizing each paragraph or each group of closely related paragraphs. This will give you a sort of outline of the essay you are reading. Then, with these summarizing sentences as a guide, you may want to write a summary of the essay. We will give some principles for summary writing after we look at George Orwell's "Shooting an Elephant" and at a student's rough outline of Orwell's essay.

Making an outline and writing a summary require effort. But these steps will give you a far better understanding of the topic and the thesis than you can gain merely by letting your eye run over the page, or even by underlining.

Here is Orwell's essay, followed by a student's rough outline and summary of it.

George Orwell   (English. 1903–1950)

SHOOTING AN ELEPHANT

In Moulmein, in Lower Burma, I was hated by large numbers of people—the only time in my life that I have been important enough for this to happen to me. I was sub-divisional police officer of the town, and in an aimless, petty kind of way anti-European feeling was very bitter. No one had the guts to raise a riot, but if a European woman went through the bazaars alone somebody would probably spit betel juice over her dress. As a police officer I was an obvious target and was baited whenever it seemed safe to do so. When a nimble Burman tripped me up on the football field and the referee (another Burman) looked the other way, the crowd yelled with hideous laughter. This happened more than once. In the end the sneering yellow faces of young men that met me everywhere, the insults hooted after me when I was at a safe distance, got badly on my nerves. The young Buddhist priests were the worst of all. There were several thousands of them in the town and none of them seemed to have anything to do except stand on street corners and jeer at Europeans.

All this was perplexing and upsetting. For at that time I had already made up my mind that imperialism was an evil thing and the sooner I chucked up my job and got out of it the better. Theoretically—and secretly, of course—I was all for the Burmese and all against their oppressors, the British. As for the job I was doing, I hated it more bitterly than I can perhaps make clear. In a job like that you see the dirty work of Empire at close quarters. The wretched prisoners huddling in the stinking cages of the lock-ups, the gray, cowed faces of the long-term convicts, the scarred buttocks of the men who had been flogged with bamboos—

all these oppressed me with an intolerable sense of guilt. But I could get nothing into perspective. I was young and ill-educated and I had had to think out my problems in the utter silence that is imposed on every Englishman in the East. I did not even know that the British Empire is dying, still less did I know that it is a great deal better than the younger empires that are going to supplant it. All I knew was that I was struck between my hatred of the empire I served and my rage against the evil-spirited little beasts who tried to make my job impossible. With one part of my mind I thought of the British Raj as an unbreakable tyranny, as something clamped down, *in saecula saeculorum,*[1] upon the will of prostrate peoples; with another part I thought that the greatest joy in the world would be to drive a bayonet into a Buddhist priest's guts. Feelings like these are the normal by-products of imperialism; ask any Anglo-Indian official, if you can catch him off duty.

One day something happened which in a roundabout way was enlightening. It was a tiny incident in itself, but it gave me a better glimpse than I had had before of the real nature of imperialism—the real motives for which despotic governments act. Early one morning the sub-inspector at a police station the other end of town rang me up on the phone and said that an elephant was ravaging the bazaar. Would I please come and do something about it? I did not know what I could do, but I wanted to see what was happening and I got on to a pony and started out. I took my rifle, an old .44 Winchester and much too small to kill an elephant, but I thought the noise might be useful *in terrorem.*[2] Various Burmans stopped me on the way and told me about the elephant's doings. It was not, of course, a wild elephant, but a tame one which had gone "must." It had been chained up, as tame elephants always are when their attack of "must" is due, but on the previous night it had broken its chain and escaped. Its mahout, the only person who could manage it when it was in that state, had set out in pursuit, but had taken the wrong direction and was now twelve hours' journey away, and in the morning the elephant had suddenly reappeared in the town. The Burmese population had no weapons and were quite helpless against it. It had already destroyed somebody's bamboo hut, killed a cow and raided some fruit-stalls and devoured the stock; also it had met the municipal rubbish van and, when the driver jumped out and took to his heels, had turned the van over and inflicted violences upon it.

The Burmese sub-inspector and some Indian constables were waiting for me in the quarter where the elephant had been seen. It was a very poor quarter, a labyrinth of squalid bamboo huts, thatched with palmleaf, winding all over a steep hillside. I remember that it was a cloudy, stuffy morning at the beginning of the rains. We began questioning the people as to where the elephant had gone and, as usual, failed to get any definite information. That is invariably the case in the East; a story always sounds clear enough at a distance, but the nearer you get to the scene of events the vaguer it becomes. Some of the people said that the elephant had gone in one direction, some said that he had gone in another, some professed

---

[1] For world without end. —ED.

[2] As a warning. —ED.

not even to have heard of any elephant. I had almost made up my mind that the whole story was a pack of lies, when we heard yells a little distance away. There was a loud, scandalized cry of "Go away, child! Go away this instant!" and an old woman with a switch in her hand came round the corner of a hut, violently shooing away a crowd of naked children. Some more women followed, clicking their tongues and exclaiming; evidently there was something that the children ought not to have seen. I rounded the hut and saw a man's dead body sprawling in the mud. He was an Indian, a black Dravidian coolie, almost naked, and he could not have been dead many minutes. The people said that the elephant had come suddenly upon him round the corner of the hut, caught him with its trunk, put its foot on his back and ground him into the earth. This was the rainy season and the ground was soft, and his face had scored a trench a foot deep and a couple of yards long. He was lying on his belly with arms crucified and head sharply twisted to one side. His face was coated with mud, the eyes wide open, the teeth bared and grinning with an expression of unendurable agony. (Never tell me, by the way, that the dead look peaceful. Most of the corpses I have seen looked devilish.) The friction of the great beast's foot had stripped the skin from his back as neatly as one skins a rabbit. As soon as I saw the dead man I sent an orderly to a friend's house nearby to borrow an elephant rifle. I had already sent back the pony, not wanting it to go mad with fright and throw me if it smelt the elephant.

The orderly came back in a few minutes with a rifle and five cartridges, and meanwhile some Burmans had arrived and told us that the elephant was in the paddy fields below, only a few hundred yards away. As I started forward practically the whole population of the quarter flocked out of the houses and followed me. They had seen the rifle and were all shouting excitedly that I was going to shoot the elephant. They had not shown much interest in the elephant when he was merely ravaging their homes, but it was different now that he was going to be shot. It was a bit of fun to them, as it would be to an English crowd; besides they wanted the meat. It made me vaguely uneasy. I had no intention of shooting the elephant—I had merely sent for the rifle to defend myself if necessary—and it is always unnerving to have a crowd following you. I marched down the hill, looking and feeling a fool, with the rifle over my shoulder and an ever-growing army of people jostling at my heels. At the bottom, when you got away from the huts, there was a metaled road and beyond that a miry waste of paddy fields a thousand yards across, not yet plowed but soggy from the first rains and dotted with coarse grass. The elephant was standing eight yards from the road, his left side towards us. He took not the slightest notice of the crowd's approach. He was tearing up bunches of grass, beating them against his knees to clean them and stuffing them into his mouth.

I had halted on the road. As soon as I saw the elephant I knew with perfect certainty that I ought not to shoot him. It is a serious matter to shoot a working elephant—it is comparable to destroying a huge and costly piece of machinery—and obviously one ought not to do it if it can possibly be avoided. And at that distance, peacefully eating, the elephant looked no more dangerous than a cow. I thought then and I think now that his attack of "must" was already passing off; in

5

which case he would merely wander harmlessly about until the mahout came back and caught him. Moreover, I did not in the least want to shoot him. I decided that I would watch him for a little while to make sure that he did not turn savage again, and then go home.

But at that moment, I glanced round at the crowd that had followed me. It was an immense crowd, two thousand at the least and growing every minute. It blocked the road for a long distance on either side. I looked at the sea of yellow faces above the garish clothes—faces all happy and excited over this bit of fun, all certain that the elephant was going to be shot. They were watching me as they would watch a conjuror about to perform a trick. They did not like me, but with the magical rifle in my hands I was momentarily worth watching. And suddenly I realized that I should have to shoot the elephant after all. The people expected it of me and I had got to do it; I could feel their two thousand wills pressing me forward, irresistibly. And it was at this moment, as I stood there with the rifle in my hands, that I first grasped the hollowness, the futility of the white man's dominion in the East. Here was I, the white man with his gun, standing in front of the unarmed native crowd—seemingly the leading actor of the piece; but in reality I was only an absurd puppet pushed to and fro by the will of those yellow faces behind. I perceived in this moment that when the white man turns tyrant it is his own freedom that he destroys. He becomes a sort of hollow, posing dummy, the conventionalized figure of a sahib. For it is the condition of his rule that he shall spend his life in trying to impress the "natives," and so in every crisis he has got to do what the "natives" expect of him. He wears a mask, and his face grows to fit it. I had got to shoot the elephant. I had committed myself to doing it when I sent for the rifle. A sahib has got to act like a sahib; he has got to appear resolute, to know his own mind and do definite things. To come all that way, rifle in hand, with two thousand people marching at my heels, and then to trail feebly away, having done nothing—no, that was impossible. The crowd would laugh at me. And my whole life, every white man's life in the East, was one long struggle not to be laughed at.

But I did not want to shoot the elephant. I watched him beating his bunch of grass against his knees, with that preoccupied grandmotherly air that elephants have. It seemed to me that it would be murder to shoot him. At that age I was not squeamish about killing animals, but I had never shot an elephant and never wanted to. (Somehow it always seems worse to kill a *large* animal.) Besides, there was the beast's owner to be considered. Alive, the elephant was worth at least a hundred pounds; dead, he would only be worth the value of his tusks, five pounds, possibly. But I had got to act quickly. I turned to some experienced-looking Burmans who had been there when we arrived, and asked them how the elephant had been behaving. They all said the same thing: he took no notice of you if you left him alone, but he might charge if you went too close to him.

It was perfectly clear to me what I ought to do. I ought to walk up to within, say, twenty-five yards of the elephant and test his behavior. If he charged, I could shoot; if he took no notice of me, it would be safe to leave him until the mahout came back. But also I knew that I was going to do no such thing. I was a poor shot with a rifle and the ground was soft mud into which one would sink at every step. If the elephant charged and I missed him, I should have about as much chance as a toad under a steam-roller. But even then I was not thinking particularly of my own skin, only of the watchful yellow faces behind. For at that moment, with the crowd watching me, I was not afraid in the ordinary sense, as I would have been if I had been alone. A white man mustn't be frightened in front of "natives"; and so, in general, he isn't frightened. The sole thought in my mind was that if anything went wrong those two thousand Burmans would see me pursued, caught, trampled on and reduced to a grinning corpse like that Indian up the hill. And if that happened it was quite probable that some of them would laugh. That would never do. There was only one alternative. I shoved the cartridges into the magazine and lay down on the road to get a better aim.

The crowd grew very still, and a deep, low, happy sigh, as of people who see   10 the theater curtain go up at last, breathed from innumerable throats. They were going to have their bit of fun after all. The rifle was a beautiful German thing with cross-hair sights. I did not then know that in shooting an elephant one would shoot to cut an imaginary bar running from ear-hole to ear-hole. I ought, therefore, as the elephant was sideways on, to have aimed straight at his ear-hole; actually I aimed several inches in front of this, thinking the brain would be further forward.

When I pulled the trigger I did not hear the bang or feel the kick—one never does when a shot goes home—but I heard the devilish roar of glee that went up from the crowd. In that instant, in too short a time, one would have thought, even for the bullet to get there, a mysterious, terrible change had come over the elephant. He neither stirred nor fell, but every line of his body had altered. He looked suddenly stricken, shrunken, immensely old, as though the frightful impact of the bullet had paralyzed him without knocking him down. At last, after what seemed a long time—it might have been five seconds, I dare say—he sagged flabbily to his knees. His mouth slobbered. An enormous senility seemed to have settled upon him. One could have imagined him thousands of years old. I fired again into the same spot. At the second shot he did not collapse but climbed with desperate slowness to his feet and stood weakly upright, with legs sagging and head drooping. I fired a third time. That was the shot that did for him. You could see the agony of it jolt his whole body and knock the last remnant of strength from his legs. But in falling he seemed for a moment to rise, for as his hind legs collapsed beneath him he seemed to tower upward like a huge rock toppling, his trunk reaching skywards like a tree. He trumpeted, for the first and only time. And then down he came, his belly towards me, with a crash that seemed to shake the ground even where I lay.

I got up. The Burmans were already racing past me across the mud. It was obvious that the elephant would never rise again, but he was not dead. He was breathing very rhythmically with long rattling gasps, his great mound of a side painfully rising and falling. His mouth was wide open. I could see far down into caverns of pale pink throat. I waited a long time for him to die, but his breathing did not weaken. Finally I fired my two remaining shots into the spot where I thought his heart must be. The thick blood welled out of him like red velvet, but still he did not die. His body did not even jerk when the shots hit him, the tortured breathing continued without a pause. He was dying, very slowly and in great agony, but in some world remote from me where not even a bullet could damage him further. I felt I had got to put an end to that dreadful noise. It seemed dreadful to see the great beast lying there, powerless to move and yet powerless to die, and not even to be able to finish him. I sent back for my small rifle and poured shot after shot into his heart and down his throat. They seemed to make no impression. The tortured gasps continued as steadily as the ticking of a clock.

In the end I could not stand it any longer and went away. I heard later that it took him half an hour to die. Burmans were bringing dahs and baskets even before I left, and I was told they had stripped his body almost to the bones by the afternoon.

Afterwards, of course, there were endless discussions about the shooting of the elephant. The owner was furious, but he was only an Indian and could do nothing. Besides, legally I had done the right thing, for a mad elephant has to be killed, like a mad dog, if its owner fails to control it. Among the Europeans opinion was divided. The older men said I was right, the younger men said it was a damn shame to shoot an elephant for killing a coolie, because the elephant was worth more than any damn Coringhee coolie. And afterwards I was very glad that the coolie had been killed; it put me legally in the right and it gave me sufficient pretext for shooting the elephant. I often wondered whether any of the others grasped that I had done it solely to avoid looking a fool.

A Student's First Responses

The student began by reading the essay, and by making a very few marginal notes—for instance, she placed question marks next to words she didn't know, such as "Dravidian" in paragraph 4. She also underlined a few sentences that struck her as especially important.

Next, she reread the essay, and in a sentence or two summarized each paragraph or group of closely related paragraphs. Here are her sentences (or phrases), preceded by the number of the paragraph.

1. Orwell, a police officer in Burma, was hated by the Burmese.

2. He was puzzled, since he was pro-Burmese and anti-British.
   He hated his job, and hated imperialism, but he was young
   and couldn't reconcile his hatred of imperialism with his
   hatred of the Burmese who tormented him.

3. He learned "the real nature of imperialism" from "a tiny
   incident"—the episode of the enraged elephant.

4. Went to site, saw dead coolie, sent for elephant gun.

5. With rifle, followed by a crowd that looked forward to the shooting; fun; meat.

6. Orwell reluctant to shoot (elephant valuable, and probably no longer a danger).

7. But crowd expected him to shoot, and he knew he must do their will. (He appeared to be "the leading actor" but really was "an absurd puppet.") ". . . when the white man turns tyrant it is his own freedom that he destroys."

8, 9. Orwell was convinced that the elephant (which took no notice of him) was now harmless. He realized he should test the elephant by approaching within 25 yards. But Orwell was a poor shot, and he imagined himself running from charging elephant, and being laughed at. So he decided to shoot.

10, 11. Prepared (to joy of crowd) to shoot. Shot, elephant staggered, Orwell fired second and third shots; elephant crashed down.

12, 13. Description of elephant's slow death (half hour).

14. Owner furious, white men crassly discuss merits of case, but Orwell knows that he shot the elephant "to avoid looking a fool."

Summarizing each stage of the essay forces a reader to be attentive and can assist the reader to formulate a **thesis sentence**, a sentence that sets forth the point of the essay. Sometimes the essay itself includes one or more sentences that assert the thesis. In "Shooting an Elephant," for example, a sentence from paragraph 7 comes quite close:

> I perceived in this moment that when the white man turns tyrant it is his own freedom that he destroys.

We asked our students to state the thesis in their own words. The student whose work has appeared so far came up with this:

> Imperialists think they are masters of their subjects, but in fact they have destroyed their own freedom, and must do what their subjects expect.

Notice that a thesis sentence states the *point* of the work. Don't confuse a thesis sentence with a summary of a narrative, such as "Orwell, pressured by the crowd into killing a harmless elephant, learned what he took to be a truth about imperialism." This sentence, though true, does not summarize the thesis or point of

Orwell's essay; rather, it summarizes what happened (the action). Of course, in writing an essay about an essay you may want to summarize the narrative (if any) and at the same time summarize the point. Thus:

> In "Shooting an Elephant," Orwell says that he shot the elephant
>
> because he dared not defy the expectations of the Burmese, and
>
> he thus learned that the tyrant really is a slave.

A thesis sentence, whether the words are your own or the author's, is a very brief summary of the argument of the work. Brief as it is, it may be sufficient (in your essay) to remind your reader of the work you are discussing, or to give the gist of an unfamiliar work.

> In "Shooting an Elephant," George Orwell argues that because in
>
> a crisis the imperialist must always do what his subjects expect
>
> him to do, he is a tyrant who has destroyed his own freedom.

Sometimes, however, a fuller summary may be useful. For instance, if an argument is complex and consists of, say, six points, you may help your reader if you provide a summary that briefly restates all six. Similarly, if you are writing about an unfamiliar work—let's say a new film, play, or novel—you may want to summarize the plot in perhaps three or four sentences. The length of your summary, then, will depend on your purpose and the needs of your audience.

The following principles may help you to write your summary:

1. First (after having written sentences that summarize each paragraph or group of paragraphs) formulate a thesis sentence. By keeping this sentence in mind, you will stay with the main point.
2. Next, write a first draft by turning your summaries of the paragraphs into fewer and better sentences. For example, the student who wrote the paragraph-by-paragraph summary of Orwell's essay turned her first three sentences (page 11), summarizing the first three paragraphs of Orwell's essay, into this:

> A policeman in Burma, Orwell hated imperialism, but he also
>
> hated the Burmese who harassed him. From "a tiny incident" he
>
> learned "the real nature of imperialism."

She turned the remaining sentences of the paragraph outline into this:

> Ordered to check out an elephant that had gone on a rampage,
>
> Orwell saw the corpse of a coolie killed by the elephant, and sent
>
> for an elephant gun. Soon after getting the gun, he found the
>
> elephant, which now was calm. Orwell was fairly sure that the

beast was no longer a menace, but the Burmese expected him to
shoot the elephant, and since he did not dare to seem irresolute,
and he could not bear the thought of the Burmese laughing at
his corpse if the elephant attacked him, he shot the creature. His
reason, in short, was not to protect the public from a mad animal,
but "to avoid looking a fool."

3. Write a lead-in sentence, probably incorporating the gist of the thesis sentence (for instance, "George Orwell, in 'Shooting an Elephant,' tells how the experience of shooting an elephant led him to perceive that the imperialist enslaves himself"), then revise the draft of your summary, eliminating needless repetition, and adding whatever may be needed to clarify the work for someone who is unfamiliar with it. You may rearrange the points if you think the rearrangement will clarify matters. For instance, although Orwell ends his essay by confessing that he shot the elephant "to avoid looking a fool," you may want to give this information near the start. Thus:

In "Shooting an Elephant," George Orwell confesses that although
the official view was that he shot the elephant in the line of
duty, he really shot it "to avoid looking a fool."

4. Edit your final draft for errors in grammar, punctuation, and spelling. Read it aloud to test it once more for readability. Sometimes only by reading aloud do we detect a needless repetition, an awkward phrase, or the need for a comma.

Writing 2 about Essays (and Other Forms of Literature)

Analyzing and Evaluating

When you read, try to read sympathetically, opening yourself to the writer's vision. When you have finished an attentive reading, and an attentive rereading, and have roughed out an outline or a summary, you are ready to *analyze* the writer's methods and to *evaluate* the piece.

In an **analysis**, you will examine the relationships between the parts. That is, you will ask such questions as:

What is the *topic* of the essay? Try to state it, preferably in writing, as specifically as possible. For example, broadly speaking one might say that the subject of Orwell's "Shooting an Elephant" (page 6) is British imperialism in India, but within this subject his topic, more specifically, is the effects of imperialism on the imperialists themselves.

What is the essay's *thesis* (either stated or implied)? If you have located a *thesis sentence* in the essay, underline it and write *thesis* in the margin. If the thesis is implied, try to formualte it in a sentence of your own.

What does the title do? What purpose does it suggest the writer holds?

What is the function of the opening paragraph (or paragraphs)? What claim on our attention or beliefs does it make?

How is the argument set forth? By logic? By drawing on personal experience? What evidence is there that the writer is an authority on the topic? Are there other appeals to authority? What other kinds of evidence support the essay's claim? What are the author's underlying assumptions? Are they stated or implied, and are they acceptable to you, or can you challenge them?

Does the tone shift as the essay progresses? If so, why does it shift?

What sort of speaker or *persona* does the writer create, and how does the writer create it? Is it created, for example, by using colloquial *diction*, or on the other hand, by using formal diction? By figurative language?

15

If the thesis is never explicitly stated, why is it not?

If there is a formal, explicit conclusion, underline or restate it. If the conclusion is not stated, but is implied, what does the writer want us to conclude?

In evaluating, you will ask such questions as:

Is the essay as clear as it can be, given the complexity of the material? For example, do specific examples help to make the generalizations clear? Are crucial terms adequately defined? If the thesis is not explicitly stated, is the essay unclear, or is it perhaps better because of the indirectness?

If the conclusion is not stated but implied, why does the writer not state it?

Is the argument (if the essay is chiefly an argument) convincing, or is it marred by faulty thinking? Look particularly for transitions such as "thus," "therefore," "then," "hence," and "finally." Trace the argument carefully. Are crucial stages missing? Do the conclusions in fact follow from the arguments, or evidence, or examples, or analogies that the writer has offered? If statistics are used, are they sound and relevant? If authorities are quoted, are they indeed authorities (rather than just big names) on this topic?

Is the essay interesting? If so, in what ways, and if not, why not?—which gets us back to analysis. If there are passages of undisguised argument, for instance, are they clear without being repetitious and boring? Do specific examples clarify and enliven general assertions?

Is the writer's tone appropriate to the topic, and does it engage rather than alienate the reader?

Exactly what devices does the writer use to make the persona engaging?

How is the essay organized? Is the organization effective? Does the essay build to a climax?

Another way of thinking about the criteria for evaluating an essay is this:

Is the essay persuasive (whether because of its logic or because of the power of the speaker's personality)? and,

Does the essay give pleasure?

Don't hesitate to demand that an essay give you pleasure. The author probably thought that he or she was writing well, and certainly hoped to hold your interest throughout the essay to make you feel that you were learning something of interest. In short, the author hoped that you would like the essay. You have every right to evaluate the essay partly by considering the degree of pleasure that it affords. Of course, in *your* essay you cannot simply say that you enjoyed an essay or that you were bored by it. You will have to support your assertions with reasons based on evidence. To support your assertions you must have read the writer's words carefully, so we are back to an earlier point: The first thing to do if you are going to write about a piece of writing is to read it attentively, pen or pencil in hand.

As you read and reread the material that you are writing about, subjecting it to the kinds of questions we have mentioned, your understanding of it will almost surely deepen. You will probably come to feel that it is better—or worse—than you had thought at first, or in any case somewhat different. As you prepare to write your own essay, and as you draft it, you are learning, feeling your way toward a considered analysis. All writers are in the position of the little girl who, told by an adult that she should think before she spoke, replied, "How do I know what I think until I say it?" But once having said something—whether in a mental question to yourself or in a note or a draft—you have to evaluate your thought, and improve it if it doesn't fit the facts.

From Pre-Writing to Writing about "Shooting an Elephant"

Suppose you are going to write about Orwell's essay (page 6). Possibly at this stage of the course your instructor is concerned with teaching a particular topic— let's say organization, or narration, or description, or the creation of a *persona*— and he or she therefore limits the scope of your essay to an examination of a given topic. Perhaps the topic is organization. In reading or rereading the essay you notice that from the third paragraph through the next-to-last paragraph Orwell is telling a story, but in the middle—not at the end—he tells us the significance of the story. And so you mark the passage, perhaps with a vertical line, perhaps with a question mark, perhaps with square brackets. (Reading with pencil in hand is a great aid to thinking.)

> ⌐And it was at this moment, as I stood there with the rifle in my hands, that I first grasped the hollowness, the futility of the white man's dominion in the East. . . .
> I perceived in this moment that when the white man turns tyrant it is his own freedom that he destroys. He becomes a sort of hollow, posing dummy, the conventionalized figure of a sahib.

You might even jot down some questions in your notebook. Why does Orwell spill the beans here, and why, pages later, does he describe at length the death throes of the elephant, since even before the elephant's lingering death he had come to his insight? Answers will vary (perhaps good reasons can be offered, or perhaps Orwell bungled the essay), but in noting and questioning this apparently unusual organization you may come to a fuller understanding of Orwell's essay, and you may also learn something about strategies of organization that you can apply to your own writing, in other courses and after you leave college.

Obviously the passages that you mark, in one way or another, will depend largely on the assigned topic. If your instructor's assignment includes words such as "summarize," "compare," "define," or "evaluate," you will be alerted to think in particular directions.

Let's say, however, that the instructor has not assigned a topic but has left the choice up to you. Again, your jottings of various sorts (lists of key phrases, underlinings, formulation of Orwell's thesis, and perhaps a summary) should suggest various possibilities. Perhaps you were puzzled by Orwell's depiction of the Burmese, which doesn't seem terribly sympathetic for someone who claims to be on their side. "Sneering yellow faces," "no one had the guts to raise a riot"—such passages may be worth thinking about and writing about. Looking at the essay again you notice that although Orwell begins with more or less the conventional attitudes of the white oppressor, he increasingly reveals his sympathy for the Burmese without sentimentalizing them. An essay on Orwell's way of depicting the Burmese (and therefore to some extent on his way of depicting his own changing attitudes) as it develops in his essay is a possibility. At this point you might try writing a few sentences in your notebook.

Let's assume that on thinking further about "Shooting an Elephant" you come to feel that your greatest interest is in Orwell's political interpretation of his action. Now, in other words, you are *settling on a topic*. You keep coming back to that passage, in the middle, about his recognition of the nature of imperialism, and somehow you don't quite feel that Orwell has correctly interpreted his own experience. You reread the essay, jotting down notes as you go from one of Orwell's paragraphs to the next, recording your chief thoughts, including your agreements and your doubts.

One student (the writer of the essay printed below) produced these notes:

O's opening parag. critical of Burmese; O self-pitying?

Admits perplexity; O anti-imperial. "wretched prisoners"; beatings.

"a tiny incident" gave him insight into "the real nature of imperialism." Elephant. Not so tiny.

shoots elephant because people expect it; when a man becomes a "tyrant," it is "his own freedom he destroys"; "hollow, posing dummy." True?

O's last parag shows cold Europeans. Is he showing his superiority (even though he acted basely) to these Europeans?

Let's say that you share this student's view, at least in part. You are bothered by what seems to be an act of cowardice on Orwell's part. Yes, the pressure on him was great—that mob at his back, his fear of losing face—and you see that Orwell has from the beginning of the essay carefully depicted the plight of the white man in Burma, but you still think that a person of greater moral fiber would have resisted the pressure and would not have shot the elephant. That is to say (and this is crucial to feeling your way toward your essay), you are *formulating a thesis statement*. At this stage you may even try to write a thesis statement, and a paragraph or two supporting it. Orwell, you come to feel, is explaining away his own failure by giving it a grand significance, by inflating it with political meaning.

Now you are *refining the thesis*, perhaps by writing another paragraph or two, in some ways modifying or amplifying what you have already jotted down.

The next step will be to work out, at least tentatively, *strategies for putting forth this thesis*. How will you begin? With a quotation from Orwell? With a statement of your initial reaction to the essay? Which passages will you quote? What tone will you adopt? Will a comparison be useful? How personal should you get? You can't hope to settle all of these questions at once, and it will almost certainly be impossible for you to write an introductory paragraph. Fortunately, the only thing you need to do at this point is to *start writing*. With a topic in mind, an idea about it (your tentative thesis), and some rough notes, you start getting as many of your ideas on paper as you can. It might be useful to sketch a very rough outline, a sort of shopping list of the points you want to make. Here is the outline with which one student began:

> Sympathy for Orwell—how he creates it
>
> His interpretation of shooting ("the system")
>
> Why I don't buy it
>
> Was he a "tyrant"?
>
> Was he a "dummy"?
>
> Maybe a coward?
>
> How I interpret shooting: Guilt
>
> Why he misinterprets: Guilt
>
> (End with something good?)

The First Draft

With some such outline in front of you, simply begin writing sentences. Don't worry about mechanical matters, such as spelling, or getting every word exactly right. Leave gaps in your sentences if you need to. What you are doing is writing a *rough draft* that no one else need ever see and that even you must not regard as sacred. You can always add or delete, or change a word, or even change your mind. If you have written a rough outline you will probably tinker with that too as your ideas take clearer shape because you find more and more evidence to support or to modify the thesis.

When you reach this point, you may want to draft an introductory paragraph. If you don't feel up to the job yet, skip it for a while. But there is much to be said, at this point, for writing a paragraph that informs the reader of the topic and the thesis. The topic is not "the essay I am writing about"—how does the reader know what essay you are writing about?—but, rather, is (for example) "George Orwell's 'Shooting an Elephant.' " The thesis should be stated clearly, but you should try to produce something a little more attractive than such a statement as "This essay will argue that . . ." Still, even such a bald statement is helpful and will encourage you to keep writing. Here is a good opening paragraph written by a student. (This student's essay dealt with the artistry of Orwell's essay, especially with Orwell's use of irony.)

> George Orwell's "Shooting an Elephant" is not, despite the implications of its title, an exciting story of a brave hunter. In this essay Orwell sets forth a reality far less glamorous than the title suggests. The essay, so to speak, disillusions the reader, just as Orwell's experience in Burma disillusioned the young English-man. The ironic undercutting of the title begins in the first paragraph and continues to the end of the essay.

Obviously the rest of the student's essay will be devoted to supporting the thesis that Orwell deliberately undercuts the reader's expectations.

Of course not every opening paragraph must name the topic and suggest the thesis. But every opening paragraph should be interesting and should make the reader want to read further.

Imagining an Audience

All writers need to imagine an audience. Consider what goes on when you write a letter: A letter asking one's parents or a friend for a loan is very different from a letter written to the college's financial aid officer, even though both letters have the same purpose. Similarly, a writer writes an essay for a particular audience, for example readers of *Ms*, or of *Time*, or of the *Quarterly Journal of Economics*, or of a college newspaper. A given reader, of course, may happen to read all four of these publications, but each publication nevertheless has its own typical readers, its own audience. The typical reader of *Ms*, for example, is a woman who is sympathetic to feminism. The typical reader of the *Quarterly Journal of Economics* is a professional economist. Thus, although an article on the economic consequences of paid leaves for pregnant women might appear in either publication, the article in *Ms* (1) will probably vigorously argue on behalf of such leaves; (2) will be intelligible to the general reader (for instance, it will not include complex statistics); and (3) will be written in a relatively informal and perhaps even a highly colloquial and personal style. On the other hand, since the *Quarterly Journal of Economics* is a scholarly magazine, its article on paid leaves for pregnant women will probably (1) appear objective; (2) be highly technical; and (3) be written in a relatively formal or impersonal style.

When you reread your draft, try to imagine someone else reading it. You may have received, with your assignment, instructions about the audience your essay should address. If not, you must define for yourself the reader you intend to persuade, and then you must keep that reader in mind as you compose and revise. We suggest that you imagine your reader to be someone like you, a classmate perhaps. But it's helpful to imagine that your reader has *not* read the essay you're writing about; it is essential to imagine that your reader knows and understands the essay less well than you do. Your reader certainly does not know what assignment you are fulfilling, and could not have arrived, unassisted, at the thesis you are prepared to argue.

With such a reader in mind—obviously not your instructor—you will be careful to be clear and to be consistent. You will take care, for example, probably in your first paragraph, to identify, at least by author and title, the essay you are analyzing. Keeping your reader in mind will also help you to decide how much summary to include, where the summary is needed, how much detail it should contain, and at what points in your analysis an additional sentence or two of summary would be helpful. Imagining a reader may also help to remind you that it is your job to analyze and to persuade. Summarize only enough to keep your reader with you, following you step by step and, we hope, agreeing with each point you make.

As you reread your draft, then, keep in mind the fact that your essay should contain two theses and two voices—Orwell's thesis and voice, and your own thesis and voice. That is, the reader should be told, early and clearly, what Orwell's point is, and should get some sense of the way Orwell makes the point. The reader should also perceive *your* point, and be able to take some pleasure in the way in which you make your point. Note, too, that the point or thesis and the voice that predominates in the essay are yours (unless the assignment has been merely to summarize a published essay). That is, your essay is, finally, *your* essay—a thoughtful *response* to someone else's essay. It probably will begin with an introductory comment, and will then give a brief summary of the essay you are responding to, but chiefly it will set forth your own views.

Revising and Editing Your Draft

And then, of course, you revise (preferably after giving the manuscript a day's rest) and revise again, perhaps adding or deleting some quotations, and checking the quotations for accuracy. Perhaps now you are ready to give your essay a title. Your title may prompt you to make still further changes: substituting one quotation for another, finding more exact verbs for your draft, perhaps even adding new material, and almost certainly revising your conclusion. At this point, try reading your essay aloud, preferably to a roommate, friend, or classmate. But if it is 3:00 A.M. and you alone are awake, read it aloud anyway (quietly). Again, imagine a real reader, or listener. You'll almost certainly find yourself deleting unnecessary repetitions and adding necessary transitions such as "but," "furthermore," and "on the other hand." Finally, check spellings of words you're not sure of in a dictionary, and check doubtful constructions in a handbook. In short, you laboriously do all the things that will make your essay seem effortless to your reader. This includes typing (or writing legibly) and, after giving yourself and your manuscript as much rest as time allows, proofreading (and making final corrections as necessary).

Sample Essay on Orwell's "Shooting an Elephant"

We have just described (partly by imagining them) the thought processes and the work of the student who wrote the following essay. Read the student's essay, ignoring our marginal comments, and then reread her essay, this time glancing back at her rough outline and our marginal notes.

Title is provocative, and implies the thesis

Is Orwell's Elephant Big Enough to Hold

Orwell's Interpretation?

Essay begins by identifying Orwell and showing appreciation of Orwell, i.e., shows fairmindedness

George Orwell's "Shooting an Elephant" is a memorable essay about his experience as a British police officer in Burma, and it is almost the exciting story the title seems to promise. The beginning of the first sentence compels our attention: "In Moulmein, in Lower

Correctly identifies Orwell's tone

Burma, I was hated by large numbers of people." And, so that on second thought this will not seem egotistical to the reader, Orwell wryly adds that this was "the only time in my life that I have been important enough for

Reference to note citing source

this to happen to me."[1] We can hardly fail to like the writer of this sentence. The next paragraph, too, with its

Summary in which brief, relevant quotations let us hear Orwell's voice

sympathy for "the wretched prisoners huddling in the stinking cages of the lock-ups" presents us with a man who, because of his sympathy for the oppressed and because of his "intolerable sense of guilt" (7), gains our

Transition ("But") lets us know that essayist will now take a somewhat different view

sympathy. But to say that we sympathize with Orwell is not to say that we have to share all of his opinions. Although we have to take his word for what happened when he shot the elephant, and we recognize that he has

Student's thesis statement

firsthand experience of imperialism, we do not have to believe that his interpretation of his experience gives us the truth about the nature of imperialism.

Repetition of "interpretation" provides transition

He first presents his interpretation just beyond the middle of the essay—just as Orwell is about to shoot the

Relevant summary

elephant (page 9). He explains not one but two things. He explains why he shot the elephant, and he also explains,

---

Citation of source, and explanation of subsequent references

[1] In <u>Literature for Composition</u>, 2nd ed., ed. Sylvan Barnet, Morton Berman, and William Burto (Glenview, Ill.: Scott, Foresman, 1988): 6. Subsequent references will be made parenthetically within the text.

Student clearly sets forth Orwell's thesis

Relevant summary

or claims to explain, the contradiction of imperialism: "When the white man turns tyrant it is his own freedom that he destroys. He becomes a sort of hollow, posing dummy" (9). Now, in "Shooting an Elephant" Orwell admits that *he* became a sort of dummy. He felt that he was forced to shoot the elephant because the Burmese wanted him to shoot, and he was afraid not to live up to their expectations. He was afraid, he says, that if he didn't shoot the elephant "some of them would laugh" (p.

Page reference given

10). Orwell has effectively prepared us for the terrible power of contemptuous laughter when, in his first paragraph, he says, "The crowd yelled with hideous laughter." Nevertheless the generalization about what happens "when the white man turns tyrant" (9) is not really supported. In the first place, Orwell does not give us any reason to believe that he was a tyrant. True, he was a British police officer in Burma, and thus he was a representative of imperial England, but nothing in the essay suggests that he was cruel or even unfair. We do know, however, that his work as a policeman produced in him "an intolerable sense of guilt" (page 7), and this, I think, is a clue to Orwell's interpretation of his act.

First sentence of new paragraph offers a clear transition

What was his act? Under pressure from a crowd, he needlessly killed an elephant. He certainly <u>should</u> feel guilt for killing a harmless beast, and also for depriving the owner of valuable property. And he should feel guilt, I think, for yielding to the pressure of the crowd. I am

Student does not overstate her criticism

not saying that I wouldn't have yielded too, but I am saying that it was wrong to yield and that a stronger person would have said to himself or herself, "Never mind what all of these people think; the elephant is harmless and I won't shoot it." Perhaps if he had refused to shoot the elephant the malicious jeers would soon have turned into cheers for the brave sahib who dared to face a crazy elephant and then walked calmly away.

Clarification of student's thesis

But Orwell did yield to the mob, and he felt guilty for doing so. It is probably this guilt, this awareness of his weakness, rather than the guilt about being a policeman in Burma, that is at the heart of the essay. But apparently he couldn't face it. Despite his modesty and his no doubt genuine sympathy for the victims of imperialism, he shifts the blame from himself to, as we now say, "the system." It isn't really his fault, Orwell says in effect, that he was a coward; it is the nature of imperialism to turn the imperialist into a coward, a "dummy."

Again, essayist tries to be fair and not seem superior to author she is analyzing; good tone

Let me say again that, judging from this essay, Orwell was in many ways a decent person, and we can admire his honesty when he admits, in the last line, that he killed the elephant "solely to avoid looking a fool." This humble confession certainly gains our sympathy, and if the essay were entirely about his deed and his awareness of his weakness there would be nothing to complain about. But Orwell tries to explain away his failure by seeing himself (no less than the Burmese) as the victim of imperialism. Finally, then, for all of his good nature and his modesty and his confession of weakness, he presents

Forceful ending

himself as innocent. He <u>had</u> to shoot the elephant, he wants us to believe, because imperialists <u>have</u> to do what their victims want them to do. His comments about the nature of imperialism may or may not be true. But it seems clear, even from his own essay, that Orwell's action

Restatement of student's thesis

in the last analysis resulted not from "the nature of imperialism," as he claims, but from Orwell's own failure of nerve.

Our marginal comments offer our chief views, but a brief restatement and amplification may be useful:

1. Although the title may be a trifle strained, it at least provides the reader with a focus, and thus it is far better than such an unhelpful title as "George Orwell's 'Shooting an Elephant'" or "On 'Shooting an Elephant.'"
2. Keeping her audience in mind, the student helpfully identifies and summarizes Orwell's essay.
3. The writer uses brief quotations, so that we hear Orwell's voice and hear the evidence. But she does not use quotations as padding.

4. The writer's tone is satisfactory. She is critical of Orwell, but she avoids overstating her case or condescending to him.

Review: A Short Guide to Writing an Essay

1. *Engage in pre-writing.* Read the work, annotating it lightly if at all, on the first reading. Then reread it, underlining or otherwise marking passages of special interest, jotting notes and queries in the margins, and writing a paragraph-by-paragraph summary, devoting a sentence to each paragraph or each group of closely related paragraphs. Try to ascertain the writer's purpose (to explain, to persuade, to amuse, or whatever), and think about how (and how well) this purpose is accomplished. In addition to annotating the text, and outlining and perhaps summarizing it, you probably will want to jot down some notes— including questions addressed to yourself—on a sheet of paper.

2. *Try to settle on a thesis.* If a topic is assigned (for instance, Orwell's attitude toward the Burmese, or Orwell's view of imperialism) start writing on it, even if you start only by stating, in writing, what the topic is, and your own doubts about what you have to say about it. At this stage, certainly, don't worry about writing a beautiful introductory paragraph; you are writing chiefly to get ideas. As you write on the topic, you probably will find your thesis—an argument related to the topic—emerging. If you must choose your own topic as well as find your own thesis, you may find it useful to start writing about what you found especially interesting or difficult or puzzling in the work you have read. Something useful may well emerge simply by writing something like "I was surprised to learn that . . . ," or "I'm trying to see why this writer is so concerned about arguing that. . . ." Probably as you write, some one point will hold your attention, and you will discover that you have an attitude toward this point. You may be able to regard this attitude, at least provisionally, as your thesis, or your controlling idea.

3. *Keep discovering ideas by writing.* If you keep jotting down material relevant to your provisional thesis, you will probably find that you are discovering new ideas. If you keep asking yourself questions ("Why does she use all those quotations?" "Why does he assume that all people share his feelings?"), you will probably find answers coming to mind.

4. *Write a draft;* When you think you know what you want to say, take what you have already written, study it to see what can be saved and to see what needs to be done, and then start writing a draft. (What you have already produced is not a first draft; it is what many writers call a "zero draft.") If writing an opening paragraph is especially difficult, skip it, and get on with the job of drafting the rest. By the time you finish a first draft, you may have a good idea for an opening paragraph—for instance, a quotation from the work you are writing about may now seem to make a good opening. Similarly, don't worry too much about a final paragraph. You can fret about that when you revise.

5. *Revise for large-scale coherence*. Try to give yourself some time—preferably a day, but in any case at least an hour or two—between writing a first draft and revising this draft. A revision ought to be a re-vision, a second (and fresh) look. Read what you have written, putting yourself in the shoes of your imagined reader. Ask yourself if the main points of your essay appear in a reasonable sequence. The best way to check the structure of the essay—the sequence of ideas—is to outline the draft, jotting down the topic idea of each paragraph. Look at your jottings to make sure the sequence is orderly and sensible and to see what can be tossed out and what must be added. (It's especially hard to toss out anything one has already written; it took fifteen minutes to write that paragraph about Orwell's life, and so one wants to keep the paragraph, even though it is irrelevant. Be strong; get rid of irrelevancies.) If you use a word processor, you can easily move passages around and add or delete. If you write by hand, or on a typewriter, you'll have to use scissors and paste to construct your revision.

6. *Revise for small-scale coherence*. (This and the following points are not so neatly separated as the previous ones. Many experienced writers engage in all of these actions more or less simultaneously, but if you do not have a method of your own, you may find it helpful, at least in writing your first few essays, to proceed by the stages given here.)

   Let's assume that you have read and revised your drafts, and that your most recent draft now has (or at least seems to you to have) a coherent and effective structure. One point leads to the next, and the whole seems to develop rather than to wander or trail off. The time has come to reread it closely, paying attention to the structure of each paragraph, and of each sentence. Is each paragraph unified and coherent? That is, does each paragraph deal with one topic (possibly announced in a topic sentence), and is this topic developed adequately, with appropriate details given step by step, sentence by sentence?

   Even if the generalizations are clear to you, ask yourself if they will be clear to your reader. Consider whether concrete examples—perhaps brief quotations from the text—are needed or not. Similarly, ask yourself if the stages in your argument are clear, or if they need to be clarified with transitions such as "moreover," "similarly," and "on the other hand."

7. *Work on an opening and a final paragraph*. Are the opening and the closing paragraphs adequate? This usually means, among other things, are they informative and interesting?

   A good opening paragraph usually identifies the topic and announces or at least implies the thesis, without the obviousness of such a statement as "In this essay I will argue that Orwell's 'Shooting an Elephant' reveals that Orwell did not really understand why he shot the elephant." Such a sentence is by no means terrible—it has the merit of identifying the topic and the thesis—but "In this essay" and "I will argue" are rather flat and colorless. Look again at the student's essay (page 22) on Orwell for a better opening. (On opening paragraphs, see especially page 19.)

Similarly, in a closing paragraph try to avoid saying something like "Thus I have shown that . . ." Such a sentence, adding nothing to what has come before, is tedious and unnecessary. On reading your last draft, you may find that a concluding paragraph, a paragraph formally drawing a conclusion, is not needed. This is especially true if the paper is fairly short, since you have been arguing a case all along, and the reader scarcely needs to be reminded of your thesis. But if you do feel that some sort of wrap-up is desirable, one of these two strategies may be useful:

a. In some way echo the opening paragraph, perhaps picking up a phrase, but now showing it in a new light;

b. Quote an effective phrase or sentence from the work you are writing about.

The first of these devices can give your essay a pleasant, conclusive symmetry; the second can enable you to end with words more evocative than any words you might produce on your own.

8. *Revise your diction.* Reread your draft yet again, now watching out especially for your choice of particular words. After all, it is through words that (1) you establish your tone, and (2) more generally, set forth your perceptions. This means that you want to be sure to use *exactly* the right word. Is Orwell "deceived," "mixed up," "mistaken," or what? Is his essay "a failure," "a mess," "a partial failure," "a fascinating example of self-deception," or what? (To comment on only one of these terms: Courtesy and good sense will probably prevent you from calling his essay a "mess." Whatever its shortcomings may be, the essay is readable and interesting, and Orwell deserves respect. The essay may have weaknesses, and Orwell as a human being was not perfect, but his achievements were considerable and it is discourteous to treat him as one's inferior.)

Reread your draft with an eye also on the effectiveness of each sentence. Probably you own a rhetoric textbook, a book that discusses such matters as wordiness, emphasis, and clarity. As you read your sentences, check them against what you learned from your rhetoric book.

9. *Edit.* Reread your draft yet again, this time checking the spelling, punctuation, grammar, and other mechanical matters—for instance, check quotations for accuracy. If you are at all unsure of the spelling of a word, check a dictionary. Similarly, if you are unsure about any punctuation in your essay, check your rhetoric textbook.

10. *Manuscript form.* In writing or typing your final version, follow the instructions on manuscript form (title, margins, etc.) given on page 767.

3 Reading and Responding in Writing: Essays

Why the Essay?

When writing, or for that matter when doing anything, probably we all feel the truth of one of Rousseau's statements: "Logically, everything ought to come first." Rousseau's truth seems especially evident when one is writing a book about two things—say, college composition and literature. This early chapter does two things—at once. It talks about essays, since you are going to write essays, and it talks about literature, since you are going to read literature and write about it. In Chapter 2 we talked briefly about the business of writing an essay. Later, in Chapter 4, we will try to offer more detailed help in writing your own analytic essays, but here we want to begin by talking about the essay that itself has literary value, the essay that one reads not simply because it explains some topic out there, but because it gives pleasure, especially the pleasure of entering another mind.

Such an essay stands more or less midway between, on the one hand, prose of the sort that you are now reading and that you will be writing, and, on the other hand, prose (or poetry) that gives us an imaginary world, such as the world of Huckleberry Finn or of Hamlet. Because literary essays have one foot in the camp of expository writing, study of them can improve your own writing (for instance, you can learn something about the techniques of exposition, persuasion, and description); because these essays have another foot in the camp of imaginative writing, they can also teach you something about the nature of literature. The two topics are, in fact, interrelated: When you study literature you are studying (among other things) the ways the masters use language, and their ways can, at least to a certain extent, be your ways, too.

It is not likely that you will become a professional writer, but it is highly likely that you will have to do some writing, not only in your English courses in college and in other courses, but after college as well. Applications for jobs, reports of committees, summaries of reports, case histories, recommendations, and proposals of all sorts are part of the work of millions of people who do not regard themselves as writers. By reading the writings of such experts as Thoreau and Orwell closely, you can learn many of the secrets of persuasive writing.

The Essay as Literature

The word *essay* entered the English language in 1597, when Francis Bacon called a small book of ten short prose pieces *Essays.* Bacon borrowed the word from Michel de Montaigne, a French writer who in 1580 had published some short prose pieces under the title *Essais*—that is, "testings" or "attempts," from the French verb *essayer,* "to try." Montaigne's title indicated that his graceful and personal jottings—the fruit of pleasant study and meditation—were not fully thought-out treatises but rather sketches that could be amplified and amended. *Macbeth,* or for that matter a limerick, is a finished thing, complete and scarcely capable of extension, but Montaigne's essays (and Bacon's) were admittedly only beginnings. Indeed, Bacon revised his several times, and though they grew they always remained fairly short, tentative pieces. Even today the essay, by its relative brevity (five or ten or even twenty or thirty pages, rather than five hundred) suggests that it is an initial exploration, a foray rather than a battle. Nevertheless, it should be readable and persuasive, coherent, thoughtful, and complete in its own way. A good essay conveys the sense that at least for the moment the topic has been effectively treated.

Each of Bacon's ten "fragments," as he spoke of them, consists for the most part of aphorisms or pithy remarks and quotations hung on a central theme. They are, he later wrote, "certain brief notes . . . which I have called Essays. The word is late, but the thing is ancient, for Seneca's *Epistles to Lucilius,* if one mark them well, are but essays—that is, dispersed meditations, though conveyed in the form of epistles." (Epistles, or letters, will concern us in the next chapter.) Here is a sample from one of Bacon's "dispersed meditations," entitled "Of Studies," that is, on reading books.

> Read not to contradict, nor to believe, but to weigh and consider. Some books are to be tasted, others to be swallowed, and some few to be chewed and digested. That is, some books are to be read only in parts; others to be read but cursorily, and some few to be read wholly and with diligence and attention. Reading maketh a full man, conference a ready man, and writing an exact man.

Notice, first of all, the figure of speech in the second sentence: "Some books are to be tasted, others to be swallowed, and some few to be chewed and digested." Figures of speech—here books are metaphorically treated as food—will be discussed at length in our comments on poetry, because they are usually most abundant in poetry, but they are part of almost all literature. Second, notice that Bacon's sentences make artful use of parallelism ("Some books are to be tasted, others to be swallowed, and some few to be chewed and digested"), and that one sentence is often closely linked to the next (for instance, by the repetition of "some" and "others" in the second and third sentences), but that a good deal of shifting around could be done without great loss—and Bacon went on to do it, in his various revisions of his essays. Even in the revised versions, however, the essays resemble the talk of a witty, cultivated gentleman, a man whose mind is well stocked and who can turn a phrase. Most of our daily talk is a good deal less—not a flow of polished sentences but a heap of rough and not always ready pauses and phrases including "I, uh, well, I mean" and "Well, you know." We can call Bacon's style conversational, but we should realize that his sentences are more shapely utterances than those that come out of our mouths. In a word, they are not talk but literature.

An essay by Bacon or (to allude to authors discussed in the first chapter) by Thoreau or Orwell, like a story, play, or poem—or, for that matter, like a good joke or a song—takes us out of the daily world of facts and gives us, instead, the writer's (or joke-teller's, or singer's) world. No one asks a joke or a song to be true; we ask only that it hold our attention. By the way, although we assume that Orwell's "Shooting an Elephant" (page 6) is true, supporting evidence is lacking. Orwell did indeed serve as a police officer in Burma between 1923 and 1928, but scholars have failed to turn up any report of the episode he narrates in the essay. Still, historically true or not, the essay holds our attention, and more or less (like any work of literature) creates its own world, a world which makes us feel, "Yes, I understand and believe in those feelings." That is, the best works hold our attention not because they embody a literal truth (of the sort that presumably stands behind every newspaper story) but because they ring true to our experience, and indeed enlarge our experience, convincing us that they do indeed accurately report feelings and beliefs—feelings and beliefs that we might not ourselves hold but that we *would* hold if we were in those circumstances. The real subject of the essay is Orwell's mind, not a piece of official business.

Some essays are purely reflective, setting forth the writer's attitudes or states of mind, and in such essays the interest is almost entirely the way the writers see things. But even in essays that are narrative—that is, in essays that recount events—our interest is, as we said in the previous chapter, more in the essayists' *responses* to the events than in the events themselves. When we read an essay we almost say, "So that's how it feels to be you," and, "Tell me more about the way you see things." The bit of history is less important to us than the memorable presence of the writer.

Even the most engaging personality, however, has to give some coherence to its utterances. We are not likely to put up with unorganized thoughts—with a disorderly mind—for very long. Pieces the length of Bacon's (a page or two) are about the limit, and one had better not write such loosely connected sentences unless one can write sentences as good as Bacon's. Doubtless you have already learned the chief ways to organize an essay—for instance, classification, chronology, comparison—and doubtless you also know that all readable writing is in some degree persuasive: It persuades the reader to stay with it and at least in some degree to accept the writer's point of view. Read each of the following essays for enjoyment, and after reading each, spend a moment imagining the kind of person who wrote it, the kind of person who seems to be speaking it. Then slowly reread the essay, seeing *how* the writer conveyed this *persona* or "voice" (even while he or she was writing about a topic "out there"): for example, by common or uncommon words, by short or long sentences, by literal or figurative language, by offering generalizations or accumulating evidence, and so forth.

Let's take a simple, familiar example of words that establish a persona. Lincoln begins the Gettysburg Address with "Four score and seven years ago." He might have said "Eighty-seven years ago"—but the language would have lacked the biblical echo, and the persona would thus have been that of an ordinary person rather than that of a man who has about him something of the tone of an Old Testament prophet. This religious tone is entirely fitting, since President Lincoln was speaking at the dedication of a cemetery for "these hallowed dead" and was urging the members of his audience to give all of their energies to ensure that the dead men had not died in vain. By such devices as the choice of words, the length of sentences, and the sorts of evidence offered, an author sounds to the reader (who, in Shakespeare's words, must "hear with eyes") solemn or agitated or witty or genial or severe. Incidentally, if you read Martin Luther King's "I Have a Dream" (page 441), you will notice that he begins his essay (originally it was a speech, delivered at the Lincoln Memorial on the one-hundredth anniversary of Lincoln's Emancipation Proclamation) with these words: "Five score years ago . . . ." King is deliberately echoing Lincoln's words, partly in tribute to Lincoln, but also to help establish himself as the spiritual descendent of Lincoln and, further back, of the founders of the Judaeo-Christian tradition.

Notice, too, as you read the essays, the ways in which the personality is developed as the essay proceeds. That is, study not only the words and the sentences but also the overall organization to see how it reveals a particular kind of person. The revelation of personality begins with the first words, but a writer may *develop* a persona as the essay proceeds; for example, a writer who seems tentative at first may become assured later in the essay, and we may come to see that the initial tentativeness was a strategy to disarm us and to achieve our good will.

Some of the questions that follow each of the next five essays are designed to help you to focus on the ways by which the writers set forth a persona. The suggestions for writing include exercises that allow you to practice some techniques exhibited in the essays. But before turning to this collection of essays, we give, by way of review, a list of questions that you can ask yourself after reading any essay. Your responses to these questions will help to stimulate ideas for your own essays.

Questions to Help Generate Essays on Essays

1. What kind of essay is it? Is it chiefly a presentation of facts (for example, an exposition, a report, or a history), or is it an argument, or a meditation?
2. What does it seem to add up to? If the essay is chiefly a presentation of facts, does it also have a larger implication? For instance, if it narrates a happening (history), does the reader draw an inference—find a meaning—in the happen-

ing? If the essay is chiefly an argument, what is the thesis? How is the thesis supported? (Is it supported, for example, by induction, deduction, analogy, or emotional appeal?) Are the assumptions (explicit and implicit) acceptable? If the essay is chiefly meditative or speculative, how much emphasis is on the persona? That is, if the essay is a sort of thinking-out-loud, is the reader's interest chiefly in the ostensible topic, or in the thinker's mood and personality?

3. What is the tone of the essay? Most expository essays are relatively impersonal, but they can range from solemn to playful. Is the tone consistent in the essay? If not, are the shifts functional, or are they signs of mere carelessness?

4. What is especially good (or bad) about the essay? For example, is it especially good because it is logically persuasive? Or because it is highly informative? Or entertaining? Or because it introduces the reader to an engaging persona? Or (if it is a narrative) because it tells a story effectively, using (where appropriate) description, dialogue, and commentary, and somehow making the reader feel that this story is worth reporting?

Jonathan Swift (English. 1667–1745)

A MODEST PROPOSAL

For Preventing the Children of Poor People in Ireland from Being a Burden to Their Parents or Country, and for Making Them Beneficial to the Public

It is a melancholy object to those who walk through this great town or travel in the country, when they see the streets, the roads, and cabin doors, crowded with beggars of the female sex, followed by three, four, or six children, all in rags and importuning every passenger for an alms. These mothers, instead of being able to work for their honest livelihood, are forced to employ all their time in strolling to beg sustenance for their helpless infants: who as they grow up either turn thieves for want of work, or leave their dear native country to fight for the Pretender in Spain, or sell themselves to the Barbadoes.

I think it is agreed by all parties that this prodigious number of children in the arms, or on the backs, or at the heels of their mothers, and frequently of their fathers, is in the present deplorable state of the kingdom a very great additional grievance; and, therefore, whoever could find out a fair, cheap, and easy method of making these children sound, useful members of the commonwealth, would deserve so well of the public as to have his statue set up for a preserver of the nation.

But my intention is very far from being confined to provide only for the children of professed beggars; it is of a much greater extent, and shall take in the whole number of infants at a certain age who are born of parents in effect as little able to support them as those who demand our charity in the streets.

As to my own part, having turned my thoughts for many years upon this important subject, and maturely weighed the several schemes of our projectors,[1] I have always found them grossly mistaken in their computation. It is true, a child just dropped from its dam may be supported by her milk for a solar year, with little other nourishment; at most not above the value of *2s.*,[2] which the mother may certainly get, or the value in scraps, by her lawful occupation of begging; and it is exactly at one year old that I propose to provide for them in such a manner as instead of being a charge upon their parents or the parish, or wanting food and raiment for the rest of their lives, they shall on the contrary contribute to the feeding, and partly to the clothing, of many thousands.

There is likewise another great advantage in my scheme, that it will prevent those voluntary abortions, and that horrid practice of women murdering their bastard children, alas! too frequent among us! sacrificing the poor innocent babes I doubt more to avoid the expense than the shame, which would move tears and pity in the most savage and inhuman breast.

The number of souls in this kingdom being usually reckoned one million and a half, of these I calculate there may be about 200,000 couple whose wives are breeders; from which number I subtract 30,000 couple who are able to maintain their own children (although I apprehend there cannot be so many, under the present distress of the kingdom); but this being granted, there will remain 170,000 breeders. I again subtract 50,000 for those women who miscarry, or whose children die by accident or disease within the year. There only remain 120,000 children of poor parents annually born. The question therefore is, how this number shall be reared and provided for? which, as I have already said, under the present situation of affairs, is utterly impossible by all the methods hitherto proposed. For we can neither employ them in handicraft or agriculture; we neither build houses (I mean in the country) nor cultivate land; they can very seldom pick up a livelihood by stealing, till they arrive at six years old, except where they are of towardly parts; although I confess they learn the rudiments much earlier; during which time they can, however, be properly looked upon only as probationers; as I have been informed by a principal gentleman in the county of Cavan, who protested to me that he never knew above one or two instances under the age of six, even in a part of the kingdom so renowned for the quickest proficiency in that art.

I am assured by our merchants, that a boy or a girl before twelve years old is no salable commodity; and even when they come to this age they will not yield above 3£. or 3£. 2*s.* 6*d.* at most on the exchange; which cannot turn to account either to the parents or kingdom, the charge of nutriment and rags having been at least four times that value.

5

---

[1] Persons who devise plans. (Notes to this selection are by the editors.)
[2] 2s. Two shillings. Later "£" is an abbreviation for pounds and "*d*" for pence.

I shall now therefore humbly propose my own thoughts, which I hope will not be liable to the least objection.

I have been assured by a very knowing American of my acquaintance in London, that a young healthy child well nursed is at a year old a most delicious, nourishing, and wholesome food, whether stewed, roasted, baked, or broiled; and I make no doubt that it will equally serve in a fricassee or a ragout.

I do therefore humbly offer it to public consideration that of the 120,000   10
children already computed, 20,000 may be reserved for breed, whereof only one-fourth part to be males; which is more than we allow to sheep, black cattle, or swine; and my reason is, that these children are seldom the fruits of marriage, a circumstance not much regarded by our savages; therefore one male will be suffi-cient to serve four females. That the remaining 100,000 may, at a year old, be offered in sale to the persons of quality and fortune through the kingdom; always advising the mother to let them suck plentifully in the last month, so as to render them plump and fat for a good table. A child will make two dishes at an entertain-ment for friends; and when the family dines alone, the fore or hind quarter will make a reasonable dish, and seasoned with a little pepper or salt will be very good boiled on the fourth day, especially in winter.

I have reckoned upon a medium that a child just born will weigh 12 pounds, and in a solar year, if tolerably nursed, will increase to 28 pounds.

I grant this food will be somewhat dear, and therefore very proper for land-lords, who, as they have already devoured most of the parents, seem to have the best title to the children.

Infant's flesh will be in season throughout the year, but more plentiful in March, and a little before and after: for we are told by a grave author, an eminent French physician, that fish being a prolific diet, there are more children born in Roman Catholic countries about nine months after Lent than at any other season; therefore, reckoning a year after Lent, the markets will be more glutted than usual, because the number of popish infants is at least three to one in this king-dom: and therefore it will have one other collateral advantage, by lessening the number of papists among us.

I have already computed the charge of nursing a beggar's child (in which list I reckon all cottagers, laborers, and four-fifths of the farmers) to be about 2s. per annum, rags included; and I believe no gentleman would repine to give 10s. for the carcass of a good fat child, which, as I have said, will make four dishes of excellent nutritive meat, when he has only some particular friend or his own family to dine with him. Thus the squire will learn to be a good landlord, and grow popular among the tenants; the mother will have 8s. net profit, and be fit for work till she produces another child.

Those who are more thrifty (as I must confess the times require) may flay   15
the carcass; the skin of which artificially dressed will make admirable gloves for ladies, and summer boots for fine gentlemen.

As to our city of Dublin, shambles[3] may be appointed for this purpose in the most convenient parts of it, and butchers we may be assured will not be wanting:

---

[3] Slaughterhouses.

although I rather recommend buying the children alive, and dressing them hot from the knife as we do roasting pigs.

A very worthy person, a true lover of his country, and whose virtues I highly esteem, was lately pleased in discoursing on this matter to offer a refinement upon my scheme. He said that many gentlemen of this kingdom, having of late destroyed their deer, he conceived that the want of venison might be well supplied by the bodies of young lads and maidens, not exceeding fourteen years of age nor under twelve; so great a number of both sexes in every country being now ready to starve for want of work and service; and these to be disposed of by their parents, if alive, or otherwise by their nearest relations. But with due deference to so excellent a friend and so deserving a patriot, I cannot be altogether in his sentiments; for as to the males, my American acquaintance assured me from frequent experience that their flesh was generally tough and lean, like that of our schoolboys by continual exercise, and their taste disagreeable; and to fatten them would not answer the charge. Then as to the females, it would, I think, with humble submission be a loss to the public, because they soon would become breeders themselves: and besides, it is not improbable that some scrupulous people might be apt to censure such a practice (although indeed very unjustly), as a little bordering upon cruelty; which, I confess, has always been with me the strongest objection against any project, how well soever intended.

But in order to justify my friend, he confessed that this expedient was put into his head by the famous Psalmanazar,[4] a native of the island Formosa, who came from thence to London about twenty years ago: and in conversation told my friend, that in his country when any young person happened to be put to death, the executioner sold the carcass to persons of quality as a prime dainty; and that in his time the body of a plump girl of fifteen, who was crucified for an attempt to poison the emperor, was sold to his imperial majesty's prime minister of state, and other great mandarins of the court, in joints from the gibbet, at 400 crowns. Neither indeed can I deny, that if the same use were made of several plump young girls in this town, who without one single groat to their fortunes cannot stir abroad without a chair, and appear at the playhouse and assemblies in foreign fineries which they never will pay for, the kingdom would not be the worse.

Some persons of a desponding spirit are in great concern about the vast number of poor people, who are aged, diseased, or maimed, and I have been desired to employ my thoughts what course may be taken to ease the nation of so grievous an encumbrance. But I am not in the least pain upon that matter, because it is very well known that they are every day dying and rotting by cold and famine, and filth and vermin, as fast as can be reasonably expected. And as to the young laborers, they are now in as hopeful a condition: they cannot get work, and consequently pine away for want of nourishment, to a degree that if at any time they are accidentally hired to common labor, they have not strength to perform it; and thus the country and themselves are happily delivered from the evils to come.

I have too long digressed, and therefore shall return to my subject. I think the   20

---

[4] Psalmanazar George Psalmanazar (c. 1679–1763), a Frenchman who claimed to be from Formosa (now Taiwan), wrote *An Historical and Geographical Description of Formosa* (1704). The hoax was exposed soon after publication.

advantages by the proposal which I have made are obvious and many, as well as of the highest importance.

For first, as I have already observed, it would greatly lessen the number of papists, with whom we are yearly overrun, being the principal breeders of the nation as well as our most dangerous enemies; and who stay at home on purpose to deliver the kingdom to the Pretender, hoping to take their advantage by the absence of so many good Protestants, who have chosen rather to leave their country than stay at home and pay tithes against their conscience to an Episcopal curate.

Secondly, The poor tenants will have something valuable of their own, which by law may be made liable to distress and help to pay their landlord's rent, their corn and cattle being already seized, and money a thing unknown.

Thirdly, Whereas the maintenance of 100,000 children from two years old and upward, cannot be computed at less than 10s. apiece per annum, the nation's stock will be thereby increased £50,000 per annum, beside the profit of a new dish introduced to the tables of all gentlemen of fortune in the kingdom who have any refinement in taste. And the money will circulate among ourselves, the goods being entirely of our own growth and manufacture.

Fourthly, The constant breeders beside the gain of 8s. sterling per annum by the sale of their children, will be rid of the charge of maintaining them after the first year.

Fifthly, This food would likewise bring great custom to taverns, where the vintners will certainly be so prudent as to procure the best receipts for dressing it to perfection, and consequently have their houses frequented by all the fine gentlemen, who justly value themselves upon their knowledge in good eating; and a skilful cook who understands how to oblige his guests, will contrive to make it as expensive as they please.   25

Sixthly, This would be a great inducement to marriage, which all wise nations have either encouraged by rewards or enforced by laws and penalties. It would increase the care and tenderness of mothers toward their children, when they were sure of a settlement for life to the poor babes, provided in some sort by the public, to their annual profit instead of expense. We should see an honest emulation among the married women, which of them would bring the fattest child to the market. Men would become as fond of their wives during the time of their pregnancy as they are now of their mares in foal, their cows in calf, their sows when they are ready to farrow; nor offer to beat or kick them (as is too frequent a practice) for fear of a miscarriage.

Many other advantages might be enumerated. For instance, the addition of some thousand carcasses in our exportation of barreled beef, the propagation of swine's flesh, and improvement in the art of making good bacon, so much wanted among us by the great destruction of pigs, too frequent at our table; which are no way comparable in taste or magnificence to a well-grown, fat, yearling child, which roasted whole will make a considerable figure at a lord mayor's feast or any other public entertainment. But this and many others I omit, being studious of brevity.

Supposing that 1,000 families in this city would be constant customers for infants' flesh, besides others who might have it at merry-meetings, particularly at weddings and christenings, I compute that Dublin would take off annually about 20,000 carcasses; and the rest of the kingdom (where probably they will be sold somewhat cheaper) the remaining 80,000.

I can think of no one objection that will possibly be raised against this proposal, unless it should be urged that the number of people will be thereby much lessened in the kingdom. This I freely own, and it was indeed one principal design in offering it to the world. I desire the reader will observe, that I calculate my remedy for this one individual kingdom of Ireland and for no other that ever was, is, or I think ever can be upon earth. Therefore let no man talk to me of other expedients: of taxing our absentees at 5s. a pound: of using neither clothes nor household furniture except what is of our own growth and manufacture: of utterly rejecting the materials and instruments that promote foreign luxury: of curing the expensiveness of pride, vanity, idleness, and gaming in our women: of introducing a vein of parsimony, prudence, and temperance: of learning to love our country, in the want of which we differ even from Laplanders and the inhabitants of Topinamboo: of quitting our animosities and factions, nor acting any longer like the Jews, who were murdering one another at the very moment their city was taken: of being a little cautious not to sell our country and conscience for nothing: of teaching landlords to have at least one degree of mercy toward their tenants: lastly, of putting a spirit of honesty, industry, and skill into our shopkeepers; who, if a resolution could now be taken to buy only our native goods, would immediately unite to cheat and exact upon us in the price, the measure, and the goodness, nor could ever yet be brought to make one fair proposal of just dealing, though often and earnestly invited to it.

Therefore I repeat, let no man talk to me of these and the like expedients, till   30
he has at least some glimpse of hope that there will be ever some hearty and sincere attempt to put them in practice.

But as to myself, having been wearied out for many years with offering vain, idle, visionary thoughts, and at length utterly despairing of success, I fortunately fell upon this proposal; which, as it is wholly new, so it has something solid and real, of no expense and little trouble, full in our own power, and whereby we can incur no danger in disobliging England. For this kind of commodity will not bear exportation, the flesh being of too tender a consistence to admit a long continuance in salt, although perhaps I could name a country which would be glad to eat up our whole nation without it.

After all, I am not so violently bent upon my own opinion as to reject any offer proposed by wise men, which shall be found equally innocent, cheap, easy, and effectual. But before something of that kind shall be advanced in contradiction to my scheme, and offering a better, I desire the author or authors will be pleased maturely to consider two points. First, as things now stand, how they will be able to find food and raiment for 100,000 useless mouths and backs. And secondly, there being a round million of creatures in human figure throughout this kingdom, whose subsistence put into a common stock would leave them in debt 2,000,000£. sterling, adding those who are beggars by profession to the bulk of farmers, cottagers, and laborers, with the wives and children who are beggars in effect; I desire those politicians who dislike my overture, and may perhaps be so bold as to attempt an answer, that they will first ask the parents of these mortals, whether they would not at this day think it a great happiness to have been sold for food at a year old in the manner I prescribe, and thereby have avoided such a perpetual scene of misfortunes as they have since gone through by the oppression of landlords, the impossibility of paying rent without money or trade, the want of common sustenance, with neither house nor clothes to cover them from the inclemencies of the weather, and the most inevitable prospect of entailing the like or greater miseries upon their breed for ever.

I profess, in the sincerity of my heart, that I have not the least personal interest in endeavoring to promote this necessary work, having no other motive than the public good of my country, by advancing our trade, providing for infants, relieving the poor, and giving some pleasure to the rich. I have no children by which I can propose to get a single penny; the youngest being nine years old, and my wife past childbearing.

QUESTIONS AND SUGGESTIONS FOR WRITING

1. In paragraph 4 the speaker of the essay mentions proposals set forth by "projectors"; that is, by advocates of other proposals or projects. On the basis of the first two paragraphs of "A Modest Proposal," how would you characterize *this* "projector," the speaker of the essay? Write your characterization in one paragraph. Then, in a second paragraph, characterize the projector as you understand him, having read the entire essay. In your second paragraph, indicate what *he thinks he is*, and also what the reader sees he really is.
2. What does the projector imply are the causes of the Irish poverty he deplores? Are there possible causes he has omitted? (If so, what are they?)
3. Imagine yourself as one of the poor parents to whom Swift refers, and write a 250-word essay explaining why you prefer not to sell your infant to the local butcher.

Henry David Thoreau (American. 1817–1862)

THE BATTLE OF THE ANTS

One day when I went out to my wood-pile, or rather my pile of stumps, I observed two large ants, the one red, the other much larger, nearly half an inch long, and black, fiercely contending with one another. Having once got hold they never let go, but struggled and wrestled and rolled on the chips incessantly. Looking farther, I was surprised to find that the chips were covered with such combatants, that it was not a *duellum*, but a *bellum*,[1] a war between two races of

---

[1] *Duellum* and *bellum* are Latin words for, respectively, a combat of two persons and a war. (Notes to this selection are by the editors.)

ants, the red always pitted against the black, and frequently two red ones to one black. The legions of these Myrmidons[2] covered all the hills and vales in my wood-yard, and the ground was already strewn with the dead and dying, both red and black. It was the only battle which I have ever witnessed, the only battle-field I ever trod while the battle was raging; internecine war; the red republicans on the one hand, and the black imperialists on the other. On every side they were engaged in deadly combat, yet without any noise that I could hear, and human soldiers never fought so resolutely. I watched a couple that were fast locked in each other's embraces, in a little sunny valley amid the chips, now at noonday prepared to fight till the sun went down, or life went out. The smaller red champion had fastened himself like a vice to his adversary's front, and through all the tumblings on that field never for an instant ceased to gnaw at one of his feelers near the root, having already caused the other to go by the board; while the stronger black one dashed him from side to side, and, as I saw on looking nearer, had already divested him of several of his members. They fought with more pertinacity than bulldogs. Neither manifested the least disposition to retreat. It was evident that their battle-cry was "Conquer or die." In the meanwhile there came along a single red ant on the hillside of this valley, evidently full of excitement, who either had despatched his foe, or had not yet taken part in the battle; probably the latter, for he had lost none of his limbs; whose mother had charged him to return with his shield or upon it. Or perchance he was some Achilles, who had nourished his wrath apart, and had now come to avenge or rescue his Patroclus.[3] He saw this unequal combat from afar—for the blacks were nearly twice the size of the red—he drew near with rapid pace till he stood on his guard within half an inch of the combatants; then, watching his opportunity, he sprang upon the black warrior, and commenced his operations near the root of his right fore leg, leaving the foe to select among his own members; and so there were three united for life, as if a new kind of attraction had been invented which put all other locks and cements to shame. I should not have wondered by this time to find that they had their respective musical bands stationed on some eminent chip, and playing their national airs the while, to excite the slow and cheer the dying combatants. I was myself excited somewhat even as if they had been men. The more you think of it, the less the difference. And certainly there is not the fight recorded in Concord history, at least, if in the history of America, that will bear a moment's comparison with this, whether for the numbers engaged in it, or for the patriotism and heroism displayed. For numbers and for carnage it was an Austerlitz or Dresden.[4] Concord Fight! Two killed on the patriots' side, and Luther Blanchard wounded! Why here every ant was a Buttrick—"Fire! for God's sake fire!"—and thousands shared the fate of Davis and Hosmer. There was not one hireling there. I have no doubt that it was a principle they fought for, as much as our ancestors, and not to avoid a three-penny tax on their tea; and the results of this battle will

---

[2] Zeus is said to have created the Myrmidons, legendary warriors in Horer's *Iliad*, out of ants. Editors' note)

[3] In the *Iliad*, Achilies avenges the death of his friend Patroclus.

[4] Battles during the Napoleonic wars.

be as important and memorable to those whom it concerns as those of the battle of Bunker Hill, at least.

I took up the chip on which the three I have particularly described were struggling, carried it into my house, and placed it under a tumbler on my window-sill, in order to see the issue. Holding a microscope to the first-mentioned red ant, I saw that, though he was assiduously gnawing at the near fore leg of his enemy, having severed his remaining feeler, his own breast was all torn away, exposing what vitals he had there to the jaws of the black warrior, whose breast-plate was apparently too thick for him to pierce; and the dark carbuncles of the sufferer's eyes shone with ferocity such as war only could excite. They struggled half an hour longer under the tumbler, and when I looked again the black soldier had severed the heads of his foes from their bodies, and the still living heads were hanging on either side of him like ghastly trophies at his saddle-bow, still apparently as firmly fastened as ever, and he was endeavoring with feeble struggles, being without feelers, and with only the remnant of a leg, and I know not how many other wounds, to divest himself of them, which at length, after half an hour more, he accomplished. I raised the glass, and he went off over the window-sill in that crippled state. Whether he finally survived that combat, and spent the remainder of his days in some Hôtel des Invalides, I do not know; but I thought that his industry would not be worth much thereafter. I never learned which party was victorious, nor the cause of the war, but I felt for the rest of that day as if I had my feelings excited and harrowed by witnessing the struggle, the ferocity and carnage, of a human battle before my door.

Kirby and Spence tell us that the battles of ants have long been celebrated and the date of them recorded, though they say that Huber[5] is the only modern author who appears to have witnessed them. "Aeneas Sylvius," say they, "after giving a very circumstantial account of one contested with great obstinacy by a great and small species on the trunk of a pear tree," adds that " 'this action was fought in the pontificate of Eugenius the Fourth, in the presence of Nicholas Pistoriensis, an eminent lawyer, who related the whole history of the battle with the greatest fidelity.' A similar engagement between great and small ants is recorded by Olaus Magnus, in which the small ones, being victorious, are said to have buried the bodies of their own soldiers, but left those of their giant enemies a prey to the birds. This event happened previous to the expulsion of the tyrant Christiern [*sic*] the Second from Sweden." The battle which I witnessed took place in the presidency of Polk, five years before the passage of Webster's Fugitive-Slave Bill.

QUESTIONS AND SUGGESTIONS FOR WRITING

1. The final sentence refers to Daniel Webster's Fugitive-Slave Bill. What is the relevance of this sentence to Thoreau's essay?
2. Are the metaphors of war serious or playful, or both? Do they glorify ants? Trivialize

---

[5] Kirby and Spence were nineteenth-century American entomologists; Huber was a Swiss entomologist.

human beings? Or what? What is Thoreau's attitude toward his material—that is, toward ants, human beings, and war? To what degree does Thoreau express his feelings directly? In what ways does he express them indirectly?

3. Thoreau says, "I have no doubt that it was a principle they fought for." Does this statement make sense?

4. In a paragraph or two, describe Thoreau's persona here, supporting your characterization with concrete references to the essay. (On persona, see page 4.)

5. In a paragraph, set forth your interpretation of Thoreau's essay. You may want to consider if the essay has a point, or if it is mere description.

6. Watching the battle, Thoreau says, "I was myself excited somewhat even as if they had been men." If you have ever felt excited by some aspect of nature, in 500 to 750 words narrate the experience and try to account for your feeling.

George Orwell (English. 1903–1950)

A HANGING

It was in Burma, a sodden morning of the rains. A sickly light, like yellow tinfoil, was slanting over the high walls into the jail yard. We were waiting outside the condemned cells, a row of sheds fronted with double bars, like small animal cages. Each cell measured about ten feet by ten and was quite bare within except for a plank bed and a pot for drinking water. In some of them brown, silent men were squatting at the inner bars, with their blankets draped round them. These were the condemned men, due to be hanged within the next week or two.

One prisoner had been brought out of his cell. He was a Hindu, a puny wisp of a man, with a shaven head and vague liquid eyes. He had a thick, sprouting mustache, absurdly too big for his body, rather like the mustache of a comic man on the films. Six tall Indian warders were guarding him and getting him ready for the gallows. Two of them stood by with rifles and fixed bayonets, while the others handcuffed him, passed a chain through his handcuffs and fixed it to their belts, and lashed his arms tight to his sides. They crowded very close about him, with their hands always on him in a careful, caressing grip, as though all the while feeling him to make sure he was there. It was like men handling a fish which is still alive and may jump back into the water. But he stood quite unresisting, yielding his arms limply to the ropes, as though he hardly noticed what was happening.

Eight o'clock struck and a bugle call, desolately thin in the wet air, floated from the distant barracks. The superintendent of the jail, who was standing apart from the rest of us, moodily prodding the gravel with his stick, raised his head at the sound. He was an army doctor, with a gray toothbrush mustache and a gruff voice. "For God's sake, hurry up, Francis," he said irritably. "The man ought to have been dead by this time. Aren't you ready yet?"

Francis, the head jailer, a fat Dravidian in a white drill suit and gold spectacles, waved his black hand. "Yes sir, yes sir," he bubbled. "All iss satisfactorily prepared. The hangman iss waiting. We shall proceed."

"Well, quick march, then. The prisoners can't get their breakfast till this job's over."

5

We set out for the gallows. Two warders marched on either side of the prisoner, with their rifles at the slope; two others marched close against him, gripping him by arm and shoulder, as though at once pushing and supporting him. The rest of us, magistrates and the like, followed behind. Suddenly, when we had gone ten yards, the procession stopped short without any order or warning. A dreadful thing had happened—a dog, come goodness knows whence, had appeared in the yard. It came bounding among us with a loud volley of barks and leapt round up wagging its whole body, wild with glee at finding so many human beings together. It was a large woolly dog, half Airedale, half pariah. For a moment it pranced around us, and then, before anyone could stop it, it had made a dash for the prisoner, and jumping up tried to lick his face. Everybody stood aghast, too taken aback even to grab the dog.

"Who let that bloody brute in here?" said the superintendent angrily. "Catch it, someone!"

A warder detached from the escort charged clumsily after the dog, but it danced and gamboled just out of his reach, taking everything as part of the game. A young Eurasian jailer picked up a handful of gravel and tried to stone the dog away, but it dodged the stones and came after us again. Its yaps echoed from the jail walls. The prisoner, in the grasp of the two warders, looked on incuriously, as though this was another formality of the hanging. It was several minutes before someone managed to catch the dog. Then we put my handkerchief through its collar and moved off once more, with the dog still straining and whimpering.

It was about forty yards to the gallows. I watched the bare brown back of the prisoner marching in front of me. He walked clumsily with his bound arms, but quite steadily, with that bobbing gait of the Indian who never straightens his knees. At each step his muscles slid neatly into place, the lock of hair on his scalp danced up and down, his feet printed themselves on the wet gravel. And once, in spite of the men who gripped him by each shoulder, he stepped lightly aside to avoid a puddle on the path.

It is curious; but till that moment I had never realized what it means to   10 destroy a healthy, conscious man. When I saw the prisoner step aside to avoid the puddle, I saw the mystery, the unspeakable wrongness, of cutting a life short when it is in full tide. This man was not dying, he was alive just as we are alive. All the organs of his body were working—bowels digesting food, skin renewing itself, nails growing, tissues forming—all toiling away in solemn foolery. His nails would still be growing when he stood on the drop, when he was falling through the air with a tenth-of-a-second to live. His eyes saw the yellow gravel and the gray walls, and his brain still remembered, foresaw, reasoned—even about puddles. He and we were a party of men walking together, seeing, hearing, feeling, understanding the same world; and in two minutes, with a sudden snap, one of us would be gone—one mind less, one world less.

The gallows stood in a small yard, separate from the main grounds of the prison, and overgrown with tall prickly weeds. It was a brick erection like three sides of a shed, with planking on top, and above that two beams and a crossbar with the rope dangling. The hangman, a grayhaired convict in the white uniform of the prison, was waiting beside his machine. He greeted us with a servile crouch as we entered. At a word from Francis the two warders, gripping the prisoner more closely than ever, half led, half pushed him to the gallows and helped him clumsily up the ladder. Then the hangman climbed up and fixed the rope round the prisoner's neck.

We stood waiting, five yards away. The warders had formed in a rough circle round the gallows. And then, when the noose was fixed, the prisoner began crying out to his god. It was a high, reiterated cry of "Ram! Ram! Ram! Ram!" not urgent and fearful like a prayer or cry for help, but steady, rhythmical, almost like the tolling of a bell. The dog answered the sound with a whine. The hangman, still standing on the gallows, produced a small cotton bag like a flour bag and drew it down over the prisoner's face. But the sound, muffled by the cloth, still persisted, over and over again: "Ram! Ram! Ram! Ram! Ram!"

The hangman climbed down and stood ready, holding the lever. Minutes seemed to pass. The steady, muffled crying from the prisoner went on and on, "Ram! Ram! Ram!" never faltering for an instant. The superintendent, his head on his chest, was slowly poking the ground with his stick; perhaps he was counting the cries, allowing the prisoner a fixed number—fifty, perhaps, or a hundred. Everyone had changed color. The Indians had gone gray like bad coffee, and one or two of the bayonets were wavering. We looked at the lashed, hooded man on the drop, and listened to his cries—each cry another second of life; the same thought was in all our minds; oh, kill him quickly, get it over, stop that abominable noise!

Suddenly the superintendent made up his mind. Throwing up his head he made a swift motion with his stick. "Chalo!" he shouted almost fiercely.

There was a clanking noise, and then dead silence. The prisoner had vanished, and the rope was twisting on itself. I let go of the dog, and it galloped immediately to the back of the gallows; but when it got there it stopped short, barked, and then retreated into a corner of the yard, where it stood among the weeds, looking timorously out at us. We went round the gallows to inspect the prisoner's body. He was dangling with his toes pointed straight downwards, very slowly revolving, as dead as a stone. 15

The superintendent reached out with his stick and poked the bare brown body; it oscillated slightly. "*He's* all right," said the superintendent. He backed out from under the gallows, and blew out a deep breath. The moody look had gone out of his face quite suddenly. He glanced at his wrist-watch. "Eight minutes past eight. Well, that's all for this morning, thank God."

The warders unfixed bayonets and marched away. The dog, sobered and conscious of having misbehaved itself, slipped after them. We walked out of the gallows yard, past the condemned cells with their waiting prisoners, into the big central yard of the prison. The convicts, under the command of warders armed with lathis, were already receiving their breakfast. They squatted in long rows, each man holding a tin pannikin, while two warders with buckets marched around ladling out rice; it seemed quite a homely, jolly scene, after the hanging. An enormous relief had come upon us now that the job was done. One felt an impulse to sing, to break into a run, to snigger. All at once everyone began chattering gaily.

The Eurasian boy walking beside me nodded towards the way we had come, with a knowing smile: "Do you know sir, our friend (he meant the dead man) when he heard his appeal had been dismissed, he pissed on the floor of his cell. From fright. Kindly take one of my cigarettes, sir. Do you not admire my new silver case, sir? From the boxwallah, two rupees eight annas. Classy European style."

Several people laughed—at what, nobody seemed certain.

Francis was walking by the superintendent, talking garrulously: "Well, sir, all has passed off with the utmost satisfactoriness. It was all finished—flick! Like that. It iss not always so—oah, no! I have known cases where the doctor wass obliged to go beneath the gallows and pull the prissoner's legs to ensure decease. Most disagreeable!" 20

"Wriggling about, eh? That's bad," said the superintendent.

"Ach, sir, it iss worse when they become refractory! One man, I recall, clung to the bars of hiss cage when we went to take him out. You will scarcely credit, sir, that it took six warders to dislodge him, three pulling at each leg. We reasoned with him, 'My dear fellow,' we said, 'think of all the pain and trouble you are causing to us!' But no, he would not listen! Ach, he wass very troublesome!"

I found that I was laughing quite loudly. Everyone was laughing. Even the superintendent grinned in a tolerant way. "You'd better all come out and have a drink," he said quite genially. "I've got a bottle of whiskey in the car. We could do with it."

We went through the big double gates of the prison into the road. "Pulling at his legs!" exclaimed a Burmese magistrate suddenly, and burst into a loud chuckling. We all began laughing again. At that moment Francis' anecdote seemed extraordinarily funny. We all had a drink together, native and European alike, quite amicably. The dead man was a hundred yards away.

QUESTIONS AND SUGGESTIONS FOR WRITING:

1. Why does Orwell give so much space to the dog? (Notice that although the dog is mentioned chiefly before the hanging, he figures again after the hanging.)
2. Orwell writes in paragraph 10, "I saw the mystery, the unspeakable wrongness, of cutting a life short when it is in full tide." Yet in the final paragraph Orwell reports that he, along with other officials, "all began laughing again" at the thought of three men pulling at the legs of a man desperately holding on to the bars of his cells, or perhaps at the thought of the doctor pulling at the legs of a dead man. How would you explain their behavior at the end?
3. Devoting a sentence or two to each, describe and characterize the prisoner, Francis, the Eurasian boy, and the superintendent.
4. Write an essay of 500 words, recounting an extremely unpleasant episode that you have witnessed—for instance, a crime, an accident, or an act of outrageous discourtesy. Editorialize only briefly, if at all; for the most part, let your report of the episode (especially your choice of details) convey your attitude.

Langston Hughes (American. 1902–1967)

SALVATION

I was saved from sin when I was going on thirteen. But not really saved. It happened like this. There was a big revival at my Auntie Reed's church. Every night for weeks there had been much preaching, singing, praying, and shouting, and some very hardened sinners had been brought to Christ, and the membership of the church had grown by leaps and bounds. Then just before the revival ended, they held a special meeting for children, "to bring the young lambs to the fold." My aunt spoke of it for days ahead. That night I was escorted to the front row and placed on the mourners' bench with all the other young sinners, who had not yet been brought to Jesus.

My aunt told me that when you were saved you saw a light, and something happened to you inside! And Jesus came into your life! And God was with you from then on! She said you could see and hear and feel Jesus in your soul. I believed her. I had heard a great many old people say the same thing and it seemed to me they ought to know. So I sat there calmly in the hot, crowded church, waiting for Jesus to come to me.

The preacher preached a wonderful rhythmical sermon, all moans and shouts and lonely cries and dire pictures of hell, and then he sang a song about the ninety and nine safe in the fold, but one little lamb was left out in the cold. Then he said: "Won't you come? Won't you come to Jesus? Young lambs, won't you come?" And he held out his arms to all us young sinners there on the mourners' bench. And the little girls cried. And some of them jumped up and went to Jesus right away. But most of us just sat there.

A great many old people came and knelt around us and prayed, old women with jet-black faces and braided hair, old men with work-gnarled hands. And the church sang a song about the lower lights are burning, some poor sinners to be saved. And the whole building rocked with prayer and song.

Still I kept waiting to *see* Jesus.

Finally all the young people had gone to the altar and were saved, but one boy and me. He was a rounder's son named Westley. Westley and I were surrounded by sisters and deacons praying. It was very hot in the church, and getting late now. Finally Westley said to me in a whisper: "God damn! I'm tired o' sitting here. Let's get up and be saved." So he got up and was saved.

Then I was left all alone on the mourners' bench. My aunt came and knelt at my knees and cried, while prayers and songs swirled all around me in the little church. The whole congregation prayed for me alone, in a mighty wail of moans and voices. And I kept waiting serenely for Jesus, waiting, waiting—but he didn't come. I wanted to see him, but nothing happened to me. Nothing! I wanted something to happen to me, but nothing happened.

I heard the songs and the minister saying: "Why don't you come? My dear child, why don't you come to Jesus? Jesus is waiting for you. He wants you. Why don't you come? Sister Reed, what is this child's name?"

"Langston," my aunt sobbed.

5

"Langston, why don't you come? Why don't you come and be saved? Oh,   10
Lamb of God! Why don't you come?"

Now it was really getting late. I began to be ashamed of myself, holding
everything up so long. I began to wonder what God thought about Westley, who
certainly hadn't seen Jesus either, but who was now sitting proudly on the platform, swinging his knickerbockered legs and grinning down at me, surrounded by
deacons and old women on their knees praying. God had not struck Westley dead
for taking his name in vain or for lying in the temple. So I decided that maybe to
save further trouble, I'd better lie, too, and say that Jesus had come, and get up
and be saved.

So I got up.

Suddenly the whole room broke into a sea of shouting, as they saw me rise.
Waves of rejoicing swept the place. Women leaped in the air. My aunt threw her
arms around me. The minister took me by the hand and led me to the platform.

When things quieted down, in a hushed silence, punctuated by a few ecstatic
"Amens," all the new young lambs were blessed in the name of God. Then joyous
singing filled the room.

That night, for the last time in my life but one—for I was a big boy   15
twelve years old—I cried. I cried, in bed alone, and couldn't stop. I buried
my head under the quilts, but my aunt heard me. She woke up and told my
uncle I was crying because the Holy Ghost had come into my life, and because
I had seen Jesus. But I was really crying because I couldn't bear to tell her that
I had lied, that I had deceived everybody in the church, and I hadn't seen Jesus,
and that now I didn't believe there was a Jesus any more, since he didn't come to
help me.

QUESTIONS AND SUGGESTIONS FOR WRITING

1. Is the piece amusing, or serious, or both? Explain.
2. How would you characterize the style or voice of the first three sentences? Childlike,
   or sophisticated, or what? How would you characterize the final sentence? How can
   you explain the change in style or tone?
3. Why does Hughes bother to tell us, in paragraph 11, that Westley was "swinging his
   knickerbockered legs and grinning"? Do you think that Westley too may have cried
   that night? Give your reasons.
4. Is the episode told from the point of view of someone "going on thirteen," or from the
   point of view of a mature man?
5. One of the Golden Rules of narrative writing is "Show, don't tell." In about 500 words,
   report an experience—for instance, a death in the family, or a severe (perhaps unjust)
   punishment, or the first day in a new school—that produced strong feelings. Like
   Hughes, you may want to draw on an experience in which you were subjected to group
   pressure. Do not explicitly state what the feelings were; rather, let the reader understand the feelings chiefly through concretely detailed actions. But, like Hughes, you
   might state your thesis or basic position in your first paragraph and then indicate when
   and where the experience took place.

Virginia Woolf (English. 1882–1941)

THE DEATH OF THE MOTH

Moths that fly by day are not properly to be called moths; they do not excite that pleasant sense of dark autumn nights and ivy-blossom which the commonest yellow-underwing asleep in the shadow of the curtain never fails to rouse in us. They are hybrid creatures, neither gay like butterflies nor somber like their own species. Nevertheless the present specimen, with his narrow hay-colored wings, fringed with a tassel of the same color, seemed to be content with life. It was a pleasant morning, mid-September, mild, benignant, yet with a keener breath than that of the summer months. The plow was already scoring the field opposite the window, and where the share had been, the earth was pressed flat and gleamed with moisture. Such vigor came rolling in from the fields and the down beyond that it was difficult to keep the eyes strictly turned upon the book. The rooks too were keeping one of their annual festivities; soaring round the tree tops until it looked as if a vast net with thousands of black knots in it had been cast up into the air; which, after a few moments, sank slowly down upon the trees until every twig seemed to have a knot at the end of it. Then, suddenly, the net would be thrown into the air again in a wider circle this time, with the utmost clamor and vocifera- tion, as though to be thrown into the air and settle slowly down upon the tree tops were a tremendously, exciting experience.

The same energy which inspired the rooks, the ploughmen, the horses, and even, it seemed, the lean bare-backed downs, sent the moth fluttering from side to side of his square of the windowpane. One could not help watching him. One was, indeed, conscious of a queer feeling of pity for him. The possibilities of pleasure seemed that morning so enormous and so various that to have only a moth's part in life, and a day moth's at that, appeared a hard fate, and his zest in enjoying his meager opportunities to the full, pathetic. He flew vigorously to one corner of his compartment, and, after waiting there a second, flew across to the other. What remained for him but to fly to a third corner and then to a fourth? That was all he could do, in spite of the size of the downs, the width of the sky, the far-off smoke of houses, and the romantic voice, now and then, of a steamer out at sea. What he could do he did. Watching him, it seemed as if a fiber, very thin but pure, of the enormous energy of the world had been thrust into his frail and diminutive body. As often as he crossed the pane, I could fancy that a thread of vital light became visible. He was little or nothing but life.

Yet, because he was so small, and so simple a form of the energy that was rolling in at the open window and driving its way through so many narrow and intricate corridors in my own brain and in those of other human beings, there was something marvelous as well as pathetic about him. It was as if someone had taken a tiny bead of pure life and decking it as lightly as possible with down and feathers, had set it dancing and zigzagging to show us the true nature of life. Thus displayed one could not get over the strangeness of it. One is apt to forget all about life, seeing it humped and bossed and garnished and cumbered so that it has to move with the greatest circumspection and dignity. Again, the thought of all that life might have been had he been born in any other shape caused one to view his simple activities with a kind of pity.

After a time, tired by his dancing apparently, he settled on the window ledge in the sun, and, the queer spectacle being at an end, I forgot about him. Then, looking up, my eye was caught by him. He was trying to resume his dancing, but seemed either so stiff or so awkward that he could only flutter to the bottom of the window-pane; and when he tried to fly across it he failed. Being intent on other matters I watched these futile attempts for a time without thinking, unconsciously waiting for him to resume his flight, as one waits for a machine, that has stopped momentarily, to start again without considering the reason of its failure. After perhaps a seventh attempt he slipped from the wooden ledge and fell, fluttering his wings, on to his back on the window sill. The helplessness of his attitude roused me. It flashed upon me that he was in difficulties; he could no longer raise himseif; his legs struggled vainly. But, as I stretched out a pencil, meaning to help him to right himself, it came over me that the failure and awkwardness were the approach of death. I laid the pencil down again.

The legs agitated themselves once more. I looked as if for the enemy against   5
which he struggled. I looked out of doors. What had happened there? Presumably it was midday, and work in the fields had stopped. Stillness and quiet had replaced the previous animation. The birds had taken themselves off to feed in the brooks. The horses stood still. Yet the power was there all the same, massed outside, indifferent, impersonal, not attending to anything in particular. Somehow it was opposed to the little hay-colored moth. It was useless to try to do anything. One could only watch the extraordinary efforts made by those tiny legs against an oncoming doom which could, had it chosen, have submerged an entire city, not merely a city, but masses of human beings; nothing, I knew, had any chance against death. Nevertheless after a pause of exhaustion the legs fluttered again. It was superb, this last protest, and so frantic that he succeeded at last in righting himself. One's sympathies, of course, were all on the side of life. Also, when there was nobody to care or to know, this gigantic effort on the part of an insignificant little moth, against a power of such magnitude, to retain what no one else valued or desired to keep, moved one strangely. Again, somehow, one saw life, a pure bead. I lifted the pencil again, useless though I knew it to be. But even as I did so, the unmistakable tokens of death showed themselves. The body relaxed, and instantly grew stiff. The struggle was over. The insignificant little creature now knew death. As I looked at the dead moth, this minute wayside triumph of so great a force over so mean an antagonist filled me with wonder. Just as life had been strange a few minutes before, so death was now as strange. The moth having righted himself now lay most decently and uncomplainingly composed. O yes, he seemed to say, death is stronger than I am.

QUESTIONS AND SUGGESTIONS FOR WRITING

1. Is the tone of the first part of the first sentence (up to the semicolon) maintained throughout the first paragraph? Set forth your answer in a detailed paragraph of your own, citing evidence to support your view.

2. What does Woolf mean in paragraph 3 when she says, "One is apt to forget all about life, seeing it humped and bossed and garnished and cumbered so that it has to move with the greatest circumspection and dignity"?

3. The author personifies the moth. (For a discussion of personification, see page 728.) She attributes to it qualities we find in human beings. For example, in the next-to-last sentence, the moth is "uncomplaining." Why does Woolf use this kind of irrational, figurative speech?

4. What is the season, and the time span covered? How are these relevant to the thesis of the essay?

5. Write an essay of 250 words, describing a creature in action (anything from an ant to an elephant or whale), connecting the creature with your sense of human life.

E. M. Forster (English. 1879–1970)

MY WOOD

A few years ago I wrote a book which dealt in part with the difficulties of the English in India. Feeling that they would have had no difficulties in India themselves, the Americans read the book freely. The more they read it the better it made them feel, and a check to the author was the result. I bought a wood with the check. It is not a large wood—it contains scarcely any trees, and it is intersected, blast it, by a public footpath. Still, it is the first property that I have owned, so it is right that other people should participate in my shame, and should ask themselves, in accents that will vary in horror, this very important question: What is the effect of property upon the character? Don't let's touch economics; the effect of private ownership upon the community as a whole is another question—a more important question, perhaps, but another one. Let's keep to psychology. If you own things, what's their effect on you? What's the effect on me of my wood?

In the first place, it makes me feel heavy. Property does have this effect. Property produces men of weight, and it was a man of weight who failed to get into the Kingdom of Heaven. He was not wicked, that unfortunate millionaire in the parable, he was only stout; he stuck out in front, not to mention behind, and as he wedged himself this way and that in the crystalline entrance and bruised his well-fed flanks, he saw beneath him a comparatively slim camel passing through the eye of a needle and being woven into the robe of God. The Gospels all through couple stoutness and slowness. They point out what is perfectly obvious, yet seldom realized: that if you have a lot of things you cannot move about a lot, that furniture requires dusting, dusters require servants, servants require insurance stamps, and the whole tangle of them makes you think twice before you accept an invitation to dinner or go for a bathe in the Jordan. Sometimes the Gospels proceed further and say with Tolstoy that property is sinful; they approach the difficult ground of asceticism here, where I cannot follow them. But as to the immediate effects of property on people, they just show straightforward logic. It produces men of weight. Men of weight cannot, by definition, move like the lightning from the East unto the West, and the ascent of a fourteen-stone[1] bishop into a pulpit is thus the exact antithesis of the coming of the Son of Man. My wood makes me feel heavy.

In the second place, it makes me feel it ought to be larger.

The other day I heard a twig snap in it. I was annoyed at first, for I thought that someone was blackberrying, and depreciating the value of the undergrowth. On coming nearer, I saw it was not a man who had trodden on the twig and snapped it, but a bird, and I felt pleased. My bird. The bird was not equally pleased. Ignoring the relation between us, it took fright as soon as it saw the shape of my face, and flew straight over the boundary hedge into a field, the property of Mrs. Henessy, where it sat down with a loud squawk. It had become Mrs. Henessy's bird. Something seemed grossly amiss here, something that would not have occurred had the wood been larger. I could not afford to buy Mrs. Henessy out, I dared not murder her, and limitations of this sort beset me on every side. Ahab did not want that vineyard—he only needed it to round off his property, preparatory to plotting a new curve—and all the land around my wood has become necessary to me in order to round off the wood. A boundary protects. But—poor little thing—the boundary ought in its turn to be protected. Noises on the edge of it. Children throw stones. A little more, and then a little more, until we reach the sea. Happy Canute! Happier Alexander! And after all, why should even the world be the limit of possession? A rocket containing a Union Jack, will, it is hoped, be shortly fired at the moon. Mars. Sirius. Beyond which . . . But these immensities ended by saddening me. I could not suppose that my wood was the destined nucleus of universal dominion—it is so very small and contains no mineral wealth beyond the blackberries. Nor was I comforted when Mrs. Henessy's bird took alarm for the second time and flew clean away from us all, under the belief that it belonged to itself.

In the third place, property makes its owner feel that he ought to do some-   5
thing to it. Yet he isn't sure what. A restlessness comes over him, a vague sense that he has a personality to express—the same sense which, without any vagueness, leads the artist to an act of creation. Sometimes I think I will cut down such trees as remain in the wood, at other times I want to fill up the gaps between them with new trees. Both impulses are pretentious and empty. They are not honest movements towards money-making or beauty. They spring from a foolish desire to express myself and from an inability to enjoy what I have got. Creation, property, enjoyment form a sinister trinity in the human mind. Creation and enjoyment are both very very good, yet they are often unattainable without a material basis, and at such moments property pushes itself in as a substitute, saying, "Accept me instead—I'm good enough for all three." It is not enough. It is, as Shakespeare said of lust, "The expense of spirit in a waste of shame": it is "Before, a joy proposed; behind, a dream." Yet we don't know how to shun it. It is forced on us by our economic system as the alternative to starvation. It is also forced on us by an internal defect in the soul, by the feeling that in property may

---

[1] A stone, an English unit of weight, is fourteen pounds; therefore, a fourteen-stone bishop would weigh 196 pounds.—ED.

lie the germs of self-development and of exquisite or heroic deeds. Our life on earth is, and ought to be, material and carnal. But we have not yet learned to manage our materialism and carnality properly; they are still entangled with the desire for ownership, where (in the words of Dante) "Possession is one with loss."

And this brings us to our fourth and final point: the blackberries.

Blackberries are not plentiful in this meager grove, but they are easily seen from the public footpath which traverses it, and all too easily gathered. Foxgloves, too—people will pull up the foxgloves, and ladies of an educational tendency even grub for toadstools to show them on the Monday in class. Other ladies, less educated, roll down the bracken in the arms of their gentlemen friends. There is paper, there are tins. Pray, does my wood belong to me or doesn't it? And, if it does, should I not own it best by allowing no one else to walk there? There is a wood near Lyme Regis, also cursed by a public footpath, where the owner has not hesitated on this point. He has built high stone walls each side of the path, and has spanned it by bridges, so that the public circulate like termites while he gorges on the blackberries unseen. He really does own his wood, this able chap. Dives in Hell did pretty well, but the gulf dividing him from Lazarus could be traversed by vision, and nothing traverses it here.[2] And perhaps I shall come to this in time. I shall wall in and fence out until I really taste the sweets of property. Enormously stout, endlessly avaricious, pseudo-creative, intensely selfish, I shall weave upon my forehead the quadruple crown of possession until those nasty Bolshies come and take it off again and thrust me aside into the outer darkness.

QUESTIONS AND SUGGESTIONS FOR WRITING

1. Much of the strength of the essay lies in its concrete presentation of generalities. Note, for example, that the essay is called "My Wood," but we might say that the general idea of the essay is "The Effect of Property on Its Owners." Forster gives four effects, chiefly through concrete statements. Put these four effects into four general statements.

2. How would you characterize Forster? Point to some sentences to support your characterization.

3. Write an essay of 500 to 750 words on the effect a new possession (perhaps a pet, a car, or a stereo set) had on you. Remember that in a good essay the author presents a persona (see page 4) as well as information or opinions. When you revise your essay, try to read it impartially to see if your readers will get a sense of a particular kind of person.

4. Write an essay of 500 to 750 words on the effect of some change in your life—say, graduating from school, or enduring a prolonged illness, or living for a while with a new member in your household (a grandparent, for example, or a stepparent). You may wish to imitate Forster's tone.

[2] According to Christ's parable in Luke 16:19–26, the rich man (unnamed, but traditionally known as *Dives*, the Latin word for "rich man") at whose gate the poor man Lazarus had begged was sent to hell, from where he could see Lazarus in heaven.—ED.

Alice Walker (American. b. 1944)

IN SEARCH OF OUR MOTHERS' GARDENS

I

I described her own nature and temperament. Told how they needed a larger life for their expression. . . . I pointed out that in lieu of proper channels, her emotions had overflowed into paths that dissipated them. I talked beautifully I thought, about an art that would be born, an art that would open the way for women the likes of her. I asked her to hope, and build up an inner life against the coming of that day. . . . I sang, with a strange quiver in my voice, a promise song.

—"Avey," Jean Toomer, *Cane*

The poet speaking to a prostitute who falls asleep while he's talking—

When the poet Jean Toomer walked through the South in the early twenties, he discovered a curious thing: Black women whose spirituality was so intense, so deep, so *unconscious*, they were themselves unaware of the richness they held. They stumbled blindly through their lives: creatures so abused and mutilated in body, so dimmed and confused by pain, that they considered themselves unworthy even of hope. In the selfless abstractions their bodies became to the men who used them, they became more than "sexual objects," more even than mere women: they became Saints. Instead of being perceived as whole persons, their bodies became shrines: what was thought to be their minds became temples suitable for worship. These crazy "Saints" stared out at the world, wildly, like lunatics—or quietly, like suicides; and the "God" that was in their gaze was as mute as a great stone.

Who were these "Saints"? These crazy, loony, pitiful women?

Some of them, without a doubt, were our mothers and grandmothers.

In the still heat of the post-Reconstruction South, this is how they seemed to   5
Jean Toomer: exquisite butterflies trapped in an evil honey, toiling away their lives in an era, a century, that did not acknowledge them, except as "the *mule* of the world." They dreamed dreams that no one knew—not even themselves, in any coherent fashion—and saw visions no one could understand. They wandered or sat about the countryside crooning lullabies to ghosts, and drawing the mother of Christ in charcoal on courthouse walls.

They forced their minds to desert their bodies and their striving spirits sought to rise, like frail whirlwinds from the hard red clay. And when those frail whirlwinds fell, in scattered particles, upon the ground, no one mourned. Instead, men lit candles to celebrate the emptiness that remained, as people do who enter a beautiful but vacant space to resurrect a God.

Our mothers and grandmothers, some of them: moving to music not yet written. And they waited.

They waited for a day when the unknown thing that was in them would be made known; but guessed, somehow in their darkness, that on the day of their revelation they would be long dead. Therefore to Toomer they walked, and even ran, in slow motion. For they were going nowhere immediate, and the future was not yet within their grasp. And men took our mothers and grandmothers, "but got no pleasure from it." So complex was their passion and their calm.

To Toomer, they lay vacant and fallow as autumn fields, with harvest time never in sight: and he saw them enter loveless marriages, without joy; and become prostitutes, without resistance; and become mothers of children without fulfillment.

For these grandmothers and mothers of ours were not "Saints," but Artists;   10 driven to a numb and bleeding madness by the springs of creativity in them for which there was no release. They were Creators, who lived lives of spiritual waste, because they were so rich in spirituality—which is the basis of Art—that the strain of enduring their unused and unwanted talent drove them insane. Throwing away this spirituality was their pathetic attempt to lighten the soul to a weight their work-worn, sexually abused bodies could bear.

What did it mean for a Black woman to be an artist in our grandmothers' time? In our great-grandmothers' day? It is a question with an answer cruel enough to stop the blood.

Did you have a genius of a great-great-grandmother who died under some ignorant and depraved white overseer's lash? Or was she required to bake biscuits for a lazy backwater tramp, when she cried out in her soul to paint watercolors of sunsets, or the rain falling on the green and peaceful pasturelands? Or was her body broken and forced to bear children (who were more often than not sold away from her)—eight, ten, fifteen, twenty children—when her one joy was the thought of modeling heroic figures of Rebellion, in stone or clay?

How was the creativity of the Black woman kept alive, year after year and century after century, when for most of the years Black people have been in America, it was a punishable crime for a Black person to read or write? And the freedom to paint, to sculpt, to expand the mind with action, did not exist. Consider, if you can bear to imagine it, what might have been the result if singing, too, had been forbidden by law. Listen to the voices of Bessie Smith, Billie Holiday, Nina Simone, Roberta Flack, and Aretha Franklin, among others, and imagine those voices muzzled for life. Then you may begin to comprehend the lives of our "crazy," "Sainted" mothers and grandmothers. The agony of the lives of women who might have been Poets, Novelists, Essayists, and Short Story Writers (over a period of centuries), who died with their real gifts stifled within them.

And, if this were the end of the story, we would have cause to cry out in my paraphrase of Okot p'Bitek's great poem:

> O, my clanswomen
> Let us all cry together!
> Come,
> Let us mourn the death of our mother,
> The death of a Queen
> The ash that was produced
> By a great fire!
> O this homestead is utterly dead
> Close the gates

With *lacari* thorns,
For our mother
The creator of the Stool is lost!
And all the young women
Have perished in the wilderness![1]

But this is not the end of the story, for all the young women—our mothers   15
and grandmothers, *ourselves*—have not perished in the wilderness. And if we ask
ourselves why, and search for and find the answer, we will know beyond all efforts
to erase it from our minds, just exactly who, and of what, we Black American
women are.

One example, perhaps the most pathetic, most misunderstood one, can provide a backdrop for our mothers' work: Phillis Wheatley, a slave in the 1700s.

Virginia Woolf, in her book, *A Room of One's Own,* wrote that in order for a
woman to write fiction she must have two things, certainly: a room of her own
(with key and lock) and enough money to support herself.

What then are we to make of Phillis Wheatley, a slave, who owned not even
herself? This sickly, frail, Black girl who required a servant of her own at times—
her health was so precarious—and who, had she been white, would have been
easily considered the intellectual superior of all the women and most of the men in
the society of her day.

Virginia Woolf wrote further, speaking of course not of our Phillis, that "any
woman born with a great gift in the sixteenth century [insert *eighteenth century,*
insert *Black woman,* insert *born or made a slave*] would certainly have gone
crazed, shot herself, or ended her days in some lonely cottage outside the village,
half witch, half wizard [insert *Saint,*] feared and mocked at. For it needs little skill
and psychology to be sure that a highly gifted girl who had tried to use her gift for
poetry would have been so thwarted and hindered by contrary instincts [add
*chains, guns, the lash, the ownership of one's body by someone else, submission to
an alien religion,*] that she must have lost her health and sanity to a certainty."

The key words, as they relate to Phillis, are "contrary instincts." For when   20
we read the poetry of Phillis Wheatley—as when we read the novels of Nella
Larsen or the oddly false-sounding autobiography of that freest of all Black women
writers, Zora Hurston—evidence of "contrary instincts" is everywhere. Her loyalties were completely divided, as was, without question, her mind.

But how could this be otherwise? Captured at seven, a slave of wealthy,
doting whites who instilled in her the "savagery" of the Africa they "rescued"
her from . . . one wonders if she was even able to remember her homeland as
she had known it, or as it really was.

Yet, because she did try to use her gift for poetry in a world that made her a
slave, she was "so thwarted and hindered by . . . contrary instincts that she . . .
lost her health. . . ." In the last years of her brief life, burdened not only with the

---

[1] Okot p'Bitek, *Song of Lawino: An Africa Lament* (Nairobi: East African Publishing House,
1966).

need to express her gift but also with a penniless, friendless "freedom" and several small children for whom she was forced to do strenuous work to feed, she lost her health, certainly. Suffering from malnutrition and neglect and who knows what mental agonies, Phillis Wheatley died.

So torn by "contrary instincts" was Black, kidnapped, enslaved Phillis that her description of "the Goddess"—as she poetically called the Liberty she did not have—is ironically, cruelly humorous. And, in fact, has held Phillis up to ridicule for more than a century. It is usually read prior to hanging Phillis's memory as that of a fool. She wrote:

> The Goddess comes, she moves divinely fair,
> Olive and laurel binds her *golden* hair:
> Wherever shines this native of the skies,
> Unnumber'd charms and recent graces rise.
>   [Emphasis mine]

It is obvious that Phillis, the slave, combed the "Goddess's" hair every morning; prior, perhaps, to bringing in the milk, or fixing her mistress's lunch. She took her imagery from the one thing she saw elevated above all others.

With the benefit of hindsight we ask, "How could she?"   25

But at last, Phillis, we understand. No more snickering when your stiff, struggling, ambivalent lines are forced on us. We know now that you were not an idiot nor a traitor; only a sickly little Black girl, snatched from your home and country and made a slave; a woman who still struggled to sing the song that was your gift, although in a land of barbarians who praised you for your bewildered tongue. It is not so much what you sang, as that you kept alive, in so many of our ancestors, *the notion of song.*

II

Black women are called, in the folklore that so aptly identifies one's status in society, "the *mule* of the world," because we have been handed the burdens that everyone else—*everyone* else—refused to carry. We have been called "Matriarchs," "Superwomen," and "Mean and Evil Bitches." Not to mention "Castrators" and "Sapphire's Mama." When we have pleaded for understanding, our character has been distorted; when we have asked for simple caring, we have been handed empty inspirational appellations, then stuck in the farthest corner. When we have asked for love, we have been given children. In short, even our plainer gifts, our labors of fidelity and love, have been knocked down our throats. To be an Artist and a Black woman, even today, lowers our status in many respects, rather than raises it: and yet, Artists we will be.

Therefore we must fearlessly pull out of ourselves and look at and identify with our lives the living creativity some of our great-grandmothers were not allowed to know. I stress *some* of them because it is well known that the majority of our great-grandmothers knew, even without "knowing" it, the reality of their spirituality, even if they didn't recognize it beyond what happened in the singing at church—and they never had any intention of giving it up.

How they did it: those millions of Black women who were not Phillis Wheatley, or Lucy Terry or Frances Harper or Zora Hurston or Nella Larsen or Bessie Smith—nor Elizabeth Catlett, nor Katherine Dunham, either—brings me to the title of this essay, "In Search of Our Mothers' Gardens," which is a personal account that is yet shared, in its theme and its meaning, by all of us. I found, while thinking about the far-reaching world of the creative Black woman, that often the truest answer to a question that really matters can be found very close.

In the late 1920s my mother ran away from home to marry my father. Marriage, if not running away, was expected of seventeen-year-old girls. By the time she was twenty, she had two children and was pregnant with a third. Five children later, I was born. And this is how I came to know my mother: she seemed a large, soft, loving-eyed woman who was rarely impatient in our home. Her quick, violent temper was on view only a few times a year, when she battled with the white landlord who had the misfortune to suggest to her that her children did not need to go to school.   30

She made all the clothes we wore, even my brothers' overalls. She made all the towels and sheets we used. She spent the summers canning vegetables and fruits. She spent the winter evenings making quilts enough to cover all our beds.

During the "working" day, she labored beside—not behind—my father in the fields. Her day began before sunup, and did not end until late at night. There was never a moment for her to sit down, undisturbed, to unravel her own private thoughts; never a time free from interruption—by work or the noisy inquiries of her many children. And yet, it is to my mother—and all our mothers who were not famous—that I went in search of the secret of what has fed that muzzled and often mutilated, but vibrant, creative spirit that the Black woman has inherited, and that pops out in wild and unlikely places to this day.

But when, you will ask, did my overworked mother have time to know or care about feeding the creative spirit?

The answer is so simple that many of us have spent years discovering it. We have constantly looked high, when we should have looked high—and low.

For example: in the Smithsonian Institution in Washington, D.C., there hangs a quilt unlike any other in the world. In fanciful, inspired, and yet simple and identifiable figures, it portrays the story of the Crucifixion. It is considered rare, beyond price. Though it follows no known pattern of quiltmaking, and though it is made of bits and pieces of worthless rags, it is obviously the work of a person of powerful imagination and deep spiritual feeling. Below this quilt I saw a note that says it was made by "an anonymous Black woman in Alabama, a hundred years ago."   35

If we could locate this "anonymous" Black woman from Alabama, she would turn out to be one of our grandmothers—an artist who left her mark in the only materials she could afford, and in the only medium her position in society allowed her to use.

As Virginia Woolf wrote further, in *A Room of One's Own:*

"Yet genius of a sort must have existed among women as it must have existed among the working class. [Change this to *slaves* and *the wives and daughters of sharecroppers*.] Now and again an Emily Brontë or a Robert Burns [change this to *a Zora Hurston or a Richard Wright*] blazes out and proves its presence. But certainly it never got itself on to paper. When, however, one reads of a witch being ducked, of a woman possessed by devils [or *Sainthood*], of a wise woman selling herbs [our rootworkers], or even a very remarkable man who had a mother, then I think we are on the track of a suppressed poet, of some mute and inglorious Jane Austen. . . . Indeed, I would venture to guess that Anon, who wrote so many poems without singing them, was often a woman. . . ."

And so our mothers and grandmothers have, more often than not anonymously, handed on the creative spark, the seed of the flower they themselves never hoped to see: or like a sealed letter they could not plainly read.

And so it is, certainly, with my own mother. Unlike Ma Rainey's songs, which   40
retained their creator's name even while blasting forth from Bessie Smith's mouth, no song or poem will bear my mother's name. Yet so many of the stories that I write, that we all write, are my mother's stories. Only recently did I fully realize this: that through years of listening to my mother's stories of her life, I have absorbed not only the stories themselves, but something of the manner in which she spoke, something of the urgency that involves the knowledge that her stories—like her life—must be recorded. It is probably for this reason that so much of what I have written is about characters whose counterparts in real life are so much older than I am.

But the telling of these stories, which came from my mother's lips as naturally as breathing, was not the only way my mother showed herself as an artist. For stories, too, were subject to being distracted, to dying without conclusion. Dinners must be started, and cotton must be gathered before the big rains. The artist that was and is my mother showed itself to me only after many years. This is what I finally noticed:

Like Mem, a character in *The Third Life of Grange Copeland,* my mother adorned with flowers whatever shabby house we were forced to live in. And not just your typical straggly country stand of zinnias, either. She planted ambitious gardens—and still does—with over fifty different varieties of plants that bloom profusely from early March until late November. Before she left home for the fields, she watered her flowers, chopped up the grass, and laid out new beds. When she returned from the fields she might divide clumps of bulbs, dig a cold pit, uproot and replant roses, or prune branches from her taller bushes or trees—until night came and it was too dark to see.

Whatever she planted grew as if by magic, and her fame as a grower of flowers spread over three counties. Because of her creativity with her flowers, even my memories of poverty are seen through a screen of blooms—sunflowers, petunias, roses, dahlias, forsythia, spirea, delphiniums, verbena . . . and on and on.

And I remember people coming to my mother's yard to be given cuttings from her flowers; I hear again the praise showered on her because whatever rocky soil she landed on, she turned into a garden. A garden so brilliant with colors, so original in its design, so magnificent with life and creativity, that to this day people drive by our house in Georgia—perfect strangers and imperfect strangers—and ask to stand or walk among my mother's art.

I notice that it is only when my mother is working in her flowers that she is   45
radiant, almost to the point of being invisible—except as Creator: hand and eye.
She is involved in work her soul must have. Ordering the universe in the image of
her personal conception of Beauty.

Her face, as she prepares the Art that is her gift, is a legacy of respect she
leaves to me, for all that illuminates and cherishes life. She has handed down
respect for the possibilities—and the will to grasp them.

For her, so hindered and intruded upon in so many ways, being an artist has
still been a daily part of her life. This ability to hold on, even in very simple ways,
is work Black women have done for a very long time.

This poem is not enough, but it is something, for the woman who literally
covered the holes in our walls with sunflowers:

> They were women then
> My mama's generation
> Husky of voice—Stout of
> Step
> With fists as well as
> Hands
> How they battered down
> Doors
> And ironed
> Starched white
> Shirts
> How they led
> Armies
> Headragged Generals
> Across mined
> Fields
> Booby-trapped
> Ditches
> To discover books
> Desks
> A place for us
> How they knew what we
> *Must* know
> Without knowing a page
> Of it
> Themselves.

Guided by my heritage of a love of beauty and a respect for strength—in
search of my mother's garden, I found my own.

And perhaps in Africa over two hundred years ago, there was just such a   50
mother; perhaps she painted vivid and daring decorations in oranges and yellows
and greens on the walls of her hut; perhaps she sang—in a voice like Roberta
Flack's—*sweetly* over the compounds of her village; perhaps she wove the most
stunning mats or told the most ingenious stories of all the village story-tellers.
Perhaps she was herself a poet—though only her daughter's name is signed to
the poems that we know.

Perhaps Phillis Wheatley's mother was also an artist.

Perhaps in more than Phillis Wheatley's biological life is her mother's signature made clear.

QUESTIONS AND SUGGESTIONS FOR WRITING

1. Can you justify the great shift in tone between "their gaze was as mute as a great stone" and "loony" (second and third paragraphs)? If so, how?
2. Explain Walker's assertion (paragraph 10) that "these grandmothers and mothers of ours were not 'Saints,' but Artists." In this view, what are the qualities of an artist?
3. Pick out two or three sentences that strike you as especially interesting, either because of what they say or because of the way they say it (or both), and try to account for their appeal.
4. Explain the last sentence of the essay.
5. Outline the organization of this essay; that is, list in order the main topics and then explain the relationships between these parts. Then, in one or two sentences, summarize Walker's thesis or argument.

Analytic Writing: An Overview

Why Write?

People write not only to communicate with others but also to clarify and to account for their responses to material that interests or excites or frustrates them. In putting words on paper you will have to take a second and a third look at what is in front of you and at what is within you. And so the process of writing is a way of learning. The last word is never said about complex thoughts and feelings, but when we write we hope to make at least a little progress in the difficult but rewarding job of talking about our responses. We learn, and then we hope to interest our reader because we are communicating our responses to material that for one reason or another is worth talking about.

When you write, you transform your responses into words that will let your reader share your perceptions, your enthusiasms, and even your doubts. This sharing is, in effect, teaching. Students often think that they are writing for the teacher, but this is a misconception. When you write, *you* are the teacher. An essay on literature is an attempt to help someone to see something as you see it.

If you are not writing for the teacher, for whom are you writing? For yourself, of course, but also for others. Occasionally, in an effort to help you develop an awareness that what you write depends partly on your audience, your instructor may specify an audience, requiring you to write for high school students, or for the readers of *The Atlantic* or *Ms*. But if an audience is not specified, write for your classmates. If you keep your classmates in mind as your audience, you will not write, "William Shakespeare, England's most famous playwright," because such a remark offensively implies that the reader does not know Shakespeare's nationality or trade. On the other hand, you *will* write, "Sei Shōnagon, a lady of the court in medieval Japan," because you can reasonably assume that your classmates do not know who she is.

Analysis

Most of the writing that you will do in college—not only in your English courses but in courses in history, sociology, economics, fine arts, and philosophy—will be analytic. **Analysis**, literally a separating of a whole into parts, is a method we commonly use in thinking about complex matters and in attempting to account for our responses. Watching John McEnroe play tennis, we may admire his serve, or his backhand, or the execution of several brilliant plays, and then think more generally about the concentration and flexibility that allow him to capitalize on his opponent's momentary weakness. Or stopping before a painting, we may take a close look at the brushwork, move a few steps back to think about the content represented, and then move even further back to take in anew the overall design. Similarly, in analyzing a literary work—a piece of fiction, for example—we commonly take a second and a third look at such components as the narrator, the other characters, the plot, the dialogue, the setting, and the overall construction. Through analysis we come to a better understanding, and a better understanding yields an increase in pleasure.

To develop an analysis, we tend, whether consciously or not, to formulate questions and then to answer them. We ask such questions as: What is the function of the setting? Why has this character been introduced here? What is the author getting at? How exactly can I describe the tone? What is the difference in tone between these two essays? This book contains a small anthology of literary works for you to practice writing about, and after most of the works we pose such questions. Later in the book we also pose more general questions on fiction (page 717), poetry (page 732), and drama (page 747). These questions may stimulate thought and thus help you to write about any literary work. Our concern as teachers of writing is not so much with the answers to these questions; we believe and we ask you to believe that there are in fact no "right answers," only more or less persuasive ones, to most questions about literature—or about life. Our aim, rather, is to help you to locate appropriate topics that will stimulate your thinking.

Choosing a Topic and Developing a Thesis

What is an appropriate topic? First, it must be a topic you can work up some interest in, or your writing will be mechanical and dull. (We say work up some interest because interest is commonly the result of some effort.) Second, an appropriate topic is compassable—that is, it is something you can cover with reasonable attention to detail in the few pages (and few days) you have to devote to it. If a work is fairly long, almost surely you will write an analysis of some part. Unless you have an enormous amount of time for reflection and revision you cannot write a meaningful essay of five hundred words or even a thousand words on "Shakespeare's *Hamlet*" or "Melville's *Moby-Dick*." You cannot even write on "Character in *Hamlet*" or "Symbolism in *Moby-Dick*." And probably you won't really want to write on such topics anyway. Probably *one* character or *one* symbol has caught your interest. Trust your feelings; you are likely onto something interesting. A "smaller" topic need not be a dull or trivial topic; treated properly, it may serve as a mine shaft that gives entry to the work. "The Role of Providence in *Hamlet*," carefully thought about, will in five hundred or a thousand words tell a reader more (and will have taught its author more) than will "*Hamlet* as a Tragedy." Similarly, "The Meanings of 'Economy' in *Walden*" is a better topic than "The Meaning of *Walden*."

Given an appropriate topic, you will find your essay easier to write and the finished version of it clearer and more persuasive, if at some point in your preparation, in note taking or in writing a first draft, you have converted your topic into a *thesis* (an argument or proposition) and constructed a *thesis statement* (a sentence stating your overall point).

Let's dwell a moment on the distinction between a topic and a thesis. It may be useful to think of it this way: A topic is a subject (for example, "The Role of Providence in *Hamlet*"); to arrive at a thesis, you have to add a predicate (for example, "The role of Providence in *Hamlet* is not obvious but it is crucial," or "The role of Providence in *Hamlet* is inconsistent"). Of course, some theses are more promising than others. For example, "The role of Providence in *Hamlet* is interesting" is a thesis, but it is vague and provides little direction, little help in generating ideas and in shaping your essay. Let's try again. It's almost always necessary to try and try again, for the process of writing is in large part a process of trial and error, of generating better and better ideas through the act of writing. "The role of Providence is not confined to the appearance of the Ghost, but is also found in the killing of Polonius, in the surprising appearance of the pirate ship, and in the presence of the poisoned chalice."

Every literary work affords its own topics for analysis, and all essayists must set forth their own theses, but a few useful generalizations may be made. As Robert Frost said, "All there is to learning to write or talk is learning how to have something to say," that is, how to have ideas. You may often find ideas—especially a thesis—by asking one of two questions:

1. *What purpose does this serve?* That is, why is this scene in the novel or play? Why is there a comic gravedigger in *Hamlet?* Why are these lines unrhymed? Why is this stanza form employed? What is the significance of the parts of the work? (Titles are often highly significant parts of the work: Henrik Ibsen's *A Doll's House* and Ken Kesey's *One Flew over the Cuckoo's Nest* would both have slightly different meanings if they had other titles.)

2. *Why do I have this response?* Why do I feel that this work is more profound (or amusing, or puzzling) than that work? How did the author make this character funny or dignified or pathetic? How did the author communicate the idea that this character is a bore without boring me?

The first of these questions, "What purpose does this serve?" requires that you identify yourself with the author, wondering, for example, whether this opening scene is the best possible for this story. The second question, "Why do I have this response?" requires that you trust your feelings. If you are amused or puzzled or annoyed, assume that these responses are appropriate and follow them up, at least until a rereading of the work provides other responses.

An Analysis of a Story

Let's look at a short story, and then at an essay analyzing one aspect of it. Later in this chapter we will look at two additional analyses, one of a character and one of a poem.

Kate Chopin (American. 1851–1904)

THE STORY OF AN HOUR

Knowing that Mrs. Mallard was afflicted with a heart trouble, great care was taken to break to her as gently as possible the news of her husband's death.

It was her sister Josephine who told her, in broken sentences, veiled hints that revealed in half concealing. Her husband's friend Richards was there, too, near her. It was he who had been in the newspaper office when intelligence of the railroad disaster was received, with Brently Mallard's name leading the list of "killed." He had only taken the time to assure himself of its truth by a second telegram, and had hastened to forestall any less careful, less tender friend in bearing the sad message.

She did not hear the story as many women have heard the same, with a paralyzed inability to accept its significance. She wept at once, with sudden, wild abandonment, in her sister's arms. When the storm of grief had spent itself she went away to her room alone. She would have no one follow her.

There stood, facing the open window, a comfortable, roomy armchair. Into this she sank, pressed down by a physical exhaustion that haunted her body and seemed to reach into her soul.

She could see in the open square before her house the tops of trees that were all aquiver with the new spring life. The delicious breath of rain was in the air. In the street below a peddler was crying his wares. The notes of a distant song which some one was singing reached her faintly, and countless sparrows were twittering in the eaves.

There were patches of blue sky showing here and there through the clouds that had met and piled above the other in the west facing her window.

She sat with her head thrown back upon the cushion of the chair quite motionless, except when a sob came up into her throat and shook her, as a child who has cried itself to sleep continues to sob in its dreams.

She was young, with a fair, calm face, whose lines bespoke repression and even a certain strength. But now there was a dull stare in her eyes, whose gaze was fixed away off yonder on one of those patches of blue sky. It was not a glance of reflection, but rather indicated a suspension of intelligent thought.

There was something coming to her and she was waiting for it, fearfully. What was it? She did not know; it was too subtle and elusive to name. But she felt it, creeping out of the sky, reaching toward her through the sounds, the scents, the color that filled the air.

Now her bosom rose and fell tumultuously. She was beginning to recognize this thing that was approaching to possess her, and she was striving to beat it back with her will—as powerless as her two white slender hands would have been.

When she abandoned herself a little whispered word escaped her slightly parted lips. She said it over and over under her breath: "Free, free, free!" The vacant stare and the look of terror that had followed it went from her eyes. They stayed keen and bright. Her pulses beat fast, and the coursing blood warmed and relaxed every inch of her body.

She did not stop to ask if it were not a monstrous joy that held her. A clear and exalted perception enabled her to dismiss the suggestion as trivial.

She knew that she would weep again when she saw the kind, tender hands folded in death; the face that had never looked save with love upon her, fixed and gray and dead. But she saw beyond that bitter moment a long procession of years to come that would belong to her absolutely. And she opened and spread her arms out to them in welcome.

There would be no one to live for during those coming years; she would live for herself. There would be no powerful will bending her in that blind persistence with which men and women believe they have a right to impose a private will upon a fellow-creature. A kind intention or a cruel intention made the act seem no less a crime as she looked upon it in that brief moment of illumination.

And yet she had loved him—sometimes. Often she had not. What did it   15
matter! What could love, the unsolved mystery, count for in face of this posses-sion of self-assertion which she suddenly recognized as the strongest impulse of her being.

"Free! Body and soul free!" she kept whispering.

Josephine was kneeling before the closed door with her lips to the keyhole, imploring for admission. "Louise, open the door! I beg; open the door—you will make yourself ill. What are you doing, Louise? For heaven's sake open the door."

"Go away. I am not making myself ill." No; she was drinking in a very elixir of life through that open window.

Her fancy was running riot along those days ahead of her. Spring days, and summer days, and all sorts of days that would be her own. She breathed a quick prayer that life might be long. It was only yesterday she had thought with a shudder that life might be long.

She arose at length and opened the door to her sister's importunities. There   20
was a feverish triumph in her eyes, and she carried herself unwittingly like a goddess of Victory. She clasped her sister's waist, and together they descended the stairs. Richards stood waiting for them at the bottom.

Some one was opening the front door with a latchkey. It was Brently Mallard who entered, a little travel-stained, composedly carrying his gripsack and um-brella. He had been far from the scene of accident, and did not even know there had been one. He stood amazed at Josephine's piercing cry; at Richards' quick motion to screen him from the view of his wife.

But Richards was too late.

When the doctors came they said she had died of heart disease—of joy that kills.

A Student's Analysis of "The Story of an Hour"

The student who wrote the essay that follows wrote on an assigned topic, "Irony in Kate Chopin's 'Story of an Hour.'" Her underlying thesis—that there are several ironies in the story—broke down into two parts: The chief irony is that Mrs. Mallard dies just as she is beginning to enjoy life, but there are also smaller ironies, such as that the "sad message" turns out (for a while) not to be sad, and that although Richards is "too late" when he tries to save her at the end, if he had been "late" at the beginning the whole mess would not have occurred. The topic ideas of the paragraphs of the essay turned out to be these:

1. The story has an ironic ending, but there are smaller ironies within it.
2. One of these smaller ironies is that the "sad message" turns out, at least for a while, to bring joy.
3. Two other bits of irony are (a) Richards's well-meaning haste at the beginning is not matched by adequate haste at the end, and (b) the doctors' comments on joy are true in a way that the speakers do not mean.
4. The central irony, however, is that Mrs. Mallard begins to live only after years of marriage, and this new life, which occurs appropriately at spring-time, is cut off even as she looks forward not only to summer but to "a long progression of years."

Some such thoughts must have preceded the following essay, but they were arrived at only after reading and rereading, and writing and rewriting. Don't let the excellence of this essay discourage you. You can do as well. Remember, this essay is the product of much work. As the writer wrote, her ideas got better and better, for in her drafts she put down a point and then realized that it needed strengthening (for instance, with a brief quotation) or that—come to think of it—the point couldn't be substantiated and ought to be deleted.

Ironies of Life in an Hour

Kate Chopin's "Story of an Hour"—which takes only a few minutes to read—turns out to have an ironic ending, but on rereading it one sees that the irony is not concentrated only in the outcome of the plot—Mrs. Mallard dies just when she is beginning to live—but is also present in many details.

After we know how the story turns out, if we reread it we find irony at the very start: Mrs. Mallard's friends and relatives all assume, mistakenly, that she was deeply in love with her husband, Brently Mallard, and so they take great care to tell her gently of his death. They mean well, and in fact they *do* well, for they bring her an hour of life, an hour of joyous freedom, but it is ironic that they think their news is sad. True, Mrs. Mallard at first expresses grief when she hears the news, but soon (unknown to her friends) she finds joy in it. So, Richards's "sad message" (63), though sad in Richards's eyes, is in fact a happy message.

Among the small but significant ironic details is the statement near the end of the story that when Mallard entered the house, Richards tries to conceal him from Mrs. Mallard, but

"Richards was too late" (64). This is ironic because almost at the start of the story, in the second paragraph, Richards with the best of motives "hastened" (63) to bring his sad message; if he had at the start been "too late," Mallard would have arrived at home first, and Mrs. Mallard's life would not have ended an hour later but would have gone on simply as it had been. Yet another irony at the end of the story is the diagnosis of the doctors. They say she had died of "heart disease—of joy that kills" (64). In one sense they are right: Mrs. Mallard has for the last hour experienced a great joy. But of course the doctors totally misunderstand the joy that kills her. It is not joy at seeing her husband alive, but her realization that the great joy she experienced during the last hour is over.

All of these ironic details add richness to the story, but the central irony resides not in the well-intentioned but ironic actions of Richards, or in the unconsciously ironic words of the doctors, but in Mrs. Mallard's own life. She has for years been alive, and yet in a way she has been dead, a body subjected to her husband's will. Now his apparent death brings her new life. Appropriately, this new life comes to her at the season of the year when "the tops of trees were all aquiver with the new spring life" (63). But, ironically, her new life will last only an hour. She is "Free, free, free" (63)—but only until her husband walks through the doorway. She looks forward to summer days, but she will not see even the end of this spring day. If her years of marriage were ironic, bringing her a sort of living death instead of joy, her new life is ironic too, not only because it grows out of her moment of grief for her supposedly dead husband, but because its vision of "a long progression of years" (64) is cut short within an hour on a spring day.

Works Cited

Chopin, Kate. "The Story of an Hour." Rpt. in Sylvan Barnet, Morton Berman, and William Burto, Literature for Composition, 2nd ed. Glenview, Ill.: Scott, Foresman 1988. Pages 63–64.

The Analysis Analyzed

Let's look at several principles illustrated by this essay.

1. The title of the essay is not merely the title of the work discussed; rather, it gives the reader a clue, a small idea of the essayist's topic.
2. The opening or introductory paragraph does not begin by saying "In this story . . ." Rather, by naming the author and the title, it lets the reader know exactly what story is being discussed. It also develops the writer's thesis a bit, so readers know where they will be going.
3. The smaller ironies are discussed in the second and third paragraphs, the central (chief) irony in the last paragraph. That is, the essay does not dwindle or become anticlimactic; rather, it builds up.
4. Some brief quotations are used, both to provide evidence and to let the reader hear—even if only fleetingly—Kate Chopin's writing.
5. The essayist, assuming that the reader has read the work, does not tell the plot in great detail. But, aware that the reader has not memorized the story, the essayist gives helpful reminders.
6. The essayist has opinions, but does not keep saying, "In my opinion" and "I feel that."
7. The present tense is used in narrating the action: "Mrs. Mallard dies"; "Mrs. Mallard's friends and relatives all assume."
8. Although a concluding paragraph is often useful—if it does more than merely summarize what has already been clearly said—it is not essential in a short analysis. In this essay, the last sentence explains the chief irony and therefore makes an acceptable ending.

Writing as a Process

The essay illustrates yet another principle—but it is invisible. Although the essay is a finished *product,* writing the essay is a *process,* a process of trial and error and success. When we read a lucid textbook, or an editorial in a newspaper, or even another student's paper, we are inclined to think that we cannot do as well, by which we mean that if we sat down at a desk we could not dash off a comparable piece. Of course not; nor did the authors of the effective writing that causes all of us to feel we simply aren't writers.

The student who wrote this essay on Chopin's story has given us permission to publish the first paragraph of an earlier draft of the essay. It runs thus:

"The Story of an Hour" ends ironically. But when one reads it a second time we see that the irony is not concentrated only in the outcome of the plot. The irony, as in many other works of literature, is also present in many details.

For comparison, here again is the revised version:

Kate Chopin's "Story of an Hour"—which takes only a few

minutes to read—turns out to have an ironic ending, but on rereading it one sees that the irony is not concentrated only in the outcome of the plot—Mrs. Mallard dies just when she is beginning to live—but is also present in many details.

Notice the following changes (all improvements):

1. The first sentence of the final version is more informative and interesting than the first sentence of the draft, because the writer
   a. identifies the author of the story,
   b. introduces a pleasant contrast between "an Hour" and "a few minutes"; and
   c. combines the first two sentences, since the first sentence (though true) was blunt and lacking in any detail. Notice also that in the second sentence of the draft the student wobbled from "one reads" to "we see." In the revision, she got rid of the shift in pronoun.
2. The final version drops the irrelevant reference to "many other works." The student realized, in revising, that her topic was Chopin's story, not its relationship to "other works." Of course, a specific comparison to another work might have been useful in illuminating Chopin's story, but since no such comparison was made, the vague allusion to "many other works of literature" was wisely deleted.

Perhaps it is best to think of a composition course not as a course in writing but as a course in revising. One revises one's thoughts as one rereads the assigned piece, and one revises further as one jots down notes, begins to arrange the notes, checks the text for supporting detail, fumbles toward a better organization, writes a first draft, rereads the draft, and perhaps starts all over. But the initial efforts are not a waste of time. They are necessary parts of the process, ideas that are modified or even abandoned but that lead a writer to better ideas, or to a more coherent presentation of the same ideas. A cook tastes the soup, and decides it needs a little more salt. The soup, in this stage, we can say, is unsatisfactory but it is scarcely a failure; it just needs some revising. The process goes on, more salt is added, maybe some parsley too, and the result is at last satisfactory.

The student's essay on Kate Chopin's story went through a fairly long cooking process. You can't see that, because you are being served only the final product, but the fact that the essay flows easily is indeed a sign that the chef did her work well, straining out (in the course of hours) all indigestible lumps. You can do as well, if while you write you remember that the secret ingredient in all good writing is rewriting.

Just for the record, we reproduce here our own next-to-last draft (it was the third draft) of the preceding paragraphs.

Writing as a Process

The essay illustrates yet another principle—but it is invisible:

Although the essay is a finished product, writing the essay was a process, a process of trial and error [*and success lucid*]. When we read a textbook or an editorial in a newspaper, or even another student's paper, we are inclined to think that we cannot do as well, by which we mean that if we sat down at a desk we could not ~~have~~ dashed off a comparable piece. Of course not; nor did the author of the [*effective*] writing that causes ~~you~~ [*all of us*] to feel ~~you~~ [*we*] simply aren't ~~a~~ writer[*s*].

Perhaps ~~we should~~ [*it is best to*] think of a composition course not as a course in writing but as a course in revising. One revises one's thoughts as one rereads the assigned story, and one revises further as one jots down notes, begins to arrange the notes, checks the text for supporting detail, fumbles toward a better organization, [*writes a first draft,*] rereads the ~~first~~ draft, and [*perhaps*] starts all over. But the initial efforts are not a waste of time. They are necessary parts of the process, ideas that are abandoned [*modified or even*] but that lead a writer to better ideas, or to a more coherent presentation of [*the same*] ideas. A cook tastes the soup, and decides it needs a little more salt. The soup, in this stage, we can say, is unsatisfactory [*(C plus at best)*], but it is scarcely a failure; it just needs ~~further work~~ [*some revising*]. The process goes on, more salt is added, [*and maybe some parsley too,*] and the result is at last satisfactory.

The student's essay on Kate Chopin's story went through a fairly long cooking process. You can't see that, because you are being served only the final product, but the fact that the essay flows easily is indeed a sign that the chef did her work well, straining out (in the course of hours) all indigestible lumps.

A Note on Summaries

One other point: The essay on "The Story of an Hour" does not include a **summary** because, as we mentioned, the writer knew that all of her readers were thoroughly familiar with Chopin's story. Sometimes, however, as we pointed out in Chapter 1, it is advisable to summarize the work you are writing about, thus reminding a reader who has not read the work recently, or even informing a reader who may never have read the work. A review of a new work of literature or of a new film, for instance, usually includes a summary, on the assumption that readers are unfamiliar with it.

A summary is a brief restatement or condensation of the plot. Consider, as an example, this summary of Chopin's "The Story of an Hour."

A newspaper office reports that Brently Mallard has been killed in a railroad accident. When the news is gently broken to

Mrs. Mallard by her sister Josephine, Mrs. Mallard weeps wildly and then shuts herself up in her room, where she sinks into an armchair. Staring dully through the window, she sees the signs of spring, and then an unnameable sensation possesses her. She tries to reject it but finally abandons herself to it. Renewed, she exults in her freedom, in the thought that at last the days will be her own. She finally comes out of the room, embraces her sister, and descends the stairs. A moment later her husband—who in fact had not been in the accident—enters. Mrs. Mallard dies—of the joy that kills, according to the doctors' diagnosis.

Remember:

1. A summary is much briefer than the original. It is *not* a paraphrase—a word-by-word translation of someone's words into your own. A paraphrase is usually at least as long as the original, whereas a summary is rarely longer than one-fourth of the original and is usually much shorter. A novel may be summarized in a few paragraphs, or even in one paragraph.
2. A summary usually achieves its brevity by omitting almost all of the concrete details of the original and by omitting minor characters and episodes. Notice that the summary of "The Story of an Hour" omits the friend of the family, omits specifying the signs of spring, omits the business of the sister imploring Mrs. Mallard to open the door, etc.
3. A summary is as accurate as possible, given the limits of space.
4. A summary of a literary work is normally written in the present tense. Thus, "A newspaper office report*s* . . . Mrs. Mallard weep*s* . . ."
5. Because a summary is openly based on someone else's writing and you do not claim that it presents your own ideas or even your own words, you need not use quotation marks around any words that you take from the original. Thus, after some such lead-in as "Kate Chopin's 'The Story of an Hour' may be summarized thus," you need not say such things as "Chopin then goes on to tell us that Mrs. Mallard . . ."
6. If the summary is brief (say, fewer than 250 words), it may be given as a single paragraph. But if you are summarizing a long work, you may feel that a longer summary is needed. In this case your reader will be grateful to you if you divide the summary into paragraphs. As you draft your summary, you may find natural divisions. For instance, the scene of the story may change midway, providing you with the opportunity to use two paragraphs. Or you may want to summarize a five-act play in five paragraphs.

Summaries have their place in essays, but be sure to remember that a summary is not an analysis; it is only a summary.

Communicating Judgments

Because a critical essay is a judicious attempt to help a reader see what is going on in a work or in a part of a work, the voice of the critic sounds, on first

Dynamic character — changes because of experience

Static — characters that don't change after circumstances

hearing, impartial; but good criticism includes—at least implicitly—the writer's evaluation. The critic may say not only that the setting changes (a neutral expression) but also that "the novelist aptly shifts the setting" or "unconvincingly describes . . ." or "effectively juxtaposes . . ." These evaluations are supported with evidence. The critic has feelings about the work under discussion and reveals them, not by continually saying "I feel" and "this moves me," but by calling attention to the degree of success or failure perceived. Nothing is wrong with occasionally using "I," and noticeable avoidances of it—"It is seen that," "this writer," "we," and the like—suggest an offensive sham modesty; but too much talk of "I" makes a writer sound like an egomaniac. Here is a sentence from the opening paragraph of a review of George Orwell's *1984:* "I do not think I have ever read a novel more frightening and depressing; and yet, such are the originality, the suspense, the speed of writing and withering indignation that it is impossible to put the book down." Fine—provided that the reviewer goes on to offer evidence that enables us to share his or her evaluations of *1984.*

Stock character — same qualities no matter what story "dizzy blondes"

flat character — stereotyped minor roles

round character — main characters depth, complexity, contradictions say and do surprising things 'human'

Analyzing Character

Writing about a Character

Later in this book we discuss writing about character in stories (pages 711–712) and in plays (pages 746–747), but here we want to offer a few general remarks and a sample essay. **Character**, of course, has two meanings: (1) a figure in a literary work, such as Hamlet, or Holden Caulfield, and (2) personality, that is, the mental and moral qualities of a figure, as when we say that X's character is strong, or weak, or immoral, or whatever. Thus, in writing about *a* character (a figure, whether Hamlet or Holden), you write about the character's character (personality, traits, characteristics).

Of course you may briefly summarize the author's description of the character's physical appearance (face, physique, gestures, clothing), but in doing so you will report these external appearances chiefly for the light that they shed on the figure's personality. For instance, the author who tells us that X is dressed in black is probably communicating something about X's state of mind. In a story (and in the stage directions in a play) the author may in fact explicitly describe the personality. But even if the author gives no direct explanation, you can perceive traits of character if, when you reread the work, you consider the following points.

1. What the character (the figure) says. (But keep in mind, of course, that the character may be hypocritical, or may be self-deceived. Thus, X may lament that he or she has bad luck, but the reader may perceive that X has, by his or her own actions, brought on trouble.)
2. What the character does.
3. What other characters (including the narrator of the story) say about the character. (Again, these comments may be accurate, or, since they are uttered by particular personalities, the comments may be biased in one way or another.)

4. What other characters do. (The figure you are writing about may be illuminated by others in the work, figures who do or do not engage in actions resembling the actions of your figure. For instance, in an effort to reveal Romeo's character, you may want to compare him briefly to Count Paris— another lover of Juliet—or even to Juliet, who, after all, is, like Romeo, a young lover.)

Understand Values + motives

Organizing an Analysis of a Character. As you read and reread, you will annotate your text and will jot down notes, recording (in whatever order they come to you) your thoughts about the character you are studying. When you set out to write a first draft, review these annotations and notes, and see if you can summarize your view of the character in one or two sentences: "X is . . . ," or "Although X is . . . , she is also . . ." That is, try to formulate a thesis sentence, a proposition that you will go on to support. You want to let your reader know early, probably in your first sentence—and almost certainly by the end of your first paragraph—which character you are writing about, and what your overall thesis is. If you can find an appropriate word or phrase in the text, you probably should quote it; it will lend authority to your assertion. Here are two examples of effective openings that identify the character and set forth a thesis:

> In the last speech of *Macbeth*, Malcolm characterizes Lady Macbeth as "fiend-like," and indeed she invokes evil spirits and prompts her husband to commit murder. But despite her bold front, her role in the murder, and her belief that she will be untroubled by guilt, she has a conscience that torments her and that ultimately drives her to suicide. She is not a mere heartless villain; she is a human being who is less strong—and more moral—than she thinks she is.

> Romeo begins as an adolescent, smitten with puppy love for Rosaline and a desire to show his friends that he knows the way a lover is supposed to act, but when he sees Juliet he experiences true love, and from this point on he steadily matures in the play, moving from a self-centered young man to a man who lives only for Juliet.

In your opening paragraph, try to avoid two common weaknesses (they are weaknesses because they make dull reading):

1. Avoid making a flat, unsupported assertion that the character is interesting ("Macbeth is the most interesting character in the play that bears his name"; "Holden Caulfield is a character well worth studying carefully"; "Montresor, in Poe's 'The Cask of Amontillado,' is a fascinating figure");

2. Avoid talking about yourself ("I think Lady Macbeth is more interesting than Macbeth"; "I feel a great kinship with Holden Caulfield"; "I believe that Romeo is a misunderstood figure"). Of course, your essay will be setting forth what you "think," "feel," and "believe," but try to begin with something more likely to engage a reader than assertions such as these.

The body of your essay will be devoted, of course, to supporting your thesis. If you have asserted that Lady Macbeth is cruel, domineering, and yet endowed with a conscience, you will go on in your essay to support those assertions with references to passages that demonstrate them. This does *not* mean that you tell the plot of the whole story or play; an essay on a character is by no means the same as a summary of the plot. But since you must support your generalizations, you will have to make brief references to episodes, and perhaps quote an occasional word or phrase.

There is no single way to organize an essay on a character; but two ways are common and effective. One is to let the organization of your essay reflect the organization of the literary work; that is, you might devote a paragraph to Lady Macbeth as we perceive her in the first act, and then in subsequent paragraphs go on to show that her character is later seen to be more complex than it at first appears. Such an essay may trace our changing responses. This does not mean that you need to write five paragraphs, one on her character in each of the five acts. But it does mean that you might begin with Lady Macbeth as we perceive her in, say, the first act, and then go on to the additional revelations of the rest of the play.

A second effective way of organizing an essay on a character is to set forth, early in the essay, the character's chief traits—let's say the chief strengths and two or three weaknesses—and then go on to study each trait you have listed. Here the organization would (in order to maintain the reader's interest) probably begin with the most obvious points and then move on to the less obvious, subtler points. The body of your essay, in any case, is devoted to offering evidence that suports your generalizations about the character.

What about a concluding paragraph? The concluding paragraph ought *not* to begin with the obviousness of "Thus we see," or "In conclusion," or "I recommend this story because . . ." In fact, after you have given what you consider a sound sketch of the character, it may be appropriate simply to quit. Especially if your essay has moved from the obvious traits to the more subtle and more important traits, and if your essay is fairly short (say, fewer than 500 words), a reader may not need a conclusion. Further, there probably is no reason to blunt what you have just said by adding an unnecessary and merely repetitive summary. But if you do feel that a conclusion is necessary, you may find it effective to write a summary of the character, somewhat as you did in your opening. For the conclusion, relate the character's character to the entire literary work—that is, try to give the reader a sense of the role that the character plays.

A Sample Essay on a Character. Here is a student's essay on Phoebe, Holden Caulfield's sister in J. D. Salinger's *The Catcher in the Rye.*

Phoebe Caulfield

Phoebe Josephine Caulfield, Holden's ten-year-old sister in J. D. Salinger's The Catcher in the Rye, is a child with a mind of her own. She doesn't care for her middle name, and so on the first page of one of her many notebooks she gives herself a new one: "Phoebe Weatherfield Caulfield." She is, we gather, playful and imaginative, but she is also in touch with reality, and able to get along well in the world. She has friends, and at school she is "good in all subjects." The quality that most impresses a reader, however, is not her academic excellence but her loyalty to Holden, and even when she criticizes Holden she does so out of deep love for him.

Since Holden is the narrator of the book, all that we know of Phoebe is seen through his eyes, but there is no reason to doubt his comments about her. Fairly early in the book, in Chapter 10, he gives us a long description, in the course of which he says that she is "pretty and smart," a redhead, "skinny," and (more important, of course) "affectionate." Later Holden tells us that she shares his taste in movies, and that she is a perfect partner when she dances with him. That is, Phoebe is on Holden's wave-length; the two can move in harmony, and not only when they dance. For instance, she is a good listener, and Holden desperately needs someone who can listen to him, since most of the people in his world are big talkers and are trying to impose their own values on him.

This is not to say, however, that Phoebe approves of all of Holden's actions. When she learns that he has left school, she is upset with him, but the reader always feels that any criticism she makes proceeds from her love for Holden. She is so loyal to him that she wants to leave school and go with him when he tells her he plans to run away from New York and hitchhike to the West. Her loyalty, her refusal to leave him, causes him to abandon his desperate plan to flee.

Her sincerity and her love for Holden are not enough to restore him to mental health (at the end of the book we learn that he "got sick and all," and is now in some sort of asylum), but the reader knows that if any character in the book can provide the human warmth that Holden requires, that character is his bright, strong-willed, loving "kid sister."

A few comments on this essay:

1. The writer does not cite pages because the instructor did not ask her to do so, but if your instructor asks you to give references, use the form prescribed. (On citations, see Appendix A.)
2. The opening paragraph announces the topic, gives a brief description of Phoebe (her age, her imaginativeness), and ends by focusing on her most important trait, her love for Holden.
3. The body of the essay (paragraphs 2 and 3) offers a few additional minor details, but chiefly it supports (by means of the comment on dancing) the earlier generalization that Phoebe is uniquely in harmony with Holden. It does not summarize the plot, but it does refer to certain episodes and it interprets them in order to show how they reveal Phoebe's character.
4. The final paragraph, the fourth, offers additional support (her plan to run away with Holden), and it concludes with a glance at the conclusion of the novel. Thus the essay more or less echoes the chronology of the book, but these last sentences are not mere plot-telling. Rather, they solidify the writer's view of Phoebe's character and her importance to Holden.

Analyzing a Poem

Later in this book we devote a chapter to analyzing poetry (pages 723–740), but here we want to give a sample essay, with a brief account of how the student came to develop his ideas.

We referred the student to our chapter, and he found it helpful in getting ideas about how to approach this poem.

Robert Herrick (English. 1591–1674)

UPON JULIA'S CLOTHES

Whenas in silk my Julia goes,
Then, then, methinks, how sweetly flows
That liquefaction of her clothes.

Next, when I cast mine eyes, and see
That brave° vibration, each way free,   *Splendid*   5
O, how that glittering taketh me.

On page 732 we give some questions that you can ask yourself in order to get some ideas for an essay on a poem. Among those questions are these:

Does the poem proceed in a straightforward way, or at some points does
   the speaker reverse course, altering his or her tone or perception?
What is the effect of the form?

With such questions in mind, the student was stimulated to see if there is
some sort of reversal or change in Herrick's poem, and if there is, how it is
related to the structure. After rereading the poem several times, thinking about it
in the light of these questions and perhaps others that came to mind, he produced
the following notes:

> Two stanzas, each of three lines, with the same structure
> Basic structure of 1st stanza: When X (one line), then Y
>
>   (two lines)
>
> Basic structure of second stanza: Next (one line), then Z
>
>   (two lines)

He noticed, too, in reading and rereading, that the last line—an exclamation
of delight ("O, how that glittering taketh me")—is much more personal than the
rest of the poem. A little further thought enabled him to refine this last perception:

> Although the pattern of stanzas is repeated, the somewhat
> analytic, detached tone of the beginning ("Whenas," "Then,"
> "Next") yields to an open, enthusiastic confession of delight in
> what the poet sees.

Further thinking led to this:

> Although the title is "Upon Julia's Clothes," and the first five
> lines describe Julia's silken dress, the poem finally is not only
> about Julia's clothing but about the effect of Julia (moving in
> silk that liquefies or seems to become a liquid) on the poet.

This is a nice observation, but when the student looked again at the poem the
next day, and started to write about it, he found that he was able to refine his
observation.

> Even at the beginning, the speaker is not entirely detached, for
> he speaks of "my Julia."

In writing about Herrick's "Upon Julia's Clothes," the student tells us, the
thoughts did not come quickly or neatly. After two or three thoughts, he started
to write. Only after drafting a paragraph, and rereading the poem, did he notice
that the personal element appears not only in the last line ("taketh *me*") but even

in the first line ("*my* Julia"). In short, for almost all of us, the only way to get to a good final essay is to read, to think, to jot down ideas, to write a draft, and to revise and revise again. Having gone through such processes, the student came up with the following excellent essay.

By the way, the student did not hit on the final version of his title ("Herrick's Julia, Julia's Herrick") until shortly before he typed his final version. His preliminary title was "Structure and Personality in Herrick's 'Upon Julia's Clothing'" (a bit heavy-handed but at least it is focused, as opposed to such an uninformative title as "On a poem"). He soon revised his tentative title to "Julia, Julia's Clothing, and Julia's poet." That's quite a good title: It is neat, and it is appropriate, since it moves (as the poem and the essay do) from Julia and her clothing to the poet. Of course it doesn't tell the reader exactly what the essay will be about, but it does stimulate the reader's interest. The essayist's final title, however, is even better: "Herrick's Julia, Julia's Herrick." Again, it is neat (the balanced structure, and structure is part of the student's topic), and it moves (as the poem itself moves) from Julia to the poet.

Herrick's Julia, Julia's Herrick

Robert Herrick's "Upon Julia's Clothes" begins as a description of Julia's clothing and ends as an expression of the poet's response not just to Julia's clothing but to Julia herself. Despite the apparently objective or detached tone of the first stanza and the first two lines of the second stanza, the poem finally conveys a strong sense of the speaker's excitement.

The first stanza seems to say, "Whenas" X (one line), "Then" Y (two lines). The second stanza repeats this basic structure of one line of assertion and two lines describing the consequence: "Next" (one line), "then" (two lines). But the coolness of "Whenas," "Then," and "Next," and of such rather scientific language as "liquefaction" (a more technical-sounding word than "melting") and "vibration," is undercut by the breathlessness or excitement of "Then, then" (that is very different from a simple "Then"). Finally, it is worth mentioning that although there is a personal rather than a fully detached note even in the first line, in "*my* Julia," this expression scarcely reveals much feeling. In fact, it is a rather complacent touch of male chauvinism, with its suggestion that the woman is a mere possession of the speaker's. Not until the last line does the speaker reveal that, far from Julia being his possession, he is possessed by Julia: "O, how that glittering taketh me." If he begins coolly, objectively, and somewhat complacently, and uses a structure that suggests a somewhat detached mind, he nevertheless at last confesses (to our delight) that he is enraptured by Julia.

Other things, of course, might be said about this poem. For instance, the writer says nothing about the changes in the meter, and their possible value in the poem. Nor does he say anything about the sounds of any of the words (he might have commented on the long vowels in "sweetly flows," and shown how the effect would have been different if instead of "sweetly flows" Herrick had written "swiftly flits"), but such topics might be material for another essay. The essay we have given is, in itself, a coherent, perceptive discussion of the way in which the poet uses a repeated structure to set forth a miniature drama, in which observation is, at the end, replaced by emotion.

Review: Writing an Analysis

Each writing assignment will require its own kind of thinking, but here are a few principles that usually are relevant:

1. Assume that your reader has already read the work you are discussing but is not thoroughly familiar with it—and of course does not know what you think and how you feel about the work.
2. Do not tell the plot (or, at most, summarize it very briefly); instead, tell your reader what the work is about (not what happens, but what the happenings add up to).
3. Whether you are writing about character or plot or meter or anything else, you will probably be telling your reader something about how the work works, that is, how it develops. The stages by which a work advances may sometimes be marked fairly clearly. For instance (to oversimplify), a poem of two stanzas may ask a question in the first, and give an answer in the second, or it may express a hope in the first, and reveal a doubt in the second. Novels, of course, are customarily divided into chapters, and even a short story (such as the one by Tolstoy on page 114) may be printed with numbered parts. Virtually all works are built up out of parts, whether or not the parts are labeled.
4. In telling the reader how each part leads to the next, or how each part arises out of what has come before, you will probably be commenting on such things as (in a story) changes in a character's state of mind—marked perhaps by a change in the setting—or (in a poem) changes in the speaker's tone of voice—for instance from eager to resigned, or from cautious to enthusiastic. Probably you will in fact be describing not only the development of character or of tone or of plot, but also (and more important) you will be advancing your own thesis.
5. Such matters as character, tone, and plot ultimately embody a theme. Remember, however, that the theme—which we often state rather abstractly—is not the heart of the work. What counts is the work as a whole—*the theme*

as it is embodied in the work, or, to reverse it, *the plot and the characters as they set forth or convey a meaning*. Every word—not simply the abstractly stated theme—counts. Your essay cannot, of course, comment on every word, but it can (and should) call attention to key words or passages, for themselves and for their power as examples.

Revising Checklist: Ten Questions to Ask Yourself

Here, as in Chapters 1 and 2, we have tried to offer a concise course in how to write essays. We will now condense even further. We think that if in the light of the following checklist you examine what you hope is your final draft, and if you then revise the draft where appropriate, you will turn in a good essay.

1. Is the title of my essay at least moderately informative?
2. What is my thesis? Do I state it soon enough (perhaps even in the title) and keep it in view?
3. Is the organization reasonable? Does each point lead into the next, without irrelevancies and without anticlimaxes?
4. Is each paragraph unified by a topic sentence or a topic idea? Are there adequate transitions from one paragraph to the next?
5. Are generalizations supported by appropriate concrete details, especially by brief quotations from the text?
6. Is the opening paragraph interesting and, by its end, have I focused on the topic? Is the concluding paragraph conclusive without being repetitive?
7. Is the tone appropriate? Do I avoid sarcasm, apologies, condescension?
8. Are the sentences clear and emphatic? Are needless words and inflated language eliminated?
9. Are the quotations accurate? Is documentation provided where necessary?
10. Are the spelling and punctuation correct? Are other mechanical matters (for instance, margins, spacing, and citations) in correct form? Have I proofread carefully?

Comparison: 5
An Analytic Tool

Analysis frequently involves comparing: Things are examined for their resemblances to and differences from other things. Strictly speaking, if one emphasizes the differences rather than the similarities, one is contrasting rather than comparing, but we need not preserve this distinction; we can call both processes **comparing**.

The point of a comparison, of course, is to help you and your reader come to a better understanding of the works being compared. To achieve this, you'll want to study things that can usefully be compared. Consider a nonliterary example. What would be the purpose of comparing a chair with an automobile? Possibly there is a point—maybe concerning stability—but if there isn't, it is hardly worth saying that a chair differs from an automobile in that a chair may be made of wood or glass or plastic or stuffed cloth, and that a chair is usually designed to be stable whereas an automobile is designed to move, and so on. It makes more sense to compare two chairs, examining them (against each other) in terms of cost, comfort, durability, beauty, and whatever other criteria come to mind. Similarly, it may not be helpful to compare two stories if the comparison merely tells a reader that one story (about war) is melodramatic, whereas a second story (about love) is humorous. There is simply no connection, no reason to juxtapose the two stories. On the other hand, if the story about war is superficially realistic (but in your view really melodramatic) and the story about love is superficially melodramatic (but in your view really plausible), you may be able to write a useful comparison, a comparison that helps the reader to see each story—and to understand melodrama and plausibility—more clearly by means of the juxtaposition.

Notice that in this example, we have focused on melodrama versus plausibility. That is, the comparison is *limited*. In comparing two literary works, you probably will not want to try to compare them in all respects. It probably is irrelevant that one story concerns three characters whereas the other concerns only two; or that one story deals with men and women, and the other deals only with women; or that one story is set in San Francisco, and the other is set in Atlanta. Possibly, of course, one or more of these points *is* relevant to your thesis. If so, you'll discuss it, but don't write a comparison in which you devote most of your space to showing that obvious differences really are obvious differences.

One other point: A comparison need not study two works; it can study two parts of one work, for instance two characters within a single story, or two kinds of irony in a play. As you read the following short story, you'll notice that the language of the first part is different from the language of the third part. A comparison might be concerned with the precise *ways* in which the language differs, and with the *reasons* for the difference. But now it's time to read the story.

Ambrose Bierce (American. 1841–1914)

AN OCCURRENCE AT OWL CREEK BRIDGE

1

A man stood upon a railroad bridge in northern Alabama, looking down into the swift water twenty feet below. The man's hands were behind his back, the wrists bound with a cord. A rope closely encircled his neck. It was attached to a stout cross-timber above his head and the slack fell to the level of his knees. Some loose boards laid upon the sleepers supporting the metals of the railway supplied a footing for him and his executioners—two private soldiers of the Federal army, directed by a sergeant who in civil life may have been a deputy sheriff. At a short remove upon the same temporary platform was an officer in the unifrom of his rank, armed. He was a captain. A sentinel at each end of the bridge stood with his rifle in the position known as "support," that is to say, vertical in front of the left shoulder, the hammer resting on the forearm thrown straight across the chest—a formal and unnatural position, enforcing an erect carriage of the body. It did not appear to be the duty of these two men to know what was occurring at the center of the bridge; they merely blockaded the two ends of the foot planking that traversed it.

Beyond one of the sentinels nobody was in sight; the railroad ran straight away into a forest for a hundred yards, then, curving, was lost to view. Doubtless there was an outpost farther long. The other bank of the stream was open ground—a gentle acclivity topped with a stockade of vertical tree trunks, loopholed for rifles, with a single embrasure through which protruded the muzzle of a brass cannon commanding the bridge. Midway of the slope between bridge and fort were the spectators—a single company of infantry in line, at "parade rest," the butts of the rifles on the ground, the barrels inclining slightly backward against the right shoulder, the hands crossed upon the stock. A lieutenant stood at the right of the line, the point of his sword upon the ground, his left hand resting upon his right. Excepting the group of four at the center of the bridge, not a man moved. The company faced the bridge, staring stonily, motionless. The sentinels, facing the banks of the stream, might have been statues to adorn the bridge. The captain stood with folded arms, silent, observing the work of his subordinates, but making no sign. Death is a dignitary who when he comes announced is to be received with formal manifestations of respect, even by those most familiar with him. In the code of military etiquette silence and fixity are forms of deference.

The man who was engaged in being hanged was apparently about thirty-five years of age. He was a civilian, if one might judge from his habit, which was that of a planter. His features were good—a straight nose, firm mouth, broad forehead, from which his long, dark hair was combed straight back, falling behind his ears to the collar of his well-fitting frock-coat. He wore a mustache and pointed beard, but no whiskers; his eyes were large and dark gray, and had a kindly expression which one would hardly have expected in one whose neck was in the hemp. Evidently this was no vulgar assassin. The liberal military code makes provision for hanging many kinds of persons, and gentlemen are not excluded.

The preparations being complete, the two private soldiers stepped aside and each drew away the plank upon which he had been standing. The sergeant turned to the captain, saluted and placed himself immediately behind that officer, who in turn moved apart one pace. These movements left the condemned man and the sergeant standing on the two ends of the same plank, which spanned three of the cross-ties of the bridge. The end upon which the civilian stood almost, but not quite, reached a fourth. This plank had been held in place by the weight of the captain; it was now held by that of the sergeant. At a signal from the former the latter would step aside, the plank would tilt and the condemned man go down between two ties. The arrangement commended itself to his judgment as simple and effective. His face had not been covered nor his eyes bandaged. He looked a moment at his "unsteadfast footing," then let his gaze wander to the swirling water of the stream racing madly beneath his feet. A piece of dancing driftwood caught his attention and his eyes followed it down the current. How slowly it appeared to move! What a sluggish stream!

He closed his eyes in order to fix his last thoughts upon his wife and children. The water, touched to gold by the early sun, the brooding mists under the banks at some distance down the stream, the fort, the soldiers, the piece of drift—all had distracted him. And now he became conscious of a new disturbance. Striking through the thought of his dear ones was a sound which he would neither ignore nor understand, a sharp, distinct, metallic percussion like the stroke of a blacksmith's hammer upon the anvil; it had the same ringing quality. He wondered what it was, and whether immeasurably distant or near by—it seemed both. Its recurrence was regular, but as slow as the tolling of a death knell. He awaited each stroke with impatience and—he knew not why—apprehension. The intervals of silence grew progressively longer; the delays became maddening. With their greater infrequency the sounds increased in strength and sharpness. They hurt his ear like the thrust of a knife; he feared he would shriek. What he heard was the ticking of his watch.

He unclosed his eyes and saw again the water below him. "If I could free my hands," he thought, "I might throw off the noose and spring into the stream. By diving I could evade the bullets and, swimming vigorously, reach the bank, take to the woods and get away home. My home, thank God, is as yet outside their lines; my wife and little ones are still beyond the invader's farthest advance."

As these thoughts, which have here to be set down in words, were flashed

5

into the doomed man's brain rather than evolved from it the captain nodded to the sergeant. The sergeant stepped aside.

2

Peyton Farquhar was a well-to-do planter, of an old and highly respected Alabama family. Being a slave owner and like other slave owners a politician he was naturally an original secessionist and ardently devoted to the Southern cause. Circumstances of an imperious nature, which it is unnecessary to relate here, had prevented him from taking service with the gallant army that had fought the disastrous campaigns ending with the fall of Corinth, and he chafed under the inglorious restraint, longing for the release of his energies, the larger life of the soldier, the opportunity for distinction. That opportunity, he felt, would come, as it comes to all in war time. Meanwhile he did what he could. No service was too humble for him to perform in aid of the South, no adventure too perilous for him to undertake if consistent with the character of a civilian who was at heart a soldier, and who in good faith and without too much qualification assented to at least a part of the frankly villainous dictum that all is fair in love and war.

One evening while Farquhar and his wife were sitting on a rustic bench near the entrance to his grounds, a gray-clad soldier rode up the gate and asked for a drink of water. Mrs. Farquhar was only too happy to serve him with her own white hands. While she was fetching the water her husband approached the dusty horseman and inquired eagerly for news from the front.

"The Yanks are repairing the railroads," said the man, "and are getting ready   10
for another advance. They have reached the Owl Creek bridge, put it in order and built a stockade on the north bank. The commandant has issued an order, which is posted everywhere, declaring that any civilian caught interfering with the railroad, its bridges, tunnels or trains will be summarily hanged. I saw the order."

"How far is it to the Owl Creek bridge?" Farquhar asked.

"About thirty miles."

"Is there no force on this side the creek?"

"Only a picket post half a mile out, on the railroad, and a single sentinel at this end of the bridge."

"Suppose a man—a civilian and student of hanging—should elude the picket   15
post and perhaps get the better of the sentinel," said Farquhar, smiling, "what could he accomplish?"

The soldier reflected. "I was there a month ago," he replied. "I observed that the flood of last winter had lodged a great quantity of driftwood against the wooden pier at this end of the bridge. It is now dry and would burn like tow."

The lady had now brought the water, which the soldier drank. He thanked her ceremoniously, bowed to her husband and rode away. An hour later, after nightfall, he repassed the plantation, going northward in the direction from which he had come. He was a Federal scout.

3

As Peyton Farquhar fell straight downward through the bridge he lost consciousness and was as one already dead. From this state he was awakened—ages later, it seemed to him—by the pain of a sharp pressure upon his throat, followed by a sense of suffocation. Keen, poignant agonies seemed to shoot from his neck downward through every fiber of his body and limbs. These pains appeared to flash along well-defined lines of ramification and to beat with an inconceivably rapid periodicity. They seemed like streams of pulsating fire heating him to an intolerable temperature. As to his head, he was conscious of nothing but a feeling of fulness—of congestion. These sensations were unaccompanied by thought. The intellectual part of his nature was already effaced; he had power only to feel, and feeling was torment. He was conscious of motion. Encompassed in a luminous cloud, of which he was now merely the fiery heart, without material substance, he swung through unthinkable arcs of oscillation, like a vast pendulum. Then all at once, with terrible suddenness, the light about him shot upward with the noise of a loud plash; a frightful roaring was in his ears, and all was cold and dark. The power of thought was restored; he knew that the rope had broken and he had fallen into the stream. There was no additional strangulation; the noose about his neck was already suffocating him and kept the water from his lungs. To die of hanging at the bottom of a river!—the idea seemed to him ludicrous. He opened his eyes in the darkness and saw above him a gleam of light, but how distant, how inaccessible! He was still sinking, for the light became fainter and fainter until it was a mere glimmer. Then it began to grow and brighten, and he knew that he was rising toward the surface—knew it with reluctance, for he was now very comfortable. "To be hanged and drowned," he thought, "that is not so bad; but I do not wish to be shot. No; I will not be shot; that is not fair."

He was not conscious of an effort, but a shrap pain in his wrist apprised him that he was trying to free his hands. He gave the struggle his attention, as an idler might observe the feat of a juggler, without interest in the outcome. What splendid effort!—what magnificent, what superhuman strength! Ah, that was a fine endeavor! Bravo! The cord fell away; his arms parted and floated upward, the hands dimly seen on each side in the growing light. He watched them with a new interest as first one and then the other pounced upon the noose at his neck. They tore it away and thrust it fiercely aside, its undulations resembling those of a water-snake. "Put it back, put it back!" He thought he shouted these words to his hands, for the undoing of the noose had been succeeded by the direst pang that he had yet experienced. His neck ached horribly; his brain was on fire; his heart, which had been fluttering faintly, gave a great leap, trying to force itself out at this mouth. His whole body was racked and wrenched with an insupportable anguish! But his disobedient hands gave no heed to the command. They beat the water vigorously with quick, downward strokes, forcing him to the surface. He felt his head emerge; his eyes were blinded by the sunlight; his chest expanded convulsively, and with a supreme and crowning agony his lungs engulfed a great draught of air, which instantly he expelled in a shriek!

He was now in full possession of his physical senses. They were, indeed, preternaturally keen and alert. Something in the awful disturbance of his organic system had so exalted and refined them that they made record of things never before perceived. He felt the ripples upon his face and heard their separate sounds as they struck. He looked at the forest on the bank of the stream, saw the individual trees, the leaves and the veining of each leaf—saw the very insects

20

upon them: the locusts, the brilliant-bodied flies, the gray spiders stretching their webs from twig to twig. He noted the prismatic colors in all the dewdrops upon a million blades of grass. The humming of the gnats that danced above the eddies of the stream, the beating of the dragon-flies' wings, the strokes of the water-spiders' legs, like oars which had lifted their boat—all these made audible music. A fish slid along beneath his eyes and he heard the rush of its body parting the water.

He had come to the surface facing down the stream; in a moment the visible world seemed to wheel slowly round, himself the pivotal point, and he saw the bridge, the fort, the soldiers upon the bridge, the captain, the sergeant, the two privates, his executioners. They were in silhouette against the blue sky. They shouted and gesticulated, pointing at him. The captain had drawn his pistol, but did not fire; the others were unarmed. Their movements were grotesque and horrible, their forms gigantic.

Suddenly he heard a sharp report and something struck the water smartly within a few inches of his head, spattering his face with spray. He heard a second report, and saw one of the sentinels with his rifle at his shoulder, a light cloud of blue smoke rising from the muzzle. The man in the water saw the eye of the man on the bridge gazing into his own through the sights of the rifle. He observed that it was a gray eye and remembered having read that gray eyes were keenest, and that all famous markmen had them. Nevertheless, this one had missed.

A counter-swirl had caught Farquhar and turned him half round; he was again looking into the forest on the bank opposite the fort. The sound of a clear, high voice in a monotonous singsong now rang out behind him and came across the water with a distinctness that pierced and subdued all other sounds, even the beating of the ripples in his ears. Although no soldier, he had frequented camps enough to know the dread significance of that deliberate, drawling, aspirated chant; the lieutenant on shore was taking a part in the morning's work. How coldly and pitilessly—with what an even, calm intonation, presaging, and enforcing tranquillity in the men—with what accurately measured intervals fell those cruel words:

"Attention, company! . . . Shoulder arms! . . . Ready! . . . Aim! . . . Fire!"

Farquhar dived—dived as deeply as he could. The water roared in his ears like the voice of Niagara, yet he heard the dulled thunder of the volley and, rising again toward the surface, met shining bits of metal, singularly flattened, oscillating slowly downward. Some of them touched him on the face and hands, then fell away, continuing their descent. One lodged between his collar and neck; it was uncomfortably warm and he snatched it out.

As he rose to the surface, gasping for breath, he saw that he had been a long time under water; he was perceptibly farther down stream—nearer to safety. The soldiers had almost finished reloading; the metal ramrods flashed all at once in the sunshine as they were drawn from the barrels, turned in the air, and thrust into their sockets. The two sentinels fired again, independently and ineffectually.

The hunted man saw all this over his shoulder; he was now swimming vigorously with the current. His brain was as energetic as his arms and legs; he thought with the rapidity of lightning.

25

"The officer," he reasoned, "will not make that martinet's error a second time. It is as easy to dodge a volley as a single shot. He has probably already given the command to fire at will. God help me, I cannot dodge them all!"

An appalling plash within two yards of him was followed by a loud, rushing sound, *diminuendo*, which seemed to travel back through the air to the fort and died in an explosion which stirred the very river to its deeps! A rising sheet of water curved over him, fell down upon him, blinded him, strangled him! The cannon had taken a hand in the game. As he shook his head free from the commotion of the smitten water he heard the deflected shot humming through the air ahead, and in an instant it was cracking and smashing the branches in the forest beyond.

"They will not do that again," he thought; "the next time they will use a charge of grape.[1] I must keep my eye upon the gun; the smoke will apprise me— the report arrives too late; it lags behind the missile. That is a good gun." 30

Suddenly he felt himself whirled round and round—spinning like a top. The water, the banks, the forests, the now distant bridge, fort and men—all were commingled and blurred. Objects were represented by their colors only; circular horizontal streaks of color—that was all he saw. He had been caught in a vortex and was being whirled on with a velocity of advance and gyration that made him giddy and sick. In a few moments he was flung upon the gravel at the foot of the left bank of the stream—the southern bank—and behind a projecting point which concealed him from his enemies. The sudden arrest of his motion, the abrasion of one of his hands on the gravel, restored him, and he wept with delight. He dug his fingers into the sand, threw it over himself in handfuls and audibly blessed it. It looked like diamonds, rubies, emeralds; he could think of nothing beautiful which it did not resemble. The trees upon the bank were giant garden plants; he noted a definite order in their arrangement, inhaled the fragrance of their blooms. A strange, roseate light shown through the spaces among their trunks and the wind made in their branches the music of aeolian harps. He had no wish to perfect his escape—was content to remain in that enchanting spot until retaken.

A whiz and rattle of grapeshot among the branches high above his head roused him from his dream. The baffled cannoneer had fired him a random farewell. He sprang to his feet, rushed up the sloping bank, and plunged into the forest.

All that day he traveled, laying his course by the rounding sun. The forest seemed interminable; nowhere did he discover a break in it, not even a woodman's road. He had not known that he lived in so wild a region. There was something uncanny in the revelation.

By nightfall he was fatigued, footsore, famishing. The thought of his wife and children urged him on. At last he found a road which led him in what he knew to be the right direction. It was as wide and straight as a city street, yet it seemed untraveled. No fields bordered it; no dwelling anywhere. Not so much as the barking of a dog suggested human habitation. The black bodies of the trees formed a straight wall on both sides, terminating on the horizon in a point, like a

---

[1] Grapeshot, a cluster of small iron balls fired from a cannon.—ED.

diagram in a lesson in perspective. Overhead, as he looked up through this rift in the wood, shone great golden stars looking unfamiliar and grouped in strange constellations. He was sure they were arranged in some order which had a secret and malign significance. The wood on either side was full of singular noises, among which—once, twice, and again—he distinctly heard whispers in an unknown tongue.

His neck was in pain and lifting his hand to it he found it horribly swollen. He knew that it had a circle of black where the rope had bruised it. His eyes felt congested; he could no longer close them. His tongue was swollen with thirst; he relieved its fever by thrusting it forward from between his teeth into the cold air. How softly the turf had carpeted the untraveled avenue—he could no longer feel the roadway beneath his feet!

Doubtless, despite his suffering, he had fallen asleep while walking, for now he sees another scene—perhaps he has merely recovered from a delirium. He stands at the gate of his own home. All is as he left it, and all bright and beautiful in the morning sunshine. He must have traveled the entire night. As he pushes open the gate and passes up the wide white walk, he sees a flutter of female garments; his wife, looking fresh and cool and sweet, steps down from the veranda to meet him. At the bottom of the steps she stands waiting, with a smile of ineffable joy, an attitude of matchless grace and dignity. Ah, how beautiful she is! He springs forward with extended arms. As he is about to clasp her he feels a stunning blow upon the back of the neck; a blinding white light blazes all about him with a sound like the shock of a cannon—then all is darkness and silence!

Peyton Farquhar was dead; his body, with a broken neck, swung gently from side to side beneath the timbers of the Owl Creek bridge.

□

Just before you began to read Bierce's story, we suggested that you might compare the style of the first part with the style of the third part. Other comparisons, of course, are possible. We don't want to be too specific here—we don't want to spoil the fun—but if you read Katherine Anne Porter's "The Jilting of Granny Weatherall" (page 613) you'll see that the plots of the two stories might be usefully compared, perhaps with the thesis that one of the two stories is psychologically truer than the other.

Or you might want to compare Bierce's story with Kate Chopin's "The Story of an Hour" in the preceding chapter (page 63). As we said earlier, in writing a comparison (1) you want to find works that are in some sense comparable, and, even then, (2) you limit the topic, since many aspects of the works are obviously not close enough to make interesting (illuminating) comparisons. Thus, if you think about "The Story of an Hour" and "An Occurrence at Owl Creek Bridge," it becomes clear that you could usefully compare the writers' reasons for withholding certain information until late in the story. Focusing on the topic of surprise, you could compare the degree to which each story can be read a second time. That is, though both stories have surprise endings, do they both offer pleasure on a second reading? Once we know how the stories end, can we read with pleasure one, or both, or neither, a second time? Or one might write a comparison of Mrs. Mallard's and Peyton Farquhar's circumstances: speaking a bit broadly, we can say that both are prisoners, both develop certain aspirations, and both are prevented from fulfilling their aspirations. But there are significant differences within these resemblances, and of course a good essay will recognize them. To take an obvious point: Mrs. Mallard and Peyton Farquhar are prisoners in different ways. Another contrast occurs between their attitudes toward their families. A good comparison does not seek to iron out the differences between the things compared. It compares, and it contrasts, in order to illuminate.

Organizing a Comparison

Something should be said about an essay organized around a comparison—say, between the settings in two stories, between two characters in a novel (or even between a character at the end of a novel and the same character at the beginning), or between the symbolism of two poems. Probably a student's first thought, after making some jottings, is to discuss one half of the comparison and then go on to the second half. Instructors and textbooks (though not this one) usually condemn such an organization, arguing that the essay breaks into two parts and that the second part involves a good deal of repetition of categories set up in the first part. Usually they recommend that the students organize their thoughts differently, somewhat along these lines:

1. First similarity
   a. first work (or character, or characteristic)
   b. second work
2. Second similarity
   a. first work
   b. second work
3. First difference
   a. first work
   b. second work
4. Second difference
   a. first work
   b. second work

and so on, for as many additional differences as seem relevant. For example, if one wishes to compare *Huckleberry Finn* with *The Catcher in the Rye*, one may organize the material thus:

1. First similarity: the narrator and his quest
   a. Huck
   b. Holden
2. Second similarity: the corrupt world surrounding the narrator
   a. society in *Huck*
   b. society in *Catcher*
3. First difference: degree to which the narrator fulfills his quest and escapes from society
   a. Huck's plan to "light out" to the frontier
   b. Holden's breakdown

Here is another way of organizing a comparison and contrast:

1. First point: the narrator and his quest
   a. similarities between Huck and Holden
   b. differences between Huck and Holden
2. Second point: the corrupt world
   a. similarities between the worlds in *Huck* and *Catcher*
   b. differences between the worlds in *Huck* and *Catcher*
3. Third point: degree of success
   a. similarities between Huck and Holden
   b. differences between Huck and Holden

But a comparison need not employ either of these structures. There is even the danger that an essay employing either of them may not come into focus until the essayist stands back from the seven-layer cake and announces, in the concluding paragraph, that the odd layers taste better. In your preparatory thinking, you may want to make comparisons in pairs (good-natured humor: the clown in *Othello*, the clownish gravedigger in *Hamlet*; social satire: the clown in *Othello*, the gravedigger in *Hamlet*; relevance to main theme: . . . ; length of role: . . . ; comments by other characters: . . .), but you must come to some conclusions about what these add up to before writing the final version. This final version should not duplicate the thought processes; rather, it should be organized so as to make the point—the thesis—clearly and effectively. After reflection, you may believe that although there are superficial similarities between the clown in *Othello* and the clownish gravedigger in *Hamlet*, there are essential differences; then in the finished essay you probably will not want to obscure the main point by jumping back and forth from play to play, working through a series of similarities and differences. It may be better to discuss the clown in *Othello*, then to point out that, although the gravedigger in *Hamlet* resembles him in *A, B,* and *C,* the gravedigger also has other functions (*D, E,* and *F*) and is of greater consequence to *Hamlet* than the clown is to *Othello*. Some repetition in the second half of the essay (for example, "The gravedigger's puns come even faster than the clown's . . .") will serve to bind the two halves into a meaningful whole, making clear the degree of similarity or difference. The point of the essay presumably is not to list pairs of similarities or differences but to illuminate a work, or works, by making thoughtful comparisons.

Although in a long essay one cannot postpone until page 30 a discussion of the second half of the comparison, in an essay of, say, fewer than ten pages there is nothing wrong with setting forth one half of the comparison and then, in light of it, the second half. The essay will break into two unrelated parts if the second half makes no use of the first, or if it fails to qualify the first half, but not if the second half looks back to the first half and calls attention to differences that the new material reveals. You ought to be able to write an essay with interwoven comparisons, but you ought also to know that there is another, simpler and clearer way to write a comparison.

PART II

A Thematic Anthology

Strange 6 Worlds

□ **ESSAYS**

Juanita Miranda (American. b. 1953)

IN DEFENSE OF FANTASY

We often hear that literature gives us an image of life. This idea is usually connected with the belief that literature teaches us. After all, if literature does not resemble life, how (one might wonder) can it teach us anything?

And since today the most popular form of literature is the novel—a form in which people who live in a recognizable society speak prose that sounds like everyday speech—it is roughly true that most of our books give us at least the illusion of life. Even today, decades after the publication of *The Catcher in the Rye,* probably millions of young people see themselves in Holden Caulfield and in Phoebe. And yet, surely we do not always want our literature to be about people like ourselves. Sometimes we want it to be about matters that apparently are remote. As Dr. Johnson said, some two hundred years ago,

> Babies do not want to hear about babies; they like to be told of giants and castles, and of somewhat which can stretch and stimulate their little minds.

But, it may be objected, we are not babies, we do not want fairy tales. Yet if we think for a moment, we will probably agree that most of the novels that please us also stretch our minds, for they strike a balance between two poles: On the one hand, they seem plausible, in one way or another lifelike, and on the other hand, they tell "a good story," that is, they stretch our minds by containing something of the unusual, the surprising, the attention-getting.

Suppose we begin by looking, very briefly, not at a novel but at the biblical story of David and Goliath, in 1 Samuel 17, a story whose chief purpose originally was to inform its audience that David was suited to become a king. The Bible tells us that the Philistine champion, Goliath, was "six cubits and a span" (nine feet, nine inches). Surely that's arresting. But, as we shall see, the story of David and

Goliath also gives us plenty of convincing details, both in its descriptions and in its dialogue.

> And there went out a champion out of the camp of the Philistines, named Goliath, of Gath, whose height was six cubits and a span. And he had an helmet of brass upon his head, and he was armed with a coat of mail; and the weight of the coat was five thousand shekels of brass. And the staff of his spear was like a weaver's beam; and his spear's head weighed six hundred shekels of iron, and one bearing a shield went before him.
>
> And he stood and cried unto the armies of Israel, and said unto them, "Why are ye come out to set your battle in array? Am not I a Philistine, and ye servants to Saul? Choose you a man for you, and let him come down to me. If he be able to fight with me, and to kill me, then will we be your servants; but if I prevail against him, and kill him, then shall ye be our servants and serve us."
>
> And the Philistine said, "I defy the armies of Israel this day; give me a man, that we may fight together."
>
> When Saul and all Israel heard those words of the Philistine, they were dismayed, and greatly afraid.

David, the young shepherd, hears Goliath, and he determines to fight this giant who insults "the living God." By the way, since many people know the story not from actually reading it but only at second hand, it's worth mentioning that the story (short as it is) is far richer than my abridgment of it. For instance, it includes an apparently irrelevant but thoroughly convincing episode that in fact serves to emphasize the obstacles that David must overcome even before he slays Goliath. David's older brother finds David near the battlefield instead of far away with the sheep, and, such is the way of older brothers, he rebukes David:

> Why camest thou down hither? And with whom hast thou left those few sheep in the wilderness? I know thy pride, and the naughtiness of thine heart, for thou art come down that thou mightest see the battle.

Other nice touches—touches not strictly necessary to the narrative but enriching it—are King Saul's initial reluctance to believe that so young and inexperienced a man could fight so great a warrior as Goliath, and (after David assures Saul that he has killed a lion) Saul's arming of David with "an helmet of brass" and "a coat of mail." But David, having never used such materials, puts them off—we may also sense that he wishes the victory to be entirely his own and not something to be shared with Saul—and so David prepares in his own way:

> He took his staff in his hand, and chose him five smooth stones out of the brook, and put them in a shepherd's bag which he had . . . and his sling was in his hand, and he drew near to the Philistine. . . .
>
> And when the Philistine looked about and saw David, he disdained him, for he was but a youth, and ruddy, and of a fair countenance. And the Philistine said unto David, "Am I a dog, that thou comest to me with staves?" And the Philistine cursed David by his gods. And the Philistine said to David, "Come to me, and I will give thy flesh unto the fowls of the air, and to the beasts of the field."
>
> Then said David to the Philistine, "Thou comest to me with a sword, and with a spear, and with a shield, but I come to thee in the name of the Lord of

hosts, the God of the armies of Israel, whom thou hast defied. This day will the Lord deliver thee into mine hand, and I will smite thee, and take thine head from thee, and I will give the carcases of the host of the Philistines this day unto the fowls of the air, and to the wild beasts of the earth, that all the earth may know that there is a God in Israel. . . .

And it came to pass, when the Philistine arose, and came and drew nigh to meet David, that David hasted, and ran toward the army to meet the Philistine. And David put his hand in his bag, and took thence a stone, and slang it, and smote the Philistine in his forehead, that the stone sunk into his forehead, and he fell upon his face to the earth.

So David prevailed over the Philistine with a sling and with a stone, and smote the Philistine, and slew him; but there was no sword in the hand of David. Therefore David ran, and stood upon the Philistine, and took his sword, and drew it out of the sheath thereof, and slew him, and cut off his head therewith.

The Philistine's scorn when he sees David, David's reply (a mixture of scorn and piety, for David announces that he comes "in the name of the Lord"), the observation that David was eager to do battle (he "*ran* toward the army to meet the Philistine"), the explanation that David cut off Goliath's head with Goliath's own sword—all of these details help us to see the scene, to believe in the characters, and yet of course the whole story is, on the literal level, remote from our experience. We don't encounter people almost ten feet tall, we don't have kings arm us, we don't fight with slingshots, and many of us don't believe that God fights on our behalf. Moreover, our daily experience may not provide us with many instances in which the underdog triumphs, or even—not quite the same thing—instances in which virtue triumphs, and yet we get all of this in the story of David and Goliath. But the writer of the story gives us not only a plot that fulfills our wishes, as "Jack the Giant-Killer" does, but also convincing details, and despite the (to the rational mind) improbability of the whole story, the story delights and continues to delight on each rereading.

Nor can even the nonbeliever feel that this is only an idle tale; it is evident that the story-teller knows too much about human psychology (remember, again, such details as the scornful older brother, Saul's initial reluctance and then his offer of superfluous help, and David's rejection of the offer) to be easily dismissed as a spinner of fantastic empty tales.

Or we can approach the matter from another side, and argue that all litera- 5
ture is fantasy. After all, Hamlet and Macbeth, like Holden and Phoebe, never existed, and even Julius Caesar, who of course did exist, did not say the things Shakespeare makes him say. All literature, then, can be thought of as "fantasy" in the sense of being something made up, imagined. Thus, Robert Frost begins a short poem, "Stopping by Woods on a Snowy Evening" [page 529], with this stanza:

Whose woods these are I think I know,
His house is in the village though;
He will not see me stopping here
To watch his woods fill up with snow.

It is of course conceivable that Frost had a thought of this sort while stopping in the woods on a snowy evening, but readers understand that the entire poem was not written in a woods. Moreover, readers are to pretend, to imagine, to fantasize, that they are with the speaker of the poem, overhearing him as he meditates, though—another fantastic bit—he doesn't seem to know they are there. The whole is fantastic—and yet the poem seems very down to earth. As we read any work of literature, then, there is the pretense that we are not in our comfortable living room but are in an imagined world. Writers themselves often use the metaphor of a work of literature as a means of travel to a new world. Emily Dickinson, for example, begins one of her most famous poems by asserting that "There is no frigate like a book / To take us lands away," and John Keats compares reading to traveling in "realms of gold." The world of literature, we are told, is different from the world of the reader.

But how different? Think again of the idea that a good story probably cannot afford utterly to neglect either of two poles: it must have enough reality in it to convince us that it is not nonsense, and it must have enough strangeness in it—it must be enough of "a good story"—to hold our interest and make us want to keep on reading. Thus, if it happens to deal with a kid named Holden Caulfield it deals with someone who in many ways resembles all of us (we are, or have been, students, have been annoyed by phonies, hold ideals, and so on) and who in many ways (most notably in his gift for expression) is not at all like us.

Some writers, for some reasons, prefer to put their characters in relatively unrealistic circumstances, and prefer to draw characters who are not especially realistic. If they are writing a short work of prose fiction, they are writing a tale rather than a story; if they are writing a long work of prose fiction, they are writing a romance rather than a novel. Hawthorne, in his preface to *The House of the Seven Gables*, speaks for such writers:

> When a writer calls his work a romance, he wishes to claim a certain lattitude, both as to its fashion and material, which he would not have felt himself entitled to assume had he professed to be writing a novel.

In the tale and the romance we are likely to feel, more than in the story and the novel, that we are in the world of myth and ritual, of symbolism. "Symbolism" is a big word with many possible meanings, but it may be enough to say that here it is used in Henry James's sense, as when he said that symbolism is the presentation "of objects casting . . . far behind them a shadow more curious . . . than the apparent figure." In the story of David and Goliath we do not quite get symbolism in this sense, because the figures themselves (except for Goliath's height) are quite convincing, but surely they cast long shadows. David's "shadow" suggests youthful piety, enthusiasm, strength, and success; Goliath's suggests the inadequacy of boasting, brute strength, and false religion. That is, because the boy and the giant are sharply etched, the story of David and Goliath does not immediately force our minds to brood about the implications (and perhaps leave David and Goliath behind), but implications or shadows are surely present and important. Further, the story of David and Goliath is none the worse for being, from a common-sense viewpoint, highly improbable. This improbability is not a weakness. If it were more probable—if Goliath were not a giant, and if David were more experienced and more heavily armed—it would be more realistic but much less memorable, less touching.

Like Hawthorne, Herman Melville was chiefly a writer of romances. In *The Confidence Man* he expresses puzzlement that people expect to find in fiction a "severe fidelity to real life." He goes on to say that he hopes his readers will read the book as "tolerantly as they sit at a play, and with much the same expectations and feelings." Melville continues:

> And as, in real life, the proprieties will not allow people to act out themselves with that unreserve permitted to the stage; so, in books of fiction, they look not only for more entertainment, but, at bottom, even for more reality, than real life itself can show. Thus, though they want novelty, they want nature, too; but nature unfettered, exhilarated, in effect transformed. In this way of thinking, the people In a fiction, like the people in a play, must dress as nobody exactly dresses, talk as nobody exactly talks, act as nobody exactly acts. It is with fiction as with religion; it should present another world, and yet one to which we feel a tie.

Melville's last words, "one to which we feel a tie," are especially important. The writer's world may be set on Mars, or it may include ghosts, but it must (if the work is to be more than a moment's idle entertainment) convince readers that it deals with human affairs. What is improbable (and boring) about so much science fiction, and what makes most of it so trivial, is not that it is set in the future, or that people have ray guns, but that it is so remote from human psychology. Writers on science fiction usually define the genre by saying, more or less, that science fiction presents with verisimilitude some enormous change in the environment. It offers much that is new, and it often succeeds in making the technology of this imagined world believable. But a convincing physical environment is not enough to make us "feel a tie." Despite all of the apparent realism (for example, some scientific language) of a science fiction work, the work may seem utterly remote from life, not because people move about in rockets rather than in automobiles but because there is so much concern with technology and so little concern with feelings. On the other hand, a fable in which animals talk, or a ghost story in which the dead come back to seek revenge, may seem to a reader close to human life.

One might contrast the remote (psychological as well as temporal) worlds of most science fiction with the world of the fairy tale. What, one might ask, can be more remote from human experience than, say, the story of Sleeping Beauty? A prophecy is uttered that at the age of fifteen the princess will prick her finger on a spindle and will fall into a deathlike sleep for a hundred years. In order to prevent the prophecy from coming true, the king bans all spindles, but the girl nevertheless pricks her finger on a spindle as predicted, and falls asleep, to be awakened at last by the handsome young man. Now, one reads this story—or, rather, first hears it told by an elder, and then treasures it ever after—for the strangeness of the story itself, for the world of royalty, prophecy, a beautiful princess and a handsome prince. Most people (since they are neither literary critics nor psychologists) never bother to analyze the story—to give it a "meaning"—but surely part of the story's appeal is that despite its apparent remoteness it sets forth a world "to which we feel a tie." What is that tie? If we stand back from the story, we can say that it reveals the adolescent's fear of new experience (especially of sexual maturing), a paralyzing withdrawal or isolation from reality, and then (after a protective interval that ends with the loving kiss of the prince), the return to reality. Max Lüthi, in *Once upon a Time: On the Nature of Fairy Tales*, puts the matter in a slightly different way, but he too sees in "Sleeping Beauty" a pattern or archetype that profoundly (if unconsciously) moves the hearer:

> The characters of the fairy tale are not personally delineated; the fairy tale is not concerned with individual destinies. Nor is it the unique process of maturation that is reflected in the fairy tale. The story of Sleeping Beauty is more than an imaginatively stylized love story portraying the withdrawal of the girl and the breaking of the spell through the young lover. One instinctively conceives of the princess as an image for the human spirit: the story portrays the endowment, peril, paralysis, and redemption not of just one girl, but of all mankind. The soul of man again and again suffers convulsions and paralysis and, each time—with luck—it can be revived, healed, redeemed. With luck! The abnormal individual, of course, can also remain in the paralyzed condition, unable to rediscover the fountainhead of life in himself and to reestablish contact with his surroundings. But the fairy tale does not portray the abnormal case, but natural development, and it fills its hearers with the confidence that a new, larger life is to come after the deathlike sleep—that, after the isolation, a new form of contact and community will follow.

It is scarcely going too far to say that "Sleeping Beauty," like many other fairy tales, alluringly sets forth our cultural values. These tales, in Dr. Johnson's words, "stretch and stimulate . . . little minds," and thus help children to grow (however unconsciously) into social adults. Allowing, of course, for great differences, something of the general pattern of "Sleeping Beauty" can be seen in Frost's "Stopping by Woods," where the movement is from a longing for extinction ("the woods are lovely, dark and deep") to the return to the larger world of life ("But I have promises to keep, / And miles to go before I sleep").

    For Edgar Allan Poe, like his contemporaries Hawthorne and Melville, a writer of romances, mere realism was "pitiable stuff," the accurate depiction of "decayed cheeses." A defense of romance or fantasy need not, however, with Poe dismiss realistic writing. For one thing, if writing is nothing but realistic, it dismisses itself; the realistic writing that endures is writing that manages to give not only a sense of the real—Poe's decayed cheeses—but also a sense of its meaning or importance to us, a sense, we might say, of the archetypal. To go back to our two poles: The realistic story that we willingly read a second and a third time has in it more than just realism, more than just convincing dialogue (a tape recorder can give us that) and descriptions of clothes and houses. It is, as one says, "a good story," which means that it has in it something of the unusual, but this unusual element is not the merely freakish; rather, it is something we feel a tie to.

10

QUESTIONS AND SUGGESTIONS FOR WRITING

1. Take one of the relatively unrealistic works in this book—any selection in this chapter will do—and test it against Miranda's essay. Does the essay help you to enjoy the work? Or does the work refute the essay?
2. Do you find Miranda's discussion of the story of David and Goliath helpful? Why, or why not?

Bruno Bettelheim (American. b. 1903)

THE THREE LITTLE PIGS:
Pleasure Principle
Versus Reality Principle

The myth of Hercules deals with the choice between following the pleasure principle or the reality principle in life. So, likewise, does the fairy story of "The Three Little Pigs."[1]

Stories like "The Three Little Pigs" are much favored by children over all "realistic" tales, particularly if they are presented with feeling by the storyteller. Children are enraptured when the huffing and puffing of the wolf at the pig's door is acted out for them. "The Three Little Pigs" teaches the nursery-age child in a most enjoyable and dramatic form that we must not be lazy and take things easy, for if we do, we may perish. Intelligent planning and foresight combined with hard labor will make us victorious over even our most ferocious enemy—the wolf! The story also shows the advantages of growing up, since the third and wisest pig is usually depicted as the biggest and oldest.

The houses the three pigs build are symbolic of man's progress in history: from a lean-to shack to a wooden house, finally to a house of solid brick. Internally, the pigs' actions show progress from the id-dominated personality to the superego-influenced but essentially ego-controlled personality.[2]

The littlest pig builds his house with the least care out of straw; the second uses sticks; both throw their shelters together as quickly and effortlessly as they

---

[1] The discussion of this tale is based on its earliest published form, printed in J. O. Halliwell, *Nursery Rhymes and Nursery Tales* (London, c. 1843). Only in some of the later renderings of the story do the two little pigs survive, which robs the tale of much of its impact. In some variations the pigs are given names, interfering with the child's ability to see them as representatives of the three stages of development. On the other hand, some renderings spell out that it was the seeking of pleasure which prevented the littler ones from building more substantial and thus safer homes, as the littlest one builds his house out of mud because it feels so pleasant to wallow in it, while the second uses cabbage to build his abode because he loves eating it.

[2] In Freudian psychology, the id stands for instinctual drives that urgently demand immediate satisfaction; the superego, chiefly unconscious and derived from parents, stands for the demands of society's morality; and the ego, the voice of reason in touch with external reality, seeks to reconcile the demands of the id with those of the superego.—ED.

can, so they can play for the rest of the day. Living in accordance with the pleasure principle, the younger pigs seek immediate gratification, without a thought for the future and the dangers of reality, although the middle pig shows some growth in trying to build a somewhat more substantial house than the youngest.

Only the third and oldest pig has learned to behave in accordance with the reality principle: he is able to postpone his desire to play, and instead acts in line with his ability to foresee what may happen in the future. He is even able to predict correctly the behavior of the wolf—the enemy, or stranger within, which tries to seduce and trap us; and therefore the third pig is able to defeat powers both stronger and more ferocious than he is. The wild and destructive wolf stands for all asocial, unconscious, devouring powers against which one must learn to protect oneself, and which one can defeat through the strength of one's ego.

"The Three Little Pigs" makes a much greater impression on children than Aesop's parallel but overtly moralistic fable of "The Ant and the Grasshopper." In this fable a grasshopper, starving in winter, begs an ant to give it some of the food which the ant had busily collected all summer. The ant asks what the grasshopper was doing during the summer. Learning that the grasshopper sang and did not work, the ant rejects his plea by saying, "Since you could sing all summer, you may dance all winter."

This ending is typical for fables, which are also folk tales handed down from generation to generation. "A fable seems to be, in its genuine state, a narrative in which beings irrational, and sometimes inanimate, are, for the purpose of moral instruction, feigned to act and speak with human interests and passions" (Samuel Johnson). Often sanctimonious, sometimes amusing, the fable always explicitly states a moral truth; there is no hidden meaning, nothing is left to our imagination.

The fairy tale, in contrast, leaves all decisions up to us, including whether we wish to make any at all. It is up to us whether we wish to make any application to our life from a fairy tale, or simply enjoy the fantastic events it tells about. Our enjoyment is what induces us to respond in our own good time to the hidden meanings, as they may relate to our life experience and present state of personal development.

A comparison of "The Three Little pigs" with "The Ant and the Grasshopper" accentuates the difference between a fairy tale and a fable. The grasshopper, much like the little pigs and the child himself, is bent on playing, with little concern for the future. In both stories the child identifies with the animals (although only a hypocritical prig can identify with the nasty ant, and only a mentally sick child with the wolf); but after having identified with the grasshopper, there is no hope left for the child, according to the fable. For the grasshopper beholden to the pleasure principle, nothing but doom awaits; it is an "either/or" situation, where having made a choice once settles things forever.

But identification with the little pigs of the fairy tale teaches that there are developments—possibilities of progress from the pleasure principle to the reality principle, which, after all, is nothing but a modification of the former. The story of the three pigs suggests a transformation in which much pleasure is retained, because now satisfaction is sought with true respect for the demands of reality. The clever and playful third pig outwits the wolf several times: first, when the wolf tries three times to lure the pig away from the safety of home by appealing to his oral greed, proposing expeditions to where the two would get delicious food. The wolf tries to tempt the pig with turnips which may be stolen, then with apples, and finally with a visit to a fair.[3]

Only after these efforts have come to naught does the wolf move in for the kill. But he has to enter the pig's house to get him, and once more the pig wins out, for the wolf falls down the chimney into the boiling water and ends up as cooked meat for the pig. Retributive justice is done: the wolf, which has devoured the other two pigs and wished to devour the third, ends up as food for the pig.

The child, who throughout the story has been invited to identify with one of its protagonists, is not only given hope, but is told that through developing his intelligence he can be victorious over even a much stronger opponent.

Since according to the primitive (and a child's) sense of justice only those who have done something really bad get destroyed, the fable seems to teach that it is wrong to enjoy life when it is good, as in summer. Even worse, the ant in this fable is a nasty animal, without any compassion for the suffering of the grasshopper—and this is the figure the child is asked to take for his example.

The wolf, on the contrary, is obviously a bad animal, because it wants to destroy. The wolf's badness is something the young child recognizes within himself: his wish to devour, and its consequence—the anxiety about possibly suffering such a fate himself. So the wolf is an externalization, a projection of the child's badness—and the story tells how this can be dealt with constructively.

The various excursions in which the oldest pig gets food in good ways are an easily neglected but significant part of the story, because they show that there is a world of difference between eating and devouring. The child subconsciously understands it as the difference between the pleasure principle uncontrolled, when one wants to devour all at once, ignoring the consequences, and the reality principle, in line with which one goes about intelligently foraging for food. The mature pig gets up in good time to bring the goodies home before the wolf appears on the scene. What better demonstration of the value of acting on the basis of the reality principle, and what it consists of, than the pig's rising very early in the morning to secure the delicious food and, in so doing, foiling the wolf's evil designs?

15

In fairy tales it is typically the youngest child who, although at first thought little of or scorned, turns out to be victorious in the end. "The Three Little Pigs" deviates from this pattern, since it is the oldest pig who is superior to the two little pigs all along. An explanation can be found in the fact that all three pigs are "little," thus immature, as is the child himself. The child identifies with each of them in turn and recognizes the progression of identity. "The Three Little Pigs" is a fairy tale because of its happy ending, and because the wolf gets what he deserves.

[3] In the version Bettelheim refers to, the wolf invites the pig to join him in stealing turnips and apples, but the pig outwits the wolf by stealing them before the appointed hour. Similarly, the pig goes alone to the fair, buys a butter churn, and rolls safely downhill past the wolf. Later the enraged wolf enters the pig's house through the chimney, but ends up in a pot of boiling water.—ED.

While the child's sense of justice is offended by the poor grasshopper having to starve although it did nothing bad, his feeling of fairness is satisfied by the punishment of the wolf. Since the three little pigs represent stages in the development of man, the disappearance of the first two little pigs is not traumatic; the child understands subconsciously that we have to shed earlier forms of existence if we wish to move on to higher ones. In talking to young children about "The Three Little Pigs," one encounters only rejoicing about the deserved punishment of the wolf and the clever victory of the oldest pig—not grief over the fate of the two little ones. Even a young child seems to understand that all three are really one and the same in different stages—which is suggested by their answering the wolf in exactly the same words: "No, no, not by the hair of my chinni-chin-chin!" If we survive in only the higher form of our identity, this is as it should be.

"The Three Little Pigs" directs the child's thinking about his own development without ever telling what it ought to be, permitting the child to draw his own conclusions. This process alone makes for true maturing, while telling the child what to do just replaces the bondage of his own immaturity with a bondage of servitude to the dicta of adults.

QUESTIONS AND SUGGESTIONS FOR WRITING

1. Does Bettelheim's interpretation of "The Three Little Pigs" seem reasonable or far-fetched to you? Or does it fall somewhere between the two? Explain.
2. Bettelheim says that we "respond in our own good time to the hidden meanings" of fairy tales. Jot down the titles of the first three or four fairy tales that come to mind, and then think about them. Did they have "meanings" to you as a child, and do you perhaps have further meanings for you now? Or are some of them simply good stories without meanings? If some of them do not seem to you to have meanings, do you assume that you are not getting at the kernel of the nut? Or is Bettelheim perhaps talking loosely when he finds such deep meanings in fairy tales? If some of the tales seem not to have meanings, do you find the ones with meanings more powerful, or is it the other way around?
3. In an essay of about 500 words, summarize and then evaluate Bettelheim's point that such fairy tales as "The Three Little Pigs" teach "possibilities of progress from the pleasure principle to the reality principle." In your essay you may want to analyze some other fairy tale that seems appropriate, such as "Cinderella" or "Hansel and Gretel," showing the degree (if any) to which it might help a child mature.

☐ FICTION

Nathaniel Hawthorne (American. 1804–1864)

DR. HEIDEGGER'S EXPERIMENT

That very singular man, old Dr. Heidegger, once invited four venerable friends to meet him in his study. There were three white-bearded gentlemen, Mr. Medbourne, Colonel Killigrew, and Mr. Gascoigne, and a withered gentlewoman, whose name was the Widow Wycherly. They were all melancholy old creatures, who had been unfortunate in life, and whose greatest misfortune it was that they were not long ago in their graves. Mr. Medbourne, in the vigor of his age, had been a prosperous merchant, but had lost his all by a frantic speculation, and was now little better than a mendicant. Colonel Killigrew had wasted his best years, and his health and substance, in the pursuit of sinful pleasures which had given birth to a brood of pains, such as the gout, and divers other torments of soul and body. Mr. Gascoigne was a ruined politician, a man of evil fame, or at least had been so, till time had buried him from the knowledge of the present generation, and made him obscure instead of infamous. As for the Widow Wycherly, tradition tells us that she was a great beauty in her day; but, for a long while past, she had lived in deep seclusion, on account of certain scandalous stories which had prejudiced the gentry of the town against her. It is a circumstance worth mentioning, that each of these three old gentlemen, Mr. Medbourne, Colonel Killigrew, and Mr. Gascoigne, were early lovers of the Widow Wycherly, and had once been on the point of cutting each other's throats for her sake. And before proceeding farther, I will merely hint that Dr. Heidegger and all his four guests were sometimes thought to be a little beside themselves; as is not unfrequently the case with old people, when worried either by present troubles or woeful recollections.

"My dear old friends," said Dr. Heidegger, motioning them to be seated, "I am desirous of your assistance in one of those little experiments with which I amuse myself here in my study."

If all stories were true, Dr. Heidegger's study must have been a very curious place. It was a dim, old-fashioned chamber, festooned with cobwebs, and besprinkled with antique dust. Around the walls stood several oaken bookcases, the lower shelves of which were filled with rows of gigantic folios and black-letter quartos, and the upper with little parchment-covered duodecimos. Over the central bookcase was a bronze bust of Hippocrates, with which, according to some authorities, Dr. Heidegger was accustomed to hold consultations in all difficult cases of his practice. In the obscurest corner of the room stood a tall and narrow oaken closet, with its door ajar, within which doubtfully appeared a skeleton. Between two of the bookcases hung a looking glass, presenting its high and dusty plate within a tarnished gilt frame. Among many wonderful stories related of this mirror, it was fabled that the spirits of all the doctor's deceased patients dwelt within its verge, and would stare him in the face whenever he looked thitherward. The opposite side of the chamber was ornamented with the full-length portrait of a young lady, arrayed in the faded magnificence of silk, satin, and brocade, and with a visage as faded as her dress. Above half a century ago, Dr. Heidegger had been on the point of marriage with this young lady; but, being affected with some slight disorder, she had swallowed one of her lover's prescriptions, and died on the bridal evening. The greatest curiosity of the study remains to be mentioned; it was a ponderous folio volume, bound in black leather, with massive silver clasps. There were no letters on the back, and nobody could tell the title of the book. But it was well known to be a book of magic; and once, when a chambermaid had lifted it, merely to brush away the dust, the skeleton had rattled in its closet, the picture of the young lady had stepped one foot upon the floor, and several ghastly faces had peeped forth from the mirror; while the brazen head of Hippocrates frowned, and said—"Forbear!"

Such was Dr. Heidegger's study. On the summer afternoon of our tale, a small round table, as black as ebony, stood in the center of the room, sustaining a cut-glass vase of beautiful form and elaborate workmanship. The sunshine came through the window, between the heavy festoons of two faded damask curtains. and fell directly across this vase; so that a mild splendor was reflected from it on the ashen visages of the five old people who sat around. Four champagne glasses were also on the table.

"My dear old friends," repeated Dr. Heidegger, "may I reckon on your aid in   5 performing an exceedingly curious experiment?"

Now Dr. Heidegger was a very strange old gentleman, whose eccentricity had become the nucleus for a thousand fantastic stories. Some of these fables, to my shame be it spoken, might possibly be traced back to mine own veracious self; and if any passages of the present tale should startle the reader's faith, I must be content to bear the stigma of a fictionmonger.

When the doctor's four guests heard him talk of his proposed experiment, they anticipated nothing more wonderful than the murder of a mouse in an air pump, or the examination of a cobweb by the microscope, or some similar nonsense, with which he was constantly in the habit of pestering his intimates. But without waiting for a reply, Dr. Heidegger hobbled across the chamber, and returned with the same ponderous folio, bound in black leather, which common report affirmed to be a book of magic. Undoing the silver clasps, he opened the volume, and took from among its black-letter pages a rose, or what was once a rose, though now the green leaves and crimson petals had assumed one brownish hue, and the ancient flower seemed ready to crumble to dust in the doctor's hands.

"This rose," said Dr. Heidegger, with a sigh, "this same withered and crumbling flower, blossomed five-and-fifty years ago. It was given me by Sylvia Ward, whose portrait hangs yonder; and I meant to wear it in my bosom at our wedding. Five-and-fifty years it has been treasured between the leaves of this old volume. Now, would you deem it possible that this rose of half a century could ever bloom again?"

"Nonsense!" said the Widow Wycherly, with a peevish toss of her head. "You might as well ask whether an old woman's wrinkled face could ever bloom again."

"See!" answered Dr. Heidegger.   10

He uncovered the vase, and threw the faded rose into the water which it contained. At first it lay lightly on the surface of the fluid, appearing to imbibe none of its moisture. Soon, however, a singular change began to be visible. The crushed and dried petals stirred, and assumed a deepening tinge of crimson, as if the flower were reviving from a deathlike slumber; the slender stalk and twigs of foliage became green; and there was the rose of half a century, looking as fresh as when Sylvia Ward had first given it to her lover. It was scarcely full blown; for some of its delicate red leaves curled modestly around its moist bosom, within which two or three dewdrops were sparkling.

"That is certainly a very pretty deception," said the doctor's friends; carelessly, however, for they had witnessed greater miracles at a conjurer's show; "pray how was it effected?"

"Did you never hear of the 'Fountain of Youth'?" asked Dr. Heidegger, "which Ponce de Leon, the Spanish adventurer, went in search of, two or three centuries ago?"

"But did Ponce de Leon ever find it?" said the Widow Wycherly.

"No," answered Dr. Heidegger, "for he never sought it in the right place.   15
The famous Fountain of Youth, if I am rightly informed, is situated in the southern part of the Floridian peninsula, not far from Lake Macaco. Its source is overshadowed by several gigantic magnolias, which, though numberless centuries old, have been kept as fresh as violets by the virtues of this wonderful water. An acquaintance of mine, knowing my curiosity in such matters, had sent me what you see in the vase."

"Ahem!" said Colonel Killigrew, who believed not a word of the doctor's story; "and what may be the effect of this fluid on the human frame?"

"You shall judge for yourself, my dear colonel," replied Dr. Heidegger; "and all of you, my respected friends, are welcome to so much of this admirable fluid as may restore to you the bloom of youth. For my own part, having had much trouble in growing old, I am in no hurry to grow young again. With your permission, therefore, I will merely watch the progress of the experiment."

While he spoke, Dr. Heidegger had been filling the four champagne glasses with the water of the Fountain of Youth. It was apparently impregnated with an effervescent gas, for little bubbles were continually ascending from the depths of the glasses, and bursting in silvery spray at the surface. As the liquor diffused a pleasant perfume, the old people doubted not that it possessed cordial and comfortable properties; and, though utter skeptics as to its rejuvenescent power, they were inclined to swallow it at once. But Dr. Heidegger besought them to stay a moment.

"Before you drink, my respectable old friends," said he, "it would be well that, with the experience of a lifetime to direct you, you should draw up a few general rules for your guidance, in passing a second time through the perils of youth. Think what a sin and a shame it would be, if with your peculiar advantages, you should not become patterns of virtue and wisdom to all the young people of the age!"

The doctor's four venerable friends made him no answer, except by a feeble   20 and tremulous laugh; so very ridiculous was the idea, that, knowing how closely repentance treads behind the steps of error, they should ever go astray again.

"Drink then," said the doctor, bowing; "I rejoice that I have so well selected the subjects of my experiment."

With palsied hands they raised the glasses to their lips. The liquor, if it really possessed such virtues as Dr. Heidegger imputed to it, could not have been bestowed on four human beings who needed it more woefully. They looked as if they had never known what youth or pleasure was, but had been the offspring of Nature's dotage, and always the gray, decrepit, sapless, miserable creatures, who now sat stooping round the doctor's table, without life enough in their souls or bodies to be animated even by the prospect of growing young again. They drank off the water, and replaced their glasses on the table.

Assuredly, there was an almost immediate improvement in the aspect of the party, not unlike what might have been produced by a glass of generous wine, together with a sudden glow of cheerful sunshine, brightening over all their visages at once. There was a healthful suffusion on their cheeks, instead of the ashen hue that had made them look so corpselike. They gazed at one another, and fancied that some magic power had really begun to smooth away the deep and sad inscription which Father Time had been so long engraving on their brows. The Widow Wycherly adjusted her cap, for she felt almost like a woman again.

"Give us more of this wondrous water!" cried they eagerly. "We are younger—but we are still too old! Quick—give us more!"

"Patience, patience!" quoth Dr. Heidegger, who sat watching the experiment   25
with philosophic coolness. "You have been a long time growing old. Surely you might be content to grow young in half an hour! But the water is at your service."

Again he filled the glasses with the liquor of youth, enough of which still remained in the vase to turn half the old people in the city to the age of their own grandchildren. While the bubbles were yet sparkling on the brim, the doctor's four guests snatched their glasses from the table, and swallowed the contents of a single gulp. Was it delusion? Even while the draught was passing down their throats, it seemed to have wrought a change on their whole systems. Their eyes grew clear and bright; a dark shade deepened among their silvery locks; they sat around the table, three gentlemen of middle age, and a woman hardly beyond her buxom prime.

"My dear widow, you are charming!" cried Colonel Killigrew, whose eyes had been fixed upon her face, while the shadows of age were flitting from it like darkness from the crimson daybreak.

The fair widow knew, of old, that Colonel Killigrew's compliments were not always measured by sober truth; so she started up and ran to the mirror, still dreading that the ugly visage of an old woman would meet her gaze. Meanwhile, the three gentlemen behaved in such a manner as proved that the water of the Fountain of Youth possessed some intoxicating qualities; unless, indeed, their exhilaration of spirits were merely a lightsome dizziness, caused by the sudden removal of the weight of years. Mr. Gascoigne's mind seemed to run on political topics, but whether relating to the past, present, or future, could not easily be determined, since the same ideas and phrases have been in vogue these fifty years. Now he rattled forth full-throated sentences about patriotism, national glory, and the people's rights; now he muttered some perilous stuff or other, in a sly and doubtful whisper, so cautiously that even his own conscience could scarcely catch the secret; and now again he spoke in measured accents, and a deeply deferential tone, as if a royal ear were listening to his well-turned periods. Colonel Killigrew all this time had been trolling forth a jolly bottle song, and ringing his glass in symphony with the chorus, while his eyes wandered towards the buxom figure of the Widow Wycherly. On the other side of the table, Mr. Medbourne was involved in a calculation of dollars and cents, with which was strangely intermingled a project for supplying the East Indies with ice, by harnessing a team of whales to the polar icebergs.

As for the Widow Wycherly, she stood before the mirror curtsying and simpering to her own image, and greeting it as the friend whom she loved better than all the world beside. She thrust her face close to the glass, to see whether some long-remembered wrinkle or crow's-foot had indeed vanished. She examined whether the snow had so entirely melted from her hair, that the venerable cap could be safely thrown aside. At last, turning briskly away, she came with a sort of dancing step to the table.

"My dear old doctor," cried she, "pray favor me with another glass!"   30

"Certainly, my dear madam, certainly!" replied the complaisant doctor; "see! I have already filled the glasses."

There, in fact, stood the four glasses, brimful of this wonderful water, the delicate spray of which, as it effervesced from the surface, resembled the tremulous glitter of diamonds. It was now so nearly sunset that the chamber had grown duskier than ever; but a mild and moonlike splendor gleamed from within the vase, and rested alike on the four guests, and on the doctor's venerable figure. He sat in a high-backed, elaborately carved, oaken armchair, with a gray dignity of aspect that might have well befitted that very Father Time whose power had never been disputed save by this fortunate company. Even while quaffing the third draught of the Fountain of Youth, they were almost awed by the expression of his mysterious visage.

But, the next moment, the exhilarating gush of young life shot through their veins. They were now in the happy prime of youth. Age, with its miserable train of cares, and sorrows, and diseases, was remembered only as the trouble of a dream from which they had joyously awoke. The fresh gloss of the soul, so early lost, and without which the world's successive scenes had been but a gallery of faded pictures, again threw its enchantment over all their prospects. They felt like new-created beings, in a new-created universe.

"We are young! We are young!" they cried, exultingly.

Youth, like the extremity of age, had effaced the strongly marked characteristics of middle life, and mutually assimilated them all. They were a group of merry youngsters, almost maddened with the exuberant frolicsomeness of their years. The most singular effect of their gaiety was an impulse to mock the infirmity and decrepitude of which they had so lately been the victims. They laughed loudly at their old-fashioned attire, the wide-skirted coats and flapped waistcoats of the young men, and the ancient cap and gown of the blooming girl. One limped across   35 the floor, like a gouty grandfather; one set a pair of spectacles astride of his nose, and pretended to pore over the black-letter pages of the book of magic; a third seated himself in an armchair, and strove to imitate the venerable dignity of Dr. Heidegger. Then all shouted mirthfully, and leaped about the room. The Widow Wycherly—if so fresh a damsel could be called a widow—tripped up to the doctor's chair, with a mischievous merriment in her rosy face.

"Doctor, you dear old soul," cried she, "get up and dance with me!" And then the four young people laughed louder than ever, to think what a queer figure the poor old doctor would cut.

"Pray excuse me," answered the doctor quietly. "I am old and rheumatic, and my dancing days were over long ago. But either of these gay young gentlemen will be glad of so pretty a partner."

"Dance with me, Clara!" cried Colonel Killigrew.

"No, no, I will be her partner!" shouted Mr. Gascoigne.

"She promised me her hand, fifty years ago!" exclaimed Mr. Medbourne.   40

They all gathered round her. One caught both her hands in his passionate grasp—another threw his arm about her waist—the third buried his hand among the glossy curls that clustered beneath the widow's cap. Blushing, panting, struggling, chiding, laughing, her warm breath fanning each of their faces by turns, she strove to disengage herself, yet still remained in their triple embrace. Never was there a livelier picture of youthful rivalship, with bewitching beauty for the prize. Yet, by a strange deception, owing to the duskiness of the chamber, and the antique dresses which they still wore, the tall mirror is said to have reflected the figures of the three old, gray, withered grandsires, ridiculously contending for the skinny ugliness of a shriveled grandam.

But they were young: their burning passions proved them so. Inflamed to madness by the coquetry of the girl-widow, who neither granted nor quite withheld her favors, the three rivals began to interchange threatening glances. Still keeping hold of the fair prize, they grappled fiercely at one another's throats. As they struggled to and fro, the table was overturned, and the vase dashed into a thousand fragments. The precious Water of Youth flowed in a bright stream across the floor, moistening the wings of a butterfly, which, grown old in the decline of summer, had alighted there to die. The insect fluttered lightly through the chamber, and settled on the snowy head of Dr. Heidegger.

"Come, come, gentlemen!—come, Madam Wycherly," exclaimed the doctor, "I really must protest against this riot."

They stood still, and shivered; for it seemed as if gray Time were calling them back from their sunny youth, far down into the chill and darksome vale of years. They looked at old Dr. Heidegger, who sat in his carved armchair, holding the rose of half a century, which he had rescued from among the fragments of the shattered vase. At the motion of his hand, the four rioters resumed their seats; the more readily, because their violent exertions had wearied them, youthful though they were.

"My poor Sylvia's rose!" ejaculated Dr. Heidegger, holding it in the light of   45
the sunset clouds; "it appears to be fading again."

And so it was. Even while the party were looking at it, the flower continued to shrivel up, till it became as dry and fragile as when the doctor had first thrown it into the vase. He shook off the few drops of moisture which clung to its petals.

"I love it as well thus as in its dewy freshness," observed he, pressing the withered rose to his withered lips. While he spoke, the butterfly fluttered down from the doctor's snowy head, and fell upon the floor.

His guests shivered again. A strange chillness, whether of the body or spirit they could not tell, was creeping gradually over them all. They gazed at one another, and fancied that each fleeting moment snatched away a charm, and left a deepening furrow where none had been before. Was it an illusion? Had the changes of a lifetime been crowded into so brief a space, and were they now four aged people, sitting with their old friend, Dr. Heidegger?

"Are we grown old again, so soon?" cried they dolefully.

In truth, they had. The Water of Youth possessed merely a virtue more 50 transient than that of wine. The delirium which it created had effervesced away. Yes! they were old again. With a shuddering impulse that showed her a woman still, the widow clasped her skinny hands before her face, and wished that the coffin lid were over it, since it could be no longer beautiful.

"Yes, friends, ye are old again," said Dr. Heidegger; "and lo! the Water of Youth is all lavished on the ground. Well—I bemoan it not; for if the fountain gushed at my very doorstep, I would not stoop to bathe my lips in it—no, though its delirium were for years instead of moments. Such is the lesson ye have taught me!"

But the doctor's four friends had taught no such lesson to themselves. They resolved forthwith to make a pilgrimage to Florida, and quaff at morning, noon, and night, from the Fountain of Youth.

QUESTIONS AND SUGGESTIONS FOR WRITING:

1. In a paragraph characterize the narrator, paying special attention to his tone.
2. Briefly describe, as objectively as possible, the furnishings of Dr. Heidegger's study. Then in a paragraph consider whether as *the narrator describes it* it is a frightening place, the dwelling of the mad scientist of horror fiction and film.
3. In a paragraph characterize Dr. Heidegger.
4. In a few sentences describe Dr. Heidegger's four visitors, and then in about 150 words characterize them.
5. In an essay of 500 words, evaluate the assertion that "Dr. Heidegger's Experiment" is a cynical story. In thinking about the topic, consider not only the plot of the story but the tone with which it is narrated. In your essay, offer a reasonable definition of cynicism, and examine the adequacy of the word as a characterization of the story.

Edgar Allan Poe (American. 1809–1849)

THE MASQUE OF THE RED DEATH

The "Red Death" had long devastated the country. No pestilence had ever been so fatal, or so hideous. Blood was its Avatar and its seal—the redness and the horror of blood. There were sharp pains, and sudden dizziness, and then profuse bleeding at the pores, with dissolution. The scarlet stains upon the body and especially upon the face of the victim, were the pest ban which shut him out from the aid and from the sympathy of his fellow-men. And the whole seizure, progress and termination of the disease, were the incidents of half an hour.

But the Prince Prospero was happy and dauntless and sagacious. When his dominions were half depopulated, he summoned to his presence a thousand hale and light-hearted friends from among the knights and dames of his court, and with these retired to the deep seclusion of one of his castellated abbeys. This was an extensive and magnificent structure, the creation of the prince's own eccentric yet august taste. A strong and lofty wall girdled it in. This wall had gates of iron. The courtiers, having entered, brought furnaces and massy hammers and welded the bolts. They resolved to leave means neither of ingress or egress to the sudden impulses of despair or of frenzy from within. The abbey was amply provisioned. With such precautions the courtiers might bid defiance to contagion. The external world could take care of itself. In the meantime it was folly to grieve, or to think. The prince had provided all the appliances of pleasure. There were buffoons, there were improvisatori, there were ballet-dancers, there were musicians, there was Beauty, there was wine. All these and security were within. Without was the "Red Death."

It was toward the close of the fifth or sixth month of his seclusion, and while the pestilence raged most furiously abroad, that the Prince Prospero entertained his thousand friends at a masked ball of the most unusual magnificence.

It was a voluptuous scene, that masquerade. But first let me tell of the rooms in which it was held. There were seven—an imperial suite. In many palaces, however, such suites form a long and straight vista, while the folding doors slide back nearly to the walls on either hand, so that the view of the whole extent is scarcely impeded. Here the case was very different; as might have been expected from the duke's love of the *bizarre*. The apartments were so irregularly disposed that the vision embraced but little more than one at a time. There was a sharp turn at every twenty or thirty yards, and at each turn a novel effect. To the right and left, in the middle of each wall, a tall and narrow Gothic window looked out upon a closed corridor which pursued the windings of the suite. These windows were of stained glass whose color varied in accordance with the prevailing hue of the decorations of the chamber into which it opened. That at the eastern extremity was hung, for example, in blue—and vividly blue went its windows. The second chamber was purple in its ornaments and tapestries, and here the panes were purple. The third was green throughout, and so were the casements. The fourth was furnished and lighted with orange—the fifth with white—the sixth with violet. The seventh apartment was closely shrouded in black velvet tapestries that hung all over the ceiling and down the walls, falling in heavy folds upon a carpet of the same material and hue. But in this chamber only, the color of the windows failed to correspond with the decorations. The panes here were scarlet—a deep blood color. Now in no one of the seven apartments was there any lamp or candelabrum, amid the profusion of golden ornaments that lay scattered to and fro or depended from the roof. There was no light of any kind emanating from lamp or candle within the suite of chambers. But in the corridors that followed the suite, there stood, opposite to each window, a heavy tripod, bearing a brazier of fire that projected its rays through the tinted glass and so glaringly illumined the room. And thus were produced a multitude of gaudy and fantastic appearances. But in the western or black chamber the effect of the fire-light that streamed upon the dark hangings through the blood-tinted panes, was ghastly in the extreme, and produced so wild a look upon the countenances of those who entered, that there were few of the company bold enough to set foot within its precincts at all.

It was in this apartment, also, that there stood against the western wall, a gigantic clock of ebony. Its pendulum swung to and fro with a dull, heavy, monotonous clang; and when the minute-hand made the circuit of the face, and the hour was to be stricken, there came from the brazen lungs of the clock a sound which was clear and loud and deep and exceedingly musical, but of so peculiar a note and emphasis that, at each lapse of an hour, the musicians of the orchestra were constrained to pause, momentarily, in their performance, to hearken to the sound; and a brief disconcert of the whole gay company; and, while the chimes of the clock yet rang, it was observed that the giddiest grew pale, and the more aged and sedate passed their hands over their brows as if in confused reverie or meditation. But when the echoes had fully ceased, a light laughter at once pervaded the assembly; the musicians looked at each other and smiled as if at their own nervousness and folly, and made whispering vows, each to the other, that the next chiming of the clock should produce in them no similar emotion: and then, after the lapse of sixty minutes, (which embrace three thousand and six hundred seconds of the Time that flies) there came yet another chiming of the clock, and then were the same disconcert and tremulousness and meditation as before.

But, in spite of these things, it was a gay and magnificent revel. The tastes of the duke were peculiar. He had a fine eye for colors and effects. He disregarded the *decora* of mere fashion. His plans were bold and fiery, and his conceptions glowed with barbaric lustre. There are some who would have thought him mad. His followers felt that he was not. It was necessary to hear and see and touch him to be *sure* that he was not.

He had directed, in great part, the moveable embellishments of the seven chambers, upon occasion of this great *fête*; and it was his own guiding taste which had given character to the masqueraders. Be sure they were grotesque. There were much glare and glitter and piquancy and phantasm—much of what has been since seen in Hernani.[1] There were arabesque figures with unsuited limbs and

---

[1] A play by Victor Hugo (1802–1885, presented in 1830.)—ED.

appointments. There were delirious fancies such as the madman fashions. There was much of the beautiful, much of the wanton, much of the *bizarre,* something of the terrible, and not a little of that which might have excited disgust. To and fro in the seven chambers there stalked, in fact, a multitude of dreams. And these—the dreams—writhed in and about, taking hue from the rooms, and causing the wild music of the orchestra to seem as the echo of their steps. And, anon, there strikes the ebony clock which stands in the hall of the velvet. And then, for a moment, all is still, and all is silent save the voice of the clock. The dreams are stiff-frozen as they stand. But the echoes of the chime die away—they have endured but an instant—and a light, half-subdued laughter floats after them as they depart. And now again the music swells, and the dreams live, and writhe to and fro more merrily than ever, taking hue from the many-tinted windows through which stream the rays from the tripods. But to the chamber which lies most westwardly of the seven, there are now none of the maskers who venture: for the night is waning away; and there flows a ruddier light through the blood-colored panes; and the blackness of the sable drapery appals: and to him whose foot falls upon the sable carpet, there comes from the near clock of ebony a muffled peal more solemnly emphatic than any which reaches *their* ears who indulge in the more remote gaieties of the other apartments.

But these other apartments were densely crowded, and in them beat feverishly the heart of life. And the revel went whirlingly on, until at length there commenced the sounding of midnight upon the clock. And then the music ceased, as I have told: and the evolutions of the waltzers were quieted: and there was an uneasy cessation of all things as before. But now there were twelve strokes to be sounded by the bell of the clock: and thus it happened, perhaps, that more of thought crept, with more of time, into the meditations of the thoughtful among those who revelled. And thus, too, it happened, perhaps, that before the last echoes of the last chimes had utterly sunk into silence, there were many individuals in the crowd who had found leisure to become aware of the presence of a masked figure which had arrested the attention of no single individual before. And the rumor of this new presence having spread itself whisperingly around, there arose at length from the whole company a buzz, finally of terror, of horror and of disgust.

In an assembly of phantasms such as I have painted, it may well be supposed that no ordinary appearance could have excited such sensation. In truth the masquerade license of the night was nearly unlimited: but the figure in question had out-Heroded Herod, and gone beyond the bounds of even the prince's indefinite decorum. There are chords in the hearts of the most reckless which cannot be touched without emotion. Even with the utterly lost, to whom life and death are equally jests, there are matters of which no jest can be made. The whole company, indeed, seemed now deeply to feel that in the costume and bearing of the stranger neither wit nor propriety existed. The figure was tall and gaunt, and shrouded from head to foot in the habiliments of the grave. The mask which concealed the visage was made so nearly to resemble the countenance of a stiffened corpse that the closest scrutiny must have had difficulty in detecting the cheat. And yet all this might have been endured, if not approved, by the mad revellers around. But the mummer had gone so far as to assume the type of the

Red Death. His vesture was dabbed in *blood*—and his broad brow, with all the features of the face, was besprinkled with the scarlet horror.

When the eyes of Prince Prospero fell upon this spectral image (which with a slow and solemn movement, as if more fully to sustain its *rôle,* stalked to and fro among the waltzers) he was seen to be convulsed, in the first moment with a strong shudder either of terror or distaste; but, in the next, his brow reddened with rage.

"Who dares?" he demanded hoarsely of the courtiers who stood near him—"who dares insult us with this blasphemous mockery? Seize him and unmask him—that we may know whom we have to hang at sunrise, from the battlements!"

It was in the eastern or blue chamber in which stood the Prince Prospero as he uttered these words. They rang throughout the seven rooms loudly and clearly—for the prince was a bold and robust man, and the music had become hushed at the waving of his hand.

It was in the blue room where stood the prince, with a group of pale courtiers by his side. At first, as he spoke, there was a slight rushing movement of this group in the direction of the intruder, who at the moment was also near at hand, and now, with deliberate and stately step, made closer approach to the speaker. But from a certain nameless awe with which the mad assumptions of the mummer had inspired the whole party, there were found none who put forth hand to seize him; so that, unimpeded, he passed within a yard of the prince's person; and, while the vast assembly, as if with one impulse, shrank from the centers of the rooms to the walls, he made his way uninterruptedly, but with the same solemn and measured step which had distinguished him from the first, through the blue chamber to the purple—through the purple to the green—through the green to the orange—through this again to the white—and even thence to the violet, ere a decided movement had been made to arrest him. It was then, however, that the Prince Prospero, maddening with rage and the shame of his own momentary cowardice, rushed hurriedly through the six chambers, while none followed him on account of a deadly terror that had seized upon all. He bore aloft a drawn dagger, and had approached, in rapid impetuosity, to within three or four feet of the retreating figure, when the latter, having attained the extremity of the velvet apartment, turned suddenly and confronted his pursuer. There was a sharp cry—and the dagger dropped gleaming upon the sable carpet, upon which, instantly afterwards, fell prostrate in death the Prince Prospero. Then, summoning the wild courage of despair, a throng of the revellers at once threw themselves into the black apartment, and, seizing the mummer, whose tall figure stood erect and motionless within the shadow of the ebony clock, gasped in unutterable horror at finding the grave-cerements and corpse-like mask which they handled with so violent a rudeness, untenanted by any tangible form.

And now was acknowledged the presence of the Red Death. He had come like a thief in the night. And one by one dropped the revellers in the blood-bedewed halls of their revel, and died each in the despairing posture of his fall. And the life of the ebony clock went out with that of the last of the gay. And the flames of the tripods expired. And Darkness and Decay and the Red Death held illimitable dominion over all.

QUESTIONS AND SUGGESTIONS FOR WRITING:

1. Why, in perilous circumstances, do the Prince and his followers engage in merrymaking?
2. Does Poe indicate, or even faintly imply, disapproval of Prince Prospero for shutting out the suffering external world?
3. Why does the striking of the clock cause such nervousness?
4. If the prince is concerned with forgetting the presence of death, why is the seventh room black, with "blood-colored panes"?
5. In a paragraph describe the prince's emotion(s) when he sees the mysterious masked figure, and orders him to be seized. In your paragraph you may occasionally quote a word or phrase from the text, but most of the writing should be your own.
6. Do you think Poe meant anything by specifying seven rooms, of which the first is the easternmost, and the seventh is the westernmost? What do you make out of the statement that the arrangement, unlike that of some other palaces, prevents a person from seeing from one end to the other?
7. In 500 words discuss and evaluate the idea that "The Masque of the Red Death" suggests that life itself is sickness.

Leo Tolstoy (Russian. 1828–1910)

HOW MUCH LAND DOES A MAN NEED?

I

An elder sister came to visit her younger sister in the country. The elder was married to a tradesman in town, the younger to a peasant in the village. As the sisters sat over their tea talking, the elder began to boast of the advantages of town life: saying how comfortably they lived there, how well they dressed, what fine clothes her children wore, what good things they ate and drank, and how she went to the theater, promenades, and entertainments.

The younger sister was piqued, and in turn disparaged the life of a tradesman, and stood up for that of a peasant.

"I would not change my way of life for yours," said she. "We may live roughly, but at least we are free from anxiety. You live in better style than we do, but though you often earn more than you need, you're very likely to lose all you have. We know the proverb, 'Loss and gain are brothers twain.' It often happens that people who are wealthy one day are begging their bread the next. Our way is safer. Though a peasant's life is not a fat one, it is long. We shall never grow rich, but we shall always have enough to eat."

The elder sister said sneeringly:

"Enough? Yes, if you like to share with the pigs and the calves! What do you know of elegance or manners! However much your good man may slave, you will die as you are living—on a dung heap—and your children the same."

"Well, what of that?" replied the younger. "Of course our work is rough and coarse. But, on the other hand, it is sure; and we need not bow to anyone. But

5

you, in your towns, are surrounded by temptations; today all may be right, but tomorrow the Evil One may tempt your husband with cards, wine, or women, and all will go to ruin. Don't such things happen often enough?"

Pahom, the master of the house, was lying on the top of the oven, and he listened to the women's chatter.

"It is perfectly true," thought he. "Busy as we are from childhood tilling mother earth, we peasants have no time to let any nonsense settle in our heads. Our only trouble is that we haven't land enough. If I had plenty of land, I shouldn't fear the Devil himself!"

The women finished their tea, chatted a while about dress, and then cleared away the tea things and lay down to sleep.

But the Devil had been sitting behind the oven, and had heard all that had   10 been said. He was pleased that the peasant's wife had led her husband into boasting, and that he had said that if he had plenty of land he would not fear the Devil himself.

"All right," thought the Devil. "We will have a tussle. I'll give you land enough; and by means of that land I will get you into my power."

II

Close to the village there lived a lady, a small landowner who had an estate of about three hundred acres or 120 *desyatins*. The *desyatina* is properly 2.7 acres; but in this story round numbers are used. She had always lived on good terms with the peasants until she engaged as her steward an old soldier, who took to burdening the people with fines. However careful Pahom tried to be, it happened again and again that now a horse of his got among the lady's oats, now a cow strayed into her garden, now his calves found their way into her meadows—and he always had to pay a fine.

Pahom paid up, but grumbled, and, going home in a temper, was rough with his family. All through that summer Pahom had much trouble because of this steward; and he was even glad when winter came and the cattle had to be stabled. Though he grudged the fodder when they could no longer graze on the pasture land, at least he was free from anxiety about them.

In the winter the news got about that the lady was going to sell her land and that the keeper of the inn on the high road was bargaining for it. When the peasants heard this they were very much alarmed.

"Well," thought they, "if the innkeeper gets the land, he will worry us with   15 fines worse than the lady's steward. We all depend on that estate."

So the peasants went on behalf of their Commune, and asked the lady not to sell the land to the innkeeper, offering her a better price for it themselves. The lady agreed to let them have it. Then the peasants tried to arrange for the Commune to buy the whole estate, so that it might be held by them all in common. They met twice to discuss it, but could not settle the matter; the Evil One sowed discord among them and they could not agree. So they decided to buy the land individually, each according to his means; and the lady agreed to this plan as she had to the other.

Presently Pahom heard that a neighbor of his was buying fifty acres, and that the lady had consented to accept one half in cash and to wait a year for the other half. Pahom felt envious.

"Look at that," thought he, "the land is all being sold, and I'll get none of it." So he spoke to his wife.

"Other people are buying," said he, "and we must also buy twenty acres or so. Life is becoming impossible. That steward is simply crushing us with his fines."

So they put their heads together and considered how they could manage to   20
buy it. They had one hundred rubles laid by. They sold a colt and one half of their bees; hired out one of their sons as a laborer, and took his wages in advance; borrowed the rest from a brother-in-law, and so scraped together half the purchase money.

Having done this, Pahom chose a farm of forty acres, some of it wooded, and went to the lady to bargain for it. They came to an agreement, and he shook hands with her upon it and paid her a deposit in advance. Then they went to town and signed the deeds; he paying half the price down, and undertaking to pay the remainder within two years.

So now Pahom had land of his own. He borrowed seed, and sowed it on the land he had bought. The harvest was a good one, and within a year he had managed to pay off his debts both to the lady and to his brother-in-law. So he became a landowner, plowing and sowing his own land, making hay on his own land, cutting his own trees, and feeding his cattle on his own pasture. When he went out to plow his fields, or to look at his growing corn, or at his grass-meadows, his heart would fill with joy. The grass that grew and the flowers that bloomed there seemed to him unlike any that grew elsewhere. Formerly, when he had passed by that land, it had appeared the same as any other land, but now it seemed quite different.

III

So Pahom was well-contented, and everything would have been right if the neighboring peasants would only not have trespassed on his cornfields and meadows. He appealed to them most civilly, but they still went on: now the Communal herdsmen would let the village cows stray into his meadows; then horses from the night pasture would get among his corn. Pahom turned them out again and again, and forgave their owners, and for a long time he forbore to prosecute anyone. But at last he lost patience and complained to the District Court. He knew it was the peasants' want of land, and no evil intent on their part, that caused the trouble, but he thought:

"I can't go on overlooking it, or they will destroy all I have. They must be taught a lesson."

So he had them up, gave them one lesson, and then another, and two or   25
three of the peasants were fined. After a time Pahom's neighbors began to bear him a grudge for this, and would now and then let their cattle on to his land on purpose. One peasant even got into Pahom's wood at night and cut down five young lime trees for their bark. Pahom, passing through the wood one day, no-

ticed something white. He came nearer and saw the stripped trunks lying on the ground, and close by stood the stumps where the trees had been. Pahom was furious.

"If he'd only cut one here and there it would have been bad enough," thought Pahom, "but the rascal has actually cut down a whole clump. If I could only find out who did this, I would pay him out."

He racked his brains as to who it could be. Finally he decided: "It must be Simon—no one else could have done it." So he went to Simon's homestead to have a look around, but he found nothing, and only had an angry scene. However, he now felt more certain than ever that Simon had done it, and he lodged a complaint. Simon was summoned. The case was tried, and retried, and at the end of it all Simon was acquitted, there being no evidence against him. Pahom felt still more aggrieved, and let his anger loose upon the Elder and the Judges.

"You let thieves grease your palms," said he. "If you were honest folk yourselves you would not let a thief go free."

So Pahom quarrelled with the judges and with his neighbors. Threats to burn his building began to be uttered. So though Pahom had more land, his place in the Commune was much worse than before.

About this time a rumor got about that many people were moving to new parts.   30

"There's no need for me to leave my land," thought Pahom. "But some of the others might leave our village and then there would be more room for us. I would take over their land myself and make my estate a bit bigger. I could then live more at ease. As it is, I'm still too cramped to be comfortable."

One day Pahom was sitting at home, when a peasant, passing through the village, happened to call in. He was allowed to stay the night, and supper was given him. Pahom had a talk with this peasant and asked him where he came from. The stranger answered that he came from beyond the Volga, where he had been working. One word led to another, and the man went on to say that many people were settling in those parts. He told how some people from his village had settled there. They had joined the Commune there and had had twenty-five acres per man granted them. The land was so good, he said, that the rye sown on it grew as high as a horse, and so thick that five cuts of a sickle made a sheaf. One peasant, he said, had brought nothing with him but his bare hands, and now he had six horses and two cows of his own.

Pahom's heart kindled with desire. He thought:

"Why should I suffer in this narrow hole, if one can live so well elsewhere? I will sell my land and my homestead here, and with the money I will start afresh over there and get everything new. In this crowded place one is always having trouble. But I must first go and find out all about it myself."

Toward summer he got ready and started. He went down the Volga on a   35 steamer to Samara, then walked another three hundred miles on foot, and at last reached the place. It was just as the stranger had said. The peasants had plenty of land: every man had twenty-five acres of Communal land given him for his use, and anyone who had money could buy, besides, at two shillings an acre (three rubles per *desyatina)* as much good freehold land as he wanted.

Having found out all he wished to know, Pahom returned home as autumn came on, and began selling off his belongings. He sold his land at a profit, sold his homestead and all his cattle, and withdrew from membership of the Commune. He only waited till the spring, and then started with his family for the new settlement.

IV

As soon as Pahom and his family arrived at their new abode, he applied for admission into the Commune of a large village. He stood treat to the Elders and obtained the necessary documents. Five shares of Communal land were given him for his own and his sons' use: that is to say—125 acres (not all together, but in different fields) besides the use of the Communal pasture. Pahom put up the buildings he needed and bought cattle. Of the Communal land alone he had three times as much as at his former home, and the land was good corn land. He was ten times better off than he had been. He had plenty of arable land and pasturage, and could keep as many head of cattle as he liked.

At first, in the bustle of building and settling down, Pahom was pleased with it all, but when he got used to it he began to think that even here he had not enough land. The first year he sowed wheat on his share of the Communal land and had a good crop. He wanted to go on sowing wheat, but had not enough Communal land for the purpose, and what he had already used was not available; for in those parts wheat is sown only on virgin soil or on fallow land. It is sown for one or two years, and then the land lies fallow till it is again overgrown with prairie grass. There were many who wanted such land, and there was not enough for all; so that people quarreled about it. Those who were better off wanted it for growing wheat, and those who were poor wanted it to let to dealers, so that they might raise money to pay their taxes. Pahom wanted to sow more wheat, so he rented land from a dealer for a year. He sowed much wheat and had a fine crop, but the land was too far from the village—the wheat had to be carted more than ten miles. After a time Pahom noticed that some peasant dealers were living on separate farms and were growing wealthy; and he thought:

"If I were to buy some freehold land and have a homestead on it, it would be a different thing altogether. Then it would all be nice and compact."

The question of buying freehold land recurred to him again and again.   40

He went on in the same way for three years, renting land and sowing wheat. The seasons turned out well and the crops were good, so that he began to lay money by. He might have gone on living contentedly, but he grew tired of having to rent other people's land every year, and having to scramble for it. Wherever there was good land to be had, the peasants would rush for it and it was taken up at once, so that unless you were sharp about it you got none. It happened in the third year that he and a dealer together rented a piece of pasture land from some peasants; and they had already plowed it up, when there was some dispute and the peasants went to law about it, and things fell out so that the labor was all lost.

"If it were my own land," thought Pahom, "I should be independent, and there would not be all this unpleasantness."

So Pahom began looking out for land which he could buy; he came across a peasant who had bought thirteen hundred acres, but having got into difficulties was willing to sell again cheap. Pahom bargained and haggled with him, and at last they settled the price at 1,500 rubles, part in cash and part to be paid later. They had all but clinched the matter when a passing dealer happened to stop at Pahom's one day to get a feed for his horses. He drank tea with Pahom, and they had a talk. The dealer said that he was just returning from the land of the Bashkirs, far away, where he had bought thirteen thousand acres of land, all for 1,000 rubles. Pahom questioned him further, and the tradesman said:

"All one need do is to make friends with the chiefs. I gave away about one hundred rubles' worth of dressing gowns and carpets, besides a case of tea, and I gave wine to those who would drink it; and I got the land for less than twopence an acre (five *kapeks* for a *desyatina*)." And he showed Pahom the title-deeds, saying:

"The land lies near a river, and the whole prairie is virgin soil."   45

Pahom plied him with questions, and the tradesman said:

"There is more land there than you could cover if you walked a year, and it all belongs to the Bashkirs. They are as simple as sheep, and land can be got almost for nothing."

"There now," thought Pahom, "with my one thousand rubles, why should I get only thirteen hundred acres, and saddle myself with a debt besides. If I take it out there, I can get more than ten times as much for the money."

V

Pahom inquired how to get to the place, and as soon as the tradesman had left him, he prepared to go there himself. He left his wife to look after the homestead, and started on his journey taking his hired man with him. They stopped at a town on their way, and bought a case of tea, some wine, and other presents, as the tradesman had advised. On and on they went until they had gone more than three hundred miles, and on the seventh day they came to a place where the Bashkirs had pitched their tents. It was all just as the tradesman had said. The people lived on the steppes, by a river, in felt-covered tents. They neither tilled the ground nor ate bread. Their cattle and horses grazed in herds on the steppe. The colts were tethered behind the tents, and the mares were driven to them twice a day. The mares were milked, and from the milk kumiss was made. It was the women who prepared kumiss, and they also made cheese. As far as the men were concerned, drinking kumiss and tea, eating mutton, and playing on their pipes was all they cared about. They were all stout and merry, and all the summer long they never thought of doing any work. They were quite ignorant, and knew no Russian, but were good-natured enough.

As soon as they saw Pahom, they came out of their tents and gathered round   50
their visitor. An interpreter was found, and Pahom told them he had come about some land. The Bashkirs seemed very glad; they took Pahom and led him into one of the best tents, where they made him sit on some down cushions placed on a carpet, while they sat round him. They gave him some tea and kumiss, and had a sheep killed, and gave him mutton to eat. Pahom took presents out of his cart and distributed them among the Bashkirs, and divided amongst them the tea. The

Bashkirs were delighted. They talked a great deal among themselves, and then told the interpreter to translate.

"They wish to tell you," said the interpreter, "that they like you, and that it is our custom to do all we can to please a guest and to repay him for his gifts. You have given us presents, now tell us which of the things we possess please you best, that we may present them to you."

"What pleases me best here," answered Pahom, "is your land. Our land is crowded and the soil is exhausted; but you have plenty of land, and it is good land. I never saw the like of it."

The interpreter translated. The Bashkirs talked among themselves for a while. Pahom could not understand what they were saying, but saw that they were much amused, and that they shouted and laughed. Then they were silent and looked at Pahom while the interpreter said:

"They wish me to tell you that in return for your presents they will gladly give you as much land as you want. You have only to point it out with your hand and it is yours."

The Bashkirs talked again for a while and began to dispute. Pahom asked what they were disputing about, and the interpreter told him that some of them thought they ought to ask their Chief about the land and not act in his absence, while others thought there was no need to wait for his return.   55

VI

While the Bashkirs were disputing, a man in a large fox fur cap appeared on the scene. They all became silent and rose to their feet. The interpreter said, "This is our Chief himself."

Pahom immediately fetched the best dressing gown and five pounds of tea, and offered these to the Chief. The Chief accepted them, and seated himself in the place of honor. The Bashkirs at once began telling him something. The Chief listened for a while, then made a sign with his head for them to be silent, and addressing himself to Pahom, said in Russian:

"Well, let it be so. Choose whatever piece of land you like; we have plenty of it."

"How can I take as much as I like?" thought Pahom. "I must get a deed to make it secure, or else they may say, 'It is yours,' and afterwards may take it away again."

"Thank you for your kind words," he said aloud. "You have much land, and I   60 only want a little. But I should like to be sure which bit is mine. Could it not be measured and made over to me? Life and death are in God's hands. You good people give it to me, but your children might wish to take it away again."

"You are quite right," said the Chief. "We will make it over to you."

"I heard that a dealer had been here," continued Pahom, "and that you gave him a little land, too, and signed title deeds to that effect. I should like to have it done in the same way."

The Chief understood.

"Yes," replied he, "that can be done quite easily. We have a scribe, and we will go to town with you and have the deed properly sealed."

"And what will be the price?" asked Pahom.   65

"Our price is always the same: one thousand rubles a day."

Pahom did not understand.

"A day? What measure is that? How many acres would that be?"

"We do not know how to reckon it out," said the Chief. "We sell it by the day. As much as you can go round on your feet in a day is yours, and the price is one thousand rubles a day."

Pahom was surprised.   70

"But in a day you can get around a large tract of land," he said.

The Chief laughed.

"It will all be yours!" said he. "But there is one condition: If you don't return on the same day to the spot whence you started, your money is lost."

"But how am I to mark the way that I have gone?"

"Why, we shall go to any spot you like, and stay there. You must start from   75
that spot and make your round, taking a spade with you. Wherever you think necessary, make a mark. At every turning, dig a hole and pile up the turf; then afterwards we will go round with a plow from hole to hole. You may make as large a circuit as you please, but before the sun sets you must return to the place you started from. All the land you cover will be yours."

Pahom was delighted. It was decided to start early next morning. They talked a while, and after drinking some more kumiss and eating some more mutton, they had tea again, and then the night came on. They gave Pahom a feather bed to sleep on, and the Bashkirs dispersed for the night, promising to assemble the next morning at daybreak and ride out before sunrise to the appointed spot.

VII

Pahom lay on the feather bed, but could not sleep. He kept thinking about the land.

"What a large tract I'll mark off!" thought he. "I can easily do thirty-five miles in a day. The days are long now, and within a circuit of thirty-five miles what a lot of land there will be! I'll sell the poorer land, or let it to peasants, but I'll pick out the best and farm it. I will buy two ox teams and hire two more laborers. About a hundred and fifty acres shall be plow land, and I will pasture cattle on the rest."

Pahom lay awake all night, and dozed off only just before dawn. Hardly were his eyes closed when he had a dream. He thought he was lying in that same tent and heard somebody chuckling outside. He wondered who it could be, and rose and went out, and he saw the Bashkir Chief sitting in front of the tent holding his sides and rolling about with laughter. Going nearer to the Chief, Pahom asked: "What are you laughing at?" But he saw that it was no longer the Chief, but the dealer who had recently stopped at his house and had told him about the land. Just as Pahom was going to ask, "Have you been here long?" he saw that it was not the dealer, but the peasant who had come up from the Volga, long ago, to Pahom's old home. Then he saw that it was not the peasant either, but the Devil himself with hoofs and horns, sitting there and chuckling, and before him lay a man barefoot, prostrate on the ground, with only trousers and a shirt on. And

Pahom dreamt that he looked more attentively to see what sort of a man it was that was lying there, and he saw that the man was dead, and that it was himself! He awoke horror struck.

"What things one does dream," thought he.   80

Looking round he saw through the open door that the dawn was breaking.

"It's time to wake them up," thought he. "We ought to be starting."

He got up, roused his man (who was sleeping in his cart), bade him harness; and went to call the Bashkirs.

"It's time to go to the steppe to measure the land," he said.

The Bashkirs rose and assembled, and the Chief came too. Then they began   85 drinking kumiss again, and offered Pahom some tea, but he would not wait.

"If we are to go, let us go. It is high time," said he.

VIII

The Bashkirs got ready and they all started: some mounted on horses and some in carts. Pahom drove in his own small cart with his servant and took a spade with him. When they reached the steppe, the morning red was beginning to kindle. They ascended a hillock (called by the Bashkirs a *shikhan*) and, dismounting from their carts and their horses, gathered in one spot. The Chief came up to Pahom and stretching out his arm towards the plain:

"See," said he, "all this, as far as your eye can reach, is ours. You may have any part of it you like."

Pahom's eyes glistened: it was all virgin soil, as flat as the palm of your hand, as black as the seed of a poppy, and in the hollows different kinds of grasses grew breast high.

The Chief took off his fox fur cap, placed it on the ground, and said: 90

"This will be the mark. Start from here, and return here again. All the land you go round shall be yours."

Pahom took out his money and put it on the cap. Then he took off his outer coat, remaining in his sleeveless undercoat. He unfastened his girdle and tied it tight below his stomach, put a little bag of bread into the breast of his coat, and tying a flask of water to his girdle, he drew up the tops of his boots, took the spade from his man, and stood ready to start. He considered for some moments which way he had better go—it was tempting everywhere.

"No matter," he concluded, "I'll go towards the rising sun."

He turned his face to the east, stretched himself, and waited for the sun to appear above the rim.

"I must lose no time," he thought, "and it is easier walking while it is still   95 cool."

The sun's rays had hardly flashed above the horizon before Pahom, carrying the spade over his shoulder, went down into the steppe.

Pahom started walking neither slowly nor quickly. After having gone a thousand yards he stopped, dug a hole, and placed pieces of turf one on another to make it more visible. Then he went on; and now that he had walked off his stiffness he quickened his pace. After a while he dug another hole.

Pahom looked back. The hillock could be distinctly seen in the sunlight, with the people on it, and the glittering tires of the cartwheels. At a rough guess Pahom concluded that he had walked three miles. It was growing warmer; he took off his undercoat, flung it across his shoulder, and went on again. It had grown quite warm now; he looked at the sun, it was time to think of breakfast.

"The first shift is done, but there are four in a day, and it is too soon yet to turn. But I will just take off my boots," said he to himself.

He sat down, took off his boots, stuck them into his girdle, and went on. It   100
was easy walking now.

"I will go on for another three miles," thought he, "and then turn to the left. This spot is so fine that it would be a pity to lose it. The further one goes, the better the land seems."

He went straight on for a while, and when he looked round, the hillock was scarcely visible and the people on it looked like black ants, and he could just see something glistening there in the sun.

"Ah," thought Pahom, "I have gone far enough in this direction, it is time to turn. Besides, I am in a regular sweat, and very thirsty."

He stopped, dug a large hole, and heaped up pieces of turf. Next he untied his flask, had a drink, and then turned sharply to the left. He went on and on; the grass was high, and it was very hot.

Pahom began to grow tired: he looked at the sun and saw that it was noon.   105

"Well," he thought, "I must have a rest."

He sat down, and ate some bread and drank some water; but he did not lie down, thinking that if he did he might fall asleep. After sitting a little while, he went on again. At first he walked easily: the food had strengthened him; but it had become terribly hot and he felt sleepy. Still he went on, thinking: "An hour to suffer, a lifetime to live."

He went a long way in this direction also, and was about to turn the left again, when he perceived a damp hollow: "It would be a pity to leave that out," he thought, "flax would do well there." So he went on past the hollow and dug a hole on the other side of it before he turned the corner. Pahom looked towards the hillock. The heat made the air hazy: it seemed to be quivering, and through the haze the people on the hillock could scarcely be seen.

"Ah," thought Pahom, "I have made the sides too long; I must make this one shorter." And he went along the third side, stepping faster. He looked at the sun: it was nearly half way to the horizon, and he had not yet done two miles of the third side of the square. He was still ten miles from the goal.

"No," he thought, "though it will make my land lopsided, I must hurry back   110
in a straight line now. I might go too far, and as it is I have a great deal of land."

So Pahom hurriedly dug a hole and turned straight towards the hillock.

IX

Pahom went straight towards the hillock, but he now walked with difficulty. He was done up with the heat, his bare feet were cut and bruised, and his legs began to fail. He longed to rest, but it was impossible if he meant to get back before sunset. The sun waits for no man, and it was sinking lower and lower.

"Oh dear," he thought, "if only I have not blundered trying for too much!

What if I am too late?"

He looked towards the hillock and at the sun. He was still far from his goal, and the sun was already near the rim.

Pahom walked on and on; it was very hard walking, but he went quicker and quicker. He pressed on, but was still far from the place. He began running, threw away his coat, his boots, his flask, and his cap, and kept only the spade which he used as a support.

"What shall I do?" he thought again. "I have grasped too much, and ruined the whole affair. I can't get there before the sun sets."

And this fear made him still more breathless. Pahom went on running, his soaking shirt and trousers stuck to him, and his mouth was parched. His breast was working like a blacksmith's bellows, his heart was beating like a hammer, and his legs were giving way as if they did not belong to him. Pahom was seized with terror lest he should die of the strain.

Though afraid of death, he could not stop.

"After having run all that way they will call me a fool if I stop now," thought he. And he ran on and on, and drew near and heard the Bashkirs yelling and shouting to him, and their cries inflamed his heart still more. He gathered his last strength and ran on.

The sun was close to the rim, and cloaked in mist, looked large, and red as blood. Now, yes now, it was about to set! The sun was quite low, but he was also quite near his aim. Pahom could already see the people on the hillock waving their arms to hurry him up. He could see the fox fur cap on the ground and the money in it, and the Chief sitting on the ground holding his sides. And Pahom remembered his dream.

"There is plenty of land," thought he, "but will God let me live on it? I have lost my life. I have lost my life! I shall never reach that spot!"

Pahom looked at the sun, which had reached the earth: one side of it had already disappeared. With all his remaining strength he rushed on, bending his body forward so that his legs could hardly follow fast enough to keep him from falling. Just as he reached the hillock it suddenly grew dark. He looked up—the sun had already set!

He gave a cry: "All my labor has been in vain," thought he, and was about to stop, but he heard the Bashkirs still shouting, and remembered that though to him, from below, the sun seemed to have set, they on the hillock could still see it. He took a long breath and ran up the hillock. It was still light there. He reached the top and saw the cap. Before it sat the Chief laughing and holding his sides. Again Pahom remembered his dream, and he uttered a cry: his legs gave way beneath him, he fell forward and reached the cap with his hands.

"Ah, that's a fine fellow!" exclaimed the Chief. "He has gained much land!"

Pahom's servant came running up and tried to raise him, but he saw that blood was flowing from his mouth. Pahom was dead.

The Bashkirs clicked their tongues to show their pity.

His servant picked up the spade and dug a grave long enough for Pahom to lie in, and buried him in it.

Six feet from his head to his heels was all he needed.

QUESTIONS AND SUGGESTIONS FOR WRITING

1. In what ways is this story like one of Aesop's fables? (If you are unfamiliar with Aesop's fables, find a volume of them in the library and read several of the fables.) In what ways is it different from a fable?
2. At the end of part V, and in part VI, the Bashkirs seem to be willing to allow Pahom the free use of as much land as he wants, but he insists on a formal agreement and on formal boundaries. What does this attitude tell us about him? Can you generalize and suggest what Tolstoy may be implying about human nature?
3. In one or two paragraphs characterize Pahom, taking account of any changes you perceive in his character as the narrative proceeds.
4. Part VII recounts a dream. What does this dream contribute to the story? Do you think the story would be better without it? Why?
5. In an essay of 500 words, set forth your understanding of Tolstoy's view about how much land a person *does* need.
6. Pahom follows the devil's way. In an essay of 500 words discuss whether in this story Tolstoy allows us to assume that there is an alternative way—God's way.

Jean Rhys (English. 1894–1979)

I USED TO LIVE HERE ONCE

She was standing by the river looking at the stepping stones and remembering each one. There was the round unsteady stone, the pointed one, the flat one in the middle—the safe stone where you could stand and look round. The next wasn't so safe for when the river was full the water flowed over it and even when it showed dry it was slippery. But after that it was easy and soon she was standing on the other side.

The road was much wider than it used to be but the work had been done carelessly. The felled trees had not been cleared away and the bushes looked trampled. Yet it was the same road and she walked along feeling extraordinarily happy.

It was a fine day, a blue day. The only thing was that the sky had a glassy look that she didn't remember. That was the only word she could think of. Glassy. She turned the corner, saw that what had been the old pavé[1] had been taken up, and there too the road was much wider, but it had the same unfinished look.

She came to the worn stone steps that led up to the house and her heart began to beat. The screw pine was gone, so was the mock summer house called the ajoupa, but the clove tree was still there and at the top of the steps the rough lawn stretched away, just as she remembered it. She stopped and looked towards the house that had been added to and painted white. It was strange to see a car standing in front of it.

There were two children under the big mango tree, a boy and a little girl, and she waved to them and called "Hello" but they didn't answer her or turn their

---

[1] Paved road. —ED.

heads. Very fair children, as Europeans born in the West Indies so often are: as if the white blood is asserting itself against all odds.

The grass was yellow in the hot sunlight as she walked towards them. When she was quite close she called again, shyly: "Hello." Then, "I used to live here once," she said.

Still they didn't answer. When she said for the third time "Hello" she was quite near them. Her arms went out instinctively with the longing to touch them.

It was the boy who turned. His gray eyes looked straight into hers. His expression didn't change. He said: "Hasn't it gone cold all of a sudden. D'you notice? Let's go in." "Yes let's," said the girl.

Her arms fell to her sides as she watched them running across the grass to the house. That was the first time she knew.

QUESTIONS AND SUGGESTIONS FOR WRITING

1. One of our students, who had lived in the West Indies (where the story is set) argued that the story is about a woman who, after having deserted the islands, returns to them and is now deliberately snubbed (that is, treated as though she doesn't exist). Do you think this is what the story is about? Are you convinced by the student's description that this is the way West Indians treat those who leave and then return?
2. What do you make out of the following details: (1) that the sky has an unfamiliar "glassy" look; (2) that the children don't reply; (3) that the boy comments on a sudden chilliness?

Elizabeth Bowen (Irish. 1899–1973)

THE DEMON LOVER

Towards the end of her day in London Mrs. Drover went round to her shut-up house to look for several things she wanted to take away. Some belonged to herself, some to her family, who were by now used to their country life. It was late August; it had been a steamy, showery day: at the moment the trees down the pavement glittered in an escape of humid yellow afternoon sun. Against the next batch of clouds, already piling up ink-dark, broken chimneys and parapets stood out. In her once familiar street, as in any unused channel, an unfamiliar queerness had silted up: a cat wove itself in and out of railings, but no human eye watched Mrs. Drover's return. Shifting some parcels under her arm, she slowly forced round her latchkey in an unwilling lock, then gave the door, which had warped, a push with her knee. Dead air came out to meet her as she went in.

The staircase window having been boarded up, no light came down into the hall. But one door, she could just see, stood ajar, so she went quickly through into the room and unshuttered the big window in there. Now the prosaic woman, looking about her, was more perplexed than she knew by everything that she saw, by traces of her long former habit of life—the yellow smoke-stain up the white marble mantelpiece, the ring left by a vase on the top of the escritoire; the bruise in the wallpaper where, on the door being thrown open widely, the china handle had always hit the wall. The piano, having gone away to be stored, had left what looked like claw-marks on its part of the parquet. Though not much dust had seeped in, each object wore a film of another kind; and, the only ventilation being the chimney, the whole drawing-room smelled of the cold hearth. Mrs. Drover put down her parcels on the escritoire and left the room to proceed upstairs; the things she wanted were in a bedroom closet.

She had been anxious to see how the house was—the part-time caretaker she shared with some neighbors was away this week on his holiday, known to be not yet back. At the best of times he did not look in often, and she was never sure that she trusted him. There were some cracks in the structure, left by the last bombing, on which she was anxious to keep an eye. Not that one could do anything—

A shaft of refracted daylight now lay across the hall. She stopped dead and stared at the hall table—on this lay a letter addressed to her.

She thought first—then the caretaker *must* be back. All the same, who, seeing the house shuttered, would have dropped a letter in at the box? It was not a circular, it was not a bill. And the post office redirected, to the address in the country, everything for her that came through the post. The caretaker (even if he *were* back) did not know she was due in London today—her call here had been planned to be a surprise—so his negligence in the manner of this letter, leaving it to wait in the dusk and the dust, annoyed her. Annoyed, she picked up the letter, which bore no stamp. But it cannot be important, or they would know . . . She took the letter rapidly upstairs with her, without a stop to look at the writing till she reached what had been her bedroom, where she let in light. The room looked over the garden and other gardens: the sun had gone in; as the clouds sharpened and lowered, the trees and rank lawns seemed already to smoke with dark. Her reluctance to look again at the letter came from the fact that she felt intruded upon—and by someone contemptuous of her ways. However, in the tenseness preceding the fall of rain she read it: it was a few lines.

> Dear Kathleen: You will not have forgotten that today is our anniversary, and the day we said. The years have gone by at once slowly and fast. In view of the fact that nothing has changed, I shall rely upon you to keep your promise. I was sorry to see you leave London, but was satisfied that you would be back in time. You may expect me, therefore, at the hour arranged. Until then . . .
>
> K.

Mrs. Drover looked for the date: it was today's. She dropped the letter on to the bed-springs, then picked it up to see the writing again—her lips, beneath the remains of lipstick, beginning to go white. She felt so much the change in her own face that she went to the mirror, polished a clear patch in it, and looked at once urgently and stealthily in. She was confronted by a woman of forty-four, with eyes starting out under a hat-brim that had been rather carelessly pulled down. She had not put on any more powder since she left the shop where she ate her solitary tea. The pearls her husband had given her on their marriage hung loose around her now rather thinner throat, slipping in the V of the pink wool jumper her sister knitted last autumn as they sat round the fire. Mrs. Drover's most normal expression was one of controlled worry, but of assent. Since the birth of the third of her little boys, attended by a quite serious illness, she had had an intermittent muscular flicker to the left of her mouth, but in spite of this she could always sustain a manner that was at once energetic and calm.

Turning from her own face as precipitately as she had gone to meet it, she went to the chest where the things were, unlocked it, threw up the lid, and knelt to search. But as rain began to come crashing down she could not keep from looking over her shoulder at the stripped bed on which the letter lay. Behind the blanket of rain the clock of the church that still stood struck six—with rapidly heightening apprehension she counted each of the slow strokes. "The hour arranged . . . My God," she said, "what hour? How should I . . . ? After twenty-five years . . ."

The young girl talking to the soldier in the garden had not ever completely seen his face. It was dark; they were saying goodbye under a tree. Now and then—for it felt, from not seeing him at this intense moment, as though she had never seen him at all—she verified his presence for these few moments longer by putting out a hand, which he each time pressed, without very much kindness, and painfully, on to one of the breast buttons of his uniform. That cut of the button on the palm of her hand was, principally, what she was to carry away. This was so near the end of a leave from France that she could only wish him already gone. It was August 1916. Being not kissed, being drawn away from and looked at intimidated Kathleen till she imagined spectral glitters in the place of his eyes. Turning away and looking back up the lawn she saw, through branches of trees, the drawing-room window light: she caught a breath for the moment when she could go running back there into the safe arms of her mother and sister, and cry: "What shall I do, what shall I do? He has gone."

Hearing her catch her breath, her fiancé said, without feeling: "Cold?"

"You're going away such a long way."

"Not so far as you think."   10

"I don't understand?"

"You don't have to," he said. "You will. You know what we said."

"But that was—suppose you—I mean, suppose."

"I shall be with you," he said, "sooner or later. You won't forget that. You need do nothing but wait."

Only a little more than a minute later she was free to run up the silent lawn.   15
Looking in through the window at her mother and sister, who did not for the moment perceive her, she already felt that unnatural promise drive down between her and the rest of all human kind. No other way of having given herself could have made her feel so apart, lost and foresworn. She could not have plighted a more sinister troth.

Kathleen behaved well when, some months later, her fiancé was reported missing, presumed killed. Her family not only supported her but were able to praise her courage without stint because they could not regret, as a husband for her, the man they knew almost nothing about. They hoped she would, in a year or two, console herself—and had it been only a question of consolation things might have gone much straighter ahead. But her trouble, behind just a little grief, was a complete dislocation from everything. She did not reject other lovers, for these failed to appear: for years she failed to attract men—and with the approach of her thirties she became natural enough to share her family's anxiousness on this score. She began to put herself out, to wonder; and at thirty-two she was very greatly relieved to find herself being courted by William Drover. She married him, and the two of them settled down in this quiet, arboreal part of Kensington: in this house the years piled up, her children were born, and they all lived till they were driven out by the bombs of the next war. Her movements as Mrs. Drover were circumscribed, and she dismissed any idea that they were still watched.

As things were—dead or living the letter-writer sent her only a threat. Unable, for some minutes, to go on kneeling with her back exposed to the empty room, Mrs. Drover rose from the chest to sit on an upright chair whose back was firmly against the wall. The desuetude of her former bedroom, her married London home's whole air of being a cracked cup from which memory, with its reassuring power, had either evaporated or leaked away, made a crisis—and at just this crisis the letter-writer had, knowledgeably, struck. The hollowness of the house this evening canceled years on years of voices, habits, and steps. Through the shut windows she only heard rain fall on the roofs around. To rally herself, she said she was in a mood—and for two or three seconds shutting her eyes, told herself that she had imagined the letter. But she opened them—there it lay on the bed.

On the supernatural side of the letter's entrance she was not permitting her mind to dwell. Who, in London, knew she meant to call at the house today? Evidently, however, this had been known. The caretaker, had he come back, had had no cause to expect her: he would have taken the letter in his pocket, to forward it, at his own time, through the post. There was no other sign that the caretaker had been in—but, if not? Letters dropped in at doors of deserted houses do not fly or walk to tables in halls. They do not sit on the dust of empty tables with the air of certainty that they will be found. There is needed some human hand—but nobody but the caretaker had a key. Under circumstances she did not care to consider, a house can be entered without a key. It was possible that she was not alone now. She might be being waited for, downstairs. Waited for—until when? Until "the hour arranged." At least that was not six o'clock: six has struck.

She rose from the chair and went over and locked the door.

The thing was, to get out. To fly? No, not that: she had to catch her train. As a woman whose utter dependability was the keystone of her family life she was not willing to return to the country, to her husband, her little boys, and her sister, without the objects she had come up to fetch. Resuming work at the chest she set about making up a number of parcels in a rapid, fumbling-decisive way. These, with her shopping parcels, would be too much to carry; these meant a taxi—at the thought of the taxi her heart went up and her normal breathing resumed. I will ring up the taxi now; the taxi cannot come too soon: I shall hear the taxi out there running its engine, till I walk calmly down to it through the hall. I'll ring up—But no: the telephone is cut off . . . She tugged at a knot she had tied wrong.

20

The idea of flight . . . He was never kind to me, not really. I don't remember him kind at all. Mother said he never considered me. He was set on me, that was what it was—not love. Not love, not meaning a person well. What did he do, to make me promise like that? I can't remember—But she found that she could.

She remembered with such dreadful acuteness that the twenty-five years since then dissolved like smoke and she instinctively looked for the weal left by the button on the palm of her hand. She remembered not only all that he said and did but the complete suspension of her existence during that August week. I was not myself—they all told me so at the time. She remembered—but with one white burning blank as where acid has dropped on a photograph: *under no conditions* could she remember his face.

So, wherever he may be waiting, I shall not know him. You have no time to run from a face you do not expect.

The thing was to get to the taxi before any clock struck what could be the hour. She would slip down the street and round the side of the square to where the square gave on the main road. She would return in the taxi, safe, to her own door, and bring the solid driver into the house with her to pick up the parcels from room to room. The idea of the taxi driver made her decisive, bold: she unlocked her door, went to the top of the staircase, and listened down.

She heard nothing—but while she was hearing nothing the *passé* air of the   25
staircase was disturbed by a draught that traveled up to her face. It emanated from the basement: down there a door or window was being opened by someone who chose this moment to leave the house.

The rain had stopped; the pavements steamily shone as Mrs. Drover let herself out by inches from her own front door into the empty street. The unoccupied houses opposite continued to meet her look with their damaged stare. Making towards the thoroughfare and the taxi, she tried not to keep looking behind. Indeed, the silence was so intense—one of those creeks of London silence exaggerated this summer by the damage of war—that no tread could have gained on hers unheard. Where her street debouched on the square where people went on living, she grew conscious of, and checked, her unnatural pace. Across the open end of the square two buses impassively passed each other: women, a perambulator, cyclists, a man wheeling a barrow signalized, once again, the ordinary flow of life. At the square's most populous corner should be—and was—the short taxi rank. This evening, only one taxi—but this, although it presented its blank rump, appeared already to be alertly waiting for her. Indeed, without looking round the driver started his engine as she panted up from behind and put her hand on the door. As she did so, the clock struck seven. The taxi faced the main road: to make the trip back to her house it would have to turn—she had settled back on the seat and the taxi *had* turned before she, surprised by its knowing movement, recollected that she had not "said where." She leaned forward to scratch at the glass panel that divided the driver's head from her own.

The driver braked to what was almost a stop, turned round, and slid the glass panel back: the jolt of this flung Mrs. Drover forward till her face was almost into the glass. Through the aperture driver and passenger, not six inches between them, remained for an eternity eye to eye. Mrs. Drover's mouth hung open for some seconds before she could issue her first scream. After that she continued to scream freely and to beat with her gloved hands on the glass all round as the taxi, accelerating without mercy, made off with her into the hinterland of deserted streets.

QUESTIONS AND SUGGESTIONS FOR WRITING

1. In a paragraph explain how Mrs. Drover's home helps to characterize her life. In a second paragraph, indicate to what degree she is a sympathetic figure. Be sure to support your view with evidence from the text.
2. Evaluate the view that the story is about a woman whose earlier frustration in love led to a nervous breakdown, and that the sight of the house now triggers hallucinations concerning a letter, a man leaving the basement, and a taxi driver.
3. In an essay of 500 words argue that the story is (1) a ghost story, *or* (2) a story about a woman with hallucinations; *or* (3) show that neither of these two views can be argued conclusively.
4. If you have read Joyce Carol Oates's "Where Are You Going" (page 143), in two paragraphs compare Bowen's demon lover and Arnold Friend.

Ray Bradbury (American. b. 1920)

OCTOBER 2026:
The Million-Year Picnic

Somehow the idea was brought up by Mom that perhaps the whole family would enjoy a fishing trip. But they weren't Mom's words; Timothy knew that. They were Dad's words, and Mom used them for him somehow.

Dad shuffled his feet in a clutter of Martian pebbles and agreed. So immediately there was a tumult and a shouting, and very quickly the camp was tucked into capsules and containers, Mom slipped into traveling jumpers and blouse, Dad stuffed his pipe full with trembling hands, his eyes on the Martian sky, and the three boys piled yelling into the motorboat, none of them really keeping an eye on Mom and Dad, except Timothy.

Dad pushed a stud. The water boat sent a humming sound up into the sky. The water shook back and the boat nosed ahead, and the family cried, "Hurrah!"

Timothy sat in the back of the boat with Dad, his small fingers atop Dad's hairy ones, watching the canal twist, leaving the crumbled place behind where they had landed in their small family rocket all the way from Earth. He remembered the night before they left Earth, the hustling and hurrying, the rocket that Dad had found somewhere, somehow, and the talk of a vacation on Mars. A long way to go for a vacation, but Timothy said nothing because of his younger brothers. They came to Mars and now, first thing, or so they said, they were going fishing.

Dad had a funny look in his eyes as the boat went up-canal. A look that

Timothy couldn't figure. It was made of strong light and maybe a sort of relief. It made the deep wrinkles laugh instead of worry or cry.

So there went the cooling rocket, around a bend, gone.

"How far are we going?" Robert splashed his hand. It looked like a small crab jumping in the violet water.

Dad exhaled. "A million years."

"Gee," said Robert.

"Look, kids." Mother pointed one soft long arm. "There's a dead city."   0

They looked with fervent anticipation and the dead city lay dead for them alone, drowsing in a hot silence of summer made on Mars by a Martian weatherman.

And Dad looked as if he was pleased that it was dead.

It was a futile spread of pink rocks sleeping on a rise of sand, a few tumbled pillars, one lonely shrine, and then the sweep of sand again. Nothing else for miles. A white desert around the canal and a blue desert over it.

Just then a bird flew up. Like a stone thrown across a blue pond, hitting, falling deep, and vanishing.

Dad got a frightened look when he saw it. "I thought it was a rocket."   15

Timothy looked at the deep ocean sky, trying to see Earth and the war and the ruined cities and the men killing each other since the day he was born. But he saw nothing. The war was as removed and far off as two flies battling to the death in the arch of a great high and silent cathedral. And just as senseless.

William Thomas wiped his forehead and felt the touch of his son's hand on his arm, like a young tarantula, thrilled. He beamed at his son. "How goes it, Timmy?"

"Fine, Dad."

Timothy hadn't quite figured out what was ticking inside the vast adult mechanism beside him. The man with the immense hawk nose, sunburnt, peeling— and the hot blue eyes like agate marbles you play with after school in summer back on Earth, and the long thick columnar legs in the loose riding breeches.

"What are you looking at so hard, Dad?"   20

"I was looking for Earthian logic, common sense, good government, peace, and responsibility."

"All that up there?"

"No. I didn't find it. It's not there any more. Maybe it'll never be there again. Maybe we fooled ourselves that it was ever there."

"Huh?"

"See the fish," said Dad, pointing.   25

There rose a soprano clamor from all three boys as they rocked the boat in arching their tender necks to see. They *oohed* and *ahed*. A silver ring fish floated by them, undulating, and closing like an iris, instantly, around food particles, to assimilate them.

Dad looked at it. His voice was deep and quiet.

"Just like war. War swims along, sees food, contracts. A moment later— Earth is gone.

"William," said Mom.

"Sorry," said Dad.   30

They sat still and felt the canal water rush cool, swift and glassy. The only sound was the motor hum, the glide of water, the sun expanding the air.

"When do we see the Martians?" cried Michael.

"Quite soon, perhaps," said Father. "Maybe tonight."

"Oh, but the Martians are a dead race now," said Mom.

"No, they're not. I'll show you some Martians, all right," Dad said presently.   35

Timothy scowled at that but said nothing. Everything was odd now. Vacations and fishing and looks between people.

The other boys were already engaged making shelves of their small hands and peering under them toward the seven-foot stone banks of the canal, watching for Martians.

"What do they look like?" demanded Michael.

"You'll know them when you see them." Dad sort of laughed, and Timothy saw a pulse beating time in his cheek.

Mother was slender and soft, with a woven plait of spun-gold hair over her   40
head in a tiara, and eyes the color of the deep cool canal water where it ran in shadow, almost purple, with flecks of amber caught in it. You could see her thoughts swimming around in her eyes, like fish—some bright, some dark, some fast, quick, some slow and easy, and sometimes, like when she looked up where Earth was, being nothing but color, and nothing else. She sat in the boat's prow, one hand resting on the side lip, the other on the lap of her dark blue breeches, and a line of sunburnt soft neck showing where her blouse opened like a white flower.

She kept looking ahead to see what was there, and, not being able to see it clearly enough, she looked backward toward her husband, and through his eyes, reflected then, she saw what was ahead; and since he added part of himself to this reflection, a determined firmness, her face relaxed and she accepted it and she turned back, knowing suddenly what to look for.

Timothy looked too. But all he saw was a straight pencil line of canal going violet through a wide shallow valley penned by low, eroded hills, and on until it fell over the sky's edge. And this canal went on and on through cities that would have rattled like beetles in a dry skull if you shook them. A hundred or two hundred cities dreaming hot summer-day dreams and cool summer-night dreams.

They had come millions of miles for this outing—fish. But there had been a gun on the rocket. This was a vacation. But why all the food, more than enough to last them years and years, left hidden back there near the rocket? Vacation. Just behind the veil of the vacation was not a soft face of laughter, but something hard and bony and perhaps terrifying. Timothy could not lift the veil, and the two other boys were busy being ten and eight years old, respectively.

"No Martians yet. Nuts." Robert put his V-shaped chin on his hands and glared at the canal.

Dad had brought an atomic radio along, strapped to his wrist. It functioned on   45
an old-fashioned principle: you held it against the bones near your ear and it vibrated singing or talking to you. Dad listened to it now. His face looked like one

of those fallen Martian cities, caved in, sucked dry, almost dead.

Then he gave it to Mom to listen. Her lips dropped open.

"What——" Timothy started to question, but never finished what he wished to say.

For at that moment there were two titanic, marrow-jolting explosions that grew upon themselves, followed by a half-dozen minor concussions.

Jerking his head up, Dad notched the boat speed higher immediately. The boat leaped and jounced and spanked. This shook Robert out of his funk and elicited yelps of frightened but esctatic joy from Michael, who clung to Mom's legs and watched the water pour by his nose in a wet torrent.

Dad swerved the boat, cut speed, and ducked the craft into a little branch   50
canal and under an ancient, crumbling stone wharf that smelled of crab flesh. The boat rammed the wharf hard enough to throw them all forward, but no one was hurt and Dad was already twisted to see if the ripples on the canal were enough to map their route into hiding. Water lines went across, lapped the stones, and rippled back to meet each other, settling, to be dappled by the sun. It all went away.

Dad listened. So did everybody.

Dad's breathing echoed like fists beating against the cold wet wharf stones. In the shadow, Mom's cat eyes just watched Father for some clue to what next.

Dad relaxed and blew out a breath, laughing at himself.

"The rocket, of course. I'm getting jumpy. The rocket."

Michael said, "What happened, Dad, what happened?"   55

"Oh, we just blew up our rocket, is all," said Timothy, trying to sound matter-of-fact. "I've heard rockets blown up before. Ours just blew."

"Why did we blow up our rocket?" asked Michael. "Huh, Dad?"

"It's part of the game, silly!" said Timothy.

"A game!" Michael and Robert loved the word.

"Dad fixed it so it would blow up and no one'd know where we landed or   60
went! In case they ever came looking, see?"

"Oh boy, a secret!"

"Scared by my own rocket," admitted Dad to Mom. "I *am* nervous. It's silly to think there'll ever be any more rockets. Except *one,* perhaps, if Edwards and his wife get through with *their* ship."

He put his tiny radio to his ear again. After two mintes he dropped his hand as you would drop a rag.

"It's over at last," he said to Mom. "The radio just went off the atomic beam. Every other world station's gone. They dwindled down to a couple in the last few years. Now the air's completely silent. It'll probably remain silent."

"For how long?" asked Robert.   65

"Maybe—your great-grandchildren will hear it again," said Dad. He just sat there, and the children were caught in the center of his awe and defeat and resignation and acceptance.

Finally he put the boat out into the canal again, and they continued in the direction in which they had originally started.

It was getting late. Already the sun was down the sky, and a series of dead cities lay ahead of them.

Dad talked very quietly and gently to his sons. Many times in the past he had been brisk, distant, removed from them, but now he patted them on the head with just a word and they felt it.

"Mike, pick a city."

"What, Dad?"

"Pick a city, Son. Any one of these cities we pass."

"All right," said Michael. "How do I pick?"

"Pick the one you like the most. You, too, Robert and Tim. Pick the city you like best."

"I want a city with Martians in it," said Michael.

"You'll have that," said Dad. "I promise." His lips were for the children, but his eyes were for Mom.

They passed six cities in twenty minutes. Dad didn't say anything more about the explosions; he seemed much more interested in having fun with his sons, keeping them happy, than anything else.

Michael liked the first city they passed, but this was vetoed because everyone doubted quick first judgments. The second city nobody liked. It was an Earth Man's settlement, built of wood and already rotting into sawdust. Timothy liked the third city because it was large. The fourth and fifth were too small and the sixth brought acclaim from everyone, including Mother, who joined in the Gees, Goshes, and Look-at-thats!

There were fifty or sixty huge structures still standing, streets were dusty but paved, and you could see one or two old centrifugal fountains still pulsing wetly in the plazas. That was the only life—water leaping in the late sunlight.

"This is the city," said everybody.

Steering the boat to a wharf, Dad jumped out.

"Here we are. This is ours. This is where we live from now on!"

"From now on?" Michael was incredulous. He stood up, looking, and then turned to blink back at where the rocket used to be. "What about the rocket? What about Minnesota?"

"Here," said Dad.

He touched the small radio to Michael's blond head. "Listen."

Michael listened.

"Nothing," he said.

"That's right. Nothing. Nothing at all any more. No more Minneapolis, no more rockets, no more Earth."

Michael considered the lethal revelation and began to sob little dry sobs.

"Wait a moment," said Dad the next instant. "I'm giving you a lot more in exchange, Mike!"

"What?" Michael held off the tears, curious, but quite ready to continue in case Dad's further revelation was as disconcerting as the original.

"I'm giving you this city, Mike. It's yours."

"Mine?"

"For you and Robert and Timothy, all three of you, to own for yourselves."

Timothy bounded from the boat. "Look, guys, all for *us!* All of *that!*" He was 95 playing the game with Dad, playing it large and playing it well. Later, after it was all over and things had settled, he could go off by himself and cry for ten minutes. But now it was still a game, still a family outing, and the other kids must be kept playing.

Mike jumped out with Robert. They helped Mom.

"Be careful of your sister," said Dad, and nobody knew what he meant until later.

They hurried into the great pink-stoned city whispering among themselves, because dead cities have a way of making you want to whisper, to watch the sun go down.

"In about five days," said Dad quietly, "I'll go back down to where our rocket was and collect the food hidden in the ruins there and bring it here; and I'll hunt for Bert Edwards and his wife and daughters there."

"Daughters?" asked Timothy. "How many?" 100

"Four."

"I can see that'll cause trouble later." Mom nodded slowly.

"Girls." Michael made a face like an ancient Martian stone image. "Girls."

"Are they coming in a rocket too?"

"Yes. If they make it. Family rockets are made for travel to the Moon, not 105 Mars. We were lucky we got through."

"Where did you get the rocket?" whispered Timothy, for the other boys were running ahead.

"I saved it. I saved it for twenty years, Tim. I had it hidden away, hoping I'd never have to use it. I suppose I should have given it to the government for the war, but I kept thinking about Mars. . . ."

"And a picnic!"

"Right. This is between you and me. When I saw everything was finishing on Earth, after I'd waited until the last moment, I packed us up. Bert Edwards had a ship hidden, too, but we decided it would be safer to take off separately, in case anyone tried to shoot us down."

"Why'd you blow up the rocket, Dad?" 110

"So we can't go back ever. And so if any of those evil men ever come to Mars they won't know we're here."

"Is that why you look up all the time?"

"Yes, it's silly. They won't follow us, ever. They haven't anything to follow with. I'm being too careful, is all."

Michael came running back. "Is this really *our* city, Dad?"

"The whole darn planet belongs to us, kids. The whole darn planet." 115

They stood there, King of the Hill, Top of the Heap, Ruler of All They Surveyed, Unimpeachable Monarchs and Presidents, trying to understand what it meant to own a world and how big a world really was.

Night came quickly in the thin atmosphere, and Dad left them in the square by the pulsing fountain, went down to the boat and came walking back carrying a stack of paper in his big hands.

He laid the papers in a clutter in an old courtyard and set them afire. To keep warm, they crouched around the blaze and laughed, and Timothy saw the little letters leap like frightened animals when the flames touched and engulfed them. The papers crinkled like an old man's skin and the cremation surrounded innumerable words:

"GOVERNMENT BONDS; Business Graph, 1999; Religious Prejudice: An Essay; The Science of Logistics; Problems of the Pan-American Unity; Stock Report for July 3, 1998; The War Digest . . ."

Dad had insisted on bringing these papers for this purpose. He sat there and fed them into the fire, one by one, with satisfaction, and told his children what it all meant.   120

"It's time I told you a few things. I don't suppose it was fair, keeping so much from you. I don't know if you'll understand, but I have to talk even if only part of it gets over to you."

He dropped a leaf in the fire.

"I'm burning a way of life, just like that way of life is being burned clean of Earth right now. Forgive me if I talk like a politician. I am, after all, a former state governor, and I was honest and they hated me for it. Life on Earth never settled down to doing anything very good. Science ran too far ahead of us too quickly, and the people got lost in a mechanical wilderness, like children making over pretty things, gadgets, helicopters, rockets; emphasizing the wrong items, emphasizing machines instead of how to run the machines. Wars got bigger and bigger and finally killed Earth. That's what the silent radio means. That's what we ran away from.

"We were lucky. There aren't any more rockets left. It's time you knew this isn't a fishing trip at all. I put off telling you. Earth is gone. Interplanetary travel won't be back for centuries, maybe never. But that way of life proved itself wrong and strangled itself with its own hands. You're young. I'll tell you this again every day until it sinks in."

He paused to feed more papers to the fire.   125

"Now we're alone. We and a handful of others who'll land in a few days. Enough to start over. Enough to turn away from all that back on Earth and strike out on a new line——"

The fire leaped up to emphasize his talking. And then all the papers were gone except one. All the laws and beliefs of Earth were burnt into small hot ashes which soon would be carried off in a wind.

Timothy looked at the last thing that Dad tossed in the fire. It was a map of the World, and it wrinkled and distorted itself hotly and went—flimpf—and was gone like a warm, black butterfly. Timothy turned away.

"Now I'm going to show you the Martians," said Dad. "Come on, all of you. Here, Alice." He took her hand.

Michael was crying loudly, and Dad picked him up and carried him, and they   130
walked down through the ruins toward the canal.

The canal. Where tomorrow or the next day their future wives would come up in a boat, small laughing girls now, with their father and mother.

The night came down around them, and there were stars. But Timothy couldn't find Earth. It had already set. That was something to think about.

A night bird called among the ruins as they walked. Dad said, "Your mother and I will try to teach you. Perhaps we'll fail. I hope not. We've had a good lot to see and learn from. We planned this trip years ago, before you were born. Even if there hadn't been a war we would have come to Mars, I think, to live and form our own standard of living. It would have been another century before Mars would have been really poisoned by the Earth civilization. Now, of course——"

They reached the canal. It was long and straight and cool and wet and reflective in the night.

"I've always wanted to see a Martian," said Michael. "Where are they, Dad?   135
You promised."

"There they are," said Dad, and he shifted Michael on his shoulder and pointed straight down.

The Martians were there. Timothy began to shiver.

The Martians were there—in the canal—reflected in the water. Timothy and Michael and Robert and Mom and Dad.

The Martians stared back up at them for a long, long silent time from the rippling water. . . .

QUESTIONS AND SUGGESTIONS FOR WRITING

1. Reread the story, marking on the first two or three pages those passages that turn out—in the light of the rest of the story—to be hints of something special that is to come.
2. Would the story be equally effective—or more so or less so—if the last sentence were omitted?

Gabriel Garcia Márquez (Colombian. b. 1928)

A VERY OLD MAN WITH ENORMOUS WINGS: A Tale for Children

Translated by Gregory Rabassa

On the third day of rain they had killed so many crabs inside the house that Pelayo had to cross his drenched courtyard and throw them into the sea, because the newborn child had a temperature all night and they thought it was due to the stench. The world had been sad since Tuesday. Sea and sky were a single ash-gray thing and the sands of the beach, which on March nights glimmered like powdered light, had become a stew of mud and rotten shellfish. The light was so weak at noon that when Pelayo was coming back to the house after throwing away the crabs, it was hard for him to see what it was that was moving and groaning in the rear of the courtyard. He had to go very close to see that it was an old man, a very old man, lying face down in the mud, who, in spite of his tremendous efforts, couldn't get up, impeded by his enormous wings.

Frightened by that nightmare, Pelayo ran to get Elisenda, his wife, who was putting compresses on the sick child, and he took her to the rear of the courtyard. They both looked at the fallen body with mute stupor. He was dressed like a ragpicker. There were only a few faded hairs left on his bald skull and very few teeth in his mouth, and his pitiful condition of a drenched great-grandfather had taken away any sense of grandeur he might have had. His huge buzzard wings, dirty and half-plucked, were forever entangled in the mud. They looked at him so long and so closely that Pelayo and Elisenda very soon overcame their surprise and in the end found him familiar. Then they dared speak to him, and he answered in an incomprehensible dialect with a strong sailor's voice. That was how they skipped over the inconvenience of the wings and quite intelligently concluded that he was a lonely castaway from some foreign ship wrecked by the storm. And yet, they called in a neighbor woman who knew everything about life and death to see him, and all she needed was one look to show them their mistake.

"He's an angel," she told them. "He must have been coming for the child, but the poor fellow is so old that the rain knocked him down."

On the following day everyone knew that a flesh-and-blood angel was held captive in Pelayo's house. Against the judgment of the wise neighbor woman, for whom angels in those times were the fugitive survivors of a celestial conspiracy, they did not have the heart to club him to death. Pelayo watched over him all afternoon from the kitchen, armed with his bailiff's club, and before going to bed he dragged him out of the mud and locked him up with the hens in the wire chicken coop. In the middle of the night, when the rain stopped, Pelayo and Elisenda were still killing crabs. A short time afterward the child woke up without a fever and with a desire to eat. Then they felt magnanimous and decided to put the angel on a raft with fresh water and provisions for three days and leave him to his fate on the high seas. But when they went out into the courtyard with the first light of dawn, they found the whole neighborhood in front of the chicken coop having fun with the angel, without the slightest reverence, tossing him things to eat through the openings in the wire as if he weren't a supernatural creature but a circus animal.

Father Gonzaga arrived before seven o'clock, alarmed at the strange news. By that time onlookers less frivolous than those at dawn had already arrived and they were making all kinds of conjectures concerning the captive's future. The simplest among them thought that he should be named mayor of the world. Others of sterner mind felt that he should be promoted to the rank of five-star general in order to win all wars. Some visionaries hoped that he could be put to stud in order to implant on earth a race of winged wise men who could take charge of the universe. But Father Gonzaga, before becoming a priest, had been a robust woodcutter. Standing by the wire, he reviewed his catechism in an instant and asked them to open the door so that he could take a close look at that pitiful man who looked more like a huge decrepit hen among the fascinated chickens. He was lying in a corner drying his open wings in the sunlight among the fruit peels and breakfast leftovers that the early risers had thrown him. Alien to the impertinences of the world, he only lifted his antiquarian eyes and murmured something in his dialect when Father Gonzaga went into the chicken coop and said good morning to him in Latin. The parish priest had his first suspicion of an imposter when he saw that he did not understand the language of God or know how to greet His ministers. Then he noticed that seen close up he was much too human: he had an unbearable smell of the outdoors, the back side of his wings was strewn with parasites and his main feathers had been mistreated by terrestrial winds, and nothing about him measured up to the proud dignity of angels. Then he came out of the chicken coop and in a brief sermon warned the curious against the risks of being ingenuous. He reminded them that the devil had the bad habit of making use of carnival tricks in order to confuse the unwary. He argued that if wings were not the essential element in determining the difference between a hawk and an airplane, they were even less so in the recognition of angels. Nevertheless, he promised to write a letter to his bishop so that the latter would write to his primate so that the latter would write to the Supreme Pontiff in order to get the final verdict from the highest courts.

His prudence fell on sterile hearts. The news of the captive angel spread with such rapidity that after a few hours the courtyard had the bustle of a marketplace and they had to call in troops with fixed bayonets to disperse the mob that was about to knock the house down. Elisenda, her spine all twisted from sweeping up so much marketplace trash, then got the idea of fencing in the yard and charging five cents admission to see the angel.

The curious came from far away. A traveling carnival arrived with a flying acrobat who buzzed over the crowd several times, but no one paid any attention to him because his wings were not those of an angel but, rather, those of a sidereal bat. The most unfortunate invalids on earth came in search of health: a poor woman who since childhood had been counting her heartbeats and had run out of numbers; a Portuguese man who couldn't sleep because the noise of the stars disturbed him; a sleepwalker who got up at night to undo the things he had done while awake; and many others with less serious ailments. In the midst of that shipwreck disorder that made the earth tremble, Pelayo and Elisenda were happy with fatigue, for in less than a week they had crammed their rooms with money and the line of pilgrims waiting their turn to enter still reached beyond the horizon.

The angel was the only one who took no part in his own act. He spent his time trying to get comfortable in his borrowed nest, befuddled by the hellish heat of the oil lamps and sacramental candles that had been placed along the wire. At first they tried to make him eat some mothballs, which, according to the wisdom of the wise neighbor woman, were the food prescribed for angels But he turned them down, just as he turned down the papal lunches that the penitents brought him, and they never found out whether it was because he was an angel or because he was an old man that in the end he ate nothing but eggplant mush. His only supernatural virtue seemed to be patience. Especially during the first days, when the hens pecked at him, searching for the stellar parasites that proliferated in his wings, and the cripples pulled out feathers to touch their defective parts with, and even the most merciful threw stones at him, trying to get him to rise so they could see him standing. The only time they succeeded in arousing him was when they burned his side with an iron for branding steers, for he had been motionless for so many hours that they thought he was dead. He awoke with a start, ranting in his hermetic language and with tears in his eyes, and he flapped his wings a couple of times, which brought on a whirlwind of chicken dung and lunar dust and a gale of panic that did not seem to be of this world. Although many thought that his reaction had been one not of rage but of pain, from then on they were careful not to annoy him, because the majority understood that his passivity was not that of a hero taking his ease but that of a cataclysm in repose.

Father Gonzaga held back the crowd's frivolity with formulas of maidservant inspiration while awaiting the arrival of a final judgment on the nature of the captive. But the mail from Rome showed no sense of urgency. They spent their time finding out if the prisoner had a navel, if his dialect had any connection with Aramaic, how many times he could fit on the head of a pin, or whether he wasn't just a Norwegian with wings. Those meager letters might have come and gone until the end of time if a providential event had not put an end to the priest's tribulations.

It so happened that during those days, among so many other carnival attrac- 10 tions, there arrived in town the traveling show of the woman who had been changed into a spider for having disobeyed her parents. The admission to see her was not only less than the admission to see the angel, but people were permitted to ask her all manner of questions about her absurd state and to examine her up and down so that no one would ever doubt the truth of her horror. She was a frightful tarantula the size of a ram and with the head of a sad maiden. What was most heart-rending, however, was not her outlandish shape but the sincere afflic-tion with which she recounted the details of her misfortune. While still practically a child she had sneaked out of her parents' house to go to a dance, and while she was coming back through the woods after having danced all night without permi-sion, a fearful thunderclap rent the sky in two and through the crack came the lightning bolt of brimstone that changed her into a spider. Her only nourishment came from the meatballs that charitable souls chose to toss into her mouth. A spectacle like that, full of so much human truth and with such a fearful lesson, was bound to defeat without even trying that of a haughty angel who scarcely deigned to look at mortals. Besides, the few miracles attributed to the angel showed a certain mental disorder, like the blind man who didn't recover his sight but grew three new teeth, or the paralytic who didn't get to walk but almost won the lottery, and the leper whose sores sprouted sunflowers. Those consolation mira-cles, which were more like mocking fun, had already ruined the angel's reputation when the woman who had been changed into a spider finally crushed him com-pletely. That was how Father Gonzaga was cured forever of his insomnia and Pelayo's courtyard went back to being as empty as during the time it had rained for three days and crabs walked through the bedrooms.

The owners of the house had no reason to lament. With the money they saved they built a two-story mansion with balconies and gardens and high netting so that crabs wouldn't get in during the winter, and with iron bars on the windows so that angels wouldn't get in. Pelayo also set up a rabbit warren close to town and gave up his job as bailiff for good, and Elisenda bought some satin pumps with high heels and many dresses of iridescent silk, the kind worn on Sunday by the most desirable women in those times. The chicken coop was the only thing that didn't receive any attention. If they washed it down with creolin and burned tears of myrrh inside it every so often, it was not in homage to the angel but to drive away the dungheap stench that still hung everywhere like a ghost and was turning the new house into an old one. At first, when the child learned to walk, they were careful that he not get too close to the chicken coop. But then they began to lose their fears and got used to the smell, and before the child got his second teeth he'd gone inside the chicken coop to play, where the wires were falling apart. The angel was no less standoffish with him than with other mortals, but he tolerated the most ingenious infamies with the patience of a dog who had no illusions. They both came down with chicken pox at the same time. The doctor who took care of the child couldn't resist the temptation to listen to the angel's heart, and he found so much whistling in the heart and so many sounds in his kidneys that it seemed impossible for him to be alive. What surprised him most, however, was the logic of his wings. They seemed so natural on that completely human organism that he couldn't understand why other men didn't have them too.

When the child began school it had been some time since the sun and rain had caused the collapse of the chicken coop. The angel went dragging himself about here and there like a stray dying man. They would drive him out of the bedroom with a broom and a moment later find him in the kitchen. He seemed to be in so many places at the same time that they grew to think that he'd been duplicated, that he was reproducing himself all through the house, and the exasperated and unhinged Elisenda shouted that it was awful living in that hell full of angels. He could scarcely eat and his antiquarian eyes had also become so foggy that he went about bumping into posts. All he had left were the bare cannulae of his last feathers. Pelayo threw a blanket over him and extended him the charity of letting him sleep in the shed, and only then did they notice that he had a temperature at night, and was delirious with the tongue twisters of an old Norwegian. That was one of the few times they became alarmed, for they thought he was going to die and not even the wise neighbor woman had been able to tell them what to do with dead angels.

And yet he not only survived his worst winter, but seemed improved with the first sunny days He remained motionless for several days in the farthest corner of the courtyard, where no one would see him, and at the beginning of December some large, stiff feathers began to grow on his wings, the feathers of a scarecrow, which looked more like another misfortune of decrepitude. But he must have known the reason for those changes, for he was quite careful that no one should notice them, that no one should hear the sea chanteys that he sometimes sang under the stars. One morning Elisenda was cutting some bunches of onions for lunch when a wind that seemed to come from the high seas blew into the kitchen. Then she went to the window and caught the angel in his first attempts at flight. They were so clumsy that his fingernails opened a furrow in the vegetable patch and he was on the point of knocking the shed down with the ungainly flapping that slipped on the light and couldn't get a grip on the air. But he did manage to gain altitude. Elisenda let out a sigh of relief, for herself and for him, when she saw him pass over the last houses, holding himself up in some way with the risky flapping of a senile vulture. She kept watching him even when she was through cutting the onions and she kept on watching until it was no longer possible for her to see him, because then he was no longer an annoyance in her life but an imaginary dot on the horizon of the sea.

QUESTIONS AND SUGGESTIONS FOR WRITING

1. The subtitle is "A Tale for Children." Do you think that the story is more suited to children than to adults? What in the story do you think children would especially like, or dislike?
2. Is the story chiefly about our inability to perceive and respect the miraculous world? Explain.
3. In a paragraph characterize the narrator of the story.
4. Devoting a paragraph to each, characterize Pelayo, Elisenda, their son, and the man with wings.

Joyce Carol Oates (American. b. 1938)

WHERE ARE YOU GOING, WHERE HAVE YOU BEEN?

To Bob Dylan

Her name was Connie. She was fifteen and she had a quick nervous giggling habit of craning her neck to glance into mirrors or checking other people's faces to make sure her own was all right. Her mother, who noticed everything and knew everything and who hadn't much reason any longer to look at her own face, always scolded Connie about it. "Stop gawking at yourself, who are you? You think you're so pretty?" she would say. Connie would raise her eyebrows at these familiar complaints and look right through her mother, into a shadowy vision of herself as she was right at that moment: she knew she was pretty and that was everything. Her mother had been pretty once too, if you could believe those old snapshots in the album, but now her looks were gone and that was why she was always after Connie.

"Why don't you keep your room clean like your sister? How've you got your hair fixed—what the hell stinks? Hair spray? You don't see your sister using that junk."

Her sister June was twenty-four and still lived at home. She was a secretary in the high school Connie attended, and if that wasn't bad enough—with her in the same building—she was so plain and chunky and steady that Connie had to hear her praised all the time by her mother and her mother's sisters. June did this, June did that, she saved money and helped clean the house and cooked and

Connie couldn't do a thing, her mind was all filled with trashy daydreams. Their father was away at work most of the time and when he came home he wanted supper and he read the newspaper at supper and after supper he went to bed. He didn't bother talking much to them, but around his bent head Connie's mother kept picking at her until Connie wished her mother were dead and she herself were dead and it were all over. "She makes me want to throw up sometimes," she complained to her friends. She had a high, breathless, amused voice which made everything she said sound a little forced, whether it was sincere or not.

There was one good thing: June went places with girlfriends of hers, girls who were just as plain and steady as she, and so when Connie wanted to do that her mother had no objections. The father of Connie's best girlfriend drove the girls the three miles to town and left them off at a shopping plaza, so that they could walk through the stores or go to a movie, and when he came to pick them up again at eleven he never bothered to ask what they had done.

They must have been familiar sights, walking around that shopping plaza in their shorts and flat ballerina slippers that always scuffed the sidewalk, with charm bracelets jingling on their thin wrists; they would lean together to whisper and laugh secretly if someone passed by who amused or interested them. Connie had long dark blond hair that drew anyone's eye to it, and she wore part of it pulled up on her head and puffed out and the rest of it she let fall down her back. She wore a pullover jersey blouse that looked one way when she was at home and another way when she was away from home. Everything about her had two sides to it, one for home and one for anywhere that was not home: her walk that could be childlike and bobbing, or languid enough to make anyone think she was hearing music in her head, her mouth which was pale and smirking most of the time, but bright and pink on these evenings out, her laugh which was cynical and drawling at home—"Ha, ha, very funny"—but high-pitched and nervous anywhere else, like the jingling of the charms on her bracelet.

Sometimes they did go shopping or to a movie, but sometimes they went across the highway, ducking fast across the busy road, to a drive-in restaurant where older kids hung out. The restaurant was shaped like a big bottle, though squatter than a real bottle, and on its cap was a revolving figure of a grinning boy who held a hamburger aloft. One night in midsummer they ran across, breathless with daring, and right away someone leaned out a car window and invited them over, but it was just a boy from high school they didn't like. It made them feel good to be able to ignore him. They went up through the maze of parked and cruising cars to the bright-lit, fly-infested restaurant, their faces pleased and expectant as if they were entering a sacred building that loomed out of the night to give them what haven and what blessing they yearned for. They sat at the counter and crossed their legs at the ankles, their thin shoulders rigid with excitement, and listened to the music that made everything so good: the music was always in the background like music at a church service, it was something to depend upon.

A boy named Eddie came in to talk with them. He sat backward on his stool, turning himself jerkily around in semicircles and then stopping and turning again, and after a while he asked Connie if she would like something to eat. She said she did and so she tapped her friend's arm on her way out—her friend pulled her face up into a brave droll look—and Connie said she would meet her at eleven, across the way. "I just hate to leave her like that," Connie said earnestly, but the boy said that she wouldn't be alone for long. So they went out to his car and on the way Connie couldn't help but let her eyes wander over the windshields and faces all around her, her face gleaming with a joy that had nothing to do with Eddie or even this place; it might have been the music. She drew her shoulders up and sucked in her breath with the pure pleasure of being alive, and just at that moment she happened to glance at a face just a few feet from hers. It was a boy with shaggy black hair, in a convertible jalopy painted gold. He stared at her and then his lips widened into a grin. Connie slit her eyes at him and turned away, but she couldn't help glancing back and there he was still watching her. He wagged a finger and laughed and said, "Gonna get you, baby," and Connie turned away again without Eddie noticing anything.

She spent three hours with him, at the restaurant where they ate hamburgers and drank Cokes in wax cups that were always sweating, and then down an alley a mile or so away, and when he left her off at five to eleven only the movie house was still open at the plaza. Her girlfriend was there, talking with a boy. When Connie came up the two girls smiled at each other and Connie said, "How was the movie?" and the girl said, "*You* should know." They rode off with the girl's father, sleepy and pleased, and Connie couldn't help but look at the darkened shopping plaza with its big empty parking lot and its signs that were faded and ghostly now, and over at the drive-in restaurant where cars were still circling tirelessly. She couldn't hear the music at this distance.

Next morning June asked her how the movie was and Connie said, "So-so."

She and that girl and occasionally another girl went out several times a week that way, and the rest of the time Connie spent around the house—it was summer vacation—getting in her mother's way and thinking, dreaming, about the boys she met. But all the boys fell back and dissolved into a single face that was not even a face, but an idea, a feeling, mixed up with the urgent insistent pounding of the music and the humid night air of July. Connie's mother kept dragging her back to the daylight by finding things for her to do or saying, suddenly, "What's this about the Pettinger girl?"

And Connie would say nervously, "Oh, her. That dope." She always drew thick clear lines between herself and such girls, and her mother was simple and kindly enough to believe her. Her mother was so simple, Connie thought, that it was maybe cruel to fool her so much. Her mother went scuffling around the house in old bedroom slippers and complained over the telephone to one sister about the other, then the other called up and the two of them complained about the third one. If June's name was mentioned her mother's tone was approving, and if Connie's name was mentioned it was disapproving. This did not really mean she disliked Connie and actually Connie thought that her mother preferred her to June because she was prettier, but the two of them kept up a pretense of exasperation, a sense that they were tugging and struggling over something of little value to either of them. Sometimes, over coffee, they were almost friends, but something would come up—some vexation that was like a fly buzzing suddenly around their heads—and their faces went hard with contempt.

10

One Sunday Connie got up at eleven—none of them bothered with church—and washed her hair so that it could dry all day long, in the sun. Her parents and sisters were going to a barbecue at an aunt's house and Connie said no, she wasn't interested, rolling her eyes to let her mother know just what she thought of it. "Stay home alone then," her mother said sharply. Connie sat out back in a lawn chair and watched them drive away, her father quiet and bald, hunched around so that he could back the car out, her mother with a look that was still angry and not at all softened through the windshield, and in the back seat poor old June all dressed up as if she didn't know what a barbecue was, with all the running yelling kids and the flies. Connie sat with her eyes closed in the sun, dreaming and dazed with the warmth about her as if this were a kind of love, the caresses of love, and her mind slipped over onto thoughts of the boy she had been with the night before and how nice he had been, how sweet it always was, not the way someone like June would suppose but sweet, gentle, the way it was in movies and promised in songs; and when she opened her eyes she hardly knew where she was, the back yard ran off into weeds and a fence line of trees and behind it the sky was perfectly blue and still. The asbestos "ranch house" that was now three years old startled her—it looked small. She shook her head as if to get awake.

It was too hot. She went inside the house and turned on the radio to drown out the quiet. She sat on the edge of her bed, barefoot, and listened for an hour and a half to a program called XYZ Sunday Jamboree, record after record of hard, fast, shrieking songs she sang along with, interspersed by exclamations from "Bobby King": "An' look here you girls at Napoleon's—Son and Charley want you to pay real close attention to this song coming up!"

And Connie paid close attention herself, bathed in a glow of slow-pulsed joy that seemed to rise mysteriously out of the music itself and lay languidly about the airless little room, breathed in and breathed out with each gentle rise and fall of her chest.

After a while she heard a car coming up the drive. She sat up at once, startled, because it couldn't be her father so soon. The gravel kept crunching all the way in from the road—the driveway was long—and Connie ran to the window. It was a car she didn't know. It was an open jalopy, painted a bright gold that caught the sunlight opaquely. Her heart began to pound and her fingers snatched at her hair, checking it, and she whispered "Christ, Christ," wondering how bad she looked. The car came to a stop at the side door and the horn sounded four short taps as if this were a signal Connie knew.   15

She went into the kitchen and approached the door slowly, then hung out the screen door, her bare toes curling down off the step. There were two boys in the car and now she recognized the driver: he had shaggy, shabby black hair that looked crazy as a wig and he was grinning at her.

"I ain't late, am I?" he said

"Who the hell do you think you are?" Connie said.

"Toldja I'd be out, didn't I?"

"I don't even know who you are."   20

She spoke sullenly, careful to show no interest or pleasure, and he spoke in a fast bright monotone. Connie looked past him to the other boy, taking her time.

He had fair brown hair, with a lock that fell onto his forehead. His sideburns gave him a fierce, embarrassed look, but so far he hadn't even bothered to glance at her. Both boys wore sunglasses. The driver's glasses were metallic and mirrored everything in miniature.

"You wanta come for a ride?" he said.

Connie smirked and let her hair fall loose over one shoulder.

"Don'tcha like my car? New paint job," he said. "Hey."

"What?"   25

"You're cute."

She pretended to fidget, chasing flies away from the door.

"Don'tcha believe me, or what?" he said.

"Look, I don't even know who you are," Connie said in disgust.

"Hey, Ellie's got a radio, see. Mine's broke down." He lifted his friend's arm   30
and showed her the little transistor the boy was holding, and now Connie began to hear the music. It was the same program that was playing inside the house.

"Bobby King?" she said.

"I listen to him all the time. I think he's great."

"He's kind of great," Connie said reluctantly.

"Listen, that guy's *great*. He knows where the action is."

Connie blushed a little, because the glasses made it impossible for her to see   35
just what this boy was looking at. She couldn't decide if she liked him or if he was just a jerk, and so she dawdled in the doorway and wouldn't come down or go back inside. She said, "What's all that stuff painted on your car?"

"Can'tcha read it?" He opened the door very carefully, as if he was afraid it might fall off. He slid out just as carefully, planting his feet firmly on the ground, the tiny metallic world in his glasses slowing down like gelatine hardening and in the midst of it Connie's bright green blouse. "This here is my name, to begin with," he said. ARNOLD FRIEND was written in tarlike black letters on the side, with a drawing of a round grinning face that reminded Connie of a pumpkin, except it wore sunglasses. "I wanta introduce myself, I'm Arnold Friend and that's my real name and I'm gonna be your friend, honey, and inside the car's Ellie Oscar, he's kinda shy." Ellie brought his transistor radio up to his shoulder and balanced it there. "Now these numbers are a secret code, honey," Arnold Friend explained. He read off the numbers 33, 19, 17 and raised his eyebrows at her to see what she thought of that, but she didn't think much of it. The left rear fender had been smashed and around it was written, on the gleaming gold background: DONE BY CRAZY WOMAN DRIVER. Connie had to laugh at that. Arnold Friend was pleased at her laughter and looked up at her. "Around the other side's a lot more—you wanta come and see them?

"No."

"Why not?"

"Why should I?"

"Don'tcha wanta see what's on the car? Don'tcha wanta go for a ride?"   40

"I don't know."

"Why not?"

"I got things to do."

"Like what?"

He laughed as if she had said something funny. He slapped his thighs. He was   45
standing in a strange way, leaning back against the car as if he were balancing
himself. He wasn't tall, only an inch or so taller than she would be if she came
down to him. Connie liked the way he was dressed, which was the way all of them
dressed: tight faded jeans stuffed into black, scuffled boots, a belt that pulled his
waist in and showed how lean he was, and a white pullover shirt that was a little
soiled and showed the hard small muscles of his arms and shoulders. He looked
as if he probably did hard work, lifting and carrying things. Even his neck looked
muscular. And his face was a familiar face, somehow: the jaw and chin and cheeks
slightly darkened, because he hadn't shaved for a day or two, and the nose long
and hawklike, sniffing as if she were a treat he was going to gobble up and it was
all a joke.

"Connie, you ain't telling the truth. This is your day set aside for a ride with
me and you know it," he said, still laughing. The way he straightened and recovered from his fit of laughing showed that it had been all fake.

"How do you know what my name is?" she said suspiciously.

"It's Connie."

"Maybe and maybe not."

"I know my Connie," he said, wagging his finger. Now she remembered him   50
even better, back at the restaurant, and her cheeks warmed at the thought of how
she sucked in her breath just at the moment she passed him—how she must have
looked at him. And he had remembered her. "Ellie and I come out here especially
for you," he said. "Ellie can sit in back. How about it?"

"Where?"

"Where what?"

"Where're we going?"

He looked at her. He took off the sunglasses and she saw how pale the skin
around his eyes was, like holes that were not in shadow but instead in light. His
eyes were like chips of broken glass that catch the light in an amiable way. He
smiled. It was as if the idea of going for a ride somewhere, to some place, was a
new idea to him.

"Just for a ride, Connie sweetheart."   55

"I never said my name was Connie," she said.

"But I know what it is. I know your name and all about you, lots of things,"
Arnold Friend said. He had not moved yet but stood still leaning back against the
side of his jalopy. "I took a special interest in you, such a pretty girl, and found
out all about you like I know your parents and sister are gone somewheres and I
know where and how long they're going to be gone, and I know who you were
with last night, and your best girlfriend's name is Betty. Right?"

He spoke in a simple lilting voice, exactly as if he were reciting the words to a
song. His smile assured her that everything was fine. In the car Ellie turned up
the volume on his radio and did not bother to look around at them.

"Ellie can sit in the back seat," Arnold Friend said. He indicated his friend
with a casual jerk of his chin, as if Ellie did not count and she should not bother
with him.

"How'd you find out all that stuff?" Connie said.   60

"Listen: Betty Schultz and Tony Fitch and Jimmy Pettinger and Nancy Pet-tinger," he said, in a chant. "Raymond Stanley and Bob Hutter—"

"Do you know all those kids?"

"I know everybody."

"Look, you're kidding. You're not from around here."

"Sure."   65

"But—how come we never saw you before?"

"Sure you saw me before," he said. He looked down at his boots, as if he were a little offended. "You just don't remember."

"I guess I'd remember you," Connie said.

"Yeah?" He looked up at this, beaming. He was pleased. He began to mark time with the music from Ellie's radio, tapping his fists lightly together. Connie looked away from his smile to the car, which was painted so bright it almost hurt her eyes to look at it. She looked at that name. ARNOLD FRIEND. And up at the front fender was an expression that was familiar—MAN THE FLYING SAUCERS. It was an expression kids had used the year before, but didn't use this year. She looked at it for a while as if the words meant something to her that she did not yet know.

"What're you thinking about? Huh?" Arnold Friend demanded. "Not worried   70
about your hair blowing around in the car, are you?"

"No."

"Think I maybe can't drive good?"

"How do I know?"

"You're a hard girl to handle. How come?" he said. "Don't you know I'm your friend? Didn't you see me put my sign in the air when you walked by?"

"What sign?"   75

"My sign." And he drew an X in the air, leaning out toward her. They were maybe ten feet apart. After his hand fell back to his side the X was still in the air, almost visible. Connie let the screen door close and stood perfectly still inside it, listening to the music from her radio and the boy's blend together. She stared at Arnold Friend. He stood there so stiffly relaxed, pretending to be relaxed, with one hand idly on the door handle as if he were keeping himself up that way and had no intention of ever moving again. She recognized most things about him, the tight jeans that showed his thighs and buttocks and the greasy leather boots and the tight shirt, and even that slippery friendly smile of his, that sleepy dreamy smile that all the boys used to get across ideas they didn't want to put into words. She recognized all this and also the singsong way he talked, slightly mocking, kidding, but serious and a little melancholy, and she recognized the way he tapped one fist against the other in homage of the perpetual music behind him. But all these things did not come together.

She said suddenly, "Hey, how old are you?"

His smile faded. She could see then that he wasn't a kid, he was much older—thirty, maybe more. At this knowledge her heart began to pound faster.

"That's a crazy thing to ask. Can'tcha see I'm your own age?"

"Like hell you are."   80

"Or maybe a coupla years older, I'm eighteen."

"Eighteen?" she said doubtfully.

He grinned to reassure her and lines appeared at the corners of his mouth. His teeth were big and white. He grinned so broadly his eyes became slits and she saw how thick the lashes were, thick and black as if painted with a black tarlike material. Then he seemed to become embarrassed, abruptly, and looked over his shoulder at Ellie. "*Him*, he's crazy," he said. "Ain't he a riot, he's a nut, a real character." Ellie was still listening to the music. His sunglasses told nothing about what he was thinking. He wore a bright orange shirt unbuttoned halfway to show his chest, which was a pale, bluish chest and not muscular like Arnold Friend's. His shirt collar was turned up all around and the very tips of the collar pointed out past his chin as if they were protecting him. He was pressing the transistor radio up against his ear and sat there in a kind of daze, right in the sun.

"He's kinda strange," Connie said

"Hey, she says you're kinda strange! Kinda strange!" Arnold Friend cried.   85
He pounded on the car to get Ellie's attention. Ellie turned for the first time and Connie saw with shock that he wasn't a kid either—he had a fair, hairless face, cheeks reddened slightly as if the veins grew too close to the surface of his skin, the face of a forty-year-old baby. Connie felt a wave of dizziness rise in her at this sight and she stared at him as if waiting for something to change the shock of the moment, make it all right again. Ellie's lips kept shaping words, mumbling along with the words blasting in his ear.

"Maybe you two better go away," Connie said faintly.

"What? How come?" Arnold Friend cried. "We come out here to take you for a ride. It's Sunday." He had the voice of the man on the radio now. It was the same voice, Connie thought. "Don'tcha know it's Sunday all day and honey, no matter who you were with last night today you're with Arnold Friend and don't you forget it!—Maybe you better step out here," he said, and this last was in a different voice. It was a little flatter, as if the heat was finally getting to him.

"No. I got things to do."

"Hey."

"You two better leave."   90

"We ain't leaving until you come with us."

"Like hell I am—"

"Connie, don't fool around with me. I mean, I mean, don't fool *around*," he said, shaking his head. He laughed incredulously. He placed his sunglasses on top of his head, carefully, as if he were indeed wearing a wig, and brought the stems down behind his ears. Connie stared at him, another wave of dizziness and fear rising in her so that for a moment he wasn't even in focus but was just a blur, standing there against his gold car, and she had the idea that he had driven up the driveway all right but had come from nowhere before that and belonged nowhere and that everything about him and even about the music that was so familiar to her was only half real.

"If my father comes and sees you—"

"He ain't coming. He's at a barbecue."   95

"How do you know that?"

"Aunt Tillie's. Right now they're—uh—they're drinking. Sitting around," he said vaguely, squinting as if he were staring all the way to town and over to Aunt Tillie's back yard. Then the vision seemed to get clear and he nodded energetically. "Yeah. Sitting around. There's your sister in a blue dress, huh? And high heels, the poor sad bitch—nothing like you, sweetheart! And your mother's helping some fat woman with the corn, they're cleaning the corn—husking the corn—"

"What fat woman?" Connie cried.

"How do I know what fat woman, I don't know every goddam fat woman in the world!" Arnold laughed.

"Oh, that's Mrs. Hornby . . . Who invited her?" Connie said. She felt a little light-headed. Her breath was coming quickly.   100

"She's too fat. I don't like them fat. I like them the way you are, honey," he said, smiling sleepily at her. They stared at each other for a while, through the screen door. He said softly, "Now what you're going to do is this: you're going to come out that door. You're going to sit up front with me and Ellie's going to sit in the back, the hell with Ellie, right? This isn't Ellie's date. You're my date. I'm your lover, honey."

"What? You're crazy—"

"Yes, I'm your lover. You don't know what that is, but you will," he said. "I know that too. I know all about you. But look: it's real nice and you couldn't ask for nobody better than me, or more polite. I always keep my word. I'll tell you how it is, I'm always nice at first, the first time. I'll hold you so tight you won't think you have to try to get away or pretend anything because you'll know you can't. And I'll come inside you where it's all secret and you'll give in to me and you'll love me—"

"Shut up! You're crazy!" Connie said. She backed away from the door. She put her hands against her ears as if she'd heard something terrible, something not meant for her. "People don't talk like that, you're crazy," she muttered. Her heart was almost too big now for her chest and its pumping made sweat break out all over her. She looked out to see Arnold Friend pause and then take a step toward the porch lurching. He almost fell. But, like a clever drunken man, he managed to catch his balance. He wobbled in his high boots and grabbed hold of one of the porch posts.

"Honey?" he said. "You still listening?"   105

"Get the hell out of here!"

"Be nice, honey. Listen."

"I'm going to call the police—"

He wobbled again and out of the side of his mouth came a fast spat curse, an aside not meant for her to hear. But even this "Christ!" sounded forced. Then he began to smile again. She watched this smile come, awkward as if he were smiling from inside a mask. His whole face was a mask, she thought wildly, tanned down onto his throat but then running out as if he had plastered makeup on his face but had forgotten about his throat.

"Honey—? Listen, here's how it is. I always tell the truth and I promise you   110
this: I ain't coming in that house after you."

"You better not! I'm going to call the police if you—if you don't—"

"Honey," he said, talking right through her voice, "honey, I'm not coming in there but you are coming out here. You know why?"

She was panting. The kitchen looked like a place she had never seen before, some room she had run inside but which wasn't good enough, wasn't going to help her. The kitchen window had never had a curtain, after three years, and there were dishes in the sink for her to do—probably—and if you ran your hand across the table you'd probably feel something sticky there.

"You listening, honey? Hey?"

"—going to call the police—"   115

"Soon as you touch the phone I don't need to keep my promise and can come inside. You won't want that."

She rushed forward and tried to lock the door. Her fingers were shaking. "But why lock it," Arnold Friend said gently, talking right into her face. "It's just a screen door. It's just nothing." One of his boots was at a strange angle, as if his foot wasn't in it. It pointed out to the left, bent at the ankle. "I mean, anybody can break through a screen door and glass and wood and iron or anything else if he needs to, anybody at all and specially Arnold Friend. If the place got lit up with a fire honey you'd come runnin, out into my arms, right into my arms an' safe at home—like you knew I was your lover and'd stopped fooling around. I don't mind a nice shy girl but I don't like no fooling around." Part of those words were spoken with a slight rhythmic lilt, and Connie somehow recognized them—the echo of a song from last year, about a girl rushing into her boyfriend's arms and coming home again—

Connie stood barefoot on the linoleum floor, staring at him. "What do you want?" she whispered.

"I want you," he said.

"What?"   120

"Seen you that night and thought, that's the one, yes sir. I never needed to look any more."

"But my father's coming back. He's coming to get me. I had to wash my hair first—" She spoke in a dry, rapid voice, hardly raising it for him to hear.

"No, your Daddy is not coming and yes, you had to wash your hair and you washed it for me. It's nice and shining and all for me, I thank you, sweetheart," he said, with a mock bow, but again he almost lost his balance. He had to bend and adjust his boots. Evidently his feet did not go all the way down; the boots must have been stuffed with something so that he would seem taller. Connie stared out at him and behind him Ellie in the car, who seemed to be looking off toward Connie's right into nothing. This Ellie said, pulling the words out of the air one after another as if he were just discovering them, "You want me to pull out the phone?"

"Shut your mouth and keep it shut," Arnold Friend said, his face red from bending over or maybe from embarrassment because Connie had seen his boots. "This ain't none of your business."

"What—what are you doing? What do you want?" Connie said. "If I call the   125
police they'll get you, they'll arrest you—"

"Promise was not to come in unless you touch that phone, and I'll keep that promise," he said. He resumed his erect position and tried to force his shoulders back. He sounded like a hero in a movie, declaring something important. He spoke too loudly and it was as if he were speaking to someone behind Connie. "I ain't made plans for coming in that house where I don't belong but just for you to come out to me, the way you should. Don't you know who I am?"

"You're crazy," she whispered. She backed away from the door but did not want to go into another part of the house, as if this would give him permission to come through the door. "What do you. . . You're crazy, you. . ."

"Huh? What're you saying, honey?"

Her eyes darted everywhere in the kitchen. She could not remember what it was, this room.

"This is how it is, honey: you come out and we'll drive away, have a nice ride.   130 But if you don't come out we're gonna wait till your people come home and then they're all going to get it."

"You want that telephone pulled out?" Ellie said. He held the radio away from his ear and grimaced, as if without the radio the air was too much for him.

"I toldja shut up, Ellie," Arnold Friend said, "you're deaf, get a hearing aid, right? Fix yourself up. This little girl's no trouble and's gonna be nice to me, so Ellie keep to yourself, this ain't your date—right? Don't hem in on me. Don't hog. Don't crush. Don't bird dog. Don't trail me," he said in a rapid meaningless voice, as if he were running through all the expressions he'd learned but was no longer sure which one of them was in style, then rushing on to new ones, making them up with his eyes closed, "Don't crawl under my fence, don't squeeze in my chipmunk hole, don't sniff my glue, suck my popsicle, keep your own greasy fingers on yourself!" He shaded his eyes and peered in at Connie, who was backed against the kitchen table. "Don't mind him honey he's just a creep. He's a dope. Right? I'm the boy for you and like I said you come out here nice like a lady and give me your hand, and nobody else gets hurt, I mean, your nice old bald-headed daddy and your mummy and your sister in her high heels. Because listen: why bring them in this?"

"Leave me alone," Connie whispered.

"Hey, you know that old woman down the road, the one with the chickens and stuff—you know her?"

"She's dead!"   135

"Dead? What? You know her?" Arnold Friend said.

"She's dead—"

"Don't you like her?"

"She's dead—she's—she isn't here any more—"

"But don't you like her, I mean, you got something against her? Some grudge   140 or something?" Then his voice dipped as if he were conscious of a rudeness. He touched the sunglasses perched on top of his head as if to make sure they were still there. "Now you be a good girl."

"What are you going to do?"

"Just two things, or maybe three," Arnold Friend said. "But I promise it won't last long and you'll like me the way you get to like people you're close to. You will. It's all over for you here, so come on out. You don't want your people in any trouble, do you?"

She turned and bumped against a chair or something, hurting her leg, but she ran into the back room and picked up the telephone. Something roared in her ear, a tiny roaring, and she was so sick with fear that she could do nothing but listen to it—the telephone was clammy and very heavy and her fingers groped down to the dial but were too weak to touch it. She began to scream into the phone, into the roaring. She cried out, she cried for her mother, she felt her breath start jerking back and forth in her lungs as if it were something Arnold Friend were stabbing her with again and again with no tenderness. A noisy sorrowful wailing rose all about her and she was locked inside it the way she was locked inside this house.

After a while she could hear again. She was sitting on the floor with her wet back against the wall.

Arnold Friend was saying from the door, "That's a good girl. Put the phone back."   145

She kicked the phone away from her.

"No, honey. Pick it up. Put it back right."

She picked it up and put it back. The dial tone stopped.

"That's a good girl. Now you come outside."

She was hollow with what had been fear, but what was now just an empti-   150 ness. All that screaming had blasted it out of her. She sat, one leg cramped under her, and deep inside her brain was something like a pinpoint of light that kept going and would not let her relax. She thought, I'm not going to see my mother again. She thought, I'm not going to sleep in my bed again. Her bright green blouse was all wet.

Arnold Friend said, in a gentle-loud voice that was like a stage voice, "The place where you came from ain't there any more, and where you had in mind to go is canceled out. This place you are now—inside your daddy's house—is nothing but a cardboard box I can knock down any time. You know that and always did know it. You hear me?"

She thought, I have got to think. I have to know what to do.

"We'll go out to a nice field, out in the country here where it smells so nice and it's sunny," Arnold Friend said. "I'll have my arms tight around you so you won't need to try to get away and I'll show you what love is like, what it does. The hell with this house! It looks solid all right," he said. He ran a fingernail down the screen and the noise did not make Connie shiver, as it would have the day before. "Now put your hand on your heart, honey. Feel that? That feels solid too, but we know better, be nice to me, be sweet like you can because what else is there for a girl like you but to be sweet and pretty and give in?—and get away before her people come back?"

She felt her pounding heart. Her hand seemed to enclose it. She thought for the first time in her life that it was nothing that was hers, that belonged to her, but just a pounding, living thing inside this body that wasn't really hers either.

"You don't want them to get hurt," Arnold Friend went on. "Now get up,   155 honey. Get up all by yourself."

She stood.

"Now turn this way. That's right. Come over here to me—Ellie, put that away, didn't I tell you? You dope. You miserable creepy dope," Arnold Friend said. His words were not angry but only part of an incantation. The incantation was kindly. "Now come out through the kitchen to me honey, and let's see a smile, try it, you're a brave sweet little girl and now they're eating corn and hot dogs cooked to bursting over an outdoor fire, and they don't know one thing about you and never did and honey you're better than them because not a one of them would have done this for you."

Connie felt the linoleum under her feet; it was cool. She brushed her hair back out of her eyes. Arnold Friend let go of the post tentatively and opened his arms for her, his elbows pointing in toward each other and his wrists limp, to show that this was an embarrassed embrace and a little mocking, he didn't want to make her self-conscious.

She put out her hand against the screen. She watched herself push the door slowly open as if she were safe back somewhere in the other doorway, watching this body and this head of long hair moving out into the sunlight where Arnold Friend waited.

"My sweet little blue-eyed girl," he said, in a half-sung sigh that had nothing   160 to do with her brown eyes but was taken up just the same by the vast sunlit reaches of the land behind him and on all sides of him, so much land that Connie had never seen before and did not recognize except to know that she was going to it.

QUESTIONS AND SUGGESTIONS FOR WRITING:

1. In a paragraph characterize Connie. Then in a second paragraph explain whether you think the early characterization of Connie prepares us for her later behavior.
2. Is Arnold Friend clairvoyant—definitely, definitely not, or maybe? Explain.
3. In an essay of 500 words evaluate the view that Arnold Friend is both Satan and the incarnation of Connie's erotic desires.
4. What do you make out of the fact that Oates dedicated the story to Bob Dylan? Is she perhaps contrasting Dylan's music with the escapist (or in some other way unwholesome) music of other popular singers?
5. In an essay of 500 words evaluate the view that Oates has given the old ballad, "The Demon Lover" (page 158), a moral interpretation.
6. If you have read Flannery O'Connor's "A Good Man Is Hard to Find" (page 126), compare and contrast Arnold Friend and the Misfit.
7. This story, like Elizabeth Bowen's "The Demon Lover" (page 126), is indebted to the ballad called "The Demon Lover" (page 158). If you have read Bowen's story, in an essay of 500 words explain why you prefer one story to the other.

□ POETRY

A Note on Popular Ballads

The first two poems are folk ballads, anonymous songs passed down orally from generation to generation. Such works are also called "popular ballads," narrative poems created for the populace rather than for a sophisticated audience. But of course sophisticated literary writers have sometimes imitated aspects of the popular ballad. For an example of a "literary ballad," see Keats's "La Belle Dame sans Merci" (page 160).

During the process of oral transmission, a folk ballad inevitably undergoes changes. Somewhat as a stone is smoothed by the force of a river, a folk ballad loses its rough spots. For example, the less memorable stanzas may simply be forgotten, and weak lines may be strengthened. So the work, whatever its origin, finally becomes a communal product. Among the chief characteristics of folk ballads are (1) abrupt transitions (probably caused by the loss of less memorable transitional stanzas), which create highly dramatic, sometimes unexplained scenes; (2) repetition of words, phrases, and even entire lines; (3) stock or conventional diction, often with alliteration, such as "red, red rose," "white, white steed," "wealthy wife," "stout and stalwart sons"; and (4) impersonality (the speaker does not offer an opinion on what happens).

Anonymous

THE WIFE OF USHER'S WELL

There lived a wife at Usher's Well,
  And a wealthy wife was she;
She had three stout and stalwart sons,
  And sent them o'er the sea.   4

They hadna been a week from her,
  A week but barely ane,
Whan word came to the carlin° wife   *Peasant*
  That her three sons were gane.   8

They hadna been a week from her,
  A week but barely three,
Whan word came to the carlin wife
  That her sons she'd never see.   12

"I wish the wind may never cease,
  Nor [fashes°] in the flood,   *Troubles*
Till my three sons come hame to me,
  In earthly flesh and blood."   16

It fell about the Martinmass,°   *November 1*
   When nights are lang and mirk,
The carlin wife's three sons came hame,
   And their hats were o' the birk.°   *Birch*   20

It neither grew in syke° nor ditch,   *Rivulet*
   Nor yet in ony sheugh;°   *Ditch*
But at the gates o Paradise,
   That birk grew fair eneugh.   24

"Blow up the fire, my maidens!
   Bring water from the well!
For a' my house shall feast this night,
   Since my three sons are well."   28

And she has made to them a bed,
   She's made it large and wide,
And she's ta'en her mantle her about,
   Sat down at the bed-side.   32

Up then crew the red, red cock,
   And up and crew the grey;
The eldest to the youngest said,
   " 'Tis time we were away."   36

The cock he hadna craw'd but once,
   And clapp'd his wings at a',
When the youngest to the eldest said,
   "Brother, we must awa'.   40

"The cock doth craw, the day doth daw,
   The channerin° worm doth chide;   *Scolding*
Gin° we be mist out o' our place,   *If*
   A sair° pain we maun° bide.   *Sore, must*   44

"Fare ye weel, my mother dear!
   Fareweel to barn and byre!°   *Shed*
And fare ye weel, the bonny lass
   That kindles my mother's fire!"   48

QUESTIONS AND SUGGESTIONS FOR WRITING

1. In a sentence or two, summarize the narrative. That is, tell the story as briefly as possible.
2. Notice that the poem does not tell how the sons were lost. We are told in line 12 that the wife learns she will never see them again, and we are told in line 23 that the birch from which their hats are made grew at "the gates o Paradise." So we infer that they are dead, but the poet does not explicitly say so. Nor, for that matter, do we get any

description of the appearance of any of the people, except for the lass in the last line, who is "bonny." Consider the mother. We are not told what she looked like, or what her thoughts or feelings are. Yet we know her thoughts and feelings, and we can characterize her.

In a sentence or two, characterize the mother. Then, in the first paragraph of an essay of 250 words, explain what your evidence is. Then try to explain the effect on the reader of the lack of explicit detail in the poem. In your final sentence or two, indicate whether you believe that the poem effectively sets the mother forth. (Most instructors in composition courses urge their students to give concrete details in their writing. Is it possible that additional details in this poem would not be useful?)

3. Medieval ghosts, for the most part, appear like ordinary mortals. They are not transparent, and they do not wear white sheets. Do you assume that the mother knows her sons are ghosts? At what point does she realize this?

4. In the last four stanzas, the sons talk about leaving, but there are no screams or tears. Do you assume they are glad to leave? Or, on the other hand, are they deeply regretful that they must leave? Exactly what, besides their mother, are they leaving? Indicate, without making excessive claims, what implications or associations may legitimately be found in the last stanza, especially in the last two lines.

Anonymous

THE DEMON LOVER

"O where have you been, my long, long love,
    This long seven years and mair?"
"O I'm come to seek my former vows
    Ye granted me before."   4

"O hold your tongue of your former vows,
    For they will breed sad strife;
O hold your tongue of your former vows,
    For I am become a wife."   8

He turned him right and round about,
    And the tear blinded his ee:
"I wad never hae trodden on Irish ground,
    If it had not been for thee.   12

"I might hae had a king's daughter,
    Far, far beyond the sea;
I might have had a king's daughter,
    Had it not been for love o thee."   16

"If ye might have had a king's daughter,
    Yer sel ye had to blame;
Ye might have taken the king's daughter,
    For ye kend° that I was nane.   *Knew*   20

"If I was to leave my husband dear,
    And my two babes also,
O what have you to take me to,
    If with you I should go?"   24

"I hae seven ships upon the sea—
    The eighth brought me to land—
With four-and-twenty bold mariners,
    And music on every hand."   28

She has taken up her two little babes,
    Kissed them baith cheek and chin:
"O fair ye weel, my ain two babes,
    For I'll never see you again."   32

She set her foot upon the ship,
    No mariners could she behold;
But the sails were o the taffetie,
    And the masts o the beaten gold.   36

They had not sailed a league, a league,
    A league but barely three,
When dismal grew his countenance,
    And drumlie° grew his ee.   *Gloomy*   40

They had not sailed a league, a league,
    A league but barely three,
Until she espied his cloven foot,
    And she wept right bitterlie.   44

"O hold your tongue of your weeping," says he,
    "Of your weeping now let me be;
I will show you how the lilies grow
    On the banks of Italy."   48

"O what hills are yon, yon pleasant hills,
    That the sun shines sweetly on?"
"O yon are the hills of heaven," he said,
    "Where you will never win."°   *Gain, get to*   52

"O whaten mountain is yon," she said,
    "All so dreary wi frost and snow?"
"O yon is the mountain of hell," he cried,
    "Where you and I will go."   56

He strack the tap-mast wi his hand,
    The fore-mast wi his knee,
And he brake that gallant ship in twain,
    And sank her in the sea.   60

QUESTIONS AND SUGGESTIONS FOR WRITING

1. What takes place between lines 28 and 29?
2. What is the first hint that supernatural forces are at work?
3. What does the "cloven foot" (line 43) signify? Is the spirit motivated by malice? By love? By both?
4. In a paragraph offer a character sketch of the Wife. You may include a brief moral judgment, but devote most of your paragraph to describing her actions in such a way that they reveal a personality. This personality may, of course, be rather complex.

John Keats (English. 1795–1821)

LA BELLE DAME SANS MERCI

O what can ail thee, knight-at-arms,
 Alone and palely loitering?
The sedge has withered from the lake,
 And no birds sing.   4

O what can ail thee, knight-at arms,
 So haggard and so woe-begone?
The squirrel's granary is full,
 And the harvest's done.   8

I see a lily on thy brow,
 With anguish moist and fever dew,
And on thy cheeks a fading rose
 Fast withereth too.   12

"I met a lady in the meads,
 Full beautiful—a faery's child,
Her hair was long, her foot was light,
 And her eyes were wild.   16

"I made a garland for her head,
 And bracelets too, and fragrant zone;°   *Belt of flowers*
She looked at me as she did love,
 And made sweet moan.   20

"I set her on my pacing steed,
 And nothing else saw all day long,
For sidelong would she bend and sing
 A faery's song.   24

"She found me roots of relish sweet,
 And honey wild, and manna dew,
And sure in language strange she said
 'I love thee true.'   28

"She took me to her elfin grot,
    And there she wept and sighed full sore,
And there I shut her wild wild eyes
    With kisses four.   32

"And there she lulléd me asleep,
    And there I dreamed—Ah! woe betide!
The latest dream I ever dreamt
    On the cold hill side.   36

"I saw pale kings and princes too,
    Pale warriors, death-pale were they all;
They cried, 'La Belle Dame sans Merci°   *The beautiful pitiless lady*
    Thee hath in thrall!'   40

"I saw their starved lips in the gloam
    With horrid warning gapéd wide,
And I awoke, and found me here,
    On the cold hill's side.   44

"And this is why I sojourn here,
    Alone and palely loitering,
Though the sedge is withered from the lake,
    And no birds sing."   48

QUESTIONS AND SUGGESTIONS FOR WRITING

1. In the first three stanzas the speaker describes the knight as pale, haggard, and so forth. In the rest of the poem the knight recounts his experience. In a few sentences summarize the knight's experience, and indicate why it has caused him to appear as he now does.
2. The *femme fatale*—the dangerously seductive woman—appears in much literature. If you are familiar with one such work, compare it with Keats's poem.
3. What characteristics of the popular ballad (see the introductory note on page 156) do you find in this poem? What characteristic does it *not* share with popular ballads? Set forth your response in an essay of 500 words.

Thomas Hardy (English. 1840–1928)
CHANNEL FIRING

That night your great guns, unawares,
Shook all our coffins as we lay,
And broke the chancel window-squares,
We thought it was the Judgment-day   4

And sat upright. While drearisome
Arose the howl of wakened hounds:
The mouse let fall the altar-crumb,
The worms drew back into the mounds,   8

The glebe cow drooled. Till God called, "No;
It's gunnery practice out at sea
Just as before you went below;
The world is as it used to be: 12

"All nations striving strong to make
Red war yet redder. Mad as hatters
They do no more for Christés sake
Than you who are helpless in such matters.   16

"That this is not the judgment-hour
For some of them's a blessed thing,
For if it were they'd have to scour
Hell's floor for so much threatening . . .   20

"Ha, ha. It will be warmer when
I blow the trumpet (if indeed
I ever do; for you are men,
And rest eternal sorely need)."   24

So down we lay again. "I wonder,
Will the world ever saner be,"
Said one, "than when He sent us under
In our indifferent century!"   28

And many a skeleton shook his head.
"Instead of preaching forty year,"
My neighbor Parson Thirdly said,
"I wish I had stuck to pipes and beer."   32

Again the guns disturbed the hour,
Roaring their readiness to avenge,
As far inland as Stourton Tower,
And Camelot, and starlit Stonehenge.   36

QUESTIONS AND SUGGESTIONS FOR WRITING

1. There are several speakers in this short poem. Identify each of them as precisely as possible. God is one of them. How would you characterize God's tone (and nature) in this poem?
2. Do you think the poem shows that Hardy had lost faith in humanity? Explain.

Walter de la Mare (English. 1873–1956)

THE LISTENERS

"Is there anybody there?" said the Traveler,
 Knocking on the moonlit door;
And his horse in the silence champed the grasses
 Of the forest's ferny floor.
And a bird flew up out of the turret,   5
 Above the Traveler's head:

And he smote upon the door again a second time;
 "Is there anybody there?" he said.
But no one descended to the Traveler;
 No head from the leaf-fringed sill   10
Leaned over and looked into his gray eyes,
 Where he stood perplexed and still.
But only a host of phantom listeners
 That dwelt in the lone house then
Stood listening in the quiet of the moonlight   15
 To that voice from the world of men:
Stood thronging the faint moonbeams on the dark stair
 That goes down to the empty hall,
Hearkening in an air stirred and shaken
 By the lonely Traveler's call.   20

And he felt in his heart their strangeness,
 Their stillness answering his cry,
While his horse moved, cropping the dark turf,
 'Neath the starred and leafy sky;
For he suddenly smote on the door, even   25
 Louder, and lifted his head:—
"Tell them I came, and no one answered,
 That I kept my word," he said.
Never the least stir made the listeners,
 Though every word he spake   30
Fell echoing through the shadowiness of the still house
 From the one man left awake:
Aye, they heard his foot upon the stirrup,
 And the sound of iron on stone,
And how the silence surged softly backward,   35
 When the plunging hoofs were gone.

QUESTIONS AND SUGGESTIONS FOR WRITING

1. Walter de la Mare is reported to have said that the Traveler is a ghost. He is also reported to have said on another occasion that the poem records a class reunion at which he found himself the only one present. Is either of these explanations convincing? Is there anything in the poem to refute the first explanation?
2. Is the poem a narrative of a man who fulfilled a promise, though the ones to whom the promise was made are dead? Is it a narrative of a man who fulfilled a promise in the face of evil forces? Of a frustrated, heroic search for the meaning of life? Of our mysterious separation from the dead? In 100 to 150 words, evaluate one of these interpretations.
3. Why are the actions of the horse described (lines 3, 23)?

□ DRAMA

W. W. Jacobs (English. 1863–1943)
Louis N. Parker (English. 1852–1944)

THE MONKEY'S PAW

Characters

MR. WHITE	SERGEANT-MAJOR MORRIS
MRS. WHITE	MR. SAMPSON
HERBERT	

Scene: The living-room of an old-fashioned cottage on the outskirts of Fulham. Set corner-wise in the left angle at the back a deep window; further front, L., three or four steps lead up to a door. Further forward a dresser, with plates, glasses, etc. R. C. at back an alcove with the street door fully visible. On the inside of the street door, a wire letter-box. On the right a cupboard, then a fireplace. In the center a round table. Against the wall, L. back, an old-fashioned piano. A comfortable armchair each side of the fireplace. Other chairs. On the mantelpiece a clock, old china figures, etc. An air of comfort pervades the room.

I

At the rise of the curtain, MRS. WHITE, *a pleasant-looking old woman, is seated in the armchair below the fire, attending to a kettle which is steaming on the fire, and keeping a laughing eye on* MR. WHITE *and* HERBERT.

These two are seated at the right angle of the table nearest the fire with a chessboard between them. MR. WHITE *is evidently losing. His hair is ruffled; his spectacles are high up on his forehead.* HERBERT, *a fine young fellow, is looking with satisfaction at the move he has just made.* MR. WHITE *makes several attempts to move, but thinks better of them. There is a shaded lamp on the table. The door is tightly shut. The curtains of the window are drawn; but every now and then the wind is heard whistling outside.*

MR. WHITE *(moving at last, and triumphant)*. There, Herbert, my boy! Got you, I think.

HERBERT. Oh, you're a deep 'un, Dad, aren't you?

MRS. WHITE. Mean to say he's beaten you at last?

HERBERT. Lor', no! Why, he's overlooked—

MR. WHITE *(very excited)*. I see it! Lemme have that back!

HERBERT. Not much. Rules of the game!

MR. WHITE *(disgusted)*. I don't hold with them scientific rules. You turn what ought to be an innocent relaxation—

MRS. WHITE. Don't talk so much, Father. You put him off—

HERBERT *(laughing)*. Not he!

MR. WHITE *(trying to distract his attention)*. Hark at the wind.

HERBERT *(drily)*. Ah! I'm listening. Check.

MR. WHITE *(still trying to distract him)*. I should hardly think Sergeant-major Morris'd come to-night.

HERBERT. Mate. *(Rises, goes up L.)*

MR. WHITE *(with an outbreak of disgust and sweeping the chessmen off the board)*. That's the worst of living so far out. Your friends can't come for a quiet chat, and you addle your brains over a confounded—

HERBERT. Now, Father! Morris'll turn up all right.

MR. WHITE *(still in a temper)*. Lovers' Lane, Fulham! Ho! of all the beastly, slushy, out-o'-the-way places to live in—! Pathway's a bog, and the road's a torrent. *(To* MRS. WHITE, *who has risen, and is at his side)* What's the County Council thinking of, that's what I want to know? Because this is the only house in the road it doesn't matter if nobody can get near it, I s'pose.

MRS. WHITE. Never mind, dear. Perhaps you'll win tomorrow. *(She moves to back of table.)*

MR. WHITE. Perhaps I'll—perhaps I'll— What d'you mean? *(Bursts out laughing.)* There! You always know what's going on inside o' me, don't you, Mother?

MRS. WHITE. Ought to, after thirty years, John.

She goes to dresser, and busies herself wiping tumblers on tray there. He rises, goes to fireplace and lights pipe.

HERBERT *(down C.)*. And it's not such a bad place, Dad, after all. One of the few old-fashioned houses left near London. None o' your stucco villas. Homelike, I call it. And so do you, or you wouldn't ha' bought it. *(Rolls a cigarette.)*

MR. WHITE *(R., growling)*. Nice job I made o' that, too! With two hundred pounds owin' on it.

HERBERT *(on back of chair, C.)*. Why, I shall work that off in no time, Dad. Matter o' three years, with the rise promised me.

MR. WHITE. If you don't get married.

HERBERT. Not me. Not that sort.

MRS. WHITE. I wish you would, Herbert. A good, steady lad—

She brings the tray with a bottle of whiskey, glasses, a lemon, spoons, buns, and a knife to the table.

HERBERT. Lots o' time, Mother. Sufficient for the day—as the sayin' goes. Just now my dynamos don't leave me any time for love-making. Jealous, they are, I tell you!

MR. WHITE *(chuckling)*. I lay awake o' nights often, and think: If Herbert took a nap, and let his what-d'you-callums— dynamos, run down, all Fulham would be in darkness. Lord! what a joke! *(Gets R. C.)*

HERBERT. Joke! And me with the sack! Pretty idea of a joke you've got, I don't think.

Knock at outer door.

MRS. WHITE. Hark!

Knock repeated, louder.

MR. WHITE *(going toward door)*. That's him. That's the Sergeant-major. *(He unlocks door, back.)*

HERBERT *(removes chessboard)*. Wonder what yarn he's got for us to-night. *(Places chessboard on piano.)*

MRS. WHITE *(goes up right, busies herself putting the other armchair nearer fire, etc.)*. Don't let the door slam, John!

MR. WHITE *opens the door a little, struggling with it. Wind.* SERGEANT-MAJOR MORRIS, *a veteran with a distinct military appearance— left arm gone—dressed as a commissionaire, is seen to enter.* MR. WHITE *helps him off with his coat, which he hangs up in the outer hall.*

MR. WHITE *(at the door)*. Slip in quick! It's as much as I can do to hold it against the wind.

SERGEANT. Awful! Awful! *(Busy taking off his cloak, etc.)* And a mile up the road—by the cemetery—it's worse. Enough to blow the hair off your head.

MR. WHITE. Give me your stick.

SERGEANT. If 'twasn't I knew what a welcome I'd get—

MR. WHITE *(preceding him into the room).* Sergeant-major Morris!

MRS. WHITE. Tut! tut! So cold you must be! Come to the fire; do'ee, now.

SERGEANT. How are you, marm? *(To HERBERT)* How's yourself, laddie? Not on duty yet, eh? Day-week, eh?

HERBERT *(C.).* No, sir. Night-week. But there's half an hour yet.

SERGEANT *(sitting in the armchair above the fire, which MRS. WHITE is motioning him toward).*

MR. WHITE *mixes grog for* MORRIS.

Thank'ee kindly, marm. That's good—hah! That's a sight better than the trenches at Chitral. That's better than settin' in a puddle with the rain pourin' down in buckets, and the natives takin' pot-shots at you.

MRS. WHITE. Didn't you have no umbrellas? *(Corner below fire, kneels before it, stirs it, etc.)*

SERGEANT. Umbrell—? Ho! ho! That's good! Eh, White? That's good. Did ye hear what she said? Umbrellas—*And* goloshes! *and* hot-water bottles!—Ho, yes! No offence, marm, but it's easy to see you was never a soldier.

HERBERT *(rather hurt).* Mother spoke out o' kindness, sir.

SERGEANT. And well I know it; and no offense intended. No, marm, 'ardship, 'ardship is the soldier's lot. Starvation, fever, and get yourself shot. That's a bit o' my own.

MRS. WHITE. You don't look to've taken much harm—except— *(Indicates his empty sleeve. She takes kettle to table, then returns to fire.)*

SERGEANT *(showing a medal hidden under his coat).* And that I got this for. No, marm. Tough. Thomas Morris is tough.

MR. WHITE *is holding a glass of grog under the* SERGEANT'S *nose.*

And sober. What's this now?

MR. WHITE. Put your nose in it; you'll see.

SERGEANT. Whiskey? And hot? And sugar? And a slice o' lemon? No. I said I'd never—but seein' the sort o' night— Well! *(Waving the glass at them)* Here's another thousand a year!

MR. WHITE *(sits R. of table, also with a glass).* Same to you and many of 'em.

SERGEANT *(to HERBERT, who has no glass).* What? Not you?

HERBERT *(laughing and sitting across chair, C.).* Oh! 'tisn't for want of being sociable. But my work don't go with it. Not if 'twas ever so little. I've got to keep a cool head, a steady eye, and a still hand. The fly-wheel might gobble me up.

MRS. WHITE. Don't, Herbert. *(Sits in armchair below fire.)*

HERBERT *(laughing).* No fear, Mother.

SERGEANT. Ah! you electricians!—Sort o' magicians, you are. Light! says you—and light it is. And, power! says you—and the trams go whizzin'. And, knowledge! says you—and words go 'ummin' to the ends o' the world. It fair beats me—and I've seen a bit in my time, too.

HERBERT *(nudges his father).* Your Indian magic? All a fake, governor. The fakir's fake.

SERGEANT. Fake, you call it? I tell you, I've *seen* it.

HERBERT *(nudging his father with his foot).* Oh, come, now! such as what? Come, now!

SERGEANT. I've seen a cove with no more clothes on than a babby, *(to* MRS. WHITE*)* if you know what I mean—take an empty basket—empty, mind!—as empty as—as this here glass—

MR. WHITE. Hand it over, Morris. *(Hands it to* HERBERT, *who goes quickly behind table and fills it.)*

SERGEANT. Which was not my intentions, but used for illustration.

HERBERT *(while mixing)*. Oh, *I've* seen the basket trick; and I've read how it was done. Why, I could do it myself, with a bit o' practice. Ladle out something stronger. (HERBERT *brings him the glass.)*

SERGEANT. Stronger?—what do you say to an old fakir chuckin' a rope up in the air—in the *air*, mind you!—and swarming up it, same as if it was 'ooked on—vanishing clean out o' sight?—I've seen that.

HERBERT *goes to table, plunges a knife into a bun, and offers it to the* SERGEANT *with exaggerated politeness.*

SERGEANT *(eyeing it with disgust).* Bun—? What for?

HERBERT. That yarn takes it.

MR. and MRS. WHITE *delighted.*

SERGEANT. Mean to say you doubt my word?

MRS. WHITE. No, no! He's only taking you off.—You shouldn't, Herbert.

MR. WHITE. Herbert always was one for a bit o' fun!

HERBERT *puts bun back on table, comes round in front, and moving the chair out of the way, sits cross-legged on the floor at his father's side.*

SERGEANT. But it's true. Why, if I chose, I could tell you things— But there! you don't get no more yarns out o' *me*.

MR. WHITE. Nonsense, old friend. *(Puts down his glass.)* You're not going to get shirty about a bit o' fun. *(Moves his chair nearer* MORRIS'S.*)* What was that you started telling me the other day about a monkey's paw, or something? *(Nudges* HERBERT, *and winks at* MRS. WHITE.*)*

SERGEANT *(gravely).* Nothing. Leastways, nothing worth hearing.

MRS. WHITE *(with astonished curiosity).* Monkey's *paw*—?

MR. WHITE. Ah—you was tellin' me—

SERGEANT. Nothing. Don't go on about it. *(Puts his empty glass to his lips—then stares at it.)* What? Empty again? There! When I begin thinkin' o' the paw, it makes me that absent-minded—

MR. WHITE *(rises and fills glass).* You said you always carried it on you.

SERGEANT. So I do, for fear o' what might happen. *(Sunk in thought)* Ay—ay!

MR. WHITE *(handing him his glass refilled).* There. *(Sits again in same chair.)*

MRS. WHITE. What's it for?

SERGEANT. You wouldn't believe me, if I was to tell you.

HERBERT. *I* will, every word.

SERGEANT. Magic, then!—Don't you laugh!

HERBERT. I'm not. Got it on you now?

SERGEANT. Of course.

HERBERT. Let's see it.

Seeing the SERGEANT *embarrassed with his glass,* MRS. WHITE *rises, takes it from him, places it on mantelpiece and remains standing.*

SERGEANT. Oh, it's nothing to look at. *(Hunting in his pocket)* Just an ordinary—little paw—dried to a mummy. *(Produces it and holds it towards* MRS. WHITE.*)* Here.

MRS. WHITE *(who has leant forward eagerly to see it, starts back with a little cry of disgust).* Oh!

HERBERT. Give us a look. (MORRIS *passes the paw to* MR. WHITE, *from whom* HERBERT *takes it.)* Why, it's all dried up!

SERGEANT. I said so.

Wind.

MRS. WHITE *(with a slight shudder).* Hark at the wind! *(Sits again in her old place.)*

MR. WHITE *(taking the paw from* HERBERT*).* And what might there be special about it?

SERGEANT *(impressively).* That there paw has had a spell put upon it!

MR. WHITE. No? *(In great alarm he thrusts the paw back into* MORRIS'S *hand.)*

SERGEANT *(pensively, holding the paw in the palm of his hand).* Ah! By an old fakir. He was a very holy man. He'd sat all doubled up in one spot, goin' on for fifteen year; thinkin' o' things. And he wanted to show that fate ruled people. That every-thing was cut and dried from the beginning, as you might say. That there warn't no get-tin' away from it. And that, if you tried to, you caught it hot. *(Pauses solemnly.)* So he put a spell on this bit of a paw. It might ha' been anything else, but he took the first thing that came handy. Ah! He put a spell on it, and made it so that three people *(looking at them and with deep meaning)* could each have three wishes.

All but MRS. WHITE *laugh rather nervously.*

MRS. WHITE. Ssh! Don't!

SERGEANT *(more gravely)*. But—! But, mark you, though the wishes was granted, those three people would have cause to wish they *hadn't* been.

MR. WHITE. But how *could* the wishes be granted?

SERGEANT. He didn't say. It would all hap-pen so natural, you might think it a coinci-dence if so disposed.

HERBERT. Why haven't you tried it, sir?

SERGEANT *(gravely, after a pause)*. I have.

HERBERT *(eagerly)*. You've had your three wishes?

SERGEANT *(gravely)*. Yes.

MRS. WHITE. Were they granted?

SERGEANT *(staring at the fire)*. They were.

A pause.

MR. WHITE. Has anybody else wished?

SERGEANT. Yes. The first owner had his three wish— *(Lost in recollection)* Yes, oh yes, he had his three wishes all right. I don't know what his first two were, *(very impressively)* but the third was for death. *(All shudder.)* That's how I got the paw.

A pause.

HERBERT *(cheerfully)*. Well! Seems to me you've only got to wish for things that *can't* have any bad luck about 'em— *(Rises.)*

SERGEANT *(shaking his head)*. Ah!

MR. WHITE *(tentatively)*. Morris—if you've had your three wishes—it's no good to you, now—what do you keep it for?

SERGEANT *(still holding the paw; looking at it)*. Fancy, I s'pose. I did have some idea of selling it, but I don't think I will. It's done mischief enough already. Besides, people won't buy. Some of 'em think it's a fairy-tale. And some want to try it first, and pay after.

Nervous laugh from the others.

MRS. WHITE. If you could have another three wishes, would you?

SERGEANT *(slowly—weighing the paw in his hand, and looking at it)*. I don't know—I don't know— *(Suddenly, with violence, flinging it in the fire)* No! I'm damned if I would!

Movement from all.

MR. WHITE *(rises and quickly snatches it out of the fire)*. What are you doing? (WHITE *goes R. C.)*

SERGEANT *(rising and following him and trying to prevent him)*. Let it burn! Let the infernal thing burn!

MRS. WHITE *(rises)*. Let it burn, Father!

MR. WHITE *(wiping it on his coat-sleeve)*. No. If you don't want it, give it to me.

SERGEANT *(violently)*. I won't! I won't! My hands are clear of it. I threw it on the fire. If you keep it, don't blame me, what-ever happens. Here! Pitch it back again.

MR. WHITE *(stubbornly)*. I'm going to keep it. What do you say, Herbert?

HERBERT *(L. C., laughing)*. I say, keep it if you want to. Stuff and nonsense, anyhow.

MR. WHITE *(looking at the paw thought-fully)*. Stuff and nonsense. Yes. I wonder— *(casually)* I wish— *(He was going to say some ordinary thing, like "I wish I were cer-tain.")*

SERGEANT *(misunderstanding him; vio-lently)*. Stop! Mind what you're doing. That's not the way.

MR. WHITE. What *is* the way?

MRS. WHITE *(moving away, up R. C. to back of table, and beginning to put the tum-blers straight, and the chairs in their places)*. Oh, don't have anything to do with it, John.

Takes glasses on tray to dresser, L., busies herself there, rinsing them in a bowl of water on the dresser, and wiping them with a cloth.

SERGEANT. That's what I say, marm. But if I warn't to tell him, he might go wishing something he didn't mean to. You hold it in your right hand, and wish aloud. But I warn you! I warn you!

MRS. WHITE. Sounds like *The Arabian Nights*. Don't you think you might wish me four pair o' hands?

MR. WHITE *(laughing)*. Right you are, Mother!—I wish—

SERGEANT *(pulling his arm down)*. Stop it! If you must wish, wish for something sensible. Look here! I can't stand this. Gets on my nerves. Where's my coat? *(Goes into alcove.)*

MR. WHITE *crosses to fireplace and carefully puts the paw on mantelpiece. He is absorbed in it to the end of the tableau.*

HERBERT. I'm coming your way, to the works, in a minute. Won't you wait? *(Goes up C., helps* MORRIS *with his coat.)*

SERGEANT *(putting on his coat)*. No. I'm all shook up. I want fresh air. I don't want to be here when you wish. And wish you will as soon's my back's turned. I know. I know. But I've warned you, mind.

MR. WHITE *(helping him into his coat)*. All right, Morris. Don't you fret about us. *(Gives him money.)* Here.

SERGEANT *(refusing it)*. No. I won't—

MR. WHITE *(forcing it into his hand)*. Yes, you will.

Opens door.

SERGEANT *(turning to the room)*. Well, good night all. *(To* WHITE*)* Put it in the fire.

ALL. Good night.   *Exit* SERGEANT.

MR. WHITE *closes door, comes towards fireplace, absorbed in the paw.*

HERBERT *(down L.)*. If there's no more in this than there is in his other stories, we shan't make much out of it.

MRS. WHITE *(comes down R. C. to* WHITE*)*. Did you give him anything for it, Father?

MR. WHITE. A trifle. He didn't want it, but I made him take it.

MRS. WHITE. There, now! You shouldn't. Throwing your money about.

MR. WHITE *(looking at the paw which he has picked up again)*. I wonder—

HERBERT. What?

MR. WHITE. I wonder, whether we hadn't better chuck it on the fire?

HERBERT *(laughing)*. Likely! Why, we're all going to be rich and famous and happy.

MRS. WHITE. Throw it on the fire, indeed, when you've given money for it! So like you, Father.

HERBERT. Wish to be an emperor, Father, to begin with. Then you can't be hen-pecked!

MRS. WHITE *(going for him front of table with a duster)*. You young—! *(Follows him to back of table.)*

HERBERT *(running away from her round behind table)*. Steady with that duster, Mother!

MR. WHITE. Be quiet, there! (HERBERT *catches* MRS. WHITE *in his arms and kisses her.)* I wonder— *(He has the paw in his hand.)* I don't know what to wish for and that's a fact. *(He looks about him with a happy smile.)* I seem to've got all I want.

HERBERT *(with his hands on the old man's shoulders)*. Old Dad! If you'd only cleared the debt on the house, you'd be quite happy, wouldn't you! *(Laughing.)* Well—go ahead!—wish for the two hundred pounds: that'll just do it.

MR. WHITE *(half laughing)*. Shall I? *(Crosses to R.C.)*

HERBERT. Go on! Here!—I'll play slow music. *(Crosses to piano.)*

MRS. WHITE. Don't 'ee, John. Don't have nothing to do with it!

HERBERT. Now, Dad! *(Plays.)*

MR. WHITE. I will! *(Holds up the paw, as if half ashamed.)* I wish for two hundred pounds.

Crash on the piano. At the same instant MR.

WHITE *utters a cry and lets the paw drop.*

MRS. WHITE and HERBERT. What's the matter?

MR. WHITE *(gazing with horror at the paw)*. It moved! As I wished, it twisted in my hand like a snake.

HERBERT *(goes down R., and picks the paw up)*. Nonsense, Dad. Why, it's as stiff as a bone. *(Lays it on the mantelpiece.)*

MRS. WHITE. Must have been your fancy, Father.

HERBERT *(laughing)*. Well—? *(Looking round the room)* I don't see the money; and I bet I never shall.

MR. WHITE *(relieved)*. Thank God, there's no harm done! But it gave me a shock.

HERBERT. Half-past eleven. I must get along. I'm on at midnight. *(Goes up C., fetches his coat, etc.)* We've had quite a merry evening.

MRS. WHITE. I'm off to bed. Don't be late for breakfast, Herbert.

HERBERT. I shall walk home as usual. Does me good. I shall be with you about nine. Don't wait, though.

MRS. WHITE. You know your father never waits.

HERBERT. Good night, Mother. *(Kisses her. She lights candle on dresser, L., goes upstairs and exits.)*

HERBERT *(coming to his father, R., who is sunk in thought)*. Good night, Dad. You'll find the cash tied up in the middle of the bed.

MR. WHITE *(staring, seizes HERBERT'S hand)*. It moved, Herbert.

HERBERT. Ah! And a monkey hanging by his tail from the bed-post, watching you count the golden sovereigns.

MR. WHITE *(accompanying him to the door)*. I wish you wouldn't joke, my boy.

HERBERT. All right, Dad. *(Opens door.)* Lord! What weather! Good night.   *(Exit.)*

The old man shakes his head, closes the door, locks it, puts the chain up, slips the lower bolt, has some difficulty with the upper bolt.

MR. WHITE. This bolt's stiff again! I must get Herbert to look to it in the morning.

Comes into the room, puts out the lamp, crosses towards steps; but is irresistibly attracted toward fireplace. Sits down and stares into the fire. His expression changes: he sees something horrible.

MR. WHITE *(with an involuntary cry)*. Mother! Mother!

MRS. WHITE *(appearing at the door at the top of the steps with candle)*. What's the matter? *(Comes down R. C.)*

MR. WHITE *(mastering himself. Rises)*. Nothing—I—haha!—I saw faces in the fire.

MRS. WHITE. Come along.

She takes his arm and draws him toward the steps. He looks back frightened toward fireplace as they reach the first step.

TABLEAU CURTAIN

II

Bright sunshine. The table, which has been moved nearer the window, is laid for breakfast. MRS. WHITE *busy about the table.* MR. WHITE *standing in the window looking off R. The inner door is open, showing the outer door.*

MR. WHITE. What a morning Herbert's got for walking home!

MRS. WHITE *(L. C.)*. What's o'clock? *(Looks at clock on mantelpiece.)* Quarter to nine, I declare. He's off at eight. *(Crosses to fire.)*

MR. WHITE. Takes him half an hour to change and wash. He's just by the cemetery now.

MRS. WHITE. He'll be here in ten minutes.

MR. WHITE *(coming to the table)*. What's for breakfast?

MRS. WHITE. Sausages. *(At the mantelpiece)* Why, if here isn't that dirty monkey's paw! *(Picks it up, looks at it with disgust, puts it back. Takes sausages in dish from before the fire and places them on table.)* Silly thing! The idea of us listening to such nonsense!

MR. WHITE *(goes up to window again)*. Ay—the Sergeant-major and his yarns! I suppose all old soldiers are alike—

MRS. WHITE. Come on, Father. Herbert hates us to wait.

They both sit and begin breakfast.

MRS. WHITE. How could wishes be granted, nowadays?

MR. WHITE. Ah! Been thinking about it all night, have you?

MRS. WHITE. You kept me awake, with your tossing and tumbling—

MR. WHITE. Ay, I had a bad night.

MRS. WHITE. It was the storm, I expect. How it blew!

MR. WHITE. I didn't hear it. I was asleep and not asleep, if you know what I mean.

MRS. WHITE. And all that rubbish about its making you unhappy if your wish *was* granted! How could two hundred pounds hurt you, eh, Father?

MR. WHITE. Might drop on my head in a lump. Don't see any other way. And I'd try to bear that. Though, mind you, Morris said it would happen so naturally that you might take it for a coincidence, if so disposed.

MRS. WHITE. Well—it hasn't happened. That's all I know. And it isn't going to. *(A letter is seen to drop in the letter-box.)* And how you can sit there and talk about it— *(Sharp postman's knock; she jumps to her feet.)* What's that?

MR. WHITE. Postman, o' course.

MRS. WHITE *(seeing the letter from a distance; in an awed whisper).* He's brought a letter, John!

MR. WHITE *(laughing).* What did you think he'd bring? Ton o' coals?

MRS. WHITE. John—! John—! Suppose—?

MR. WHITE. Suppose what?

MRS. WHITE. Suppose it was two hundred pounds!

MR. WHITE *(suppressing his excitement).* Eh!—Here! Don't talk nonsense. Why don't you fetch it?

MRS. WHITE *(crosses and takes letter out of the box).* It's thick, John—*(feels it)*—and—and it's got something crisp inside it. *(Takes letter to* WHITE, *R. C.)*

MR. WHITE. Who—who's it for?

MRS. WHITE. You.

MR. WHITE. Hand it over, then. *(Feeling and examining it with ill-concealed excitement)* The idea! What a superstitious old woman you are! Where are my specs?

MRS. WHITE. Let me open it.

MR. WHITE. Don't you touch it. Where are my specs? *(Goes to R.)*

MRS. WHITE. Don't let sudden wealth sour your temper, John.

MR. WHITE. *Will* you find my specs?

MRS. WHITE *(taking them off mantelpiece).* Here, John, here. *(As he opens the letter)* Take care! Don't tear it!

MR. WHITE. Tear what?

MRS. WHITE. If it was banknotes, John!

MR. WHITE *(taking a thick, formal document out of the envelope and a crisp-looking slip).* You've gone dotty.—You've made me nervous. *(Reads.)* "Sir, Enclosed please find receipt for interest on the mortgages of £200 on your house, duly received."

They look at each other, MR. WHITE *sits down to finish his breakfast silently.* MRS. WHITE *goes to the window.*

MRS. WHITE. That comes of listening to tipsy old soldiers.

MR. WHITE *(pettish).* What does?

MRS. WHITE. You thought there was banknotes in it.

MR. WHITE *(injured).* I didn't. I said all along—

MRS. WHITE. How Herbert will laugh, when I tell him!

MR. WHITE *(with gruff good-humor).* You're not going to tell him. You're going to keep your mouth shut. That's what you're going to do. Why, I should never hear the last of it.

MRS. WHITE. Serve you right. I shall tell him. You know you like his fun. See how he joked you last night when you said the paw moved. *(She is looking through the window towards R.)*

MR. WHITE. So it did. It did move. That I'll swear to.

MRS. WHITE *(abstractedly: she is watching something outside).* You thought it did.

MR. WHITE. I say it did. There was no thinking about it. You saw how it upset me, didn't you?

She doesn't answer.

Didn't you?—Why don't you listen? (Turns round.) What is it?

MRS. WHITE. Nothing.

MR. WHITE *(turns back to his breakfast).* Do you see Herbert coming?

MRS. WHITE. No.

MR. WHITE. He's about due. What *is* it?

MRS. WHITE. Nothing. Only a man. Looks like a gentleman. Leastways, he's in black, and he's got a top-hat on.

MR. WHITE. What about him? *(He is not interested; goes on eating.)*

MRS. WHITE. He stood at the garden-gate as if he wanted to come in. But he couldn't seem to make up his mind.

MR. WHITE. Oh, go on! You're full o' fancies.

MRS. WHITE. He's going—no; he's coming back.

MR. WHITE. Don't let him see you peeping.

MRS. WHITE *(with increasing excitement).* He's looking at the house. He's got his hand on the latch. No. He turns away again. *(Eagerly)* John! He looks like a sort of lawyer.

MR. WHITE. What of it?

MRS. WHITE. Oh, you'll only laugh again. But suppose—suppose he's coming about the two hundred—

MR. WHITE. You're not to mention it again!—You're a foolish old woman.—Come and eat your breakfast. *(Eagerly)* Where is he now?

MRS. WHITE. Gone down the road. He has turned back. He seems to've made up his mind. Here he comes!—Oh, John, and me all untidy! *(Crosses to fire R.)*

Knock.

MR. WHITE *(to* MRS. WHITE, *who is hastily smoothing her hair, etc.).* What's it matter? He's made a mistake. Come to the wrong house. *(Crosses to fireplace.)*

MRS. WHITE *opens the door.* MR. SAMPSON, *dressed from head to foot in solemn black, with a top-hat, stands in the doorway.*

SAMPSON *(outside).* Is this Mr. White's?

MRS. WHITE. Come in, sir. Please step in.

She shows him into the room; goes R.; he is awkward and nervous.

You must overlook our being so untidy; and the room all anyhow; and John in his garden-coat. *(To* MR. WHITE, *reproachfully)* Oh, John.

SAMPSON *(to* MR. WHITE). Morning. My name is Sampson.

MRS. WHITE *(offering a chair).* Won't you please be seated?

SAMPSON *stands quite still up C.*

SAMPSON. Ah—thank you—no, I think not—I think not. *(Pause.)*

MR. WHITE *(awkwardly, trying to help him).* Fine weather for the time o' year.

SAMPSON. Ah—yes—yes— *(Pause; he makes a renewed effort.)* My name is Sampson—I've come—

MRS. WHITE. Perhaps you was wishful to see Herbert; he'll be home in a minute. *(Pointing)* Here's his breakfast waiting—

SAMPSON *(interrupting her hastily).* No, no! *(Pause.)* I've come from the electrical works—

MRS. WHITE. Why, you might have come *with* him.

MR. WHITE *sees something is wrong, tenderly puts his hand on her arm.*

SAMPSON. No—no—I've come—*alone.*

MRS. WHITE *(with a little anxiety).* Is anything the matter?

SAMPSON. I was asked to call—

MRS. WHITE *(abruptly).* Herbert! Has anything happened? Is he hurt? Is he hurt?

MR. WHITE *(soothing her).* There, there, Mother. Don't you jump to conclusions. Let the gentleman speak. You've not brought bad news, I'm sure, sir.

SAMPSON. I'm—sorry—

MRS. WHITE. Is he hurt?

SAMPSON *bows.*

MRS. WHITE. Badly?

SAMPSON. Very badly. *(Turns away.)*

MRS. WHITE *(with a cry).* John—! *(She instinctively moves towards* MR. WHITE.)

MR. WHITE. Is he in pain?

SAMPSON. He is not in pain.

MRS. WHITE. Oh, thank God! Thank God for that! Thank— *(She looks in a startled fashion at* MR. WHITE—*realizes what* SAMPSON *means, catches his arm and tries to turn him towards her.)* Do you mean—?

SAMPSON *avoids her look; she gropes for her husband: he takes her two hands in his, and gently lets her sink into the armchair above the fireplace, then he stands on her right, between her and* SAMPSON.

MR. WHITE *(hoarsely).* Go on, sir.

SAMPSON. He was telling his mates a story. Something that had happened here last night. He was laughing, and wasn't noticing and—and—*(hushed)* the machinery caught him—

A little cry from MRS. WHITE, *her face shows her horror and agony.*

MR. WHITE *(vague, holding* MRS. WHITE'S *hand).* The machinery caught him—yes—and him the only child—it's hard, sir—very hard—

SAMPSON *(subdued).* The Company wished me to convey their sincere sympathy with you in your great loss—

MR. WHITE *(staring blankly).* Our—great—loss—!

SAMPSON. I was to say further—*(as if apologizing)* I am only their servant—I am only obeying orders—

MR. WHITE. Our—great—loss—

SAMPSON *(laying an envelope on the table and edging towards the door).* I was to say, the Company disclaim all responsibility, but, in consideration of your son's services, they wish to present you with a certain sum as compensation. *(Gets to door.)*

MR. WHITE. Our—great—loss— *(Suddenly, with horror)* How—how much?

SAMPSON *(in the doorway).* Two hundred pounds. *(Exit.)*

MRS. WHITE *gives a cry. The old man takes no heed of her, smiles faintly, puts out his hands like a sightless man, and drops, a senseless heap, to the floor.* MRS. WHITE *stares at him blankly and her hands go out*

helplessly towards him.

TABLEAU CURTAIN

III

Night. On the table a candle is flickering at its last gasp. The room looks neglected. MR. WHITE *is dozing fitfully in the armchair.* MRS. WHITE *is in the window peering through the blinds towards L.*

MR. WHITE *starts, wakes, looks around him.*

MR. WHITE *(fretfully).* Jenny—Jenny.

MRS. WHITE *(in the window).* Yes.

MR. WHITE. Where are you?

MRS. WHITE. At the window.

MR. WHITE. What are you doing?

MRS. WHITE. Looking up the road.

MR. WHITE *(falling back).* What the use, Jenny? What's the use?

MRS. WHITE. That's where the cemetery is; that's where we've laid him.

MR. WHITE. Ay—ay—a week to-day— what o'clock is it?

MRS. WHITE. I don't know.

MR. WHITE. We don't take much account of time now, Jenny, do we?

MRS. WHITE. Why should we? He don't come home. He'll never come home again. There's nothing to think about—

MR. WHITE. Or to talk about. *(Pause.)* Come away from the window; you'll get cold.

MRS. WHITE. It's colder where *he* is.

MR. WHITE. Ay—gone for ever—

MRS. WHITE. And taken all our hopes with him—

MR. WHITE. And all our *wishes*—

MRS. WHITE. Ay, and all our— *(With a sudden cry)* John!

She comes quickly to him; he rises.

MR. WHITE. Jenny! For God's sake! What's the matter?

MRS. WHITE *(with dreadful eagerness).* The *paw!* The monkey's paw!

MR. WHITE *(bewildered).* Where? Where is it? What's wrong with it?

MRS. WHITE. I want it! You haven't done away with it?

MR. WHITE. I haven't seen it—since—why?

MRS. WHITE. I want it! Find it! Find it!

MR. WHITE (*groping on the mantelpiece*). Here! Here it is! What do you want of it? (*He leaves it there.*)

MRS. WHITE. Why didn't I think of it? Why didn't *you* think of it?

MR. WHITE. Think of what?

MRS. WHITE. The *other two* wishes!

MR. WHITE (*with horror*). What?

MRS. WHITE. We've only had one.

MR. WHITE (*tragically*). Wasn't that enough?

MRS. WHITE. No! We'll have one more. (WHITE *crosses to R. C.* MRS. WHITE *takes the paw and follows him.*) Take it. Take it quickly. And wish—

MR. WHITE (*avoiding the paw*). Wish what?

MRS. WHITE. Oh, John! John! Wish our boy alive again!

MR. WHITE. Good God! Are you mad?

MRS. WHITE. Take it. Take it and wish. (*With a paroxysm of grief*) Oh, my boy! My boy!

MR. WHITE. Get to bed. Get to sleep. You don't know what you're saying.

MRS. WHITE. We had the first wish granted—why not the second?

MR. WHITE (*hushed*). He's been dead ten days, and—Jenny! Jenny! I only knew him by his clothing—if you wasn't allowed to see him then—how could you bear to see him *now?*

MRS. WHITE. I don't care. Bring him back.

MR. WHITE (*shrinking from the paw*). I daren't touch it!

MRS. WHITE (*thrusting it in his hand*). Here! Here! Wish!

MR. WHITE (*trembling*). Jenny!

MRS. WHITE (*fiercely*). Wish. (*She goes on frantically whispering "Wish."*)

MR. WHITE (*shuddering, but overcome by her insistence*). I—I—wish—my—son—alive again.

He drops it with a cry. The candle goes out. Utter darkness. He sinks into a chair. MRS. WHITE *hurries to the window and draws the blind back. She stands in the moonlight. Pause.*

MRS. WHITE (*drearily*). Nothing.

MR. WHITE. Thank God! Thank God!

MRS. WHITE. Nothing at all. Along the whole length of the road not a living thing. (*Closes blind.*) And nothing, nothing, nothing left in our lives, John.

MR. WHITE. Except each other, Jenny—and memories.

MRS. WHITE (*coming back slowly to the fireplace*). We're too old. We were only alive in him. We can't begin again. We can't feel anything now, John, but emptiness and darkness. (*She sinks into armchair.*)

MR. WHITE. 'Tisn't for long, Jenny. There's that to look forward to.

MRS. WHITE. Every minute's long, now.

MR. WHITE (*rising*). I can't bear the darkness!

MRS. WHITE. It's dreary—dreary.

MR. WHITE (*crosses to dresser*). Where's the candle? (*Finds it and brings it to table.*) And the matches? Where are the matches? We mustn't sit in the dark. 'Tisn't wholesome. (*Lights match; the other candlestick is close to him.*) There. (*Turning with the lighted match toward* MRS. WHITE, *who is rocking and moaning*) Don't take on so, Mother.

MRS. WHITE. I'm a mother no longer.

MR. WHITE (*lights candle*). There now; there now. Go on up to bed. Go on, now—I'm a-coming.

MRS. WHITE. Whether I'm here or in bed, or wherever I am, I'm with my boy, I'm with—

A low single knock at the street door.

MRS. WHITE (*starting*). What's that!

MR. WHITE (*mastering his horror*). A rat. The house is full of 'em.

A louder single knock; she starts up. He catches her by the arm.

Stop! What are you going to do?

MRS. WHITE (*wildly*). It's my boy! It's Herbert! I forgot it was a mile away! What are you holding me for? I must open the door!

The knocking continues in single knocks at irregular intervals, constantly growing louder and more insistent.

MR. WHITE *(still holding her)*. For God's sake!

MRS. WHITE *(struggling)*. Let me go!

MR. WHITE. Don't open the door! *(He drags her towards left front.)*

MRS. WHITE. Let me go!

MR. WHITE. Think what you might see!

MRS. WHITE *(struggling fiercely)*. Do you think I fear the child I bore! Let me go! *(She wrenches herself loose and rushes to the door which she tears open.)* I'm coming, Herbert! I'm coming!

MR. WHITE *(cowering in the extreme corner, left front.)* Don't 'ee do it! Don't 'ee do it!

MRS. WHITE *is at work on the outer door, where the knocking still continues. She slips the chain, slips the lower bolt, unlocks the door.*

MR. WHITE *(suddenly)*. The paw! Where's the monkey's paw? *(He gets on his knees and feels along the floor for it.)*

MRS. WHITE *(tugging at the top bolt)*. John! The top bolt's stuck. I can't move it. Come and help. Quick!

MR. WHITE *(wildly groping)*. The paw! There's a wish left.

The knocking is now loud, and in groups of increasing length between the speeches.

MRS. WHITE. D'ye hear him? John! Your child's knocking!

MR. WHITE. Where is it? Where did it fall?

MRS. WHITE *(tugging desperately at the bolt)*. Help! Help! Will you keep your child from his home?

MR. WHITE. Where did it fall? I can't find it—I can't find—

The knocking is now tempestuous, and there are blows upon the door as of a body beating against it.

MRS. WHITE. Herbert! Herbert! My boy! Wait! Your mother's opening to you! Ah! It's moving! It's moving!

MR. WHITE. God forbid! *(Finds the paw.)* Ah!

MRS. WHITE *(slipping the bolt)*. Herbert!

MR. WHITE *(has raised himself to his knees; he holds the paw high)*. I wish him dead. *(The knocking stops abruptly.)* I wish him dead and at peace!

MRS. WHITE *(flinging the door open simultaneously)*. Herb—

A flood of moonlight. Emptiness. The old man sways in prayer on his knees. The old woman lies half swooning, wailing against the door-post.

CURTAIN

QUESTIONS AND SUGGESTIONS FOR WRITING

1. In a paragraph, characterize Mr. White and Herbert, basing your remarks only on what they reveal of themselves during the game of chess at the start of the play.

2. Sergeant-major Morris tells the Whites that the fakir who put a spell on the paw had a purpose: "And he wanted to show that fate ruled people. That everything was cut and dried from the beginning, as you might say. That there warn't no gettin' away from it. And that, if you tried to, you caught it hot." In a paragraph explain how the plot of the play illustrates this point.

3. In the third scene, Mrs. White persuades Mr. White to wish that Herbert return alive. Imagine, for a moment, that the playwright handled the story differently. In this imagined version, Mr. White wants Herbert to return, but Mrs. White tries to dissuade him. Despite her pleas, he makes the wish—but then, when he hears the

knocking at the door, he realizes that she is right not to want to bring Herbert back from the dead. In an essay of 250 words explain why you think one version—the printed one, or the one we have sketched—is superior to the other.

Innocence and Experience

7

☐ **ESSAY**

Maya Angelou (American. b. 1928)

GRADUATION

The children in Stamps trembled visibly with anticipation. Some adults were excited too, but to be certain the whole young population had come down with graduation epidemic. Large classes were graduating from both the grammar school and the high school. Even those who were years removed from their own day of glorious release were anxious to help with preparations as a kind of dry run. The junior students who were moving into the vacating classes' chairs were tradition-bound to show their talents for leadership and management. They strutted through the school and around the campus exerting pressure on the lower grades. Their authority was so new that occasionally if they pressed a little too hard it had to be overlooked. After all, next term was coming, and it never hurt a sixth grader to have a play sister in the eighth grade, or a tenth-year student to be able to call a twelfth grader Bubba. So all was endured in a spirit of shared understanding. But the graduating classes themselves were the nobility. Like travelers with exotic destinations on their minds, the graduates were remarkably forgetful. They came to school without their books, or tablets or even pencils. Volunteers fell over themselves to secure replacements for the missing equipment. When accepted, the willing workers might or might not be thanked, and it was of no importance to the pregraduation rites. Even teachers were respectful of the now quiet and aging seniors, and tended to speak to them, if not as equals, as beings only slightly lower than themselves. After tests were returned and grades given, the student body, which acted like an extended family, knew who did well, who excelled, and what piteous ones had failed.

Unlike the white high school, Lafayette County Training School distinguished itself by having neither lawn, nor hedges, nor tennis court, nor climbing ivy. Its two buildings (main classrooms, the grade school and home economics) were set on a dirt hill with no fence to limit either its boundaries or those of bordering farms. There was a large expanse to the left of the school which was used alternately as a baseball diamond or a basketball court. Rusty hoops on the swaying poles represented the permanent recreational equipment, although bats and balls could be borrowed from the P.E. teacher if the borrower was qualified and if the diamond wasn't occupied.

Over this rocky area relieved by a few shady tall persimmon trees the graduating class walked. The girls often held hands and no longer bothered to speak to the lower students. There was a sadness about them, as if this old world was not their home and they were bound for higher ground. The boys, on the other hand, had become more friendly, more outgoing. A decided change from the closed attitude they projected while studying for finals. Now they seemed not ready to give up the old school, the familiar paths and classrooms. Only a small percentage would be continuing on to college—one of the South's A & M (agricultural and mechanical) schools, which trained Negro youths to be carpenters, farmers, handymen, masons, maids, cooks and baby nurses. Their future rode heavily on their shoulders, and blinded them to the collective joy that had pervaded the lives of the boys and girls in the grammar school graduating class.

Parents who could afford it had ordered new shoes and ready-made clothes for themselves from Sears and Roebuck or Montgomery Ward. They also engaged the best seamstresses to make the floating graduating dresses and to cut down secondhand pants which would be pressed to a military slickness for the important event.

Oh, it was important, all right. Whitefolks would attend the ceremony, and two or three would speak of God and home, and the Southern way of life, and Mrs. Parsons, the principal's wife, would play the graduation march while the lower-grade graduates paraded down the aisles and took their seats below the platform. The high school seniors would wait in empty classrooms to make their dramatic entrance.   5

In the Store I was the person of the moment. The birthday girl. The center. Bailey had graduated the year before, although to do so he had had to forfeit all pleasures to make up for his time lost in Baton Rouge.

My class was wearing butter-yellow piqué dresses, and Momma launched out on mine. She smocked the yoke into tiny crisscrossing puckers, then shirred the rest of the bodice. Her dark fingers ducked in and out of the lemony cloth as she embroidered raised daisies around the hem. Before she considered herself finished she had added a crocheted cuff on the puff sleeves, and a pointy crocheted collar.

I was going to be lovely. A walking model of all the various styles of fine hand sewing and it didn't worry me that I was only twelve years old and merely graduating from the eighth grade. Besides, many teachers in Arkansas Negro schools had only that diploma and were licensed to impart wisdom.

The days had become longer and more noticeable. The faded beige of former times had been replaced with strong and sure colors. I began to see my classmates' clothes, their skin tones, and the dust that waved off pussy willows.

Clouds that lazed across the sky were objects of great concern to me. Their shiftier shapes might have held a message that in my new happiness and with a little bit of time I'd soon decipher. During that period I looked at the arch of heaven so religiously my neck kept a steady ache. I had taken to smiling more often, and my jaws hurt from the unaccustomed activity. Between the two physical sore spots, I suppose I could have been uncomfortable, but that was not the case. As a member of the winning team (the graduating class of 1940) I had outdistanced unpleasant sensations by miles. I was headed for the freedom of open fields.

Youth and social approval allied themselves with me and we trammeled memories of slights and insults. The wind of our swift passage remodeled my features. Lost tears were pounded to mud and then to dust. Years of withdrawal were brushed aside and left behind, as hanging ropes of parasitic moss.

My work alone had awarded me a top place and I was going to be one of the first called in the graduating ceremonies. On the classroom blackboard, as well as on the bulletin board in the auditorium, there were blue stars and white stars and red stars. No absences, no tardinesses, and my academic work was among the best of the year. I could say the preamble to the Constitution even faster than Bailey. We timed ourselves often: "We the people of the United States in order to form a more perfect union . . ." I had memorized the Presidents of the United States from Washington to Roosevelt in chronological as well as alphabetical order.

My hair pleased me too. Gradually the black mass had lengthened and thickened, so that it kept at last to its braided pattern, and I didn't have to yank my scalp off when I tried to comb it.

Louise and I had rehearsed the exercises until we tired out ourselves. Henry Reed was class valedictorian. He was a small, very black boy with hooded eyes, a long, broad nose and an oddly shaped head. I had admired him for years because each term he and I vied for the best grades in our class. Most often he bested me, but instead of being disappointed I was pleased that we shared top places between us. Like many Southern Black children, he lived with his grandmother, who was as strict as Momma and as kind as she knew how to be. He was courteous, respectful and soft-spoken to elders, but on the playground he chose to play the roughest games. I admired him. Anyone, I reckoned, sufficiently afraid or sufficiently dull could be polite. But to be able to operate at a top level with both adults and children was admirable.

His valedictory speech was entitled "To Be or Not To Be." The rigid tenth-grade teacher had helped him to write it. He'd been working on the dramatic stresses for months.

The weeks until graduation were filled with heady activities. A group of small children were to be presented in a play about buttercups and daisies and bunny rabbits. They could be heard throughout the building practicing their hops and their little songs that sounded like silver bells. The older girls (non-graduates, of course) were assigned the task of making refreshments for the night's festivities. A tangy scent of ginger, cinnamon, nutmeg and chocolate wafted around the home economics building as the budding cooks made samples for themselves and their teachers.

In every corner of the workshop, axes and saws split fresh timber as the woodshop boys made sets and stage scenery. Only the graduates were left out of the general bustle. We were free to sit in the library at the back of the building or look in quite detachedly, naturally, on the measures being taken for our event.

Even the minister preached on graduation the Sunday before. His subject was, "Let your light so shine that men will see your good works and praise your Father, Who is in Heaven." Although the sermon was purported to be addressed to us, he used the occasion to speak to backsliders, gamblers, and general ne'er-do-wells. But since he had called our names at the beginning of the service we were mollified.

Among Negroes the tradition was to give presents to children going only from one grade to another. How much more important this was when the person was graduating at the top of the class. Uncle Willie and Momma had sent away for a Mickey Mouse watch like Bailey's. Louise gave me four embroidered handkerchiefs. (I gave her three crocheted doilies.) Mrs. Sneed, the minister's wife, made me an underskirt to wear for graduation, and nearly every customer gave me a nickel or maybe even a dime with the instruction "Keep on moving to higher ground," or some such encouragement.

Amazingly the great day finally dawned and I was out of bed before I knew it. I threw open the back door to see it more clearly, but Momma said, "Sister, come away from that door and put your robe on."

I hoped the memory of that morning would never leave me. Sunlight was   20
itself still young, and the day had none of the insistence maturity would bring it in a few hours. In my robe and barefoot in the backyard, under cover of going to see about my new beans, I gave myself up to the gentle warmth and thanked God that no matter what evil I had done in my life He had allowed me to live to see this day. Somewhere in my fatalism I had expected to die, accidentally, and never have the chance to walk up the stairs in the auditorium and gracefully receive my hard-earned diploma. Out of God's merciful bosom I had won reprieve.

Bailey came out in his robe and gave me a box wrapped in Christmas paper. He said he had saved his money for months to pay for it. It felt like a box of chocolates, but I knew Bailey wouldn't save money to buy candy when we had all we could want under our noses.

He was as proud of the gift as I. It was a soft-leather-bound copy of a collection of poems by Edgar Allan Poe, or, as Bailey and I called him, "Eap." I turned to "Annabel Lee" and we walked up and down the garden rows, the cool dirt between our toes, reciting the beautifully sad lines.

Momma made a Sunday breakfast although it was only Friday. After we finished the blessing, I opened my eyes to find the watch on my plate. It was a dream of a day. Everything went smoothly and to my credit, I didn't have to be reminded or scolded for anything. Near evening I was too jittery to attend to chores, so Bailey volunteered to do all before his bath.

Days before, we had made a sign for the Store and as we turned out the lights Momma hung the cardboard over the doorknob. It read clearly: CLOSED. GRADUATION.

My dress fitted perfectly and everyone said that I looked like a sunbeam in it.   25
On the hill, going toward the school, Bailey walked behind with Uncle Willie, who
muttered, "Go on, Ju." He wanted him to walk ahead with us because it embarrassed him to have to walk so slowly. Bailey said he'd let the ladies walk together,
and the men would bring up the rear. We all laughed, nicely.

Little children dashed by out of the dark like fireflies. Their crepe-paper
dresses and butterfly wings were not made for running and we heard more than
one rip, dryly, and the regretful "uh uh" that followed.

The school blazed without gaiety. The windows seemed cold and unfriendly
from the lower hill. A sense of ill-fated timing crept over me, and if Momma hadn't
reached for my hand I would have drifted back to Bailey and Uncle Willie, and
possibly beyond. She made a few slow jokes about my feet getting cold, and
tugged me along to the now-strange building.

Around the front steps, assurance came back. There were my fellow
"greats," the graduating class. Hair brushed back, legs oiled, new dresses and
pressed pleats, fresh pocket handkerchiefs and little handbags, all homesewn.
Oh, we were up to snuff, all right. I joined my comrades and didn't even see my
family go in to find seats in the crowded auditorium.

The school band struck up a march and all classes filed in as had been
rehearsed. We stood in front of our seats, as assigned, and on a signal from the
choir director, we sat. No sooner had this been accomplished than the band
started to play the national anthem. We rose again and sang the song, after which
we recited the pledge of allegiance. We remained standing for a brief minute
before the choir director and the principal signaled to us, rather desperately I
thought, to take our seats. The command was so unusual that our carefully rehearsed and smooth-running machine was thrown off. For a full minute we fumbled for our chairs and bumped into each other awkwardly. Habits change or
solidify under pressure, so in our state of nervous tension we had been ready to
follow our usual assembly pattern: the American National Anthem, then the
pledge of allegiance, then the song every Black person I knew called the Negro
National Anthem. All done in the same key, with the same passion and most often
standing on the same foot.

Finding my seat at last, I was overcome with a presentiment of worse things   30
to come. Something unrehearsed, unplanned, was going to happen, and we were
going to be made to look bad. I distinctly remember being explicit in the choice of
pronoun. It was "we," the graduating class, the unit, that concerned me then.

The principal welcomed "parents and friends" and asked the Baptist minister
to lead us in prayer. His invocation was brief and punchy, and for a second I
thought we were getting back on the high road to right action. When the principal
came back to the dais, however, his voice had changed. Sounds always affected
me profoundly and the principal's voice was one of my favorites. During assembly
it melted and lowed weakly into the audience. It had not been in my plan to listen
to him, but my curiosity was piqued and I straightened up to give him my attention.

He was talking about Booker T. Washington, our "late great leader," who said we can be as close as the fingers on the hand, etc. . . . Then he said a few vague things about friendship and the friendship of kindly people to those less fortunate than themselves. With that his voice nearly faded, thin, away. Like a river diminishing to a stream and then to a trickle. But he cleared his throat and said, "Our speaker tonight, who is also our friend, came from Texarkana to deliver the commencement address, but due to the irregularity of the train schedule, he's going to, as they say, 'speak and run.' " He said that we understood and wanted the man to know that we were most grateful for the time he was able to give us and then something about how we were willing always to adjust to another's program, and without more ado—"I give you Mr. Edward Donleavy."

Not one but two white men came through the door offstage. The shorter one walked to the speaker's platform, and the tall one moved over to the center seat and sat down. But that was our principal's seat, and already occupied. The dislodged gentleman bounced around for a long breath or two before the Baptist minister gave him his chair, then with more dignity than the situation deserved, the minister walked off the stage.

Donleavy looked at the audience once (on reflection, I'm sure that he wanted only to reassure himself that we were really there), adjusted his glasses and began to read from a sheaf of papers.

He was glad "to be here and to see the work going on just as it was in the other schools."   35

At the first "Amen" from the audience I willed the offender to immediate death by choking on the word. But Amen's and Yes, sir's began to fall around the room like rain through a ragged umbrella.

He told us of the wonderful changes we children in Stamps had in store. The Central School (naturally, the white school was Central) had already been granted improvements that would be in use in the fall. A well-known artist was coming from Little Rock to teach art to them. They were going to have the newest microscopes and chemistry equipment for their laboratory. Mr. Donleavy didn't leave us long in the dark over who made these improvements available to Central High. Nor were we to be ignored in the general betterment scheme he had in mind.

He said that he had pointed out to people at a very high level that one of the first-line football tacklers at Arkansas Agricultural and Mechanical College had graduated from good old Lafayette County Training School. Here fewer Amen's were heard. Those few that did break through lay dully in the air with the heaviness of habit.

He went on to praise us. He went on to say how he had bragged that "one of the best basketball players at Fisk sank his first ball right here at Lafayette County Training School."

The white kids were going to have a chance to become Galileos and Madame   40
Curies and Edisons and Gauguins, and our boys (the girls weren't even in on it) would try to be Jesse Owenses and Joe Louises.

Owens and the Brown Bomber were great heroes in our world, but what school official in the white-goddom of Little Rock had the right to decide that those two men must be our only heroes? Who decided that for Henry Reed to become a scientist he had to work like George Washington Carver, as a bootblack, to buy a lousy microscope? Bailey was obviously always going to be too small to be an athlete, so which concrete angel glued to what country seat had decided that if my brother wanted to become a lawyer he had to first pay penance for his skin by picking cotton and hoeing corn and studying correspondence books at night for twenty years?

The man's dead words fell like bricks around the auditorium and too many settled in my belly. Constrained by hard-learned manners I couldn't look behind me, but to my left and right the proud graduating class of 1940 had dropped their heads. Every girl in my row had found something new to do with her handkerchief. Some folded the tiny squares into love knots, some into triangles, but most were wadding them, then pressing them flat on their yellow laps.

On the dais, the ancient tragedy was being replayed. Professor Parsons sat, a sculptor's reject, rigid. His large, heavy body seemed devoid of will or willingness, and his eyes said he was no longer with us. The other teachers examined the flag (which was draped stage right) or their notes, or the windows which opened on our now-famous playing diamond.

Graduation, the hush-hush magic time of frills and gifts and congratulations and diplomas, was finished for me before my name was called. The accomplishment was nothing. The meticulous maps, drawn in three colors of ink, learning and spelling decasyllabic words, memorizing the whole of *The Rape of Lucrece*—it was nothing. Donleavy had exposed us.

We were maids and farmers, handymen and washerwomen, and anything higher that we aspired to was farcical and presumptuous. Then I wished that Gabriel Prosser and Nat Turner had killed all whitefolks in their beds and that Abraham Lincoln had been assassinated before the signing of the Emancipation Proclamation, and that Harriet Tubman had been killed by that blow on her head and Christopher Columbus had drowned in the *Santa Maria*. 45

It was awful to be Negro and have no control over my life. It was brutal to be young and already trained to sit quietly and listen to charges brought against my color with no chance of defense. We should all be dead. I thought I should like to see us all dead, one on top of the other. A pyramid of flesh with the whitefolks on the bottom, as the broad base, then the Indians with their silly tomahawks and teepees and wigwams and treaties, the Negroes with their mops and recipes and cotton sacks and spirituals sticking out of their mouths. The Dutch children should all stumble in their wooden shoes and break their necks. The French should choke to death on the Louisiana Purchase (1803) while silkworms ate all the Chinese with their stupid pigtails. As a species, we were an abomination. All of us.

Donleavy was running for election, and assured our parents that if he won we could count on having the only colored paved playing field in that part of Arkansas. Also—he never looked up to acknowledge the grunts of acceptance—also, we were bound to get some new equipment for the home economics building and the workshop.

He finished, and since there was no need to give any more than the most perfunctory thank-you's, he nodded to the men on the stage, and the tall white man who was never introduced joined him at the door. They left with the attitude that now they were off to something really important. (The graduation ceremonies at Lafayette County Training School had been a mere preliminary.)

The ugliness they left was palpable. An uninvited guest who wouldn't leave. The choir was summoned and sang a modern arrangement of "Onward, Christian Soldiers," with new words pertaining to graduates seeking their place in the world. But it didn't work. Elouise, the daughter of the Baptist minister, recited "Invictus," and I could have cried at the impertinence of "I am the master of my fate, I am the captain of my soul."

My name had lost its ring of familiarity and I had to be nudged to go and receive my diploma. All my preparations had fled. I neither marched up to the stage like a conquering Amazon, nor did I look in the audience for Bailey's nod of approval. Marguerite Johnson, I heard the name again, my honors were read, there were noises in the audience of appreciation, and I took my place on the stage as rehearsed.

50

I thought about colors I hated: ecru, puce, lavender, beige and black.

There was shuffling and rustling around me, then Henry Reed was giving his valedictory address, "To Be or Not to Be." Hadn't he heard the whitefolks? We couldn't *be*, so the question was a waste of time. Henry's voice came out clear and strong. I feared to look at him. Hadn't he got the message? There was no "nobler in the mind" for Negroes because the world didn't think we had minds, and they let us know it. "Outrageous fortune"? Now, that was a joke. When the ceremony was over I had to tell Henry Reed some things. That is, if I still cared. Not "rub," Henry, "erase." "Ah, there's the erase." Us.

Henry had been a good student in elocution. His voice rose on tides of promise and fell on waves of warnings. The English teacher had helped him to create a sermon winging through Hamlet's soliloquy. To be a man, a doer, a builder, a leader, or to be a tool, an unfunny joke, a crusher of funky toadstools. I marveled that Henry could go through with the speech as if we had a choice.

I had been listening and silently rebutting each sentence with my eyes closed; then there was a hush, which in an audience warns that something unplanned is happening. I looked up and saw Henry Reed, the conservative, the proper, the A student, turn his back to the audience and turn to us (the proud graduating class of 1940) and sing, nearly speaking,

> Lift ev'ry voice and sing
> Till earth and heaven ring
> Ring with the harmonies of Liberty . . .

It was the poem written by James Weldon Johnson. It was the music composed by J. Rosamond Johnson. It was the Negro National Anthem. Out of habit we were singing it.

Our mothers and fathers stood in the dark hall and joined the hymn of encouragement. A kindergarten teacher led the small children onto the stage and the buttercups and daisies and bunny rabbits marked time and tried to follow:

55

Stony the road we trod
Bitter the chastening rod
Felt in the days when hope, unborn, had died.
Yet with a steady beat
Have not our weary feet
Come to the place for which our fathers sighed?

Every child I knew had learned that song with his ABC's and along with "Jesus Loves Me This I Know." But I personally had never heard it before. Never heard the words, despite the thousands of times I had sung them. Never thought they had anything to do with me.

On the other hand, the words of Patrick Henry had made such an impression on me that I had been able to stretch myself tall and trembling and say, "I know not what course others may take, but as for me, give me liberty or give me death."

And now I heard, really for the first time:

We have come over a way that with tears has been watered,
We have come, treading our path through the blood of the slaughtered.

While echoes of the song shivered in the air, Henry Reed bowed his head, said "Thank you," and returned to his place in the line. The tears that slipped down many faces were not wiped away in shame.

We were on top again. As always, again. We survived. The depths had been 60 icy and dark, but now a bright sun spoke to our souls. I was no longer simply a member of the proud graduating class of 1940; I was a proud member of the wonderful, beautiful Negro race.

Oh, Black known and unknown poets, how often have your auctioned pains sustained us? Who will compute the lonely nights made less lonely by your songs, or the empty pots made less tragic by your tales?

If we were a people much given to revealing secrets, we might raise monuments and sacrifice to the memories of our poets, but slavery cured us of that weakness. It may be enough, however, to have it said that we survive in exact relationship to the dedication of our poets (include preachers, musicians and blues singers).

QUESTIONS AND SUGGESTIONS FOR WRITING

1. In the first paragraph notice such overstatements as "glorious release," "the graduating classes themselves were the nobility," and "exotic destinations." Find further examples in the next few pages. What is the function of this diction?
2. How would you define "poets" as Angelou uses the word in the last sentence?
3. Characterize the writer as you perceive her up to the middle of page 181. Support your characterization with references to specific passages. Next, characterize her in the paragraph beginning "It was awful to be Negro" (paragraph 46). Next, characterize her on the basis of the entire essay. Finally, in a sentence, try to describe the change, telling the main attitudes or moods that she goes through.

□ FICTION

Nathaniel Hawthorne (American. 1804–1864)

MY KINSMAN, MAJOR MOLINEUX

After the kings of Great Britain had assumed the right of appointing the colonial governors, the measures of the latter seldom met with the ready and generous approbation which had been paid to those of their predecessors, under the original charters. The people looked with most jealous scrutiny to the exercise of power which did not emanate from themselves, and they usually rewarded their rulers with slender gratitude for the compliances by which, in softening their instructions from beyond the sea, they had incurred the reprehension of those who gave them. The annals of Massachusetts Bay will inform us, that of six governors in the space of about forty years from the surrender of the old charter, under James II., two were imprisoned by a popular insurrection; a third, as Hutchinson inclines to believe, was driven from the province by the whizzing of a musket-ball; a fourth, in the opinion of the same historian, was hastened to his grave by continual bickerings with the House of Representatives; and the remaining two, as well as their successors, till the Revolution, were favored with few and brief intervals of peaceful sway. The inferior members of the court party, in times of high political excitement, led scarcely a more desirable life. These remarks may serve as a preface to the following adventures, which chanced upon a summer night, not far from a hundred years ago. The reader, in order to avoid a long and dry detail of colonial affairs, is requested to dispense with an account of the train of circumstances that had caused much temporary inflammation of the popular mind.

It was near nine o'clock of a moonlight evening, when a boat crossed the ferry with a single passenger, who had obtained his conveyance at that unusual hour by the promise of an extra fare. While he stood on the landing-place, searching in either pocket for the means of fulfilling his agreement, the ferryman lifted a lantern, by the aid of which, and the newly risen moon, he took a very accurate survey of the stranger's figure. He was a youth of barely eighteen years, evidently country-bred, and now, as it should seem, upon his first visit to town. He was clad in a coarse gray coat, well worn, but in excellent repair; his under garments were durably constructed of leather, and fitted tight to a pair of serviceable and well-shaped limbs; his stockings of blue yarn were the incontrovertible work of a mother or a sister; and on his head was a three-cornered hat, which in its better days had perhaps sheltered the graver brow of the lad's father. Under his left arm was a heavy cudgel formed of an oak sapling, and retaining a part of the hardened root; and his equipment was completed by a wallet, not so abundantly stocked as to incommode the vigorous shoulders on which it hung. Brown, curly hair, well-shaped features, and bright, cheerful eyes were nature's gifts, and worth all that art could have done for his adornment.

The youth, one of whose names was Robin, finally drew from his pocket the half of a little province bill of five shillings, which, in the depreciation in that sort of currency, did but satisfy the ferryman's demand, with the surplus of a sexangular piece of parchment, valued at three pence. He then walked forward into the town, with as light a step as if his day's journey had not already exceeded thirty miles, and with as eager an eye as if he were entering London city, instead of the little metropolis of a New England colony. Before Robin had proceeded far, however, it occurred to him that he knew not whither to direct his steps; so he paused, and looked up and down the narrow street, scrutinizing the small and mean wooden buildings that were scattered on either side.

"This low hovel cannot be my kinsman's dwelling," thought he, "nor yonder old house, where the moonlight enters at the broken casement; and truly I see none hereabouts that might be worthy of him. It would have been wise to inquire my way of the ferryman, and doubtless he would have gone with me, and earned a shilling from the Major for his pains. But the next man I meet will do as well."

He resumed his walk, and was glad to perceive that the street now became 5 wider, and the houses more respectable in their appearance. He soon discerned a figure moving on moderately in advance, and hastened his steps to overtake it. As Robin drew nigh, he saw that the passenger was a man in years, with a full periwig of gray hair, a wide-skirted coat of dark cloth, and silk stockings rolled above his knees. He carried a long and polished cane, which he struck down perpendicularly before him at every step; and at regular intervals he uttered two successive hems, of a peculiarly solemn and sepulchral intonation. Having made these observations, Robin laid hold of the skirt of the old man's coat, just when the light from the open door and windows of a barber's shop fell upon both their figures.

"Good evening to you, honored sir," said he, making a low bow, and still retaining his hold of the skirt. "I pray you tell me whereabouts is the dwelling of my kinsman, Major Molineux."

The youth's question was uttered very loudly; and one of the barbers, whose razor was descending on a well-soaped chin and another who was dressing a Ramillies wig, left their occupations, and came to the door. The citizen, in the mean time, turned a long-favored countenance upon Robin, and answered him in a tone of excessive anger and annoyance. His two sepulchral hems, however, broke into the very center of his rebuke, with most singular effect, like a thought of the cold grave obtruding among wrathful passions.

"Let go my garment, fellow! I tell you, I know not the man you speak of. What! I have authority, I have—hem, hem—authority; and if this be the respect you show for your betters, your feet shall be brought acquainted with the stocks by daylight, tomorrow morning!"

Robin released the old man's skirt, and hastened away, pursued by an ill-mannered roar of laughter from the barber's shop. He was at first considerably surprised by the result of his question, but, being a shrewd youth, soon thought himself able to account for the mystery.

"This is some country representative," was his conclusion, "who has never 10 seen the inside of my kinsman's door, and lacks the breeding to answer a stranger civilly. The man is old, or verily—I might be tempted to turn back and smite him on the nose. Ah, Robin, Robin! even the barber's boys laugh at you for choosing such a guide! You will be wiser in time, friend Robin."

He now became entangled in a succession of crooked and narrow streets, which crossed each other, and meandered at no great distance from the waterside. The smell of tar was obvious to his nostrils, the masts of vessels pierced the moonlight above the tops of the buildings, and the numerous signs, which Robin paused to read, informed him that he was near the center of business. But the streets were empty, the shops were closed, and lights were visible only in the second stories of a few dwelling-houses. At length, on the corner of a narrow lane, through which he was passing, he beheld the broad countenance of a British hero swinging before the door of an inn, whence proceeded the voices of many guests. The casement of one of the lower windows was thrown back, and a very thin curtain permitted Robin to distinguish a party at supper, round a well-furnished table. The fragrance of the good cheer steamed forth into the outer air, and the youth could not fail to recollect that the last remnant of his traveling stock of provision had yielded to his morning appetite, and that noon had found and left him dinnerless.

"Oh, that a parchment three-penny might give me a right to sit down at yonder table!" said Robin, with a sigh. "But the Major will make me welcome to the best of his victuals; so I will even step boldly in, and inquire my way to his dwelling."

He entered the tavern, and was guided by the murmur of voices and the fumes of tobacco to the public-room. It was a long and low apartment, with oaken walls, grown dark in the continual smoke, and a floor which was thickly sanded, but of no immaculate purity. A number of persons—the larger part of whom appeared to be mariners, or in some way connected with the sea—occupied the wooden benches, or leather-bottomed chairs, conversing on various matters, and occasionally lending their attention to some topic of general interest. Three or four little groups were draining as many bowls of punch, which the West India trade had long since made a familiar drink in the colony. Others, who had the appearance of men who lived by regular and laborious handicraft, preferred the insulated bliss of an unshared potation, and became more taciturn under its influence. Nearly all, in short, evinced a predilection for the Good Creature in some of its various shapes, for this is a vice to which, as Fast Day sermons of a hundred years ago will testify, we have a long hereditary claim. The only guests to whom Robin's sympathies inclined him were two or three sheepish countrymen, who were using the inn somewhat after the fashion of a Turkish caravansary; they had gotten themselves into the darkest corner of the room, and heedless of the Nicotian atmosphere, were supping on the bread of their own ovens, and the bacon cured in their own chimney-smoke. But though Robin felt a sort of brotherhood with these strangers, his eyes were attracted from them to a person who stood near the door, holding whispered conversation with a group of ill-dressed associates. His features were separately striking almost to grotesqueness, and the whole face left a deep impression on the memory. The forehead bulged out into a double prominence, with a vale between; the nose came boldly forth in an irregular curve, and its bridge was of more than a finger's breadth; the eyebrows were deep and shaggy, and the eyes glowed beneath them like fire in a cave.

While Robin deliberated of whom to inquire respecting his kinsman's dwelling, he was accosted by the innkeeper, a little man in a stained white apron, who had come to pay his professional welcome to the stranger. Being in the second generation from a French Protestant, he seemed to have inherited the courtesy of his parent nation; but no variety of circumstances was ever known to change his voice from the one shrill note in which he now addressed Robin.

"From the country, I presume, sir?" said he, with a profound bow. "Beg   15
leave to congratulate you on your arrival, and trust you intend a long stay with us. Fine town here, sir, beautiful buildings, and much that may interest a stranger. May I hope for the honor of your commands in respect to supper?"

"The man sees a family likeness! the rogue has guessed that I am related to the Major!" thought Robin, who had hitherto experienced little superfluous civility.

All eyes were now turned on the country lad, standing at the door, in his worn three-cornered hat, gray coat, leather breeches, and blue yarn stockings, leaning on an oaken cudgel, and bearing a wallet on his back.

Robin replied to the courteous innkeeper, with such an assumption of confidence as befitted the Major's relative. "My honest friend," he said, "I shall make it a point to patronize your house on some occasion, when"—here he could not help lowering his voice—"when I may have more than a parchment three-pence in my pocket. My present business," continued he, speaking with lofty confidence, "is merely to inquire my way to the dwelling of my kinsman, Major Molineux."

There was a sudden and general movement in the room which Robin interpreted as expressing the eagerness of each individual to become his guide. But the innkeeper turned his eyes to a written paper on the wall, which he read, or seemed to read, with occasional recurrences to the young man's figure.

"What have we here?" said he, breaking his speech into little dry fragments.   20
" 'Left the house of the subscriber, bounden servant, Hezekiah Mudge,—had on, when he went away, gray coat, leather breeches, master's third-best hat. One pound currency reward to whosoever shall lodge him in any jail of the providence.' Better trudge, boy; better trudge!"

Robin had begun to draw his hand towards the lighter end of the oak cudgel, but a strange hostility in every countenance induced him to relinquish his purpose of breaking the courteous innkeeper's head. As he turned to leave the room, he encountered a sneering glance from the bold-featured personage whom he had before noticed; and no sooner was he beyond the door, than he heard a general laugh, in which the innkeeper's voice might be distinguished, like the dropping of small stones into a kettle.

"Now, is it not strange," thought Robin, with his usual shrewdness,—"is it not strange that the confession of an empty pocket should outweigh the name of my kinsman, Major Molineux? Oh, if I had one of those grinning rascals in the woods, where I and my oak sapling grew up together, I would teach him that my arm is heavy though my purse be light!"

On turning the corner of the narrow lane, Robin found himself in a spacious street, with an unbroken line of lofty houses on each side, and a steepled building at the upper end, whence the ringing of a bell announced the hour of nine. The light of the moon, and the lamps from the numerous shop-windows, discovered people promenading on the pavement, and amongst them Robin had hoped to recognize his hitherto inscrutable relative. The result of his former inquiries made him unwilling to hazard another, in a scene of such publicity, and he determined to walk slowly and silently up the street, thrusting his face close to that of every elderly gentleman, in search of the Major's lineaments. In his progress, Robin encountered many gay and gallant figures. Embroidered garments of showy colors, enormous periwigs, gold-laced hats, and silver-hilted swords glided past him and dazzled his optics. Traveled youths, imitators of the European fine gentlemen of the period, trod jauntily along, half dancing to the fashionable tunes which they hummed, and making poor Robin ashamed of his quiet and natural gait. At length, after many pauses to examine the gorgeous display of goods in the shop-windows, and after suffering some rebukes for the impertinence of his scrutiny into people's faces, the Major's kinsman found himself near the steepled building, still unsuccessful in his search. As yet, however, he had seen only one side of the thronged street; so Robin crossed, and continued the same sort of inquisition down the opposite pavement, with stronger hopes than the philosopher seeking an honest man, but with no better fortune. He had arrived about midway towards the lower end, from which his course began, when he overheard the approach of some one who struck down a cane on the flag-stones at every step, uttering at regular intervals, two sepulchral hems.

"Mercy on us!" quoth Robin, recognizing the sound.

Turning a corner, which chanced to be close at his right hand, he hastened to pursue his researches in some other part of the town. His patience now was wearing low, and he seemed to feel more fatigue from his rambles since he crossed the ferry, than from his journey of several days on the other side. Hunger also pleaded loudly within him, and Robin began to balance the propriety of demanding, violently, and with lifted cudgel, the necessary guidance from the first solitary passenger whom he should meet. While a resolution to this effect was gaining strength, he entered a street of mean appearance, on either side of which a row of ill-built houses was straggling towards the harbor. The moonlight fell upon no passenger along the whole extent, but in the third domicile which Robin passed there was a half-opened door, and his keen glance detected a woman's garment within.

"My luck may be better here," said he to himself.

Accordingly, he approached the door and beheld it shut closer as he did so; yet an open space remained, sufficing for the fair occupant to observe the stranger, without a corresponding display on her part. All that Robin could discern was a strip of scarlet petticoat, and the occasional sparkle of an eye, as if the moonbeams were trembling on some bright thing.

"Pretty mistress," for I may call her so with a good conscience, thought the shrewd youth, since I know nothing to the contrary, — "my sweet pretty mistress, will you be kind enough to tell me whereabouts I must seek the dwelling of my kinsman, Major Molineux?"

Robin's voice was plaintive and winning, and the female, seeing nothing to be shunned in the handsome country youth, thrust open the door, and came forth into the moonlight. She was a dainty little figure, with a white neck, round arms, and a slender waist, at the extremity of which her scarlet petticoat jutted out over a hoop, as if she were standing in a balloon. Moreover, her face was oval and pretty, her hair dark beneath the little cap, and her bright eyes possessed a sly freedom, which triumphed over those of Robin.

"Major Molineux dwells here," said this fair woman.   30

Now, her voice was the sweetest Robin had heard that night, yet he could not help doubting whether that sweet voice spoke Gospel truth. He looked up and down the mean street, and then surveyed the house before which they stood. It was a small, dark edifice of two stories, the second of which projected over the lower floor, and the front apartment had the aspect of a shop for petty commodities.

"Now, truly, I am in luck," replied Robin, cunningly, "and so indeed is my kinsman, the Major, in having so pretty a housekeeper. But I prithee trouble him to step to the door; I will deliver him a message from his friends in the country, and then go back to my lodgings at the inn."

"Nay, the Major has been abed this hour or more," said the lady of the scarlet petticoat; "and it would be to little purpose to disturb him tonight, seeing his evening draught was of the strongest. But he is a kind-hearted man, and it would be as much as my life's worth to let a kinsman of his turn away from the door. You are the good old gentleman's very picture, and I could swear that was his rainy-weather hat. Also he has garments very much resembling those leather small-clothes. But come in, I pray, for I bid you hearty welcome in his name."

So saying, the fair and hospitable dame took our hero by the hand; and the touch was light, and the force was gentleness, and though Robin read in her eyes what he did not hear in her words, yet the slender-waisted woman in the scarlet petticoat proved stronger than the athletic country youth. She had drawn his half-willing footsteps nearly to the threshold, when the opening of a door in the neighborhood startled the Major's housekeeper, and, leaving the Major's kinsman, she vanished speedily into her own domicile. A heavy yawn preceded the appearance of a man, who, like the Moonshine of Pyramus and Thisbe, carried a lantern, needlessly aiding his sister luminary in the heavens. As he walked sleepily up the street, he turned his broad, dull face on Robin, and displayed a long staff, spiked at the end.

"Home, vagabond, home!" said the watchman, in accents that seemed to fall   35
asleep as soon as they were uttered. "Home, or we'll set you in the stocks by peep of day!"

"This is the second hint of the kind," thought Robin. "I wish they would end my difficulties, by setting me there tonight."

Nevertheless, the youth felt an instinctive antipathy towards the guardian of midnight order, which at first prevented him from asking his usual question. But just when the man was about to vanish behind the corner, Robin resolved not to lose the opportunity, and shouted lustily after him,—

"I say, friend! will you guide me to the house of my kinsman, Major Molineux?"

The watchman made no reply, but turned the corner and was gone; yet Robin seemed to hear the sound of drowsy laughter stealing along the solitary street. At that moment, also, a pleasant titter saluted him from the open window above his head; he looked up, and caught the sparkle of a saucy eye; a round arm beckoned to him, and next he heard light footsteps descending the staircase within. But Robin, being of the household of a New England clergyman, was a good youth, as well as a shrewd one; so he resisted temptation, and fled away.

He now roamed desperately, and at random, through the town, almost ready   40
to believe that a spell was on him, like that by which a wizard of his country had once kept three pursuers wandering, a whole winter night, within twenty paces of the cottage which they sought. The streets lay before him, strange and desolate, and the lights were extinguished in almost every house. Twice, however, little parties of men, among whom Robin distinguished individuals in outlandish attire, came hurrying along; but, though on both occasions, they paused to address him, such intercourse did not at all enlighten his perplexity. They did but utter a few words in some language of which Robin knew nothing, and perceiving his inability to answer, bestowed a curse upon him in plain English and hastened away. Finally, the lad determined to knock at the door of every mansion that might appear worthy to be occupied by his kinsman, trusting that perseverance would overcome the fatality that had hitherto thwarted him. Firm in this resolve, he was passing beneath the walls of a church, which formed the corner of two streets, when, as he turned into the shade of its steeple, he encountered a bulky stranger, muffled in a cloak. The man was proceeding with the speed of earnest business, but Robin planted himself full before him, holding the oak cudgel with both hands across his body as a bar to further passage.

"Halt, honest man, and answer me a question," said he, very resolutely. "Tell me, this instant, whereabouts is the dwelling of my kinsman, Major Molineux!"

"Keep your tongue between your teeth, fool, and let me pass!" said a deep, gruff voice, which Robin partly remembered. "Let me pass, or I'll strike you to the earth!"

"No, no, neighbor!" cried Robin, flourishing his cudgel, and then thrusting its larger end close to the man's muffled face. "No, no, I'm not the fool you take me for, nor do you pass till I have an answer to my question. Whereabouts is the dwelling of my kinsman, Major Molineux?"

The stranger, instead of attempting to force his passage, stepped back into the moonlight, unmuffled his face, and stared full into that of Robin.

"Watch here an hour, and Major Molineux will pass by," said he.   45

Robin gazed with dismay and astonishment on the unprecedented physiognomy of the speaker. The forehead with its double prominence, the broad hooked nose, the shaggy eyebrows, and fiery eyes were those which he had noticed at the inn, but the man's complexion had undergone a singular, or, more properly, a twofold change. One side of the face blazed an intense red, while the other was black as midnight, the division line being in the broad bridge of the nose; and a mouth which seemed to extend from ear to ear was black or red in contrast to the color of the cheek. The effect was as if two individual devils, a fiend of fire and a fiend of darkness, had united themselves to form this infernal visage. The stranger grinned in Robin's face, muffled his party-colored features, and was out of sight in a moment.

"Strange things we travelers see!" ejaculated Robin.

He seated himself, however, upon the steps of the church-door, resolving to wait the appointed time for his kinsman. A few moments were consumed in philosophical speculations upon the species of man who had just left him; but having settled this point shrewdly, rationally, and satisfactorily, he was compelled to look elsewhere for his amusement. And first he threw his eyes along the street. It was of more respectable appearance than most of those into which he had wandered; and the moon, creating, like the imaginative power, a beautiful strangeness in familiar objects, gave something of romance to a scene that might not have possessed it in the light of day. The irregular and often quaint architecture of the houses, some of whose roofs were broken into numerous little peaks, while others ascended, steep and narrow, into a single point, and others again were square; the pure snow-white of some of their complexions, the aged darkness of others, and the thousand sparklings, reflected from bright substances in the walls of many; these matters engaged Robin's attention for a while, and then began to grow wearisome. Next he endeavored to define the forms of distant objects, starting away, with almost ghostly indistinctness, just as his eye appeared to grasp them; and finally he took a minute survey of an edifice which stood on the opposite side of the street, directly in front of the church-door, where he was stationed. It was a large, square mansion, distinguished from its neighbors by a balcony, which rested on tall pillars, and by an elaborate Gothic window, communicating therewith.

"Perhaps this is the very house I have been seeking," thought Robin.

Then he strove to speed away the time, by listening to a murmur which swept   50
continually along the street, yet was scarcely audible, except to an unaccustomed ear like his; it was a low, dull, dreamy sound, compounded of many noises, each of which was at too great a distance to be separately heard. Robin marveled at this snore of a sleeping town, and marveled more whenever its continuity was broken by now and then a distant shout, apparently loud where it originated. But altogether it was a sleep-inspiring sound, and, to shake off its drowsy influence, Robin arose, and climbed a window-frame, that he might view the interior of the church. There the moonbeams came trembling in, and fell down upon the deserted pews, and extended along the quiet aisles. A fainter yet more awful radiance was hovering around the pulpit, and one solitary ray had dared to rest upon the open page of the great Bible. Had nature, in that deep hour, become a worshiper in the house which man had builded? Or was that heavenly light the visible sanctity of the place,—visible because no earthly and impure feet were within the walls? The scene made Robin's heart shiver with a sensation of loneliness stronger than he had ever felt in the remotest depths of his native woods; so he turned away and sat down again before the door. There were graves around the church, and now an uneasy thought obtruded into Robin's breast. What if the

object of his search, which had been so often and so strangely thwarted, were all the time moldering in his shroud? What if his kinsman should glide through yonder gate, and nod and smile to him in dimly passing by?

"Oh that any breathing thing were here with me!" said Robin.

Recalling his thoughts from this uncomfortable track, he sent them over forest, hill, and stream, and attempted to imagine how that evening of ambiguity and weariness had been spent by his father's household. He pictured them assembled at the door, beneath the tree, the great old tree, which had been spared for its huge twisted trunk and venerable shade, when a thousand leafy brethren fell. There, at the going down of the summer sun, it was his father's custom to perform domestic worship, that the neighbors might come and join with him like brothers of the family, and that the wayfaring man might pause to drink at that fountain, and keep his heart pure by freshening the memory of home. Robin distinguished the seat of every individual of the little audience; he saw the good man in the midst, holding the Scriptures in the golden light that fell from the western clouds; he beheld him close the book and all rise up to pray. He heard the old thanksgivings for daily mercies, the old supplications for their continuance, to which he had so often listened in weariness, but which were now among his dear remembrances. He perceived the slight inequality of his father's voice when he came to speak of the absent one; he noted how his mother turned her face to the broad and knotted trunk; how his elder brother scorned, because the beard was rough upon his upper lip, to permit his features to be moved; how the younger sister drew down a low hanging branch before her eyes; and how the little one of all, whose sports had hitherto broken the decorum of the scene, understood the prayer for her playmate, and burst into clamorous grief. Then he saw them go in at the door; and when Robin would have entered also, the latch tinkled into its place, and he was excluded from his home.

"Am I here, or there?" cried Robin, starting; for all at once, when his thoughts had become visible and audible in a dream, the long, wide, solitary street shone out before him.

He aroused himself, and endeavored to fix his attention steadily upon the large edifice which he had surveyed before. But still his mind kept vibrating between fancy and reality; by turns, the pillars of the balcony lengthened into the tall, bare stems of pines, dwindled down to human figures, settled again into their true shape and size, and then commenced a new succession of changes. For a single moment, when he deemed himself awake, he could have sworn that a visage—one which he seemed to remember, yet could not absolutely name as his kinsman's—was looking towards him from the Gothic window. A deeper sleep wrestled with and nearly overcame him, but fled at the sound of footsteps along the opposite pavement. Robin rubbed his eyes, discerned a man passing at the foot of the balcony, and addressed him in a loud, peevish, and lamentable cry.

"Hallo, friend! must I wait here all night for my kinsman, Major Molineux?"   55

The sleeping echoes awoke, and answered the voice; and the passenger, barely able to discern a figure sitting in the oblique shade of the steeple, traversed the street to obtain a nearer view. He was himself a gentleman in his prime, of open, intelligent, cheerful, and altogether prepossessing countenance. Perceiving a country youth, apparently homeless and without friends, he accosted him in a tone of real kindness, which had become strange to Robin's ears.

"Well, my good lad, why are you sitting here?" inquired he. "Can I be of service to you in any way?"

"I am afraid not, sir," replied Robin, despondingly; "yet I shall take it kindly, if you'll answer me a single question. I've been searching, half the night, for one Major Molineux; now, sir, is there really such a person in these parts, or am I dreaming?"

"Major Molineux! The name is not altogether strange to me," said the gentleman, smiling. "Have you any objection to telling me the nature of your business with him?"

Then Robin briefly related that his father was a clergyman, settled on a small salary, at a long distance back in the country, and that he and Major Molineux were brothers' children. The Major, having inherited riches, and acquired civil and military rank, had visited his cousin, in great pomp, a year or two before; had manifested much interest in Robin and an elder brother, and, being childless himself, had thrown out hints respecting the future establishment of one of them in life. The elder brother was destined to succeed to the farm which his father cultivated in the interval of sacred duties; it was therefore determined that Robin should profit by his kinsman's generous intentions, especially as he seemed to be rather the favorite, and was thought to possess other necessary endowments.

"For I have the name of being a shrewd youth," observed Robin, in this part of his story.

"I doubt not you deserve it," replied his new friend, good-naturedly; "but pray proceed."

"Well, sir, being nearly eighteen years old, and well grown, as you see," continued Robin, drawing himself up to his full height, "I thought it high time to begin in the world. So my mother and sister put me in handsome trim, and my father gave me half the remnant of his last year's salary, and five days ago I started for this place, to pay the Major a visit. But, would you believe it, sir! I crossed the ferry a little after dark, and have yet found nobody that would show me the way to his dwelling; only, an hour or two since, I was told to wait here, and Major Molineux would pass by."

"Can you describe the man who told you this?" inquired the gentleman.

"Oh, he was a very ill-favored fellow, sir," replied Robin, "with two great bumps on his forehead, a hook nose, fiery eyes; and, what struck me as the strangest, his face was of two different colors. Do you happen to know such a man, sir?"

"Not intimately," answered the stranger, "but I chanced to meet him a little time previous to your stopping me. I believe you may trust his word, and that the Major will very shortly pass through this street. In the mean time, as I have a singular curiosity to witness your meeting, I will sit down here upon the steps and bear you company."

He seated himself accordingly, and soon engaged his companion in animated discourse. It was but of brief continuance, however, for a noise of shouting, which had long been remotely audible, drew so much nearer that Robin inquired its cause.

"What may be the meaning of this uproar?" asked he. "Truly, if your town be always as noisy, I shall find little sleep while I am an inhabitant."

"Why, indeed, friend Robin, there do appear to be three or four riotous fellows abroad to-night," replied the gentleman. "You must not expect all the stillness of your native woods here in our streets. But the watch will shortly be at the heels of these lads and"—

"Ay, and set them in the stocks by peep of day," interrupted Robin, recollect-   70
ing his own encounter with the drowsy lantern-bearer. "But, dear sir, if I may trust my ears, an army of watchmen would never make head against such a multitude of rioters. There were at least a thousand voices went up to make that one shout."

"May not a man have several voices, Robin, as well as two complexions?" said his friend.

"Perhaps a man may; but Heaven forbid that a woman should!" responded the shrewd youth, thinking of the seductive tones of the Major's housekeeper.

The sounds of a trumpet in some neighboring street now became so evident and continual, that Robin's curiosity was strongly excited. In addition to the shouts, he heard frequent bursts from many instruments of discord, and a wild and confused laughter filled up the intervals. Robin rose from the steps, and looked wistfully towards a point whither people seemed to be hastening.

"Surely some prodigious merry-making is going on," exclaimed he. "I have laughed very little since I left home, sir, and should be sorry to lose an opportunity. Shall we step round the corner by that darkish house, and take our share of the fun?"

"Sit down again, sit down, good Robin," replied the gentleman, laying his   75
hand on the skirt of the gray coat. "You forget that we must wait here for your kinsman; and there is reason to believe that he will pass by, in the course of a very few moments."

The near approach of the uproar had now disturbed the neighborhood; windows flew open on all sides; and many heads, in the attire of the pillow, and confused by sleep suddenly broken, were protruded to the gaze of whoever had leisure to observe them. Eager voices hailed each other from house to house, all demanding the explanation, which not a soul could give. Half-dressed men hurried towards the unknown commotion, stumbling as they went over the stone steps that thrust themselves into the narrow foot-walk. The shouts, the laughter, and the tuneless bray, the antipodes of music, came onwards with increasing din, till scattered individuals, and then denser bodies, began to appear round a corner at the distance of a hundred yards.

"Will you recognize your kinsman, if he passes in this crowd?" inquired the gentleman.

"Indeed, I can't warrant it, sir; but I'll take my stand here, and keep a bright lookout," answered Robin, descending to the outer edge of the pavement.

A mighty stream of people now emptied into the street, and came rolling slowly towards the church. A single horseman wheeled the corner in the midst of them, and close behind him came a band of fearful wind-instruments, sending forth a fresher discord now that no intervening buildings kept it from the ear. Then a redder light disturbed the moonbeams, and a dense multitude of torches shone along the street, concealing, by their glare, whatever object they illuminated. The single horseman, clad in a military dress, and bearing a drawn sword, rode onward as the leader, and, by his fierce and variegated countenance, appeared like war personified; the red of one cheek was an emblem of fire and sword; the blackness of the other betokened the mourning that attends them. In his train were wild figures in the Indian dress, and many fantastic shapes without a model, giving the whole march a visionary air, as if a dream had broken forth from some feverish brain, and were sweeping visibly through the midnight streets. A mass of people, inactive, except as applauding spectators, hemmed the procession in; and several women ran along the sidewalk, piercing the confusion of heavier sounds with their shrill voices of mirth or terror.

"The double-faced fellow has his eye upon me," muttered Robin, with an indefinite but an uncomfortable idea that he was himself to bear a part in the pageantry.   80

The leader turned himself in the saddle, and fixed his glance full upon the country youth, as the steed went slowly by. When Robin had freed his eyes from those fiery ones, the musicians were passing before him, and the torches were close at hand; but the unsteady brightness of the latter formed a veil which he could not penetrate. The rattling of wheels over the stones sometimes found its way to his ear, and confused traces of a human form appeared at intervals, and then melted into the vivid light. A moment more, and the leader thundered a command to halt: the trumpets vomited a horrid breath, and then held their peace; the shouts and laughter of the people died away, and there remained only a universal hum, allied to silence. Right before Robin's eyes was an uncovered cart. There the torches blazed the brightest, there the moon shone out like day, and there, in tar-and-feathery dignity, sat his kinsman, Major Molineux!

He was an elderly man, of large and majestic person, and strong, square features, betokening a steady soul; but steady as it was, his enemies had found means to shake it. His face was pale as death, and far more ghastly; the broad forehead was contracted in his agony, so that his eyebrows formed one grizzled line; his eyes were red and wild, and the foam hung white upon his quivering lip. His whole frame was agitated by a quick and continual tremor, which his pride strove to quell, even in those circumstances of overwhelming humiliation. But perhaps the bitterest pang of all was when his eyes met those of Robin; for he evidently knew him on the instant, as the youth stood witnessing the foul disgrace of a head grown gray in honor. They stared at each other in silence, and Robin's knees shook, and his hair bristled, with a mixture of pity and terror. Soon, however, a bewildering excitement began to seize upon his mind; the preceding adventures of the night, the unexpected appearance of the crowd, the torches, the confused din and the hush that followed, the specter of his kinsman reviled by that great multitude,—all this, and, more than all, a perception of tremendous ridicule in the whole scene, affected him with a sort of mental inebriety. At that moment a voice of sluggish merriment saluted Robin's ears; he turned instinctively, and just behind the corner of the church stood the lantern-bearer, rubbing his eyes, and drowsily enjoying the lad's amazement. Then he heard a peal of laughter like the ringing of silvery bells; a woman twitched his arm, a saucy eye met his, and he saw the lady of the scarlet petticoat. A sharp, dry cachinnation appealed to his memory, and, standing on tiptoe in the crowd, with his white apron over his head, he beheld the courteous little innkeeper. And lastly, there sailed over the heads of the multitude a great, broad laugh, broken in the midst by two sepulchral hems; thus, "Haw, haw, haw,—hem, hem,—haw, haw, haw, haw!"

The sound proceeded from the balcony of the opposite edifice, and thither Robin turned his eyes. In front of the Gothic window stood the old citizen, wrapped in a wide gown, his gray periwig exchanged for a nightcap, which was thrust back from his forehead, and his silk stockings hanging about his legs. He supported himself on his polished cane in a fit of convulsive merriment, which manifested itself on his solemn old features like a funny inscription on a tombstone. Then Robin seemed to hear the voices of the barbers, of the guests of the inn, and of all who had made sport of him that night. The contagion was spreading among the multitude, when all at once, it seized upon Robin, and he sent forth a shout of laughter that echoed through the street,—every man shook his sides, every man emptied his lungs, but Robin's shout was the loudest there. The cloud-spirits peeped from their silvery islands, as the congregated mirth went roaring up the sky! The Man in the Moon heard the far bellow. "Oho," quoth he, "the old earth is frolicsome to-night!"

When there was a momentary calm in that tempestuous sea of sound, the leader gave the sign, the procession resumed its march. On they went, like fiends that throng in mockery around some dead potentate, mighty no more, but majestic still in his agony. On they went, in counterfeited pomp, in senseless uproar, in frenzied merriment, trampling all on an old man's heart. On swept the tumult, and left a silent street behind.

"Well, Robin, are you dreaming?" inquired the gentleman, laying his hand on   85
the youth's shoulder.

Robin started, and withdrew his arm from the stone post to which he had instinctively clung, as the living stream rolled by him. His cheek was somewhat pale, and his eye not quite as lively as in the earlier part of the evening.

"Will you be kind enough to show me the way to the ferry?" said he, after a moment's pause.

"You have, then, adopted a new subject of inquiry?" observed his companion, with a smile.

"Why, yes, sir," replied Robin, rather dryly. "Thanks to you, and to my other friends, I have at last met my kinsman, and he will scarce desire to see my face again. I begin to grow weary of a town life, sir. Will you show me the way to the ferry?"

"No, my good friend Robin,—not to-night, at least," said the gentleman.   90
"Some few days hence, if you wish it, I will speed you on your journey. Or, if you

prefer to remain with us, perhaps, as you are a shrewd youth, you may rise in the world without the help of your kinsman, Major Molineux."

QUESTIONS AND SUGGESTIONS FOR WRITING

1. In a paragraph characterize Robin as he sees himself in the first half of the story, up through the scene in which he encounters the man with the strange forehead, hooked nose, and shaggy eyebrows. In a second paragraph, characterize Robin as *we* see him in this encounter.
2. Major Molineux is described sympathetically: "He was an elderly man, of large and majestic person, and strong, square features, betokening a steady soul." Why, then, does Robin join in the laughter at the Major's plight? Is the story about Robin's corruption? Or is it perhaps about the necessity of experiencing evil if one is to do good? Or what?
3. In an essay of 500 words evaluate the view that the story is about Robin's perception of the universality of evil, which he comes (when he laughs) to see in himself.
4. In an essay of 500 words evaluate the view that the story is about the colonies'—and Robin's—transition from dependence upon authority to independence.

Sherwood Anderson (American. 1876–1941)

I WANT TO KNOW WHY

We got up at four in the morning, that first day in the east. On the evening before we had climbed off a freight train at the edge of town, and with the true instinct of Kentucky boys had found our way across town and to the race track and the stables at once. Then we knew we were all right. Hanley Turner right away found a nigger we knew. It was Bildad Johnson who in the winter works at Ed Becker's livery barn in our home town, Beckersville. Bildad is a good cook as almost all our niggers are and of course he, like everyone in our part of Kentucky who is anyone at all, likes the horses. In the spring Bildad begins to scratch around. A nigger from our country can flatter and wheedle anyone into letting him do most anything he wants. Bildad wheedles the stable men and the trainers from the horse farms in our country around Lexington. The trainers come into town in the evening to stand around and talk and maybe get into a poker game. Bildad gets in with them. He is always doing little favors and telling about things to eat, chicken browned in a pan, and how is the best way to cook sweet potatoes and corn bread. It makes your mouth water to hear him.

When the racing season comes on and the horses go to the races and there is all the talk on the streets in the evenings about the new colts, and everyone says when they are going over to Lexington or to the spring meeting at Churchill Downs or to Latonia, and the horsemen that have been down to New Orleans or maybe at the winter meeting at Havana in Cuba come home to spend a week before they start out again, at such a time when everything talked about in Beckersville is just horses and nothing else and the outfits start out and horse racing is in every breath of air you breathe, Bildad shows up with a job as cook for some outfit. Often when I think about it, his always going all season to the races and working in the livery barn in the winter where horses are and where men like to come and talk about horses, I wish I was a nigger. It's a foolish thing to say, but that's the way I am about being around horses, just crazy. I can't help it.

Well, I must tell you about what we did and let you in on what I'm talking about. Four of us boys from Beckersville, all whites and sons of men who live in Beckersville regular, made up our minds we were going to the races, not just to Lexington or Louisville, I don't mean, but to the big eastern track we were always hearing our Beckersville men talk about, to Saratoga. We were all pretty young then. I was just turned fifteen and I was the oldest of the four. It was my scheme. I admit that and I talked the others into trying it. There was Hanley Turner and Henry Rieback and Tom Tumberton and myself. I had thirty-seven dollars I had earned during the winter working nights and Saturdays in Enoch Myer's grocery. Henry Rieback had eleven dollars and the others, Hanley and Tom, had only a dollar or two each. We fixed it all up and laid low until the Kentucky spring meetings were over and some of our men, the sportiest ones, the ones we envied the most, had cut out—then we cut out too.

I won't tell you the trouble we had beating our way on freights and all. We went through Cleveland and Buffalo and other cities and saw Niagara Falls. We bought things there, souvenirs and spoons and cards and shells with pictures of the falls on them for our sisters and mothers, but thought we had better not send any of the things home. We didn't want to put the folks on our trail and maybe be nabbed.

We got into Saratoga as I said at night and went to the track. Bildad fed us up. He showed us a place to sleep in hay over a shed and promised to keep still. Niggers are all right about things like that. They won't squeal on you. Often a white man you might meet, when you had run away from home like that, might appear to be all right and give you a quarter or a half-dollar or something, and then go right and give you away. White men will do that, but not a nigger. You can trust them. They are squarer with kids. I don't know why.

At the Saratoga meeting that year there were a lot of men from home. Dave Williams and Arthur Mulford and Jerry Myers and others. Then there was a lot from Louisville and Lexington Henry Rieback knew but I didn't. They were professional gamblers and Henry Rieback's father is one too. He is what is called a sheet writer and goes away most of the year to tracks. In the winter when he is home in Beckersville he don't stay there much but goes away to cities and deals faro. He is a nice man and generous, is always sending Henry presents, a bicycle and a gold watch and a boy scout suit of clothes and things like that.

My own father is a lawyer. He's all right, but don't make much money and can't buy me things and anyway I'm getting so old now I don't expect it. He never said nothing to me against Henry, but Hanley Turner and Tom Tumberton's fathers did. They said to their boys that money so come by is no good and they didn't want their boys brought up to hear gamblers' talk and be thinking about such things and maybe embrace them.

5

That's all right and I guess the men know what they are talking about, but I don't see what it's got to do with Henry or with horses either. That's what I'm writing this story about. I'm puzzled. I'm getting to be a man and want to think straight and be O. K., and there's something I saw at the race meeting at the eastern track I can't figure out.

I can't help it, I'm crazy about thoroughbred horses. I've always been that way. When I was ten years old and saw I was growing to be big and couldn't be a rider I was so sorry I nearly died. Harry Hellinfinger in Beckersville, whose father is Postmaster, is grown up and too lazy to work, but likes to stand around in the street and get up jokes on boys like sending them to a hardware store for a gimlet to bore square holes and other jokes like that. He played one on me. He told me that if I would eat a half a cigar I would be stunted and not grow any more and maybe could be a rider. I did it. When father wasn't looking I took a cigar out of his pocket and gagged it down some way. It made me awful sick and the doctor had to be sent for, and then it did no good. I kept right on growing. It was a joke. When I told what I had done and why most fathers would have whipped me but mine didn't.

Well, I didn't get stunted and didn't die. It serves Harry Hellinfinger right. Then I made up my mind I would like to be a stable boy, but had to give that up too. Mostly niggers do that work and I knew father wouldn't let me go into it. No use to ask him.

If you've never been crazy about thoroughbreds it's because you've never been around where they are much and don't know any better. They're beautiful. There isn't anything so lovely and clean and full of spunk and honest and everything as some race horses. On the big horse farms that are all around our town Beckersville there are tracks and the horses run in the early morning. More than a thousand times I've got out of bed before daylight and walked two or three miles to the tracks. Mother wouldn't of let me go but father always says, "Let him alone." So I got some bread out of the bread box and some butter and jam, gobbled it and lit out.

At the tracks you sit on the fence with men, whites and niggers, and they chew tobacco and talk, and then the colts are brought out. It's early and the grass is covered with shiny dew and in another field a man is plowing and they are frying things in a shed where the track niggers sleep, and you know how a nigger can giggle and laugh and say things that make you laugh. A white man can't do it and some niggers can't but a track nigger can every time.

And so the colts are brought out and some are just galloped by stable boys, but almost every morning on a big track owned by a rich man who lives maybe in New York, there are always, nearly every morning, a few colts and some of the old race horses and geldings and mares that are cut loose.

It brings a lump up into my throat when a horse runs. I don't mean all horses but some. I can pick them nearly every time. It's in my blood like in the blood of race track niggers and trainers. Even when they just go slob-jogging along with a little nigger on their backs I can tell a winner. If my throat hurts and it's hard for me to swallow, that's him. He'll run like Sam Hill when you let him out. If he don't win every time it'll be a wonder and because they've got him in a pocket behind

10

another or he was pulled or got off bad at the post or something. If I wanted to be a gambler like Henry Rieback's father I could get rich. I know I could and Henry says so, too. All I would have to do is to wait 'til that hurt comes when I see a horse and then bet every cent. That's what I would do if I wanted to be a gambler, but I don't.

When you're at the tracks in the morning—not the race tracks but the train-　15
ing tracks around Beckersville—you don't see a horse, the kind I've been talking about, very often, but it's nice anyway. Any thoroughbred, that is sired right and out of a good mare and trained by a man that knows how, can run. If he couldn't what would he be there for and not pulling a plow?

Well, out of the stables they come and the boys are on their backs and it's lovely to be there. You hunch down on top of the fence and itch inside you. Over in the sheds the niggers giggle and sing. Bacon is being fried and coffee made. Everything smells lovely. Nothing smells better than coffee and manure and horses and niggers and bacon frying and pipes being smoked out of doors on a morning like that. It just gets you, that's what it does.

But about Saratoga. We was there six days and not a soul from home seen us and everything came off just as we wanted it to, fine weather and horses and races and all. We beat our way home and Bildad gave us a basket with fried chicken and bread and other eatables in, and I had eighteen dollars when we got back to Beckersville. Mother jawed and cried but Pop didn't say much. I told everything we done except one thing. I did and saw that alone. That's what I'm writing about. It got me upset, I think about it at night. Here it is.

At Saratoga we laid up nights in the hay in the shed Bildad had showed us and ate with the niggers early and at night when the race people had all gone away. The men from home stayed mostly in the grandstand and betting field, and didn't come out around the places where the horses are kept except to the paddocks just before a race when the horses are saddled. At Saratoga they don't have paddocks under an open shed as at Lexington and Churchill Downs and other tracks down in our country, but saddle the horses right out in an open place under trees on a lawn as smooth and nice as Banker Bohon's front yard here in Beckersville. It's lovely. The horses are sweaty and nervous and shine and the men come out and smoke cigars and look at them and the trainers are there and the owners, and your heart thumps so you can hardly breathe.

Then the bugle blows for post and the boys that ride come running out with their silk clothes on and you run to get a place by the fence with the niggers.

I always am wanting to be a trainer or owner, and at the risk of being seen　20
and caught and sent home I went to the paddocks before every race. The other boys didn't but I did.

We got to Saratoga on a Friday and on Wednesday the next week the big Mullford Handicap was to be run. Middlestride was in it and Sunstreak. The weather was fine and the track fast. I couldn't sleep the night before.

What had happened was that both these horses are the kind it makes my throat hurt to see. Middlestride is long and looks awkward and is a gelding. He belongs to Joe Thompson, a little owner from home who only has a half-dozen horses. The Mullford Handicap is for a mile and Middlestride can't untrack fast.

He goes away slow and is always way back at the half, then he begins to run and if the race is a mile and a quarter he'll just eat up everything and get there.

Sunstreak is different. He is a stallion and nervous and belongs on the biggest farm we've got in our country, the Van Riddle place that belongs to Mr. Van Riddle of New York. Sunstreak is like a girl you think about sometimes but never see. He is hard all over and lovely too. When you look at his head you want to kiss him. He is trained by Jerry Tillford who knows me and has been good to me lots of times, lets me walk into a horse's stall to look at him close and other things. There isn't anything as sweet as that horse. He stands at the post quiet and not letting on, but he is just burning up inside. Then when the barrier goes up he is off like his name, Sunstreak. It makes you ache to see him. It hurts you. He just lays down and runs like a bird dog. There can't anything I ever see run like him except Middlestride when he gets untracked and stretches himself.

Gee! I ached to see that race and those two horses run, ached and dreaded it too. I didn't want to see either of our horses beaten. We had never sent a pair like that to the races before. Old men in Beckersville said so and the niggers said so. It was a fact.

Before the race I went over to the paddocks to see. I looked a last look at Middlestride, who isn't such a much standing in a paddock that way, then I went to Sunstreak.

It was his day. I knew when I see him. I forgot all about being seen myself and walked right up. All the men from Beckersville were there and no one noticed me except Jerry Tillford. He saw me and something happened. I'll tell you about that.

I was standing looking at that horse and aching. In some way, I can't tell how, I knew just how Sunstreak felt inside. He was quiet and letting the niggers rub his legs and Mr. Van Riddle himself put the saddle on, but he was just a raging torrent inside. He was like the water in the river at Niagara Falls just before it goes plunk down. That horse wasn't thinking about running. He don't have to think about that. He was just thinking about holding himself back 'til the time for the running came. I knew that. I could just in a way see right inside him. He was going to do some awful running and I knew it. He wasn't bragging or letting on much or prancing or making a fuss, but just waiting. I knew it and Jerry Tillford his trainer knew. I looked up and then that man and I looked into each other's eyes. Something happened to me. I guess I loved the man as much as I did the horse because he knew what I knew. Seemed to me there wasn't anything in the world but that man and the horse and me. I cried and Jerry Tillford had a shine in his eyes. Then I came away to the fence to wait for the race. The horse was better than me, more steadier, and now I know better than Jerry. He was the quietest and he had to do the running.

Sunstreak ran first of course and he busted the world's record for a mile. I've seen that if I never see anything more. Everything came out just as I expected. Middlestride got left at the post and was way back and closed up to be second, just as I knew he would. He'll get a world's record too some day. They can't skin the Beckersville country on horses.

I watched the race calm because I knew what would happen. I was sure.

25

Hanley Turner and Henry Rieback and Tom Tumberton were all more excited than me.

A funny thing had happened to me. I was thinking about Jerry Tillford the   30
trainer and how happy he was all through the race. I liked him that afternoon even more than I ever liked my own father. I almost forgot the horses thinking that way about him. It was because of what I had seen in his eyes as he stood in the paddocks beside Sunstreak before the race started. I knew he had been watching and working with Sunstreak since the horse was a baby colt, had taught him to run and be patient and when to let himself out and not to quit, never. I knew that for him it was like a mother seeing her child do something brave or wonderful. It was the first time I ever felt for a man like that.

After the race that night I cut out from Tom and Hanley and Henry. I wanted to be by myself and I wanted to be near Jerry Tillford if I could work it. Here is what happened.

The track in Saratoga is near the edge of town. It is all polished up and trees around, the evergreen kind, and grass and everything painted and nice. If you go past the track you get to a hard road made of asphalt for automobiles, and if you go along this for a few miles there is a road turns off to a little rummy-looking farm house set in a yard.

That night after the race I went along that road because I had seen Jerry and some other men go that way in an automobile. I didn't expect to find them. I walked for a ways and then sat down by a fence to think. It was the direction they went in. I wanted to be as near Jerry as I could. I felt close to him. Pretty soon I went up the side road—I don't know why—and came to the rummy farm house. I was just lonesome to see Jerry, like wanting to see your father at night when you are a young kid. Just then an automobile came along and turned in. Jerry was in it and Henry Rieback's father, and Arthur Bedford from home, and Dave Williams and two other men I didn't know. They got out of the car and went into the house, all but Henry Rieback's father who quarreled with them and said he wouldn't go. It was only about nine o'clock, but they were all drunk and the rummy-looking farm house was a place for bad women to stay in. That's what it was. I crept up along a fence and looked through a window and saw.

It's what give me the fantods. I can't make it out. The women in the house were all ugly mean-looking women, not nice to look at or be near. They were homely too, except one who was tall and looked a little like the gelding Middle-stride, but not clean like him, but with a hard ugly mouth. She had red hair. I saw everything plain. I got up by an old rose bush by an open window and looked. The women had on loose dresses and sat around in chairs. The men came in and some sat on the women's laps. The place smelled rotten and there was rotten talk, the kind a kid hears around a livery stable in a town like Beckersville in the winter but don't ever expect to hear talked when there are women around. It was rotten. A nigger wouldn't go into such a place.

I looked at Jerry Tillford. I've told you how I had been feeling about him on   35
account of his knowing what was going on inside of Sunstreak in the minute before he went to the post for the race in which he made a world's record.

Jerry bragged in that bad woman house as I know Sunstreak wouldn't never have bragged. He said that he made that horse, that it was him that won the race and made the record. He lied and bragged like a fool. I never heard such silly talk.

And then, what do you suppose he did! He looked at the woman in there, the one that was lean and hard-mouthed and looked a little like the gelding Middle-stride, but not clean like him, and his eyes began to shine just as they did when he looked at me and at Sunstreak in the paddocks at the track in the afternoon. I stood there by the window—gee!—but I wished I hadn't gone away from the tracks, but had stayed with the boys and the niggers and the horses. The tall rotten-looking woman was between us just as Sunstreak was in the paddocks in the afternoon.

Then, all of a sudden, I began to hate that man. I wanted to scream and rush in the room and kill him. I never had such a feeling before. I was so mad clean through that I cried and my fists were doubled up so my finger nails cut my hands.

And Jerry's eyes kept shining and he waved back and forth, and then he went and kissed that woman and I crept away and went back to the tracks and to bed and didn't sleep hardly any, and then next day I got the other kids to start home with me and never told them anything I seen.

I been thinking about it ever since. I can't make it out. Spring has come again   40 and I'm nearly sixteen and go to the tracks mornings same as always, and I see Sunstreak and Middlestride and a new colt named Strident I'll bet will lay them all out, but no one thinks so but me and two or three niggers.

But things are different. At the tracks the air don't taste as good or smell as good. It's because a man like Jerry Tillford, who knows what he does, could see a horse like Sunstreak run, and kiss a woman like that the same day. I can't make it out. Darn him, what did he want to do like that for? I keep thinking about it and it spoils looking at horses and smelling things and hearing niggers laugh and everything. Sometimes I'm so mad about it I want to fight someone. It gives me the fantods. What did he do it for? I want to know why.

QUESTIONS AND SUGGESTIONS FOR WRITING

1. How does the scene of Tillford in the farmhouse connect with the earlier scene at the paddock? What parallels or contrasts do you see?
2. In a sentence or two explain *why* the boy tells his story.
3. In paragraph 8, about one-third of the way through the story, the boy says, "I'm getting to be a man and want to think straight and be O. K." Drawing only on what he has said up to this point, in a paragraph or two set forth what you think the "straight" thoughts (the accepted values) of the white society he is born into are. In what ways do the boy's values differ from these?
4. The boy sees blacks as different from whites. Putting aside your own views—and drawing only on the story—discuss the differences. How, again using only the story as evidence, can the distinction be explained?
5. The narrator "wants to know why." If you were able to talk to him, what explanation would you offer? If you believe that his question is unanswerable, explain your belief.

James Joyce (Irish. 1882–1941)

ARABY

North Richmond Street, being blind, was a quiet street except at the hour when the Christian Brothers' School set the boys free. An uninhabited house of two stories stood at the blind end, detached from its neighbors in a square ground. The other houses of the street, conscious of decent lives within them, gazed at one another with brown imperturbable faces.

The former tenant of our house, a priest, had died in the back drawing-room. Air, musty from having been long enclosed, hung in all the rooms, and the waste room behind the kitchen was littered with old useless papers. Among these I found a few paper-covered books, the pages of which were curled and damp: *The Abbot,* by Walter Scott, *The Devout Communicant* and *The Memoirs of Vidocq.* I liked the last best because its leaves were yellow. The wild garden behind the house contained a central apple-tree and a few straggling bushes under one of which I found the late tenant's rusty bicycle-pump. He had been a very charitable priest; in his will he had left all his money to institutions and the furniture of his house to his sister.

When the short days of winter came dusk fell before we had well eaten our dinners. When we met in the street the houses had grown somber. The space of sky above us was the color of ever-changing violet and towards it the lamps of the street lifted their feeble lanterns. The cold air stung us and we played till our bodies glowed. Our shouts echoed in the silent street. The career of our play brought us through the dark muddy lanes behind the houses where we ran the gantlet of the rough tribes from the cottages, to the back doors of the dark dripping gardens where odors arose from the ashpits, to the dark odorous stables where a coachman smoothed and combed the horse or shook music from the buckled harness. When we returned to the street light from the kitchen windows had filled the areas. If my uncle was seen turning the corner we hid in the shadow until we had seen him safely housed. Or if Mangan's sister came out on the doorstep to call her brother in to his tea we watched her from our shadow peer up and down the street. We waited to see whether she would remain or go in and, if she remained, we left our shadow and walked up to Mangan's steps resignedly. She was waiting for us, her figure defined by the light from the half-opened door. Her brother always teased her before he obeyed and I stood by the railings looking at her. Her dress swung as she moved her body and the soft rope of her hair tossed from side to side.

Every morning I lay on the floor in the front parlor watching her door. The blind was pulled down to within an inch of the sash so that I could not be seen. When she came out on the doorstep my heart leaped. I ran to the hall, seized my books and followed her. I kept her brown figure always in my eye and, when we came near the point at which our ways diverged, I quickened my pace and passed her. This happened morning after morning. I had never spoken to her, except for a few casual words, and yet her name was like a summons to all my foolish blood.

Her image accompanied me even in places the most hostile to romance. On

5

Saturday evenings when my aunt went marketing I had to go to carry some of the parcels. We walked through the flaring streets, jostled by drunken men and bargaining women, amid the curses of laborers, the shrill litanies of shop-boys who stood on guard by the barrels of pigs' cheeks, the nasal chanting of street-singers, who sang a *come-all-you* about O'Donovan Rossa, or a ballad about the troubles in our native land. These noises converged in a single sensation of life for me: I imagined that I bore my chalice safely through a throng of foes. Her name sprang to my lips at moments in strange prayers and praises which I myself did not understand. My eyes were often full of tears (I could not tell why) and at times a flood from my heart seemed to pour itself out into my bosom. I thought little of the future. I did not know whether I would ever speak to her or not or, if I spoke to her, how I could tell her of my confused adoration. But my body was like a harp and her words and gestures were like fingers running upon the wires.

One evening I went into the back drawing-room in which the priest had died. It was a dark rainy evening and there was no sound in the house. Through one of the broken panes I heard the rain impinge upon the earth, the fine incessant needles of water playing in the sodden beds. Some distant lamp or lighted window gleamed below me. I was thankful that I could see so little. All my senses seemed to desire to veil themselves and, feeling that I was about to slip from them, I pressed the palms of my hands together until they trembled, murmuring: *O love! O love!* many times.

At last she spoke to me. When she addressed the first words to me I was so confused that I did not know what to answer. She asked me was I going to *Araby.* I forget whether I answered yes or no. It would be a splendid bazaar, she said; she would love to go.

—And why can't you? I asked.

While she spoke she turned a silver bracelet round and round her wrist. She could not go, she said, because there would be a retreat that week in her convent. Her brother and two other boys were fighting for their caps and I was alone at the railings. She held one of the spikes, bowing her head towards me. The light from the lamp opposite our door caught the white curve of a neck, lit up her hair that rested there and, falling, lit up the hand upon the railing. It fell over one side of her dress and caught the white border of a petticoat, just visible as she stood at ease.

—It's well for you, she said.

—If I go, I said, I will bring you something.

What innumerable follies laid waste my waking and sleeping thoughts after that evening! I wished to annihilate the tedious intervening days. I chafed against the work of school. At night in my bedroom and by day in the classroom her image came between me and the page I strove to read. The syllables of the word *Araby* were called to me through the silence in which my soul luxuriated and cast an Eastern enchantment over me. I asked for leave to go to the bazaar on Saturday night. My aunt was surprised and hoped it was not some Freemason affair. I answered few questions in class. I watched my master's face pass from amiability to sternness; he hoped I was not beginning to idle. I could not call my wandering thoughts together. I had hardly any patience with the serious work of life which,

10

now that it stood between me and my desire, seemed to me child's play, ugly monotonous child's play.

On Saturday morning I reminded my uncle that I wished to go to the bazaar in the evening. He was fussing at the hall-stand, looking for the hat-brush, and answered me curtly:

—Yes, boy, I know.

As he was in the hall I could not go into the front parlor and lie at the window. 15
I left the house in bad humor and walked slowly towards the school. The air was pitilessly raw and already my heart misgave me.

When I came home to dinner my uncle had not yet been home. Still it was early. I sat staring at the clock for some time and, when its ticking began to irritate me, I left the room. I mounted the staircase and gained the upper part of the house. The high cold empty gloomy rooms liberated me and I went from room to room singing. From the front window I saw my companions playing below in the street. Their cries reached me weakened and indistinct and, leaning my forehead against the cool glass, I looked over at the dark house where she lived. I may have stood there for an hour, seeing nothing but the brown-clad figure cast by my imagination, touched discreetly by the lamplight at the curved neck, at the hand upon the railings and at the border below the dress.

When I came downstairs again I found Mrs. Mercer sitting at the fire. She was an old garrulous woman, a pawnbroker's widow, who collected used stamps for some pious purpose. I had to endure the gossip of the tea-table. The meal was prolonged beyond an hour and still my uncle did not come. Mrs. Mercer stood up to go: she was sorry she couldn't wait any longer, but it was after eight o'clock and she did not like to be out late, as the night air was bad for her. When she had gone I began to walk up and down the room, clenching my fists. My aunt said:

—I'm afraid you may put off your bazaar for this night of Our Lord.

At nine o'clock I heard my uncle's latchkey in the halldoor. I heard him talking to himself and heard the hall-stand rocking when it had received the weight of his overcoat. I could interpret these signs. When he was midway through his dinner I asked him to give me the money to go to the bazaar. He had forgotten.

—The people are in bed and after their first sleep now, he said. 20

I did not smile. My aunt said to him energetically:

—Can't you give him the money and let him go? You've kept him late enough as it is.

My uncle said he was very sorry he had forgotten. He said he believed in the old saying: *All work and no play makes Jack a dull boy.* He asked me where I was going and, when I had told him a second time he asked me did I know *The Arab's Farewell to His Steed.* When I left the kitchen he was about to recite the opening lines of the piece to my aunt.

I held a florin tightly in my hand as I strode down Buckingham Street towards the station. The sight of the streets thronged with buyers and glaring with gas recalled to me the purpose of my journey. I took my seat in a third-class carriage of a deserted train. After an intolerable delay the train moved out of the station slowly. It crept onward among ruinous houses and over the twinkling river. At Westland Row Station a crowd of people pressed to the carriage doors; but the porters moved them back, saying that it was a special train for the bazaar. I remained alone in the bare carriage. In a few minutes the train drew up beside an improvised wooden platform. I passed out on to the road and saw by the lighted dial of a clock that it was ten minutes to ten. In front of me was a large building which displayed the magical name.

I could not find any sixpenny entrance and, fearing that the bazaar would be   25
closed, I passed in quickly through a turnstile, handing a shilling to a weary-looking man. I found myself in a big hall girdled at half its height by a gallery. Nearly all the stalls were closed and the greater part of the hall was in darkness. I recognized a silence like that which pervades a church after a service. I walked into the center of the bazaar timidly. A few people were gathered about the stalls which were still open. Before a curtain, over which the words *Café Chantant* were written in colored lamps, two men were counting money on a salver. I listened to the fall of the coins.

Remembering with difficulty why I had come I went over to one of the stalls and examined porcelain vases and flowered tea-sets. At the door of the stall a young lady was talking and laughing with two young gentlemen. I remarked their English accents and listened vaguely to their conversation.

—O, I never said such a thing!

—O, but you did!

—O, but I didn't!

—Didn't she say that?   30

—Yes. I heard her.

—O, there's a . . . fib!

Observing me the young lady came over and asked me did I wish to buy anything. The tone of her voice was not encouraging; she seemed to have spoken to me out of a sense of duty. I looked humbly at the great jars that stood like eastern guards at either side of the dark entrance to the stall and murmured:

—No, thank you.

The young lady changed the position of one of the vases and went back to the   35
two young men. They began to talk of the same subject. Once or twice the young lady glanced at me over her shoulder.

I lingered before her stall, though I knew my stay was useless, to make my interest in her wares seem the more real. Then I turned away slowly and walked down the middle of the bazaar. I allowed the two pennies to fall against the sixpence in my pocket. I heard a voice call from one end of the gallery that the light was out. The upper part of the hall was now completely dark.

Gazing up into the darkness I saw myself as a creature driven and derided by vanity; and my eyes burned with anguish and anger.

QUESTIONS AND SUGGESTIONS FOR WRITING

1. Joyce wrote a novel called *A Portrait of the Artist as a Young Man*. Write an essay of about 500 words on "Araby" as a portrait of the artist as a boy.
2. In an essay of about 500 words, consider the role of images of darkness and blindness

and what they reveal to us about "Araby" as a story of the fall from innocence into painful awareness.

3. This story about a boy is told in the first person, but the language is not that of a boy. Find some passages that clearly indicate that the narrator is an adult, looking back on his youth. What is the narrator's attitude toward the experience he narrates?

4. The boy, apparently an only child, lives with an uncle and aunt, rather than with parents. Why do you suppose Joyce put him in this family setting rather than some other?

5. The story is rich in images of religion. This in itself is not surprising, for the story is set in Roman Catholic Ireland, but the religious images are not simply references to religious persons or objects. In an essay of 500 to 750 words, discuss the function of these images.

William Carlos Williams (American. 1883–1963)
THE USE OF FORCE

They were new patients to me, all I had was the name, Olson. Please come down as soon as you can, my daughter is very sick.

When I arrived I was met by the mother, a big startled looking woman, very clean and apologetic who merely said, Is this the doctor? and let me in. In the back, she added. You must excuse us, doctor, we have her in the kitchen where it is warm. It is very damp here sometimes.

The child was fully dressed and sitting on her father's lap near the kitchen table. He tried to get up, but I motioned for him not to bother, took off my overcoat and started to look things over. I could see that they were all very nervous, eyeing me up and down distrustfully. As often, in such cases, they weren't telling me more than they had to, it was up to me to tell them; that's why they were spending three dollars on me.

The child was fairly eating me up with her cold, steady eyes, and no expression to her face whatever. She did not move and seemed, inwardly, quiet; an unusually attractive little thing, and as strong as a heifer in appearance. But her face was flushed, she was breathing rapidly, and I realized that she had a high fever. She had magnificent blonde hair, in profusion. One of those picture children often reproduced in advertising leaflets and the photogravure sections of the Sunday papers.

She'd had a fever for three days, began the father and we don't know what it comes from. My wife has given her things, you know, like people do, but it don't do no good. And there's been a lot of sickness around. So we tho't you'd better look her over and tell us what is the matter.

As doctors often do I took a trial shot at it as a point of departure. Has she had a sore throat?

Both parents answered me together, No . . . No, she says her throat don't hurt her.

Does your throat hurt you? added the mother to the child. But the little girl's expression didn't change nor did she move her eyes from my face.

5

Have you looked?

I tried to, said the mother, but I couldn't see.   10

As it happens we had been having a number of cases of diphtheria in the school to which this child went during that month and we were all, quite apparently, thinking of that, though no one had as yet spoken of the thing.

Well, I said, suppose we take a look at the throat first. I smiled in my best professional manner and for asking the child's first name I said, come on, Mathilda, open your mouth and let's take a look at your throat.

Nothing doing.

Aw, come on, I coaxed, just open your mouth wide and let me take a look. Look, I said opening both hands wide, I haven't anything in my hands. Just open up and let me see.

Such a nice man, put in the mother. Look how kind he is to you. Come on, do   15
what he tells you to. He won't hurt you.

At that I ground my teeth in disgust. If only they wouldn't use the word "hurt" I might be able to get somewhere. But I did not allow myself to be hurried or disturbed but speaking quietly and slowly I approached the child again.

As I moved my chair a little nearer suddenly with one catlike movement both her hands clawed instinctively for my eyes and she almost reached them too. In fact she knocked my glasses flying and they fell, though unbroken, several feet away from me on the kitchen floor.

Both the mother and father almost turned themselves inside out in embarrassment and apology. You bad girl, said the mother, taking her and shaking her by one arm. Look what you've done. The nice man . . .

For heaven's sake, I broke in. Don't call me a nice man to her. I'm here to look at her throat on the chance that she might have diphtheria and possibly die of it. But that's nothing to her. Look here, I said to the child, we're going to look at your throat. You're old enough to understand what I'm saying. Will you open it now by yourself or shall we have to open it for you?

Not a move. Even her expression hadn't changed. Her breaths however were   20
coming faster and faster. Then the battle began. I had to do it. I had to have a throat culture for her own protection. But first I told the parents that it was entirely up to them. I explained the danger but said that I would not insist on a throat examination so long as they would take the responsibility.

If you don't do what the doctor says you'll have to go to the hospital, the mother admonished her severely.

Oh yeah? I had to smile to myself. After all, I had already fallen in love with the savage brat, the parents were contemptible to me. In the ensuing struggle they grew more and more abject, crushed, exhausted while she surely rose to magnificent heights of insane fury of effort bred of her terror of me.

The father tried his best, and he was a big man but the fact that she was his daughter, his shame at her behavior and his dread of hurting her made him release her just at the critical times when I had almost achieved success, till I wanted to kill him. But his dread also that she might have diphtheria made him tell me to go on, go on though he himself was almost fainting, while the mother moved back and forth behind us raising and lowering her hands in an agony of apprehension.

Put her in front of you on your lap, I ordered, and hold both her wrists.

But as soon as he did the child let out a scream. Don't, you're hurting me. 25
Let go of my hands. Let them go I tell you. Then she shrieked terrifyingly,
hysterically. Stop it! Stop it! You're killing me!

Do you think she can stand it, doctor! said the mother.

You get out, said the husband to his wife. Do you want her to die of diphtheria?

Come on now, hold her, I said.

Then I grasped the child's head with my left hand and tried to get the wooden
tongue depressor between her teeth. She fought, with clenched teeth, desperately! But now I also had grown furious—at a child. I tried to hold myself down
but I couldn't. I know how to expose a throat for inspection. And I did my best.
When finally I got the wooden spatula behind the last teeth and just the point of it
into the mouth cavity, she opened up for an instant but before I could see anything
she came down again and gripping the wooden blade between her molars she
reduced it to splinters before I could get it out again.

Aren't you ashamed, the mother yelled at her. Aren't you ashamed to act like 30
that in front of the doctor?

Get me a smooth-handled spoon of some sort, I told the mother. We're going
through with this. The child's mouth was already bleeding. Her tongue was cut
and she was screaming in wild hysterical shrieks. Perhaps I should have desisted
and come back in an hour or more. No doubt it would have been better. But I have
seen at least two children lying dead in bed of neglect in such cases, and feeling
that I must get a diagnosis now or never I went at it again. But the worst of it was
that I too had got beyond reason. I could have torn the child apart in my own fury
and enjoyed it. It was pleasure to attack her. My face was burning with it.

The dammed little brat must be protected against her own idiocy, one says to
one's self at such times. Others must be protected against her. It is a social
necessity. And all these things are true. But a blind fury, a feeling of adult shame,
bred of a longing for muscular release are the operatives. One goes on to the end.

In a final unreasoning assault I overpowered the child's neck and jaws. I
forced the heavy silver spoon back of her teeth and down her throat till she
gagged. And there it was—both tonsils covered with membrane. She had fought
valiantly to keep me from knowing her secret. She had been hiding that sore
throat for three days at least and lying to her parents in order to escape just such
an outcome as this.

Now truly she was furious. She had been on the defensive before but now she
attacked. Tried to get off her father's lap and fly at me while tears of defeat
blinded her eyes.

QUESTIONS AND SUGGESTIONS FOR WRITING

1. In a paragraph, characterize the narrator, including a comment on the narrator's degree of self-awareness as he writes the piece.
2. Fiction usually deals with conflict. In this story there is an obvious conflict between

the doctor and the girl. Is there also a conflict between the sexes? Would the story be different if the sick child were a boy rather than a girl?

3. To what extent is "The Use of Force" about the doctor as well as about the child? Is there a conflict within the doctor?

4. In 1,000 words, rewrite the story, telling it from the point of the girl, who is now a young woman remembering the episode. If you have read "Araby" (page 206), you may want to treat the experience as the narrator of that story treats his experience— an adult recalling a sort of initiation into the adult world.

5. Given the title, we are inclined to search the story for a thesis concerning "the use of force." In 500 words, evaluate the view that Williams is saying that when one uses force (even for a good purpose) one is corrupted. Or evaluate the view that he is dramatizing an alternative thesis: that even a civilized society must sometimes resort to force.

Frank O'Connor (Irish. 1903–1966)

GUESTS OF THE NATION

I

At dusk the big Englishman, Belcher, would shift his long legs out of the ashes and say "Well, chums, what about it?" and Noble or me would say "All right, chum" (for we had picked up some of their curious expressions), and the little Englishman, Hawkins, would light the lamp and bring out the cards. Sometimes Jeremiah Donovan would come up and supervise the game and get excited over Hawkins's cards, which he always played badly, and shout at him as if he was one of our own "Ah, you divil, you, why didn't you play the tray?"

But ordinarily Jeremiah was a sober and contented poor devil like the big Englishman, Belcher, and was looked up to only because he was a fair hand at documents, though he was slow enough even with them. He wore a small cloth hat and big gaiters over his long pants, and you seldom saw him with his hands out of his pockets. He reddened when you talked to him, tilting from toe to heel and back, and looking down all the time at his big farmer's feet. Noble and me used to make fun of his broad accent, because we were from the town.

I couldn't at the time see the point of me and Noble guarding Belcher and Hawkins at all, for it was my belief that you could have planted that pair down anywhere from this to Claregalway and they'd have taken root there like a native weed. I never in my short experience seen two men to take to the country as they did.

They were handed on to us by the Second Battalion when the search for them became too hot, and Noble and myself, being young, took over with a natural feeling of responsibility, but Hawkins made us look like fools when he showed that he knew the country better than we did.

"You're the bloke they calls Bonaparte," he says to me. "Mary Brigid O'Connell told me to ask you what you done with the pair of her brother's socks you borrowed."

For it seemed, as they explained it, that the Second used to have little

5

evenings, and some of the girls of the neighborhood turned in, and, seeing they were such decent chaps, our fellows couldn't leave the two Englishmen out of them. Hawkins learned to dance "The Walls of Limerick," "The Siege of Ennis," and "The Waves of Tory" as well as any of them, though, naturally, we couldn't return the compliment, because our lads at that time did not dance foreign dances on principle.

So whatever privileges Belcher and Hawkins had with the Second they just naturally took with us, and after the first day or two we gave up all pretense of keeping a close eye on them. Not that they could have got far, for they had accents you could cut with a knife and wore khaki tunics and overcoats with civilian pants and boots. But it's my belief that they never had any idea of escaping and were quite content to be where they were.

It was a treat to see how Belcher got off with the old woman of the house where we were staying. She was a great warrant to scold, and cranky even with us, but before ever she had a chance of giving our guests, as I may call them, a lick of her tongue, Belcher had made her his friend for life. She was breaking sticks, and Belcher, who hadn't been more than ten minutes in the house, jumped up from his seat and went over to her.

"Allow me, madam," he says, smiling his queer little smile, "please allow me"; and he takes the bloody hatchet. She was struck too paralytic to speak, and after that, Belcher would be at her heels, carrying a bucket, a basket, or a load of turf, as the case might be. As Noble said, he got into looking before she leapt, and hot water, or any little thing she wanted, Belcher would have it ready for her. For such a huge man (and though I am five foot ten myself I had to look up at him) he had an uncommon shortness—or should I say lack?—of speech. It took us some time to get used to him, walking in and out, like a ghost, without a word. Especially because Hawkins talked enough for a platoon, it was strange to hear big Belcher with his toes in the ashes come out with a solitary "Excuse me, chum," or "That's right, chum." His one and only passion was cards, and I will say for him that he was a good cardplayer. He could have fleeced myself and Noble, but whatever we lost to him Hawkins lost to us, and Hawkins played with the money Belcher gave him.

Hawkins lost to us because he had too much old gab, and we probably lost to   10
Belcher for the same reason. Hawkins and Noble would spit at one another about religion into the early hours of the morning, and Hawkins worried the soul out of Noble, whose brother was a priest, with a string of questions that would puzzle a cardinal. To make it worse, even in treating of holy subjects, Hawkins had a deplorable tongue. I never in all my career met a man who could mix such a variety of cursing and bad language into an argument. He was a terrible man, and a fright to argue. He never did a stroke of work, and when he had no one else to talk to, he got stuck in the old woman.

He met his match in her, for one day when he tried to get her to complain profanely of the drought, she gave him a great comedown by blaming it entirely on Jupiter Pluvius (a deity neither Hawkins nor I had ever heard of, though Noble said that among the pagans it was believed that he had something to do with the rain). Another day he was swearing at the capitalists for starting the German war when the old lady laid down her iron, puckered up her little crab's mouth, and said: "Mr. Hawkins, you can say what you like about the war, and think you'll deceive me because I'm only a simple poor countrywoman, but I know what started the war. It was the Italian Count that stole the heathen divinity out of the temple in Japan. Believe me, Mr. Hawkins, nothing but sorrow and want can follow the people that disturb the hidden powers."

A queer old girl, all right.

II

We had our tea one evening, and Hawkins lit the lamp and we all sat into cards. Jeremiah Donovan came in too, and sat down and watched us for a while, and it suddenly struck me that he had no great love for the two Englishmen. It came as a great surprise to me, because I hadn't noticed anything about him before.

Late in the evening a really terrible argument blew up between Hawkins and Noble, about capitalists and priests and love of your country.

"The capitalists," says Hawkins with an angry gulp, "pays the priests to tell you about the next world so as you won't notice what the bastards are up to in this."

"Nonsense, man!" says Noble, losing his temper. "Before ever a capitalist was thought of, people believed in the next world."

Hawkins stood up as though he was preaching a sermon.

"Oh, they did, did they?" he says with a sneer. "They believed all the things you believe, isn't that what you mean? And you believe that God created Adam, and Adam created Shem, and Shem created Jehoshaphat. You believe all that silly old fairytale about Eve and Eden and the apple. Well, listen to me, chum. If you're entitled to hold a silly belief like that, I'm entitled to hold my silly belief—which is that the first thing your God created was a bleeding capitalist, with morality and Rolls-Royce complete. Am I right, chum?" he says to Belcher.

"You're right, chum," says Belcher with his amused smile, and got up from the table to stretch his long legs into the fire and stroke his moustache. So, seeing that Jeremiah Donovan was going, and that there was no knowing when the argument about religion would be over, I went out with him. We strolled down to the village together, and then he stopped and started blushing and mumbling and saying I ought to be behind, keeping guard on the prisoners. I didn't like the tone he took with me, and anyway I was bored with life in the cottage, so I replied by asking him what the hell we wanted guarding them at all for. I told him I'd talked it over with Noble, and that we'd both rather be out with a fighting column.

"What use are those fellows to us?" says I.

He looked at me in surprise and said: "I thought you knew we were keeping them as hostages."

"Hostages?" I said.

"The enemy have prisoners belonging to us," he says, "and now they're talking of shooting them. If they shoot our prisoners, we'll shoot theirs."

"Shoot them?" I said.

"What else did you think we were keeping them for?" he says.   25

"Wasn't it very unforeseen of you not to warn Noble and myself of that in the beginning?" I said.

"How was it?" says he. "You might have known it."

"We couldn't know it, Jeremiah Donovan," says I. "How could we when they were on our hands so long?"

"The enemy have our prisoners as long and longer," says he.

"That's not the same thing at all," says I.   30

"What difference is there?" says he.

I couldn't tell him, because I knew he wouldn't understand. If it was only an old dog that was going to the vet's, you'd try and not get too fond of him, but Jeremiah Donovan wasn't a man that would ever be in danger of that.

"And when is this thing going to be decided?" says I.

"We might hear tonight," he says. "Or tomorrow or the next day at latest. So if it's only hanging round here that's a trouble to you, you'll be free soon enough."

It wasn't the hanging round that was a trouble to me at all by this time. I had   35
worse things to worry about. When I got back to the cottage the argument was still on. Hawkins was holding forth in his best style, maintaining that there was no next world, and Noble was maintaining that there was; but I could see that Hawkins had had the best of it.

"Do you know what, chum?" he was saying with a saucy smile. "I think you're just as big a bleeding unbeliever as I am. You say you believe in the next world, and you know just as much about the next world as I do, which is sweet damn-all. What's heaven? You don't know. Where's heaven? You don't know. You know sweet damn-all! I ask you again, do they wear wings?"

"Very well, then," says Noble, "they do. Is that enough for you? They do wear wings."

"Where do they get them, then? Who makes them? Have they a factory for wings? Have they a sort of store where you hands in your chit and takes your bleeding wings?"

"You're an impossible man to argue with," says Noble. "Now, listen to me—" And they were off again.

It was long after midnight when we locked up and went to bed. As I blew out   40
the candle I told Noble what Jeremiah Donovan was after telling me. Noble took it very quietly. When we'd been in bed about an hour he asked me did I think we ought to tell the Englishmen. I didn't think we should, because it was more than likely that the English wouldn't shoot our men, and even if they did, the brigade officers, who were always up and down with the Second Battalion and knew the Englishmen well, wouldn't be likely to want them plugged. "I think so too," says Noble. "It would be great cruelty to put the wind up them now."

"It was very unforeseen of Jeremiah Donovan anyhow," says I.

It was next morning that we found it so hard to face Belcher and Hawkins. We went about the house all day scarcely saying a word. Belcher didn't seem to notice; he was stretched into the ashes as usual, with his usual look of waiting in quietness for something unforeseen to happen, but Hawkins noticed and put it down to Noble's being beaten in the argument of the night before.

"Why can't you take a discussion in the proper spirit?" he says severely. "You and your Adam and Eve! I'm a Communist, that's what I am. Communist or anarchist, it all comes to much the same thing." And for hours he went round the house, muttering when the fit took him. "Adam and Eve! Adam and Eve! Nothing better to do with their time than picking bleeding apples!"

III

I don't know how we got through that day, but I was very glad when it was over, the tea things were cleared away, and Belcher said in his peaceable way: "Well, chums, what about it?" We sat round the table and Hawkins took out the cards, and just then I heard Jeremiah Donovan's footstep on the path and a dark presentiment crossed my mind. I rose from the table and caught him before he reached the door.

"What do you want?" I asked.   45

"I want those two soldier friends of yours," he says, getting red.

"Is that the way, Jeremiah Donovan?" I asked.

"That's the way. There were four of our lads shot this morning, one of them a boy of sixteen."

"That's bad," I said.

At that moment Noble followed me out, and the three of us walked down the   50
path together, talking in whispers. Feeney, the local intelligence officer, was standing by the gate.

"What are you going to do about it?" I asked Jeremiah Donovan.

"I want you and Noble to get them out; tell them they're being shifted again; that'll be the quietest way."

"Leave me out of that," says Noble under his breath.

Jeremiah Donovan looks at him hard.

"All right," he says. "You and Feeney get a few tools from the shed and dig a   55
hole by the far end of the bog. Bonaparte and myself will be after you. Don't let anyone see you with the tools. I wouldn't like it to go beyond ourselves."

We saw Feeney and Noble go round to the shed and went in ourselves. I left Jeremiah Donovan to do the explanations. He told them that he had orders to send them back to the Second Battalion. Hawkins let out a mouthful of curses, and you could see that though Belcher didn't say anything, he was a bit upset too. The old woman was for having them stay in spite of us, and she didn't stop advising them until Jeremiah Donovan lost his temper and turned on her. He had a nasty temper, I noticed. It was pitch-dark in the cottage by this time, but no one thought of lighting the lamp, and in the darkness the two Englishmen fetched their topcoats and said good-bye to the old woman.

"Just as a man makes a home of a bleeding place, some bastard at headquarters thinks you're too cushy and shunts you off," says Hawkins, shaking her hand.

"A thousand thanks, madam," says Belcher. "A thousand thanks for everything"—as though he'd made it up.

We went round to the back of the house and down towards the bog, it was only then that Jeremiah Donovan told them. He was shaking with excitement.

"There were four of our fellows shot in Cork this morning and now you're to   60
be shot as a reprisal."

"What are you talking about?" snaps Hawkins. "It's bad enough being
mucked about as we are without having to put up with your funny jokes."

"It isn't a joke," says Donovan. "I'm sorry, Hawkins, but it's true," and
begins on the usual rigmarole about duty and how unpleasant it is.

I never noticed that people who talk a lot about duty find it much of a trouble
to them.

"Oh, cut it out!" says Hawkins.

"Ask Bonaparte," says Donovan, seeing that Hawkins isn't taking him seri-   65
ously. "Isn't it true, Bonaparte?"

"It is," I say, and Hawkins stops.

"Ah, for Christ's sake, chum."

"I mean it, chum," I say.

"You don't sound as if you meant it."

"If he doesn't mean it, I do," says Donovan, working himself up.   70

"What have you against me, Jeremiah Donovan?"

"I never said I had anything against you. But why did your people take out
four of our prisoners and shoot them in cold blood?"

He took Hawkins by the arm and dragged him on, but it was impossible to
make him understand that we were in earnest. I had the Smith and Wesson in my
pocket and I kept fingering it and wondering what I'd do if they put up a fight for it
or ran, and wishing to God they'd do one or the other. I knew if they did run for
it, that I'd never fire on them. Hawkins wanted to know was Noble in it, and when
we said yes, he asked us why Noble wanted to plug him. Why did any of us want
to plug him? What had he done to us? Weren't we all chums? Didn't we understand him and didn't he understand us? Did we imagine for an instant that he'd
shoot us for all the so-and-so officers in the so-and-so British Army?

By this time we'd reached the bog, and I was so sick I couldn't even answer
him. We walked along the edge of it in the darkness, and every now and then
Hawkins would call a halt and begin all over again, as if he was wound up, about
our being chums, and I knew that nothing but the sight of the grave would convince him that we had to do it. And all the time I was hoping that something would
happen; that they'd run for it or that Noble would take over the responsibility
from me. I had the feeling that it was worse on Noble than on me.

IV

At last we saw the lantern in the distance and made towards it. Noble was   75
carrying it, and Feeney was standing somewhere in the darkness behind him, and
the picture of them so still and silent in the bogland brought it home to me that we
were in earnest, and banished the last bit of hope I had.

Belcher, on recognizing Noble, said: "Hallo, chum," in his quiet way, but
Hawkins flew at him at once, and the argument began all over again, only this
time Noble had nothing to say for himself and stood with his head down, holding
the lantern between his legs.

It was Jeremiah Donovan who did the answering. For the twentieth time, as though it was haunting his mind, Hawkins asked if anybody thought he'd shoot Noble.

"Yes, you would," says Jeremiah Donovan.

"No, I wouldn't, damn you!"

"You would, because you'd know you'd be shot for not doing it."   80

"I wouldn't, not if I was to be shot twenty times over. I wouldn't shoot a pal. And Belcher wouldn't—isn't that right, Belcher?"

"That's right, chum," Belcher said, but more by way of answering the question than of joining in the argument. Belcher sounded as though whatever unforeseen thing he'd always been waiting for had come at last.

"Anyway, who says Noble would be shot if I wasn't? What do you think I'd do if I was in his place, out in the middle of a blasted bog?"

"What would you do?" asks Donovan.

"I'd go with him wherever he was going, of course. Share my last bob with   85 him and stick by him through thick and thin. No one can ever say of me that I let down a pal."

"We had enough of this," says Jeremiah Donovan, cocking his revolver. "Is there any message you want to send?"

"No, there isn't."

"Do you want to say your prayers?"

Hawkins came out with a cold-blooded remark that even shocked me and turned on Noble again.

"Listen to me, Noble," he says. "You and me are chums. You can't come over   90 to my side, so I'll come over to your side. That show you I mean what I say? Give me a rifle and I'll go along with you and the other lads."

Nobody answered him. We knew that was no way out.

"Hear what I'm saying?" he says. "I'm through with it. I'm a deserter or anything else you like. I don't believe in your stuff, but it's no worse than mine. That satisfy you?"

Noble raised his head, but Donovan began to speak and he lowered it again without replying.

"For the last time, have you any messages to send?" says Donovan in a cold, excited sort of voice.

"Shut up, Donovan! You don't understand me, but these lads do. They're not   95 the sort to make a pal and kill a pal. They're not the tools of any capitalist."

I alone of the crowd saw Donovan raise his Webley to the back of Hawkins's neck, and as he did so I shut my eyes and tried to pray. Hawkins had begun to say something else when Donovan fired, and as I opened my eyes at the bang, I saw Hawkins stagger at the knees and lie out flat at Noble's feet, slowly and as quiet as a kid falling asleep, with the lantern-light on his lean legs and bright farmer's boots. We all stood very still, watching him settle out in the last agony.

Then Belcher took out a handkerchief and began to tie it about his own eyes (in our excitement we'd forgotten to do the same for Hawkins), and, seeing it wasn't big enough, turned and asked for the loan of mine. I gave it to him and he knotted the two together and pointed with his foot at Hawkins.

"He's not quite dead," he says. "Better give him another."

Sure enough, Hawkins's left knee is beginning to rise. I bend down and put my gun to his head; then, recollecting myself, I get up again. Belcher understands what's in my mind.

"Give him his first," he says. "I don't mind. Poor bastard, we don't know   100
what's happening to him now."

I knelt and fired. By this time I didn't seem to know what I was doing. Belcher, who was fumbling a bit awkwardly with the handkerchiefs, came out with a laugh as he heard the shot. It was the first time I heard him laugh and it sent a shudder down my back; it sounded so unnatural.

"Poor bugger!" he said quietly. "And last night he was so curious about it all. It's very queer, chums, I always think. Now he knows as much about it as they'll ever let him know, and last night he was all in the dark."

Donovan helped him to tie the handkerchiefs about his eyes. "Thanks, chum," he said. Donovan asked if there were any messages he wanted sent.

"No, chum," he says. "Not for me. If any of you would like to write to Hawkins's mother, you'll find a letter from her in his pocket. He and his mother were great chums. But my missus left me eight years ago. Went away with another fellow and took the kid with her. I like the feeling of a home, as you may have noticed, but I couldn't start again after that."

It was an extraordinary thing, but in those few minutes Belcher said more   105
than in all the weeks before. It was just as if the sound of the shot had started a flood of talk in him and he could go on the whole night like that, quite happily, talking about himself. We stood round like fools now that he couldn't see us any longer. Donovan looked at Noble, and Noble shook his head. Then Donovan raised his Webley, and at that moment Belcher gives his queer laugh again. He may have thought we were talking about him, or perhaps he noticed the same thing I'd noticed and couldn't understand it.

"Excuse me, chums," he says. "I feel I'm talking the hell of a lot, and so silly, about my being so handy about a house and things like that. But this thing came on me suddenly. You'll forgive me, I'm sure."

"You don't want to say a prayer?" asked Donovan.

"No, chum," he says. "I don't think it would help. I'm ready, and you boys want to get it over."

"You understand that we're only doing our duty?" says Donovan.

Belcher's head was raised like a blind man's, so that you could only see his   110
chin and the tip of his nose in the lantern-light.

"I never could make out what duty was myself," he said. "I think you're all good lads, if that's what you mean. I'm not complaining."

Noble, just as if he couldn't bear any more of it, raised his fist at Donovan, and in a flash Donovan raised his gun and fired. The big man went over like a sack of meal, and this time there was no need of a second shot.

I don't remember much about the burying, but that it was worse than all the rest because we had to carry them to the grave. It was all mad lonely with nothing but a patch of lantern-light between ourselves and the dark, and birds hooting and screeching all round, disturbed by the guns. Noble went through Hawkins's belongings to find the letter from his mother, and then joined his hands together. He did the same with Belcher. Then, when we'd filled in the grave, we separated from Jeremiah Donovan and Feeney and took our tools back to the shed. All the way we didn't speak a word. The kitchen was dark and cold as we'd left it, and the old woman was sitting over the hearth, saying her beads. We walked past her into the room, and Noble struck a match to light the lamp. She rose quietly and came to the doorway with all her cantankerousness gone.

"What did ye do with them?" she asked in a whisper, and Noble started so that the match went out in his hand.

"What's that?" he asked without turning round.   115

"I heard ye," she said.

"What did you hear?" asked Noble.

"I heard ye. Do ye think I didn't hear ye, putting the spade back in the houseen?"

Noble struck another match and this time the lamp lit for him.

"Was that what ye did to them?" she asked.   120

Then, by God, in the very doorway, she fell on her knees and began praying, and after looking at her for a minute or two Noble did the same by the fireplace. I pushed my way out past her and left them at it. I stood at the door, watching the stars and listening to the shrieking of the birds dying out over the bogs. It is so strange what you feel at times like that you can't describe it. Noble says he saw everything ten times the size, as though there were nothing in the whole world but that little patch of bog with the two Englishmen stiffening into it, but with me it was as if the patch of bog where the Englishmen were was a million miles away, and even Noble and the old woman, mumbling behind me, and the birds and the bloody stars were all far away, and I was somehow very small and very lost and lonely like a child astray in the snow. And anything that happened to me afterwards, I never felt the same about again.

QUESTIONS AND SUGGESTIONS FOR WRITING

1. Although the narrator, Noble, and Donovan are all patriotic Irishmen, Donovan's attitude toward the English prisoners is quite different from that of the other two. How does that difference in attitude help point up the story's theme?
2. How does the constant bickering between Noble and Hawkins help to prepare us for the conclusion of the story? How does it contribute to the theme?
3. When he hears he is about to be shot, Hawkins, to save his life, volunteers to join the Irish cause. Is his turnabout simply evidence of his cowardice and hypocrisy? Explain.
4. Throughout most of the story Belcher is shy and speaks little; just before his execution, however, he suddenly becomes loquacious. Is he trying to stall for time? Would it have been more in character for Belcher to have remained stoically taciturn to the end, or do the narrator's remarks about Belcher's change make it plausible?
5. Does the old woman's presence in the story merely furnish local color or picturesqueness? If so, is it necessary or desirable? Or does her presence further contribute to the story's meaning? If so, how?
6. The following is the last paragraph of an earlier version. Which is the more effective conclusion? Why?

So then, by God, she fell on her two knees by the door, and began telling her beads, and after a minute or two Noble went on his knees by the fireplace, so I pushed my way past her, and stood at the door, watching the stars and listening to the damned shrieking of the birds. It is so strange what you feel at such moments, and not to be written afterwards. Noble says he felt he seen everything ten times as big, perceiving nothing around him but the little patch of black bog with the two Englishmen stiffening into it; but with me it was the other way, as though the patch of bog where the two Englishmen were was a thousand miles away from me, and even Noble mumbling just behind me and the old woman and the birds and the bloody stars were all far away, and I was somehow very small and very lonely. And nothing that ever happened me after I never felt the same about again.

7. How does the point of view (see page 714) help to emphasize the narrator's development from innocence to awareness? If the story had been told in the third person, how would it have affected the story's impact?

□ POETRY

William Blake (English. 1757–1827)

THE LAMB

Little Lamb, who made thee?
  Dost thou know who made thee?
Gave thee life, and bid thee feed?
By the stream and o'er the mead;
Give thee clothing of delight,   5
Softest clothing, wooly, bright;
Gave thee such a tender voice,
Making all the vales rejoice?
  Little Lamb, who made thee?
  Dost thou know who made thee?   10

Little Lamb, I'll tell thee,
  Little Lamb, I'll tell thee:
He is calléd by thy name,
For he calls himself a Lamb.
He is meek, and he is mild;   15
He became a little child.
I a child, and thou a lamb,
We are calléd by his name.
  Little Lamb, God bless thee!
  Little Lamb, God bless thee!   20

William Blake (English. 1757–1827)

THE TYGER

Tyger! Tyger! burning bright
In the forests of the night,
What immortal hand or eye
Could frame thy fearful symmetry?   4

In what distant deeps or skies
Burnt the fire of thine eyes?
On what wings dare he aspire?
What the hand dare seize the fire?   8

And what shoulder, and what art,
Could twist the sinews of thy heart?
And, when thy heart began to beat,
What dread hand? and what dread feet?   12

What the hammer? what the chain?
In what furnace was thy brain?
What the anvil? what dread grasp
Dare its deadly terrors clasp?   16

When the stars threw down their spears,
And watered heaven with their tears,
Did he smile his work to see?
Did he who made the lamb make thee?   20

Tyger! Tyger! burning bright
In the forests of the night,
What immortal hand or eye,
Dare frame thy fearful symmetry?   24

QUESTION

Why does Blake answer his question in "The Lamb" but not in "The Tyger"?

John Keats (English. 1795–1821)

ODE ON A GRECIAN URN

I

Thou still unravished bride of quietness,
    Thou foster-child of silence and slow time,
Sylvan historian, who canst thus express
    A flowery tale more sweetly than our rhyme:

What leaf-fringed legend haunts about thy shape   5
    Of deities or mortals, or of both,
        In Tempe or the dales of Arcady?
    What men or gods are these? What maidens loth?
What mad pursuit? What struggle to escape?
        What pipes and timbrels? What wild ecstasy?   10

II

Heard melodies are sweet, but those unheard
    Are sweeter; therefore, ye soft pipes, play on;
Not to the sensual° ear, but, more endeared,   *Sensuous*
    Pipe to the spirit ditties of no tone:
Fair youth, beneath the trees, thou canst not leave   15
    Thy song, nor ever can those trees be bare;
        Bold Lover, never, never canst thou kiss,
Though winning near the goal—yet, do not grieve;
        She cannot fade, though thou hast not thy bliss,
    For ever wilt thou love, and she be fair!   20

III

Ah, happy, happy boughs! that cannot shed
    Your leaves, nor ever bid the Spring adieu;
And, happy melodist, unwearied,
    For ever piping songs for ever new;
More happy love! more happy, happy love!   25
    For ever warm and still to be enjoyed,
        For ever panting, and for ever young;
All breathing human passion far above,
    That leaves a heart high-sorrowful and cloyed,
        A burning forehead, and a parching tongue.   30

IV

Who are these coming to the sacrifice?
    To what green altar, O mysterious priest,
Lead'st thou that heifer lowing at the skies,
    And all her silken flanks with garlands drest?
What little town by river or sea shore,   35
    Or mountain-built with peaceful citadel,
        Is emptied of this folk, this pious morn?
And, little town, thy streets for evermore
    Will silent be; and not a soul to tell
        Why thou art desolate can e'er return.   40

V

O Attic shape! Fair attitude! with brede°   *Design*
    Of marble men and maidens overwrought,

With forest branches and the trodden weed;
     Thou, silent form, dost tease us out of thought
As doth eternity: Cold Pastoral!   45
When old age shall this generation waste,
     Thou shalt remain, in midst of other woe
     Than ours, a friend to man, to whom thou say'st,
"Beauty is truth, truth beauty,"—that is all
     Ye know on earth, and all ye need to know.   50

QUESTIONS AND SUGGESTIONS FOR WRITING

1. Why "sylvan" historian (line 3)? As the poem continues, what evidence is there that the urn cannot "express" (line 3) a tale so sweetly as the speaker said?
2. What do you interpret lines 11–14 to mean?
3. What might the urn stand for in the first three stanzas? In the third stanza is the speaker caught up in the urn's world or is he sharply aware of his own?
4. Does "tease us out of thought" (line 44) mean "draw us into a realm of imaginative experience superior to that of reason," or "draw us into futile and frustrating questions"? Or both, or neither? What are the suggestions in "Cold Pastoral" (line 45)?
5. Do lines 49–50 perhaps mean that imagination, stimulated by the urn, achieves a realm richer than the daily world? Or perhaps that art, the highest earthly wisdom, suggests there is a realm wherein earthly troubles are resolved?

Gerard Manley Hopkins (English. 1844–1889)

SPRING AND FALL:
To a Young Child

Margaret, are you grieving
Over Goldengrove unleaving?
Leaves, like the things of man, you
With your fresh thoughts care for, can you?   5
Áh! as the heart grows older
It will come to such sights colder
By and by, nor spare a sigh
Though worlds of wanwood leafmeal lie;
And yet you will weep and know why.   10
Now no matter, child, the name:
Sorrow's springs are the same.
Nor mouth had, no nor mind, expressed   *Spirit*
What heart heard of, ghost° guessed:
It is the blight man was born for,   15
It is Margaret you mourn for.

QUESTIONS AND SUGGESTIONS FOR WRITING

1. What is the speaker's age? His tone? What is the relevance of the title to the speaker and to Margaret? What meanings are in "Fall"?
2. What is meant by Margaret's "fresh thoughts" (line 4)? Paraphrase lines 3–4 and lines 12–13.
3. "Wanwood" and "leafmeal" are words coined by Hopkins. What are their suggestions?
4. Why is it not contradictory for the speaker to say that Margaret weeps for herself (line 15) after saying that she weeps for "Goldengrove unleaving" (line 2)?

A. E. Housman (English. 1859–1936)

WHEN I WAS ONE-AND-TWENTY

When I was one-and-twenty
  I heard a wise man say,
"Give crowns and pounds and guineas
  But not your heart away;
Give pearls away and rubies   5
  But keep your fancy free."
But I was one-and-twenty,
  No use to talk to me.

When I was one-and-twenty
  I heard him say again,   10
"The heart out of the bosom
  Was never given in vain;
'Tis paid with sighs a plenty
  And sold for endless rue."
And I am two-and-twenty,   15
  And oh, 'tis true, 'tis true.

QUESTIONS AND SUGGESTIONS FOR WRITING

1. In your own words, what is the advice of the "wise man"?
2. In a paragraph, indicate what you think the speaker's attitude is toward himself. In a second paragraph, indicate what *our* attitude toward him is.

Robert Hayden (American. 1913–1980)

THOSE WINTER SUNDAYS

Sundays too my father got up early
and put his clothes on in the blueblack cold,
then with cracked hands that ached

from labor in the weekday weather made
banked fires blaze. No one ever thanked him.   5

I'd wake and hear the coal splintering, breaking.
When the rooms were warm, he'd call,
and slowly I would rise and dress,
fearing the chronic angers of that house,

Speaking indifferently to him,   10
who had driven out the cold
and polished my good shoes as well.
What did I know, what did I know
of love's austere and lonely offices?

QUESTION

What is the meaning of "offices" in the last line?

Louise Glück (American. b. 1943)

GRETEL IN DARKNESS

This is the world we wanted. All who would have seen us dead
Are dead. I hear the witch's cry
Break in the moonlight through a sheet of sugar: God rewards.
Her tongue shrivels into gas. . . .
                              Now, far from women's arms   5
And memory of women, in our father's hut
We sleep, are never hungry.
Why do I not forget?
My father bars the door, bars harm
From this house, and it is years.   10

No one remembers. Even you, my brother,
Summer afternoons you look at me as though you meant
To leave, as though it never happened. But I killed for you.
I see armed firs, the spires of that gleaming kiln come back, come back—

Nights I turn to you to hold me but you are not there.   15
Am I alone? Spies
Hiss in the stillness, Hansel we are there still, and it is real, real,
That black forest, and the fire in earnest.

QUESTIONS AND SUGGESTIONS FOR WRITING

1. If you are not thoroughly familiar with the story of Hansel and Gretel, read the story
   in *Grimm's Fairy Tales*. Why, according to the poem, does the episode with the witch
   mean so much more to Gretel than to Hansel?
2. How, as the poem develops, is the first sentence of the poem modified?

□ DRAMA

A Note on the Elizabethan Theater

Shakespeare's theater was wooden, round or polygonal (the Chorus in *Henry V* calls it a "wooden O"). About eight hundred spectators could stand in the yard in front of—and perhaps along the two sides of—the stage that jutted from the rear wall, and another fifteen hundred or so spectators could sit in the three roofed galleries that ringed the stage. That portion of the galleries that was above the rear of the stage was sometimes used by actors. Entry to the stage was normally gained by doors at the rear but some use was made of a curtained alcove—or perhaps a booth—between the doors, which allowed characters to be "discovered" (revealed) as in the modern proscenium theater, which normally employs a curtain. A performance was probably uninterrupted by intermissions or by long pauses for the changing of scenery; a group of characters leaves the stage, another enters, and if the locale has changed, the new characters somehow tell us. (Modern editors customarily add indications of locales to help a reader, but it should be understood that the action on the Elizabethan stage was continuous.)

A Note on the Text of *Hamlet*

Shakespeare's *Hamlet* comes to us in three versions. The first, known as the First Quarto (Q1), was published in 1603. It is an illegitimate garbled version, perhaps derived from the memory of the actor who played Marcellus (this part is conspicuously more accurate than the rest of the play) in a short version of the play. The second printed version (Q2), which appeared in 1604, is almost twice as long as Q1; all in all, it is the best text we have, doubtless published (as Q1 was not) with the permission of Shakespeare's theatrical company. The third printed version, in the First Folio (the collected edition of Shakespeare's plays, published in 1623), is also legitimate, but it seems to be an acting version, for it lacks some two hundred lines of Q2. On the other hand, the Folio text includes some ninety lines not found in Q2. Because Q2 is the longest version, giving us more of the play as Shakespeare conceived it than either of the other texts, it serves as the basic version for this text. Unfortunately, the printers of it often worked carelessly: words and phrases are omitted, there are plain misreadings of what must have been in Shakespeare's manuscript, and speeches are sometimes wrongly assigned. It was therefore necessary to turn to the First Folio for many readings. It has been found useful, also, to divide the play into acts and scenes; these divisions, not found in Q2 (and only a few are found in the Folio), are purely editorial additions, and they are therefore enclosed in square brackets.

William Shakespeare (English. 1564–1616)

THE TRAGEDY OF HAMLET
Prince of Denmark

[Dramatis Personae

CLAUDIUS, *King of Denmark*
HAMLET, *son to the late, and nephew to the present, King*
POLONIUS, *Lord Chamberlain*
HORATIO, *friend to Hamlet*
LAERTES, *son to Polonius*
VOLTEMAND ⎫
CORNELIUS ⎪
ROSENCRANTZ ⎬ *courtiers*
GUILDENSTERN ⎪
OSRIC ⎪
A GENTLEMAN ⎭
A PRIEST
MARCELLUS ⎫ *officers*
BARNARDO ⎭
FRANCISCO, *a soldier*
REYNALDO, *servant to Polonius*
PLAYERS
TWO CLOWNS, *gravediggers*
FORTINBRAS, *Prince of Norway*
A NORWEGIAN CAPTAIN
ENGLISH AMBASSADORS
GERTRUDE, *Queen of Denmark, mother to Hamlet*
OPHELIA, *daughter to Polonius*
GHOST OF HAMLET'S FATHER
LORDS, LADIES, OFFICERS, SOLDIERS, SAILORS,
    MESSENGERS, ATTENDANTS

Scene. *Elsinore]*

[ACT I

Scene I. *A guard platform of the castle.]*

Enter BARNARDO *and* FRANCISCO, *two sentinels.*

BARNARDO. Who's there?
FRANCISCO. Nay, answer me. Stand and unfold°* yourself.
BARNARDO. Long live the King!°

FRANCISCO. Barnardo?   5
BARNARDO. He.
FRANCISCO. You come most carefully upon your hour.
BARNARDO. 'Tis now struck twelve. Get thee to bed, Francisco.   10
FRANCISCO. For this relief much thanks.
    'Tis bitter cold,
And I am sick at heart.
BARNARDO. Have you had quiet guard?
FRANCISCO.   Not a mouse stirring.
BARNARDO. Well, good night.
If you do meet Horatio and Marcellus,   15

*The notes are Edward Hubler's for the Signet edition of *Hamlet.* I.i. ³ **unfold** disclose ⁴ **Long live the King** (perhaps a password, perhaps a greeting)

The rivals° of my watch, bid them make
  haste.

Enter HORATIO *and* MARCELLUS.

  FRANCISCO. I think I hear them. Stand,
  ho! Who is there?
  HORATIO. Friends to this ground.
  MARCELLUS. And liegemen to the Dane.°
  FRANCISCO. Give you° good night.
  MARCELLUS. O, farewell, honest soldier.
Who hath relieved you?
20   FRANCISCO.   Barnardo hath my place
Give you good night.   *Exit* FRANCISCO.
  MARCELLUS.   Holla, Barnardo!
  BARNARDO.   Say——
What, is Horatio there?
  HORATIO.   A piece of him.
  BARNARDO. Welcome, Horatio. Wel-
  come, good Marcellus.
  MARCELLUS. What, has this thing ap-
  peared again tonight?
25   BARNARDO. I have seen nothing.
  MARCELLUS. Horatio says 'tis but our
  fantasy,
And will not let belief take hold of him
Touching this dreaded sight twice seen of
  us;
Therefore I have entreated him along
30 With us to watch the minutes of this night,
That, if again this apparition come,
He may approve° our eyes and speak to it.
  HORATIO. Tush, tush, 'twill not appear.
  BARNARDO.   Sit down awhile,
And let us once again assail your ears,
35 That are so fortified against our story,
What we have two nights seen.
  HORATIO.   Well, sit we down,
And let us hear Barnardo speak of this.
  BARNARDO. Last night of all,
When yond same star that's westward
  from the pole°
Had made his course t' illume that part of
40   heaven
Where now it burns, Marcellus and my-
  self,
The bell then beating one——

Enter GHOST.

  MARCELLUS. Peace, break thee off. Look
  where it comes again.
  BARNARDO. In the same figure like the
  king that's dead.
  MARCELLUS. Thou art a scholar; speak
  to it, Horatio.   45
  BARNARDO. Looks 'a not like the king?
  Mark it, Horatio.
  HORATIO. Most like: it harrows me with
  fear and wonder.
  BARNARDO. It would be spoke to.
  MARCELLUS.   Speak to it, Horatio.
  HORATIO. What art thou that usurp'st
  this time of night,
Together with that fair and warlike form   50
In which the majesty of buried Denmark°
Did sometimes march? By heaven I charge
  thee, speak.
  MARCELLUS. It is offended.
  BARNARDO.   See, it stalks away.
  HORATIO. Stay! Speak, speak. I charge
  thee, speak.   *Exit* GHOST.
  MARCELLUS. 'Tis gone and will not an-
  swer.   55
  BARNARDO. How now, Horatio? You
  tremble and look pale.
Is not this something more than fantasy?
What think you on't?
  HORATIO. Before my God, I might not
  this believe
Without the sensible and true avouch°   60
Of mine own eyes.
  MARCELLUS.   Is it not like the King?
  HORATIO. As thou art to thyself.
Such was the very armor he had on
When he the ambitious Norway° com-
  bated:
So frowned he once, when, in an angry
  parle,°   65
He smote the sledded Polacks° on the ice.
'Tis strange.
  MARCELLUS. Thus twice before, and
  jump° at this dead hour,

---

[16] **rivals** partners [18] **liegemen to the Dane**
loyal subjects to the King of Denmark [19] **Give
you** God give you [32] **approve** confirm [39] **pole**
polestar

[51] **buried Denmark** the buried king of Denmark
[60] **sensible and true avouch** sensory and true
proof [64] **Norway** King of Norway [65] **parle** parley
[66] **sledded Polacks** Poles in sledges [68] **jump**
just

With martial stalk hath he gone by our
    watch.
  HORATIO. In what particular thought to
70   work I know not;
But, in the gross and scope° of my opin-
    ion,
This bodes some strange eruption to our
    state.
  MARCELLUS. Good now, sit down, and
    tell me he that knows,
Why this same strict and most observant
    watch
75 So nightly toils the subject° of the land,
And why such daily cast of brazen cannon
And foreign mart° for implements of war,
Why such impress° of shipwrights, whose
    sore task
Does not divide the Sunday from the
    week,
What might be toward° that this sweaty
80   haste
Doth make the night joint-laborer with the
    day?
Who is't that can inform me?
  HORATIO.   That can I.
At least the whisper goes so: our last
    king,
Whose image even but now appeared to
    us,
Was, as you know, by Fortinbras of Nor-
85   way,
Thereto pricked on by a most emulate
    pride,
Dared to the combat; in which our valiant
    Hamlet
(For so this side of our known world es-
    teemed him)
Did slay this Fortinbras, who, by a sealed
    compact
90 Well ratified by law and heraldry,°
Did forfeit, with his life, all those his lands
Which he stood seized° of, to the con-
    queror;
Against the which a moiety competent°

Was gagèd° by our King, which had re-
    turned
To the inheritance of Fortinbras,   95
Had he been vanquisher, as, by the same
    comart°
And carriage of the article designed,°
His fell to Hamlet. Now, sir, young Fortin-
    bras,
Of unimprovèd° mettle hot and full,
Hath in the skirts° of Norway here and
    there   100
Sharked up° a list of lawless resolutes,°
For food and diet, to some enterprise
That hath a stomach in't;° which is no
    other,
As it doth well appear unto our state,
But to recover of us by strong hand   105
And terms compulsatory, those foresaid
    lands
So by his father lost; and this, I take it,
Is the main motive of our preparations,
The source of this our watch, and the
    chief head°
Of this posthaste and romage° in the land.   110
  BARNARDO. I think it bè no other but
    e'en so;
Well may it sort° that this portentous
    figure
Comes armèd through our watch so like
    the King
That was and is the question of these
    wars.
  HORATIO. A mote it is to trouble the
    mind's eye: 115
In the most high and palmy state of Rome,
A little ere the mightiest Julius fell,
The graves stood tenantless, and the
    sheeted dead
Did squeak and gibber in the Roman
    streets;°

---

71 **gross and scope** general drift 75 **toils the subject** makes the subjects toil 77 **mart** trading 78 **impress** forced service 80 **toward** in preparation 90 **law and heraldry** heraldic law (governing the combat) 92 **seized** possessed 93 **moiety competent** equal portion

94 **gagèd** engaged, pledged 96 **comart** agreement 97 **carriage of the article designed** import of the agreement drawn up 99 **unimprovèd** untried 100 **skirts** borders 101 **Sharked up** collected indiscriminately (as a shark gulps its prey) 101 **resolutes** desperadoes 103 **hath a stomach in't** i.e., requires courage 109 **head** fountainhead, origin 110 **romage** bustle 112 **sort** befit 119 **Did squeak . . . Roman streets** (the break in the sense which follows this line suggests that a line has dropped out)

As stars with trains of fire and dews of
120   blood,
Disasters° in the sun; and the moist star,°
Upon whose influence Neptune's empire
    stands,
Was sick almost to doomsday with eclipse.
And even the like precurse° of feared
    events,
125   As harbingers° preceding still° the fates
And prologue to the omen° coming on,
Have heaven and earth together demon-
    strated
Unto our climatures° and countrymen.

Enter GHOST.

But soft, behold, lo where it comes again!
I'll cross it,° though it blast me.—Stay,
130   illusion.

It spreads his° arms.

If thou hast any sound or use of voice,
Speak to me.
If there be any good thing to be done
That may to thee do ease and grace to
    me,
135   Speak to me.
If thou art privy to thy country's fate,
Which happily° foreknowing may avoid,
O, speak!
Or if thou hast uphoarded in thy life
140   Extorted° treasure in the womb of earth,
For which, they say, you spirits oft walk in
    death,

The cock crows.

Speak of it. Stay and speak. Stop it, Mar-
    cellus.
    MARCELLUS. Shall I strike at it with my
        partisan°?
    HORATIO. Do, if it will not stand.

BARNARDO.   'Tis here.
HORATIO.   'Tis here.
MARCELLUS. 'Tis gone.   *Exit* GHOST.   145
We do it wrong, being so majestical,
To offer it the show of violence,
For it is as the air, invulnerable,
And our vain blows malicious mockery.
    BARNARDO. It was about to speak when
        the cock crew.   150
    HORATIO. And then it started, like a
        guilty thing
Upon a fearful summons. I have heard,
The cock, that is the trumpet to the
    morn,
Doth with his lofty and shrill-sounding
    throat
Awake the god of day, and at his warning,   155
Whether in sea or fire, in earth or air,
Th' extravagant and erring° spirit hies
To his confine; and of the truth herein
This present object made probation.°
    MARCELLUS. It faded on the crowing of
        the cock.   160
Some say that ever 'gainst° that season
    comes
Wherein our Savior's birth is celebrated,
This bird of dawning singeth all night long,
And then, they say, no spirit dare stir
    abroad,
The nights are wholesome, then no plan-
    ets strike,°   165
No fairy takes,° nor witch hath power to
    charm:
So hallowed and so gracious is that time.
    HORATIO. So have I heard and do in part
        believe it.
But look, the morn in russet mantle clad
Walks o'er the dew of yon high eastward
    hill.   170
Break we our watch up, and by my advice
Let us impart what we have seen tonight
Unto young Hamlet, for upon my life
This spirit, dumb to us, will speak to him.
Do you consent we shall acquaint him with
    it,   175

---

121 **Disasters** threatening signs 121 **moist star**
moon 124 **precurse** precursor, foreshadowing
125 **harbingers** forerunners 125 **still** always
126 **omen** calamity 128 **climatures** regions
130 **cross it** (1) cross its path, confront it, (2)
make the sign of the cross in front of it 130 s.d. **his**
i.e., its, the ghost's (though possibly what is
meant is that Horatio spreads his own arms,
making a cross of himself) 137 **happily** haply, perhaps 140 **Extorted** ill-won 143 **partisan** pike (a
long-handled weapon)

---

157 **extravagant and erring** out of bounds and
wandering 159 **probation** proof 161 **'gainst** just
before 165 **strike** exert an evil influence 166 **takes**
bewitches

As needful in our loves, fitting our duty?
MARCELLUS. Let's do't, I pray, and I
   this morning know
Where we shall find him most convenient.
                        Exeunt.

[Scene II. *The castle.]*

Flourish.° *Enter* CLAUDIUS, *King of Den-*
mark, GERTRUDE *the Queen, Councilors,*
POLONIUS *and his son* LAERTES, HAMLET,
cum aliis° *[including* VOLTEMAND *and* COR-
NELIUS*].*

  KING. Though yet of Hamlet our dear
    brother's death
The memory be green, and that it us
   befitted
To bear our hearts in grief, and our whole
   kingdom
To be contracted in one brow of woe,
Yet so far hath discretion fought with
5   nature
That we with wisest sorrow think on him
Together with remembrance of ourselves.
Therefore our sometime sister,° now our
   Queen,
Th' imperial jointress° to this warlike
   state,
10 Have we, as 'twere, with a defeated joy,
With an auspicious° and a dropping eye,
With mirth in funeral, and with dirge in
   marriage,
In equal scale weighing delight and dole,
Taken to wife. Nor have we herein barred
Your better wisdoms, which have freely
15   gone
With this affair along. For all, our thanks.
Now follows that you know young Fortin-
   bras,
Holding a weak supposal of our worth,
Or thinking by our late dear brother's
   death
20 Our state to be disjoint and out of frame,°
Colleaguèd with this dream of his advan-
   tage,°

He hath not failed to pester us with mes-
   sage,
Importing the surrender of those lands
Lost by his father, with all bands of law,
To our most valiant brother. So much for
   him.   25
Now for ourself and for this time of meet-
   ing.
Thus much the business is: we have here
   writ
To Norway, uncle of young Fortinbras—
Who, impotent and bedrid, scarcely hears
Of this his nephew's purpose—to sup-
   press   30
His further gait° herein, in that the levies,
The lists, and full proportions° are all
   made
Out of his subject;° and we here dispatch
You, good Cornelius, and you, Voltemand,
For bearers of this greeting to old Norway,   35
Giving to you no further personal power
To business with the King, more than the
   scope
Of these delated articles° allow.
Farewell, and let your haste commend
   your duty.
  CORNELIUS, VOLTEMAND. In that, and all
    things, will we show our duty.   40
  KING. We doubt it nothing. Heartily
    farewell.

      Exeunt VOLTEMAND *and* CORNELIUS.

And now, Laertes, what's the news with
   you?
You told us of some suit. What is't,
   Laertes?
You cannot speak of reason to the Dane
And lose your voice.° What wouldst thou
   beg, Laertes,   45
That shall not be my offer, not thy asking?
The head is not more native° to the heart,
The hand more instrumental to the mouth,
Than is the throne of Denmark to thy
   father.

I.ii. ˢ·ᵈ· **Flourish** fanfare of trumpets ˢ·ᵈ· **cum aliis** with others (Latin) ⁸ **our sometime sister** my (the royal "we") former sister-in-law ⁹ **jointress** joint tenant, partner ¹¹ **auspicious** joyful ²⁰ **frame** order ²¹ **advantage** superiority

³¹ **gait** proceeding ³² **proportions** supplies for war ³³ **Out of his subject** i.e., out of old Norway's subjects and realm ³⁸ **delated articles** detailed documents ⁴⁵ **lose your voice** waste your breath ⁴⁷ **native** related

What wouldst thou have, Laertes?
50   LAERTES.   My dread lord,
Your leave and favor to return to France,
From whence, though willingly I came to
    Denmark
To show my duty in your coronation,
Yet now I must confess, that duty done,
My thoughts and wishes bend again to-
55   ward France
And bow them to your gracious leave and
    pardon.
    KING. Have you your father's leave?
    What says Polonius?
    POLONIUS. He hath, my lord, wrung
    from me my slow leave
By laborsome petition, and at last
60   Upon his will I sealed my hard consent.°
I do beseech you give him leave to go.
    KING. Take thy fair hour, Laertes. Time
    be thine,
And thy best graces spend it at thy will.
But now, my cousin° Hamlet, and my
    son——
    HAMLET *[aside]*. A little more than kin,
65   and less than kind!°
    KING. How is it that the clouds still hang
    on you?
    HAMLET. Not so, my lord. I am too
    much in the sun.°
    QUEEN. Good Hamlet, cast thy nighted
    color off,
And let thine eye look like a friend on
    Denmark.
70   Do not forever with thy vailèd lids
Seek for thy noble father in the dust.
Thou know'st 'tis common; all that lives
    must die,
Passing through nature to eternity.
    HAMLET. Ay, madam, it is common.°
    QUEEN.   If it be,

Why seems it so particular with thee?   75
    HAMLET. Seems, madam? Nay, it is. I
    know not "seems."
'Tis not alone my inky cloak, good
    mother,
Nor customary suits of solemn black,
Nor windy suspiration° of forced breath,   80
No, nor the fruitful river in the eye,
Nor the dejected havior of the visage,
Together with all forms, moods, shapes of
    grief,
That can denote me truly. These indeed
    seem,
For they are actions that a man might play,   85
But I have that within which passes show;
These but the trappings and the suits of
    woe.
    KING. 'Tis sweet and commendable in
    your nature, Hamlet,
To give these mourning duties to your
    father,
But you must know your father lost a
    father,
That father lost, lost his, and the survivor   90
    bound
In filial obligation for some term
To do obsequious° sorrow. But to per-
    sever
In obstinate condolement° is a course
Of impious stubbornness. 'Tis unmanly
    grief.   95
It shows a will most incorrect to heaven,
A heart unfortified, a mind impatient,
An understanding simple and unschooled.
For what we know must be and is as
    common
As any the most vulgar° thing to sense,   100
Why should we in our peevish opposition
Take it to heart? Fie, 'tis a fault to
    heaven,
A fault against the dead, a fault to nature,
To reason most absurd, whose common
    theme
Is death of fathers, and who still hath
    cried,

⁶⁰ **Upon his . . . hard consent** to his desire I
gave my reluctant consent ⁶⁴ **cousin** kinsman
⁶⁵ **kind** (pun on the meanings "kindly" and "natural"; though doubly related—*more than kin*—
Hamlet asserts that he neither resembles
Claudius in nature nor feels kindly toward him)
⁶⁷ **sun** sunshine of royal favor (with a pun on
"son") ⁷⁰ **vailèd** lowered ⁷⁴ **common** (1) universal, (2) vulgar

⁷⁹ **windy suspiration** heavy sighing ⁹² **obsequi-
ous** suitable to obsequies (funerals) ⁹³ **condole-
ment** mourning ⁹⁹ **vulgar** common

From the first corse° till he that died
105   today,
"This must be so." We pray you throw to
    earth
This unprevailing° woe, and think of us
As of a father, for let the world take note
You are the most immediate to our throne,
110 And with no less nobility of love
Than that which dearest father bears his
    son
Do I impart toward you. For your intent
In going back to school in Wittenberg,
It is most retrograde° to our desire,
115 And we beseech you, bend you° to remain
Here in the cheer and comfort of our eye,
Our chiefest courtier, cousin, and our son.
    QUEEN. Let not thy mother lose her
        prayers, Hamlet.
I pray thee stay with us, go not to Witten-
    berg.
    HAMLET. I shall in all my best obey you,
120   madam.
    KING. Why, 'tis a loving and a fair reply.
Be as ourself in Denmark. Madam, come.
This gentle and unforced accord of Hamlet
Sits smiling to my heart, in grace whereof
No jocund health that Denmark drinks
125   today,
But the great cannon to the clouds shall
    tell,
And the King's rouse° the heaven shall
    bruit° again,
Respeaking earthly thunder. Come away.

Flourish. Exeunt all but HAMLET.

    HAMLET. O that this too too sullied°
        flesh would melt,
130
Thaw, and resolve itself into a dew,
Or that the Everlasting had not fixed
His canon° 'gainst self-slaughter. O God,
    God,
How weary, stale, flat, and unprofitable

Seem to me all the uses of this world!
Fie on't, ah, fie, 'tis an unweeded garden   135
That grows to seed. Things rank and
    gross in nature
Possess it merely.° That it should come to
    this:
But two months dead, nay, not so much,
    not two,
So excellent a king, that was to this
Hyperion° to a satyr, so loving to my
    mother   140
That he might not beteem° the winds of
    heaven
Visit her face too roughly. Heaven and
    earth,
Must I remember? Why, she would hang
    on him
As if increase of appetite had grown
By what it fed on; and yet within a
    month—   145
Let me not think on't; frailty, thy name is
    woman—
A little month, or ere those shoes were
    old
With which she followed my poor father's
    body
Like Niobe,° all tears, why she, even
    she—
O God, a beast that wants discourse of
    reason°   150
Would have mourned longer—married with
    my uncle,
My father's brother, but no more like my
    father
Than I to Hercules. Within a month,
Ere yet the salt of most unrighteous tears
Had left the flushing° in her gallèd eyes,   155
She married. O, most wicked speed, to
    post°
With such dexterity to incestuous° sheets!
It is not, nor it cannot come to good.

---

105 **corse** corpse 107 **unprevailing** unavailing
114 **retrograde** contrary 115 **bend you** incline
127 **rouse** deep drink 127 **bruit** announce noisily
129 **sullied** (Q2 has *sallied*, here modernized to
sullied, which makes sense and is therefore
given; but the Folio reading, *solid*, which fits better with *melt*, is quite possibly correct) 132 **canon**
law

137 **merely** entirely 140 **Hyperion** the sun god, a
model of beauty 141 **beteem** allow 149 **Niobe** (a
mother who wept profusely at the death of her
children) 150 **wants discourse of reason** lacks
reasoning power 155 **left the flushing** stopped
reddening 156 **post** hasten 157 **incestuous** (canon
law considered marriage with a deceased brother's widow to be incestuous)

But break my heart, for I must hold my
    tongue.

Enter HORATIO, MARCELLUS, *and* BAR-
NARDO.

    HORATIO. Hail to your lordship!
160   HAMLET.   I am glad to see you well.
Horatio—or I do forget myself.
    HORATIO. The same, my lord, and your
    poor servant ever.
    HAMLET. Sir, my good friend, I'll
    change° that name with you.
And what make you from Wittenberg,
165   Horatio? Marcellus.
    MARCELLUS. My good lord!
    HAMLET. I am very glad to see you *[To*
    BARNARDO.*]* Good even, sir.
But what, in faith, make you from Witten-
    berg?
    HORATIO. A truant disposition, good my
    lord.
    HAMLET. I would not hear your enemy
170   say so,
Nor shall you do my ear that violence
To make it truster° of your own report
Against yourself. I know you are no tru-
    ant.
But what is your affair in Elsinore?
We'll teach you to drink deep ere you
175   depart.
    HORATIO. My lord, I came to see your
    father's funeral.
    HAMLET. I prithee do not mock me,
    fellow student.
I think it was to see my mother's wedding.
    HORATIO. Indeed, my lord, it followed
    hard upon.
    HAMLET. Thrift, thrift, Horatio. The
180   funeral baked meats
Did coldly furnish forth the marriage ta-
    bles.
Would I had met my dearest° foe in
    heaven
Or ever I had seen that day, Horatio!
My father, methinks I see my father.
    HORATIO. Where, my lord?
185   HAMLET.   In my mind's eye, Horatio.

    HORATIO. I saw him once. 'A° was a
    goodly king.
    HAMLET. 'A was a man, take him for all
    in all,
I shall not look upon his like again.
    HORATIO. My lord, I think I saw him
    yesternight.
    HAMLET. Saw? Who?   190
    HORATIO. My lord, the King your father.
    HAMLET.   The King my father?
    HORATIO. Season your admiration° for a
    while
With an attent ear till I may deliver
Upon the witness of these gentlemen
This marvel to you.
    HAMLET.   For God's love let me hear!   195
    HORATIO. Two nights together had these
    gentlemen,
Marcellus and Barnardo, on their watch
In the dead waste and middle of the night
Been thus encountered. A figure like your
    father,
Armèd at point exactly, cap-a-pe,°   200
Appears before them, and with solemn
    march
Goes slow and stately by them. Thrice he
    walked
By their oppressed and fear-surprisèd
    eyes,
Within his truncheon's length,° whilst they,
    distilled°
Almost to jelly with the act° of fear,   205
Stand dumb and speak not to him. This to
    me
In dreadful° secrecy impart they did,
And I with them the third night kept the
    watch,
Where, as they had delivered, both in
    time,
Form of the thing, each word made true
    and good,   210
The apparition comes. I knew your father.
These hands are not more like.
    HAMLET.   But where was this?

---

163 **change** exchange 172 **truster** believer
182 **dearest** most intensely felt

186 **'A** he 192 **Season your admiration** control
your wonder 200 **cap-a-pe** head to foot 204 **truncheon's length** space of a short staff 204 **distilled** reduced 205 **act** action 207 **dreadful**
terrified

MARCELLUS. My lord, upon the platform
    where we watched.
HAMLET. Did you not speak to it?
HORATIO.   My lord, I did;
But answer made it none. Yet once me-
215   thought
It lifted up it° head and did address
Itself to motion like as it would speak:
But even then the morning cock crew
    loud,
And at the sound it shrunk in haste away
And vanished from our sight.
220   HAMLET.   'Tis very strange.
HORATIO. As I do live, my honored lord,
    'tis true,
And we did think it writ down in our duty
To let you know of it.
    HAMLET. Indeed, indeed, sirs, but this
        troubles me.
Hold you the watch tonight?
225   ALL.   We do, my lord.
HAMLET. Armed, say you?
ALL. Armed, my lord.
HAMLET. From top to toe?
ALL.   My lord, from head to foot.
HAMLET. Then saw you not his face.
HORATIO. O, yes, my lord. He wore his
230   beaver° up.
HAMLET. What, looked he frowningly?
HORATIO. A countenance more in sorrow
    than in anger.
HAMLET. Pale or red?
HORATIO. Nay, very pale.
HAMLET.   And fixed his eyes upon you?
HORATIO. Most constantly.
235   HAMLET.   I would I had been there.
HORATIO. It would have much amazed
    you.
HAMLET. Very like, very like. Stayed it
    long?
HORATIO. While one with moderate
    haste might tell° a hundred.
BOTH. Longer, longer.
HORATIO. Not when I saw't.
240   HAMLET.   His beard was grizzled,° no?
HORATIO. It was as I have seen it in his
    life,

A sable silvered.°
    HAMLET.   I will watch tonight.
Perchance 'twill walk again.
    HORATIO.   I warr'nt it will.
    HAMLET. If it assume my noble father's
        person,
I'll speak to it though hell itself should
    gape   245
And bid me hold my peace. I pray you all,
If you have hitherto concealed this sight,
Let it be tenable° in your silence still,
And whatsomever else shall hap tonight,
Give it an understanding but no tongue;   250
I will requite your loves. So fare you well.
Upon the platform 'twixt eleven and
    twelve
I'll visit you.
    ALL.   Our duty to your honor.
    HAMLET. Your loves, as mine to you.
        Farewell.   *Exeunt [all but* HAMLET*].*
My father's spirit—in arms? All is not
    well.   255
I doubt° some foul play. Would the night
    were come!
Till then sit still, my soul. Foul deeds will
    rise,
Though all the earth o'erwhelm them, to
    men's eyes.   *Exit.*

[Scene III. A room.]

Enter LAERTES *and* OPHELIA, *his sister.*

    LAERTES. My necessaries are em-
        barked. Farewell.
And, sister, as the winds give benefit
And convoy° is assistant, do not sleep,
But let me hear from you.
    OPHELIA.   Do you doubt that?
    LAERTES. For Hamlet, and the trifling of
        his favor,   5
Hold it a fashion and a toy° in blood,
A violet in the youth of primy° nature,
Forward,° not permanent, sweet, not
    lasting,

---

²¹⁶ **it** its ²³⁰ **beaver** visor, face guard ²³⁸ **tell** count
²⁴⁰ **grizzled** gray

²⁴² **sable silvered** black mingled with white
²⁴⁸ **tenable** held ²⁵⁶ **doubt** suspect I.iii. ³ **convoy**
conveyance ⁶ **toy** idle fancy ⁷ **primy** springlike
⁸ **Forward** premature

The perfume and suppliance° of a minute,
No more.
    OPHELIA. No more but so?
10   LAERTES.   Think it no more.
For nature crescent° does not grow alone
In thews° and bulk, but as this temple°
    waxes,
The inward service of the mind and soul
Grows wide withal. Perhaps he loves you
    now,
15 And now no soil nor cautel° doth besmirch
The virtue of his will; but you must fear,
His greatness weighed,° his will is not his
    own.
For he himself is subject to his birth.
He may not, as unvalued° persons do,
Carve for himself; for on his choice de-
20   pends
The safety and health of this whole state;
And therefore must his choice be circum-
    scribed
Unto the voice and yielding of that body
Whereof he is the head. Then if he says
    he loves you,
25 It fits your wisdom so far to believe it
As he in his particular act and place
May give his saying deed, which is no
    further
Than the main voice of Denmark goes
    withal.
Then weigh what loss your honor may
    sustain
30 If with too credent° ear you list his songs,
Or lose your heart, or your chaste trea-
    sure open
To his unmastered importunity.
Fear it, Ophelia, fear it, my dear sister,
And keep you in the rear of your affection,
35 Out of the shot and danger of desire.
The chariest maid is prodigal enough
If she unmask her beauty to the moon.
Virtue itself scapes not calumnious
    strokes.
The canker° galls the infants of the spring

Too oft before their buttons° be disclosed,   40
And in the morn and liquid dew of youth
Contagious blastments are most imminent.
Be wary then; best safety lies in fear;
Youth to itself rebels, though none else
    near.
    OPHELIA. I shall the effect of this good
    lesson keep   45
As watchman to my heart, but, good my
    brother,
Do not, as some ungracious° pastors do,
Show me the steep and thorny way to
    heaven,
Whiles, like a puffed and reckless liber-
    tine,
Himself the primrose path of dalliance
    treads   50
And recks not his own rede.°

Enter POLONIUS.

    LAERTES.   O, fear me not.
I stay too long. But here my father comes.
A double blessing is a double grace;
Occasion smiles upon a second leave.
    POLONIUS. Yet here, Laertes? Aboard,
    aboard, for shame!   55
The wind sits in the shoulder of your sail,
And you are stayed for. There—my bless-
    ing with thee,
And these few precepts in thy memory
Look thou character.° Give thy thoughts
    no tongue,
Nor any unproportioned° thought his act.   60
Be thou familiar, but by no means vulgar.
Those friends thou hast, and their adop-
    tion tried,
Grapple them unto thy soul with hoops of
    steel,
But do not dull thy palm with entertain-
    ment
Of each new-hatched, unfledged courage.°
    Beware   65
Of entrance to a quarrel; but being in,
Bear't that th' opposèd may beware of
    thee.

---

⁹ **suppliance** diversion ¹¹ **crescent** growing
¹² **thews** muscles and sinews ¹² **temple** i.e., the
body ¹⁵ **cautel** deceit ¹⁷ **greatness weighed**
high rank considered ¹⁹ **unvalued** of low rank
³⁰ **credent** credulous ³⁹ **canker** cankerworm

⁴⁰ **buttons** buds ⁴⁷ **ungracious** lacking grace
⁵² **recks not his own rede** does not heed his
own advice ⁵⁹ **character** inscribe ⁶⁰ **unpropor-
tioned** unbalanced ⁶⁵ **courage** gallant youth

Give every man thine ear, but few thy
  voice;
Take each man's censure,° but reserve thy
  judgment.
70 Costly thy habits as thy purse can buy,
But not expressed in fancy; rich, not
  gaudy,
For the apparel oft proclaims the man,
And they in France of the best rank and
  station
Are of a most select and generous, chief
  in that.°
75 Neither a borrower nor a lender be,
For loan oft loses both itself and friend,
And borrowing dulleth edge of husbandry.°
This above all, to thine own self be true,
And it must follow, as the night the day,
80 Thou canst not then be false to any man.
Farewell. My blessing season this° in
  thee!
  LAERTES. Most humbly do I take my
  leave, my lord.
  POLONIUS. The time invites you. Go,
  your servants tend.°
  LAERTES. Farewell, Ophelia, and re-
  member well
What I have said to you.
85   OPHELIA.   'Tis in my memory locked,
And you yourself shall keep the key of it.
  LAERTES. Farewell.   *Exit* LAERTES.
  POLONIUS. What is't, Ophelia, he hath
  said to you?
  OPHELIA. So please you, something
  touching the Lord Hamlet.
90   POLONIUS. Marry,° well bethought.
'Tis told me he hath very oft of late
Given private time to you, and you your-
  self
Have of your audience been most free and
  bounteous.
If it be so—as so 'tis put on me,
95 And that in way of caution—I must tell you
You do not understand yourself so clearly

As it behooves my daughter and your
  honor.
What is between you? Give me up the
  truth.
  OPHELIA. He hath, my lord, of late made
  many tenders°
Of his affection to me.   100
  POLONIUS. Affection pooh! You speak
  like a green girl,
Unsifted° in such perilous circumstance.
Do you believe his tenders, as you call
  them?
  OPHELIA. I do not know, my lord, what I
  should think.
  POLONIUS. Marry, I will teach you.
  Think yourself a baby   105
That you have ta'en these tenders for true
  pay
Which are not sterling. Tender yourself
  more dearly,
Or (not to crack the wind of the poor
  phrase)
Tend'ring it thus you'll tender me a fool.°
  OPHELIA. My lord, he hath importuned
  me with love   110
In honorable fashion.
  POLONIUS. Ay, fashion you may call it.
  Go to, go to.
  OPHELIA. And hath given countenance to
  his speech, my lord,
With almost all the holy vows of heaven.
  POLONIUS. Ay, springes to catch wood-
  cocks.° I do know,   115
When the blood burns, how prodigal the
  soul
Lends the tongue vows. These blazes,
  daughter,
Giving more light than heat, extinct in
  both,
Even in their promise, as it is a-making,
You must not take for fire. From this time   120

---

⁶⁹ **censure** opinion ⁷⁴ **Are of . . . in that** show their fine taste and their gentlemanly instincts more in that than in any other point of manners (Kittredge) ⁷⁷ **husbandry** thrift ⁸¹ **season this** make fruitful this (advice) ⁸³ **tend** attend ⁹⁰ **Marry** (a light oath, from "By the Virgin Mary") ⁹⁹ **tenders** offers (in line 103 it has the same meaning, but in line 106 Polonius speaks of *tenders* in the sense of counters or chips; in line 109 *Tend'ring* means "holding," and *tender* means "give," "present") ¹⁰² **Unsifted** untried ¹⁰⁸ **tender me a fool** (1) present me with a fool, (2) present me with a baby ¹¹⁵ **springes to catch woodcocks** snares to catch stupid birds

Be something scanter of your maiden
    presence.
Set your entreatments° at a higher rate
Than a command to parley. For Lord
    Hamlet,
Believe so much in him that he is young,
125 And with a larger tether may he walk
Than may be given you. In few, Ophelia,
Do not believe his vows, for they are
    brokers,°
Not of that dye° which their investments°
    show,
But mere implorators° of unholy suits,
130 Breathing like sanctified and pious bonds,°
The better to beguile. This is for all:
I would not, in plain terms, from this time
    forth
Have you so slander° any moment leisure
As to give words or talk with the Lord
    Hamlet.
135 Look to't, I charge you. Come your ways.
    OPHELIA. I shall obey, my lord.   *Exeunt.*

[Scene IV. A guard platform.]

Enter HAMLET, HORATIO, *and* MARCELLUS.

    HAMLET. The air bites shrewdly;° it is
    very cold.
    HORATIO. It is a nipping and an eager°
    air.
    HAMLET. What hour now?
    HORATIO.   I think it lacks of twelve.
    MARCELLUS. No, it is struck.
    HORATIO. Indeed? I heard it not. It then
5   draws near the season
Wherein the spirit held his wont to walk.

A flourish of trumpets, and two pieces go off.

What does this mean, my lord?
    HAMLET. The King doth wake° tonight
    and takes his rouse,°
Keeps wassail, and the swagg'ring up-
    spring° reels,

And as he drains his draughts of Rhenish°
    down   10
The kettledrum and trumpet thus bray out
The triumph of his pledge.°
    HORATIO.   Is it a custom?
    HAMLET. Ay, marry, is't,
But to my mind, though I am native here
And to the manner born, it is a custom   15
More honored in the breach than the
    observance.
This heavy-headed revel east and west
Makes us traduced and taxed of° other
    nations.
They clepe° us drunkards and with swin-
    ish phrase
Soil our addition,° and indeed it takes   20
From our achievements, though performed
    at height,
The pith and marrow of our attribute.°
So oft it chances in particular men
That for some vicious mole° of nature in
    them,
As in their birth, wherein they are not
    guilty,   25
(Since nature cannot choose his origin)
By the o'ergrowth of some complexion,°
Oft breaking down the pales° and forts of
    reason,
Or by some habit that too much o'er-
    leavens°
The form of plausive° manners, that
    (these men,   30
Carrying, I say, the stamp of one defect,
Being nature's livery, or fortune's star°)
Their virtues else, be they as pure as
    grace,
As infinite as man may undergo,
Shall in the general censure° take corrup-
    tion   35

---

¹²² **entreatments** interviews ¹²⁷ **brokers** procur-
ers ¹²⁸ **dye** i.e., kind ¹²⁸ **investments** garments
¹²⁹ **implorators** solicitors ¹³⁰ **bonds** pledges
¹³³ **slander** disgrace I.iv ¹ **shrewdly** bitterly
² **eager** sharp ⁸ **wake** hold a revel by night
⁸ **takes his rouse** carouses ⁹ **upspring** (a
dance)

¹⁰ **Rhenish** Rhine wine ¹² **The triumph of his
pledge** the achievement (of drinking a wine cup
in one draught) of his toast ¹⁸ **taxed of** blamed by
¹⁹ **clepe** call ²⁰ **addition** reputation (literally, "title of honor") ²² **attribute** reputation ²⁴ **mole**
blemish ²⁷ **complexion** natural disposition
²⁸ **pales** enclosures ²⁹ **o'erleavens** mixes with,
corrupts ³⁰ **plausive** pleasing ³² **nature's livery, or fortune's star** nature's equipment (i.e.,
"innate"), or a person's destiny determined by
the stars ³⁵ **general censure** popular judgment

From that particular fault. The dram of
evil
Doth all the noble substance of a doubt,
To his own scandal.°

Enter GHOST.

HORATIO.   Look, my lord, it comes.
HAMLET. Angels and ministers of grace
defend us!
Be thou a spirit of health° or goblin
40   damned,
Bring with thee airs from heaven or blasts
from hell,
Be thy intents wicked or charitable,
Thou com'st in such a questionable° shape
That I will speak to thee. I'll call thee
Hamlet,
45   King, father, royal Dane. O, answer me!
Let me not burst in ignorance, but tell
Why thy canonized° bones, hearsèd in
death,
Have burst their cerements,° why the
sepulcher
Wherein we saw thee quietly interred
50   Hath oped his ponderous and marble jaws
To cast thee up again. What may this
mean
That thou, dead corse, again in complete
steel,
Revisits thus the glimpses of the moon,
Making night hideous, and we fools of
nature
55   So horridly to shake our disposition°
With thoughts beyond the reaches of our
souls?
Say, why is this? Wherefore? What should
we do?

GHOST *beckons* HAMLET.

HORATIO. It beckons you to go away
with it,

As if it some impartment° did desire
To you alone.
MARCELLUS.   Look with what courteous
action   60
It waves you to a more removèd ground.
But do not go with it.
HORATIO.   No, by no means.
HAMLET. It will not speak. Then I will
follow it.
HORATIO. Do not, my lord.
HAMLET.   Why, what should be the fear?
I do not set my life at a pin's fee,   65
And for my soul, what can it do to that,
Being a thing immortal as itself?
It waves me forth again. I'll follow it.
HORATIO. What if it tempt you toward
the flood, my lord,
Or to the dreadful summit of the cliff   70
That beetles° o'er his base into the sea,
And there assume some other horrible
form,
Which might deprive your sovereignty of
reason°
And draw you into madness? Think of it.
The very place puts toys° of desperation,   75
Without more motive, into every brain
That looks so many fathoms to the sea
And hears it roar beneath.
HAMLET.   It waves me still.
Go on; I'll follow thee.
MARCELLUS. You shall not go, my lord.
HAMLET.   Hold off your hands.   80
HORATIO. Be ruled. You shall not go.
HAMLET.   My fate cries out
And makes each petty artere° in this body
As hardy as the Nemean lion's nerve.°
Still am I called! Unhand me, gentlemen.
By heaven, I'll make a ghost of him that
lets° me!   85
I say, away! Go on. I'll follow thee.
              Exit GHOST, *and* HAMLET.
HORATIO. He waxes desperate with
imagination.

---

³⁶⁻³⁸ **The dram . . . own scandal** (though the
drift is clear, there is no agreement as to the
exact meaning of these lines) ⁴⁰ **spirit of health**
good spirit ⁴³ **questionable** (1) capable of discourse, (2) dubious ⁴⁷ **canonized** buried according to the canon or ordinance of the church
⁴⁸ **cerements** waxed linen shroud ⁵⁵ **shake our
disposition** disturb us

⁵⁹ **impartment** communication ⁷¹ **beetles** juts
out ⁷³ **deprive your sovereignty of reason**
destroy the sovereignty of your reason ⁷⁵ **toys**
whims, fancies ⁸² **artere** artery ⁸³ **Nemean lion's nerve** sinews of the mythical lion slain by
Hercules ⁸⁵ **lets** hinders

MARCELLUS. Let's follow. 'Tis not fit
  thus to obey him.
HORATIO. Have after! To what issue will
  this come?
MARCELLUS. Something is rotten in the
90 state of Denmark.
HORATIO. Heaven will direct it.
MARCELLUS. Nay, let's follow him.
                              Exeunt.

[Scene V. *The battlements.]*

Enter GHOST *and* HAMLET.

HAMLET. Whither wilt thou lead me?
  Speak; I'll go no further.
GHOST. Mark me.
HAMLET.   I will.
GHOST.   My hour is almost come,
When I to sulf'rous and tormenting flames
Must render up myself.
HAMLET.   Alas, poor ghost.
GHOST. Pity me not, but lend thy seri-
5   ous hearing
To what I shall unfold.
HAMLET.   Speak. I am bound to hear.
GHOST. So art thou to revenge, when
  thou shalt hear.
HAMLET. What?
GHOST. I am thy father's spirit,
Doomed for a certain term to walk the
10   night,
And for the day confined to fast in fires,
Till the foul crimes° done in my days of
  nature
Are burnt and purged away. But that I am
  forbid
To tell the secrets of my prison house,
15 I could a tale unfold whose lightest word
Would harrow up thy soul, freeze thy
  young blood,
Make thy two eyes like stars start from
  their spheres,°
Thy knotted and combinèd locks to part,
And each particular hair to stand on end
20 Like quills upon the fearful porpentine.°

But this eternal blazon° must not be
To ears of flesh and blood. List, list, O,
  list!
If thou didst ever thy dear father love——
HAMLET. O God!
GHOST. Revenge his foul and most un-
  natural murder.   25
HAMLET. Murder?
GHOST. Murder most foul, as in the best
  it is,
But this most foul, strange, and unnatural.
HAMLET. Haste me to know't, that I,
  with wings as swift
As meditation° or the thoughts of love,   30
May sweep to my revenge.
GHOST.   I find thee apt,
And duller shouldst thou be than the fat
  weed
That roots itself in ease on Lethe wharf,°
Wouldst thou not stir in this. Now, Ham-
  let, hear.
'Tis given out that, sleeping in my or-
  chard,   35
A serpent stung me. So the whole ear of
  Denmark
Is by a forgèd process° of my death
Rankly abused. But know, thou noble
  youth,
The serpent that did sting thy father's life
Now wears his crown.
HAMLET.   O my prophetic soul! 40
My uncle?
GHOST. Ay, that incestuous, that adulter-
  ate° beast,
With witchcraft of his wits, with traitorous
  gifts—
O wicked wit and gifts, that have the
  power
So to seduce!—won to his shameful lust 45
The will of my most seeming-virtuous
  queen.
O Hamlet, what a falling-off was there,
From me, whose love was of that dignity
That it went hand in hand even with the
  vow

I.v. ¹² **crimes** sins ¹⁷ **spheres** (in Ptolemaic astronomy, each planet was fixed in a hollow transparent shell concentric with the earth) ²⁰ **fearful porpentine** timid porcupine

²¹ **eternal blazon** revelation of eternity ³⁰ **meditation** thought ³³ **Lethe wharf** bank of the river of forgetfulness in Hades ³⁷ **forged process** false account ⁴² **adulterate** adulterous

50 I made to her in marriage, and to decline
Upon a wretch whose natural gifts were
    poor
To those of mine.
But virtue, as it never will be moved,
Though lewdness° court it in a shape of
    heaven,
55 So lust, though to a radiant angel linked,
Will sate itself in a celestial bed
And prey on garbage.
But soft, methinks I scent the morning
    air;
Brief let me be. Sleeping within my or-
    chard,
60 My custom always of the afternoon,
Upon my secure hour thy uncle stole
With juice of cursed hebona° in a vial,
And in the porches of my ears did pour
The leperous distillment, whose effect
65 Holds such an enmity with blood of man
That swift as quicksilver it courses
    through
The natural gates and alleys of the body,
And with a sudden vigor it doth posset°
And curd, like eager° droppings into milk,
The thin and wholesome blood. So did it
70   mine,
And a most instant tetter° barked about
Most lazarlike° with vile and loathsome
    crust
All my smooth body.
Thus was I, sleeping, by a brother's hand
Of life, of crown, of queen at once dis-
75   patched,
Cut off even in the blossoms of my sin,
Unhouseled, disappointed, unaneled,°
No reck'ning made, but sent to my ac-
    count
With all my imperfections on my head.
80 O, horrible! O, horrible! Most horrible!
If thou hast nature in thee, bear it not.
Let not the royal bed of Denmark be
A couch for luxury° and damnèd incest.

But howsomever thou pursues this act,
Taint not thy mind, nor let thy soul con-
    trive   85
Against thy mother aught. Leave her to
    heaven
And to those thorns that in her bosom
    lodge
To prick and sting her. Fare thee well at
    once.
The glowworm shows the matin° to be
    near
And 'gins to pale his uneffectual fire.   90
Adieu, adieu, adieu. Remember me. *Exit.*
  HAMLET. O all you host of heaven! O
    earth! What else?
And shall I couple hell? O fie! Hold, hold,
    my heart,
And you, my sinews, grow not instant old,
But bear me stiffly up. Remember thee?   95
Ay, thou poor ghost, whiles memory holds
    a seat
In this distracted globe.° Remember thee?
Yea, from the table° of my memory
I'll wipe away all trivial fond° records,
All saws° of books, all forms, all pres-
    sures° past   100
That youth and observation copied there,
And thy commandment all alone shall live
Within the book and volume of my brain,
Unmixed with baser matter. Yes, by
    heaven!
O most pernicious woman!   105
O villain, villain, smiling, damnèd villain!
My tables—meet it is I set it down
That one may smile, and smile, and be a
    villain.
At least I am sure it may be so in Den-
    mark. *[Writes.]*
So, uncle, there you are. Now to my
    word: 110
It is "Adieu, adieu, remember me."
I have sworn't.
  HORATIO and MARCELLUS *(within).* My lord,
    my lord!

Enter HORATIO *and* MARCELLUS.

---

⁵⁴ **lewdness** lust ⁶¹ **secure** unsuspecting ⁶² **he-
bona** a poisonous plant ⁶⁸ **posset** curdle ⁶⁹ **eager** acid ⁷¹ **tetter** scab ⁷² **lazarlike** leperlike
⁷⁷ **Unhouseled, disappointed, unaneled**
without the sacrament of communion, unab-
solved, without extreme unction ⁸³ **luxury** lust

⁸⁹ **matin** morning ⁹⁷ **globe** i.e., his head ⁹⁸ **table**
tablet, notebook ⁹⁹ **fond** foolish ¹⁰⁰ **saws** maxims
¹⁰⁰ **pressures** impressions

MARCELLUS. Lord Hamlet!

HORATIO.   Heavens secure him!

HAMLET. So be it!

115   MARCELLUS. Illo, ho, ho,° my lord!

HAMLET. Hillo, ho, ho, boy! Come, bird,
    come.

MARCELLUS. How is't, my noble lord?

HORATIO.   What news, my lord?

HAMLET. O, wonderful!

HORATIO. Good my lord, tell it.

HAMLET.   No, you will reveal it.

HORATIO. Not I, my lord, by heaven.

120   MARCELLUS.   Nor I, my lord.

HAMLET. How say you then? Would
    heart of man once think it?

But you'll be secret?

BOTH.   Ay, by heaven, my lord.

HAMLET. There's never a villain dwelling
    in all Denmark

But he's an arrant knave.

HORATIO. There needs no ghost, my

125   lord, come from the grave

To tell us this.

HAMLET. Why, right, you are in the right;

And so, without more circumstance° at all,

I hold it fit that we shake hands and part:

You, as your business and desire shall
    point you,

130   For every man hath business and desire

Such as it is, and for my own poor part,

Look you, I'll go pray.

HORATIO. These are but wild and whirl-
    ing words, my lord.

HAMLET. I am sorry they offend you,
    heartily;

Yes, faith, heartily.

135   HORATIO.   There's no offense, my lord.

HAMLET. Yes, by Saint Patrick, but there
    is, Horatio,

And much offense too. Touching this vi-
    sion here,

It is an honest ghost,° that let me tell
    you.

For your desire to know what is between
    us,

O'ermaster't as you may. And now, good
    friends,   140

As you are friends, scholars, and soldiers,

Give me one poor request.

HORATIO. What is't, my lord? We will.

HAMLET. Never make known what you
    have seen tonight.

BOTH. My lord, we will not.

HAMLET.   Nay, but swear't.

HORATIO.   In faith,   145

My lord, not I.

MARCELLUS. Nor I, my lord—in faith.

HAMLET. Upon my sword.

MARCELLUS.   We have sworn, my lord,
    already.

HAMLET. Indeed, upon my sword, in-
    deed.

GHOST *cries under the stage.*

GHOST. Swear.

HAMLET. Ha, ha, boy, say'st thou so?
    Art thou there, truepenny?°   150

Come on. You hear this fellow in the cel-
    larage.

Consent to swear.

HORATIO.   Propose the oath, my lord.

HAMLET. Never to speak of this that you
    have seen.

Swear by my sword.

GHOST *[beneath].* Swear.   155

HAMLET. *Hic et ubique?*° Then we'll shift
    our ground;

Come hither, gentlemen,

And lay your hands again upon my sword.

Swear by my sword

Never to speak of this that you have
    heard.   160

GHOST *[beneath].* Swear by his sword.

HAMLET. Well said, old mole! Canst
    work i' th' earth so fast?

A worthy pioner!° Once more remove,
    good friends.

HORATIO. O day and night, but this is
    wondrous strange!

HAMLET. And therefore as a stranger
    give it welcome.   165

---

¹¹⁵ **Illo, ho, ho** (falconer's call to his hawk)
¹²⁷ **circumstance** details ¹²⁸ **honest ghost** i.e.,
not a demon in his father's shape

¹⁵⁰ **truepenny** honest fellow ¹⁵⁶ **Hic et ubique**
here and everywhere (Latin) ¹⁶³ **pioner** digger of
mines

There are more things in heaven and
    earth, Horatio,
Than are dreamt of in your philosophy.
But come:
Here as before, never, so help you mercy,
170 How strange or odd some'er I bear myself
(As I perchance hereafter shall think meet
To put an antic disposition° on),
That you, at such times seeing me, never
    shall
With arms encumb'red° thus, or this
    headshake,
Or by pronouncing of some doubtful
175   phrase,
As "Well, well, we know," or "We could,
    an if we would,"
Or "If we list to speak," or "There be, an
    if they might,"
Or such ambiguous giving out, to note
That you know aught of me—this do
    swear,
So grace and mercy at your most need
180   help you.
    GHOST *[beneath]*. Swear.

[They swear.]

    HAMLET. Rest, rest, perturbèd spirit.
    So, gentlemen,
With all my love I do commend me° to
    you,
And what so poor a man as Hamlet is
May do t' express his love and friending to
185   you,
God willing, shall not lack. Let us go in
    together,
And still your fingers on your lips, I pray.
The time is out of joint. O cursèd spite,
That ever I was born to set it right!
190 Nay, come, let's go together.   *Exeunt.*

*[*ACT II

Scene I. A room.]

Enter old POLONIUS, *with his man* REY-
NALDO.

POLONIUS. Give him this money and
    these notes, Reynaldo.
REYNALDO. I will, my lord.
POLONIUS. You shall do marvell's°
    wisely, good Reynaldo,
Before you visit him, to make inquire
Of his behavior.
    REYNALDO.   My lord, I did intend it.   5
POLONIUS. Marry, well said, very well
    said. Look you sir,
Inquire me first what Danskers° are in
    Paris,
And how, and who, what means, and
    where they keep,°
What company, at what expense; and
    finding
By this encompassment° and drift of ques-
    tion   10
That they do know my son, come you
    more nearer
Than your particular demands° will touch
    it.
Take you as 'twere some distant knowl-
    edge of him,
As thus, "I know his father and his
    friends,
And in part him." Do you mark this, Rey-
    naldo?   15
    REYNALDO. Ay, very well, my lord.
POLONIUS. "And in part him, but," you
    may say, "not well,
But if 't be he I mean, he's very wild,
Addicted so and so." And there put on him
What forgeries° you please; marry, none
    so rank   20
As may dishonor him—take heed of that—
But, sir, such wanton, wild, and usual slips
As are companions noted and most known
To youth and liberty.
    REYNALDO.   As gaming, my lord.
POLONIUS. Ay, or drinking, fencing,
    swearing, quarreling,   25
Drabbing.° You may go so far.
    REYNALDO. My lord, that would dis-
    honor him.

---

172 **antic disposition** fantastic behavior 174 **encumb'red** folded 183 **commend me** entrust myself

II.i. 3 **marvell's** marvelous(ly) 7 **Danskers**
Danes 8 **keep** dwell 10 **encompassment** circling
12 **demands** questions 20 **forgeries** inventions
26 **Drabbing** wenching

POLONIUS. Faith, no, as you may season
   it in the charge.
You must not put another scandal on him,
30 That he is open to incontinency.°
That's not my meaning. But breathe his
   faults so quaintly°
That they may seem the taints of liberty,
The flash and outbreak of a fiery mind,
A savageness in unreclaimèd blood,
Of general assault.°
35 REYNALDO.   But, my good lord——
POLONIUS. Wherefore should you do
   this?
REYNALDO.   Ay, my lord,
I would know that.
   POLONIUS.   Marry, sir, here's my drift,
And I believe it is a fetch of warrant.°
You laying these slight sullies on my son
As 'twere a thing a little soiled i' th' work-
40   ing,
Mark you,
Your party in converse, him you would
   sound,
Having ever seen in the prenominate
   crimes°
The youth you breathe of guilty, be as-
   sured
45 He closes with you in this consequence:
"Good sir," or so, or "friend," or
   "gentleman"—
According to the phrase or the addition°
Of man and country—
   REYNALDO.   Very good, my lord.
   POLONIUS. And then, sir, does 'a° this—
   'a does—
50   What was I about to say? By the mass, I
was about to say something! Where did I
leave?
   REYNALDO. At "closes in the consequence," at "friend or so," and "gentlemen."
   POLONIUS. At "closes in the consequence"—Ay, marry!
55

He closes thus: "I know the gentleman;
I saw him yesterday, or t'other day,
Or then, or then, with such or such, and,
   as you say,
There was 'a gaming, there o'ertook in's
   rouse,
There falling out at tennis"; or perchance,   60
"I saw him enter such a house of sale,"
Videlicet,° a brothel, or so forth.
See you now—
Your bait of falsehood take this carp of
   truth,
And thus do we of wisdom and of reach,°   65
With windlasses° and with assays of bias,°
By indirections find directions out.
So, by my former lecture and advice,
Shall you my son. You have me, have you
   not?
REYNALDO. My lord, I have.
POLONIUS.   God bye ye, fare ye well.   70
REYNALDO. Good my lord.
POLONIUS. Observe his inclination in
   yourself.°
REYNALDO. I shall, my lord.
POLONIUS. And let him ply his music.
REYNALDO.   Well, my lord.
POLONIUS. Farewell.   *Exit* REYNALDO.

Enter OPHELIA.

   How now, Ophelia, what's the matter?   75
OPHELIA. O my lord, my lord, I have
   been so affrighted!
POLONIUS. With what, i' th' name of
   God?
OPHELIA. My lord, as I was sewing in
   my closet,°
Lord Hamlet, with his doublet all un-
   braced,°
No hat upon his head, his stockings
   fouled,   80
Ungartered, and down-gyvèd° to his an-
   kle,

---

[30] **incontinency** habitual licentiousness
[31] **quaintly** ingeniously, delicately [35] **Of general assault** common to all men [38] **fetch of warrant** justifiable device [43] **Having . . . crimes** if he has ever seen in the aforementioned crimes [45] **He closes . . . this consequence** he falls in with you in this conclusion [47] **addition** title [49] **'a** he

[61] **Videlicet** namely [64] **reach** far-reaching awareness (?) [65] **windlasses** circuitous courses [65] **assays of bias** indirect attempts (metaphor from bowling; *bias* = curved course) [71] **in yourself** for yourself [77] **closet** private room [78] **doublet all unbraced** jacket entirely unlaced [90] **downgived** hanging down like fetters

Pale as his shirt, his knees knocking each
    other,
And with a look so piteous in purport,°
As if he had been loosèd out of hell
To speak of horrors—he comes before
85   me.
    POLONIUS. Mad for thy love?
    OPHELIA.   My lord, I do not know,
But truly I do fear it.
    POLONIUS.   What said he?
    OPHELIA. He took me by the wrist and
    held me hard;
Then goes he to the length of all his arm,
And with his other hand thus o'er his
90   brow
He falls to such perusal of my face
As 'a would draw it. Long stayed he so.
At last, a little shaking of mine arm,
And thrice his head thus waving up and
    down,
95 He raised a sigh so piteous and profound
As it did seem to shatter all his bulk
And end his being. That done, he lets me
    go,
And, with his head over his shoulder
    turned,
He seemed to find his way without his
    eyes,
For out o' doors he went without their
100   helps,
And to the last bended their light on me.
    POLONIUS. Come, go with me. I will go
    seek the King.
This is the very ecstasy° of love,
Whose violent property fordoes° itself
And leads the will to desperate undertak-
105   ings
As oft as any passions under heaven
That does afflict our natures. I am sorry.
What, have you given him any hard words
    of late?
    OPHELIA. No, my good lord; but as you
    did command,
110 I did repel his letters and denied
His access to me.

    POLONIUS.   That hath made him mad.
I am sorry that with better heed and
    judgment
I had not quoted° him. I feared he did but
    trifle
And meant to wrack thee; but beshrew
    my jealousy.°
By heaven, it is as proper° to our age   115
To cast beyond ourselves° in our opinions
As it is common for the younger sort
To lack discretion. Come, go we to the
    King.
This must be known, which, being kept
    close, might move
More grief to hide than hate to utter
    love.°   120
Come.   *Exeunt.*

[Scene II. *The castle.*]

Flourish. Enter KING *and* QUEEN, ROSEN-
CRANTZ, *and* GUILDENSTERN *[with others].*

    KING. Welcome, dear Rosencrantz and
    Guildenstern.
Moreover that° we much did long to see
    you,
The need we have to use you did provoke
Our hasty sending. Something have you
    heard
Of Hamlet's transformation: so call it,   5
Sith° nor th' exterior nor the inward man
Resembles that it was. What it should be,
More than his father's death, that thus
    hath put him
So much from th' understanding of himself,
I cannot dream of. I entreat you both
That, being of so° young days brought up   10
    with him,
And sith so neighbored to his youth and
    havior,°

---

¹¹³ **quoted** noted ¹¹⁴ **beshrew my jealousy**
curse on my suspicious ¹¹⁵ **proper** natural ¹¹⁶ **To
cast beyond ourselves** to be overcalculating
¹¹⁸⁻¹²⁰ **Come, go . . . utter love** (the general
meaning is that while telling the King of Hamlet's
love may anger the King, more grief would come
from keeping it secret) II.ii. ² **Moreover that**
beside the fact that ⁶ **Sith** since ¹¹ **of so** from
such ¹² **youth and havior** behavior in his youth

---

⁸³ **purport** expression ¹⁰³ **ecstasy** madness
¹⁰⁴ **property fordoes** quality destroys

That you vouchsafe your rest° here in our
    court
Some little time, so by your companies
To draw him on to pleasures, and to
15   gather
So much as from occasion you may glean,
Whether aught to us unknown afflicts him
    thus,
That opened° lies within our remedy.
    QUEEN. Good gentlemen, he hath much
      talked of you,
20 And sure I am, two men there is not living
To whom he more adheres. If it will
    please you
To show us so much gentry° and good will
As to expend your time with us awhile
For the supply and profit of our hope,
25 Your visitation shall receive such thanks
As fits a king's remembrance.
    ROSENCRANTZ.   Both your Majesties
Might, by the sovereign power you have of
    us,
Put your dread pleasures more into com-
    mand
Than to entreaty.
    GUILDENSTERN. But we both obey,
And here give up ourselves in the full
30   bent°
To lay our service freely at your feet,
To be commanded.
    KING. Thanks, Rosencrantz and gentle
      Guildenstern.
    QUEEN. Thanks, Guildenstern and gen-
      tle Rosencrantz.
35 And I beseech you instantly to visit
My too much changèd son. Go, some of
    you,
And bring these gentlemen where Hamlet
    is.
    GUILDENSTERN. Heavens make our
      presence and our practices
Pleasant and helpful to him!
    QUEEN.   Ay, amen!
Exeunt ROSENCRANTZ *and* GUILDENSTERN
    [with some Attendants].

Enter POLONIUS.

    POLONIUS. Th' ambassadors from Nor-
      way, my good lord,   40
Are joyfully returned.
    KING. Thou still° hast been the father of
      good news.
    POLONIUS. Have I, my lord? Assure you,
      my good liege,
I hold my duty, as I hold my soul,
Both to my God and to my gracious king; 45
And I do think, or else this brain of mine
Hunts not the trail of policy so sure°
As it hath used to do, that I have found
The very cause of Hamlet's lunacy.
    KING. O, speak of that! That do I long
      to hear.   50
    POLONIUS. Give first admittance to th'
      ambassadors.
My news shall be the fruit to that great
    feast.
    KING. Thyself do grace to them and
      bring them in.   *[Exit* POLONIUS.*]*
He tells me, my dear Gertrude, he hath
    found
The head and source of all your son's
    distemper.   55
    QUEEN. I doubt° it is no other but the
      main,°
His father's death and our o'erhasty mar-
    riage.
    KING. Well, we shall sift him.

Enter POLONIUS, VOLTEMAND, *and* CORNÈ-
LIUS.

              Welcome, my good friends.
Say, Voltemand, what from our brother
    Norway?
    VOLTEMAND. Most fair return of greet-
      ings and desires.   60
Upon our first,° he sent out to suppress
His nephew's levies, which to him ap-
    peared
To be a preparation 'gainst the Polack;
But better looked into, he truly found

---

¹³ **vouchsafe your rest** consent to remain
¹⁸ **opened** revealed ²² **gentry** courtesy ³⁰ **in the
full bent** entirely (the figure is of a bow bent to
its capacity)

⁴² **still** always ⁴⁷ **Hunts not . . . so sure** does
not follow clues of political doings with such sureness ⁵⁶ **doubt** suspect ⁵⁶ **main** principal point
⁶¹ **first** first audience

It was against your Highness, whereat
65   grieved,
That so his sickness, age, and impotence
Was falsely borne in hand,° sends out
    arrests
On Fortinbras; which he, in brief, obeys,
Receives rebuke from Norway, and in
    fine,°
70 Makes vow before his uncle never more
To give th' assay° of arms against your
    Majesty.
Whereon old Norway, overcome with joy,
Gives him threescore thousand crowns in
    annual fee
And his commission to employ those
    soldiers,
75 So levied as before, against the Polack,
With an entreaty, herein further shown,
    [gives a paper]
That it might please you to give quiet pass
Through your dominions for this enter-
    prise,
On such regards of safety and allowance°
As therein are set down.
80   KING.   It likes us well;
And at our more considered time° we'll
    read,
Answer, and think upon this business.
Meantime, we thank you for your well-
    took labor.
Go to your rest; at night we'll feast to-
    gether.
Most welcome home!
                    Exeunt AMBASSADORS.
85   POLONIUS.   This business is well ended.
My liege and madam, to expostulate°
What majesty should be, what duty is,
Why day is day, night night, and time is
    time,
Were nothing but to waste night, day, and
    time.
Therefore, since brevity is the soul of
90   wit,°

And tediousness the limbs and outward
    flourishes,
I will be brief. Your noble son is mad.
Mad call I it, for, to define true madness,
What is't but to be nothing else but mad?
But let that go.
    QUEEN.   More matter, with less art.   95
    POLONIUS. Madam, I swear I use no art
    at all.
That he's mad, 'tis true: 'tis true 'tis pity,
And pity 'tis 'tis true—a foolish figure.°
But farewell it, for I will use no art.
Mad let us grant him then; and now re-
    mains   100
That we find out the cause of this effect,
Or rather say, the cause of this defect,
For this effect defective comes by cause.
Thus it remains, and the remainder thus.
Perpend.°   105
I have a daughter: have, while she is mine,
Who in her duty and obedience, mark,
Hath given me this. Now gather, and
    surmise.

[Reads] the letter.

    "To the celestial, and my soul's idol, the
    most beautified Ophelia"—   110

That's an ill pharse, a vile phrase; "beauti-
fied" is a vile phrase. But you shall hear.
Thus:

    "In her excellent white bosom, these,
    &c."   115

    QUEEN. Came this from Hamlet to her?
    POLONIUS. Good madam, stay awhile. I
    will be faithful.

    "Doubt thou the stars are fire,
        Doubt that the sun doth move;
    Doubt° truth to be a liar,   120
        But never doubt I love.

    O dear Ophelia, I am ill at these num-
    bers.° I have not art to reckon my
    groans; but that I love thee best, O most
    best, believe it. Adieu.   125

---

⁶⁷ **borne in hand** deceived ⁶⁹ **in fine** finally
⁷¹ **assay** trial ⁷⁹ **regards of safety and allowance** i.e., conditions ⁸¹ **considered time** time
proper for considering ⁸⁶ **expostulate** discuss
⁹⁰ **wit** wisdom, understanding

⁹⁶ **figure** figure of rhetoric ¹⁰⁵ **Perpend** consider
carefully ¹²⁰ **Doubt** suspect ¹²²⁻¹²³ **ill at these
numbers** unskilled in verses

Thine evermore, most dear lady, whilst this machine° is to him,

HAMLET."

This in obedience hath my daughter shown
130 me,
And more above° hath his solicitings,
As they fell out by time, by means, and
place,
All given to mine ear.
KING.   But how hath she
Received his love?
POLONIUS.   What do you think of me?
KING. As of a man faithful and honorable.
POLONIUS. I would fain prove so. But
135   what might you think,
When I had seen this hot love on the wing
(As I perceived it, I must tell you that,
Before my daughter told me), what might
you,
Or my dear Majesty your Queen here,
think,
140 If I had played the desk or table book,°
Or given my heart a winking,° mute and
dumb,
Or looked upon this love with idle sight?
What might you think? No, I went round
to work
And my young mistress thus I did be-
speak:
145 "Lord Hamlet is a prince, out of thy star.°
This must not be." And then I prescripts
gave her,
That she should lock herself from his
resort,
Admit no messengers, receive no tokens.
Which done, she took the fruits of my
advice,
150 And he, repellèd, a short tale to make,
Fell into a sadness, then into a fast,
Thence to a watch,° thence into a weakness,
Thence to a lightness,° and, by this de-
clension,

Into the madness wherein now he raves,
And all we mourn for.
KING.   Do you think 'tis this?   155
QUEEN. It may be, very like.
POLONIUS. Hath there been such a time,
I would fain know that,
That I have positively said "'Tis so,"
When it proved otherwise?
KING.   Not that I know.
POLONIUS *[pointing to his head and
shoulder].* Take this from this, if this
be otherwise.   160
If circumstances lead me, I will find
Where truth is hid, though it were hid
indeed
Within the center.°
KING.   How may we try it further?
POLONIUS. You know sometimes he
walks four hours together
Here in the lobby.
QUEEN.   So he does indeed.   165
POLONIUS. At such a time I'll loose my
daughter to him.
Be you and I behind an arras° then.
Mark the encounter. If he love her not,
And be not from his reason fall'n thereon,
Let me be no assistant for a state   170
But keep a farm and carters.
KING.   We will try it.

Enter HAMLET *reading on a book.*

QUEEN. But look where sadly the poor
wretch comes reading.
POLONIUS. Away, I do beseech you both,
away.
                    Exit KING *and* QUEEN.
I'll board him presently.° O, give me
leave.
How does my good Lord Hamlet?   175
HAMLET. Well, God-a-mercy.
POLONIUS. Do you know me, my lord?
HAMLET. Excellent well. You are a fish-
monger.°
POLONIUS. Not I, my lord.   180

---

[127] **machine** complex device (here, his body)
[130] **more above** in addition [140] **played the desk
or table book** i.e., been a passive recipient of
secrets [141] **winking** closing of the eyes [145] **star**
sphere [152] **watch** wakefulness [153] **lightness**
mental derangement

[163] **center** center of the earth [167] **arras** tapestry
hanging in front of a wall [174] **board him presently** accost him at once [178-179] **fishmonger**
dealer in fish (slang for a procurer)

HAMLET. Then I would you were so honest a man.

POLONIUS. Honest, my lord?

HAMLET. Ay, sir. To be honest, as this world goes, is to be one man picked out of ten thousand.

POLONIUS. That's very true, my lord.

HAMLET. For if the sun breed maggots in a dead dog, being a good kissing carrion°——Have you a daughter?

POLONIUS. I have, my lord.

HAMLET. Let her not walk i' th' sun. Conception° is a blessing, but as your daughter may conceive, friend, look to't.

POLONIUS *[aside].* How say you by that? Still harping on my daughter. Yet he knew me not at first. 'A said I was a fishmonger. 'A is far gone, far gone. And truly in my youth I suffered much extremity for love, very near this. I'll speak to him again.—What do you read, my lord?

HAMLET. Words, words, words.

POLONIUS. What is the matter,° my lord?

HAMLET. Between who?

POLONIUS. I mean the matter that you read, my lord.

HAMLET. Slanders, sir; for the satirical rogue says here that old men have gray beards, that their faces are wrinkled, their eyes purging thick amber and plumtree gum, and that they have a plentiful lack of wit, together with most weak hams. All which, sir, though I most powerfully and potently believe, yet I hold it not honesty° to have it thus set down; for you yourself, sir, should be old as I am if, like a crab, you could go backward.

POLONIUS *[aside].* Though this be madness, yet there is method in't. Will you walk out of the air, my lord?

HAMLET. Into my grave.

POLONIUS. Indeed, that's out of the air.

[Aside.] How pregnant° sometimes his replies are! A happiness° that often madness hits on, which reason and sanity could not so prosperously be delivered of. I will leave him and suddenly contrive the means of meeting between him and my daughter.—My lord, I will take my leave of you.

HAMLET. You cannot take from me anything that I will more willingly part withal—except my life, except my life, except my life.

Enter GUILDENSTERN *and* ROSENCRANTZ.

POLONIUS. Fare you well, my lord.

HAMLET. These tedious old fools!

POLONIUS. You go to seek the Lord Hamlet? There he is.

ROSENCRANTZ *[to Polonius].* God save you, sir!

[Exit POLONIUS.*]*

GUILDENSTERN. My honored lord!

ROSENCRANTZ. My most dear lord!

HAMLET. My excellent good friends! How dost thou, Guildenstern? Ah, Rosencrantz! Good lads, how do you both?

ROSENCRANTZ. As the indifferent° children of the earth.

GUILDENSTERN. Happy in that we are not overhappy. On Fortune's cap we are not the very button.

HAMLET. Nor the soles of her shoe?

ROSENGRANTZ. Neither, my lord.

HAMLET. Then you live about her waist, or in the middle of her favors?

GUILDENSTERN. Faith, her privates° we.

HAMLET. In the secret parts of Fortune? O, most true! She is a strumpet. What news?

ROSENCRANTZ. None, my lord, but that the world's grown honest.

HAMLET. Then is doomsday near. But your news is not true. Let me question more in particular. What have you, my good friends, deserved at the hands of Fortune that she sends you to prison hither?

---

[189] **a good kissing carrion** (perhaps the meaning is "a good piece of flesh to kiss," but many editors emend *good* to *god*, taking the word to refer to the sun) [193] **Conception** (1) understanding, (2) becoming pregnant [203] **matter** (Polonius means "subject matter," but Hamlet pretends to take the word in the sense of "quarrel") [214] **honesty** decency

[223] **pregnant** meaningful [224] **happiness** apt turn of phrase [245] **indifferent** ordinary [254] **privates** ordinary men (with a pun on "private parts")

265 GUILDENSTERN. Prison, my lord?

HAMLET. Denmark's a prison.

ROSENCRANTZ. Then is the world one.

HAMLET. A goodly one, in which there are many confines, wards,° and dungeons, 270 Denmark being one o' th' worst.

ROSENCRANTZ. We think not so, my lord.

HAMLET. Why, then 'tis none to you, for there is nothing either good or bad but thinking makes it so. To me it is a prison.

275 ROSENCRANTZ. Why then your ambition makes it one. 'Tis too narrow for your mind.

HAMLET. O God, I could be bounded in a nutshell and count myself a king of infinite 280 space, were it not that I have bad dreams.

GUILDENSTERN. Which dreams indeed are ambition, for the very substance of the ambitious is merely the shadow of a dream.

HAMLET. A dream itself is but a shadow.

285 ROSENCRANTZ. Truly, and I hold ambition of so airy and light a quality that it is but a shadow's shadow.

HAMLET. Then are our beggars bodies, and our monarchs and outstretched heroes 290 the beggars' shadows.° Shall we to th' court? For, by my fay,° I cannot reason.

BOTH. We'll wait upon you.

HAMLET. No such matter. I will not sort you with the rest of my servants, for, to 295 speak to you like an honest man, I am most dreadfully attended. But in the beaten way of friendship, what make you at Elsinore?

ROSENCRANTZ. To visit you, my lord; no other occasion.

300 HAMLET. Beggar that I am, I am even poor in thanks, but I thank you; and sure, dear friends, my thanks are too dear a halfpenny.° Were you not sent for? Is it your own inclining? Is it a free visitation? Come, 305 come, deal justly with me. Come, come; nay, speak.

GUILDENSTERN. What should we say, my lord?

HAMLET. Why anything—but to th' pur-310 pose. You were sent for, and there is a kind of confession in your looks, which your modesties have not craft enough to color. I know the good King and Queen have sent for you.

315 ROSENCRANTZ. To what end, my lord?

HAMLET. That you must teach me. But let me conjure you by the rights of our fellowship, by the consonancy of our youth, by the obligation of our ever preserved love, 320 and by what more dear a better proposer can charge you withal, be even and direct with me, whether you were sent for or no.

ROSENCRANTZ *[aside to* GUILDENSTERN*]*. What say you?

325 HAMLET *[aside]*. Nay then, I have an eye of you.—If you love me, hold not off.

GUILDENSTERN. My lord, we were sent for.

HAMLET. I will tell you why; so shall my 330 anticipation prevent your discovery,° and your secrecy to the King and Queen molt no feather. I have of late, but wherefore I know not, lost all my mirth, forgone all custom of exercises; and indeed, it goes so 335 heavily with my disposition that this goodly frame, the earth, seems to me a sterile promontory; this most excellent canopy, the air, look you, this brave o'erhanging firmament, this majestical roof fretted° with 340 golden fire: why, it appeareth nothing to me but a foul and pestilent congregation of vapors. What a piece of work is a man, how noble in reason, how infinite in faculties, in form and moving how express° and admira-345 ble, in action how like an angel, in apprehension how like a god: the beauty of the world, the paragon of animals; and yet to me, what is this quintessence of dust? Man delights not me; nor woman neither, though 350 by your smiling you seem to say so.

ROSENCRANTZ. My lord, there was no such stuff in my thoughts.

HAMLET. Why did ye laugh then, when I said "Man delights not me"?

355 ROSENCRANTZ. To think, my lord, if you

---

²⁶⁹ **wards** cells ²⁸⁸⁻²⁹⁰ **Then are . . . beggars' shadows** i.e., by your logic, beggars (lacking ambition) are substantial, and great men are elongated shadows ²⁹¹ **fay** faith ³⁰²⁻³⁰³ **too dear a halfpenny** i.e., not worth a halfpenny

³³⁰ **prevent your discovery** forestall your disclosure ³³⁹ **fretted** adorned ³⁴⁴ **express** exact

delight not in man, what lenten° entertainment the players shall receive from you. We coted° them on the way, and hither are they coming to offer you service.

360 HAMLET. He that plays the king shall be welcome; his Majesty shall have tribute of me; the adventurous knight shall use his foil and target;° the lover shall not sigh gratis; the humorous man° shall end his part in

365 peace; the clown shall make those laugh whose lungs are tickle o' th' sere;° and the lady shall say her mind freely, or° the blank verse shall halt° for't. What players are they?

370 ROSENCRANTZ. Even those you were wont to take such delight in, the tragedians of the city.

HAMLET. How chances it they travel? Their residence, both in reputation and

375 profit, was better both ways.

ROSENCRANTZ. I think their inhibition° comes by the means of the late innovation.°

HAMLET. Do they hold the same estimation they did when I was in the city? Are

380 they so followed?

ROSENCRANTZ. No indeed, are they not.

HAMLET. How comes it? Do they grow rusty?

ROSENCRANTZ. Nay, their endeavor

385 keeps in the wonted pace, but there is, sir, an eyrie° of children, little eyases, that cry out on the top of question° and are most tyrannically° clapped for't. These are now the fashion, and so berattle the common

390 stages° (so they call them) that many wearing rapiers are afraid of goosequills° and dare scarce come thither.

HAMLET. What, are they children? Who maintains 'em? How are they escoted?° Will

395 they pursue the quality° no longer than they can sing? Will they not say afterwards, if they should grow themselves to common players (as it is most like, if their means are no better), their writers do them wrong to

400 make them exclaim against their own succession?°

ROSENCRANTZ. Faith, there has been much to-do on both sides, and the nation holds it no sin to tarre° them to contro-

405 versy. There was, for a while, no money bid for argument° unless the poet and the player went to cuffs in the question.

HAMLET. Is't possible?

GUILDENSTERN. O, there has been much throwing about of brains.

410

HAMLET. Do the boys carry it away?

ROSENCRANTZ. Ay, that they do, my lord—Hercules and his load° too.

HAMLET. It is not very strange, for my

415 uncle is King of Denmark, and those that would make mouths at him while my father lived give twenty, forty, fifty, a hundred ducats apiece for his picture in little. 'Sblood,° there is something in this more

420 than natural, if philosophy could find it out.

A flourish.

GUILDENSTERN. There are the players.

HAMLET. Gentlemen, you are welcome to Elsinore. Your hands, come then. Th' appurtenance of welcome is fashion and

425 ceremony. Let me comply° with you in this garb,° lest my extent° to the players (which I tell you must show fairly outwards) should more appear like entertainment than yours.

---

³⁵⁶ **lenten** meager ³⁵⁸ **coted** overtook ³⁶³ **target** shield ³⁶⁴ **humorous man** i.e., eccentric man (among stock characters in dramas were men dominated by a "humor" or odd trait) ³⁶⁶ **tickle o' th' sere** on hair trigger (*sere* = part of the gunlock) ³⁶⁷ **or** else ³⁶⁸ **halt** limp ³⁷⁶ **inhibition** hindrance ³⁷⁷ **innovation** (probably an allusion to the companies of child actors that had become popular and were offering serious competition to the adult actors) ³⁸⁶ **eyrie** nest ³⁸⁶⁻³⁸⁷ **eyases, that . . . of question** unfledged hawks that cry shrilly above others in matter of debate ³⁸⁸ **tyrannically** violently ³⁸⁹⁻³⁹⁰ **berattle the common stages** cry down the public theaters (with the adult acting companies)

³⁹¹ **goosequills** pens (of satirists who ridicule the public theaters and their audiences) ³⁹⁴ **escoted** financially supported ³⁹⁵ **quality** profession of acting ⁴⁰⁰⁻⁴⁰¹ **succession** future ⁴⁰⁴ **tarre** incite ⁴⁰⁶ **argument** plot of a play ⁴¹³ **Hercules and his load** i.e., the whole world (with a reference to the Globe Theatre, which had a sign that represented Hercules bearing the globe) ⁴¹⁹ **'Sblood** by God's blood ⁴²⁵ **comply** be courteous ⁴²⁶ **garb** outward show ⁴²⁶ **extent** behavior

430 You are welcome. But my uncle-father and aunt-mother are deceived.

GUILDENSTERN. In what, my dear lord?

HAMLET. I am but mad north-north-west:° when the wind is southerly I know a hawk from a handsaw.°

Enter POLONIUS.

435 POLONIUS. Well be with you, gentlemen.

HAMLET. Hark you, Guildenstern, and you too; at each ear a hearer. That great baby you see there is not yet out of his swaddling clouts.

440 ROSENCRANTZ. Happily° he is the second time come to them, for they say an old man is twice a child.

HAMLET. I will prophesy he comes to tell me of the players. Mark it.—You say right, 445 sir; a Monday morning, 'twas then indeed.

POLONIUS. My lord, I have news to tell you.

HAMLET. My lord, I have news to tell you. When Roscius° was an actor in 450 Rome——

POLONIUS. The actors are come hither, my lord.

HAMLET. Buzz, buzz.°

POLONIUS. Upon my honor——

455 HAMLET. Then came each actor on his ass——

POLONIUS. The best actors in the world, either for tragedy, comedy, history, pastoral, pastoral-comical, historical-pastoral, 460 tragical-historical, tragical-comical-historical-pastoral; scene individable,° or poem unlimited.° Seneca° cannot be too heavy, nor Plautus° too light. For the law of

writ and the liberty,° these are the only 465 men.

HAMLET. O Jeptha, judge of Israel,° what a treasure hadst thou!

POLONIUS. What a treasure had he, my lord?

HAMLET. Why, 470

"One fair daughter, and no more,
    The which he lovèd passing well."

POLONIUS *[aside].* Still on my daughter.

HAMLET. Am I not i' th' right, old Jeptha? 475

POLONIUS. If you call me Jeptha, my lord, I have a daughter that I love passing well.

HAMLET. Nay, that follows not.

POLONIUS. What follows then, my lord?

HAMLET. Why, 480

"As by lot, God wot,"

and then, you know,

"It came to pass, as most like it was."

The first row of the pious chanson° will show you more, for look where my abridg- 485 ment° comes.

Enter the PLAYERS.

You are welcome, masters, welcome, all. I am glad to see thee well. Welcome, good friends. O, old friend, why, thy face is valanced° since I saw thee last. Com'st thou 490 to beard me in Denmark? What, my young lady° and mistress? By'r Lady, your ladyship is nearer to heaven than when I saw you last by the altitude of a chopine.° Pray God your voice, like a piece of uncurrent 495

---

⁴³²⁻⁴³³ **north-northwest** i.e., on one point of the compass only ⁴³⁴ **hawk from a handsaw** (*hawk* can refer not only to a bird but to a kind of pickax; *handsaw*—a carpenter's tool—may involve a similar pun on "hernshaw," a heron) ⁴⁴⁰ **Happily** perhaps ⁴⁴⁹ **Roscius** (a famous Roman comic actor) ⁴⁵³ **Buzz, buzz** (an interjection, perhaps indicating that the news is old) ⁴⁶¹ **scene individable** plays observing the unities of time, place, and action ⁴⁶² **poem unlimited** plays not restricted by the tenets of criticism ⁴⁶² **Seneca** (Roman tragic dramatist) ⁴⁶³ **Plautus** (Roman comic dramatist)

⁴⁶⁴ **For the law of writ and the liberty** (perhaps "for sticking to the text and for improvising"; perhaps "for classical plays and for modern loosely written plays") ⁴⁶⁶ **Jeptha, judge of Israel** (the title of a ballad on the Hebrew judge who sacrificed his daughter; see Judges 11) ⁴⁸⁴ **row of the pious chanson** stanza of the scriptural song ⁴⁸⁵⁻⁴⁸⁶ **abridgment** (1) i.e., entertainers, who abridge the time, (2) interrupters ⁴⁸⁹⁻⁴⁹⁰ **valanced** fringed (with a beard) ⁴⁹¹⁻⁴⁹² **young lady** i.e., boy for female roles ⁴⁹⁴ **chopine** thick-soled shoe

gold, be not cracked within the ring.°—
Masters, you are all welcome. We'll e'en
to't like French falconers, fly at anything we
see. We'll have a speech straight. Come,
500   give us a taste of your quality. Come, a passionate speech.

PLAYER. What speech, my good lord?

HAMLET. I heard thee speak me a speech
once, but it was never acted, or if it was,
505   not above once, for the play, I remember,
pleased not the million; 'twas caviary to the
general,° but it was (as I received it, and
others, whose judgments in such matters
cried in the top of° mine) an excellent play,
510   well digested in the scenes, set down with
as much modesty as cunning.° I remember
one said there were no sallets° in the lines
to make the matter savory; nor no matter
in the phrase that might indict the author of
515   affectation, but called it an honest method,
as wholesome as sweet, and by very much
more handsome than fine.° One speech in't
I chiefly loved.'Twas Aeneas' tale to Dido,
and thereabout of it especially when he
520   speaks of Priam's slaughter. If it live in your
memory, begin at this line—let me see, let
me see:

"The rugged Pyrrhus, like th' Hyrcanian
    beast°—"

'Tis not so; it begins with Pyrrhus:

"The rugged Pyrrhus, he whose sable°
525   arms,
Black as his purpose, did the night resem-
    ble
When he lay couchèd in th' ominous
    horse,°

Hath now this dread and black complexion
    smeared
With heraldry more dismal.° Head to foot
Now is he total gules, horridly tricked°   530
With blood of fathers, mothers, daughters,
    sons,
Baked and impasted° with the parching
    streets,
That lend a tyrannous and a damnèd light
To their lord's murder. Roasted in wrath
    and fire,
And thus o'ersizèd° with coagulate gore,   535
With eyes like carbuncles, the hellish
    Pyrrhus
Old grandsire Priam seeks."

So, proceed you.

POLONIUS. Fore God, my lord, well spoken, with good accent and good discretion.   540

PLAYER.   "Anon he finds him,
Striking too short at Greeks. His antique
    sword,
Rebellious to his arm, lies where it falls,
Repugnant to command.° Unequal
    matched,
Pyrrhus at Priam drives, in rage strikes
    wide,   545
But with the whiff and wind of his fell
    sword
Th' unnervèd father falls. Then senseless
    Ilium,°
Seeming to feel this blow, with flaming top
Stoops to his base,° and with a hideous
    crash
Takes prisoner Pyrrhus' ear. For lo, his
    sword,   550
Which was declining on the milky head
Of reverend Priam, seemed i' th' air to
    stick.
So as a painted tyrant° Pyrrhus stood,
And like a neutral to his will and matter°
Did nothing.   555

495-496 **like a piece . . . the ring** (a coin was unfit for legal tender if a crack extended from the
edge through the ring enclosing the monarch's
head. Hamlet, punning on *ring*, refers to the
change of voice that the boy actor will undergo)
506-507 **caviary to the general** i.e., too choice
for the multitude 509 **in the top of** overtopping
511 **modesty as cunning** restraint as art 512 **sal-
lets** salads, spicy jests 517 **more handsome
than fine** well-proportioned rather than ornamented 523 **Hyrcanian beast** i.e., tiger (Hyrca-
nia was in Asia) 525 **sable** black 527 **ominous
horse** i.e., wooden horse at the siege of Troy

529 **dismal** ill omened 530 **total gules, horridly
tricked** all red, horridly adorned 532 **impasted**
encrusted 535 **o'ersizèd** smeared over 544 **Repugnant to command** disobedient 547 **senseless
Ilium** insensate Troy 549 **Stoops to his base**
collapses (*his* = its) 553 **painted tyrant** tyrant in
a picture 554 **matter** task

But as we often see, against° some storm,
A silence in the heavens, the rack° stand
    still,
The bold winds speechless, and the orb
    below
As hush as death, anon the dreadful thun-
    der
Doth rend the region, so after Pyrrhus'
560   pause,
A rousèd vengeance sets him new awork,
And never did the Cyclops' hammers fall
On Mars's armor, forged for proof eterne,°
With less remorse than Pyrrhus' bleeding
    sword
565 Now falls on Priam.
Out, out, thou strumpet Fortune! All you
    gods,
In general synod° take away her power,
Break all the spokes and fellies° from her
    wheel,
And bowl the round nave° down the hill of
    heaven,
570 As low as to the fiends."

    POLONIUS. This is too long.
    HAMLET. It shall to the barber's, with
your beard.—Prithee say on. He's for a jig
or a tale of bawdry, or he sleeps. Say on;
575 come to Hecuba.

    PLAYER. "But who (ah woe!) had seen
    the mobled° queen—',

    HAMLET. "The mobled queen"?
    POLONIUS. That's good. "Mobled queen"
is good.

    PLAYER. "Run barefoot up and down,
580   threat'ning the flames
With bisson rheum;° a clout° upon that
    head
Where late the diadem stood, and for a
    robe,
About her lank and all o'erteemèd° loins,
A blanket in the alarm of fear caught up—

Who this had seen, with tongue in venom
    steeped   585
'Gainst Fortune's state would treason have
    pronounced.
But if the gods themselves did see her
    then,
When she saw Pyrrhus make malicious
    sport
In mincing with his sword her husband's
    limbs,
The instant burst of clamor that she made   590
(Unless things mortal move them not at
    all)
Would have made milch° the burning eyes
    of heaven
And passion in the gods."

    POLONIUS. Look, whe'r° he has not
turned his color, and has tears in's eyes.   595
Prithee no more.
    HAMLET. 'Tis well. I'll have thee speak
out the rest of this soon. Good my lord, will
you see the players well bestowed?° Do you
hear? Let them be well used, for they are   600
the abstract and brief chronicles of the
time. After your death you were better
have a bad epitaph than their ill report while
you live.
    POLONIUS. My lord, I will use them ac-   605
cording to their desert.
    HAMLET. God's bodkin,° man, much bet-
ter! Use every man after his desert, and
who shall scape whipping? Use them after
your own honor and dignity. The less they   610
deserve, the more merit is in your bounty.
Take them in.
    POLONIUS. Come, sirs.
    HAMLET. Follow him, friends. We'll hear
a play tomorrow. *[Aside to* PLAYER.*]* Dost   615
thou hear me, old friend? Can you play *The
Murder of Gonzago?*
    PLAYER. Ay, my lord.
    HAMLET. We'll ha't tomorrow night. You
could for a need study a speech of some   620
dozen or sixteen lines which I would set
down and insert in't, could you not?

---

556 **against** just before 557 **rack** clouds 563 **proof
eterne** eternal endurance 567 **synod** council
568 **fellies** rims 569 **nave** hub 576 **mobled** muffled
581 **bisson rheum** blinding tears 581 **clout** rag
583 **o'erteemèd** exhausted with childbearing

592 **milch** moist (literally, "milk-giving")
594 **whe'r** whether 599 **bestowed** housed
607 **God's bodkin** by God's little body

PLAYER. Ay, my lord.

HAMLET. Very well. Follow that lord, and
625 look you mock him not. My good friends,
I'll leave you till night. You are welcome to
Elsinore.

Exeunt POLONIUS *and* PLAYERS.

ROSENCRANTZ. Good my lord.

*Exeunt [*ROSENCRANTZ *and*
GUILDENSTERN*].*

HAMLET. Ay, so, God bye to you.—Now
I am alone.

630 O, what a rogue and peasant slave am I!
Is it not monstrous that this player here,
But in a fiction, in a dream of passion,°
Could force his soul so to his own conceit°
That from her working all his visage
wanned,
635 Tears in his eyes, distraction in his aspect,
A broken voice, and his whole function°
suiting
With forms° to his conceit? And all for
nothing!
For Hecuba!
What's Hecuba to him, or he to Hecuba,
That he should weep for her? What would
640 he do
Had he the motive and the cue for passion
That I have? He would drown the stage
with tears
And cleave the general ear with horrid
speech,
Make mad the guilty and appall the free,°
645 Confound the ignorant, and amaze indeed
The very faculties of eyes and ears.
Yet I,
A dull and muddy-mettled° rascal, peak
Like John-a-dreams,° unpregnant of° my
cause,
650 And can say nothing. No, not for a king,
Upon whose property and most dear life
A damned defeat was made. Am I a cow-
ard?

Who calls me villain? Breaks my pate
across?
Plucks off my beard and blows it in my
face?
Tweaks me by the nose? Gives me the lie
i' th' throat   655
As deep as to the lungs? Who does me
this?
Ha, 'swounds,° I should take it, for it
cannot be
But I am pigeon-livered° and lack gall
To make oppression bitter, or ere this
I should ha' fatted all the region kites°   660
With this slave's offal. Bloody, bawdy
villain!
Remorseless, treacherous, lecherous,
kindless° villain!
O, vengeance!
Why, what an ass am I! This is most
brave,°
That I, the son of a dear father murdered,   665
Prompted to my revenge by heaven and
hell,
Must, like a whore, unpack my heart with
words
And fall a-cursing like a very drab,°
A stallion!° Fie upon't, foh! About,° my
brains.
Hum——   -   670
I have heard that guilty creatures sitting at
a play
Have by the very cunning of the scene
Been struck so to the soul that presently°
They have proclaimed their malefactions.
For murder, though it have no tongue, will
speak   675
With most miraculous organ. I'll have
these players
Play something like the murder of my
father
Before mine uncle. I'll observe his looks,
I'll tent° him to the quick. If 'a do blench,°

---

632 **dream of passion** imaginary emotion 633 **conceit** imagination 636 **function** action 637 **forms**
bodily expressions 644 **appall the free** terrify
(make pale?) the guiltless 648 **muddy-mettled**
weak-spirited 648–649 **peak/Like John-a-dreams**
mope like a dreamer 649 **unpregnant of** unquick-
ened by

657 **'swounds** by God's wounds 658 **pigeon-
livered** gentle as a dove 660 **region kites** kites
(scavenger birds) of the sky 662 **kindless** unnatural 664 **brave** fine 668 **drab** prostitute 669 **stallion**
male prostitute (perhaps one should adopt the
Folio reading, *scullion* = kitchen wench)
669 **About** to work 673 **presently** immediately
679 **tent** probe 679 **blench** flinch

I know my course. The spirit that I have
680 seen
May be a devil, and the devil hath power
T' assume a pleasing shape, yea, and
  perhaps
Out of my weakness and my melancholy,
As he is very potent with such spirits,
685 Abuses me to damn me. I'll have grounds
More relative° than this. The play's the
  thing
Wherein I'll catch the conscience of the
  King.   *Exit*.

/ACT III

Scene I. The castle.]

Enter KING, QUEEN, POLONIUS, OPHELIA,
ROSENCRANTZ, GUILDENSTERN, LORDS.

  KING. And can you by no drift of confer-
    ence°
Get from him why he puts on this confu-
  sion,
Grating so harshly all his days of quiet
With turbulent and dangerous lunacy?
5   ROSENCRANTZ. He does confess he feels
    himself distracted,
But from what cause 'a will by no means
  speak.
  GUILDENSTERN. Nor do we find him
    forward to be sounded,°
But with a crafty madness keeps aloof
When we would bring him on to some
  confession
Of his true state.
10   QUEEN.   Did he receive you well?
  ROSENCRANTZ. Most like a gentleman.
  GUILDENSTERN. But with much forcing
    of his disposition.°
  ROSENCRANTZ. Niggard of question,° but
    of our demands
Most free in his reply.

  QUEEN.   Did you assay° him
    To any pastime?   15
  ROSENCRANTZ. Madam, it so fell out
    that certain players
We o'erraught° on the way; of these we
  told him,
And there did seem in him a kind of joy
To hear of it. They are here about the
  court,
And, as I think, they have already order   20
This night to play before him.
  POLONIUS.   'Tis most true,
And he beseeched me to entreat your
  Majesties
To hear and see the matter.
  KING. With all my heart, and it doth
    much content me
To hear him so inclined.   25
Good gentlemen, give him a further edge
And drive his purpose into these delights.
  ROSENCRANTZ. We shall, my lord.
  Exeunt ROSENCRANTZ *and* GUILDENSTERN.
  KING.   Sweet Gertrude, leave us too,
For we have closely° sent for Hamlet
  hither,
That he, as 'twere by accident, may here   30
Affront° Ophelia.
Her father and myself (lawful espials°)
Will so bestow ourselves that, seeing
  unseen,
We may of their encounter frankly judge
And gather by him, as he is behaved,   35
If't be th' affliction of his love or no
That thus he suffers for.
  QUEEN.   I shall obey you.
And for your part, Ophelia, I do wish
That your good beauties be the happy
  cause
Of Hamlet's wildness. So shall I hope your
  virtues   40
Will bring him to his wonted way again,
To both your honors.
  OPHELIA.   Madam, I wish it may.
                              [Exit QUEEN.]

---

⁶⁸⁶ **relative** (probably "pertinent," but possibly
"able to be related plausibly") III.i. ¹ **drift of
conference** management of conversation ⁷ **forward to be sounded** willing to be questioned
¹² **forcing of his disposition** effort ¹³ **Niggard
of question** uninclined to talk

¹⁴ **assay** tempt ¹⁷ **o'erraught** overtook
²⁹ **closely** secretly ³¹ **Affront** meet face to face
³² **espials** spies

POLONIUS. Ophelia, walk you here.—
   Gracious, so please you,
We will bestow ourselves. *[To* OPHELIA.*]*
   Read on this book,
45 That show of such an exercise may color°
Your loneliness. We are oft to blame in
   this,
'Tis too much proved, that with devotion's
   visage
And pious action we do sugar o'er
The devil himself.
   KING *[aside].*   O, 'tis too true.
How smart a lash that speech doth give
50   my conscience!
The harlot's cheek, beautied with plas-
   t'ring art,
Is not more ugly to the thing that helps it
Than is my deed to my most painted
   word.
O heavy burden!
   POLONIUS. I hear him coming. Let's
55   withdraw, my lord.
       [Exeunt KING *and* POLONIUS.*]*

Enter HAMLET.

   HAMLET. To be, or not to be: that is the
   question:
Whether 'tis nobler in the mind to suffer
The slings and arrows of outrageous for-
   tune,
Or to take arms against a sea of troubles,
And by opposing end them. To die, to
60   sleep—
No more—and by a sleep to say we end
The heartache, and the thousand natural
   shocks
That flesh is heir to! 'Tis a consummation
Devoutly to be wished. To die, to sleep—
To sleep—perchance to dream: ay, there's
65   the rub,°
For in that sleep of death what dreams
   may come
When we have shuffled off this mortal
   coil,°

Must give us pause. There's the respect°
That makes calamity of so long life:°
For who would bear the whips and scorns
   of time, 70
Th' oppressor's wrong, the proud man's
   contumely,
The pangs of despised love, the law's
   delay,
The insolence of office, and the spurns
That patient merit of th' unworthy takes,
When he himself might his quietus° make 75
With a bare bodkin?° Who would fardels°
   bear,
To grunt and sweat under a weary life,
But that the dread of something after
   death,
The undiscovered country, from whose
   bourn°
No traveler returns, puzzles the will, 80
And makes us rather bear those ills we
   have,
Than fly to others that we know not of?
Thus conscience° does make cowards of
   us all,
And thus the native hue of resolution
Is sicklied o'er with the pale cast° of
   thought, 85
And enterprises of great pitch° and mo-
   ment,
With this regard° their currents turn awry,
And lose the name of action.—Soft you
   now,
The fair Ophelia!—Nymph, in thy orisons°
Be all my sins remembered.
   OPHELIA.   Good my lord, 90
How does your honor for this many a day?
   HAMLET. I humbly thank you; well, well,
   well.
   OPHELIA. My lord, I have remembrances
   of yours
That I have longèd long to redeliver.
I pray you now, receive them.

---

⁴⁵ **exercise may color** act of devotion may give
a plausible hue to (the book is one of devotion)
⁶⁵ **rub** impediment (obstruction to a bowler's ball)
⁶⁷ **coil** (1) turmoil, (2) a ring of rope (here the
flesh encircling the soul)

⁶⁸ **respect** consideration ⁶⁹ **makes calamity of
so long life** (1) makes calamity so long-lived,
(2) makes living so long a calamity ⁷⁵ **quietus** full
discharge (a legal term) ⁷⁶ **bodkin** dagger ⁷⁶ **far-
dels** burdens ⁷⁹ **bourn** region ⁸³ **conscience**
self-consciousness, introspection ⁸⁵ **cast** color
⁸⁶ **pitch** height (a term from falconry) ⁸⁷ **regard**
consideration ⁸⁹ **orisons** prayers

95   HAMLET.   No, not I,
I never gave you aught.
   OPHELIA. My honored lord, you know
     right well you did,
And with them words of so sweet breath
     composed
As made these things more rich. Their
     perfume lost,
100   Take these again, for to the noble mind
Rich gifts wax poor when givers prove
     unkind.
There, my lord.
   HAMLET. Ha, ha! Are you honest?°
   OPHELIA. My lord?
105   HAMLET. Are you fair?
   OPHELIA. What means your lordship?
   HAMLET. That if you be honest and fair,
your honesty should admit no discourse to
your beauty.°
110   OPHELIA. Could beauty, my lord, have
better commerce than with honesty?
   HAMLET. Ay, truly; for the power of
beauty will sooner transform honesty from
what it is to a bawd° than the force of hon-
115   esty can translate beauty into his likeness.
This was sometime a paradox, but now the
time gives it proof. I did love you once.
   OPHELIA. Indeed, my lord, you made me
believe so.
120   HAMLET. You should not have believed
me, for virtue cannot so inoculate° our old
stock but we shall relish of it.° I loved you
not.
   OPHELIA. I was the more deceived.
125   HAMLET. Get thee to a nunnery. Why
wouldst thou be a breeder of sinners? I am
myself indifferent honest,° but yet I could
accuse me of such things that it were better
my mother had not borne me: I am very
130   proud, revengeful, ambitious, with more offenses at my beck° than I have thoughts to
put them in, imagination to give them

shape, or time to act them in. What should
such fellows as I do crawling between earth
and heaven? We are arrant knaves all; be-   135
lieve none of us. Go thy ways to a nunnery.
Where's your father?
   OPHELIA. At home, my lord.
   HAMLET. Let the doors be shut upon
him, that he may play the fool nowhere but   140
in's own house. Farewell.
   OPHELIA. O help him, you sweet heavens!
   HAMLET. If thou dost marry, I'll give
thee this plague for thy dowry: be thou as   145
chaste as ice, as pure as snow, thou shalt
not escape calumny. Get thee to a nunnery.
Go, farewell. Or if thou wilt needs marry,
marry a fool, for wise men know well
enough what monsters° you make of them.   150
To a nunnery, go, and quickly too. Farewell.
   OPHELIA. Heavenly powers, restore him!
   HAMLET. I have heard of your paintings,
well enough. God hath given you one face,
and you make yourselves another. You jig   155
and amble, and you lisp; you nickname
God's creatures and make your wantonness
your ignorance.° Go to, I'll no more on't; it
hath made me mad. I say we will have no
moe° marriage. Those that are married   160
already—all but one—shall live. The rest
shall keep as they are. To a nunnery, go.
                             Exit.
  OPHELIA. O what a noble mind is here
    o'erthrown!
The courtier's, soldier's, scholar's, eye,
    tongue, sword,
Th' expectancy and rose° of the fair state,   165
The glass of fashion, and the mold of
    form,°
Th' observed of all observers, quite, quite
    down!
And I, of ladies most deject and wretched,

---

³ **Are you honest** (1) are you modest, (2) are
you chaste, (3) have you integrity ¹⁰⁸⁻¹⁰⁹ **your
honesty . . . to your beauty** your modesty
should permit no approach to your beauty
¹¹⁴ **bawd** procurer ¹²¹ **inoculate** graft ¹²² **relish
of it** smack of it (our old sinful nature) ¹²⁷ **indifferent honest** moderately virtuous ¹³¹ **beck** call

¹⁵⁰ **monsters** horned beasts, cuckolds
¹⁵⁷⁻¹⁵⁸ **make your wantonness your ignorance** excuse your wanton speech by pretending
ignorance ¹⁶⁰ **moe** more ¹⁶⁵ **expectancy and
rose** i.e., fair hope ¹⁶⁶ **The glass . . . of form**
the mirror of fashion, and the pattern of excellent
behavior

That sucked the honey of his musicked
    vows,
Now see that noble and most sovereign
170   reason
Like sweet bells jangled, out of time and
    harsh,
That unmatched form and feature of
    blown° youth
Blasted with ecstasy.° O, woe is me
T' have seen what I have seen, see what I
    see!

Enter KING *and* POLONIUS.

    KING. Love? His affections° do not that
175   way tend,
Nor what he spake, though it lacked form
    a little,
Was not like madness. There's something
    in his soul
O'er which his melancholy sits on brood,
And I do doubt° the hatch and the disclose
180 Will be some danger; which for to prevent,
I have in quick determination
Thus set it down: he shall with speed to
    England
For the demand of our neglected tribute.
Haply the seas, and countries different,
185 With variable objects, shall expel
This something-settled° matter in his
    heart,
Whereon his brains still beating puts him
    thus
From fashion of himself. What think you
    on't?
    POLONIUS. It shall do well. But yet do I
    believe
190 The origin and commencement of his grief
Sprung from neglected love. How now,
    Ophelia?
You need not tell us what Lord Hamlet
    said;
We heard it all. My lord, do as you please,
But if you hold it fit, after the play,
195 Let his queen mother all alone entreat him

To show his grief. Let her be round° with
    him,
And I'll be placed, so please you, in the
    ear
Of all their conference. If she find him
    not,°
To England send him, or confine him
    where
Your wisdom best shall think.
    KING.   It shall be so.   200
Madness in great ones must not un-
    watched go.   *Exeunt.*

[Scene II. The castle.]

Enter HAMLET *and three of the* PLAYERS.

    HAMLET. Speak the speech, I pray you,
as I pronounced it to you, trippingly on the
tongue. But if you mouth it, as many of our
players do, I had as lief the town crier
spoke my lines. Nor do not saw the air too   5
much with your hand, thus, but use all gently, for in the very torrent, tempest, and (as
I may say) whirlwind of your passion, you
must acquire and beget a temperance that
may give it smoothness. O, it offends me to   10
the soul to hear a robustious periwig-pated°
fellow tear a passion to tatters, to very
rags, to split the ears of the groundlings,°
who for the most part are capable of° nothing but inexplicable dumb shows° and noise.   15
I would have such a fellow whipped for o'er-
doing Termagant. It out-herods Herod.°
Pray you avoid it.
    PLAYER. I warrant your honor.
    HAMLET. Be not too tame neither, but let   20
your own discretion be your tutor. Suit the
action to the word, the word to the action,
with this special observance, that you o'er-
step not the modesty of nature. For any-

---

196 **round** blunt 198 **find him not** does not find
him out III.ii. 11 **robustious periwig-pated**
boisterous wig-headed 13 **groundlings** those
who stood in the pit of the theater (the poorest
and presumably most ignorant of the audience)
14 **are capable of** are able to understand
15 **dumb shows** (it had been the fashion for actors to preface plays or parts of plays with silent
mime) 17 **Termagant . . . Herod** (boisterous
characters in the old mystery plays)

---

172 **blown** blooming 173 **ecstasy** madness 175 **af-
fections** inclinations 179 **doubt** fear
186 **somethng-settled** somewhat settled

25 thing so o'erdone is from° the purpose of
playing, whose end, both at the first and
now, was and is, to hold, as 'twere, the
mirror up to nature; to show virtue her own
feature, scorn her own image, and the very
30 age and body of the time his form and pressure.° Now, this overdone, or come tardy
off, though it makes the unskillful laugh,
cannot but make the judicious grieve, the
censure of the which one must in your al-
35 lowance o'erweigh a whole theater of others. O, there be players that I have seen
play, and heard others praise, and that
highly (not to speak it profanely), that neither having th' accent of Christians, nor the
40 gait of Christian, pagan, nor man, have so
strutted and bellowed that I have thought
some of Nature's journeymen° had made
men, and not made them well, they imitated humanity so abominably.
45   PLAYER. I hope we have reformed that in-
differently° with us, sir.
    HAMLET. O, reform it altogether! And let
those that play your clowns speak no more
than is set down for them, for there be of
50 them that will themselves laugh, to set on
some quantity of barren spectators to laugh
too, though in the meantime some necessary question of the play be then to be considered. That's villainous and shows a most
55 pitiful ambition in the fool that uses it. Go
make you ready.   *Exit* PLAYERS.

Enter POLONIUS, GUILDENSTERN, *and* RO-
SENCRANTZ.

    How now, my lord? Will the King hear
this piece of work?
    POLONIUS. And the Queen too, and that
60 presently.
    HAMLET. Bid the players make haste.
                        Exit POLONIUS.
Will you two help to hasten them?
ROSENCRANTZ. Ay, my lord.
                    Exeunt they two.
HAMLET. What, ho, Horatio!

Enter HORATIO.

HORATIO. Here, sweet lord, at your   65
service.
    HAMLET. Horatio, thou art e'en as just a
man
As e'er my conversation coped withal.°
    HORATIO. O, my dear lord——
    HAMLET.   Nay, do not think I flatter.
For what advancement° may I hope from
    thee,   70
That no revenue hast but thy good spirits
To feed and clothe thee? Why should the
    poor be flattered?
No, let the candied° tongue lick absurd
    pomp,
And crook the pregnant° hinges of the
    knee
Where thrift° may follow fawning. Dost
    thou hear?   75
Since my dear soul was mistress of her
    choice
And could of men distinguish her election,
S' hath sealed thee° for herself, for thou
    hast been
As one, in suff'ring all, that suffers noth-
    ing,
A man that Fortune's buffets and rewards   80
Hast ta'en with equal thanks; and blest
    are those
Whose blood° and judgment are so well
    commeddled°
That they are not a pipe for Fortune's
    finger
To sound what stop she please. Give me
    that man
That is not passion's slave, and I will wear
    him   85
In my heart's core, ay, in my heart of
    heart,
As I do thee. Something too much of
    this——
There is a play tonight before the King.
One scene of it comes near the circum-
    stance

---

⁶⁷ **coped withal** met with ⁷⁰ **advancement** promotion ⁷³ **candied** sugared, flattering ⁷⁴ **pregnant** (1) pliant, (2) full of promise of good
fortune ⁷⁵ **thrift** profit ⁷⁸ **S' hath sealed thee**
she (the soul) has set a mark on you ⁸² **blood**
passion ⁸² **commeddled** blended

²⁵ **from** contrary to ³⁰⁻³¹ **pressure** image, impress ⁴² **journeymen** workers not yet masters
of their craft ⁴⁵⁻⁴⁶ **indifferently** tolerably

Which I have told thee, of my father's
90   death.
I prithee, when thou seest that act afoot,
Even with the very comment° of thy soul
Observe my uncle. If his occulted° guilt
Do not itself unkennel in one speech,
95 It is a damnèd ghost that we have seen,
And my imaginations are as foul
As Vulcan's stithy.° Give him heedful note,
For I mine eyes will rivet to his face,
And after we will both our judgments join
In censure of his seeming.°
100   HORATIO.   Well, my lord.
If 'a steal aught the whilst this play is
      playing,
And scape detecting, I will pay the theft.

Enter TRUMPETS *and* KETTLEDRUMS, KING,
QUEEN, POLONIUS, OPHELIA, ROSENCRANTZ,
GUILDENSTERN, *and other* LORDS *attendant
with his* GUARD *carrying torches. Danish
March. Sound a Flourish.*

      HAMLET. They are coming to the play: I
            must be idle;°
Get you a place.
105   KING. How fares our cousin Hamlet?
      HAMLET. Excellent, i' faith, of the cha-
meleon's dish;° I eat the air, promise-
crammed; you cannot feed capons so.
      KING. I have nothing with this answer,
110 Hamlet; these words are not mine.
      HAMLET. No, nor mine now. *[To* POLO-
NIUS.*]* My lord, you played once i' th' university, you say?
      POLONIUS. That did I, my lord, and was
115 accounted a good actor.
      HAMLET. What did you enact?
      POLONIUS. I did enact Julius Caesar. I
was killed i' th' Capitol; Brutus killed me.
      HAMLET. It was a brute part of him to kill
120 so capital a calf there. Be the players
ready?
      ROSENCRANTZ. Ay, my lord. They stay
upon your patience.

QUEEN. Come hither, my dear Hamlet,
sit by me.   125
      HAMLET. No, good mother. Here's metal
more attractive.°
      POLONIUS *[to the* KING*]*. O ho! Do you
mark that?
      HAMLET. Lady, shall I lie in your lap?   130

[He lies at OPHELIA'S *feet.]*

      OPHELIA. No, my lord.
      HAMLET. I mean, my head upon your lap?
      OPHELIA. Ay, my lord.
      HAMLET. Do you think I meant country
matters?°   135
      OPHELIA. I think nothing, my lord.
      HAMLET. That's a fair thought to lie be-
tween maids' legs.
      OPHELIA. What is, my lord?
      HAMLET. Nothing.   140
      OPHELIA. You are merry, my lord.
      HAMLET. Who, I?
      OPHELLA. Ay, my lord.
      HAMLET. O God, your only jig-maker!°
What should a man do but be merry? For   145
look you how cheerfully my mother looks,
and my father died within's two hours.
      OPHELIA. Nay, 'tis twice two months, my
lord.
      HAMLET. So long? Nay then, let the devil 150
wear black, for I'll have a suit of sables.° O
heavens! Die two months ago, and not forgotten yet? Then there's hope a great man's
memory may outlive his life half a year. But,
by'r Lady, 'a must build churches then, or   155
else shall 'a suffer not thinking on, with the
hobbyhorse,° whose epitaph is "For O, for
O, the hobbyhorse is forgot!"

The trumpets sound. Dumb show follows:
      Enter a KING *and a* QUEEN *very lov-
ingly, the* QUEEN *embracing him, and he her.
She kneels; and makes show of protestation
unto him. He takes her up, and declines his*

---

⁹² **very comment** deepest wisdom ⁹³ **occulted**
hidden ⁹⁷ **stithy** forge, smithy ¹⁰⁰ **censure of his
seeming** judgment on his looks ¹⁰³ **be idle** play
the fool ¹⁰⁶⁻¹⁰⁷ **the chameleon's dish** air (on
which chameleons were thought to live)

¹²⁶ **attractive** magnetic ¹³⁵ **country matters**
rustic doings (with a pun on the vulgar word for
the pudendum) ¹⁴⁴ **jig-maker** composer of songs
and dances (often a Fool, who performed them)
¹⁵¹ **sables** (Pun on "black" and "luxurious furs")
¹⁵⁷ **hobbyhorse** mock horse worn by a per-
former in the morris dance

head upon her neck. He lies him down upon a bank of flowers. She, seeing him asleep, leaves him. Anon come in another man: takes off his crown, kisses it, pours poison in the sleeper's ears, and leaves him. The QUEEN *returns, finds the* KING *dead, makes passionate action. The poisoner, with some three or four, come in again, seem to condole with her. The dead body is carried away. The poisoner woos the* QUEEN *with gifts; she seems harsh awhile, but in the end accepts love.*

Exeunt.

OPHELIA. What means this, my lord?

160   HAMLET. Marry, this is miching mallecho;° it means mischief.

OPHELIA. Belike this show imports the argument° of the play.

Enter PROLOGUE.

HAMLET. We shall know by this fellow.
165   The players cannot keep counsel; they'll tell all.

OPHELIA. Will 'a tell us what this show meant?

HAMLET. Ay, or any show that you will
170   show him. Be not you ashamed to show, he'll not shame to tell you what it means.

OPHELIA. You are naught,° you are naught; I'll mark the play.

PROLOGUE. For us, and for our tragedy,
175   Here stooping to your clemency,
We beg your hearing patiently.   *[Exit.]*

HAMLET. Is this a prologue, or the posy of a ring?°

OPHELIA. 'Tis brief, my lord.

HAMLET. As woman's love.

Enter [two PLAYERS *as]* KING *and* QUEEN.

PLAYER KING. Full thirty times hath
180   Phoebus' cart° gone round
Neptune's salt wash° and Tellus'° orbèd ground,

And thirty dozen moons with borrowed sheen
About the world have times twelve thirties been,
Since love our hearts, and Hymen did our hands,
Unite commutual in most sacred bands.   185

PLAYER QUEEN. So many journeys may the sun and moon
Make us again count o'er ere love be done!
But woe is me, you are so sick of late,
So far from cheer and from your former state,
That I distrust° you. Yet, though I distrust,   190
Discomfort you, my lord, it nothing must.
For women fear too much, even as they love,
And women's fear and love hold quantity,
In neither aught, or in extremity.°
Now what my love is, proof° hath made you know,   195
And as my love is sized, my fear is so.
Where love is great, the littlest doubts are fear;
Where little fears grow great, great love grows there.

PLAYER KING. Faith, I must leave thee, love, and shortly too;
My operant° powers their functions leave to do: 200
And thou shalt live in this fair world behind,
Honored, beloved, and haply one as kind
For husband shalt thou——

PLAYER QUEEN.   O, confound the rest!
Such love must needs be treason in my breast.
In second husband let me be accurst!   205
None wed the second but who killed the first.

HAMLET *[aside]*. That's wormwood.°

160-161 **miching mallecho** sneaking mischief
163 **argument** plot 172 **naught** wicked, improper
177 **posy of a ring** motto inscribed in a ring
180 **Phoebus' cart** the sun's chariot 181 **Neptune's salt wash** the sea 181 **Tellus** Roman goddess of the earth

190 **distrust** am anxious about 193-194 **And women's . . . in extremity** (perhaps the idea is that women's anxiety is great or little in proportion to their love. The previous line, unrhymed, may be a false start that Shakespeare neglected to delete) 193 **proof** experience 200 **operant** active 207 **wormwood** a bitter herb

PLAYER QUEEN. The instances° that second marriage move°
Are base respects of thrift,° but none of love.
300 A second time I kill my husband dead
When second husband kisses me in bed.
PLAYER KING. I do believe you think what now you speak,
But what we do determine oft we break.
Purpose is but the slave to memory,
305 Of violent birth, but poor validity,°
Which now like fruit unripe sticks on the tree,
But fall unshaken when they mellow be.
Most necessary 'tis that we forget.
To pay ourselves what to ourselves is debt.
310 What to ourselves in passion we propose,
The passion ending, doth the purpose lose.
The violence of either grief or joy
Their own enactures° with themselves destroy:
Where joy most revels, grief doth most lament;
Grief joys, joy grieves, on slender acci-
315   dent.
This word is not for aye, nor 'tis not strange
That even our loves should with our for-tunes change,
For 'tis a question left us yet to prove,
Whether love lead fortune, or else fortune love.
The great man down, you mark his favor-
320   ite flies;
The poor advanced makes friends of ene-mies;
And hitherto doth love on fortune tend,
For who not needs shall never lack a friend;
And who in want a hollow friend doth try,
325 Directly seasons him° his enemy.
But, orderly to end where I begun,
Our wills and fates do so contrary run
That our devices still are overthrown;

Our thoughts are ours, their ends none of our own.
So think thou wilt no second husband wed,   330
But die thy thoughts when thy first lord is dead.
PLAYER QUEEN. Nor earth to give me food, nor heaven light,
Sport and repose lock from me day and night,
To desperation turn my trust and hope,
An anchor's° cheer in prison be my scope,   335
Each opposite that blanks° the face of joy
Meet what I would have well, and it de-stroy:
Both here and hence pursue me lasting strife,
If, once a widow, ever I be wife!
HAMLET. If she should break it now!   340
PLAYER KING. 'Tis deeply sworn. Sweet, leave me here awhile;
My spirits grow dull, and fain I would beguile
The tedious day with sleep.
PLAYER QUEEN.   Sleep rock thy brain,

[He] sleeps.

And never come mischance between us twain!   *Exit.*
HAMLET. Madam, how like you this play?   345
QUEEN. The lady doth protest too much, methinks.
HAMLET. O, but she'll keep her word.
KING. Have you heard the argument?° Is there no offense in't?   350
HAMLET. No, no, they do but jest, poison in jest; no offense i' th' world.
KING. What do you call the play?
HAMLET. *The Mousetrap.* Marry, how? Tropically.° This play is the image of a mur-   355
der done in Vienna: Gonzago is the Duke's name; his wife, Baptista. You shall see anon. 'Tis a knavish piece of work, but what of that? Your Majesty, and we that have free° souls, it touches us not. Let the   360

---

²⁹⁸ **instances** motives ²⁹⁸ **move** induce ²⁹⁹ **re-spects of thrift** considerations of profit ³⁰⁵ **va-lidity** strength ³¹³ **enactures** acts ³²⁵ **seasons him** ripens him into

³³⁵ **anchor's** anchorite's, hermit's ³³⁶ **opposite that blanks** adverse thing that blanches ³⁴⁹ **ar-gument** plot ³⁵⁵ **Tropically** figuratively (with a pun on "trap") ³⁶⁰ **free** innocent

galled jade winch;° our withers are un-
wrung.

Enter LUCIANUS.

This is one Lucianus, nephew to the
King.

365   OPHELIA. You are as good as a chorus,
my lord.

HAMLET. I could interpret° between you
and your love, if I could see the puppets
dallying.

370   OPHELIA. You are keen,° my lord, you
are keen.

HAMLET. It would cost you a groaning to
take off mine edge.

OPHELIA. Still better, and worse.

375   HAMLET. So you mistake° your husbands.—Begin, murderer. Leave thy damnable faces and begin. Come, the croaking
raven doth bellow for revenge.

LUCIANUS. Thoughts black, hands apt,
drugs fit, and time agreeing,
Confederate season,° else no creature
380   seeing,
Thou mixture rank, of midnight weeds
collected,
With Hecate's ban° thrice blasted, thrice
infected,
Thy natural magic and dire property°
On wholesome life usurps immediately.

Pours the poison in his ears.

385   HAMLET. 'A poisons him i' th' garden for
his estate. His name's Gonzago. The story
is extant, and written in very choice Italian.
You shall see anon how the murderer gets
the love of Gonzago's wife.

390   OPHELIA. The King rises.

HAMLET. What, frighted with false fire?°

QUEEN. How fares my lord?

POLONIUS. Give o'er the play.

KING. Give me some light. Away!

POLONIUS. Lights, lights, lights!   395

Exeunt all but HAMLET *and* HORATIO.

HAMLET. Why, let the strucken deer go
weep,
The hart ungallèd play:
For some must watch, while some must
sleep;
Thus runs the world away.

Would not this, sir, and a forest of   400
feathers°—if the rest of my fortunes turn
Turk° with me—with two Provincial roses°
on my razed° shoes, get me a fellowship in
a cry° of players?

HORATIO. Half a share.   405

HAMLET. A whole one, I.

For thou dost know, O Damon dear,
This realm dismantled was
Of Jove himself; and now reigns here
A very, very—pajock.°   410

HORATIO. You might have rhymed.°

HAMLET. O good Horatio, I'll take the
ghost's word for a thousand pound. Didst
perceive?

HORATIO. Very well, my lord.   415

HAMLET. Upon the talk of poisoning?

HORATIO. I did very well note him.

HAMLET. Ah ha! Come, some music!
Come, the recorders!°

For if the king like not the comedy,   420
Why then, belike he likes it not,
perdy.°

Come, some music!

Enter ROSENCRANTZ *and* GUILDENSTERN.

GUILDENSTERN. Good my lord, vouchsafe
me a word with you.

HAMLET. Sir, a whole history.   425

GUILDENSTERN. The King, sir——

---

361 **galled jade winch** chafed horse wince 367 **interpret** (like a showman explaining the action of
puppets) 370 **keen** (1) sharp, (2) sexually aroused
375 **mistake** err in taking 380 **Confederate season** the opportunity allied with me 382 **Hecate's
ban** the curse of the goddess of sorcery
383 **property** nature 391 **false fire** blank discharge
of firearms

401 **feathers** (plumes were sometimes part of a
costume) 402 **turn Turk** i.e., go bad, treat me
badly 402 **Provincial roses** rosettes like the
roses of Provence (?) 403 **razed** ornamented with
slashes 404 **cry** pack, company 410 **pajock** peacock
411 **You might have rhymed** i.e., rhymed "was"
with "ass" 419 **recorders** flutelike instruments
421 **perdy** by God (French: *par dieu*)

HAMLET. Ay, sir, what of him?

GUILDENSTERN. Is in his retirement marvelous distemp'red.

430 HAMLET. With drink, sir?

GUILDENSTERN. No, my lord, with choler.°

HAMLET. Your wisdom should show itself more richer to signify this to the doctor, for
435 for me to put him to his purgation would perhaps plunge him into more choler.

GUILDENSTERN. Good my lord, put your discourse into some frame,° and start not so wildly from my affair.

440 HAMLET. I am tame, sir; pronounce.

GUILDENSTERN. The Queen, your mother, in most great affliction of spirit hath sent me to you.

HAMLET. You are welcome.

445 GUILDENSTERN. Nay, good my lord, this courtesy is not of the right breed. If it shall please you to make me a wholesome answer, I will do your mother's commandment: if not, your pardon and my return
450 shall be the end of my business.

HAMLET. Sir, I cannot.

ROSENCRANTZ. What, my lord?

HAMLET. Make you a wholesome° answer; my wit's diseased. But, sir, such an-
455 swer as I can make, you shall command, or rather, as you say, my mother. Therefore no more, but to the matter. My mother, you say——

ROSENCRANTZ. Then thus she says: your
460 behavior hath struck her into amazement and admiration.°

HAMLET. O wonderful son, that can so stonish a mother! But is there no sequel at the heels of this mother's admiration? Im-
465 part.

ROSENCRANTZ. She desires to speak with you in her closet ere you go to bed.

HAMLET. We shall obey, were she ten times our mother. Have you any further
470 trade with us?

ROSENCRANTZ. My lord, you once did love me.

HAMLET. And do still, by these pickers and stealers.°

ROSENCRANTZ. Good my lord, what is 475 your cause of distemper? You do surely bar the door upon your own liberty, if you deny your griefs to your friend.

HAMLET. Sir, I lack advancement.°

ROSENCRANTZ. How can that be, when 480 you have the voice of the King himself for your succession in Denmark?

Enter the PLAYERS *with recorders.*

HAMLET. Ay, sir, but "while the grass grows"—the proverb° is something musty. O, the recorders. Let me see one. To with- 485 draw° with you—why do you go about to recover the wind° of me as if you would drive me into a toil?°

GUILDENSTERN. O my lord, if my duty be too bold, my love is too unmannerly.° 490

HAMLET. I do not well understand that. Will you play upon this pipe?

GUILDENSTERN. My lord, I cannot.

HAMLET. I pray you.

GUILDENSTERN. Believe me, I cannot. 495

HAMLET. I pray you.

GUILDENSTERN. Believe me, I cannot.

HAMLET. I do beseech you.

GUILDENSTERN. I know no touch of it, my lord. 500

HAMLET. It is as easy as lying. Govern these ventages° with your fingers and thumb, give it breath with your mouth, and it will discourse most eloquent music. Look you, these are the stops. 505

GUILDENSTERN. But these cannot I command to any utt'rance of harmony; I have not the skill.

431-432 **choler** anger (but Hamlet pretends to take the word in its sense of "biliousness") 438 **frame** order, control 453 **wholesome** sane 461 **admiration** wonder

473-474 **pickers and stealers** i.e., hands (with reference to the prayer): "Keep my hands from picking and stealing") 479 **advancement** promotion 484 **proverb** ("While the grass groweth, the horse starveth") 485-486 **withdraw** speak in private 487 **recover the wind** get on the windward side (as in hunting) 488 **toil** snare 489-490 **if my duty . . . too unmannerly** i.e., if these questions seem rude, it is because my love for you leads me beyond good manners 502 **ventages** vents, stops on a recorder

HAMLET. Why, look you now, how unworthy a thing you make of me! You would play upon me; you would seem to know my stops; you would pluck out the heart of my mystery; you would sound me from my lowest note to the top of my compass;° and there is much music, excellent voice, in this little organ,° yet cannot you make it speak. 'Sblood, do you think I am easier to be played on than a pipe? Call me what instrument you will, though you can fret° me, you cannot play upon me.

Enter POLONIUS.

God bless you, sir!
POLONIUS. My lord, the Queen would speak with you, and presently.
HAMLET. Do you see yonder cloud that's almost in shape of a camel?
POLONIUS. By th' mass and 'tis, like a camel indeed.
HAMLET. Methinks it is like a weasel.
POLONIUS. It is backed like a weasel.
HAMLET. Or like a whale.
POLONIUS. Very like a whale.
HAMLET. Then I will come to my mother by and by. *[Aside.]* They fool me to the top of my bent.°—I will come by and by.°
POLONIUS. I will say so.   *Exit.*
HAMLET. "By and by" is easily said. Leave me, friends.

                    [Exeunt all but HAMLET.*]*
'Tis now the very witching time of night,
When churchyards yawn, and hell itself breathes out
Contagion to this world. Now could I drink hot blood
And do such bitter business as the day
Would quake to look on. Soft, now to my mother.
O heart, lose not thy nature; let not ever
The soul of Nero° enter this firm bosom.

Let me be cruel, not unnatural;   545
I will speak daggers to her, but use none.
My tongue and soul in this be hypocrites:
How in my words somever she be shent,°
To give them seals° never, my soul, consent!   *Exit.*

[Scene III. The castle.]

Enter KING, ROSENCRANTZ, *and* GUILDENSTERN.

KING. I like him not, nor stands it safe with us
To let his madness range. Therefore prepare you.
I your commission will forthwith dispatch,
And he to England shall along with you.
The terms° of our estate may not endure   5
Hazard so near's° as doth hourly grow
Out of his brows.
GUILDENSTERN. We will ourselves provide.
Most holy and religious fear it is
To keep those many many bodies safe
That live and feed upon your Majesty.   10
ROSENCRANTZ. The single and peculiar° life is bound
With all the strength and armor of the mind
To keep itself from noyance,° but much more
That spirit upon whose weal depends and rests
The lives of many. The cess of majesty°   15
Dies not alone, but like a gulf° doth draw
What's near it with it; or it is a massy wheel
Fixed on the summit of the highest mount,
To whose huge spokes ten thousand lesser things
Are mortised and adjoined, which when it falls,   20
Each small annexment, petty consequence,
Attends° the boist'rous ruin. Never alone

---

⁵¹⁴ **compass** range of voice ⁵¹⁶ **organ** i.e., the recorder ⁵¹⁹ **fret** vex (with a pun alluding to the frets, or ridges, that guide the fingering on some instruments) ⁵³³⁻⁵³⁴ **They fool . . . my bent** they compel me to play the fool to the limit of my capacity ⁵³⁴ **by and by** very soon ⁵⁴⁴ **Nero** (Roman emperor who had his mother murdered)

⁵⁴⁸ **shent** rebuked ⁵⁴⁹ **give them seals** confirm them with deeds III.iii. ⁵ **terms** conditions ⁶ **near's** near us ¹¹ **peculiar** individual, private ¹³ **noyance** injury ¹⁵ **cess of majesty** cessation (death) of a king ¹⁶ **gulf** whirlpool ²² **Attends** waits on, participates in

Did the King sigh, but with a general
   groan.
   KING. Arm° you, I pray you, to this
     speedy voyage,
25 For we will fetters put about this fear,
Which now goes too free-footed.
   ROSENCRANTZ.   We will haste us.
                 Exeunt GENTLEMEN.

Enter POLONIUS.

   POLONIUS. My lord, he's going to his
     mother's closet.°
Behind the arras I'll convey myself
To hear the process.° I'll warrant she'll
   tax him home,°
30 And, as you said, and wisely was it said,
'Tis meet that some more audience than a
   mother,
Since nature makes them partial, should
   o'erhear
The speech of vantage.° Fare you well, my
   liege.
I'll call upon you ere you go to bed
And tell you what I know.
35   KING.   Thanks, dear my lord.
                   *Exit [*POLONIUS*].*
O, my offense is rank, it smells to heaven;
It hath the primal eldest curse° upon't,
A brother's murder. Pray can I not,
Though inclination be as sharp as will.
My stronger guilt defeats my strong in-
40   tent,
And like a man to double business bound
I stand in pause where I shall first begin,
And both neglect. What if this cursèd hand
Were thicker than itself with brother's
   blood,
Is there not rain enough in the sweet
45   heavens
To wash it white as snow? Whereto serves
   mercy
But to confront° the visage of offense?
And what's in prayer but this twofold
   force,
To be forestallèd ere we come to fall,

Or pardoned being down? Then I'll look
   up.   50
My fault is past. But, O, what form of
   prayer
Can serve my turn? "Forgive me my foul
   murder"?
That cannot be, since I am still possessed
Of those effects° for which I did the mur-
   der,
My crown, mine own ambition, and my
   queen.   55
May one be pardoned and retain th' of-
   fense?
In the corrupted currents of this world
Offense's gilded hand may shove by jus-
   tice,
And oft 'tis seen the wicked prize itself
Buys out the law. But 'tis not so above.   60
There is no shuffling;° there the action lies
In his true nature, and we ourselves com-
   pelled,
Even to the teeth and forehead of our
   faults,
To give in evidence. What then? What
   rests?°
Try what repentance can. What can it not?   65
Yet what can it when one cannot repent?
O wretched state! O bosom black as
   death!
O limèd° soul, that struggling to be free
Art more engaged!° Help, angels! Make
   assay.°
Bow, stubborn knees, and, heart with
   strings of steel,   70
Be soft as sinews of the newborn babe.
All may be well. *[He kneels.]*

Enter HAMLET.

   HAMLET. Now might I do it pat, now 'a
     is a-praying,
And now I'll do't. And so 'a goes to
   heaven,
And so am I revenged. That would be
   scanned.°   75

---

²⁴ **Arm** prepare ²⁷ **closet** private room ²⁹ **proc-ess** proceedings ²⁹ **tax him home** censure him sharply ³³ **of vantage** from an advantageous place ³⁷ **primal eldest curse** (curse of Cain, who killed Abel) ⁴⁷ **confront** oppose

⁵⁴ **effects** things gained ⁶¹ **shuffling** trickery ⁶⁴ **rests** remains ⁶⁸ **limèd** caught (as with bird-lime, a sticky substance spread on boughs to snare birds) ⁶⁹ **engaged** ensnared ⁶⁹ **assay** an at-tempt ⁷⁵ **would be scanned** ought to be looked into

A villain kills my father, and for that
I, his sole son, do this same villain send
To heaven.
Why, this is hire and salary, not revenge.
80 'A took my father grossly, full of bread,°
With all his crimes broad blown,° as flush°
    as May;
And how his audit° stands, who knows
    save heaven?
But in our circumstance and course of
    thought,
'Tis heavy with him; and am I then re-
    venged,
85 To take him in the purging of his soul,
When he is fit and seasoned for his pas-
    sage?
No.
Up, sword, and know thou a more horrid
    hent.°
When he is drunk asleep, or in his rage,
90 Or in th' incestuous pleasure of his bed,
At game a-swearing, or about some act
That has no relish° of salvation in't—
Then trip him, that his heels may kick at
    heaven,
And that his soul may be as damned and
    black
As hell, whereto it goes. My mother
95   stays.
This physic° but prolongs thy sickly days.
                              Exit.

    KING *[rises].* My words fly up, my
        thoughts remain below.
Words without thoughts never to heaven
    go.   *Exit.*

[Scene IV. The Queen's closet.]

Enter [QUEEN] GERTRUDE *and* POLONIUS.

    POLONIUS. 'A will come straight. Look
        you lay home° to him.
Tell him his pranks have been too broad°
    to bear with,

And that your Grace hath screened and
    stood between
Much heat and him. I'll silence me even
    here.
Pray you be round with him.   5
    HAMLET *[within].* Mother, Mother,
        Mother!
    QUEEN. I'll warrant you; fear me not.
        Withdraw; I hear him coming.
        [POLONIUS hides behind the arras.]

Enter HAMLET.

    HAMLET. Now, Mother, what's the mat-
        ter?
    QUEEN. Hamlet, thou hast thy father
        much offended.
    HAMLET. Mother, you have my father
        much offended.   10
    QUEEN. Come, come, you answer with
        an idle° tongue.
    HAMLET. Go, go, you question with a
        wicked tongue.
    QUEEN. Why, how now, Hamlet?
    HAMLET.   What's the matter now?
    QUEEN. Have you forgot me?
    HAMLET.   No, by the rood,° not so!
You are the Queen, your husband's broth-
    er's wife,   15
And, would it were not so, you are my
    mother.
    QUEEN. Nay, then I'll set those to you
        that can speak.
    HAMLET. Come, come, and sit you
        down. You shall not budge.
You go not till I set you up a glass°
Where you may see the inmost part of
    you!   20
    QUEEN. What wilt thou do? Thou wilt
        not murder me?
Help, ho!
    POLONIUS *[behind].* What, ho! Help!
    HAMLET *[draws].* How now? A rat?
        Dead for a ducat, dead!

[Makes a pass through the arras and] kills
POLONIUS.

    POLONIUS *[behind].* O, I am slain!
    QUEEN.   O me, what hast thou done? 25

---

80 bread i.e., wordly gratification ⁸¹ **crimes broad blown** sins in full bloom ⁸¹ **flush** vigorous ⁸² **audit** account ⁸⁸ **hent** grasp (here, occasion for seizing) ⁹² **relish** flavor ⁹⁶ **physic** (Claudius' purgation by prayer, as Hamlet thinks in line 85) III.iv. ¹ **lay home** thrust (rebuke) him sharply ² **broad** unrestrained

¹² **idle** foolish ¹⁴ **rood** cross ¹⁹ **glass** mirror

HAMLET. Nay, I know not. Is it the King?

QUEEN. O, what a rash and bloody deed
is this!

HAMLET. A bloody deed—almost as bad,
good Mother,

As kill a king, and marry with his brother.

QUEEN. As kill a king?

HAMLET.   Ay, lady, it was
30   my word.

[Lifts up the arras and sees POLONIUS.*]*

Thou wretched, rash, intruding fool, farewell!

I took thee for thy better. Take thy fortune.

Thou find'st to be too busy is some
danger.—

Leave wringing of your hands. Peace, sit
you down

35   And let me wring your heart, for so I shall
If it be made of penetrable stuff,
If damnèd custom have not brazed° it so
That it be proof° and bulwark against
sense.°

QUEEN. What have I done that thou
dar'st wag thy tongue
In noise so rude against me?

40   HAMLET.   Such an act
That blurs the grace and blush of mod-
esty,
Calls virtue hypocrite, takes off the rose
From the fair forehead of an innocent love,
And sets a blister° there, makes marriage
vows

45   As false as dicers' oaths. O, such a deed
As from the body of contraction° plucks
The very soul, and sweet religion makes
A rhapsody° of words! Heaven's face does
glow
O'er this solidity and compound mass

50   With heated visage, as against the doom
Is thoughtsick at the act.°

QUEEN.   Ay me, what act,
That roars so loud and thunders in the
index?°

HAMLET. Look here upon this picture,
and on this,
The counterfeit presentment° of two
brothers.

See what a grace was seated on this brow: 55
Hyperion's curls, the front° of Jove him-
self,
An eye like Mars, to threaten and com-
mand,
A station° like the herald Mercury
New lighted on a heaven-kissing hill—
A combination and a form indeed   60
Where every god did seem to set his seal
To give the world assurance of a man.
This was your husband. Look you now
what follows.
Here is your husband, like a mildewed ear
Blasting his wholesome brother. Have you
eyes?   65
Could you on this fair mountain leave to
feed,
And batten° on this moor? Ha! Have you
eyes?
You cannot call it love, for at your age
The heyday° in the blood is tame, it's
humble,
And waits upon the judgment, and what
judgment   70
Would step from this to this? Sense° sure
you have,
Else could you not have motion, but sure
that sense
Is apoplexed,° for madness would not err,
Nor sense to ecstasy° was ne'er so
thralled
But it reserved some quantity of choice   75
To serve in such a difference. What devil
wast
That thus hath cozened you at hoodman-
blind?°
Eyes without feeling, feeling without sight,

---

37 **brazed** hardened like brass ³⁸ **proof** armor
³⁸ **sense** feeling ⁴⁴ **sets a blister** brands (as a
harlot) ⁴⁶ **contraction** marriage contract
⁴⁸ **rhapsody** senseless string ⁴⁸⁻⁵¹ **Heaven's
face . . . the act** i.e., the face of heaven
blushes over this earth (compounded of four elements), the face hot, as if Judgment Day were
near, and it is thoughtsick at the act

⁵² **index** prologue ⁵⁴ **counterfeit presentment**
represented image ⁵⁶ **front** forehead ⁵⁸ **station**
bearing ⁶⁷ **batten** feed gluttonously ⁶⁹ **heyday**
excitement ⁷¹ **Sense** feeling ⁷³ **apoplexed** paralyzed ⁷⁴ **ecstasy** madness ⁷⁷ **cozened you at
hoodman-blind** cheated you at blindman's buff

Ears without hands or eyes, smelling
    sans° all,
80 Or but a sickly part of one true sense
Could not so mope.°
O shame, where is thy blush? Rebellious
    hell,
If thou canst mutine in a matron's bones,
To flaming youth let virtue be as wax
And melt in her own fire. Proclaim no
85   shame
When the compulsive ardor° gives the
    charge,
Since frost itself as actively doth burn,
And reason panders will.°
    QUEEN.   O Hamlet, speak no more.
Thou turn'st mine eyes into my very soul,
And there I see such black and grainèd°
90   spots
As will not leave their tinct.°
    HAMLET.   Nay, but to live
In the rank sweat of an enseamèd° bed,
Stewed in corruption, honeying and mak-
    ing love
Over the nasty sty——
    QUEEN.   O, speak to me no more.
These words like daggers enter in my
95   ears.
No more, sweet Hamlet.
    HAMLET.   A murderer and a villain,
A slave that is not twentieth part the
    tithe°
Of your precedent lord, a vice° of kings,
A cutpurse of the empire and the rule,
That from a shell the precious diadem
100   stole
And put it in his pocket——
    QUEEN.   No more.

Enter GHOST.

    HAMLET. A king of shreds and patches——

Save me and hover o'er me with your
    wings,
You heavenly guards! What would your
    gracious figure?
    QUEEN. Alas, he's mad.   105
    HAMLET. Do you not come your tardy
    son to chide,
That, lapsed in time and passion, lets go
    by
Th' important acting of your dread com-
    mand?
O, say!
    GHOST. Do not forget. This visitation   110
Is but to whet thy almost blunted purpose.
But look, amazement on thy mother sits.
O, step between her and her fighting soul!
Conceit° in weakest bodies strongest
    works.
Speak to her, Hamlet.
    HAMLET.   How is it with you, lady?   115
    QUEEN. Alas, how is't with you,
That you do bend your eye on vacancy,
And with th' incorporal° air do hold dis-
    course?
Forth at your eyes your spirits wildly
    peep,
And as the sleeping soldiers in th' alarm   120
Your bedded hair° like life in excrements°
Start up and stand an end.° O gentle son,
Upon the heat and flame of thy distemper
Sprinkle cool patience. Whereon do you
    look?
    HAMLET. On him, on him!
Look you, how pale he glares!   125
His form and cause conjoined, preaching
    to stones,
Would make them capable.°—Do not look
    upon me,
Lest with this piteous action you convert
My stern effects.°—Then what I have to
    do
Will want true color; tears perchance for
    blood.   130
    QUEEN. To whom do you speak this?
    HAMLET.   Do you see nothing there?

QUEEN. Nothing at all; yet all that is I
    see.

HAMLET. Nor did you nothing hear?

QUEEN.   No, nothing but ourselves.

HAMLET. Why, look you there! Look how
    it steals away!

135 My father, in his habit° as he lived!

Look where he goes even now at the
    portal!   *Exit* GHOST.

QUEEN. This is the very coinage of your
    brain.

This bodiless creation ecstasy

Is very cunning in.

HAMLET.   Ecstasy?

My pulse as yours doth temperately keep

140   time

And makes as healthful music. It is not
    madness

That I have uttered. Bring me to the test,

And I the matter will reword, which mad-
    ness

Would gambol° from. Mother, for love of
    grace,

Lay not that flattering unction° to your

145   soul,

That not your trespass but my madness
    speaks.

It will but skin and film the ulcerous place

Whiles rank corruption, mining° all within,

Infects unseen. Confess yourself to
    heaven,

Repent what's past, avoid what is to

150   come,

And do not spread the compost° on the
    weeds

To make them ranker. Forgive me this my
    virtue.

For in the fatness of these pursy° times

Virtue itself of vice must pardon beg,

Yea, curb° and woo for leave to do him

155   good.

QUEEN. O Hamlet, thou hast cleft my
    heart in twain.

HAMLET. O, throw away the worser part
    of it,

And live the purer with the other half.

Good night—but go not to my uncle's bed.

Assume a virtue, if you have it not.   160

That monster custom, who all sense doth
    eat,

Of habits devil, is angel yet in this,

That to the use° of actions fair and good

He likewise gives a frock or livery°

That aptly is put on. Refrain tonight,   165

And that shall lend a kind of easiness

To the next abstinence; the next more
    easy;

For use almost can change the stamp of
    nature,

And either° the devil, or throw him out

With wondrous potency. Once more, good
    night,   170

And when you are desirous to be blest,

I'll blessing beg of you.—For this same
    lord,

I do repent; but heaven hath pleased it so,

To punish me with this, and this with me,

That I must be their° scourge and minis-
    ter.   175

I will bestow° him and will answer well

The death I gave him. So again, good
    night.

I must be cruel only to be kind.

Thus bad begins, and worse remains
    behind.

One word more, good lady.

QUEEN.   What shall I do?   180

HAMLET. Not this, by no means, that I
    bid you do:

Let the bloat King tempt you again to bed,

Pinch wanton on your cheek, call you his
    mouse,

And let him, for a pair of reechy° kisses,

Or paddling in your neck with his damned
    fingers,   185

---

[135] **habit** garment (Q1, though a "bad" quarto, is probably correct in saying that at line 102 the ghost enters "in his nightgown," i.e., dressing gown) [144] **gambol** start away [145] **unction** ointment [148] **mining** undermining [151] **compost** fertilizing substance [153] **pursy** bloated [155] **curb** bow low

[153] **use** practice [164] **livery** characteristic garment (punning on "habits" in line 162) [169] **either** (probably a word is missing after *either*; among suggestions are "master," "curb," and "house"; but possibly *either* is a verb meaning "make easier") [175] **their** i.e., the heavens' [176] **bestow** stow, lodge [184] **reechy** foul (literally "smoky")

Make you to ravel° all this matter out,
That I essentially am not in madness,
But mad in craft. 'Twere good you let him
    know,
For who that's but a queen, fair, sober,
    wise,
190 Would from a paddock,° from a bat, a gib,°
Such dear concernings hide? Who would
    do so?
No, in despite of sense and secrecy,
Unpeg the basket on the house's top,
Let the birds fly, and like the famous ape,
195 To try conclusions,° in the basket creep
And break your own neck down.
    QUEEN. Be thou assured, if words be
        made of breath,
And breath of life, I have no life to breathe
What thou hast said to me.
    HAMLET. I must to England; you know
        that?
200   QUEEN.   Alack,
I had forgot. 'Tis so concluded on.
    HAMLET. There's letters sealed, and my
        two school-fellows,
Whom I will trust as I will adders fanged,
They bear the mandate;° they must sweep
    my way
205 And marshal me to knavery. Let it work;
For 'tis the sport to have the enginer
Hoist with his own petar,° and 't shall go
    hard
But I will delve one yard below their
    mines
And blow them at the moon. O, 'tis most
    sweet
When in one line two crafts° directly
210   meet.
This man shall set me packing:
I'll lug the guts into the neighbor room.
Mother, good night. Indeed, this counselor
Is now most still, most secret, and most
    grave,

Who was in life a foolish prating knave.   215
Come, sir, to draw toward an end with
    you.
Good night, Mother.
    [Exit the QUEEN. *Then] exit* HAMLET,
              tugging in POLONIUS.

/ACT IV

Scene I. The castle.]

Enter KING *and* QUEEN, *with* ROSENCRANTZ
and GUILDENSTERN.

    KING. There's matter in these sighs.
        These profound heaves
You must translate; 'tis fit we understand
    them.
Where is your son?
    QUEEN. Bestow this place on us a little
        while.   *[Exeunt* ROSENCRANTZ
              and GUILDENSTERN.]

Ah, mine own lord, what have I seen
    tonight!   5
    KING. What, Gertrude? How does Ham-
        let?
    QUEEN. Mad as the sea and wind when
        both contend
Which is the mightier. In his lawless fit,
Behind the arras hearing something stir,
Whips out his rapier, cries, "A rat, a rat!"   10
And in this brainish apprehension° kills
The unseen good old man.
    KING.   O heavy deed!
It had been so with us, had we been
    there.
His liberty is full of threats to all,
To you yourself, to us, to every one.   15
Alas, how shall this bloody deed be an-
    swered?
It will be laid to us, whose providence°
Should have kept short, restrained, and
    out of haunt°

---

186 **ravel** unravel, reveal 190 **paddock** toad 190 **gib**
tomcat 195 **To try conclusions** to make experiments 204 **mandate** command 207 **petar** bomb
210 **crafts** (1) boats, (2) acts of guile, crafty
schemes

IV.i. 11 **brainish apprehension** mad imagination 17 **providence** foresight 18 **out of haunt**
away from association with others

This mad young man. But so much was
    our love
We would not understand what was most
20   fit,
But, like the owner of a foul disease,
To keep it from divulging, let it feed
Even on the pith of life. Where is he
    gone?
    QUEEN. To draw apart the body he hath
    killed;
O'er whom his very madness, like some
25   ore
Among a mineral° of metals base,
Shows itself pure. 'A weeps for what is
    done.
    KING. O Gertrude, come away!
The sun no sooner shall the mountains
    touch
But we will ship him hence, and this vile
30   deed
We must with all our majesty and skill
Both countenance and excuse. Ho,
    Guildenstern!

Enter ROSENCRANTZ *and* GUILDENSTERN.

Friends both, go join you with some fur-
    ther aid:
Hamlet in madness hath Polonius slain,
And from his mother's closet hath he
35   dragged him.
Go seek him out; speak fair, and bring the
    body
Into the chapel. I pray you haste in this.
    [Exeunt ROSENCRANTZ *and*
        GUILDENSTERN.*]*
Come, Gertrude, we'll call up our wisest
    friends
And let them know both what we mean to
    do
40   And what's untimely done. . .°
Whose whisper o'er the world's diameter,
As level as the cannon to his blank°
Transports his poisoned shot, may miss
    our name

And hit the woundless° air. O, come away!
My soul is full of discord and dismay.   45
          Exeunt.

[Scene II. The castle.]

Enter HAMLET.

  HAMLET. Safely stowed.
  GENTLEMEN *[within]*. Hamlet! Lord
    Hamlet!
  HAMLET. But soft, what noise? Who calls
    on Hamlet? O, here they come.

Enter ROSENCRANTZ *and* GUILDENSTERN.

  ROSENCRANTZ. What have you done, my
    lord, with the dead body?
  HAMLET. Compounded it with dust,
    whereto 'tis kin.   5
  ROSENCRANTZ.   Tell us where 'tis, that
we may take it thence and bear it to the
chapel.
  HAMLET. Do not believe it.
  ROSENCRANTZ. Believe what?   10
  HAMLET. That I can keep your counsel
and not mine own. Besides, to be demanded of° a sponge, what replication°
should be made by the son of a king?
  ROSENCRANTZ. Take you me for a   15
sponge, my lord?
  HAMLET. Ay, sir, that soaks up the King's
countenance,° his rewards, his authorities.
But such officers do the King best service
in the end. He keeps them, like an ape, in   20
the corner of his jaw, first mouthed, to be
last swallowed. When he needs what you
have gleaned, it is but squeezing you and,
sponge, you shall be dry again.
  ROSENCRANTZ. I understand you not, my   25
lord.
  HAMLET. I am glad of it: a knavish
speech sleeps in a foolish ear.
  ROSENCRANTZ. My lord, you must tell us
where the body is and go with us to the   30
King.

---

²⁵⁻²⁶ **ore/Among a mineral** vein of gold in a
mine ⁴⁰ **done . . .** (evidently something has
dropped out of the text. Cappell's conjecture,
"So, haply slander," is usually printed) ⁴² **blank**
white center of a target

⁴⁴ **woundless** invulnerable IV.ii. ¹²⁻¹³ **demanded
of** questioned by ¹³ **replication** reply ¹⁸ **countenance** favor

HAMLET. The body is with the King, but the King is not with the body.° The King is a thing——

35   GUILDENSTERN. A thing, my lord?

HAMLET. Of nothing. Bring me to him. Hide fox, and all after.°   *Exeunt.*

[Scene III. The castle.]

Enter KING, *and two or three.*

KING. I have sent to seek him and to find the body:
How dangerous is it that this man goes loose!
Yet must not we put the strong law on him:
He's loved of the distracted° multitude,
5   Who like not in their judgment, but their eyes,
And where 'tis so, th' offender's scourge is weighed,
But never the offense. To bear° all smooth and even,
This sudden sending him away must seem
Deliberate pause.° Diseases desperate grown
10   By desperate appliance are relieved,
Or not at all.

Enter ROSENCRANTZ, *[*GUILDENSTERN,*] and all the rest.*

How now? What hath befall'n?
ROSENCRANTZ. Where the dead body is bestowed, my lord,
We cannot get from him.
KING.   But where is he?
ROSENCRANTZ. Without, my lord;
    guarded, to know your pleasure.
KING. Bring him before us.
15   ROSENCRANTZ.   Ho! Bring in the lord.

They enter.

KING. Now, Hamlet, where's Polonius?

HAMLET. At supper.

KING. At supper? Where?

HAMLET. Not where he eats, but where 'a is eaten. A certain convocation of politic° 20 worms are e'en at him. Your worm is your only emperor for diet. We fat all creatures else to fat us, and we fat ourselves for maggots. Your fat king and your lean beggar is but variable service°—two dishes, but to 25 one table. That's the end.

KING. Alas, alas!

HAMLET. A man may fish with the worm that hath eat of a king, and eat of the fish that hath fed of that worm.   30

KING. What dost thou mean by this?

HAMLET. Nothing but to show you how a king may go a progress° through the guts of a beggar.

KING. Where is Polonius?   35

HAMLET. In heaven. Send thither to see. If your messenger find him not there, seek him i' th' other place yourself. But if indeed you find him not within this month, you shall nose him as you go up the stairs into 40 the lobby.

KING *[to* ATTENDANTS*]*. Go seek him there.

HAMLET. 'A will stay till you come.

                [Exeunt ATTENDANTS.*]*

KING. Hamlet, this deed, for thine especial safety,   45
Which we do tender° as we dearly grieve
For that which thou hast done, must send thee hence
With fiery quickness. Therefore prepare thyself.
The bark is ready and the wind at help,
Th' associates tend,° and everything is bent   50
For England.

HAMLET.   For England?

KING.   Ay, Hamlet.

HAMLET.   Good.

KING. So is it, if thou knew'st our purposes.

---

³²⁻³³ **The body . . . body** i.e., the body of authority is with Claudius, but spiritually he is not the true king ³⁷ **Hide fox, and all after** (a cry in a game such as hide-and-seek; Hamlet runs from the stage) IV.iii. ⁴ **distracted** bewildered, senseless ⁷ **bear** carry out ⁹ **pause** planning

²⁰ **politic** statesmanlike, shrewd ²⁵ **variable service** different courses ³³ **progress** royal journey ⁴⁶ **tender** hold dear ⁵⁰ **tend** wait

HAMLET. I see a cherub° that sees them.
But come, for England! Farewell, dear
55 Mother.
    KING. Thy loving father, Hamlet.
    HAMLET. My mother—father and mother
is man and wife, man and wife is one flesh,
and so, my mother. Come, for England!
                              Exit.
    KING. Follow him at foot;° tempt him
60   with speed abroad.
Delay it not; I'll have him hence tonight.
Away! For everything is sealed and done
That else leans° on th' affair. Pray you
    make haste. *[Exeunt all but the* KING.*]*

And, England, if my love thou hold'st at
    aught—
As my great power thereof may give thee
65   sense,
Since yet thy cicatrice° looks raw and red
After the Danish sword, and thy free awe°
Pays homage to us—thou mayst not coldly
    set
Our sovereign process,° which imports at
    full
70 By letters congruing to that effect
The present° death of Hamlet. Do it,
    England,
For like the hectic° in my blood he rages,
And thou must cure me. Till I know 'tis
    done,
How'er my haps,° my joys were ne'er
    begun.   *Exit.*

[Scene IV. A plain in Denmark.]

Enter FORTINBRAS *with his Army over the
stage.*

    FORTINBRAS. Go, Captain, from me
    greet the Danish king.
Tell him that by his license Fortinbras
Craves the conveyance of° a promised
    march

Over his kingdom. You know the rendez-
    vous.
If that his Majesty would aught with us,   5
We shall express our duty in his eye;°
And let him know so.
    CAPTAIN.   I will do't, my lord.
    FORTINBRAS. Go softly° on.
        [Exeunt all but the CAPTAIN.*]*

Enter HAMLET, ROSENCRANTZ, *&c.*

    HAMLET. Good sir, whose powers° are
    these?
    CAPTAIN. They are of Norway, sir.   10
    HAMLET. How purposed, sir, I pray you?
    CAPTAIN. Against some part of Poland.
    HAMLET. Who commands them, sir?
    CAPTAIN. The nephew to old Norway,
    Fortinbras.
    HAMLET. Goes it against the main° of
    Poland, sir,   15
Or for some frontier?
    CAPTAIN. Truly to speak, and with no
    addition,°
We go to gain a little patch of ground
That hath in it no profit but the name.
To pay five ducats, five, I would not farm
    it,   20
Nor will it yield to Norway or the Pole
A ranker° rate, should it be sold in fee.°
    HAMLET. Why, then the Polack never will
    defend it.
    CAPTAIN. Yes, it is already garrisoned.
    HAMLET. Two thousand souls and twenty
    thousand ducats   25
Will not debate° the question of this straw.
This is th' imposthume° of much wealth
    and peace,
That inward breaks, and shows no cause
    without
Why the man dies. I humbly thank you,
    sir.
    CAPTAIN. God bye you, sir.   *[Exit.]*
    ROSENCRANTZ.   Will't please you go, my
    lord?   30

---

⁵³ **cherub** angel of knowledge ⁶⁰ **at foot** closely
⁶³ **leans** depends ⁶⁶ **cicatrice** scar ⁶⁷ **free awe**
uncompelled submission ⁶⁸⁻⁶⁹ **coldly set/Our
sovereign process** regard slightly our royal
command ⁷¹ **present** instant ⁷² **hectic** fever
⁷⁴ **haps** chances, fortunes IV.iv. ³ **conveyance
of** escort for

⁶ **in his eye** before his eyes (i.e., in his presence) ⁸ **softly** slowly ⁹ **powers** forces ¹⁵ **main**
main part ¹⁷ **with no addition** plainly ²² **ranker**
higher ²² **in fee** outright ²⁶ **debate** settle ²⁷ **im-
posthume** abscess, ulcer

HAMLET. I'll be with you straight. Go a
    little before. *[Exeunt all but* HAMLET.*]*
How all occasions do inform against me
And spur my dull revenge! What is a man,
If his chief good and market° of his time
Be but to sleep and feed? A beast, no
35   more.
Sure he that made us with such large
    discourse,°
Looking before and after, gave us not
That capability and godlike reason
To fust° in us unused. Now, whether it be
40 Bestial oblivion,° or some craven scruple
Of thinking too precisely on th' event°—
A thought which, quartered, hath but one
    part wisdom
And ever three parts coward—I do not
    know
Why yet I live to say, "This thing's to do,"
Sith I have cause, and will, and strength,
45   and means
To do't. Examples gross° as earth exhort
    me.
Witness this army of such mass and
    charge,°
Led by a delicate and tender prince,
Whose spirit, with divine ambition puffed,
50 Makes mouths at the invisible event,°
Exposing what is mortal and unsure
To all that fortune, death, and danger
    dare,
Even for an eggshell. Rightly to be great
Is not° to stir without great argument,°
55 But greatly° to find quarrel in a straw
When honor's at the stake. How stand I
    then,
That have a father killed, a mother
    stained,
Excitements° of my reason and my blood,
And let all sleep, while to my shame I see

The imminent death of twenty thousand
    men   60
That for a fantasy and trick of fame°
Go to their graves like beds, fight for a
    plot
Whereon the numbers cannot try the
    cause,   65
Which is not tomb enough and continent°
To hide the slain? O, from this time forth,
My thoughts be bloody, or be nothing
    worth!   *Exit.*

[Scene V. *The castle.*]

Enter HORATIO, *[*QUEEN*]* GERTRUDE, *and a*
GENTLEMAN.

  QUEEN. I will not speak with her.
  GENTLEMAN. She is importunate, indeed
    distract.
Her mood will needs be pitied.
  QUEEN.   What would she have?
  GENTLEMAN. She speaks much of her
    father, says she hears
There's tricks i' th' world, and hems, and
    beats her heart,   5
Spurns enviously at straws,° speaks things
    in doubt°
That carry but half sense. Her speech is
    nothing,
Yet the unshapèd use of it doth move
The hearers to collection;° they yawn° at
    it,
And botch the words up fit to their own
    thoughts,   10
Which, as the winks and nods and ges-
    tures yield them,
Indeed would make one think there might
    be thought,
Though nothing sure, yet much unhappily.
  HORATIO. 'Twere good she were spoken
    with, for she may strew
Dangerous conjectures in ill-breeding
    minds.   15

---

³⁴ **market** profit ³⁶ **discourse** understanding
³⁹ **fust** grow moldy ⁴⁰ **oblivion** forgetfulness
⁴¹ **event** outcome ⁴⁶ **gross** large, obvious
⁴⁷ **charge** expense ⁵⁰ **Makes mouths at the
invisible event** makes scornful faces (is contemptuous of) the unseen outcome ⁵⁴ **not** (the
sense seems to require "not not") ⁵⁴ **argument**
reason ⁵⁵ **greatly** i.e., nobly ⁵⁸ **Excitements** in-
centives

⁶¹ **fantasy and trick of fame** illusion and trifle
of reputation ⁶⁴ **continent** receptacle, container
IV.v. ⁶ **Spurns enviously at straws** objects
spitefully to insignificant matters ⁶ **in doubt** uncertainly ⁸⁻⁹ **Yet the . . . to collection** i.e., yet
the formless manner of it moves her listeners to
gather up some sort of meaning ⁹ **yawn** gape (?)

QUEEN. Let her come in.

                [Exit GENTLEMAN.*]*

[Aside.] To my sick soul (as sin's true
    nature is)

Each toy seems prologue to some great
    amiss;°

So full of artless jealousy° is guilt

20 It spills° itself in fearing to be spilt.

Enter OPHELIA *[distracted].*

  OPHELIA. Where is the beauteous majesty of Denmark?

  QUEEN. How now, Ophelia?

  OPHELIA. *(She sings.)*

How should I your truelove know
    From another one?

25 By his cockle hat° and staff
    And his sandal shoon.°

  QUEEN. Alas, sweet lady, what imports
this song?

  OPHELIA. Say you? Nay, pray you mark.

He is dead and gone, lady,   *(Song.)*

30   He is dead and gone;

At his head a grass-green turf,
    At his heels a stone.

O, ho!

  QUEEN. Nay, but Ophelia——

35 OPHELIA. Pray you mark. *(Sings.)*

White his shroud as the mountain
    snow——

Enter KING.

  QUEEN. Alas, look here, my lord.

  OPHELIA.

    Larded° all with sweet flowers *(Song.)*
Which bewept to the grave did not go

40   With truelove showers.

  KING. How do you, pretty lady?

  OPHELIA. Well, God dild° you! They say

the owl was a baker's daughter.° Lord, we
know what we are, but know not what we
may be. God be at your table!   45

  KING. Conceit° upon her father.

  OPHELIA. Pray let's have no words of
this, but when they ask you what it means,
say you this:

Tomorrow is Saint Valentine's day.°

                  (Song.) 50
    All in the morning betime,
And I a maid at your window,
    To be your Valentine.
Then up he rose and donned his clothes
    And dupped° the chamber door, 55
Let in the maid, that out a maid
    Never departed more.

  KING. Pretty Ophelia.

  OPHELIA. Indeed, la, without an oath, I'll
make an end on't: 60

[Sings.]

  By Gis° and by Saint Charity,
    Alack, and fie for shame!
Young men will do't if they come to't,
    By Cock,° they are to blame.
Quoth she, "Before you tumbled me, 65
    You promised me to wed."

He answers:

"So would I 'a' done, by yonder sun,
    An thou hadst not come to my bed."

  KING. How long hath she been thus? 70

  OPHELIA. I hope all will be well. We must
be patient, but I cannot choose but weep to
think they would lay him i' th' cold ground.
My brother shall know of it; and so I thank
you for your good counsel. Come, my 75
coach! Good night, ladies, good night.
Sweet ladies, good night, good night. *Exit.*

  KING. Follow her close; give her good
watch, I pray you.   *[Exit* HORATIO.*]*

---

¹⁸ **amiss** misfortune ¹⁹ **artless jealousy** crude
suspicion ²⁰ **spills** destroys ²⁵ **cockle hat** (a
cockleshell on the hat was the sign of a pilgrim
who had journeyed to shrines overseas. The association of lovers and pilgrims was a common
one) ²⁶ **shoon** shoes ³⁸ **Larded** decorated ⁴² **dild**
yield, i.e., reward

⁴³ **baker's daughter** (an allusion to a tale of a
baker's daughter who begrudged bread to Christ
and was turned into an owl) ⁴⁶ **Conceit** brooding
⁵⁰ **Saint Valentine's day** Feb. 14 (the notion
was that a bachelor would become the truelove of
the first girl he saw on this day) ⁵⁵ **dupped**
opened (did up) ⁶¹ **Gis** (contraction of "Jesus")
⁶⁴ **Cock** (1) God, (2) phallus

O, this is the poison of deep grief; it
springs
All from her father's death—and now
behold!
O Gertrude, Gertrude,
When sorrows come, they come not single
spies,
But in battalions; first, her father slain;
Next, your son gone, and he most violent
author
Of his own just remove; the people mud-
died,°
Thick and unwholesome in their thoughts
and whispers
For good Polonius' death, and we have
done but greenly°
In huggermugger° to inter him; poor
Ophelia
Divided from herself and her fair judg-
ment,
Without the which we are pictures or
mere beasts;
Last, and as much containing as all these,
Her brother is in secret come from
France,
Feeds on his wonder,° keeps himself in
clouds,
And wants not buzzers° to infect his ear
With pestilent speeches of his father's
death,
Wherein necessity, of matter beggared,°
Will nothing stick° our person to arraign
In ear and ear. O my dear Gertrude, this,
Like a murd'ring piece,° in many places
Gives me superfluous death.
                        A noise within.

Enter a MESSENGER.

QUEEN.   Alack, what noise is this?
KING. Attend, where are my Switzers?°
        Let them guard the door.
What is the matter?
MESSENGER.   Save yourself, my lord.

The ocean, overpeering of his list,°
Eats not the flats with more impiteous
haste
Than young Laertes, in a riotous head,°
O'erbears your officers. The rabble call
him lord,
And, as the world were now but to begin,
Antiquity forgot, custom not known,
The ratifiers and props of every word,
They cry, "Choose we! Laertes shall be
king!"
Caps, hands, and tongues applaud it to the
clouds,
"Laertes shall be king! Laertes king!"
                        A noise within.
QUEEN. How cheerfully on the false trail
they cry!
O, this is counter,° you false Danish dogs!

Enter LAERTES *with others.*

KING. The doors are broke.
LAERTES. Where is this king?—Sirs,
stand you all without.
ALL. No, let's come in.
LAERTES.   I pray you give me leave.
ALL. We will, we will.
LAERTES. I thank you. Keep the door.
                [Exeunt his FOLLOWERS.*]*
                        O thou vile King,
Give me my father.
QUEEN.   Calmly, good Laertes.
LAERTES. That drop of blood that's calm
proclaims me bastard,
Cries cuckold° to my father, brands the
harlot
Even here between the chaste unsmirchèd
brow
Of my true mother.
KING.   What is the cause, Laertes,
That thy rebellion looks so giantlike?
Let him go, Gertrude. Do not fear° our
person.
There's such divinity doth hedge a king
That treason can but peep to° what it
would,

86 **muddied** muddled 88 **greenly** foolishly 89 **hug-
germugger** secret haste 94 **wonder** suspicion
95 **wants not buzzers** does not lack talebearers
97 **of matter beggared** unprovided with facts
98 **Will nothing stick** will not hesitate
100 **murd'ring piece** (a cannon that shot a kind
of shrapnel) 102 **Switzers** Swiss guards

104 **list** shore 106 **in a riotous head** with a rebellious force 115 **counter** (a hound runs counter
when he follows the scent backward from the
prey) 123 **cuckold** man whose wife is unfaithful
127 **fear** fear for 129 **peep to** i.e., look at from a
distance

130 Acts little of his will. Tell me, Laertes,
Why thou art thus incensed. Let him go,
  Gertrude.
Speak, man.

LAERTES. Where is my father?

KING. Dead.

QUEEN. But not by him.

KING. Let him demand his fill.

LAERTES. How came he dead? I'll not be
135 juggled with.
To hell allegiance, vows to the blackest
  devil,
Conscience and grace to the profoundest
  pit!
I dare damnation. To this point I stand,
That both the worlds I give to negli-
  gence,°
Let come what comes, only I'll be re-
140 venged
Most throughly for my father.

KING. Who shall stay you?

LAERTES. My will, not all the world's.
And for my means, I'll husband them° so
  well
They shall go far with little.

KING. Good Laertes,
145 If you desire to know the certainty
Of your dear father, is't writ in your revenge
That swoopstake° you will draw both
  friend and foe,
Winner and loser?

LAERTES. None but his enemies.

KING. Will you know them then?

LAERTES. To his good friends thus wide
150 I'll ope my arms
And like the kind life-rend'ring pelican°
Repast° them with my blood.

KING. Why, now you speak
Like a good child and a true gentleman.
That I am guiltless of your father's death,
155 And am most sensibly° in grief for it,

It shall as level to your judgment 'pear
As day does to your eye.

A noise within: "Let her come in."

LAERTES. How now? What noise is that?

Enter OPHELIA.

O heat, dry up my brains; tears seven
  times salt
Burn out the sense and virtue° of mine
  eye! 160
By heaven, thy madness shall be paid with
  weight
Till our scale turn the beam.° O rose of
  May,
Dear maid, kind sister, sweet Ophelia!
O heavens, is't possible a young maid's
  wits
Should be as mortal as an old man's life? 165
Nature is fine° in love, and where 'tis fine,
It sends some precious instance° of itself
After the thing it loves.

OPHELIA. *(Song.)*

They bore him barefaced on the bier
  Hey non nony, nony, hey nony 170
  And in his grave rained many a tear——

Fare you well, my dove!

LAERTES. Hadst thou thy wits, and didst
  persuade revenge,
It could not move thus.

OPHELIA. You must sing "A-down a- 175
down, and you call him a-down-a." O, how
the wheel° becomes it! It is the false steward, that stole his master's daughter.

LAERTES. This nothing's more than matter.° 180

OPHELIA. There's rosemary, that's for
remembrance. Pray you, love, remember.
And there is pansies, that's for thoughts.

LAERTES. A document° in madness,
thoughts and remembrance fitted. 185

---

¹³⁹ **That both . . . to negligence** i.e., I care
not what may happen (to me) in this world or the
next ¹⁴³ **husband them** use them economically
¹⁴⁷ **swoopstake** in a clean sweep ¹⁵¹ **pelican**
(thought to feed its young with its own blood)
¹⁵² **Repast** feed ¹⁵⁵ **sensibly** acutely

¹⁵⁸ **virtue** power ¹⁶⁰ **turn the beam** weigh down
the bar (of the balance) ¹⁶⁶ **fine** refined, delicate
¹⁶⁷ **instance** sample ¹⁷⁷ **wheel** (of uncertain
meaning, but probably a turn or dance of Ophelia's, rather than Fortune's wheel) ¹⁷⁹⁻¹⁸⁰ **This
nothing's more than matter** this nonsense
has more meaning than matters of consequence
¹⁸⁴ **document** lesson

OPHELIA. There's fennel° for you, and columbines. There's rue for you, and here's some for me. We may call it herb of grace o' Sundays. O, you must wear your rue

190 with a difference. There's a daisy. I would give you some violets, but they withered all when my father died. They say 'a made a good end. *[Sings.]*

For bonny sweet Robin is all my joy.

LAERTES. Thought and affliction, pas-
195   sion, hell itself,
She turns to favor° and to prettiness.
OPHELIA.

And will 'a not come again?   *(Song.)*
And will 'a not come again?
     No, no, he is dead,
200   Go to thy deathbed,
He never will come again.

His beard was as white as snow,
All flaxen was his poll.°
     He is gone, he is gone,
205   And we cast away moan.
God 'a' mercy on his soul!

And of all Christian souls, I pray God. God bye you.   *[Exit.]*
LAERTES. Do you see this, O God?
KING. Laertes, I must commune with
210   your grief,
Or you deny me right. Go but apart,
Make choice of whom your wisest friends you will,
And they shall hear and judge 'twixt you and me.
If by direct or by collateral° hand
They find us touched,° we will our king-
215   dom give,

Our crown, our life, and all that we call ours,
To you in satisfaction; but if not,
Be you content to lend your patience to us,
And we shall jointly labor with your soul
To give it due content.
LAERTES.   Let this be so.   220
His means of death, his obscure funeral—
No trophy, sword, nor hatchment° o'er his bones,
No noble rite nor formal ostentation°—
Cry to be heard, as 'twere from heaven to earth,
Then I must call't in question.
KING.   So you shall;   225
And where th' offense is, let the great ax fall.
I pray you go with me.   *Exeunt.*

[Scene VI. The castle.]

Enter HORATIO *and others.*

HORATIO. What are they that would
     speak with me?
GENTLEMAN. Seafaring men, sir. They say they have letters for you.
HORATIO. Let them come in.
                    [Exit ATTENDANT.*]*
I do not know from what part of the world   5
I should be greeted, if not from Lord
     Hamlet.

Enter SAILORS.

SAILOR. God bless you, sir.
HORATIO. Let Him bless thee too.
SAILOR. 'A shall, sir, an't please Him. There's a letter for you, sir—it came from   10
th' ambassador that was bound for England—if your name be Horatio, as I am let to know it is.
HORATIO *[reads the letter].*

"Horatio, when thou shalt have over-looked° this, give these fellows some   15

---

¹⁸⁶ **fennel** (the distribution of flowers in the ensuing lines has symbolic meaning, but the meaning is disputed. Perhaps *fennel*, flattery; *columbines*, cuckoldry; *rue*, sorrow for Ophelia and repentance for the Queen; *daisy*, dissembling; *violets*, faithfulness. For other interpretations, see J. W. Lever in *Review of English Studies*, New Series 3 [1952], pp. 123–129) ¹⁹⁶ **favor** charm, beauty ²⁰³ **All flaxen was his poll** white as flax was his head ²¹⁴ **collateral** indirect ²¹⁵ **touched** implicated

²²² **hatchment** tablet bearing the coat of arms of the dead ²²³ **ostentation** ceremony IV.vi. ¹⁴⁻¹⁵ **overlooked** surveyed

means to the King. They have letters for
him. Ere we were two days old at sea, a
pirate of very warlike appointment° gave us
chase. Finding ourselves too slow of sail,
20 we put on a compelled valor, and in the
grapple I boarded them. On the instant they
got clear of our ship; so I alone became
their prisoner. They have dealt with me like
thieves of mercy, but they knew what they
25 did: I am to do a good turn for them. Let
the King have the letters I have sent, and
repair thou to me with as much speed as
thou wouldest fly death. I have words to
speak in thine ear will make thee dumb; yet
30 are they much too light for the bore° of the
matter. These good fellows will bring thee
where I am. Rosencrantz and Guildenstern
hold their course for England. Of them I
have much to tell thee. Farewell.
35   He that thou knowest thine, HAMLET."

Come, I will give you way for these your
    letters,
And do't the speedier that you may direct
    me
To him from whom you brought them.
                                    Exeunt.

[Scene VII. The castle.]

Enter KING *and* LAERTES.

    KING. Now must your conscience my
        acquittance seal,
And you must put me in your heart for
    friend,
Sith you have heard, and with a knowing
    ear,
That he which hath your noble father slain
Pursued my life.
5   LAERTES.   It well appears. But tell me
Why you proceeded not against these feats
So criminal and so capital° in nature,
As by your safety, greatness, wisdom, all
    things else,
You mainly° were stirred up.
        KING.   O, for two special reasons,

Which may to you perhaps seem much
    unsinewed,°   10
But yet to me they're strong. The Queen
    his mother
Lives almost by his looks, and for
    myself—
My virtue or my plague, be it either
    which—
She is so conjunctive° to my life and soul,
That, as the star moves not but in his
    sphere,   15
I could not but by her. The other motive
Why to a public count° I might not go
Is the great love the general gender° bear
    him,
Who, dipping all his faults in their affec-
    tion,
Would, like the spring that turneth wood
    to stone,°   20
Convert his gyves° to graces; so that my
    arrows,
Too slightly timbered° for so loud a wind,
Would have reverted to my bow again,
And not where I had aimed them.
    LAERTES. And so have I a noble father
        lost,   25
A sister driven into desp'rate terms°
Whose worth, if praises may go back
    again,°
Stood challenger on mount of all the age
For her perfections. But my revenge will
    come.
    KING. Break not your sleeps for that.
        You must not think   30
That we are made of stuff so flat and dull
That we can let our beard be shook with
    danger,
And think it pastime. You shortly shall
    hear more.
I loved your father, and we love ourself,

¹⁰ **unsinewed** weak ¹⁴ **conjunctive** closely
united ¹⁷ **count** reckoning ¹⁸ **general gender**
common people ²⁰ **spring that turneth wood
to stone** (a spring in Shakespeare's county was
so charged with lime that it would petrify wood
placed in it) ²¹ **gyves** fetters ²² **timbered** shafted
²⁶ **terms** conditions ²⁷ **go back again** revert to
what is past

¹⁸ **appointment** equipment ³⁰ **bore** caliber
(here, "importance") IV.vii. ⁷ **capital** deserving
death ⁹ **mainly** powerfully

And that, I hope, will teach you to
35   imagine——

Enter a MESSENGER *with letters.*

How now? What news?
   MESSENGER.   Letters, my lord, from
   Hamlet:
These to your Majesty; this to the Queen.
   KING. From Hamlet? Who brought
   them?
   MESSENGER. Sailors, my lord, they say; I
   saw them not.
They were given me by Claudio; he re-
40   ceived them
Of him that brought them.
   KING.   Laertes, you shall hear them.—
Leave us. *[Reads.]*   *Exit* MESSENGER.

   "High and mighty, you shall know I am
set naked° on your kingdom. Tomorrow
45 shall I beg leave to see your kingly eyes;
when I shall (first asking your pardon there-
unto) recount the occasion of my sudden
and more strange return.   HAMLET."
What should this mean? Are all the rest
   come back?
Or is it some abuse,° and no such thing?
50
   LAERTES. Know you the hand?
   KING.   'Tis Hamlet's character.° "Naked"!
And in a postscript here, he says, "alone."
Can you devise° me?
   LAERTES. I am lost in it, my lord. But
   let him come.
It warms the very sickness in my heart
55 That I shall live and tell him to his teeth,
"Thus did'st thou."
   KING.   If it be so, Laertes
(As how should it be so? How other-
   wise?),
Will you be ruled by me?
   LAERTES.   Ay, my lord,
So you will not o'errule me to a peace.
60
   KING. To thine own peace. If he be now
   returned,
As checking at° his voyage, and that he
   means

No more to undertake it, I will work him
To an exploit now ripe in my device,   65
Under the which he shall not choose but
   fall;
And for his death no wind of blame shall
   breathe,
But even his mother shall uncharge the
   practice°
And call it accident.
   LAERTES.   My lord, I will be ruled;
The rather if you could devise it so   70
That I might be the organ.
   KING.   It falls right.
You have been talked of since your travel
   much,
And that in Hamlet's hearing, for a quality
Wherein they say you shine. Your sum of
   parts
Did not together pluck such envy from him   75
As did that one, and that, in my regard,
Of the unworthiest siege.°
   LAERTES.   What part is that, my lord?
   KING. A very riband in the cap of youth,
Yet needful too, for youth no less becomes
The light and careless livery that it wears   80
Than settled age his sables and his
   weeds,°
Importing health and graveness. Two
   months since
Here was a gentleman of Normandy.
I have seen myself, and served against,
   the French,
And they can° well on horseback, but this
   gallant   85
Had witchcraft in't. He grew unto his seat,
And to such wondrous doing brought his
   horse
As had he been incorpsed and demina-
   tured
With the brave beast. So far he topped my
   thought
That I, in forgery° of shapes and tricks,   90
Come short of what he did.

---

⁴⁴ **naked** destitute ⁵¹ **abuse** deception ⁵² **character** handwriting ⁵⁴ **devise** advise ⁶³ **checking
at** turning away from (a term in falconry)

⁶⁸ **uncharge the practice** not charge the device
with treachery ⁷⁷ **siege** rank ⁸¹ **sables and his
weeds** i.e., sober attire ⁸⁵ **can** do ⁹⁰ **forgery** in-
vention

LAERTES. A Norman was't?

KING.   A Norman.

LAERTES. Upon my life, Lamord.

KING.   The very same.

LAERTES. I know him well. He is the brooch° indeed

95 And gem of all the nation.

KING. He made confession° of you,
And gave you such a masterly report,
For art and exercise in your defense,
And for your rapier most especial,
That he cried out 'twould be a sight in-
100   deed
If one could match you. The scrimers° of their nation
He swore had neither motion, guard, nor eye,
If you opposed them. Sir, this report of his
Did Hamlet so envenom with his envy
105 That he could nothing do but wish and beg
Your sudden coming o'er to play with you.
Now, out of this——

LAERTES.   What out of this, my lord?

KING. Laertes, was your father dear to you?
Or are you like the painting of a sorrow,
A face without a heart?

110 LAERTES.   Why ask you this?

KING. Not that I think you did not love your father,
But that I know love is begun by time,
And that I see, in passages of proof.°
Time qualifies° the spark and fire of it.
115 There lives within the very flame of love
A kind of wick or snuff° that will abate it,
And nothing is at a like goodness still,°
For goodness, growing to a plurisy,°
Dies in his own too-much. That we would do
We should do when we would, for this
120   "would" changes,
And hath abatements and delays as many

As there are tongues, are hands, are accidents,
And then this "should" is like a spend-thrift sigh,°
That hurts by easing. But to the quick° of th' ulcer—
Hamlet comes back; what would you undertake 125
To show yourself in deed your father's son
More than in words?

LAERTES.   To cut his throat i' th' church!

KING. No place indeed should murder sanctuarize;°
Revenge should have no bounds. But, good Laertes,
Will you do this? Keep close within your chamber. 130
Hamlet returned shall know you are come home.
We'll put on those° shall praise your excellence
And set a double varnish on the fame
The Frenchman gave you, bring you in fine° together
And wager on your heads. He, being remiss, 135
Most generous, and free from all contriv-ing,
Will not peruse the foils, so that with ease,
Or with a little shuffling, you may choose
A sword unbated,° and, in a pass of prac-tice,°
Requite him for your father.

LAERTES.   I will do't, 140
And for that purpose I'll anoint my sword.
I bought an unction of a mountebank,°
So mortal that, but dip a knife in it,
Where it draws blood, no cataplasm° so rare,

---

[123] **spendthrift sigh** (sighing provides ease, but because it was thought to thin the blood and so shorten life it was spendthrift) [124] **quick** sensitive flesh [128] **sanctuarize** protect [132] **We'll put on those** we'll incite persons who [134] **in fine** finally [139] **unbated** not blunted [139] **pass of practice** treacherous thrust [142] **mountebank** quack [144] **cataplasm** poultice

[94] **brooch** ornament [96] **confession** report [101] **scrimers** fencers [113] **passages of proof** proved cases [114] **qualifies** diminishes [116] **snuff** residue of burnt wick (which dims the light) [117] **still** always [118] **plurisy** fullness, excess

Collected from all simples° that have vir-
145   tue°
Under the moon, can save the thing from
      death
That is but scratched withal. I'll touch my
      point
With this contagion, that, if I gall him
      slightly,
It may be death.
        KING.   Let's further think of this,
Weigh what convenience both of time and
150   means
May fit us to our shape.° If this should
      fail,
And that our drift look through° our bad
      performance,
'Twere better not assayed. Therefore this
      project
Should have a back or second, that might
      hold
155 If this did blast in proof.° Soft, let me see.
We'll make a solemn wager on your
      cunnings—
I ha't!
When in your motion you are hot and
      dry—
As make your bouts more violent to that
      end—
And that he calls for drink, I'll have pre-
160   pared him
A chalice for the nonce,° whereon but
      sipping,
If he by chance escape your venomed
      stuck,°
Our purpose may hold there.—But stay,
      what noise?

Enter QUEEN.

      QUEEN. One woe doth tread upon an-
            other's heel.
So fast they follow. Your sister's drowned,
165   Laertes.
      LAERTES. Drowned! O, where?
      QUEEN. There is a willow grows askant°
            the brook,

That shows his hoar° leaves in the glassy
      stream:
Therewith° fantastic garlands did she
      make
Of crowflowers, nettles, daisies, and long
      purples,   170
That liberal° shepherds give a grosser
      name,
But our cold maids do dead men's fingers
      call them.
There on the pendent boughs her
      crownet° weeds
Clamb'ring to hang, an envious sliver°
      broke,
When down her weedy trophies and her-
      self   175
Fell in the weeping brook. Her clothes
      spread wide,
And mermaidlike awhile they bore her up,
Which time she chanted snatches of old
      lauds,°
As one incapable° of her own distress,
Or like a creature native and indued°   180
Unto that element. But long it could not
      be
Till that her garments, heavy with their
      drink,
Pulled the poor wretch from her melodi-
      ous lay
To muddy death.
      LAERTES.   Alas, then she is drowned?
      QUEEN. Drowned, drowned.   185
      LAERTES. Too much of water hast thou,
            poor Ophelia,
And therefore I forbid my tears; but yet
It is our trick;° nature her custom holds,
Let shame say what it will: when these
      are gone,
The woman° will be out. Adieu, my lord.   190
I have a speech o' fire, that fain would
      blaze,
But that this folly drowns it.   *Exit.*
      KING.   Let's follow, Gertrude.

How much I had to do to calm his rage!
Now fear I this will give it start again;
195   Therefore let's follow.   *Exeunt.*

/ACT V

Scene I. A churchyard.]

Enter two CLOWNS.°

CLOWN. Is she to be buried in Christian burial when she willfully seeks her own salvation?

OTHER. I tell thee she is. Therefore
5   make her grave straight.° The crowner° hath sate on her, and finds it Christian burial.

CLOWN. How can that be, unless she drowned herself in her own defense?

10   OTHER. Why, 'tis found so.

CLOWN. It must be *se offendendo;*° it cannot be else. For here lies the point: if I drown myself wittingly, it argues an act, and an act hath three branches—it is to act,
15   to do, to perform. Argal,° she drowned herself wittingly.

OTHER. Nay, but hear you, Goodman Delver.

CLOWN. Give me leave. Here lies the
20   water—good. Here stands the man—good. If the man go to this water and drown himself, it is, will he nill he,° he goes; mark you that. But if the water come to him and drown him, he drowns not himself. Argal,
25   he that is not guilty of his own death, shortens not his own life.

OTHER. But is this law?

CLOWN. Ay marry, is't—crowner's quest° law.

30   OTHER. Will you ha' the truth on't? If this had not been a gentlewoman, she should have been buried out o' Christian burial.

CLOWN. Why, there thou say'st. And the more pity that great folk should have

count'nance° in this world to drown or hang   35
themselves more than their even-Christen.° Come, my spade. There is no ancient gentlemen but gard'ners, ditchers, and gravemakers. They hold up° Adam's profession.   40

OTHER. Was he a gentleman?

CLOWN. 'A was the first that ever bore arms.°

OTHER. Why, he had none.

CLOWN. What, art a heathen? How dost   45
thou understand the Scripture? The Scripture says Adam digged. Could he dig without arms? I'll put another question to thee. If thou answerest me not to the purpose, confess thyself——   50

OTHER. Go to.

CLOWN. What is he that builds stronger than either the mason, the shipwright, or the carpenter?

OTHER. The gallowsmaker, for that   55
frame outlives a thousand tenants.

CLOWN. I like thy wit well, in good faith. The gallows does well. But how does it well? It does well to those that do ill. Now thou dost ill to say the gallows is built   60
stronger than the church. Argal, the gallows may do well to thee. To't again, come.

OTHER. Who builds stronger than a mason, a shipwright, or a carpenter?

CLOWN. Ay, tell me that, and unyoke.°   65

OTHER. Marry, now I can tell.

CLOWN. To't.

OTHER. Mass,° I cannot tell.

Enter HAMLET *and* HORATIO *afar off.*

CLOWN. Cudgel thy brains no more about it, for your dull ass will not mend his pace   70
with beating. And when you are asked this question next, say "a gravemaker." The houses he makes lasts till doomsday. Go, get thee in, and fetch me a stoup° of liquor.   *[Exit* OTHER CLOWN.]   75

In youth when I did love, did love, *(Song.)*

V.i. ˢ·ᵈ· **Clowns** rustics ⁵ **straight** straightway ⁵ **crowner** coroner ¹¹ **se offendendo** (blunder for *se defendendo,* a legal term meaning "in self-defense") ¹⁵ **Argal** (blunder for Latin *ergo,* "therefore") ²² **will he nill he** will he or will he not (whether he will or will not) ²⁹ **quest** inquest

³⁵ **count'nance** privilege ³⁶⁻³⁷ **even-Christen** fellow Christian ³⁹ **hold up** keep up ⁴²⁻⁴³ **bore arms** had a coat of arms (the sign of a gentleman) ⁶⁵ **unyoke** i.e., stop work for the day ⁶⁸ **Mass** by the mass ⁷⁴ **stoup** tankard

Methought it was very sweet
To contract—O—the time for—a—
   my behove,
O, methought there—a—was
   nothing—a—meet.

80   HAMLET. Has this fellow no feeling of his
business? 'A sings in gravemaking.
   HORATIO. Custom hath made it in him a
property of easiness.°
   HAMLET. 'Tis e'en so. The hand of little
85   employment hath the daintier sense.°

(Song.)

CLOWN. But age with his stealing steps
   Hath clawed me in his clutch,
And hath shipped me into the land,
   As if I had never been such.

[Throws up a skull.]

90   HAMLET. That skull had a tongue in it,
and could sing once. How the knave jowls°
it to the ground, as if 'twere Cain's jaw-
bone, that did the first murder! This might
be the pate of a politician, which this ass
95   now o'erreaches,° one that would circumvent God, might it not?
   HORATIO. It might, my lord.
   HAMLET. Or of a courtier, which could
say "Good morrow, sweet lord! How dost
100   thou, sweet lord?" This might be my Lord
Such-a-one, that praised my Lord Such-a-
one's horse when 'a went to beg it, might it
not?
   HORATIO. Ay, my lord.
105   HAMLET. Why, e'en so, and now my Lady
Worm's, chapless,° and knocked about the
mazzard° with a sexton's spade. Here's fine
revolution, an we had the trick to see't. Did
these bones cost no more than breeding
110   but to play at loggets° with them? Mine
ache to think on't.

(Song.)

CLOWN. A pickax and a spade, a spade,
   For and a shrouding sheet;
O, a pit of clay for to be made
   For such a guest is meet.   115

[Throws up another skull.]

   HAMLET. There's another. Why may not
that be the skull of a lawyer? Where be his
quiddities° now, his quillities,° his cases, his
tenures,° and his tricks? Why does he suffer this mad knave now to knock him about   120
the sconce° with a dirty shovel, and will not
tell him of his action of battery? Hum! This
fellow might be in's time a great buyer of
land, with his statutes, his recognizances,
his fines,° his double vouchers, his recover-   125
ies. Is this the fine° of his fines, and the
recovery of his recoveries, to have his fine
pate full of fine dirt? Will his vouchers vouch
him no more of his purchases, and double
ones too, than the length and breadth of a   130
pair of indentures?° The very conveyances°
of his lands will scarcely lie in this box, and
must th' inheritor himself have no more,
ha?
   HORATIO. Not a jot more, my lord.   135
   HAMLET. Is not parchment made of
sheepskins?
   HORATIO. Ay, my lord, and of calveskins
too.
   HAMLET. They are sheep and calves   140
which seek out assurance° in that. I will
speak to this fellow. Whose grave's this, sirrah?
   CLOWN. Mine, sir. *[Sings.]*

O, a pit of clay for to be made   145
   For such a guest is meet.

---

⁷⁸ **behove** advantage ⁸²⁻⁸³ **in him a property of easiness** easy for him ⁸⁵ **hath the daintier sense** is more sensitive (because it is not cal-loused) ⁹¹ **jowls** hurls ⁹⁴⁻⁹⁵ **o'erreaches** (1) reaches over, (2) has the advantage over ¹⁰⁶ **chapless** lacking the lower jaw ¹⁰⁷ **mazzard** head ¹¹⁰ **loggets** (a game in which small pieces of wood were thrown at an object)

¹¹⁸ **quiddities** subtle arguments (from Latin *quidditas*, "whatness") ¹¹⁸ **quillities** fine distinc-tions ¹¹⁹ **tenures** legal means of holding land ¹²¹ **sconce** head ¹²⁴⁻¹²⁵ **his statutes, his recog-nizances, his fines** his documents giving a creditor control of a debtor's land, his bonds of surety, his documents changing an entailed es-tate into fee simple (unrestricted ownership) ¹²⁶ **fine** end ¹³¹ **indentures** contracts ¹³¹ **convey-ances** legal documents for the transference of land ¹⁴¹ **assurance** safety

HAMLET. I think it be thine indeed, for thou liest in't.

CLOWN. You lie out on't sir, and therefore
150 'tis not yours. For my part, I do not lie in't, yet it is mine.

HAMLET. Thou dost lie in't, to be in't and say it is thine. 'Tis for the dead, not for the quick;° therefore thou liest.

155 CLOWN. 'Tis a quick lie, sir; 'twill away again from me to you.

HAMLET. What man dost thou dig it for?

CLOWN. For no man, sir.

HAMLET. What woman then?

160 CLOWN. For none neither.

HAMLET. Who is to be buried in't?

CLOWN. One that was a woman, sir; but, rest her soul, she's dead.

HAMLET. How absolute° the knave is! We
165 must speak by the card,° or equivocation° will undo us. By the Lord, Horatio, this three years I have took note of it, the age is grown so picked° that the toe of the peasant comes so near the heel of the courtier
170 he galls his kibe.° How long hast thou been a gravemaker?

CLOWN. Of all the days i' th' year, I came to't that day that our last king Hamlet overcame Fortinbras.

175 HAMLET. How long is that since?

CLOWN. Cannot you tell that? Every fool can tell that. It was that very day that young Hamlet was born—he that is mad, and sent into England.

180 HAMLET. Ay, marry, why was he sent into England?

CLOWN. Why, because 'a was mad. 'A shall recover his wits there; or, if 'a do not, 'tis no great matter there.

185 HAMLET. Why?

CLOWN. 'Twill not be seen in him there. There the men are as mad as he.

HAMLET. How came he mad?

CLOWN. Very strangely, they say.

190 HAMLET. How strangely?

CLOWN. Faith, e'en with losing his wits.

HAMLET. Upon what ground?

CLOWN. Why, here in Denmark. I have been sexton here, man and boy, thirty years. 195

HAMLET. How long will a man lie i' th' earth ere he rot?

CLOWN. Faith, if 'a be not rotten before 'a die (as we have many pocky corses° nowadays that will scarce hold the laying 200 in), 'a will last you some eight year or nine year. A tanner will last you nine year.

HAMLET. Why he, more than another?

CLOWN. Why, sir, his hide is so tanned with his trade that 'a will keep out water a 205 great while, and your water is a sore decayer of your whoreson dead body. Here's a skull now hath lien you i' th' earth three and twenty years.

HAMLET. Whose was it? 210

CLOWN. A whoreson mad fellow's it was. Whose do you think it was?

HAMLET. Nay, I know not.

CLOWN. A pestilence on him for a mad rogue! 'A poured a flagon of Rhenish on my 215 head once. This same skull, sir, was, sir, Yorick's skull, the King's jester.

HAMLET. This?

CLOWN. E'en that.

HAMLET. Let me see. *[Takes the skull.]* 220 Alas, poor Yorick! I knew him, Horatio, a fellow of infinite jest, of most excellent fancy. He hath borne me on his back a thousand times. And now how abhorred in my imagination it is! My gorge rises at it. Here 225 hung those lips that I have kissed I know not how oft. Where be your gibes now? Your gambols, your songs, your flashes of merriment that were wont to set the table on a roar? Not one now to mock your own 230 grinning? Quite chapfall'n?° Now get you to my lady's chamber, and tell her, let her paint an inch thick, to this favor° she must come. Make her laugh at that. Prithee, Horatio, tell me one thing. 235

HORATIO. What's that, my lord?

154 **quick** living 164 **absolute** positive, decided 165 **by the card** by the compass card, i.e., exactly 165 **equivocation** ambiguity 168 **picked** refined 170 **kibe** sore on the back of the heel

199 **pocky corses** bodies of persons who had been infected with the pox (syphilis) 231 **chapfall'n** (1) down in the mouth, (2) jawless 233 **favor** facial appearance

HAMLET. Dost thou think Alexander looked o' this fashion i' th' earth?

HORATIO. E'en so.

240   HAMLET. And smelt so? Pah!

[Puts down the skull.]

HORATIO. E'en so, my lord.

HAMLET. To what base uses we may return, Horatio! Why may not imagination trace the noble dust of Alexander till 'a find

245   it stopping a bunghole?

HORATIO. 'Twere to consider too curiously,° to consider so.

HAMLET. No, faith, not a jot, but to follow him thither with modesty enough,° and

250   likelihood to lead it; as thus: Alexander died, Alexander was buried. Alexander returneth to dust; the dust is earth; of earth we make loam; and why of that loam whereto he was converted might they not

255   stop a beer barrel?

Imperious Caesar, dead and turned to clay.
Might stop a hole to keep the wind away.
O, that that earth which kept the world in
    awe
Should patch a wall t' expel the winter's
    flaw!°
But soft, but soft awhile! Here comes the
260   King.

Enter KING, QUEEN, LAERTES, *and a coffin,
with* LORDS *attendant [and a* DOCTOR OF DI-
VINITY].*

The Queen, the courtiers. Who is this
    they follow?
And with such maimèd° rites? This doth
    betoken
The corse they follow did with desp'rate
    hand
Fordo it° own life. 'Twas of some estate.°
265   Couch° we awhile, and mark.

[Retires with HORATIO.]

LAERTES. What ceremony else?

HAMLET.   That is Laertes,
A very noble youth. Mark.

LAERTES. What ceremony else?

DOCTOR. Her obsequies have been as far
    enlarged
As we have warranty. Her death was
    doubtful,°   270
And, but that great command o'ersways
    the order,
She should in ground unsanctified been
    lodged
Till the last trumpet. For charitable pray-
    ers,
Shards,° flints, and pebbles should be
    thrown on her.
Yet here she is allowed her virgin crants,°   275
Her maiden strewments,° and the bringing
    home
Of bell and burial.

LAERTES. Must there no more be done?

DOCTOR.   No more be done.
We should profane the service of the dead
To sing a requiem and such rest to her   280
As to peace-parted souls.

LAERTES.   Lay her i' th' earth,
And from her fair and unpolluted flesh
May violets spring! I tell thee, churlish
    priest,
A minist'ring angel shall my sister be
When thou liest howling!

HAMLET.   What, the fair Ophelia?   285

QUEEN. Sweets to the sweet! Farewell.

[Scatters flowers.]

I hoped thou shouldst have been my Ham-
    let's wife.
I thought thy bride bed to have decked,
    sweet maid,
And not have strewed thy grave.

LAERTES.   O, treble woe   290
Fall ten times treble on that cursèd head
Whose wicked deed thy most ingenious
    sense°
Deprived thee of! Hold off the earth
    awhile,
Till I have caught her once more in mine
    arms.

Leaps in the grave.

---

²⁴⁶⁻²⁴⁷ **curiously** minutely ²⁴⁹ **with modesty enough** without exaggeration ²⁵⁹ **flaw** gust ²⁶² **maimèd** incomplete ²⁶⁴ **Fordo it** destroy its ²⁶⁴ **estate** high rank ²⁶⁵ **Couch** hide

²⁷⁰ **doubtful** suspicious ²⁷⁴ **Shards** broken pieces of pottery ²⁷⁵ **crants** garlands ²⁷⁶ **strewments** i.e., of flowers ²⁹¹ **most ingenious sense** finely endowed mind

Now pile your dust upon the quick and
   dead
295 Till of this flat a mountain you have made
T' o'ertop old Pelion° or the skyish head
Of blue Olympus.
    HAMLET *[coming forward].* What is he
      whose grief
Bears such an emphasis, whose phrase of
   sorrow
Conjures the wand'ring stars,° and makes
300   them stand
Like wonder-wounded hearers? This is I,
Hamlet the Dane.
    LAERTES.   The devil take thy soul!

[Grapples with him.]°

    HAMLET. Thou pray'st not well.
I prithee take thy fingers from my throat,
305 For, though I am not splenitive° and rash,
Yet have I in me something dangerous,
Which let thy wisdom fear. Hold off thy
   hand.
    KING. Pluck them asunder.
    QUEEN.   Hamlet, Hamlet!
    ALL. Gentlemen!
    HORATIO.   Good my lord, be quiet.

[ATTENDANTS part them.]

    HAMLET. Why, I will fight with him upon
310   this theme
Until my eyelids will no longer wag.
    QUEEN. O my son, what theme?
    HAMLET. I loved Ophelia. Forty thousand
   brothers
Could not with all their quantity of love
Make up my sum. What wilt thou do for
315   her?

---

²⁹⁶ **Pelion** (according to classical legend, giants in
their fight with the gods sought to reach heaven
by piling Mount Pelion and Mount Ossa on
Mount Olympus) ³⁰⁰ **wand'ring stars** planets ³⁰²
ˢ·ᵈ· **Grapples with him** (Q1, a bad quarto, presumably reporting a version that toured, has a
previous direction saying "Hamlet leaps in after
Laertes." Possibly he does so, somewhat hysterically. But such a direction—absent from the two
good texts, Q2 and F—makes Hamlet the ag-
gressor, somewhat contradicting his next
speech. Perhaps Laertes leaps out of the grave
to attack Hamlet) ³⁰⁵ **splenitive** fiery (the spleen
was thought to be the seat of anger)

    KING. O, he is mad, Laertes.
    QUEEN. For love of God forbear him.
    HAMLET. 'Swounds, show me what
      thou't do.
Woo't weep? Woo't fight? Woo't fast?
Woo't tear thyself?   320
Woo't drink up eisel?° Eat a crocodile?
I'll do't. Dost thou come here to whine?
To outface me with leaping in her grave?
Be buried quick with her, and so will I.
And if thou prate of mountains, let them
   throw   325
Millions of acres on us, till our ground,
Singeing his pate against the burning
   zone,°
Make Ossa like a wart! Nay, an thou'lt
   mouth,
I'll rant as well as thou.
    QUEEN.   This is mere madness;
And thus a while the fit will work on him.   330
Anon, as patient as the female dove
When that her golden couplets are dis-
   closed,°
His silence will sit drooping.
    HAMLET.   Hear you, sir.
What is the reason that you use me thus?
I loved you ever. But it is no matter.   335
Let Hercules himself do what he may,
The cat will mew, and dog will have his
   day.
    KING. I pray thee, good Horatio, wait
      upon him. *Exit* HAMLET *and* HORATIO.
[To LAERTES.*]* Strengthen your patience in
    our last night's speech.
We'll put the matter to the present push.°   340
Good Gertrude, set some watch over your
   son.
This grave shall have a living° monument.
An hour of quiet shortly shall we see;
Till then in patience our proceeding be.
                      Exeunt.

---

³²¹ **eisel** vinegar ³²⁷ **burning zone** sun's orbit
³³² **golden couplets are disclosed** (the dove
lays two eggs, and the newly hatched [*disclosed*]
young are covered with golden down) ³⁴⁰ **present
push** immediate test ³⁴² **living** lasting (with perhaps also a reference to the plot against Hamlet's
life)

[Scene II. The castle.]

Enter HAMLET *and* HORATIO.

HAMLET. So much for this, sir; now shall
   you see the other.
You do remember all the circumstance?
   HORATIO. Remember it, my lord!
   HAMLET. Sir, in my heart there was a
      kind of fighting
That would not let me sleep. Methought I
5   lay
Worse than the mutines in the bilboes.°
   Rashly
(And praised be rashness for it) let us
   know,
Our indiscretion sometime serves us well
When our deep plots do pall,° and that
   should learn us
10 There's a divinity that shapes our ends,
Rough-hew them how we will.
   HORATIO.   That is most certain.
   HAMLET. Up from my cabin,
My sea gown scarfed about me, in the
   dark
Groped I to find out them, had my desire,
Fingered° their packet, and in fine° with-
15   drew
To mine own room again, making so bold,
My fears forgetting manners, to unseal
Their grand commission; where I found,
   Horatio—
Ah, royal knavery!—an exact command,
Larded° with many several sorts of rea-
20   sons,
Importing Denmark's health, and En-
   gland's too,
With, ho, such bugs and goblins in my
   life,°
That on the supervise,° no leisure bated,°
No, not to stay the grinding of the ax,
My head should be struck off.
25   HORATIO.   Is't possible?
   HAMLET. Here's the commission; read it
      at more leisure.

But wilt thou hear now how I did proceed?
   HORATIO. I beseech you.
   HAMLET. Being thus benetted round with
      villains,
Or° I could make a prologue to my brains, 30
They had begun the play. I sat me down,
Devised a new commission, wrote it fair.
I once did hold it, as our statists° do,
A baseness to write fair,° and labored
   much
How to forget that learning, but, sir, now 35
It did me yeoman's service. Wilt thou
   know
Th' effect° of what I wrote?
   HORATIO.   Ay, good my lord.
   HAMLET. An earnest conjuration from
      the King,
As England was his faithful tributary,
As love between them like the palm might
   flourish,   40
As peace should still her wheaten garland
   wear
And stand a comma° 'tween their amities,
And many suchlike as's of great charge,°
That on the view and knowing of these
   contents,
Without debatement further, more or less, 45
He should those bearers put to sudden
   death,
Not shriving° time allowed.
   HORATIO.   How was this sealed?
   HAMLET. Why, even in that was heaven
      ordinant.°
I had my father's signet in my purse,
Which was the model° of that Danish seal, 50
Folded the writ up in the form of th'
   other,
Subscribed it, gave't th' impression,
   placed it safely,
The changeling never known. Now, the
   next day
Was our sea fight, and what to this was
   sequent
Thou knowest already.   55

V.ii. ⁶ **mutines in the bilboes** mutineers in fetters ⁹ **pall** fail ¹⁵ **Fingered** stole ¹⁵ **in fine** finally
²⁰ **Larded** enriched ²² **such bugs and goblins
in my life** such bugbears and imagined terrors if
I were allowed to live ²³ **supervise** reading ²³ **leisure bated** delay allowed

³⁰ **Or** ere ³³ **statists** statesmen ³⁴ **fair** clearly
³⁷ **effect** purport ⁴² **comma** link ⁴³ **great charge**
(1) serious exhortation, (2) heavy burden (punning on *as's* and "asses") ⁴⁷ **shriving** absolution
⁴⁸ **ordinant** ruling ⁵⁰ **model** counterpart

HORATIO. So Guildenstern and Rosencrantz go to't.

HAMLET. Why, man, they did make love
to this employment.

They are not near my conscience; their
defeat

Does by their own insinuation° grow.

'Tis dangerous when the baser nature
comes

60   Between the pass° and fell° incensèd
points

Of mighty opposites.

HORATIO.   Why, what a king is this!

HAMLET. Does it not, think thee, stand
me now upon°—

He that hath killed my king, and whored
my mother,

Popped in between th' election° and my

65   hopes,

Thrown out his angle° for my proper life,°

And with such coz'nage°—is't not perfect
conscience

To quit° him with this arm? And is't not to
be damned

To let this canker of our nature come

70   In further evil?

HORATIO. It must be shortly known to
him from England

What is the issue of the business there.

HAMLET. It will be short; the interim's
mine,

And a man's life's no more than to say
"one."

75   But I am very sorry, good Horatio,

That to Laertes I forgot myself,

For by the image of my cause I see

The portraiture of his. I'll court his favors.

But sure the bravery° of his grief did put
me

Into a tow'ring passion.

80   HORATIO.   Peace, who comes here?

Enter young OSRIC, *a courtier.*

OSRIC. Your lordship is right welcome
back to Denmark.

HAMLET. I humbly thank you, sir. *[Aside
to* HORATIO.*]* Dost know this waterfly?

HORATIO *[aside to* HAMLET*]*. No, my good   85
lord.

HAMLET *[aside to* HORATIO*]*. Thy state is
the more gracious, for 'tis a vice to know
him. He hath much land, and fertile. Let a
beast be lord of beasts, and his crib shall   90
stand at the king's mess.° 'Tis a chough,°
but, as I say, spacious° in the possession of
dirt.

OSRIC. Sweet lord, if your lordship were
at leisure, I should impart a thing to you   95
from his Majesty.

HAMLET. I will receive it, sir, with all diligence of spirit. Put your bonnet to his right
use. 'Tis for the head.

OSRIC. I thank your lordship, it is very   100
hot.

HAMLET. No, believe me, 'tis very cold;
the wind is northerly.

OSRIC. It is indifferent cold, my lord, indeed.   105

HAMLET. But yet methinks it is very sultry and hot for my complexion.°

OSRIC. Exceedingly, my lord; it is very
sultry, as 'twere—I cannot tell how. But,
my lord, his Majesty bade me signify to you   110
that 'a has laid a great wager on your head.
Sir, this is the matter—

HAMLET. I beseech you remember.

*[*HAMLET *moves him to put on his hat.]*

OSRIC. Nay, good my lord; for my ease,
in good faith. Sir, here is newly come to   115
court Laertes—believe me, an absolute
gentleman, full of most excellent differences,° of very soft society and great showing. Indeed, to speak feelingly° of him, he
is the card° or calendar of gentry; for you   120
shall find in him the continent° of what part
a gentleman would see.

---

59 **insinuation** meddling 61 **pass** thrust 61 **fell**
cruel 63 **stand me now upon** become incum-
bent upon me 65 **election** (the Danish monarchy
was elective) 66 **angle** fishing line 66 **my proper
life** my own life 67 **coz'nage** trickery 68 **quit** pay
back 79 **bravery** bravado

91 **mess** table 91 **chough** jackdaw (here chat-
terer) 92 **spacious** well off 107 **complexion** temperament 117-118 **differences** distinguishing
characteristics 119 **feelingly** justly 120 **card** chart
121 **continent** summary

HAMLET. Sir, his definement° suffers no perdition° in you, though, I know, to divide
125 him inventorially would dozy° th' arithmetic of memory, and yet but yaw neither in respect of his quick sail.° But, in the verity of extolment, I take him to be a soul of great article,° and his infusion° of such dearth
130 and rareness as, to make true diction° of him, his semblable° is his mirror, and who else would trace him, his umbrage,° nothing more.

OSRIC. Your lordship speaks most infalli-
135 bly of him.

HAMLET. The concernancy,° sir? Why do we wrap the gentleman in our more rawer breath?

OSRIC. Sir?
140 HORATIO. Is't not possible to understand in another tongue? You will to't,° sir, really.

HAMLET. What imports the nomination of this gentleman?

OSRIC. Of Laertes?
145 HORATIO *[aside to* HAMLET*]*. His purse is empty already. All's golden words are spent.

HAMLET. Of him, sir.

OSRIC. I know you are not ignorant—
150 HAMLET. I would you did, sir; yet, in faith, if you did, it would not much approve° me. Well, sir?

OSRIC. You are not ignorant of what excellence Laertes is—
155 HAMLET. I dare not confess that, lest I should compare with him in excellence; but to know a man well were to know himself.

OSRIC. I mean, sir, for his weapon; but in the imputation° laid on him by them, in his
160 meed° he's unfellowed.

HAMLET. What's his weapon?

OSRIC. Rapier and dagger.

---

[123] **definement** description [124] **perdition** loss [125] **dozy** dizzy [126] [127]**and yet . . . quick sail** i.e., and yet only stagger despite all (*yaw neither*) in trying to overtake his virtues [129] **article** (literally, "item," but here perhaps "traits" or "importance") [129] **infusion** essential quality [130] **diction** description [131] **semblable** likeness [132] **umbrage** shadow [136] **concernancy** meaning [141] **will to't** will get there [151] **approve** commend [159] **imputation** reputation [160] **meed** merit

HAMLET. That's two of his weapons—but well.

OSRIC. The King, sir, hath wagered with 165 him six Barbary horses, against the which he has impawned,° as I take it, six French rapiers and poniards, with their assigns,° as girdle, hangers,° and so. Three of the carriages,° in faith, are very dear to fancy, 170 very responsive° to the hilts, most delicate carriages, and of very liberal conceit.°

HAMLET. What call you the carriages?

HORATIO *[aside to* HAMLET*]*. I knew you must be edified by the margent° ere you 175 had done.

OSRIC. The carriages, sir, are the hangers.

HAMLET. The phrase would be more germane to the matter if we could carry a can- 180 non by our sides. I would it might be hangers till then. But on! Six Barbary horses against six French swords, their assigns, and three liberal-conceited carriages—that's the French bet against 185 the Danish. Why is this all impawned, as you call it?

OSRIC. The King, sir, hath laid, sir, that in a dozen passes between yourself and him he shall not exceed you three hits; he hath 190 laid on twelve for nine, and it would come to immediate trial if your lordship would vouchsafe the answer.

HAMLET. How if I answer no?

OSRIC. I mean, my lord, the opposition 195 of your person in trial.

HAMLET. Sir, I will walk here in the hall. If it please his Majesty, it is the breathing time of day with me.° Let the foils be brought, the gentleman willing, and the 200 King hold his purpose, I will win for him an I can; if not, I will gain nothing but my shame and the odd hits.

OSRIC. Shall I deliver you e'en so?

---

[167] **impawned** wagered [168] **assigns** accompaniments [169] **hangers** straps hanging the sword to the belt [170] **carriages** (an affected word for hangers) [171] **responsive** corresponding [172] **liberal conceit** elaborate design [175] **margent** i.e., marginal (explanatory comment) [198]-[199] **breathing time of day with me** time when I take exercise

205 HAMLET. To this effect, sir, after what flourish your nature will.

OSRIC. I commend my duty to your lordship.

HAMLET. Yours, yours.   *[Exit* OSRIC.*]*

210 He does well to commend it himself; there are no tongues else for's turn.

HORATIO. This lapwing° runs away with the shell on his head.

HAMLET. 'A did comply, sir, with his dug°
215 before 'a sucked it. Thus has he, and many more of the same breed that I know the drossy age dotes on, only got the tune of the time and, out of an habit of encounter,° a kind of yeasty° collection, which carries
220 them through and through the most fanned and winnowed opinions; and do but blow them to their trial, the bubbles are out.°

Enter a LORD.

LORD. My lord, his Majesty commended him to you by young Osric, who brings back
225 to him that you attend him in the hall. He sends to know if your pleasure hold to play with Laertes, or that you will take longer time.

HAMLET. I am constant to my purposes;
230 they follow the King's pleasure. If his fitness speaks, mine is ready; now or whensoever, provided I be so able as now.

LORD. The King and Queen and all are coming down.

235 HAMLET. In happy time.

LORD. The Queen desires you to use some gentle entertainment° to Laertes before you fall to play.

HAMLET. She well instructs me.

      [Exit LORD.*]*

240 HORATIO. You will lose this wager, my lord.

HAMLET. I do not think so. Since he went into France I have been in continual practice. I shall win at the odds. But thou wouldst not think how ill all's here about my 245 heart. But it is no matter.

HORATIO. Nay, good my lord——

HAMLET. It is but foolery, but it is such a kind of gain-giving° as would perhaps trouble a woman. 250

HORATIO. If your mind dislike anything, obey it. I will forestall their repair hither and say you are not fit.

HAMLET. Not a whit, we defy augury. There is special providence in the fall of a 255 sparrow.° If it be now, 'tis not to come; if it be not to come, it will be now; if it be not now, yet it will come. The readiness is all. Since no man of aught he leaves knows, what is't to leave betimes?° Let be. 260

A table prepared. [Enter] TRUMPETS, DRUMS, *and* OFFICERS *with cushions;* KING, QUEEN, *[*OSRIC,*] and all the* STATE, *[with] foils, daggers, [and stoups of wine borne in]; and* LAERTES.

KING. Come, Hamlet, come, and take
    this hand from me.

[The KING *puts* LAERTES' *hand into* HAMLET'S.*]*

HAMLET. Give me your pardon, sir. I
    have done you wrong,
But pardon't, as you are a gentleman.
This presence° knows, and you must
    needs have heard,
How I am punished with a sore distraction. 265
What I have done
That might your nature, honor, and exception°
Roughly awake, I here proclaim was madness.
Was't Hamlet wronged Laertes? Never
    Hamlet.

---

[212] **lapwing** (the new-hatched lapwing was thought to run around with half its shell on its head) [214] **'A did comply, sir, with his dug** he was ceremoniously polite to his mother's breast [218] **out of an habit of encounter** out of his own superficial way of meeting and conversing with people [219] **yeasty** frothy [222] **the bubbles are out** i.e., they are blown away (the reference is to the "yeasty collection") [236-237] **to use some gentle entertainment** to be courteous

[249] **gain-giving** misgiving [255-256] **the fall of a sparrow** (cf. Matthew 10:29 "Are not two sparrows sold for a farthing? and one of them shall not fall on the ground without your Father") [260] **betimes** early [264] **presence** royal assembly [267] **exception** disapproval

270 If Hamlet from himself be ta'en away,
And when he's not himself does wrong Laertes,
Then Hamlet does it not, Hamlet denies it.
Who does it then? His madness. If 't be so,
Hamlet is of the faction° that is wronged;
275 His madness is poor Hamlet's enemy.
Sir, in this audience,
Let my disclaiming from a purposed evil
Free me so far in your most generous thoughts
That I have shot my arrow o'er the house
And hurt my brother.
280   LAERTES.   I am satisfied in nature,
Whose motive in this case should stir me most
To my revenge. But in my terms of honor
I stand aloof, and will no reconcilement
Till by some elder masters of known honor
285 I have a voice and precedent° of peace
To keep my name ungored. But till that time
I do receive your offered love like love,
And will not wrong it.
       HAMLET.   I embrace it freely,
And will this brother's wager frankly play.
Give us the foils. Come on.
290   LAERTES.   Come, one for me.
HAMLET. I'll be your foil,° Laertes. In mine ignorance
Your skill shall, like a star i' th' darkest night,
Stick fiery off° indeed.
       LAERTES.   You mock me, sir.
HAMLET. No, by this hand.
       KING. Give them the foils, young Osric.
295   Cousin Hamlet,
You know the wager?
       HAMLET.   Very well, my lord.
Your grace has laid the odds o' th' weaker side.

KING. I do not fear it, I have seen you both;
But since he is bettered,° we have there-fore odds.
LAERTES. This is too heavy; let me see another.   300
HAMLET. This likes me well. These foils have all a length?

Prepare to play.

OSRIC. Ay, my good lord.
KING. Set me the stoups of wine upon that table.
If Hamlet give the first or second hit,
Or quit° in answer of the third exchange,   305
Let all the battlements their ordnance fire.
The King shall drink to Hamlet's better breath,
And in the cup an union° shall he throw
Richer than that which four successive kings
In Denmark's crown have worn. Give me the cups,   310
And let the kettle° to the trumpet speak,
The trumpet to the cannoneer without,
The cannons to the heavens, the heaven to earth,
"Now the King drinks to Hamlet." Come, begin.

Trumpets the while.
                                                                                             315
And you, the judges, bear a wary eye.
HAMLET. Come on, sir.
LAERTES.   Come, my lord!

       They play.

HAMLET.   One!
LAERTES.   No.
HAMLET.   Judgment?
OSRIC. A hit, a very palpable hit.

Drum, trumpets, and shot. Flourish, a piece goes off.

LAERTES.   Well, again.
KING. Stay, give me drink. Hamlet, this pearl is thine.
Here's to thy health. Give him the cup.

---

²⁷⁴ **faction** party, side ²⁸⁵ **voice and precedent** authoritative opinion justified by precedent ²⁹¹ **foil** (1) blunt sword, (2) background (of metal-lic leaf) for a jewel ²⁹³ **Stick fiery off** stand out brilliantly

²⁹⁹ **bettered** has improved (in France) ³⁰⁵ **quit** re-pay, hit back ³⁰⁸ **union** pearl ³¹¹ **kettle** kettle-drum

HAMLET. I'll play this bout first; set it by
320 a while.
Come.

[They play.]

Another hit. What say you?
LAERTES. A touch, a touch; I do con-
fess't.
KING. Our son shall win.
QUEEN.   He's fat,° and scant of breath.
Here, Hamlet, take my napkin, rub thy
brows.
The Queen carouses to thy fortune, Ham-
325 let.
HAMLET. Good madam!
KING.   Gertrude, do not drink.
QUEEN. I will, my lord; I pray you par-
don me. *[Drinks.]*
KING *[aside]*. It is the poisoned cup; it is
too late.
HAMLET. I dare not drink yet, madam—
by and by.
330 QUEEN. Come, let me wipe thy face.
LAERTES. My lord, I'll hit him now.
KING.   I do not think't.
LAERTES *[aside]*. And yet it is almost
against my conscience.
HAMLET. Come for the third, Laertes.
You do but dally.
I pray you pass with your best violence;
335 I am sure you make a wanton° of me.

[They] play.

LAERTES. Say you so? Come on.
OSRIC. Nothing neither way.
LAERTES. Have at you now!

*In scuffling they change rapiers, [and both
are wounded].*

KING.   Part them. They are incensed.
HAMLET. Nay, come—again!

[The QUEEN *falls.]*

OSRIC.   Look to the Queen there, ho!
HORATIO. They bleed on both sides.
340   How is it, my lord?

OSRIC. How is't, Laertes?
LAERTES. Why, as a woodcock to mine
own springe,° Osric.
I am justly killed with mine own treachery.
HAMLET. How does the Queen?
KING.   She sounds° to see them bleed.
QUEEN. No, no, the drink, the drink! O
my dear Hamlet!   345
The drink, the drink! I am poisoned.

[Dies.]

HAMLET. O villainy! Ho! Let the door be
locked.
Treachery! Seek it out.

*[*LAERTES *falls.]*

LAERTES. It is here, Hamlet. Hamlet,
thou art slain;
No med'cine in the world can do thee
good.   350
In thee there is not half an hour's life.
The treacherous instrument is in thy hand,
Unbated and envenomed. The foul prac-
tice°
Hath turned itself on me. Lo, here I lie,
Never to rise again. Thy mother's poi-
soned.   355
I can no more. The King, the King's to
blame.
HAMLET. The point envenomed too?
Then, venom, to thy work.

Hurts the KING.

ALL. Treason! Treason!
KING. O, yet defend me, friends. I am
but hurt.   360
HAMLET. Here, thou incestuous, mur-
d'rous damnèd Dane,
Drink off this potion. Is thy union here?
Follow my mother.   KING *dies.*
LAERTES.   He is justly served.
It is a poison tempered° by himself.
Exchange forgiveness with me, noble
Hamlet.   365
Mine and my father's death come not upon
thee,
Nor thine on me!   *Dies.*
HAMLET. Heaven make thee free of it! I
follow thee.

---

³²³ **fat** (1) sweaty, (2) out of training ³³⁵ **wanton**
spoiled child

³⁴² **springe** snare ³⁴⁴ **sounds** swoons ³⁵³ **practice** deception ³⁶⁴ **tempered** mixed

I am dead, Horatio. Wretched Queen,
   adieu!
You that look pale and tremble at this
370   chance,
That are but mutes° or audience to this
   act,
Had I but time (as this fell sergeant,°
   Death,
Is strict in his arrest) O, I could tell you—
But let it be. Horatio, I am dead;
Thou livest; report me and my cause
375   aright
To the unsatisfied.°
    HORATIO.   Never believe it.
I am more an antique Roman° than a
   Dane.
Here's yet some liquor left.
    HAMLET.   As th' art a man,
Give me the cup. Let go. By heaven, I'll
   ha't!
380 O God, Horatio, what a wounded name,
Things standing thus unknown, shall live
   behind me!
If thou didst ever hold me in thy heart,
Absent thee from felicity° awhile,
And in this harsh world draw thy breath in
   pain,
To tell my story.

A march afar off.   *[Exit* OSRIC.*]*

385   What warlike noise is this?

Enter OSRIC.

    OSRIC. Young Fortinbras, with conquest
       come from Poland,
To th' ambassadors of England gives
This warlike volley.
    HAMLET.   O, I die, Horatio!
The potent poison quite o'ercrows° my
   spirit.
I cannot live to hear the news from En-
390   gland,
But I do prophesy th' election lights

On Fortinbras. He has my dying voice.
So tell him, with th' occurrents,° more
   and less,
Which have solicited°—the rest is silence.
                     Dies.
    HORATIO. Now cracks a noble heart.
      Good night, sweet prince,   395
And flights of angels sing thee to thy
   rest.   *[March within.]*
Why does the drum come hither?

Enter FORTINBRAS, *with the* AMBASSADORS
with drum, colors, and ATTENDANTS.

    FORTINBRAS. Where is this sight?
    HORATIO.   What is it you would see?
If aught of woe or wonder, cease your
   search.
    FORTINBRAS. This quarry° cries on
     havoc.° O proud Death,   400
What feast is toward° in thine eternal cell
That thou so many princes at a shot
So bloodily hast struck?
    AMBASSADOR.   The sight is dismal;
And our affairs from England come too late.
The ears are senseless that should give us
   hearing   405
To tell him his commandment is fulfilled,
That Rosencrantz and Guildenstern are
   dead.
Where should we have our thanks?
    HORATIO.   Not from his° mouth,
Had it th' ability of life to thank you.
He never gave commandment for their
   death.   410
But since, so jump° upon this bloody
   question,
You from the Polack wars, and you from
   England,
Are here arrived, give order that these
   bodies
High on a stage° be placèd to the view,

---

³⁷¹ **mutes** performers who have no words to
speak ³⁷² **fell sergeant** dread sheriff's officer
³⁷⁶ **unsatisfied** uninformed ³⁷⁷ **antique Roman**
(with reference to the old Roman fashion of suicide) ³⁸³ **felicity** i.e., the felicity of death
³⁸⁹ **o'ercrows** overpowers (as a triumphant cock
crows over its weak opponent)

³⁹³ **occurrents** occurrences ³⁹⁴ **solicited** incited
⁴⁰⁰ **quarry** heap of slain bodies ⁴⁰⁰ **cries on
havoc** proclaims general slaughter ⁴⁰¹ **toward** in
preparation ⁴⁰⁸ **his** (Claudius') ⁴¹¹ **jump** precisely
⁴¹⁴ **stage** platform

And let me speak to th' yet unknowing
415   world
How these things came about. So shall
    you hear
Of carnal, bloody, and unnatural acts,
Of accidental judgments, casual° slaugh-
    ters,
Of deaths put on by cunning and forced
    cause,
420 And, in this upshot, purposes mistook
Fall'n on th' inventors' heads. All this
    can I
Truly deliver.
    FORTINBRAS.   Let us haste to hear it,
And call the noblest to the audience.
For me, with sorrow I embrace my for-
    tune.
I have some rights of memory° in this
425   kingdom,
Which now to claim my vantage doth invite
    me.
    HORATIO. Of that I shall have also cause
    to speak,

And from his mouth whose voice will draw
    on° more.
But let this same be presently performed,
Even while men's minds are wild, lest
    more mischance   430
On° plots and errors happen.
    FORTINBRAS.   Let four captains
Bear Hamlet like a soldier to the stage,
For he was likely, had he been put on,°
To have proved most royal; and for his
    passage°
The soldiers' music and the rite of war   435
Speak loudly for him.
Take up the bodies. Such a sight as this
Becomes the field,° but here shows much
    amiss.
Go, bid the soldiers shoot.
        *Exeunt marching; after the which
        a peal of ordnance are shot off.*

Finis

---

[418] **casual** not humanly planned, chance
[425] **rights of memory** remembered claims

[428] **voice will draw on** vote will influence [431] **On** on top of [433] **put on** advanced (to the throne) [434] **passage** death [438] **field** battlefield

QUESTIONS AND SUGGESTIONS FOR WRITING

Act I

1. The first scene (like many other scenes in this play) is full of expressions of uncertainty. What are some of these uncertainties? The Ghost first appears at I.i. 42. Does his appearance surprise us, or have we been prepared for it? Or is there both preparation and surprise? Do the last four speeches of I.i help to introduce a note of hope? If so, how?

2. Does the King's opening speech in I.ii reveal him to be an accomplished public speaker—or are lines 10–14 offensive? In his second speech (lines 41–49), what is the effect of naming Laertes four times? Claudius sometimes uses the royal pronouns ("we," "our"), sometimes the more intimate "I" and "my." Study his use of these in lines 1–4 and in 106–117. What do you think he is getting at?

3. Hamlet's first soliloquy (I.ii. 129–159) reveals that more than just his father's death distresses him. Be as specific as possible about the causes of Hamlet's anguish here. What traits does Hamlet reveal in his conversation with Horatio (I.ii. 160–254)?

4. What do you make of Polonius's advice to Laertes (I.iii. 55–80)? Is it sound? Sound advice, but here uttered by a fool? Ignoble advice? How would one follow the advice of line 78: "to thine own self be true"? In his words to Ophelia in I.iii. 101–135, what does he reveal about himself?

5. Can I.iv. 17–38 reasonably be taken as a speech on the "tragic flaw"? (On this idea,

see page 742.) Or is the passage a much more limited discussion, a comment simply on Danish drinking habits?

6. Hamlet is convinced in I.v. 95–104 that the Ghost has told the truth, indeed, the only important truth. But do we detect in 105–112 a hint of a tone suggesting that Hamlet delights in hating villainy? If so, can it be said that later this delight grows, and that in some scenes (e.g., III.iii) we feel that Hamlet has almost become a diabolic revenger? Explain.

Act II

1. Characterize Polonius on the basis of II.i. 1–74.
2. In light of what we have seen of Hamlet, is Ophelia's report of his strange behavior when he visits her understandable?
3. Why does II.ii. 33–34 seem almost comic? How do these lines help us to form a view about Rosencrantz and Guildenstern?
4. Is "the hellish Pyrrhus" (II.ii. 536) Hamlet's version of Claudius? Or is he Hamlet, who soon will be responsible for the deaths of Polonius, Rosencrantz and Guildenstern, Claudius, Gertrude, Ophelia, and Laertes? Explain.
5. Is the player's speech (II.ii. 541ff) a huffing speech? If so, why? To distinguish it from the poetry of the play itself? To characterize the bloody deeds that Hamlet cannot descend to?
6. In II.ii. 629–687 Hamlet rebukes himself for not acting. Why has he not acted? Because he is a coward (line 513)? Because he has a conscience? Because no action can restore his father and his mother's purity? Because he doubts the Ghost? What reason(s) can you offer?

Act III

1. What do you make out of Hamlet's assertion to Ophelia: "I loved you not" (III.i. 122)? Of his characterization of himself as full of "offenses" (III.i. 130–131)? Why is Hamlet so harsh to Ophelia?
2. In III.iii. 36–72 Claudius's conscience afflicts him. But is he repentant? What makes you say so?
3. Is Hamlet other than abhorrent in III.iii. 73–96? Do we want him to kill Claudius at this moment, when Claudius (presumably with his back to Hamlet) is praying? Why?
4. The Ghost speaks of Hamlet's "almost blunted purpose" (III.iv. 112). Is the accusation fair? Explain.
5. How would you characterize the Hamlet who speaks in III.iv. 203–218?

Act IV

1. Is Gertrude protecting Hamlet when she says he is mad (IV.i. 7), or does she believe that he is mad? If she believes he is mad, does it follow that she no longer feels ashamed and guilty? Explain.
2. Why should Hamlet hide Polonius's body (in IV.ii)? Is he feigning madness? Is he on the edge of madness? Explain.
3. How can we explain Hamlet's willingness to go to England (IV.iii. 52)?
4. Judging from IV.v, what has driven Ophelia mad? Is Laertes heroic, or somewhat foolish? Consider also the way Claudius treats him in IV.vii.

Act V

1. Would anything be lost if the Gravediggers in V.i were omitted?
2. To what extent do we judge Hamlet severely for sending Rosencrantz and Guilden-

stern to their deaths, as he reports in V.ii? On the whole, do we think of Hamlet as an intriguer? What other intrigues has he engendered? How successful were they?

3. Does V.ii. 254–260 show a paralysis of the will, or a wise recognition that more is needed than mere human scheming? Explain.

4. Does V.ii. 336 suggest that Laertes takes advantage of a momentary pause and unfairly stabs Hamlet? Is the exchange of weapons accidental, or does Hamlet (as in Olivier's film version), realizing that he has been betrayed, deliberately get possession of Laertes's deadly weapon?

5. Fortinbras is often cut from the play. How much is lost by the cut? Explain.

6. Fortinbras gives Hamlet a soldier's funeral. Is this ridiculous? Can it fairly be said that, in a sense, Hamlet has been at war? Explain.

General Questions

1. Hamlet in V.ii. 10–11 speaks of a "divinity that shapes our ends." To what extent does "divinity" (or Fate or mysterious Chance) play a role in the happenings?

2. How do Laertes, Fortinbras, and Horatio help to define Hamlet for us?

3. T. S. Eliot says (in "Shakespeare and the Stoicism of Seneca") that Hamlet, having made a mess, "dies fairly well pleased with himself." Evaluate.

Love and Hate

8

□ **ESSAYS**

James Thurber (American. 1894–1961)

COURTSHIP THROUGH THE AGES

Surely nothing in the astonishing scheme of life can have nonplussed Nature so much as the fact that none of the females of any of the species she created really cared very much for the male, as such. For the past ten million years Nature has been busily inventing ways to make the male attractive to the female, but the whole business of courtship, from the marine annelids up to man, still lumbers heavily along, like a complicated musical comedy. I have been reading the sad and absorbing story in Volume 6 (Cole to Dama) of the *Encyclopaedia Britannica*. In this volume you can learn all about cricket, cotton, costume designing, crocodiles, crown jewels, and Coleridge, but none of these subjects is so interesting as the Courtship of Animals, which recounts the sorrowful lengths to which all males must go to arouse the interest of a lady.

We all know, I think, that Nature gave man whiskers and a mustache with the quaint idea in mind that these would prove attractive to the female. We all know that, far from attracting her, whiskers and mustaches only made her nervous and gloomy, so that man had to go in for somersaults, tilting with lances, and performing feats of parlor magic to win her attention; he also had to bring her candy, flowers, and the furs of animals. It is common knowledge that in spite of all these "love displays" the male is constantly being turned down, insulted, or thrown out of the house. It is rather comforting, then, to discover that the peacock, for all his gorgeous plumage, does not have a particularly easy time in courtship; none of the males in the world do. The first peahen, it turned out, was only faintly stirred by her suitor's beautiful train. She would often go quietly to sleep while he was whisking it around. The *Britannica* tells us that the peacock actually had to learn a certain little trick to wake her up and revive her interest: he had to learn to

302

vibrate his quills so as to make a rustling sound. In ancient times man himself, observing the ways of the peacock, probably tried vibrating his whiskers to make a rustling sound; if so, it didn't get him anywhere. He had to go in for something else; so, among other things, he went in for gifts. It is not unlikely that he got this idea from certain flies and birds who were making no headway at all with rustling sounds.

One of the flies of the family Empidae, who had tried everything, finally hit on something pretty special. He contrived to make a glistening transparent balloon which was even larger than himself. Into this he would put sweetmeats and tidbits and he would carry the whole elaborate envelope through the air to the lady of his choice. This amused her for a time, but she finally got bored with it. She demanded silly little colorful presents, something that you couldn't eat but that would look nice around the house. So the male Empis had to go around gathering flower petals and pieces of bright paper to put into his balloon. On a courtship flight a male Empis cuts quite a figure now, but he can hardly be said to be happy. He never knows how soon the female will demand heavier presents, such as Roman coins and gold collar buttons. It seems probable that one day the courtship of the Empidae will fall down, as man's occasionally does, of its own weight.

The bowerbird is another creature that spends so much time courting the female that he never gets any work done. If all the male bowerbirds became nervous wrecks within the next ten or fifteen years, it would not surprise me. The female bowerbird insists that a playground be built for her with a specially constructed bower at the entrance. This bower is much more elaborate than an ordinary nest and is harder to build: it costs a lot more, too. The female will not come to the playground until the male has filled it up with a great many gifts: silvery leaves, red leaves, rose petals, shells, beads, berries, bones, dice, buttons, cigar bands, Christmas seals, and the Lord knows what else. When the female finally condescends to visit the playground, she is in a coy and silly mood and has to be chased in and out of the bower and up and down the playground before she will quit giggling and stand still long enough even to shake hands. The male bird is, of course, pretty well done in before the chase starts, because he has worn himself out hunting for eyeglass lenses and begonia blossoms. I imagine that many a bowerbird, after chasing a female for two or three hours, says the hell with it and goes home to bed. Next day, of course, he telephones someone else and the same trying ritual is gone through with again. A male bowerbird is as exhausted as a night-club habitué before he is out of his twenties.

The male fiddler crab has a somewhat easier time, but it can hardly be said that he is sitting pretty. He has one enormously large and powerful claw, usually brilliantly colored, and you might suppose that all he had to do was reach out and grab some passing cutie. The very earliest fiddler crabs may have tried this, but, if so, they got slapped for their pains. A female fiddler crab will not tolerate any caveman stuff: she never has and she doesn't intend to start now. To attract a female, a fiddler crab has to stand on tiptoe and brandish his claw in the air. If any female in the neighborhood is interested—and you'd be surprised how many are not—she comes over and engages him in light badinage, for which he is not in the mood. As many as a hundred females may pass the time of day with him and go on

5

about their business. By nightfall of an average courting day, a fiddler crab who has been standing on tiptoe for eight or ten hours waving a heavy claw in the air is in pretty sad shape. As in the case of the males of all species, however, he gets out of bed next morning, dashes some water on his face, and tries again.

The next time you encounter a male web-spinning spider, stop and reflect that he is too busy worrying about his love life to have any desire to bite you. Male web-spinning spiders have a tougher life than any other males in the animal kingdom. This is because the female web-spinning spiders have very poor eyesight. If a male lands on a female's web, she kills him before he has time to lay down his cane and gloves, mistaking him for a fly or a bumblebee who has tumbled into her trap. Before the species figured out what to do about this, millions of males were murdered by ladies they called on. It is the nature of spiders to perform a little dance in front of the female, but before a male spinner could get near enough for the female to see who he was and what he was up to, she would lash out at him with a flat-iron or a pair of garden shears. One night, nobody knows when, a very bright male spinner lay awake worrying about calling on a lady who had been killing suitors right and left. It came to him that this business of dancing as a love display wasn't getting anybody anywhere except the grave. He decided to go in for web-twitching, or strand-vibrating. The next day he tried it on one of the nearsighted girls. Instead of dropping in on her suddenly, he stayed outside the web and began monkeying with one of its strands. He twitched it up and down and in and out with such a lilting rhythm that the female was charmed. The serenade worked beautifully; the female let him live. The *Britannica*'s spider-watchers, however, report that this system is not always successful. Once in a while, even now, a female will fire three bullets into a suitor or run him through with a kitchen knife. She keeps threatening him from the moment he strikes the first low notes on the outside strings, but usually by the time he has got up to the high notes played around the center of the web, he is going to town and she spares his life.

Even the butterfly, as handsome a fellow as he is, can't always win a mate merely by fluttering around and showing off. Many butterflies have to have scent scales on their wings. Hepialus carries a powder puff in a perfumed pouch. He throws perfume at the ladies when they pass. The male tree cricket, Oecanthus, goes Hepialus one better by carrying a tiny bottle of wine with him and giving drinks to such doxies as he has designs on. One of the male snails throws darts to entertain the girls. So it goes, through the long list of animals, from the bristle worm and his rudimentary dance steps to man and his gift of diamonds and sapphires. The golden-eye drake raises a jet of water with his feet as he flies over a lake; Hepialus has his powder puff, Oecanthus his wine bottle, man his etchings. It is a bright and melancholy story, the age-old desire of the male for the female, the age-old desire of the female to be amused and entertained. Of all the creatures on earth, the only males who could be figured as putting any irony into their courtship are the grebes and certain other diving birds. Every now and then a courting grebe slips quietly down to the bottom of a lake and then, with a mighty "Whoosh!," pops out suddenly a few feet from his girl friend, splashing water all over her. She seems to be persuaded that this is a purely loving display, but I like to think that the grebe always has a faint hope of drowning her or scaring her to death.

I will close this investigation into the mournful burdens of the male with the *Britannica*'s story about a certain Argus pheasant. It appears that the Argus displays himself in front of a female who stands perfectly still without moving a feather. . . . The male Argus the *Britannica* tells about was confined in a cage with a female of another species, a female who kept moving around, emptying ashtrays and fussing with lampshades all the time the male was showing off his talents. Finally, in disgust, he stalked away and began displaying in front of his water trough. He reminds me of a certain male (Homo sapiens) of my acquaintance who one night after dinner asked his wife to put down her detective magazine so that he could read a poem of which he was very fond. She sat quietly enough until he was well into the middle of the thing, intoning with great ardor and intensity. Then suddenly there came a sharp, disconcerting *slap!* It turned out that all during the male's display, the female had been intent on a circling mosquito and had finally trapped it between the palms of her hands. The male in this case did not stalk away and display in front of a water trough; he went over to Tim's and had a flock of drinks and recited the poem to the fellas. I am sure they all told bitter stories of their own about how their displays had been interrupted by females. I am also sure that they all ended up singing "Honey, Honey, Bless Your Heart."

QUESTIONS AND SUGGESTIONS FOR WRITING

1. In a paragraph describe the persona Thurber presents here.
2. The essay is amusing, and we need not say that it seriously represents Thurber's ideas about courtship. Nevertheless, can one reasonably say that some serious point is hinted at, or is set forth playfully? If so, what might this point (or these points) be?
3. Find out something about the mating behavior of bees, or geese, or penguins, or a subject of your own choice, and write an essay of 500 words in Thurber's style. Notice that Thurber clearly (and comically) writes from the point of view of a male. You may, if you wish (whether you are a male or a female), write from a female point of view.

Erich Fromm (American. 1900–1980)

EROTIC LOVE

Brotherly love is love among equals; motherly love is love for the helpless. Different as they are from each other, they have in common that they are by their very nature not restricted to one person. If I love my brother, I love all my brothers; if I love my child, I love all my children; no, beyond that, I love all children, all that are in need of my help. In contrast to both types of love is *erotic love;* it is the craving for complete fusion, for union with one other person. It is by its very nature exclusive and not universal; it is also perhaps the most deceptive form of love there is.

First of all, it is often confused with the explosive experience of "falling" in love, the sudden collapse of the barriers which existed until that moment between two strangers. But . . . this experience of sudden intimacy is by its very nature short-lived. After the stranger has become an intimately known person there are no more barriers to be overcome, there is no more sudden closeness to be achieved. The "loved" person becomes as well known as oneself. Or, perhaps I should better say as little known. If there were more depth in the experience of the other person, if one could experience the infiniteness of his personality, the other person would never be so familiar—and the miracle of overcoming the barriers might occur every day anew. But for most people their own person, as well as others, is soon explored and soon exhausted. For them intimacy is established primarily through sexual contact. Since they experience the separateness of the other person primarily as physical separateness, physical union means overcoming separateness.

Beyond that, there are other factors which to many people denote the overcoming of separateness. To speak of one's own personal life, one's hopes and anxieties, to show oneself with one's childlike or childish aspects, to establish a common interest vis-à-vis the world—all this is taken as overcoming separateness. Even to show one's anger, one's hate, one's complete lack of inhibition is taken for intimacy, and this may explain the perverted attraction married couples often have for each other, who seem intimate only when they are in bed or when they give vent to their mutual hate and rage. But all these types of closeness tend to become reduced more and more as time goes on. The consequence is one seeks love with a new person, with a new stranger. Again the stranger is transformed into an "intimate" person, again the experience of falling in love is exhilarating and intense, and again it slowly becomes less and less intense, and ends in the wish for a new conquest, a new love—always with the illusion that the new love will be different from the earlier ones. These illusions are greatly helped by the deceptive character of sexual desire.

Sexual desire aims at fusion—and is by no means only a physical appetite, the relief of a painful tension. But sexual desire can be stimulated by the anxiety of aloneness, by the wish to conquer or be conquered, by vanity, by the wish to hurt and even to destroy, as much as it can be stimulated by love. It seems that sexual desire can easily blend with and be stimulated by any strong emotion, of which love is only one. Because sexual desire is in the minds of most people coupled with the idea of love, they are easily misled to conclude that they love each other when they want each other physically. Love can inspire the wish for sexual union; in this case the physical relationship is lacking in greediness, in a wish to conquer or to be conquered, but is blended with tenderness. If the desire for physical union is not stimulated by love, if erotic love is not also brotherly love, it never leads to union in more than an orgiastic, transitory sense. Sexual attraction creates, for the moment, the illusion of union, yet without love this "union" leaves strangers as far apart as they were before—sometimes it makes them ashamed of each other, or even makes them hate each other, because when the illusion has gone they feel their estrangement even more markedly than before. Tenderness is by no means, as Freud believed, a sublimation of the sexual instinct; it is the direct outcome of brotherly love, and exists in physical as well as in nonphysical forms of love.

In erotic love there is an exclusiveness which is lacking in brotherly love and motherly love. This exclusive character of erotic love warrants some further discussion. Frequently the exclusiveness of erotic love is misinterpreted as meaning possessive attachment. One can often find two people "in love" with each other who feel no love for anybody else. Their love is, in fact, an egotism *à deux;* they are two people who identify themselves with each other, and who solve the problem of separateness by enlarging the single individual into two. They have the experience of overcoming aloneness, yet, since they are separated from the rest of mankind, they remain separated from each other and alienated from themselves; their experience of union is an illusion. Erotic love is exclusive, but it loves in the other person all of mankind, all that is alive. It is exclusive only in the sense that I can fuse myself fully and intensely with one person only. Erotic love excludes the love for others only in the sense of erotic fusion, full commitment in all aspects of life—but not in the sense of deep brotherly love.

Erotic love, if it is love, has one premise. That I love from the essence of my being—and experience the other person in the essence of his or her being. In essence, all human beings are identical. We are all part of One; we are One. This being so, it should not make any difference whom we love. Love should be essentially an act of will, of decision to commit my life completely to that of one other person. This is, indeed, the rationale behind the idea of the insolubility of marriage, as it is behind the many forms of traditional marriage in which the two partners never choose each other, but are chosen for each other—and yet are expected to love each other. In contemporary Western culture this idea appears altogether false. Love is supposed to be the outcome of a spontaneous, emotional reaction, of suddenly being gripped by an irresistible feeling. In this view, one sees only the peculiarities of the two individuals involved—and not the fact that all men are part of Adam, and all women part of Eve. One neglects to see an important factor in erotic love, that of *will*. To love somebody is not just a strong feeling—it is a decision, it is a judgment, it is a promise. If love were only a feeling, there would be no basis for the promise to love each other forever. A feeling comes and it may go. How can I judge that it will stay forever, when my act does not involve judgment and decision?

Taking these views into account one may arrive at the position that love is exclusively an act of will and commitment, and that therefore fundamentally it does not matter who the two persons are. Whether the marriage was arranged by others, or the result of individual choice, once the marriage is concluded, the act of will should guarantee the continuation of love. This view seems to neglect the paradoxical character of human nature and of erotic love. We are all One—yet every one of us is a unique, unduplicable entity. In our relationships to others the same paradox is repeated. Inasmuch as we are all one, we can love everybody in the same way in the sense of brotherly love. But inasmuch as we are all also different, erotic love requires certain specific, highly individual elements which exist between some people but not between all.

Both views then, that of erotic love as completely individual attraction, unique between two specific persons, as well as the other view that erotic love is nothing but an act of will, are true—or, as it may be put more aptly, the truth is neither this nor that. Hence the idea of a relationship which can be easily dissolved if one is not successful with it is as erroneous as the idea that under no circumstances must the relationship be dissolved.

QUESTIONS AND SUGGESTIONS FOR WRITING

1. Summarize Fromm's argument. (Suggestions: Carefully read his last paragraph, in which he states his conclusion, and then reread the essay, tracing the argument that allows for this conclusion.)
2. Evaluate Fromm's remark (paragraph 6): "Love should be essentially an act of will, of decision to commit my life completely to that of one other person."
3. In paragraph 5 Fromm says, "Erotic love is exclusive, but it loves in the other person all of mankind, all that is alive." Does this strike you as true? Support or reject the idea in an essay of 500 to 750 words.

Henry Fairlie (American. b. 1924)

LUST OR LUXURIA[1]

Lust is not interested in its partners, but only in the gratification of its own craving: not even in the satisfaction of our whole natures, but in the appeasement merely of an appetite which we are unable to subdue. It is therefore a form of self-subjection; in fact of self-emptying. The sign it wears is: "This property is vacant." Anyone may take possession of it for a while. Lustful people may think that they can choose a partner at will for sexual gratification. But they do not really choose; they accept what is available. Lust accepts any partner for a momentary service; anyone may squat in its groin.

Love has meaning only insofar as it includes the idea of its continuance. Even what we rather glibly call a love affair, if it comes to an end, may continue as a memory that is pleasing in our lives, and we can still renew the sense of privilege and reward of having been allowed to know someone with such intimacy and sharing. But Lust dies at the next dawn and, when it returns in the evening, to search where it may, it is with its own past erased. Love wants to enjoy in other ways the human being whom it has enjoyed in bed. But in the morning Lust is always furtive. It dresses as mechanically as it undressed, and heads straight for the door, to return to its own solitude. Like all the sins, it makes us solitary. It is a self-abdication at the very heart of one's own being, of our need and ability to give and receive.

Love is involvement as well as continuance; but Lust will not get involved. This is one of the forms in which we may see it today. If people now engage in indiscriminate and short-lived relationships more than in the past, it is not really for some exquisite sexual pleasure that is thus gained, but because they refuse to become involved and to meet the demands that love makes. They are asking for

---

[1]*Luxuria* is Latin for "lust." (Notes to this selection are by the editors.)

little more than servicing, such as they might get at a gas station. The fact that it may go to bed with a lot of people is less its offense than the fact that it goes to bed with people for whom it does not care. The characteristic of the "singles" today is not the sexual freedom they supposedly enjoy, but the fact that this freedom is a deception. They are free with only a fraction of their natures. The full array of human emotions is hardly involved. The "singles bar" does not have an obnoxious odor because its clients, before the night is over, may hop into bed with someone whom they have just met, but because they do not even consider that, beyond the morning, either of them may care for the other. As they have made deserts of themselves, so they make deserts of their beds. This is the sin of Lust. Just as it dries up human beings, so it dries up human relationships. The word that comes to mind, when one thinks of it, is that it is parched. Everyone in a "singles bar" seems to have lost moisture, and this is peculiarly the accomplishment of Lust, to make the flesh seem parched, to deprive it of all real dewiness, shrivelling it to no more than a husk.

Lust is not a sin of the flesh so much as a sin *against* it. We are present in our flesh to the rest of creation, and particularly we are present in it to each other, revealing and exposing, sensitive to others and even vulnerable to them. When one hears people talk today of the sexual act as if it were rather like emptying one's bladder, one wishes to remind them that people still get hurt. They get hurt in their bodies, not merely from slappings and beatings and whippings, but from more subtle humiliations of which our sexual feelings are registers. Lust is a humiliation of the flesh, of another's and of one's own; and it is a perversity of our time that, in the name of a freedom which is delusive, we not only tolerate this humiliation, but exalt it as a wonder of the modern age.

We have reduced love to sex, sex to the act, and the act to a merely quantitative measurement of it. Sexual love can have infinite expressions, not all of which need to be consummated in the act, and it is this variety of expression that Lust will always diminish. It is not only solitary but uninventive in the slaking of its thirst. Whatever may be said for the sexual investigations that we today pursue and read so avidly, it cannot be denied that they are a little single-minded in their approach to the questions they raise. "People now seem to have sex on their minds," Malcolm Muggeridge once said, "which is a peculiar place to have it." Our obsession with sex is in fact a misplacing and a trivialization of it: a preoccupation with it which has no association with the rest of our lives.

More than we care to admit, we all have become voyeurs. "We live in an age in which voyeurism is no longer the side line of the solitary deviate," writes William F. May, "but rather a national pastime, fully institutionalized and naturalized in the mass media." The puritan makes the mistake of thinking that to have sex continually on view is an incitement to it. But it in fact weakens the feelings and passions that sex can and should arouse. Pornographic literature and films do not incite us to strenuous emulation. On the contrary, they are substitutes, evidence not of the strength of our sexual feelings, but of their weakness. We can and usually do indulge in them by ourselves; no one else has to be there; and we have to do nothing with even our own sexuality, except possibly to manipulate ourselves. They are again substitutes for involvement with another person. If they make us Lust at all, it is not for sexual experience with someone else, but merely for the empty cravings and gratifications of Lust itself. We reduce ourselves to the final absurdity: that we will lust after Lust.

What is left to Lust when its cravings at last subside, as subside in the end they will? It is alone. It has died. It has made no bonds, and is in the desert which it has made, with no longer even a craving. It is in its own black hole, where no vice can reach it, and from which its own voice cannot get out. It has collapsed into nothingness. It has burned itself out. Our excessive fear of old age is the fear that must be expected in a society in which Lust has been made a dominating motive. We would not fear it so much, if we did not fear that it will be empty; and we would not fear so much that it will be empty, if we had not emptied our lives already in the pursuit of mere cravings.

To be interested only in pursuit and not in the attainment, to give so much of one's energy only to the seduction, is a prescription for making a desert of one's world and oneself. "Promiscuous love necessitates hypocrisy," Christopher Sykes has said. "To play the part of Don Juan you have to be word-perfect in that of Tartuffe as well."[2] Such hypocrisy is again a form of self-emptying. We become only the words and roles in which we are so practiced, and at last we cannot find who we are behind them. The play of seduction, if it is to be rewarding to the seducer as well as the seduced, requires that their whole personalities be engaged. If love is a journey into another land, then seduction ought to be part of a mutual exploration, to see if the land may be entered and enjoyed together. Lust is incapable of this play, it is not interested in exploring, it does not want to enter any land. But perhaps above all, it has no personality of its own to bring to the encounter, with which to bring into play the personality of the other.

If love is continuance and involvement, perhaps no less it is attention, a constancy of gaze on the object of one's love, so that one may grow to know how to love it as the Other, in all the richness and variety of its aspects. Lust is incapable of this constancy; it has no attention to give. The time span of its interest is determined by the clockwork to which it has reduced its desires. The trouble with sexual infidelity is that it distracts the constancy of our attention to someone else. We remove a part of our gaze, and turn it elsewhere. In fact we remove a part of ourselves, and give it elsewhere. What comes between a couple when one of them is unfaithful is not the other woman, or the other man, *but what now cannot be shared by them.* If a mere sexual act were all that is involved, unfaithfulness would not be such an everlasting problem. Even if it is possible to "have sex" (the phrase is revealing) with someone else without loving that person, the fact that no love may have been bestowed elsewhere does not mean that none has been withdrawn.

It is rare for unfaithfulness to do its damage in a single affair. Its danger is that it erodes. Piecemeal it chips away at a relationship, not only at the constancy of

10

---

[2]Christopher Sykes is a contemporary English writer. Don Juan, a fourteenth-century libertine, is the subject of a play by Molière. Tartuffe, the subject of another play by Molière, is a religious hypocrite who disguises self-indulgence with a mask of piety.

our love, but at last at our capacity to love. It empties us of our capacity for loyalty, until we become incapable of forming an enduring relationship with any one individual, whom we have singled out. Our relationships are frayed from the start, like cutoff jeans, because we are no longer capable of discovering the unconditional worth of another human being, or ultimately of oneself. Love requires some effort, but our age encourages us to escape from it. At the first itch of dissatisfaction, the first rankle of difficulty, we can sever the knot, with as little ado as possible, and go to the other side of the fence, where we know that it will be greener.

Perhaps there are few things after which we lust more today than the experiences which we have not so far enjoyed or endured. Since Lust will not take the time or the trouble to explore or develop any relationship to the full, none can satisfy it, and it will whip itself (perhaps an appropriate term in the context) to try anything that will revive its jaded feelings. It is tired of fellatio. Then it will try its hand (hardly the appropriate word in the context) at a little sodomy. Weary of only one partner, it will advance to group sex. Unsure at last of its own sexuality, it will have recourse to bisexuality. Bored with the flesh, it will call for chains and leather jackets. Who knows when, abandoning the last shred of its humanity, it will turn to bestiality? All of this is again often interpreted as a proof that our age is more actively sexual than any before, whereas it is evidence rather that the lustfulness of our age has reduced our sexuality to impotence.

Even the more restrained workouts that are outlined in *The Joy of Sex* amount to instruction for those who live in a time in which the theme and fear of sexual impotence dominate our lives and much of our literature. Our sexuality has been animalized, stripped of the intricacy of feeling with which human beings have endowed it, leaving us to contemplate only the act, and our fear of our impotence in it. It is this animalization from which the sexual manuals cannot escape because they are reflections of it. They might be textbooks for veterinarians, and it is to precisely this kind of dejection that Lust has reduced our sexuality. What ought to be a mutual enchantment, something not on our minds but in our whole beings, is drained of its spontaneous gladness, and the rewards of a long and intricate relationship.

The fascination today with sadism, masochism, and fetishism suggests that, just as they reflect a hideous emptiness in the individuals who practice them, they reflect a no less terrible emptiness in our societies. We have said that Lust is a form of self-emptying, but there has been emptiness there already. In no other sin does one feel so much of a void, and this void is not only inside, it is also outside in the society. There is a profound failure of our societies to make continuing individual relationships seem part of the much wider social bonds that tie us to them. It is only in and for themselves that they are given any significance, and they are thus emptied of some of their satisfaction. Our fascination with various forms of sexual perversion is a direct result of the fact that our personal relationships now rest only on their own self-justification. It is not surprising that, in such a situation, we say that "anything goes."

There is no more pat shibboleth of our time than the idea that what consenting adults do in private is solely their own business. This is false. What we do in private has repercussions on ourselves, and what we are and believe has repercussions on others. What we do in our own homes will inevitably affect, not only our own behavior outside them, but what we expect and tolerate in the behavior of others. A change in manners or discipline in the family will not leave unchanged the manners and discipline in the wider society. When we recognize how deeply our sexual feelings are registers of our whole beings, it is mere trifling to say that our societies ought not to be constantly alert to the manner in which we employ them.

But if our societies have good reason to be interested in our sexual attitudes   15
and behavior, we have no less reason as individuals to be interested in why our societies have encouraged us to look to sex for such prurient and morbid delectations. The lustful person usually will be found to have only a terrible hollowness at the center of his life, and he is agitated to fill it, not daring to desist lest he should have to confront the desert he has made of himself and his life. He has no spiritual resource to which to turn. But is this not the condition of our societies? They do not know why they are there, except to continue; we hardly know why we are members of them, except to survive. It is all but inevitable in such a condition, with nothing very much outside ourselves to hold our attention for long, that we should agitate the most easily aroused and placable of our physical and emotional urges, if only to reassure ourselves that we are still alive and sentient beings. When our societies reduce most of the rest of life to little more than a series of disconnected episodes, commotions that only distract us, they cannot be surprised that their members reduce their own lives to a series of disconnected encounters, to find distraction in the commotions of their sexual organs.

We do not see how parched our social landscape has become, because it is studded with gawdy and erotogenic allurements to what we conceive to be a pleasure that is within the easy reach of us all. The managers of our society much prefer that we are infatuated with our sexuality, than that we look long and steadily at what they contrive from day to day. They have little to fear as long as we define ourselves by Kinsey, or Masters and Johnson, or Hite,[3] and find our most revolutionary tract in *The Joy of Sex*. They have discovered that, now that religion has been displaced, sex can be made the opiate of the masses. When the entire society is at last tranquilly preoccupied in the morbid practices of onanism, they will know that there is nothing more for them to do but rule forever over the dead.

QUESTIONS AND SUGGESTIONS FOR WRITING

1. Jot down a list of similes or metaphors (on these figures of speech, see pages 727–729) that Fairlie uses in his first three or four paragraphs, and evaluate them. Are they fresh? Are they appropriate? Do they help to clarify his argument?
2. The essay is largely an extended definition of lust and of love. In a paragraph, summarize Fairlie's definition of lust, and in another summarize his definition of love.

[3]Kinsey, Masters, Johnson, and Hite are comtemporary sociologists.

3. Fairlie occasionally uses "we," as for example in paragraph 5, beginning "We have reduced love to sex." Is he offensively blaming the reader for a fault that the reader may not be guilty of? If not, how does he manage to chastise the reader and yet keep the reader's good will?

4. Fairlie argues, especially in paragraph 11, that our age is *not* more active sexually than earlier ages. In a paragraph state the basis of his argument, and then in about 500 words evaluate it.

☐ FICTION

Edgar Allan Poe (American. 1809–1849)

THE CASK OF AMONTILLADO

The thousand injuries of Fortunato I had borne as I best could, but when he ventured upon insult, I vowed revenge. You, who so well know the nature of my soul, will not suppose, however, that I gave utterance to a threat. *At length* I would be avenged; this was a point definitely settled—but the very definitiveness with which it was resolved precluded the idea of risk. I must not only punish, but punish with impunity. A wrong is unredressed when retribution overtakes its redresser. It is equally unredressed when the avenger fails to make himself felt as such to him who has done the wrong.

It must be understood that neither by word nor deed had I given Fortunato cause to doubt my good will. I continued, as was my wont, to smile in his face, and he did not perceive that my smile *now* was at the thought of his immolation.

He had a weak point—this Fortunato—although in other regards he was a man to be respected and even feared. He prided himself on his connoisseurship in wine. Few Italians have the true virtuoso spirit. For the most part their enthusiasm is adopted to suit the time and opportunity to practice imposture upon the British and Austrian *millionaires*. In painting and gemmary Fortunato, like his countrymen, was a quack, but in the matter of old wines he was sincere. In this respect I did not differ from him materially;—I was skillful in the Italian vintages myself, and bought largely whenever I could.

It was about dusk, one evening during the supreme madness of the carnival season, that I encountered my friend. He accosted me with excessive warmth, for he had been drinking much. The man wore motley. He had on a tight-fitting parti-striped dress, and his head was surmounted by the conical cap and bells. I was so pleased to see him, that I thought I should never have done wringing his hand.

I said to him—"My dear Fortunato, you are luckily met. How remarkably well you are looking to-day! But I have received a pipe[1] of what passes for Amontillado, and I have my doubts."

5

[1]Wine cask. (Notes to this selection are by the editors.)

"How?" said he. "Amontillado? A pipe? Impossible! And in the middle of the carnival?"

"I have my doubts," I replied; "and I was silly enough to pay the full Amontillado price without consulting you in the matter. You were not to be found, and I was fearful of losing a bargain."

"Amontillado!"

"I have my doubts."

"Amontillado!"

"And I must satisfy them." 10

"Amontillado!"

"As you are engaged, I am on my way to Luchesi. If any one has a critical turn, it is he. He will tell me—"

"Luchesi cannot tell Amontillado from Sherry."

"And yet some fools will have it that his taste is a match for your own." 15

"Come, let us go."

"Whither?"

"To your vaults."

"My friend, no; I will not impose upon your good nature. I perceive you have an engagement. Luchesi—"

"I have no engagement; come." 20

"My friend, no. It is not the engagement, but the severe cold with which I perceive you are afflicted. The vaults are insufferably damp. They are encrusted with niter."

"Let us go, nevertheless. The cold is merely nothing. Amontillado! You have been imposed upon; and as for Luchesi, he cannot distinguish Sherry from Amontillado."

Thus speaking, Fortunato possessed himself of my arm. Putting on a mask of black silk, and drawing a *roquelaure*[2] closely about my person, I suffered him to hurry me to my palazzo.

There were no attendants at home; they had absconded to make merry in honor of the time. I had told them that I should not return until the morning, and had given them explicit orders not to stir from the house. These orders were sufficient, I well knew, to insure their immediate disappearance, one and all, as soon as my back was turned.

I took from their sconces two flambeaux, and giving one to Fortunato, bowed 25 him through several suites of rooms to the archway that led into the vaults. I passed down a long and winding staircase, requesting him to be cautious as he followed. We came at length to the foot of the descent, and stood together on the damp ground of the catacombs of the Montresors.

The gait of my friend was unsteady, and the bells upon his cap jingled as he strode.

"The pipe," said he.

"It is farther on," said I; "but observe the white web-work which gleams from these cavern walls."

[2]A short cloak.

He turned towards me, and looked into my eyes with two filmy orbs that distilled the rheum of intoxication.

"Niter?" he asked, at length.   30

"Niter," I replied. "How long have you had that cough?"

"Ugh! ugh! ugh!—ugh! ugh! ugh!—ugh! ugh! ugh!—ugh! ugh! ugh!— ugh! ugh! ugh!"

My poor friend found it impossible to reply for many minutes.

"It is nothing," he said, at last.

"Come," I said, with decision, "we will go back; your health is precious. You   35 are rich, respected, admired, beloved; you are happy, as once I was. You are a man to be missed. For me it is no matter. We will go back; you will be ill, and I cannot be responsible. Besides, there is Luchesi—"

"Enough," he said; "the cough is a mere nothing: it will not kill me. I shall not die of a cough."

"True—true," I replied; "and, indeed, I had no intention of alarming you unnecessarily—but you should use all proper caution. A draught of this Medoc will defend us from the damps."

Here I knocked off the neck of a bottle which I drew from a long row of its fellows that lay upon the mould.

"Drink," I said, presenting him the wine.

He raised it to his lips with a leer. He paused and nodded to me familiarly,   40 while his bells jingled.

"I drink," he said, "to the buried that repose around us."

"And I to your long life."

He again took my arm, and we proceeded.

"These vaults," he said, "are extensive."

"The Montresors," I replied, "were a great and numerous family."   45

"I forget your arms."

"A huge human foot d'or, in a field azure; the foot crushes a serpent rampant whose fangs are imbedded in the heel."

"And the motto?"

"Nemo me impune lacessit."[3]

"Good!" he said.   50

The wine sparkled in his eyes and the bells jingled. My own fancy grew warm with the Medoc. We had passed through walls of piled bones, with casks and puncheons intermingling, into the inmost recesses of the catacombs. I paused again, and this time I made bold to seize Fortunato by an arm above the elbow.

"The niter!" I said; "see, it increases. It hangs like moss upon the vaults. We are below the river's bed. The drops of moisture trickle among the bones. Come, we will go back ere it is too late. Your cough—"

"It is nothing," he said; "let us go on. But first, another draught of the Medoc."

I broke and reached him a flagon of De Grâve. He emptied it at a breath. His

---

[3] "No one dare attack me with impunity"—the motto of Scotland.

eyes flashed with a fierce light. He laughed and threw the bottle upwards with a gesticulation I did not understand.

I looked at him in surprise. He repeated the movement—a grotesque one.   55

"You do not comprehend?" he said.

"Not I," I replied.

"Then you are not of the brotherhood."

"How?"

"You are not of the masons."   60

"Yes, yes," I said, "yes, yes."

"You? Impossible! A mason?"

"A mason," I replied.

"A sign," he said.

"It is this," I answered, producing a trowel from beneath the folds of my   65
roquelaure.

"You jest," he exclaimed, recoiling a few paces. "But let us proceed to the Amontillado."

"Be it so," I said, replacing the tool beneath the cloak, and again offering him my arm. He leaned upon it heavily. We continued our route in search of the Amontillado. We passed through a range of low arches, descended, passed on, and descending again, arrived at a deep crypt, in which the foulness of the air caused our flambeaux rather to glow than flame.

At the most remote end of the crypt there appeared another less spacious. Its walls had been lined with human remains piled to the vault overhead, in the fashion of the great catacombs of Paris. Three sides of this interior crypt were still ornamented in this manner. From the fourth the bones had been thrown down, and lay promiscuously upon the earth, forming at one point a mound of some size. Within the wall thus exposed by the displacing of the bones, we perceived a still interior recess, in depth about four feet, in width three, in height six or seven. It seemed to have been constructed for no especial use within itself, but formed merely the interval between two of the colossal supports of the roof of the catacombs, and was backed by one of their circumscribing walls of solid granite.

It was in vain that Fortunato, uplifting his dull torch, endeavored to pry into the depths of the recess. Its termination the feeble light did not enable us to see.

"Proceed," I said; "herein is the Amontillado. As for Luchesi—"   70

"He is an ignoramus," interrupted my friend, as he stepped unsteadily forward, while I followed immediately at his heels. In an instant he had reached the extremity of the niche, and finding his progress arrested by the rock, stood stupidly bewildered. A moment more and I had fettered him to the granite. In its surface were two iron staples, distant from each other about two feet, horizontally. From one of these depended a short chain, from the other a padlock. Throwing the links about his waist, it was but the work of a few seconds to secure it. He was too much astounded to resist. Withdrawing the key I stepped back from the recess.

"Pass your hand," I said, "over the wall; you cannot help feeling the niter. Indeed it is *very* damp. Once more let me *implore* you to return. No? Then I must positively leave you. But I must first render you all the little attentions in my power."

"The Amontillado!" ejaculated my friend, not yet recovered from his astonishment.

"True," I replied; "the Amontillado."

As I said these words I busied myself among the pile of bones of which I have   75
before spoken. Throwing them aside, I soon uncovered a quantity of building-stone and mortar. With these materials and with the aid of my trowel, I began vigorously to wall up the entrance of the niche.

I had scarcely laid the first tier of masonry when I discovered that the intoxication of Fortunato had in a great measure worn off. The earliest indication I had of this was a low moaning cry from the depth of the recess. It was *not* the cry of a drunken man. There was then a long and obstinate silence. I laid the second tier, and the third, and the fourth; and then I heard the furious vibrations of the chain. The noise lasted for several minutes, during which, that I might hearken to it with the more satisfaction, I ceased my labors and sat down upon the bones. When at last the clanking subsided, I resumed the trowel, and finished without interruption the fifth, the sixth, and the seventh tier. The wall was now nearly upon a level with my breast. I again paused, and holding the flambeaux over the masonwork, threw a few feeble rays upon the figure within.

A succession of loud and shrill screams, bursting suddenly from the throat of the chained form, seemed to thrust me violently back. For a brief moment I hesitated—I trembled. Unsheathing my rapier, I began to grope with it about the recess; but the thought of an instant reassured me. I placed my hand upon the solid fabric of the catacombs, and felt satisfied. I reapproached the wall. I replied to the yells of him who clamored. I re-echoed—I aided—I surpassed them in volume and in strength. I did this, and the clamorer grew still.

It was now midnight, and my task was drawing to a close. I had completed the eighth, the ninth, and the tenth tier. I had finished a portion of the last and the eleventh; there remained but a single stone to be fitted and plastered in. I struggled with its weight; I placed it partially in its destined position. But now there came from out the niche a low laugh that erected the hairs upon my head. It was succeeded by a sad voice, which I had difficulty in recognizing as that of the noble Fortunato. The voice said—

"Ha! ha! ha!—he! he! he!—a very good joke indeed—an excellent jest. We will have many a rich laugh about it at the palazzo—he! he! he!—over our wine—he! he! he!"

"The Amontillado!" I said.   80

"He! he! he!—he! he! he!—yes, the Amontillado. But is it not getting late? Will not they be awaiting us at the palazzo, the Lady Fortunato and the rest? Let us be gone."

"Yes," I said, "let us be gone."

"For the love of God, Montresor!"

"Yes," I said, "for the love of God!"

But to these words I hearkened in vain for a reply. I grew impatient. I called   85
aloud:

"Fortunato!"

No answer. I called again:

"Fortunato!"

No answer still. I thrust a torch through the remaining aperture and let it fall within. There came forth in return only a jingling of the bells. My heart grew sick—on account of the dampness of the catacombs. I hastened to make an end of my labor. I forced the last stone into its position; I plastered it up. Against the new masonry I re-erected the old rampart of bones. For the half of a century no mortal has disturbed them. *In pace requiescat!*[4]

QUESTIONS AND SUGGESTIONS FOR WRITING

1. Construct a definition of madness (you may want to do a little research, but if you make use of your findings be sure to give credit to your sources), and write an essay of 500 to 750 words arguing whether or not Montresor is mad. Note: You may want to distinguish between Montresor at the time of the murder, and Montresor at the time he is telling the story.

2. Consult the entry on "irony" in the glossary on page 778, then consult the pages referred to in Question 1, and write an essay of 500 words on irony in this story. Develop your thesis—for instance, "There are three kinds of irony here," or "Only one sort of irony is really important here," or "The story begins with one kind of irony and ends with another." Do not simply offer definitions of irony with examples.

Edith Wharton (American. 1862–1937)

ROMAN FEVER

I

From the table at which they had been lunching two American ladies of ripe but well-cared-for middle age moved across the lofty terrace of the Roman restaurant and, leaning on its parapet, looked first at each other, and then down on the outspread glories of the Palatine and the Forum, with the same expression of vague but benevolent approval.

As they leaned there a girlish voice echoed up gaily from the stairs leading to the court below. "Well, come along, then," it cried, not to them but to an invisible companion, "and let's leave the young things to their knitting"; and a voice as fresh laughed back: "Oh, look here, Babs, not actually *knitting*—" "Well, I mean figuratively," rejoined the first. "After all, we haven't left our poor parents much else to do . . ." and at that point the turn of the stairs engulfed the dialogue.

The two ladies looked at each other again, this time with a tinge of smiling embarrassment, and the smaller and paler one shook her head and colored slightly.

"Barbara!" she murmured, sending an unheard rebuke after the mocking voice in the stairway.

[4]Latin for "May he rest in peace."

The other lady, who was fuller, and higher in color, with a small determined nose supported by vigorous black eyebrows, gave a good-humored laugh. "That's what our daughters think of us!"

Her companion replied by a deprecating gesture. "Not of us individually. We must remember that. It's just the collective modern idea of Mothers. And you see—" Half guiltily she drew from her handsomely mounted black hand-bag a twist of crimson silk run through by two fine knitting needles. "One never knows," she murmured. "The new system has certainly given us a good deal of time to kill; and sometimes I get tired just looking—even at this." Her gesture was now addressed to the stupendous scene at their feet.

The dark lady laughed again, and they both relapsed upon the view, contemplating it in silence, with a sort of diffused serenity which might have been borrowed from the spring effulgence of the Roman skies. The luncheon-hour was long past, and the two had their end of the vast terrace to themselves. At this opposite extremity a few groups, detained by a lingering look at the outspread city, were gathering up guide-books and fumbling for tips. The last of them scattered, and the two ladies were alone on the air-washed height.

"Well, I don't see why we shouldn't just stay here," said Mrs. Slade, the lady of the high color and energetic brows. Two derelict basket-chairs stood near, and she pushed them into the angle of the parapet, and settled herself in one, her gaze upon the Palatine. "After all, it's still the most beautiful view in the world."

"It always will be, to me," assented her friend Mrs. Ansley, with so slight a stress on the "me" that Mrs. Slade, though she noticed it, wondered if it were not merely accidental, like the random underlinings of old-fashioned letter-writers.

"Grace Ansley was always old-fashioned," she thought; and added aloud, with a retrospective smile: "It's a view we've both been familiar with for a good many years. When we first met here we were younger than our girls are now. You remember?"

"Oh, yes, I remember," murmured Mrs. Ansley, with the same undefinable stress.—"There's that head-waiter wondering," she interpolated. She was evidently far less sure than her companion of herself and of her rights in the world.

"I'll cure him of wondering," said Mrs. Slade, stretching her hand toward a bag as discreetly opulent-looking as Mrs. Ansley's. Signing to the head-waiter, she explained that she and her friend were old lovers of Rome, and would like to spend the end of the afternoon looking down on the view—that is, if it did not disturb the service? The head-waiter, bowing over her gratuity, assured her that the ladies were most welcome, and would be still more so if they would condescend to remain for dinner. A full moon night, they would remember. . . .

Mrs. Slade's black brows drew together, as though references to the moon were out-of-place and even unwelcome. But she smiled away her frown as the head-waiter retreated. "Well, why not? We might do worse. There's no knowing, I suppose, when the girls will be back. Do you even know back from *where*? I don't!"

Mrs. Ansley again colored slightly. "I think those young Italian aviators we met at the Embassy invited them to fly to Tarquinia for tea. I suppose they'll want to wait and fly back by moonlight."

"Moonlight—moonlight! What a part it still plays. Do you suppose they're as   15
sentimental as we were?"

"I've come to the conclusion that I don't in the least know what they are,"
said Mrs. Ansley. "And perhaps we didn't know much more about each other."

"No; perhaps we didn't."

Her friend gave her a shy glance. "I never should have supposed you were
sentimental, Alida."

"Well, perhaps I wasn't." Mrs. Slade drew her lids together in retrospect;
and for a few moments the two ladies, who had been intimate since childhood,
reflected how little they knew each other. Each one, of course, had a label ready
to attach to the other's name; Mrs. Delphin Slade, for instance, would have told
herself, or any one who asked her, that Mrs. Horace Ansley, twenty-five years
ago, had been exquisitely lovely—no, you wouldn't believe it, would you? . . .
though, of course, still charming, distinguished . . . Well, as a girl she had been
exquisite; far more beautiful than her daughter Barbara, though certainly Babs,
according to the new standards at any rate, was more effective—had more edge,
as they say. Funny where she got it, with those two nullities as parents. Yes;
Horace Ansley was—well, just the duplicate of his wife. Museum specimens of
old New York. Good-looking, irreproachable, exemplary. Mrs. Slade and Mrs.
Ansley had lived opposite each other—actually as well as figuratively—for years.
When the drawing-room curtains in No. 20 East 73rd Street were renewed, No.
23, across the way, was always aware of it. And of all the movings, buyings,
travels, anniversaries, illnesses—the tame chronicle of an estimable pair. Little of
it escaped Mrs. Slade. But she had grown bored with it by the time her husband
made his big *coup* in Wall Street, and when they bought in upper Park Avenue had
already begun to think: "I'd rather live opposite a speak-easy for a change; at
least one might see it raided." The idea of seeing Grace raided was so amusing
that (before the move) she launched it at a woman's lunch. It made a hit, and went
the rounds—she sometimes wondered if it had crossed the street, and reached
Mrs. Ansley. She hoped not, but didn't much mind. Those were the days when
respectability was at a discount, and it did the irreproachable no harm to laugh at
them a little.

A few years later, and not many months apart, both ladies lost their hus-   20
bands. There was an appropriate exchange of wreaths and condolences, and a
brief renewal of intimacy in the half-shadow of their mourning; and now, after
another interval, they had run across each other in Rome, at the same hotel, each
of them the modest appendage of a salient daughter. The similarity of their lot
again drawn them together, lending itself to mild jokes, and the mutual confession
that, if in old days it must have been tiring to "keep up" with daughters, it was
now, at times, a little dull not to.

No doubt, Mrs. Slade reflected, she felt her unemployment more than poor
Grace ever would. It was a big drop from being the wife of Delphin Slade to being
his widow. She had always regarded herself (with a certain conjugal pride) as his
equal in social gifts, as contributing her full share to the making of the exceptional
couple they were: but the difference after his death was irremediable. As the wife
of the famous corporation lawyer, always with an international case or two on

hand, every day brought its exciting and unexpected obligation: the impromptu entertaining of eminent colleagues from abroad, the hurried dashes on legal business to London, Paris or Rome, where the entertaining was so handsomely reciprocated; the amusement of hearing in her wake: "What, that handsome woman with the good clothes and eyes is Mrs. Slade—*the* Slade's wife? Really? Generally the wives of celebrities are such frumps."

Yes; being *the* Slade's widow was a dullish business after that. In living up to such a husband all her faculties had been engaged; now she had only her daughter to live up to, for the son who seemed to have inherited his father's gifts had died suddenly in boyhood. She had fought through that agony because her husband was there, to be helped and to help; now, after the father's death, the thought of the boy had become unbearable. There was nothing left but to mother her daughter; and dear Jenny was such a perfect daughter that she needed no excessive mothering. "Now with Babs Ansley I don't know that I *should* be so quiet," Mrs. Slade sometimes half-enviously reflected; but Jenny, who was younger than her brilliant friend, was that rare accident, an extremely pretty girl who somehow made youth and prettiness seem as safe as their absence. It was all perplexing—and to Mrs. Slade a little boring. She wished that Jenny would fall in love—with the wrong man, even; that she might have to be watched, out-maneuvered, rescued. And instead, it was Jenny who watched her mother, kept her out of draughts, made sure that she had taken her tonic . . .

Mrs. Ansley was much less articulate than her friend, and her mental portrait of Mrs. Slade was slighter, and drawn with fainter touches. "Alida Slade's awfully brilliant; but not as brilliant as she thinks," would have summed it up; though she would have added, for the enlightenment of strangers, that Mrs. Slade had been an extremely dashing girl; much more so than her daughter, who was pretty, of course, and clever in a way, but had none of her mother's—well, "vividness," some one had once called it. Mrs. Ansley would take up current words like this, and cite them in quotation marks, as unheard-of audacities. No; Jenny was not like her mother. Sometimes Mrs. Ansley thought Alida Slade was disappointed; on the whole she had had a sad life. Full of failures and mistakes; Mrs. Ansley had always been rather sorry for her . . .

So these two ladies visualized each other, each through the wrong end of her little telescope.

II

For a long time they continued to sit side by side without speaking. It seemed as though, to both, there was a relief in laying down their somewhat futile activities in the presence of the vast Memento Mori which faced them. Mrs. Slade sat quite still, her eyes fixed on the golden slope of the Palace of the Caesars, and after a while Mrs. Ansley ceased to fidget with her bag, and she too sank into meditation. Like many intimate friends, the two ladies had never before had occasion to be silent together, and Mrs. Ansley was slightly embarrassed by what seemed, after so many years, a new stage in their intimacy, and one with which she did not yet know how to deal.

Suddenly the air was full of that deep clangor of bells which periodically

25

covers Rome with a roof of silver. Mrs. Slade glanced at her wrist-watch. "Five o'clock already," she said, as though surprised.

Mrs. Ansley suggested interrogatively: "There's bridge at the Embassy at five." For a long time Mrs. Slade did not answer. She appeared to be lost in contemplation, and Mrs. Ansley thought the remark had escaped her. But after a while she said, as if speaking out of a dream: "Bridge, did you say? Not unless you want to . . . But I don't think I will, you know."

"Oh, no," Mrs. Ansley hastened to assure her. "I don't care to at all. It's so lovely here; and so full of old memories, as you say." She settled herself in her chair, and almost furtively drew forth her knitting. Mrs. Slade took sideways note of this activity, but her own beautifully cared-for hands remained motionless on her knee.

"I was just thinking," she said slowly, "what different things Rome stands for to each generation of travelers. To our grandmothers, Roman fever; to our mothers, sentimental dangers—how we used to be guarded!—to our daughters, no more dangers than the middle of Main Street. They don't know it—but how much they're missing!"

The long golden light was beginning to pale, and Mrs. Ansley lifted her knitting a little closer to her eyes. "Yes; how we were guarded!"   30

"I always used to think," Mrs. Slade continued, "that our mothers had a much more difficult job than our grandmothers. When Roman fever stalked the streets it must have been comparatively easy to gather in the girls at the danger hour; but when you and I were young, with such beauty calling us, and the spice of disobedience thrown in, and no worse risk than catching cold during the cool hour after sunset, the mothers used to be put to it to keep us in—didn't they?"

She turned again toward Mrs. Ansley, but the latter had reached a delicate point in her knitting. "One, two, three—slip two; yes, they must have been," she assented, without looking up.

Mrs. Slade's eyes rested on her with a deepened attention. "She can knit—in the face of *this!* How like her . . ."

Mrs. Slade leaned back, brooding, her eyes ranging from the ruins which faced her to the long green hollow of the Forum, the fading glow of the church fronts beyond it, and the outlying immensity of the Colosseum. Suddenly she thought: "It's all very well to say that our girls have done away with sentiment and moonlight. But if Babs Ansley isn't out to catch that young aviator—the one who's a Marchese—then I don't know anything. And Jenny has no chance beside her. I know that too. I wonder if that's why Grace Ansley likes the two girls to go everywhere together? My poor Jenny as a foil—!" Mrs. Slade gave a hardly audible laugh, and at the sound Mrs. Ansley dropped her knitting.

"Yes—?"

"I—oh, nothing. I was only thinking how your Babs carries everything before her. That Campolieri boy is one of the best matches in Rome. Don't look so innocent, my dear—you know he is. And I was wondering, ever so respectfully, you understand . . . wondering how two such exemplary characters as you and Horace had managed to produce anything quite so dynamic." Mrs. Slade laughed again, with a touch of asperity.   35

Mrs. Ansley's hands lay inert across her needles. She looked straight out at the great accumulated wreckage of passion and splendor at her feet. But her small profile was almost expressionless. At length she said: "I think you overrate Babs, my dear."

Mrs. Slade's tone grew easier. "No; I don't. I appreciate her. And perhaps envy you. Oh, my girl's perfect; if I were a chronic invalid I'd—well, I think I'd rather be in Jenny's hands. There must be times . . . but there! I always wanted a brilliant daughter . . . and never quite understood why I got an angel instead."

Mrs. Ansley echoed her laugh in a faint murmur. "Babs is an angel too."

"Of course—of course! But she's got rainbow wings. Well, they're wandering by the sea with their young men; and here we sit . . . and it all brings back the past a little too acutely."   40

Mrs. Ansley had resumed her knitting. One might almost have imagined (if one had known her less well, Mrs. Slade reflected) that, for her also, too many memories rose from the lengthening shadows of those august ruins. But no; she was simply absorbed in her work. What was there for her to worry about? She knew that Babs would almost certainly come back engaged to the extremely eligible Campolieri. "And she'll sell the New York house, and settle down near them in Rome, and never be in their way . . . she's much too tactful. But she'll have an excellent cook, and just the right people in for bridge and cocktails . . . and a perfectly peaceful old age among her grandchildren."

Mrs. Slade broke off this prophetic flight with a recoil of self-disgust. There was no one of whom she had less right to think unkindly than of Grace Ansley. Would she never cure herself of envying her? Perhaps she had begun too long ago.

She stood up and leaned against the parapet, filling her troubled eyes with the tranquilizing magic of the hour. But instead of tranquilizing her the sight seemed to increase her exasperation. Her gaze turned toward the Colosseum. Already its golden flank was drowned in purple shadow, and above it the sky curved crystal clear, without light or color. It was the moment when afternoon and evening hang balanced in mid-heaven.

Mrs. Slade turned back and laid her hand on her friend's arm. The gesture was so abrupt that Mrs. Ansley looked up, startled.

"The sun's set. You're not afraid, my dear?"   45

"Afraid—?"

"Of Roman fever or pneumonia? I remember how ill you were that winter. As a girl you had a very delicate throat, hadn't you?"

"Oh, we're all right up here. Down below, in the Forum, it does get deathly cold, all of a sudden . . . but not here."

"Ah, of course you know because you had to be so careful." Mrs. Slade turned back to the parapet. She thought: "I must make one more effort not to hate her." Aloud she said: "Whenever I look at the Forum from up here, I remember that story about a great-aunt of yours, wasn't she? A dreadfully wicked great-aunt?"

"Oh, yes; Great-aunt Harriet. The one who was supposed to have sent her   50
young sister out to the Forum after sunset to gather a night-blooming flower for

her album. All our great-aunts and grandmothers used to have albums of dried flowers."

Mrs. Slade nodded. "But she really sent her because they were in love with the same man—"

"Well, that was the family tradition. They said Aunt Harriet confessed it years afterward. At any rate, the poor little sister caught the fever and died. Mother used to frighten us with the story when we were children."

"And you frightened *me* with it, that winter when you and I were here as girls. The winter I was engaged to Delphin."

Mrs. Ansley gave a faint laugh. "Oh, did I? Really frightened you? I don't believe you're easily frightened."

"Not often; but I was then. I was easily frightened because I was too happy. I wonder if you know what that means?"   55

"I—yes . . ." Mrs. Ansley faltered.

"Well, I suppose that was why the story of your wicked aunt made such an impression on me. And I thought: 'There's no more Roman fever, but the Forum is deathly cold after sunset—especially after a hot day. And the Colosseum's even colder and damper.'"

"The Colosseum—?"

"Yes. It wasn't easy to get in, after the gates were locked for the night. Far from easy. Still, in those days it could be managed; it was managed, often. Lovers met there who couldn't meet elsewhere. You knew that?"

"I—I daresay. I don't remember."   60

"You don't remember? You don't remember going to visit some ruins or other one evening, just after dark, and catching a bad chill? You were supposed to have gone to see the moon rise. People always said that expedition was what caused your illness."

There was a moment's silence; then Mrs. Ansley rejoined: "Did they? It was all so long ago."

"Yes. And you got well again—so it didn't matter. But I suppose it struck your friends—the reason given for your illness, I mean—because everybody knew you were so prudent on account of your throat, and your mother took such care of you . . . You *had* been out late sightseeing, hadn't you, that night?"

"Perhaps I had. The most prudent girls aren't always prudent. What made you think of it now?"

Mrs. Slade seemed to have no answer ready. But after a moment she broke out: "Because I simply can't bear it any longer—!"   65

Mrs. Ansley lifted her head quickly. Her eyes were wide and very pale. "Can't bear what?"

"Why—your not knowing that I've always known why you went."

"Why I went?"

"Yes. You think I'm bluffing, don't you? Well, you went to meet the man I was engaged to—and I can repeat every word of the letter that took you there."

While Mrs. Slade spoke Mrs. Ansley had risen unsteadily to her feet. Her bag, her knitting and gloves, slid in a panic-stricken heap to the ground. She   70 looked at Mrs. Slade as though she were looking at a ghost.

"No, no—don't," she faltered out.

"Why not? Listen, if you don't believe me. 'My one darling, things can't go on like this. I must see you alone. Come to the Colosseum immediately after dark tomorrow. There will be somebody to let you in. No one whom you need fear will suspect'—but perhaps you've forgotten what the letter said?"

Mrs. Ansley met the challenge with an unexpected composure. Steadying herself against the chair she looked at her friend, and replied: "No, I know it by heart too."

"And the signature? 'Only *your* D.S.' Was that it? I'm right, am I? That was the letter that took you out that evening after dark?"

Mrs. Ansley was still looking at her. It seemed to Mrs. Slade that a slow struggle was going on behind the voluntarily controlled mask of her small quiet face. "I shouldn't have thought she had herself so well in hand," Mrs. Slade reflected, almost resentfully. But at this moment Mrs. Ansley spoke. "I don't know how you knew. I burnt that letter at once."

"Yes; you would, naturally—you're so prudent!" The sneer was open now. "And if you burnt the letter you're wondering how on earth I know what was in it. That's it, isn't it?"

Mrs. Slade waited, but Mrs. Ansley did not speak.

"Well, my dear, I know what was in that letter because I wrote it!"

"You wrote it?"

"Yes."

The two women stood for a minute staring at each other in the last, golden light. Then Mrs. Ansley dropped back into her chair. "Oh," she murmured, and covered her face with her hands.

Mrs. Slade waited nervously for another word or movement. None came, and at length she broke out: "I horrify you."

Mrs. Ansley's hands dropped to her knee. The face they uncovered was streaked with tears. "I wasn't thinking of you. I was thinking—it was the only letter I ever had from him!"

"And I wrote it. Yes; I wrote it! But I was the girl he was engaged to. Did you happen to remember that?"

Mrs. Ansley's head dropped again. "I'm not trying to excuse myself . . . I remembered . . ."

"And still you went?"

"Still I went."

Mrs. Slade stood looking down on the small bowed figure at her side. The flame of her wrath had already sunk, and she wondered why she had ever thought there would be any satisfaction in inflicting so purposeless a wound on her friend. But she had to justify herself.

"You do understand? I found out—and I hated you, hated you. I knew you were in love with Delphin—and I was afraid; afraid of you, of your quiet ways, your sweetness . . . your . . . well, I wanted you out of the way, that's all. Just for a few weeks; just till I was sure of him. So in a blind fury I wrote that letter . . . I don't know why I'm telling you now."

75

80

85

"I suppose," said Mrs. Ansley slowly, "it's because you've always gone on   90
hating me."

"Perhaps. Or because I wanted to get the whole thing off my mind." She
paused. "I'm glad you destroyed the letter. Of course I never thought you'd die."

Mrs. Ansley relapsed into silence, and Mrs. Slade, leaning above her, was
conscious of a strange sense of isolation, of being cut off from the warm current of
human communion. "You think me a monster!"

"I don't know . . . It was the only letter I had, and you say he didn't write
it?"

"Ah, how you care for him still!"

"I cared for that memory," said Mrs. Ansley.   95

Mrs. Slade continued to look down on her. She seemed physically reduced by
the blow—as if, when she got up, the wind might scatter her like a puff of dust.
Mrs. Slade's jealousy suddenly leapt up again at the sight. All these years the
woman had been living on that letter. How she must have loved him, to treasure
the mere memory of its ashes! The letter of the man her friend was engaged to.
Wasn't it she who was the monster?

"You tried your best to get him away from me, didn't you? But you failed; and
I kept him. That's all."

"Yes. That's all."

"I wish now I hadn't told you. I'd no idea you'd feel about it as you do; I
thought you'd be amused. It all happened so long ago, as you say; and you must
do me the justice to remember that I had no reason to think you'd ever taken it
seriously. How could I, when you were married to Horace Ansley two months
afterward? As soon as you could get out of bed your mother rushed you off to
Florence and married you. People were rather surprised—they wondered at its
being done so quickly; but I thought I knew. I had an idea you did it out of *pique*—
to be able to say you'd got ahead of Delphin and me. Girls have such silly reasons
for doing the most serious things. And your marrying so soon convinced me that
you'd never really cared."

"Yes, I suppose it would," Mrs. Ansley assented.   100

The clear heaven overhead was emptied of all its gold. Dusk spread over it,
abruptly darkening the Seven Hills. Here and there lights began to twinkle
through the foliage at their feet. Steps were coming and going on the deserted
terrace—waiters looking out of the doorway at the head of the stairs, then reap-
pearing with trays and napkins and flasks of wine. Tables were moved, chairs
straightened. A feeble string of electric lights flickered out. Some vases of faded
flowers were carried away, and brought back replenished. A stout lady in a dust-
coat suddenly appeared, asking in broken Italian if any one had seen the elastic
band which held together her tattered Baedeker. She poked with her stick under
the table at which she had lunched, the waiters assisting.

The corner where Mrs. Slade and Mrs. Ansley sat was still shadowy and
deserted. For a long time neither of them spoke. At length Mrs. Slade began
again: "I suppose I did it as a sort of joke—"

"A joke?"

"Well, girls are ferocious sometimes, you know. Girls in love especially. And I remember laughing to myself all that evening at the idea that you were waiting around there in the dark, dodging out of sight, listening for every sound, trying to get in—. Of course I was upset when I heard you were so ill afterward."

Mrs. Ansley had not moved for a long time. But now she turned slowly   105
toward her companion. "But I didn't wait. He'd arranged everything. He was there. We were let in at once," she said.

Mrs. Slade sprang up from her leaning position. "Delphin there? They let you in?—Ah, now you're lying!" she burst out with violence.

Mrs. Ansley's voice grew clearer, and full of surprise. "But of course he was there. Naturally he came—"

"Came? How did he know he'd find you there? You must be raving!"

Mrs. Ansley hesitated, as though reflecting. "But I answered the letter. I told him I'd be there. So he came."

Mrs. Slade flung her hands up to her face. "Oh, God—you answered! I never   110
thought of your answering . . ."

"It's odd you never thought of it, if you wrote the letter."

"Yes. I was blind with rage."

Mrs. Ansley rose, and drew her fur scarf about her. "It is cold here. We'd better go . . . I'm sorry for you," she said, as she clasped the fur about her throat.

The unexpected words sent a pang through Mrs. Slade. "Yes; we'd better go." She gathered up her bag and cloak. "I don't know why you should be sorry for me," she muttered.

Mrs. Ansley stood looking away from her toward the dusky secret mass of   115
the Colosseum. "Well—because I didn't have to wait that night."

Mrs. Slade gave an unquiet laugh. "Yes; I was beaten there. But I oughtn't to begrudge it to you, I suppose. At the end of all these years. After all, I had everything; I had him for twenty-five years. And you had nothing but that one letter that he didn't write."

Mrs. Ansley was again silent. At length she turned toward the door of the terrace. She took a step, and turned back, facing her companion.

"I had Barbara," she said, and began to move ahead of Mrs. Slade toward the stairway.

QUESTIONS AND SUGGESTIONS FOR WRITING

1. In a paragraph indicate whether the setting—Rome—is especially significant. Would London or St. Louis be equally effective settings?
2. In a paragraph explain the last line of the story, calling attention to what it reveals about Mrs. Ansley.

D. H. Lawrence (English. 1885–1930)

THE HORSE DEALER'S DAUGHTER

"Well, Mabel, and what are you going to do with yourself?" asked Joe, with foolish flippancy. He felt quite safe himself. Without listening for an answer, he turned aside, worked a grain of tobacco to the tip of his tongue and spat it out. He did not care about anything, since he felt safe himself.

The three brothers and the sister sat round the desolate breakfast table, attempting some sort of desultory consultation. The morning's post had given the final tap to the family fortune, and all was over. The dreary dining room itself, with its heavy mahogany furniture, looked as if it were waiting to be done away with.

But the consultation amounted to nothing. There was a strange air of ineffectuality about the three men, as they sprawled at table, smoking and reflecting vaguely on their own condition. The girl was alone, a rather short, sullen-looking young woman of twenty-seven. She did not share the same life as her brothers. She would have been good-looking, save for the impassive fixity of her face, "bulldog," as her brothers called it.

There was a confused tramping of horses' feet outside. The three men all sprawled round in their chairs to watch. Beyond the dark holly bushes that separated the strip of lawn from the highroad, they could see a cavalcade of shire horses swinging out of their own yard, being taken for exercise. This was the last time. These were the last horses that would go through their hands. The young men watched with critical, callous looks. They were all frightened at the collapse of their lives, and the sense of disaster in which they were involved left them no inner freedom.

Yet they were three fine, well-set fellows enough. Joe, the eldest, was a man of thirty-three, broad and handsome in a hot, flushed way. His face was red, he twisted his black moustache over a thick finger, his eyes were shallow and restless. He had a sensual way of uncovering his teeth when he laughed, and his bearing was stupid. Now he watched the horses with a glazed look of helplessness in his eyes, a certain stupor of downfall.

The great draft-horses swung past. They were tied head to tail, four of them, and they heaved along to where a lane branched off from the highroad, planting their great hoofs floutingly in the fine black mud, swinging their great rounded haunches sumptuously, and trotting a few sudden steps as they were led into the lane, round the corner. Every movement showed a massive, slumbrous strength, and a stupidity which held them in subjection. The groom at the head looked back, jerking the leading rope. And the cavalcade moved out of sight up the lane, the tail of the last horse, bobbed up tight and stiff, held out taut from the swinging great haunches as they rocked behind the hedges in a motion-like sleep.

Joe watched with glazed hopeless eyes. The horses were almost like his own body to him. He felt he was done for now. Luckily he was engaged to a woman as old as himself, and therefore her father, who was steward of a neighboring estate, would provide him with a job. He would marry and go into harness. His life was over, he would be a subject animal now.

5

He turned uneasily aside, the retreating steps of the horses echoing in his ears. Then, with foolish restlessness, he reached for the scraps of bacon rind from the plates, and making a faint whistling sound, flung them to the terrier that lay against the fender. He watched the dog swallow them, and waited till the creature looked into his eyes. Then a faint grin came on his face, and in a high, foolish voice he said:

"You won't get much more bacon, shall you, you little bitch?"

The dog faintly and dismally wagged its tail, then lowered its haunches, cir- cled round, and lay down again.

There was another helpless silence at the table. Joe sprawled uneasily in his seat, not willing to go till the family conclave was dissolved. Fred Henry, the second brother, was erect, clean-limbed, alert. He had watched the passing of the horses with more sang-froid. If he was an animal, like Joe, he was an animal which controls, not one which is controlled. He was master of any horse, and he carried himself with a well-tempered air of mastery. But he was not master of the situa- tions of life. He pushed his coarse brown moustache upwards, off his lip, and glanced irritably at his sister, who sat impassive and inscrutable.

"You'll go and stop with Lucy for a bit, shan't you?" he asked. The girl did not answer.

"I don't see what else you can do," persisted Fred Henry.

"Go as a skivvy," Joe interpolated laconically.

The girl did not move a muscle.

"If I was her, I should go in for training for a nurse," said Malcolm, the youngest of them all. He was the baby of the family, a young man of twenty-two, with a fresh, jaunty *museau*.[1]

But Mabel did not take any notice of him. They had talked at her and round her for so many years, that she hardly heard them at all.

The marble clock on the mantelpiece softly chimed the half-hour, the dog rose uneasily from the hearthrug and looked at the party at the breakfast table. But still they sat on in effectual conclave.

"Oh, all right," said Joe suddenly, apropos of nothing. "I'll get a move on."

He pushed back his chair, straddled his knees with a downward jerk, to get them free, in horsey fashion, and went to the fire. Still he did not go out of the room; he was curious to know what the others would do or say. He began to charge his pipe, looking down at the dog and saying, in a high, affected voice:

"Going wi' me? Going wi' me are ter? Tha'rt goin' further tha that counts on just now, dost hear?"

The dog faintly wagged its tail, the man stuck out his jaw and covered his pipe with his hands, and puffed intently, losing himself in the tobacco, looking down all the while at the dog with an absent brown eye. The dog looked at him in mournful distrust. Joe stood with his knees stuck out, in real horsey fashion.

"Have you had a letter from Lucy?" Fred Henry asked of his sister.

"Last week," came the neutral reply.

---

[1] Jaw; literally, muzzle or snout of a beast. —ED.

"And what does she say?"   25

There was no answer.

"Does she *ask* you to go and stop there?" persisted Fred Henry.

"She says I can if I like."

"Well, then, you'd better. Tell her you'll come on Monday."

This was received in silence.   30

"That's what you'll do then, is it?" said Fred Henry, in some exasperation.

But she made no answer. There was a silence of futility and irritation in the room. Malcolm grinned fatuously.

"You'll have to make up your mind between now and next Wednesday," said Joe loudly, "or else find yourself lodgings on the curbstone."

The face of the young woman darkened, but she sat on immutable.

"Here's Jack Fergusson!" exclaimed Malcolm, who was looking aimlessly out   35
of the window.

"Where?" exclaimed Joe, loudly.

"Just gone past."

"Coming in?"

Malcolm craned his neck to see the gate.

"Yes," he said.   40

There was a silence. Mabel sat on like one condemned, at the head of the table. Then a whistle was heard from the kitchen. The dog got up and barked sharply. Joe opened the door and shouted:

"Come on."

After a moment a young man entered. He was muffled up in overcoat and a purple woolen scarf, and his tweed cap, which he did not remove, was pulled down on his head. He was of medium height, his face was rather long and pale, his eyes looked tired.

"Hello, Jack! Well, Jack!" exclaimed Malcolm and Joe. Fred Henry merely said, "Jack."

"What's doing?" asked the newcomer, evidently addressing Fred Henry.   45

"Same. We've got to be out by Wednesday. Got a cold?"

"I have—got it bad, too."

"Why don't you stop in?"

"*Me* stop in? When I can't stand on my legs, perhaps I shall have a chance." The young man spoke huskily. He had a slight Scotch accent.

"It's a knock-out, isn't it," said Joe, boisterously, "if a doctor goes round   50
croaking with a cold. Looks bad for the patients, doesn't it?"

The young doctor looked at him slowly.

"Anything the matter with *you,* then?" he asked sarcastically.

"Not as I know of. Damn your eyes, I hope not. Why?"

"I thought you were very concerned about the patients, wondered if you might be one yourself."

"Damn it, no, I've never been patient to no flaming doctor, and hope I never   55
shall be," returned Joe.

At this point Mabel rose from the table, and they all seemed to become aware of her existence. She began putting the dishes together. The young doctor looked at her, but did not address her. He had not greeted her. She went out of the room with the tray, her face impassive and unchanged.

"When are you off then, all of you?" asked the doctor.

"I'm catching the eleven-forty," replied Malcolm. "Are you goin' down wi' th' trap, Joe?"

"Yes, I've told you I'm going down wi' th' trap, haven't I?"

"We'd better be getting her in then. So long, Jack, if I don't see you before I go," said Malcolm, shaking hands.

He went out, followed by Joe, who seemed to have his tail between his legs.

"Well, this is the devil's own," exclaimed the doctor, when he was left alone with Fred Henry. "Going before Wednesday, are you?"

"That's the orders," replied the other.

"Where, to Northampton?"

"That's it."

"The devil!" exclaimed Fergusson, with quiet chagrin.

And there was silence between the two.

"All settled up, are you?" asked Fergusson.

"About."

There was another pause.

"Well, I shall miss yer, Freddy, boy," said the young doctor.

"And I shall miss thee, Jack," returned the other.

"Miss you like hell," mused the doctor.

Fred Henry turned aside. There was nothing to say. Mabel came in again, to finish clearing the table.

"What are *you* going to do, then, Miss Pervin?" asked Fergusson. "Going to your sister's, are you?"

Mabel looked at him with her steady, dangerous eyes, that always made him uncomfortable, unsettling his superficial ease.

"No," she said.

"Well, what in the name of fortune *are* you going to do? Say what you mean to do," cried Fred Henry, with futile intensity.

But she only averted her head, and continued her work. She folded the white table-cloth, and put on the chenille cloth.

"The sulkiest bitch that ever trod!" muttered her brother.

But she finished her task with perfectly impassive face, the young doctor watching her interestedly all the while. Then she went out.

Fred Henry stared after her, clenching his lips, his blue eyes fixing in sharp antagonism, as he made a grimace of sour exasperation.

"You could bray her into bits, and that's all you'd get out of her," he said in a small, narrowed tone.

The doctor smiled faintly.

"What's she *going* to do, then?" he asked.

"Strike me if *I* know!" returned the other.

There was a pause. Then the doctor stirred.

"I'll be seeing you to-night, shall I?" he said to his friend.

"Ay—where's it to be? Are we going over to Jessdale?"

"I don't know. I've got such a cold on me. I'll come round to the Moon and Stars, anyway."

"Let Lizzie and May miss their night for once, eh?"

"That's it—if I feel as I do now."

"All's one—"

The two young men went through the passage and down to the back door together. The house was large, but it was servantless now, and desolate. At the back was a small bricked house-yard, and beyond that a big square, graveled fine and red, and having stables on two sides. Sloping, dank, winter-dark fields stretched away on the open sides.

But the stables were empty. Joseph Pervin, the father of the family, had been   95
a man of no education, who had become a fairly large horse dealer. The stables had been full of horses, there was a great turmoil and come-and-go of horses and of dealers and grooms. Then the kitchen was full of servants. But of late things had declined. The old man had married a second time, to retrieve his fortunes. Now he was dead and everything was gone to the dogs, there was nothing but debt and threatening.

For months, Mabel had been servantless in the big house, keeping the home together in penury for her ineffectual brothers. She had kept house for ten years. But previously it was with unstinted means. Then, however brutal and coarse everything was, the sense of money had kept her proud, confident. The men might be foul-mouthed, the women in the kitchen might have bad reputations, her brothers might have illegitimate children. But so long as there was money, the girl felt herself established, and brutally proud, reserved.

No company came to the house, save dealers and coarse men. Mabel had no associates of her own sex, after her sister went away. But she did not mind. She went regularly to church, she attended to her father. And she lived in the memory of her mother, who had died when she was fourteen, and whom she had loved. She had loved her father, too, in a different way, depending upon him, and feeling secure in him, until at the age of fifty-four he married again. And then she had set hard against him. Now he had died and left them all hopelessly in debt.

She had suffered badly during the period of poverty. Nothing, however, could shake the curious sullen, animal pride that dominated each member of the family. Now, for Mabel, the end had come. Still she would not cast about her. She would follow her own way just the same. She would always hold the keys of her own situation. Mindless and persistent, she endured from day to day. Why should she think? Why should she answer anybody? It was enough that this was the end, and there was no way out. She need not pass any more darkly along the main street of the small town, avoiding every eye. She need not demean herself any more, going into the shops and buying the cheapest food. This was at an end. She thought of nobody, not even of herself. Mindless and persistent, she seemed in a sort of ecstasy to be coming nearer to her fulfillment, her own glorification, approaching her dead mother, who was glorified.

In the afternoon she took a little bag, with shears and sponge and a small scrubbing brush, and went out. It was a gray, wintry day, with saddened, dark green fields and an atmosphere blackened by the smoke of foundries not far off. She went quickly, darkly along the causeway, heeding nobody, through the town to the churchyard.

There she always felt secure, as if no one could see her, although as a matter 100
of fact she was exposed to the stare of every one who passed along under the
churchyard wall. Nevertheless, once under the shadow of the great looming
church, among the graves, she felt immune from the world, reserved within the
thick churchyard wall as in another country.

Carefully she clipped the grass from the grave, and arranged the pinky white,
small chrysanthemums in the tin cross. When this was done, she took an empty
jar from a neighboring grave, brought water, and carefully, most scrupulously
sponged the marble headstone and the coping-stone.

It gave her sincere satisfaction to do this. She felt in immediate contact with
the world of her mother. She took minute pains, went through the park in a state
bordering on pure happiness, as if in performing this task she came into a subtle,
intimate connection with her mother. For the life she followed here in the world
was far less real than the world of death she inherited from her mother.

The doctor's house was just by the church. Fergusson, being a mere hired
assistant, was slave to the countryside. As he hurried now to attend to the outpa-
tients in the surgery, glancing across the graveyard with his quick eyes, he saw
the girl at her task at the grave. She seemed so intent and remote, it was like
looking into another world. Some mystical element was touched in him. He
slowed down as he walked, watching her as if spellbound.

She lifted her eyes, feeling him looking. Their eyes met. And each looked
away again at once, each feeling, in some way, found out by the other. He lifted his
cap and passed on down the road. There remained distinct in his consciousness,
like a vision, the memory of her face, lifted from the tombstone in the churchyard,
and looking at him with slow, large, portentous eyes. It *was* portentous, her face.
It seemed to mesmerize him. There was a heavy power in her eyes which laid
hold of his whole being, as if he had drunk some powerful drug. He had been
feeling weak and done before. Now the life came back into him, he felt delivered
from his own fretted, daily self.

He finished his duties at the surgery as quickly as might be, hastily filling up 105
the bottles of the waiting people with cheap drugs. Then, in perpetual haste, he
set off again to visit several cases in another part of his round, before teatime. At
all times he preferred to walk if he could, but particularly when he was not well.
He fancied the motion restored him.

The afternoon was falling. It was gray, deadened, and wintry, with a slow,
moist, heavy coldness sinking in and deadening all the faculties. But why should
he think or notice? He hastily climbed the hill and turned across the dark green
fields, following the black cindertrack. In the distance, across a shallow dip in the
country, the small town was clustered like smoldering ash, a tower, a spire, a
heap of low, raw, extinct houses. And on the nearest fringe of the town, sloping
into the dip, was Oldmeadow, the Pervins's house. He could see the stables and
the outbuildings distinctly, as they lay towards him on the slope. Well, he would
not go there many more times! Another resource would be lost to him, another
place gone: the only company he cared for in the alien, ugly little town he was
losing. Nothing but work, drudgery, constant hastening from dwelling to dwelling
among the colliers and the iron-workers. It wore him out, but at the same time he

had a craving for it. It was a stimulant to him to be in the homes of the working people, moving as it were through the innermost body of their life. His nerves were excited and gratified. He could come so near, into the very lives of the rough, inarticulate, powerfully emotional men and women. He grumbled, he said he hated the hellish hole. But as a matter of fact it excited him, the contact with the rough, strongly-feeling people was a stimulant applied direct to his nerves.

Below Oldmeadow, in the green, shallow, soddened hollow of fields, lay a square, deep pond. Roving across the landscape, the doctor's quick eye detected a figure in black passing through the gate of the field, down towards the pond. He looked again. It would be Mabel Pervin. His mind suddenly became alive and attentive.

Why was she going down there? He pulled up on the path on the slope above, and stood staring. He could just make sure of the small black figure moving in the hollow of the failing day. He seemed to see her in the midst of such obscurity, that he was like a clairvoyant, seeing rather with the mind's eye than with ordinary sight. Yet he could see her positively enough, while he kept his eye attentive. He felt, if he looked away from her, in the thick, ugly falling dusk, he would lose her altogether.

He followed her minutely as she moved, direct and intent, like something transmitted rather than stirring in voluntary activity, straight down the field towards the pond. There she stood on the bank for a moment. She never raised her head. Then she waded slowly into the water.

He stood motionless as the small black figure walked slowly and deliberately towards the center of the pond, very slowly, gradually moving deeper into the motionless water, and still moving forward as the water got up to her breast. Then he could see her no more in the dusk of the dead afternoon.

110

"There!" he exclaimed. "Would you believe it?"

And he hastened straight down, running over the wet, soddened fields, pushing through the hedges, down into the depression of callous wintry obscurity. It took him several minutes to come to the pond. He stood on the bank, breathing heavily. He could see nothing. His eyes seemed to penetrate the dead water. Yes, perhaps that was the dark shadow of her black clothing beneath the surface of the water.

He slowly ventured into the pond. The bottom was deep, soft clay, he sank in, and the water clasped dead cold round his legs. As he stirred he could smell the cold, rotten clay that fouled up into the water. It was objectionable in his lungs. Still, repelled and yet not heeding, he moved deeper into the pond. The cold water rose over his thighs, over his loins, upon his abdomen. The lower part of his body was all sunk in the hideous cold element. And the bottom was so deeply soft and uncertain he was afraid of pitching with his mouth underneath. He could not swim, and was afraid.

He crouched a little, spreading his hands under the water and moving them round, trying to feel for her. The dead cold pond swayed upon his chest. He moved again, a little deeper, and again, with his hands underneath, he felt all around under the water. And he touched her clothing. But it evaded his fingers. He made a desperate effort to grasp it.

And so doing he lost his balance and went under, horribly, suffocating in the   115
foul earthy water, struggling madly for a few moments. At last, after what seemed
an eternity, he got his footing, rose again into the air and looked around. He
gasped, and knew he was in the world. Then he looked at the water. She had
risen near him. He grasped her clothing, and drawing her nearer, turned to take
his way to land again.

He went very slowly, carefully, absorbed in the slow progress. He rose
higher, climbing out of the pond. The water was now only about his legs; he was
thankful, full of relief to be out of the clutches of the pond. He lifted her and
staggered on to the bank, out of the horror of wet, gray clay.

He laid her down on the bank. She was quite unconscious and running with
water. He made the water come from her mouth, he worked to restore her. He
did not have to work very long before he could feel the breathing begin again in
her; she was breathing naturally. He worked a little longer. He could feel her live
beneath his hands; she was coming back. He wiped her face, wrapped her in his
overcoat, looked round into the dim, dark gray world, then lifted her and staggered down the bank and across the fields.

It seemed an unthinkably long way, and his burden so heavy he felt he would
never get to the house. But at last he was in the stableyard, and then in the
house-yard. He opened the door and went into the house. In the kitchen he laid
her down on the hearthrug, and called. The house was empty. But the fire was
burning in the grate.

Then again he kneeled to attend to her. She was breathing regularly, her eyes
were wide open and as if conscious, but there seemed something missing in her
look. She was conscious in herself, but unconscious of her surroundings.

He ran upstairs, took blankets from a bed, and put them before the fire to   120
warm. Then he removed her saturated, earthy-smelling clothing, rubbed her dry
with a towel, and wrapped her naked in the blankets. Then he went into the
dining-room, to look for spirits. There was a little whiskey. He drank a gulp
himself, and put some into her mouth.

The effect was instantaneous. She looked full into his face, as if she had been
seeing him for some time, and yet had only just become conscious of him.

"Dr. Fergusson?" she said.

"What?" he answered.

He was divesting himself of his coat, intending to find some dry clothing
upstairs. He could not bear the smell of the dead, clayey water, and he was
mortally afraid of his own health.

"What did I do?" she asked.   125

"Walked into the pond," he replied. He had begun to shudder like one sick,
and could hardly attend to her. Her eyes remained full on him, he seemed to be
going dark in his mind, looking back at her helplessly. The shuddering became
quieter in him, his life came back in him, dark and unknowing, but strong again.

"Was I out of my mind?" she asked, while her eyes were fixed on him all the
time.

"Maybe, for the moment," he replied. He felt quiet, because his strength
came back. The strange fretful strain had left him.

"Am I out of my mind now?" she asked.

"Are you?" he reflected a moment. "No," he answered truthfully, "I don't   130
see that you are." He turned his face aside. He was afraid now, because he felt
dazed, and felt dimly that her power was stronger than his, in this issue. And she
continued to look at him fixedly all the time. "Can you tell me where I shall find
some dry things to put on?" he asked.

"Did you dive into the pond for me?" she asked.

"No," he answered. "I walked in. But I went in overhead as well."

There was silence for a moment. He hesitated. He very much wanted to go
upstairs to get into dry clothing. But there was another desire in him. And she
seemed to hold him. His will seemed to have gone to sleep, and left him, standing
there slack before her. But he felt warm inside himself. He did not shudder at all,
though his clothes were sodden on him.

"Why did you?" she asked.

"Because I didn't want you to do such a foolish thing," he said.   135

"It wasn't foolish," she said, still gazing at him as she lay on the floor, with a
sofa cushion under her head. "It was the right thing to do. *I* knew best, then."

"I'll go and shift these wet things," he said. But still he had not the power to
move out of her presence, until she sent him. It was as if she had the life of his
body in her hands, and he could not extricate himself. Or perhaps he did not want
to.

Suddenly she sat up. Then she became aware of her own immediate condition. She felt the blankets about her, she knew her own limbs. For a moment it
seemed as if her reason were going. She looked round, with wild eye, as if
seeking something. He stood still with fear. She saw her clothing lying scattered.

"Who undressed me?" she asked, her eyes resting full and inevitable on his
face.

"I did," he replied, "to bring you round." For some moments she sat and   140
gazed at him awfully, her lips parted.

"Do you love me, then?" she asked.

He only stood and stared at her, fascinated. His soul seemed to melt.

She shuffled forward on her knees, and put her arms round him, round his
legs, as he stood there, pressing her breasts against his knees and thighs, clutching him with strange, convulsive certainty, pressing his thighs against her, drawing
him to her face, her throat, as she looked up at him with flaring, humble eyes of
transfiguration, triumphant in first possession.

"You love me," she murmured, in strange transport, yearning and triumphant
and confident. "You love me. I know you love me, I know."

And she was passionately kissing his knees, through the wet clothing, pas-   145
sionately and indiscriminately kissing his knees, his legs, as if unaware of everything.

He looked down at the tangled wet hair, the wild, bare, animal shoulders. He
was amazed, bewildered, and afraid. He had never thought of loving her. He had
never wanted to love her. When he rescued her and restored her, he was a doctor,
and she was a patient. He had had no single personal thought of her. Nay, this
introduction of the personal element was very distasteful to him, a violation of his

professional honor. It was horrible to have her there embracing his knees. It was horrible. He revolted from it, violently. And yet—and yet—he had not the power to break away.

She looked at him again, with the same supplication of powerful love, and that same transcendent, frightening light of triumph. In view of the delicate flame which seemed to come from her face like a light, he was powerless. And yet he had never intended to love her. He had never intended. And something stubborn in him could not give way.

"You love me," she repeated, in a murmur of deep, rhapsodic assurance. "You love me."

Her hands were drawing him, drawing him down to her. He was afraid, even a little horrified. For he had, really, no intention of loving her. Yet her hands were drawing him towards her. He put out his hand quickly to steady himself, and grasped her bare shoulder. A flame seemed to burn the hand that grasped her soft shoulder. He had no intention of loving her: his whole will was against his yielding. It was horrible. And yet wonderful was the touch of her shoulders, beautiful the shining of her face. Was she perhaps mad? He had a horror of yielding to her. Yet something in him ached also.

He had been staring away at the door, away from her. But his hand remained on her shoulder. She had gone suddenly very still. He looked down at her. Her eyes were now wide with fear, with doubt, the light was dying from her face, a shadow of terrible grayness was returning. He could not bear the touch of her eyes' question upon him, and the look of death behind the question.   150

With an inward groan he gave way, and let his heart yield towards her. A sudden gentle smile came on his face. And her eyes, which never left his face, slowly, slowly filled with tears. He watched the strange water rise in her eyes, like some slow fountain coming up. And his heart seemed to burn and melt away in his breast.

He could not bear to look at her any more. He dropped on his knees and caught her head with his arms and pressed her face against his throat. She was very still. His heart, which seemed to have broken, was burning with a kind of agony in his breast. And he felt her slow, hot tears wetting his throat. But he could not move.

He felt the hot tears wet his neck and the hollows of his neck, and he remained motionless, suspended through one of man's eternities. Only now it had become indispensable to him to have her face pressed close to him; he could never let her go again. He could never let her head go away from the close clutch of his arm. He wanted to remain like that for ever, with his heart hurting him in a pain that was also life to him. Without knowing, he was looking down on her damp, soft brown hair.

Then, as it were suddenly, he smelt the horrid stagnant smell of that water. And at the same moment she drew away from him and looked at him. Her eyes were wistful and unfathomable. He was afraid of them, and he fell to kissing her, not knowing what he was doing. He wanted her eyes not to have that terrible, wistful, unfathomable look.

When she turned her face to him again, a faint delicate flush was glowing, and   155 there was again dawning that terrible shining of joy in her eyes, which really terrified him, and yet which he now wanted to see, because he feared the look of doubt still more.

"You love me?" she said, rather faltering.

"Yes." The word cost him a painful effort. Not because it wasn't true. But because it was too newly true, the *saying* seemed to tear open again his newly torn heart. And he hardly wanted it to be true, even now.

She lifted her face to him, and he bent forward and kissed her on the mouth, gently, with the one kiss that is an eternal pledge. And as he kissed her his heart strained again in his breast. He never intended to love her. But now it was over. He had crossed over the gulf to her, and all that he had left behind had shriveled and become void.

After the kiss, her eyes again slowly filled with tears. She sat still, away from him, with her face drooped aside, and her hands folded in her lap. The tears fell very slowly. There was complete silence. He too sat there motionless and silent on the hearthrug. The strange pain of his heart that was broken seemed to consume him. That he should love her? That this was love! That he should be ripped open in this way! Him, a doctor! How they would all jeer if they knew! It was agony to him to think they might know.

In the curious naked pain of the thought he looked again to her. She was   160
sitting there drooped into a muse. He saw a tear fall, and his heart flared hot. He saw for the first time that one of her shoulders was quite uncovered, one arm bare, he could see one of her small breasts; dimly, because it had become almost dark in the room.

"Why are you crying?" he asked, in an altered voice.

She looked up at him, and behind her tears the consciousness of her situation for the first time brought a dark look of shame to her eyes.

"I'm not crying, really," she said, watching him half frightened.

He reached his hand, and softly closed it on her bare arm.

"I love you! I love you!" he said in a soft, low vibrating voice, unlike himself.   165

She shrank, and dropped her head. The soft, penetrating grip of his hand on her arm distressed her. She looked up at him.

"I want to go," she said. "I want to go and get you some dry things."

"Why?" he said. "I'm all right."

"But I want to go," she said. "And I want you to change your things."

He released her arm, and she wrapped herself in the blanket, looking at him   170
rather frightened. And still she did not rise.

"Kiss me," she said wistfully.

He kissed her, but briefly, half in anger.

Then, after a second, she rose nervously, all mixed up in the blanket. He watched her in her confusion, as she tried to extricate herself and wrap herself up so that she could walk. He watched her relentlessly, as she knew. And as she went, the blanket trailing, and as he saw a glimpse of her feet and her white leg, he tried to remember her as she was when he had wrapped her in the blanket. But then he didn't want to remember, because she had been nothing to him then, and his nature revolted from remembering her as she was when she was nothing to him.

A tumbling, muffled noise from within the dark house startled him. Then he heard her voice: — "There are clothes." He rose and went to the foot of the stairs, and gathered up the garments she had thrown down. Then he came back to the fire, to rub himself down and dress. He grinned at his own appearance when he had finished.

The fire was sinking, so he put on coal. The house was now quite dark, save   175
for the light of a street-lamp that shone in faintly from beyond the holly trees. He lit the gas with matches he found on the mantelpiece. Then he emptied the pockets of his own clothes, and threw all his wet things in a heap into the scullery. After which he gathered up her sodden clothes, gently, and put them in a separate heap on the copper-top in the scullery.

It was six o'clock on the clock. His own watch had stopped. He ought to go back to the surgery. He waited, and still she did not come down. So he went to the foot of the stairs and called:

"I shall have to go."

Almost immediately he heard her coming down. She had on her best dress of black voile, and her hair was tidy, but still damp. She looked at him—and in spite of herself, smiled.

"I don't like you in those clothes," she said.

"Do I look a sight?" he answered.   180

They were shy of one another.

"I'll make you some tea," she said.

"No, I must go."

"Must you?" And she looked at him again with the wide, strained, doubtful eyes. And again, from the pain of his breast, he knew how he loved her. He went and bent to kiss her, gently, passionately, with his heart's painful kiss.

"And my hair smells so horrible," she murmured in distraction. "And I'm so   185
awful, I'm so awful! Oh, no, I'm too awful." And she broke into bitter, heart-broken sobbing. "You can't want to love me, I'm horrible."

"Don't be silly, don't be silly," he said, trying to comfort her, kissing her, holding her in his arms. "I want you, I want to marry you, we're going to be married, quickly, quickly—tomorrow if I can."

But she only sobbed terribly, and cried:

"I feel awful. I feel awful. I feel I'm horrible to you."

"No, I want you, I want you," was all he answered, blindly, with that terrible intonation which frightened her almost more than her horror lest he should *not* want her.

QUESTIONS AND SUGGESTIONS FOR WRITING

1. In the opening scene, what is the attitude of the men toward Mabel? In the context of the entire story, why is it important that the family is breaking up?
2. Briefly characterize each of Mabel's brothers, and then, more fully, characterize Ma-

bel, pointing out the ways in which she differs from them. You may want to emphasize the ways in which her relations with her mother and father help to differentiate her from the brothers.

3. Drawing only on this story, set forth in an essay of 250 to 500 words what you take to be Lawrence's concept of love.

4. Many psychologists and sociologists say that love is not an instinct but a learned behavior. Basing your views on "The Horse Dealer's Daughter," indicate in an essay of about 500 words whether or not, in your opinion, Lawrence would have subscribed to such a view.

William Faulkner (American. 1897–1962)

A ROSE FOR EMILY

I

When Miss Emily Grierson died, our whole town went to her funeral: the men through a sort of respectful affection for a fallen monument, the women mostly out of curiosity to see the inside of her house, which no one save an old manservant—a combined gardener and cook—had seen in at least ten years.

It was a big, squarish frame house that had once been white, decorated with cupolas and spires and scrolled balconies in the heavily lightsome style of the seventies, set on what had once been our most select street. But garages and cotton gins had encroached and obliterated even the august names of that neighborhood; only Miss Emily's house was left, lifting its stubborn and coquettish decay above the cotton wagons and the gasoline pumps—an eyesore among eyesores. And now Miss Emily had gone to join the representatives of those august names where they lay in the cedar-bemused cemetery among the ranked and anonymous graves of Union and Confederate soldiers who fell at the battle of Jefferson.

Alive, Miss Emily had been a tradition, a duty, and a care; a sort of hereditary obligation upon the town, dating from that day in 1894 when Colonel Sartoris, the mayor—he who fathered the edict that no Negro woman should appear on the streets without an apron—remitted her taxes, the dispensation dating from the death of her father on into perpetuity. Not that Miss Emily would have accepted charity. Colonel Sartoris invented an involved tale to the effect that Miss Emily's father had loaned money to the town, which the town, as a matter of business, preferred this way of repaying. Only a man of Colonel Sartoris' generation and thought could have invented it, and only a woman could have believed it.

When the next generation, with its more modern ideas, became mayors and aldermen, this arrangement created some little dissatisfaction. On the first of the year they mailed her a tax notice. February came, and there was no reply. They wrote her a formal letter, asking her to call at the sheriff's office at her convenience. A week later the mayor wrote her himself, offering to call or to send his car for her, and received in reply a note on paper of an archaic shape, in a thin, flowing calligraphy in faded ink, to the effect that she no longer went out at all. The tax notice was also enclosed, without comment.

They called a special meeting of the Board of Aldermen. A deputation waited upon her, knocked at the door through which no visitor had passed since she ceased giving china-painting lessons eight or ten years earlier. They were admitted by the old Negro into a dim hall from which a staircase mounted into still more shadow. It smelled of dust and disuse—a close, dank smell. The Negro led them into the parlor. It was furnished in heavy, leather-covered furniture. When the Negro opened the blinds of one window, a faint dust rose sluggishly about their thighs, spinning with slow motes in the single sunray. On a tarnished gilt easel before the fireplace stood a crayon portrait of Miss Emily's father.

They rose when she entered—a small, fat woman in black, with a thin gold chain descending to her waist and vanishing into her belt, leaning on an ebony cane with a tarnished gold head. Her skeleton was small and spare; perhaps that was why what would have been merely plumpness in another was obesity in her. She looked bloated, like a body long submerged in motionless water, and of that pallid hue. Her eyes, lost in the fatty ridges of her face, looked like two small pieces of coal pressed into a lump of dough as they moved from one face to another while the visitors stated their errand.

She did not ask them to sit. She just stood in the door and listened quietly until the spokesman came to a stumbling halt. Then they could hear the invisible watch ticking at the end of the gold chain.

Her voice was dry and cold. "I have no taxes in Jefferson. Colonel Sartoris explained it to me. Perhaps one of you can gain access to the city records and satisfy yourselves."

"But we have. We are the city authorities, Miss Emily. Didn't you get a notice from the sheriff, signed by him?"

"I received a paper, yes," Miss Emily said. "Perhaps he considers himself the sheriff. . . . I have no taxes in Jefferson."

"But there is nothing on the books to show that, you see. We must go by the—"

"See Colonel Sartoris. I have no taxes in Jefferson."

"But, Miss Emily—"

"See Colonel Sartoris." (Colonel Sartoris had been dead almost ten years.) "I have no taxes in Jefferson. Tobe!" The Negro appeared. "Show these gentlemen out."

II

So she vanquished them, horse and foot, just as she had vanquished their fathers thirty years before about the smell. That was two years after her father's death and a short time after her sweetheart—the one we believed would marry her—had deserted her. After her father's death she went out very little; after her sweetheart went away, people hardly saw her at all. A few of the ladies had the temerity to call, but were not received, and the only sign of life about the place was the Negro man—a young man then—going in and out with a market basket.

"Just as if a man—any man—could keep a kitchen properly," the ladies said; so they were not surprised when the smell developed. It was another link between the gross, teeming world and the high and mighty Griersons.

A neighbor, a woman, complained to the mayor, Judge Stevens, eighty years old.

"But what will you have me do about it, madam?" he said.

"Why, send her word to stop it," the woman said. "Isn't there a law?"

"I'm sure that won't be necessary," Judge Stevens said. "It's probably just a 20 snake or a rat that nigger of hers killed in the yard. I'll speak to him about it."

The next day he received two more complaints, one from a man who came in diffident deprecation. "We really must do something about it, Judge. I'd be the last one in the world to bother Miss Emily, but we've got to do something." That night the Board of Aldermen met—three gray-beards and one younger man, a member of the rising generation.

"It's simple enough," he said. "Send her word to have her place cleaned up. Give her a certain time to do it in, and if she don't . . ."

"Dammit, sir," Judge Stevens said, "will you accuse a lady to her face of smelling bad?"

So the next night, after midnight, four men crossed Miss Emily's lawn and slunk about the house like burglars, sniffing along the base of the brickwork and at the cellar openings while one of them performed a regular sowing motion with his hand out of a sack slung from his shoulder. They broke open the cellar door and sprinkled lime there, and in all the out-buildings. As they recrossed the lawn, a window that had been dark was lighted and Miss Emily sat in it, the light behind her, and her upright torso motionless as that of an idol. They crept quietly across the lawn and into the shadow of the locusts that lined the street. After a week or two the smell went away.

That was when people had begun to feel really sorry for her. People in our 25 town remembering how old lady Wyatt, her great-aunt, had gone completely crazy at last, believed that the Griersons held themselves a little too high for what they really were. None of the young men were quite good enough for Miss Emily and such. We had long thought of them as a tableau; Miss Emily a slender figure in white in the background, her father a spraddled silhouette in the foreground, his back to her and clutching a horsewhip, the two of them framed by the back-flung front door. So when she got to be thirty and was still single, we were not pleased exactly, but vindicated; even with insanity in the family she wouldn't have turned down all of her chances if they had really materialized.

When her father died, it got about that the house was all that was left to her; and in a way, people were glad. At last they could pity Miss Emily. Being left alone, and a pauper, she had become humanized. Now she too would know the old thrill and the old despair of a penny more or less.

The day after his death all the ladies prepared to call at the house and offer condolence and aid, as is our custom. Miss Emily met them at the door, dressed as usual and with no trace of grief on her face. She told them that her father was not dead. She did that for three days, with the ministers calling on her, and the doctors, trying to persuade her to let them dispose of the body. Just as they were about to resort to law and force, she broke down, and they buried her father quickly.

We did not say she was crazy then. We believed she had to do that. We remembered all the young men her father had driven away, and we knew that with nothing left, she would have to cling to that which had robbed her, as people will.

III

She was sick for a long time. When we saw her again, her hair was cut short, making her look like a girl, with a vague resemblance to those angels in colored church windows—sort of tragic and serene.

The town had just let the contracts for paving the sidewalks, and in the summer after her father's death they began to work. The construction company came with niggers and mules and machinery, and a foreman named Homer Barron, a Yankee—a big, dark, ready man, with a big voice and eyes lighter than his face. The little boys would follow in groups to hear him cuss the niggers, and the niggers singing in time to the rise and fall of picks. Pretty soon he knew everybody in town. Whenever you heard a lot of laughing anywhere about the square, Homer Barron would be in the center of the group. Presently we began to see him and Miss Emily on Sunday afternoons driving in the yellow-wheeled buggy and the matched team of bays from the livery stable.

At first we were glad that Miss Emily would have an interest, because the ladies all said, "Of course a Grierson would not think seriously of a Northerner, a day laborer." But there were still others, older people, who said that even grief could not cause a real lady to forget *noblesse oblige*—without calling it *noblesse oblige*. They just said, "Poor Emily. Her kinsfolk should come to her." She had some kin in Alabama; but years ago her father had fallen out with them over the estate of old lady Wyatt, the crazy woman, and there was no communication between the two families. They had not even been represented at the funeral.

And as soon as the old people said, "Poor Emily," the whispering began. "Do you suppose it's really so?" they said to one another. "Of course it is. . . ." This behind their hands; rustling of craned silk and satin behind jalousies closed upon the sun of Sunday afternoon as the thin, swift clop-clop-clop of the matched team passed: "Poor Emily."

She carried her head high enough—even when we believed that she was fallen. It was as if she demanded more than ever the recognition of her dignity as the last Grierson; as if it had wanted that touch of earthiness to reaffirm her imperviousness. Like when she bought the rat poison, the arsenic. That was over a year after they had begun to say "Poor Emily," and while the two female cousins were visiting her.

"I want some poison," she said to the druggist. She was over thirty then, still a slight woman, though thinner than usual, with cold, haughty black eyes in a face the flesh of which was strained across the temples and about the eyesockets as you imagine a lighthousekeeper's face ought to look. "I want some poison," she said.

"Yes, Miss Emily. What kind? For rats and such? I'd recom—"

"I want the best you have. I don't care what kind."

The druggist named several. "They'll kill anything up to an elephant. But what you want is—"

"Arsenic," Miss Emily said. "Is that a good one?"

"Is . . . arsenic? Yes ma'am. But what you want—"

"I want arsenic."

The druggist looked down at her. She looked back at him, erect, her face like a strained flag. "Why, of course," the druggist said. "If that's what you want. But the law requires you to tell what you are going to use it for."

Miss Emily just stared at him, her head tilted back in order to look him eye for eye, until he looked away and went and got the arsenic and wrapped it up. The Negro delivery boy brought her the package; the druggist didn't come back. When she opened the package at home there was written on the box, under the skull and bones: "For rats."

IV

So the next day we all said, "She will kill herself"; and we said it would be the best thing. When she had first begun to be seen with Homer Barron, we had said, "She will marry him." Then we said, "She will persuade him yet," because Homer himself had remarked—he liked men, and it was known that he drank with the younger men in the Elks' Club—that he was not a marrying man. Later we said, "Poor Emily," behind the jalousies as they passed on Sunday afternoon in the glittering buggy, Miss Emily with her head high and Homer Barron with his hat cocked and a cigar in his teeth, reins and whip in a yellow glove.

Then some of the ladies began to say that it was a disgrace to the town and a bad example to the young people. The men did not want to interfere, but at last the ladies forced the Baptist minister—Miss Emily's people were Episcopal—to call upon her. He would never divulge what happened during that interview, but he refused to go back again. The next Sunday they again drove about the streets, and the following day the minister's wife wrote to Miss Emily's relations in Alabama.

So she had blood-kin under her roof again and we sat back to watch developments. At first nothing happened. Then we were sure that they were to be married. We learned that Miss Emily had been to the jeweler's and ordered a man's toilet set in silver, with the letters H.B. on each piece. Two days later we learned that she had bought a complete outfit of men's clothing, including a nightshirt, and we said, "They are married." We were really glad. We were glad because the two female cousins were even more Grierson than Miss Emily had ever been.

So we were surprised when Homer Barron—the streets had been finished some time since—was gone. We were a little disappointed that there was not a public blowing-off, but we believed that he had gone on to prepare for Miss Emily's coming, or to give a chance to get rid of the cousins. (By that time it was a cabal, and we were all Miss Emily's allies to help circumvent the cousins.) Sure enough, after another week they departed. And, as we had expected all along, within three days Homer Barron was back in town. A neighbor saw the Negro man admit him at the kitchen door at dusk one evening.

And that was the last we saw of Homer Barron. And of Miss Emily for some time. The Negro man went in and out with the market basket, but the front door remained closed. Now and then we would see her at a window for a moment, as the men did that night when they sprinkled the lime, but for almost six months she did not appear on the streets. Then we knew that this was to be expected too; as if that quality of her father which had thwarted her woman's life so many times had been too virulent and too furious to die.

When we next saw Miss Emily, she had grown fat and her hair was turning gray. During the next few years it grew grayer and grayer until it attained an even pepper-and-salt iron-gray, when it ceased turning. Up to the day of her death at seventy-four it was still that vigorous iron-gray, like the hair of an active man.

From that time on her front door remained closed, save for a period of six or seven years, when she was about forty, during which she gave lessons in china-painting. She fitted up a studio in one of the downstairs rooms, where the daughters and granddaughters of Colonel Sartoris' contemporaries were sent to her with the same regularity and in the same spirit that they were sent on Sundays with a twenty-five cent piece for the collection plate. Meanwhile her taxes had been remitted.

Then the newer generation became the backbone and the spirit of the town, and the painting pupils grew up and fell away and did not send their children to her with boxes of color and tedious brushes and pictures cut from the ladies' magazines. The front door closed upon the last one and remained closed for good. When the town got free postal delivery Miss Emily alone refused to let them fasten the metal numbers above her door and attach a mailbox to it. She would not listen to them.

Daily, monthly, yearly we watched the Negro grow grayer and more stooped, going in and out with the market basket. Each December we sent her a tax notice, which would be returned by the post office a week later, unclaimed. Now and then we would see her in one of the downstairs windows—she had evidently shut up the top floor of the house—like the carven torso of an idol in a niche, looking or not looking at us, we could never tell which. Thus she passed from generation to generation—dear, inescapable, impervious, tranquil, and perverse.

And so she died. Fell ill in the house filled with dust and shadows, with only a doddering Negro man to wait on her. We did not even know she was sick; we had long since given up trying to get any information from the Negro. He talked to no one, probably not even to her, for his voice had grown harsh and rusty, as if from disuse.

She died in one of the downstairs rooms, in a heavy walnut bed with a curtain, her gray head propped on a pillow yellow and moldy with age and lack of sunlight.

V

The Negro met the first of the ladies at the front door and let them in, with their hushed, sibilant voices and their quick, curious glances, and then he disappeared. He walked right through the house and out the back and was not seen again.

The two female cousins came at once. They held the funeral on the second day, with the town coming to look at Miss Emily beneath a mass of bought flowers, with the crayon face of her father musing profoundly above the bier and the ladies sibilant and macabre; and the very old men—some in their brushed Confederate uniforms—on the porch and the lawn, talking of Miss Emily as if she had been a contemporary of theirs, believing that they had danced with her and courted her perhaps, confusing time with its mathematical progression, as the old do, to whom all the past is not a diminishing road, but, instead, a huge meadow which no winter ever quite touches, divided from them now by the narrow bottle-neck of the most recent decade of years.

Already we knew that there was one room in that region above stairs which no one had seen in forty years, and which would have to be forced. They waited until Miss Emily was decently in the ground before they opened it.

The violence of breaking down the door seemed to fill this room with pervad-ing dust. A thin, acrid pall as of the tomb seemed to lie everywhere upon this room decked and furnished as for a bridal: upon the valance curtains of faded rose color, upon the rose-shaded lights, upon the dressing table, upon the delicate array of crystal and the man's toilet things backed with tarnished silver, silver so tarnished that the monogram was obscured. Among them lay a collar and tie, as if they had just been removed, which, lifted, left upon the surface a pale crescent in the dust. Upon a chair hung the suit, carefully folded; beneath it the two mute shoes and the discarded socks.

The man himself lay in the bed.

For a long while we just stood there, looking down at the profound and fleshless grin. The body had apparently once lain in the attitude of an embrace, but now the long sleep that outlasts love, that conquers even the grimace of love, had cuckolded him. What was left of him, rotted beneath what was left of the nightshirt, had become inextricable from the bed in which he lay; and upon him and upon the pillow beside him lay that even coating of the patient and biding dust.

Then we noticed that in the second pillow was the indentation of a head. One of us lifted something from it, and leaning forward, that faint and invisible dust dry and acrid in the nostrils, we saw a long strand of iron-gray hair. 60

QUESTIONS AND SUGGESTIONS FOR WRITING

1. Why does the narrator begin with what is almost the end of the story—the death of Miss Emily—rather than save this information for later? What devices does Faulkner use to hold the reader's interest throughout?

2. In a paragraph, offer a conjecture about Miss Emily's attitudes toward Homer Barron after he was last seen alive.

3. In a paragraph or two, characterize Miss Emily, calling attention not only to her eccentricities or even craziness, but also to what you conjecture to be her moral values.

4. In paragraph 44 we are told that the Baptist minister "would never divulge what happened" during the interview with Miss Emily. Why do you suppose that Faulkner does not narrate or describe the interview? Let's assume that in his first draft of the story he *did* give a paragraph of narration or a short dramatic scene. Write such an episode.

John Steinbeck (American. 1902–1968)

THE CHRYSANTHEMUMS

The high grey-flannel fog of winter closed off the Salinas Valley from the sky and from all the rest of the world. On every side it sat like a lid on the mountains and made of the great valley a closed pot. On the broad, level land floor the gang plows bit deep and left the black earth shining like metal where the shares had cut. On the foothill ranches across the Salinas River, the yellow stubble fields seemed to be bathed in pale cold sunshine, but there was no sunshine in the valley now in December. The thick willow scrub along the river flamed with sharp and positive yellow leaves.

It was a time of quiet and of waiting. The air was cold and tender. A light wind blew up from the southwest so that the farmers were mildly hopeful of a good rain before long; but fog and rain do not go together.

Across the river, on Henry Allen's foothill ranch there was little work to be done, for the hay was cut and stored and the orchards were plowed up to receive the rain deeply when it should come. The cattle on the higher slopes were becoming shaggy and rough-coated.

Elisa Allen, working in her flower garden, looked down across the yard and saw Henry, her husband, talking to two men in business suits. The three of them stood by the tractor shed, each man with one foot on the side of the little Fordson. They smoked cigarettes and studied the machine as they talked.

Elisa watched them for a moment and then went back to her work. She was thirty-five. Her face was lean and strong and her eyes were as clear as water. Her figure looked blocked and heavy in her gardening costume, a man's black hat pulled low down over her eyes, clod-hopper shoes, a figured print dress almost completely covered by a big corduroy apron with four big pockets to hold the snips, the trowel and scratcher, the seeds and the knife she worked with. She wore heavy leather gloves to protect her hands while she worked.

She was cutting down the old year's chrysanthemum stalks with a pair of short and powerful scissors. She looked down toward the men by the tractor shed now and then. Her face was eager and mature and handsome; even her work with the scissors was over-eager, over-powerful. The chrysanthemum stems seemed too small and easy for her energy.

She brushed a cloud of hair out of her eyes with the back of her glove, and left a smudge of earth on her cheek in doing it. Behind her stood the neat white farm house with red geraniums close-banked around it as high as the windows. It was a hard-swept looking little house with hard-polished windows, and a clean mud-mat on the front steps.

Elisa cast another glance toward the tractor shed. The strangers were getting into their Ford coupe. She took off a glove and put her strong fingers down into the forest of new green chrysanthemum sprouts that were growing around the old roots. She spread the leaves and looked down among the close-growing stems. No aphids were there, no sowbugs or snails or cutworms. Her terrier fingers destroyed such pests before they could get started.

Elisa started at the sound of her husband's voice. He had come near quietly,

5

and he leaned over the wire fence that protected her flower garden from cattle and dogs and chickens.

"At it again," he said. "You've got a strong new crop coming."   10

Elisa straightened her back and pulled on the gardening glove again. "Yes. They'll be strong this coming year." In her tone and on her face there was a little smugness.

"You've got a gift with things," Henry observed. "Some of those yellow chrysanthemums you had this year were ten inches across. I wish you'd work out in the orchard and raise some apples that big."

Her eyes sharpened. "Maybe I could do it, too. I've a gift with things, all right. My mother had it. She could stick anything in the ground and make it grow. She said it was having planters' hands that knew how to do it."

"Well, it sure works with flowers," he said.

"Henry, who were those men you were talking to?"   15

"Why, sure, that's what I came to tell you. They were from the Western Meat Company. I sold those thirty head of three-year-old steers. Got nearly my own price, too."

"Good," she said. "Good for you."

"And I thought," he continued, "I thought how it's Saturday afternoon, and we might go into Salinas for dinner at a restaurant, and then to a picture show—to celebrate, you see."

"Good," she repeated. "Oh, yes. That will be good."

Henry put on his joking tone. "There's fights tonight. How'd you like to go to   20
the fights?"

"Oh, no," she said breathlessly. "No, I wouldn't like fights."

"Just fooling, Elisa. We'll go to a movie. Let's see. It's two now. I'm going to take Scotty and bring down those steers from the hill. It'll take us maybe two hours. We'll go in town about five and have dinner at the Cominos Hotel. Like that?"

"Of course I'll like it. It's good to eat away from home."

"All right, then. I'll go get up a couple of horses."

She said, "I'll have plenty of time to transplant some of these sets, I guess."   25

She heard her husband calling Scotty down by the barn. And a little later she saw the two men ride up the pale yellow hillside in search of the steers.

There was a little square sandy bed kept for rooting the chrysanthemums. With her trowel she turned the soil over and over, and smoothed it and patted it firm. Then she dug ten parallel trenches to receive the sets. Back at the chrysanthemum bed she pulled out the little crisp shoots, trimmed off the leaves of each one with her scissors and laid it on a small orderly pile.

A squeak of wheels and plod of hoofs came from the road. Elisa looked up. The country road ran along the dense bank of willows and cottonwoods that bordered the river, and up this road came a curious vehicle, curiously drawn. It was an old springwagon, with a round canvas top on it like the cover of a prairie schooner. It was drawn by an old bay horse and a little grey-and-white burro. A big stubble-bearded man sat between the cover flaps and drove the crawling team. Underneath the wagon, between the hind wheels, a lean and rangy mongrel dog walked sedately. Words were painted on the canvas, in clumsy, crooked letters. "Pots, pans, knives, sisors, lawn mores, Fixed." Two rows of articles, and the triumphantly definitive "Fixed" below. The black paint had run down in little sharp points beneath each letter.

Elisa, squatting on the ground, watched to see the crazy, loose-jointed wagon pass by. But it didn't pass. It turned into the farm road in front of her house, crooked old wheels skirling and squeaking. The rangy dog darted from between the wheels and ran ahead. Instantly the two ranch shepherds flew out at him. Then all three stopped, and with stiff and quivering tails, with taut straight legs, with ambassadorial dignity, they slowly circled, sniffing daintily. The caravan pulled up to Elisa's wire fence and stopped. Now the newcomer dog, feeling outnumbered, lowered his tail and retired under the wagon with raised hackles and bared teeth.

The man on the wagon seat called out, "That's a bad dog in a fight when he gets started."   30

Elisa laughed. "I see he is. How soon does he generally get started?"

The man caught up her laughter and echoed it heartily. "Sometimes not for weeks and weeks," he said. He climbed stiffly down, over the wheel. The horse and the donkey drooped like unwatered flowers.

Elisa saw that he was a very big man. Although his hair and beard were greying, he did not look old. His worn black suit was wrinkled and spotted with grease. The laughter had disappeared from his face and eyes the moment his laughing voice ceased. His eyes were dark, and they were full of the brooding that gets in the eyes of teamsters and of sailors. The calloused hands he rested on the wire fence were cracked, and every crack was a black line. He took off his battered hat.

"I'm off my general road, ma'am," he said. "Does this dirt road cut over across the river to the Los Angeles highway?"

Elisa stood up and shoved the thick scissors in her apron pocket. "Well, yes,   35
it does, but it winds around and then fords the river. I don't think your team could pull through the sand."

He replied with some asperity, "It might surprise you what them beasts can pull through."

"When they get started?" she asked.

He smiled for a second. "Yes. When they get started."

"Well," said Elisa, "I think you'll save time if you go back to the Salinas road and pick up the highway there."

He drew a big finger down the chicken wire and made it sing. "I ain't in any   40
hurry, ma'am. I go from Seattle to San Diego and back every year. Takes all my time. About six months each way. I aim to follow nice weather."

Elisa took off her gloves and stuffed them in the apron pocket with the scissors. She touched the under edge of her man's hat, searching for fugitive hairs. "That sounds like a nice kind of a way to live," she said.

He leaned confidentially over the fence. "Maybe you noticed the writing on my wagon. I mend pots and sharpen knives and scissors. You got any of them things to do?"

"Oh, no," she said quickly. "Nothing like that." Her eyes hardened with resistance.

"Scissors is the worst thing," he explained. "Most people just ruin scissors trying to sharpen 'em, but I know how. I got a special tool. It's a little bobbit kind of thing, and patented. But it sure does the trick."

"No. My scissors are all sharp." 45

"All right, then. Take a pot," he continued earnestly, "a bent pot, or a pot with a hole. I can make it like new so you don't have to buy no new ones. That's a saving for you."

"No," she said shortly. "I tell you I have nothing like that for you to do."

His face fell to an exaggerated sadness. His voice took on a whining undertone. "I ain't had a thing to do today. Maybe I won't have no supper tonight. You see I'm off my regular road. I know folks on the highway clear from Seattle to San Diego. They save their things for me to sharpen up because they know I do it so good and save them money."

"I'm sorry," Elisa said irritably. "I haven't anything for you to do."

His eyes left her face and fell to searching the ground. They roamed about 50 until they came to the chrysanthemum bed where she had been working. "What's them plants, ma'am?"

The irritation and resistance melted from Elisa's face. "Oh, those are chrysanthemums, giant whites and yellows. I raise them every year, bigger than anybody around here."

"Kind of a long-stemmed flower? Looks like a quick puff of colored smoke?" he asked.

"That's it. What a nice way to describe them."

"They smell kind of nasty till you get used to them," he said.

"It's a good bitter smell," she retorted, "not nasty at all." 55

He changed his tone quickly. "I like the smell myself."

"I had ten-inch blooms this year," she said.

The man leaned farther over the fence. "Look. I know a lady down the road a piece, has got the nicest garden you ever seen. Got nearly every kind of flower but no chrysantheums. Last time I was mending a copper-bottom wash-tub for her (that's a hard job but I do it good), she said to me, 'If you ever run acrost some nice chrysantheums I wish you'd try to get me a few seeds.' That's what she told me."

Elisa's eyes grew alert and eager. "She couldn't have known much about chrysanthemums. You *can* raise them from seed, but it's much easier to root the little sprouts you see there."

"Oh," he said. "I s'pose I can't take none to her, then." 60

"Why yes you can," Elisa cried. "I can put some in damp sand, and you can carry them right along with you. They'll take root in the pot if you keep them damp. And then she can transplant them."

"She'd sure like to have some, ma'am. You say they're nice ones?"

"Beautiful," she said. "Oh, beautiful." Her eyes shone. She tore off the battered hat and shook out her dark pretty hair. "I'll put them in a flower pot, and you can take them right with you. Come into the yard."

While the man came through the picket gate Elisa ran excitedly along the geranium-bordered path to the back of the house. And she returned carrying a big red flower pot. The gloves were forgotten now. She kneeled on the ground by the starting bed and dug up the sandy soil with her fingers and scooped it into the bright new flower pot. Then she picked up the little pile of shoots she had prepared. With her strong fingers she pressed them into the sand and tamped around them with her knuckles. The man stood over her. "I'll tell you what to do," she said. "You remember so you can tell the lady."

"Yes, I'll try to remember." 65

"Well, look. These will take root in about a month. Then she must set them out, about a foot apart in good rich earth like this, see?" She lifted a handful of dark soil for him to look at. "They'll grow fast and tall. Now remember this: In July tell her to cut them down, about eight inches from the ground."

"Before they bloom?" he asked.

"Yes, before they bloom." Her face was tight with eagerness. "They'll grow right up again. About the last of September the buds will start."

She stopped and seemed perplexed. "It's the budding that takes the most care," she said hesitantly. "I don't know how to tell you." She looked deep into his eyes, searchingly. Her mouth opened a little, and she seemed to be listening. "I'll try to tell you," she said. "Did you ever hear of planting hands?"

"Can't say I have, ma'am." 70

"Well, I can only tell you what it feels like. It's when you're picking off the buds you don't want. Everything goes right down into your fingertips. You watch your fingers work. They do it themselves. You can feel how it is. They pick and pick the buds. They never make a mistake. They're with the plant. Do you see? Your fingers and the plant. You can feel that, right up your arm. They know. They never make a mistake. You can feel it. When you're like that you can't do anything wrong. Do you see that? Can you understand that?"

She was kneeling on the ground looking up at him. Her breast swelled passionately.

The man's eyes narrowed. He looked away self-consciously. "Maybe I know," he said. "Sometimes in the night in the wagon there—"

Elisa's voice grew husky. She broke in on him, "I've never lived as you do, but I know what you mean. When the night is dark—why, the stars are sharp-pointed, and there's quiet. Why, you rise up and up! Every pointed star gets driven into your body. It's like that. Hot and sharp and—lovely."

Kneeling there, her hand went out toward his legs in the greasy black trousers. Her hesitant fingers almost touched the cloth. Then her hand dropped to the ground. She crouched low like a fawning dog. 75

He said, "It's nice, just like you say. Only when you don't have no dinner, it ain't."

She stood up then, very straight, and her face was ashamed. She held the flower pot out to him and placed it gently in his arms. "Here. Put it in your wagon, on the seat, where you can watch it. Maybe I can find something for you to do."

At the back of the house she dug in the can pile and found two old and battered aluminum saucepans. She carried them back and gave them to him. "Here, maybe you can fix these."

His manner changed. He became professional. "Good as new I can fix them." At the back of his wagon he set a little anvil, and out of an oily tool box dug a small machine hammer. Elisa came through the gate to watch him while he pounded out the dents in the kettles. His mouth grew sure and knowing. At a difficult part of the work he sucked his under-lip.

"You sleep right in the wagon?" Elisa asked.   80

"Right in the wagon, ma'am. Rain or shine I'm dry as a cow in there."

"It must be nice," she said. "It must be very nice. I wish women could do such things."

"It ain't the right kind of life for a woman."

Her upper lip raised a little, showing her teeth. "How do you know? How can you tell?" she said.

"I don't know, ma'am," he protested. "Of course I don't know. Now here's   85 your kettles, done. You don't have to buy no new ones.

"How much?"

"Oh, fifty cents'll do. I keep my prices down and my work good. That's why I have all them satisfied customers up and down the highway."

Elisa brought him a fifty-cent piece from the house and dropped it in his hand. "You might be surprised to have a rival some time. I can sharpen scissors, too. And I can beat the dents out of little pots. I could show you what a woman might do."

He put his hammer back in the oily box and shoved the little anvil out of sight. "It would be a lonely life for a woman, ma'am, and a scarey life, too, with animals creeping under the wagon all night." He climbed over the singletree, steadying himself with a hand on the burro's white rump. He settled himself in the seat, picked up the lines. "Thank you kindly, ma'am," he said. "I'll do like you told me; I'll go back and catch the Salinas road."

"Mind," she called, "if you're long in getting there, keep the sand damp."   90

"Sand, ma'am? . . . Sand? Oh, sure. You mean around the chrysantheums. Sure I will." He clucked his tongue. The beasts leaned luxuriously into their collars. The mongrel dog took his place between the back wheels. The wagon turned and crawled out the entrance road and back the way it had come, along the river.

Elisa stood in front of her wire fence watching the slow progress of the caravan. Her shoulders were straight, her head thrown back, her eyes half-closed, so that the scene came vaguely into them. Her lips moved silently, forming the words "Good-bye—good-bye." Then she whispered, "That's a bright direction. There's a glowing there." The sound of her whisper startled her. She shook herself free and looked about to see whether anyone had been listening. Only the dogs had heard. They lifted their heads toward her from their sleeping in the dust, and then stretched out their chins and settled asleep again. Elisa turned and ran hurriedly into the house.

In the kitchen she reached behind the stove and felt the water tank. It was full of hot water from the noonday cooking. In the bathroom she tore off her soiled clothes and flung them into the corner. And then she scrubbed herself with a little block of pumice, legs and thighs, loins and chest and arms, until her skin was scratched and red. When she had dried herself she stood in front of a mirror in her bedroom and looked at her body. She tightened her stomach and threw out her chest. She turned and looked over her shoulder at her back.

After a while she began to dress, slowly. She put on her newest underclothing and her nicest stockings and the dress which was the symbol of her prettiness. She worked carefully on her hair, penciled her eyebrows and rouged her lips.

Before she was finished she heard the little thunder hoofs and the shouts of Henry and his helper as they drove the red steers into the corral. She heard the gate bang shut and set herself for Henry's arrival.   95

His step sounded on the porch. He entered the house calling, "Elisa, where are you?"

"In my room, dressing. I'm not ready. There's hot water for your bath. Hurry up. It's getting late."

When she heard him splashing in the tub, Elisa laid his dark suit on the bed, and shirt and socks and tie beside it. She stood his polished shoes on the floor beside the bed. Then she went to the porch and sat primly and stiffly down. She looked toward the river road where the willow-line was still yellow with frosted leaves so that under the high grey fog they seemed a thin band of sunshine. This was the only color in the grey afternoon. She sat unmoving for a long time. Her eyes blinked rarely.

Henry came banging out of the door shoving his tie inside his vest as he came. Elisa stiffened and her face grew tight. Henry stopped short and looked at her. "Why—why, Elisa. You look so nice!"

"Nice? You think I look nice? What do you mean by 'nice'?"   100

Henry blundered on. "I don't know. I mean you look different, strong and happy."

"I am strong? Yes, strong. What do you mean 'strong'?"

He looked bewildered. "You're playing some kind of a game," he said helplessly. "It's a kind of a play. You look strong enough to break a calf over your knee, happy enough to eat it like a watermelon."

For a second she lost her rigidity. "Henry! Don't talk like that. You didn't know what you said." She grew complete again. "I'm strong," she boasted. "I never knew before how strong."

Henry looked down toward the tractor shed, and when he brought his eyes back to her, they were his own again. "I'll get out the car. You can put on your coat while I'm starting."   105

Elisa went into the house. She heard him drive to the gate and idle down his motor, and then she took a long time to put on her hat. She pulled it here and pressed it there. When Henry turned the motor off she slipped into her coat and went out.

The little roadster bounced along on the dirt road by the river, raising the birds and driving the rabbits into the brush. Two cranes flapped heavily over the willow-line and dropped into the river-bed.

Far ahead on the road Elisa saw a dark speck. She knew.

She tried not to look as they passed it, but her eyes would not obey. She whispered to herself sadly, "He might have thrown them off the road. That wouldn't have been much trouble, not very much. But he kept the pot," she explained. "He had to keep the pot. That's why he couldn't get them off the road."

The roadster turned a bend and she saw the caravan ahead. She swung full   110
around toward her husband so she could not see the little covered wagon and the mismatched team as the car passed them.

In a moment it was over. The thing was done. She did not look back.

She said loudly, to be heard above the motor, "It will be good, tonight, a good dinner."

"Now you're changed again," Henry complained. He took one hand from the wheel and patted her knee. "I ought to take you in to dinner oftener. It would be good for both of us. We get so heavy out on the ranch."

"Henry," she asked, "could we have wine at dinner?"

"Sure we could. Say! That will be fine."   115

She was silent for a while; then she said, "Henry, at those prize fights, do the men hurt each other very much?"

"Sometimes a little, not often. Why?"

"Well, I've read how they break noses, and blood runs down their chests. I've read how the fighting gloves get heavy and soggy with blood."

He looked around at her. "What's the matter, Elisa? I didn't know you read things like that." He brought the car to a stop, then turned to the right over the Salinas River bridge.

"Do any women ever go to the fights?" she asked.   120

"Oh, sure, some. What's the matter, Elisa? Do you want to go? I don't think you'd like it, but I'll take you if you really want to go."

She relaxed limply in the seat. "Oh, no. No. I don't want to go. I'm sure I don't." Her face was turned away from him. "It will be enough if we can have wine. It will be plenty." She turned up her coat collar so he could not see that she was crying weakly—like an old woman.

QUESTIONS AND SUGGESTIONS FOR WRITING

1. In the first paragraph of the story, the valley, shut off by fog, is said to be "a closed pot." Is this setting significant? Would any other setting do equally well?
2. What physical descriptions in the story—literal or figurative—suggest that Elisa is frustrated?
3. In a paragraph describe Elisa's and Henry's marriage. Your paragraph should include supporting evidence drawn from the text.
4. Write an essay of 500 words, evaluating the view that Elisa is responsible for her troubles.

Frank O'Connor (Irish. 1903–1966)

MY OEDIPUS COMPLEX

Father was in the army all through the war—the first war, I mean—so, up to the age of five, I never saw much of him, and what I saw did not worry me. Sometimes I woke and there was a big figure in khaki peering down at me in the candlelight. Sometimes in the early morning I heard the slamming of the front door and the clatter of nailed boots down the cobbles of the lane. These were Father's entrances and exits. Like Santa Claus he came and went mysteriously.

In fact, I rather liked his visits, though it was an uncomfortable squeeze between Mother and him when I got into the big bed in the early morning. He smoked, which gave him a pleasant musty smell, and shaved, an operation of astounding interest. Each time he left a trail of souvenirs—model tanks and Gurkha knives with handles made of bullet cases, and German helmets and cap badges and button-sticks, and all sorts of military equipment—carefully stowed away in a long box on top of the wardrobe, in case they ever came in handy. There was a bit of the magpie about Father; he expected everything to come in handy. When his back was turned, Mother let me get a chair and rummage through his treasures. She didn't seem to think so highly of them as he did.

The war was the most peaceful period of my life. The window of my attic faced southeast. My mother had curtained it, but that had small effect. I always woke with the first light and, with all the responsibilities of the previous day melted, feeling myself rather like the sun, ready to illumine and rejoice. Life never seemed so simple and clear and full of responsibilities as then. I put my feet out from under the clothes—I called them Mrs. Left and Mrs. Right—and invented dramatic situations for them in which they discussed the problems of the day. At least Mrs. Right did; she was very demonstrative, but I hadn't the same control of Mrs. Left, so she mostly contented herself with nodding agreement.

They discussed what Mother and I should do during the day, what Santa Claus should give a fellow for Christmas, and what steps should be taken to brighten the home. There was that little matter of the baby, for instance. Mother and I could never agree about that. Ours was the only house in the terrace without a new baby, and Mother said we couldn't afford one till Father came back from the war because they cost seventeen and six. That showed how simple she was. The Geneys up the road had a baby, and everyone knew they couldn't afford seventeen and six. It was probably a cheap baby, and Mother wanted something really good, but I felt she was too exclusive. The Geneys' baby would have done us fine.

Having settled my plans for the day, I got up, put a chair under the attic window, and lifted the frame high enough to stick out my head. The window overlooked the front gardens of the terrace behind ours, and beyond these it looked over a deep valley to the tall, red-brick houses terraced up the opposite hillside, which were all still in shadow, while those at our side of the valley were all lit up, though with long strange shadows that made them seem unfamiliar; rigid and painted.

5

After that I went into Mother's room and climbed into the big bed. She woke and I began to tell her of my schemes. By this time, though I never seem to have noticed it, I was petrified in my nightshirt, and I thawed as I talked until, the last frost melted, I fell asleep beside her and woke again only when I heard her below in the kitchen, making the breakfast.

After breakfast we went into town; heard Mass at St. Augustine's and said a prayer for Father, and did the shopping. If the afternoon was fine we either went for a walk in the country or a visit to Mother's great friend in the convent, Mother St. Dominic. Mother had them all praying for Father, and every night, going to bed, I asked God to send him back safe from the war to us. Little, indeed, did I know what I was praying for!

One morning, I got into the big bed, and there, sure enough, was Father in his usual Santa Claus manner, but later, instead of uniform, he put on his best blue suit, and Mother was as pleased as anything. I saw nothing to be pleased about, because, out of uniform, Father was altogether less interesting, but she only beamed, and explained that our prayers had been answered, and off we went to Mass to thank God for having brought Father safely home.

The irony of it! That very day when he came in to dinner he took off his boots and put on his slippers, donned the dirty old cap he wore about the house to save him from colds, crossed his legs, and began to talk gravely to Mother, who looked anxious. Naturally, I disliked her looking anxious, because it destroyed her good looks, so I interrupted him.

"Just a moment, Larry!" she said gently.   10

This was only what she said when we had boring visitors, so I attached no importance to it and went on talking.

"Do be quiet, Larry!" she said impatiently. "Don't you hear me talking to Daddy?"

This was the first time I had heard those ominous words, "talking to Daddy," and I couldn't help feeling that if this was how God answered prayers, he couldn't listen to them very attentively.

"Why are you talking to Daddy?" I asked with as great a show of indifference as I could muster.

"Because Daddy and I have business to discuss. Now, don't interrupt again!"   15

In the afternoon, at Mother's request, Father took me for a walk. This time we went into town instead of out to the country, and I thought at first, in my usual optimistic way, that it might be an improvement. It was nothing of the sort. Father and I had quite different notions of a walk in town. He had no proper interest in trams, ships, and horses, and the only thing that seemed to divert him was talking to fellows as old as himself. When I wanted to stop he simply went on, dragging me behind him by the hand; when he wanted to stop I had no alternative but to do the same. I noticed that it seemed to be a sign that he wanted to stop for a long time whenever he leaned against a wall. The second time I saw him do it I got wild. He seemed to be settling himself forever. I pulled him by the coat and trousers, but, unlike Mother who, if you were too persistent, got into a wax and said: "Larry, if you don't behave yourself, I'll give you a good slap," Father had an extraordinary capacity for amiable inattention. I sized him up and wondered would

I cry, but he seemed to be too remote to be annoyed even by that. Really, it was like going for a walk with a mountain! He either ignored the wrenching and pummeling entirely, or else glanced down with a grin of amusement from his peak. I had never met anyone so absorbed in himself as he seemed.

At teatime, "talking to Daddy" began again, complicated this time by the fact that he had an evening paper, and every few minutes he put it down and told Mother something new out of it. I felt this was foul play. Man for man, I was prepared to compete with him any time for Mother's attention, but when he had it all made up for him by other people it left me no chance. Several times I tried to change the subject without success.

"You must be quiet while Daddy is reading, Larry," Mother said impatiently.

It was clear that she either genuinely liked talking to Father better than talking to me, or else that he had some terrible hold on her which made her afraid to admit the truth.

"Mummy," I said that night when she was tucking me up, "do you think if I prayed hard God would send Daddy back to the war?"   20

She seemed to think about that for a moment.

"No, dear," she said with a smile. "I don't think he would."

"Why wouldn't he, Mummy?"

"Because there isn't a war any longer, dear."

"But, Mummy, couldn't God make another war, if he liked?"   25

"He wouldn't like to, dear. It's not God who makes wars, but bad people."

"Oh!" I said.

I was disappointed about that. I began to think that God wasn't quite what he was cracked up to be.

Next morning I woke at my usual hour, feeling like a bottle of champagne. I put out my feet and invented a long conversation in which Mrs. Right talked of the trouble she had with her own father till she put him in the Home. I didn't quite know what the Home was but it sounded the right place for Father. Then I got my chair and stuck my head out of the attic window. Dawn was just breaking, with a guilty air that made me feel I had caught it in the act. My head bursting with stories and schemes, I stumbled in next door, and in the half-darkness scrambled into the big bed. There was no room at Mother's side so I had to get between her and Father. For the time being I had forgotten about him, and for several minutes I sat bolt upright, racking my brains to know what I could do with him. He was taking up more than his fair share of the bed, and I couldn't get comfortable, so I gave him several kicks that made him grunt and stretch. He made room all right, though. Mother waked and felt for me. I settled back comfortably in the warmth of the bed with my thumb in my mouth.

"Mummy!" I hummed, loudly and contentedly.   30

"Sssh! dear," she whispered. "Don't wake Daddy!"

This was a new development, which threatened to be even more serious than "talking to Daddy." Life without my early-morning conferences was unthinkable.

"Why?" I asked severely.

"Because poor Daddy is tired."

This seemed to me a quite inadequate reason, and I was sickened by the   35 sentimentality of her "poor Daddy." I never liked that sort of gush; it always struck me as insincere.

"Oh!" I said lightly. Then in my most winning tone: "Do you know where I want to go with you today, Mummy?"

"No, dear," she sighed.

"I want to go down the Glen and fish for thornybacks with my new net, and then I want to go out to the Fox and Hounds, and—"

"Don't-wake-Daddy!" she hissed angrily, clapping her hand across my mouth.

But it was too late. He was awake, or nearly so. He grunted and reached for   40
the matches. Then he stared incredulously at his watch.

"Like a cup of tea, dear?" asked Mother in a meek, hushed voice I had never heard her use before. It sounded almost as though she were afraid.

"Tea?" he exclaimed indignantly. "Do you know what the time is?"

"And after that I want to go up the Rathcooney Road," I said loudly, afraid I'd forget something in all those interruptions.

"Go to sleep at once, Larry!" she said sharply.

I began to snivel. I couldn't concentrate, the way that pair went on, and   45
smothering my early-morning schemes was like burying a family from the cradle.

Father said nothing, but lit his pipe and sucked it, looking out into the shadows without minding Mother or me. I knew he was mad. Every time I made a remark Mother hushed me irritably. I was mortified. I felt it wasn't fair; there was even something sinister in it. Every time I had pointed out to her the waste of making two beds when we could both sleep in one, she had told me it was healthier like that, and now here was this man, this stranger, sleeping with her without the least regard for her health!

He got up early and made tea, but though he brought Mother a cup he brought none for me.

"Mummy," I shouted, "I want a cup of tea, too."

"Yes, dear," she said patiently. "You can drink from Mummy's saucer."

That settled it. Either Father or I would have to leave the house. I didn't want   50
to drink from Mother's saucer; I wanted to be treated as an equal in my own home, so, just to spite her, I drank it all and left none for her. She took that quietly, too.

But that night when she was putting me to bed she said gently:

"Larry, I want you to promise me something."

"What is it?" I asked.

"Not to come in and disturb poor Daddy in the morning. Promise?"

"Poor Daddy" again! I was becoming suspicious of everything involving that   55
quite impossible man.

"Why?" I asked.

"Because poor Daddy is worried and tired and he doesn't sleep well."

"Why doesn't he, Mummy?"

"Well, you know, don't you, that while he was at the war Mummy got the pennies from the Post Office?"

"From Miss MacCarthy?"   60

"That's right. But now, you see, Miss MacCarthy hasn't any more pennies, so Daddy must go out and find us some. You know what would happen if he couldn't?"

"No," I said, "tell us."

"Well, I think we might have to go out and beg for them like the poor old woman on Fridays. We wouldn't like that, would we?"

"No," I agreed. "We wouldn't."

"So you'll promise not to come in and wake him?"   65

"Promise."

Mind you, I meant that. I knew pennies were a serious matter, and I was all against having to go out and beg like the old woman on Fridays. Mother laid out all my toys in a complete ring round the bed so that, whatever way I got out, I was bound to fall over one of them.

When I woke I remembered my promise all right. I got up and sat on the floor and played—for hours, it seemed to me. Then I got my chair and looked out the attic window for more hours. I wished it was time for Father to wake; I wished someone would make me a cup of tea. I didn't feel in the least like the sun; instead, I was bored and so very, very cold! I simply longed for the warmth and depth of the big featherbed.

At last I could stand it no longer. I went into the next room. As there was still no room at Mother's side I climbed over her and she woke with a start.

"Larry," she whispered, gripping my arm very tightly, "what did you promise?"   70

"But I did, Mummy," I wailed, caught in the very act. "I was quiet for ever so long."

"Oh, dear, and you're perished!" she said sadly, feeling me all over. "Now, if I let you stay will you promise not to talk?"

"But I want to talk, Mummy," I wailed.

"That has nothing to do with it," she said with a firmness that was new to me. "Daddy wants to sleep. Now, do you understand that?"

I understood it only too well. I wanted to talk, he wanted to sleep—whose house was it, anyway?   75

"Mummy," I said with equal firmness, "I think it would be healthier for Daddy to sleep in his own bed."

That seemed to stagger her, because she said nothing for a while.

"Now, once for all," she went on, "you're to be perfectly quiet or go back to your own bed. Which is it to be?"

The injustice of it got me down. I had convicted her out of her own mouth of inconsistency and unreasonableness, and she hadn't even attempted to reply. Full of spite, I gave Father a kick, which she didn't notice but which made him grunt and open his eyes in alarm.

"What time is it?" he asked in a panic-stricken voice, not looking at Mother   80
but the door, as if he saw someone there.

"It's early yet," she replied soothingly. "It's only the child. Go to sleep again.
. . . Now, Larry," she added, getting out of bed, "you've wakened Daddy and you must go back."

This time, for all her quiet air, I knew she meant it, and knew that my principal rights and privileges were as good as lost unless I asserted them at once. As she lifted me, I gave a screech, enough to wake the dead, not to mind Father. He groaned.

"That damn child! Doesn't he ever sleep?"

"It's only a habit, dear," she said quietly, though I could see she was vexed.

"Well, it's time he got out of it," shouted Father, beginning to heave in the bed. He suddenly gathered all the bedclothes about him, turned to the wall, and then looked back over his shoulder with nothing showing only two small, spiteful, dark eyes. The man looked very wicked.

To open the bedroom door, Mother had to let me down, and I broke free and dashed for the farthest corner, screeching. Father sat bolt upright in bed.

"Shut up, you little puppy!" he said in a choking voice.

I was so astonished that I stopped screeching. Never, never had anyone spoken to me in that tone before. I looked at him incredulously and saw his face convulsed with rage. It was only then that I fully realized how God had codded me, listening to my prayers for the safe return of this monster.

"Shut up, you!" I bawled, beside myself.

"What's that you said?" shouted Father, making a wild leap out of bed.

"Mick, Mick!" cried Mother. "Don't you see the child isn't used to you?"

"I see he's better fed than taught," snarled Father, waving his arms wildly. "He wants his bottom smacked."

All his previous shouting was as nothing to these obscene words referring to my person. They really made my blood boil.

"Smack your own!" I screamed hysterically. "Smack your own! Shut up! Shut up!"

At this he lost his patience and let fly at me. He did it with the lack of conviction you'd expect of a man under Mother's horrified eyes, and it ended up as a mere tap, but the sheer indignity of being struck at all by a stranger, a total stranger who had cajoled his way back from the war into our big bed as a result of my innocent intercession, made me completely dotty. I shrieked and shrieked, and danced in my bare feet, and Father, looking awkward and hairy in nothing but a short gray army shirt, glared down at me like a mountain out for murder. I think it must have been then that I realized he was jealous too. And there stood Mother in her nightdress, looking as if her heart was broken between us. I hoped she felt as she looked. It seemed to me that she deserved it all.

From that morning out my life was a hell. Father and I were enemies, open and avowed. We conducted a series of skirmishes against one another, he trying to steal my time with Mother and I his. When she was sitting on my bed, telling me a story, he took to looking for some pair of old boots which he alleged he had left behind him at the beginning of the war. While he talked to Mother I played loudly with my toys to show my total lack of concern. He created a terrible scene one evening when he came in from work and found me at his box, playing with his regimental badges, Gurkha knives and button-sticks. Mother got up and took the box from me.

"You mustn't play with Daddy's toys unless he lets you, Larry," she said severely. "Daddy doesn't play with yours."

For some reason Father looked at her as if she had struck him and then turned away with a scowl.

"Those are not toys," he growled, taking down the box again to see had I lifted anything. "Some of those curios are very rare and valuable."

But as time went on I saw more and more how he managed to alienate Mother and me. What made it worse was that I couldn't grasp his method or see what attraction he had for Mother. In every possible way he was less winning than I. He had a common accent and made noises at his tea. I thought for a while that it might be the newspapers she was interested in, so I made up bits of news of my own to read to her. Then I thought it might be the smoking, which I personally thought attractive, and took his pipes and went round the house dribbling into them till he caught me. I even made noises at my tea, but Mother only told me I was disgusting. It all seemed to hinge round that unhealthy habit of sleeping together, so I made a point of dropping into their bedroom and nosing round, talking to myself, so that they wouldn't know I was watching them, but they were never up to anything that I could see. In the end it beat me. It seemed to depend on being grown-up and giving people rings, and I realized I'd have to wait.

But at the same time I wanted him to see that I was only waiting, not giving up the fight. One evening when he was being particularly obnoxious, chattering away well above my head, I let him have it.

"Mummy," I said, "do you know what I'm going to do when I grow up?"

"No, dear," she replied. "What?"

"I'm going to marry you," I said quietly.

Father gave a great guffaw out of him, but he didn't take me in. I knew it must only be pretense. And Mother, in spite of everything, was pleased. I felt she was probably relieved to know that one day Father's hold on her would be broken.

"Won't that be nice?" she said with a smile.

"It'll be very nice," I said confidently. "Because we're going to have lots and lots of babies."

"That's right, dear," she said placidly. "I think we'll have one soon, and then you'll have plenty of company."

I was no end pleased about that because it showed that in spite of the way she gave in to Father she still considered my wishes. Besides, it would put the Geneys in their place.

It didn't turn out like that, though. To begin with, she was very preoccupied—I supposed about where she would get the seventeen and six—and though Father took to staying out late in the evenings it did me no particular good. She stopped taking me for walks, became as touchy as blazes, and smacked me for nothing at all. Sometimes I wished I'd never mentioned the confounded baby—I seemed to have a genius for bringing calamity on myself.

And calamity it was! Sonny arrived in the most appalling hullabaloo—even that much he couldn't do without a fuss—and from the first moment I disliked him. He was a difficult child—so far as I was concerned he was always difficult—and demanded far too much attention. Mother was simply silly about him, and couldn't see when he was only showing off. As company he was worse than useless. He slept all day, and I had to go round the house on tiptoe to avoid waking him. It wasn't any longer a question of not waking Father. The slogan now was "Don't-wake-Sonny!" I couldn't understand why the child wouldn't sleep at the proper time, so whenever Mother's back was turned I woke him. Sometimes to keep him awake I pinched him as well. Mother caught me at it one day and gave me a most unmerciful flaking.

One evening, when Father was coming in from work, I was playing trains in the front garden. I let on not to notice him; instead, I pretended to be talking to myself, and said in a loud voice: "If another bloody baby comes into this house, I'm going out."

Father stopped dead and looked at me over his shoulder.

"What's that you said?" he asked sternly.

"I was only talking to myself," I replied, trying to conceal my panic. "It's   115
private."

He turned and went in without a word. Mind you, I intended it as a solemn warning, but its effect was quite different. Father started being quite nice to me. I could understand that, of course. Mother was quite sickening about Sonny. Even at mealtimes she'd get up and gawk at him in the cradle with an idiotic smile, and tell Father to do the same. He was always polite about it, but he looked so puzzled you could see he didn't know what she was talking about. He complained of the way Sonny cried at night, but she only got cross and said that Sonny never cried except when there was something up with him—which was a flaming lie, because Sonny never had anything up with him, and only cried for attention. It was really painful to see how simple-minded she was. Father wasn't attractive, but he had a fine intelligence. He saw through Sonny, and now he knew that I saw through him as well.

One night I woke with a start. There was someone beside me in the bed. For one wild moment I felt sure it must be Mother, having come to her senses and left Father for good, but then I heard Sonny in convulsions in the next room, and Mother saying: "There! There! There!" and knew it wasn't she. It was Father. He was lying beside me, wide awake, breathing hard and apparently as mad as hell.

After a while it came to me what he was mad about. It was his turn now. After turning me out of the big bed, he had been turned out himself. Mother had no consideration now for anyone but that poisonous pup, Sonny. I couldn't help feeling sorry for Father. I had been through it all myself, and even at that age I was magnanimous. I began to stroke him down and say: "There! There!" He wasn't exactly responsive.

"Aren't you asleep either?" he snarled.

"Ah, come on and put your arm around us, can't you?" I said, and he did, in a   120
sort of way. Gingerly, I suppose, is how you'd describe it. He was very bony but better than nothing.

At Christmas he went out of his way to buy me a really nice model railway.

QUESTIONS AND SUGGESTIONS FOR WRITING

1. The boy is immensely egotistical. Why do we not detest him?
2. Is "My Oedipus Complex" a story or only a character sketch? Explain.

3. At the end of the piece, is the narrator still possessed by an Oedipus complex, or is he released from it? Explain. (If you don't know what an Oedipus complex is, begin by checking a dictionary or an encyclopedia.)
4. Write a narrative of 500 to 750 words setting forth an episode in which, resenting an apparent lack of loving attention, you sought to divert interest from a parent or sibling toward yourself. Let the reader understand your behavior from the action, not from explicit comment.

Eudora Welty (American. b. 1909)

A WORN PATH

It was December—a bright frozen day in the early morning. Far out in the country there was an old Negro woman with her head tied in a red rag, coming along a path through the pinewoods. Her name was Phoenix Jackson. She was very old and small and she walked slowly in the dark pine shadows, moving a little from side to side in her steps, with the balanced heaviness and lightness of a pendulum in a grandfather clock. She carried a thin, small cane made from an umbrella, and with this she kept tapping the frozen earth in front of her. This made a grave and persistent noise in the still air, that seemed meditative like the chirping of a solitary little bird.

She wore a dark striped dress reaching down to her shoe tops, and an equally long apron of bleached sugar sacks, with a full pocket: all neat and tidy, but every time she took a step she might have fallen over her shoe-laces, which dragged from her unlaced shoes. She looked straight ahead. Her eyes were blue with age. Her skin had a pattern all its own of numberless branching wrinkles and as though a whole little tree stood in the middle of her forehead, but a golden color ran underneath, and the two knobs of her cheeks were illuminated by a yellow burning under the dark. Under the red rag her hair came down on her neck in the frailest of ringlets, still black, and with an odor like copper.

Now and then there was a quivering in the thicket. Old Phoenix said, "Out of my way, all you foxes, owls, beetles, jack rabbits, coons, and wild animals! . . . Keep out from under these feet, little bob-whites. . . . Keep the big wild hogs out of my path. Don't let none of those come running my direction. I got a long way." Under her small black-freckled hand her cane, limber as a buggy whip, would switch at the brush as if to rouse up any hiding things.

On she went. The woods were deep and still. The sun made the pine needles almost too bright to look at, up where the wind rocked. The cones dropped as light as feathers. Down in the hollow was the mourning dove—it was not too late for him.

The path ran up a hill. "Seem like there is chains about my feet, time I get this far," she said, in the voice of argument old people keep to use with themselves. "Something always take a hold of me on this hill—pleads I should stay."

After she got to the top she turned and gave a full, severe look behind her where she had come. "Up through pines," she said at length. "Now down through oaks."

5

Her eyes opened their widest, and she started down gently. But before she got to the bottom of the hill a bush caught her dress.

Her fingers were busy and intent, but her skirts were full and long, so that before she could pull them free in one place they were caught in another. It was not possible to allow the dress to tear. "I in the thorny bush," she said. "Thorns, you doing your appointed work. Never want to let folks pass—no sir. Old eyes thought you was a pretty little *green* bush."

Finally, trembling all over, she stood free, and after a moment dared to stoop for her cane.

"Sun so high!" she cried, leaning back and looking, while the thick tears went over her eyes. "The time getting all gone here."   10

At the foot of this hill was a place where a log was laid across the creek.

"Now comes the trial," said Phoenix.

Putting her right foot out, she mounted the log and shut her eyes. Lifting her skirt, levelling her cane fiercely before her, like a festival figure in some parade, she began to march across. Then she opened her eyes and she was safe on the other side.

"I wasn't as old as I thought," she said.

But she sat down to rest. She spread her skirts on the bank around her and   15
folded her hands over her knees. Up above her was a tree in a pearly cloud of mistletoe. She did not dare to close her eyes, and when a little boy brought her a little plate with a slice of marble-cake on it she spoke to him. "That would be acceptable," she said. But when she went to take it there was just her own hand in the air.

So she left that tree, and had to go through a barbed-wire fence. There she had to creep and crawl, spreading her knees and stretching her fingers like a baby trying to climb the steps. But she talked loudly to herself: she could not let her dress be torn now, so late in the day, and she could not pay for having her arm or her leg sawed off if she got caught fast where she was.

At last she was safe through the fence and risen up out in the clearing. Big dead trees, like black men with one arm, were standing in the purple stalks of the withered cotton field. There sat a buzzard.

"Who you watching?"

In the furrow she made her way along.

"Glad this not the season for bulls," she said, looking sideways, "and the   20
good Lord made his snakes to curl up and sleep in the winter. A pleasure I don't see no two-headed snake coming around that tree, where it come once. It took a while to get by him, back in the summer."

She passed through the old cotton and went into a field of dead corn. It whispered and shook and was taller than her head. "Through the maze now," she said, for there was no path.

Then there was something tall, black, and skinny there, moving before her.

At first she took it for a man. It could have been a man dancing in the field. But she stood still and listened, and it did not make a sound. It was as silent as a ghost.

"Ghost," she said sharply, "who be you the ghost of? For I have heard of nary death close by."

But there was no answer—only the ragged dancing in the wind.   25

She shut her eyes, reached out her hand, and touched a sleeve. She found a coat and inside that an emptiness, cold as ice.

"You scarecrow," she said. Her face lighted. "I ought to be shut up for good," she said with laughter. "My senses is gone, I too old. I the oldest people I ever know. Dance, old scarecrow," she said, "while I dancing with you."

She kicked her foot over the furrow, and with mouth drawn down, shook her head once or twice in a little strutting way. Some husks blew down and whirled in streamers about her skirts.

Then she went on, parting her way from side to side with the cane, through the whispering field. At last she came to the end, to a wagon track where the silver grass blew between the red ruts. The quail were walking around like pullets, seeming all dainty and unseen.

"Walk pretty," she said. "This the easy place. This the easy going."   30

She followed the track, swaying through the quiet bare fields, through the little strings of trees silver in their dead leaves, past cabins silver from weather, with the doors and windows boarded shut, all like old women under a spell sitting there. "I walking in their sleep," she said, nodding her head vigorously.

In a ravine she went where a spring was silently flowing through a hollow log. Old Phoenix bent and drank. "Sweet-gum makes the water sweet," she said, and drank more. "Nobody know who made this well, for it was here when I was born."

The track crossed a swampy part where the moss hung as white as lace from every limb. "Sleep on, alligators, and blow your bubbles." Then the track went into the road.

Deep, deep the road went down between the high green-colored banks. Overhead the live-oaks met, and it was as dark as a cave.

A black dog with a lolling tongue came up out of the weeds by the ditch. She   35
was meditating, and not ready, and when he came at her she only hit him a little with her cane. Over she went in the ditch, like a little puff of milk-weed.

Down there, her senses drifted away. A dream visited her, and she reached her hand up, but nothing reached down and gave her a pull. So she lay there and presently went to talking. "Old woman," she said to herself, "that black dog come up out of the weeds to stall you off, and now there he sitting on his fine tail, smiling at you."

A white man finally came along and found her—a hunter, a young man, with his dog on a chain.

"Well, Granny!" he laughed. "what are you doing there?"

"Lying on my back like a June-bug waiting to be turned over, mister," she said, reaching up her hand.

He lifted her up, gave her a swing in the air, and set her down. "Anything   40
broken, Granny?"

"No sir, them old dead weeds is springy enough," said Phoenix, when she had got her breath. "I thank you for your trouble."

"Where do you live, Granny?" he asked, while the two dogs were growling at each other.

"Away back yonder, sir, behind the ridge. You can't even see it from here."

"On your way home?"

"No, sir, I going to town."   45

"Why, that's too far! That's as far as I walk when I come out myself, and I get something for my trouble." He patted the stuffed bag he carried, and there hung down a little closed claw. It was one of the bob-whites, with its beak hooked bitterly to show it was dead. "Now you go on home, Granny!"

"I bound to go to town, mister," said Phoenix. "The time come around."

He gave another laugh, filling the whole landscape. "I know you old colored people! Wouldn't miss going to town to see Santa Claus!"

But something held Old Phoenix very still. The deep lines in her face went into a fierce and different radiation. Without warning, she had seen with her own eyes a flashing nickel fall out of the man's pocket onto the ground.

"How old are you, Granny?" he was saying.   50

"There is no telling, mister," she said, "no telling."

Then she gave a little cry and clapped her hands and said, "Git on away from here, dog! Look! Look at that dog!" She laughed as if in admiration. "He ain't scared of nobody. He a big black dog." She whispered, "Sic him!"

"Watch me get rid of that cur," said the man. "Sic him, Pete! Sic him!"

Phoenix heard the dogs fighting, and heard the man running and throwing sticks. She even heard a gunshot. But she was slowly bending forward by that time, further and further forward, the lids stretched down over her eyes, as if she were doing this in her sleep. Her chin was lowered almost to her knees. The yellow palm of her hand came out from the fold of her apron. Her fingers slid down and along the ground under the piece of money with the grace and care they would have in lifting an egg from under a sitting hen. Then she slowly straightened up, she stood erect, and the nickel was in her apron pocket. A bird flew by. Her lips moved. "God watching me the whole time. I come to stealing."

The man came back, and his own dog panted about them. "Well, I scared him   55
off that time," he said, and then he laughed and lifted his gun and pointed it at Phoenix.

She stood straight and faced him.

"Doesn't the gun scare you?" he said, still pointing it.

"No, sir, I seen plenty go off closer by, in my day, and for less than what I done," she said, holding utterly still.

He smiled, and shouldered the gun. "Well, Granny," he said, "You must be a hundred years old, and scared of nothing. I'd give you a dime if I had any money with me. But you take my advice and stay home, and nothing will happen to you."

"I bound to go on my way, mister," said Phoenix. She inclined her head in the   60
red rag. Then they went in different directions, but she could hear the gun shooting again and again over the hill.

She walked on. The shadows hung from the oak trees to the road like curtains. Then she smelled wood-smoke, and smelled the river, and she saw a steeple and the cabins on their steep steps. Dozens of little black children whirled around her. There ahead was Natchez shining. Bells were ringing. She walked on.

In the paved city it was Christmas time. There were red and green electric lights strung and crisscrossed everywhere, and all turned on in the daytime. Old Phoenix would have been lost if she had not distrusted her eyesight and depended on her feet to know where to take her.

She paused quietly on the sidewalk where people were passing by. A lady came along in the crowd, carrying an armful of red-, green-, and silver-wrapped presents; she gave off perfume like the red roses in hot summer, and Phoenix stopped her.

"Please, missy, will you lace up my shoe?" She held up her foot.

"What do you want, Grandma?"   65

"See my shoe," said Phoenix. "Do all right for out in the country, but wouldn't look right to go in a big building."

"Stand still then, Grandma," said the lady. She put her packages down on the sidewalk beside her and laced and tied both shoes tightly.

"Can't lace 'em with a cane," said Phoenix. "Thank you, missy. I doesn't mind asking a nice lady to tie up my shoe, when I gets out on the street."

Moving slowly and from side to side, she went into the big building and into a tower of steps, where she walked up and around and around until her feet knew to stop.

She entered a door, and there she saw nailed up on the wall the document   70
that had been stamped with the gold seal and framed in the gold frame, which matched the dream that was hung up in her head.

"Here I be," she said. There was a fixed and ceremonial stiffness over her body.

"A charity case, I suppose," said an attendant who sat at the desk before her.

But Phoenix only looked above her head. There was sweat on her face, the wrinkles in her skin shone like a bright net.

"Speak up, Grandma," the woman said. "What's your name? We must have your history, you know. Have you been here before? What seems to be the trouble with you?"

Old Phoenix only gave a twitch to her face as if a fly were bothering her.   75

"Are you deaf?" cried the attendant.

But then the nurse came in.

"Oh, that's just old Aunt Phoenix," she said. "She doesn't come for herself— she has a little grandson. She makes these trips just as regular as clockwork. She lives away back off the old Natchez Trace." She bent down. "Well, Aunt Phoenix, why don't you just take a seat? We won't keep you standing after your long trip." She pointed.

The old woman sat down, bolt upright in the chair.

"Now, how is the boy?" asked the nurse.   80

Old Phoenix did not speak.

"I said, how is the boy?"

But Phoenix only waited and stared straight ahead, her face very solemn and withdrawn into rigidity.

"Is his throat any better?" asked the nurse. "Aunt Phoenix, don't you hear me? Is your grandson's throat any better since the last time you came for the medicine?"

With her hands on her knees, the old woman waited, silent, erect and motionless, just as if she were in armor.

"You mustn't take up our time this way, Aunt Phoenix," the nurse said. "Tell us quickly about your grandson, and get it over. He isn't dead, is he?"

At last there came a flicker and then a flame of comprehension across her face, and she spoke.

"My grandson. It was my memory had left me. There I sat and forgot why I made my long trip."

"Forgot?" The nurse frowned. "After you came so far?"

Then Phoenix was like an old woman begging a dignified forgiveness for waking up frightened in the night. "I never did go to school, I was too old at the Surrender," she said in a soft voice. "I'm an old woman without an education. It was my memory fail me. My little grandson, he is just the same, and I forgot it in the coming."

"Throat never heals, does it?" said the nurse, speaking in a loud, sure voice to Old Phoenix. By now she had a card with something written on it, a little list. "Yes. Swallowed lye. When was it—January—two-three years ago—"

Phoenix spoke unasked now. "No, missy, he not dead, he just the same. Every little while his throat begin to close up again, and he not able to swallow. He not get his breath. He not able to help himself. So the time come around, and I go on another trip for the soothing medicine."

"All right. The doctor said as long as you came to get it, you could have it," said the nurse. "But it's an obstinate case."

"My little grandson, he sit up there in the house all wrapped up, waiting by himself," Phoenix went on. "We is the only two left in the world. He suffer and it don't seem to put him back at all. He got a sweet look. He going to last. He wear a little patch quilt and peep out holding his mouth open like a little bird. I remembers so plain now. I not going to forget him again, no, the whole enduring time. I could tell him from all the others in creation."

"All right." The nurse was trying to hush her now. She brought her a bottle of medicine. "Charity," she said, making a check mark in a book.

Old Phoenix held the bottle close to her eyes and then carefully put it into her pocket.

"I thank you," she said.

"It's Christmas time, Grandma," said the attendant. "Could I give you a few pennies out of my purse?"

"Five pennies is a nickel," said Phoenix stiffly.

"Here's a nickel," said the attendant.

Phoenix rose carefully and held out her hand. She received the nickel and then fished the other nickel out of her pocket and laid it beside the new one. She stared at her palm closely, with her head on one side.

Then she gave a tap with her cane on the floor.

"This is what come to me to do," she said. "I going to the store and buy my child a little windmill they sells, made out of paper. He going to find it hard to believe there such a thing in the world. I'll march myself back where he waiting, holding it straight up in this hand."

She lifted her free hand, gave a little nod, turned round, and walked out of the doctor's office. Then her slow step began on the stairs, going down.

QUESTIONS AND SUGGESTIONS FOR WRITING

1. If you do not know the legend of the phoenix, look it up in a dictionary or, better, in an encyclopedia. Then carefully reread the story, to learn whether the story in any way connects with the legend.
2. Characterize the hunter.
3. What would be lost if the episode (with all of its dialogue) of Phoenix falling into the ditch and being helped out of it by the hunter were omitted?
4. Is Christmas a particularly appropriate time in which to set the story? Why or why not?
5. Some readers believe that the grandson is dead, or that in any case the story would be better if the grandson were dead. Evaluate this view.
6. What do you make of the title?

☐ POETRY

William Shakespeare (English. 1564–1616)
SONNET 29

times are hard

When, in disgrace with Fortune and men's eyes,
I all alone beweep my outcast state,
And trouble deaf heaven with my bootless° cries,   *Useless*
And look upon myself and curse my fate,   —   4
Wishing me like to one more rich in hope,
Featured like him, like him° with friends possessed,   *Like a second*
Desiring this man's art and that man's scope,   *man, like a third man*
With what I most enjoy contented least;   8
Yet in these thoughts myself almost despising,
Haply° I think on thee, and then my state,   *Perchance*
Like to the lark at break of day arising
From sullen earth, sings hymns at heaven's gate;   12
    For thy sweet love rememb'red such wealth brings,
    That then I scorn to change my state with kings.

QUESTIONS AND SUGGESTIONS FOR WRITING

1. Disregarding for the moment the last two lines (or *couplet*), where does the sharpest turn or shift occur? In a sentence, summarize the speaker's state of mind before this turn, and in another sentence, the state of mind after it.
2. In the last two lines of a sonnet Shakespeare often summarizes the lines that pre-

ceded. In this sonnet, how does the structure of the summary differ from that of the statement in the first twelve lines? Why?

3. The "thee" of this poem is almost certainly a man, not a woman. Is the "love" of the poem erotic love *(eros),* or can it be taken as something like brotherly love or even as the loving-kindness of Paul in I Corinthians (page 591)?

William Shakespeare (English. 1564–1616)

SONNET 116

Let me not to the marriage of true minds
Admit impediments; love is not love
Which alters when it alteration finds,
Or bends with the remover to remove.   4
O, no, it is an ever-fixèd mark°   *Seamark, guide to mariners*
That looks on tempests and is never shaken;
It is the star° to every wand'ring bark,   *The North Star*
Whose worth's unknown, although his height be taken.   8
Love's not Time's fool,° though rosy lips and cheeks   *Plaything*
Within his bending sickle's compass° come;   *Range, circle*
Love alters not with his° brief hours and weeks   *Time's*
But bears° it out even to the edge of doom.°   *Survives   Judgment Day*   12
    If this be error and upon° me proved,   *Against*
    I never writ, nor no man ever loved.

QUESTIONS AND SUGGESTIONS FOR WRITING

1. Notice that the poem celebrates "the marriage of true minds," not of bodies. In a sentence, using only your own words, summarize Shakespeare's idea of the nature of such love.
2. Does this love resemble the "charity" that Paul speaks of in I Corinthians (page 591)? Explain.

John Donne (English. 1572–1631)

A VALEDICTION: FORBIDDING MOURNING

As virtuous men pass mildly away;
    And whisper to their souls, to go,
Whilst some of their sad friends do say,
    "The breath goes now," and some say, "No":   4

So let us melt, and make no noise.
    No tear-floods, nor sigh-tempests move.
'Twere profanation of our joys
    To tell the laity our love.   8

Moving of the earth° brings harms and fears,   *An earthquake*
    Men reckon what it did and meant;
But trepidation of the spheres,
    Though greater far, is innocent.*   12

Dull sublunary° lovers' love   *Under the moon, i.e., earthly*
    (Whose soul is sense) cannot admit
Absence, because it doth remove
    Those things which elemented it.   16

But we, by a love so much refined
    That our selves know not what it is,
Inter-assurèd of the mind,
    Care less, eyes, lips, and hands to miss.   20

Our two souls therefore, which are one,
    Though I must go, endure not yet
A breach, but an expansion,
    Like gold to airy thinness beat.   24

If they be two, they are two so
    As stiff twin compasses° are two: *I.e., a carpenter's compass*
Thy soul, the fixed foot, makes no show
    To move, but doth, if the other do.   28

And though it in the center sit,
    Yet when the other far doth roam,
It leans, and hearkens after it,
    And grows erect, as that comes home.   32

Such wilt thou be to me, who must
    Like the other foot, obliquely run:
Thy firmness makes my circle just,
    And makes me end where I begun.   36

QUESTIONS AND SUGGESTIONS FOR WRITING

1. Donne contrasts the love of "dull sublunary lovers" (i.e., ordinary mortals) with the love he and his beloved share. What is the difference? What is the meaning of "laity" in line 8, and what does it say, implicitly, about the speaker and his beloved?
2. In the figure of the carpenter's or draftsperson's compass (lines 25–36) the speaker offers reasons—some stated clearly, some not so clearly—why he will end where he began. In 250 words explain these reasons.
3. Paraphrase the first two stanzas, making clear the relation of the simile that asserts a resemblance between the death of virtuous men (lines 1–4) and the parting of lovers (lines 5–8).
4. In line 35 Donne speaks of his voyage as a "circle." Explain in a paragraph why the circle is traditionally a symbol of perfection.

*But the movement of the heavenly spheres (in Ptolemaic astronomy), though far greater, is harmless.

Robert Herrick (English. 1591–1674)

TO THE VIRGINS, TO MAKE MUCH OF TIME

Gather ye rosebuds while ye may,
    Old time is still a-flying;
And this same flower that smiles today
    Tomorrow will be dying.   4

The glorious lamp of heaven, the sun,
    The higher he's a-getting,
The sooner will his race be run,
    And nearer he's to setting.   8

That age is best which is the first,
    When youth and blood are warmer;
But being spent, the worse, and worst
    Times still succeed the former.   12

Then be not coy, but use your time,
    And, while ye may, go marry;
For, having lost but once your prime,
    You may forever tarry.   16

QUESTIONS AND SUGGESTIONS FOR WRITING

1. Who do you think is speaking in the poem—a man or a woman? Is the speaker old or young? In a paragraph or two explain your view.
2. In two paragraphs explain the connection between the virgins and flowers, and between the virgins and the progress of a day.
3. This seventeenth-century poem suggests that a woman finds fulfillment only in marriage. Can the poem, then, be of any interest to a society in which women may choose careers in preference to marriage?

Andrew Marvell (English. 1621–1678)

TO HIS COY MISTRESS

Had we but world enough, and time,
This coyness, lady, were no crime.
We would sit down, and think which way
To walk, and pass our long love's day.
Thou by the Indian Ganges' side   5
Should'st rubies find: I by the tide
Of Humber° would complain.° I   *River in England   Write love poems*
Love you ten years before the Flood,
And you should, if you please, refuse   10

Till the conversion of the Jews.
My vegetable° love should grow   *I.e., unconsciously growing*
Vaster than empires, and more slow.
An hundred years should go to praise
Thine eyes, and on thy forehead gaze:
Two hundred to adore each breast: 15
But thirty thousand to the rest.
An age at least to every part,
And the last age should show your heart.
For, lady, you deserve this state,
Nor would I love at lower rate.   20
    But at my back I always hear
Time's wingèd chariot hurrying near;
And yonder all before us lie
Deserts of vast eternity.
Thy beauty shall no more be found,   25
Nor in thy marble vault shall sound
My echoing song; then worms shall try
That long preserved virginity,
And your quaint honor turn to dust,
And into ashes all my lust.   30
The grave's a fine and private place,
But none, I think, do there embrace.
    Now therefore, while the youthful hue
Sits on thy skin like morning dew,
And while thy willing soul transpires   35
At every pore with instant fires,
Now let us sport us while we may;
And now, like am'rous birds of prey,
Rather at once our time devour,
Than languish in his slow-chapt° power,   *Slowly devouring*   40
Let us roll all our strength, and all
Our sweetness, up into one ball;
And tear our pleasures with rough strife
Thorough° the iron gates of life.   *Through*
Thus, though we cannot make our sun   45
Stand still, yet we will make him run.

QUESTIONS AND SUGGESTIONS FOR WRITING

1. Are the assertions in lines 1–20 so inflated that we detect behind them a playfully ironic tone? Explain. Why does the speaker say, in line 8, that he would love "ten years before the Flood," rather than merely "since the Flood"?
2. Explain lines 21–24. Why is time behind the speaker, and eternity in front of him? Is this "eternity" the same as the period discussed in lines 1–20? Discuss the change in the speaker's tone after line 20.

3. Why "am'rous birds of prey" (line 38) rather than the conventional doves? How is the idea of preying continued in the poem?
4. What is meant by "slow-chapt" (line 40)? Consult a dictionary for various meanings of "chap." In the seventeenth century, a cannonball was simply called a "ball." Could lines 42–44 suggest a cannonball ripping through a city's fortifications?
5. Is there any verbal irony in lines 33–46? (On irony, see page 730.) Explain the last two lines, and characterize the speaker's tone. Are the lines anticlimactic?
6. The poem is organized in the form of an argument. Trace the steps.

Robert Browning (English. 1812–1889)
PORPHYRIA'S LOVER

The rain set early in tonight,
    The sullen wind was soon awake,
It tore the elm-tops down for spite,
    And did its worst to vex the lake:
I listened with heart fit to break.   5
When glided in Porphyria; straight
    She shut the cold out and the storm,
And kneeled and made the cheerless grate
    Blaze up, and all the cottage warm;
Which done, she rose, and from her form   10
Withdrew the dripping cloak and shawl,
    And laid her soiled gloves by, untied
Her hat and let the damp hair fall,
    And, last, she sat down by my side
And called me. When no voice replied,   15
She put my arm about her waist,
    And made her smooth white shoulder bare
And all her yellow hair displaced,
    And stooping, made my cheek lie there,
And spread, o'er all, her yellow hair,   20
Murmuring how she loved me—she
    Too weak, for all her heart's endeavor,
To set its struggling passion free
    From pride, and vainer ties dissever,
And give herself to me forever.   25
But passion sometimes would prevail,
    Nor could tonight's gay feast restrain
A sudden thought of one so pale
    For love of her, and all in vain:
So, she was come through wind and rain.   30
Be sure I looked up at her eyes
    Happy and proud; at last I knew
Porphyria worshiped me; surprise

Made my heart swell, and still it grew
While I debated what to do.   35
That moment she was mine, mine, fair,
    Perfectly pure and good: I found
A thing to do, and all her hair
    In one long yellow string I wound   40
Three times her little throat around,
And strangled her. No pain felt she;
    I am quite sure she felt no pain.
As a shut bud that holds a bee,
    I warily oped her lids: again   45
Laughed the blue eyes without a stain.
And I untightened next the tress
    About her neck; her cheek once more
Blushed bright beneath my burning kiss:
    I propped her head up as before,   50
Only, this time my shoulder bore
Her head, which droops upon it still:
    The smiling rosy little head,
So glad it has its utmost will,
    That all it scorned at once is fled,   55
And I, its love, am gained instead!
Porphyria's love: she guessed not how
    Her darling one wish would be heard.
And thus we sit together now,
    And all night long we have not stirred,   60
And yet God has not said a word!

QUESTIONS AND SUGGESTIONS FOR WRITING

1. Exactly why did the speaker murder Porphyria?
2. You are a lawyer assigned to defend the speaker against the charge of murder. In 500 to 750 words, write your defense.

Robert Browning (English 1812–1889)
MY LAST DUCHESS lyric

Ferrara°   *Town in Italy*

That's my last Duchess painted on the wall,
Looking as if she were alive. I call
That piece a wonder, now; Frà Pandolf's° hands   *A fictitious painter*
Worked busily a day, and there she stands.
Will't please you sit and look at her? I said   5
"Frà Pandolf" by design, for never read

Strangers like you that pictured countenance,
The depth and passion of its earnest glance,
But to myself they turned (since none puts by
The curtain I have drawn for you, but I)   10
And seemed as they would ask me, if they durst,
How such a glance came there; so, not the first
Are you to turn and ask thus. Sir, 'twas not
Her husband's presence only, called that spot
Of joy into the Duchess' cheek; perhaps   15
Frà Pandolf chanced to say "Her mantle laps
Over my Lady's wrist too much," or, "Paint
Must never hope to reproduce the faint
Half-flush that dies along her throat." Such stuff
Was courtesy, she thought, and cause enough   20
For calling up that spot of joy. She had
A heart—how shall I say?—too soon made glad,
Too easily impressed; she liked whate'er
She looked on, and her looks went everywhere.
Sir, 'twas all one! My favor at her breast,   25
The dropping of the daylight in the west,
The bough of cherries some officious fool
Broke in the orchard for her, the white mule
She rode with round the terrace—all and each
Would draw from her alike the approving speech,   30
Or blush, at least. She thanked men—good! but thanked
Somehow—I know not how—as if she ranked
My gift of a nine-hundred-years-old name
With anybody's gift. Who'd stoop to blame
This sort of trifling? Even had you skill   35
In speech—(which I have not)—to make your will
Quite clear to such an one, and say, "Just this
Or that in you disgusts me; here you miss,
Or there exceed the mark"—and if she let
Herself be lessoned so, nor plainly set   40
Her wits to yours, forsooth, and made excuse,
—E'en then would be some stooping; and I choose
Never to stoop. Oh, Sir, she smiled, no doubt,
Whene'er I passed her; but who passed without
Much the same smile? This grew; I gave commands;   45
Then all smiles stopped together. There she stands
As if alive. Will't please you rise? We'll meet
The company below, then. I repeat,
The Count your master's known munificence
Is ample warrant that no just pretense   50
Of mine for dowry will be disallowed;
Though his fair daughter's self, as I avowed

At starting, is my object. Nay, we'll go
Together down, Sir. Notice Neptune, though,   55
Taming a sea-horse, thought a rarity,
Which Claus of Innsbruck° cast in bronze for me!   *A fictitious sculptor*

QUESTIONS AND SUGGESTIONS FOR WRITING

1. Who is speaking to whom? On what occasion?
2. What words or lines especially convey the speaker's arrogance? What is our attitude toward the speaker? Loathing? Fascination? Respect? Explain.
3. The time and place are Renaissance Italy; how do they affect our attitude toward the duke? What would be the effect if the poem were set in the twentieth century?
4. Years after writing this poem, Browning explained that the duke's "commands" (line 45) were "that she should be put to death, or he might have had her shut up in a convent." Should the poem have been more explicit? Does Browning's later uncertainty indicate that the poem is badly thought out? Suppose we did not have Browning's comment on line 45; could the line then mean only that he commanded her to stop smiling and that she obeyed? Explain.
5. Elizabeth Barrett (not yet Mrs. Browning) wrote to Robert Browning that it was not "by the dramatic medium that poets teach most impressively. . . . It is too difficult for the common reader to analyze, and to discern between the vivid and the earnest." She went on, urging him to teach "in the directest and most impressive way, the mask thrown off." What teaching, if any, is in this poem? If there is any teaching here, would it be more impressive if Browning had not used the mask of a Renaissance duke? Explain.
6. You are the envoy, writing to the Count, your master, a 500-word report of your interview with the duke. What do you write?

Matthew Arnold (English. 1822–1888)
DOVER BEACH

The sea is calm to-night.
The tide is full, the moon lies fair
Upon the straits;—on the French coast the light
Gleams and is gone; the cliffs of England stand,
Glimmering and vast, out in the tranquil bay.   5
Come to the window, sweet is the night-air!
Only, from the long line of spray
Where the sea meets the moon-blanch'd land,
Listen! you hear the grating roar
Of pebbles which the waves draw back, and fling,   10
At their return, up the high strand,
Begin, and cease, and then again begin,
With tremulous cadence slow, and bring
The eternal note of sadness in.

Sophocles long ago   15
Heard it on the Aegean, and it brought
Into his mind the turbid ebb and flow
Of human misery; we
Find also in the sound a thought,
Hearing it by this distant northern sea.   20

The Sea of Faith
Was once, too, at the full, and round earth's shore
Lay like the folds of a bright girdle furl'd.
But now I only hear
Its melancholy, long, withdrawing roar,   25
Retreating, to the breath
Of the night-wind, down the vast edges drear
And naked shingles° of the world.   *Pebbled beaches*

Ah, love, let us be true
To one another! for the world, which seems   30
To lie before us like a land of dreams,
So various, so beautiful, so new,
Hath really neither joy, nor love, nor light,
Nor certitude, nor peace, nor help for pain;
And we are here as on a darkling plain   35
Swept with confused alarms of struggle and flight,
Where ignorant armies clash by night.

QUESTIONS AND SUGGESTIONS FOR WRITING

1. The sea, described in the first stanza, puts the speaker in mind of two metaphors, one in the second stanza and one in the third. Explain each of these metaphors in your own words. (On metaphor, see pages 727–729.) In commenting on the first, be sure to include a remark about "turbid" in line 17.
2. In the last stanza the sea is omitted, but one can argue that the first stanza prepared us for much in the last stanza. What connections do you find?

Robert Frost (American. 1874–1963)

THE SILKEN TENT

She is as in a field a silken tent
At midday when a sunny summer breeze
Has dried the dew and all its ropes relent,
So that in guys it gently sways at ease,   4
And its supporting central cedar pole,
That is its pinnacle to heavenward
And signifies the sureness of the soul,
Seems to owe naught to any single cord,   8

But strictly held by none, is loosely bound
By countless silken ties of love and thought
To everything on earth the compass round,
And only by one's going slightly taut   12
In the capriciousness of summer air
Is of the slightest bondage made aware.

QUESTIONS AND SUGGESTIONS FOR WRITING

1. The tent is supported by "guys" (not men, but the cords or "ties" of line 10) and by
   its "central cedar pole." What does Frost tell us about these ties? What does he tell
   us about the pole?
2. What do you make of lines 12–14?

Sylvia Plath (American. 1932–1963)
DADDY   *confessional*

You do not do, you do not do
Any more, black shoe
In which I have lived like a foot
For thirty years, poor and white,
Barely daring to breathe or Achoo.   5

Daddy, I have had to kill you.
You died before I had time—
Marble-heavy, a bag full of God,
Ghastly statue with one gray toe
Big as a Frisco seal   10

And a head in the freakish Atlantic
Where it pours bean green over blue
In the waters off beautiful Nauset.
I used to pray to recover you.
Ach, du°   *Ah, you (German)*   15

In the German tongue, in the Polish town
Scraped flat by the roller
Of wars, wars, wars.
But the name of the town is common.
My Polack friend   20

Says there are a dozen or two.
So I never could tell where you
Put your foot, your root,
I never could talk to you.
The tongue stuck in my jaw.   25

It stuck in a barb wire snare.
Ich, ich, ich, ich,
I could hardly speak.
I thought every German was you.
And the language obscene   30

An engine, an engine
Chuffing me off like a Jew.
A Jew to Dachau, Auschwitz, Belsen.°   *Concentration camps where*
I began to talk like a Jew.   *Germans exterminated Jews*
I think I may well be a Jew.   35

The snows of the Tyrol, the clear beer of Vienna
Are not very pure or true.
With my gypsy ancestress and my weird luck
And my Taroc pack and my Taroc pack
I may be a bit of a Jew.   40

I have always been scared of *you,*
With your Luftwaffe,° your gobbledygoo.   *German air force*
And your neat moustache
And your Aryan eye, bright blue,
Panzer-man, panzer-man,° O You—   *Armored tank soldier*   45

Not God but a swastika
So black no sky could squeak through.
Every woman adores a Fascist,
The boot in the face, the brute
Brute heart of a brute like you.   50

You stand at the blackboard, daddy,
In the picture I have of you,
A cleft in your chin instead of your foot
But no less a devil for that, no not
Any less the black man who   55

Bit my pretty red heart in two.
I was ten when they buried you.
At twenty I tried to die
And get back, back, back to you.
I thought even the bones would do.   60

But they pulled me out of the sack,
And they stuck me together with glue,
And then I knew what to do.
I made a model of you,
A man in black with a Meinkampf* look   65

*My Struggle was Adolf Hitler's major statement of his political and racial views, published in two
volumes in 1925 and 1927.

And a love of the rack and the screw.
And I said I do, I do.
So daddy, I'm finally through.
The black telephone's off at the root,
The voices just can't worm through.   70

If I've killed one man, I've killed two—
The vampire who said he was you
And drank my blood for a year,
Seven years, if you want to know.
Daddy, you can lie back now.   75

There's a stake in your fat black heart
And the villagers never liked you.
They are dancing and stamping on you.
They always *knew* it was you.
Daddy, daddy, you bastard, I'm through.   80

QUESTION AND SUGGESTION FOR WRITING

The speaker expresses her hatred for her father by identifying him with the Nazis,
herself with the Jews. Is it irresponsible for a poet to compare her sense of torment
with that of Jews who were gassed in Dachau, Auschwitz, and Belsen?

Margaret Atwood (Canadian. b. 1939)
SIREN SONG   *Confessional*

This is the one song everyone
would like to learn: the song
that is irresistible:

the song that forces men
to leap overboard in squadrons   5
even though they see the beached skulls

the song nobody knows
because anyone who has heard it
is dead, and the others can't remember.

Shall I tell you the secret   10
and if I do, will you get me
out of this bird suit?

I don't enjoy it here
squatting on this island
looking picturesque and mythical   15

with these two feathery maniacs,
I don't enjoy singing
this trio, fatal and valuable.

I will tell the secret to you,
to you, only to you.   20
Come closer. This song

is a cry for help: Help me!
Only you, only you can,
you are unique

at last. Alas   25
it is a boring song
but it works every time.

QUESTION AND SUGGESTION FOR WRITING

In Greek mythology, the sirens were sea nymphs whose sweet singing lured mariners
to destruction on the rocks surrounding their islands. In this poem, what is the gist of
the song? Why does it "work every time"?

□ DRAMA

William Shakespeare (English. 1564–1616)
THE TAMING OF THE SHREW

[Dramatis Personae

Induction (and ending of Act I, Scene I)

CHRISTOPHER SLY, *a tinker*
HOSTESS *of an alehouse*
A LORD
HUNTSMEN *and* SERVANTS *of the Lord*
PLAYERS *in a traveling company*
BARTHOLOMEW, *a page*

Acts I–V

BAPTISTA MINOLA, *of Padua, father of Kate and Bianca*
KATE, *the shrew*
BIANCA
PETRUCHIO, *of Verona, suitor of Kate*
LUCENTIO *(Cambio)* ⎫
GREMIO, *a pantaloon* ⎬ *suitors of Bianca*
HORTENSIO *(Litio)* ⎭
VINCENTIO, *of Pisa, father of Lucentio*
A PEDANT *(impersonating Vincentio)*
TRANIO *(later impersonating* ⎫
   Lucentio) ⎬ *servants of Lucentio*
BIONDELLO ⎭
GRUMIO ⎫
CURTIS ⎪
NATHANIEL, NICHOLAS ⎬ *servants of Petruchio*
JOSEPH, PHILIP, PETER ⎪
A TAILOR ⎭
A HABERDASHER
A WIDOW
SERVANTS of *Baptista and Lucentio*

Scene: *Warwick (Induction); Padua;
the country near Verona]*

[INDUCTION]

Scene I. *[Outside rural alehouse.]*

Enter HOSTESS *and* BEGGAR, CHRISTOPHER
SLY.

   SLY. I'll pheeze° you, in faith.
   HOSTESS. A pair of stocks,° you rogue!

   SLY. Y'are a baggage, the Slys are no
rogues. Look in the chronicles: we came in
with Richard° Conqueror. Therefore,   5
paucas pallabris;° let the world slide.°
Sessa!°

Ind.i. ¹ **pheeze** do for (cf. *faze*) ² **stocks** (threatened punishment)

⁵ **Richard** (he means William) ⁶ **paucas pallabris** few words (Spanish *pocas palabras*) ⁶ **slide** go by (proverb; cf. Ind.ii.150) ⁷ **Sessa** scram (?), shut up (?)

HOSTESS. You will not pay for the glasses you have burst?

10 SLY. No, not a denier.° Go, by St. Jeronimy,° go to thy cold bed and warm thee.

HOSTESS. I know my remedy: I must go fetch the thirdborough.°   *[Exit.]*

15 SLY. Third or fourth or fifth borough, I'll answer him by law. I'll not budge an inch, boy;° let him come and kindly.°*Falls asleep.*

Wind° *horns. Enter a* LORD *from hunting, with his train.*

LORD. Huntsman, I charge thee, tender° well my hounds.
Broach° Merriman—the poor cur is embossed°—
And couple Clowder with the deep-
20 mouthed brach.°
Saw'st thou not, boy, how Silver made it good
At the hedge-corner in the coldest fault?°
I would not lose the dog for twenty pound.
FIRST HUNTSMAN. Why, Bellman is as good as he, my lord;
25 He cried upon it at the merest loss°
And twice today picked out the dullest scent
Trust me, I take him for the better dog.
LORD. Thou art a fool. If Echo were as fleet,
I would esteem him worth a dozen such.
30 But sup them well and look unto them all.
Tomorrow I intend to hunt again.
FIRST HUNTSMAN. I will, my lord.
LORD. What's here? One dead or drunk? See, doth he breathe?
SECOND HUNTSMAN. He breathes, my lord. Were he not warmed with ale,

This were a bed but cold to sleep so soundly.   35
LORD. O monstrous beast, how like a swine he lies!
Grim death, how foul and loathsome is thine image!
Sirs, I will practice on° this drunken man.
What think you, if he were conveyed to bed,
Wrapped in sweet clothes, rings put upon his fingers,   40
A most delicious banquet by his bed,
And brave° attendants near him when he wakes—
Would not the beggar then forget himself?
FIRST HUNTSMAN. Believe me, lord, I think he cannot choose.
SECOND HUNTSMAN. It would seem strange unto him when he waked.   45
LORD. Even as a flatt'ring dream or worthless fancy.
Then take him up and manage well the jest.
Carry him gently to my fairest chamber
And hang it round with all my wanton° pictures;
Balm° his foul head in warm distillèd wa-
ters   50
And burn sweet wood to make the lodging sweet.
Procure me music ready when he wakes
To make a dulcet° and a heavenly sound;
And if he chance to speak, be ready straight°
And with a low submissive reverence   55
Say, "What is it your honor will com-
mand?"
Let one attend him with a silver basin
Full of rose water and bestrewed with flowers;
Another bear the ewer, the third a diaper,°
And say, "Will't please your lordship cool your hands?"   60
Some one be ready with a costly suit

---

10 **denier** very small coin (cf. "a copper")
11 **Jeronimy** (Sly's oath inaccurately reflects a line in Kyd's *Spanish Tragedy*) 14 **thirdborough** constable 17 **boy** wretch 17 **kindly** by all means 17 s.d. **Wind** blow 18 **tender** look after 19 **Broach** bleed, i.e., medicate (some editors emend to *Breathe*) 19 **embossed** foaming at the mouth 20 **brach** hunting bitch 22 **fault** lost ("cold") scent 25 **cried . . . loss** gave cry despite complete loss (of scent)

---

38 **practice on** play a trick on 42 **brave** well dressed 49 **wanton** gay 50 **Balm** bathe 53 **dulcet** sweet 54 **straight** without delay 59 **diaper** towel

And ask him what apparel he will wear,
Another tell him of his hounds and horse
And that his lady mourns at his disease.
65 Persuade him that he hath been lunatic,
And when he says he is,° say that he
       dreams,
For he is nothing but a mighty lord.
This do, and do it kindly,° gentle sirs.
It will be pastime passing excellent
70 If it be husbanded with modesty.°
       FIRST HUNTSMAN. My lord, I warrant
          you we will play our part
As° he shall think by our true diligence
He is no less than what we say he is.
       LORD. Take him up gently and to bed
          with him,
And each one to his office° when he
75   wakes.   *[SLY is carried out.]*

Sound trumpets.

Sirrah,° go see what trumpet 'tis that
       sounds.   *[Exit SERVINGMAN.]*
Belike° some noble gentleman that means,
Traveling some journey, to repose him
       here.

Enter SERVINGMAN.

How now? Who is it?
       SERVINGMAN.   An't° please your
          honor, players
80 That offer service to your lordship.

Enter PLAYERS.

       LORD. Bid them come near. Now, fel-
          lows, you are welcome.
       PLAYERS. We thank your honor.
       LORD. Do you intend to stay with me to-
night?
85   A PLAYER. So please your lordship to accept our duty.°
       LORD. With all my heart. This fellow I
          remember

Since once he played a farmer's eldest
       son;
'Twas where you wooed the gentlewoman
       so well.
I have forgot your name, but sure that
       part   90
Was aptly fitted° and naturally performed.
       SECOND PLAYER. I think 'twas Soto° that
          your honor means.
       LORD. 'Tis very true; thou didst it excel-
lent.
Well, you are come to me in happy° time,
The rather for° I have some sport in hand   95
Wherein your cunning° can assist me
       much.
There is a lord will hear you play tonight.
But I am doubtful of your modesties,°
Lest over-eyeing° of his odd behavior—
For yet his honor never heard a play—   100
You break into some merry passion°
And so offend him, for I tell you, sirs,
If you should smile he grows impatient.
       A PLAYER. Fear not, my lord, we can
          contain ourselves
Were he the veriest antic° in the world.   105
       LORD. Go, sirrah, take them to the
          buttery°
And give them friendly welcome every
       one.
Let them want° nothing that my house
       affords.   *Exit one with the* PLAYERS.
Sirrah, go you to Barthol'mew my page
And see him dressed in all suits° like a
       lady.
That done, conduct him to the drunkard's   110
       chamber
And call him "madam"; do him obeisance.
Tell him from me—as he will° win my
       love—
He bear himself with honorable action

---

⁹¹ **aptly fitted** well suited (to you) ⁹² **Soto** (in
John Fletcher's *Women Pleased*, 1620; reference
possibly inserted here later) ⁹⁴ **in happy** at the
right ⁹⁵ **The rather for** especially because
⁹⁶ **cunning** talent ⁹⁸ **modesties** self-restraint
⁹⁹ **over-eyeing** seeing ¹⁰¹ **merry passion** fit of
merriment ¹⁰⁵ **antic** odd person ¹⁰⁶ **buttery** liquor pantry, bar ¹⁰⁸ **want** lack ¹¹⁰ **suits** respects
(with pun) ¹¹³ **as he will** if he wishes to

⁶⁶ **is** i.e., is "lunatic" now ⁶⁸ **kindly** naturally
⁷⁰ **husbanded with modesty** carried out with
moderation ⁷² **As** so that ⁷⁵ **office** assignment
⁷⁶ **Sirrah** (term of address used to inferiors)
⁷⁷ **Belike** likely ⁷⁹ **An't** if it ⁸⁶ **duty** respectful
greeting

115 Such as he hath observed in noble ladies
    Unto their lords, by them accomplishèd.°
    Such duty to the drunkard let him do
    With soft low tongue and lowly courtesy,
    And say, "What is't your honor will com-
        mand
120 Wherein your lady and your humble wife
    May show her duty and make known her
        love?"
    And then, with kind embracements,
        tempting kisses,
    And with declining head into his bosom,
    Bid him shed tears, as being overjoyed
125 To see her noble lord restored to health
    Who for this seven years hath esteemèd
        him
    No better than a poor and loathsome
        beggar.
    And if the boy have not a woman's gift
    To rain a shower of commanded tears,
130 An onion will do well for such a shift,°
    Which in a napkin° being close conveyed°
    Shall in despite° enforce a watery eye.
    See this dispatched with all the haste thou
        canst;
    Anon° I'll give thee more instructions.
                          Exit a SERVINGMAN.
135 I know the boy will well usurp° the grace,
    Voice, gait, and action of a gentlewoman.
    I long to hear him call the drunkard hus-
        band,
    And how my men will stay themselves
        from laughter
    When they do homage to this simple
        peasant.
    I'll in to counsel them; haply° my pres-
140   ence
    May well abate the over-merry spleen°
    Which otherwise would grow into ex-
        tremes.   *[Exeunt.]*

[Scene II. Bedroom in the Lord's house.]

Enter aloft° *the Drunkard* [SLY] *with*

ATTENDANTS—*some with apparel, basin and
ewer, and other appurtenances*—*and* LORD.

SLY. For God's sake, a pot of small° ale!
FIRST SERVINGMAN. Will't please your
lordship drink a cup of sack?°
SECOND SERVINGMAN. Will't please your
honor taste of these conserves?°   5
THIRD SERVINGMAN. What raiment will
your honor wear today?
SLY. I am Christophero Sly; call not me
"honor" nor "lordship." I ne'er drank sack
in my life, and if you give me any con-   10
serves, give me conserves of beef.° Ne'er
ask me what raiment I'll wear, for I have no
more doublets° than backs, no more stockings than legs nor no more shoes than
feet—nay, sometime more feet than shoes   15
or such shoes as my toes look through the
overleather.
LORD. Heaven cease this idle humor° in
    your honor!
O that a mighty man of such descent,
Of such possessions and so high esteem,   20
Should be infusèd with so foul a spirit!
SLY. What, would you make me mad? Am
not I Christopher Sly, old Sly's son of
Burton-heath,° by birth a peddler, by education a cardmaker,° by transmutation a   25
bearherd,° and now by present profession a
tinker? Ask Marian Hacket, the fat ale-wife
of Wincot,° if she know me not. If she say I
am not fourteen pence on the score° for
sheer ale,° score me up for the lying'st   30
knave in Christendom. What, I am not bestraught!° Here's—
THIRD SERVINGMAN. O, this it is that
    makes your lady mourn.

---

116 **by them accomplished** i.e., as carried out by the ladies ¹³⁰ **shift** purpose ¹³¹ **napkin** handkerchief ¹³¹ **close conveyed** secretly carried ¹³² **Shall in despite** can't fail to ¹³⁴ **Anon** then ¹³⁵ **usurp** take on ¹⁴⁰ **haply** perhaps ¹⁴¹ **spleen** spirit Ind.ii. ˢ·ᵈ· **aloft** (on balcony above stage at back)

¹ **small** thin, diluted (inexpensive) ³ **sack** imported sherry (costly) ⁵ **conserves** i.e., of fruit ¹¹ **conserves of beef** salt beef ¹³ **doublets** close-fitting jackets ¹⁸ **idle humor** unreasonable fantasy ²⁴ **Barton-heath** (probably Barton-on-the-Heath, south of Stratford) ²⁵ **cardmaker** maker of cards, or combs, for arranging wool fibers before spinning ²⁶ **bearherd** leader of a tame bear ²⁸ **Wincot** village near Stratford (some Hackets lived there) ²⁹ **score** charge account ³⁰ **sheer ale** ale alone (?), undiluted ale (?) ³¹·³² **bestraught** distraught, crazy

SECOND SERVINGMAN. O, this is it that
     makes your servants droop.
     LORD. Hence comes it that your kindred
35   shuns your house
     As beaten hence by your strange lunacy.
     O noble lord, bethink thee of thy birth,
     Call home thy ancient thoughts° from
          banishment
     And banish hence these abject lowly
          dreams.
40   Look how thy servants do attend on thee,
     Each in his office ready at thy beck.
     Wilt thou have music? Hark, Apollo°
          plays,   *(Music.)*
     And twenty cagèd nightingales do sing.
     Or wilt thou sleep? We'll have thee to a
          couch
45   Softer and sweeter than the lustful bed
     On purpose trimmed up for Semiramis.°
     Say thou wilt walk, we will bestrow° the
          ground.
     Or wilt thou ride? Thy horses shall be
          trapped,°
     Their harness studded all with gold and
          pearl.
     Dost thou love hawking? Thou hast hawks
50   will soar
     Above the morning lark. Or wilt thou
          hunt?
     Thy hounds shall make the welkin° answer
          them
     And fetch shrill echoes from the hollow
          earth.
     FIRST SERVINGMAN. Say thou wilt
          course,° thy greyhounds are as swift
     As breathèd° stags, ay, fleeter than the
55   roe.°
     SECOND SERVINGMAN. Dost thou love
          pictures? We will fetch thee straight
     Adonis° painted by a running brook
     And Cytherea all in sedges° hid,

Which seem to move and wanton° with her
     breath
Even as the waving sedges play with wind.   60
     LORD. We'll show thee Io° as she was a
          maid
And how she was beguilèd and surprised,
As lively° painted as the deed was done.
     THIRD SERVINGMAN. Or Daphne° roam-
          ing through a thorny wood,
Scratching her legs that one shall swear
     she bleeds,   65
And at that sight shall sad Apollo weep,
So workmanly the blood and tears are
     drawn.
     LORD. Thou art a lord and nothing but a
          lord.
Thou hast a lady far more beautiful
Than any woman in this waning° age.   70
     FIRST SERVINGMAN. And till the tears
          that she hath shed for thee
Like envious floods o'errun her lovely
     face,
She was the fairest creature in the world,
And yet° she is inferior to none.
     SLY. Am I a lord, and have I such a
          lady?   75
Or do I dream? Or have I dreamed till
     now?
I do not sleep: I see, I hear, I speak,
I smell sweet savors and I feel soft things.
Upon my life, I am a lord indeed
And not a tinker nor Christopher Sly.   80
Well, bring our lady hither to our sight,
And once again a pot o' th' smallest° ale.
     SECOND SERVINGMAN. Will't please your
          mightiness to wash your hands?
O, how we joy to see your wit° restored!
O, that once more you knew but what you
     are!   85
These fifteen years you have been in a
     dream,
Or when you waked so waked as if you
     slept.

---

³⁸ **ancient thoughts** original sanity ⁴² **Apollo**
here, god of music ⁴⁶ **Semiramis** mythical As-
syrian queen, noted for beauty and sexuality (cf.
Titus Andronicus, II.i.22, II.iii.118) ⁴⁷ **bestrow**
cover ⁴⁸ **trapped** decorated ⁵¹ **welkin** sky
⁵⁴ **course** hunt hares ⁵⁵ **breathèd** having good
wind ⁵⁵ **roe** small deer ⁵⁷ **Adonis** young hunter
loved by Venus (Cytherea) and killed by wild boar
⁵⁸ **sedges** grasslike plant growing in marshy
places

⁵⁹ **wanton** sway sinuously ⁶¹ **Io** mortal loved by
Zeus and changed into a heifer ⁶³ **lively** lifelike
⁶⁴ **Daphne** nymph loved by Apollo and changed
into laurel to evade him ⁷⁰ **waning** decadent
⁷⁴ **yet** now, still ⁸² **smallest** weakest ⁸⁴ **wit** mind

SLY. These fifteen years! By my fay,° a
   goodly nap.
But did I never speak of° all that time?
   FIRST SERVINGMAN. O yes, my lord, but
90   very idle words,
For though you lay here in this goodly
   chamber,
Yet would you say ye were beaten out of
   door
And rail upon the hostess of the house°
And say you would present her at the
   leet°
Because she brought stone jugs and no
95   sealed° quarts.
Sometimes you would call out for Cicely
   Hacket.
   SLY. Ay, the woman's maid of the house.
   THIRD SERVINGMAN. Why, sir, you know
   no house nor no such maid
Nor no such men as you have reckoned
   up,
As Stephen Sly° and old John Naps of
100   Greece,°
And Peter Turph and Henry Pimpernell,
And twenty more such names and men as
   these
Which never were nor no man ever saw.
   SLY. Now, Lord be thankèd for my good
   amends!°
105   ALL. Amen.

Enter [the PAGE, *as a] Lady, with* ATTEN-
DANTS.

   SLY. I thank thee; thou shalt not lose by
   it.
   PAGE. How fares my noble lord?
   SLY. Marry,° I fare well, for here is
   cheer enough. Where is my wife?
   PAGE. Here, noble lord. What is thy will
   with her?
   SLY. Are you my wife and will not call
110   me husband?

My men should call me "lord"; I am your
   goodman.°
   PAGE. My husband and my lord, my lord
   and husband,
I am your wife in all obedience.
   SLY. I know it well. What must I call
   her?
   LORD. Madam.   115
   SLY. Al'ce madam or Joan madam?
   LORD. Madam and nothing else. So
   lords call ladies.
   SLY. Madam wife, they say that I have
   dreamed
And slept above some fifteen year or
   more.
   PAGE. Ay, and the time seems thirty
   unto me,   120
Being all this time abandoned° from your
   bed.
   SLY. 'Tis much. Servants, leave me and
   her alone.
Madam, undress you and come now to
   bed.
   PAGE. Thrice noble lord, let me entreat
   of you
To pardon me yet for a night or two   125
Or, if not so, until the sun be set.
For your physicians have expressly
   charged,
In peril to incur° your former malady,
That I should yet absent me from your
   bed.
I hope this reason stands for my excuse.   130
   SLY. Ay, it stands so° that I may hardly
tarry so long, but I would be loath to fall
into my dreams again. I will therefore tarry
in despite of the flesh and the blood.

Enter a MESSENGER.

   MESSENGER. Your Honor's players,
   hearing your amendment,
Are come to play a pleasant comedy.   135
For so your doctors hold it very meet,

---

⁸⁸ **fay** faith ⁸⁹ **of** in ⁹³ **house** inn ⁹⁴ **present her
at the leet** accuse her at the court under lord of
a manor ⁹⁵ **sealed** marked by a seal guaranteeing
quantity ¹⁰⁰ **Stephen Sly** Stratford man (Naps,
etc., may also be names of real persons)
¹⁰⁰ **Greece** the Green (?) Greet, hamlet not far
from Stratford (?) ¹⁰⁴ **amends** recovery ¹⁰⁸ **Marry**
in truth (originally, [by St.] Mary)

---

¹¹¹ **goodman** husband ¹²¹ **abandoned** excluded
¹²⁸ **In peril to incur** because of the danger of a
return of ¹³¹ **stands so** will do (with phallic pun,
playing on "reason," which was pronounced
much like "raising")

Seeing too much sadness hath congealed
your blood,
And melancholy is the nurse of frenzy.°
Therefore they thought it good you hear a
140   play
And frame your mind to mirth and merriment,
Which bars a thousand harms and length-
ens life.
    SLY. Marry, I will let them play it. Is not a
comontie° a Christmas gambold° or a tum-
145 bling trick?
    PAGE. No, my good lord, it is more
pleasing stuff.
    SLY. What, household stuff?°
    PAGE. It is a kind of history.
    SLY. Well, we'll see't. Come, madam
wife, sit by my side
And let the world slip.° We shall ne'er be
150   younger.

[ACT I

Scene I. *Padua. A street.*]

Flourish.° Enter LUCENTIO *and his man*°
TRANIO.

    LUCENTIO. Tranio, since for the great
desire I had
To see fair Padua,° nursery of arts,
I am arrived for fruitful Lombardy,
The pleasant garden of great Italy,
And by my father's love and leave am
5   armed
With his good will and thy good company,
My trusty servant well approved° in all,
Here let us breathe and haply institute
A course of learning and ingenious° stud-
ies.
10 Pisa, renownèd for grave citizens,
Gave me my being and my father first,°

A merchant of great traffic° through the
world,
Vincentio, come of the Bentivolii.
Vincentio's son, brought up in Florence,
It shall become to serve° all hopes con-
ceived,   15
To deck his fortune with his virtuous
deeds;
And therefore, Tranio, for the time I
study,
Virtue and that part of philosophy
Will I apply° that treats of happiness
By virtue specially to be achieved.   20
Tell me thy mind, for I have Pisa left
And am to Padua come, as he that leaves
A shallow plash° to plunge him in the deep
And with satiety seeks to quench his
thirst.
    TRANIO. *Mi perdonato,*° gentle master
mine,   25
I am in all affected° as yourself,
Glad that you thus continue your resolve
To suck the sweets of sweet philosophy.
Only, good master, while we do admire
This virtue and this moral discipline,   30
Let's be no stoics nor no stocks,° I pray,
Or so devote° to Aristotle's checks°
As° Ovid° be an outcast quite abjured.
Balk logic° with acquaintance that you have
And practice rhetoric in your common
talk.   35
Music and poesy use to quicken° you.
The mathematics and the metaphysics,
Fall to them as you find your stomach°
serves you.
No profit grows where is no pleasure
ta'en.
In brief, sir, study what you most affect.° 40
    LUCENTIO. Gramercies,° Tranio, well
dost thou advise.

---

¹³⁹ **frenzy** mental illness ¹⁴⁴ **comontie** comedy (as pronounced by Sly) ¹⁴⁴ **gambold** gambol (game, dance, frolic) ¹⁴⁷ **stuff** (with sexual innuendo; see Eric Partridge, *Shakespeare's Bawdy*) ¹⁴³ **slip** go by I.i.ˢ·ᵈ· **Flourish** fanfare of trumpets ˢ·ᵈ· **man** servant ² **Padua** (noted for its university) ⁷ **approved** proved, found reliable ⁹ **ingenious** mind-training ¹¹ **first** i.e., before that

¹² **traffic** business ¹⁵ **serve** work for ¹⁹ **apply** apply myself to ²³ **plash** pool ²⁵ **Mi perdonato** pardon me ²⁶ **affected** inclined ³¹ **stocks** sticks (with pun on Stoics) ³² **devote** devoted ³² **checks** restraints ³³ **As** so that ³³ **Ovid** Roman love poet (cf. III.i.28–29, IV.ii.8) ³⁴ **Balk logic** engage in arguments ³⁶ **quicken** make alive ³⁸ **stomach** taste, preference ⁴⁰ **affect** like ⁴¹ **Gramercies** many thanks

If, Biondello, thou wert come ashore,
We could at once put us in readiness
And take a lodging fit to entertain
45　Such friends as time in Padua shall beget.
But stay awhile, what company is this?
　　TRANIO. Master, some show to welcome
　　　us to town.

Enter BAPTISTA *with his two daughters*, KATE
and BIANCA; GREMIO, *a pantaloon;*° *[and]*
HORTENSIO, *suitor to* BIANCA. LUCENTIO
[and] TRANIO *stand by.*°

　　BAPTISTA. Gentlemen, importune me no
　　　farther,
For how I firmly am resolved you know,
That is, not to bestow my youngest daugh-
50　　ter
Before I have a husband for the elder.
If either of you both love Katherina,
Because I know you well and love you
　　well,
Leave shall you have to court her at your
　　pleasure.
　　GREMIO. To cart° her rather. She's too
55　　rough for me.
There, there, Hortensio, will you any
　　wife?
　　KATE. I pray you, sir, is it your will
To make a stale° of me amongst these
　　mates?°
　　HORTENSIO. Mates, maid? How mean
　　　you that? No mates for you
60　Unless you were of gentler, milder mold.
　　KATE. I' faith, sir, you shall never need
　　　to fear:
Iwis° it° is not halfway to her° heart.
But if it were, doubt not her care should
　　be
To comb your noddle with a three-legged
　　stool

And paint° your face and use you like a
　　fool.　　　　　　　　　　　　　　　65
　　HORTENSIO. From all such devils, good
　　　Lord deliver us!
　　GREMIO. And me too, good Lord!
　　TRANIO *[aside]*. Husht, master, here's
　　　some good pastime toward.°
That wench is stark mad or wonderful
　　froward.°
　　LUCENTIO *[aside]*. But in the other's
　　　silence do I see　　　　　　　　　70
Maid's mild behavior and sobriety.
Peace, Tranio.
　　TRANIO *[aside]*. Well said, master. Mum,
　　　and gaze your fill.
　　BAPTISTA. Gentlemen, that I may soon
　　　make good
What I have said: Bianca, get you in,　　75
And let it not displease thee, good Bianca,
For I will love thee ne'er the less, my girl.
　　KATE. A pretty peat!° It is best
Put finger in the eye,° and° she knew why.
　　BIANCA. Sister, content you in my dis-
　　　content.　　　　　　　　　　　80
Sir, to your pleasure humbly I subscribe.
My books and instruments shall be my
　　company,
On them to look and practice by myself.
　　LUCENTIO *[aside]*. Hark, Tranio, thou
　　　mayst hear Minerva° speak.
　　HORTENSIO. Signior Baptista, will you be
　　　so strange?°　　　　　　　　　85
Sorry am I that our good will effects Bian-
　　ca's grief.
　　GREMIO.　Why will you mew° her up,
Signior Baptista, for this fiend of hell
And make her bear the penance of her
　　tongue?
　　BAPTISTA. Gentlemen, content ye. I am
　　　resolved.　　　　　　　　　　90
Go in, Bianca.　　　　　*[Exit* BIANCA.*]*
And for° I know she taketh most delight
In music, instruments, and poetry,

47 s.d. **pantaloon** laughable old man (a stock character with baggy pants, in Italian Renaissance
comedy) 47 s.d. **by** nearby 55 **cart** drive around in
an open cart (a punishment for prostitutes)
58 **stale** (1) laughingstock, (2) prostitute
58 **mates** low fellows (with pun on *stalemate* and
leading to pun on *mate* = husband) 62 **Iwis** certainly 62 **It** i.e., getting a mate 62 **her** Kate's

65 **paint** i.e., red with blood 68 **toward** coming up
69 **froward** willful 78 **peat** pet (cf. "teacher's
pet") 79 **Put finger in the eye** cry 79 **and** if
84 **Minerva** goddess of wisdom 85 **strange** rigid
87 **mew** cage (falconry term) 92 **for** because

Schoolmasters will I keep within my
   house,
Fit to instruct her youth. If you, Horten-
95   sio,
Or Signior Gremio, you, know any such,
Prefer° them hither; for to cunning° men
I will be very kind, and liberal
To mine own children in good bringing up.
100 And so, farewell. Katherina, you may stay,
For I have more to commune with° Bianca.   *Exit.*
   KATE. Why, and I trust I may go too,
    may I not?
What, shall I be appointed hours, as
   though, belike,°
I knew not what to take and what to
   leave? Ha!   *Exit.*
105 GREMIO. You may go to the devil's dam;°
your gifts are so good, here's none will hold
you. Their love is not so great,° Hortensio,
but we may blow our nails together° and
fast it fairly out. Our cake's dough on both
110 sides.° Farewell. Yet for the love I bear my
sweet Bianca, if I can by any means light on
a fit man to teach her that wherein she delights, I will wish° him to her father.
   HORTENSIO. So will I, Signior Gremio.
115 But a word, I pray. Though the nature of
our quarrel yet never brooked parle,° know
now, upon advice,° it toucheth° us both—
that we may yet again have access to our
fair mistress and be happy rivals in Bianca's
120 love—to labor and effect one thing specially.
   GREMIO. What's that, I pray?
   HORTENSIO. Marry, sir, to get a husband
for her sister.
125 GREMIO. A husband! A devil.
   HORTENSIO. I say, a husband.

   GREMIO. I say, a devil. Think'st thou,
Hortensio, though her father be very rich,
any man is so very° a fool to° be married to
hell?   130
   HORTENSIO. Tush, Gremio, though it
pass your patience and mine to endure her
loud alarums,° why, man, there be good fellows in the world, and° a man could light on
them, would take her with all faults, and 135
money enough.
   GREMIO. I cannot tell, but I had as lief°
take her dowry with this condition, to be
whipped at the high cross° every morning.
   HORTENSIO. Faith, as you say, there's 140
small choice in rotten apples. But come,
since this bar in law° makes us friends, it
shall be so far forth° friendly maintained, till
by helping Baptista's eldest daughter to a
husband, we set his youngest free for a 145
husband, and then have to't° afresh. Sweet
Bianca! Happy man be his dole!° He that
runs fastest gets the ring. How say you,
Signior Gremio?
   GREMIO. I am agreed, and would I had 150
given him the best horse in Padua to begin
his wooing, that° would thoroughly woo her,
wed her, and bed her and rid the house of
her. Come on.   *Exeunt ambo.*°
      Manet° TRANIO *and* LUCENTIO.

   TRANIO. I pray, sir, tell me, is it possible
That love should of a sudden take such   155
   hold?
   LUCENTIO. O Tranio, till I found it to be
   true
I never thought it possible or likely.
But see, while idly I stood looking on,

---

⁹⁷ **Prefer** recommend ⁹⁷ **cunning** talented
¹⁰¹ **commune with** communicate to ¹⁰³ **belike** it
seems likely ¹⁰⁵ **dam** mother (used of animals)
¹⁰⁷ **great** important ¹⁰⁸ **blow our nails together**
i.e., wait patiently ¹⁰⁹⁻¹¹⁰ **Our cake's dough on
both sides** we've both failed (proverbial)
¹¹³ **wish** commend ¹¹⁶ **brooked parle** allowed
negotiation ¹¹⁷ **advice** consideration ¹¹⁸ **toucheth**
concerns

¹²⁹ **very** thorough ¹²⁹ **to** as to ¹³³ **alarums** out-
cries ¹³⁴ **and** if ¹³⁷ **had as lief** would as willingly
¹³⁹ **high cross** market cross (prominent spot)
¹⁴² **bar in law** legal action of preventive sort
¹⁴³ **so far forth** so long ¹⁴⁶ **have to't** renew our
competition ¹⁴⁷ **Happy man be his dole** let being a happy man be his (the winner's) destiny
¹⁵² **that** (antecedent is *his*) ¹⁵⁴ ˢ·ᵈ· **ambo** both
¹⁵⁴ ˢ·ᵈ· **Manet** remain (though the Latin plural is
properly *manent*, the singular with a plural subject is common in Elizabethan texts)

160 I found the effect of love-in-idleness°
And now in plainness do confess to thee,
That art to me as secret° and as dear
As Anna° to the Queen of Carthage was,
Tranio, I burn, I pine, I perish, Tranio,
165 If I achieve not this young modest girl.
Counsel me, Tranio, for I know thou
    canst.
Assist me, Tranio, for I know thou wilt.
    TRANIO. Master, it is no time to chide
        you now.
Affection is not rated° from the heart.
If love have touched you, naught remains
170   but so,°
"Redime te captum, quam queas minimo."°
    LUCENTIO. Gramercies,° lad, go for-
        ward. This contents.
The rest will comfort, for thy counsel's
    sound.
    TRANIO. Master, you looked so longly°
        on the maid,
Perhaps you marked not what's the pith of
175   all.°
    LUCENTIO. O yes, I saw sweet beauty in
        her face,
Such as the daughter of Agenor° had,
That made great Jove to humble him to
    her hand
When with his knees he kissed the Cretan
    strond.°
    TRANIO. Saw you no more? Marked you
180   not how her sister
Began to scold and raise up such a storm
That mortal ears might hardly endure the
    din?

---

¹⁶⁰ **love-in-idleness** popular name for pansy
(believed to have mysterious power in love; cf.
Midsummer Night's Dream, II.i. 165 ff.) ¹⁶² **to
me as secret** as much in my confidence
¹⁶³ **Anna** sister and confidante of Queen Dido
¹⁶⁹ **rated** scolded ¹⁷⁰ **so** to act thus ¹⁷¹ **Redime
. . . minimo** ransom yourself, a captive, at the
smallest possible price (from Terence's play *The
Eunuch*, as quoted inaccurately in Lilly's *Latin
Grammar*) ¹⁷² **Gramercies** many thanks
¹⁷⁴ **longly** (1) longingly, (2) interminably ¹⁷⁵ **pith
of all** heart of the matter ¹⁷⁷ **daughter of
Agenor** Europa, loved by Jupiter, who, in the
form of a bull, carried her to Crete ¹⁷⁹ **strond**
strand, shore

    LUCENTIO. Tranio, I saw her coral lips
        to move
And with her breath she did perfume the
    air.
Sacred and sweet was all I saw in her.   185
    TRANIO. Nay, then, 'tis time to stir him
        from his trance.
I pray, awake, sir. If you love the maid,
Bend thoughts and wits to achieve her.
    Thus it stands:
Her elder sister is so curst and shrewd°
That till the father rid his hands of her,   190
Master, your love must live a maid at
    home;
And therefore has he closely mewed° her
    up,
Because° she will not be annoyed with
    suitors.
    LUCENTIO. Ah, Tranio, what a cruel
        father's he!
But art thou not advised° he took some
    care   195
To get her cunning° schoolmasters to
    instruct her?
    TRANIO. Ay, marry, am I, sir—and now
        'tis plotted!°
    LUCENTIO. I have it, Tranio!
    TRANIO.   Master, for°
        my hand,
Both our inventions° meet and jump in
    one.°
    LUCENTIO. Tell me thine first.
    TRANIO.   You will be
        schoolmaster   200
And undertake the teaching of the maid.
That's your device.
    LUCENTIO.   It is. May it be done?
    TRANIO. Not possible, for who shall
        bear° your part
And be in Padua here Vincentio's son?
Keep house and ply his book, welcome his
    friends,   205
Visit his countrymen and banquet them?

---

¹⁸⁹ **curst and shrewd** sharp-tempered and
shrewish ¹⁹² **mewed** caged ¹⁹³ **Because** so that
¹⁹⁵ **advised** informed ¹⁹⁶ **cunning** knowing
¹⁹⁷ **'tis plotted** I've a scheme ¹⁹⁸ **for** I bet ¹⁹⁹ **inventions** schemes ¹⁹⁹ **jump in one** are identical
²⁰³ **bear** act

LUCENTIO. *Basta,*° content thee, for I
    have it full.°
We have not yet been seen in any house,
Nor can we be distinguished by our faces
210 For man or master. Then it follows thus:
Thou shalt be master, Tranio, in my stead,
Keep house and port° and servants as I
    should.
I will some other be—some Florentine,
Some Neapolitan, or meaner° man of Pisa.
'Tis hatched and shall be so. Tranio, at
215   once
Uncase° thee, take my colored° hat and
    cloak.
When Biondello comes he waits on thee,
But I will charm° him first to keep his
    tongue.
    TRANIO. So had you need.
220 In brief, sir, sith° it your pleasure is
And I am tied° to be obedient—
For so your father charged me at our
    parting;
"Be serviceable to my son," quoth he,
Although I think 'twas in another sense—
225 I am content to be Lucentio
Because so well I love Lucentio.
    LUCENTIO. Tranio, be so, because Lu-
    centio loves,
And let me be a slave, t'achieve that maid
Whose sudden sight hath thralled° my
    wounded eye.

Enter BIONDELLO.

Here comes the rogue. Sirrah, where have
230   you been?
    BIONDELLO. Where have I been? Nay,
    how now, where are you?
Master, has my fellow Tranio stol'n your
    clothes,
Or you stol'n his, or both? Pray, what's
    the news?
    LUCENTIO. Sirrah, come hither. 'Tis no
    time to jest,

And therefore frame your manners to the
    time.°   235
Your fellow Tranio, here, to save my life,
Puts my apparel and my count'nance° on,
And I for my escape have put on his,
For in a quarrel since I came ashore
I killed a man and fear I was descried.°   240
Wait you on him, I charge you, as be-
    comes,
While I make way from hence to save my
    life.
You understand me?
    BIONDELLO.   I, sir? Ne'er a whit.
    LUCENTIO. And not a jot of Tranio in
    your mouth.
Tranio is changed into Lucentio.   245
    BIONDELLO. The better for him. Would I
    were so too.
    TRANIO. So could I, faith, boy, to have
    the next wish after,
That Lucentio indeed had Baptista's
    youngest daughter.
But sirrah, not for my sake but your mas-
    ter's, I advise
You use your manners discreetly in all kind
    of companies.   250
When I am alone, why, then I am Tranio,
But in all places else your master, Lucen-
    tio.
    LUCENTIO. Tranio, let's go.
One thing more rests,° that thyself
    execute°—
To make one among these wooers. If thou
    ask me why,   255
Sufficeth my reasons are both good and
    weighty.   *Exeunt.*

The Presenters° *above speaks.*

    FIRST SERVINGMAN. My lord, you nod;
    you do not mind° the play.
    SLY. Yes, by Saint Anne, do I. A good
    matter, surely.

---

²⁰⁷ **Basta** enough (Italian) ²⁰⁷ **full** fully (worked
out) ²¹² **port** style ²¹⁴ **meaner** of lower rank
²¹⁶ **Uncase** undress ²¹⁶ **colored** (masters
dressed colorfully; servants wore dark blue)
²¹⁸ **charm** exercise power over (he tells him a
fanciful tale, lines 234–243). ²²⁰ **sith** since
²²¹ **tied** obligated ²²⁹ **thralled** enslaved

²³⁵ **frame your manners to the time** adjust
your conduct to the situation ²³⁷ **count'nance**
demeanor ²⁴⁰ **descried** seen, recognized
²⁵⁴ **rests** remains ²⁵⁴ **execute** are to perform
²⁵⁶ ˢ·ᵈ· **Presenters** commentators, actors thought
of collectively, hence the singular verb ²⁵⁷ **mind**
pay attention to

Comes there any more of it?

260 PAGE. My lord, 'tis but begun.

SLY. 'Tis a very excellent piece of work,
      madam lady.

Would 'twere done!   *They sit and mark.*°

[**Scene II.** *Padua. The street in front of*
HORTENSIO's *house.]*

Enter PETRUCHIO° *and his man* GRUMIO.

PETRUCHIO. Verona, for a while I take
      my leave

To see my friends in Padua, but of all

My best belovèd and approvèd friend,

Hortensio, and I trow° this is his house.

5   Here, sirrah Grumio, knock, I say.

GRUMIO. Knock, sir? Whom should I
knock? Is there any man has rebused° your
worship?

PETRUCHIO. Villain, I say, knock me
      here° soundly.

10   GRUMIO. Knock you here, sir? Why, sir,
what am I, sir, that I should knock you
here, sir?

PETRUCHIO. Villain, I say, knock me at
      this gate°

And rap me well or I'll knock your knave's
      pate.°

GRUMIO. My master is grown quarrel-

15   some. I should knock you first,

And then I know after who comes by the
      worst.

PETRUCHIO. Will it not be?

Faith, sirrah, and° you'll not knock, I'll
      ring° it;

I'll try how you can *sol, fa,*° and sing it.

He wrings him by the ears.

GRUMIO. Help, masters, help! My mas-   20
ter is mad.

PETRUCHIO. Now, knock when I bid you,
sirrah villain.

Enter HORTENSIO.

HORTENSIO. How now, what's the matter? My old friend Grumio, and my good   25
friend Petruchio! How do you all at Verona?

PETRUCHIO. Signior Hortensio, come
      you to part the fray?

Con tutto il cuore ben trovato,° may I say.

HORTENSIO. *Alla nostra casa ben venuto,*
molto honorato signior mio Petruchio.°   30

Rise, Grumio, rise. We will compound°
      this quarrel.

GRUMIO. Nay, 'tis no matter, sir, what he
'leges° in Latin.° If this be not a lawful
cause for me to leave his service—look
you, sir, he bid me knock him and rap him   35
soundly, sir. Well, was it fit for a servant to
use his master so, being perhaps, for aught
I see, two-and-thirty, a peep out?°

Whom would to God I had well knocked at
      first,

Then had not Grumio come by the worst.   40

PETRUCHIO. A senseless villain! Good
      Hortensio,

I bade the rascal knock upon your gate

And could not get him for my heart° to do
      it.

GRUMIO. Knock at the gate? O heavens!

Spake you not these words plain, "Sirrah,   45
knock me here, rap me here, knock me
well, and knock me soundly"? And come
you now with "knocking at the gate"?

PETRUCHIO. Sirrah, be gone or talk not,
      I advise you.

---

²⁶² ˢ·ᵈ· **mark** observe   I.ii. ˢ·ᵈ· **Petruchio** (correct
form *Petrucio*, with *c* pronounced *tch*) ⁴ **trow**
think ⁷ **rebused** (Grumio means *abused*)
⁹ **knock me here** knock here for me (Grumio
plays game of misunderstanding, taking "me
here" as "my ear") ¹³ **gate** door ¹⁴ **pate** head
¹⁸ **and if** ¹⁸ **ring** (pun on *wring*) ¹⁹ **sol, fa** go up
and down the scales (possibly with puns on
meanings now lost)

²⁸ **Con . . . trovato** with all [my] heart well
found (i.e., welcome) ²⁹·³⁰ **Alla . . . Petruchio**
welcome to our house, my much honored Signor
Petruchio ³¹ **compound** settle ³³ **'leges** alleges
³³ **Latin** (as if he were English, Grumio does not
recognize Italian) ³⁸ **two-and-thirty, a peep
out** (1) an implication that Petruchio is aged, (2)
a term from cards, slang for "drunk" (*peep* is an
old form of *pip*, a marking on a card) ⁴³ **heart** life

HORTENSIO. Petruchio, patience, I am
Grumio's pledge.
50
Why, this's a heavy chance° 'twixt him and
you,
Your ancient, trusty, pleasant servant
Grumio.
And tell me now, sweet friend, what
happy gale
Blows you to Padua here from old Verona?
PETRUCHIO. Such wind as scatters
young men through the world
55
To seek their fortunes farther than at
home,
Where small experience grows. But in a
few,°
Signior Hortensio, thus it stands with
me:
Antonio my father is deceased,
60
And I have thrust myself into this maze,°
Happily° to wive and thrive as best I may.
Crowns in my purse I have and goods at
home
And so am come abroad to see the world.
HORTENSIO. Petruchio, shall I then come
roundly° to thee
And wish thee to a shrewd ill-favored°
65
wife?
Thou'ldst thank me but a little for my
counsel—
And yet I'll promise thee she shall be
rich,
And very rich—but thou'rt too much my
friend,
And I'll not wish thee to her.
PETRUCHIO. Signior Hortensio, 'twixt
70
such friends as we
Few words suffice; and therefore if thou
know
One rich enough to be Petruchio's wife—
As wealth is burthen° of my wooing
dance—

Be she as foul° as was Florentius'° love,
As old as Sibyl,° and as curst and shrewd   75
As Socrates' Xanthippe° or a worse,
She moves me not, or not removes, at
least,
Affection's edge in me, were she as rough
As are the swelling Adriatic seas.
I come to wive it wealthily in Padua;   80
If wealthily, then happily in Padua.
GRUMIO. Nay, look you, sir, he tells you
flatly what his mind is. Why, give him gold
enough and marry him to a puppet or an
aglet-baby° or an old trot° with ne'er a   85
tooth in her head, though she have as many
diseases as two-and-fifty horses. Why,
nothing comes amiss so money comes
withal.°
HORTENSIO. Petruchio, since we are
stepped thus far in,   90
I will continue that° I broached in jest.
I can, Petruchio, help thee to a wife
With wealth enough and young and beauteous,
Brought up as best becomes a gentlewoman.
Her only fault—and that is faults enough—   95
Is that she is intolerable curst°
And shrewd and froward,° so beyond all
measure
That were my state° far worser than it is,
I would not wed her for a mine of gold.
PETRUCHIO. Hortensio, peace. Thou
know'st not gold's effect.   100
Tell me her father's name, and 'tis
enough,
For I will board° her though she chide as
loud

---

⁷⁴ **foul** homely ⁷⁴ **Florentius** knight in Gower's
Confessio Amantis (cf. Chaucer's Wife of Bath's
Tale: knight marries hag who turns into beautiful
girl) ⁷⁵ **Sibyl** prophetess in Greek and Roman
myth ⁷⁶ **Xanthippe** Socrates' wife, legendarily
shrewish ⁸⁵ **aglet-baby** small female figure forming metal tip of cord or lace (French *aiguillette*,
point) ⁸⁵ **trot** hag ⁸⁹ **withal** with it ⁹¹ **that** what
⁹⁶ **intolerable curst** intolerably sharp-tempered
⁹⁷ **froward** willful ⁹⁸ **state** estate, revenue
¹⁰² **board** naval term, with double sense: (1) ac-
cost, (2) go on board

⁵¹ **heavy chance** sad happening ⁵⁷ **few** i.e.,
words ⁶⁰ **maze** traveling; uncertain course
⁶¹ **Happily** haply, perchance ⁶⁴ **come roundly**
talk frankly ⁶⁵ **shrewd ill-favored** shrewish,
poorly qualified ⁷³ **burthen** burden (music ac-
companiment)

As thunder when the clouds in autumn
   crack.°
  HORTENSIO. Her father is Baptista
  Minola,
105 An affable and courteous gentleman.
Her name is Katherina Minola,
Renowned in Padua for her scolding
   tongue.
  PETRUCHIO. I know her father though I
  know not her,
And he knew my deceasèd father well.
110 I will not sleep, Hortensio, till I see her,
And therefore let me be thus bold with
   you,
To give you over° at this first encounter
Unless you will accompany me thither.
  GRUMIO. I pray you, sir, let him go while
115 the humor° lasts. A° my word, and° she
knew him as well as I do, she would think
scolding would do little good° upon him.
She may perhaps call him half a score
knaves or so—why, that's nothing. And he
120 begin once, he'll rail in his rope-tricks.° I'll
tell you what, sir, and she stand° him but a
little, he will throw a figure in her face and
so disfigure her with it that she shall have
no more eyes to see withal than a cat. You
125 know him not, sir.
  HORTENSIO. Tarry, Petruchio, I must go
  with thee,
For in Baptista's keep° my treasure is.
He hath the jewel of my life in hold,°
His youngest daughter, beautiful Bianca,
And her withholds from me and other
130   more,
Suitors to her and rivals in my love,
Supposing it a thing impossible,
For° those defects I have before re-
  hearsed,
That ever Katherina will be wooed.

Therefore this order° hath Baptista ta'en, 135
That none shall have access unto Bianca
Till Katherine the curst have got a hus-
  band.
  GRUMIO. Katherine the curst!
A title for a maid of all titles the worst.
  HORTENSIO. Now shall my friend Petru-
  chio do me grace° 140
And offer° me, disguised in sober robes,
To old Baptista as a schoolmaster
Well seen° in music, to instruct Bianca,
That so I may, by this device, at least
Have leave and leisure to make love to her 145
And unsuspected court her by herself.

Enter GREMIO, *and* LUCENTIO *disguised [as
a schoolmaster, Cambio].*

  GRUMIO. Here's no knavery! See, to beguile the old folks, how the young folks lay
their heads together! Master, master, look
about you. Who goes there, ha? 150
  HORTENSIO. Peace, Grumio. It is the
  rival of my love.
Petruchio, stand by awhile.

[They eavesdrop.]

  GRUMIO. A proper stripling,° and an
  amorous!
  GREMIO. O, very well, I have perused
  the note.°
Hark you, sir, I'll have them very fairly 155
  bound—
All books of love, see that at any hand,°
And see you read no other lectures° to
  her.
You understand me. Over and beside
Signior Baptista's liberality,
I'll mend it with a largess.° Take your 160
  paper° too
And let me have them° very well per-
  fumed,

---

103 crack make explosive roars **112 give you over** leave you **115 humor** mood **115 A** on **115 and** if (also at lines 119 and 121) **117 do little good** have little effect **120 rope-tricks** (1) Grumio's version of *rhetoric* going with *figure* just below, (2) rascally conduct, deserving hanging, (3) possible sexual innuendo, as in following lines **121 stand** withstand **127 keep** heavily fortified inner tower of castle **128 hold** stronghold **133 For** because of

135 order step **140 grace** a favor **141 offer** present, introduce **143 seen** trained **153 proper stripling** handsome youth (sarcastic comment on Gremio) **154 note** memorandum (reading list for Bianca) **156 at any hand** in any case **157 read no other lectures** assign no other readings **160 mend it with a largess** add a gift of money to it **160 paper** note (line 154) **161 them** i.e., the books

For she is sweeter than perfume itself
To whom they go to. What will you read
    to her?
    LUCENTIO. Whate'er I read to her, I'll
    plead for you
165 As for my patron, stand you so assured,
As firmly as° yourself were still in place°—
Yea, and perhaps with more successful
    words
Than you unless you were a scholar, sir.
    GREMIO. O this learning, what a thing it
    is!
    GRUMIO *[aside].* O this woodcock,° what
170   an ass it is!
    PETRUCHIO. Peace, sirrah!
    HORTENSIO. Grumio, mum! *[Coming*
    forward.] God save you, Signior Gre-
    mio.
    GREMIO. And you are well met, Signior
    Hortensio.
Trow° you whither I am going? To Baptista
    Minola.
175 I promised to inquire carefully
About a schoolmaster for the fair Bianca,
And, by good fortune, I have lighted well
On this young man—for° learning and
    behavior
Fit for her turn,° well read in poetry
180 And other books, good ones I warrant ye.
    HORTENSIO. 'Tis well. And I have met a
    gentleman
Hath promised me to help me to° another,
A fine musician to instruct our mistress.
So shall I no whit be behind in duty
185 To fair Bianca, so beloved of me.
    GREMIO. Beloved of me, and that my
    deeds shall prove.
    GRUMIO *[aside].* And that his bags° shall
    prove.
    HORTENSIO. Gremio, 'tis now no time to
    vent° our love.
Listen to me, and if you speak me fair,

I'll tell you news indifferent° good for
    either.   190
Here is a gentleman whom by chance I
    met,
Upon agreement from us to his liking,°
Will undertake° to woo curst Katherine,
Yea, and to marry her if her dowry please.
    GREMIO. So said, so done, is well.   195
Hortensio, have you told him all her faults?
    PETRUCHIO. I know she is an irksome,
    brawling scold;
If that be all, masters, I hear no harm.
    GREMIO. No, say'st me so, friend? What
    countryman?
    PETRUCHIO. Born in Verona, old Anto-
    nio's son.   200
My father dead, my fortune lives for me,
And I do hope good days and long to see.
    GREMIO. O, sir, such a life with such a
    wife were strange.
But if you have a stomach,° to't a° God's
    name;
You shall have me assisting you in all.   205
But will you woo this wildcat?
    PETRUCHIO.   Will I live?
    GRUMIO *[aside].* Will he woo her? Ay, or
    I'll hang her.
    PETRUCHIO. Why came I hither but to
    that intent?
Think you a little din can daunt mine ears?
Have I not in my time heard lions roar?   210
Have I not heard the sea, puffed up with
    winds,
Rage like an angry boar chafèd with
    sweat?
Have I not heard great ordnance° in the
    field
And heaven's artillery thunder in the
    skies?
Have I not in a pitchèd battle heard   215
Loud 'larums,° neighing steeds, and trum-
    pets' clang?
And do you tell me of a woman's tongue,
That gives not half so great a blow to hear

---

166 **as** as if you   166 **in place** present   170 **woodcock**
bird easily trapped, so considered silly   174 **Trow**
know   178 **for** in   179 **turn** situation (with unconscious bawdy pun on the sense of "copulation")
182 **help me to** (1) find, (2) become (Hortensio's
jest)   187 **bags** i.e., of money   188 **vent** express

190 **indifferent** equally   192 **Upon . . . liking** if we
agree to his terms (paying costs)   193 **undertake**
promise   204 **stomach** inclination   204 **a** in   213 **ord-**
nance cannon   216 **'larums** calls to arms, sudden
attacks

As will a chestnut in a farmer's fire?
Tush, tush, fear° boys with bugs.°
220   GRUMIO *[aside].*   For he fears none.
GREMIO. Hortensio, hark.
This gentleman is happily arrived,
My mind presumes, for his own good and
    ours.
    HORTENSIO. I promised we would be
    contributors
And bear his charge of° wooing, what-
225   soe'er.
    GREMIO. And so we will, provided that
    he win her.
    GRUMIO *[aside].* I would I were as sure
    of a good dinner.

Enter TRANIO *brave*° *[as Lucentio] and*
BIONDELLO.

    TRANIO. Gentlemen, God save you. If I
    may be bold,
Tell me, I beseech you, which is the readi-
    est way
230   To the house of Signior Baptista Minola?
    BIONDELLO. He that has the two fair
    daughters? Is't he you mean?
    TRANIO. Even he, Biondello.
    GREMIO. Hark you, sir. You mean not
    her to—
    TRANIO. Perhaps, him and her, sir. What
    have you to do?°
    PETRUCHIO. Not her that chides, sir, at
235   any hand,° I pray.
    TRANIO. I love no chiders, sir. Bion-
    dello, let's away.
    LUCENTIO *[aside].* Well begun, Tranio.
    HORTENSIO.   Sir,
    a word ere you go.
Are you a suitor to the maid you talk of,
    yea or no?
    TRANIO. And if I be, sir, is it any of-
    fense?
    GREMIO. No, if without more words you
240   will get you hence.
    TRANIO. Why, sir, I pray, are not the
    streets as free
For me as for you?

GREMIO.   But so is not she.
TRANIO. For what reason, I beseech
    you?
GREMIO. For this reason, if you'll know,
That she's the choice° love of Signior
    Gremio.   245
    HORTENSIO. That she's the chosen of
    Signior Hortensio.
    TRANIO. Softly, my masters! If you be
    gentlemen,
Do me this right: hear me with patience.
Baptista is a noble gentleman
To whom my father is not all unknown,   250
And were his daughter fairer than she is,
She may more suitors have, and me for
    one.
Fair Leda's daughter° had a thousand
    wooers;
Then well one more may fair Bianca have.
And so she shall. Lucentio shall make
    one,   255
Though Paris° came° in hope to speed°
    alone.
    GREMIO. What, this gentleman will out-
    talk us all.
    LUCENTIO. Sir, give him head. I know
    he'll prove a jade.°
    PETRUCHIO. Hortensio, to what end are
    all these words?
    HORTENSIO. Sir, let me be so bold as
    ask you,   260
Did you yet ever see Baptista's daughter?
    TRANIO. No, sir, but hear I do that he
    hath two,
The one as famous for a scolding tongue
As is the other for beauteous modesty.
    PETRUCHIO. Sir, sir, the first's for me;
    let her go by.   265
    GREMIO. Yea, leave that labor to great
    Hercules,
And let it be more than Alcides'° twelve.
    PETRUCHIO. Sir, understand you this of
    me in sooth:°

---

²⁴⁵ **choice** chosen ²⁵³ **Leda's daughter** Helen of
Troy ²⁵⁶ **Paris** lover who took Helen to Troy (legendary cause of Trojan War) ²⁵⁶ **came** should
come ²⁵⁶ **speed** succeed ²⁵⁸ **prove a jade** soon
tire (cf. "jaded") ²⁶⁷ **Alcides** Hercules (after Al-
caeus, a family ancestor) ²⁶⁸ **sooth** truth

---

²²⁰ **fear** frighten ²²⁰ **bugs** bugbears ²²⁵ **his charge
of** the cost of his ²²⁷ ˢ·ᵈ· **brave** elegantly attired
²³⁴ **to do** i.e., to do with this ²³⁵ **at any hand** in
any case

The youngest daughter, whom you
hearken° for,
270 Her father keeps from all access of suitors
And will not promise her to any man
Until the elder sister first be wed.
The younger then is free, and not before.
   TRANIO. If it be so, sir, that you are the
man
Must stead° us all, and me amongst the
275   rest,
And if you break the ice and do this feat,
Achieve° the elder, set the younger free
For our access, whose hap° shall be to
have her
Will not so graceless be to be ingrate.°
   HORTENSIO. Sir, you say well, and well
280   you do conceive,°
And since you do profess to be a suitor,
You must, as we do, gratify° this gentle-
man
To whom we all rest° generally beholding.°
   TRANIO. Sir, I shall not be slack, in sign
whereof,
285 Please ye we may contrive° this afternoon
And quaff carouses° to our mistress'
health
And do as adversaries° do in law,
Strive mightily but eat and drink as
friends.
   GRUMIO, BIONDELLO. O excellent motion!
Fellows, let's be gone.
   HORTENSIO. The motion's good indeed,
290   and be it so.
Petruchio, I shall be your *ben venuto.*°
                              Exeunt.

[ACT II

Scene I. In BAPTISTA*'s house.]*

Enter KATE *and* BIANCA *[with her hands
tied].*

   BIANCA. Good sister, wrong me not nor
wrong yourself

²⁶⁹ **hearken** long ²⁷⁵ **stead** aid ²⁷⁷ **Achieve** suc-
ceed with ²⁷⁸ **whose hap** the man whose luck
²⁷⁹ **to be ingrate** as to be ungrateful ²⁸⁰ **con-
ceive** put the case ²⁸² **gratify** compensate
²⁸³ **rest** remain ²⁸³ **beholding** indebted ²⁸⁵ **con-
trive** pass ²⁸⁶ **quaff carouses** empty our cups
²⁸⁷ **adversaries** attorneys ²⁹¹ **ben venuto** wel-
come (i.e., host)

To make a bondmaid and a slave of me.
That I disdain. But for these other
gawds,°
Unbind my hands, I'll pull them off myself,
Yea, all my raiment, to my petticoat,   5
Or what you will command me will I do,
So well I know my duty to my elders.
   KATE. Of all thy suitors, here I charge
thee, tell
Whom thou lov'st best. See thou dissem-
ble not.
   BIANCA. Believe me, sister, of all the
men alive   10
I never yet beheld that special face
Which I could fancy more than any other.
   KATE. Minion,° thou liest. Is't not Hor-
tensio?
   BIANCA. If you affect° him, sister, here I
swear
I'll plead for you myself but you shall have
him.   15
   KATE. O then, belike,° you fancy riches
more:
You will have Gremio to keep you fair.°
   BIANCA. Is it for him you do envy° me
so?
Nay, then you jest, and now I well per-
ceive
You have but jested with me all this while. 20
I prithee, sister Kate, untie my hands.
   KATE. If that be jest then all the rest
was so.   *Strikes her.*

Enter BAPTISTA.

   BAPTISTA. Why, how now, dame, whence
grows this insolence?
Bianca, stand aside. Poor girl, she weeps.
Go ply thy needle; meddle not with her.   25
For shame, thou hilding° of a devilish
spirit,
Why dost thou wrong her that did ne'er
wrong thee?
When did she cross thee with a bitter
word?

II.i.³ **gawds** adornments ¹³ **Minion** impudent
creature ¹⁴ **affect** like ¹⁶ **belike** probably ¹⁷ **fair
in fine** clothes ¹⁸ **envy** hate ²⁶ **hilding** base
wretch

KATE. Her silence flouts me and I'll be
   revenged.   *Flies after* BIANCA.
BAPTISTA. What, in my sight? Bianca,
30   get thee in.   *Exit [*BIANCA*].*
KATE. What, will you not suffer° me?
   Nay, now I see
She is your treasure, she must have a
   husband;
I must dance barefoot on her wedding
   day,°
And, for your love to her, lead apes in
   hell.°
35   Talk not to me; I will go sit and weep
Till I can find occasion of revenge.   *[Exit.]*
BAPTISTA. Was ever gentleman thus
   grieved as I?
But who comes here?

Enter GREMIO, LUCENTIO *in the habit of a
mean° man [Cambio],* PETRUCHIO, *with
[*HORTENSIO *as a music teacher, Litio, and]*
TRANIO *[as Lucentio], with his boy [*BION-
DELLO*] bearing a lute and books.*

   GREMIO. Good morrow, neighbor Bap-
tista.
40   BAPTISTA. Good morrow, neighbor Gre-
mio. God save you, gentlemen.
   PETRUCHIO. And you, good sir. Pray,
   have you not a daughter
Called Katherina, fair and virtuous?
   BAPTISTA. I have a daughter, sir, called
   Katherina.
   GREMIO *[aside].* You are too blunt; go to
45   it orderly.°
   PETRUCHIO *[aside].* You wrong me,
   Signior Gremio, give me leave.
[To BAPTISTA.*]* I am a gentleman of Verona,
   sir,
That, hearing of her beauty and her wit,
Her affability and bashful modesty,
50   Her wondrous qualities and mild behavior,
Am bold to show myself a forward° guest

Within your house, to make mine eye the
   witness
Of that report which I so oft have heard.
And, for an entrance to° my entertain-
   ment,°
I do present you with a man of mine,   55
[presenting HORTENSIO*]*
Cunning in music and the mathematics,
To instruct her fully in those sciences,
Whereof I know she is not ignorant.
Accept of him, or else you do me wrong.
His name is Litio, born in Mantua.   60
   BAPTISTA. Y'are welcome, sir, and he for
   your good sake.
But for my daughter Katherine, this I
   know,
She is not for your turn,° the more my
   grief.
   PETRUCHIO. I see you do not mean to
   part with her,
Or else you like not of my company.   65
   BAPTISTA. Mistake me not; I speak but
   as I find.
Whence are you, sir? What may I call your
   name?
   PETRUCHIO. Petruchio is my name,
   Antonio's son,
A man well known throughout all Italy.
   BAPTISTA. I know him well. You are
   welcome for his sake.   70
   GREMIO. Saving° your tale, Petruchio, I
   pray,
Let us, that are poor petitioners, speak
   too.
Backare,° you are marvelous° forward.
   PETRUCHIO. O pardon me, Signior Gre-
   mio, I would fain° be doing.°
   GREMIO. I doubt it not, sir, but you will
   curse your wooing.   75
Neighbor, this is a gift very grateful,° I am
sure of it. To express the like kindness my-
self, that° have been more kindly beholding

---

[31] **suffer** permit (i.e., to deal with you) [33] **dance
. . . day** (expected of older maiden sisters)
[34] **lead apes in bell** (proverbial occupation of old
maids; cf. *Much Ado About Nothing* , II.i.41) [38 s.d.]
mean lower class [45] **orderly** gradually [51] **forward** eager

[54] **entrance to** price of admission for [54] **entertainment** reception [63] **turn** purpose (again, with
bawdy pun) [71] **Saving** with all respect for
[73] **Backare** back (proverbial quasi-Latin) [73] **marvelous** very [74] **would fain** am eager to [74] **doing**
(with a sexual jest) [76] **grateful** worthy of gratitude [77-78] **myself, that** I myself, who

to you than any, freely give unto you this
80 young scholar *[presenting* LUCENTIO*]* that
hath been long studying at Rheims—as
cunning in Greek, Latin, and other languages, as the other in music and mathematics. His name is Cambio.° Pray accept
85 his service.
 BAPTISTA. A thousand thanks, Signior
Gremio. Welcome, good Cambio. *[To* TRA-
NIO.*]* But, gentle sir, methinks you walk
like° a stranger. May I be so bold to know
90 the cause of your coming?
 TRANIO. Pardon me, sir, the boldness is
  mine own,
That,° being a stranger in this city here,
Do make myself a suitor to your daughter,
Unto Bianca, fair and virtuous.
95 Nor is your firm resolve unknown to me
In the preferment of° the eldest sister.
This liberty is all that I request,
That, upon knowledge of my parentage,
I may have welcome 'mongst the rest that
  woo
100 And free access and favor° as the rest.
And, toward the education of your daugh-
  ters
I here bestow a simple instrument,°
And this small packet of Greek and Latin
  books.
If you accept them, then their worth is
  great.
 BAPTISTA *[looking at books].* Lucentio is
105   your name. Of whence, I pray?
 TRANIO. Of Pisa, sir, son to Vincentio.
 BAPTISTA. A mighty man of Pisa; by
  report
I know him° well. You are very welcome,
  sir.
[To HORTENSIO.*]* Take you the lute, *[to*
  LUCENTIO*]* and you the set of books;
110 You shall go see your pupils presently.°
Holla, within!

Enter a SERVANT.

   Sirrah, lead these gentlemen
To my daughters and tell them both
These are their tutors; bid them use them
  well. *[Exit* SERVANT, *with* LUCENTIO,
     HORTENSIO, *and* BIONDELLO
        following.]
We will go walk a little in the orchard°
And then to dinner. You are passing° wel-
  come,   115
And so I pray you all to think yourselves.
 PETRUCHIO. Signior Baptista, my busi-
  ness asketh haste,
And every day I cannot come to woo.
You knew my father well, and in him me,
Left solely heir to all his lands and goods, 120
Which I have bettered rather than de-
  creased.
Then tell me, if I get your daughter's love
What dowry shall I have with her to wife?
 BAPTISTA. After my death the one half of
  my lands,
And in possession° twenty thousand
  crowns.   125
 PETRUCHIO. And, for that dowry, I'll
  assure her of
Her widowhood,° be it that she survive
  me,
In all my lands and leases whatsoever.
Let specialties° be therefore drawn be-
  tween us
That covenants may be kept on either
  hand.   130
 BAPTISTA. Ay, when the special thing is
  well obtained,
That is, her love, for that is all in all.
 PETRUCHIO. Why, that is nothing, for I
  tell you, father,
I am as peremptory° as she proud-
  minded.
And where two raging fires meet together 135

---

⁸⁴ **Cambio** (Italian for "exchange") ⁸⁸⁻⁸⁹ **walk like** have the bearing of ⁹² **That** who ⁹⁶ **preferment of** giving priority to ¹⁰⁰ **favor** countenance, acceptance ¹⁰² **instrument** i.e., the lute ¹⁰⁸ **him** his name ¹¹⁰ **presently** at once   ¹¹⁴ **orchard** garden ¹¹⁵ **passing** very ¹²⁵ **possession** i.e., at the time of marriage ¹²⁷ **widowhood** estate settled on a widow (Johnson) ¹²⁹ **specialties** special contracts ¹³⁴ **peremptory** resolved

They do consume the thing that feeds
  their fury.
Though little fire grows great with little
  wind,
Yet extreme gusts will blow out fire and
  all.
So I to her, and so she yields to me,
140 For I am rough and woo not like a babe.
  BAPTISTA. Well mayst thou woo, and
    happy be thy speed!°
But be thou armed for some unhappy
  words.
  PETRUCHIO. Ay, to the proof,° as moun-
    tains are for winds
That shakes not, though they blow perpet-
  ually.

Enter HORTENSIO *with his head broke.*

  BAPTISTA. How now, my friend, why
145   dost thou look so pale?
  HORTENSIO. For fear, I promise you, if I
    look pale.
  BAPTISTA. What, will my daughter prove
    a good musician?
  HORTENSIO. I think she'll sooner prove a
    soldier.
Iron may hold with her,° but never lutes.
  BAPTISTA. Why, then thou canst not
150   break° her to the lute?
  HORTENSIO. Why, no, for she hath broke
    the lute to me.
I did but tell her she mistook her frets°
And bowed° her hand to teach her finger-
  ing,
When, with a most impatient devilish
  spirit,
"Frets, call you these?" quoth she; "I'll
155   fume with them."
And with that word she stroke° me on the
  head,
And through the instrument my pate made
  way.
And there I stood amazèd for a while
As on a pillory,° looking through the lute,

While she did call me rascal, fiddler,   160
And twangling Jack,° with twenty such vile
  terms
As° had she studied° to misuse me so.
  PETRUCHIO. Now, by the world, it is a
    lusty° wench!
I love her ten times more than e'er I did.
O how I long to have some chat with her! 165
  BAPTISTA. *[To* HORTENSIO.*]* Well, go with
    me, and be not so discomfited.
Proceed in practice° with my younger
  daughter;
She's apt° to learn and thankful for good
  turns.
Signior Petruchio, will you go with us
Or shall I send my daughter Kate to you? 170
    *Exit [*BAPTISTA, *with* GREMIO, TRANIO,
      and HORTENSIO*]. Manet Petruchio.*°
  PETRUCHIO. I pray you do. I'll attend°
    her here
And woo her with some spirit when she
  comes.
Say that she rail,° why then I'll tell her
  plain
She sings as sweetly as a nightingale.
Say that she frown, I'll say she looks as
  clear 175
As morning roses newly washed with dew.
Say she be mute and will not speak a
  word,
Then I'll commend her volubility
And say she uttereth piercing eloquence.
If she do bid me pack,° I'll give her
  thanks 180
As though she bid me stay by her a week.
If she deny° to wed, I'll crave the day
When I shall ask the banns° and when be
  marrièd.
But here she comes, and now, Petruchio,
  speak.

Enter KATE.

---

¹⁴¹ **speed** progress ¹⁴³ **to the proof** in tested steel armor ¹⁴⁹ **hold with her** stand her treatment ¹⁵⁰ **break** train ¹⁵² **frets** ridges where strings are pressed ¹⁵³ **bowed** bent ¹⁵⁶ **stroke** struck ¹⁵⁹ **pillory** i.e., with a wooden collar (old structure for public punishment)

¹⁶¹ **Jack** (term of contempt) ¹⁶² **As** as if ¹⁶² **studied** prepared ¹⁶³ **lusty** spirited ¹⁶⁷ **practice** instruction ¹⁶⁸ **apt** disposed ^{170 s.d.} (is in the F position, which need not be changed; Petruchio speaks to the departing Baptista) ¹⁷¹ **attend** wait for ¹⁷³ **rail** scold, scoff ¹⁸⁰ **pack** go away ¹⁸² **deny** refuse ¹⁸³ **banns** public announcement in church of intent to marry

Good morrow, Kate, for that's your name,
185   I hear.
        KATE. Well have you heard,° but some-
        thing hard of hearing.
They call me Katherine that do talk of me.
        PETRUCHIO. You lie, in faith, for you are
        called plain Kate,
And bonny° Kate, and sometimes Kate the
        curst.
But, Kate, the prettiest Kate in Christen-
190   dom,
Kate of Kate Hall,° my super-dainty Kate,
For dainties° are all Kates,° and therefore,
        Kate,
Take this of me, Kate of my consolation.
Hearing thy mildness praised in every
        town,
Thy virtues spoke of, and thy beauty
195   sounded°—
Yet not so deeply as to thee belongs—
Myself am moved to woo thee for my
        wife.
        KATE. Moved! In good time,° let him
        that moved you hither
Remove you hence. I knew you at the first
You were a movable.°
200   PETRUCHIO.   Why, what's a movable?
        KATE. A joint stool.°
        PETRUCHIO.   Thou hast hit it;
        come sit on me.
        KATE. Asses are made to bear° and so
        are you.
        PETRUCHIO. Women are made to bear°
        and so are you.
        KATE. No such jade° as you, if me you
        mean.
        PETRUCHIO. Alas, good Kate, I will not
205   burden thee,

For, knowing thee to be but young and
        light—
        KATE. Too light for such a swain° as you
        to catch
And yet as heavy as my weight should be.
        PETRUCHIO. Should be!° Should—buzz!
        KATE.   Well ta'en, and like a buzzard.°
        PETRUCHIO. O slow-winged turtle,° shall
        a buzzard take° thee?   210
        KATE. Ay, for a turtle, as he takes a
        buzzard.°
        PETRUCHIO. Come, come, you wasp, i'
        faith you are too angry.
        KATE. If I be waspish, best beware my
        sting.
        PETRUCHIO. My remedy is then to pluck
        it out.
        KATE. Ay, if the fool could find it where
        it lies.   215
        PETRUCHIO. Who knows not where a
        wasp does wear his sting?
In his tail.
        KATE.   In his tongue.
        PETRUCHIO.   Whose tongue?
        KATE. Yours, if you talk of tales,° and so
        farewell.
        PETRUCHIO. What, with my tongue in
        your tail? Nay, come again.
Good Kate, I am a gentleman—
        KATE.   That I'll try.   220

She strikes him.

        PETRUCHIO. I swear I'll cuff you if you
        strike again.
        KATE. So may you lose your arms:°
If you strike me you are no gentleman,
And if no gentleman, why then no arms.
        PETRUCHIO. A herald,° Kate? O, put me
        in thy books.°   225

---

¹⁸⁶ **heard** (pun: pronounced like *hard*) ¹⁸⁹ **bonny**
big, fine (perhaps with pun on *bony*, the F spelling) ¹⁹¹ **Kate Hall** (possible topical reference;
several places have been proposed) ¹⁹² **dainties**
delicacies ¹⁹² **Kates** i.e., *cates*, delicacies
¹⁹⁵ **sounded** (1) measured (effect of deeply), (2)
spoken of (pun) ¹⁹⁸ **In good time** indeed ²⁰⁰ **movable** article of furniture (with pun) ²⁰¹ **joint stool**
stool made by a joiner (standard term of dispar-
agement) ²⁰² **bear** carry ²⁰³ **bear** i.e., bear children (with second sexual meaning in Petruchio's
"I will not burden thee") ²⁰⁴ **jade** worn-out horse
(Kate has now called him both "ass" and "sorry
horse")

²⁰⁷ **swain** country boy ²⁰⁸ **be** (pun on *bee* ; hence
buzz, scandal, i.e., about "light" woman) ²⁰⁹ **buzzard** hawk unteachable in falconry (hence idiot)
²¹⁰ **turtle** turtledove, noted for affectionateness
²¹⁰ **take** capture (with pun, "mistake for," in next
line) ²¹¹ **buzzard** buzzing insect (hence "wasp")
²¹⁸ **of tales** idle tales (leading to bawdy pun on
tail =pudend) ²²² **arms** (pun on "coat of arms")
²²⁵ **herald** one skilled in heraldry ²²⁵ **books** registers of heraldry (with pun on "in your good
books")

KATE. What is your crest?° A coxcomb?°

PETRUCHIO. A combless° cock, so° Kate
will be my hen.

KATE. No cock of mine; you crow too
like a craven.°

PETRUCHIO. Nay, come, Kate, come,
you must not look so sour.

230 KATE. It is my fashion when I see a
crab.°

PETRUCHIO. Why, here's no crab, and
therefore look not sour.

KATE. There is, there is.

PETRUCHIO. Then show it me.

KATE.   Had I a glass° I would.

PETRUCHIO. What, you mean my face?

KATE. Well aimed of° such a young one.

235 PETRUCHIO. Now, by Saint George, I am
too young for you.

KATE. Yet you are withered.

PETRUCHIO.   'Tis with cares.

KATE.   I care not.

PETRUCHIO. Nay, hear you, Kate, in
sooth° you scape° not so.

KATE. I chafe° you if I tarry. Let me go.

PETRUCHIO. No, not a whit. I find you
passing gentle.

'Twas told me you were rough and coy°
240 and sullen,

And now I find report a very liar,

For thou art pleasant, gamesome, passing
courteous,

But slow in speech, yet sweet as spring-
time flowers.

Thou canst not frown, thou canst not look
askance,

245 Nor bite the lip as angry wenches will,

Nor hast thou pleasure to be cross in talk,

But thou with mildness entertain'st thy
wooers,

With gentle conference,° soft and affable.

Why does the world report that Kate doth
limp?

O sland'rous world! Kate like the hazel-
twig   250

Is straight and slender, and as brown in
hue

As hazelnuts and sweeter than the ker-
nels.

O, let me see thee walk. Thou dost not
halt.°

KATE. Go, fool, and whom thou keep'st°
command.

PETRUCHIO. Did ever Dian° so become a
grove   255

As Kate this chamber with her princely
gait?

O, be thou Dian and let her be Kate,

And then let Kate be chaste and Dian
sportful!°

KATE. Where did you study all this
goodly speech?

PETRUCHIO. It is extempore, from my
mother-wit.°   260

KATE. A witty mother! Witless else° her
son.

PETRUCHIO. Am I not wise?

KATE.   Yes,° keep you warm.

PETRUCHIO. Marry, so I mean, sweet
Katherine, in thy bed.

And therefore, setting all this chat aside,

Thus in plain terms: your father hath
consented   265

That you shall be my wife, your dowry
'greed on,

And will you, nill° you, I will marry you.

Now, Kate, I am a husband for your turn,°

For, by this light, whereby I see thy
beauty—

Thy beauty that doth make me like thee
well—   270

Thou must be married to no man but me.

Enter BAPTISTA, GREMIO, TRANIO.

---

²²⁶ **crest** heraldic device ²²⁶ **coxcomb** identifying
feature of court Fool's cap; the cap itself
²²⁷ **combless** i.e., unwarlike ²²⁷ **so** if ²²⁸ **craven**
defeated cock ²³⁰ **crab** crab apple ²³³ **glass** mirror
²³⁴ **well aimed of** a good shot (in the dark)
²³⁷ **sooth** truth ²³⁷ **scape** escape ²³⁸ **chafe** (1) annoy, (2) warm up ²⁴⁰ **coy** offish ²⁴⁸ **conference**
conversation

²⁵³ **halt** limp ²⁵⁴ **whom thou keep'st** i.e., your
servants ²⁵⁵ **Dian** Diana, goddess of hunting and
virginity ²⁵⁸ **sportful** (i.e., in the game of love)
²⁶⁰ **mother-wit** natural intelligence ²⁶¹ **else** otherwise would be ²⁶² **Yes** yes, just enough to (refers to a proverbial saying) ²⁶⁷ **nill** won't ²⁶⁸ **turn**
advantage (with bawdy second meaning)

For I am he am born to tame you, Kate,
And bring you from a wild Kate° to a Kate
Conformable° as other household Kates.
Here comes your father. Never make
275   denial;
I must and will have Katherine to my wife.
    BAPTISTA. Now, Signior Petruchio, how
        speed° you with my daughter?
    PETRUCHIO. How but well sir? How but
        well?
It were impossible I should speed amiss.
    BAPTISTA. Why, how now, daughter
280   Katherine, in your dumps?°
    KATE. Call you me daughter? Now, I
        promise° you
You have showed a tender fatherly regard
To wish me wed to one half lunatic,
A madcap ruffian and a swearing Jack
That thinks with oaths to face° the matter
285   out.
    PETRUCHIO. Father, 'tis thus: yourself
        and all the world
That talked of her have talked amiss of
    her.
If she be curst it is for policy,°
For she's not froward but modest as the
    dove.
She is not hot° but temperate as the
290   morn;
For patience she will prove a second Gris-
    sel°
And Roman Lucrece° for her chastity.
And to conclude, we have 'greed so well
    together
That upon Sunday is the wedding day.
    KATE. I'll see thee hanged on Sunday
295   first.
    GREMIO. Hark, Petruchio, she says
        she'll see thee hanged first.
    TRANIO. Is this your speeding?° Nay,
        then good night our part!
    PETRUCHIO. Be patient, gentlemen, I
        choose her for myself.

If she and I be pleased, what's that to
    you?
'Tis bargained 'twixt us twain, being
    alone,   300
That she shall still be curst in company.
I tell you, 'tis incredible to believe
How much she loves me. O, the kindest
    Kate,
She hung about my neck, and kiss on kiss
She vied° so fast, protesting oath on oath,   305
That in a twink° she won me to her love.
O, you are novices. 'Tis a world° to see
How tame, when men and women are
    alone,
A meacock° wretch can make the curstest
    shrew.
Give me thy hand, Kate. I will unto Venice   310
To buy apparel 'gainst° the wedding day.
Provide the feast, father, and bid the
    guests;
I will be sure my Katherine shall be fine.°
    BAPTISTA. I know not what to say, but
        give me your hands.
God send you joy, Petruchio! 'Tis a match.   315
    GREMIO, TRANIO. Amen, say we. We will
        be witnesses.
    PETRUCHIO. Father, and wife, and gen-
        tlemen, adieu.
I will to Venice; Sunday comes apace.
We will have rings and things and fine
    array,
And, kiss me, Kate, "We will be married a
    Sunday."°   Exit PETRUCHIO and KATE.   320
    GREMIO. Was ever match clapped° up so
        suddenly?
    BAPTISTA. Faith, gentlemen, now I play
        a merchant's part
And venture madly on a desperate mart.°
    TRANIO. 'Twas a commodity° lay fret-
        ting° by you;

273 **wild Kate** (pun on "wildcat") 274 **Conform-
able** submissive 277 **speed** get on 280 **dumps** low
spirits 281 **promise** tell 285 **face** brazen 288 **policy**
tactics 290 **hot** intemperate 291 **Grissel** Griselda
(patient wife in Chaucer's Clerk's Tale) 292 **Lucrece** (killed herself after Tarquin raped her)
297 **speeding** success

305 **vied** made higher bids (card-playing terms),
i.e., kissed more frequently 306 **twink** twinkling
307 **world** wonder 309 **meacock** timid 311 **'gainst**
in preparation for 313 **fine** well dressed 320 **"We
. . . Sunday"** (line from a ballad) 321 **clapped**
fixed 323 **mart** "deal" 324 **commodity** (here a
coarse term for women; see Partridge, *Shakespeare's Bawdy*) 324 **fretting** decaying in storage
(with pun)

'Twill bring you gain or perish on the
   seas.
   BAPTISTA. The gain I seek is quiet in
   the match.
   GREMIO. No doubt but he hath got a
   quiet catch.
But now, Baptista, to your younger daugh-
   ter;
Now is the day we long have lookèd for.
I am your neighbor and was suitor first.
   TRANIO. And I am one that love Bianca
   more
Than words can witness or your thoughts
   can guess.
   GREMIO. Youngling, thou canst not love
   so dear as I.
   TRANIO. Graybeard, thy love doth
   freeze.
   GREMIO.   But thine doth fry.
Skipper,° stand back, 'tis age that
   nourisheth.
   TRANIO. But youth in ladies' eyes that
   flourisheth.
   BAPTISTA. Content you, gentlemen; I
   will compound° this strife.
'Tis deeds must win the prize, and he of
   both°
That can assure my daughter greatest
   dower°
Shall have my Bianca's love.
Say, Signior Gremio, what can you assure
   her?
   GREMIO. First, as you know, my house
   within the city
Is richly furnishèd with plate and gold,
Basins and ewers to lave° her dainty
   hands;
My hangings all of Tyrian° tapestry;
In ivory coffers I have stuffed my crowns,
In cypress chests my arras counterpoints,°
Costly apparel, tents,° and canopies,
Fine linen, Turkey cushions bossed° with
   pearl,

Valance° of Venice gold in needlework,
Pewter and brass, and all things that be-
   longs
To house or housekeeping. Then, at my
   farm
I have a hundred milch-kine to the pail,°
Six score fat oxen standing in my stalls
And all things answerable to this portion.°
Myself am struck° in years, I must con-
   fess,
And if I die tomorrow, this is hers,
If whilst I live she will be only mine.
   TRANIO. That "only" came well in. Sir,
   list to me.
I am my father's heir and only son.
If I may have your daughter to my wife,
I'll leave her houses three or four as
   good,
Within rich Pisa walls, as any one
Old Signior Gremio has in Padua,
Besides two thousand ducats° by the year
Of° fruitful land, all which shall be her
   jointure.°
What, have I pinched° you, Signior Gre-
   mio?
   GREMIO *[aside].* Two thousand ducats by
   the year of land!
My land amounts not to so much in all.
[To others.] That she shall have besides an
   argosy°
That now is lying in Marcellus' road.°
What, have I choked you with an argosy?
   TRANIO. Gremio, 'tis known my father
   hath no less
Than three great argosies, besides two
   galliasses°
And twelve tight° galleys. These I will
   assure her
And twice as much, whate'er thou off'rest
   next.
   GREMIO. Nay, I have off'red all. I have
   no more,

325
330
335
340
345

350
355
360
365
370
375

And she can have no more than all I have.
If you like me, she shall have me and
    mine.
    TRANIO. Why, then the maid is mine
380   from all the world
By your firm promise. Gremio is outvied.°
    BAPTISTA. I must confess your offer is
    the best,
And let your father make her the assur-
    ance,°
She is your own; else you must pardon
    me.
If you should die before him, where's her
385   dower?
    TRANIO. That's but a cavil.° He is old, I
    young.
    GREMIO. And may not young men die as
    well as old?
    BAPTISTA. Well, gentlemen,
I am thus resolved. On Sunday next, you
    know,
390 My daughter Katherine is to be married.
Now on the Sunday following shall Bianca
Be bride to you if you make this assur-
    ance;
If not, to Signior Gremio.
And so I take my leave and thank you
    both.   *Exit.*
    GREMIO. Adieu, good neighbor. Now I
395   fear thee not.
Sirrah° young gamester,° your father
    were° a fool
To give thee all and in his waning age
Set foot under thy table.° Tut, a toy!°
An old Italian fox is not so kind, my boy.
                                Exit.
    TRANIO. A vengeance on your crafty
400   withered hide!
Yet I have faced it with a card of ten.°
'Tis in my head to do my master good.
I see no reason but supposed Lucentio
Must get° a father, called "supposed
    Vincentio,"
405 And that's a wonder. Fathers commonly

Do get their children, but in this case of
    wooing
A child shall get a sire if I fail not of my
    cunning.   *Exit.*

ACT III

[Scene I. Padua. In Baptista's house.]

Enter LUCENTIO *[as Cambio],* HORTENSIO
[as Litio], and BIANCA.

    LUCENTIO. Fiddler, forbear. You grow
    too forward, sir.
Have you so soon forgot the entertain-
    ment°
Her sister Katherine welcomed you
    withal?
    HORTENSIO. But, wrangling pedant, this
    is
The patroness of heavenly harmony.   5
Then give me leave to have prerogative,°
And when in music we have spent an hour,
Your lecture° shall have leisure for as
    much.
    LUCENTIO. Preposterous° ass, that
    never read so far
To know the cause why music was or-
    dained!   10
Was it not to refresh the mind of man
After his studies or his usual pain?°
Then give me leave to read° philosophy,
And while I pause, serve in your harmony.
    HORTENSIO. Sirrah, I will not bear these
    braves° of thine.   15
    BIANCA. Why, gentlemen, you do me
    double wrong
To strive for that which resteth in my
    choice.
I am no breeching° scholar° in the
    schools.
I'll not be tied to hours nor 'pointed
    times,
But learn my lessons as I please myself.   20

---

381 **outvied** outbid 383 **assurance** guarantee
386 **cavil** small point 396 **Sirrah** (used contemptuously) 396 **gamester** gambler 396 **were** would be
398 **Set foot under thy table** be dependent on
you 398 **a toy** a joke 401 **faced it with a card of
ten** bluffed with a tenspot 404 **get** beget

III.i.² **entertainment** i.e., "pillorying" him with
the lute 6 **prerogative** priority 8 **lecture** instruction 9 **Preposterous** putting later things
(*post-*) first (*pre-*) 12 **pain** labor 13 **read** give a lesson in 15 **braves** defiances 18 **breeching** (1) in
breeches (young), (2) whippable 18 **scholar**
schoolboy

And, to cut off all strife, here sit we
   down.
[To Hortensio.] Take you your instrument,
   play you the whiles;°
His lecture will be done ere you have
   tuned.
  HORTENSIO. You'll leave his lecture when
    I am in tune?
  LUCENTIO. That will be never. Tune
25   your instrument.
  BIANCA. Where left we last?
  LUCENTIO. Here, madam:
    Hic ibat Simois, hic est Sigeia tellus,
    Hic steterat Priami regia celsa senis.°
30 BIANCA. Conster° them.
  LUCENTIO. *Hic ibat,* as I told you before,
  Simois, I am Lucentio, *hic est,* son unto
  Vincentio of Pisa, *Sigeia tellus,* disguised
  thus to get your love, *Hic steterat,* and that
35 Lucentio that comes a wooing, *Priami,* is
  my man Tranio, *regia,* bearing my port,°
  celsa senis, that we might beguile the old
  pantaloon.°
  HORTENSIO *[breaks in].* Madam, my
    instrument's in tune.
  BIANCA. Let's hear. O fie, the treble
40   jars.°
  LUCENTIO. Spit in the hole, man, and
    tune again.
  BIANCA. Now let me see if I can conster
  it. *Hic ibat Simois,* I know you not, *hic est*
  Sigeia tellus, I trust you not, *Hic steterat*
45 *Priami,* take heed he hear us not, *regia,*
  presume not, *celsa senis,* despair not.
  HORTENSIO *[breaks in again].* Madam,
    'tis now in tune.
  LUCENTIO.   All but the bass.
  HORTENSIO. The bass is right; 'tis the
    base knave that jars.
[Aside.] How fiery and forward our pedant
   is!

Now, for my life, the knave doth court my
   love.   50
Pedascule,° I'll watch you better yet.
  BIANCA. In time I may believe, yet I
    mistrust.
  LUCENTIO. Mistrust it not, for sure
    Aeacides
Was Ajax,° called so from his grandfather.
  BIANCA. I must believe my master; else,
    I promise you,   55
I should be arguing still upon that doubt.
But let it rest. Now, Litio, to you.
Good master, take it not unkindly, pray,
That I have been thus pleasant° with you
   both.
  HORTENSIO *[to LUCENTIO].* You may go
    walk and give me leave° a while.   60
My lessons make no music in three
   parts.°
  LUCENTIO. Are you so formal, sir?
  [Aside.] Well, I must wait
And watch withal,° for but° I be deceived,
Our fine musician groweth amorous.
  HORTENSIO. Madam, before you touch
    the instrument,   65
To learn the order of my fingering,
I must begin with rudiments of art
To teach you gamut° in a briefer sort,
More pleasant, pithy, and effectual,
Than hath been taught by any of my trade; 70
And there it is in writing, fairly drawn.
  BIANCA. Why, I am past my gamut long
    ago.
  HORTENSIO. Yet read the gamut of Hor-
    tensio.
  BIANCA *[reads].*

Gamut I am, the ground° of all accord.°
  A re, to plead Hortensio's passion: 75

---

²² **the whiles** meanwhile ²⁸⁻²⁹ **Hic . . . senis**
here flowed the Simois, here is the Sigeian (Trojan) land, here had stood old Priam's high palace
(Ovid) ³⁰ **Conster** construe ³⁶ **bearing my port**
taking on my style ³⁸ **pantaloon** Gremio (see
I.i.47.s.d. note) ⁴⁰ **treble jars** highest tone is off

⁵¹ **Pedascule** little pedant (disparaging quasi-
Latin) ⁵³⁻⁵⁴ **Aeacides/Was Ajax** Ajax, Greek
warrior at Troy, was grandson of Aeacus (Lucentio comments on next passage in Ovid) ⁵⁹ **pleasant** merry ⁶⁰ **give me leave** leave me alone ⁶¹ **in
three parts** for three voices ⁶³ **withal** besides
⁶³ **but** unless ⁶⁸ **gamut** the scale ⁷⁴ **ground** beginning, first note ⁷⁴ **accord** harmony

B mi, Bianca, take him for thy lord,
  C fa ut, that loves with all affection;
D sol re, one clef, two notes have I:
  E la mi, show pity or I die.

80 Call you this gamut? Tut, I like it not.
Old fashions please me best; I am not so
  nice°
To change true rules for odd inventions.

Enter a MESSENGER.

  MESSENGER. Mistress, your father prays
    you leave your books
And help to dress your sister's chamber
  up.
85 You know tomorrow is the wedding day.
  BIANCA. Farewell, sweet masters both, I
    must be gone.
       [Exeunt BIANCA *and* MESSENGER.*]*
  LUCENTIO. Faith, mistress, then I have
    no cause to stay.   *[Exit.]*
  HORTENSIO. But I have cause to pry into
    this pedant.
Methinks he looks as though he were in
  love.
90 Yet if thy thoughts, Bianca, be so humble
To cast thy wand'ring eyes on every
  stale,°
Seize thee that list.° If once I find thee
  ranging,°
Hortensio will be quit with thee by chang-
  ing.°   *Exit.*

[Scene II. Padua. The street in front of
BAPTISTA'S *house.]*

Enter BAPTISTA, GREMIO, TRANIO *[as Lucen-
tio]*, KATE, BIANCA, *[*LUCENTIO *as Cambio]
and others,* ATTENDANTS.

  BAPTISTA *[to* TRANIO*]*. Signior Lucentio,
    this is the 'pointed day
That Katherine and Petruchio should be
  marrièd,
And yet we hear not of our son-in-law.
What will be said? What mockery will it be

To want° the bridegroom when the priest
  attends   5
To speak the ceremonial rites of marriage!
What says Lucentio to this shame of ours?
  KATE. No shame but mine. I must,
    forsooth, be forced
To give my hand opposed against my heart
Unto a mad-brain rudesby,° full of spleen,° 10
Who wooed in haste and means to wed at
  leisure.
I told you, I, he was a frantic fool,
Hiding his bitter jests in blunt behavior.
And to be noted for° a merry man,
He'll woo a thousand, 'point the day of
  marriage,   15
Make friends. invite,° and proclaim the
  banns,
Yet never means to wed where he hath
  wooed.
Now must the world point at poor
  Katherine
And say, "Lo, there is mad Petruchio's
  wife,
If it would please him come and marry
  her."   20
  TRANIO. Patience, good Katherine, and
    Baptista too.
Upon my life, Petruchio means but well,
Whatever fortune stays° him from his
  word.
Though he be blunt, I know him passing°
  wise;
Though he be merry, yet withal he's hon-
  est.   25
  KATE. Would Katherine had never seen
    him though! *Exit weeping [followed by*
                  BIANCA *and others].*
  BAPTISTA. Go, girl, I cannot blame thee
    now to weep.
For such an injury would vex a very saint,
Much more a shrew of thy impatient hu-
  mor.°

---

81 **nice** whimsical 91 **stale** lure (as in hunting)
92 **Seize thee that list** let him who likes capture you 92 **ranging** going astray 93 **changing**
i.e., sweethearts

III.ii. 5 **want** be without 10 **rudesby** uncouth fellow 10 **spleen** caprice 14 **noted for** reputed
16 **Make friends, invite** (some editors emend
to "Make feast, invite friends") 23 **stays** keeps
24 **passing** very 29 **humor** temper

Enter BIONDELLO.

30　BIONDELLO. Master, master, news! And such old° news as you never heard of!

BAPTISTA. Is it new and old too? How may that be?

BIONDELLO. Why, is it not news to hear
35　of Petruchio's coming?

BAPTISTA. Is he come?

BIONDELLO. Why, no, sir.

BAPTISTA. What then?

BIONDELLO. He is coming.

40　BAPTISTA. When will he be here?

BIONDELLO. When he stands where I am and sees you there.

TRANIO. But, say, what to thine old news?

45　BIONDELLO. Why, Petruchio is coming in a new hat and an old jerkin;° a pair of old breeches thrice turned;° a pair of boots that have been candle-cases,° one buckled, another laced; an old rusty sword ta'en out of
50　the town armory, with a broken hilt and chapeless;° with two broken points;° his horse hipped° (with an old mothy saddle and stirrups of no kindred),° besides, possessed with the glanders° and like to mose
55　in the chine;° troubled with the lampass,° infected with the fashions,° full of windgalls,° sped with spavins,° rayed° with the yellows,° past cure of the fives,° stark spoiled with the staggers,° begnawn with
60　the bots,° swayed° in the back, and

shoulder-shotten;° near-legged before,° and with a half-cheeked° bit and a head-stall° of sheep's leather,° which, being restrained° to keep him from stumbling, hath been often burst and now repaired with　65 knots; one girth° six times pieced,° and a woman's crupper° of velure,° which hath two letters for her name fairly set down in studs,° and here and there pieced with packthread.°　70

BAPTISTA. Who comes with him?

BIONDELLO. O sir, his lackey, for all the world caparisoned° like the horse: with a linen stock° on one leg and a kersey boot-hose° on the other, gart'red with a red and　75 blue list;° an old hat, and the humor of forty fancies° pricked° in't for a feather—a monster, a very monster in apparel, and not like a Christian footboy° or a gentleman's lackey.　80

TRANIO. 'Tis some odd humor° pricks° him to this fashion
Yet oftentimes he goes but mean-
　　appareled.

BAPTISTA. I am glad he's come, how-
　　soe'er he comes.

BIONDELLO. Why, sir, he comes not.

BAPTISTA. Didst thou not say he comes?　85

BIONDELLO. Who? That Petruchio came?

BAPTISTA. Ay, that Petruchio came.

BIONDELLO. No, sir, I say his horse comes, with him on his back.

---

[31] **old** strange [46] **jerkin** short outer coat [47] **turned** i.e., inside out (to conceal wear and tear) [48] **candle-cases** worn-out boots used to keep candle ends in [51] **chapeless** lacking the metal mounting at end of scabbard [51] **points** laces to fasten hose to garment above [52] **hipped** with dislocated hip [53] **of no kindred** not matching [54] **glanders** bacterial disease affecting mouth and nose [54-55] **mose in the chine** (1) glanders, (2) nasal discharge [55] **lampass** swollen mouth [56] **fashions** tumors (related to glanders) [57] **windgalls** swellings on lower leg [57] **spavins** swellings on upper hind leg [57] **rayed** soiled [58] **yellows** jaundice [58] **fives** vives: swelling of submaxillary glands [59] **staggers** nervous disorder causing loss of balance [59-60] **begnawn with the bots** gnawed by parasitic worms (larvae of the botfly) [60] **swayed** sagging

[61] **shoulder-shotten** with dislocated shoulder [61] **near-legged before** with forefeet knocking together [62] **half-cheeked** wrongly adjusted to bridle and affording less control [62-63] **head-stall** part of bridle which surrounds head [63] **sheep's leather** (weaker than pigskin) [64-65] **restrained** pulled back [66] **girth** saddle strap under belly [66] **pieced** patched [67] **crupper** leather loop under horse's tail to help steady saddle [67] **velure** velvet [69] **studs** large-headed nails of brass or silver [69-70] **pieced with packthread** tied together with coarse thread [73] **caparisoned** outfitted [74] **stock** stocking [74-75] **kersey boot-hose** coarse stocking worn with riding boot [76] **list** strip of discarded border-cloth [76-77] **humor of forty fancies** fanciful decoration (in place of feather) [77] **pricked** pinned [79] **footboy** page in livery [81] **humor** mood, fancy [81] **pricks** incites

90   BAPTISTA. Why, that's all one.°
      BIONDELLO *[sings]*.

            Nay, by Saint Jamy,
            I hold° you a penny,
            A horse and a man
            Is more than one
95   And yet not many.

      Enter PETRUCHIO *and* GRUMIO.

      PETRUCHIO. Come, where be these
          gallants?° Who's at home?
      BAPTISTA. You are welcome, sir.
      PETRUCHIO.   And yet
          I come not well.
      BAPTISTA. And yet you halt° not.
      TRANIO.   Not so
          well appareled
      As I wish you were.
      PETRUCHIO. Were it better,° I should
100   rush in thus.
      But where is Kate? Where is my lovely
          bride?
      How does my father? Gentles,° methinks
          you frown.
      And wherefore gaze this goodly company
      As if they saw some wondrous monu-
          ment,°
105   Some comet or unusual prodigy?°
      BAPTISTA. Why, sir, you know this is
          your wedding day.
      First were we sad, fearing you would not
          come,
      Now sadder that you come so unpro-
          vided.°
      Fie, doff this habit,° shame to your es-
          tate,°
110   An eyesore to our solemn festival.
      TRANIO. And tell us what occasion of
          import°
      Hath all so long detained you from your
          wife
      And sent you hither so unlike yourself.

      PETRUCHIO. Tedious it were to tell and
          harsh to hear.
      Sufficeth, I am come to keep my word   115
      Though in some part enforcèd to digress,°
      Which, at more leisure, I will so excuse
      As you shall well be satisfied with all.
      But where is Kate? I stay too long from
          her.
      The morning wears, 'tis time we were at
          church.   120
      TRANIO. See not your bride in these
          unreverent robes.
      Go to my chamber; put on clothes of
          mine.
      PETRUCHIO. Not I, believe me; thus I'll
          visit her.
      BAPTISTA. But thus, I trust, you will not
          marry her.
      PETRUCHIO. Good sooth,° even thus;
          therefore ha' done with words.   125
      To me she's married, not unto my clothes.
      Could I repair what she will wear° in me
      As I can change these poor accoutre-
          ments,
      'Twere well for Kate and better for my-
          self.
      But what a fool am I to chat with you   130
      When I should bid good morrow to my
          bride
      And seal the title° with a lovely° kiss.
                        Exit [with GRUMIO*].*
      TRANIO. He hath some meaning in his
          mad attire.
      We will persuade him, be it possible,
      To put on better ere he go to church.   135
      BAPTISTA. I'll after him and see the
          event° of this.
                Exit [with GREMIO *and* ATTENDANTS*].*
      TRANIO. But to her love concerneth us
          to add
      Her father's liking, which to bring to pass,
      As I before imparted to your worship,
      I am to get a man—whate'er he be   140

---

⁹⁰ **all one** the same thing ⁹² **hold** bet ⁹⁶ **gallants** men of fashion ⁹⁸ **halt** limp (pun on *come* meaning "walk") ¹⁰⁰ **Were it better** even if I were better ¹⁰² **Gentles** sirs ¹⁰⁴ **monument** warning sign ¹⁰⁵ **prodigy** marvel ¹⁰⁸ **unprovided** ill-outfitted ¹⁰⁹ **habit** costume ¹⁰⁹ **estate** status ¹¹¹ **of import** important

¹¹⁶ **enforcèd to digress** forced to depart (perhaps from his plan to "buy apparel 'gainst the wedding day," II.i.311) ¹²⁵ **Good sooth** yes indeed ¹²⁷ **wear** wear out ¹³² **title** i.e., as of ownership ¹³² **lovely** loving ¹³⁶ **event** upshot, outcome

It skills° not much, we'll fit him to our
    turn°—
And he shall be Vincentio of Pisa,
And make assurance° here in Padua
Of greater sums than I have promisèd.
145 So shall you quietly enjoy your hope
And marry sweet Bianca with consent.
    LUCENTIO. Were it not that my fellow
      schoolmaster
Doth watch Bianca's steps so narrowly,
'Twere good, methinks, to steal our mar-
    riage,°
Which once performed, let all the world
150   say no,
I'll keep mine own despite of all the world.
    TRANIO. That by degrees we mean to
      look into
And watch our vantage° in this business.
We'll overreach° the graybeard, Gremio,
155 The narrow-prying father, Minola,
The quaint° musician, amorous Litio—
All for my master's sake, Lucentio.

Enter GREMIO.

Signior Gremio, came you from the
    church?
    GREMIO. As willingly as e'er I came
      from school.
    TRANIO. And is the bride and bride-
160   groom coming home?
    GREMIO. A bridegroom say you? 'Tis a
    groom° indeed,
A grumbling groom, and that the girl shall
    find.
    TRANIO. Curster than she? Why, 'tis
    impossible.
    GREMIO. Why, he's a devil, a devil, a
    very fiend.
    TRANIO. Why, she's a devil, a devil, the
165   devil's dam.°
    GREMIO. Tut, she's a lamb, a dove, a
    fool to° him.
I'll tell you, Sir Lucentio, when the priest

Should ask, if Katherine should be his
    wife,
"Ay, by goggs woones!"° quoth he and
    swore so loud
That, all amazed, the priest let fall the
    book,   170
And as he stooped again to take it up,
This mad-brained bridegroom took° him
    such a cuff
That down fell priest and book and book
    and priest.
"Now, take them up," quoth he, "if any
    list."°
    TRANIO. What said the wench when he
    rose again?   175
    GREMIO. Trembled and shook, for why°
    he stamped and swore
As if the vicar meant to cozen° him.
But after many ceremonies done
He calls for wine. "A health!" quoth he as
    if
He had been aboard, carousing° to his
    mates   180
After a storm; quaffed off the muscadel°
And threw the sops° all in the sexton's
    face,
Having no other reason
But that his beard grew thin and hun-
    gerly,°
And seemed to ask him sops as he was
    drinking.   185
This done, he took the bride about the
    neck
And kissed her lips with such a clamorous
    smack
That at the parting all the church did
    echo,
And I, seeing this, came thence for very
    shame.
And after me, I know, the rout° is coming. 190
Such a mad marriage never was before.
Hark, hark, I hear the minstrels play.
                          Music plays.

---

141 **skills** matters 141 **turn** purpose 143 **assurance** guarantee 149 **steal our marriage** elope 153 **vantage** advantage 154 **overreach** get the better of 156 **quaint** artful 161 **groom** menial (i.e., coarse fellow) 165 **dam** mother 166 **fool to** harmless person compared with

169 **goggs woones** by God's wounds (a common oath) 172 **took** gave 174 **list** pleases to 176 **for why** because 177 **cozen** cheat 180 **carousing** calling "Bottoms up" 181 **muscadel** sweet wine, conventionally drunk after marriage service 182 **sops** pieces of cake soaked in wine; dregs 184 **hungerly** as if poorly nourished 190 **rout** crowd

Enter PETRUCHIO, KATE, BIANCA, HORTENSIO *[as Litio]*, BAPTISTA *[with* GRUMIO *and others].*

PETRUCHIO. Gentlemen and friends, I thank you for your pains.
I know you think to dine with me today
And have prepared great store of wedding
195   cheer,°
But so it is, my haste doth call me hence
And therefore here I mean to take my leave.
BAPTISTA. Is't possible you will away tonight?
PETRUCHIO. I must away today, before night come.
Make it no wonder;° if you knew my
200   business,
You would entreat me rather go than stay.
And, honest company, I thank you all
That have beheld me give away myself
To this most patient, sweet, and virtuous wife.
205 Dine with my father, drink a health to me,
For I must hence, and farewell to you all.
TRANIO. Let us entreat you stay till after dinner.
PETRUCHIO. It may not be.
GREMIO.   Let me entreat you.
PETRUCHIO. It cannot be.
KATE.   Let me entreat you.
PETRUCHIO. I am content.
KATE.   Are you content
210   to stay?
PETRUCHIO. I am content you shall entreat me stay,
But yet not stay, entreat me how you can.
KATE. Now if you love me, stay.
PETRUCHIO.   Grumio, my horse!°
GRUMIO. Ay, sir, they be ready; the oats
215 have eaten the horses.°

KATE. Nay then,
Do what thou canst, I will not go today,
No, nor tomorrow, not till I please myself.
The door is open, sir, there lies your way.
You may be jogging whiles your boots are
        green;°   220
For me, I'll not be gone till I please myself.
'Tis like you'll prove a jolly° surly groom,
That take it on you° at the first so roundly.°
PETRUCHIO. O Kate, content thee; prithee,° be not angry.
KATE. I will be angry. What hast thou to
        do?°   225
Father, be quiet; he shall stay my leisure.°
GREMIO. Ay, marry, sir, now it begins to work.
KATE. Gentlemen, forward to the bridal dinner.
I see a woman may be made a fool
If she had not a spirit to resist.   230
PETRUCHIO. They shall go forward, Kate, at thy command.
Obey the bride, you that attend on her.
Go to the feast, revel and domineer,°
Carouse full measure to her maidenhead,
Be mad and merry, or go hang yourselves.   235
But for my bonny Kate, she must with me.
Nay, look not big,° nor stamp, nor stare,° nor fret;
I will be master of what is mine own.
She is my goods, my chattels; she is my house,
My household stuff, my field, my barn,   240
My horse, my ox, my ass, my anything,°
And here she stands. Touch her whoever dare,
I'll bring mine action° on the proudest he

---

²²⁰ **You . . . green** (proverbial way of suggesting departure to a guest, *green* = new, cleaned) ²²² **jolly** domineering ²²³ **take it on you** do as you please ²²³ **roundly** roughly ²²⁴ **prithee** I pray thee ²²⁵ **What hast thou to do** what do you have to do with it ²²⁶ **stay my leisure** await my willingness ²³³ **domineer** cut up in a lordly fashion ²³⁷ **big** challenging ²³⁷ **stare** swagger ²⁴¹ **My horse . . . anything** (echoing Tenth Commandment) ²⁴³ **action** lawsuit

---

¹⁹⁵ **cheer** food and drink ²⁰⁰ **Make it no wonder** don't be surprised ²¹³ **horse** horses ²¹⁴⁻²¹⁵ **oats have eaten the horses** (1) a slip of the tongue or (2) an ironic jest

That stops my way in Padua. Grumio,
Draw forth thy weapon, we are beset with
245   thieves.
Rescue thy mistress, if thou be a man.
Fear not, sweet wench; they shall not
        touch thee, Kate.
I'll buckler° thee against a million.
    Exeunt PETRUCHIO, KATE *[and* GRUMIO*].*
BAPTISTA. Nay, let them go, a couple of
    quiet ones.
GREMIO. Went they not quickly, I should
250   die with laughing.
TRANIO. Of all mad matches never was
    the like.
LUCENTIO. Mistress, what's your opin-
    ion of your sister?
BIANCA. That being mad herself, she's
    madly mated.
GREMIO. I warrant him, Petruchio is
    Kated.
BAPTISTA. Neighbors and friends, though
255   bride and bridegroom wants°
For to supply the places at the table,
You know there wants no junkets° at the
    feast.
[To Tranio.] Lucentio, you shall supply the
    bridegroom's place,
And let Bianca take her sister's room.
TRANIO. Shall sweet Bianca practice how
260   to bride it?
BAPTISTA. She shall, Lucentio. Come,
    gentlemen, let's go.   *Exeunt.*

/ACT IV

Scene I. PETRUCHIO'S *country house.]*

Enter GRUMIO.

GRUMIO. Fie, fie, on all tired jades,° on
all mad masters, and all foul ways!° Was
ever man so beaten? Was ever man so
rayed?° Was ever man so weary? I am sent
5   before to make a fire, and they are coming
after to warm them. Now were not I a little

pot and soon hot,° my very lips might
freeze to my teeth, my tongue to the roof of
my mouth, my heart in my belly, ere I
should come by a fire to thaw me. But I
10 with blowing the fire shall warm myself, for
considering the weather, a taller° man than
I will take cold. Holla, ho, Curtis!

Enter CURTIS *[a Servant].*

CURTIS. Who is that calls so coldly?
GRUMIO. A piece of ice. If thou doubt it,
15 thou mayst slide from my shoulder to my
heel with no greater a run° but my head and
my neck. A fire, good Curtis.
CURTIS. Is my master and his wife coming, Grumio?
20 GRUMIO. O ay, Curtis, ay, and therefore
fire, fire; cast on no water.°
CURTIS. Is she so hot a shrew as she's
reported?
GRUMIO. She was, good Curtis, before
25 this frost, but thou know'st winter tames
man, woman, and beast; for it hath tamed
my old master, and my new mistress, and
myself, fellow Curtis.
CURTIS. Away, you three-inch° fool! I am
30 no beast.
GRUMIO. Am I but three inches? Why,
thy horn° is a foot, and so long am I at the
least. But wilt thou make a fire, or shall I
complain on thee to our mistress, whose
35 hand—she being now at hand—thou shalt
soon feel, to thy cold comfort, for being
slow in thy hot office?°
CURTIS. I prithee, good Grumio, tell me,
how goes the world?
40 GRUMIO. A cold world, Curtis, in every
office but thine, and therefore, fire. Do thy
duty and have thy duty,° for my master and
mistress are almost frozen to death.

---

248 **buckler** shield 255 **wants** are lacking 257 **jun-kets** sweetmeats, confections IV.i. 1 **jades** worthless horses 2 **foul ways** bad roads 4 **rayed** befouled

6-7 **little pot and soon hot** (proverbial for small person of short temper) 11 **taller** sturdier (with allusion to "little pot") 16 **run** running start 21 **cast on no water** (alters "Cast on more wa-ter" in a well-known round) 29 **three-inch** (1) another allusion to Grumio's small stature, (2) a phallic jest, the first of several 32 **horn** (symbol of cuckold) 37 **hot office** job of making a fire 42 **thy duty** what is due thee

CURTIS. There's fire ready, and there-
45 fore, good Grumio, the news.

GRUMIO. Why, "Jack boy, ho boy!"° and
as much news as wilt thou.

CURTIS. Come, you are so full of cony-
catching.°

50 GRUMIO. Why therefore fire, for I have
caught extreme cold. Where's the cook? Is
supper ready, the house trimmed, rushes
strewed,° cobwebs swept, the servingmen
in their new fustian,° the white stockings,
55 and every officer° his wedding garment on?
Be the jacks° fair within, the jills° fair without, the carpets° laid and everything in order?

CURTIS. All ready, and therefore, I pray
60 thee, news.

GRUMIO. First, know my horse is tired,
my master and mistress fall'n out.

CURTIS. How?

GRUMIO. Out of their saddles into the
65 dirt—and thereby hangs a tale.

CURTIS. Let's ha't, good Grumio.

GRUMIO. Lend thine ear.

CURTIS. Here.

GRUMIO. There.   *[Strikes him.]*
70 CURTIS. This 'tis to feel a tale, not to
hear a tale.

GRUMIO. And therefore 'tis called a sen-
sible° tale, and this cuff was but to knock at
your ear and beseech list'ning. Now I be-
75 gin. *Imprimis,*° we came down a foul° hill,
my master riding behind my mistress—

CURTIS. Both of° one horse?

GRUMIO. What's that to thee?

CURTIS. Why, a horse.

80 GRUMIO. Tell thou the tale. But hadst
thou not crossed° me thou shouldst have
heard how her horse fell and she under her
horse. Thou shouldst have heard in how
miry a place, how she was bemoiled,° how
he left her with the horse upon her, how he   85
beat me because her horse stumbled, how
she waded through the dirt to pluck him off
me; how he swore, how she prayed that
never prayed before; how I cried, how the
horses ran away, how her bridle was burst,   90
how I lost my crupper, with many things of
worthy memory which now shall die in oblivion, and thou return unexperienced° to
thy grave.

CURTIS. By this reck'ning° he is more   95
shrew than she.

GRUMIO. Ay, and that thou and the
proudest of you all shall find when he
comes home. But what° talk I of this? Call
forth Nathaniel, Joseph, Nicholas, Philip,   100
Walter, Sugarsop, and the rest. Let their
heads be slickly° combed, their blue° coats
brushed, and their garters of an indifferent°
knit. Let them curtsy with their left legs
and not presume to touch a hair of my mas-   105
ter's horsetail till they kiss their hands. Are
they all ready?

CURTIS. They are.

GRUMIO. Call them forth.

CURTIS. Do you hear, ho? You must meet   110
my master to countenance° my mistress.

GRUMIO. Why, she hath a face of her
own.

CURTIS. Who knows not that?

GRUMIO. Thou, it seems, that calls for   115
company to countenance her.

CURTIS. I call them forth to credit° her.

GRUMIO. Why, she comes to borrow
nothing of them.

Enter four or five SERVINGMEN.

NATHANIEL. Welcome home, Grumio!   120
PHILIP. How now, Grumio?
JOSEPH. What, Grumio!

---

46 **"Jack boy, ho boy!"** (from another round or
catch) 48-49 **cony-catching** rabbit-catching (i.e.,
tricking simpletons; with pun on *catch* , the song)
53 **strewed** i.e., on floor (for special occasion)
54 **fustian** coarse cloth (cotton and flax) 55 **officer** servant 56 **jacks** (1) menservants, (2) half-
pint leather drinking cups 56 **jills** (1) maids, (2)
gill-size metal drinking cups 57 **carpets** table covers 72-73 **sensible** (1) rational, (2) "feel"-able
75 **Imprimis** first 75 **foul** muddy 76 **of** on
81 **crossed** interrupted

84 **bemoiled** muddied 92 **unexperienced** uninformed 95 **reck'ning** account 99 **what** why
102 **slickly** smoothly 102 **blue** (usual color of servants' clothing) 103 **indifferent** matching (?), appropriate (?) 111 **countenance** show respect to
(with puns following) 117 **credit** honor

NICHOLAS. Fellow Grumio!

NATHANIEL. How now, old lad!

125 GRUMIO. Welcome, you; how now, you;
what, you; fellow, you; and thus much for
greeting. Now, my spruce companions, is
all ready and all things neat?

NATHANIEL. All things is ready. How near
130 is our master?

GRUMIO. E'en at hand, alighted by this,°
and therefore be not—Cock's° passion, silence! I hear my master.

Enter PETRUCHIO *and* KATE.

PETRUCHIO. Where be these knaves?
What, no man at door
135 To hold my stirrup nor to take my horse?
Where is Nathaniel, Gregory, Philip?

ALL SERVINGMEN. Here, here, sir, here,
sir.

PETRUCHIO. Here, sir, here, sir, here,
sir, here, sir!
You loggerheaded° and unpolished grooms!
What, no attendance? No regard? No
140   duty?
Where is the foolish knave I sent before?

GRUMIO. Here, sir, as foolish as I was
before.

PETRUCHIO. You peasant swain!° You
whoreson° malt-horse drudge!°
Did I not bid thee meet me in the park°
And bring along these rascal knaves with
145   thee?

GRUMIO. Nathaniel's coat, sir, was not
fully made
And Gabrel's pumps were all unpinked° i'
th' heel.
There was no link° to color Peter's hat,
And Walter's dagger was not come from
sheathing.°
There were none fine but Adam, Rafe, and
150   Gregory;

The rest were ragged, old, and beggarly.
Yet, as they are, here are they come to
meet you.

PETRUCHIO. Go, rascals, go, and fetch
my supper in.   *Exeunt* SERVANTS.
[Sings] "Where is the life that late I led?"°
Where are those°—Sit down, Kate, and
welcome.   155
Soud,° soud, soud, soud!

Enter SERVANTS *with supper.*

Why, when,° I say?—Nay, good sweet
Kate, be merry.—
Off with my boots, you rogues, you vil-
lains! When?
[Sings.] "It was the friar of orders gray,
As he forth walkèd on his way"°—   160
Out, you rogue, you pluck my foot awry!
Take that, and mend° the plucking of the
other. *[Strikes him.]*
Be merry, Kate. Some water here! What
ho!

Enter one with water.

Where's my spaniel Troilus? Sirrah, get
you hence
And bid my cousin Ferdinand come
hither—   *[Exit* SERVANT.*]*   165
One, Kate, that you must kiss and be
acquainted with.
Where are my slippers? Shall I have some
water?
Come, Kate, and wash, and welcome
heartily.
You whoreson villain, will you let it fall?
[Strikes him.]

KATE. Patience, I pray you. 'Twas a
fault unwilling.   170

PETRUCHIO. A whoreson, beetle-
headed,° flap-eared knave!
Come, Kate, sit down; I know you have a
stomach.°

131 **this** now   132 **Cock's** God's (i.e., Christ's)
139 **loggerheaded** blockheaded   143 **swain** bump-
kin   143 **whoreson** bastardly   143 **malt-horse
drudge** slow horse on brewery treadmill   144 **park**
country-house grounds   147 **unpinked** lacking em-
bellishment made by pinking (making small holes
in leather)   148 **link** torch, providing blacking
149 **sheathing** repairing scabbard

154 **"Where . . . led?"** (from an old ballad)
155 **those** servants   156 **Soud** (exclamation variously explained: some editors emend to Food)
157 **when** (exclamation of annoyance, as in next
line)   159-160 **"It was . . . his way"** (from another
old song)   162 **mend** improve   171 **beetle-headed**
mallet-headed   172 **stomach** (1) hunger, (2) irascibility

Will you give thanks,° sweet Kate, or else
    shall I?
What's this? Mutton?
    FIRST SERVINGMAN. Ay.
    PETRUCHIO.   Who brought it?
    PETER.   I.
    PETRUCHIO. 'Tis burnt, and so is all the
175   meat.
What dogs are these! Where is the rascal
    cook?
How durst you, villains, bring it from the
    dresser,°
And serve it thus to me that love it not?
There, take it to you, trenchers,° cups,
    and all,
           [Throws food and dishes at them.]
You heedless joltheads° and unmannered
180   slaves!
What, do you grumble? I'll be with° you
    straight.°
    KATE. I pray you, husband, be not so
    disquiet.
The meat was well if you were so con-
    tented.°
    PETRUCHIO. I tell thee, Kate, 'twas
    burnt and dried away,
185 And I expressly am forbid to touch it,
For it engenders choler,° planteth anger,
And better 'twere that both of us did
    fast—
Since of ourselves, ourselves are
    choleric°—
Than feed it° with such overroasted flesh.
190 Be patient. Tomorrow't shall be mended,°
And for this night we'll fast for company.°
Come, I will bring thee to thy bridal cham-
    ber.   *Exeunt.*

Enter SERVANTS *severally.*

    NATHANIEL. Peter, didst ever see the
    like?

    PETER. He kills her in her own humor.°

Enter CURTIS, *a Servant.*

    GRUMIO. Where is he?   195
    CURTIS. In her chamber, making a ser-
    mon of continency to her,
And rails and swears and rates,° that she,
    poor soul,
Knows not which way to stand, to look, to
    speak,
And sits as one new-risen from a dream.
Away, away, for he is coming hither.   200
                    [Exeunt.]

Enter PETRUCHIO.

    PETRUCHIO. Thus have I politicly° begun
    my reign,
And 'tis my hope to end successfully.
My falcon° now is sharp° and passing
    empty,
And till she stoop° she must not be full
    gorged,°
For then she never looks upon her lure.°   205
Another way I have to man° my haggard,°
To make her come and know her keeper's
    call,
That is, to watch° her as we watch these
    kites°
That bate and beat° and will not be obedi-
    ent.
She eat° no meat today, nor none shall
    eat.   210
Last night she slept not, nor tonight she
    shall not.
As with the meat, some undeservèd fault
I'll find about the making of the bed,

---

173 **give thanks** say grace 177 **dresser** sideboard
179 **trenchers** wooden platters 180 **joltheads**
boneheads (*jolt* is related to *jaw* or *jowl*) 181 **with**
even with 181 **straight** directly 183 **so conten7ed**
willing to see it as it was 186 **choler** bile, the "humor" (fluid) supposed to produce anger 188 **choleric** bilious, i.e., hot-tempered 189 **it** i.e., their
choler 190 **'t shall be mended** things will be better 191 **for company** together

194 **kills her in her own humor** conquers her
by using her own disposition 197 **rates** scolds
201 **politicly** with a calculated plan 203 **falcon**
hawk trained for hunting (falconry figures continue for seven lines) 203 **sharp** pinched with hunger 204 **stoop** (1) obey, (2) swoop to the lure
204 **full gorged** fully fed 205 **lure** device used in
training a hawk to return from flight 206 **man** (1)
tame, (2) be a man to 206 **haggard** hawk captured
after reaching maturity 208 **watch** keep from
sleep 208 **kites** type of small hawk 209 **bate and
beat** flap and flutter (i.e., in jittery resistance to
training) 210 **eat** ate (pronounced *et* , as still in
Britain)

And here I'll fling the pillow, there the
　　bolster,°
This way the coverlet, another way the
215　　sheets.
Ay, and amid this hurly° I intend°
That all is done in reverent care of her,
And in conclusion she shall watch° all
　　night.
And if she chance to nod I'll rail and brawl
220　And with the clamor keep her still awake.
This is a way to kill a wife with kindness,°
And thus I'll curb her mad and headstrong
　　humor.
He that knows better how to tame a
　　shrew,°
Now let him speak—'tis charity to
　　show.　　　　　　　　　　　*Exit.*

[Scene II. Padua. The street in front of
BAPTISTA'S *house.]*

Enter TRANIO *[as Lucentio] and* HORTENSIO
[as Litio].

TRANIO. Is't possible, friend Litio, that
　　Mistress Bianca
Doth fancy° any other but Lucentio?
I tell you, sir, she bears me fair in hand.°
　　HORTENSIO. Sir, to satisfy you in what I
　　have said,
Stand by and mark the manner of his
5　　teaching.

[They eavesdrop.]

Enter BIANCA *[and* LUCENTIO *as Cambio].*

LUCENTIO. Now mistress, profit you in
　　what you read?
BIANCA. What, master, read you? First
　　resolve° me that.
LUCENTIO. I read that° I profess,° the
　　Art to Love.°

BIANCA. And may you prove, sir, master
　　of your art.
LUCENTIO. While you, sweet dear, prove
　　mistress of my heart.　　*[They court.]*　10
HORTENSIO. Quick proceeders,° marry!°
　　Now, tell me, I pray,
You that durst swear that your mistress
　　Bianca
Loved none in the world so well as Lucen-
　　tio.
TRANIO. O despiteful° love! Unconstant
　　womankind!
I tell thee, Litio, this is wonderful.°　　　　15
　　HORTENSIO. Mistake no more. I am not
　　Litio,
Nor a musician, as I seem to be,
But one that scorn to live in this disguise,
For such a one as leaves a gentleman
And makes a god of such a cullion.°　　　　20
Know, sir, that I am called Hortensio.
　　TRANIO. Signior Hortensio, I have often
　　heard
Of your entire affection to Bianca,
And since mine eyes are witness of her
　　lightness,°
I will with you, if you be so contented,　　　25
Forswear° Bianca and her love forever.
　　HORTENSIO. See, how they kiss and
　　court! Signior Lucentio,
Here is my hand and here I firmly vow
Never to woo her more, but do forswear
　　her,
As one unworthy all the former favors°　　　30
That I have fondly° flattered her withal.
　　TRANIO. And here I take the like un-
　　feignèd oath,
Never to marry with her though she would
　　entreat.
Fie on her! See how beastly° she doth
　　court him.

---

²¹⁴ **bolster** cushion extending width of bed as
under-support for pillows ²¹⁶ **hurly** disturbance
²¹⁶ **intend** profess ²¹⁸ **watch** stay awake ²²¹ **kill a
wife with kindness** (ironic allusion to proverb
on ruining a wife by pampering) ²²³ **shrew**
(rhymes with "show") IV.ii. ² **fancy** like
³ **bears me fair in hand** leads me on ⁷ **resolve**
answer ⁸ **that** what ⁸ **profess** avow, practice
⁸ **Art to Love** (i.e., Ovid's *Ars Amandi*)

¹¹ **proceeders** (pun on idiom "proceed Master of
Arts"; cf. line 9) ¹¹ **marry** by Mary (mild exclamation) ¹⁴ **despiteful** spiteful ¹⁵ **wonderful**
causing wonder ²⁰ **cullion** low fellow (literally,
testicle) ²⁴ **lightness** (cf. "light woman") ²⁶ **Forswear** "swear off" ³⁰ **favors** marks of esteem
³¹ **fondly** foolishly ³⁴ **beastly** unashamedly

HORTENSIO. Would all the world but he
35   had quite forsworn.°
For me, that I may surely keep mine oath,
I will be married to a wealthy widow
Ere three days pass, which° hath as long
          loved me
As I have loved this proud disdainful hag-
          gard.°
40 And so farewell, Signior Lucentio.
Kindness in women, not their beauteous
          looks,
Shall win my love, and so I take my leave
In resolution as I swore before.   *[Exit.]*
          TRANIO. Mistress Bianca, bless you
          with such grace
45 As 'longeth to a lover's blessèd case.
Nay, I have ta'en you napping,° gentle
          love,
And have forsworn you with Hortensio.
          BIANCA. Tranio, you jest. But have you
          both forsworn me?
          TRANIO. Mistress, we have.
          LUCENTIO.   Then we are
          rid of Litio.
          TRANIO. I' faith, he'll have a lusty°
50   widow now,
That shall be wooed and wedded in a day.
          BIANCA. God give him joy!
          TRANIO. Ay, and he'll tame her.
          BIANCA.   He says
          so, Tranio.
          TRANIO. Faith, he is gone unto the
          taming school.
          BIANCA. The taming school! What, is
55   there such a place?
          TRANIO. Ay, mistress, and Petruchio is
          the master,
That teacheth tricks eleven and twenty
          long°
To tame a shrew and charm her chattering
          tongue.

Enter BIONDELLO.

          BIONDELLO. Master, master, I have
          watched so long
That I am dog-weary, but at last I spied   60
An ancient angel° coming down the hill
Will serve the turn.°
          TRANIO.   What° is he, Biondello?
          BIONDELLO. Master, a mercatante° or a
          pedant,°
I know not what, but formal in apparel,
In gait and countenance° surely like a
          father.   65
          LUCENTIO. And what of him, Tranio?
          TRANIO. If he be credulous and trust my
          tale,
I'll make him glad to seem Vincentio,
And give assurance to Baptista Minola
As if he were the right Vincentio.   70
Take in your love and then let me alone.
          [Exeunt LUCENTIO *and* BIANCA.*]*

Enter a PEDANT.

          PEDANT. God save you, sir.
          TRANIO.   And you, sir.
          You are welcome.
Travel you far on, or are you at the far-
          thest?
          PEDANT. Sir, at the farthest for a week
          or two,
But then up farther and as far as Rome,   75
And so to Tripoli if God lend me life.
          TRANIO. What countryman,° I pray?
          PEDANT.   Of Mantua.
          TRANIO. Of Mantua, sir? Marry, God
          forbid!
And come to Padua, careless of your life?
          PEDANT. My life, sir? How, I pray? For
          that goes hard.°   80
          TRANIO. 'Tis death for anyone in Mantua
To come to Padua. Know you not the
          cause?

---

[61] **ancient angel** man of good old stamp (*angel*
= coin; cf. "gentleman of the old school")
[62] **Will serve the turn** who will do for our purposes [62] **What** what kind of man [63] **mercatante**
merchant [63] **pedant** schoolmaster [65] **gait and
countenance** bearing and style [77] **What coun-
tryman** a man of what country [80] **goes hard** (cf.
"is rough")

[35] **Would . . . forsworn** i.e., would she had only
one lover [38] **which** who [39] **haggard** (cf. IV.i.206)
[46] **ta'en you napping** seen you "kiss and court"
(line 27) [50] **lusty** lively [57] **tricks eleven and
twenty long** (1) many tricks, (2) possibly an
allusion to card game "thirty-one" (cf.I.ii.38)

Your ships are stayed° at Venice and the
    Duke,
For private quarrel 'twixt your duke and
    him,
85 Hath published and proclaimed it openly.
'Tis marvel, but that you are but newly
    come,
You might have heard it else proclaimed
    about.
    PEDANT. Alas, sir, it is worse for me
    than so,°
For I have bills for money by exchange
From Florence and must here deliver
90   them.
    TRANIO. Well, sir, to do you courtesy,
This will I do and this I will advise° you.
First tell me, have you ever been at Pisa?
    PEDANT. Ay, sir, in Pisa have I often
    been—
95 Pisa, renownèd for grave citizens.
    TRANIO. Among them, know you one
    Vincentio?
    PEDANT. I know him not but I have
    heard of him—
A merchant of incomparable wealth.
    TRANIO. He is my father, sir, and, sooth
    to say,
In count'nance somewhat doth resemble
100   you.
    BIONDELLO *[aside].* As much as an apple
doth an oyster, and all one.°
    TRANIO. To save your life in this extrem-
    ity,
This favor will I do you for his sake,
And think it not the worst of all your
105   fortunes
That you are like to Sir Vincentio.
His name and credit° shall you undertake,°
And in my house you shall be friendly
    lodged.
Look that you take upon you° as you
    should.
110 You understand me, sir? So shall you stay
Till you have done your business in the
    city.

If this be court'sy, sir, accept of it.
    PEDANT. O sir, I do, and will repute° you
    ever
The patron of my life and liberty.
    TRANIO. Then go with me to make the
    matter good.   115
This, by the way,° I let you understand:
My father is here looked for every day
To pass assurance° of a dower in marriage
'Twixt me and one Baptista's daughter
    here.
In all these circumstances I'll instruct you. 120
Go with me to clothe° you as becomes
    you.   *Exeunt.*

[Scene III. In PETRUCHIO'S *house.]*

Enter KATE *and* GRUMIO.

    GRUMIO. No, no, forsooth, I dare not
    for my life.
    KATE. The more my wrong,° the more
    his spite appears.
What, did he marry me to famish me?
Beggars that come unto my father's door,
Upon entreaty have a present° alms;   5
If not, elsewhere they meet with charity.
But I, who never knew how to entreat
Nor never needed that I should entreat,
Am starved for meat,° giddy for lack of
    sleep,
With oaths kept waking and with brawling
    fed.   10
And that which spites me more than all
    these wants,
He does it under name of perfect love,
As who should say,° if I should sleep or
    eat
'Twere deadly sickness or else present
    death.
I prithee go and get me some repast,   15
I care not what, so° it be wholesome
    food.
    GRUMIO. What say you to a neat's° foot?

---

83 **stayed** held 88 **than so** than it appears so far
92 **advise** explain to 102 **all one** no difference
107 **credit** standing 107 **undertake** adopt 109 **take
upon you** assume your role

113 **repute** esteem 116 **by the way** as we walk
along 118 **pass assurance** give a guarantee IV.iii.
2 **The more my wrong** the greater the wrong
done me 5 **present** prompt 9 **meat** food 13 **As
who should say** as if to say 16 **so** as long as
17 **neat's** ox's or calf's

KATE. 'Tis passing good; prithee let me
   have it.
GRUMIO. I fear it is too choleric° a
   meat.
20 How say you to a fat tripe finely broiled?
KATE. I like it well. Good Grumio, fetch
   it me.
GRUMIO. I cannot tell, I fear 'tis choleric.
What say you to a piece of beef and mustard?
KATE. A dish that I do love to feed
   upon.
GRUMIO. Ay, but the mustard is too hot
25   a little.
KATE. Why then, the beef, and let the
   mustard rest.
GRUMIO. Nay then, I will not. You shall
   have the mustard
Or else you get no beef of Grumio.
KATE. Then both or one, or anything
   thou wilt.
GRUMIO. Why then, the mustard without
30   the beef.
KATE. Go, get thee gone, thou false
   deluding slave,   *Beats him.*
That feed'st me with the very name° of
   meat.
Sorrow on thee and all the pack of you
That triumph thus upon my misery.
35 Go, get thee gone, I say.

Enter PETRUCHIO *and* HORTENSIO *with
meat.*

PETRUCHIO. How fares my Kate? What,
   sweeting, all amort?°
HORTENSIO. Mistress, what cheer?°
KATE.   Faith, as cold° as can be.
PETRUCHIO. Pluck up thy spirits; look
   cheerfully upon me.
Here, love, thou seest how diligent I am
To dress thy meat° myself and bring it
40   thee.

I am sure, sweet Kate, this kindness
   merits thanks.
What, not a word? Nay then, thou lov'st it
   not,
And all my pains is sorted to no proof.°
Here, take away this dish.
KATE.   I pray you, let it
   stand.
PETRUCHIO. The poorest service is
   repaid with thanks,   45
And so shall mine before you touch the
   meat.
KATE. I thank you, sir.
HORTENSIO. Signior Petruchio, fie, you
   are to blame.
Come, Mistress Kate, I'll bear you com-
   pany.
PETRUCHIO *[aside].* Eat it up all, Hor-
   tensio, if thou lovest me;   50
Much good do it unto thy gentle heart.
Kate, eat apace. And now, my honey love,
Will we return unto thy father's house
And revel it as bravely° as the best,
With silken coats and caps and golden
   rings,   55
With ruffs° and cuffs and fardingales° and
   things,
With scarfs and fans and double change of
   brav'ry,°
With amber bracelets, beads, and all this
   knav'ry.°
What, hast thou dined? The tailor stays
   thy leisure°
To deck thy body with his ruffling° trea-
   sure.   60

Enter TAILOR.

Come, tailor, let us see these ornaments.

Enter HABERDASHER.

Lay forth the gown. What news with
   you, sir?

---

19 **choleric** temper-producing 32 **very name** name only 36 **all amort** depressed, lifeless (cf. "mortified") 37 **what cheer** how are things 37 **cold** (cf. "not so hot": "cold comfort," IV.i.36) 40 **To dress thy meat** in fixing your food

43 **sorted to no proof** have come to nothing 54 **bravely** handsomely dressed 56 **ruffs** stiffly starched, wheelshaped collars 56 **fardingales** farthingales, hooped skirts of petticoats 57 **brav'ry** handsome clothes 58 **knav'ry** girlish things 59 **stays thy leisure** awaits your permission 60 **ruffling** gaily ruffled

HABERDASHER. Here is the cap your
Worship did bespeak.°

PETRUCHIO. Why, this was molded on a
porringer°—

A velvet dish. Fie, fie, 'tis lewd° and
65   filthy.

Why, 'tis a cockle° or a walnut shell,

A knack,° a toy, a trick,° a baby's cap.

Away with it! Come, let me have a bigger.

KATE. I'll have no bigger. This doth fit
the time,°

And gentlewomen wear such caps as
70   these.

PETRUCHIO. When you are gentle you
shall have one too,

And not till then.

HORTENSIO *[aside].*   That will not be in
haste.

KATE. Why, sir, I trust I may have leave
to speak,

And speak I will. I am no child, no babe.

Your betters have endured me say my
75   mind,

And if you cannot, best you stop your
ears.

My tongue will tell the anger of my heart,

Or else my heart, concealing it, will break,

And rather than it shall I will be free

Even to the uttermost, as I please, in
80   words.

PETRUCHIO. Why, thou sayst true. It is
a paltry cap,

A custard-coffin,° a bauble, a silken pie.°

I love thee well in that thou lik'st it not.

KATE. Love me or love me not, I like
the cap,

85   And it I will have or I will have none.
[Exit HABERDASHER.*]*

PETRUCHIO. Thy gown? Why, ay. Come,
tailor, let us see't.

O mercy, God! What masquing° stuff is
here?

What's this? A sleeve? 'Tis like a demi-
cannon.°

What, up and down,° carved like an apple
tart?

Here's snip and nip and cut and slish and
slash,   90

Like to a censer° in a barber's shop.

Why, what, a° devil's name, tailor, call'st
thou this?

HORTENSIO *[aside].* I see she's like to
have neither cap nor gown.

TAILOR. You bid me make it orderly and
well,

According to the fashion and the time.   95

PETRUCHIO. Marry, and did, but if you
be rememb'red,

I did not bid you mar it to the time.°

Go, hop me over every kennel° home,

For you shall hop without my custom, sir.

I'll none of it. Hence, make your best of
it.   100

KATE. I never saw a better-fashioned
gown,

More quaint,° more pleasing, nor more
commendable.

Belike° you mean to make a puppet of me.

PETRUCHIO. Why, true, he means to
make a puppet of thee.

TAILOR. She says your worship means to
make a puppet of her.   105

PETRUCHIO. O monstrous arrogance!

Thou liest, thou thread, thou thimble,

Thou yard, three-quarters, half-yard,
quarter, nail!°

Thou flea, thou nit,° thou winter cricket
thou!

Braved° in mine own house with° a skein
of thread!   110

Away, thou rag, thou quantity,° thou remnant,

Or I shall so bemete° thee with thy yard

°° **demi-cannon** big cannon °° **up and down** entirely °¹ **censer** incense burner with perforated
top °² **a** in the °⁷ **to the time** for all time (cf. line
95, in which "the time" is "the contemporary
style") °⁸ **kennel** gutter (canal) ¹⁰² **quaint** skill-
fully made ¹⁰³ **Belike** no doubt ¹⁰⁸ **nail** 1/16 of a
yard ¹⁰⁹ **nit** louse's egg ¹¹⁰ **Braved** defied ¹¹⁰ **with**
by ¹¹¹ **quantity** fragment ¹¹² **bemete** (1) measure, (2) beat

---

⁶³ **bespeak** order ⁶⁴ **porringer** soup bowl
⁶⁵ **lewd** vile ⁶⁶ **cockle** shell of a mollusk ⁶⁷ **knack**
knickknack ⁶⁷ **trick** plaything ⁶⁹ **doth fit the
time** is in fashion ⁸² **custard-coffin** custard
crust ⁸² **pie** meat pie ⁸⁷ **masquing** for masquer-
ades or actors' costumes

As thou shalt think on prating° whilst thou
   liv'st.
I tell thee, I, that thou hast marred her
   gown.
   TAILOR. Your worship is deceived. The
115   gown is made
Just as my master had direction.°
Grumio gave order how it should be done.
   GRUMIO. I gave him no order; I gave him
the stuff.
120   TAILOR. But how did you desire it should
be made?
   GRUMIO. Marry, sir, with needle and
thread.
   TAILOR. But did you not request to have
125 it cut?
   GRUMIO. Thou hast faced° many things.
   TAILOR. I have.
   GRUMIO. Face° not me. Thou hast
braved° many men; brave° not me. I will
130 neither be faced nor braved. I say unto
thee, I bid thy master cut out the gown, but
I did not bid him cut it to pieces. *Ergo,*°
thou liest.
   TAILOR. Why, here is the note° of the
135 fashion to testify.
   PETRUCHIO. Read it.
   GRUMIO. The note lies in's throat° if he°
say I said so.
   TAILOR. *"Imprimis,*° a loose-bodied
140 gown."°
   GRUMIO. Master, if ever I said loose-
bodied gown, sew me in the skirts of it and
beat me to death with a bottom° of brown
thread. I said, a gown.
145   PETRUCHIO. Proceed.
   TAILOR. "With a small compassed°
cape."
   GRUMIO. I confess the cape.

   TAILOR. "With a trunk° sleeve."
   GRUMIO. I confess two sleeves.   150
   TAILOR. "The sleeves curiously° cut."
   PETRUCHIO. Ay, there's the villainy.
   GRUMIO. Error i' th' bill,° sir, error i' th'
bill. I commanded the sleeves should be cut
out and sewed up again, and that I'll prove   155
upon° thee, though thy little finger be
armed in a thimble.
   TAILOR. This is true that I say. And° I
had thee in place where,° thou shouldst
know it.   160
   GRUMIO. I am for° thee straight.° Take
thou the bill,° give me thy mete-yard,° and
spare not me.
   HORTENSIO. God-a-mercy, Grumio, then
he shall have no odds.   165
   PETRUCHIO. Well, sir, in brief, the gown
is not for me.
   GRUMIO. You are i' th' right, sir; 'tis for
my mistress.
   PETRUCHIO. Go, take it up unto° thy   170
master's use.°
   GRUMIO. Villain, not for thy life! Take up
my mistress' gown for thy master's use!
   PETRUCHIO. Why sir, what's your con-
ceit° in that?   175
   GRUMIO. O sir, the conceit is deeper
      than you think for.
Take up my mistress' gown to his master's
      use!
O, fie, fie, fie!
   PETRUCHIO *[aside].* Hortensio, say thou
      wilt see the tailor paid.
[To TAILOR.*]* Go take it hence; be gone
      and say no more.   180
   HORTENSIO. Tailor, I'll pay thee for thy
      gown tomorrow;
Take no unkindness of his hasty words.
Away, I say, commend me to thy master.
                           Exit TAILOR.

---

¹¹³ **think on prating** remember your silly talk
¹¹⁶ **had direction** received orders ¹²⁶ **faced**
trimmed ¹²⁸ **Face** challenge ¹²⁹ **braved** equipped
with finery ¹²⁹ **brave** defy ¹³² **Ergo** therefore
¹³⁴ **note** written notation ¹³⁷ **in's throat** from the
heart, with premeditation ¹³⁷ **he** it ¹³⁹ **Imprimis**
first ¹³⁹⁻¹⁴⁰ **loose-bodied gown** (worn by prostitutes, with *loose* in pun) ¹⁴³ **bottom** spool
¹⁴⁶ **compassed** with circular edge

¹⁴⁹ **trunk** full (cf. line 88) ¹⁵¹ **curiously** painstakingly ¹⁵³ **bill** i.e., the "note" ¹⁵⁵⁻¹⁵⁶ **prove upon**
test by dueling with ¹⁵⁸ **And** if ¹⁵⁹ **place where**
the right place ¹⁶¹ **for** ready for ¹⁶¹ **straight** right
now ¹⁶² **bill** (1) written order, (2) long-handled
weapon ¹⁶² **mete-yard** yardstick ¹⁷⁰ **up unto** away
for ¹⁷¹ **use** i.e., in whatever way he can; Grumio
uses these words for a sex joke ¹⁷⁴⁻¹⁷⁵ **conceit**
idea

PETRUCHIO. Well, come, my Kate, we
    will unto your father's,
Even in these honest mean habiliments.°
Our purses shall be proud, our garments
185   poor,
For 'tis the mind that makes the body
    rich,
And as the sun breaks through the darkest
    clouds
So honor peereth° in the meanest habit.°
What, is the jay more precious than the
    lark
190   Because his feathers are more beautiful?
Or is the adder better than the eel
Because his painted skin contents the eye?
O no, good Kate, neither art thou the
    worse
For this poor furniture° and mean array.
195   If thou account'st it shame, lay° it on me,
And therefore frolic. We will hence forth-
    with
To feast and sport us at thy father's
    house.
[To Grumio.] Go call my men, and let us
    straight to him;
And bring our horses unto Long-lane end.
There will we mount, and thither walk on
200   foot.
Let's see, I think 'tis now some seven
    o'clock,
And well we may come there by dinner-
    time.°
    KATE. I dare assure you, sir, 'tis almost
    two,
And 'twill be suppertime ere you come
    there.
    PETRUCHIO. It shall be seven ere I go to
205   horse.
Look what° I speak or do or think to do,
You are still crossing° it. Sirs, let 't alone:
I will not go today, and ere I do,
It shall be what o'clock I say it is.
    HORTENSIO *[aside].* Why, so this gallant
210   will command the sun.   *[Exeunt.]*

[Scene IV. Padua. The street in front of
BAPTISTA'S *house.]*

Enter TRANIO *[as Lucentio] and the* PEDANT
dressed like Vincentio.

    TRANIO. Sir, this is the house. Please it
    you that I call?
    PEDANT. Ay, what else? And but° I be
    deceived,
Signior Baptista may remember me
Near twenty years ago in Genoa,
Where we were lodgers at the Pegasus.°   5
    TRANIO. 'Tis well, and hold your own° in
    any case
With such austerity as 'longeth to a father.
    PEDANT. I warrant° you. But sir, here
    comes your boy;
'Twere good he were schooled.°

Enter BIONDELLO.

    TRANIO. Fear you not him. Sirrah Bion-
    dello,   10
Now do your duty throughly,° I advise
    you.
Imagine 'twere the right Vincentio.
    BIONDELLO. Tut, fear not me.
    TRANIO. But hast thou done thy errand
    to Baptista?
    BIONDELLO. I told him that your father
    was at Venice   15
And that you looked for him this day in
    Padua.
    TRANIO. Th' art a tall° fellow. Hold thee
    that° to drink.
Here comes Baptista. Set your counte-
    nance, sir.

Enter BAPTISTA *and* LUCENTIO *[as Cambio].*
PEDANT *booted and bareheaded.°*

Signior Baptista, you are happily met.

IV.iv. ² **but** unless ³⁻⁵ **Signior Baptista . . .**
Pegasus (the Pedant is practicing as Vincentio)
⁵ **Pegasus** common English inn name (after
mythical winged horse symbolizing poetic inspiration) ⁶ **hold your own** act your role ⁸ **warrant**
guarantee ⁹ **schooled** informed (about his role)
¹¹ **throughly** thoroughly ¹⁷ **tall** excellent ¹⁷ **Hold
thee that** i.e., take this tip ¹⁸ ˢ·ᵈ· **booted and
bareheaded** i.e., arriving from a journey and
courteously greeting Baptista

---

¹⁸⁴ **habiliments** clothes ¹⁸⁸ **peereth** is recognized ¹⁸⁸ **habit** clothes ¹⁹⁴ **furniture** outfit ¹⁹⁵ **lay**
blame ²⁰² **dinnertime** midday ²⁰⁶ **Look what**
whatever ²⁰⁷ **crossing** obstructing, going counter
to

[To the PEDANT.*]* Sir, this is the gentleman
20   I told you of.
I pray you, stand good father to me now,
Give me Bianca for my patrimony.
        PEDANT. Soft,° son.
Sir, by your leave. Having come to Padua
25   To gather in some debts, my son Lucentio
Made me acquainted with a weighty
        cause°
Of love between your daughter and him-
        self.
And—for the good report I hear of you,
And for the love he beareth to your daugh-
        ter,
And she to him—to stay° him not too
30   long,
I am content, in a good father's care,
To have him matched. And if you please to
        like°
No worse than I, upon some agreement
Me shall you find ready and willing
With one consent to have her so be-
35   stowed,
For curious° I cannot be with you,
Signior Baptista, of whom I hear so well.
        BAPTISTA. Sir, pardon me in what I have
        to say.
Your plainness and your shortness° please
        me well.
40   Right true it is, your son Lucentio here
Doth love my daughter and she loveth
        him—
Or both dissemble deeply their
        affections—
And therefore, if you say no more than
        this,
That like a father you will deal with him
45   And pass° my daughter a sufficient dower,
The match is made, and all is done.
Your son shall have my daughter with
        consent.
        TRANIO. I thank you, sir. Where, then,
        do you know° best
We be affied° and such assurance ta'en

As shall with either part's° agreement
        stand?   50
        BAPTISTA. Not in my house, Lucentio,
        for you know
Pitchers have ears, and I have many ser-
        vants.
Besides, old Gremio is heark'ning still,°
And happily° we might be interrupted.
        TRANIO. Then at my lodging and it like°
        you.   55
There doth my father lie,° and there this
        night
We'll pass° the business privately and well.
Send for your daughter by your servant
        here;
My boy shall fetch the scrivener° pres-
        ently.
The worst is this, that at so slender warn-
        ing°   60
You are like to have a thin and slender
        pittance.°
        BAPTISTA. It likes° me well. Cambio, hie
        you home
And bid Bianca make her ready straight,
And, if you will, tell what hath happenèd:
Lucentio's father is arrived in Padua,   65
And how she's like to be Lucentio's wife.
                        [Exit LUCENTIO.*]*
        BIONDELLO. I pray the gods she may
        with all my heart!   *Exit.*
        TRANIO. Dally not with the gods, but
        get thee gone.
Signior Baptista, shall I lead the way?
Welcome, one mess° is like to be your
        cheer.°   70
Come, sir, we will better it in Pisa.
        BAPTISTA. I follow you.   *Exeunt.*

Enter LUCENTIO *[as Cambio] and* BION-
DELLO.

        BIONDELLO. Cambio!
        LUCENTIO. What sayst thou, Biondello?

²³ **Soft** take it easy ²⁶ **weighty cause** important
matter ³⁰ **stay** delay ³² **like** i.e., the match ³⁶ **curious** overinsistent on fine points ³⁹ **shortness**
conciseness ⁴⁵ **pass** legally settle upon ⁴⁸ **know**
think ⁴⁹ **affied** formally engaged

⁵⁰ **part's** party's ⁵³ **heark'ning still** listening
constantly ⁵⁴ **happily** perchance ⁵⁵ **and it like** if
it please ⁵⁶ **lie** stay ⁵⁷ **pass** settle ⁵⁹ **scrivener**
notary ⁶⁰ **slender warning** short notice ⁶¹ **pit-
tance** meal ⁶² **likes** pleases ⁷⁰ **mess** dish
⁷⁰ **cheer** entertainment

75   BIONDELLO. You saw my master° wink
and laugh upon you?

LUCENTIO. Biondello, what of that?

BIONDELLO. Faith, nothing, but has° left
me here behind to expound the meaning or
80   moral of his signs and tokens.

LUCENTIO. I pray thee, moralize° them.

BIONDELLO. Then thus. Baptista is safe,
talking with the deceiving father of a deceit-
ful son.

85   LUCENTIO. And what of him?

BIONDELLO. His daughter is to be
brought by you to the supper.

LUCENTIO. And then?

BIONDELLO. The old priest at Saint
90   Luke's church is at your command at all
hours.

LUCENTIO. And what of all this?

BIONDELLO. I cannot tell, except they are
busied about a counterfeit assurance.° Take
95   you assurance° of her, *"cum previlegio ad
impremendum solem."°* To th' church! Take
the priest, clerk, and some sufficient honest witnesses.

If this be not that you look for, I have no
        more to say,
100   But bid Bianca farewell forever and a day.

LUCENTIO. Hear'st thou, Biondello?

BIONDELLO. I cannot tarry. I knew a
wench married in an afternoon as she went
to the garden for parsley to stuff a rabbit.
105   And so may you, sir. And so adieu, sir. My
master hath appointed me to go to Saint
Luke's, to bid the priest be ready to come
against you come° with your appendix.°
                                        Exit.

LUCENTIO. I may, and will, if she be so
110   contented. She will be pleased; then

wherefore should I doubt? Hap what hap
may, I'll roundly° go about° her. It shall go
hard if Cambio go without her.   *Exit.*

[Scene V. *The road to Padua.*]

Enter PETRUCHIO, KATE, HORTENSIO *[with*
SERVANTS.]

PETRUCHIO. Come on, a° God's name,
    once more toward our father's.
Good Lord, how bright and goodly shines
    the moon.

KATE. The moon? The sun. It is not
    moonlight now.

PETRUCHIO. I say it is the moon that
    shines so bright.   5

KATE. I know it is the sun that shines
    so bright.

PETRUCHIO. Now, by my mother's son,
    and that's myself,
It shall be moon or star or what I list,°
Or ere° I journey to your father's house.
[To SERVANTS.] Go on and fetch our horses
    back again.
Evermore crossed and crossed, nothing
    but crossed!°   10

HORTENSIO *[to* KATE]. Say as he says or
    we shall never go.

KATE. Forward, I pray, since we have
    come so far,
And be it moon or sun or what you
    please.
And if you please to call it a rush-candle,°
Henceforth I vow it shall be so for me.   15

PETRUCHIO. I say it is the moon.

KATE.   I know
    it is the moon.

PETRUCHIO. Nay, then you lie. It is the
    blessèd sun.

KATE. Then God be blessed, it is the
    blessèd sun.
But sun it is not when you say it is not,
And the moon changes even as your mind.   20

---

⁷⁵ **my master** i.e., Tranio; cf. line 59 ⁷⁸ **has** he
has ⁸¹ **moralize** "expound" ⁹⁴ **assurance** be-
trothal document ⁹⁴⁻⁹⁵ **Take you assurance**
make sure ⁹⁵⁻⁹⁶ **cum . . . solem** (Biondello's version of *cum previlegio ad imprimendum solum,*
"with right of sole printing," a licensing phrase,
with sexual pun in *imprimendum* , literally
"pressing upon") ¹⁰⁸ **against you come** in preparing for your coming ¹⁰⁸ **appendix** (1) servant,
(2) wife (another metaphor from printing)

¹¹² **roundly** directly ¹¹² **about** after IV.v. ¹ **a** in
⁷ **list** please ⁸ **Or ere** before ¹⁰ **crossed** opposed, challenged ¹⁴ **rush-candle** rush dipped in
grease and used as candle

What you will have it named, even that it
    is,
And so it shall be so for Katherine.
    HORTENSIO *[aside]*. Petruchio, go thy
      ways. The field is won.
    PETRUCHIO. Well, forward, forward!
      Thus the bowl° should run
25 And not unluckily against the bias.°
But soft,° company° is coming here.

Enter VINCENTIO.

[To VINCENTIO.*]* Good morrow, gentle
    mistress; where away?
Tell me, sweet Kate, and tell me truly too,
Hast thou beheld a fresher° gentlewoman?
Such war of white and red within her
30   cheeks!
What stars do spangle heaven with such
    beauty
As those two eyes become that heavenly
    face?
Fair lovely maid, once more good day to
    thee.
Sweet Kate, embrace her for her beauty's
    sake.
35   HORTENSIO *[aside]*. 'A° will make the man
mad, to make a woman of him.
    KATE. Young budding virgin, fair and
      fresh and sweet,
Whither away, or where is thy abode?
Happy the parents of so fair a child!
40 Happier the man whom favorable stars
Allots thee for his lovely bedfellow!
    PETRUCHIO. Why, how now, Kate, I
      hope thou are not mad.
This is a man, old, wrinkled, faded, with-
    ered,
And not a maiden, as thou sayst he is.
    KATE. Pardon, old father, my mistaking
45   eyes
That have been so bedazzled with the sun
That everything I look on seemeth green.°

Now I perceive thou art a reverend father;
Pardon, I pray thee, for my mad mistak-
    ing.
    PETRUCHIO. Do, good old grandsire, and 50
      withal make known
Which way thou travelest. If along with us,
We shall be joyful of thy company.
    VINCENTIO. Fair sir, and you my merry
      mistress,
That with your strange encounter° much
    amazed me,
My name is called Vincentio, my dwelling 55
    Pisa,
And bound I am to Padua, there to visit
A son of mine which long I have not seen.
    PETRUCHIO. What is his name?
    VINCENTIO.   Lucentio, gentle sir.
    PETRUCHIO. Happily met, the happier
      for thy son.   60
And now by law as well as reverend age,
I may entitle thee my loving father.
The sister to my wife, this gentlewoman,
Thy son by this° hath married. Wonder not
Nor be not grieved. She is of good es-
    teem,   65
Her dowry wealthy, and of worthy birth;
Beside, so qualified° as may beseem°
The spouse of any noble gentleman.
Let me embrace with old Vincentio
And wander we to see thy honest son,   70
Who will of thy arrival be full joyous.
    VINCENTIO. But is this true, or is it else
      your pleasure,
Like pleasant° travelers, to break a jest
Upon the company you overtake?
    HORTENSIO. I do assure thee, father, so
      it is.
    PETRUCHIO. Come, go along, and see   75
      the truth hereof,
For our first merriment hath made thee
    jealous.°   *Exeunt [all but* HORTENSIO*]*.
    HORTENSIO. Well, Petruchio, this has put
      me in heart.

---

[24] **bowl** bowling ball [25] **against the bias** not in
the planned curving route, made possible by a
lead insertion (bias) weighting one side of the ball
[26] **soft** hush [26] **company** someone [29] **fresher**
more radiant [35] **'A** he [47] **green** young

[54] **encounter** mode of address [63] **this** now [65] **so
qualified** having qualities [66] **beseem** befit
[72] **pleasant** addicted to pleasantries [76] **jealous**
suspicious

Have to° my widow, and if she be froward,°
Then hast thou taught Hortensio to be
untoward.°   *Exit.*

[ACT V

Scene I. *Padua. The street in front of* LU-
CENTIO's *house.]*

Enter BIONDELLO, LUCENTIO *[as Cambio],*
and BIANCA; GREMIO *is out before.*°

BIONDELLO. Softly and swiftly, sir, for
the priest is ready.
LUCENTIO. I fly, Biondello. But they may
chance to need thee at home; therefore
5   leave us.   *Exit [with* BIANCA].
BIONDELLO. Nay, faith, I'll see the
church a your back,° and then come back to
my master's as soon as I can.   *[Exit.]*
GREMIO. I marvel Cambio comes not all
10 this while.

Enter PETRUCHIO, KATE, VINCENTIO, *[and]*
GRUMIO, *with* ATTENDANTS.

PETRUCHIO. Sir, here's the door, this is
Lucentio's house.
My father's bears° more toward the mar-
ketplace;
Thither must I, and here I leave you, sir.
VINCENTIO. You shall not choose but
drink before you go.
I think I shall command your welcome
15 here,
And by all likelihood some cheer is to-
ward.°   *Knock.*
GREMIO. They're busy within. You were
best knock louder.

PEDANT *[as Vincentio] looks out of the win-*
dow [above].

PEDANT. What's° he that knocks as he
would beat down the gate?   20
VINCENTIO. Is Signior Lucentio within,
sir?
PEDANT. He's within, sir, but not to be
spoken withal.°
VINCENTIO. What if a man bring him a   25
hundred pound or two, to make merry
withal?
PEDANT. Keep your hundred pounds to
yourself; he shall need none so long as I
live.   30
PETRUCHIO. Nay, I told you your son was
well beloved in Padua. Do you hear, sir? To
leave frivolous circumstances,° I pray you
tell Signior Lucentio that his father is come
from Pisa and is here at the door to speak 35
with him.
PEDANT. Thou liest. His father is come
from Padua° and here looking out at the
window.
VINCENTIO. Art thou his father?   40
PEDANT. Ay sir, so his mother says, if I
may believe her.
PETRUCHIO *[to* VINCENTIO]. Why how
now, gentleman? Why this is flat° knavery,
to take upon you another man's name.   45
PEDANT. Lay hands on the villain. I believe 'a° means to cozen° somebody in this
city under my countenance.°

Enter BIONDELLO.

BIONDELLO. I have seen them in the
church together; God send 'em good ship-   50
ping!° But who is here? Mine old master,
Vincentio! Now we are undone° and
brought to nothing.°
VINCENTIO. Come hither, crack-hemp.°
BIONDELLO. I hope I may choose,° sir.   55

⁷⁸ **Have to** on to ⁷⁸ **froward** fractious ⁷⁹ **untoward** difficult V.i. ˢ·ᵈ· **out before** precedes, and
does not see, the others ⁷ **a your back** on your
back (see you enter the church? or, married?)
¹² **bears** lies ¹⁶ **toward** at hand

¹⁹ **What's** who is ²⁴ **withal** with ³³ **frivolous
circumstances** trivial matters ³⁸ **Padua** (perhaps Shakespeare's slip of the pen for *Pisa*,
home of the real Vincentio, or *Mantua*, where
the Pedant comes from; cf. IV.ii.77) ⁴⁴ **flat** unvar-
nished ⁴⁷ **'a** he ⁴⁷ **cozen** defraud ⁴⁸ **countenance**
identity ⁵⁰·⁵¹ **shipping** journey ⁵² **undone** defeated ⁵³ **brought to nothing** (cf. "annihilated")
⁵⁴ **crack-hemp** rope-stretcher (i.e., subject for
hanging)

VINCENTIO. Come hither, you rogue. What, have you forgot me?

BIONDELLO. Forgot you? No, sir. I could not forget you, for I never saw you before in all my life.

VINCENTIO. What, you notorious° villain, didst thou never see thy master's father, Vincentio?

BIONDELLO. What, my old worshipful old master? Yes, marry, sir, see where he looks out of the window.

VINCENTIO. Is't so, indeed?

He beats BIONDELLO.

BIONDELLO. Help, help, help! Here's a madman will murder me.   *[Exit.]*

PEDANT. Help, son! Help, Signior Baptista!   *[Exit from above.]*

PETRUCHIO. Prithee, Kate, let's stand aside and see the end of this controversy.

[They stand aside.]

　　Enter PEDANT *[below] with* SERVANTS, BAPTISTA, *[and]* TRANIO *[as Lucentio].*

TRANIO. Sir, what are you that offer° to beat my servant?

VINCENTIO. What am I, sir? Nay, what are you, sir? O immortal gods! O fine° villain! A silken doublet, a velvet hose, a scarlet cloak, and a copatain° hat! O, I am undone, am undone! While I play the good husband° at home, my son and my servant spend all at the university.

TRANIO. How now, what's the matter?

BAPTISTA. What, is the man lunatic?

TRANIO. Sir, you seem a sober ancient gentleman by your habit,° but your words show you a madman. Why sir, what 'cerns° it you if I wear pearl and gold? I thank my good father, I am able to maintain it.

VINCENTIO. Thy father! O villain, he is a sailmaker in Bergamo.

BAPTISTA. You mistake, sir, you mistake, sir. Pray, what do you think is his name?

VINCENTIO. His name! As if I knew not his name! I have brought him up ever since he was three years old, and his name is Tranio.

PEDANT. Away, away, mad ass! His name is Lucentio, and he is mine only son and heir to the lands of me, Signior Vincentio.

VINCENTIO. Lucentio! O he hath murd'red his master. Lay hold on him, I charge you in the Duke's name. O my son, my son! Tell me, thou villain, where is my son Lucentio?

TRANIO. Call forth an officer.

[Enter an OFFICER.*]*

Carry this mad knave to the jail. Father Baptista, I charge you see that he be forthcoming.°

VINCENTIO. Carry me to the jail!

GREMIO. Stay, officer. He shall not go to prison.

BAPTISTA. Talk not, Signior Gremio. I say he shall go to prison.

GREMIO. Take heed, Signior Baptista, lest you be cony-catched° in this business. I dare swear this is the right Vincentio.

PEDANT. Swear, if thou dar'st.

GREMIO. Nay, I dare not swear it.

TRANIO. Then thou wert best° say that I am not Lucentio.

GREMIO. Yes, I know thee to be Signior Lucentio.

BAPTISTA. Away with the dotard,° to the jail with him!

VINCENTIO. Thus strangers may be haled° and abused. O monstrous villain!

Enter BIONDELLO, LUCENTIO, *and* BIANCA.

BIONDELLO. O we are spoiled°—and yonder he is. Deny him, forswear him, or else we are all undone.

　　　　　Exit BIONDELLO, TRANIO,
　　　　　and PEDANT *as fast*
　　　　　as may be.

---

⁵⁵ **choose** have some choice (in the matter) ⁶¹ **notorious** extraordinary ⁷⁴ **offer** attempt ⁷⁷ **fine** well dressed ⁷⁹ **copatain** high comical ⁸¹ **husband** manager ⁸⁶ **habit** manner ⁸⁷ **'cerns** concerns

¹¹¹ **forthcoming** available (for trial) ¹¹⁸**cony-catched** fooled ¹²² **thou wert best** maybe you'll dare ¹²⁶ **dotard** old fool ¹²⁹ **haled** pulled about ¹³⁰ **spoiled** ruined

LUCENTIO. Pardon, sweet father. *Kneel.*
VINCENTIO.   Lives
  my sweet son?
BIANCA. Pardon, dear father.
BAPTISTA.   How hast
  thou offended?
Where is Lucentio?
135   LUCENTIO.   Here's Lucentio,
Right son to the right Vincentio,
That have by marriage made thy daughter
  mine
While counterfeit supposes° bleared thine
  eyne.°
  GREMIO. Here's packing,° with a wit-
  ness,° to deceive us all!
  VINCENTIO. Where is that damnèd villain
140   Tranio
That faced and braved° me in this matter
  so?
BAPTISTA. Why, tell me, is not this my
  Cambio?
BIANCA. Cambio is changed into Lucen-
  tio.
LUCENTIO. Love wrought these miracles.
  Bianca's love
145   Made me exchange my state with Tranio
While he did bear my countenance° in the
  town,
And happily I have arrived at the last
Unto the wishèd haven of my bliss.
What Tranio did, myself enforced him to.
Then pardon him, sweet father, for my
150   sake.
VINCENTIO. I'll slit the villain's nose that
would have sent me to the jail.
BAPTISTA *[to* LUCENTIO*]*. But do you hear,
sir? Have you married my daughter without
155   asking my good will?
VINCENTIO. Fear not, Baptista; we will
content you, go to.° But I will in, to be re-
venged for this villainy.   *Exit.*

BAPTISTA. And I, to sound the depth° of
this knavery.   *Exit.*   160
LUCENTIO. Look not pale, Bianca. Thy
father will not frown.   *Exeunt [*LUCENTIO
  and BIANCA*].*
GREMIO. My cake is dough,° but I'll in
  among the rest
Out of hope of all but my share of the
  feast.   *[Exit.]*
KATE. Husband, let's follow, to see the
  end of this ado.   165
PETRUCHIO. First kiss me, Kate, and we
  will.
KATE. What, in the midst of the street?
PETRUCHIO. What, art thou ashamed of
  me?
KATE. No sir, God forbid, but ashamed
  to kiss.
PETRUCHIO. Why, then let's home again.
[To GRUMIO*.]* Come sirrah, let's away.   170
KATE. Nay, I will give thee a kiss. Now
  pray thee, love, stay.
PETRUCHIO. Is not this well? Come, my
  sweet Kate.
Better once° than never, for never too
  late.°   *Exeunt.*

*[**Scene II.** Padua. In* LUCENTIO'S *house.]*

Enter BAPTISTA, VINCENTIO, GREMIO, *the*
PEDANT, LUCENTIO, *and* BIANCA, *[*PETRU-
CHIO, KATE, HORTENSIO,*]* TRANIO, BION-
DELLO, GRUMIO, *and* WIDOW*; the* SER-
VINGMEN *with* TRANIO *bringing in a ban-
quet.°*

LUCENTIO. At last, though long,° our
  jarring notes agree,
And time it is, when raging war is done,
To smile at 'scapes and perils overblown.°
My fair Bianca, bid my father welcome

---

138 **supposes** pretendings (evidently an allusion to Gascoigne's play *Supposes*, one of Shakespeare's sources) 138 **eyne** eyes 139 **packing** plotting 139 **with a witness** outright, unabashed 141 **faced and braved** impudently challenged and defied 146 **bear my countenance** take on my identity

157 **go to** (mild remonstrance; cf. "go on," "come, come," "don't worry") 159 **sound the depth** get to the bottom of 163 **cake is dough** project hasn't worked out (proverbial; cf. I.i.109–110) 173 **once** at some time 173 **Better . . . late** better late than never V.ii. s.d.**banquet** dessert 1 **At last, though long** at long last 3 **overblown** that have blown over

While I with self-same kindness welcome
5   thine.
Brother Petruchio, sister Katherina,
And thou, Hortensio, with thy loving
        widow,
Feast with the best and welcome to my
        house.
My banquet is to close our stomachs° up
After our great good cheer.° Pray you, sit
10   down,
For now we sit to chat as well as eat.
    PETRUCHIO. Nothing but sit and sit, and
        eat and eat.
    BAPTISTA. Padua affords this kindness,
        son Petruchio.
    PETRUCHIO. Padua affords nothing but
        what is kind.
    HORTENSIO. For both our sakes I would
15   that word were true.
    PETRUCHIO. Now, for my life, Hortensio
        fears° his widow.
    WIDOW. Then never trust me if I be
        afeard.°
    PETRUCHIO. You are very sensible and
        yet you miss my sense:
I mean Hortensio is afeard of you.
    WIDOW. He that is giddy thinks the
20   world turns round.
    PETRUCHIO. Roundly° replied.
    KATE.   Mistress,
        how mean you that?
    WIDOW. Thus I conceive by° him.
    PETRUCHIO. Conceives by° me! How
        likes Hortensio that?
    HORTENSIO. My widow says, thus she
        conceives her tale.°
    PETRUCHIO. Very well mended. Kiss him
25   for that, good widow.
    KATE. "He that is giddy thinks the
        world turns round."
I pray you, tell me what you meant by
        that.

    WIDOW. Your husband, being troubled
        with a shrew,
Measures° my husband's sorrow by his°
        woe,
And now you know my meaning.   30
    KATE. A very mean° meaning.
    WIDOW.   Right, I
        mean you.
    KATE. And I am mean° indeed, respect-
        ing you.
    PETRUCHIO. To her, Kate!
    HORTENSIO. To her, widow!
    PETRUCHIO. A hundred marks, my Kate
        does put her down.°   35
    HORTENSIO. That's my office.°
    PETRUCHIO. Spoke like an officer. Ha'°
        to thee, lad.   *Drinks to* HORTENSIO.
    BAPTISTA. How likes Gremio these
        quick-witted folks?
    GREMIO. Believe me, sir, they butt°
        together well.
    BIANCA. Head and butt!° An hasty-
        witted body   40
Would say your head and butt were head
        and horn.°
    VINCENTIO. Ay, mistress bride, hath that
        awakened you?
    BIANCA. Ay, but not frighted me; there-
        fore I'll sleep again.
    PETRUCHIO. Nay, that you shall not.
        Since you have begun,
Have at you° for a bitter° jest or two.   45
    BIANCA. Am I your bird?° I mean to
        shift my bush,
And then pursue me as you draw your
        bow.
You are welcome all.
        Exit BIANCA *[with* KATE *and* WIDOW*].*
    PETRUCHIO. She hath prevented me.°
        Here, Signior Tranio,

---

⁹ **stomachs** (with pun on "irascibility"; cf. IV.i.172) ¹⁰ **cheer** (reception at Baptista's) ¹⁶ **fears** is afraid of (the Widow puns on the meaning "frightens") ¹⁷ **afeard** (1) frightened, (2) suspected ²¹ **Roundly** outspokenly ²² **conceive by** understand ²³ **Conceives by** is made pregnant by ²⁴ **conceives her tale** understands her statement (with another pun)

²⁹ **Measures** estimates ²⁹ **his** his own ³¹ **mean** paltry ³² **am mean** (1) am moderate, (2) have a low opinion ³⁵ **put her down** defeat her (with sexual pun by Hortensio) ³⁶ **office** job ³⁷ **Ha'** here's, hail ³⁹ **butt** (perhaps also "but," i.e., argue or differ) ⁴⁰ **butt** (with pun on "bottom") ⁴¹ **horn** (1) butting instrument, (2) symbol of cuckoldry, (3) phallus ⁴⁵ **Have at you** let's have ⁴⁵ **bitter** biting (but good-natured) ⁴⁶ **bird** prey ⁴⁹ **prevented me** beaten me to it

This bird you aimed at, though you hit her
50   not;°
Therefore a health to all that shot and
        missed.
    TRANIO. O sir, Lucentio slipped° me,
        like his greyhound,
Which runs himself and catches for his
        master.
    PETRUCHIO. A good swift° simile but
        something currish.
    TRANIO. 'Tis well, sir, that you hunted
55   for yourself;
'Tis thought your deer° does hold you at a
        bay.°
    BAPTISTA. O, O, Petruchio, Tranio hits
        you now.
    LUCENTIO. I thank thee for that gird,°
        good Tranio.
    HORTENSIO. Confess, confess, hath he
        not hit you here?
    PETRUCHIO. 'A has a little galled° me, I
60   confess,
And as the jest did glance away from me,
'Tis ten to one it maimed you two out-
        right.
    BAPTISTA. Now, in good sadness,° son
        Petruchio,
I think thou hast the veriest° shrew of all.
    PETRUCHIO. Well, I say no. And there-
65   fore, for assurance,°
Let's each one send unto his wife,
And he whose wife is most obedient
To come at first when he doth send for
        her
Shall win the wager which we will pro-
        pose.
    HORTENSIO. Content. What's the wager?
70 LUCENTIO.   Twenty crowns.
    PETRUCHIO. Twenty crowns!
I'll venture so much of° my hawk or
        hound,
But twenty times so much upon my wife.
    LUCENTIO. A hundred then.

    HORTENSIO.   Content.°
    PETRUCHIO.   A match,° 'tis done.
    HORTENSIO. Who shall begin?
    LUCENTIO.   That will I.°   75
Go Biondello, bid your mistress come to
    me.
    BIONDELLO. I go.   *Exit.*
    BAPTISTA. Son, I'll be your half,° Bianca
        comes.
    LUCENTIO. I'll have no halves; I'll bear it
        all myself.

Enter BIONDELLO.

How now,° what news?
    BIONDELLO.   Sir, my mistress
        sends you word   80
That she is busy and she cannot come.
    PETRUCHIO. How?° She's busy and she
        cannot come?
Is that an answer?
    GREMIO.   Ay, and a kind one too.
Pray God, sir, your wife send you not a
        worse.
    PETRUCHIO. I hope, better.   85
    HORTENSIO. Sirrah Biondello, go and
        entreat my wife
To come to me forthwith.°
                          Exit BIONDELLO.
    PETRUCHIO.   O ho, entreat her!
Nay, then she must needs come.
    HORTENSIO.   I am afraid, sir,
Do what you can, yours will not be en-
        treated.

Enter BIONDELLO.

Now where's my wife?   90
    BIONDELLO. She says you have some
        goodly jest in hand.
She will not come. She bids you come to
    her.
    PETRUCHIO. Worse and worse. She will
        not come. O vile,
Intolerable, not to be endured!
Sirrah Grumio, go to your mistress; say°   95

---

52 **slipped** unleashed 54 **swift** quick-witted
56 **deer** (1) doe, (2) dear 56 **at a bay** at bay (i.e.,
backed up at a safe distance) 58 **gird** gibe
60 **galled** chafed 63 **sadness** seriousness 64 **veriest** most genuine 65 **assurance** proof 72 **of** on

74 **Content** agreed 74 **A match** (it's) a bet 78 **be
your half** assume half your bet 80 **How now**
(mild exclamation; cf. "well") 82 **How** what
87 **forthwith** right away

I command her come to me.
                              *Exit [*GRUMIO*].*
HORTENSIO. I know her answer.
PETRUCHIO.   What?
HORTENSIO.   She will not.
PETRUCHIO. The fouler fortune mine,
    and there an end.

Enter KATE.

BAPTISTA. Now, by my holidame,° here
    comes Katherina.
KATE. What is your will, sir, that you
100   send for me?
PETRUCHIO. Where is your sister and
    Hortensio's wife?
KATE. They sit conferring° by the parlor
    fire.
PETRUCHIO. Go fetch them hither. If
    they deny° to come,
Swinge° me them soundly° forth unto
    their husbands.
Away, I say, and bring them hither
105   straight.   *[Exit* KATE.*]*
LUCENTIO. Here is a wonder, if you talk
    of a wonder.
HORTENSIO. And so it is. I wonder what
    it bodes.
PETRUCHIO. Marry, peace it bodes, and
    love, and quiet life,
An awful° rule and right supremacy;
And, to be short, what not° that's sweet
110   and happy.
BAPTISTA. Now fair befall° thee, good
    Petruchio.
The wager thou hast won, and I will add
Unto their losses twenty thousand crowns,
Another dowry to another daughter,
For she is changed as she had never
115   been.
PETRUCHIO. Nay, I will win my wager
    better yet
And show more sign of her obedience,
Her new-built virtue and obedience.

Enter KATE, BIANCA, *and* WIDOW.

See where she comes and brings your
    froward° wives
As prisoners to her womanly persuasion.°   120
Katherine, that cap of yours becomes you
    not
Off with that bauble, throw it under foot.

[She throws it.]

WIDOW. Lord, let me never have a cause
    to sigh
Till I be brought to such a silly pass.°
BIANCA. Fie, what a foolish—duty call
    you this?   125
LUCENTIO. I would your duty were as
    foolish too.
The wisdom of your duty, fair Bianca,
Hath cost me five hundred° crowns since
    supper-time.
BIANCA. The more fool you for laying°
    on my duty.
PETRUCHIO. Katherine, I charge thee,
    tell these head-strong women°   130
What duty they do owe their lords and
    husbands.
WIDOW. Come, come, you're mocking.
    We will have no telling.
PETRUCHIO. Come on, I say, and first
    begin with her.
WIDOW. She shall not.
PETRUCHIO. I say she shall—and first
    begin with her.°   135
KATE. Fie, fie, unknit that threatening
    unkind° brow
And dart not scornful glances from those
    eyes
To wound thy lord, thy king, thy governor.
It blots thy beauty as frosts do bite the
    meads,
Confounds thy fame° as whirlwinds shake°
    fair buds,°   140

---

⁹⁹ **holidame** holy dame (some editors emend to *halidom*, sacred place or relic) ¹⁰² **conferring** conversing ¹⁰³ **deny** refuse ¹⁰⁴ **Swinge** thrash ¹⁰⁴ **soundly** thoroughly (cf. "sound beating") ¹⁰⁹ **awful** inspiring respect ¹¹⁰ **what not** i.e., everything ¹¹¹ **fair befall** good luck to

¹¹⁹ **froward** uncooperative ¹²⁴ **pass** situation ¹²⁸ **five hundred** (1) Lucentio makes it look worse than it is, or (2) he made several bets, or (3) the text errs (some editors emend to "a hundred," assuming that the manuscript's "a" was misread as the Roman numeral v) ¹²⁹ **laying** betting ¹³⁶ **unkind** hostile ¹⁴⁰ **Confounds thy fame** spoils people's opinion of you ¹⁴⁰ **shake** shake off

And in no sense is meet or amiable.
A woman moved° is like a fountain trou-
      bled,
Muddy, ill-seeming, thick, bereft of
      beauty,
And while it is so, none so dry or thirsty
145 Will deign to sip or touch one drop of it.
Thy husband is thy lord, thy life, thy
      keeper,
Thy head, thy sovereign—one that cares
      for thee,
And for thy maintenance commits his body
To painful labor both by sea and land,
To watch° the night in storms, the day in
150   cold,
Whilst thou li'st warm at home, secure
      and safe;
And craves no other tribute at thy hands
But love, fair looks, and true obedience:
Too little payment for so great a debt.
155 Such duty as the subject owes the prince,
Even such a woman oweth to her hus-
      band,
And when she is froward, peevish, sullen,
      sour,
And not obedient to his honest° will,
What is she but a foul contending rebel
160 And graceless traitor to her loving lord?
I am ashamed that women are so simple°
To offer war where they should kneel for
      peace,
Or seek for rule, supremacy, and sway,
When they are bound to serve, love, and
      obey.
Why are our bodies soft and weak and
165   smooth,
Unapt to° toil and trouble in the world,
But that our soft conditions° and our
      hearts
Should well agree with our external parts?

Come, come, you froward and unable
      worms,°
My mind hath been as big° as one of
      yours,   170
My heart as great, my reason haply more,
To bandy word for word and frown for
      frown.
But now I see our lances are but straws,
Our strength as weak, our weakness past
      compare,
That seeming to be most which we indeed
      least are.   175
Then vail your stomachs,° for it is no
      boot,°
And place your hands below your hus-
      band's foot,
In token of which duty, if he please,
My hand is ready, may it° do him ease.
    PETRUCHIO. Why, there's a wench!
      Come on and kiss me, Kate.   180
    LUCENTIO. Well, go thy ways, old lad,
      for thou shalt ha't.
    VINCENTIO. 'Tis a good hearing° when
      children are toward.°
    LUCENTIO. But a harsh hearing when
      women are froward.
    PETRUCHIO. Come, Kate, we'll to bed.
We three are married, but you two are
      sped.°   185
'Twas I won the wager, *[to* LUCENTIO*]*
      though you hit the white,°
And, being a winner, God give you good
      night.   *Exit* PETRUCHIO *[with* KATE*].*
    HORTENSIO. Now, go thy ways; thou
      hast tamed a curst shrow.
    LUCENTIO. 'Tis a wonder, by your leave,
      she will be tamèd so.   *[Exeunt.]*

---

[149] **unable worms** weak, lowly creatures [170] **big**
inflated (cf. "think big") [176] **vail your stomachs**
fell your pride [176] **no boot** useless, profitless
[179] **may it** (1) I hope it may, (2) if it may [182] **hearing** thing to hear; report [182] **toward** tractable
[185] **sped** done for [186] **white** (1) bull's eye, (2)
Bianca means white

---

[142] **moved** i.e., by ill temper [150] **watch** stay
awake, be alert during [158] **honest** honorable
[161] **simple** silly [166] **Unapt to** unfitted for [167] **conditions** qualities

QUESTIONS AND SUGGESTIONS FOR WRITING

1. In a paragraph characterize Lucentio. In a second paragraph explain why you do or do not find him comic.
2. In a paragraph characterize Bianca. In your characterization, be sure to take account of III.i.16–20.
3. In an essay of 250 words, characterize Gremio (*not* Grumio), paying special attention to his romantic pretensions. In your discussion, compare Gremio to his rival, Lucentio.
4. One critic (a male) has said that Petruchio "is every woman's dream of a kind of ideal lover—coming to take her by storm, to club her to his cave, and then to become gentle." First, what do you think he means by this, and, second, do you think he is correct?
5. *The Taming of the Shrew* is a play, not a case history. Do you suppose that watching the play you would be offended by Petruchio's treatment of Kate? Why, or why not?
6. One critic has said that the play is a criticism of the Elizabethan view that marriage is a commercial arrangement, and a celebration of another Elizabethan view, that marriage is a true union of hearts and minds. Evaluate this opinion.
7. An anonymous play called *The Taming of a Shrew* (customarily called *A Shrew*, in contrast to Shakespeare's *The Shrew*), ends with a return to the characters of the induction. We print this ending here. Read it, and then write an essay of 500 words in which you explain why, if you were staging Shakespeare's play, you would or would not add this ending.

Then enter two bearing of SLY *in his own apparel again, and leaves him where they found him, and then gets out. Then enter the* TAPSTER.

TAPSTER. Now that the darksome night
    is overpast,
And dawning day appears in crystal sky,
Now must I haste abroad. But soft, who's this?
What, Sly? O wondrous, hath he lain here all night?
5 I'll wake him; I think he's starved by this
But that his belly was so stuffed with ale.
What now, Sly, awake for shame!
    SLY. Sim, gi's some more wine. What's all the players gone? Am not I a lord?
10   TAPSTER. A lord with a murrain.° Come, art thou drunken still?

SLY. Who's this? Tapster? O Lord, sirrah, I have had the bravest° dream tonight° that ever thou heardest in all thy life.
    TAPSTER. Ay, marry,° but you had best 15 get you home, for your wife will corse you for dreaming here tonight.
    SLY. Will she? I know now how to tame a shrew: I dreamt upon it all this night till now, and thou hast waked me out of the 20 best dream that ever I had in my life. But I'll to my wife presently and tame her too an if she anger me.
    TAPSTER. Nay tarry, Sly, for I'll go home
    with thee,
And hear the rest that thou hast dreamt
    tonight.   *[Exit all.]* 25

---

¹⁰ **murrain** plague

¹³ **bravest** most splendid ¹³**tonight** last night
¹⁵ **Ay, marry** a mild oath, from "By Mary"

American Dreams and Nightmares

9

☐ ESSAYS

Thomas Jefferson (American. 1743–1826)

THE DECLARATION OF INDEPENDENCE

In CONGRESS, July 4, 1776.

THE UNANIMOUS DECLARATION
OF THE THIRTEEN UNITED STATES OF AMERICA.

When in the Course of human events, it becomes necessary for one people to dissolve the political bands which have connected them with another, and to assume among the powers of the earth, the separate and equal station to which the Laws of Nature and of Nature's God entitle them, a decent respect to the opinions of mankind requires that they should declare the causes which impel them to the separation.

We hold these truths to be self-evident, that all men are created equal, that they are endowed by their Creator with certain unalienable Rights, that among these are Life, Liberty and the pursuit of Happiness.

That to secure these rights, Governments are instituted among Men, deriving their just powers from the consent of the governed.

That whenever any Form of Government becomes destructive of these ends, it is the Right of the people to alter or to abolish it, and to institute new Government, laying its foundation on such principles and organizing its powers in such form, as to them shall seem most likely to effect their Safety and Happiness. Prudence, indeed, will dictate that Governments long established should not be changed for light and transient causes; and accordingly all experience hath shewn, that mankind are more disposed to suffer, while evils are sufferable, than to right themselves by abolishing the forms to which they are accustomed. But when a long train of abuses and usurpations, pursuing invariably the same Object evinces a design to reduce them under absolute Despotism, it is their right, it is their duty, to throw off such Government, and to provide new Guards for their future security.

Such has been the patient sufferance of these Colonies; and such is now the   5
necessity which constrains them to alter their former Systems of Government.
The history of the present King of Great Britain is a history of repeated injuries
and usurpations, all having in direct object the establishment of an absolute Tyranny over these States. To prove this, let Facts be submitted to a candid world.

He has refused his Assent to Laws, the most wholesome and necessary for
the public good.

He has forbidden his Governors to pass Laws of immediate and pressing
importance, unless suspended in their operation till his Assent should be obtained; and when so suspended, he has utterly neglected to attend to them.

He has refused to pass other Laws for the accommodation of large districts of
people, unless those people would relinquish the right of Representation in the
Legislature, a right inestimable to them and formidable to tyrants only.

He has called together legislative bodies at places unusual, uncomfortable,
and distant from the depository of their public Records, for the sole purpose of
fatiguing them into compliance with his measures.

He has dissolved Representative Houses repeatedly, for opposing with manly   10
firmness his invasions on the rights of people.

He has refused for a long time, after such dissolutions, to cause others to be
elected; whereby the Legislative powers, incapable of Annihilation, have returned
to the people at large for their exercise; the State remaining in the mean time
exposed to all the dangers of invasion from without, and convulsions within.

He has endeavoured to prevent the population of these States; for that purpose obstructing the Laws for Naturalization of Foreigners; refusing to pass others to encourage their migrations hither, and raising the conditions of new
Appropriations of Lands.

He has obstructed the Administration of Justice, by refusing his Assent to
Laws for establishing Judiciary powers.

He has made Judges dependent on his Will alone, for the tenure of their
offices, and the amount and payment of their salaries.

He has erected a multitude of New Offices, and sent hither swarms of Offi-   15
cers to harass our people, and eat out their substance.

He has kept among us, in times of peace, Standing Armies without the
Consent of our legislatures.

He has affected to render the Military independent of and superior to the
Civil power.

He has combined with others to subject us to a jurisdiction foreign to our
constitution, and unacknowledged by our laws; giving his Assent to their Acts of
pretended Legislation:

For Quartering large bodies of armed troops among us:

For protecting them, by a mock Trial, from punishment for any Murders   20
which they should commit on the Inhabitants of these States:

For cutting off our Trade with all parts of the world:

For imposing Taxes on us without our Consent:

For depriving us in many cases, of the benefits of Trial by Jury:

For transporting us beyond Seas to be tried for pretended offenses:

For abolishing the free System of English Laws in a neighbouring Province, establishing therein an Arbitrary government, and enlarging its Boundaries so as to render it at once an example and fit instrument for introducing the same absolute rule into these Colonies:

For taking away our Charters, abolishing our most valuable Laws, and altering fundamentally the Forms of our Governments:

For suspending our own Legislatures, and declaring themselves invested with power to legislate for us in all cases whatsoever.

He has abdicated Government here, by declaring us out of his Protection and waging War against us:

He has plundered our seas, ravaged our Coasts, burnt our towns, and destroyed the lives of our people.

He is at this time transporting large Armies of foreign Mercenaries to compleat the works of death, desolation and tyranny, already begun with circumstances of Cruelty & perfidy scarcely paralleled in the most barbarous ages, and totally unworthy the Head of a civilized nation.

He has constrained our fellow Citizens taken Captive on the high Seas to bear Arms against their Country, to become the executioners of their friends and Brethren, or to fall themselves by their Hands.

He has excited domestic insurrections amongst us, and has endeavoured to bring on the inhabitants of our frontiers, the merciless Indian Savages, whose known rule of warfare, is an undistinguished destruction of all ages, sexes and conditions. In every stage of these Oppressions We have Petitioned for Redress in the most humble terms: Our repeated Petitions have been answered only by repeated injury. A Prince, whose character is thus marked by every act which may define a Tyrant, is unfit to be the ruler of a free people. Nor have We been wanting in attentions to our British brethren. We have warned them from time to time of attempts by their legislature to extend an unwarrantable jurisdiction over us. We have reminded them of the circumstances of our emigration and settlement here. We have appealed to their native justice and magnanimity, and we have conjured them by the ties of our common kindred to disavow these usurpations, which, would inevitably interrupt our connections and correspondence. They too have been deaf to the voice of justice and of consanguinity. We must, therefore, acquiesce in the necessity, which denounces our Separation, and hold them, as we hold the rest of mankind, Enemies in War, in Peace Friends.

WE, THEREFORE, the Representatives of the UNITED STATES OF AMERICA, in General Congress Assembled, appealing to the Supreme Judge of the world for the rectitude of our intentions, do, in the Name and by Authority of the good People of these Colonies, solemnly publish and declare, That these United Colonies are, and of Right ought to be FREE AND INDEPENDENT STATES; that they are Absolved from all Allegiance to the British Crown, and that all political connection between them and the State of Great Britain, is and ought to be totally dissolved; and that as Free and Independent States, they have full Power to levy War, conclude Peace, contract Alliances, establish Commerce, and to do all other Acts and Things which Independent States may of right do.

And for the support of this Declaration, with a firm reliance on the protection of divine Providence, we mutually pledge to each other our Lives, our Fortunes and our sacred Honor.

QUESTIONS AND SUGGESTIONS FOR WRITING

1. In a paragraph, define "happiness," and then in a second paragraph explain why, in your opinion, Jefferson spoke of a right to "the pursuit of happiness" rather than of a right to "happiness."
2. In a paragraph, argue that the assertion that "all men are created equal" is clearly nonsense, or, on the other hand, that it makes sense.
3. Write a persuasive Declaration of Independence for some imagined group. Some possible examples include adolescents who declare that their parents have no right to govern them; young adolescents who declare that they should not be compelled to attend school; parents who declare that the state has no right to regulate the education of their children; college students who declare that they should not be required to take certain courses.
4. You are one of King George's trusted ministers. Draft a reply to the colonists for the king to sign.

Chief Seattle (Native American. c. 1786–1866)

MY PEOPLE

Yonder sky that has wept tears of compassion upon my people for centuries untold, and which to us appears changeless and eternal, may change. Today is fair. Tomorrow may be overcast with clouds. My words are like the stars that never change. Whatever Seattle says the great chief at Washington can rely upon with as much certainty as he can upon the return of the sun or the seasons. The White Chief says that Big Chief at Washington sends us greetings of friendship and goodwill. That is kind of him for we know he has little need of our friendship in return. His people are many. They are like the grass that covers vast prairies. My people are few. They resemble the scattering trees of a storm swept plain. The great, and—I presume—good, White Chief sends us word that he wishes to buy our lands but is willing to allow us enough to live comfortably. This indeed appears just, even generous, for the Red Man no longer has rights that he need respect, and the offer may be wise also, as we are no longer in need of an extensive country. I will not dwell on, nor mourn over, our untimely decay, nor reproach our paleface brothers with hastening it, as we too may have been somewhat to blame. . . .

Our good father at Washington—for I presume he is now our father as well as yours, since King George has moved his boundaries further north—our great good father, I say, sends us word that if we do as he desires he will protect us. His brave warriors will be to us a bristling wall of strength, and his wonderful ships of war will fill our harbors so that our ancient enemies far to the northward—the

Hydas and Tsimpsians—will cease to frighten our women, children, and old men. Then in reality will he be our father and we his children. But can that ever be? Your God is not our God! Your God loves your people and hates mine. He folds his strong and protecting arms lovingly about the paleface and leads him by the hand as a father leads his infant son—but He has forsaken His red children—if they really are his. Our God, the Great Spirit, seems also to have forsaken us. Your God makes your people wax strong every day. Soon they will fill the land. Our people are ebbing away like a rapidly receding tide that will never return. The white man's God cannot love our people or He would protect them. They seem to be orphans who can look nowhere for help. How then can we be brothers? How can your God become our God and renew our prosperity and awaken in us dreams of returning greatness? If we have a common heavenly father He must be partial—for He came to his paleface children. We never saw Him. He gave you laws but He had no word for His red children whose teeming multitudes once filled this vast continent as stars fill the firmament. No; we are two distinct races with separate origins and separate destinies. There is little in common between us.

To us the ashes of our ancestors are sacred and their resting place is hallowed ground. You wander far from the graves of your ancestors and seemingly without regret. Your religion was written upon tables of stone by the iron finger of your God so that you could not forget. The Red Man could never comprehend nor remember it. Our religion is the traditions of our ancestors—the dreams of our old men, given them in solemn hours of night by the Great Spirit; and the visions of our sachems;[1] and it is written in the hearts of our people.

Your dead cease to love you and the land of their nativity as soon as they pass the portals of the tomb and wander way beyond the stars. They are soon forgotten and never return. Our dead never forget the beautiful world that gave them being.

Day and night cannot dwell together. The Red man has ever fled the approach of the White Man, as the morning mist flees before the morning sun. However, your proposition seems fair and I think that my people will accept it and will retire to the reservation you offer them. Then we will dwell apart in peace, for the words of the Great White Chief seem to be the words of nature speaking to my people out of dense darkness.   5

It matters little where we pass the remnant of our days. They will not be many. A few more moons; a few more winters—and not one of the descendants of the mighty hosts that once moved over this broad land or lived in happy homes, protected by the Great Spirit, will remain to mourn over the graves of a people once more powerful and hopeful than yours. But why should I mourn at the untimely fate of my people? Tribe follows tribe, and nation follows nation, like the waves of the sea. It is the order of nature, and regret is useless. Your time of decay may be distant, but it will surely come, for even the White Man whose God

---

[1] Indian chiefs.—ED.

walked and talked with him as friend with friend, cannot be exempt from the common destiny. We may be brothers after all. We will see.

We will ponder your proposition, and when we decide we will let you know. But should we accept it, I here and now make this condition that we will not be denied the privilege without molestation of visiting at any time the tombs of our ancestors, friends and children. Every part of this soil is sacred in the estimation of my people. Every hillside, every valley, every plain and grove, has been hallowed by some sad or happy event in days long vanished. The very dust upon which you now stand responds more lovingly to their footsteps than to yours, because it is rich with the blood of our ancestors and our bare feet are conscious of the sympathetic touch. Even the little children who lived here and rejoiced here for a brief season will love these somber solitudes and at eventide they greet shadowy returning spirits. And when the last Red Man shall have perished, and the memory of my tribe shall have become a myth among the White Men, these shores will swarm with the invisible dead of my tribe, and when your children's children think themselves alone in the field, the store, the shop, upon the highway, or in the silence of the pathless woods, they will not be alone. At night when the streets of your cities and villages are silent and you think them deserted, they will throng with the returning hosts that once filled and still love this beautiful land. The White Man will never be alone.

Let him be just and deal kindly with my people, for the dead are not powerless. Dead, did I say? There is not death, only a change of worlds.

QUESTIONS AND SUGGESTIONS FOR WRITING

1. In a paragraph explain why Chief Seattle believes white people have a different God from that of Native Americans.
2. Chief Seattle says that he thinks the offer of the whites is "fair," and that he thinks his people will accept the offer and retire to the reservation. Judging from his speech, do you think his main reason for approving the proposal is that it is fair?
3. In 250 words explain why Chief Seattle believes that whites and Native Americans can never be reconciled, and evaluate his view.
4. Chief Seattle's speech is rich in metaphors and other figures of speech. (On these terms, see page 726.) List three of his figures. From what areas are most of his figures drawn?

Martin Luther King, Jr. (American. 1929–1968)

I HAVE A DREAM

Five score years ago, a great American, in whose symbolic shadow we stand, signed the Emancipation Proclamation. This momentous decree came as a great beacon light of hope to millions of Negro slaves who had been seared in the flames of withering injustice. It came as a joyous daybreak to end the long night of captivity.

But one hundred years later, we must face the tragic fact that the Negro is still not free. One hundred years later, the life of the Negro is still sadly crippled by the manacles of segregation and the chains of discrimination. One hundred years later, the Negro lives on a lonely island of poverty in the midst of a vast ocean of material prosperity. One hundred years later, the Negro is still languishing in the corners of American society and finds himself an exile in his own land. So we have come here today to dramatize an appalling condition.

In a sense we have come to our nation's Capitol to cash a check. When the architects of our republic wrote the magnificent words of the Constitution and the Declaration of Independence, they were signing a promissory note to which every American was to fall heir. This note was a promise that all men would be guaranteed the unalienable rights of life, liberty, and the pursuit of happiness.

It is obvious today that America has defaulted on this promissory note insofar as her citizens of color are concerned. Instead of honoring this sacred obligation, America has given the Negro people a bad check; a check which has come back marked "insufficient funds." But we refuse to believe that the bank of justice is bankrupt. We refuse to believe that there are insufficient funds in the great vaults of opportunity of this nation. So we have come to cash this check—a check that will give us upon demand the riches of freedom and the security of justice. We have also come to this hallowed spot to remind America of the fierce urgency of *now*. This is no time to engage in the luxury of cooling off or to take the tranquilizing drug of gradualism. *Now* is the time to make real the promises of Democracy. *Now* is the time to rise from the dark and desolate valley of segregation to the sunlit path of racial justice. *Now* is the time to open the doors of opportunity to all of God's children. *Now* is the time to lift our nation from the quicksands of racial injustice to the solid rock of brotherhood.

It would be fatal for the nation to overlook the urgency of the moment and to underestimate the determination of the Negro. This sweltering summer of the Negro's legitimate discontent will not pass until there is an invigorating autumn of freedom and equality. 1963 is not an end, but a beginning. Those who hope that the Negro needed to blow off steam and will now be content will have a rude awakening if the nation returns to business as usual. There will be neither rest nor tranquility in America until the Negro is granted his citizenship rights. The whirlwinds of revolt will continue to shake the foundations of our nation until the bright day of justice emerges.

But there is something I must say to my people who stand on the warm threshold which leads into the palace of justice. In the process of gaining our rightful place we must not be guilty of wrongful deeds. Let us not seek to satisfy our thirst for freedom by drinking from the cup of bitterness and hatred. We must forever conduct our struggle on the high plane of dignity and discipline. We must not allow our creative protest to degenerate into physical violence. Again and again we must rise to the majestic heights of meeting physical force with soul force. The marvelous new militancy which has engulfed the Negro community must not lead us to a distrust of all white people, for many of our white brothers, as evidenced by their presence here today, have come to realize that their destiny is tied up with our destiny and their freedom is inextricably bound to our freedom. We cannot walk alone.

And as we walk, we must make the pledge that we shall march ahead. We cannot turn back. There are those who are asking the devotees of civil rights, "When will you be satisfied?" We can never be satisfied as long as the Negro is the victim of the unspeakable horrors of police brutality. We can never be satisfied as long as our bodies, heavy with the fatigue of travel, cannot gain lodging in the motels of the highways and the hotels of the cities. We cannot be satisfied as long as the Negro's basic mobility is from a smaller ghetto to a larger one. We can never be satisfied as long as a Negro in Mississippi cannot vote and a Negro in New York believes he has nothing for which to vote. No, no, we are not satisfied, and we will not be satisfied until justice rolls down like waters and righteousness like a mighty stream.

I am not unmindful that some of you have come here out of great trials and tribulations. Some of you have come fresh from narrow jail cells. Some of you have come from areas where your quest for freedom left you battered by the storms of persecution and staggered by the winds of police brutality. You have been the veterans of creative suffering. Continue to work with the faith that unearned suffering is redemptive.

Go back to Mississippi, go back to Alabama, go back to South Carolina, go back to Georgia, go back to Louisiana, go back to the slums and ghettoes of our northern cities, knowing that somehow this situation can and will be changed. Let us not wallow in the valley of despair.

I say to you today, my friends, that in spite of the difficulties and frustrations 10
of the moment I still have a dream. It is a dream deeply rooted in the American dream.

I have a dream that one day this nation will rise up and live out the true meaning of its creed: "We hold these truths to be self-evident; that all men are created equal."

I have a dream that one day on the red hills of Georgia the sons of former slaves and the sons of former slaveowners will be able to sit down together at the table of brotherhood.

I have a dream that the state of Mississippi, a desert state sweltering with the heat of injustice and oppression, will be transformed into an oasis of freedom and justice.

I have a dream that my four little children will one day live in a nation where they will not be judged by the color of their skin but by the content of their character.

I have a dream today. 15

I have a dream that the state of Alabama, whose governor's lips are presently dripping with the words of interposition and nullification, will be transformed into a situation where little black boys and black girls will be able to join hands with little white boys and white girls and walk together as sisters and brothers.

I have a dream today.

I have dream that one day every valley shall be exalted, every hill and mountain shall be made low, the rough places will be made plain, and the crooked places will be made straight, and the glory of the Lord shall be revealed, and all flesh shall see it together.

This is our hope. This is the faith with which I return to the South. With this faith we will be able to hew out of the mountain of despair a stone of hope. With this faith we will be able to transform the jangling discords of our nation into a beautiful symphony of brotherhood. With this faith we will be able to work together, to pray together, to struggle together, to go to jail together, to stand up for freedom together, knowing that we will be free one day.

This will be the day when all of God's children will be able to sing with new   20
meaning.

> My country, tis of thee
> Sweet land of liberty,
>   Of thee I sing:
> Land where my fathers died,   115
> Land of the pilgrims' pride,
> From every mountainside
>   Let freedom ring.

And if America is to be a great nation this must become true. So let freedom ring from the prodigious hilltops of New Hampshire. Let freedom ring from the mighty mountains of New York. Let freedom ring from the heightening Alleghenies of Pennsylvania!

Let freedom ring from the snowcapped Rockies of Colorado!

Let freedom ring from the curvaceous peaks of California!

But not only that; let freedom ring from Stone Mountain of Georgia!

Let freedom ring from Lookout Mountain of Tennessee!

Let freedom ring from every hill and molehill of Mississippi. From every mountainside, let freedom ring.

When we let freedom ring, when we let it ring from every village and every   25
hamlet, from every state and every city, we will be able to speed up that day when all of God's children, black men and white men, Jews and Gentiles, Protestants and Catholics, will be able to join hands and sing in the words of the old Negro spiritual, "Free at last! free at last! thank God almighty, we are free at last!"

QUESTIONS AND SUGGESTIONS FOR WRITING

1. "I Have a Dream" was originally a speech, not an essay. What words in the speech indicate King's relationship to his audience?

2. Clearly this is not ordinary talk, of the sort that can be heard on a bus. How does it differ? What devices do you find that might also be found in a poem?

3. In a paragraph, examine the analogy (in the second and third paragraphs) of the check King and his audience have come to cash. Is it effective, and if so, why?

4. Consider the organization of the talk. In a sentence, summarize the gist of the first four paragraphs. Next, summarize the gist of the next four paragraphs (through the

paragraph beginning "Go back to Mississippi"). Finally, summarize the remainder of the speech. Then consider what purpose the first part serves.

5. Exactly what is King asking for on behalf of blacks?
6. King delivered this speech in 1963. Do you believe that his dream has been fulfilled? Or is near fulfillment? Explain.

Studs Terkel (American. b. 1912)

ARNOLD SCHWARZENEGGER'S DREAM[1]

Call me Arnold.

I was born in a little Austrian town, outside Graz. It was a 300-year-old house.

When I was ten years old, I had the dream of being the best in the world in something. When I was fifteen, I had a dream that I wanted to be the best body builder in the world and the most muscular man. It was not only a dream I dreamed at night. It was also a daydream. It was so much in my mind that I felt it had to become a reality. It took me five years of hard work. Five years later, I turned this dream into reality and became Mr. Universe, the best-built man in the world.

"Winning" is a very important word. There is one that achieves what he wanted to achieve and there are hundreds of thousands that failed. It singles you out: the winner.

I came out second three times, but that is not what I call losing. The bottom   5 line for me was: Arnold has to be the winner. I have to win more often the Mr. Universe title than anybody else. I won it five times consecutively. I hold the record as Mr. Olympia, the top professional body-building championship. I won it six times. That's why I retired. There was nobody even close to me. Everybody gave up competing against me. That's what I call a winner.

When I was a small boy, my dream was not to be big physically, but big in a way that everybody listens to me when I talk, that I'm a very important person, that people recognize me and see me as something special. I had a big need for being singled out.

Also my dream was to end up in America. When I was ten years old, I dreamed of being an American. At the time I didn't know much about America, just that it was a wonderful country. I felt it was where I belonged. I didn't like being in a little country like Austria. I did everything possible to get out. I did so in 1968, when I was twenty-one years old.

If I would believe in life after death, I would say my before-life I was living in America. That's why I feel so good here. It is the country where you can turn your dream into reality. Other countries don't have those things. When I came

---

[1] Terkel's *American Dreams* presents transcriptions of interviews that Terkel recorded. —ED.

over here to America, I felt I was in heaven. In America, we don't have an obstacle. Nobody's holding you back.

Number One in America pretty much takes care of the rest of the world. You kind of run through the rest of the world like nothing. I'm trying to make people in America aware that they should appreciate what they have here. You have the best tax advantages here and the best prices here and the best products here.

One of the things I always had was a business mind. When I was in high   10
school, a majority of my classes were business classes. Economics and accounting and mathematics. When I came over here to this country, I really didn't speak English almost at all. I learned English and then started taking business courses, because that's what America is best known for: business. Turning one dollar into a million dollars in a short period of time. Also when you make money, how do you keep it?

That's one of the most important things when you have money in your hand, how can you keep it? Or make more out of it? Real estate is one of the best ways of doing that. I own apartment buildings, office buildings, and raw land. That's my love, real estate.

I have emotions. But what you do, you keep them cold or you store them away for a time. You must control your emotions, you must have command over yourself. Three, four months before a competition, I could not be interfered by other people's problems. This is sometimes called selfish. It's the only way you can be if you want to achieve something. Any emotional things inside me, I try to keep cold so it doesn't interfere with my training.

Many times things really touched me. I felt them and I felt sensitive about them. But I had to talk myself out of it. I had to suppress those feelings in order to go on. Sport is one of those activities where you really have to concentrate. You must play attention a hundred percent to the particular thing you're doing. There must be nothing else on your mind. Emotions must not interfere. Otherwise, you're thinking about your girlfriend. You're in love, your positive energies get channeled into another direction rather than going into your weight room or making money.

You have to choose at a very early date what you want: a normal life or to achieve things you want to achieve. I never wanted to win a popularity contest in doing things the way people want me to do it. I went the road I thought was best for me. A few people thought I was cold, selfish. Later they found out that's not the case. After I achieve my goal, I can be Mr. Nice Guy. You know what I mean?

California is to me a dreamland. It is the absolute combination of everything I   15
was always looking for. It has all the money in the world there, show business there, wonderful weather there, beautiful country, ocean is there. Snow skiing in the winter, you can go in the desert the same day. You have beautiful-looking people there. They all have a tan.

I believe very strongly in the philosophy of staying hungry. If you have a dream and it becomes a reality, don't stay satisfied with it too long. Make up a new dream and hunt after that one and turn it into reality. When you have that dream achieved, make up a new dream.

I am a strong believer in Western philosophy, the philosophy of success, of progress, of getting rich. The Eastern philosophy is passive, which I believe in maybe three percent of the times, and the ninety-seven percent is Western, conquering and going on. It's a beautiful philosophy, and America should keep it up.

QUESTIONS AND SUGGESTIONS FOR WRITING

1. After saying that America "is the country where you can turn your dream into reality. Other countries don't have those things," Schwarzenegger goes on to say, "In America, . . . nobody's holding you back." What do you suppose he means by "those things," and by saying that here "nobody's holding you back"?
2. If you have some firsthand knowledge of another country, in an essay of 250–500 words indicate in what ways that country might differ from America in the matter of allowing individuals to fulfill their dreams. By the way, is it your guess that Schwarzenegger's particular dream ("to be the best body builder in the world") is more easily fulfilled in the United States than elsewhere—say in Canada, or Cuba, or Russia, or Austria? Why?
3. In a paragraph set forth what you think Schwarzenegger's view of America is.
4. In one paragraph, sketch Schwarzenegger as objectively as possible, as you perceive him in this interview. In a second paragraph, again drawing only on this interview, evaluate him, calling attention to what you think are his strengths and weaknesses.
5. If you have read Arthur Miller's *Death of a Salesman*, write an essay of 500 words comparing Arnold Schwarzenegger and Willy Loman.

☐ FICTION

Sherwood Anderson (American. 1876–1941)

THE EGG

My father was, I am sure, intended by nature to be a cheerful, kindly man. Until he was thirty-four years old he worked as a farmhand for a man named Thomas Butterworth whose place lay near the town of Bidwell, Ohio. He had then a horse of his own, and on Saturday evenings drove into town to spend a few hours in social intercourse with other farmhands. In town he drank several glasses of beer and stood about in Ben Head's saloon—crowded on Saturday evenings with visiting farmhands. Songs were sung and glasses thumped on the bar. At ten o'clock father drove home along a lonely country road, made his horse comfortable for the night, and himself went to bed, quite happy in his position in life. He had at that time no notion of trying to rise in the world.

It was in the spring of his thirty-fifth year that father married my mother, then a country school-teacher, and in the following spring I came wriggling and crying into the world. Something happened to the two people. They became ambitious. The American passion for getting up in the world took possession of them.

It may have been that mother was responsible. Being a school-teacher she had no doubt read books and magazines. She had, I presume, read of how Garfield, Lincoln, and other Americans rose from poverty to fame and greatness, and as I lay beside her—in the days of her lying-in—she may have dreamed that I would some day rule men and cities. At any rate she induced father to give up his place as a farmhand, sell his horse, and embark on an independent enterprise of his own. She was a tall silent woman with a long nose and troubled gray eyes. For herself she wanted nothing. For father and myself she was incurably ambitious.

The first venture into which the two people went turned out badly. They rented ten acres of poor stony land on Grigg's Road, eight miles from Bidwell, and launched into chicken-raising. I grew into boyhood on the place and got my first impressions of life there. From the beginning they were impressions of disaster, and if, in my turn, I am a gloomy man inclined to see the darker side of life, I attribute it to the fact that what should have been for me the happy joyous days of childhood were spent on a chicken farm.

One unversed in such matters can have no notion of the many and tragic   5
things that can happen to a chicken. It is born out of an egg, lives for a few weeks as a tiny fluffy thing such as you will see pictured on Easter cards, then becomes hideously naked, eats quantities of corn and meal bought by the sweat of your father's brow, gets diseases called pip, cholera, and other names, stands looking with stupid eyes at the sun, becomes sick and dies. A few hens and now and then a rooster, intended to serve God's mysterious ends, struggle through to maturity. The hens lay eggs out of which come other chickens and the dreadful cycle is thus made complete. It is all unbelievably complex. Most philosophers must have been raised on chicken farms. One hopes for so much from a chicken and is so dreadfully disillusioned. Small chickens, just setting out on the journey of life, look so bright and alert and they are in fact so dreadfully stupid. They are so much like people they mix one up in one's judgments of life. If disease does not kill them, they wait until your expectations are thoroughly aroused and then walk under the wheels of a wagon—to go squashed and dead back to their maker. Vermin infest their youth, and fortunes must be spent for curative powders. In later life I have seen how a literature has been built up on the subject of fortunes to be made out of the raising of chickens. It is intended to be read by the gods who have just eaten of the tree of the knowledge of good and evil. It is a hopeful literature and declares that much may be done by simple ambitious people who own a few hens. Do not be led astray by it. It was not written for you. Go hunt for gold on the frozen hills of Alaska, put your faith in the honesty of a politician, believe if you will that the world is daily growing better and that good will triumph over evil, but do not read and believe the literature that is written concerning the hen. It was not written for you.

I, however, digress. My tale does not primarily concern itself with the hen. If correctly told it will center on the egg. For ten years my father and mother struggled to make our chicken farm pay and then they gave up their struggle and began another. They moved into the town of Bidwell, Ohio, and embarked in the restaurant business. After ten years of worry with incubators that did not hatch, and with tiny—and in their own way lovely—balls of fluff that passed on into semi-naked pullethood and from that into dead henhood, we threw all aside and, packing our belongings on a wagon, drove down Grigg's Road toward Bidwell, a tiny caravan of hope looking for a new place from which to start on our upward journey through life.

We must have been a sad-looking lot, not, I fancy, unlike refugees fleeing from a battlefield. Mother and I walked in the road. The wagon that contained our goods had been borrowed for the day from Mr. Albert Griggs, a neighbor. Out of its side stuck the legs of cheap chairs, and at the back of the pile of beds, tables, and boxes filled with kitchen utensils was a crate of live chickens, and on top of that the baby carriage in which I had been wheeled about in my infancy. Why we stuck to the baby carriage I don't know. It was unlikely other children would be born and the wheels were broken. People who have few possessions cling tightly to those they have. That is one of the facts that make life so discouraging.

Father rode on top of the wagon. He was then a bald-headed man of forty-five, a little fat, and from long association with mother and the chickens he had become habitually silent and discouraged. All during our ten years on the chicken farm he had worked as a laborer on neighboring farms and most of the money he had earned had been spent for remedies to cure chicken diseases, on Wilmer's White Wonder Cholera Cure or Professor Bidlow's Egg Producer or some other preparations that mother found advertised in the poultry papers. There were two little patches of hair on father's head just above his ears. I remember that as a child I used to sit looking at him when he had gone to sleep in a chair before the stove on Sunday afternoons in the winter. I had at that time already begun to read books and have notions of my own, and the bald path that led over the top of his head was, I fancied, something like a broad road, such a road as Caesar might have made on which to lead his legions out of Rome and into the wonders of an unknown world. The tufts of hair that grew above father's ears were, I thought, like forests. I fell into a half-sleeping, half-waking state and dreamed I was a tiny thing going along the road into a far beautiful place where there were no chicken farms and where life was a happy eggless affair.

One might write a book concerning our flight from the chicken farm into town. Mother and I walked the entire eight miles—she to be sure that nothing fell from the wagon and I to see the wonders of the world. On the seat of the wagon beside father was his greatest treasure. I will tell you of that.

On a chicken farm, where hundreds and even thousands of chickens come out 10 of eggs, surprising things sometimes happen. Grotesques are born out of eggs as out of people. The accident does not often occur—perhaps once in a thousand births. A chicken is, you see, born that has four legs, two pairs of wings, two heads, or what not. The things do not live. They go quickly back to the hand of their maker that has for a moment trembled. The fact that the poor little things could not live was one of the tragedies of life to father. He had some sort of notion that if he could but bring into henhood or roosterhood a five-legged hen or a two-headed rooster his fortune would be made. He dreamed of taking the wonder about the county fairs and of growing rich by exhibiting it to other farmhands.

At any rate, he saved all the little monstrous things that had been born on our chicken farm. They were preserved in alcohol and put each in its own glass bottle. These he had carefully put into a box, and on our journey into town it was carried on the wagon seat beside him. He drove the horses with one hand and with the other clung to the box. When we got to our destination, the box was taken down at once and the bottles removed. All during our days as keepers of a restaurant in the town of Bidwell, Ohio, the grotesques in their little glass bottles sat on a shelf back of the counter. Mother sometimes protested, but father was a rock on the subject of his treasure. The grotesques were, he declared, valuable. People, he said, liked to look at strange and wonderful things.

Did I say that we embarked in the restaurant business in the town of Bidwell, Ohio? I exaggerated a little. The town itself lay at the foot of a low hill and on the shore of a small river. The railroad did not run through the town and the station was a mile away to the north at a place called Pickleville. There had been a cider mill and pickle factory at the station, but before the time of our coming they had both gone out of business. In the morning and in the evening busses came down to the station along a road called Turner's Pike from the hotel on the main street of Bidwell. Our going to the out-of-the-way place to embark in the restaurant business was mother's idea. She talked of it for a year and then one day went off and rented an empty store building opposite the railroad station. It was her idea that the restaurant would be profitable. Traveling men, she said, would be always waiting around to take trains out of town and town people would come to the station to await incoming trains. They would come to the restaurant to buy pieces of pie and drink coffee. Now that I am older I know that she had another motive in going. She was ambitious for me. She wanted me to rise in the world, to get into a town school and become a man of the towns.

At Pickleville father and mother worked hard, as they always had done. At first there was the necessity of putting our place into shape to be a restaurant. That took a month. Father built a shelf on which he put tins of vegetables. He painted a sign on which he put his name in large red letters. Below his name was the sharp command—"EAT HERE"—that was so seldom obeyed. A showcase was bought and filled with cigars and tobacco. Mother scrubbed the floors and the walls of the room. I went to school in the town and was glad to be away from the farm, from the presence of the discouraged, sad-looking chickens. Still I was not very joyous. In the evening I walked home from school along Turner's Pike and remembered the children I had seen playing in the town school yard. A troop of little girls had gone hopping about and singing. I tried that. Down along the frozen road I went hopping solemnly on one leg. "Hippity Hop To The Barber Shop," I sang shrilly. Then I stopped and looked doubtfully about. I was afraid of being seen in my gay mood. It must have seemed to me that I was doing a thing that should not be done by one who, like myself, had been raised on a chicken farm where death was a daily visitor.

Mother decided that our restaurant should remain open at night. At ten in the evening a passenger train went north past our door followed by a local freight. The freight crew had switching to do in Pickleville, and when the work was done they came to our restaurant for hot coffee and food. Sometimes one of them ordered a fried egg. In the morning at four they returned north-bound and again visited us. A little trade began to grow up. Mother slept at night and during the day tended the restaurant and fed our boarders while father slept. He slept in the same bed mother had occupied during the night and I went off to the town of Bidwell and to school. During the long nights, while mother and I slept, father cooked meats that were to go into sandwiches for the lunch baskets of our boarders. Then an idea in regard to getting up in the world came into his head. The American spirit took hold of him. He also became ambitious.

In the long nights when there was little to do, father had time to think. That was his undoing. He decided that he had in the past been an unsuccessful man because he had not been cheerful enough and that in the future he would adopt a cheerful outlook on life. In the early morning he came upstairs and got into bed with mother. She woke and the two talked. From my bed in the corner I listened.

It was father's idea that both he and mother should try to entertain the people who came to eat at our restaurant. I cannot now remember his words, but he gave the impression of one about to become in some obscure way a kind of public entertainer. When people, particularly young people from the town of Bidwell, came into our place, as on very rare occasions they did, bright entertaining conversation was to be made. From father's words I gathered that something of the jolly innkeeper effect was to be sought. Mother must have been doubtful from the first, but she said nothing discouraging. It was father's notion that a passion for the company of himself and mother would spring up in the breasts of the younger people of the town of Bidwell. In the evening bright happy groups would come singing down Turner's Pike. They would troop shouting with joy and laughter into our place. There would be song and festivity. I do not mean to give the impression that father spoke so elaborately of the matter. He was, as I have said, an uncommunicative man. "They want some place to go. I tell you they want some place to go," he said over and over. That was as far as he got. My own imagination has filled in the blanks.

For two or three weeks this notion of father's invaded our house. We did not talk much, but in our daily lives tried earnestly to make smiles take the place of glum looks. Mother smiled at the boarders and I, catching the infection, smiled at our cat. Father became a little feverish in his anxiety to please. There was, no doubt, lurking somewhere in him, a touch of the spirit of the showman. He did not waste much of his ammunition on the railroad men he served at night, but seemed to be waiting for a young man or woman from Bidwell to come in to show what he could do. On the counter in the restaurant there was a wire basket kept always filled with eggs, and it must have been before his eyes when the idea of being entertaining was born in his brain. There was something pre-natal about the way eggs kept themselves connected with the development of his idea. At any rate, an egg ruined his new impulse in life. Late one night I was awakened by a roar of anger coming from father's throat. Both mother and I sat upright in our beds. With trembling hands she lighted a lamp that stood on a table by her head. Downstairs the front door of our restaurant went shut with a bang and in a few minutes father tramped up the stairs. He held an egg in his hand and his hand trembled as though he were having a chill. There was a half-insane light in his eyes. As he stood glaring at us I was sure he intended throwing the egg at either mother or me. Then he laid it gently on the table beside the lamp and dropped on his knees beside mother's bed. He began to cry like a boy, and I, carried away by his grief, cried with him. The two of us filled the little upstairs room with our wailing voices. It is ridiculous, but of the picture we made I can remember only the fact that mother's hand continually stroked the bald path that ran across the top of his head. I have forgotten what mother said to him and how she induced him to tell her of what had happened downstairs. His explanation also has gone out of my mind. I remember only my own grief and fright and the shiny path over father's head glowing in the lamplight as he knelt by the bed.

As to what happened downstairs. For some unexplainable reason I know the story as well as though I had been a witness to my father's discomfiture. One in time gets to know many unexplainable things. On that evening young Joe Kane, son of a merchant of Bidwell, came to Pickleville to meet his father, who was expected on the ten-o'clock evening train from the South. The train was three hours late and Joe came into our place to loaf about and to wait for its arrival. The local freight train came in and the freight crew were fed. Joe was left alone in the restaurant with father.

From the moment he came into our place the Bidwell young man must have been puzzled by my father's actions. It was his notion that father was angry at him for hanging around. He noticed that the restaurant-keeper was apparently disturbed by his presence and he thought of going out. However, it began to rain and he did not fancy the long walk to town and back. He bought a five-cent cigar and ordered a cup of coffee. He had a newspaper in his pocket and took it out and began to read. "I'm waiting for the evening train. It's late," he said apologetically.

For a long time father, whom Joe Kane had never seen before, remained silently gazing at his visitor. He was no doubt suffering from an attack of stage fright. As so often happens in life he had thought so much and so often of the situation that now confronted him that he was somewhat nervous in its presence.   20

For one thing, he did not know what to do with his hands. He thrust one of them nervously over the counter and shook hands with Joe Kane. "How-de-do," he said. Joe Kane put his newspaper down and stared at him. Father's eyes lighted on the basket of eggs that sat on the counter and he began to talk. "Well," he began hesitatingly, "well, you have heard of Christopher Columbus, eh?" He seemed to be angry. "That Christopher Columbus was a cheat," he declared emphatically. "He talked of making an egg stand on its end. He talked, he did, and then he went and broke the end of the egg."

My father seemed to his visitor to be beside himself at the duplicity of Christopher Columbus. He muttered and swore. He declared it was wrong to teach children that Christopher Columbus was a great man when, after all, he cheated at the critical moment. He had declared he would make an egg stand on end and then, when his bluff had been called, he had done a trick. Still grumbling at Columbus, father took an egg from the basket on the counter and began to walk up and down. He rolled the egg between the palms of his hands. He smiled genially. He began to mumble words regarding the effect to be produced on an egg by the electricity that comes out of the human body. He declared that, without breaking its shell and by virtue of rolling it back and forth in his hands, he could stand the egg on its end. He explained that the warmth of his hands and the gentle rolling movement he gave the egg created a new center of gravity, and Joe Kane was mildly interested. "I have handled thousands of eggs," father said. "No one knows more about eggs than I do."

He stood the egg on the counter and it fell on its side. He tried the trick again and again, each time rolling the egg between the palms of his hands and saying the words regarding the wonders of electricity and the laws of gravity. When after a half-hour's effort he did succeed in making the egg stand for a moment, he looked up to find that his visitor was no longer watching. By the time he had succeeded in calling Joe Kane's attention to the success of his effort, the egg had again rolled over and lay on its side.

Afire with the showman's passion and at the same time a good deal disconcerted by the failure of his first effort, father now took the bottles containing the poultry monstrosities down from their place on the shelf and began to show them to his visitor. "How would you like to have seven legs and two heads like this fellow?" he asked, exhibiting the most remarkable of his treasures. A cheerful smile played over his face. He reached over the counter and tried to slap Joe Kane on the shoulder as he had seen men do in Ben Head's saloon when he was a young farmhand and drove to town on Saturday evenings. His visitor was made a little ill by the sight of the body of the terribly deformed bird floating in the alcohol in the bottle and got up to go. Coming from behind the counter, father took hold of the young man's arm and led him back to his seat. He grew a little angry and for a moment had to turn his face away and force himself to smile. Then he put the bottles back on the shelf. In an outburst of generosity he fairly compelled Joe Kane to have a fresh cup of coffee and another cigar at his expense. Then he took a pan and filling it with vinegar, taken from a jug that sat beneath the counter, he declared himself about to do a new trick. "I will heat this egg in this pan of vinegar," he said. "Then I will put it through the neck of a bottle without breaking the shell. When the egg is inside the bottle it will resume its normal shape and the shell will become hard again. Then I will give the bottle with the egg in it to you. You can take it about with you wherever you go. People will want to know how you got the egg in the bottle. Don't tell them. Keep them guessing. That is the way to have fun with this trick."

Father grinned and winked at his visitor. Joe Kane decided that the man who confronted him was mildly insane but harmless. He drank the cup of coffee that had been given him and began to read his paper again. When the egg had been heated in vinegar, father carried it on a spoon to the counter and going into a back room got an empty bottle. He was angry because his visitor did not watch him as he began to do his trick, but nevertheless went cheerfully to work. For a long time he struggled, trying to get the egg to go through the neck of the bottle. He put the pan of vinegar back on the stove, intending to reheat the egg, then picked it up and burned his fingers. After a second bath in the hot vinegar, the shell of the egg had been softened a little, but not enough for his purpose. He worked and worked and a spirit of desperate determination took possession of him. When he thought that at last the trick was about to be consummated, the delayed train came in at the station and Joe Kane started to go nonchalantly out at the door. Father made a last desperate effort to conquer the egg and make it do the thing that would establish his reputation as one who knew how to entertain guests who came into his restaurant. He worried the egg. He attempted to be somewhat rough with it. He swore and the sweat stood out on his forehead. The egg broke under his hand. When the contents spurted over his clothes, Joe Kane, who had stopped at the door, turned and laughed.

A roar of anger rose from my father's throat. He danced and shouted a string of inarticulate words. Grabbing another egg from the basket on the counter, he threw it, just missing the head of the young man as he dodged through the door and escaped.

Father came upstairs to mother and me with an egg in his hand. I do not know what he intended to do. I imagine he had some idea of destroying it, of destroying all eggs, and that he intended to let mother and me see him begin. When, however, he got into the presence of mother, something happened to him. He laid the egg gently on the table and dropped on his knees by the bed as I have already explained. He later decided to close the restaurant for the night and to come upstairs and get into bed. When he did so, he blew out the light and after much muttered conversation both he and mother went to sleep. I suppose I went to sleep also, but my sleep was troubled. I awoke at dawn and for a long time looked at the egg that lay on the table. I wondered why eggs had to be and why from the egg came the hen who again laid the egg. The question got into my blood. It has stayed there, I imagine, because I am the son of my father. At any rate, the problem remains unsolved in my mind. And that, I conclude, is but another evidence of the complete and final triumph of the egg—at least as far as my family is concerned.

QUESTIONS AND SUGGESTIONS FOR WRITING

1. In a paragraph or two characterize the father, including in your discussion a comment on whether or not he is hypocritical. Then discuss, in an additional paragraph or two, whether his failure is based on his own inadequacies.
2. What do you make out of the narrator's statement that the story "if correctly told . . . will center on the egg"?
3. In a sentence state the theme of the story. Then in the remainder of the paragraph, offer support for your view of the theme.
4. Characterize the narrator.
5. In 250–500 words, recount a story of someone you know. The story should reveal the person's character, and convey to the reader a sense of the character's view of life. Your own view—for example, admiration, amusement, or sorrow—should be implicit, but do not state this view explicitly.

James Thurber (American. 1894–1961)

THE SECRET LIFE
OF WALTER MITTY

"We're going through!" The Commander's voice was like thin ice breaking. He wore his full-dress uniform, with the heavily braided white cap pulled down rakishly over one cold gray eye. "We can't make it, sir. It's spoiling for a hurricane, if you ask me." "I'm not asking you, Lieutenant Berg," said the Commander. "Throw on the power lights! Rev her up to 8,500! We're going through!" The pounding of the cylinders increased; ta-pocketa-pocketa-pocketa-*pocketa-pocketa*. The Commander stared at the ice forming on the pilot window. He walked over and twisted a row of complicated dials. "Switch on No. 8 auxiliary!" he shouted. "Switch on No. 8 auxiliary!" repeated Lieutenant Berg. "Full strength in No. 3 turret!" shouted the Commander. "Full strength in No. 3 turret!" The crew, bending to their various tasks in the huge, hurtling eight-engined Navy hydroplane, looked at each other and grinned. "The Old Man'll get us through," they said to one another. "The Old Man ain't afraid of Hell!" . . .

"Not so fast! You're driving too fast!" said Mrs. Mitty. "What are you driving so fast for?"

"Hmm?" said Walter Mitty. He looked at his wife, in the seat beside him, with shocked astonishment. She seemed grossly unfamiliar, like a strange woman who had yelled at him in a crowd. "You were up to fifty-five," she said. "You know I don't like to go more than forty. You were up to fifty-five." Walter Mitty drove on toward Waterbury in silence, the roaring of the SN202 through the worst storm in twenty years of Navy flying fading in the remote, intimate airways of his mind. "You're tensed up again," said Mrs. Mitty. "It's one of your days. I wish you'd let Dr. Renshaw look you over."

Walter Mitty stopped the car in front of the building where his wife went to have her hair done. "Remember to get those overshoes while I'm having my hair done," she said. "I don't need overshoes," said Mitty. She put her mirror back into her bag. "We've been all through that," she said, getting out of the car. "You're not a young man any longer." He raced the engine a little. "Why don't you wear your gloves? Have you lost your gloves?" Walter Mitty reached in a pocket and brought out the gloves. He put them on, but after she had turned and gone into the building and he had driven on to a red light, he took them off again. "Pick it up, brother," snapped a cop as the light changed, and Mitty hastily pulled on his gloves and lurched ahead. He drove around the streets aimlessly for a time, and then he drove past the hospital on his way to the parking lot.

. . . "It's the millionaire banker, Wellington McMillan," said the pretty nurse. "Yes?" said Walter Mitty, removing his gloves slowly. "Who has the case?" "Dr. Renshaw and Dr. Benbow, but there are two specialists here, Dr. Remington from New York and Dr. Pritchard-Mitford from London. He flew over." A door opened down a long, cool corridor and Dr. Renshaw came out. He looked distraught and

5

haggard. "Hello, Mitty," he said. "We're having the devil's own time with McMillan, the millionaire banker and close personal friend of Roosevelt. Obstreosis of
the ductal tract. Tertiary. Wish you'd take a look at him." "Glad to," said Mitty.

In the operating room there were whispered introductions: "Dr. Remington,
Dr. Mitty. Dr. Pritchard-Mitford, Dr. Mitty." "I've read your book on streptothri-
cosis," said Pritchard-Mitford, shaking hands. "A brilliant performance, sir."
"Thank you," said Walter Mitty. "Didn't know you were in the States, Mitty,"
grumbled Remington. "Coals to Newcastle, bringing Mitford and me up here for a
tertiary." "You are very kind," said Mitty. A huge, complicated machine, connected to the operating table, with many tubes and wires, began at this moment
to go pocketa-pocketa-pocketa. "The new anaesthetizer is giving away!" shouted
an intern. "There is no one in the East who knows how to fix it!" "Quiet, man!"
said Mitty, in a low, cool voice. He sprang to the machine, which was now going
pocketa-pocketa-queep-pocketa-queep. He began fingering delicately a row of
glistening dials. "Give me a fountain pen!" he snapped. Someone handed him a
fountain pen. He pulled a faulty piston out of the machine and inserted the pen in
its place. "That will hold for ten minutes," he said. "Get on with the operation." A
nurse hurried over and whispered to Renshaw, and Mitty saw the man turn pale.
"Coreopsis has set in," said Renshaw nervously. "If you would take over, Mitty?"
Mitty looked at him and at the craven figure of Benbow, who drank, and at the
grave, uncertain faces of the two great specialists. "If you wish," he said. They
slipped a white gown on him; he adjusted a mask and drew on thin gloves; nurses
handed him shining . . .

"Back it up, Mac! Look out for that Buick!" Walter Mitty jammed on the
brakes. "Wrong lane, Mac," said the parking-lot attendant, looking at Mitty
closely. "Gee. Yeh," muttered Mitty. He began cautiously to back out of the lane
marked "Exit Only." "Leave her sit there," said the attendant. "I'll put her away."
Mitty got out of the car. "Hey, better leave the key." "Oh," said Mitty, handing
the man the ignition key. The attendant vaulted into the car, backed it up with
insolent skill, and put it where it belonged.

They're so damn cocky, thought Walter Mitty, walking along Main Street;
they think they know everything. Once he had tried to take his chains off, outside
New Milford, and he had got them wound around the axles. A man had had to
come out in a wrecking car and unwind them, a young, grinning garage man. Since
then Mrs. Mitty always made him drive to a garage to have the chains taken off.
The next time, he thought, I'll wear my right arm in a sling; they won't grin at me
then. I'll have my right arm in a sling and they'll see I couldn't possibly take the
chains off myself. He kicked at the slush on the sidewalk. "Overshoes," he said to
himself, and he began looking for a shoe store.

When he came out into the street again, with the overshoes in a box under
his arm, Walter Mitty began to wonder what the other thing was his wife had told
him to get. She had told him, twice before they set out from their house for
Waterbury. In a way he hated these weekly trips to town—he was always getting
something wrong. Kleenex, he thought, Squibb's, razor blades? No. Toothpaste,
toothbrush, bicarbonate, carborundum, initiative and referendum? He gave it up.

But she would remember it. "Where's the what's-its-name?" she would ask. "Don't tell me you forgot the what's-its-name." A newsboy went by shouting something about the Waterbury trial.

   . . . "Perhaps this will refresh your memory." The District Attorney sud-   10 denly thrust a heavy automatic at the quiet figure on the witness stand. "Have you ever seen this before?" Walter Mitty took the gun and examined it expertly. "This is my Webley-Vickers 50.-80," he said calmly. An excited buzz ran around the courtroom. The judge rapped for order. "You are a crack shot with any sort of firearms, I believe?" said the District Attorney, insinuatingly. "Objection!" shouted Mitty's attorney. "We have shown that the defendant could not have fired the shot. We have shown that he wore his right arm in a sling on the night of the fourteenth of July." Walter Mitty raised his hand briefly and the bickering attorneys were stilled. "With any known make of gun," he said evenly, "I could have killed Gregory Fitzhurst at three hundred feet *with my left hand*." Pandemonium broke loose in the courtroom. A woman's scream rose above the bedlam and suddenly a lovely, dark-haired girl was in Walter Mitty's arms. The District Attorney struck at her savagely. Without rising from his chair, Mitty let the man have it on the point of the chin. "You miserable cur!"

   "Puppy biscuit," said Walter Mitty. He stopped walking and the buildings of Waterbury rose up out of the misty courtroom and surrounded him again. A woman who was passing laughed. "He said 'puppy biscuit,' " she said to her companion. "That man said 'puppy biscuit' to himself." Walter Mitty hurried on. He went into an A. & P., not the first one he came to but a smaller one farther up the street. "I want some biscuit for small, young dogs," he said to the clerk. "Any special brand, sir?" The greatest pistol shot in the world thought a moment. "It says 'Puppies Bark for It' on the box," said Walter Mitty.

   His wife would be through at the hairdresser's in fifteen minutes, Mitty saw in looking at his watch, unless they had trouble drying it; sometimes they had trouble drying it. She didn't like to get to the hotel first; she would want him to be there waiting for her as usual. He found a big leather chair in the lobby, facing a window, and he put the overshoes and the puppy biscuit on the floor beside it. He picked up an old copy of *Liberty* and sank down into the chair. "Can Germany Conquer the World through the Air?" Walter Mitty looked at the pictures of bombing planes and of ruined streets.

   . . . "The cannonading has got the wind up in young Raleigh, sir," said the sergeant. Captain Mitty looked up at him through tousled hair. "Get him to bed," he said wearily, "with the others. I'll fly alone." "But you can't, sir," said the sergeant anxiously. "It takes two men to handle that bomber and the Archies are pounding hell out of the air. Von Richtman's circus is between here and Saulier." "Somebody's got to get that ammunition dump," said Mitty. "I'm going over. Spot of brandy?" He poured a drink for the sergeant and one for himself. War thundered and whined around the dugout and battered at the door. There was a rending of wood and splinters flew through the room. "A bit of a near thing," said Captain Mitty carelessly. "The box barrage is closing in," said the sergeant. "We only live once, sergeant," said Mitty with his faint, fleeting smile. "Or do we?"

He poured another brandy and tossed it off. "I never see a man could hold his brandy like you, sir," said the sergeant. "Begging your pardon, sir." Captain Mitty stood up and strapped on his huge Webley-Vickers automatic. "It's forty kilometers through hell, sir," said the sergeant. Mitty finished one last brandy. "After all," he said softly, "what isn't?" The pounding of the cannon increased; there was the rat-tat-tatting of machine guns, and from somewhere came the menacing pocketa-pocketa-pocketa of the new flame-throwers. Walter Mitty walked to the door of the dugout humming "Auprès de Ma Blonde." He turned and waved to the sergeant. "Cheerio!" he said. . . .

Something struck his shoulder. "I've been looking all over this hotel for you," said Mrs. Mitty. "Why do you have to hide in this old chair? How did you expect me to find you?" "Things close in," said Walter Mitty vaguely. "What?" Mrs. Mitty said. "Did you get the what's-its-name? The puppy biscuit? What's in that box?" "Overshoes," said Mitty. "Couldn't you have put them on in the store?" "I was thinking," said Walter Mitty. "Does it ever occur to you that I am sometimes thinking?" She looked at him. "I'm going to take your temperature when I get you home," she said.

They went out through the revolving doors that made a faintly derisive whis-   15 tling sound when you pushed them. It was two blocks to the parking lot. At the drugstore on the corner she said, "Wait here for me. I forgot something. I won't be a minute." She was more than a minute. Walter Mitty lighted a cigarette. It began to rain, rain with sleet in it. He stood up against the wall of the drugstore, smoking. . . . He put his shoulders back and his heels together. "To hell with the handkerchief," said Walter Mitty scornfully. He took one last drag on his cigarette and snapped it away. Then, with that faint, fleeting smile playing about his lips, he faced the firing squad; erect and motionless, proud and disdainful, Walter Mitty the Undefeated, inscrutable to the last.

QUESTIONS AND SUGGESTIONS FOR WRITING

1. Why does Mitty have daydreams? From what sources has he derived the substance of his daydreams?
2. We may sympathize with Mitty, but we laugh at him, too. Why do we find this story primarily comic instead of pathetic? If it were intended to move us deeply, rather than to amuse us, what kinds of changes would have to be made in Mitty's daydreams? What other changes would have to be made in the characterization of Mitty and of his wife?
3. In the last sentence Mitty imagines himself facing a firing squad, "Mitty the Undefeated, inscrutable to the last." To what degree can it be argued that he is undefeated and inscrutable?
4. In a paragraph characterize Mrs. Mitty.
5. In an essay of 500 words evaluate the view that Mrs. Mitty is exactly the sort of woman whom Walter Mitty needs.

E. B. White (American. 1899–1985)

THE SECOND TREE FROM THE CORNER

"Ever have any bizarre thoughts?" asked the doctor.

Mr. Trexler failed to catch the word. "What kind?" he said.

"Bizarre," repeated the doctor, his voice steady. He watched his patient for any slight change of expression, any wince. It seemed to Trexler that the doctor was not only watching him closely but was creeping slowly toward him, like a lizard toward a bug. Trexler shoved his chair back an inch and gathered himself for a reply. He was about to say "Yes" when he realized that if he said yes the next question would be unanswerable. Bizarre thoughts, bizarre thoughts? Ever have any bizarre thoughts? What kind of thoughts *except* bizarre had he had since the age of two?

Trexler felt the time passing, the necessity for an answer. These psychiatrists were busy men, overloaded, not to be kept waiting. The next patient was probably already perched out there in the waiting room, lonely, worried, shifting around on the sofa, his mind stuffed with bizarre thoughts and amorphous fears. Poor bastard, thought Trexler. Out there all alone in that misshapen antechamber, staring at the filing cabinet and wondering whether to tell the doctor about that day on the Madison Avenue bus.

Let's see, bizarre thoughts. Trexler dodged back along the dreadful corridor   5
of the years to see what he could find. He felt the doctor's eyes upon him and knew that time was running out. Don't be so conscientious, he said to himself. If a bizarre thought is indicated here, just reach into the bag and pick anything at all. A man as well supplied with bizarre thoughts as you are should have no difficulty producing one for the record. Trexler darted into the bag, hung for a moment before one of his thoughts, as a hummingbird pauses in the delphinium. No, he said, not that one. He darted to another (the one about the rhesus monkey), paused, considered. No, he said, not that.

Trexler knew he must hurry. He had already used up pretty nearly four seconds since the question had been put. But it was an impossible situation—just one more lousy, impossible situation such as he was always getting himself into. When, he asked himself, are you going to quit maneuvering yourself into a pocket? He made one more effort. This time he stopped at the asylum, only the bars were lucite—fluted, retractable. Not here, he said. Not this one.

He looked straight at the doctor. "No," he said quietly. "I never have any bizarre thoughts."

The doctor sucked in on his pipe, blew a plume of smoke toward the rows of medical books. Trexler's gaze followed the smoke. He managed to make out one of the titles, "The Genito-Urinary System." A bright wave of fear swept cleanly over him, and he winced under the first pain of kidney stones. He remembered when he was a child, the first time he ever entered a doctor's office, sneaking a look at the titles of the books—and the flush of fear, the shirt wet under the arms, the book on t.b., the sudden knowledge that he was in the advanced stages of consumption, the quick vision of the hemorrhage. Trexler sighed wearily. Forty years, he thought, and I still get thrown by the title of a medical book. Forty years and I still can't stay on life's little bucky horse. No wonder I'm sitting here in this dreary joint at the end of this woebegone afternoon, lying about my bizarre thoughts to a doctor who looks, come to think of it, rather tired.

The session dragged on. After about twenty minutes, the doctor rose and knocked his pipe out. Trexler got up, knocked the ashes out of his brain, and waited. The doctor smiled warmly and stuck out his hand. "There's nothing the matter with you—you're just scared. Want to know how I know you're scared?"

"How?" asked Trexler.   10

"Look at the chair you've been sitting in! See how it has moved back away from my desk? You kept inching away from me while I asked you questions. That means you're scared."

"Does it?" said Trexler, faking a grin. "Yeah, I suppose it does."

They finished shaking hands. Trexler turned and walked out uncertainly along the passage, then into the waiting room and out past the next patient, a ruddy pin-striped man who was seated on the sofa twirling his hat nervously and staring straight ahead at the files. Poor, frightened guy, thought Trexler, he's probably read in the *Times* that one American male out of every two is going to die of heart disease by twelve o'clock next Thursday. It says that in the paper almost every morning. And he's also probably thinking about that day on the Madison Avenue bus.

A week later, Trexler was back in the patient's chair. And for several weeks thereafter he continued to visit the doctor, always toward the end of the after-noon, when the vapors hung thick above the pool of the mind and darkened the whole region of the East Seventies.[1] He felt no better as time went on, and he found it impossible to work. He discovered that the visits were becoming routine and that although the routine was one to which he certainly did not look forward, at least he could accept it with cool resignation, as once, years ago, he had accepted a long spell with a dentist who had settled down to a steady fooling with a couple of dead teeth. The visits, moreover, were now assuming a pattern recognizable to the patient.

Each session would begin with a *résumé* of symptoms—the dizziness in the   15
streets, the constricting pain in the back of the neck, the apprehensions, the tightness of the scalp, the inability to concentrate, the despondency and the melancholy times, the feeling of pressure and tension, the anger at not being able to work, the anxiety over work not done, the gas on the stomach. Dullest set of neurotic symptoms in the world, Trexler would think, as he obediently trudged back over them for the doctor's benefit. And then, having listened attentively to the recital, the doctor would spring his question: "Have you ever found anything that gives you relief?" And Trexler would answer. "Yes. A drink." And the doctor would nod his head knowingly.

[1] An expensive neighborhood in Manhattan.—ED.

As he became familiar with the pattern Trexler found that he increasingly tended to identify himself with the doctor, transferring himself into the doctor's seat—probably (he thought) some rather slick form of escapism. At any rate, it was nothing new for Trexler to identify himself with other people. Whenever he got into a cab, he instantly became the driver, saw everything from the hackman's angle (and the reaching over with the right hand, the nudging of the flag, the pushing it down, all the way down along the side of the meter), saw everything— traffic, fare, everything—through the eyes of Anthony Rocco, or Isidore Freedman, or Matthew Scott. In a barbershop, Trexler was the barber, his fingers curled around the comb, his hand on the tonic. Perfectly natural, then, that Trexler should soon be occupying the doctor's chair, asking the questions, waiting for the answers. He got quite interested in the doctor, in this way. He liked him, and he found him a not too difficult patient.

It was on the fifth visit, about halfway through, that the doctor turned to Trexler and said, suddenly. "What do you want?" He gave the word "want" special emphasis.

"I d'know," replied Trexler uneasily. "I guess nobody knows the answer to that one."

"Sure they do," replied the doctor.

"Do *you* know what *you* want?" asked Trexler narrowly.   20

"Certainly," said the doctor. Trexler noticed that at this point the doctor's chair slid slightly backward, away from him. Trexler stifled a small, internal smile. Scared as a rabbit, he said to himself. Look at him scoot!

"What *do* you want?" continued Trexler, pressing his advantage, pressing it hard.

The doctor glided back another inch away from his inquisitor. "I want a wing on the small house I own in Westport. I want more money, and more leisure to do the things I want to do."

Trexler was just about to say, "And what are those things you want to do, Doctor?" when he caught himself. Better not go too far, he mused. Better not lose possession of the ball. And besides, he thought, what the hell goes on here, anyway—me paying fifteen bucks a throw for these *séances* and then doing the work myself, asking the questions, weighing the answers. So he wants a new wing! There's a fine piece of theatrical gauze for you! A new wing.

Trexler settled down again and resumed the role of patient for the rest of the   25
visit. It ended on a kindly, friendly note. The doctor reassured him that his fears were the cause of his sickness, and that his fears were unsubstantial. They shook hands, smiling.

Trexler walked dizzily through the empty waiting room and the doctor followed along to let him out. It was late; the secretary had shut up shop and gone home. Another day over the dam. "Goodbye," said Trexler. He stepped into the street, turned west toward Madison, and thought of the doctor all alone there, after hours, in that desolate hole—a man who worked longer hours than his secretary. Poor, scared, overworked bastard, thought Trexler. And that new wing!

It was an evening of clearing weather, the Park showing green and desirable in the distance, the last daylight applying a high lacquer to the brick and brownstone walls and giving the street scene a luminous and intoxicating splendor. Trexler meditated, as he walked, on what he wanted. "What do you want?" he heard again. Trexler knew what he wanted, and what, in general, all men wanted; and he was glad, in a way, that it was both inexpressible and unattainable, and that it wasn't a wing. He was satisfied to remember that it was deep, formless, enduring, and impossible of fulfillment, and that it made men sick, and that when you sauntered along Third Avenue and looked through the doorways into the dim saloons, you could sometimes pick out from the unregenerate ranks the ones who had not forgotten, gazing steadily into the bottoms of the glasses on the long chance that they could get another little peek at it. Trexler found himself renewed by the remembrance that what he wanted was at once great and microscopic, and that although it borrowed from the nature of large deeds and of youthful love and of old songs and early intimations, it was not any one of these things, and that it had not been isolated or pinned down, and that a man who attempted to define it in the privacy of a doctor's office would fall flat on his face.

Trexler felt invigorated. Suddenly his sickness seemed health, his dizziness stability. A small tree, rising between him and the light, stood there saturated with the evening, each gilt-edged leaf perfectly drunk with excellence and delicacy. Trexler's spine registered an ever so slight tremor as it picked up his natural disturbance in the lovely scene. "I want the second tree from the corner, just as it stands," he said, answering an imaginary question from an imaginary physician. And he felt a slow pride in realizing that what he wanted none could bestow, and that what he had none could take away. He felt content to be sick, unembarrassed at being afraid; and in the jungle of his fear he glimpsed (as he had so often glimpsed them before) the flashy tail feathers of the bird courage.

Then he thought once again of the doctor, and of his being left there all alone, tired, frightened. (The poor, scared guy, thought Trexler.) Trexler began humming "Moonshine Lullaby," his spirit reacting instantly to the hypodermic of Merman's[2] healthy voice. He crossed Madison, boarded a downtown bus, and rode all the way to Fifty-second Street before he had a thought that could rightly have been called bizarre.

QUESTIONS AND SUGGESTIONS FOR WRITING

1. Except for telling us that Trexler wants the second tree from the corner, White does not set forth Trexler's "bizarre thoughts" in detail. Do you think the story would have been better if such detail had been given? Why, or why not?

2. Toward the end of the story we are told that "Trexler knew what he wanted." In a paragraph state, as specifically as you can, what you think he wanted.

3. In the next-to-last paragraph White says of Trexler, "Suddenly his sickness seemed health, his dizziness stability." Explain why Trexler comes to this perception.

---

[2] Ethel Merman, a musical comedy star. —ED.

4. Check the meanings of "neurotic" and "psychotic" in a dictionary. Then in one or two paragraphs state whether, and why, you think White regards Trexler as neurotic, psychotic, or neither. You may want to distinguish between Trexler at the beginning of the story and Trexler at the end of the story.
5. In a paragraph characterize the doctor.

Shirley Jackson (American. 1919–1965)

THE LOTTERY

The morning of June 27th was clear and sunny, with the fresh warmth of a full-summer day; the flowers were blossoming profusely and the grass was richly green. The people of the village began to gather in the square, between the post office and the bank, around ten o'clock; in some towns there were so many people that the lottery took two days and had to be started on June 26th, but in this village, where there were only about three hundred people, the whole lottery took less than two hours, so it could begin at ten o'clock in the morning and still be through in time to allow the villagers to get home for noon dinner.

The children assembled first, of course. School was recently over for the summer, and the feeling of liberty sat uneasily on most of them; they tended to gather together quietly for a while before they broke into boisterous play, and their talk was still of the classroom and the teacher, of books and reprimands. Bobby Martin had already stuffed his pockets full of stones, and the other boys soon followed his example, selecting the smoothest and roundest stones; Bobby and Harry Jones and Dickie Delacroix—the villagers pronounced this name "Dellacroy"—eventually made a great pile of stones in one corner of the square and guarded it against the raids of the other boys. The girls stood aside, talking among themselves, looking over their shoulders at the boys, and the very small children rolled in the dust or clung to the hands of their older brothers or sisters.

Soon the men began to gather, surveying their own children, speaking of planting and rain, tractors and taxes. They stood together, away from the pile of stones in the corner, and their jokes were quiet and they smiled rather than laughed. The women, wearing faded house dresses and sweaters, came shortly after their menfolk. They greeted one another and exchanged bits of gossip as they went to join their husbands. Soon the women, standing by their husbands, began to call to their children, and the children came reluctantly, having to be called four or five times. Bobby Martin ducked under his mother's grasping hand and ran, laughing, back to the pile of stones. His father spoke up sharply, and Bobby came quickly and took his place between his father and his oldest brother.

The lottery was conducted—as were the square dances, the teenage club, the Halloween program—by Mr. Summers, who had time and energy to devote to civic activities. He was a round-faced, jovial man and he ran the coal business, and people were sorry for him, because he had no children and his wife was a scold.

When he arrived in the square, carrying the black wooden box, there was a murmur of conversation among the villagers and he waved and called, "Little late today, folks." The postmaster, Mr. Graves, followed him, carrying a three-legged stool, and the stool was put in the center of the square and Mr. Summers set the black box down on it. The villagers kept their distance, leaving a space between themselves and the stool, and when Mr. Summers said, "Some of you fellows want to give me a hand?" there was a hesitation before two men, Mr. Martin and his oldest son, Baxter, came forward to hold the box steady on the stool while Mr. Summers stirred up the papers inside it.

The original paraphernalia for the lottery had been lost long ago, and the 5 black box now resting on the stool had been put into use even before Old Man Warner, the oldest man in town, was born. Mr. Summers spoke frequently to the villagers about making a new box, but no one liked to upset even as much tradition as was represented by the black box. There was a story that the present box had been made with some pieces of the box that had preceded it, the one that had been constructed when the first people settled down to make a village here. Every year, after the lottery, Mr. Summers began talking again about a new box, but every year the subject was allowed to fade off without anything's being done. The black box grew shabbier each year; by now it was no longer completely black but splintered badly along one side to show the original wood color, and in some places faded or stained.

Mr. Martin and his oldest son, Baxter, held the black box securely on the stool until Mr. Summers had stirred the papers thoroughly with his hand. Because so much of the ritual had been forgotten or discarded, Mr. Summers had been successful in having slips of paper substituted for the chips of wood that had been used for generations. Chips of wood, Mr. Summers had argued, had been all very well when the village was tiny, but now that the population was more than three hundred and likely to keep on growing, it was necessary to use something that would fit more easily into the black box. The night before the lottery, Mr. Summers and Mr. Graves made up the slips of paper and put them in the box, and it was then taken to the safe of Mr. Summers's coal company and locked up until Mr. Summers was ready to take it to the square next morning. The rest of the year, the box was put away, sometimes one place, sometimes another; it had spent one year in Mr. Graves's barn and another year underfoot in the post office, and sometimes it was set on a shelf in the Martin grocery and left there.

There was a great deal of fussing to be done before Mr. Summers declared the lottery open. There were lists to make up—of heads of families, heads of households in each family, members of each household in each family. There was the proper swearing-in of Mr. Summers by the postmaster, as the official of the lottery; at one time, some people remembered, there had been a recital of some sort, performed by the official of the lottery, a perfunctory, tuneless chant that had been rattled off duly each year; some people believed that the official of the lottery used to stand just so when he said or sang it, others believed that he was supposed to walk among the people, but years and years ago this part of the ritual had been allowed to lapse. There had been, also, a ritual salute, which the official of the lottery had had to use in addressing each person who came up to draw from the box, but this also had changed with time, until now it was felt necessary only for the official to speak to each person approaching. Mr. Summers was very good at all this; in his clean white shirt and blue jeans, with one hand resting carelessly on the black box, he seemed very proper and important as he talked interminably to Mr. Graves and the Martins.

Just as Mr. Summers finally left off talking and turned to the assembled villagers, Mrs. Hutchinson came hurriedly along the path to the square, her sweater thrown over her shoulders, and slid into place in the back of the crowd. "Clean forgot what day it was," she said to Mrs. Delacroix, who stood next to her, and they both laughed softly. "Thought my old man was out back stacking wood," Mrs. Hutchinson went on, "and then I looked out the window and the kids were gone, and then I remembered it was the twenty-seventh and came a-running." She dried her hands on her apron, and Mrs. Delacroix said, "You're in time, though. They're still talking away up there."

Mrs. Hutchinson craned her neck to see through the crowd and found her husband and children standing near the front. She tapped Mrs. Delacroix on the arm as a farewell and began to make her way through the crowd. The people separated goodhumoredly to let her through; two or three people said, in voices just loud enough to be heard across the crowd, "Here comes your Missus, Hutchinson," and "Bill, she made it after all." Mrs. Hutchinson reached her husband, and Mr. Summers, who had been waiting, said cheerfully, "Thought we were going to have to get on without you, Tessie." Mrs. Hutchinson said, grinning, "Wouldn't have me leave m'dishes in the sink, now would you, Joe?," and soft laughter ran through the crowd as the people stirred back into position after Mrs. Hutchinson's arrival.

"Well, now," Mr. Summers said soberly, "guess we better get started, get   10 this over with, so's we can go back to work. Anybody ain't here?"

"Dunbar," several people said. "Dunbar, Dunbar."

Mr. Summers consulted his list. "Clyde Dunbar," he said. "That's right. He's broke his leg, hasn't he? Who's drawing for him?"

"Me, I guess," a woman said, and Mr. Summers turned to look at her. "Wife draws for her husband," Mr. Summers said. "Don't you have a grown boy to do it for you, Janey?" Although Mr. Summers and everyone else in the village knew the answer perfectly well, it was the business of the official of the lottery to ask such questions formally. Mr. Summers waited with an expression of polite interest while Mrs. Dunbar answered.

"Horace's not but sixteen yet," Mrs. Dunbar said regretfully. "Guess I gotta fill in for the old man this year."

"Right," Mr. Summers said. He made a note on the list he was holding. Then   15 he asked, "Watson boy drawing this year?"

A tall boy in the crowd raised his hand. "Here," he said. "I'm drawing for m'mother and me." He blinked his eyes nervously and ducked his head as several voices in the crowd said things like "Good fellow, Jack," and "Glad to see your mother's got a man to do it."

"Well," Mr. Summers said, "guess that's everyone. Old Man Warner make it?"

"Here," a voice said, and Mr. Summers nodded.

A sudden hush fell on the crowd as Mr. Summers cleared his throat and looked at the list. "All ready?" he called. "Now, I'll read the names—heads of families first—and the men come up and take a paper out of the box. Keep the paper folded in your hand without looking at it until everyone has had a turn. Everything clear?"

The people had done it so many times that they only half listened to the directions, most of them were quiet, wetting their lips, not looking around. Then Mr. Summers raised one hand high and said, "Adams." A man disengaged himself from the crowd and came forward. "Hi, Steve," Mr. Summers said, and Mr. Adams said, "Hi, Joe." They grinned at one another humorlessly and nervously. Then Mr. Adams reached into the black box and took out a folded paper. He held it firmly by one corner as he turned and went hastily back to his place in the crowd, where he stood a little apart from his family, not looking down at his hand.   20

"Allen," Mr. Summers said. "Anderson. . . . Bentham."

"Seems like there's no time at all between lotteries any more," Mrs. Delacroix said to Mrs. Graves in the back row. "Seems like we got through with the last one only last week."

"Time sure goes fast," Mrs. Graves said.

"Clark. . . . Delacroix."

"There goes my old man," Mrs. Delacroix said. She held her breath while her husband went forward.   25

"Dunbar," Mr. Summers said, and Mrs. Dunbar went steadily to the box while one of the women said, "Go on, Janey," and another said, "There she goes."

"We're next," Mrs. Graves said. She watched while Mr. Graves came around from the side of the box, greeted Mr. Summers gravely, and selected a slip of paper from the box. By now, all through the crowd there were men holding the small folded papers in their large hands, turning them over and over nervously. Mrs. Dunbar and her two sons stood together, Mrs. Dunbar holding the slip of paper.

"Harburt. . . . Hutchinson."

"Get up there, Bill," Mrs. Hutchinson said, and the people near her laughed.

"Jones."   30

"They do say," Mr. Adams said to Old Man Warner, who stood next to him, "that over in the north village they're talking of giving up the lottery."

Old Man Warner snorted, "Pack of crazy fools," he said. "Listening to the young folks, nothing's good enough for *them*. Next thing you know, they'll be wanting to go back to living in caves, nobody work any more, live *that* way for a while. Used to be a saying about 'Lottery in June, corn be heavy soon.' First thing you know, we'd all be eating stewed chickweed and acorns. There's *always* been a lottery," he added petulantly. "Bad enough to see young Joe Summers up there joking with everybody."

"Some places have already quit lotteries," Mrs. Adams said.

"Nothing but trouble in *that*," Old Man Warner said stoutly. "Pack of young fools."

"Martin." And Bobby Martin watched his father go forward. "Overdyke. . . . Percy."   35

"I wish they'd hurry," Mrs. Dunbar said to her older son. "I wish they'd hurry."

"They're almost through," her son said.

"You get ready to run tell Dad," Mrs. Dunbar said.

Mr. Summers called his own name and then stepped forward precisely and selected a slip from the box. Then he called, "Warner."

"Seventy-seventh year I been in the lottery," Old Man Warner said as he   40 went through the crowd. "Seventy-seventh time."

"Watson." The tall boy came awkwardly through the crowd. Someone said, "Don't be nervous, Jack," and Mr. Summers said, "Take your time, son."

"Zanini."

After that, there was a long pause, a breathless pause, until Mr. Summers, holding his slip of paper in the air, said, "All right, fellows." For a minute, no one moved, and then all the slips of paper were opened. Suddenly, all women began to speak at once, saying, "Who is it?," "Who's got it?," "Is it the Dunbars?," "Is it the Watsons?" Then the voices began to say, "It's Hutchinson. It's Bill." "Bill Hutchinson's got it."

"Go tell your father," Mrs. Dunbar said to her older son.

People began to look around to see the Hutchinsons. Bill Hutchinson was   45 standing quiet, staring down at the paper in his hand. Suddenly, Tessie Hutchinson shouted to Mr. Summers, "You didn't give him time enough to take any paper he wanted. I saw you. It wasn't fair!"

"Be a good sport, Tessie," Mrs. Delacroix called, and Mrs. Graves said, "All of us took the same chance."

"Shut up, Tessie," Bill Hutchinson said.

"Well, everyone," Mr. Summers said, "that was done pretty fast, and now we've got to be hurrying a little more to get done in time." He consulted his next list. "Bill," he said, "you draw for the Hutchinson family. You got any other households in the Hutchinsons?"

"There's Don and Eva," Mrs. Hutchinson yelled. "Make *them* take their chance!"

"Daughters draw with their husbands' families, Tessie," Mr. Summers said   50 gently. "You know that as well as anyone else."

"It wasn't fair," Tessie said.

"I guess not, Joe," Bill Hutchinson said regretfully. "My daughter draws with her husband's family, that's only fair. And I've got no other family except the kids."

"Then, as far as drawing for families is concerned, it's you," Mr. Summers said in explanation, "and as far as drawing for households is concerned, that's you, too. Right?"

"Right," Bill Hutchinson said.

"How many kids, Bill?" Mr. Summers asked formally.   55

"Three," Bill Hutchinson said. "There's Bill, Jr., and Nancy, and little Dave. And Tessie and me."

"All right, then," Mr. Summers said. "Harry, you got their tickets back?"

Mr. Graves nodded and held up the slips of paper. "Put them in the box, then," Mr. Summers directed. "Take Bill's and put it in."

"I think we ought to start over," Mrs. Hutchinson said, as quietly as she could. "I tell you it wasn't *fair*. You didn't give him time enough to choose. *Everybody* saw that."

Mr. Graves had selected the five slips and put them in the box, and he   60
dropped all the papers but those onto the ground, where the breeze caught them and lifted them off.

"Listen, everybody," Mrs. Hutchinson was saying to the people around her.

"Ready, Bill?" Mr. Summers asked, and Bill Hutchinson, with one quick glance around at his wife and children, nodded.

"Remember," Mr. Summers said, "take the slips and keep them folded until each person has taken one. Harry, you help little Dave." Mr. Graves took the hand of the little boy, who came willingly with him up to the box. "Take a paper out of the box, Davy," Mr. Summers said. Davy put his hand into the box and laughed. "Take just *one* paper," Mr. Summers said. "Harry, you hold it for him." Mr. Graves took the child's hand and removed the folded paper from the tight fist and held it while little Dave stood next to him and looked up at him wonderingly.

"Nancy next," Mr. Summers said. Nancy was twelve, and her school friends breathed heavily as she went forward, switching her skirt, and took a slip daintily from the box. "Bill, Jr.," Mr. Summers said, and Billy, his face red and his feet over-large, nearly knocked the box over as he got a paper out. "Tessie," Mr. Summers said. She hesitated for a minute, looking around defiantly, and then set her lips and went up to the box. She snatched a paper out and held it behind her.

"Bill," Mr. Summers said, and Bill Hutchinson reached into the box and felt   65
around, bringing his hand out at last with the slip of paper in it.

The crowd was quiet. A girl whispered, "I hope it's not Nancy," and the sound of the whisper reached the edges of the crowd.

"It's not the way it used to be," Old Man Warner said clearly. "People ain't the way they used to be."

"All right," Mr. Summers said. "Open the papers. Harry, you open little Dave's."

Mr. Graves opened the slip of paper and there was a general sigh through the crowd as he held it up and everyone could see that it was blank. Nancy and Bill, Jr., opened theirs at the same time, and both beamed and laughed, turning around to the crowd and holding their slips of paper above their heads.

"Tessie," Mr. Summers said. There was a pause, and then Mr. Summers   70
looked at Bill Hutchinson, and Bill unfolded his paper and showed it. It was blank.

"It's Tessie," Mr. Summers said, and his voice was hushed. "Show us her paper, Bill."

Bill Hutchinson went over to his wife and forced the slip of paper out of her hand. It had a black spot on it, the black spot Mr. Summers had made the night before with the heavy pencil in the coal-company office. Bill Hutchinson held it up, and there was a stir in the crowd.

"All right, folks," Mr. Summers said, "let's finish quickly."

Although the villagers had forgotten the ritual and lost the original black box, they still remembered to use stones. The pile of stones the boys had made earlier was ready; there were stones on the ground with the blowing scraps of paper that had come out of the box. Mrs. Delacroix selected a stone so large she had to pick it up with both hands and turned to Mrs. Dunbar. "Come on," she said. "Hurry up."

Mrs. Dunbar had small stones in both hands, and she said, gasping for   75
breath, "I can't run at all. You'll have to go ahead and I'll catch up with you."

The children had stones already, and someone gave little Davy Hutchinson a few pebbles.

Tessie Hutchinson was in the center of a cleared space by now, and she held her hands out desperately as the villagers moved in on her. "It isn't fair," she said. A stone hit her on the side of the head.

Old Man Warner was saying, "Come on, come on, everyone." Steve Adams was in the front of the crowd of villagers, with Mrs. Graves beside him.

"It isn't fair, it isn't right," Mrs. Hutchinson screamed, and then they were upon her.

QUESTIONS AND SUGGESTIONS FOR WRITING

1. What is the community's attitude toward tradition?
2. Doubtless a good writer could tell this story effectively from the point of view of a participant, but Jackson chose a nonparticipant point of view. What does she gain?
3. Let's say you were writing this story, and you had decided to write it from Tessie's point of view. What would your first paragraph, or your first 250 words, be?
4. Suppose someone claimed that the story is an attack on religious orthodoxy. What might be your response? (Whether you agree or disagree, set forth your reasons.)

Toni Cade Bambara (American. b. 1939)

THE LESSON

Back in the days when everyone was old and stupid or young and foolish and me and Sugar were the only ones just right, this lady moved on our block with nappy hair and proper speech and no makeup. And quite naturally we laughed at her, laughed the way we did at the junk man who went about his business like he was some big-time president and his sorry-ass horse his secretary. And we kinda hated her too, hated the way we did the winos who cluttered up our parks and pissed on our handball walls and stank up our hallways and stairs so you couldn't halfway play hide-and-seek without a goddamn gas mask. Miss Moore was her name. The only woman on the block with no first name. And she was black as hell, cept for her feet, which were fish-white and spooky. And she was always planning these boring-ass things for us to do, us being my cousin, mostly, who lived on the block cause we all moved North the same time and to the same apartment then spread out gradual to breathe. And our parents would yank our heads into some kinda shape and crisp up our clothes so we'd be presentable for travel with Miss Moore, who always looked like she was going to church, though she never did. Which is just one of the things the grownups talked about when they talked behind her back like a dog. But when she came calling with some sachet she'd sewed up or some gingerbread she'd made or some book, why then they'd all be too embarrassed to turn her down and we'd get handed over all spruced up. She'd been to college and said it was only right that she should take responsibility for the young ones' education, and she not even related by marriage or blood. So they'd go for it. Specially Aunt Gretchen. She was the main gofer in the family. You got some ole dumb shit foolishness you want somebody to go for, you send for Aunt Gretchen. She been screwed into the go-along for so long, it's a blood-deep natural thing with her. Which is how she got saddled with me and Sugar and Junior in the first place while our mothers were in a la-de-da apartment up the block having a good ole time.

So this one day Miss Moore rounds us all up at the mailbox and it's puredee hot and she's knockin herself out about arithmetic. And school suppose to let up in summer I heard, but she don't never let up. And the starch in my pinafore scratching the shit outta me and I'm really hating this nappy-head bitch and her goddamn college degree. I'd much rather go to the pool or to the show where it's cool. So me and Sugar leaning on the mailbox being surly, which is a Miss Moore word. And Flyboy checking out what everybody brought for lunch. And Fat Butt already wasting his peanut-butter-and-jelly sandwich like the pig he is. And June-bug punchin on Q.T.'s arm for potato chips. And Rosie Giraffe shifting from one hip to the other waiting for somebody to step on her foot or ask her if she from Georgia so she can kick ass, preferably Mercedes'. And Miss Moore asking us do we know what money is, like we a bunch of retards. I mean real money, she say, like it's only poker chips or monopoly papers we lay on the grocer. So right away I'm tired of this and say so. And would much rather snatch Sugar and go to the Sunset and terrorize the West Indian kids and take their hair ribbons and their money too. And Miss Moore files that remark away for next week's lesson on brotherhood, I can tell. And finally I say we oughta get to the subway cause it's cooler and besides we might meet some cute boys. Sugar done swiped her mama's lipstick, so we ready.

So we heading down the street and she's boring us silly about what things cost and what our parents make and how much goes for rent and how money ain't divided up right in this country. And then she gets to the part about we all poor and live in the slums, which I don't feature. And I'm ready to speak on that, but she steps out in the street and hails two cabs just like that. Then she hustles half the crew in with her and hands me a five-dollar bill and tells me to calculate 10 percent tip for the driver. And we're off. Me and Sugar and Junebug and Flyboy hangin out the window and hollering to everybody, putting lipstick on each other cause Flyboy a faggot anyway, and making farts with our sweaty armpits. But I'm mostly trying to figure how to spend this money. But they all fascinated with the meter ticking and Junebug starts laying bets as to how much it'll read when Flyboy can't hold his breath no more. Then Sugar lays bets as to how much it'll be when we get there. So I'm stuck. Don't nobody want to go for my plan, which is to jump out at the next light and run off to the first bar-b-que we can find. Then the driver tells us to get the hell out cause we there already. And the meter reads eighty-five cents. And I'm stalling to figure out the tip and Sugar say give him a dime. And I decide he don't need it bad as I do, so later for him. But then he tries to take off with Junebug foot still in the door so we talk about his mama something ferocious. Then we check out that we on Fifth Avenue and everybody dressed up in stockings. One lady in a fur coat, hot as it is. White folks crazy.

"This is the place," Miss Moore say, presenting it to us in the voice she uses at the museum. "Let's look in the windows before we go in."

"Can we steal?" Sugar asks very serious like she's getting the ground rules   5
squared away before she plays. "I beg your pardon," say Miss Moore, and we fall out. So she leads us around the windows of the toy store and me and Sugar screamin, "This is mine, that's mine, I gotta have that, that was made for me, I was born for that," till Big Butt drowns us out.

"Hey, I'm goin to buy that there."

"That there? You don't even know what it is, stupid."

"I do so," he say punchin on Rosie Giraffe. "It's a microscope."

"Whatcha gonna do with a microscope, fool?"

"Look at things."   10

"Like what, Ronald?" ask Miss Moore. And Big Butt ain't got the first notion. So here go Miss Moore gabbing about the thousands of bacteria in a drop of water and the somethinorother in a speck of blood and the million and one living things in the air around us is invisible to the naked eye. And what she say that for? Junebug go to town on that "naked" and we rolling. Then Miss Moore ask what it cost. So we all jam into the window smudgin it up and the price tag say $300. So then she ask how long'd take for Big Butt and Junebug to save up their allowances. "Too long," I say. "Yeh," adds Sugar, "outgrown it by that time." And Miss Moore say no, you never outgrow learning instruments. "Why, even medical students and interns and," blah, blah, blah. And we ready to choke Big Butt for bringing it up in the first damn place.

"This here costs four hundred eighty dollars," say Rosie Giraffe. So we pile up all over her to see what she pointin out. My eyes tell me it's a chunk of glass cracked with something heavy, and different-color inks dripped into the splits, then the whole thing put into a oven or something. But for $480 it don't make sense.

"That's a paperweight made of semi-precious stones fused together under tremendous pressure," she explains slowly, with her hands doing the mining and all the factory work.

"So what's a paperweight?" asks Rosie Giraffe.

"To weigh paper with, dumbbell," say Flyboy, the wise man from the East.   15

"Not exactly," say Miss Moore, which is what she say when you warm or way off too. "It's to weigh paper down so it won't scatter and make your desk untidy." So right away me and Sugar curtsy to each other and then to Mercedes who is more the tidy type.

"We don't keep paper on top of the desk in my class," say Junebug, figuring Miss Moore crazy or lyin one.

"At home, then," she say. "Don't you have a calendar and a pencil case and a blotter and a letter-opener on your desk at home where you do your homework?" And she know damn well what our homes look like cause she nosys around in them every chance she gets.

"I don't even have a desk," say Junebug. "Do we?"

"No. And I don't get no homework neither," says Big Butt.   20

"And I don't even have a home," say Flyboy like he do at school to keep the white folks off his back and sorry for him. Send this poor kid to camp posters, is his specialty.

"I do," says Mercedes. "I have a box of stationery on my desk and a picture of my cat. My godmother bought the stationery and the desk. There's a big rose on each sheet and the envelopes smell like roses."

"Who wants to know about your smelly-ass stationery," say Rosie Giraffe fore I can get my two cents in.

"It's important to have a work area all your own so that . . ."

"Will you look at this sailboat, please," say Flyboy, cuttin her off and pointin   25
to the thing like it was his. So once again we tumble all over each other to gaze at this magnificent thing in the toy store which is just big enough to maybe sail two kittens across the pond if you strap them to the posts tight. We all start reciting the price tag like we in assembly. "Hand-crafted sailboat of fiberglass at one thousand one hundred ninety-five dollars."

"Unbelievable," I hear myself say and am really stunned. I read it again for myself just in case the group recitation put me in a trance. Same thing. For some reason this pisses me off. We look at Miss Moore and she lookin at us, waiting for I dunno what.

"Who'd pay all that when you can buy a sailboat set for a quarter at Pop's, a tube of glue for a dime, and a ball of string for eight cents? It must have a motor and a whole lot else besides," I say. "My sailboat cost me about fifty cents."

"But will it take water?" say Mercedes with her smart ass.

"Took mine to Alley Pond Park once," say Flyboy. "String broke. Lost it. Pity."

"Sailed mine in Central Park and it keeled over and sank. Had to ask my   30
father for another dollar."

"And you got the strap," laugh Big Butt. "The jerk didn't even have a string on it. My old man wailed on his behind."

Little Q.T. was staring hard at the sailboat and you could see he wanted it bad. But he too little and somebody'd just take it from him. So what the hell. "This boat for kids, Miss Moore?"

"Parents silly to buy something like that just to get all broke up," say Rosie Giraffe.

"That much money it should last forever," I figure.

"My father'd buy it for me if I wanted it." 35

"Your father, my ass," say Rosie Giraffe getting a chance to finally push Mercedes.

"Must be rich people shop here," say Q.T.

"You are a very bright boy," say Flyboy. "What was your first clue?" And he rap him on the head with the back of his knuckles, since Q.T. the only one he could get away with. Though Q.T. liable to come up behind you years later and get his licks in when you half expect it.

"What I want to know is," I says to Miss Moore though I never talk to her, I wouldn't give the bitch that satisfaction, "is how much a real boat costs? I figure a thousand'd get you a yacht any day."

"Why don't you check that out," she says, "and report back to the group?" 40 Which really pains my ass. If you gonna mess up a perfectly good swim day least you could do is have some answers. "Let's go in," she say like she got something up her sleeve. Only she don't lead the way. So me and Sugar turn the corner to where the entrance is, but when we get there I kinda hang back. Not that I'm scared, what's there to be afraid of, just a toy store. But I feel funny, shame. But what I got to be shamed about? Got as much right to go in as anybody. But somehow I can't seem to get hold of the door, so I step away for Sugar to lead. But she hangs back too. And I look at her and she looks at me and this is ridiculous. I mean, damn, I have never ever been shy about doing nothing or going nowhere. But then Mercedes steps up and then Rosie Giraffe and Big Butt crowd in behind and shove, and next thing we all stuffed into the doorway with only Mercedes squeezing past us, smoothing out her jumper and walking right down the aisle. Then the rest of us tumble in like a glued-together jigsaw done all wrong. And people lookin at us. And it's like the time me and Sugar crashed into the Catholic church on a dare. But once we got in there and everything so hushed and holy and the candles and the bowin and the handkerchiefs on all the drooping heads, I just couldn't go through with the plan. Which was for me to run up to the altar and do a tap dance while Sugar played the nose flute and messed around in the holy water. And Sugar kept givin me the elbow. Then later teased me so bad I tied her up in the shower and turned it on and locked her in. And she'd be there till this day if Aunt Gretchen hadn't finally figured I was lyin about the boarder takin a shower.

Same thing in the store. We all walkin on tiptoe and hardly touchin the games and puzzles and things. And I watched Miss Moore who is steady watchin us like she waitin for a sign. Like Mama Drewery watches the sky and sniffs the air and takes note of just how much slant is in the bird formation. Then me and Sugar bump smack into each other, so busy gazing at the toys, 'specially the sailboat. But we don't laugh and go into our fat-lady bump-stomach routine. We just stare at that price tag. Then Sugar run a finger over the whole boat. And I'm jealous and want to hit her. Maybe not her, but I sure want to punch somebody in the mouth.

"Watcha bring us here for, Miss Moore?"

"You sound angry, Sylvia. Are you mad about something?" Givin me one of them grins like she tellin a grown-up joke that never turns out to be funny. And she's lookin very closely at me like maybe she plannin to do my portrait from memory. I'm mad, but I won't give her that satisfaction. So I slouch around the store bein very bored and say, "Let's go."

Me and Sugar at the back of the train watchin the tracks whizzin by large then small then gettin gobbled up in the dark. I'm thinkin about this tricky toy I saw in the store. A clown that somersaults on a bar then does chin-ups just cause you yank lightly at his leg. Cost $35. I could see me askin my mother for a $35 birthday clown. "You wanna who that costs what?" she'd say, cocking her head to the side to get a better view of the hole in my head. Thirty-five dollars could buy new bunk beds for Junior and Gretchen's boy. Thirty-five dollars and the whole household could go visit Granddaddy Nelson in the country. Thirty-five dollars would pay for the rent and the piano bill too. Who are these people that spend that much for performing clowns and $1000 for toy sailboats? What kinda work they do and how they live and how come we ain't in on it? Where we are is who we are, Miss Moore always pointin out. But it don't necessarily have to be that way, she always adds then waits for somebody to say that poor people have to wake up and demand their share of the pie and don't none of us know what kind of pie she talkin about in the first damn place. But she ain't so smart cause I still got her four dollars from the taxi and she sure ain't gettin it. Messin up my day with this shit. Sugar nudges me in my pocket and winks.

Miss Moore lines us up in front of the mailbox where we started from, seem   45
like years ago, and I got a headache for thinkin so hard. And we lean all over each other so we can hold up under the draggy-ass lecture she always finishes us off with at the end before we thank her for borin us to tears. But she just looks at us like she readin tea leaves. Finally she say, "Well, what did you think of F. A. O. Schwarz?"

Rosie Giraffe mumbles, "White folks crazy."

"I'd like to go there again when I get my birthday money," says Mercedes, and we shove her out the pack so she has to lean on the mailbox by herself.

"I'd like a shower. Tiring day," say Flyboy.

Then Sugar surprises me by sayin, "You know, Miss Moore, I don't think all of us here put together eat in a year what that sailboat costs." And Miss Moore lights up like somebody goosed her. "And?" she say, urging Sugar on. Only I'm standin on her foot so she don't continue.

"Imagine for a minute what kind of society it is in which some people can   50
spend on a toy what it would cost to feed a family of six or seven. What do you think?"

"I think," say Sugar pushing me off her feet like she never done before, cause I whip her ass in a minute, "that this is not much of a democracy if you ask me. Equal chance to pursue happiness means an equal crack at the dough, don't it?" Miss Moore is besides herself and I am disgusted with Sugar's treachery. So I stand on her foot one more time to see if she'll shove me. She shuts up, and Miss Moore looks at me, sorrowfully I'm thinkin. And somethin weird is goin on, I can feel it in my chest.

"Anybody else learn anything today?" lookin dead at me. I walk away and Sugar has to run to catch up and don't even seem to notice when I shrug her arm off my shoulder.

"Well, we got four dollars anyway," she says.

"Uh hunh."

"We could go to Hascombs and get half a chocolate layer and then go to the   55 Sunset and still have plenty money for potato chips and ice cream sodas."

"Uh hunh."

"Race you to Hascombs," she say.

We start down the block and she gets ahead which is O.K. by me cause I'm going to the West End and then over to the Drive to think this day through. She can run if she want to and even run faster. But ain't nobody gonna beat me at nuthin.

QUESTIONS AND SUGGESTIONS FOR WRITING

1. What is the point of Miss Moore's lesson? Why does Sylvia resist it?
2. Describe the relationship between Sugar and Sylvia. What is Sugar's function in the story?
3. What does the last line of the story suggest?
4. In a paragraph or two, characterize the narrator. Do not summarize the story— assume that your reader is familiar with it—but support your characterization by some references to episodes in the story and perhaps by a few brief quotations.

☐ POETRY

Edwin Arlington Robinson (American. 1869–1935)
RICHARD CORY

Whenever Richard Cory went down town,
We people on the pavement looked at him:
He was a gentleman from sole to crown,
Clean favored, and imperially slim.   4

And he was always quietly arrayed,
And he was always human when he talked;
But still he fluttered pulses when he said,
"Good-morning," and he glittered when he walked.   8

And he was rich—yes, richer than a king—
And admirably schooled in every grace:
In fine,° we thought that he was everything   *In short*
To make us wish that we were in his place.   12

So on we worked, and waited for the light,
And went without the meat, and cursed the bread;
And Richard Cory, one calm summer night,
Went home and put a bullet through his head.   16

SUGGESTION FOR WRITING

Consult the entry on "irony" in the glossary. Then read the pages referred to in the entry. Finally, write an essay of 500 words on irony in "Richard Cory."

Robert Frost (American. 1874–1963)

THE GIFT OUTRIGHT

The land was ours before we were the land's.
She was our land more than a hundred years
Before we were her people. She was ours
In Massachusetts, in Virginia,
But we were England's, still colonials,   5
Possessing what we still were unpossessed by,
Possessed by what we now no more possessed.
Something we were withholding made us weak
Until we found it was ourselves
We were withholding from our land of living,   10
And forthwith found salvation in surrender.
Such as we were we gave ourselves outright
(The deed of gift was many deeds of war)
To the land vaguely realizing westward,
But still unstoried, artless, unenhanced,   15
Such as she was, such as she would become.

QUESTIONS AND SUGGESTIONS FOR WRITING

1. Paraphrase the poem. (If you find lines 6–7 especially difficult, consider the possibility that "possess" may have multiple meanings: (1) to own; (2) to enchant. Thus, for instance, "possessed by" can mean "owned by" or "enchanted by, obsessed with.")
2. What is the gift referred to in the title? (In rereading the poem, pay special attention to lines 12–13.)
3. If you have read Chief Seattle's "My People" (page 439), consider the degree to which Seattle's view of whites resembles Frost's view of the settlers.
4. Consult the entry on "paradox" in the glossary. Then read the pages referred to in the entry, and write an essay of 500 words on paradox in "The Gift Outright."

Langston Hughes (American. 1902–1967)
HARLEM (A DREAM DEFERRED)

What happens to a dream deferred?

Does it dry up
like a raisin in the sun?
Or fester like a sore—
And then run?   5
Does it stink like rotten meat?
Or crust and sugar over—
like a syrupy sweet?

Maybe it just sags
like a heavy load.   10

Or does it explode?

QUESTION AND SUGGESTION FOR WRITING

One might keep the first line where it is, and then rearrange the other stanzas—for
instance, putting lines 2–8 after 9–11. Which version (Hughes's or the one just mentioned) do you prefer? Why?

☐ DRAMA

Edward Albee (American. b. 1928)
THE SANDBOX

The Players

THE YOUNG MAN, *25, a good looking, well-built boy in a bathing suit*
MOMMY, *55, a well-dressed, imposing woman*
DADDY, *60, a small man; gray, thin*
GRANDMA, *86, a tiny, wizened woman with bright eyes*
THE MUSICIAN, *no particular age, but young would be nice*

Note: When, in the course of the play, MOMMY *and* DADDY *call each other by these names, there should be no suggestion of regionalism. These names are of empty affection and point up the pre-senility and vacuity of their characters.*

The Scene *A bare stage, with only the following: Near the footlights, far stage-right, two simple chairs set side by side, facing the audience; near the footlights, far stage-left, a chair facing stage-right with a music stand before it; farther back, and stage-center, slightly elevated and raked, a large child's sandbox with a toy pail and shovel; the background is the sky, which alters from brightest day to deepest night.*

At the beginning, it is brightest day, the YOUNG MAN *is alone on stage, to the rear of the sandbox, and to one side. He is doing calisthenics; he does calisthenics until quite at the very end of the play. These calisthenics, employing the arms only, should suggest the beating and fluttering of wings. The* YOUNG MAN *is, after all, the Angel of Death.*

MOMMY *and* DADDY *enter from stage-left,* MOMMY *first.*

MOMMY *(motioning to* DADDY*)*. Well, here we are; this is the beach.

DADDY *(whining)*. I'm cold.

MOMMY *(dismissing him with a little laugh)*. Don't be silly; it's as warm as toast. Look at that nice young man over there: *he* doesn't think it's cold. *(Waves to the* YOUNG MAN.*)* Hello.

YOUNG MAN *(with an endearing smile)*. Hi!

MOMMY *(looking about)*. This will do perfectly . . . don't you think so, Daddy? There's sand there . . . and the water beyond. What do you think, Daddy?

DADDY *(vaguely)*. Whatever you say, Mommy.

MOMMY *(with the same little laugh)*. Well, of course . . . whatever I say. Then, it's settled, is it?

DADDY *(shrugs)*. She's *your* mother, not mine.

MOMMY. *I* know she's my mother. What do you take me for? *(A pause.)* All right, now; let's get on with it. *(She shouts into the wings, stage-left.)* You! Out there! You can come in now.

The MUSICIAN *enters, seats himself in the chair, stage-left, places music on the music stand, is ready to play.* MOMMY *nods approvingly.*

MOMMY. Very nice; very nice. Are you ready, Daddy? Let's go get Grandma.

DADDY. Whatever you say, Mommy.

MOMMY *(leading the way out, stage-left)*. Of course, whatever I say. *(To the* MUSICIAN.*)* You can begin now.

The MUSICIAN *begins playing;* MOMMY *and* DADDY *exit; the* MUSICIAN, *all the while playing, nods to the* YOUNG MAN.

YOUNG MAN *(with the same endearing smile)*. Hi!

After a moment, MOMMY *and* DADDY *re-enter, carrying* GRANDMA. *She is borne in by their hands under her armpits; she is quite*

rigid; her legs are drawn up; her feet do not touch the ground; the expression on her ancient face is that of puzzlement and fear.

DADDY. Where do we put her?

MOMMY *(the same little laugh)*. Wherever I say, of course. Let me see . . . well . . . all right, over there . . . in the sandbox. *(Pause.)* Well, what are you waiting for, Daddy? . . . The sandbox!

Together they carry GRANDMA *over to the sandbox and more or less dump her in.*

GRANDMA *(righting herself to a sitting position; her voice a cross between a baby's laugh and cry)*. Ahhhhhh! Graaaaa!

DADDY *(dusting himself)*. What do we do now?

MOMMY *(to the* MUSICIAN*)*. You can stop now. *(The* MUSICIAN *stops.)* *(Back to* DADDY.*)* What do you mean, what do we do now? We go over there and sit down, of course. *(To the* YOUNG MAN.*)* Hello there.

YOUNG MAN *(again smiling)*. Hi!

MOMMY *and* DADDY *move to the chairs, stage-right, and sit down. A pause.*

GRANDMA *(same as before)*. Ahhhhhh! Ah-haaaaaa! Graaaaaa!

DADDY. Do you think . . . do you think she's . . . comfortable?

MOMMY *(impatiently)*. How would I know?

DADDY *(pause)*. What do we do now?

MOMMY *(as if remembering)*. We . . . wait. We . . . sit here . . . and we wait . . . that's what we do.

DADDY *(after a pause)*. Shall we talk to each other?

MOMMY *(with that little laugh; picking something off her dress)*. Well, *you* can talk, if you want to . . . if you can think of anything to *say* . . . if you can think of anything *new*.

DADDY *(thinks)*. No . . . I suppose not.

MOMMY *(with a triumphant laugh)*. Of course not!

GRANDMA *(banging the toy shovel against the pail)*. Haaaaaa! Ah-haaaaaa!

MOMMY *(out over the audience)*. Be quiet, Grandma . . . just be quiet, and wait.

GRANDMA *throws a shovelful of sand at* MOMMY.

MOMMY *(still out over the audience)*. She's throwing sand at me! You stop that, Grandma; you stop throwing sand at Mommy! *(To* DADDY.*)* She's throwing sand at me.

DADDY *looks around at* GRANDMA, *who screams at him.*

GRANDMA. GRAAAAA!

MOMMY. Don't look at her. Just . . . sit here . . . be very still . . . and wait. *(To the* MUSICIAN.*)* You . . . uh . . . you go ahead and do whatever it is you do.

The MUSICIAN *plays.*

MOMMY *and* DADDY *are fixed, staring out beyond the audience.* GRANDMA *looks at them, looks at the* MUSICIAN, *looks at the sandbox, throws down the shovel.*

GRANDMA. Ah-haaaaaa! Graaaaaa! *(Looks for reaction; gets none. Now . . . directly to the audience.)* Honestly! What a way to treat an old woman! Drag her out of the house . . . stick her in a car . . . bring her out here from the city . . . dump her in a pile of sand . . . and leave her here to set. I'm eighty-six years old! I was married when I was seventeen. To a farmer. He died when I was thirty. *(To the* MUSICIAN.*)* Will you stop that, please?

The MUSICIAN *stops playing.*

I'm a feeble old woman . . . how do you expect anybody to hear me over that peep! peep! peep! *(To herself.)* There's no respect around here. *(To the* YOUNG MAN.*)* There's no respect around here!

YOUNG MAN *(same smile)*. Hi!

GRANDMA *(after a pause, a mild double-take, continues, to the audience)*. My husband died when I was thirty *(indicates* MOMMY*)*, and I had to raise that big cow over there all by my lonesome. You can imagine what *that* was like. Lordy! *(To the* YOUNG MAN.*)* Where'd they get *you?*

YOUNG MAN. Oh . . . I've been around for a while.

GRANDMA. I'll bet you have! Heh, heh, heh. Will you look at you!

YOUNG MAN *(flexing his muscles)*. Isn't that something? *(Continues his calisthenics.)*

GRANDMA. Boy, oh boy; I'll say. Pretty good.

YOUNG MAN *(sweetly)*. I'll say.

GRANDMA. Where ya from?

YOUNG MAN. Southern California.

GRANDMA *(nodding)*. Figgers, figgers. What's your name, honey?

YOUNG MAN. I don't know. . . .

GRANDMA *(to the audience)*. Bright, too!

YOUNG MAN. I mean . . . I mean, they haven't given me one yet . . . the studio . . .

GRANDMA *(giving him the once-over)*. You don't say . . . you don't say. Well . . . uh, I've got to talk some more . . . don't you go 'way.

YOUNG MAN. Oh, no.

GRANDMA *(turning her attention back to the audience)*. Fine; fine. *(Then, once more, back to the* YOUNG MAN.*)* You're . . . you're an actor, hunh?

YOUNG MAN *(beaming)*. Yes. I am.

GRANDMA *(to the audience again; shrugs)*. I'm smart that way. *Anyhow,* I had to raise . . . *that* over there all by my lonesome; and what's next to her there . . . that's what she married. Rich? I tell you . . . money, money, money. They took me off the *farm* . . . which was real decent of them . . . and they moved me into the big town house with *them* . . . fixed a nice place for me under the stove . . . gave me an army blanket . . . and my own dish . . . my very own dish! So, what have I got to complain about? Nothing, of course. I'm not complaining. *(She looks up at the sky, shouts to someone offstage.)* Shouldn't it be getting dark now, dear?

The lights dim; night comes on. The MUSICIAN *begins to play; it becomes deepest night. There are spots on all the players, including the* YOUNG MAN, *who is, of course, continuing his calisthenics.*

DADDY *(stirring)*. It's nighttime.

MOMMY. Shhhh. Be still . . . wait.

DADDY *(whining)*. It's so hot.

MOMMY. Shhhhhh. Be still . . . wait.

GRANDMA *(to herself)*. That's better. Night. *(To the* MUSICIAN.*)* Honey, do you play all through this part?

The MUSICIAN *nods.*

Well, keep it nice and soft; that's a good boy.

The MUSICIAN *nods again; plays softly.*

That's nice.

There is an off-stage rumble.

DADDY *(starting)*. What was that?

MOMMY *(beginning to weep)*. It was nothing.

DADDY. It was . . . it was . . . thunder . . . or a wave breaking . . . or something.

MOMMY *(whispering, through her tears)*. It was an off-stage rumble . . . and you know what *that* means. . . .

DADDY. I forget. . . .

MOMMY *(barely able to talk)*. It means the time has come for poor Grandma . . . and I can't bear it!

DADDY *(vacantly)*. I . . . I suppose you've got to be brave.

GRANDMA *(mocking)*. That's right, kid; be brave. You'll bear up; you'll get over it. *(Another off-stage rumble . . . louder.)*

MOMMY. Ohhhhhhhhhh . . . poor Grandma . . . poor Grandma. . . .

GRANDMA *(to* MOMMY*)*. I'm fine! I'm all right! It hasn't happened yet!

A violent off-stage rumble. All the lights go out, save the spot on the YOUNG MAN; *the* MUSICIAN *stops playing.*

MOMMY. Ohhhhhhhhhh.   .   .   . Ohhhhhhhhhh. . . .

Silence.

GRANDMA. Don't put the lights up yet . . . I'm not ready; I'm not quite ready. *(Silence.)* All right, dear . . . I'm about done.

The lights come up again, to brightest day; the MUSICIAN *begins to play.* GRANDMA *is discovered, still in the sandbox, lying on her side, propped up on an elbow, half covered, busily shoveling sand over herself.*

GRANDMA *(muttering)*. I don't know how I'm supposed to do anything with this goddam toy shovel. . . .

DADDY. Mommy! It's daylight!

MOMMY *(brightly)*. So it is! Well! Our long night is over. We must put away our tears, take off our mourning . . . and face the future. It's our duty.

GRANDMA *(still shoveling; mimicking)*. . . . take off our mourning . . . face the future. . . . Lordy!

MOMMY *and* DADDY *rise, stretch.* MOMMY *waves to the* YOUNG MAN.

YOUNG MAN *(with that smile)*. Hi!

GRANDMA *plays dead.* (!) MOMMY *and* DADDY *go over to look at her; she is a little more than half buried in the sand; the toy shovel is in her hands, which are crossed on her breast.*

MOMMY *(before the sandbox; shaking her head)*. Lovely! It's . . . it's hard to be sad . . . she looks . . . so happy. *(With pride and conviction.)* It pays to do things well. *(To the* MUSICIAN.*)* All right, you can stop now, if you want to. I mean, stay around for a swim, or something; it's all right with us. *(She sighs heavily.)* Well, Daddy . . . off we go.

DADDY. Brave Mommy!

MOMMY. Brave Daddy!

They exit, stage-left.

GRANDMA *(after they leave; lying quite still)*. It pays to do things well. . . . Boy, oh boy! *(She tries to sit up)* . . . well, kids . . . *(but she finds she can't.)* . . . I . . . I can't get up, I . . . I can't move. . . .

The YOUNG MAN *stops his calisthenics, nods to the* MUSICIAN, *walks over to* GRANDMA, *kneels down by the sandbox.*

GRANDMA. I . . . can't move. . . .

YOUNG MAN. Shhhhh . . . be very still . . .

GRANDMA. I . . . I can't move. . . .

YOUNG MAN. Uh . . . ma'am; I . . . I have a line here.

GRANDMA. Oh, I'm sorry, sweetie; you go right ahead.

YOUNG MAN. I am . . . uh . . .

GRANDMA. Take your time, dear.

YOUNG MAN *(prepares; delivers the line like a real amateur).* I am the Angel of Death. I am . . . uh . . . I am come for you.

GRANDMA. What . . . wha . . . *(Then, with resignation.)* . . . ohhhh . . . ohhhh, I see.

The YOUNG MAN *bends over, kisses* GRANDMA *gently on the forehead.*

GRANDMA *(her eyes closed, her hands folded on her breast again, the shovel between her hands, a sweet smile on her face).*

Well . . . that was very nice, dear. . . .

YOUNG MAN *(still kneeling).* Shhhhhh . . . be still. . . .

GRANDMA. What I meant was . . . you did that very well, dear. . . .

YOUNG MAN *(blushing).* . . . . oh . . .

GRANDMA. No; I mean it. You've got that . . . you've got a quality.

YOUNG MAN *(with his endearing smile).* Oh . . . thank you; thank you very much . . . ma'am.

GRANDMA *(slowly; softly—as the* YOUNG MAN *puts his hands on top of* GRANDMA's). You're . . . you're welcome . . . dear.

Tableau. The MUSICIAN *continues to play as the curtain slowly comes down.*

Curtain

QUESTIONS AND SUGGESTIONS FOR WRITING

1. In a sentence characterize Mommy, and in another sentence characterize Daddy.
2. Of the four characters in the play, which is the most sympathetic? Set forth your answer, with supporting evidence, in two paragraphs, devoting the first to the three less sympathetic characters, the second to the most sympathetic character.
3. In a longer play, *The American Dream*, Albee uses the same four characters that he uses in *The Sandbox*. Of *The American Dream* he wrote:

The play is . . . a condemnation of complacency, cruelty, emasculation and vacuity; it is a stand against the fiction that everything in this slipping land of ours is peachy-keen.

To what extent does this statement help you to understand (and to enjoy) *The Sandbox*?

4. In *The New York Times Magazine*, 25 February 1962, Albee protested against the view that his plays, and others of the so-called Theater of the Absurd, are depressing. He includes a quotation from Martin Esslin's book, *The Theatre of the Absurd*:

Ultimately . . . the Theatre of the Absurd does not reflect despair or a return to dark irrational forces but expresses modern man's endeavor to come to terms with the world in which he lives. It attempts to make him face up to the human condition as it really is, to free him from illusions that are bound to cause constant maladjustment and disappointment. . . . For the dignity of man lies in his ability to face reality in all its senselessness; to accept it freely, without fear, without illusions—and to laugh at it.

In what ways is this statement helpful? In what ways is it not helpful? Explain.

The Individual and 10
Society

☐ ESSAYS

May Sarton (American. b. 1912)

THE REWARDS OF
LIVING A SOLITARY LIFE

The other day an acquaintance of mine, a gregarious and charming man, told me he had found himself unexpectedly alone in New York for an hour or two between appointments. He went to the Whitney and spent the "empty" time looking at things in solitary bliss. For him it proved to be a shock nearly as great as falling in love to discover that he could enjoy himself so much alone.

What had he been afraid of, I asked myself? That, suddenly alone, he would discover that he bored himself, or that there was, quite simply, no self there to meet? But having taken the plunge, he is now on the brink of adventure; he is about to be launched into his own inner space, space as immense, unexplored, and sometimes frightening as outer space to the astronaut. His every percepti will come to him with a new freshness and, for a time, seem startlingly original. For anyone who can see things for himself with a naked eye becomes, for a moment or two, something of a genius. With another human being present vision becomes double vision, inevitably. We are busy wondering, what does my companion see or think of this, and what do I think of it? The original impact gets lost, or diffused.

"Music I heard with you was more than music." Exactly. And therefore music *itself* can only be heard alone. Solitude is the salt of personhood. It brings out the authentic flavor of every experience.

"Alone one is never lonely: the spirit adventures, walking/In a quiet garden, in a cool house, abiding single there."

Loneliness is most acutely felt with other people, for with others, even with a   5
lover sometimes, we suffer from our differences of taste, temperament, mood. Human intercourse often demands that we soften the edge of perception, or withdraw at the very instant of personal truth for fear of hurting, or of being inappropriately present, which is to say naked, in a social situation. Alone we can

afford to be wholly whatever we are, and to feel whatever we feel absolutely. That is a great luxury!

For me the most interesting thing about a solitary life, and mine has been that for the last twenty years, is that it becomes increasingly rewarding. When I can wake up and watch the sun rise over the ocean, as I do most days, and know that I have an entire day ahead, uninterrupted, in which to write a few pages, take a walk with my dog, lie down in the afternoon for a long think (why does one think better in a horizontal position?), read and listen to music, I am flooded with happiness.

I am lonely only when I am overtired, when I have worked too long without a break, when for the time being I feel empty and need filling up. And I am lonely sometimes when I come back home after a lecture trip, when I have seen a lot of people and talked a lot, and am full to the brim with experience that needs to be sorted out.

Then for a little while the house feels huge and empty, and I wonder where my self is hiding. It has to be recaptured slowly by watering the plants, perhaps, and looking again at each one as though it were a person, by feeding the two cats, by cooking a meal.

It takes a while, as I watch the surf blowing up in fountains at the end of the field, but the moment comes when the world falls away, and the self emerges again from the deep unconscious, bringing back all I have recently experienced to be explored and slowly understood, when I can converse again with my hidden powers, and so grow, and so be renewed, till death do us part.

QUESTIONS AND SUGGESTIONS FOR WRITING

1. What does Sarton mean when she says: "Anyone who can see things for himself with a naked eye becomes, for a moment or two, something of a genius"? Does your own experience confirm her comment? Explain.
2. Drawing on Sarton's essay, explain in 500 words the distinction between being "alone" and being "lonely."
3. What phrase in the last paragraph connects the ending with the first paragraph?

Andy Rooney (American. b. 1920)

IN AND OF OURSELVES WE TRUST

Last night I was driving from Harrisburg to Lewisburg, Pa., a distance of about 80 miles. It was late, I was late, and if anyone asked me how fast I was driving, I'd have to plead the Fifth Amendment to avoid self-incrimination.

At one point along an open highway, I came to a crossroads with a traffic light. I was alone on the road by now, but as I approached the light, it turned red, and I breaked to a halt. I looked left, right, and behind me. Nothing. Not a car, no suggestion of headlights, but there I sat, waiting for the light to change, the only human being for at least a mile in any direction.

I started wondering why I refused to run the light. I was not afraid of being arrested, because there was obviously no cop anywhere around and there certainly would have been no danger in going through it.

Much later that night, after I'd met with a group in Lewisburg and had climbed into bed near midnight, the question of why I'd stopped for that light came back to me. I think I stopped because it's part of a contract we all have with each other. It's not only the law, but it's an agreement we have, and we trust each other to honor it: We don't go through red lights. Like most of us, I'm more apt to be restrained from doing something bad by the social convention that disapproves of it than by any law against it.

It's amazing that we ever trust each other to do the right thing, isn't it? And we do, too. Trust is our first inclination. We have to make a deliberate decision to mistrust someone or to be suspicious or skeptical.   5

It's a darn good thing, too, because the whole structure of our society depends on mutual trust, not distrust. This whole thing we have going for us would fall apart if we didn't trust each other most of the time. In Italy they have an awful time getting any money for the government because many people just plain don't pay their income tax. Here, the Internal Revenue Service makes some gestures toward enforcing the law, but mostly they just have to trust that we'll pay what we owe. There has often been talk of a tax revolt in this country, most recently among unemployed auto workers in Michigan, and our government pretty much admits that if there were a widespread tax revolt here, they wouldn't be able to do anything about it.

We do what we say we'll do. We show up when we say we'll show up.

I was so proud of myself for stopping for that red light. And inasmuch as no one would ever have known what a good person I was on the road from Harrisburg to Lewisburg, I had to tell someone.

QUESTIONS AND SUGGESTIONS FOR WRITING

1. In a sentence, state Rooney's thesis. (If you find a thesis sentence in the essay, simply quote it.)
2. In his first paragraph Rooney admits that he was exceeding the speed limit. Does this fact contradict his basic point? If not, why not?
3. What does the last paragraph contribute to the essay?

Judy Syfers (American. b. 1937)

I WANT A WIFE

I belong to that classification of people known as wives. I am A Wife. And, not altogether incidentally, I am a mother.

Not too long ago a male friend of mine appeared on the scene fresh from a recent divorce. He had one child, who is, of course, with his ex-wife. He is looking for another wife. As I thought about him while I was ironing one evening, it suddenly occurred to me that I, too, would like to have a wife. Why do I want a wife?

I would like to go back to school so that I can become economically independent, support myself, and, if need be, support those dependent upon me. I want a wife who will work and send me to school. And while I am going to school I want a wife to take care of my children. I want a wife to keep track of the children's doctor and dentist appointments. And to keep track of mine, too. I want a wife to make sure my children eat properly and are kept clean. I want a wife who will wash the children's clothes and keep them mended. I want a wife who is a good nurturant attendant to my children, who arranges for their schooling, makes sure that they have an adequate social life with their peers, takes them to the park, the zoo, etc. I want a wife who takes care of the children when they are sick, a wife who arranges to be around when the children need special care, because, of course, I cannot miss classes at school. My wife must arrange to lose time at work and not lose the job. It may mean a small cut in my wife's income from time to time, but I guess I can tolerate that. Needless to say, my wife will arrange and pay for the care of the children while my wife is working.

I want a wife who will take care of *my* physical needs. I want a wife who will keep my house clean. A wife who will pick up after my children, a wife who will pick up after me. I want a wife who will keep my clothes clean, ironed, mended, replaced when need be, and who will see to it that my personal things are kept in their proper place so that I can find what I need the minute I need it. I want a wife who cooks the meals, a wife who is a *good* cook. I want a wife who will plan the menus, do the necessary grocery shopping, prepare the meals, serve them pleasantly, and then do the cleaning up while I do my studying. I want a wife who will care for me when I am sick and sympathize with my pain and loss of time from school. I want a wife to go along when our family takes a vacation so that someone can continue to care for me and my children when I need a rest and change of scene.

I want a wife who will not bother me with rambling complaints about a wife's   5 duties. But I want a wife who will listen to me when I feel the need to explain a rather difficult point I have come across in my course of studies. And I want a wife who will type my papers for me when I have written them.

I want a wife who will take care of the details of my social life. When my wife and I are invited out by my friends, I want a wife who will take care of the babysitting arrangements. When I meet people at school that I like and want to entertain, I want a wife who will have the house clean, will prepare a special meal, serve it to me and my friends, and not interrupt when I talk about things that interest me and my friends. I want a wife who will have arranged that the children are fed and ready for bed before my guests arrive so that the children do not bother us. I want a wife who takes care of the needs of my guests so that they feel comfortable, who makes sure that they have an ashtray, that they are passed the hors d'oeuvres, that they are offered a second helping of the food, that their wine glasses are replenished when necessary, that their coffee is served to them as they like it. And I want a wife who knows that sometimes I need a night out by myself.

I want a wife who is sensitive to my sexual needs, a wife who makes love passionately and eagerly when I feel like it, a wife who makes sure that I am satisfied. And, of course, I want a wife who will not demand sexual attention when I am not in the mood for it. I want a wife who assumes the complete responsibility for birth control, because I do not want more children. I want a wife who will remain sexually faithful to me so that I do not have to clutter up my intellectual life with jealousies. And I want a wife who understands that *my* sexual needs may entail more than strict adherence to monogamy. I must, after all, be able to relate to people as fully as possible.

If, by chance, I find another person more suitable as a wife than the wife I already have, I want the liberty to replace my present wife with another one. Naturally, I will expect a fresh, new life; my wife will take the children and be solely responsible for them so that I am left free.

When I am through with school and have a job, I want my wife to quit working and remain at home so that my wife can more fully and completely take care of a wife's duties.

My God, who *wouldn't* want a wife?   10

QUESTIONS AND SUGGESTIONS FOR WRITING

1. If the constant repetition of "I want a wife who . . ." is not boring, what keeps it from being boring?
2. Drawing on your experience as observer of the world around you (and perhaps as wife, husband, or ex-spouse), do you think that Syfers's picture of a wife's role is grossly exaggerated? If so, is it meaningless?
3. Whether or not you agree with Syfers's vision of marriage, write an essay of 500 words entitled "I Want a Husband," imitating Syfers's style and approach.

☐ FICTION

Nathaniel Hawthorne (American. 1804–1864)

THE MAYPOLE OF MERRY MOUNT

There is an admirable foundation for a philosophic romance in the curious history of the early settlement of Mount Wollaston, or Merry Mount. In the slight sketch here attempted, the facts, recorded on the grave pages of our New England annalists, have wrought themselves, almost spontaneously, into a sort of allegory. The masques, mummeries, and festive customs, described in the text, are in accordance with the manners of the age. Authority on these points may be found in Strutt's Book of English Sports and Pastimes.

Bright were the days at Merry Mount, when the Maypole was the banner staff of that gay colony! They who reared it, should their banner be triumphant, were to pour sunshine over New England's rugged hills, and scatter flower seeds throughout the soil. Jollity and gloom were contending for an empire. Midsummer eve had come, bringing deep verdure to the forest, and roses in her lap, of a more vivid hue than the tender buds of Spring. But May, or her mirthful spirit, dwelt all the year round at Merry Mount, sporting with the Summer months, and revelling with Autumn, and basking in the glow of Winter's fireside. Through a world of toil and care she flitted with a dreamlike smile, and came hither to find a home among the lightsome hearts of Merry Mount.

Never had the Maypole been so gayly decked as at sunset on midsummer eve. This venerated emblem was a pine-tree, which had preserved the slender grace of youth, while it equalled the loftiest height of the old wood monarchs. From its top streamed a silken banner, colored like the rainbow. Down nearly to the ground the pole was dressed with birchen boughs, and others of the liveliest green, and some with silvery leaves, fastened by ribbons that fluttered in fantastic knots of twenty different colors, but no sad ones. Garden flowers, and blossoms of the wilderness, laughed gladly forth amid the verdure, so fresh and dewy that they must have grown by magic on that happy pine-tree. Where this green and flowery splendor terminated, the shaft of the Maypole was stained with the seven brilliant hues of the banner at its top. On the lowest green bough hung an abundant wreath of roses, some that had been gathered in the sunniest spots of the forest, and others, of still richer blush, which the colonists had reared from English seed. O, people of the Golden Age, the chief of your husbandry was to raise flowers!

But what was the wild throng that stood hand in hand about the Maypole? It could not be that the fauns and nymphs, when driven from their classic groves and homes of ancient fable, had sought refuge, as all the persecuted did, in the fresh woods of the West. These were Gothic monsters, though perhaps of Grecian ancestry. On the shoulders of a comely youth uprose the head and branching antlers of a stag; a second, human in all other points, had the grim visage of a wolf; a third, still with the trunk and limbs of a mortal man, showed the beard and horns of a venerable he-goat. There was the likeness of a bear erect, brute in all but his hind legs, which were adorned with pink silk stockings. And here again, almost as wondrous, stood a real bear of the dark forest, lending each of his fore paws to the grasp of a human hand, and as ready for the dance as any in that circle. His inferior nature rose half way, to meet his companions as they stooped. Other faces wore the similitude of man or woman, but distorted or extravagant, with red noses pendulous before their mouths, which seemed of awful depth, and stretched from ear to ear in an eternal fit of laughter. Here might be seen the Savage Man, well known in heraldry, hairy as a baboon, and girdled with green leaves. By his side, a noble figure, but still a counterfeit, appeared an Indian hunter, with feathery crest and wampum belt. Many of this strange company wore foolscaps, and had little bells appended to their garments, tinkling with a silvery sound, responsive to the inaudible music of their gleesome spirits. Some youths and maidens were of soberer garb, yet well maintained their places in the irregular throng by the expression of wild revelry upon their features. Such were the colonists of Merry Mount, as they stood in the broad smile of sunset round their venerated Maypole.

Had a wanderer, bewildered in the melancholy forest, heard their mirth, and stolen a half-affrighted glance, he might have fancied them the crew of Comus,[1] some already transformed to brutes, some midway between man and beast, and the others rioting in the flow of tipsy jollity that foreran the change. But a band of Puritans, who watched the scene, invisible themselves, compared the masques to those devils and ruined souls with whom their superstition peopled the black wilderness.

Within the ring of monsters appeared the two airiest forms that had ever   5
trodden on any more solid footing than a purple and golden cloud. One was a youth in glistening apparel, with a scarf of the rainbow pattern crosswise on his breast. His right hand held a gilded staff, the ensign of high dignity among the revellers, and his left grasped the slender fingers of a fair maiden, not less gayly decorated than himself. Bright roses glowed in contrast with the dark and glossy curls of each, and were scattered round their feet, or had sprung up spontaneously there. Behind this lightsome couple, so close to the Maypole that its boughs shaded his jovial face, stood the figure of an English priest, canonically dressed, yet decked with flowers, in heathen fashion, and wearing a chaplet of the native vine leaves. By the riot of his rolling eye, and the pagan decorations of his holy garb, he seemed the wildest monster there, and the very Comus of the crew.

"Votaries of the Maypole," cried the flower-decked priest, "merrily, all day long, have the woods echoed to your mirth. But be this your merriest hour, my hearts! Lo, here stand the Lord and Lady of the May, whom I, a clerk of Oxford, and high priest of Merry Mount, am presently to join in holy matrimony. Up with your nimble spirits, ye morris-dancers, green men, and glee maidens, bears and wolves, and horned gentlemen! Come; a chorus now, rich with the old mirth of Merry England, and the wilder glee of this fresh forest; and then a dance, to show the youthful pair what life is made of, and how airily they should go through it! All ye that love the Maypole, lend your voices to the nuptial song of the Lord and Lady of the May!"

This wedlock was more serious than most affairs of Merry Mount, where jest and delusion, trick and fantasy, kept up a continual carnival. The Lord and Lady of the May, though their titles must be laid down at sunset, were really and truly to be partners for the dance of life, beginning the measure that same bright eve. The wreath of roses, that hung from the lowest green bough of the Maypole, had been twined for them, and would be thrown over both their heads, in symbol of their flowery union. When the priest had spoken, therefore, a riotous uproar burst from the rout of monstrous figures.

"Begin you the stave, reverend Sir," cried they all; "and never did the woods ring to such a merry peal as we of the Maypole shall send up!"

Immediately a prelude of pipe, cithern, and viol, touched with practised minstrelsy, began to play from a neighboring thicket, in such a mirthful cadence that the boughs of the Maypole quivered to the sound. But the May Lord, he of the gilded staff, chancing to look into his Lady's eyes, was wonder struck at the almost pensive glance that met his own.

[1] A classical deity of revelry. —ED.

"Edith, sweet Lady of the May," whispered he reproachfully, "is yon wreath   10
of roses a garland to hang above our graves, that you look so sad? O, Edith, this is
our golden time! Tarnish it not by any pensive shadow of the mind; for it may be
that nothing of futurity will be brighter than the mere remembrance of what is
now passing."

"That was the very thought that saddened me! How came it in your mind
too?" said Edith, in a still lower tone than he, for it was high treason to be sad at
Merry Mount. "Therefore do I sigh amid this festive music. And besides, dear
Edgar, I struggle as with a dream, and fancy that these shapes of our jovial
friends are visionary, and their mirth unreal, and that we are no true Lord and
Lady of the May. What is the mystery in my heart?"

Just then, as if a spell had loosened them, down came a little shower of
withering rose leaves from the Maypole. Alas, for the young lovers! No sooner
had their hearts glowed with real passion than they were sensible of something
vague and unsubstantial in their former pleasures, and felt a dreary presentiment
of inevitable change. From the moment that they truly loved, they had subjected
themselves to earth's doom of care and sorrow, and troubled joy, and had no more
a home at Merry Mount. That was Edith's mystery. Now leave we the priest to
marry them, and the masquers to sport round the Maypole, till the last sunbeam
be withdrawn from its summit, and the shadows of the forest mingle gloomily in
the dance. Meanwhile, we may discover who these gay people were.

Two hundred years ago, and more, the old world and its inhabitants became
mutually weary of each other. Men voyaged by thousands to the West: some to
barter glass beads, and such like jewels, for the furs of the Indian hunter; some to
conquer virgin empires; and one stern band to pray. But none of these motives
had much weight with the colonists of Merry Mount. Their leaders were men
who had sported so long with life, that when Thought and Wisdom came, even
these unwelcome guests were led astray by the crowd of vanities which they
should have put to flight. Erring Thought and perverted Wisdom were made to
put on masques, and play the fool. The men of whom we speak, after losing the
heart's fresh gayety, imagined a wild philosophy of pleasure, and came hither to
act out their latest day-dream. They gathered followers from all that giddy tribe
whose whole life is like the festal days of soberer men. In their train were minstrels, not unknown in London streets; wandering players, whose theatres had
been the halls of noblemen; mummers, rope-dancers, and mountebanks, who
would long be missed at wakes, church ales, and fairs; in a word, mirth makers of
every sort, such as abounded in that age, but now began to be discountenanced
by the rapid growth of Puritanism. Light had their footsteps been on land, and as
lightly they came across the sea. Many had been maddened by their previous
troubles into a gay despair; others were as madly gay in the flush of youth, like
the May Lord and his Lady; but whatever might be the quality of their mirth, old
and young were gay at Merry Mount. The young deemed themselves happy. The
elder spirits, if they knew that mirth was but the counterfeit of happiness, yet
followed the false shadow wilfully, because at least her garments glittered brightest. Sworn triflers of a lifetime, they would not venture among the sober truths of
life not even to be truly blest.

All the hereditary pastimes of Old England were transplanted hither. The King of Christmas was duly crowned, and the Lord of Misrule bore potent sway. On the Eve of St. John, they felled whole acres of the forest to make bonfires, and danced by the blaze all night, crowned with garlands, and throwing flowers into the flame. At harvest time, though their crop was of the smallest, they made an image with the sheaves of Indian corn, and wreathed it with autumnal garlands, and bore it home triumphantly. But what chiefly characterized the colonists of Merry Mount was their veneration for the Maypole. It has made their true history a poet's tale. Spring decked the hallowed emblem with young blossoms and fresh green boughs; Summer brought roses of the deepest blush, and the perfected foliage of the forest; Autumn enriched it with that red and yellow gorgeousness which converts each wildwood leaf into a painted flower; and Winter silvered it with sleet, and hung it round with icicles, till it flashed in the cold sunshine, itself a frozen sunbeam. Thus each alternate season did homage to the Maypole, and paid it a tribute of its own richest splendor. Its votaries danced round it, once, at least, in every month; sometimes they called it their religion, or their altar; but always, it was the banner staff of Merry Mount.

Unfortunately, there were men in the new world of a sterner faith than those Maypole worshippers. Not far from Merry Mount was a settlement of Puritans, most dismal wretches, who said their prayers before daylight, and then wrought in the forest or the cornfield till evening made it prayer time again. Their weapons were always at hand to shoot down the straggling savage. When they met in conclave, it was never to keep up the old English mirth, but to hear sermons three hours long, or to proclaim bounties on the heads of wolves and the scalps of Indians. Their festivals were fast days, and their chief pastime the singing of psalms. Woe to the youth or maiden who did but dream of a dance! The selectman nodded to the constable; and there sat the light-heeled reprobate in the stocks; or if he danced, it was round the whipping-post, which might be termed the Puritan Maypole.

A party of these grim Puritans, toiling through the difficult woods, each with a horseload of iron armor to burden his footsteps, would sometimes draw near the sunny precincts of Merry Mount. There were the silken colonists, sporting round their Maypole; perhaps teaching a bear to dance, or striving to communicate their mirth to the grave Indian; or masquerading in the skins of deer and wolves, which they had hunted for that especial purpose. Often, the whole colony were playing at blindman's buff, magistrates and all, with their eyes bandaged, except a single scapegoat, whom the blinded sinners pursued by the tinkling of the bells at his garments. Once, it is said, they were seen following a flower-decked corpse, with merriment and festive music, to his grave. But did the dead man laugh? In their quietest times, they sang ballads and told tales, for the edification of their pious visitors; or perplexed them with juggling tricks; or grinned at them through horse collars; and when sport itself grew wearisome, they made game of their own stupidity, and began a yawning match. At the very least of these enormities, the men of iron shook their heads and frowned so darkly that the revellers looked up imagining that a momentary cloud had overcast the sunshine, which was to be perpetual there. On the other hand, the Puritans affirmed that, when a psalm was pealing from their place of worship, the echo which the forest sent them back

15

seemed often like the chorus of a jolly catch, closing with a roar of laughter. Who but the fiend, and his bond slaves, the crew of Merry Mount, had thus disturbed them? In due time, a feud arose, stern and bitter on one side, and as serious on the other as anything could be among such light spirits as had sworn allegiance to the Maypole. The future complexion of New England was involved in this important quarrel. Should the grizzly saints establish their jurisdiction over the gay sinners, then would their spirits darken all the clime, and make it a land of clouded visages, of hard toil, of sermon and psalm forever. But should the banner staff of Merry Mount be fortunate, sunshine would break upon the hills, and flowers would beautify the forest, and late posterity do homage to the Maypole.

After these authentic passages from history, we return to the nuptials of the Lord and Lady of the May. Alas! we have delayed too long, and must darken our tale too suddenly. As we glance again at the Maypole, a solitary sunbeam is fading from the summit, and leaves only a faint, golden tinge blended with the hues of the rainbow banner. Even that dim light is now withdrawn, relinquishing the whole domain of Merry Mount to the evening gloom, which has rushed so instantaneously from the black surrounding woods. But some of these black shadows have rushed forth in human shape.

Yes, with the setting sun, the last day of mirth had passed from Merry Mount. The ring of gay masquers was disordered and broken; the stag lowered his antlers in dismay; the wolf grew weaker than a lamb; the bells of the morris-dancers tinkled with tremulous affright. The Puritans had played a characteristic part in the Maypole mummeries. Their darksome figures were intermixed with the wild shapes of their foes, and made the scene a picture of the moment, when waking thoughts start up amid the scattered fantasies of a dream. The leader of the hostile party stood in the centre of the circle, while the route of monsters cowered around him, like evil spirits in the presence of a dread magician. No fantastic foolery could look him in the face. So stern was the energy of his aspect, that the whole man, visage, frame, and soul, seemed wrought of iron, gifted with life and thought, yet all of one substance with his headpiece and breastplate. It was the Puritan of Puritans; it was Endicott himself!

"Stand off, priest of Baal!" said he, with a grim frown, and laying no reverent hand upon the surplice. "I know thee, Blackstone![2] Thou art the man who couldst not abide the rule even of thine own corrupted church, and hast come hither to preach iniquity, and to give example of it in thy life. But now shall it be seen that the Lord hath sanctified this wilderness for his peculiar people. Woe unto them that would defile it! And first, for this flower-decked abomination, the altar of thy worship!"

And with his keen sword Endicott assaulted the hallowed Maypole. Nor long did it resist his arm. It groaned with a dismal sound; it showered leaves and rosebuds upon the remorseless enthusiast; and finally, with all its green boughs and ribbons and flowers, symbolic of departed pleasures, down fell the banner

20

---

[2] Did Governor Endicott speak less positively, we should suspect a mistake here. The Rev. Mr. Blackstone, though an eccentric, is not known to have been an immoral man. We rather doubt his identity with the priest of Merry Mount.

staff of Merry Mount. As it sank, tradition says, the evening sky grew darker, and the woods threw forth a more sombre shadow.

"There," cried Endicott, looking triumphantly on his work, "there lies the only Maypole in New England! The thought is strong within me that, by its fall, is shadowed forth the fate of light and idle mirth makers, amongst us and our posterity. Amen, saith John Endicott."

"Amen!" echoed his followers.

But the votaries of the Maypole gave one groan for their idol. At the sound, the Puritan leader glanced at the crew of Comus, each a figure of broad mirth, yet, at this moment, strangely expressive of sorrow and dismay.

"Valiant captain," quoth Peter Palfrey, the Ancient of the band, "what order shall be taken with the prisoners?"

"I thought not to repent me of cutting down a Maypole," replied Endicott,   25 "yet now I could find in my heart to plant it again, and give each of these bestial pagans one other dance round their idol. It would have served rarely for a whipping-post!"

"But there are pine-trees enow," suggested the lieutenant.

"True, good Ancient," said the leader. "Wherefore, bind the heathen crew, and bestow on them a small matter of stripes apiece, as earnest of our future justice. Set some of the rogues in the stocks to rest themselves, so soon as Providence shall bring us to one of our own well-ordered settlements where such accommodations may be found. Further penalties, such as branding and cropping of ears, shall be thought of hereafter."

"How many stripes for the priest?" inquired Ancient Palfrey.

"None as yet," answered Endicott, bending his iron frown upon the culprit. "It must be for the Great and General Court to determine, whether stripes and long imprisonment, and other grievous penalty, may atone for his transgressions. Let him look to himself! For such as violate our civil order, it may be permitted us to show mercy. But woe to the wretch that troubleth our religion."

"And this dancing bear," resumed the officer. "Must he share the stripes of   30 his fellows?"

"Shoot him through the head!" said the energetic Puritan. "I suspect witchcraft in the beast."

"Here be a couple of shining ones," continued Peter Palfrey, pointing his weapon at the Lord and Lady of the May. "They seem to be of high station among these misdoers. Methinks their dignity will not be fitted with less than a double share of stripes."

Endicott rested on his sword, and closely surveyed the dress and aspect of the hapless pair. There they stood, pale, downcast, and apprehensive. Yet there was an air of mutual support and of pure affection, seeking aid and giving it, that showed them to be man and wife, with the sanction of a priest upon their love. The youth, in the peril of the moment, had dropped his gilded staff, and thrown his arm about the Lady of the May, who leaned against his breast, too lightly to burden him, but with weight enough to express that their destinies were linked together, for good or evil. They looked first at each other, and then into the grim captain's face. There they stood, in the first hour of wedlock, while the idle pleasures, of which their companions were the emblems, had given place to the sternest cares of life, personified by the dark Puritans. But never had their youthful beauty seemed so pure and high as when its glow was chastened by adversity.

"Youth," said Endicott, "ye stand in an evil case thou and thy maiden wife. Make ready presently, for I am minded that ye shall both have a token to remember your wedding day!"

"Stern man," cried the May Lord, "how can I move thee? Were the means at   35 hand, I would resist to the death. Being powerless, I entreat! Do with me as thou wilt, but let Edith go untouched!"

"Not so," replied the immitigable zealot. "We are not wont to show an idle courtesy to that sex, which requireth the stricter discipline. What sayest thou, maid? Shall thy silken bridegroom suffer thy share of the penalty, besides his own?"

"Be it death," said Edith, "and lay it all on me!"

Truly, as Endicott had said, the poor lovers stood in a woful case. Their foes were triumphant, their friends captive and abased, their home desolate, the benighted wilderness around them, and a rigorous destiny, in the shape of the Puritan leader, their only guide. Yet the deepening twilight could not altogether conceal that the iron man was softened; he smiled at the fair spectacle of early love; he almost sighed for the inevitable blight of early hopes.

"The troubles of life have come hastily on this young couple," observed Endicott. "We will see how they comport themselves under their present trials ere we burden them with greater. If, among the spoil, there be any garments of a more decent fashion, let them be put upon this May Lord and his Lady, instead of their glistening vanities. Look to it, some of you."

"And shall not the youth's hair be cut?" asked Peter Palfrey, looking with   40 abhorrence at the lovelock and long glossy curls of the young man.

"Crop it forthwith, and that in the true pumpkin-shell fashion," answered the captain. "Then bring them along with us, but more gently than their fellows. There be qualities in the youth, which may make him valiant to fight, and sober to toil, and pious to pray; and in the maiden, that may fit her to become a mother in our Israel, bringing up babes in better nurture than her own hath been. Nor think ye, young ones, that they are the happiest, even in our lifetime of a moment, who misspend it in dancing round a Maypole!"

And Endicott, the severest Puritan of all who laid the rock foundation of New England, lifted the wreath of roses from the ruin of the Maypole, and threw it, with his own gauntleted hand, over the heads of the Lord and Lady of the May. It was a deed of prophecy. As the moral gloom of the world overpowers all systematic gayety, even so was their home of wild mirth made desolate amid the sad forest. They returned to it no more. But as their flowery garland was wreathed of the brightest roses that had grown there, so, in the tie that united them, were intertwined all the purest and best of their early joys. They went heavenward, supporting each other along the difficult path which it was their lot to tread, and never wasted one regretful thought on the vanities of Merry Mount.

QUESTIONS AND SUGGESTIONS FOR WRITING

1. In his brief headnote, Hawthorne says that the facts as "recorded on the grave pages of our New England annalists, have wrought themselves, almost spontaneously, into a sort of allegory." In a paragraph or two explain the allegory.
2. What words or phrases in the first two paragraphs suggest that there is something illusory or insubstantial or transient in the life of Merry Mount?
3. In a paragraph, characterize Endicott.

Mary E. Wilkins Freeman (American. 1852–1930)

THE REVOLT OF "MOTHER"

"Father!"

"What is it?"

"What are them men diggin' over there in the field for?"

There was a sudden dropping and enlarging of the lower part of the old man's face, as if some heavy weight had settled therein; he shut his mouth tight, and went on harnessing the great bay mare. He hustled the collar on to her neck with a jerk.

"Father!"   5

The old man slapped the saddle upon the mare's back.

"Look here, father, I want to know what them men are diggin' over in the field for, an' I'm goin' to know."

"I wish you'd go into the house, mother, an' 'tend to your own affairs," the old man said then. He ran his words together, and his speech was almost as inarticulate as a growl.

But the woman understood; it was her most native tongue. "I ain't goin' into the house till you tell me what them men are doin' over there in the field," said she.

Then she stood waiting. She was a small woman, short and straight-waisted   10
like a child in her brown cotton gown. Her forehead was mild and benevolent between the smooth curves of gray hair; there were meek downward lines about her nose and mouth; but her eyes, fixed upon the old man, looked as if the meekness had been the result of her own will, never of the will of another.

They were in the barn, standing before the wide open doors. The spring air, full of the smell of growing grass and unseen blossoms, came in their faces. The deep yard in front was littered with farm wagons and piles of wood; on the edges, close to the fence and the house, the grass was a vivid green, and there were some dandelions.

The old man glanced doggedly at his wife as he tightened the last buckles on the harness. She looked as immovable to him as one of the rocks in his pasture land, bound to the earth with generations of blackberry vines. He slapped the reins over the horse, and started forth from the barn.

"*Father!*" said she.

The old man pulled up. "What is it?"

"I want to know what them men are diggin' over there in that field for."   15
"They're diggin' a cellar, I s'pose, if you've got to know."
"A cellar for what?"
"A barn."
"A barn? You ain't goin' to build a barn over there where we was goin' to have a house, father?"

The old man said not another word. He hurried the horse into the farm   20
wagon, and clattered out of the yard, jouncing as sturdily on his seat as a boy.

The woman stood a moment looking after him, then she went out of the barn
across a corner of the yard to the house. The house, standing at right angles with
the great barn and a long reach of sheds and out-buildings, was infinitesimal
compared with them. It was scarcely as commodious for people as the little boxes
under the barn eaves were for doves.

A pretty girl's face, pink and delicate as a flower, was looking out of one of
the house windows. She was watching three men who were digging over in the
field which bounded the yard near the road line. She turned quietly when the
woman entered.

"What are they digging for, mother?" said she. "Did he tell you?"
"They're diggin' for—a cellar for a new barn."
"Oh, mother, he ain't going to build another barn?"   25
"That's what he says."

A boy stood before the kitchen glass combing his hair. He combed slowly and
painstakingly, arranging his brown hair in a smooth hillock over his forehead. He
did not seem to pay any attention to the conversation.

"Sammy, did you know father was going to build a new barn?" asked the girl.
The boy combed assiduously.
"Sammy!"   30

He turned, and showed a face like his father's under his smooth crest of hair.
"Yes, I s'pose I did," he said, reluctantly.
"How long have you known it?" asked his mother.
"'Bout three months, I guess."
"Why didn't you tell of it?"
"Didn't think 'twould do no good."   35

"I don't see what father wants another barn for," said the girl, in her sweet,
slow voice. She turned again to the window, and stared out at the digging men in
the field. Her tender, sweet face was full of a gentle distress. Her forehead was as
bald and innocent as a baby's, with the light hair strained back from it in a row of
curl-papers. She was quite large, but her soft curves did not look as if they
covered muscles.

Her mother looked sternly at the boy. "Is he goin' to buy more cows?" said
she.

The boy did not reply; he was tying his shoes.
"Sammy, I want you to tell me if he's going' to buy more cows."
"I s'pose he is."   40
"How many?"
"Four, I guess."

His mother said nothing more. She went up into the pantry, and there was a clatter of dishes. The boy got his cap from a nail behind the door, took an old arithmetic from the shelf, and started for school. He was lightly built, but clumsy. He went out of the yard with a curious spring in his hips, that made his loose home-made jacket tilt up in the rear.

The girl went to the sink, and began to wash the dishes that were piled up there. Her mother came promptly out of the pantry, and shoved her aside. "You wipe 'em," said she; "I'll wash. There's a good many this mornin'."

The mother plunged her hands vigorously into the water, the girl wiped the   45
plates slowly and dreamily. "Mother," said she, "don't you think it's too bad father's going to build that new barn, much as we need a decent house to live in?"

Her mother scrubbed a dish fiercely. "You ain't found out yet we're women-folks, Nanny Penn," said she. "You ain't seen enough of men-folks yet to. One of these days you'll find it out, an' then you'll know that we know only what men-folks think we do, so far as any use of it goes, an' how we'd ought to reckon men-folks in with Providence, an' not complain of what they do any more than we do of the weather."

"I don't care; I don't believe George is anything like that, anyhow," said Nanny. Her delicate face flushed pink, her lips pouted softly, as if she were going to cry.

"You wait an' see. I guess George Eastman ain't no better than other men. You hadn't ought to judge father, though. He can't help it, 'cause he don't look at things jest the way we do. An' we've been pretty comfortable here, after all. The roof don't leak—ain't never but once—that's one thing. Father's kept it shingled right up."

"I do wish we had a parlor."

"I guess it won't hurt George Eastman any to come to see you in a nice clean   50
kitchen. I guess a good many girls don't have as good a place as this. Nobody's ever heard me complain."

"I ain't complained either, mother."

"Well, I don't think you'd better, a good father an' a good home as you've got. S'pose your father made you go out an' work for your livin'? Lots of girls have to that ain't no stronger an' better able to than you be."

Sarah Penn washed the frying pan with a conclusive air. She scrubbed the outside of it as faithfully as the inside. She was a masterly keeper of her box of a house. Her one living room never seemed to have in it any of the dust which the friction of life with inanimate matter produces. She swept, and there seemed to be no dirt to go before the broom; she cleaned, and one could see no difference. She was like an artist so perfect that he has apparently no art. To-day she got out a mixing bowl and a board, and rolled some pies, and there was no more flour upon her than upon her daughter who was doing finer work. Nanny was to be married in the fall, and she was sewing on some white cambric and embroidery. She sewed industriously while her mother cooked, her soft milk-white hands and wrists showed whiter than her delicate work.

"We must have the stove moved out in the shed before long," said Mrs. Penn. "Talk about not havin' things, it's been a real blessin' to be able to put a stove up in that shed in hot weather. Father did one good thing when he fixed that stove-pipe out there."

Sarah Penn's face as she rolled her pies had that expression of meek vigor which might have characterized one of the New Testament saints. She was making mince-pies. Her husband, Adoniram Penn, liked them better than any other kind. She baked twice a week. Adoniram often liked a piece of pie between meals. She hurried this morning. It had been later than usual when she began, and she wanted to have a pie baked for dinner. However deep a resentment she might be forced to hold against her husband, she would never fail in sedulous attention to his wants.

Nobility of character manifests itself at loop-holes when it is not provided with large doors. Sarah Penn's showed itself to-day in flaky dishes of pastry. So she made the pies faithfully, while across the table she could see, when she glanced up from her work, the sight that rankled in her patient and steadfast soul—the digging of the cellar of the new barn in the place where Adoniram forty years ago had promised her their new house should stand.

The pies were done for dinner. Adoniram and Sammy were home a few minutes after twelve o'clock. The dinner was eaten with serious haste. There was never much conversation at the table in the Penn family. Adoniram asked a blessing, and they ate promptly, then rose up and went about their work.

Sammy went back to school, taking soft sly lopes out of the yard like a rabbit. He wanted a game of marbles before school, and feared his father would give him some chores to do. Adoniram hastened to the door and called after him, but he was out of sight.

"I don't see what you let him go for, mother," said he. "I wanted him to help me unload that wood."

Adoniram went to work out in the yard unloading wood from the wagon. Sarah put away the dinner dishes, while Nanny took down her curl-papers and changed her dress. She was going down to the store to buy some more embroidery and thread.

When Nanny was gone, Mrs. Penn went to the door. "Father!" she called.

"Well, what is it!"

"I want to see you jest a minute, father."

"I can't leave this wood nohow. I've got to git it unloaded an' go for a load of gravel afore two o'clock. Sammy had ought to helped me. You hadn't ought to let him go to school so early."

"I want to see you jest a minute."

"I tell ye I can't, nohow, mother."

"Father, you come here." Sarah Penn stood in the door like a queen; she held her head as if it bore a crown; there was that patience which makes authority royal in her voice. Adoniram went.

Mrs. Penn led the way into the kitchen, and pointed to a chair. "Sit down, father," said she; "I've got somethin' I want to say to you."

He sat down heavily; his face was quite stolid, but he looked at her with restive eyes. "Well, what is it, mother?"

"I want to know what you're buildin' that new barn for, father?"

"I ain't got nothin' to say about it."

"It can't be you think you need another barn?"

"I tell ye I ain't got nothin' to say about it, mother; an' I ain't goin' to say nothin'."

"Be you goin' to buy more cows?"

Adoniram did not reply; he shut his mouth tight.   75

"I know you be, as well as I want to. Now, father, look here"—Sarah Penn had not sat down; she stood before her husband in the humble fashion of a Scripture woman[1]—"I'm goin' to talk real plain to you; I never have sence I married you, but I'm goin' to now. I ain't never complained, an' I ain't goin' to complain now, but I'm goin' to talk plain. You see this room here, father; you look at it well. You see there ain't no carpet on the floor, an' you see the paper is all dirty, an' droppin' off the walls. We ain't had no new paper on it for ten year, an' then I put it on myself, an' it didn't cost but ninepence a roll. You see this room, father; it's all the one I've had to work in an' eat in an' set in sence we was married. There ain't another woman in the whole town whose husband ain't got half the means you have but what's got better. It's all the room Nanny's got to have her company in; an' there ain't one of her mates but what's got better, an' their fathers not so able as hers is. It's all the room she'll have to be married in. What would you have thought, father, if we had had our weddin' in a room no better than this? I was married in my mother's parlor, with a carpet on the floor, an' stuffed furniture, an' a mahogany card-table. An' this is all the room my daughter will have to be married in. Look here, father!"

Sarah Penn went across the room as though it were a tragic stage. She flung open a door and disclosed a tiny bedroom, only large enough for a bed and bureau, with a path between. "There, father," said she—"there's all the room I've had to sleep in forty year. All my children were born there—the two that died, an' the two that's livin.' I was sick with a fever there."

She stepped to another door and opened it. It led into the small, ill-lighted pantry. "Here," said she, "is all the buttery[2] I've got—every place I've got for my dishes, to set away my victuals in, an' to keep my milk-pans in. Father, I've been takin' care of the milk of six cows in this place, an' now you're goin' to build a new barn, an' keep more cows, an' give me more to do in it."

She threw open another door. A narrow crooked flight of stairs wound upward from it. "There, father," said she, "I want you to look at the stairs that go up to them two unfinished chambers that are all the places our son an' daughter have had to sleep in all their lives. There ain't a prettier girl in town nor a more ladylike one than Nanny, an' that's the place she has to sleep in. It ain't so good as your horse's stall; it ain't so warm an' tight."

Sarah Penn went back and stood before her husband.   80

"Now, father," said she, "I want to know if you think you're doin' right an' accordin' to what you profess. Here, when we was married, forty year ago, you

---

[1] I.e., like an obedient wife in the Old Testament. (Notes to this selection are by the editors.)
[2] Pantry.

promised me faithful that we should have a new house built in that lot over in the field before the year was out. You said you had money enough, an' you wouldn't ask me to live in no such place as this. It is forty year now, an' you've been makin' more money, an' I've been savin' of it for you ever since, an' you ain't built no house yet. You've built sheds an' cow-houses an' one new barn, an' now you're goin' to build another. Father, I want to know if you think it's right. You're lodgin' your dumb beasts better than you are your own flesh an' blood. I want to know if you think it's right."

"I ain't got nothin' to say."

"You can't say nothin' without ownin' it ain't right, father. An' there's another thing—I ain't complained; I've got along forty year, an' I s'pose I should forty more, if it wa'n't for that—if we don't have another house. Nanny she can't live with us after she's married. She'll have to go somewheres else to live away from us, an' it don't seem as if I could have it so, noways, father. She wa'n't ever strong. She's got considerable color, but there wa'n't never any backbone to her. I've always took the heft of everything off her, an' she ain't fit to keep house an' do everything herself. She'll be all worn out inside of a year. Think of her doin' all the washin' an' ironin' an' bakin' with them soft white hands an' arms, an' sweepin'! I can't have it so, noways, father."

Mrs. Penn's face was burning, her mild eyes gleamed. She had pleaded her little cause like a Webster;[3] she had ranged from severity to pathos; but her opponent employed that obstinate silence which makes eloquence futile with mocking echoes. Adoniram arose clumsily.

"Father, ain't you got nothin' to say?" said Mrs. Penn.   85

"I've got to go off after that load of gravel. I can't stan' here talkin' all day."

"Father, won't you think it over, an' have a house built there instead of a barn?"

"I ain't got nothin' to say."

Adoniram shuffled out. Mrs. Penn went into her bedroom. When she came out, her eyes were red. She had a roll of unbleached cotton cloth. She spread it out on the kitchen table, and began cutting out some shirts for her husband. The men over in the field had a team to help them this afternoon; she could hear their halloos. She had a scanty pattern for the shirts; she had to plan and piece the sleeves.

Nanny came home with her embroidery, and sat down with her needlework.   90
She had taken down her curl papers, and there was a soft roll of fair hair like an aureole over her forehead; her face was as delicately fine and clear as porcelain. Suddenly she looked up, and the tender red flamed all over her face and neck. "Mother," said she.

"What say?"

"I've been thinking—I don't see how we're goin' to have any—wedding in this room. I'd be ashamed to have his folks come if we didn't have anybody else."

"Mebbe we can have some new paper before then; I can put it on. I guess you won't have no call to be ashamed of your belongin's."

---

[3] I.e., Daniel Webster (1782–1852), American orator.

"We might have the wedding in the new barn," said Nanny, with gentle pet-
tishness. "Why, mother, what makes you look so?"

Mrs. Penn had started, and was staring at her with a curious expression. She   95
turned again to her work, and spread out a pattern carefully on the cloth.
"Nothin'," said she.

Presently Adoniram clattered out of the yard in his two-wheeled dump cart,
standing as proudly upright as a Roman charioteer. Mrs. Penn opened the door
and stood there a minute looking out; the halloos of the men sounded louder.

It seemed to her all through the spring months that she heard nothing but the
halloos and the noises of the saws and hammers. The new barn grew fast. It was
a fine edifice for this little village. Men came on pleasant Sundays, in their meeting suits and clean shirt bosoms, and stood around it admiringly. Mrs. Penn did
not speak of it, and Adoniram did not mention it to her, although sometimes, upon
a return from inspecting it, he bore himself with injured dignity.

"It's a strange thing how your mother feels about the new barn," he said,
confidentially, to Sammy one day.

Sammy only grunted after an odd fashion for a boy; he had learned it from his
father.

The barn was all completed ready for use by the third week in July. Adoniram   100
had planned to move his stock in on Wednesday; on Tuesday he received a letter
which changed his plans. He came in with it early in the morning. "Sammy's been
to the post-office," said he, "an' I've got a letter from Hiram." Hiram was Mrs.
Penn's brother, who lived in Vermont.

"Well," said Mrs. Penn, "what does he say about the folks?"

"I guess they're all right. He says he thinks if I come up country right off
there's a chance to buy jest the kind of a horse I want." He stared reflectively out
of the window at the new barn.

Mrs. Penn was making pies. She went on clapping the rolling-pin into the
crust, although she was very pale, and her heart beat loudly.

"I dun' know but what I'd beter go," said Adoniram. "I hate to go off jest.
now, right in the midst of hayin', but the ten-acre lot's cut, an' I guess Rufus an'
the others can git along without me three or four days. I can't get a horse round
here to suit me, nohow, an' I've got to have another for all the wood-haulin' in the
fall. I told Hiram to watch out, an' if he got wind of a good horse to let me know. I
guess I'd better go."

"I'll get out your clean shirt an' collar," said Mrs. Penn calmly.   105

She laid out Adoniram's Sunday suit and his clean clothes on the bed in the
little bedroom. She got his shaving-water and razor ready. At last she buttoned on
his collar and fastened his black cravat.

Adoniram never wore his collar and cravat except on extra occasions. He held
his head high, with a rasped dignity. When he was all ready, with his coat and hat
brushed, and a lunch of pie and cheese in a paper bag, he hesitated on the
threshold of the door. He looked at his wife, and his manner was defiantly apologetic. "*If* them cows come to day, Sammy can drive 'em into the new barn," said
he; "an' when they bring the hay up, they can pitch it in there."

"Well," replied Mrs. Penn.

Adoniram set his shaven face ahead and started. When he had cleared the door-step, he turned and looked back with a kind of nervous solemnity. "I shall be back by Saturday if nothin' happens," said he.

"Do be careful, father," returned his wife.   110

She stood in the door with Nanny at her elbow and watched him out of sight. Her eyes had a strange, doubtful expression in them; her peaceful forehead was contracted. She went in, and about her baking again. Nanny sat sewing. Her wedding day was drawing nearer, and she was getting pale and thin with her steady sewing. Her mother kept glancing at her.

"Have you got that pain in your side this mornin'?" she asked.

"A little."

Mrs. Penn's face, as she worked, changed, her perplexed forehead smoothed, her eyes were steady, her lips firmly set. She formed a maxim for herself, although incoherently with her unlettered thoughts. "Unsolicited opportunities are the guide posts of the Lord to the new roads of life," she repeated in effect, and she made up her mind to her course of action.

"S'posin' I *had* wrote to Hiram," she muttered once, when she was in the   115
pantry—"s'posin' I had wrote, an' asked him if he knew of any horse? But I didn't, an' father's goin' wa'n't none of my doin'. It looks like a providence." Her voice rang out quite loud at the last.

"What you talkin' about, mother?" called Nanny.

"Nothin'."

Mrs. Penn hurried her baking; at eleven o'clock it was all done. The load of hay from the west field came slowly down the cart track, and drew up at the new barn. Mrs. Penn ran out. "Stop!" she screamed—"stop!"

The men stopped and looked; Sammy upreared from the top of the load, and stared at his mother.

"Stop!" she cried out again. "Don't you put the hay in that barn; put it in the   120
old one."

"Why, he said to put it in here," returned one of the haymakers, wonderingly. He was a young man, a neighbor's son, whom Adoniram hired by the year to help on the farm.

"Don't you put the hay in the new barn; there's room enough in the old one, ain't there?" said Mrs. Penn.

"Room enough," returned the hired man, in his thick, rustic tones. "Didn't need the new barn, nohow, far as room's concerned. Well, I s'pose he changed his mind." He took hold of the horses' bridles.

Mrs. Penn went back to the house. Soon the kitchen windows were darkened, and a fragrance like warm honey came into the room.

Nanny laid down her work. "I thought father wanted them to put the hay into   125
the new barn?" she said, wonderingly.

"It's all right," replied her mother.

Sammy slid down from the load of hay, and came in to see if dinner was ready.

"I ain't goin' to get a regular dinner to-day, as long as father's gone," said his mother. "I've let the fire go out. You can have some bread an' milk an' pie. I thought we could get along." She set out some bowls of milk, some bread, and a pie on the kitchen table. "You'd better eat your dinner now," said she. "You might jest as well get through with it. I want you to help me afterward."

Nanny and Sammy stared at each other. There was something strange in their mother's manner. Mrs. Penn did not eat anything herself. She went into the pantry, and they heard her moving dishes while they ate. Presently she came out with a pile of plates. She got the clothes-basket out of the shed, and packed them in it. Nanny and Sammy watched. She brought out cups and saucers, and put them in with the plates.

"What you goin' to do, mother?" inquired Nanny, in a timid voice. A sense of   130
something unusual made her tremble, as if it were a ghost. Sammy rolled his eyes over his pie.

"You'll see what I'm going to do," replied Mrs. Penn. "If you're through, Nanny, I want you to go up-stairs an' pack up your things; an' I want you, Sammy, to help me take down the bed in the bedroom."

"Oh, mother, what for?" gasped Nanny.

"You'll see."

During the next few hours a feat was performed by this simple, pious New England mother which was equal in its way to Wolfe's storming of the Heights of Abraham.[4] It took no more genius and audacity of bravery for Wolfe to cheer his wondering soldiers up those steep precipices, under the sleeping eyes of the enemy, than for Sarah Penn, at the head of her children, to move all their little household goods into the new barn while her husband was away.

Nanny and Sammy followed their mother's instructions without a murmur;   135
indeed, they were overawed. There is a certain uncanny and superhuman quality about all such purely original undertakings as their mother's was to them. Nanny went back and forth with her light loads, and Sammy tugged with sober energy.

At five o'clock in the afternoon the little house in which the Penns had lived for forty years had emptied itself into the new barn.

Every builder builds somewhat for unknown purposes, and is in a measure a prophet. The architect of Adoniram Penn's barn, while he designed it for the comfort of four-footed animals, had planned better than he knew for the comfort of humans. Sarah Penn saw at a glance its possibilities. Those great box-stalls, with quilts hung before them, would make better bedrooms than the one she had occupied for forty years, and there was a tight carriage-room. The harness room, with its chimney and shelves, would make a kitchen of her dreams. The great middle space would make a parlor, by and by, fit for a palace. Upstairs there was as much room as down. With partitions and windows, what a house would there be! Sarah looked at the row of stanchions before the allotted space for cows, and reflected that she would have her front entry there.

At six o'clock the stove was up in the harness-room, the kettle was boiling,

---

[4] James Wolfe, British general, scaled the Plains of Abraham and led his forces to victory over the French at Quebec in September 1759, but he died in battle.

and the table set for tea. It looked almost as homelike as the abandoned house across the yard had ever done. The young hired man milked, and Sarah directed him calmly to bring the milk to the new barn. He came gaping, dropping little blots of foam from the brimming pails on the grass. Before the next morning he had spread the story of Adoniram Penn's wife moving into the new barn all over the little village. Men assembled in the store and talked it over, women with shawls over their heads scuttled into each other's houses before their work was done. Any deviation from the ordinary course of life in this quiet town was enough to stop all progress in it. Everybody paused to look at the staid, independent figure on the side track. There was a difference of opinion with regard to her. Some held her to be insane; some, of a lawless and rebellious spirit.

Friday the minister went to see her. It was in the forenoon, and she was at the barn door shelling pease for dinner. She looked up and returned his salutation with dignity, then she went on with her work. She did not invite him in. The saintly expression of her face remained fixed, but there was an angry flush over it.

The minister stood awkwardly before her, and talked. She handled the pease   140
as if they were bullets. At last she looked up, and her eyes showed the spirit that her meek front had covered for a lifetime.

"There ain't no use talkin', Mr. Hersey," said she. "I've thought it all over an' over, an' I believe I'm doin' what's right. I've made it the subject of prayer, an' it's betwixt me an' the Lord an' Adoniram. There ain't no call for nobody else to worry about it."

"Well, of course, if you have brought it to the Lord in prayer, and feel satisfied that you are doing right, Mrs. Penn," said the minister, helplessly. His thin gray-bearded face was pathetic. He was a sickly man; his youthful confidence had cooled; he had to scourge himself up to some of his pastoral duties as relentlessly as a Catholic ascetic, and then he was prostrated by the smart.

"I think it's right jest as much as I think it was right for our forefathers to come over from the old country 'cause they didn't have what belonged to 'em," said Mrs. Penn. She arose. The barn threshold might have been Plymouth Rock from her bearing. "I don't doubt you mean well, Mr. Hersey," said she, "but there are things people hadn't ought to interfere with. I've been a member of the church for over forty year. I've got my own mind an' my own feet, an' I'm goin' to think my own thoughts an' go my own ways, an' nobody but the Lord is goin' to dictate to me unless I've a mind to have him. Won't you come in an' set down? How is Mis' Hersey?"

"She is well, I thank you," replied the minister. He added some more perplexed apologetic remarks; then he retreated.

He could expound the intricacies of every character study in the Scriptures,   145
he was competent to grasp the Pilgrim Fathers and all historical innovators, but Sarah Penn was beyond him. He could deal with primal cases, but parallel ones worsted him. But, after all, although it was aside from his province, he wondered more how Adoniram Penn would deal with his wife than how the Lord would. Everybody shared the wonder. When Adoniram's four new cows arrived, Sarah ordered three to be put in the old barn, the other in the house shed where the

cooking-stove had stood. That added to the excitement. It was whispered that all four cows were domiciled in the house.

Towards sunset on Saturday, when Adoniram was expected home, there was a knot of men in the road near the new barn. The hired man had milked, but he still hung around the premises. Sarah Penn had supper all ready. There was brown-bread and baked beans and a custard pie; it was the supper that Adoniram loved on a Saturday night. She had on a clean calico, and she bore herself imperturbably. Nanny and Sammy kept close at her heels. Their eyes were large, and Nanny was full of nervous tremors. Still there was to them more pleasant excitement than anything else. An inborn confidence in their mother over their father asserted itself.

Sammy looked out of the harness-room window. "There he is," he announced, in an awed whisper. He and Nanny peeped around the casing. Mrs. Penn kept on about her work. The children watched Adoniram leave the new horse standing in the drive while he went to the house door. It was fastened. Then he went around to the shed. That door was seldom locked, even when the family was away. The thought how her father would be confronted by the cow flashed upon Nanny. There was a hysterical sob in her throat. Adoniram emerged from the shed and stood looking about in a dazed fashion. His lips moved; he was saying something, but they could not hear what it was. The hired man was peeping around a corner of the old barn, but nobody saw him.

Adoniram took the new horse by the bridle and led him across the yard to the new barn. Nanny and Sammy slunk close to their mother. The barn doors rolled back, and there stood Adoniram, with the long mild face of the great Canadian farm horse looking over his shoulder.

Nanny kept behind her mother, but Sammy stepped suddenly forward, and stood in front of her.

Adoniram stared at the group. "What on airth you all down here for?" said he. "What's the matter over to the house?" 150

"We've come here to live, father," said Sammy. His shrill voice quavered out bravely.

"What"—Adoniram sniffed—"what is it smells like cookin'?" said he. He stepped forward and looked in the open door of the harness-room. Then he turned to his wife. His old bristling face was pale and frightened. "What on airth does this mean, mother?" he gasped.

"You come in here, father," said Sarah. She led the way into the harness-room and shut the door. "Now, father," said she, "you needn't be scared. I ain't crazy. There ain't nothin' to be upset over. But we've come here to live, an' we're goin' to live here. We've got jest as good a right here as new horses an' cows. The house wa'n't fit for us to live in any longer, an' I made up my mind I wa'n't goin' to stay there. I've done my duty by you forty year, an' I'm goin' to do it now; but I'm goin' to live here. You've got to put in some windows and partitions; an' you'll have to buy some furniture."

"Why, mother!" the old man gasped.

"You'd better take your coat off an' get washed—there's the wash-basin—an'   155
then we'll have supper."

"Why, mother!"

Sammy went past the window, leading the new horse to the old barn. The old
man saw him, and shook his head speechlessly. He tried to take off his coat, but
his arms seemed to lack the power. His wife helped him. She poured some water
into the tin basin, and put in a piece of soap. She got the comb and brush, and
smoothed his thin gray hair after he had washed. Then she put the beans, hot
bread, and tea on the table. Sammy came in, and the family drew up. Adoniram
sat looking dazedly at his plate, and they waited.

"Ain't you goin' to ask a blessin', father?" said Sarah.

And the old man bent his head and mumbled.

All through the meal he stopped eating at intervals, and stared furtively at his   160
wife; but he ate well. The home food tasted good to him, and his old frame was
too sturdily healthy to be affected by his mind. But after supper he went out, and
sat down on the step of the smaller door at the right of the barn, through which
he had meant his Jerseys to pass in stately file, but which Sarah designed for her
front house door, and he leaned his head on his hands.

After supper dishes were cleared away and the milk-pans washed, Sarah went
out to him. The twilight was deepening. There was a clear green glow in the sky.
Before them stretched the smooth level of field; in the distance was a cluster of
hay-stacks like the huts of a village; the air was very cool and calm and sweet.
The landscape might have been an ideal one of peace.

Sarah bent over and touched her husband on one of his thin, sinewy shoulders. "Father!"

The old man's shoulders heaved: he was weeping.

"Why, don't do so, father," said Sarah.

"I'll put up the—partitions, an'—everything you—want, mother."   165

Sarah put her apron up to her face; she was overcome by her own triumph.

Adoniram was like a fortress whose walls had no active resistance, and went
down the instant the right besieging tools were used. "Why, mother," he said,
hoarsely, "I hadn't no idee you was so set on't as all this comes to."

QUESTIONS AND SUGGESTIONS FOR WRITING

1. In paragraph 53 Freeman says of Mother, "She was like an artist so perfect that he
   has apparently no art." In an essay of 250 words, clarify this point, by pointing out the
   apparently artless artistry of some aspect of this story, or of another story of your
   choice.
2. Mother argues forcefully against Father, yet she then goes on to bake a pie for him. In
   a paragraph explain why.
3. Compare and contrast Mother's relation to her son with her relation to her daughter.
4. Do you find any passages in the story that are at least mildly amusing? If so, specify
   some, and indicate why you find them amusing.

William Faulkner (American. 1897–1962)

SPOTTED HORSES

I

Yes, sir. Flem Snopes has filled that whole country full of spotted horses. You can hear folks running them all day and all night, whooping and hollering, and the horses running back and forth across them little wooden bridges ever now and then kind of like thunder. Here I was this morning pretty near half way to town, with the team ambling along and me setting in the buckboard about half asleep, when all of a sudden something come swurging up outen the bushes and jumped the road clean, without touching hoof to it. It flew right over my team, big as a billboard and flying through the air like a hawk. It taken me thirty minutes to stop my team and untangle the harness and the buckboard and hitch them up again.

That Flem Snopes. I be dog if he ain't a case, now. One morning about ten years ago, the boys was just getting settled down on Varner's porch for a little talk and tobacco, when here come Flem out from behind the counter, with his coat off and his hair all parted, like he might have been clerking for Varner for ten years already. Folks all knowed him; it was a big family of them about five miles down the bottom. That year, at least. Share-cropping. They never stayed on any place over a year. Then they would move on to another place, with the chap or maybe the twins of that year's litter. It was a regular nest of them. But Flem. The rest of them stayed tenant farmers, moving ever year, but here come Flem one day, walking out from behind Jody Varner's counter like he owned it. And he wasn't there but a year or two before folks knowed that, if him and Jody was both still in that store in ten years more, it would be Jody clerking for Flem Snopes. Why, that fellow could make a nickel where it wasn't but four cents to begin with. He skun me in two trades, myself, and the fellow that can do that, I just hope he'll get rich before I do; that's all.

All right. So here Flem was, clerking at Varner's, making a nickel here and there and not telling nobody about it. No, sir. Folks never knowed when Flem got the better of somebody lessen the fellow he beat told it. He'd just set there in the store-chair, chewing his tobacco and keeping his own business to hisself, until about a week later we'd find out it was somebody else's business he was keeping to hisself—provided the fellow he trimmed was mad enough to tell it. That's Flem.

We give him ten years to own ever thing Jody Varner had. But he never waited no ten years. I reckon you-all know that gal of Uncle Billy Varner's, the youngest one; Eula. Jody's sister. Ever Sunday ever yellow-wheeled buggy and curried riding horse in that country would be hitched to Bill Varner's fence, and the young bucks setting on the porch, swarming around Eula like bees around a honey pot. One of these here kind of big, soft-looking gals that could giggle richer than plowed new-ground. Wouldn't none of them leave before the others, and so they would set there on the porch until time to go home, with some of them with nine and ten miles to ride and then get up tomorrow and go back to the field. So they would all leave together and they would ride in a clump down to the creek ford and hitch them curried horses and yellow-wheeled buggies and get out and fight one another. Then they would get in the buggies again and go on home.

Well, one day about a year ago, one of them yellow-wheeled buggies and one of them curried saddle-horses quit this country. We heard they was heading for Texas. The next day Uncle Billy and Eula and Flem come in to town in Uncle Bill's surrey, and when they come back, Flem and Eula was married. And on the next day we heard that two more of them yellow-wheeled buggies had left the country. They mought have gone to Texas, too. It's a big place.

Anyway, about a month after the wedding, Flem and Eula went to Texas, too. They was gone pretty near a year. Then one day last month, Eula come back, with a baby. We figgered up, and we decided that it was as well-growed a three-months-old baby as we ever see. It can already pull up on a chair. I reckon Texas makes big men quick, being a big place. Anyway, if it keeps on like it started, it'll be chewing tobacco and voting time it's eight years old.

And so last Friday here come Flem himself. He was on a wagon with another fellow. The other fellow had one of these two-gallon hats and a ivory-handled pistol and a box of ginger snaps sticking out of his hind pocket, and tied to the tail-gate of the wagon was about two dozen of them Texas ponies, hitched to one another with barbed wire. They was colored like parrots and they was quiet as doves, and ere a one of them would kill you quick as a rattlesnake. Nere a one of them had two eyes the same color, and nere a one of them had ever see a bridle, I reckon; and when that Texas man got down offen the wagon and walked up to them to show how gentle they was, one of them cut his vest clean offen him, same as with a razor.

Flem had done already disappeared; he had went on to see his wife, I reckon, and to see if that ere baby had done gone on to the field to help Uncle Billy plow, maybe. It was the Texas man that taken the horses on to Mrs. Littlejohn's lot. He had a little trouble at first, when they come to the gate, because they hadn't never see a fence before, and when he finally got them in and taken a pair of wire cutters and unhitched them and got them into the barn and poured some shell corn into the trough, they durn nigh tore down the barn. I reckon they thought that shell corn was bugs, maybe. So he left them in the lot and he announced that the auction would begin at sunup to-morrow.

That night we was setting on Mrs. Littlejohn's porch. You-all mind the moon was nigh full that night, and we could watch them spotted varmints swirling along the fence and back and forth across the lot same as minnows in a pond. And then now and then they would all kind of huddle up against the barn and rest themselves by biting and kicking one another. We would hear a squeal, and then a set of hoofs would go Bam! against the barn, like a pistol. It sounded just like a fellow with a pistol, in a nest of cattymounts, taking his time.

II

It wasn't ere a man knowed yet if Flem owned them things or not. They just knowed one thing: that they wasn't never going to know for sho if Flem did or not, or if maybe he didn't just get on that wagon at the edge of town, for the ride or not. Even Eck Snopes didn't know, Flem's own cousin. But wasn't nobody surprised at that. We knowed that Flem would skin Eck quick as he would ere a one of us.

They was there by sunup next morning, some of them come twelve and sixteen miles, with seed-money tied up in tobacco sacks in their overalls, standing along the fence, when the Texas man come out of Mrs. Littlejohn's after breakfast and clumb onto the gate post with that ere white pistol butt sticking outen his hind pocket. He taken a new box of gingersnaps outen his pocket and bit the end offen it like a cigar and spit out the paper, and said the auction was open. And still they was coming up in wagons and a horse and mule-back and hitching the teams across the road and coming to the fence. Flem wasn't nowhere in sight.

But he couldn't get them started. He begun to work on Eck, because Eck holp him last night to get them into the barn and feed them that shell corn. Eck got out just in time. He come outen that barn like a chip on the crest of a busted dam of water, and clumb into the wagon just in time.

He was working on Eck when Henry Armstid come up in his wagon. Eck was saying he was skeered to bid on one of them, because he might get it, and the Texas man says, "Them ponies? Them little horses?" He clumb down offen the gate post and went toward the horses. They broke and run, and him following them, kind of chirping to them, with his hand out like he was fixing to catch a fly, until he got three or four of them cornered. Then he jumped into them, and then we couldn't see nothing for a while because of the dust. It was a big cloud of it, and them blare-eyed, spotted things swoaring outen it twenty foot to a jump, in forty directions without counting up. Then the dust settled and there they was, that Texas man and the horse. He had its head twisted clean around like a owl's head. Its legs was braced and it was trembling like a new bride and groaning like a saw mill, and him holding its head wrung clean around on its neck so it was snuffing sky. "Look it over," he says, with his heels dug too and that white pistol sticking outen his pocket and his neck swole up like a spreading adder's until you could just tell what he was saying, cussing the horse and talking to us all at once: "Look him over, the fiddleheaded son of fourteen fathers. Try him, buy him; you will get the best—" Then it was all dust again, and we couldn't see nothing but spotted hide and mane, and that ere Texas man's boot-heels like a couple of walnuts on two strings, and after a while that two-gallon hat come sailing out like a fat old hen crossing a fence.

When the dust settled again, he was just getting outen the far fence corner, brushing himself off. He come and got his hat and brushed it off and come and clumb onto the gate post again. He was breathing hard. He taken the gingersnap box outen his pocket and et one, breathing hard. The hammer-head horse was still running round and round the lot like a merry-go-round at a fair. That was when Henry Armstid come shoving up to the gate in them patched overalls and one of them dangle-armed shirts of hisn. Hadn't nobody noticed him until then. We was all watching the Texas man and the horses. Even Mrs. Littlejohn; she had done come out and built a fire under the wash-pot in her back yard, and she would stand at the fence a while and then go back into the house and come out again with a arm full of wash and stand at the fence again. Well, here come Henry shoving up, and then we see Mrs. Armstid right behind him, in that ere faded wrapper and sunbonnet and them tennis shoes. "Git on back to that wagon," Henry says.

"Henry," she says.

"Here, boys," the Texas man says; "make room for missus to git up and see. Come on, Henry," he says; "here's your chance to buy that saddle-horse missus has been wanting. What about ten dollars, Henry?"

"Henry," Mrs. Armstid says. She put her hand on Henry's arm. Henry knocked her hand down.

"Git on back to that wagon, like I told you," he says.

Mrs. Armstid never moved. She stood behind Henry, with her hands rolled into her dress, not looking at nothing. "He hain't no more despair than to buy one of them things," she says. "And us not five dollars ahead of the pore house, he hain't no more despair." It was the truth, too. They ain't never made more than a bare living offen that place of theirs, and them with four chaps and the very clothes they wears she earns by weaving by the firelight at night while Henry's asleep.

"Shut your mouth and git on back to that wagon," Henry says. "Do you want I taken a wagon stake to you here in the big road?"

Well, that Texas man taken one look at her. Then he begun on Eck again, like Henry wasn't even there. But Eck was skeered. "I can git me a snapping turtle or a water moccasin for nothing. I ain't going to buy none."

So the Texas man said he would give Eck a horse. "To start the auction, and because you holp me last night. If you'll start the bidding on the next horse," he says, "I'll give you that fiddle-head horse."

I wish you could have seen them, standing there with their seed-money in their pockets, watching that Texas man give Eck Snopes a live horse, all fixed to call him a fool if he taken it or not. Finally Eck says he'll take it. "Only I just starts the bidding," he says. "I don't have to buy the next one lessen I ain't over-topped." The Texas man said all right, and Eck bid a dollar on the next one, with Henry Armstid standing there with his mouth already open, watching Eck and the Texas man like a mad-dog or something. "A dollar," Eck says.

The Texas man looked at Eck. His mouth was already open too, like he had started to say something and what he was going to say had up and died on him. "A dollar?" he says. "One dollar? You mean, *one* dollar, Eck?"

"Durn it," Eck says; "two dollars, then."

Well, sir, I wish you could a seen that Texas man. He taken out that ginger-snap box and held it up and looked into it, careful, like it might have been a diamond ring in it, or a spider. Then he threwed it away and wiped his face with a bandanna. "Well," he says. "Well. Two dollars. Two dollars. Is your pulse all right, Eck?" he says. "Do you have ager-sweats at night, maybe?" he says. "Well," he says, "I got to take it. But are you boys going to stand there and see Eck get two horses at a dollar a head?"

That done it. I be dog if he wasn't nigh as smart as Flem Snopes. He hadn't no more than got the words outen his mouth before here was Henry Armstid, waving his hand. "Three dollars," Henry says. Mrs. Armstid tried to hold him again. He knocked her hand off, shoving up to the gate post.

"Mister," Mrs. Armstid says, "we got chaps in the house and not corn to feed the stock. We got five dollars I earned my chaps a-weaving after dark, and him snoring in the bed. And he hain't no more despair."

"Henry bids three dollars," the Texas man says. "Raise him a dollar, Eck, and the horse is yours."

"Henry," Mrs. Armstid says.   30

"Raise him, Eck," the Texas man says.

"Four dollars," Eck says.

"Five dollars," Henry says, shaking his fist. He shoved up right under the gate post. Mrs. Armstid was looking at the Texas man too.

"Mister," she says, "if you take that five dollars I earned my chaps a-weaving for one of them things, it'll be a curse onto you and yourn during all the time of man."

But it wasn't no stopping Henry. He had shoved up, waving his fist at the   35
Texas man. He opened it; the money was in nickels and quarters, and one dollar bill that looked like a cow's cud. "Five dollars," he says. "And the man that raises it'll have to beat my head off, or I'll beat hisn."

"All right," the Texas man says. "Five dollars is bid. But don't you shake your hand at me."

III

It taken till nigh sundown before the last one was sold. He got them hotted up once and the bidding got up to seven dollars and a quarter, but most of them went around three or four dollars, him setting on the gate post and picking the horses out one at a time by mouth-word, and Mrs. Littlejohn pumping up and down at the tub and stopping and coming to the fence for a while and going back to the tub again. She had done got done too, and the wash was hung on the line in the back yard, and we could smell supper cooking. Finally they was all sold; he swapped the last two and the wagon for a buckboard.

We was all kind of tired, but Henry Armstid looked more like a mad-dog than ever. When he bought, Mrs. Armstid had went back to the wagon, setting in it behind them two rabbit-sized, bone-pore mules, and the wagon itself looking like it would fall all to pieces soon as the mules moved. Henry hadn't even waited to pull it outen the road; it was still in the middle of the road and her setting in it, not looking at nothing, ever since this morning.

Henry was right up against the gate. He went up to the Texas man. "I bought a horse and I paid cash," Henry says. "And yet you expect me to stand around here until they are all sold before I can get my horse. I'm going to take my horse outen that lot."

The Texas man looked at Henry. He talked like he might have been asking for   40
a cup of coffee at the table. "Take your horse," he says.

Then Henry quit looking at the Texas man. He begun to swallow, holding onto the gate. "Ain't you going to help me?" he says.

"It ain't my horse," the Texas man says.

Henry never looked at the Texas man again, he never looked at nobody. "Who'll help me catch my horse?" he says. Never nobody said nothing. "Bring the plowline," Henry says. Mrs. Armstid got outen the wagon and brought the plowline. The Texas man got down offen the post. The woman made to pass him, carrying the rope.

"Don't you go in there, missus," the Texas man says.

Henry opened the gate. He didn't look back. "Come on here," he says.   45

"Don't you go in there, missus," the Texas man says.

Mrs. Armstid wasn't looking at nobody, neither, with her hands across her middle, holding the rope. "I reckon I better," she says. Her and Henry went into the lot. The horses broke and run. Henry and Mrs. Armstid followed.

"Get him into the corner," Henry says. They got Henry's horse cornered finally, and Henry taken the rope, but Mrs. Armstid let the horse get out. They hemmed it up again, but Mrs. Armstid let it get out again, and Henry turned and hit her with the rope. "Why didn't you head him back?" Henry says. He hit her again. "Why didn't you?" It was about that time I looked around and see Flem Snopes standing there.

It was the Texas man that done something. He moved fast for a big man. He caught the rope before Henry could hit the third time, and Henry whirled and made like he would jump at the Texas man. But he never jumped. The Texas man went and taken Henry's arm and led him outen the lot. Mrs. Armstid come behind them and the Texas man taken some money outen his pocket and he give it into Mrs. Armstid's hand. "Get him into the wagon and take him on home," the Texas man says, like he might have been telling them he enjoyed his supper.

Then here come Flem. "What's that for, Buck?" Flem says.   50

"Thinks he bought one of them ponies," the Texas man says. "Get him on away, missus."

But Henry wouldn't go. "Give him back that money," he says. "I bought that horse and I aim to have him if I have to shoot him."

And there was Flem, standing there with his hands in his pockets, chewing, like he had just happened to be passing.

"You take your money and I take my horse," Henry says. "Give it back to him," he says to Mrs. Armstid.

"You don't own no horse of mine," the Texas many says. "Get him on home,   55 missus."

Then Henry seen Flem. "You got something to do with these horses," he says. "I bought one. Here's the money for it." He taken the bill outen Mrs. Armstid's hand. He offered it to Flem. "I bought one. Ask him. Here. Here's the money," he says, giving the bill to Flem.

When Flem taken the money, the Texas man dropped the rope he had snatched outen Henry's hand. He had done sent Eck Snopes's boy up to the store for another box of gingersnaps, and he taken the box outen his pocket and looked into it. It was empty and he dropped it on the ground. "Mr. Snopes will have your money for you to-morrow," he says to Mrs. Armstid. "You can get it from him to-morrow. He don't own no horse. You get him into the wagon and get him on home." Mrs. Armstid went back to the wagon and got in. "Where's that ere buckboard I bought?" the Texas man says. It was after sundown then. And then Mrs. Littlejohn come out on the porch and rung the supper bell.

IV

I come on in and et supper. Mrs. Littlejohn would bring in a pan of bread or something, then she would go out to the porch a minute and come back and tell us. The Texas man had hitched his team to the buckboard he had swapped them last tow horses for, and him and Flem had gone, and then she told that the rest of them that never had ropes had went back to the store with I. O. Snopes to get some ropes, and wasn't nobody at the gate but Henry Armstid, and Mrs. Armstid setting in the wagon in the road, and Eck Snopes and that boy of hisn. "I don't care how many of them fool men gets killed by them things," Mrs. Littlejohn says, "but I ain't going to let Eck Snopes take that boy into that lot again." So she went down to the gate, but she come back without the boy or Eck neither.

"It ain't no need to worry about that boy," I says. "He's charmed." He was right behind Eck last night when Eck went to help feed them. The whole drove of them jumped clean over that boy's head and never touched him. It was Eck that touched him. Eck snatched him into the wagon and taken a rope and frailed the tar outen him.

So I had done et and went to my room and was undressing, long as I had a long trip to make next day; I was trying to sell a machine to Mrs. Bundren up past Whiteleaf; when Henry Armstid opened that gate and went in by hisself. They couldn't make him wait for the balance of them to get back with their ropes. Eck Snopes said he tried to make Henry wait, but Henry wouldn't do it. Eck said Henry walked right up to them and that when they broke, they run clean over Henry like a hay-mow breaking down. Eck said he snatched that boy of hisn out of the way just in time and that them things went through that gate like a creek flood and into the wagons and teams hitched side the road, busting wagon tongues and snapping harness like it was fishing-line, with Mrs. Armstid still setting in their wagon in the middle of it like something carved outen wood. Then they scattered, wild horses and tame mules with pieces of harness and single trees dangling offen them, both ways up and down the road.

"There goes ourn, paw!" Eck says his boy said. "There it goes, into Mrs. Littlejohn's house." Eck says it run right up the steps and into the house like a boarder late for supper. I reckon so. Anyway, I was in my room, in my under-clothes, with one sock on and one sock in my hand, leaning out the window when the commotion busted out, when I heard something run into the melodeon in the hall; it sounded like a railroad engine. Then the door to my room come sailing in like when you throw a tin bucket top into the wind and I looked over my shoulder and see something that looked like a fourteen-foot pinwheel a-blaring its eyes at me. It had to blare them fast, because I was already done jumped out the window.

I reckon it was anxious, too. I reckon it hadn't never seen barbed wire or shell corn before, but I know it hadn't never seen underclothes before, or maybe

60

it was a sewing-machine agent it hadn't never seen. Anyway, it swirled and turned to run back up the hall and outen the house, when it met Eck Snopes and that boy just coming in, carrying a rope. It swirled again and run down the hall and out the back door just in time to meet Mrs. Littlejohn. She had just gathered up the clothes she had washed, and she was coming onto the back porch with a armful of washing in one hand and a scrubbing-board in the other, when the horse skidded up to her, trying to stop and swirl again. It never taken Mrs. Littlejohn no time a-tall.

"Git outen here, you son," she says. She hit it across the face with the scrubbing-board; that ere scrubbing-board split as neat as ere a axe could have done it, and when the horse swirled to run back up the hall, she hit it again with what was left of the scrubbing-board, not on the head this time. "And stay out," she says.

Eck and that boy was half-way down the hall by this time. I reckon that horse looked like a pinwheel to Eck too. "Git to hell outen here, Ad!" Eck says. Only there wasn't time. Eck dropped flat on his face, but the boy never moved. The boy was about a yard tall maybe, in overhalls just like Eck's; that horse swoared over his head without touching a hair. I saw that, because I was just coming back up the front steps, still carrying that ere sock and still in my underclothes, when the horse come onto the porch again. It taken one look at me and swirled again and run to the end of the porch and jumped the banisters and the lot fence like a henhawk and lit in the lot runnng and went out the gate again and jumped eight or ten upside-down wagons and went on down the road. It was a full moon then. Mrs. Armstid was still setting in the wagon like she had done been carved outen wood and left there and forgot.

That horse. It ain't never missed a lick. It was going about forty miles a hour when it come to the bridge over the creek. It would have had a clear road, but it so happened that Vernon Tull was already using the bridge when it got there. He was coming back from town; he hadn't heard about the auction; him and his wife and three daughters and Mrs. Tull's aunt, all setting in chairs in the wagon bed, and all asleep, including the mules. They waked up when the horse hit the bridge one time, but Tull said the first he knew was when the mules tried to turn the wagon around in the middle of the bridge and he seen that spotted varmint run right twixt the mules and run up the wagon tongue like a squirrel. He said he just had time to hit it across the face with his whip-stock, because about that time the mules turned the wagon around on that ere one-way bridge and that horse clumb across one of the mules and jumped down onto the bridge again and went on, with Vernon standing up in the wagon and kicking at it.

Tull said the mules turned in the harness and clumb back into the wagon too, with Tull trying to beat them out again, with the reins wrapped around his wrist. After that he says all he seen was overturned chairs and women folks' legs and white drawers shining in the moonlight, and his mules and that spotted horse going on up the road like a ghost.

The mules jerked Tull outen the wagon and drug him a spell on the bridge before the reins broke. They thought at first that he was dead, and while they was kneeling around him, picking the bridge splinters outen him, here come Eck and that boy, still carrying the rope. They was running and breathing a little hard. "Where'd he go?" Eck says.

V

I went back and got my pants and shirt and shoes on just in time to go and help get Henry Armstid outen the trash in the lot. I be dog if he didn't look like he was dead, with his head hanging back and his teeth showing in the moonlight, an a little rim of white under his eyelids. We could still hear them horses, here and there; hadn't none of them got more than four—five miles away yet, not knowing the country, I reckon. So we could hear them and folks yelling now and then: "Whooey. Head him!"

We toted Henry into Mrs. Littlejohn's. She was in the hall; she hadn't put down the armful of clothes. She taken one look at us, and she laid down the busted scrubbing-board and taken up the lamp and opened a empty door. "Bring him in here," she says.

We toted him in and laid him on the bed. Mrs. Littlejohn set the lamp on the   70 dresser, still carrying the clothes. "I'll declare, you men," she says. Our shadows was way up the wall, tiptoeing too; we could hear ourselves breathing. "Better get his wife," Mrs. Littlejohn says. She went out, carrying the clothes.

"I reckon we had," Quick says. "Go get her, somebody."

"Whyn't you go?" Winterbottom says.

"Let Ernest git her," Durley says. "He lives neighbors with them."

Ernest went to fetch her. I be dog if Henry didn't look like he was dead. Mrs. Littlejohn come back, with a kettle and some towels. She went to work on Henry, and then Mrs. Armstid and Ernest come in. Mrs. Armstid come to the foot of the bed and stood there, with her hands rolled into her apron, watching what Mrs. Littlejohn was doing, I reckon.

"You men get outen the way," Mrs. Littlejohn says. "Git outside," she says.   75 "See if you can't find something else to play with that will kill some more of you."

"Is he dead?" Winterbottom says.

"It ain't your fault if he ain't," Mrs. Littlejohn says. "Go tell Will Varner to come up here. I reckon a man ain't so different from a mule, come long come short. Except maybe a mule's got more sense."

We went to get Uncle Billy. It was a full moon. We could hear them, now and then, four mile away: "Whooey. Head him." The country was full of them, one on ever wooden bridge in the land, running across it like thunder: "Whooey. There he goes. Head him."

We hadn't got far before Henry begun to scream. I reckon Mrs. Littlejohn's water had brung him to; anyway, he wasn't dead. We went on to Uncle Billy's. The house was dark. We called to him, and after a while the window opened and Uncle Billy put his head out, peart as a peckerwood, listening. "Are they still trying to catch them durn rabbits?" he says.

He come down, with his britches on over his night-shirt and his suspenders   80 dangling, carrying his horse-doctoring grip. "Yes, sir," he says, cocking his head like a woodpecker; "they're still a-trying."

We could hear Henry before we reached Mrs. Littlejohn's. He was going Ah-

Ah-Ah. We stopped in the yard. Uncle Billy went on in. We could hear Henry. We stood in the yard, hearing them on the bridges, this-a-way and that: "Whooey. Whooey."

"Eck Snopes ought to caught hisn," Ernest says.

"Looks like he ought," Winterbottom said.

Henry was going Ah-Ah-Ah steady in the house; then he begun to scream. "Uncle Billy's started," Quick says. We looked into the hall. We could see the light where the door was. Then Mrs. Littlejohn come out.

"Will needs some help," she says. "You, Ernest. You'll do." Ernest went into   85 the house.

"Hear them?" Quick said. "That one was on Four Mile bridge." We could hear them; it sounded like thunder a long way off; it didn't last long:

"Whooey."

We could hear Henry: "Ah-Ah-Ah-Ah-Ah."

"They are both started now," Winterbottom says. "Ernest too."

That was early in the night. Which was a good thing, because it taken a long   90 night for folks to chase them things right and for Henry to lay there and holler, being as Uncle Billy never had none of this here chloryfoam to set Henry's leg with. So it was considerate in Flem to get them started early. And what do you reckon Flem's com-ment was?

That's right. Nothing. Because he wasn't there. Hadn't nobody see him since that Texas man left.

VI

That was Saturday night. I reckon Mrs. Armstid got home about daylight, to see about the chaps. I don't know where they thought her and Henry was. But lucky the oldest one was a gal, about twelve, big enough to take care of the little ones. Which she did for the next two days. Mrs Armstid would nurse Henry all night and work in the kitchen for hern and Henry's keep, and in the afternoon she would drive home (it was about four miles) to see to the chaps. She would cook up a pot of victuals and leave it on the stove, and the gal would bar the house and keep the little ones quiet. I would hear Mrs. Littlejohn and Mrs. Armstid talking in the kitchen. "How are the chaps making out?" Mrs. Littlejohn says.

"All right," Mrs. Armstid says.

"Don't they git skeered at night?" Mrs. Littlejohn says.

"Ina May bars the door when I leave," Mrs. Armstid says. "She's got the axe   95 in bed with her. I reckon she can make out."

I reckon they did. And I reckon Mrs. Armstid was waiting for Flem to come back to town; hadn't nobody seen him until this morning; to get her money the Texas man said Flem was keeping for her. Sho. I reckon she was.

Anyway, I heard Mrs. Armstid and Mrs. Littlejohn talking in the kitchen this morning while I was eating breakfast. Mrs. Littlejohn had just told Mrs. Armstid that Flem was in town. "You can ask him for that five dollars," Mrs. Littlejohn says.

"You reckon he'll give it to me?" Mrs. Armstid says.

Mrs. Littlejohn was washing dishes, washing them like a man, like they was made out of iron. "No," she says. "But asking him won't do no hurt. It might shame him. I don't reckon it will, but it might."

"If he wouldn't give it back, it ain't no use to ask," Mrs. Armstid says.   100

"Suit yourself," Mrs. Littlejohn says. "It's your money."

I could hear the dishes.

"Do you reckon he might give it back to me?" Mrs. Armstid says. "That Texas man said he would. He said I could get it from Mr. Snopes later."

"Then go and ask him for it," Mrs. Littlejohn says.

I could hear the dishes.   105

"He won't give it back to me," Mrs. Armstid says.

"All right," Mrs. Littlejohn says. "Don't ask him for it, then."

I could hear the dishes; Mrs. Armstid was helping. "You don't reckon he would, do you?" she says. Mrs. Littlejohn never said nothing. It sounded like she was throwing the dishes at one another. "Maybe I better go and talk to Henry about it," Mrs. Armstid says.

"I would," Mrs. Littlejohn says. I be dog if it didn't sound like she had two plates in her hands, beating them together. "Then Henry can buy another five-dollar horse with it. Maybe he'll buy one next time that will out and out kill him. If I thought that, I'd give you back the money, myself."

"I reckon I better talk to him first," Mrs. Armstid said. Then it sounded like   110
Mrs. Littlejohn taken up all the dishes and throwed them at the cook-stove, and I come away.

That was this morning. I had been up to Bundren's and back, and I thought that things would have kind of settled down. So after breakfast, I went up to the store. And there was Flem, setting in the store chair and whittling, like he might not have ever moved since he come to clerk for Jody Varner. I. O. was leaning in the door, in his shirt sleeves and with his hair parted too, same as Flem was before he turned the clerking job over to I. O. It's a funny thing about them Snopes: they all looks alike, yet there ain't ere a two of them that claims brothers. They're always just cousins, like Flem and Eck and Flem and I. O. Eck was there too, squatting against the wall, him and that boy, eating cheese and crackers outen a sack; they told me that Eck hadn't been home a-tall. And that Lon Quick hadn't got back to town, even. He followed his horse clean down to Samson's Bridge, with a wagon and a camp outfit. Eck finally caught one of hisn. It run into a blind lane at Freeman's and Eck and the boy taken and tied their rope across the end of the lane, about three foot high. The horse come to the end of the lane and whirled and run back without ever stopping. Eck says it never seen the rope a-tall. He says it looked just like one of these here Christmas pinwheels. "Didn't it try to run again?" I says.

"No," Eck says, eating a bit of cheese offen his knife balde. "Just kicked some."

"Kicked some?" I says.

"It broke its neck," Eck says.

Well, they was squatting there, about six of them, talking, talking at Flem;   115
never nobody knowed yet if Flem had ere a interest in them horses or not. So finally I come right out and asked him. "Flem's done skun all of us so much," I

says, "that we're proud of him. Come on, Flem," I says, "how much did you and that Texas man make offen them horses? You can tell us. Ain't nobody here but Eck that bought one of them; the others ain't got back to town yet, and Eck's your own cousin; he'll be proud to hear, too. How much did you-all make?"

They was all whittling, not looking at Flem, making like they was studying. But you could a heard a pin drop. And I. O. He had been rubbing his back up and down on the door, but he stopped now, watching Flem like a pointing dog. Flem finished cutting the sliver offen his stick. He spit across the porch, into the road. "'Twarn't none of my horses," he says.

I. O. cackled, like a hen, slapping his legs with both hands. "You boys might just as well quit trying to get ahead of Flem," he said.

Well, about that time I see Mrs. Armstid come outen Mrs. Littlejohn's gate, coming up the road. I never said nothing. I says, "Well, if a man can't take care of himself in a trade, he can't blame the man that trims him."

Flem never said nothing, trimming at the stick. He hadn't seen Mrs. Armstid. "Yes, sir," I says. "A fellow like Henry Armstid ain't got nobody but hisself to blame."

"Course he ain't," I. O. says. He ain't seen her, neither. "Henry Armstid's a born fool. Always is been. If Flem hadn't a got his money, somebody else would."   120

We looked at Flem. He never moved. Mrs. Armstid come on up the road.

"That's right," I says. "But, come to think of it, Henry never bought no horse." We looked at Flem; you could a heard a match drop. "That Texas man told her to get that five dollars back from Flem next day. I reckon Flem's done already taken that money to Mrs. Littlejohn's and give it to Mrs. Armstid."

We watched Flem. I. O. quit rubbing his back against the door again. After a while Flem raised his head and spit across the porch, into the dust. I. O. cackled, just like a hen. "Ain't he a beating fellow, now?" I. O. says.

Mrs. Armstid was getting closer, so I kept on talking, watching to see if Flem would look up and see her. But he never looked up. I went on talking about Tull, about how he was going to sue Flem, and Flem setting there, whittling his stick, not saying nothing else after he said they wasn't none of his horses.

Then I. O. happened to look around. He seen Mrs. Armstid. "Psssst!" he   125
says. Flem looked up. "Here she comes!" I. O says. "Go out the back. I'll tell here you done went in to town to-day."

But Flem never moved. He just set there, whittling, and we watched Mrs. Armstid come up onto the porch, in that ere faded sunbonnet and wrapper and them tennis shoes that made a kind of hissing noise on the porch. She come onto the porch and stopped, her hands rolled into her dress in front, not looking at nothing.

"He said Saturday," she says, "that he wouldn't sell Henry no horse. He said I could get the money from you."

Flem looked up. The knife never stopped. It went on trimming off a sliver same as if he was watching it. "He taken that money off with him when he left," Flem says.

Mrs. Armstid never looked at nothing. We never looked at her, neither, except that boy of Eck's. He had a half-et cracker in his hand, watching her, chewing.

"He said Henry hadn't bought no horse," Mrs. Armstid says. "He said for   130
me to get the money from you today."

"I reckon he forgot about it," Flem said. "He taken that money off with him
Saturday." He whittled again. I. O. kept on rubbing his back, slow. He licked his
lips. After a while the woman looked up the road, where it went on up the hill,
toward the graveyard. She looked up that way for a while, with that boy of Eck's
watching her and I. O. rubbing his back slow against the door. Then she turned
back toward the steps.

"I reckon it's time to get dinner started," she says.

"How's Henry this morning, Mrs. Armstid?" Winterbottom says.

She looked at Winterbottom; she almost stopped. "He's resting, I thank you
kindly," she says.

Flem got up, outen the chair, putting his knife away. He spit across the porch.   135
"Wait a minute, Mrs. Armstid," he says. She stopped again. She didn't look at
him. Flem went on into the store, with I. O. done quit rubbing his back now, with
his head craned after Flem, and Mrs. Armstid standing there with her hands
rolled into her dress, not looking at nothing. A wagon come up the road and
passed; it was Freeman, on the way to town. Then Flem come out again, with
I. O. still watching him. Flem had one of these little striped sacks of Jody Varner's
candy; I bet he still owns Jody that nickel, too. He put the sack into Mrs. Armstid's hand, like he would have put it into a hollow stump. He spit again across the
porch. "A little sweetening for the chaps," he says.

"You're right kind," Mrs. Armstid says. She held the sack of candy in her
hand, not looking at nothing. Eck's boy was watching the sack, the half-et cracker
in his hand; he wasn't chewing now. He watched Mrs. Armstid roll the sack into
her apron. "I reckon I better get on back and help with dinner," she says. She
turned and went back across the porch. Flem set down in the chair again and
opened his knife. He spit across the porch again, past Mrs. Armstid where she
hadn't went down the steps yet. Then she went on, in that ere sunbonnet and
wrapper all the same color, back down the road toward Mrs. Littlejohn's. You
couldn't see her dress move, like a natural woman walking. She looked like a old
snag still standing up and moving along on a high water. We watched her turn in at
Mrs. Littlejohn's and go outen sight. Flem was whittling. I. O. begun to rub his
back on the door. Then he begun to cackle, just like a durn hen.

"You boys might just as well quit trying," I. O. says. "You can't git ahead of
Flem. You can't touch him. Ain't he a sight, now?"

I be dog if he ain't. If I had brung a herd of wild cattymounts into town and
sold them to my neighbors and kinfolks, they would have lynched me. Yes, sir.

QUESTIONS AND SUGGESTIONS FOR WRITING

1. Characterize the narrator, paying special attention to his attitude toward Flem.
2. In an essay of 250–350 words compare and contrast Flem and the Texas man.
3. Why does Faulkner include Mrs. Littlejohn in the story?

4. Are there passages in the story that you find funny? If so, point out a few, and explain in some detail why one passage seems to you to be especially comic.

5. The story is in the tradition of the tall tale (think of stories of Davy Crockett or Paul Bunyan), in which obvious lies are stated with a straight face. Is "Spotted Horses" merely a fanciful joke? Explain.

Alice Munro (Canadian. b. 1931)

BOYS AND GIRLS

My father was a fox farmer. That is, he raised silver foxes, in pens; and in the fall and early winter, when their fur was prime, he killed them and skinned them and sold their pelts to the Hudson's Bay Company or the Montreal Fur Traders. These companies supplied us with heroic calendars to hang, one on each side of the kitchen door. Against a background of cold blue sky and black pine forests and treacherous northern rivers, plumed adventurers planted the flags of England or of France; magnificent savages bent their backs to the portage.

For several weeks before Christmas, my father worked after supper in the cellar of our house. The cellar was whitewashed, and lit by a hundred-watt bulb over the worktable. My brother Laird and I sat on the top step and watched. My father removed the pelt inside-out from the body of the fox, which looked surprisingly small, mean and rat-like, deprived of its arrogant weight of fur. The naked, slippery bodies were collected in a sack and buried at the dump. One time the hired man, Henry Bailey, had taken a swipe at me with this sack, saying, "Christmas present!" My mother thought that was not funny. In fact she disliked the whole pelting operation—that was what the killing, skinning, and preparation of the furs was called—and wished it did not have to take place in the house. There was the smell. After the pelt had been stretched inside-out on a long board my father scraped away delicately, removing the little clotted webs of blood vessels, the bubbles of fat; the smell of blood and animal fat, with the strong primitive odor of the fox itself, penetrated all parts of the house. I found it reassuringly seasonal, like the smell of oranges and pine needles.

Henry Bailey suffered from bronchial troubles. He would cough and cough until his narrow face turned scarlet, and his light blue, derisive eyes filled up with tears; then he took the lid off the stove, and, standing well back, shot out a great clot of phlegm—hsss—straight into the heart of the flames. We admired him for this performance and for his ability to make his stomach growl at will, and for his laughter, which was full of high whistlings and gurglings and involved the whole faulty machinery of his chest. It was sometimes hard to tell what he was laughing at, and always possible that it might be us.

After we had been sent to bed we could still smell fox and still hear Henry's laugh, but these things, reminders of the warm, safe, brightly lit downstairs world, seemed lost and diminished, floating on the stale cold air upstairs. We were afraid at night in the winter. We were not afraid of *outside* though this was the time of year when snowdrifts curled around our house like sleeping whales and the wind harassed us all night, coming up from the buried fields, the frozen swamp, with its old bugbear chorus of threats and misery. We were afraid of *inside*, the room where we slept. At this time the upstairs of our house was not finished. A brick chimney went up one wall. In the middle of the floor was a square hole, with a wooden railing around it; that was where the stairs came up. On the other side of the stairwell were the things that nobody had any use for any more—a soldiery roll of linoleum, standing on end, a wicker baby carriage, a fern basket, china jugs and basins with cracks in them, a picture of the Battle of Balaclava, very sad to look at. I had told Laird, as soon as he was old enough to understand such things, that bats and skeletons lived over there; whenever a man escaped from the county jail, twenty miles away, I imagined that he had somehow let himself in the window and was hiding behind the linoleum. But we had rules to keep us safe. When the light was on, we were safe as long as we did not step off the square of worn carpet which defined our bedroom-space; when the light was off no place was safe but the beds themselves. I had to turn out the light kneeling on the end of my bed, and stretching as far as I could to reach the cord.

In the dark we lay on our beds, our narrow life rafts, and fixed our eyes on   5
the faint light coming up the stairwell, and sang songs. Laird sang "Jingle Bells," which he would sing any time, whether it was Christmas or not, and I sang "Danny Boy." I loved the sound of my own voice, frail and supplicating, rising in the dark. We could make out the tall frosted shapes of the windows now, gloomy and white. When I came to the part, *When I am dead, as dead I well may be*—a fit of shivering caused not by the cold sheets but by pleasurable emotion almost silenced me. *You'll kneel and say, an Ave there above me*—What was an Ave? Every day I forgot to find out.

Laird went straight from singing to sleep. I could hear his long, satisfied, bubbly breaths. Now for the time that remained to me, the most perfectly private and perhaps the best time of the whole day, I arranged myself tightly under the covers and went on with one of the stories I was telling myself from night to night. These stories were about myself, when I had grown a little older; they took place in a world that was recognizably mine, yet one that presented opportunities for courage, boldness and self-sacrifice, as mine never did. I rescued people from a bombed building (it discouraged me that the real war had gone on so far away from Jubilee). I shot two rabid wolves who were menacing the schoolyard (the teachers cowered terrified at my back). I rode a fine horse spiritedly down the main street of Jubilee, acknowledging the townspeople's gratitude for some yet-to-be-worked-out piece of heroism (nobody ever rode a horse there, except King Billy in the Orangemen's Day[1] parade). There was always riding and shooting in these stories, though I had only been on a horse twice—bareback because we did not own a saddle—and the second time I had slid right around and dropped under the horse's feet; it had stepped placidly over me. I really was learning to shoot, but I could not hit anything yet, not even tin cans on fence posts.

---

[1] The Orange Society is named for William of Orange, who, as King William III of England, defeated James II of England at the Battle of the Boyne on 12 July 1609. It sponsors an annual procession on 12 July. (Notes to this selection are by the editors.)

*   *   *   *   *

Alive, the foxes inhabited a world my father made for them. It was surrounded by a high guard fence, like a medieval town, with a gate that was padlocked at night. Along the streets of this town were ranged large, sturdy pens. Each of them had a real door that a man could go through, a wooden ramp along the wire, for the foxes to run up and down on, and a kennel—something like a clothes chest with airholes—where they slept and stayed in winter and had their young. There were feeding and watering dishes attached to the wire in such a way that they could be emptied and cleaned from the outside. The dishes were made of old tin cans, and the ramps and kennels of odds and ends of old lumber. Everything was tidy and ingenious; my father was tirelessly inventive and his favorite book in the world was Robinson Crusoe. He had fitted a tin drum on a wheelbarrow, for bringing water down to the pens. This was my job in summer, when the foxes had to have water twice a day. Between nine and ten o'clock in the morning, and again after supper, I filled the drum at the pump and trundled it down through the barnyard to the pens, where I parked it, and filled my watering can and went along the streets. Laird came too, with his little cream and green gardening can, filled too full and knocking against his legs and slopping water on his canvas shoes. I had the real watering can, my father's, though I could only carry it three-quarters full.

The foxes all had names, which were printed on a tin plate and hung beside their doors. They were not named when they were born, but when they survived the first year's pelting and were added to the breeding stock. Those my father had named were called names like Prince, Bob, Wally and Betty. Those I had named were called Star or Turk, or Maureen or Diana. Laird named one Maud after a hired girl we had when he was little, one Harold after a boy at school, and one Mexico, he did not say why.

Naming them did not make pets out of them, or anything like it. Nobody but my father ever went into the pens, and he had twice had blood-poisoning from bites. When I was bringing them their water they prowled up and down on the paths they had made inside their pens, barking seldom—they saved that for nighttime, when they might get up a chorus of community frenzy—but always watching me, their eyes burning, clear gold, in their pointed, malevolent faces. They were beautiful for their delicate legs and heavy, aristocratic tails and the bright fur sprinkled on dark down their backs—which gave them their name—but especially for their faces, drawn exquisitely sharp in pure hostility, and their golden eyes.

Besides carrying water I helped my father when he cut the long grass, and the lamb's quarter and flowering money-musk, that grew between the pens. He cut with the scythe and I raked into piles. Then he took a pitchfork and threw fresh-cut grass all over the top of the pens to keep the foxes cooler and shade their coats, which were browned by too much sun. My father did not talk to me unless it was about the job we were doing. In this he was quite different from my mother, who, if she was feeling cheerful, would tell me all sorts of things—the name of a dog she had had when she was a little girl, the names of boys she had gone out with later on when she was grown up, and what certain dresses of hers had looked like—she could not imagine now what had become of them. Whatever

10

thoughts and stories my father had were private, and I was shy of him and would never ask him questions. Nevertheless I worked willingly under his eyes, and with a feeling of pride. One time a feed salesman came down into the pens to talk to him and my father said, "Like to have you meet my new hired man." I turned away and raked furiously, red in the face with pleasure.

"Could of fooled me," said the salesman. "I thought it was only a girl."

After the grass was cut, it seemed suddenly much later in the year. I walked on stubble in the earlier evening, aware of the reddening skies, the entering silences, of fall. When I wheeled the tank out of the gate and put the padlock on, it was almost dark. One night at this time I saw my mother and father standing talking on the little rise of ground we called the gangway, in front of the barn. My father had just come from the meathouse; he had his stiff bloody apron on, and a pail of cut-up meat in his hand.

It was an odd thing to see my mother down at the barn. She did not often come out of the house unless it was to do something—hang out the wash or dig potatoes in the garden. She looked out of place, with her bare lumpy legs, not touched by the sun, her apron still on and damp across the stomach from the supper dishes. Her hair was tied up in a kerchief, wisps of it falling out. She would tie her hair up like this in the morning, saying she did not have time to do it properly, and it would stay tied up all day. It was true, too; she really did not have time. These days our back porch was piled with baskets of peaches and grapes and pears, bought in town, and onions and tomatoes and cucumbers grown at home, all waiting to be made into jelly and jam and preserves, pickles and chili sauce. In the kitchen there was a fire in the stove all day, jars clinked in boiling water, sometimes a cheesecloth bag was strung on a pole between two chairs straining blue-black grape pulp for jelly. I was given jobs to do and I would sit at the table peeling peaches that had been soaked in the hot water, or cutting up onions, my eyes smarting and streaming. As soon as I was done I ran out of the house, trying to get out of earshot before my mother thought of what she wanted me to do next. I hated the hot dark kitchen in summer, the green blinds and the flypapers, the same old oilcloth table and wavy mirror and bumpy linoleum. My mother was too tired and preoccupied to talk to me, she had no heart to tell about the Normal School Graduation Dance; sweat trickled over her face and she was always counting under her breath, pointing at jars, dumping cups of sugar. It seemed to me that work in the house was endless, dreary and peculiarly depressing; work done out of doors, and in my father's service, was ritualistically important.

I wheeled the tank up to the barn, where it was kept, and I heard my mother saying, "Wait till Laird gets a little bigger, then you'll have a real help."

What my father said I did not hear. I was pleased by the way he stood listening, politely as he would to a salesman or a stranger, but with an air of wanting to get on with his real work. I felt my mother had no business down here and I wanted him to feel the same way. What did she mean about Laird? He was no help to anybody. Where was he now? Swinging himself sick on the swing, going around in circles, or trying to catch caterpillars. He never once stayed with me till I was finished.

15

"And then I can use her more in the house," I heard my mother say. She had a dead-quiet, regretful way of talking about me that always made me uneasy. "I just get my back turned and she runs off. It's not like I had a girl in the family at all."

I went and sat on a feed bag in the corner of the barn, not wanting to appear when this conversation was going on. My mother, I felt, was not to be trusted. She was kinder than my father and more easily fooled, but you could not depend on her, and the real reasons for the things she said and did were not to be known. She loved me, and she sat up late at night making a dress of the difficult style I wanted, for me to wear when school started, but she was also my enemy. She was always plotting. She was plotting now to get me to stay in the house more, although she knew I hated it (*because* she knew I hated it) and keep me from working for my father. It seemed to me she would do this simply out of perversity, and to try her power. It did not occur to me that she could be lonely, or jealous. No grown-up could be; they were too fortunate. I sat and kicked my heels monotonously against a feed bag, raising dust, and did not come out till she was gone.

At any rate, I did not expect my father to pay any attention to what she said. Who could imagine Laird doing my work—Laird remembering the padlock and cleaning out the watering dishes with a leaf on the end of a stick, or even wheeling the tank without it tumbling over? It showed how little my mother knew about the way things really were.

I have forgotten to say what the foxes were fed. My father's bloody apron reminded me. They were fed horsemeat. At this time most farmers still kept horses, and when a horse got too old to work, or broke a leg or got down and would not get up, as they sometimes did, the owner would call my father, and he and Henry went out to the farm in the truck. Usually they shot and butchered the horse there, paying the farmer from five to twelve dollars. If they had already too much meat on hand, they would bring the horse back alive, and keep it for a few days or weeks in our stable, until the meat was needed. After the war the farmers were buying tractors and gradually getting rid of horses altogether, so it sometimes happened that we got a good healthy horse, that there was just no use for any more. If this happened in the winter we might keep the horse in our stable till spring, for we had plenty of hay and if there was a lot of snow—and the plow did not always get our road cleared—it was convenient to be able to go to town with a horse and cutter.[2]

The winter I was eleven years old we had two horses in the stable. We did   20
not know what names they had had before, so we called them Mack and Flora. Mack was an old black workhorse, sooty and indifferent. Flora was a sorrel mare, a driver. We took them both out in the cutter. Mack was slow and easy to handle. Flora was given to fits of violent alarm, veering at cars and even at other horses, but we loved her speed and high-stepping, her general air of gallantry and abandon. On Saturdays we went down to the stable and as soon as we opened the door

[2] A small sleigh.

on its cosy, animal-smelling darkness Flora threw up her head, rolled her eyes, whinnied despairingly and pulled herself through a crisis of nerves on the spot. It was not safe to go into her stall; she would kick.

This winter also I began to hear a great deal more on the theme my mother had sounded when she had been talking in front of the barn. I no longer felt safe. It seemed that in the minds of the people around me there was a steady undercurrent of thought, not to be deflected, on this one subject. The word *girl* had formerly seemed to me innocent and unburdened, like the word *child*; now it appeared that it was no such thing. A girl was not, as I had supposed, simply what I was; it was what I had to become. It was a definition, always touched with emphasis, with reproach and disappointment. Also it was a joke on me. Once Laird and I were fighting, and for the first time ever I had to use all my strength against him; even so, he caught and pinned my arm for a moment, really hurting me. Henry saw this, and laughed, saying, "Oh, that there Laird's gonna show you, one of these days!" Laird was getting a lot bigger. But I was getting bigger too.

My grandmother came to stay with us for a few weeks and I heard other things. "Girls don't slam doors like that." "Girls keep their knees together when they sit down." And worse still, when I asked some questions, "That's none of girls' business." I continued to slam the doors and sit as awkwardly as possible, thinking that by such measures I kept myself free.

When spring came, the horses were let out in the barnyard. Mack stood against the barn wall trying to scratch his neck and haunches, but Flora trotted up and down and reared at the fences, clattering her hooves against the rails. Snow drifts dwindled quickly, revealing the hard gray and brown earth, the familiar rise and fall of the ground, plain and bare after the fantastic landscape of winter. There was a great feeling of opening-out, of release. We just wore rubbers now, over our shoes; our feet felt ridiculously light. One Saturday we went to the stable and found all the doors open, letting in the unaccustomed sunlight and fresh air. Henry was there, just idling around looking at his collection of calendars which were tacked up behind the stalls in a part of the stable my mother had probably never seen.

"Come to say goodbye to your old friend Mack?" Henry said. "Here, you give him a taste of oats." He poured some oats into Laird's cupped hands and Laird went to feed Mack. Mack's teeth were in bad shape. He ate very slowly, patiently shifting the oats around in his mouth, trying to find a stump of a molar to grind it on. "Poor old Mack," said Henry mournfully. "When a horse's teeth's gone, he's gone. That's about the way."

"Are you going to shoot him today?" I said. Mack and Flora had been in the   25 stable so long I had almost forgotten they were going to be shot.

Henry didn't answer me. Instead he started to sing in a high, trembly, mocking-sorrowful voice. *Oh, there's no more work, for poor Uncle Ned, he's gone where the good darkies go.* Mack's thick, blackish tongue worked diligently at Laird's hand. I went out before the song was ended and sat down on the gangway.

I had never seen them shoot a horse, but I knew where it was done. Last summer Laird and I had come upon a horse's entrails before they were buried. We had thought it was a big black snake, coiled up in the sun. That was around in the field that ran up beside the barn. I thought that if we went inside the barn, and found a wide crack or a knothole to look through, we would be able to see them do it. It was not something I wanted to see; just the same, if a thing really happened, it was better to see, and know.

My father came down from the house, carrying the gun.

"What are you doing here?" he said.

"Nothing."   30

"Go on up and play around the house."

He sent Laird out of the stable. I said to Laird, "Do you want to see them shoot Mack?" and without waiting for an answer led him around to the front door of the barn, opened it carefully, and went in. "Be quiet or they'll hear us," I said. We could hear Henry and my father talking in the stable; then the heavy, shuffling steps of Mack being backed out of his stall.

In the loft it was cold and dark. Thin crisscrossed beams of sunlight fell through the cracks. The hay was low. It was a rolling country, hills and hollows, slipping under our feet. About four feet up was a beam going around the walls. We piled hay up in one corner and I boosted Laird up and hoisted myself. The beam was not very wide; we crept along it with our hands flat on the barn walls. There were plenty of knotholes, and I found one that gave me the view I wanted—a corner of the barnyard, the gate, part of the field. Laird did not have a knothole and began to complain.

I showed him a widened crack between two boards. "Be quiet and wait. If they hear you you'll get us in trouble."

My father came in sight carrying the gun. Henry was leading Mack by the   35
halter. He dropped it and took out his cigarette papers and tobacco; he rolled cigarettes for my father and himself. While this was going on Mack nosed around in the old, dead grass along the fence. Then my father opened the gate and they took Mack through. Henry led Mack way from the path to a patch of ground and they talked together, not loud enough for us to hear. Mack again began searching for a mouthful of fresh grass, which was not to be found. My father walked away in a straight line, and stopped short at a distance which seemed to suit him. Henry was walking away from Mack too, but sideways, still negligently holding on to the halter. My father raised the gun and Mack looked up as if he had noticed something and my father shot him.

Mack did not collapse at once but swayed, lurched sideways and fell, first on his side; then he rolled over on his back and, amazingly, kicked his legs for a few seconds in the air. At this Henry laughed, as if Mack had done a trick for him. Laird, who had drawn a long, groaning breath of surprise when the shot was fired, said out loud, "He's not dead." And it seemed to me it might be true. But his legs stopped, he rolled on his side again, his muscles quivered and sank. The two men walked over and looked at him in a businesslike way; they bent down and examined his forehead where the bullet had gone in, and now I saw his blood on the brown grass.

"Now they just skin him and cut him up," I said. "Let's go." My legs were a little shaky and I jumped gratefully down into the hay. "Now you've seen how they shoot a horse," I said in a congratulatory way, as if I had seen it many times before. "Let's see if any barn cat's had kittens in the hay." Laird jumped. He seemed young and obedient again. Suddenly I remembered how, when he was little, I had brought him into the barn and told him to climb the ladder to the top beam. That was in the spring, too, when the hay was low. I had done it out of a need for excitement, a desire for something to happen so that I could tell about it. He was wearing a little bulky brown and white checked coat, made down from one of mine. He went all the way up just as I told him, and sat down on the top beam with the hay far below him on one side, and the barn floor and some old machinery on the other. Then I ran screaming to my father, "Laird's up on the top beam!" My father came, my mother came, my father went up the ladder talking very quietly and brought Laird down under his arm, at which my mother leaned against the ladder and began to cry. They said to me, "Why weren't you watching him?" but nobody ever knew the truth. Laird did not know enough to tell. But whenever I saw the brown and white checked coat hanging in the closet, or at the bottom of the rag bag, which was where it ended up, I felt a weight in my stomach, the sadness of unexorcised guilt.

I looked at Laird, who did not even remember this, and I did not like the look on this thin, winter-pale face. His expression was not frightened or upset, but remote, concentrating. "Listen," I said, in an unusually bright and friendly voice, "you aren't going to tell, are you?"

"No," he said absently.

"Promise."

"Promise," he said. I grabbed the hand behind his back to make sure he was not crossing his fingers. Even so, he might have a nightmare; it might come out that way. I decided I had better work hard to get all thoughts of what he had seen out of his mind—which, it seemed to me, could not hold very many things at a time. I got some money I had saved and that afternoon we went into Jubilee and saw a show, with Judy Canova,[3] at which we both laughed a great deal. After that I thought it would be all right.

Two weeks later I knew they were going to shoot Flora. I knew from the night before, when I heard my mother ask if the hay was holding out all right, and my father said, "Well, after tomorrow there'll just be the cow, and we should be able to put her out to grass in another week." So I knew it was Flora's turn in the morning.

This time I didn't think of watching it. That was something to see just one time. I had not thought about it very often since, but sometimes when I was busy, working at school, or standing in front of the mirror combing my hair and wondering if I would be pretty when I grew up, the whole scene would flash into my mind: I would see the easy, practiced way my father raised the gun, and hear

40

---

[3] American comedian, popular in films of the 1940s.

Henry laughing when Mack kicked his legs in the air. I did not have any great feeling of horror and opposition, such as a city child might have had; I was too used to seeing the death of animals as a necessity by which we lived. Yet I felt a little ashamed, and there was a new wariness, a sense of holding-off, in my attitude to my father and his work.

It was a fine day, and we were going around the yard picking up tree branches that had been torn off in winter storms. This was something we had been told to do, and also we wanted to use them to make a teepee. We heard Flora whinny, and then my father's voice and Henry's shouting, and we ran down to the barnyard to see what was going on.

The stable door was open. Henry had just brought Flora out, and she had broken away from him. She was running free in the barnyard, from one end to the other. We climbed up on the fence. It was exciting to see her running, whinnying, going up on her hind legs, prancing and threatening like a horse in a Western movie, an unbroken ranch horse, though she was just an old driver, an old sorrel mare. My father and Henry ran after her and tried to grab the dangling halter. They tried to work her into a corner, and they had almost succeeded when she made a run between them, wild-eyed, and disappeared around the corner of the barn. We heard the rails clatter down as she got over the fence, and Henry yelled. "She's into the field now!"

That meant she was in the long L-shaped field that ran up by the house. If she got around the center, heading towards the lane, the gate was open; the truck had been driven into the field this morning. My father shouted to me, because I was on the other side of the fence, nearest the lane, "Go shut the gate!"

I could run very fast. I ran across the garden, past the tree where our swing was hung, and jumped across a ditch into the lane. There was the open gate. She had not got out, I could not see her up on the road; she must have run to the other end of the field. The gate was heavy. I lifted it out of the gravel and carried it across the roadway. I had it halfway across when she came in sight, galloping straight toward me. There was just time to get the chain on. Laird came scrambling through the ditch to help me.

Instead of shutting the gate, I opened it as wide as I could. I did not make any decision to do this, it was just what I did. Flora never slowed down; she galloped straight past me, and Laird jumped up and down, yelling, "Shut it, shut it!" even after it was too late. My father and Henry appeared in the field a moment too late to see what I had done. They only saw Flora heading for the township road. They would think I had not got there in time.

They did not waste any time asking about it. They went back to the barn and got the gun and the knives they used, and put these in the truck; then they turned the truck around and came bouncing up the field toward us. Laird called to them, "Let me go too, let me go too!" and Henry stopped the truck and they took him in. I shut the gate after they were all gone.

I supposed Laird would tell. I wondered what would happen to me. I had never disobeyed my father before, and I could not understand why I had done it. Flora would not really get away. They would catch up with her in the truck. Or if they did not catch her this morning somebody would see her and telephone us this afternoon or tomorrow. There was no wild country here for her to run to, only farms. What was more, my father had paid for her, we needed the meat to feed the foxes, we needed the foxes to make our living. All I had done was make more work for my father who worked hard enough already. And when my father found out about it he was not going to trust me any more; he would know that I was not entirely on his side. I was on Flora's side, and that made me no use to anybody, not even to her. Just the same, I did not regret it; when she came running at me and I held the gate open, that was the only thing I could do.

I went back to the house, and my mother said. "What's all the commotion?" I told her that Flora had kicked down the fence and got away. "Your poor father," she said, "now he'll have to go chasing over the countryside. Well, there isn't any use planning dinner before one." She put up the ironing board. I wanted to tell her, but thought better of it and went upstairs and sat on my bed.

Lately I had been trying to make my part of the room fancy, spreading the bed with old lace curtains, and fixing myself a dressing table with some leftovers of cretonne for a skirt. I planned to put up some kind of barricade between my bed and Laird's, to keep my section separate from his. In the sunlight, the lace curtains were just dusty rags. We did not sing at night any more. One night when I was singing Laird said, "You sound silly," and I went right on but the next night I did not start. There was not so much need to anyway, we were no longer afraid. We knew it was just old furniture over there, old jumble and confusion. We did not keep to the rules. I still stayed awake after Laird was asleep and told myself stories, but even in these stories something different was happening, mysterious alterations took place. A story might start off in the old way, with a spectacular danger, a fire or wild animals, and for a while I might rescue people; then things would change around, and instead, somebody would be rescuing me. It might be a boy from our class at school, or even Mr. Campbell, our teacher, who tickled girls under the arms. And at this point the story concerned itself at great length with what I looked like—how long my hair was, and what kind of dress I had on; by the time I had these details worked out the real excitement of the story was lost.

It was later than one o'clock when the truck came back. The tarpaulin was over the back, which meant there was meat in it. My mother had to heat dinner up all over again. Henry and my father had changed from their bloody overalls into ordinary working overalls in the barn, and they washed their arms and necks and faces at the sink, and splashed water on their hair and combed it. Laird lifted his arm to show off a streak of blood. "We shot old Flora," he said, "and cut her up in fifty pieces."

"Well I don't want to hear about it," my mother said. "And don't come to my table like that."

My father made him go and wash the blood off.   55

We sat down and my father said grace and Henry pasted his chewing gum on the end of his fork, the way he always did; when he took it off he would have us admire the pattern. We began to pass the bowls of steaming, overcooked vegetables. Laird looked across the table at me and said proudly, distinctly, "Anyway it was her fault Flora got away."

"What?" my father said.

"She could of shut the gate and she didn't. She just open' it up and Flora run out."

"Is that right?" my father said.

Everybody at the table was looking at me. I nodded, swallowing food with great difficulty. To my shame, tears flooded my eyes.   60

My father made a curt sound of disgust. "What did you do that for?"

I did not answer. I put down my fork and waited to be sent from the table, still not looking up.

But this did not happen. For some time nobody said anything, then Laird said matter-of-factly, "She's crying."

"Never mind," my father said. He spoke with resignation, even good humor, the words which absolved and dismissed me for good. "She's only a girl," he said.

I didn't protest that, even in my heart. Maybe it was true.   65

QUESTIONS AND SUGGESTIONS FOR WRITING

1. Explain, in a paragraph, what the narrator means when she says (paragraph 21), "The word *girl* had formerly seemed to me innocent and unburdened, like the word *child*; now it appeared that it was no such thing. A girl was not, as I had supposed, simply what I was; it was what I had to become."
2. The narrator says that she "could not understand" why she disobeyed her father and allowed the horse to escape. Can you explain her action to her? If so, do so.
3. In a paragraph, characterize the mother.

☐ POETRY

Robert Frost (American. 1874–1963)

STOPPING BY WOODS
ON A SNOWY EVENING

Whose woods these are I think I know.
His house is in the village though;
He will not see me stopping here
To watch his woods fill up with snow.   4

My little horse must think it queer
To stop without a farmhouse near
Between the woods and frozen lake
The darkest evening of the year.   8

He gives his harness bells a shake
To ask if there is some mistake.
The only other sound's the sweep
Of easy wind and downy flake.   12

The woods are lovely, dark and deep.
But I have promises to keep,
And miles to go before I sleep,
And miles to go before I sleep.   16

QUESTIONS AND SUGGESTIONS FOR WRITING

1. Line 5 originally read: "The steaming horses think it queer." Line 7 read: "Between a forest and a lake." Evaluate the changes.
2. The rhyming words in the first stanza can be indicated by *aaba;* the second stanza picks up the *b* rhyme: *bbcb.* Indicate the rhymes for the third stanza. For the fourth. Why is it appropriate that the rhyme scheme differs in the fourth stanza?
3. Hearing that the poem had been interpreted as a "death poem," Frost said, "I never intended that, but I did have the feeling it was loaded with ulteriority." What "ulteriority" is implicit? How is the time of day and year significant? How does the horse's attitude make a contrast with the man's?

Robert Frost (American. 1874–1963)

MENDING WALL

Something there is that doesn't love a wall,
That sends the frozen-ground-swell under it,
And spills the upper boulder, in the sun;
And makes gaps even two can pass abreast.
The work of hunters is another thing: 5
I have come after them and made repair
Where they have left not one stone on a stone,
But they would have the rabbit out of hiding,
To please the yelping dogs. The gaps I mean,
No one has seen them made or heard them made,   10
But at spring mending-time we find them there.
I let my neighbor know beyond the hill;
And on a day we meet to walk the line
And set the wall between us once again.
We keep the wall between us as we go.   15
To each the boulders that have fallen to each.
And some are loaves and some so nearly balls
We have to use a spell to make them balance:
"Stay where you are until our backs are turned!"
We wear our fingers rough with handling them.   20
Oh, just another kind of outdoor game,
One on a side. It comes to little more:
There where it is we do not need the wall:
He is all pine and I am apple orchard.
My apple trees will never get across   25
And eat the cones under his pines, I tell him.

He only says, "Good fences make good neighbors."
Spring is the mischief in me, and I wonder
If I could put a notion in his head:
"*Why* do they make good neighbors? Isn't it   30
Where there are cows? But here there are no cows.
Before I built a wall I'd ask to know
What I was walling in or walling out,
And to whom I was like to give offense.
Something there is that doesn't love a wall,   35
That wants it down." I could say "Elves" to him,
But it's not elves exactly, and I'd rather
He said it for himself. I see him there
Bringing a stone grasped firmly by the top
In each hand, like an old-stone savage armed.   40
He moves in darkness as it seems to me,
Not of woods only and the shade of trees.
He will not go behind his father's saying,
And he likes having thought of it so well
He says again, "Good fences make good neighbors."   45

QUESTIONS AND SUGGESTIONS FOR WRITING

1. Compare and contrast the speaker and the neighbor.
2. Notice that the speaker, not the neighbor, initiates the business of repairing the wall (line 12). Why do you think he does this?
3. Write an essay of 500 words, telling of an experience in which you came to conclude that "good fences make good neighbors." Or tell of an experience that led you to conclude that fences (they can be figurative fences, of course) are detrimental.

Robert Frost (American. 1874–1963)

THE ROAD NOT TAKEN

Two roads diverged in a yellow wood, *A*
And sorry I could not travel both *B*
And be one traveler, long I stood *A*
And looked down one as far as I could *B*
To where it bent in the undergrowth; *B*   5

Then took the other, as just as fair, *A*
And having perhaps the better claim, *B*
Because it was grassy and wanted wear; *A*
Though as for that the passing there *A*
Had worn them really about the same, *B*   10

And both that morning equally lay
In leaves no step had trodden black.

Oh, I kept the first for another day!
Yet knowing how way leads on to way,
I doubted if I should ever come back.   15

I shall be telling this with a sigh
Somewhere ages and ages hence:
Two roads diverged in a wood, and I—
I took the one less traveled by,
And that has made all the difference.   20

QUESTIONS AND SUGGESTIONS FOR WRITING

1. Suppose that someone said to you that the poem is simply about walking in the woods and choosing one road rather than another. In an essay of 250 words set forth your response. (You may, of course, agree with the view, in which case you will offer supporting evidence.)
2. In a paragraph discuss whether it would make any difference if instead of "yellow" in the first line the poet had written "bright green" (or "dark green").
3. Why do you think that Frost says he (or, more strictly, the speaker of the poem) will later be telling this story "with a sigh"? Set forth your response in a paragraph.

Robert Frost (American. 1874–1963)

THE WOOD-PILE

Out walking in the frozen swamp one gray day,
I paused and said, "I will turn back from here.
No, I will go on farther—and we shall see."
The hard snow held me, save where now and then
One foot went through. The view was all in lines   5
Straight up and down of tall slim trees
Too much alike to mark or name a place by
So as to say for certain I was here
Or somewhere else: I was just far from home.
A small bird flew before me. He was careful   10
To put a tree between us when he lighted,
And say no word to tell me who he was
Who was so foolish as to think what *he* thought.
He thought that I was after him for a feather—
The white one in his tail; like one who takes   15
Everything said as personal to himself.
One flight out sideways would have undeceived him.
And then there was a pile of wood for which
I forgot him and let his little fear
Carry him off the way I might have gone,   20
Without so much as wishing him good-night.

He went behind it to make his last stand.
It was a cord of maple, cut and split
And piled—and measured, four by four by eight.
And not another like it could I see.   25
No runner tracks in this year's snow looped near it.
And it was older sure than this year's cutting,
Or even last year's or the year's before.
The wood was gray and the bark warping off it
And the pile somewhat sunken. Clematis   30
Had wound strings round and round it like a bundle.
What held it though on one side was a tree
Still growing, and on one a stake and prop,
These latter about to fall. I thought that only
Someone who lived in turning to fresh tasks   35
Could so forget his handiwork in which
He spent himself, the labor of his axe,
And leave it there far from a useful fireplace
To warm the frozen swamp as best it could
With the slow smokeless burning of decay.   40

QUESTIONS AND SUGGESTIONS FOR WRITING

1. What is the contrast that Frost makes between human beings and nature?
2. What does he say about the relationship between human beings and nature?

T. S. Eliot (English. 1888–1965)

THE LOVE SONG OF J. ALFRED PRUFROCK

S'io credesse che mia risposta fosse
A persona che mai tornasse al mondo,
Questa fiamma staria senza piu scosse.
Ma perciocche giammai di questo fondo
Non torno vivo alcun, s' i' odo il vero,
Senza tema d'infama ti rispondo.*

*In Dante's *Inferno* XXVII:61–66, a damned soul who had sought absolution before committing a crime addresses Dante, thinking that his words will never reach the earth: "If I believed that my answer were to a person who could ever return to the world, this flame would no longer quiver. But because no one ever returned from this depth, if what I hear is true, without fear of infamy, I answer you."

Explanations of allusions in the poem may be helpful. "Works and days" (line 29) is the title of a poem on farm life by Hesiod (eighth century B.C.); "dying fall" (line 52) echoes Shakespeare's *Twelfth Night* I.i.4; lines 81–83 allude to John the Baptist (see Matthew 14:1–11); line 92 echoes lines 41–42 of Marvell's "To His Coy Mistress" (see page 372); for "Lazarus" (line 94) see Luke 16 and John 11; lines 112–117 allude to Polonius and perhaps to other figures in *Hamlet*; "full of high sentence" (line 117) comes from Chaucer's description of the Clerk of Oxford in the *Canterbury Tales*.—ED.

Let us go then, you and I,
When the evening is spread out against the sky
Like a patient etherized upon a table;
Let us go, through certain half-deserted streets,
The muttering retreats   5
Of restless nights in one-night cheap hotels
And sawdust restaurants with oyster-shells:
Streets that follow like a tedious argument
Of insidious intent
To lead you to an overwhelming question . . .   10
Oh, do not ask, "What is it?"
Let us go and make our visit.

In the room the women come and go
Talking of Michelangelo.

The yellow fog that rubs its back upon the window-panes,   15
The yellow smoke that rubs its muzzle on the window-panes
Licked its tongue into the corners of the evening,
Lingered upon the pools that stand in drains,
Let fall upon its back the soot that falls from chimneys,
Slipped by the terrace, made a sudden leap,   20
And seeing that it was a soft October night,
Curled once about the house, and fell asleep.

And indeed there will be time
For the yellow smoke that slides along the street,
Rubbing its back upon the window-panes;   25
There will be time, there will be time
To prepare a face to meet the faces that you meet;
There will be time to murder and create,
And time for all the works and days of hands
That lift and drop a question on your plate;   30
Time for you and time for me,
And time yet for a hundred indecisions,
And for a hundred visions and revisions,
Before the taking of a toast and tea.

In the room the women come and go   35
Talking of Michelangelo.

And indeed there will be time
To wonder, "Do I dare?" and, "Do I dare?"
Time to turn back and descend the stair,
With a bald spot in the middle of my hair—   40
[They will say: "How his hair is growing thin!"]
My morning coat, my collar mounting firmly to the chin,
My necktie rich and modest, but asserted by a simple pin—

[They will say: "But how his arms and legs are thin!"]
Do I dare   45
Disturb the universe?
In a minute there is time
For decisions and revisions which a minute will reverse.

For I have known them all already, known them all: —
Have known the evenings, mornings, afternoons,   50
I have measured out my life with coffee spoons;
I know the voices dying with a dying fall
Beneath the music from a farther room.
        So how should I presume?

And I have known the eyes already, known them all—   55
The eyes that fix you in a formulated phrase,
And when I am formulated, sprawling on a pin,
When I am pinned and wriggling on the wall,
Then how should I begin
To spit out all the butt-ends of my days and ways?   60
        And how should I presume?

And I have known the arms already, known them all—
Arms that are braceleted and white and bare
[But in the lamplight, downed with light brown hair!]

Is it perfume from a dress   65
That makes me so digress?
Arms that lie along a table, or wrap about a shawl.
        And should I then presume?
        And how should I begin?

                    .   .   .   .   .

Shall I say, I have gone at dusk through narrow streets   70
And watched the smoke that rises from the pipes
Of lonely men in shirt-sleeves, leaning out of windows? . . .

I should have been a pair of ragged claws
Scuttling across the floors of silent seas.

                    .   .   .   .   .

And the afternoon, the evening, sleeps so peacefully!   75
Smoothed by long fingers,
Asleep . . . tired . . . or it malingers,
Stretched on the floor, here beside you and me.
Should I, after tea and cakes and ices,
Have the strength to force the moment to its crisis?   80
But though I have wept and fasted, wept and prayed,
Though I have seen my head [grown slightly bald]
        brought in upon a platter,

I am no prophet—and here's no great matter;
I have seen the moment of my greatness flicker,
And I have seen the eternal Footman hold my coat, and snicker,   85
And in short, I was afraid.

And would it have been worth it, after all,
After the cups, the marmalade, the tea,
Among the porcelain, among some talk of you and me,
Would it have been worth while,   90
To have bitten off the matter with a smile,
To have squeezed the universe into a ball
To roll it toward some overwhelming question,
To say: "I am Lazarus, come from the dead,
Come back to tell you all, I shall tell you all"—   95
If one, settling a pillow by her head,
        Should say: "That is not what I meant at all.
        That is not it, at all."

And would it have been worth it, after all,
Would it have been worth while,   100
After the sunsets and the dooryards and the sprinkled streets,
After the novels, after the teacups, after the skirts
        that trail along the floor—
And this, and so much more?—
It is impossible to say just what I mean!
But as if a magic lantern threw the nerves in patterns
        on a screen: 105
Would it have been worth while
If one, settling a pillow or throwing off a shawl,
And turning toward the window, should say:
        "That is not it at all,
        That is not what I meant, at all."   110

                    ·   ·   ·   ·   ·

No! I am not Prince Hamlet, nor was meant to be;
Am an attendant lord, one that will do
To swell a progress, start a scene or two,
Advise the prince; no doubt, an easy tool,
Deferential, glad to be of use,   115
Politic, cautious, and meticulous;
Full of high sentence, but a bit obtuse;
At times, indeed, almost ridiculous—
Almost, at times, the Fool.

I grow old . . . I grow old . . .   120
I shall wear the bottoms of my trousers rolled.

Shall I part my hair behind? Do I dare to eat a peach?
I shall wear white flannel trousers, and walk upon the beach.
I have heard the mermaids singing, each to each.
I do not think that they will sing to me.   125

I have seen them riding seaward on the waves
Combing the white hair of the waves blown back
When the wind blows the water white and black.

We have lingered in the chambers of the sea   130
By sea-girls wreathed with seaweed red and brown
Till human voices wake us, and we drown.

QUESTIONS AND SUGGESTIONS FOR WRITING

1. Consider the possibility that the "you" whom Prufrock is addressing is not a listener
   but is one aspect of Prufrock, and the "I" is another. Given this possibility, in a
   paragraph characterize the "you," and in another paragraph characterize the "I."
2. In a paragraph, characterize Prufrock as he might be characterized by one of the
   women in the poem, and then, in a paragraph or two, offer your own characterization
   of him.

W. H. Auden (American. 1907–1973)
MUSÉE DES BEAUX ARTS

About suffering they were never wrong,
The Old Masters: how well they understood
Its human position; how it takes place
While someone else is eating or opening a window or just walking dully along;
How, when the aged are reverently, passionately waiting   5
For the miraculous birth, there always must be
Children who did not specially want it to happen, skating
On a pond at the edge of the wood:
They never forgot
That even the dreadful martyrdom must run its course   10
Anyhow in a corner, some untidy spot
Where the dogs go on with their doggy life and the torturer's horse
Scratches its innocent behind on a tree.

In Brueghel's *Icarus,** for instance: how everything turns away
Quite leisurely from the disaster; the plowman may   15

*Painting by the Flemish painter Pieter Brueghel (c. 1522–1569) that now hangs in the Brussels
Museum of Fine Arts.

Have heard the splash, the forsaken cry,
But for him it was not an important failure; the sun shone
As it had to on the white legs disappearing into the green
Water; and the expensive delicate ship that must have seen
Something amazing, a boy falling out of the sky,   20
Had somewhere to get to and sailed calmly on.

QUESTIONS AND SUGGESTIONS FOR WRITING

1. Reread the poem (preferably over the course of several days) a number of times, jotting down your chief responses after each reading. Then, in connection with a final reading, study your notes, and write an essay of 500 words setting forth the history of your final response to the poem. For example, you may want to report that certain difficulties soon were clarified, and that your enjoyment increased. Or, conversely, you may want to report that the poem became less interesting (for reasons you will set forth) the more you studied it. Probably your history will be somewhat more complicated than these simple examples. Try to find a chief pattern in your experience, and shape it into a thesis.
2. Consider a picture, either in a local museum or reproduced in a book, and write a 500-word reflection on it. If the picture is not well known, include a reproduction (a postcard from the museum, or a photocopy of a page of the book) with your essay.

W. H. Auden (American. 1907–1973)

THE UNKNOWN CITIZEN
(To JS/07/M/378
This Marble Monument
Is Erected by the State)

He was found by the Bureau of Statistics to be
One against whom there was no official complaint,
And all the reports on his conduct agree
That, in the modern sense of an old-fashioned word, he was a saint,
For in everything he did he served the Greater Community.   5
Except for the War till the day he retired
He worked in a factory and never got fired,
But satisfied his employers, Fudge Motors Inc.
Yet he wasn't a scab or odd in his views,
For his Union reports that he paid his dues,   10
(Our report on his Union shows it was sound)
And our Social Psychology workers found
That he was popular with his mates and liked a drink.
The press are convinced that he bought a paper every day
And that his reactions to advertisements were normal in every way.   15

Policies taken out in his name prove that he was fully insured,
And his Health-card shows he was once in hospital but left it cured.
Both Producers Research and High-Grade Living declare
He was fully sensible to the advantages of the Installment Plan
And had everything necessary to the Modern Man, 20
A phonograph, radio, a car and a frigidaire.
Our researches into Public Opinion are content
That he held the proper opinions for the time of year;
When there was peace, he was for peace; when there was war, he went.
He was married and added five children to the population, 25
Which our Eugenist says was the right number for a parent of his generation,
And our teachers report that he never interfered with their education.
Was he free? Was he happy? The question is absurd:
Had anything been wrong, we should certainly have heard.

QUESTIONS AND SUGGESTIONS FOR WRITING

1. Was he free? Was he happy? Explain.
2. In a paragraph or two, sketch the values of the speaker of the poem, and then sum them up in a sentence or two. Finally, in as much space as you feel you need, judge these values.

Marge Piercy (Canadian. b. 1936)
BARBIE DOLL

This girlchild was born as usual
and presented dolls that did pee-pee
and miniature GE stoves and irons
and wee lipsticks the color of cherry candy.
Then in the magic of puberty, a classmate said: 5
You have a great big nose and fat legs.

She was healthy, tested intelligent,
possessed strong arms and back,
abundant sexual drive and manual dexterity.
She went to and fro apologizing. 10
Everyone saw a fat nose on thick legs.

She was advised to play coy,
exhorted to come on hearty,
exercise, diet, smile and wheedle. 15
Her good nature wore out
like a fan belt.
So she cut off her nose and her legs
and offered them up.

In the casket displayed on satin she lay
with the undertaker's cosmetics painted on,   20
a turned-up putty nose,
dressed in a pink and white nightie.
Doesn't she look pretty? everyone said.
Consummation at last.
To every woman a happy ending.   25

QUESTIONS AND SUGGESTIONS FOR WRITING

1. Do you have any particular attitude(s) toward Barbie Dolls? Do you find them attractive? Repellent? Whatever your response, set it forth in a paragraph.
2. In a paragraph explain why the poem is called "Barbie Doll."
3. What voice do you hear in lines 1–4? Line 6 is, we are told, the voice of "a classmate." How do these voices differ? What voice do you hear in the first three lines of the second stanza?
4. Explain in your own words what Piercy is saying about women in this poem. Does her view seem to you fair, slightly exaggerated, or greatly exaggerated?

Marge Piercy (Canadian. b. 1936)

WHAT'S THAT SMELL IN THE KITCHEN?

All over America women are burning dinners.
It's lambchops in Peoria; it's haddock
in Providence; it's steak in Chicago;
tofu delight in Big Sur; red
rice and beans in Dallas.   5
All over America women are burning
food they're supposed to bring with calico
smile on platters glittering like wax.
Anger sputters in her brainpan, confined
but spewing out missiles of hot fat.   10
Carbonized despair presses like a clinker
from a barbecue against the back of her eyes.
If she wants to grill anything, it's
her husband spitted over a slow fire.
If she wants to serve him anything   15
it's a dead rat with a bomb in its belly
ticking like the heart of an insomniac.
Her life is cooked and digested,
nothing but leftovers in Tupperware.
Look, she says, once I was roast duck   20
on your platter with parsley but now I am Spam.
Burning dinner is not incompetence but war.

QUESTIONS AND SUGGESTIONS FOR WRITING

1. Suppose a friend told you that she didn't understand lines 20–21. How would you paraphrase the lines?
2. Who speaks the title?
3. If a poem begins, "All over America women are . . . ," what words might a reader reasonably expect next?
4. Do you take the poem to be chiefly comic? Superficially but essentially comic but a work with a serious purpose? Or what?

□ DRAMA

Henrik Ibsen (Norwegian. 1828–1906)

A DOLL'S HOUSE

Translated by Otto Reinert

List of Characters

TORVALD HELMER, *a lawyer*
NORA, *his wife*
DR. RANK
MRS. LINDE
KROGSTAD
THE HELMERS' THREE SMALL CHILDREN
ANNE-MARIE, *the children's nurse*
A HOUSEMAID
A PORTER

Scene: *The Helmers' living room.*

ACT I

A pleasant, tastefully but not expensively furnished, living room. A door on the rear wall, right, leads to the front hall, another door, left, to HELMER's *study. Between the two doors a piano. A third door in the middle of the left wall; further front a window. Near the window a round table with easy chairs and a small couch. Toward the rear of the right wall a fourth door; further front a tile stove with a rocking chair and a couple of armchairs in front of it. Between the stove and the side door a small table. Copperplate etchings on the walls. A whatnot with porcelain figurines and other small objects. A small bookcase with de luxe editions. A rug on the floor; fire in the stove. Winter day. The doorbell rings, then the sound of the front door opening.* NORA, *dressed for out-doors, enters, humming cheerfully. She carries several packages, which she puts down on the table, right. She leaves the door to the front hall open; there a* PORTER *is seen holding a Christmas tree and a basket. He gives them to the* MAID, *who has let them in.*

NORA. Be sure to hide the Christmas tree, Helene. The children mustn't see it before tonight when we've trimmed it. *(Opens her purse; to the* PORTER.) How much?

PORTER. Fifty øre.

NORA. Here's a crown. No, keep the change. *(The* PORTER *thanks her, leaves.* NORA *closes the door. She keeps laughing quietly to herself as she takes off her coat, etc. She takes a bag of macaroons from her pocket and eats a couple. She walks cautiously over to the door to the study and listens.)* Yes, he's home. *(Resumes her humming, walks over to the table, right.)*

HELMER *(in his study).* Is that my little lark twittering out there?

NORA *(opening some of the packages).* That's right.

HELMER. My squirrel bustling about?

NORA. Yes.

HELMER. When did squirrel come home?

NORA. Just now. *(Puts the bag of macaroons back in her pocket, wipes her mouth.)* Come out here, Torvald. I want to show you what I've bought.

HELMER. I'm busy! *(After a little while he opens the door and looks in, pen in hand.)* Bought, eh? All that? So little wastrel has been throwing money around again?

NORA. Oh but Torvald, this Christmas we can be a little extravagant, can't we? It's the first Christmas we don't have to scrimp.

HELMER. I don't know about that. We certainly don't have money to waste.

NORA. Yes, Torvald, we do. A little, anyway. Just a tiny little bit? Now that you're going to get that big salary and make lots and lots of money.

HELMER. Starting at New Year's, yes. But payday isn't till the end of the quarter.

NORA. That doesn't matter. We can always borrow.

HELMER. Nora! *(Goes over to her and playfully pulls her ear.)* There you go being irresponsible again. Suppose I borrowed a thousand crowns today and you spent it all for Christmas and on New Year's Eve a tile hit me in the head and laid me out cold.

NORA *(putting her hand over his mouth).* I won't have you say such horrid things.

HELMER. But suppose it happened. Then what?

NORA. If it did, I wouldn't care whether we owed money or not.

HELMER. But what about the people I had borrowed from?

NORA. Who cares about them! They are strangers.

HELMER. Nora, Nora, you *are* a woman.

No, really! You know how I feel about that. No debts! A home in debt isn't a free home, and if it isn't free it isn't beautiful. We've managed nicely so far, you and I, and that's the way we'll go on. It won't be for much longer.

NORA *(walks over toward the stove).* All right, Torvald. Whatever you say.

HELMER *(follows her).* Come, come, my little songbird mustn't droop her wings. What's this? Can't have a pouty squirrel in the house, you know. *(Takes out his wallet.)* Nora, what do you think I have here?

NORA *(turns around quickly).* Money!

HELMER. Here. *(Gives her some bills.)* Don't you think I know Christmas is expensive?

NORA *(counting).* Ten—twenty—thirty—forty. Thank you, thank you, Torvald. This helps a lot.

HELMER. I certainly hope so.

NORA. It does, it does. But I want to show you what I got. It was cheap, too. Look. New clothes for Ivar. And a sword. And a horse and trumpet for Bob. And a doll and a little bed for Emmy. It isn't any good, but it wouldn't last, anyway. And here's some dress material and scarves for the maids. I feel bad about old Anne-Marie, though. She really should be getting much more.

HELMER. And what's in here?

NORA *(cries).* Not till tonight!

HELMER. I see. But now what does my little prodigal have in mind for herself?

NORA. Oh, nothing. I really don't care.

HELMER. Of course you do. Tell me what you'd like. Within reason.

NORA. Oh, I don't know. Really, I don't. The only thing—

HELMER. Well?

NORA *(fiddling with his buttons, without looking at him).* If you really want to give me something, you might—you could—

HELMER. All right, let's have it.

NORA *(quickly).* Some money, Torvald. Just as much as you think you can spare. Then I'll buy myself something one of these days.

HELMER. No, really Nora—

NORA. Oh yes, please, Torvald. Please? I'll wrap the money in pretty gold paper and hang it on the tree. Won't that be nice?

HELMER. What's the name for little birds that are always spending money?

NORA. Wastrels, I know. But please let's do it my way, Torvald. Then I'll have time to decide what I need most. Now that's sensible, isn't it?

HELMER *(smiling)*. Oh, very sensible. That is, if you really bought yourself something you could use. But it all disappears in the household expenses or you buy things you don't need. And then you come back to me for more.

NORA. Oh, but Torvald—

HELMER. That's the truth, dear little Nora, and you know it. *(Puts his arm around her.)* My wastrel is a little sweetheart, but she *does* go through an awful lot of money awfully fast. You've no idea how expensive it is for a man to keep a wastrel.

NORA. That's not fair, Torvald. I really save all I can.

HELMER *(laughs)*. Oh, I believe that. All you can. Meaning, exactly nothing!

NORA *(hums, smiles mysteriously)*. You don't know all the things we songbirds and squirrels need money for, Torvald.

HELMER. You know, you're funny. Just like your father. You're always looking for ways to get money, but as soon as you do it runs through your fingers and you can never say what you spent it for. Well, I guess I'll just have to take you the way you are. It's in your blood. Yes, that sort of thing is hereditary, Nora.

NORA. In that case, I wish I had inherited many of Daddy's qualities.

HELMER. And I don't want you any different from just what you are—my own sweet little songbird. Hey!—I think I just noticed something. Aren't you looking—what's the word?—a little—sly—?

NORA. I am?

HELMER. You definitely are. Look at me.

NORA *(looks at him)*. Well?

HELMER *(wagging a finger)*. Little sweettooth hasn't by any chance been on a rampage today, has she?

NORA. Of course not. Whatever makes you think that?

HELMER. A little detour by the pastryshop maybe?

NORA. No, I assure you, Torvald—

HELMER. Nibbled a little jam?

NORA. Certainly not!

HELMER. Munched a macaroon or two?

NORA. No, really, Torvald, I honestly—

HELMER. All right. Of course I was only joking.

NORA *(walks toward the table, right)*. You know I wouldn't do anything to displease you.

HELMER. I know. And I have your promise. *(Over to her.)* All right, keep your little Christmas secrets to yourself, Nora darling. They'll all come out tonight, I suppose, when we light the tree.

NORA. Did you remember to invite Rank?

HELMER. No, but there's no need to. He knows he'll have dinner with us. Anyway, I'll see him later this morning. I'll ask him then. I did order some good wine. Oh Nora, you've no idea how much I'm looking forward to tonight!

NORA. Me too. And the children, Torvald! They'll have such a good time!

HELMER. You know, it *is* nice to have a good, safe job and a comfortable income. Feels good just thinking about it. Don't you agree?

NORA. Oh, it's wonderful!

HELMER. Remember last Christmas? For three whole weeks you shut yourself up every evening till long after midnight, making ornaments for the Christmas tree and I don't know what else. Some big surprise for all of us, anyway. I'll be damned if I've ever been so bored in my whole life!

NORA. I wasn't bored at all.

HELMER *(smiling)*. But you've got to admit you didn't have much to show for it in the end.

NORA. Oh, don't tease me again about that! Could I help it that the cat got in and tore up everything?

HELMER. Of course you couldn't, my poor little Nora. You just wanted to please the rest of us, and that's the important thing. But I *am* glad the hard times are behind us. Aren't you?

NORA. Oh yes. I think it's just wonderful.

HELMER. This year I won't be bored and lonely. And you won't have to strain your dear eyes and your delicate little hands—

NORA *(claps her hands).* No I won't will I, Torvald? Oh, how wonderful, how lovely, to hear you say that! *(Puts her arm under his.)* Let me tell you how I think we should arrange things, Torvald. Soon as Christmas is over— *(The doorbell rings.)* Someone's at the door. *(Straightens things up a bit.)* A caller, I suppose. Bother!

HELMER. Remember, I'm not home for visitors.

THE MAID *(in the door to the front hall).* Ma'am, there's a lady here—

NORA. All right. Ask her to come in.

THE MAID *(to* HELMER*).* And the Doctor just arrived.

HELMER. Is he in the study?

THE MAID. Yes, sir.

HELMER *exits into his study. The* MAID *shows* MRS. LINDE *in and closes the door behind her as she leaves.* MRS. LINDE *is in travel dress.*

MRS. LINDE *(timid and a little hesitant).* Good morning, Nora.

NORA *(uncertainly).* Good morning.

MRS. LINDE. I don't believe you know who I am.

NORA. No—I'm not sure—Though I know I should—Of course! Kristine! It's you!

MRS. LINDE. Yes, it's me.

NORA. And I didn't even recognize you! I had no idea! *(In a lower voice.)* You've changed, Kristine.

MRS. LINDE. I'm sure I have. It's been nine or ten long years.

NORA. Has it really been that long? Yes, you're right. I've been so happy these last eight years. And now you're here. Such a long trip in the middle of winter. How brave!

MRS. LINDE. I got in on the steamer this morning.

NORA. To have some fun over the holidays, of course. That's lovely. For we *are* going to have fun. But take off your coat! You aren't cold, are you? *(Helps her.)* There, now! Let's sit down here by the fire and just relax and talk. No, you sit there. I want the rocking chair. *(Takes her hands.)* And now you've got your old face back. It was just for a minute, right at first— Though you are a little more pale, Kristine. And maybe a little thinner.

MRS. LINDE. And much, much older, Nora.

NORA. Maybe a little older. Just a teeny-weeny bit, not much. *(Interrupts herself, serious.)* Oh, but how thoughtless of me, chatting away like this! Sweet, good Kristine, can you forgive me?

MRS. LINDE. Forgive you what, Nora?

NORA *(in a low voice).* You poor dear, you lost your husband, didn't you?

MRS. LINDE. Three years ago, yes.

NORA. I know. I saw it in the paper. Oh please believe me, Kristine. I really meant to write you, but I never got around to it. Something was always coming up.

MRS. LINDE. Of course, Nora. I understand.

NORA. No, that wasn't very nice of me. You poor thing, all you must have been through. And he didn't leave you much, either, did he?

MRS. LINDE. No.

NORA. And no children?

MRS. LINDE. No.

NORA. Nothing at all, in other words?

MRS. LINDE. Not so much as a sense of loss—a grief to live on—

NORA *(incredulous).* But Kristine, how can that *be?*

MRS. LINDE *(with a sad smile, strokes* NORA*'s hair).* That's the way it sometimes is, Nora.

NORA. All alone. How awful for you. I have three darling children. You can't see them right now, though; they're out with their nurse. But now you must tell me everything—

MRS. LINDE. No, no; I'd rather listen to you.

NORA. No, you begin. Today I won't be selfish. Today I'll think only of you. Except there's one thing I've just got to tell you first. Something marvelous that's happened to us just these last few days. You haven't heard, have you?

MRS. LINDE. No; tell me.

NORA. Just think. My husband's been made manager of the Mutual Bank.

MRS. LINDE. Your husband—! Oh, I'm so glad!

NORA. Yes, isn't that great? You see, private law practice is so uncertain, especially when you won't have anything to do with cases that aren't—you know—quite nice. And of course Torvald won't do that, and I quite agree with him. Oh, you've no idea how delighted we are! He takes over at New Year's, and he'll be getting a big salary and all sorts of extras. From now on we'll be able to live in quite a different way— exactly as we like. Oh, Kristine! I feel so carefree and happy! It's lovely to have lots and lots of money and not have to worry about a thing! Don't you agree?

MRS. LINDE. It would be nice to have enough, at any rate.

NORA. No, I don't mean just enough. I mean lots and lots!

MRS. LINDE *(smiles)*. Nora, Nora, when are you going to be sensible? In school you spent a great deal of money.

NORA *(quietly laughing)*. Yes, and Torvald says I still do. *(Raises her finger at* MRS. LINDE.*)* But "Nora, Nora" isn't so crazy as you all think. Believe me, we've had nothing to be extravagant with. We've both had to work.

MRS. LINDE. You too?

NORA. Yes. Oh, it's been little things mostly—sewing, crocheting, embroidery— that sort of thing. *(Casually.)* And other things too. You know, of course, that Torvald left government service when we got married? There was no chance of promotion in his department, and of course he had to make more money than he had been making. So for the first few years he worked altogether too hard. He had to take jobs on the side and work night and day. It turned out to be too much for him. He became seriously ill. The doctors told him he needed to go south.

MRS. LINDE. That's right; you spent a year in Italy, didn't you?

NORA. Yes, we did. But you won't believe how hard it was to get away. Ivar had just been born. But of course we had to go. Oh, it was a wonderful trip. And it saved Torvald's life. But it took a lot of money, Kristine.

MRS. LINDE. I'm sure it did.

NORA. Twelve hundred specie dollars. Four thousand eight hundred crowns. That's a lot of money.

MRS. LINDE. Yes. So it's lucky you have it when something like that happens.

NORA. Well, actually we got the money from Daddy.

MRS. LINDE. I see. That was about the time your father died, I believe.

NORA. Yes, just about then. And I couldn't even go and take care of him. I was expecting little Ivar any day. And I had poor Torvald to look after, desperately sick and all. My dear, good Daddy! I never saw him again, Kristine. That's the saddest thing that's happened to me since I got married.

MRS. LINDE. I know you were very fond of him. But then you went to Italy?

NORA. Yes, for now we had the money, and the doctors urged us to go. So we left about a month later.

MRS. LINDE. And when you came back your husband was well again?

NORA. Healthy as a horse!

MRS. LINDE. But—the doctor?

NORA. What do you mean?

MRS. LINDE. I thought the maid said it was the doctor, that gentleman who came the same time I did.

NORA. Oh, that's Dr. Rank. He doesn't come as a doctor. He's our closest friend. He looks in at least once every day. No, Torvald hasn't been sick once since then. And the children are strong and healthy, too, and so am I. *(Jumps up and claps her hands.)* Oh God, Kristine! Isn't it wonderful to be alive and happy! Isn't it just lovely!—But now I'm being mean again, talking only about myself and my things. *(Sits down on a footstool close to* MRS. LINDE *and puts her arms on her lap.)* Please, don't be angry with me! Tell me, is it really true that you didn't care for your husband? Then why did you marry him?

MRS. LINDE. Mother was still alive then, but she was bedridden and helpless. And I had my two younger brothers to look after. I didn't think I had the right to turn him down.

NORA. No, I suppose not. So he had money then?

MRS. LINDE. He was quite well off, I think. But it was an uncertain business, Nora. When he died, the whole thing collapsed and there was nothing left.

NORA. And then—?

MRS. LINDE. Well, I had to manage as best I could. With a little store and a little school and anything else I could think of. The last three years have been one long work day for me, Nora, without any rest. But now it's over. My poor mother doesn't need me any more. She passed away. And the boys are on their own too. They've both got jobs and support themselves.

NORA. What a relief for you—

MRS. LINDE. No, not relief. Just a great emptiness. Nobody to live for any more. *(Gets up, restlessly.)* That's why I couldn't stand it any longer in that little hole. Here in town it has to be easier to find something to keep me busy and occupy my thoughts. With a little luck I should be able to find a permanent job, something in an office—

NORA. Oh but Kristine, that's exhausting work, and you look worn out already. It would be much better for you to go to a resort.

MRS. LINDE *(walks over to the window)*. I don't have a Daddy who can give me the money, Nora.

NORA *(getting up)*. Oh, don't be angry with me.

MRS. LINDE *(over to her)*. Dear Nora, don't *you* be angry with *me*. That's the worst thing about my kind of situation: you

become so bitter. You've nobody to work for, and yet you have to look out for yourself, somehow. You've got to keep on living, and so you become selfish. Do you know—when you told me about your husband's new position I was delighted not so much for your sake as for my own.

NORA. Why was that? Oh, I see. You think maybe Torvald can give you a job?

MRS. LINDE. That's what I had in mind.

NORA. And he will too, Kristine. Just leave it to me. I'll be ever so subtle about it. I'll think of something nice to tell him, something he'll like. Oh I so much want to help you.

MRS. LINDE. That's very good of you, Nora—making an effort like that for me. Especially since you've known so little trouble and hardship in your own life.

NORA. I—?—have known so little—?

MRS. LINDE *(smiling)*. Oh well, a little sewing or whatever it was. You're still a child, Nora.

NORA *(with a toss of her head, walks away)*. You shouldn't sound so superior.

MRS. LINDE. I shouldn't?

NORA. You're just like all the others. None of you think I'm good for anything really serious.

MRS. LINDE. Well, now—

NORA. That I've never been through anything difficult.

MRS. LINDE. But Nora! You just told me all your troubles!

NORA. That's nothing. *(Lowers her voice.)* I haven't told you about *it*.

MRS. LINDE. It? What's that? What do you mean?

NORA. You patronize me, Kristine, and that's not fair. You're proud that you worked so long and so hard for your mother.

MRS. LINDE. I don't think I patronize anyone. But it *is* true that I'm both proud and happy that I could make mother's last years comparatively easy.

NORA. And you're proud of all you did for your brothers.

MRS. LINDE. I think I have the right to be.

NORA. And so do I. But now I want to

tell you something, Kristine. I have something to be proud and happy about too.

MRS. LINDE. I don't doubt that for a moment. But what exactly do you mean?

NORA. Not so loud! Torvald mustn't hear—not for anything in the world. Nobody must know about this, Kristine. Nobody but you.

MRS. LINDE. But what is it?

NORA. Come here. *(Pulls her down on the couch beside her.)* You see, I *do* have something to be proud and happy about. I've saved Torvald's life.

MRS. LINDE. Saved—? How do you mean—"saved"?

NORA. I told you about our trip to Italy. Torvald would have died if he hadn't gone.

MRS. LINDE. I understand that. And so your father gave you the money you needed.

NORA *(smiles)*. Yes, that's what Torvald and all the others think. But—

MRS. LINDE. But what?

NORA. Daddy didn't give us a penny. *I* raised that money.

MRS. LINDE. *You* did? That whole big amount?

NORA. Twelve hundred specie dollars. Four thousand eight hundred crowns. *Now* what do you say?

MRS. LINDE. But Nora, how could you? Did you win in the state lottery?

NORA *(contemptuously)*. State lottery! *(Snorts.)* What is so great about that?

MRS. LINDE. Where did it come from then?

NORA *(humming and smiling, enjoying her secret)*. Hmmm. Tra-la-la-la-la!

MRS. LINDE. You certainly couldn't have borrowed it.

NORA. Oh? And why not?

MRS. LINDE. A wife can't borrow money without her husband's consent.

NORA *(with a toss of her head)*. Oh, I don't know—take a wife with a little bit of a head for business—a wife who knows how to manage things—

MRS. LINDE. But Nora, I don't understand at all—

NORA. You don't have to. I didn't say I borrowed the money, did I? I could have gotten it some other way. *(Leans back.)* An admirer may have given it to me. When you're as tolerably goodlooking as I am—

MRS. LINDE. Oh, you're crazy.

NORA. I think you're dying from curiosity, Kristine.

MRS. LINDE. I'm beginning to think you've done something very foolish, Nora.

NORA *(sits up)*. Is it foolish to save your husband's life?

MRS. LINDE. I say it's foolish to act behind his back.

NORA. But don't you see: he couldn't be told! You're missing the whole point, Kristine. We couldn't even let him know how seriously ill he was. The doctors came to *me* and told me his life was in danger, that nothing could save him but a stay in the south. Don't you think I tried to work on him? I told him how lovely it would be if I could go abroad like other young wives. I cried and begged. I said he'd better remember what condition I was in, that he had to be nice to me and do what I wanted. I even hinted he could borrow the money. But that almost made him angry with me. He told me I was being irresponsible and that it was his duty as my husband not to give in to my moods and whims—I think that's what he called it. All right, I said to myself, you've got to be saved somehow, and so I found a way—

MRS. LINDE. And your husband never learned from your father that the money didn't come from him?

NORA. Never. Daddy died that same week. I thought of telling him all about it and ask him not to say anything. But since he was so sick—It turned out I didn't have to—

MRS. LINDE. And you've never told your husband?

NORA. Of course not! Good heavens, how could I? He, with his strict principles! Besides, you know how men are. Torvald would find it embarrassing and humiliating to learn that he owed me anything. It would upset our whole relationship. Our happy, beautiful home would no longer be what it is.

MRS. LINDE. Aren't you ever going to tell him?

NORA *(reflectively, half smiling).* Yes— one day, maybe. Many, many years from now, when I'm no longer young and pretty. Don't laugh! I mean when Torvald no longer feels about me the way he does now, when he no longer thinks it's fun when I dance for him and put on costumes and recite for him. Then it will be good to have something in reserve— *(Interrupts herself.)* Oh, I'm just being silly! That day will never come.— Well, now, Kristine, what do you think of my great secret? Don't you think I'm good for something too?—By the way, you wouldn't believe all the worry I've had because of it. It's been very hard to meet my obligations on schedule. You see, in business there's something called quarterly interest and something called installments on the principal, and those are terribly hard to come up with. I've had to save a little here and a little there, whenever I could. I couldn't use much of the housekeeping money, for Torvald has to eat well. And I couldn't use what I got for clothes for the children. They have to look nice, and I didn't think it would be right to spend less than I got—the sweet little things!

MRS. LINDE. Poor Nora! So you had to take it from your own allowance?

NORA. Yes, of course. After all, it was my affair. Every time Torvald gave me money for a new dress and things like that, I never used more than half of it. I always bought the cheapest, simplest things for myself. Thank God, everything looks good on me, so Torvald never noticed. But it was hard many times, Kristine, for it's fun to have pretty clothes. Don't you think?

MRS. LINDE. Certainly.

NORA. Anyway, I had other ways of making money too. Last winter I was lucky enough to get some copying work. So I locked the door and sat up writing every night till quite late. God! I often got so tired—! But it was great fun, too, working and making money. It was almost like being a man.

MRS. LINDE. But how much have you been able to pay off this way?

NORA. I couldn't tell you exactly. You see, it's very difficult to keep track of business like that. All I know is I have been paying off as much as I've been able to scrape together. Many times I just didn't know what to do. *(Smiles.)* Then I used to imagine a rich old gentleman had fallen in love with me—

MRS. LINDE. What! What old gentleman?

NORA. Phooey! And now he was dead and they were reading his will, and there it said in big letters, "All my money is to be paid in cash immediately to the charming Mrs. Nora Helmer."

MRS. LINDE. But dearest Nora—who *was* this old gentleman?

NORA. For heaven's sake, Kristine, don't you see! There *was* no old gentleman. He was just somebody I made up when I couldn't think of any way to raise the money. But never mind him. The old bore can be anyone he likes to for all I care. I have no use for him or his last will, for now I don't have a single worry in the world. *(Jumps up.)* Dear God, what a lovely thought that is! To be able to play and have fun with the children, to have everything nice and pretty in the house, just the way Torvald likes it! Not a care! And soon spring will be here, and the air will be blue and high. Maybe we can travel again. Maybe I'll see the ocean again! Oh, yes, yes!—it's wonderful to be alive and happy!

The doorbell rings.

MRS. LINDE *(getting up).* There's the doorbell. Maybe I better be going.

NORA. No, please stay. I'm sure it's just someone for Torvald—

THE MAID *(in the hall door).* Excuse me, ma'am. There's a gentleman here who'd like to see Mr. Helmer.

NORA. You mean the bank manager.

THE MAID. Sorry, ma'am; the bank man-ger. But I didn't know—since the Doctor is with him—

NORA. Who is the gentleman?

KROGSTAD *(appearing in the door).* It's just me, Mrs. Helmer.

Mrs. Linde starts, looks, turns away toward the window.

NORA *(takes a step toward him, tense, in a low voice).* You? What do you want? What do you want with my husband?

KROGSTAD. Bank business—in a way. I have a small job in the Mutual, and I understand your husband is going to be our new manager—

NORA. So it's just—

KROGSTAD. Just routine business, ma'am. Nothing else.

NORA. All right. In that case, why don't you go through the door to the office.

Dismisses him casually as she closes the door. Walks over to the stove and tends the fire.

MRS. LINDE. Nora—who was that man?

NORA. His name's Krogstad. He's a lawyer.

MRS. LINDE. So it *was* him.

NORA. Do you know him?

MRS. LINDE. I used to—many years ago. For a while he clerked in our part of the country.

NORA. Right. He did.

MRS. LINDE. He has changed a great deal.

NORA. I believe he had a very unhappy marriage.

MRS. LINDE. And now he's a widower, isn't he?

NORA. With many children. There now; it's burning nicely again. *(Closes the stove and moves the rocking chair a little to the side.)*

MRS. LINDE. They say he's into all sorts of business.

NORA. Really? Maybe so. I wouldn't know. But let's not think about business. It's such a bore.

DR. RANK *(appears in the door to* HELMER'*s study).* No, I don't want to be in the way. I'd rather talk to your wife a bit. *(Closes the door and notices* MRS. LINDE.*)* Oh, I beg your pardon. I believe I'm in the way here too.

NORA. No, not at all. *(Introduces them.)* Dr. Rank. Mrs. Linde.

RANK. Aha. A name often heard in this house. I believe I passed you on the stairs coming up.

MRS. LINDE. Yes. I'm afraid I climb stairs very slowly. They aren't good for me.

RANK. I see. A slight case of inner decay, perhaps?

MRS. LINDE. Overwork, rather.

RANK. Oh, is that all? And now you've come to town to relax at all the parties?

MRS. LINDE. I have come to look for a job.

RANK. A proven cure for overwork, I take it?

MRS. LINDE. One has to live, Doctor.

RANK. Yes, that seems to be the common opinion.

NORA. Come on, Dr. Rank—you want to live just as much as the rest of us.

RANK. Of course I do. Miserable as I am, I prefer to go on being tortured as long as possible. All my patients feel the same way. And that's true of the moral invalids too. Helmer is talking with a specimen right this minute.

MRS. LINDE *(in a low voice).* Ah!

NORA. What do you mean?

RANK. Oh, this lawyer, Krogstad. You don't know him. The roots of his character are decayed. But even he began by saying something about having *to live*—as if it were a matter of the highest importance.

NORA. Oh? What did he want with Torvald?

RANK. I don't really know. All I heard was something about the bank.

NORA. I didn't know that Krog—that this Krogstad had anything to do with the Mutual Bank.

RANK. Yes, he seems to have some kind of job there. *(To* MRS. LINDE.*)* I don't know if you are familiar in your part of the country with the kind of person who is always running around trying to sniff out cases of moral decrepitude and as soon as he finds one puts the individual under observation in some excellent position or other. All the healthy ones are left out in the cold.

MRS. LINDE. I should think it's the sick who need looking after the most.

RANK *(shrugs his shoulders)*. There we are. That's the attitude that turns society into a hospital.

NORA, *absorbed in her own thoughts, suddenly starts giggling and clapping her hands.*

RANK. What's so funny about that? Do you even know what society is?

NORA. What do I care about your stupid society! I laughed at something entirely different—something terribly amusing. Tell me, Dr. Rank—all the employees in the Mutual Bank, from now on they'll all be dependent on Torvald, right?

RANK. Is that what you find so enormously amusing?

NORA *(smiles and hums)*. That's my business, that's my business! *(Walks around.)* Yes, I do think it's fun that we— that Torvald is going to have so much influence on so many people's lives. *(Brings out the bag of macaroons.)* Have a macaroon, Dr. Rank.

RANK. Well, well—macaroons. I thought they were banned around here.

NORA. Yes, but these were some that Kristine gave me.

MRS. LINDE. What! I?

NORA. That's all right. Don't look so scared. You couldn't know that Torvald won't let me have them. He's afraid they'll ruin my teeth. But who cares! Just once in a while—! Right, Dr. Rank? Have one! *(Puts a macaroon into his mouth.)* You too, Kristine. And one for me. A very small one. Or at most two. *(Walks around again.)* Yes, I really feel very, very happy. Now there's just one thing I'm dying to do.

RANK. Oh? And what's that?

NORA. Something I'm dying to say so Torvald could hear.

RANK. And why can't you?

NORA. I don't dare to, for it's not nice.

MRS. LINDE. Not nice?

RANK. In that case, I guess you'd better not. But surely to the two of us—? What is it you'd like to say for Helmer to hear?

NORA. I want to say, "Goddammit!"

RANK. Are you out of your mind!

MRS. LINDE. For heaven's sake, Nora!

RANK. Say it. Here he comes.

NORA *(hiding the macaroons)*. Shhh!

HELMER *enters from his study, carrying his hat and overcoat.*

NORA *(going to him)*. Well, dear, did you get rid of him?

HELMER. Yes, he just left.

NORA. Torvald, I want you to meet Kristine. She's just come to town.

HELMER. Kristine—? I'm sorry; I don't think—

NORA. Mrs. Linde, Torvald dear. Mrs. Kristine Linde.

HELMER. Ah, yes. A childhood friend of my wife's, I suppose.

MRS. LINDE. Yes, we've known each other for a long time.

NORA. Just think; she has come all this way just to see you.

HELMER. I'm not sure I understand—

MRS. LINDE. Well, not really—

NORA. You see, Kristine is an absolutely fantastic secretary, and she would so much like to work for a competent executive and learn more than she knows already—

HELMER. Very sensible, I'm sure, Mrs. Linde.

NORA. So when she heard about your appointment—they got a wire about it—she came here as fast as she could. How about it, Torvald? Couldn't you do something for Kristine? For my sake. Please?

HELMER. Quite possibly. I take it you're a widow, Mrs. Linde?

MRS. LINDE. Yes.

HELMER. And you've had office experience?

MRS. LINDE. Some—yes.

HELMER. In that case I think it's quite likely that I'll be able to find you a position.

NORA *(claps her hands).* I knew it! I knew it!

HELMER. You've arrived at a most opportune time, Mrs. Linde.

MRS. LINDE. Oh, how can I ever thank you—

HELMER. Not at all, not at all. *(Puts his coat on.)* But today you'll have to excuse me—

RANK. Wait a minute; I'll come with you. *(Gets his fur coat from the front hall, warms it by the stove.)*

NORA. Don't be long, Torvald.

HELMER. An hour or so; no more.

NORA. Are you leaving, too, Kristine?

MRS. LINDE *(putting on her things).* Yes, I'd better go and find a place to stay.

HELMER. Good. Then we'll be going the same way.

NORA *(helping her).* I'm sorry this place is so small, but I don't think we very well could—

MRS. LINDE. Of course! Don't be silly, Nora. Goodbye, and thank you for everything.

NORA. Goodbye. We'll see you soon. You'll be back this evening, of course. And you too, Dr. Rank; right? If you feel well enough? Of course you will. Just wrap yourself up.

General small talk as all exit into the hall. Children's voices are heard on the stairs.

NORA. There they are! There they are! *(She runs and opens the door. The nurse Anne-Marie enters with the children.)*

NORA. Come in! Come in! *(Bends over and kisses them.)* Oh, you sweet, sweet darlings! Look at them, Kristine! Aren't they beautiful?

RANK. No standing around in the draft!

HELMER. Come along, Mrs. Linde. This place isn't fit for anyone but mothers right now.

DR. RANK, HELMER, *and* MRS. LINDE *go down the stairs. The* NURSE *enters the living room with the children.* NORA *follows, closing the door behind her.*

NORA. My, how nice you all look! Such red cheeks! Like apples and roses. *(The children all talk at the same time.)* You've had so much fun? I bet you have. Oh, isn't that nice! You pulled both Emmy and Bob on your sleigh? Both at the same time? That's very good, Ivar. Oh, let me hold her for a minute, Anne-Marie. My sweet little doll baby! *(Takes the smallest of the children from the* NURSE *and dances with her.)* Yes, yes, of course; Mama'll dance with you too, Bob. What? You threw snowballs? Oh, I wish I'd been there! No, no; *I* want to take their clothes off, Anne-Marie. Please let me; I think it's so much fun. You go on in. You look frozen. There's hot coffee on the stove.

The NURSE *exits into the room to the left.* NORA *takes the children's wraps off and throws them all around. They all keep telling her things at the same time.*

NORA. Oh, really? A big dog ran after you? But it didn't bite you. Of course not. Dogs don't bite sweet little doll babies. Don't peek at the packages, Ivar! What's in them? Wouldn't you like to know! No, no; that's something terrible! play? You want to play? What do you want to play? Okay, let's play hide-and-seek. Bob hides first. You want *me* to? All right. I'll go first.

Laughing and shouting, NORA *and the children play in the living room and in the adjacent room, right. Finally,* NORA *hides herself under the table; the children rush in, look for her, can't find her. They hear her low giggle, run to the table, lift the rug that covers it, see her. General hilarity. She crawls out, pretends to scare them. New delight. In the meantime there has been a knock on the door between the living room and the front hall, but nobody has noticed. Now the door is opened halfway;* KROGSTAD *appears. He waits a little. The playing goes on.*

KROGSTAD. Pardon me, Mrs. Helmer—

NORA *(with a muted cry turns around, jumps up).* Ah! What do you want?

KROGSTAD. I'm sorry. The front door was open. Somebody must have forgotten to close it—

NORA *(standing up)*. My husband isn't here, Mr. Krogstad.

KROGSTAD. I know.

NORA. So what do you want?

KROGSTAD. I'd like a word with you.

NORA. With—? *(To the children in a low voice.)* Go in to Anne-Marie. What? No, the strange man won't do anything bad to Mama. When he's gone we'll play some more.

She takes the children into the room to the left and closes the door.

NORA *(tense, troubled)*. You want to speak with me?

KROGSTAD. Yes I do.

NORA. Today—? It isn't the first of the month yet.

KROGSTAD. No, it's Christmas Eve. It's up to you what kind of holiday you'll have.

NORA. What do you want? I can't possibly—

KROGSTAD. Let's not talk about that just yet. There's something else. You do have a few minutes, don't you?

NORA. Yes. Yes, of course. That is—

KROGSTAD. Good. I was sitting in Olsen's restaurant when I saw your husband go by.

NORA. Yes—?

KROGSTAD. —with a lady.

NORA. What of it?

KROGSTAD. May I be so free as to ask: wasn't that lady Mrs. Linde?

NORA. Yes.

KROGSTAD. Just arrived in town?

NORA. Yes, today.

KROGSTAD. She's a good friend of yours, I understand?

NORA. Yes, she is. But I fail to see—

KROGSTAD. I used to know her myself.

NORA. I know that.

KROGSTAD. So you know about that. I thought as much. In that case, let me ask you a simple question. Is Mrs. Linde going to be employed in the bank?

NORA. What makes you think you have the right to cross-examine me like this, Mr. Krogstad—you, one of my husband's employees? But since you ask, I'll tell you. Yes, Mrs. Linde is going to be working in the bank. And it was I who recommended her, Mr. Krogstad. Now you know.

KROGSTAD. So I was right.

NORA *(walks up and down)*. After all, one does have a little influence, you know. Just because you're a woman, it doesn't mean that—Really, Mr. Krogstad, people in a subordinate position should be careful not to offend someone who—oh well—

KROGSTAD. —has influence?

NORA. Exactly.

KROGSTAD *(changing his tone)*. Mrs. Helmer, I must ask you to be good enough to use your influence on my behalf.

NORA. What do you mean?

KROGSTAD. I want you to make sure that I am going to keep my subordinate position in the bank.

NORA. I don't understand. Who is going to take your position away from you?

KROGSTAD. There's no point in playing ignorant with me, Mrs. Helmer. I can very well appreciate that your friend would find it unpleasant to run into me. So now I know who I can thank for my dismissal.

NORA. But I assure you—

KROGSTAD. Never mind. Just want to say you still have time. I advise you to use your influence to prevent it.

NORA. But Mr. Krogstad, I don't have any influence—none at all.

KROGSTAD. No? I thought you just said—

NORA. Of course I didn't mean it that way. I! Whatever makes you think that I have any influence of that kind on my husband?

KROGSTAD. I went to law school with your husband. I have no reason to think that the bank manager is less susceptible than other husbands.

NORA. If you're going to insult my husband, I'll ask you to leave.

KROGSTAD. You're brave, Mrs. Helmer.

NORA. I'm not afraid of you any more. After New Year's I'll be out of this thing with you.

KROGSTAD *(more controlled)*. Listen, Mrs. Helmer. If necessary, I'll fight as for my life to keep my little job in the bank.

NORA. So it seems.

KROGSTAD. It isn't just the money; that's really the smallest part of it. There is something else—Well, I guess I might as well tell you. It's like this. I'm sure you know, like everybody else, that some years ago I committed—an impropriety.

NORA. I believe I've heard it mentioned.

KROGSTAD. The case never came to court, but from that moment all doors were closed to me. So I took up the kind of business you know about. I had to do something, and I think I can say about myself that I have not been among the worst. But now I want to get out of all that. My sons are growing up. For their sake I must get back as much of my good name as I can. This job in the bank was like the first rung on the ladder. And now your husband wants to kick me down and leave me back in the mud again.

NORA. But I swear to you, Mr. Krogstad; it's not at all in my power to help you.

KROGSTAD. That's because you don't want to. But I have the means to force you.

NORA. You don't mean you're going to tell my husband I owe you money?

KROGSTAD. And if I did?

NORA. That would be a mean thing to do. *(Almost crying.)* That secret, which is my joy and my pride—for him to learn about it in such a coarse and ugly manner—to learn it from *you*—! It would be terribly unpleasant for me.

KROGSTAD. Just unpleasant?

NORA *(heatedly)*. But go ahead! Do it! It will be worse for you than for me. When my husband realizes what a bad person you are, you'll be sure to lose your job.

KROGSTAD. I asked you if it was just domestic unpleasantness you were afraid of?

NORA. When my husband finds out, of course he'll pay off the loan, and then we won't have anything more to do with you.

KROGSTAD *(stepping closer)*. Listen, Mrs. Helmer—either you have a very bad memory, or you don't know much about business. I think I had better straighten you out on a few things.

NORA. What do you mean?

KROGSTAD. When your husband was ill, you came to me to borrow twelve hundred dollars.

NORA. I knew nobody else.

KROGSTAD. I promised to get you the money—

NORA. And you did.

KROGSTAD. I promised to get you the money on certain conditions. At the time you were so anxious about your husband's health and so set on getting him away that I doubt very much that you paid much attention to the details of our transaction. That's why I remind you of them now. Anyway, I promised to get you the money if you would sign an I.O.U., which I drafted.

NORA. And which I signed.

KROGSTAD. Good. But below your signature I added a few lines, making your father security for the loan. Your father was supposed to put his signature to those lines.

NORA. Supposed to—? He did.

KROGSTAD. I had left the date blank. That is, your father was to date his own signature. You recall that, don't you, Mrs. Helmer?

NORA. I guess so—

KROGSTAD. I gave the note to you. You were to mail it to your father. Am I correct?

NORA. Yes.

KROGSTAD. And of course you did so right away, for no more than five or six days later you brought the paper back to me, signed by your father. Then I paid you the money.

NORA. Well? And haven't I been keeping up with the payments?

KROGSTAD. Fairly well, yes. But to get back to what we were talking about—those were difficult days for you, weren't they, Mrs. Helmer?

NORA. Yes, they were.

KROGSTAD. Your father was quite ill, I believe.

NORA. He was dying.

KROGSTAD. And died shortly afterwards?

NORA. That's right.

KROGSTAD. Tell me, Mrs. Helmer; do you happen to remember the date of your father's death? I mean the exact day of the month?

NORA. Daddy died on September 29.

KROGSTAD. Quite correct. I have ascertained that fact. That's why there is something peculiar about this *(takes out a piece of paper),* which I can't account for.

NORA. Peculiar? How? I don't understand—

KROGSTAD. It seems very peculiar, Mrs. Helmer, that your father signed this promissory note three days after his death.

NORA. How so? I don't see what—

KROGSTAD. Your father died on September 29. Now look. He has dated his signature October 2. Isn't that odd?

NORA *remains silent.*

KROGSTAD. Can you explain it?

NORA *is still silent.*

KROGSTAD. I also find it striking that the date and the month and the year are not in your father's handwriting but in a hand I think I recognize. Well, that might be explained. Your father may have forgotten to date his signature and somebody else may have done it here, guessing at the date before he had learned of your father's death. That's all right. It's only the signature itself that matters. And that is genuine, isn't it, Mrs. Helmer? Your father *did* put his name to this note?

NORA *(after a brief silence tosses her head back and looks defiantly at him).* No, he didn't. *I* wrote Daddy's name.

KROGSTAD. Mrs. Helmer—do you realize what a dangerous admission you just made?

NORA. Why? You'll get your money soon.

KROGSTAD. Let me ask you something. Why didn't you mail this note to your father?

NORA. Because it was impossible. Daddy was sick—you know that. If I had asked him to sign it, I would have had to tell him what the money was for. But I couldn't tell him, as sick as he was, that my husband's life was in danger. That was impossible. Surely you can see that.

KROGSTAD. Then it would have been better for you if you had given up your trip abroad.

NORA. No, that was impossible! That trip was to save my husband's life. I couldn't give it up.

KROGSTAD. But didn't you realize that what you did amounted to fraud against me?

NORA. I couldn't let that make any difference. I didn't care about you at all. I hated the way you made all those difficulties for me, even though you knew the danger my husband was in. I thought you were cold and unfeeling.

KROGSTAD. Mrs. Helmer, obviously you have no clear idea of what you have done. Let me tell you that what I did that time was no more and no worse. And it ruined my name and reputation.

NORA. You! Are you trying to tell me that you did something brave once in order to save your wife's life?

KROGSTAD. The law doesn't ask about motives.

NORA. Then it's a bad law.

KROGSTAD. Bad or not—if I produce this note in court you'll be judged according to the law.

NORA. I refuse to believe you. A daughter shouldn't have the right to spare her dying old father worry and anxiety? A wife shouldn't have the right to save her husband's life? I don't know the laws very well, but I'm sure that somewhere they make allowance for cases like that. And you, a lawyer, don't know that? I think you must be a bad lawyer, Mr. Krogstad.

KROGSTAD. That may be. But business— the kind of business you and I have with one another—don't you think I know something about that? Very well. Do what you like. But let me tell you this: if I'm going to be kicked out again, you'll keep me company. *(He bows and exits through the front hall.)*

NORA *(pauses thoughtfully; then, with a defiant toss of her head).* Oh, nonsense! Trying to scare me like that! I'm not all that silly. *(Starts picking up the children's clothes; soon stops.)* But—? No! That's impossible! I did it for love!

THE CHILDREN *(in the door to the left).*

Mama, the strange man just left. We saw him.

NORA. Yes, yes; I know. But don't tell anybody about the strange man. Do you hear? Not even Daddy.

THE CHILDREN. We won't. But now you'll play with us again, won't you, Mama?

NORA. No, not right now.

THE CHILDREN. But Mama—you promised.

NORA. I know, but I can't just now. Go to your own room. I've so much to do. Be nice now, my little darlings. Do as I say. *(She nudges them gently into the other room and closes the door. She sits down on the couch, picks up a piece of embroidery, makes a few stitches, then stops.)* No! *(Throws the embroidery down, goes to the hall door and calls out.)* Helene! Bring the Christmas tree in here, please! *(Goes to the table, left, opens the drawer, halts.)* No—that's impossible!

THE MAID *(with the Christmas tree).* Where do you want it, ma'am?

NORA. There. The middle of the floor.

THE MAID. You want anything else?

NORA. No, thanks. I have everything I need. *(*THE MAID *goes out.* NORA *starts trimming the tree.)* I want candles—and flowers—That awful man! Oh, nonsense! There's nothing wrong. This will be a lovely tree. I'll do everything you want me to, Torvald. I'll sing for you—dance for you—

HELMER, *a bundle of papers under his arm, enters from outside.*

NORA. Ah—you're back already?

HELMER. Yes. Has anybody been here?

NORA. Here? No.

HELMER. That's funny. I saw Krogstad leaving just now.

NORA. Oh? Oh yes, that's right. Krogstad was here for just a moment.

HELMER. I can tell from your face that he came to ask you to put in a word for him.

NORA. Yes.

HELMER. And it was supposed to be your own idea, wasn't it? You were not to tell me he'd been here. He asked you that too, didn't he?

NORA. Yes, Torvald, but—

HELMER. Nora, Nora, how could you! Talk to a man like that and make him promises! And lying to me about it afterwards—!

NORA. Lying—?

HELMER. Didn't you say nobody had been here? *(Shakes his finger at her.)* My little songbird must never do that again. Songbirds are supposed to have clean beaks to chirp with—no false notes. *(Puts his arm around her waist.)* Isn't that so? Of course it is. *(Lets her go.)* And that's enough about that. *(Sits down in front of the fireplace.)* Ah, it's nice and warm in here. *(Begins to leaf through his papers.)*

NORA *(busy with the tree; after a brief pause).* Torvald.

HELMER. Yes.

NORA. I'm looking forward so much to the Stenborgs' costume party day after tomorrow.

HELMER. And I can't wait to find out what you're going to surprise me with.

NORA. Oh, that silly idea!

HELMER. Oh?

NORA. I can't think of anything. It all seems so foolish and pointless.

HELMER. Ah, my little Nora admits that?

NORA *(behind his chair, her arms on the back of the chair).* Are you very busy, Torvald?

HELMER. Well—

NORA. What are all those papers?

HELMER. Bank business.

NORA. Already?

HELMER. I've asked the board to give me the authority to make certain changes in organization and personnel. That's what I'll be doing over the holidays. I want it all settled before New Year's.

NORA. So that's why this poor Krogstad—

HELMER. Hm.

NORA *(leisurely playing with the hair on his neck).* If you weren't so busy, Torvald, I'd ask you for a great big favor.

HELMER. Let's hear it, anyway.

NORA. I don't know anyone with better taste than you, and I want so much to look nice at the party. Couldn't you sort of take charge of me, Torvald, and decide what I'll wear—Help me with my costume?

HELMER. Aha! Little Lady Obstinate is looking for someone to rescue her?

NORA. Yes, Torvald. I won't get anywhere without your help.

HELMER. All right. I'll think about it. We'll come up with something.

NORA. Oh, you *are* nice! *(Goes back to the Christmas tree. A pause.)* Those red flowers look so pretty.—Tell me, was it really all that bad what this Krogstad fellow did?

HELMER. He forged signatures. Do you have any idea what that means?

NORA. Couldn't it have been because he felt he had to?

HELMER. Yes, or like so many others he may simply have been thoughtless. I'm not so heartless as to condemn a man absolutely because of a single imprudent act.

NORA. Of course not, Torvald!

HELMER. People like him can redeem themselves morally by openly confessing their crime and taking their punishment.

NORA. Punishment—?

HELMER. But that was not the way Krogstad chose. He got out of it with tricks and evasions. That's what has corrupted him.

NORA. So you think that if—?

HELMER. Can't you imagine how a guilty person like that has to lie and fake and dissemble wherever he goes—putting on a mask before everybody he's close to, even his own wife and children. It's this thing with the children that's the worst part of it, Nora.

NORA. Why is that?

HELMER. Because when a man lives inside such a circle of stinking lies he brings infection into his own home and contaminates his whole family. With every breath of air his children inhale the germs of something ugly.

NORA *(moving closer behind him)*. Are you so sure of that?

HELMER. Of course I am. I have seen enough examples of that in my work. Nearly all young criminals have had mothers who lied.

NORA. Why mothers—particularly?

HELMER. Most often mothers. But of course fathers tend to have the same influence. Every lawyer knows that. And yet, for years this Krogstad has been poisoning his own children in an atmosphere of lies and deceit. That's why I call him a lost soul morally. *(Reaches out for her hands.)* And that's why my sweet little Nora must promise me never to take his side again. Let's shake on that.—What? What's this? Give me your hand. There! Now that's settled. I assure you, I would find it impossible to work in the same room with that man. I feel literally sick when I'm around people like that.

NORA *(withdraws her hand and goes to the other side of the Christmas tree)*. It's so hot in here. And I have so much to do.

HELMER *(gets up and collects his papers)*. Yes, and I really should try to get some of this reading done before dinner. I must think about your costume too. And maybe just possibly I'll have something to wrap in gilt paper and hang on the Christmas tree. *(Puts his hand on her head.)* Oh my adorable little songbird! *(Enters his study and closes the door.)*

NORA *(after a pause, in a low voice)*. It's all a lot of nonsense. It's not that way at all. It's impossible. It has to be impossible.

THE NURSE *(in the door, left)*. The little ones are asking ever so nicely if they can't come in and be with their mamma.

NORA. No, no, no! Don't let them in here! You stay with them, Anne-Marie.

THE NURSE. If you say so, ma'am. *(Closes the door.)*

NORA *(pale with terror)*. Corrupt my little children—! Poison my home—? *(Brief pause; she lifts her head.)* That's not true. Never. Never in a million years.

ACT II

The same room. The Christmas tree is in the corner by the piano, stripped and shabby-looking, with burnt-down candles. NORA's outside clothes are on the couch. NORA is alone. She walks around restlessly. She stops by the couch and picks up her coat.

NORA *(drops the coat again)*. There's somebody now! *(Goes to the door, listens.)* No. Nobody. Of course not—not on Christmas. And not tomorrow either[1]—But perhaps—*(Opens the door and looks.)* No, nothing in the mailbox. All empty. *(Comes forward.)* How silly I am! Of course he isn't serious. Nothing like that could happen. After all, I have three small children.

THE NURSE *enters from the room, left, carrying a big carton.*

THE NURSE. Well, at last I found it—the box with your costume.

NORA. Thanks. Just put it on the table.

NURSE *(does so)*. But it's all a big mess, I'm afraid.

NORA. Oh, I wish I could tear the whole thing to little pieces!

NURSE. Heavens! It's not as bad as all that. It can be fixed all right. All it takes is a little patience.

NORA. I'll go over and get Mrs. Linde to help me.

NURSE. Going out again? In this awful weather? You'll catch a cold.

NORA. That might not be such a bad thing. How are the children?

NURSE. The poor little dears are playing with their presents, but—

NORA. Do they keep asking for me?

NURSE. Well, you know, they're used to being with their mamma.

NORA. I know. But Anne-Marie, from now on I can't be with them as much as before.

NURSE. Oh well. Little children get used to everything.

NORA. You think so? Do you think they'll forget their mamma if I were gone altogether?

NURSE. Goodness me—gone altogether?

NORA. Listen, Anne-Marie—something

I've wondered about. How could you bring yourself to leave your child with strangers?

NURSE. But I had to, if I were to nurse you.

NORA. Yes, but how could you *want* to?

NURSE. When I could get such a nice place? When something like that happens to a poor young girl, she'd better be grateful for whatever she gets. For *he* didn't do a thing for me—the louse!

NORA. But your daughter has forgotten all about you, hasn't she?

NURSE. Oh no! Not at all! She wrote to me both when she was confirmed and when she got married.

NORA *(putting her arms around her neck)*. You dear old thing—you were a good mother to me when I was little.

NURSE. Poor little Nora had no one else, you know.

NORA. And if my little ones didn't, I know you'd—oh, I'm being silly! *(Opens the carton.)* Go in to them, please. I really should—Tomorrow you'll see how pretty I'll be.

NURSE. I know. There won't be anybody at that party half as pretty as you, ma'am. *(Goes out, left.)*

NORA *(begins to take clothes out of the carton; in a moment she throws it all down)*. If only I dared to go out. If only I knew nobody would come. That nothing would happen while I was gone.—How silly! Nobody'll come. Just don't think about it. Brush the muff. Beautiful gloves. Beautiful gloves. Forget it. Forget it. One, two, three, four, five, six— *(Cries out.)* There they are! *(Moves toward the door, stops irresolutely.)*

MRS. LINDE *enters from the hall. She has already taken off her coat.*

NORA. Oh, it's you, Kristine. There's no one else out there, is there? I'm so glad you're here.

MRS. LINDE. They told me you'd asked for me.

NORA. I just happened to walk by. I need your help with something—badly. Let's sit here on the couch. Look. Torvald and I are

[1] In Norway both December 25 and 26 are legal holidays.—ED.

going to a costume party tomorrow night—at Consul Stenborg's upstairs—and Torvald wants me to go as a Neapolitan fisher girl and dance the tarantella. I learned it when we were on Capri.

MRS. LINDE. Well, well! So you'll be putting on a whole show?

NORA. Yes. Torvald thinks I should. Look, here's the costume. Torvald had it made for me while we were there. But it's also torn and everything. I just don't know—

MRS. LINDE. Oh, that can be fixed. It's not that much. The trimmings have come loose in a few places. Do you have needle and thread? Ah, here we are. All set.

NORA. I really appreciate it, Kristine.

MRS. LINDE *(sewing)*. So you'll be in disguise tomorrow night, eh? You know—I may come by for just a moment, just to look at you.—Oh dear. I haven't even thanked you for the nice evening last night.

NORA *(gets up, moves around)*. Oh, I don't know. I don't think last night was as nice as it usually is.—You should have come to town a little earlier, Kristine.—Yes, Torvald knows how to make it nice and pretty around here.

MRS. LINDE. You too, I should think. After all, you're your father's daughter. By the way, is Dr. Rank always as depressed as he was last night?

NORA. No, last night was unusual. He's a very sick man, you know—very sick. Poor Rank, his spine is rotting away. Tuberculosis, I think. You see, his father was a nasty old man with mistresses and all that sort of thing. Rank has been sickly ever since he was a little boy.

MRS. LINDE *(dropping her sewing to her lap)*. But dearest Nora, where have you learned about things like that?

NORA *(still walking about)*. Oh, you know—with three children you sometimes get to talk with—other wives. Some of them know quite a bit about medicine. So you pick up a few things.

MRS. LINDE *(resumes her sewing; after a brief pause)*. Does Dr. Rank come here every day?

NORA. Every single day. He's Torvald's oldest and best friend, after all. And my friend too, for that matter. He's part of the family, almost.

MRS. LINDE. But tell me, is he quite sincere? I mean, isn't he the kind of man who likes to say nice things to people?

NORA. No, not at all. Rather the opposite, in fact. What makes you say that?

MRS. LINDE. When you introduced us yesterday, he told me he'd often heard my name mentioned in this house. But later on it was quite obvious that your husband really had no idea who I was. So how could Dr. Rank—?

NORA. You're right, Kristine, but I can explain that. You see, Torvald loves me so very much that he wants me all to himself. That's what he says. When we were first married he got almost jealous when I as much as mentioned anybody from back home that I was fond of. So of course I soon stopped doing that. But with Dr. Rank I often talk about home. You see, he likes to listen to me.

MRS. LINDE. Look here, Nora. In many ways you're still a child. After all, I'm quite a bit older than you and have had more experience. I want to give you a piece of advice. I think you should get out of this thing with Dr. Rank.

NORA. Get out of what thing?

MRS. LINDE. Several things in fact, if you want my opinion. Yesterday you said something about a rich admirer who was going to give you money—

NORA. One who doesn't exist, unfortunately. What of it?

MRS. LINDE. Does Dr. Rank have money?

NORA. Yes, he does.

MRS. LINDE. And no dependents?

NORA. No. But—?

MRS. LINDE. And he comes here every day?

NORA. Yes, I told you that already.

MRS. LINDE. But how can that sensitive man be so tactless?

NORA. I haven't the slightest idea what you're talking about.

MRS. LINDE. Don't play games with me,

Nora. Don't you think I know who you borrowed the twelve hundred dollars from?

NORA. Are you out of your mind! The very idea—! A friend of both of us who sees us every day—! What a dreadfully uncomfortable position that would be!

MRS. LINDE. So it really isn't Dr. Rank?

NORA. Most certainly not! I would never have dreamed of asking him—not for a moment. Anyway, he didn't have any money then. He inherited it afterwards.

MRS. LINDE. Well, I still think it may have been lucky for you, Nora dear.

NORA. The idea! It would never have occurred to me to ask Dr. Rank—Though I'm sure that if I *did* ask him—

MRS. LINDE. But of course you wouldn't.

NORA. Of course not. I can't imagine that that would ever be necessary. But I am quite sure that if I told Dr. Rank—

MRS. LINDE. Behind your husband's back?

NORA. I must get out of—this other thing. That's also behind his back. I *must* get out of it.

MRS. LINDE. That's what I told you yesterday. But—

NORA *(walking up and down)*. A man manages these things so much better than a woman—

MRS. LINDE. One's husband, yes.

NORA. Silly, silly! *(Stops.)* When you've paid off all you owe, you get your I.O.U. back; right?

MRS. LINDE. Yes, of course.

NORA. And you can tear it into a hundred thousand little pieces and burn it—that dirty, filthy paper!

MRS. LINDE *(looks hard at her, puts down her sewing, rises slowly)*. Nora—you're hiding something from me.

NORA. Can you tell?

MRS. LINDE. Something's happened to you, Nora, since yesterday morning. What is it?

NORA *(going to her)*. Kristine! *(Listens.)* Shhh. Torvald just came back. Listen. Why don't you go in to the children for a while. Torvald can't stand having sewing around. Get Anne-Marie to help you.

MRS. LINDE *(gathers some of the sewing things together)*. All right, but I'm not leaving here till you and I have talked.

She goes out left, just as HELMER *enters from the front hall.*

NORA *(toward him)*. I have been waiting and waiting for you, Torvald.

HELMER. Was that the dressmaker?

NORA. No, it was Kristine. She's helping me with my costume. Oh Torvald, just wait till you see how nice I'll look!

HELMER. I told you. Pretty good idea I had, wasn't it?

NORA. Lovely! And wasn't it nice of me to go along with it?

HELMER *(his hand under her chin)*. Nice? To do what your husband tells you? All right, you little rascal; I know you didn't mean it that way. But don't let me interrupt you. I suppose you want to try it on.

NORA. And you'll be working?

HELMER. Yes. *(Shows her a pile of papers.)* Look. I've been down to the bank. *(Is about to enter his study.)*

NORA. Torvald.

HELMER *(halts)*. Yes?

NORA. What if your little squirrel asked you ever so nicely—

HELMER. For what?

NORA. Would you do it?

HELMER. Depends on what it is.

NORA. Squirrel would run around and do all sorts of fun tricks if you'd be nice and agreeable.

HELMER. All right. What is it?

NORA. Lark would chirp and twitter in all the rooms, up and down—

HELMER. So what? Lark does that anyway.

NORA. I'll be your elfmaid and dance for you in the moonlight, Torvald.

HELMER. Nora, don't tell me it's the same thing you mentioned this morning?

NORA *(closer to him)*. Yes, Torvald. I beg you!

HELMER. You really have the nerve to bring that up again?

NORA. Yes. You've just got to do as I say. You *must* let Krogstad keep his job.

HELMER. My dear Nora. It's his job I intend to give to Mrs. Linde.

NORA. I know. And that's ever so nice of you. But can't you just fire somebody else?

HELMER. This is incredible! You just don't give up, do you? Because you make some foolish promise, *I* am supposed to—!

NORA. That's not the reason, Torvald. It's for your own sake. That man writes for the worst newspapers. You've said so yourself. There's no telling what he may do to you. I'm scared to death of him.

HELMER. Ah, I understand. You're afraid because of what happened before.

NORA. What do you mean?

HELMER. You're thinking of your father, of course.

NORA. Yes. Yes, you're right. Remember the awful things they wrote about Daddy in the newspapers. I really think they might have forced him to resign if the ministry hadn't sent you to look into the charges and if you hadn't been so helpful and understanding.

HELMER. My dear little Nora, there is a world of difference between your father and me. Your father's official conduct was not above reproach. Mine is, and I intend for it to remain that way as long as I hold my position.

NORA. Oh, but you don't know what vicious people like that may think of. Oh, Torvald! Now all of us could be so happy together here in our own home, peaceful and carefree. Such a good life, Torvald, for you and me and the children! That's why I implore you—

HELMER. And it's exactly because you plead for him that you make it impossible for me to keep him. It's already common knowledge in the bank that I intend to let Krogstad go. If it gets out that the new manager has changed his mind because of his wife—

NORA. Yes? What then?

HELMER. No, of course, that wouldn't matter at all as long as little Mrs. Pighead here got her way! Do you want me to make myself look ridiculous before my whole staff—make people think I can be swayed by just anybody—by outsiders? Believe me. I would soon enough find out what the consequences would be! Besides, there's another thing that makes it absolutely impossible for Krogstad to stay on in the bank now that I'm in charge.

NORA. What's that?

HELMER. I suppose in a pinch I could overlook his moral shortcomings—

NORA. Yes, you could; couldn't you, Torvald?

HELMER. And I understand he's quite a good worker, too. But we've known each other for a long time. It's one of those imprudent relationships you get into when you're young that embarrass you for the rest of your life. I guess I might as well be frank with you: he and I are on a first name basis. And that tactless fellow never hides the fact even when other people are around. Rather, he seems to think it entitles him to be familiar with me. Every chance he gets he comes out with his damn "Torvald, Torvald." I'm telling you, I find it most awkward. He would make my position in the bank intolerable.

NORA. You don't really mean any of this, Torvald.

HELMER. Oh? I don't? And why not?

NORA. No, for it's all so petty.

HELMER. What! Petty? You think I'm being petty!

NORA. No, I *don't* think you are petty, Torvald dear. That's exactly why I—

HELMER. Never mind. You think my reasons are petty, so it follows that I must be petty too. Petty! Indeed! By God, I'll put an end to this right now! *(Opens the door to the front hall and calls out.)* Helene!

NORA. What are you doing?

HELMER *(searching among his papers)*. Making a decision. (THE MAID enters.) Here. Take this letter. Go out with it right away. Find somebody to deliver it. But quick. The address is on the envelope. Wait. Here's money.

THE MAID. Very good, sir. *(She takes the letter and goes out.)*

HELMER *(collecting his papers)*. There now, little Mrs. Obstinate!

NORA *(breathless)*. Torvald—what was that letter?

HELMER. Krogstad's dismissal.

NORA. Call it back, Torvald! There's still time! Oh Torvald, please—call it back! For my sake, for your own sake, for the sake of the children! Listen to me, Torvald! Do it! You don't know what you're doing to all of us!

HELMER. Too late.

NORA. Yes. Too late.

HELMER. Dear Nora, I forgive you this fear you're in, although it really is an insult to me. Yes, it is! It's an insult to think that I am scared of a shabby scrivener's revenge. But I forgive you, for it's such a beautiful proof how much you love me. *(Takes her in his arms.)* And that's the way it should be, my sweet darling. Whatever happens, you'll see that when things get really rough I have both strength and courage. You'll find out that I am man enough to shoulder the whole burden.

NORA *(terrified)*. What do you mean by that?

HELMER. All of it, I tell you—

NORA *(composed)*. You'll never have to do that.

HELMER. Good. Then we'll share the burden, Nora—like husband and wife, the way it ought to be. *(Caresses her.)* Now are you satisfied? There, there, there. Not that look in your eyes—like a frightened dove. It's all your own foolish imagination.—Why don't you practice the tarantella— and your tambourine, too. I'll be in the inner office and close both doors, so I won't hear you. You can make as much noise as you like. *(Turning in the doorway.)* And when Rank comes, tell him where to find me. *(He nods to her, enters his study carrying his papers, and closes the door.)*

NORA *(transfixed by terror, whispers)*. He would do it. He'll do it. He'll do it in spite of the whole world.—No, this mustn't happen. Anything rather than that! There must be a way—! *(The doorbell rings.)* Dr. Rank! Anything rather than that! Anything—anything at all!

She passes her hand over her face, pulls herself together, and opens the door to the hall. DR. RANK *is out there, hanging up his coat. Darkness begins to fall during the following scene.*

NORA. Hello there, Dr. Rank. I recognized your ringing. Don't go in to Torvald yet. I think he's busy.

RANK. And you?

NORA *(as he enters and she closes the door behind him)*. You know I always have time for you.

RANK. Thanks. I'll make use of that as long as I can.

NORA. What do you mean by that—As long as you can?

RANK. Does that frighten you?

NORA. Well, it's a funny expression. As if something was going to happen.

RANK. Something is going to happen that I've long been expecting. But I admit I hadn't thought it would come quite so soon.

NORA *(seizes his arm)*. What is it you've found out? Dr. Rank—tell me!

RANK *(sits down by the stove)*. I'm going downhill fast. There's nothing to do about that.

NORA *(with audible relief)*. So it's *you*—

RANK. Who else? No point in lying to myself. I'm in worse shape than any of my other patients, Mrs. Helmer. These last few days I've been conducting an audit on my inner condition. Bankrupt. Chances are that within a month I'll be rotting up in the cemetery.

NORA. Shame on you! Talking that horrid way!

RANK. The thing itself is horrid—damn horrid. The worst of it, though, is all that other horror that comes first. There is only one more test I need to make. After that I'll have a pretty good idea when I'll start coming apart. There is something I want to say to you. Helmer's refined nature can't stand anything hideous. I don't want him in my sick room.

NORA. Oh, but Dr. Rank—

RANK. I don't want him there. Under no circumstance. I'll close my door to him. As soon as I have full certainty that the worst is about to begin I'll give you my card with a black cross on it. Then you'll know the last horror of destruction has started.

NORA. Today you're really quite impossible. And I had hoped you'd be in a particularly good mood.

RANK. With death on my hands? Paying for someone else's sins? Is there justice in that? And yet there isn't a single family that isn't ruled by that same law of ruthless retribution, in one way or another.

NORA *(puts her hands over her ears)*. Poppycock! Be fun! Be fun!

RANK. Well, yes. You may just as well laugh at the whole thing. My poor, innocent spine is suffering for my father's frolics as a young lieutenant.

NORA *(over by the table, left)*. Right. He was addicted to asparagus and goose liver pâté, wasn't he?

RANK. And truffles.

NORA. Of course. Truffles. And oysters too, I think.

RANK. And oysters. Obviously.

NORA. And all the port and champagne that go with it. It's really too bad that goodies like that ruin your backbone.

RANK. Particularly an unfortunate backbone that never enjoyed any of it.

NORA. Ah yes, that's the saddest part of it all.

RANK *(looks searchingly at her)*. Hm—

NORA *(after a brief pause)*. Why did you smile just then?

RANK. No, it was you that laughed.

NORA. No, it was you that smiled, Dr. Rank!

RANK *(gets up)*. You're more of a mischief-maker than I thought.

NORA. I feel in the mood for mischief today.

RANK. So it seems.

NORA *(with both her hands on his shoulders)*. Dear, dear Dr. Rank, don't you go and die and leave Torvald and me.

RANK. Oh, you won't miss me for very long. Those who go away are soon forgotten.

NORA *(with an anxious look)*. Do you believe that?

RANK. You'll make new friends, and then—

NORA. Who'll make new friends?

RANK. Both you and Helmer, once I'm gone. You yourself seem to have made a good start already. What was this Mrs. Linde doing here last night?

NORA. Aha—Don't tell me you're jealous of poor Kristine?

RANK. Yes, I am. She'll be my successor in this house. As soon as I have made my excuses, that woman is likely to—

NORA. Shh—not so loud. She's in there.

RANK. Today too? There you are!

NORA. She's mending my costume. My God, you really *are* unreasonable. *(Sits down on the couch.)* Now be nice, Dr. Rank. Tomorrow you'll see how beautifully I'll dance, and then you are to pretend I'm dancing just for you—and for Torvald too, of course. *(Takes several items out of the carton.)* Sit down, Dr. Rank; I want to show you something.

RANK *(sitting down)*. What?

NORA. Look.

RANK. Silk stockings.

NORA. Flesh-colored. Aren't they lovely? Now it's getting dark in here, but tomorrow—No, no. You only get to see the foot. Oh well, you might as well see all of it.

RANK. Hmm.

NORA. Why do you look so critical? Don't you think they'll fit?

RANK. That's something I can't possibly have a reasoned opinion about.

NORA *(looks at him for a moment)*. Shame on you. *(Slaps his ear lightly with the stocking.)* That's what you get. *(Puts the things back in the carton.)*

RANK. And what other treasures are you going to show me?

NORA. Nothing at all, because you're naughty. *(She hums a little and rummages in the carton.)*

RANK *(after a brief silence)*. When I sit

here like this, talking confidently with you, I can't imagine—I can't possibly imagine what would have become of me if I hadn't had you and Helmer.

NORA *(smiles)*. Well, yes—I do believe you like being with us.

RANK *(in a lower voice, lost in thought)*. And then to have to go away from it all—

NORA. Nonsense. You are not going anywhere.

RANK *(as before)*. —and not to leave behind as much as a poor little token of gratitude, hardly a brief memory of someone missed, nothing but a vacant place that anyone can fill.

NORA. And what if I were to ask you—? No—

RANK. Ask me what?

NORA. For a great proof of your friendship—

RANK. Yes, yes—?

NORA. No, I mean—for an enormous favor—

RANK. Would you really for once make me as happy as all that?

NORA. But you don't even know what it is.

RANK. Well, then; tell me.

NORA. Oh, but I can't, Dr. Rank. It's altogether too much to ask—It's advice and help and a favor—

RANK. So much the better. I can't even begin to guess what it is you have in mind. So for heaven's sake tell me! Don't you trust me?

NORA. Yes, I trust you more than anyone else I know. You are my best and most faithful friend. I know that. So I will tell you. All right, Dr. Rank. There is something you can help me prevent. You know how much Torvald loves me—beyond all words. Never for a moment would he hesitate to give his life for me.

RANK *(leaning over to her)*. Nora—do you really think he's the only one—?

NORA *with a slight start)*. Who—?

RANK. —would gladly give his life for you.

NORA *(heavily)*. I see.

RANK. I have sworn an oath to myself to tell you before I go. I'll never find a better occasion.—All right, Nora; now you know. And now you also know that you can confide in me more than in anyone else.

NORA *(gets up; in a calm, steady voice)*. Let me get by.

RANK *(makes room for her but remains seated)*. Nora—

NORA *(in the door to the front hall)*. Helene, bring the lamp in here, please. *(Walks over to the stove.)* Oh, dear Dr. Rank. That really wasn't very nice of you.

RANK *(gets up)*. That I have loved you as much as anybody—was that not nice?

NORA. No, not that. But that you told me. There was no need for that.

RANK. What do you mean? Have you known—?

THE MAID *enters with the lamp, puts it on the table, and goes out.*

RANK. Nora—Mrs. Helmer—I'm asking you: did you know?

NORA. Oh, how can I tell what I knew and didn't know! I really can't say—But that you could be so awkward, Dr. Rank! Just when everything was so comfortable.

RANK. Well, anyway, now you know that I'm at your service with my life and soul. And now you must speak.

NORA *(looks at him)*. After what just happened?

RANK. I beg of you—let me know what it is.

NORA. There is nothing I can tell you now.

RANK. Yes, yes. You mustn't punish me this way. Please let me do for you whatever anyone *can* do.

NORA. Now there is nothing you can do. Besides, I don't think I really need any help, anyway. It's probably just my imagination. Of course that's all it is. I'm sure of it! *(Sits down in the rocking chair, looks at him, smiles.)* Well, well, well, Dr. Rank! What a fine gentleman you turned out to be! Aren't you ashamed of yourself, now that we have light?

RANK. No, not really. But perhaps I ought to leave—and not come back?

NORA. Don't be silly; of course not! You'll come here exactly as you have been doing. You know perfectly well that Torvald can't do without you.

RANK. Yes, but what about you?

NORA. Oh, I always think it's perfectly delightful when you come.

RANK. That's the very thing that misled me. You are a riddle to me. It has often seemed to me that you'd just as soon be with me as with Helmer.

NORA. Well, you see, there are people you love, and then there are other people you'd almost rather be with.

RANK. Yes, there is something in that.

NORA. When I lived at home with Daddy, of course I loved him most. But I always thought it was so much fun to sneak off down to the maids' room, for they never gave me good advice and they always talked about such fun things.

RANK. Aha! So it's *their* place I have taken.

NORA *(jumps up and goes over to him)*. Oh dear, kind Dr. Rank, you know very well I didn't mean it that way. Can't you see that with Torvald it is the way it used to be with Daddy?

THE MAID *enters from the front hall.*

THE MAID. Ma'am! *(Whispers to her and gives her a caller's card.)*

NORA *(glances at the card)*. Ah! *(Puts it in her pocket.)*

RANK. Anything wrong?

NORA. No, no; not at all. It's nothing— just my new costume—

RANK. But your costume is lying right there!

NORA. Oh yes, that one. But this is another one. I ordered it. Torvald mustn't know—

RANK. Aha. So that's the great secret.

NORA. That's it. Why don't you go in to him, please. He's in the inner office. And keep him there for a while—

RANK. Don't worry. He won't get away. *(Enters* HELMER'*s study.)*

NORA *(to* THE MAID*)*. You say he's waiting in the kitchen?

THE MAID. Yes. He came up the back stairs.

NORA. But didn't you tell him there was somebody with me?

THE MAID. Yes, but he wouldn't listen.

NORA. He won't leave?

THE MAID. No, not till he's had a word with you, ma'am.

NORA. All right. But try not to make any noise. And, Helene—don't tell anyone he's here. It's supposed to be a surprise for my husband.

THE MAID. I understand, ma'am—*(She leaves.)*

NORA. The terrible is happening. It's happening, after all. No, no, no. It can't happen. It won't happen. *(She bolts the study door.)*

THE MAID *opens the front hall door for* KROG-STAD *and closes the door behind him. He wears a fur coat for traveling, boots, and a fur hat.*

NORA *(toward him)*. Keep your voice down. My husband's home.

KROGSTAD. That's all right.

NORA. What do you want?

KROGSTAD. To find out something.

NORA. Be quick, then. What is it?

KROGSTAD. I expect you know I've been fired.

NORA. I couldn't prevent it, Mr. Krogstad. I fought for you as long and as hard as I could, but it didn't do any good.

KROGSTAD. Your husband doesn't love you any more than that? He knows what I can do to you, and yet he runs the risk—

NORA. Surely you didn't think I'd tell him?

KROGSTAD. No, I really didn't. It wouldn't be like Torvald Helmer to show that kind of guts—

NORA. Mr. Krogstad, I insist that you show respect for my husband.

KROGSTAD. By all means. All due respect. But since you're so anxious to keep this a secret, may I assume that you are a little better informed than yesterday about exactly what you have done?

NORA. Better than *you* could ever teach me.

KROGSTAD. Of course. Such a bad lawyer as I am—

NORA. What do you want of me?

KROGSTAD. I just wanted to find out how you are, Mrs. Helmer. I've been thinking about you all day. You see, even a bill collector, a pen pusher, a—anyway, someone like me—even he has a little of what they call a heart.

NORA. Then show it. Think of my little children.

KROGSTAD. Have you and your husband thought of mine? Never mind. All I want to tell you is that you don't need to take this business too seriously. I have no intention of bringing charges right away.

NORA. Oh no, you wouldn't; would you? I knew you wouldn't.

KROGSTAD. The whole thing can be settled quite amiably. Nobody else needs to know anything. It will be between the three of us.

NORA. My husband must never find out about this.

KROGSTAD. How are you going to prevent that? Maybe you can pay me the balance on the loan?

NORA. No, not right now.

KROGSTAD. Or do you have a way of raising the money one of these next few days?

NORA. None I intend to make use of.

KROGSTAD. It wouldn't do you any good, anyway. Even if you had the cash in your hand right this minute, I wouldn't give you your note back. It wouldn't make any difference *how* much money you offered me.

NORA. Then you'll have to tell me what you plan to use the note *for*.

KROGSTAD. Just keep it; that's all. Have it on hand, so to speak. I won't say a word to anybody else. So if you've been thinking about doing something desperate—

NORA. I have.

KROGSTAD. —like leaving house and home—

NORA. I have!

KROGSTAD. —or even something worse—

NORA. How did you know?

KROGSTAD. —then: don't.

NORA. How did you know I was thinking of *that*?

KROGSTAD. Most of us do, right at first. I did, too, but when it came down to it I didn't have the courage—

NORA *(tonelessly)*. Nor do I.

KROGSTAD *(relieved)*. See what I mean? I thought so. You don't either.

NORA. I don't. I don't.

KROGSTAD. Besides, it would be very silly of you. Once that first domestic blow-up is behind you—. Here in my pocket is a letter for your husband.

NORA. Telling him everything?

KROGSTAD. As delicately as possible.

NORA *(quickly)*. He mustn't get that letter. Tear it up. I'll get you the money somehow.

KROGSTAD. Excuse me, Mrs. Helmer. I thought I just told you—

NORA. I'm not talking about the money I owe you. Just let me know how much money you want from my husband, and I'll get it for you.

KROGSTAD. I want no money from your husband.

NORA. Then, what *do* you want?

KROGSTAD. I'll tell you, Mrs. Helmer. I want to rehabilitate myself; I want to get up in the world; and your husband is going to help me. For a year and a half I haven't done anything disreputable. All that time I have been struggling with the most miserable circumstances. I was content to work my way up step by step. Now I've been kicked out, and I'm no longer satisfied just getting my old job back. I want more than that; I want to get to the top. I'm being quite serious. I want the bank to take me back but in a higher position. I want your husband to create a new job for me—

NORA. He'll never do that!

KROGSTAD. He will. I know him. He won't dare not to. And once I'm back inside and he and I are working together, you'll see! Within a year I'll be the manager's right hand. It will be Nils Krogstad and not Torvald Helmer who'll be running the Mutual Bank!

NORA. You'll never see that happen!

KROGSTAD. Are you thinking of—?

NORA. Now I *do* have the courage.

KROGSTAD. You can't scare me. A fine, spoiled lady like you—

NORA. You'll see, you'll see!

KROGSTAD. Under the ice, perhaps? Down into that cold, black water? Then spring comes, and you float up again—hideous, can't be identified, hair all gone—

NORA. You don't frighten me.

KROGSTAD. Nor you me. One doesn't do that sort of thing, Mrs. Helmer. Besides, what good would it do? He'd still be in my power.

NORA. Afterwards? When I'm no longer—?

KROGSTAD. Aren't you forgetting that your reputation would be in my hands?

NORA *stares at him, speechless.*

KROGSTAD. All right; now I've told you what to expect. So don't do anything foolish. When Helmer gets my letter I expect to hear from him. And don't you forget that it's your husband himself who forces me to use such means again. That I'll never forgive him. Goodbye, Mrs. Helmer. *(Goes out through the hall.)*

NORA *(at the door, opens it a little, listens).* He's going. And no letter. Of course not! That would be impossible! *(Opens the door more.)* What's he doing? He's still there. Doesn't go down. Having second thoughts—? Will he—?

The sound of a letter dropping into the mailbox. Then KROGSTAD'*s steps are heard going down the stairs, gradually dying away.*

NORA *(with a muted cry runs forward to the table by the couch; brief pause).* In the mailbox. *(Tiptoes back to the door to the front hall.)* There it is. Torvald, Torvald—now we're lost!

MRS. LINDE *(enters from the left, carrying* NORA'*s Capri costume).* There now. I think it's all fixed. Why don't we try it on you—

NORA *(in a low, hoarse voice).* Kristine, come here.

MRS. LINDE. What's wrong with you? You look quite beside yourself.

NORA. Come over here. Do you see that letter? There, look—through the glass in the mailbox.

MRS. LINDE. Yes, yes; I see it.

NORA. That letter is from Krogstad.

MRS. LINDE. Nora—it was Krogstad who lent you the money!

NORA. Yes, and now Torvald will find out about it.

MRS. LINDE. Oh believe me, Nora. That's the best thing for both of you.

NORA. There's more to it than you know. I forged a signature—

MRS. LINDE. Oh my God—!

NORA. I just want to tell you this, Kristine, that you must be my witness.

MRS. LINDE. Witness? How? Witness to what?

NORA. If I lose my mind—and that could very well happen—

MRS. LINDE. Nora!

NORA. —or if something were to happen to me—something that made it impossible for me to be here—

MRS. LINDE. Nora, Nora! You're not yourself!

NORA. —and if someone were to take all the blame, assume the whole responsibility—Do you understand—?

MRS. LINDE. Yes, yes; but how can you think—!

NORA. —then you are to witness that that's not so, Kristine. I am not beside myself. I am perfectly rational, and what I'm telling you is that nobody else has known about this. I've done it all by myself, the whole thing. Just remember that.

MRS. LINDE. I will. But I don't understand any of it.

NORA. Oh, how could you! For it's the wonderful that's about to happen.

MRS. LINDE. The wonderful?

NORA. Yes, the wonderful. But it's so terrible, Kristine. It mustn't happen for anything in the whole world!

MRS. LINDE. I'm going over to talk to Krogstad right now.

NORA. No, don't. Don't go to him. He'll do something bad to you.

MRS. LINDE. There was a time when he would have done anything for me.

NORA. He!

MRS. LINDE. Where does he live?

NORA. Oh, I don't know—Yes, wait a minute— *(Reaches into her pocket.)* here's his card.—But the letter, the letter—!

HELMER *(in his study, knocks on the door)*. Nora!

NORA *(cries out in fear)*. Oh, what is it? What do you want?

HELMER. That's all right. Nothing to be scared about. We're not coming in. For one thing, you've bolted the door, you know. Are you modeling your costume?

NORA. Yes, yes; I am. I'm going to be so pretty, Torvald.

MRS. LINDE *(having looked at the card)*. He lives just around the corner.

NORA. Yes, but it's no use. Nothing can save us now. The letter is in the mailbox.

MRS. LINDE. And your husband has the key?

NORA. Yes. He always keeps it with him.

MRS. LINDE. Krogstad must ask for his letter back, unread. He's got to think up some pretext or other—

NORA. But this is just the time of day when Torvald—

MRS. LINDE. Delay him. Go in to him. I'll be back as soon as I can. *(She hurries out through the hall door.)*

NORA *(walks over to Helmer's door, opens it, and peeks in)*. Torvald!

HELMER *(still offstage)*. Well, well! So now one's allowed in one's own living room again. Come on, Rank. Now we'll see— *(In the doorway.)* But what's this?

NORA. What, Torvald dear?

HELMER. Rank prepared me for a splendid metamorphosis.

RANK *(in the doorway)*. That's how I understood it. Evidently I was mistaken.

NORA. Nobody gets to admire me in my costume before tomorrow.

HELMER. But, dearest Nora—you look all done in. Have you been practicing too hard?

NORA. No, I haven't practiced at all.

HELMER. But you'll have to, you know.

NORA. I know it, Torvald. I simply must. But I can't do a thing unless you help me. I have forgotten everything.

HELMER. Oh it will all come back. We'll work on it.

NORA. Oh yes, please, Torvald. You just have to help me. Promise? I am so nervous. That big party—. You mustn't do anything else tonight. Not a bit of business. Don't even touch a pen. Will you promise, Torvald?

HELMER. I promise. Tonight I'll be entirely at your service—you helpless little thing.—Just a moment, though. First I want to— *(Goes to the door to the front hall.)*

NORA. What are you doing out there?

HELMER. Just looking to see if there's any mail.

NORA. No, no! Don't, Torvald!

HELMER. Why not?

NORA. Torvald, I beg you. There is no mail.

HELMER. Let me just look, anyway. *(Is about to go out.)*

NORA *by the piano, plays the first bars of the tarantella dance.*

HELMER *(halts at the door)*. Aha!

NORA. I won't be able to dance tomorrow if I don't get to practice with you.

HELMER *(goes to her)*. Are you really all that scared, Nora dear?

NORA. Yes, so terribly scared. Let's try it right now. There's still time before we eat. Oh please, sit down and play for me, Torvald. Teach me, coach me, the way you always do.

HELMER. Of course I will, my darling, if that's what you want. *(Sits down at the piano.)*

NORA *takes the tambourine out of the carton, as well as a long, many-colored shawl. She quickly drapes the shawl around herself, then leaps into the middle of the floor.*

NORA. Play for me! I want to dance!

HELMER *plays and* NORA *dances.* DR. RANK *stands by the piano behind* HELMER *and watches.*

HELMER *(playing).* Slow down, slow down!

NORA. Can't!

HELMER. Not so violent, Nora!

NORA. It has to be this way.

HELMER *(stops playing).* No, no. This won't do at all.

NORA *(laughing, swinging her tambourine).* What did I tell you?

RANK. Why don't you let me play?

HELMER *(getting up).* Good idea. Then I can direct her better.

RANK *sits down at the piano and starts playing.* NORA *dances more and more wildly.* HELMER *stands over by the stove, repeatedly correcting her. She doesn't seem to hear. Her hair comes loose and falls down over her shoulders. She doesn't notice but keeps on dancing.* MRS. LINDE *enters.*

MRS. LINDE *(stops by the door, dumbfounded).* Ah—!

NORA *(dancing).* We're having such fun, Kristine!

HELMER. My dearest Nora, you're dancing as if it were a matter of life and death!

NORA. It is! It is!

HELMER. Rank, stop. This is sheer madness. Stop it, I say!

RANK *stops playing;* NORA *suddenly stops dancing.*

HELMER *(goes over to her).* If I hadn't seen it I wouldn't have believed it. You've forgotten every single thing I ever taught you.

NORA *(tosses away the tambourine).* See? I told you.

HELMER. Well! You certainly need coaching.

NORA. Didn't I tell you I did? Now you've seen for yourself. I'll need your help till the very minute we're leaving for the party. Will you promise, Torvald?

HELMER. You can count on it.

NORA. You're not to think of anything except me—not tonight and not tomorrow. You're not to read any letters—not to look in the mailbox—

HELMER. Ah, I see. You're still afraid of that man.

NORA. Yes—yes, that too.

HELMER. Nora, I can tell from looking at you. There's a letter from him out there.

NORA. I don't know. I think so. But you're not to read it now. I don't want anything ugly to come between us before it's all over.

RANK *(to* HELMER *in a low voice).* Better not argue with her.

HELMER *(throws his arm around her).* The child shall have her way. But tomorrow night, when you've done your dance—

NORA. Then you'll be free.

THE MAID *(in the door, right).* Dinner can be served any time, ma'am.

NORA. We want champagne, Helene.

THE MAID. Very good, ma'am. *(Goes out.)*

HELMER. Aha! Having a party, eh?

NORA. Champagne from now till sunrise! *(Calls out.)* And some macaroons, Helene. Lots!—just this once.

HELMER *(taking her hands).* There, there—I don't like this wild—frenzy—Be my own sweet little lark again, the way you always are.

NORA. Oh, I will. But you go on in. You too, Dr. Rank. Kristine, please help me put up my hair.

RANK *(in a low voice to* HELMER *as they go out).* You don't think she is—you know—expecting—?

HELMER. Oh no. Nothing like that. It's just this childish fear I was telling you about. *(They go out, right.)*

NORA. Well?

MRS. LINDE. Left town.

NORA. I saw it in your face.

MRS. LINDE. He'll be back tomorrow night. I left him a note.

NORA. You shouldn't have. I don't want you to try to stop anything. You see, it's a kind of ecstasy, too, this waiting for the wonderful.

MRS. LINDE. But what is it you're waiting *for?*

NORA. You wouldn't understand. Why don't you go in to the others. I'll be there in a minute.

MRS. LINDE *enters the dining room, right.*

NORA *(stands still for a little while, as if collecting herself, she looks at her watch).* Five o'clock. Seven hours till midnight. Twenty-four more hours till next midnight. Then the tarantella is over. Twenty-four plus seven—thirty-one more hours to live.

HELMER *(in the door, right).* What's happening to my little lark?

NORA *(to him, with open arms).* Here's your lark!

ACT III

The same room. The table by the couch and the chairs around it have been moved to the middle of the floor. A lighted lamp is on the table. The door to the front hall is open. Dance music is heard from upstairs.

MRS. LINDE is seated by the table, idly leafing through the pages of a book. She tries to read but seems unable to concentrate. Once or twice she turns her head in the direction of the door, anxiously listening.

MRS. LINDE *(looks at her watch).* Not yet. It's almost too late. If only he hasn't— *(Listens again.)* Ah! There he is. *(She goes to the hall and opens the front door carefully. Quiet footsteps on the stairs. She whispers.)* Come in. There's nobody here.

KROGSTAD *(in the door).* I found your note when I got home. What's this all about?

MRS. LINDE. I've got to talk to you.

KROGSTAD. Oh? And it has to be here?

MRS. LINDE. It couldn't be at my place. My room doesn't have a separate entrance. Come in. We're all alone. The maid is asleep and the Helmers are at a party upstairs.

KROGSTAD *(entering).* Really? The Helmers are dancing tonight, are they?

MRS. LINDE. And why not?

KROGSTAD. You're right. Why not, indeed.

MRS. LINDE. All right, Krogstad. Let's talk, you and I.

KROGSTAD. I didn't know we had anything to talk about.

MRS. LINDE. We have much to talk about.

KROGSTAD. I didn't think so.

MRS. LINDE. No, because you've never really understood me.

KROGSTAD. What was there to understand? What happened was perfectly commonplace. A heartless woman jilts a man when she gets a more attractive offer.

MRS. LINDE. Do you think I'm all that heartless? And do you think it was easy for me to break with you?

KROGSTAD. No?

MRS. LINDE. You really thought it was?

KROGSTAD. If it wasn't, why did you write the way you did that time?

MRS. LINDE. What else could I do? If I had to make a break, I also had the duty to destroy whatever feelings you had for me.

KROGSTAD *(clenching his hands).* So that's the way it was. And you did—*that*—just for money!

MRS. LINDE. Don't forget I had a helpless mother and two small brothers. We couldn't wait for you, Krogstad. You know yourself how uncertain your prospects were then.

KROGSTAD. All right. But you still didn't have the right to throw me over for somebody else.

MRS. LINDE. I don't know. I have asked myself that question many times. Did I have that right?

KROGSTAD *(in a lower voice).* When I lost you I lost my footing. Look at me now. A shipwrecked man on a raft.

MRS. LINDE. Rescue may be near.

KROGSTAD. It *was* near. Then you came between.

MRS. LINDE. I didn't know that, Krogstad. Only today did I find out it's your job I'm taking over in the bank.

KROGSTAD. I believe you when you say so. But now that you *do* know, aren't you going to step aside?

MRS. LINDE. No, for it wouldn't do you any good.

KROGSTAD. Whether it would or not—*I* would do it.

MRS. LINDE. I have learned common sense. Life and hard necessity have taught me that.

KROGSTAD. And life has taught me not to believe in pretty speeches.

MRS. LINDE. Then life has taught you a very sensible thing. But you do believe in actions, don't you?

KROGSTAD. How do you mean?

MRS. LINDE. You referred to yourself just now as a shipwrecked man.

KROGSTAD. It seems to me I had every reason to do so.

MRS. LINDE. And I am a shipwrecked woman. No one to grieve for, no one to care for.

KROGSTAD. You made your choice.

MRS. LINDE. I had no other choice that time.

KROGSTAD. Let's say you didn't. What then?

MRS. LINDE. Krogstad, how would it be if we two shipwrecked people got together?

KROGSTAD. What's this!

MRS. LINDE. Two on one wreck are better off than each on his own.

KROGSTAD. Kristine!

MRS. LINDE. Why do you think I came to town?

KROGSTAD. Surely not because of me?

MRS. LINDE. If I'm going to live at all I must work. All my life, for as long as I can remember, I have worked. That's been my one and only pleasure. But now that I'm all alone in the world I feel nothing but this terrible emptiness and desolation. There is no joy in working just for yourself. Krogstad—give me someone and something to work for.

KROGSTAD. I don't believe this. Only hysterical females go in for that kind of high-minded self-sacrifice.

MRS. LINDE. Did you ever know me to be hysterical?

KROGSTAD. You really could do this? Listen—do you know about my past? All of it?

MRS. LINDE. Yes, I do.

KROGSTAD. Do you also know what people think of me around here?

MRS. LINDE. A little while ago you sounded as if you thought that together with me you might have become a different person.

KROGSTAD. I'm sure of it.

MRS. LINDE. Couldn't that still be?

KROGSTAD. Kristine—do you know what you are doing? Yes, I see you do. And you think you have the courage—

MRS. LINDE. I need someone to be a mother to, and your children need a mother. You and I need one another. Nils, I believe in you—in the real you. Together with you I dare to do anything.

KROGSTAD *(seizes her hands)*. Thanks, thanks, Kristine—now I know I'll raise myself in the eyes of others.—Ah, but I forget—!

MRS. LINDE *(listening)*. Shh!—There's the tarantella. You must go; hurry!

KROGSTAD. Why? What is it?

MRS. LINDE. Do you hear what they're playing up there? When that dance is over they'll be down.

KROGSTAD. All right. I'm leaving. The whole thing is pointless, anyway. Of course you don't know what I'm doing to the Helmers.

MRS. LINDE. Yes, Krogstad; I do know.

KROGSTAD. Still, you're brave enough—?

MRS. LINDE. I very well understand to what extremes despair can drive a man like you.

KROGSTAD. If only it could be undone!

MRS. LINDE. It could, for your letter is still out there in the mailbox.

KROGSTAD. Are you sure?

MRS. LINDE. Quite sure. But—

KROGSTAD *(looks searchingly at her)*. Maybe I'm beginning to understand. You want to save your friend at any cost. Be honest with me. That's it, isn't it?

MRS. LINDE. Krogstad, you may sell yourself once for somebody else's sake, but you don't do it twice.

KROGSTAD. I'll demand my letter back.

MRS. LINDE. No, no.

KROGSTAD. Yes, of course. I'll wait here till Helmer comes down. Then I'll ask him for my letter. I'll tell him it's just about my dismissal—that he shouldn't read it.

MRS. LINDE. No, Krogstad. You are not to ask for that letter back.

KROGSTAD. But tell me—wasn't that the real reason you wanted to meet me here?

MRS. LINDE. At first it was, because I was so frightened. But that was yesterday. Since then I have seen the most incredible things going on in this house. Helmer must learn the whole truth. This miserable secret must come out in the open; those two must come to a full understanding. They simply can't continue with all this concealment and evasion.

KROGSTAD. All right; if you want to take that chance. But there is one thing I *can* do, and I'll do that right now.

MRS. LINDE *(listening)*. But hurry! Go! The dance is over. We aren't safe another minute.

KROGSTAD. I'll be waiting for you downstairs.

MRS. LINDE. Yes, do. You must see me home.

KROGSTAD. I've never been so happy in my whole life. *(He leaves through the front door. The door between the living room and the front hall remains open.)*

MRS. LINDE *(straightens up the room a little and gets her things ready)*. What a change! Oh yes!—what a change! People to work for—to live for—a home to bring happiness to. I can't wait to get to work—! If only they'd come soon— *(Listens.)* Ah, there they are. Get my coat on— *(Puts on her coat and hat.)*

HELMER'*s and* NORA'*s voices are heard outside. A key is turned in the lock, and* HELMER *almost forces* NORA *into the hall. She is dressed in her Italian costume, with a big black shawl over her shoulders. He is in evening dress under an open black cloak.*

NORA *(in the door, still resisting)*. No, no, no! I don't want to! I want to go back upstairs. I don't want to leave so early.

HELMER. But dearest Nora—

NORA. Oh please, Torvald—please! I'm asking you as nicely as I can—just another hour!

HELMER. Not another minute, sweet. You know we agreed. There now. Get inside. You'll catch a cold out here. *(She still resists, but he guides her gently into the room.)*

MRS. LINDE. Good evening.

NORA. Kristine!

HELMER. Ah, Mrs. Linde. Still here?

MRS. LINDE. I know. I really should apologize, but I so much wanted to see Nora in her costume.

NORA. You've been waiting up for me?

MRS. LINDE. Yes, unfortunately I didn't get here in time. You were already upstairs, but I just didn't feel like leaving till I had seen you.

HELMER *(removing* NORA'*s shawl)*. Yes, do take a good look at her, Mrs. Linde. I think I may say she's worth looking at. Isn't she lovely?

MRS. LINDE. She certainly is—

HELMER. Isn't she a miracle of loveliness, though? That was the general opinion at the party, too. But dreadfully obstinate—that she is, the sweet little thing. What can we do about that? Will you believe it—I practically had to use force to get her away.

NORA. Oh Torvald, you're going to be sorry you didn't give me even half an hour more.

HELMER. See what I mean, Mrs. Linde? She dances the tarantella—she is a tremendous success—quite deservedly so, though perhaps her performance was a little too natural—I mean, more than could be reconciled with the rules of art. But all right! The point is: she's a success, a tremendous success. So should I let her stay after that? Spoil the effect? Of course not. So I take my lovely little Capri girl—I might say, my capricious little Capri girl—under my arm—a quick turn around the room—a graceful bow in all directions, and—as they say in the novels—the beautiful apparition is gone. A finale should always be done for effect, Mrs. Linde, but there doesn't seem to be any way of getting that into Nora's head. Poooh—! It's hot in here. *(Throws his cloak down on a chair and opens the door to his room.)* Why, it's dark in here! Of course. Excuse me— *(Goes inside and lights a couple of candles.)*

NORA *(in a hurried, breathless whisper)*. Well?

MRS. LINDE *(in a low voice)*. I have talked to him.

NORA. And—?

MRS. LINDE. Nora—you've got to tell your husband everything.

NORA *(no expression in her voice)*. I knew it.

MRS. LINDE. You have nothing to fear from Krogstad. But you must speak.

NORA. I'll say nothing.

MRS. LINDE. Then the letter will.

NORA. Thank you, Kristine. Now I know what I have to do. Shh!

HELMER *(returning)*. Well, Mrs. Linde, have you looked your fill?

MRS. LINDE. Yes. And now I'll say good-night.

HELMER. So soon? Is that your knitting?

MRS. LINDE *(takes it)*. Yes, thank you. I almost forgot.

HELMER. So you knit, do you?

MRS. LINDE. Oh yes.

HELMER. You know—you ought to take up embroidery instead.

MRS. LINDE. Oh? Why?

HELMER. Because it's so much more beautiful. Look. You hold the embroidery so—in your left hand. Then with your right you move the needle—like this—in an easy, elongated arc—you see?

MRS. LINDE. Maybe you're right—

HELMER. Knitting, on the other hand, can never be anything but ugly. Look here: arms pressed close to the sides—the needles going up and down—there's something Chinese about it somehow—. That really was an excellent champagne they served us tonight.

MRS. LINDE. Well, goodnight, Nora. And don't be obstinate any more.

HELMER. Well said, Mrs. Linde!

MRS. LINDE. Goodnight, sir.

HELMER *(sees her to the front door)*. Goodnight, goodnight. I hope you'll get home all right? I'd be very glad to—but of course you don't have far to walk, do you? Goodnight, goodnight. *(She leaves. He closes the door behind her and returns to the living room.)* There! At last we got rid of her. She really is an incredible bore, that woman.

NORA. Aren't you very tired, Torvald?

HELMER. No, not in the least.

NORA. Not sleepy either?

HELMER. Not at all. Quite the opposite. I feel enormously—animated. How about you? Yes, you do look tired and sleepy.

NORA. Yes I am very tired. Soon I'll be asleep.

HELMER. What did I tell you? I was right, wasn't I? Good thing I didn't let you stay any longer.

NORA. Everything you do is right.

HELMER *(kissing her forehead)*. Now my little lark is talking like a human being. But did you notice what splendid spirits Rank was in tonight?

NORA. Was he? I didn't notice. I didn't get to talk with him.

HELMER. Nor did I—hardly. But I haven't seen him in such a good mood for a long time. *(Looks at her, comes closer to her.)* Ah! It does feel good to be back in our own home again, to be quite alone with you—my young, lovely, ravishing woman!

NORA. Don't look at me like that, Torvald!

HELMER. Am I not to look at my most precious possession? All that loveliness that is mine, nobody's but mine, all of it mine.

NORA *(walks to the other side of the table)*. I won't have you talk to me like that tonight.

HELMER *(follows her)*. The tarantella is still in your blood. I can tell. That only makes you all the more alluring. Listen! The guests are beginning to leave. *(Softly.)* Nora—soon the whole house will be quiet.

NORA. Yes, I hope so.

HELMER. Yes, don't you, my darling? Do you know—when I'm at a party with you, like tonight—do you know why I hardly ever talk to you, why I keep away from you, only look at you once in a while—a few stolen glances—do you know why I do that? It's because I pretend that you are my secret love, my young, secret bride-to-be, and nobody has the slightest suspicion that there is anything between us.

NORA. Yes, I know. All your thoughts are with me.

HELMER. Then when we're leaving and I

lay your shawl around your delicate young shoulders—around that wonderful curve of your neck—then I imagine you're my young bride, that we're coming away from the wedding, that I am taking you to my home for the first time—that I am alone with you for the first time—quite alone with you, you young, trembling beauty! I have desired you all evening—there hasn't been a longing in me that hasn't been for you. When you were dancing the tarantella, chasing, inviting—my blood was on fire; I couldn't stand it any longer—that's why I brought you down so early—

NORA. Leave me now, Torvald. Please! I don't want all this.

HELMER. What do you mean? You're only playing your little teasing bird game with me; aren't you, Nora? Don't want to? I'm your husband, aren't I?

There is a knock on the front door.

NORA *(with a start)*. Did you hear that—?

HELMER *(on his way to the hall)*. Who is it?

RANK *(outside)*. It's me. May I come in for a moment?

HELMER *(in a low voice, annoyed)*. Oh, what does he want now? *(Aloud.)* Just a minute. *(Opens the door.)* Well! How good of you not to pass by our door.

RANK. I thought I heard your voice, so I felt like saying hello. *(Looks around.)* Ah yes—this dear, familiar room. What a cozy, comfortable place you have here, you two.

HELMER. Looked to me as if you were quite comfortable upstairs too.

RANK. I certainly was. Why not? Why not enjoy all you can in this world? As much as you can for as long as you can, anyway. Excellent wine.

HELMER. The champagne, particularly.

RANK. You noticed that too? Incredible how much I managed to put away.

NORA. Torvald drank a lot of champagne tonight, too.

RANK. Did he?

NORA. Yes, he did, and then he's always so much fun afterwards.

RANK. Well, why not have some fun in the evening after a well spent day?

HELMER. Well spent? I'm afraid I can't claim that.

RANK *(slapping him lightly on the shoulder)*. But you see, I can!

NORA. Dr. Rank, I believe you must have been conducting a scientific test today.

RANK. Exactly.

HELMER. What do you know—little Nora talking about scientific tests!

NORA. May I congratulate you on the result?

RANK. You may indeed.

NORA. It was a good one?

RANK. The best possible for both doctor and patient—certainty.

NORA *(a quick query)*. Certainty?

RANK. Absolute certainty. So why shouldn't I have myself an enjoyable evening afterwards?

NORA. I quite agree with you, Dr. Rank. You should.

HELMER. And so do I. If only you don't pay for it tomorrow.

RANK. Oh well—you get nothing for nothing in this world.

NORA. Dr. Rank—you are fond of costume parties, aren't you?

RANK. Yes, particularly when there is a reasonable number of amusing disguises.

NORA. Listen—what are the two of us going to be the next time?

HELMER. You frivolous little thing! Already thinking about the next party!

RANK. You and I? That's easy. You'll be Fortune's Child.

HELMER. Yes, but what is a fitting costume for that?

RANK. Let your wife appear just the way she always is.

HELMER. Beautiful. Very good indeed. But how about yourself? Don't you know what you'll go as?

RANK. Yes, my friend. I know precisely what I'll be.

HELMER. Yes?

RANK. At the next masquerade I'll be invisible.

HELMER. That's a funny idea.

RANK. There's a certain big, black hat— you've heard about the hat that makes you invisible, haven't you? You put that on, and nobody can see you.

HELMER *(suppressing a smile)*. I guess that's right.

RANK. But I'm forgetting what I came for. Helmer, give me a cigar—one of your dark Havanas.

HELMER. With the greatest pleasure. *(Offers him his case.)*

RANK *(takes one and cuts off the tip)*. Thanks.

NORA *(striking a match)*. Let me give you a light.

RANK. Thanks. *(She holds the match; he lights his cigar.)* And now goodbye!

HELMER. Goodbye, goodbye, my friend.

NORA. Sleep well, Dr. Rank.

RANK. I thank you.

NORA. Wish me the same.

RANK. You? Well, if you really want me to—. Sleep well. And thanks for the light. *(He nods to both of them and goes out.)*

HELMER *(in a low voice)*. He had had quite a bit to drink.

NORA *(absently)*. Maybe so.

HELMER *takes out his keys and goes out into the hall.*

NORA. Torvald—what are you doing out there?

HELMER. Got to empty the mailbox. It is quite full. There wouldn't be room for the newspapers in the morning—

NORA. Are you going to work tonight?

HELMER. You know very well I won't.— Say! What's this? Somebody's been at the lock.

NORA. The lock?

HELMER. Yes. Why, I wonder. I hate to think that any of the maids—. Here's a broken hairpin. It's one of yours, Nora.

NORA *(quickly)*. Then it must be one of the children.

HELMER. You better make damn sure they stop that. Hm, hm.—There! I got it open, finally. *(Gathers up the mail, calls out to the kitchen.)* Helene?—Oh Helene—turn out the light here in the hall, will you? *(He*

comes back into the living room and closes the door.)* Look how it's been piling up. *(Shows her the bundle of letters. Starts leafing through it.)* What's this?

NORA *(by the window)*. The letter! Oh no, no, Torvald!

HELMER. Two calling cards—from Rank.

NORA. From Dr. Rank?

HELMER *(looking at them)*. "Doctor medicinae Rank." They were on top. He must have put them there when he left just now.

NORA. Anything written on them?

HELMER. A black cross above the name. Look. What a macabre idea. Like announcing his own death.

NORA. That's what it is.

HELMER. Hm? You know about this? Has he said anything to you?

NORA. That card means he has said goodbye to us. He'll lock himself up to die.

HELMER. My poor friend. I knew of course he wouldn't be with me very long. But so soon—. And hiding himself away like a wounded animal—

NORA. When it has to be, it's better it happens without words. Don't you think so, Torvald?

HELMER *(walking up and down)*. He'd grown so close to us. I find it hard to think of him as gone. With his suffering and loneliness he was like a clouded background for our happy sunshine. Well, it may be better this way. For him, at any rate. *(Stops.)* And perhaps for us, too, Nora. For now we have nobody but each other. *(Embraces her.)* Oh you—my beloved wife! I feel I just can't hold you close enough. Do you know, Nora—many times I have wished some great danger threatened you, so I could risk my life and blood and everything— everything, for your sake.

NORA *(frees herself and says in a strong and firm voice)*. I think you should go and read your letters now, Torvald.

HELMER. No, no—not tonight. I want to be with you, my darling.

NORA. With the thought of your dying friend—?

HELMER. You are right. This has shaken both of us. Something not beautiful has come between us. Thoughts of death and dissolution. We must try to get over it—out of it. Till then—we'll each go to our own room.

NORA *(her arms around his neck)*. Torvald—goodnight! Goodnight!

HELMER *(kisses her forehead)*. Goodnight, my little songbird. Sleep well, Nora. Now I'll read my letters. *(He goes into his room, carrying the mail. Closes the door.)*

NORA *(her eyes desperate, her hands groping, finds* HELMER*'s domino and throws it around her; she whispers, quickly, brokenly, hoarsely)*, Never see him again. Never. Never. Never. *(Puts her shawl over her head.)* And never see the children again, either. Never; never.—The black, icy water—fathomless—this—! If only it was all over.—Now he has it. Now he's reading it. No, no; not yet. Torvald—goodbye—you—the children—

She is about to hurry through the hall, when HELMER *flings open the door to his room and stands there with an open letter in his hand.*

HELMER. Nora!

NORA *(cries out)*. Ah—!

HELMER. What is it? You know what's in this letter?

NORA. Yes, I do! Let me go! Let me out!

HELMER *(holds her back)*. Where do you think you're going?

NORA *(trying to tear herself loose from him)*. I won't let you save me, Torvald!

HELMER *(tumbles back)*. True! Is it true what he writes? Oh my God! No, no—this can't possibly be true.

NORA. It is true. I have loved you more than anything else in the whole world.

HELMER. Oh, don't give me any silly excuses.

NORA *(taking a step toward him)*. Torvald—!

HELMER. You wretch! What have you done!

NORA. Let me go. You are not to sacrifice yourself for me. You are not to take the blame.

HELMER. No more playacting. *(Locks the door to the front hall.)* You'll stay here and answer me. Do you understand what you have done? Answer me! Do you understand?

NORA *(gazes steadily at him with an increasingly frozen expression)*. Yes. Now I'm beginning to understand.

HELMER *(walking up and down)*. What a dreadful awakening. All these years—all these eight years—she, my pride and my joy—a hypocrite, a liar—oh worse! worse!—a criminal! Oh, the bottomless ugliness in all this! Damn! Damn! Damn!

NORA, *silent, keeps gazing at him.*

HELMER *(stops in front of her)*. I ought to have guessed that something like this would happen. I should have expected it. All your father's loose principles—Silence! You have inherited every one of your father's loose principles. No religion, no morals, no sense of duty—. Now I am being punished for my leniency with him. I did it for your sake, and this is how you pay me back.

NORA. Yes. This is how.

HELMER. You have ruined all my happiness. My whole future—that's what you have destroyed. Oh, it's terrible to think about. I am at the mercy of an unscrupulous man. He can do with me whatever he likes, demand anything of me, command me and dispose of me just as he pleases—I dare not say a word! To go down so miserably, to be destroyed—all because of an irresponsible woman!

NORA. When I am gone from the world, you'll be free.

HELMER. No noble gestures, please. Your father was always full of such phrases too. What good would it do me if you were gone from the world, as you put it? Not the slightest good at all. He could still make the whole thing public, and if he did I wouldn't be surprised if people thought I'd put you up to it. They might even think it was my idea—that it was I who urged you to do it! And for all this I have you to thank—you, whom I've borne on my hands through all the years of our marriage. *Now* do you understand what you've done to me?

NORA *(with cold calm)*. Yes.

HELMER. I just can't get it into my head that this is happening; it's all so incredible. But we have to come to terms with it somehow. Take your shawl off. Take it off, I say! I have to satisfy him one way or another. The whole affair must be kept quiet at whatever cost.—And as far as you and I are concerned, nothing must seem to have changed. I'm talking about appearances, of course. You'll go on living here; that goes without saying. But I won't let you bring up the children; I dare not trust you with them.—Oh! Having to say this to one I have loved so much, and whom I still—! But all that is past. It's not a question of happiness any more but of hanging on to what can be salvaged—pieces, appearances— *(The doorbell rings.)*

HELMER *(jumps)*. What's that? So late. Is the worst—? Has he—! Hide, Nora! Say you're sick.

NORA *doesn't move.* HELMER *opens the door to the hall.*

THE MAID *(half dressed, out in the hall).* A letter for your wife, sir.

HELMER. Give it to me. *(Takes the letter and closes the door.)* Yes, it's from him. But I won't let you have it. I'll read it myself.

NORA. Yes—you read it.

HELMER *(by the lamp).* I hardly dare. Perhaps we're lost, both you and I. No; I've got to know. *(Tears the letter open, glances through it, looks at an enclosure; a cry of joy.)* Nora!

NORA *looks at him with a question in her eyes.*

HELMER. Nora!—No, I must read it again.—Yes, yes, it is so! I'm saved! Nora, I'm saved!

NORA. And I?

HELMER. You too, of course; we're both saved, both you and I. Look! He's returning your note. He writes that he's sorry, he regrets, a happy turn in his life—oh, it doesn't matter what he writes. We're saved, Nora! Nobody can do anything to you now. Oh Nora, Nora—. No, I want to get rid of this disgusting thing first. Let me see— *(Looks at the signature.)* No, I don't want to see it. I don't want it to be more than a bad dream, the whole thing. *(Tears up the note and both letters, throws the pieces in the stove, and watches them burn.)* There! Now it's gone.—He wrote that ever since Christmas Eve—. Good God, Nora, these must have been three terrible days for you.

NORA. I have fought a hard fight these last three days.

HELMER. And been in agony and seen no other way out than—. No, we won't think of all that ugliness. We'll just rejoice and tell ourselves it's over, it's all over! Oh, listen to me, Nora. You don't seem to understand. It's over. What *is* it? Why do you look like that—that frozen expression on your face? Oh my poor little Nora, don't you think I know what it is? You can't make yourself believe that I have forgiven you. But I have, Nora; I swear to you, I have forgiven you for everything. Of course I know that what you did was for love of me.

NORA. That is true.

HELMER. You have loved me the way a wife ought to love her husband. You just didn't have the wisdom to judge the means. But do you think I love you any less because you don't know how to act on your own? Of course not. Just lean on me. I'll advise you; I'll guide you. I wouldn't be a man if I didn't find you twice as attractive because of your womanly helplessness. You mustn't pay any attention to the hard words I said to you right at first. It was just that first shock when I thought everything was collapsing all around me. I have forgiven you, Nora. I swear to you—I really have forgiven you.

NORA. I thank you for your forgiveness. *(She goes out through the door, right.)*

HELMER. No, stay— *(Looks into the room she entered.)* What are you doing in there?

NORA *(within).* Getting out of my costume.

HELMER *(by the open door).* Good, good. Try to calm down and compose yourself, my poor little frightened songbird. Rest safely; I have broad wings to cover you with. *(Walks around near the door.)* What a nice and cozy home we have, Nora. Here's shelter for you. Here I'll keep you safe like a hunted dove I have rescued from the hawk's talons. Believe me: I'll know how to quiet your beating heart. It will happen by and by, Nora; you'll see. Why, tomorrow you'll look at all this in quite a different light. And soon everything will be just the way it was before. I won't need to keep reassuring you that I have forgiven you; you'll feel it yourself. Did you really think I could have abandoned you, or even reproached you? Oh, you don't know a real man's heart, Nora. There is something unspeakably sweet and satisfactory for a man to know deep in himself that he has forgiven his wife—forgiven her in all the fullness of his honest heart. You see, that way she becomes his very own all over again—in a double sense, you might say. He has, so to speak, given her a second birth; it is as if she had become his wife and his child, both. From now on that's what you'll be to me, you lost and helpless creature. Don't worry about a thing, Nora. Only be frank with me, and I'll be your will and your conscience.—What's this? You're not in bed? You've changed your dress—!

NORA *(in an everyday dress)*. Yes, Torvald. I have changed my dress.

HELMER. But why—now—this late—?

NORA. I'm not going to sleep tonight.

HELMER. But my dear Nora—

NORA *(looks at her watch)*. It isn't all that late. Sit down here with me, Torvald. You and I have much to talk about. *(Sits down at the table.)*

HELMER. Nora—what is this all about? That rigid face—

NORA. Sit down. This will take a while. I have much to say to you.

HELMER *(sits down, facing her across the table)*. You worry me, Nora. I don't understand you.

NORA. No, that's just it. You don't understand me. And I have never understood you—not till tonight. No, don't interrupt me. Just listen to what I have to say.—This is a settling of accounts, Torvald.

HELMER. What do you mean by that?

NORA *(after a brief silence)*. Doesn't one thing strike you, now that we are sitting together like this?

HELMER. What would that be?

NORA. We have been married for eight years. Doesn't it occur to you that this is the first time that you and I, husband and wife, are having a serious talk?

HELMER. Well—serious—. What do you mean by that?

NORA. For eight whole years—longer, in fact—ever since we first met, we have never talked seriously to each other about a single serious thing.

HELMER. You mean I should forever have been telling you about worries you couldn't have helped me with anyway?

NORA. I am not talking about worries. I'm saying we have never tried seriously to get to the bottom of anything together.

HELMER. But dearest Nora, I hardly think that would have been something *you*—

NORA. That's the whole point. You have never understood me. Great wrong has been done to me, Torvald. First by Daddy and then by you.

HELMER. What! By us two? We who have loved you more deeply than anyone else?

NORA *(shakes her head)*. You never loved me—neither Daddy nor you. You only thought it was fun to be in love with me.

HELMER. But, Nora—what an expression to use!

NORA. That's the way it has been, Torvald. When I was home with Daddy, he told me all his opinions, and so they became my opinions too. If I disagreed with him I kept it to myself, for he wouldn't have liked that. He called me his little doll baby, and he played with me the way I played with my dolls. Then I came to your house—

HELMER. What a way to talk about our marriage!

NORA *(imperturbably)*. I mean that I passed from Daddy's hands into yours. You arranged everything according to your taste, and so I came to share it—or I pretended to; I'm not sure which. I think it was a little of both, now one and now the other. When I look back on it now, it seems to me I've been living here like a pauper— just a hand-to-mouth kind of existence. I have earned my keep by doing tricks for you, Torvald. But that's the way you wanted it. You have great sins against me to answer for, Daddy and you. It's your fault that nothing has become of me.

HELMER. Nora, you're being both unreasonable and ungrateful. Haven't you been happy here?

NORA. No, never. I thought I was, but I wasn't.

HELMER. Not—not happy!

NORA. No; just having fun. And you have always been very good to me. But our home has never been more than a playroom. I have been your doll wife here, just the way I used to be Daddy's doll child. And the children have been my dolls. I thought it was fun when you played with me, just as they thought it was fun when I played with them. That's been our marriage, Torvald.

HELMER. There is something in what you are saying—exaggerated and hysterical though it is. But from now on things will be different. Playtime is over; it's time for growing up.

NORA. Whose growing up—mine or the children's?

HELMER. Both yours and the children's, Nora darling.

NORA. Oh Torvald, you're not the man to bring me up to be the right kind of wife for you.

HELMER. How can you say that?

NORA. And I—? What qualifications do I have for bringing up the children?

HELMER. Nora!

NORA. You said so yourself a minute ago—that you didn't dare to trust me with them.

HELMER. In the first flush of anger, yes. Surely, you're not going to count that.

NORA. But you were quite right. I am *not* qualified. Something else has to come first. Somehow I have to grow up myself. And you are not the man to help me do that. That's a job I have to do by myself. And that's why I'm leaving you.

HELMER (*jumps up*). What did you say!

NORA. I have to be by myself if I am to find out about myself and about all the other things too. So I can't stay here with you any longer.

HELMER. Nora, Nora!

NORA. I'm leaving now. I'm sure Kristine will put me up for tonight.

HELMER. You're out of your mind! I won't let you! I forbid you!

NORA. You can't forbid me anything any more; it won't do any good. I'm taking my own things with me. I won't accept anything from you, either now or later.

HELMER. But this is madness!

NORA. Tomorrow I'm going home—I mean back to my old hometown. It will be easier for me to find some kind of job there.

HELMER. Oh, you blind, inexperienced creature—!

NORA. I must see to it that I get experience, Torvald.

HELMER. Leaving your home, your husband, your children! Not a thought of what people will say!

NORA. I can't worry about that. All I know is that I have to leave.

HELMER. Oh, this is shocking! Betraying your most sacred duties like this!

NORA. And what do you consider my most sacred duties?

HELMER. Do I need to tell you that? They are your duties to your husband and your children.

NORA. I have other duties equally sacred.

HELMER. You do not. What duties would they be?

NORA. My duties to myself.

HELMER. You are a wife and a mother before you are anything else.

NORA. I don't believe that any more. I believe I am first of all a human being, just as much as you—or at any rate that I must try to become one. Oh, I know very well that most people agree with you, Torvald, and that it says something like that in all the books. But what people say and what the books say is no longer enough for me. I have to think about these things myself and see if I can't find the answers.

HELMER. You mean to tell me you don't know what your proper place in your own home is? Don't you have a reliable guide in such matters? Don't you have religion?

NORA. Oh but Torvald—I don't really know what religion is.

HELMER. What are you saying!

NORA. All I know is what the Reverend Hansen told me when he prepared me for confirmation. He said that religion was *this* and it was *that*. When I get by myself, away from here, I'll have to look into that, too. I have to decide if what the Reverend Hansen said was right, or anyway if it is right for *me*.

HELMER. Oh, this is unheard of in a young woman! If religion can't guide you, let me appeal to your conscience. For surely you have moral feelings? Or—answer me—maybe you don't?

NORA. Well, you see, Torvald, I don't really know what to say. I just don't know. I am confused about these things. All I know is that my ideas are quite different from yours. I have just found out that the laws are different from what I thought they were, but in no way can I get it into my head that those laws are right. A woman shouldn't have the right to spare her dying old father or save her husband's life! I just can't believe that.

HELMER. You speak like a child. You don't understand the society you live in.

NORA. No, I don't. But I want to find out about it. I have to make up my mind who is right, society or I.

HELMER. You are sick, Nora; you have a fever. I really don't think you are in your right mind.

NORA. I have never felt so clearheaded and sure of myself as I do tonight.

HELMER. And clearheaded and sure of yourself you're leaving your husband and children?

NORA. Yes.

HELMER. Then there is only one possible explanation.

NORA. What?

HELMER. You don't love me any more.

NORA. No, that's just it.

HELMER. Nora! Can you say that?

NORA. I am sorry, Torvald, for you have always been so good to me. But I can't help it. I don't love you any more.

HELMER *(with forced composure)*. And this too is a clear and sure conviction?

NORA. Completely clear and sure. That's why I don't want to stay here any more.

HELMER. And are you ready to explain to me how I came to forfeit your love?

NORA. Certainly I am. It was tonight, when the wonderful didn't happen. That was when I realized you were not the man I thought you were.

HELMER. You have to explain. I don't understand.

NORA. I have waited patiently for eight years, for I wasn't such a fool that I thought the wonderful is something that happens any old day. Then this—thing—came crashing in on me, and then there wasn't a doubt in my mind that now—now comes the wonderful. When Krogstad's letter was in that mailbox, never for a moment did it even occur to me that you would submit to his conditions. I was so absolutely certain that you would say to him: make the whole thing public—tell everybody. And when that had happened—

HELMER. Yes, then what? When I had surrendered my own wife to shame and disgrace—!

NORA. When that had happened, I was absolutely certain that you would stand up and take the blame and say, "I'm the guilty one."

HELMER. Nora!

NORA. You mean I never would have accepted such a sacrifice from you? Of course not. But what would my protests have counted against yours? *That* was the wonderful I was waiting for in hope and terror. And to prevent that I was going to kill myself.

HELMER. I'd gladly work nights and days for you, Nora—endure sorrow and want for your sake. But nobody sacrifices his *honor* for his love.

NORA. A hundred thousand women have done so.

HELMER. Oh, you think and talk like a silly child.

NORA. All right. But you don't think and talk like the man I can live with. When you had gotten over your fright—not because of what threatened *me* but because of the risk to *you*—and the whole danger was past, then you acted as if nothing at all had happened. Once again I was your little songbird, your doll, just as before, only now you had to handle her even more carefully, because she was so frail and weak. *(Rises.)* Torvald—that moment I realized that I had been living here for eight years with a stranger and had borne him three children—Oh, I can't stand thinking about it! I feel like tearing myself to pieces!

HELMER *(heavily)*. I see it, I see it. An abyss has opened up between us.—Oh but Nora—surely it can be filled?

NORA. The way I am now I am no wife for you.

HELMER. I have it in me to change.

NORA. Perhaps—if your doll is taken from you.

HELMER. To part—to part from you! No, no, Nora! I can't grasp that thought!

NORA *(goes out, right)*. All the more reason why it has to be. *(She returns with her outdoor clothes and a small bag, which she sets down on the chair by the table.)*

HELMER. Nora, Nora! Not now! Wait till tomorrow.

NORA *(putting on her coat)*. I can't spend the night in a stranger's rooms.

HELMER. But couldn't we live here together like brother and sister—?

NORA *(tying on her hat)*. You know very well that wouldn't last long—. *(Wraps her shawl around her.)* Goodbye, Torvald. I don't want to see the children. I know I leave them in better hands than mine. The way I am now I can't be anything to them.

HELMER. But some day, Nora—some day—?

NORA. How can I tell? I have no idea what's going to become of me.

HELMER. But you're still my wife, both as you are now and as you will be.

NORA. Listen, Torvald—when a wife leaves her husband's house, the way I am doing now, I have heard he has no more legal responsibilities for her. At any rate, I now release you from all responsibility. You are not to feel yourself obliged to me for anything, and I have no obligations to you. There has to be full freedom on both sides. Here is your ring back. Now give me mine.

HELMER. Even this?

NORA. Even this.

HELMER. Here it is.

NORA. There. So now it's over. I'm putting the keys here. The maids know everything about the house—better than I. Tomorrow, after I'm gone, Kristine will come over and pack my things from home. I want them sent after me.

HELMER. Over! It's all over! Nora, will you never think of me?

NORA. I'm sure I'll often think of you and the children and this house.

HELMER. May I write to you, Nora?

NORA. No—never. I won't have that.

HELMER. But send you things—? You must let me.

NORA. Nothing, nothing.

HELMER. —help you, when you need help—

NORA. I told you, no; I won't have it. I'll accept nothing from strangers.

HELMER. Nora—can I never again be more to you than a stranger?

NORA *(picks up her bag)*. Oh Torvald—then the most wonderful of all would have to happen—

HELMER. Tell me what that would be—!

NORA. For that to happen, both you and I would have to change so that—Oh Torvald; I no longer believe in the wonderful.

HELMER. But I *will* believe. Tell me! Change, so that—?

NORA. So that our living together would become a true marriage. Goodbye. *(She goes out through the hall.)*

HELMER *(sinks down on a chair near the door and covers his face with his hands)*. Nora! Nora! *(Looks around him and gets up.)* All empty. She's gone. *(With sudden hope.)* The most wonderful—?!

From downstairs comes the sound of a heavy door slamming shut.

QUESTIONS AND SUGGESTIONS FOR WRITING

1. Near the beginning of the play, how does Mrs. Linde's presence help to define Nora's character? How does Nora's response to Krogstad's entrance tell us something about Nora?

2. What does Dr. Rank contribute to the play? If he were eliminated, what would be lost?

3. Ibsen very reluctantly acceded to a request for an alternate ending for a German production. In the new ending Helmer forces Nora to look at their sleeping children and reminds her that "tomorrow, when they wake up and call for their mother, they will be—motherless." Nora "struggles with herself" and concludes by saying, "Oh, this is a sin against myself, but I cannot leave them." In view of the fact that the last act several times seems to be moving toward a "happy ending" (e.g., Krogstad promises to recall his letter), what is wrong with this alternate ending?

4. Can it be argued that although at the end Nora goes out to achieve self-realization, her abandonment of her children—especially to Torvald's loathsome conventional morality—is a crime? (By the way, exactly why does Nora leave the children? She seems to imply, in some passages, that because she forged a signature she is unfit to bring them up. But do you agree with her?)

5. Michael Meyer, in his splendid biography *Henrik Ibsen,* says that the play is not so much about women's rights as about "the need of every individual to find out the kind of person he or she really is, and to strive to become that person." What evidence can you offer to support this interpretation?

6. In *The Quintessence of Ibsenism,* Bernard Shaw says that Ibsen, reacting against a common theatrical preference for strange situations, "saw that . . . the more familiar the situation, the more interesting the play. Shakespear had put ourselves on the stage but not our situations. Our uncles seldom murder our fathers and . . . marry our mothers. . . . Ibsen . . . gives us not only ourselves, but ourselves in our own situations. The things that happen to his stage figures are things that happen to us. One consequence is that his plays are much more important to us than Shakespear's. Another is that they are capable both of hurting us cruelly and of filling us with excited hopes of escape from idealistic tyrannies, and with visions of intenser life in the future." How much of this do you believe?

7. In about 250 words (perhaps two paragraphs), sketch Nora's character. In your discussion, indicate to what degree she may be a victim, and to what degree she may be at fault.

Susan Glaspell (American. 1882–1948)

TRIFLES

Scene: *The kitchen in the now abandoned farmhouse of John Wright, a gloomy kitchen, and left without having been put in order— the walls covered with a faded wall paper. Down right is a door leading to the parlor. On the right wall above this door is a built-in kitchen cupboard with shelves in the upper portion and drawers below. In the rear wall at right, up two steps is a door opening onto stairs leading to the second floor. In the rear wall at left is a door to the shed and from there to the outside. Between these two doors is an old-fashioned black iron stove. Running along the left wall from the shed door is an old iron sink and sink shelf, in which is set a hand pump. Downstage of the sink is an uncurtained window. Near the window is an old wooden rocker. Center stage is an unpainted wooden kitchen table with straight chairs on either side. There is a small chair* *down right. Unwashed pans under the sink, a loaf of bread outside the breadbox, a dish towel on the table—other signs of incompleted work. At the rear the shed door opens and the* SHERIFF *comes in followed by the* COUNTY ATTORNEY *and* HALE. *The* SHERIFF *and* HALE *are men in middle life, the* COUNTY ATTORNEY *is a young man; all are much bundled up and go at once to the stove. They are followed by the two women—the Sheriff's wife,* MRS. PETERS, *first: she is a slight wiry woman, a thin nervous face.* MRS. HALE *is larger and would ordinarily be called more comfortable looking, but she is disturbed now and looks fearfully about as she enters. The women have come in slowly, and stand close together near the door.*

COUNTY ATTORNEY (*at stove rubbing his hands*). This feels good. Come up to the fire, ladies.

MRS. PETERS (*after taking a step forward*). I'm not—cold.

SHERIFF (*unbuttoning his overcoat and stepping away from the stove to right of table as if to mark the beginning of official business*). Now, Mr. Hale, before we move things about, you explain to Mr. Henderson just what you saw when you came here yesterday morning.

COUNTY ATTORNEY (*crossing down to left of the table*). By the way, has anything been moved? Are things just as you left them yesterday?

SHERIFF (*looking about*). It's just about the same. When it dropped below zero last night I thought I'd better send Frank out this morning to make a fire for us—(*sits right of center table*) no use getting pneumonia with a big case on, but I told him not to touch anything except the stove—and you know Frank.

COUNTY ATTORNEY. Somebody should have been left here yesterday.

SHERIFF. Oh—yesterday. When I had to send Frank to Morris Center for that man who went crazy—I want you to know I had my hands full yesterday. I knew you could get back from Omaha by today and as long as I went over everything here myself——

COUNTY ATTORNEY. Well, Mr. Hale, tell just what happened when you came here yesterday morning.

HALE (*crossing down to above table*). Harry and I had started to town with a load of potatoes. We came along the road from my place and as I got here I said, "I'm going to see if I can't get John Wright to go in with me on a party telephone." I spoke to Wright about it once before and he put me off, saying folks talked too much anyway, and all he asked was peace and quiet—I guess you know about how much he talked himself, but I thought maybe if I went to the house and talked about it before his wife, though I said to Harry that I didn't know as what his wife wanted made much difference to John——

COUNTY ATTORNEY. Let's talk about that later, Mr. Hale. I do want to talk about that, but tell now just what happened when you got to the house.

HALE. I didn't hear or see anything; I knocked at the door, and still it was all quiet inside. I knew they must be up, it was past eight o'clock. So I knocked again, and I thought I heard somebody say, "Come in." I wasn't sure, I'm not sure yet, but I opened the door—this door (*indicating the door by which the two women are still standing*) and there in that rocker—(*pointing to it*) sat Mrs. Wright. (*They all look at the rocker down left.*)

COUNTY ATTORNEY. What—was she doing?

HALE. She was rockin' back and forth. She had her apron in her hand and was kind of—pleating it.

COUNTY ATTORNEY. And how did she—look?

HALE. Well, she looked queer.

COUNTY ATTORNEY. How do you mean—queer?

HALE. Well, as if she didn't know what she was going to do next. And kind of done up.

COUNTY ATTORNEY (*takes out notebook and pencil and sits left of center table*). How did she seem to feel about your coming?

HALE. Why, I don't think she minded—

one way or other. She didn't pay much attention. I said, "How do, Mrs. Wright, it's cold, ain't it?' And she said, "Is it?"—and went on kind of pleating at her apron. Well, I was surprised; she didn't ask me to come up to the stove, or to set down, but just sat there, not even looking at me, so I said, "I want to see John." And then she—laughed. I guess you would call it a laugh. I thought of Harry and the team outside, so I said a little sharp: "Can't I see John?" "No," she says, kind o' dull like. "Ain't he home?" says I. "Yes," says she, "he's home." "Then why can't I see him?" I asked her, out of patience. " 'Cause he's dead," says she. *"Dead?"* says I. She just nodded her head, not getting a bit excited, but rockin' back and forth. "Why—where is he?" says I, not knowing what to say. She just pointed upstairs—like that. (*Himself pointing to the room above.*) I started for the stairs, with the idea of going up there. I walked from there to here—then I says, "Why, what did he die of?" "He died of a rope round his neck," says she, and just went on pleatin' at her apron. Well, I went out and called Harry. I thought I might—need help. We went upstairs and there he was lyin'——

COUNTY ATTORNEY. I think I'd rather have you go into that upstairs, where you can point it all out. Just go on now with the rest of the story.

HALE. Well, my first thought was to get that rope off. It looked . . . (*stops, his face twitches*) . . . but Harry, he went up to him, and he said, "No, he's dead all right, and we'd better not touch anything." So we went back downstairs. She was still sitting that same way. "Has anybody been notified?" I asked. "No," says she, unconcerned. "Who did this, Mrs. Wright?" said Harry. He said it business-like—and she stopped pleatin' of her apron. "I don't know," she says. "You don't *know?*" says Harry. "No," says she. "Weren't you sleepin' in the bed with him?" says Harry. "Yes," says she, "but I was on the inside." "Somebody slipped a rope round his neck and strangled him and you didn't wake up?" says Harry. "I didn't wake up," she said af-

ter him. We must 'a' looked as if we didn't see how that could be, for after a minute she said, "I sleep sound." Harry was going to ask her more questions but I said maybe we ought to let her tell her story first to the coroner, or the sheriff. So Harry went fast as he could to Rivers' place, where there's a telephone.

COUNTY ATTORNEY. And what did Mrs. Wright do when she knew that you had gone for the coroner?

HALE. She moved from the rocker to that chair over there (*pointing to a small chair in the down right corner*) and just sat there with her hands held together and looking down. I got a feeling that I ought to make some conversation, so I said I had come in to see if John wanted to put in a telephone, and at that she started to laugh, and then she stopped and looked at me—scared. (*The* COUNTY ATTORNEY, *who has had his notebook out, makes a note.*) I dunno, maybe it wasn't scared. I wouldn't like to say it was. Soon Harry got back, and then Dr. Lloyd came and you, Mr. Peters, and so I guess that's all I know that you don't.

COUNTY ATTORNEY (*rising and looking around*). I guess we'll go upstairs first—and then out to the barn and around there. (*To the* SHERIFF.) You're convinced that there was nothing important here—nothing that would point to any motive?

SHERIFF Nothing here but kitchen things. (*The* COUNTY ATTORNEY, *after again looking around the kitchen, opens the door of a cupboard closet in right wall. He brings a small chair from right—gets on it and looks on a shelf. Pulls his hand away, sticky.*)

COUNTY ATTORNEY. Here's a nice mess. (*The women draw nearer up center.*)

MRS. PETERS (*to the other woman*). Oh, her fruit; it did freeze. (*To the lawyer.*) She worried about that when it turned so cold. She said the fire'd go out and her jars would break.

SHERIFF (*rises*). Well, can you beat the woman! Held for murder and worryin' about her preserves.

COUNTY ATTORNEY (*getting down from chair*). I guess before we're through she may have something more serious than preserves to worry about. (*Crosses down right center.*)

HALE. Well, women are used to worrying over trifles. (*The two women move a little closer together.*)

COUNTY ATTORNEY (*with the gallantry of a young politician*). And yet, for all their worries, what would we do without the ladies? (*The women do not unbend. He goes below the center table to the sink, takes a dipperful of water from the pail and pouring it into a basin, washes his hands. While he is doing this the* SHERIFF *and* HALE *cross to cupboard, which they inspect. The* COUNTY ATTORNEY *starts to wipe his hands on the roller towel, turns it for a cleaner place.*) Dirty towels! (*Kicks his foot against the pans under the sink.*) Not much of a housekeeper, would you say, ladies?

MRS. HALE (*stiffly*). There's a great deal of work to be done on a farm.

COUNTY ATTORNEY. To be sure. And yet (*with a little bow to her*) I know there are some Dickson County farmhouses which do not have such roller towels. (*He gives it a pull to expose its full length again.*)

MRS. HALE. Those towels get dirty awful quick. Men's hands aren't always as clean as they might be.

COUNTY ATTORNEY. Ah, loyal to your sex, I see. But you and Mrs. Wright were neighbors. I suppose you were friends, too.

MRS. HALE (*shaking her head*). I've not seen much of her of late years. I've not been in this house—it's more than a year.

COUNTY ATTORNEY (*crossing to women up center*). And why was that? You didn't like her?

MRS. HALE. I liked her all well enough. Farmers' wives have their hands full, Mr. Henderson. And then——

COUNTY ATTORNEY. Yes——?

MRS. HALE (*looking about*). It never seemed a very cheerful place.

COUNTY ATTORNEY. No—it's not cheerful. I shouldn't say she had the homemaking instinct.

MRS. HALE. Well, I don't know as Wright had, either.

COUNTY ATTORNEY. You mean that they didn't get on very well?

MRS. HALE. No, I don't mean anything. But I don't think a place'd be any cheerfuller for John Wright's being in it.

COUNTY ATTORNEY. I'd like to talk more of that a little later. I want to get the lay of things upstairs now. (*He goes past the women to up right where steps lead to a stair door.*)

SHERIFF. I suppose anything Mrs. Peters does'll be all right. She was to take in some clothes for her, you know, and a few little things. We left in such a hurry yesterday.

COUNTY ATTORNEY. Yes, but I would like to see what you take, Mrs. Peters, and keep an eye out for anything that might be of use to us.

MRS. PETERS. Yes, Mr. Henderson. (*The men leave by up right door to stairs. The women listen to the men's steps on the stairs, then look about the kitchen.*)

MRS. HALE (*crossing left to sink*). I'd hate to have men coming into my kitchen, snooping around and criticizing. (*She arranges the pans under sink which the lawyer had shoved out of place.*)

MRS. PETERS. Of course it's no more than their duty. (*Crosses to cupboard up right.*)

MRS. HALE. Duty's all right, but I guess that deputy sheriff that came out to make the fire might have got a little of this on. (*Gives the roller towel a pull.*) Wish I'd thought of that sooner. Seems mean to talk about her for not having things slicked up when she had to come away in such a hurry. (*Crosses right to* MRS. PETERS *at cupboard.*)

MRS. PETERS (*who has been looking through cupboard, lifts one end of towel that covers a pan*). She had bread set. (*Stands still.*)

MRS. HALE (*eyes fixed on a loaf of bread beside the breadbox, which is on a low shelf the cupboard.*) She was going to put this in there. (*Picks up loaf, then abruptly drops it. In a manner of returning to familiar things.*) It's a shame about her fruit. I wonder if it's all gone. (*Gets up on the chair and looks.*) I think there's some here that's all right,

Mrs. Peters. Yes—here; (*holding it toward the window*) this is cherries, too. (*Looking again.*) I declare I believe that's the only one. (*Gets down, jar in her hand. Goes to the sink and wipes it off on the outside.*) She'll feel awful bad after all her hard work in the hot weather. I remember the afternoon I put up my cherries last summer.

She puts the jar on the big kitchen table, center of the room. With a sigh, is about to sit down in the rocking chair. Before she is seated realizes what chair it is; with a slow look at it, steps back. The chair which she has touched rocks back and forth. Mrs. Peters moves to center table and they both watch the chair rock for a moment or two.

MRS. PETERS (*shaking off the mood which the empty rocking chair has evoked. Now in a business-like manner she speaks*). Well I must get those things from the front room closet. (*She goes to the door at the right but, after looking into the other room, steps back.*) You coming with me, Mrs. Hale? You could help me carry them. (*They go in the other room; reappear,* MRS. PETERS *carrying a dress, petticoat and skirt,* MRS. HALE *following with a pair of shoes.*) My, it's cold in there. (*She puts the clothes on the big table, and hurries to the stove.*)

MRS. HALE (*right of center table examining the skirt*). Wright was close. I think maybe that's why she kept so much to herself. She didn't even belong to the Ladies' Aid. I suppose she felt she couldn't do her part, and then you don't enjoy things when you feel shabby. I heard she used to wear pretty clothes and be lively, when she was Minnie Foster, one of the town girls singing in the choir. But that—oh, that was thirty years ago. This all you want to take in?

MRS. PETERS. She said she wanted an apron. Funny thing to want, for there isn't much to get you dirty in jail, goodness knows. But I suppose just to make her feel more natural. (*Crosses to cupboard.*) She said they was in the top drawer in this cupboard. Yes, here. And then her little shawl that always hung behind the door. (*Opens stair door and looks.*) Yes, here it is. (*Quickly shuts door leading upstairs.*)

MRS. HALE (*abruptly moving toward her*). Mrs. Peters?

MRS. PETERS. Yes, Mrs. Hale? (*At up right door.*)

MRS. HALE. Do you think she did it?

MRS. PETERS (*in a frightened voice*). Oh, I don't know.

MRS. HALE. Well, I don't think she did. Asking for an apron and her little shawl. Worrying about her fruit.

MRS. PETERS (*starts to speak, glances up, where footsteps are heard in the room above. In a low voice*). Mr. Peters says it looks bad for her. Mr. Henderson is awful sarcastic in a speech and he'll make fun of her sayin' she didn't wake up.

MRS. HALE. Well, I guess John Wright didn't wake when they was slipping that rope under his neck.

MRS. PETERS (*crossing slowly to table and placing shawl and apron on table with other clothing*). No, it's strange. It must have been done awful crafty and still. They say it was such a—funny way to kill a man, rigging it all up like that.

MRS. HALE (*crossing to left of* MRS. PETERS *at table*). That's just what Mr. Hale said. There was a gun in the house. He says that's what he can't understand.

MRS. PETERS. Mr. Henderson said coming out that what was needed for the case was a motive; something to show anger, or—sudden feeling.

MRS. HALE (*who is standing by the table*). Well, I don't see any signs of anger around here. (*She puts her hand on the dish towel which lies on the table, stands looking down at table, one-half of which is clean, the other half messy.*) It's wiped to here. (*Makes a move as if to finish work, then turns and looks at loaf of bread outside the breadbox. Drops towel. In that voice of coming back to familiar things.*) Wonder how they are finding things upstairs. (*Crossing below table to down right.*) I hope she had it a little more red-up up there. You know, it seems kind of *sneaking*. Locking her up in town and then coming out here and trying to get her own house to turn against her!

MRS. PETERS. But, Mrs. Hale, the law is the law.

MRS. HALE. I s'pose 'tis. (*Unbuttoning her coat.*) Better loosen up your things, Mrs. Peters. You won't feel them when you go out.

Mrs. Peters takes off her fur tippet, goes to hang it on chair back left of table, stands looking at the work basket on floor near down left window.

MRS. PETERS. She was piecing a quilt.

She brings the large sewing basket to the center table and they look at the bright pieces, MRS. HALE *above the table and* MRS. PETERS *left of it.*

MRS. HALE. It's a log cabin pattern. Pretty, isn't it? I wonder if she was goin' to quilt it or just knot it? (*Footsteps have been heard coming down the stairs. The* SHERIFF *enters followed by* HALE *and the* COUNTY ATTORNEY.)

SHERIFF. They wonder if she was going to quilt it or just knot it! (*The men laugh, the women look abashed.*)

COUNTY ATTORNEY (*rubbing his hands over the stove*). Frank's fire didn't do much up there, did it? Well, let's go out to the barn and get that cleared up. (*The men go outside by up left door.*)

MRS. HALE (*resentfully*). I don't know as there's anything so strange, our takin' up our time with little things while we're waiting for them to get the evidence. (*She sits in chair right of table smoothing out a block with decision.*) I don't see as it's anything to laugh about.

MRS. PETERS (*apologetically*). Of course they've got awful important things on their minds. (*Pulls up a chair and joins* MRS. HALE *at the left of the table.*)

MRS. HALE (*examining another block*). Mrs. Peters, look at this one. Here, this is the one she was working on, and look at the sewing! All the rest of it has been so nice and even. And look at this! It's all over the place! Why, it looks as if she didn't know what she was about! (*After she has said this they look at each other, then start to glance back at the door. After an instant* MRS. HALE *has pulled at a knot and ripped the sewing.*)

MRS. PETERS. Oh, what are you doing, Mrs. Hale?

MRS. HALE (*mildly*). Just pulling out a stitch or two that's not sewed very good. (*Threading a needle.*) Bad sewing always made me fidgety.

MRS. PETERS (*with a glance at door, nervously*). I don't think we ought to touch things.

MRS. HALE. I'll just finish up this end. (*Suddenly stopping and leaning forward.*) Mrs. Peters?

MRS. PETERS. Yes, Mrs. Hale?

MRS. HALE. What do you suppose she was so nervous about?

MRS. PETERS. Oh—I don't know. I don't know as she was nervous. I sometimes sew awful queer when I'm just tired. (MRS. HALE *starts to say something, looks at* MRS. PETERS, *then goes on sewing.*) Well, I must get these things wrapped up. They may be through sooner than we think. (*Putting apron and other things together.*) I wonder where I can find a piece of paper, and string. (*Rises.*)

MRS. HALE. In that cupboard, maybe.

MRS. PETERS (*crosses right looking in cupboard*). Why, here's a bird-cage. (*Holds it up.*) Did she have a bird, Mrs. Hale?

MRS. HALE. Why, I don't know whether she did or not—I've not been here for so long. There was a man around last year selling canaries cheap, but I don't know as she took one; maybe she did. She used to sing real pretty herself.

MRS. PETERS (*glancing around*). Seems funny to think of a bird here. But she must have had one, or why would she have a cage? I wonder what happened to it?

MRS. HALE. I s'pose maybe the cat got it.

MRS. PETERS. No, she didn't have a cat. She's got that feeling some people have about cats—being afraid of them. My cat got in her room and she was real upset and asked me to take it out.

MRS. HALE. My sister Bessie was like that. Queer, ain't it?

MRS. PETERS (*examining the cage*). Why, look at this door. It's broke. One hinge is pulled apart. (*Takes a step down to* MRS. HALE'S *right.*)

MRS. HALE (*looking too*). Looks as if someone must have been rough with it.

MRS. PETERS. Why, yes. (*She brings the cage forward and puts it on the table.*)

MRS. HALE (*glancing toward up left door*). I wish if they're going to find any evidence they'd be about it. I don't like this place.

MRS. PETERS. But I'm awful glad you came with me, Mrs. Hale. It would be lonesome for me sitting here alone.

MRS. HALE. It would, wouldn't it? (*Dropping her sewing.*) But I tell you what I do wish, Mrs. Peters. I wish I had come over sometimes when *she* was here. I—(*looking around the room*)—wish I had.

MRS. PETERS. But of course you were awful busy, Mrs. Hale—your house and your children.

MRS. HALE (*rises and crosses left*). I could've come. I stayed away because it weren't cheerful—and that's why I ought to have come. I—(*looking out left window*)—I've never liked this place. Maybe because it's down in a hollow and you don't see the road. I dunno what it is, but it's a lonesome place and always was. I wish I had come over to see Minnie Foster sometimes. I can see now— (*Shakes her head.*)

MRS. PETERS (*left of table and above it*). Well, you mustn't reproach yourself, Mrs. Hale. Somehow we just don't see how it is with other folks until—something turns up.

MRS. HALE. Not having children makes less work—but it makes a quiet house, and Wright out to work all day, and no company when he did come in. (*Turning from window.*) Did you know John Wright, Mrs. Peters?

MRS. PETERS. Not to know him; I've seen him in town. They say he was a good man.

MRS. HALE. Yes—good; he didn't drink, and kept his word as well as most, I guess, and paid his debts. But he was a hard man,

Mrs. Peters. Just to pass the time of day with him—(*Shivers.*) Like a raw wind that gets to the bone. (*Pauses, her eye falling on the cage.*) I should think she would 'a' wanted a bird. But what do you suppose went with it?

MRS. PETERS. I don't know, unless it got sick and died. (*She reaches over and swings the broken door, swings it again, both women watch it.*)

MRS. HALE. You weren't raised round here, were you? (MRS. PETERS *shakes her head.*) You didn't know—her?

MRS. PETERS. Not till they brought her yesterday.

MRS. HALE. She—come to think of it, she was kind of like a bird herself—real sweet and pretty, but kind of timid and—fluttery. How—she—did—change. (*Silence: then as if struck by a happy thought and relieved to get back to everyday things. Crosses right above* MRS. PETERS *to cupboard, replaces small chair used to stand on to its original place down right.*) Tell you what, Mrs. Peters, why don't you take the quilt in with you? It might take up her mind.

MRS. PETERS. Why, I think that's a real nice idea, Mrs. Hale. There couldn't possibly be any objection to it could there? Now, just what would I take? I wonder if her patches are in here—and her things. (*They look in the sewing basket.*)

MRS. HALE (*crosses to right of table*). Here's some red. I expect this has got sewing things in it. (*Brings out a fancy box.*) What a pretty box. Looks like something somebody would give you. Maybe her scissors are in here. (*Opens box. Suddenly puts her hand to her nose.*) Why——(MRS. PETERS *bends nearer, then turns her face away.*) There's something wrapped up in this piece of silk.

MRS. PETERS. Why, this isn't her scissors.

MRS. HALE (*lifting the silk*). Oh, Mrs. Peters—it's——(MRS. PETERS *bends closer.*)

MRS. PETERS. It's the bird.

MRS. HALE. But, Mrs. Peters—look at it! Its neck! Look at its neck! It's all—other side *to.*

MRS. PETERS. Somebody—wrung—its—neck.

Their eyes meet. A look of growing comprehension, of horror. Steps are heard outside. MRS. HALE slips box under quilt pieces, and sinks into her chair. Enter SHERIFF and COUNTY ATTORNEY. MRS. PETERS steps down left and stands looking out of window.

COUNTY ATTORNEY *(as one turning from serious things to little pleasantries).* Well, ladies, have you decided whether she was going to quilt it or knot it? *(Crosses to center above table.)*

MRS. PETERS. We think she was going to—knot it. *(SHERIFF crosses to right of stove, lifts stove lid and glances at fire, then stands warming hands at stove.)*

COUNTY ATTORNEY. Well, that's interesting, I'm sure. *(Seeing the bird-cage.)* Has the bird flown?

MRS. HALE *(putting more quilt pieces over the box).* We think the—cat got it.

COUNTY ATTORNEY *(preoccupied).* Is there a cat? *(MRS. HALE glances in a quick covert way at MRS. PETERS.)*

MRS. PETERS *(turning from window, takes a step in).* Well, not *now.* They're superstitious, you know. They leave.

COUNTY ATTORNEY *(to SHERIFF PETERS, continuing an interrupted conversation).* No sign at all of anyone having come from the outside. Their own rope. Now let's go up again and go over it piece by piece. *(They start upstairs.)* It would have to have been someone who knew just the——

MRS. PETERS *sits down left of table. The two women sit there not looking at one another, but as if peering into something and at the same time holding back. When they talk now it is in the manner of feeling their way over strange ground, as if afraid of what they are saying, but as if they cannot help saying it.*

MRS. HALE *(hesitatively and in hushed voice).* She liked the bird. She was going to bury it in that pretty box.

MRS. PETERS *(in a whisper).* When I was a girl—my kitten—there was a boy took a hatchet, and before my eyes—and before I could get there——*(Covers her face an instant.)* If they hadn't held me back I would have—*(catches herself, looks upstairs where steps are heard, falters weakly)*—hurt him.

MRS. HALE *(with a slow look around her).* I wonder how it would seem never to have had any children around. *(Pause.)* No, Wright wouldn't like the bird—a thing that sang. She used to sing. He killed that, too.

MRS. PETERS *(moving uneasily).* We don't know who killed the bird.

MRS. HALE. I knew John Wright.

MRS. PETERS. It was an awful thing was done in this house that night, Mrs. Hale. Killing a man while he slept, slipping a rope around his neck that choked the life out of him.

MRS. HALE. His neck. Choked the life out of him. *(Her hand goes out and rests on the bird-cage.)*

MRS. PETERS *(with rising voice).* We don't know who killed him. We don't *know.*

MRS. HALE *(her own feeling not interrupted).* If there'd been years and years of nothing, then a bird to sing to you, it would be awful—still, after the bird was still.

MRS. PETERS *(something within her speaking).* I know what stillness is. When we homesteaded in Dakota, and my first baby died——after he was two years old, and me with no other then——

MRS. HALE *(moving).* How soon do you suppose they'll be through looking for the evidence?

MRS. PETERS. I know what stillness is. *(Pulling herself back.)* The law has got to punish crime, Mrs. Hale.

MRS. HALE *(not as if answering that).* I wish you'd seen Minnie Foster when she wore a white dress with blue ribbons and stood up there in the choir and sang. *(A look around the room.)* Oh I *wish* I'd come over here once in a while! That was a crime! That was a crime! Who's going to punish that?

MRS. PETERS *(looking upstairs).* We mustn't—take on.

MRS. HALE. I might have known she needed help! I know how things can be—for women. I tell you, it's queer, Mrs. Peters. We live close together and we live far apart. We all go through the same things— it's all just a different kind of the same thing. (*Brushes her eyes, noticing the jar of fruit, reaches out for it.*) If I was you I wouldn't tell her her fruit was gone. Tell her it *ain't.* Tell her it's all right. Take this in to prove it to her. She—she may never know whether it was broke or not.

MRS. PETERS (*takes the jar, looks about for something to wrap it in; takes petticoat from the clothes brought from the other room, very nervously begins winding this around the jar. In a false voice*). My, it's a good thing the men couldn't hear us. Wouldn't they just laugh! Getting all stirred up over a little thing like a—dead canary. As if that could have anything to do with—with— wouldn't they *laugh!* (*The men are heard coming downstairs.*)

MRS. HALE (*under her breath*). Maybe they would—maybe they wouldn't.

COUNTY ATTORNEY. No, Peters, it's all perfectly clear except a reason for doing it. But you know juries when it comes to women. If there was some definite thing. (*Crosses slowly to above table.* SHERIFF *crosses down right.* MRS. HALE *and* MRS. PETERS *remain seated at either side of table.*) Something to show—something to make a story about—a thing that would connect up with this strange way of doing it——(*The women's eyes meet for an instant. Enter* HALE *from outer door.*)

HALE (*remaining by door*). Well, I've got the team around. Pretty cold out there.

COUNTY ATTORNEY. I'm going to stay awhile by myself. (*To the* SHERIFF.) You can send Frank out for me, can't you? I want to go over everything. I'm not satisfied that we can't do better.

SHERIFF Do you want to see what Mrs. Peters is going to take in? (*The lawyer picks up the apron, laughs.*)

COUNTY ATTORNEY. Oh, I guess they're not very dangerous things the ladies have picked out. (*Moves a few things about, disturbing the quilt pieces which cover the box. Steps back.*) No, Mrs. Peters doesn't need supervising. For that matter a sheriff's wife is married to the law. Ever think of it that way, Mrs. Peters?

MRS. PETERS. Not—just that way.

SHERIFF (*chuckling*). Married to the law. (*Moves to down right door to the other room.*) I just want you to come in here a minute, George. We ought to take a look at these windows.

COUNTY ATTORNEY (*scoffingly*). Oh, windows!

SHERIFF. We'll be right out, Mr. Hale.

HALE *goes outside. The* SHERIFF *follows the* COUNTY ATTORNEY *into the room. Then* MRS. HALE *rises, hands tight together, looking intensely at* MRS. PETERS, *whose eyes make a slow turn, finally meeting* MRS. HALE's. *A moment* MRS. HALE *holds her, then her own eyes point the way to where the box is concealed. Suddenly* MRS. PETERS *throws back quilt pieces and tries to put the box in the bag she is carrying. It is too big. She opens box, starts to take bird out, cannot touch it, goes to pieces, stands there helpless. Sound of a knob turning in the other room.* MRS. HALE *snatches the box and puts it in the pocket of her big coat. Enter* COUNTY ATTORNEY *and* SHERIFF, *who remains down right.*

COUNTY ATTORNEY (*crosses to up left door facetiously*). Well, Henry, at least we found out that she was not going to quilt it. She was going to—what is it you call it, ladies?

MRS. HALE (*standing center below table facing front, her hand against her pocket*). We call it—knot it, Mr. Henderson.

Curtain

QUESTIONS AND SUGGESTIONS FOR WRITING

1. How would you characterize Mr. Henderson, the County Attorney?
2. In what way or ways are Mrs. Peters and Mrs. Hale different?
3. Several times the men "laugh" or "chuckle." In their contexts, what do these expressions of amusement convey?
4. On page 589, *"the women's eyes meet for an instant."* What does this bit of action "say"? What do we understand by the exchange of glances?
5. On page 588, when Mrs. Peters tells of the boy who killed her cat, she says, "If they hadn't held me back I would have—(*catches herself, looks upstairs where steps are heard, falters weakly*)—hurt him." What was she about to say before she faltered? Why does Glaspell include this speech about Mrs. Peters's girlhood?
6. On page 586 Mrs. Hale, looking at a quilt, wonders whether Mrs. Wright "was goin' to quilt it or just knot it." The men are amused by the women's concern with this topic, and the last line of the play returns to this issue. What is the point?
7. In what way or ways is the play ironic? (Consult the entry on "irony" in the glossary).
8. Can it reasonably be argued that this play is immoral? Explain.

Men, Women, God, and Gods

11

☐ ESSAYS

Paul (5?–67?)

I CORINTHIANS 13

Though I speak with the tongues of men and of angels, and have not charity, I am become as sounding brass, or a tinkling cymbal. And though I have the gift of prophecy, and understand all mysteries, and all knowledge; and though I have all faith, so that I could remove mountains, and have not charity, I am nothing. And though I bestow all my goods to feed the poor, and though I give my body to be burned, and have not charity, it profiteth me nothing.

Charity suffereth long, and is kind; charity envieth not; charity vaunteth not itself, is not puffed up, doth not behave itself unseemly, seeketh not her own, is not easily provoked, thinketh no evil; rejoiceth not in iniquity, but rejoiceth in the truth; beareth all things, believeth all things, hopeth all things, endureth all things.

Charity never faileth: but whether there be prophecies, they shall fail; whether there be tongues, they shall cease; whether there be knowledge, it shall vanish away. For we know in part, and we prophesy in part. But when that which is perfect is come, then that which is in part shall be done away. When I was a child, I spake as a child, I understood as a child, I thought as a child: but when I became a man, I put away childish things. For now we see through a glass,[1] darkly; but then face to face: now I know in part; but then shall I know even as also I am known. And now abideth faith, hope, charity, these three; but the greatest of these is charity.

QUESTIONS AND SUGGESTIONS FOR WRITING

1. Consult a reference work such as *The Interpreter's Bible*, volume 10, to see the special meaning of the word (*agape* in Greek) here translated as "charity" and usually translated in later versions as "love." How does it differ from erotic love? From the usual modern sense of charity?

---

[1] Mirror. —ED.

2. Paul defines charity both negatively and positively: Charity is *not* this and that; it *is* such and such. In your own words, set forth Paul's definition of charity.
3. Paul uses "I" rather than "you." From a persuasive point of view, what is the effect of this choice?
4. Put into your own words what is here translated as: "And though I bestow all my goods to feed the poor, and though I give my body to be burned, and have not charity, it profiteth me nothing."

William James (American. 1842–1910)

RELIGIOUS FAITH[1]

Religion has meant many things in human history; but when from now onward I use the word I mean to use it in the supernaturalist sense, as declaring that the so-called order of nature, which constitutes this world's experience, is only one portion of the total universe, and that there stretches beyond this visible world an unseen world of which we now know nothing positive, but in its relation to which the true significance of our present mundane life consists. A man's religious faith (whatever more special items of doctrine it may involve) means for me essentially his faith in the existence of an unseen order of some kind in which the riddles of the natural order may be found explained. In the more developed religions the natural world has always been regarded as the mere scaffolding or vestibule of a truer, more eternal world, and affirmed to be a sphere of education, trial, or redemption. In these religions, one must in some fashion die to the natural life before one can enter into life eternal. The notion that this physical world of wind and water, when the sun rises and the moon sets, is absolutely and ultimately the divinely aimed-at and established thing, is one which we find only in very early religions. . . . It is this natural religion (primitive still, in spite of the fact that poets and men of science whose good-will exceeds their perspicacity keep publishing it in new editions tuned to our contemporary ears) that, as I said a while ago, has suffered definitive bankruptcy in the opinion of a circle of persons, among whom I must count myself, and who are growing more numerous every day. For such persons the physical order of nature, taken simply as science knows it, cannot be held to reveal any one harmonious spiritual intent. It is mere *weather,* as Chauncey Wright called it, doing and undoing without end.

Now, I wish to make you feel, if I can in the short remainder of this hour, that we have a right to believe the physical order to be only a partial order; that we have a right to supplement it by an unseen spiritual order which we assume on trust, if only thereby life may seem to us better worth living again. But as such a trust will seem to some of you sadly mystical and execrably unscientific, I must first say a word or two to weaken the veto which you may consider that science opposes to our act.

There is included in human nature an ingrained naturalism and materialism of

[1] Editors' title. From *The Will to Believe.*

mind which can only admit facts that are actually tangible. Of this sort of mind the entity called "science" is the idol. Fondness for the word "scientist" is one of the notes by which you may know its votaries; and its short way of killing any opinion that it disbelieves in is to call it "unscientific." It must be granted that there is no slight excuse for this. Science has made such glorious leaps in the last three hundred years, and extended our knowledge of nature so enormously both in general and in detail; men of science, moreover, have as a class displayed such admirable virtues—that it is no wonder if the worshippers of science lose their head. In this very University, accordingly, I have heard more than one teacher say that all the fundamental conceptions of truth have already been found by science, and that the future has only the details of the picture to fill in. But the slightest reflection on the real conditions will suffice to show how barbaric such notions are. They show such a lack of scientific imagination, that it is hard to see how one who is actively advancing any part of science can make a mistake so crude. Think how many absolutely new scientific conceptions have arisen in our own generation, how many new problems have been formulated that were never thought of before, and then cast an eye upon the brevity of science's career. It began with Galileo, not three hundred years ago. Four thinkers since Galileo, each informing his successor of what discoveries his own lifetime had seen achieved, might have passed the torch of science into our hands as we sit here in this room. Indeed, for the matter of that, an audience much smaller than the present one, an audience of some five or six score people, if each person in it could speak for his own generation, would carry us away to the black unknown of the human species, to days without a document or monument to tell their tale. Is it credible that such a mushroom knowledge, such a growth overnight as this, *can* represent more than the minutest glimpse of what the universe will really prove to be when adequately understood? No! our science is a drop, our ignorance a sea. Whatever else be certain, this at least is certain—that the world of our present natural knowledge *is* enveloped in a larger world of *some* sort of whose residual properties we at present can frame no positive idea.

Agnostic positivism,[2] of course, admits this principle theoretically in the most cordial terms, but insists that we must not turn it to any practical use. We have no right, this doctrine tells us, to dream dreams, or suppose anything about the unseen part of the universe, merely because to do so may be for what we are pleased to call our highest interests. We must always wait for sensible evidence for our beliefs; and where such evidence is inaccessible we must frame no hypotheses whatever. Of course this is a safe enough position *in abstracto*. If a thinker had no stake in the unknown, no vital needs, to live or languish according to what the unseen world contained, a philosophic neutrality and refusal to believe either one way or the other would be his wisest cue. But, unfortunately, neutrality is not only inwardly difficult, it is also outwardly unrealizable, where our relations to an alternative are practical and vital. This is because, as the psychologists tell us, belief and doubt are living attitudes, and involve conduct on our part. Our

[2] A belief that human knowledge must be based on sense perceptions.—ED.

only way, for example, of doubting, or refusing to believe, that a certain thing *is,* is continuing to act as if it were *not.* If, for instance, I refuse to believe that the room is getting cold, I leave the windows open and light no fire just as if it still were warm. If I doubt that you are worthy of my confidence, I keep you uninformed of all my secrets just as if you were *un*worthy of the same. If I doubt the need of insuring my house, I leave it uninsured as much as if I believed there were no need. And so if I must not believe that the world is divine, I can only express that refusal by declining ever to act distinctively as if it were so, which can only mean acting on certain critical occasions as if it were *not* so, or in an irreligious way. There are, you see, inevitable occasions in life when inaction is a kind of action, and must count as action, and when not to be for is to be practically against; and in all such cases strict and consistent neutrality is an unattainable thing.

And, after all, is not this duty of neutrality where only our inner interests   5
would lead us to believe, the most ridiculous of commands? Is it not sheer dog-matic folly to say that our inner interests can have no real connection with the forces that the hidden world may contain? In other cases divinations based on inner interests have proved prophetic enough. Take science itself! Without an imperious inner demand on our part for ideal logical and mathematical harmonies, we should never have attained to proving that such harmonies lie hidden between all the chinks and interstices of the crude natural world. Hardly a law has been established in science, hardly a fact ascertained, which was not first sought after, often with sweat and blood, to gratify an inner need. Whence such needs come from we do not know: we find them in us, and biological psychology so far only classes them with Darwin's "accidental variations." But the inner need of believ-ing that this world of nature is a sign of something more spiritual and eternal than itself is just as strong and authoritative in those who feel it, as the inner need of uniform laws of causation ever can be in a professionally scientific head. The toil of many generations has proved the latter need prophetic. Why *may* not the former one be prophetic, too? And if needs of ours outrun the visible universe, why *may* not that be a sign that an invisible universe is there? What, in short, has authority to debar us from trusting our religious demands? Science as such assuredly has no authority, for she can only say what is, not what is not; and the agnostic "thou shalt not believe without coercive sensible evidence" is simply an expression (free to any one to make) of private personal appetite for evidence of a certain peculiar kind.

Now, when I speak of trusting our religious demands, just what do I mean by "trusting"? Is the word to carry with it license to define in detail an invisible world, and to anathematize and excommunicate those whose trust is different? Certainly not! Our faculties of belief were not primarily given us to make ortho-doxies and heresies withal; they were given us to live by. And to trust our reli-gious demands means first of all to live in the light of them, and to act as if the invisible world which they suggest were real. It is a fact of human nature, that men can live and die by the help of a sort of faith that goes without a single dogma or definition. The bare assurance that this natural order is not ultimate but a mere sign or vision, the external staging of a many-storied universe, in which spiritual forces have the last word and are eternal—this bare assurance is to such men enough to make life seem worth living in spite of every contrary presumption suggested by its circumstances on the natural plane. Destroy this inner assurance, however, vague as it is, and all the light and radiance of existence is extinguished for these persons at a stroke. Often enough the wild-eyed look at life—the suicidal mood—will then set in.

And now the application comes directly home to you and me. Probably to almost every one of us here the most adverse life would seem well worth living, if we only could be *certain* that our bravery and patience with it were terminating and eventuating and bearing fruit somewhere in an unseen spiritual world. But granting we are not certain, does it then follow that a bare trust in such a world is a fool's paradise and lubberland, or rather that it is a living attitude in which we are free to indulge? Well, we are free to trust at our own risks anything that is not impossible, and that can bring analogies to bear in its behalf. That the world of physics is probably not absolute, all the converging multitude of arguments that make in favor of idealism tend to prove; and that our whole physical life may lie soaking in a spiritual atmosphere, a dimension of being that we at present have no organ for apprehending, is vividly suggested to us by the analogy of the life of our domestic animals. Our dogs, for example, are in our human life but not of it. They witness hourly the outward body of events whose inner meaning cannot, by any possible operation, be revealed to their intelligence—events in which they themselves often play the cardinal part. My terrier bites a teasing boy, for example, and the father demands damages. The dog may be present at every step of the negotiations, and see the money paid, without an inkling of what it all means, without a suspicion that it has anything to do with *him;* and he never *can* know in his natural dog's life. Or take another case which used greatly to impress me in my medical-student days. Consider a poor dog whom they are vivisecting in a laboratory. He lies strapped on a board and shrieking at his executioners, and to his own dark consciousness is literally in a sort of hell. He cannot see a single redeeming ray in the whole business; and yet all these diabolical-seeming events are often controlled by human intentions with which, if his poor benighted mind could only be made to catch a glimpse of them, all that is heroic in him would religiously acquiesce. Healing truth, relief to future sufferings of beast and man, are to be bought by them. It may be genuinely a process of redemption. Lying on his back on the board there he may be performing a function incalculably higher than any that prosperous canine life admits of; and yet, of the whole performance, this function is the one portion that must remain absolutely beyond his ken.

Now turn from this to the life of man. In the dog's life we see the world invisible to him because we live in both worlds. In human life, although we only see our world, and his within it, yet encompassing both these worlds a still wider world may be there, as unseen by us as our world is by him; and to believe in that world *may* be the most essential function that our lives in this world have to perform. But "*may* be! *may* be!" one now hears the positivist contemptuously exclaim; "what use can a scientific life have for maybes?" Well, I reply, the "scientific" life itself has much to do with maybes, and human life at large has everything to do with them. So far as man stands for anything, and is productive or originative at all, his entire vital function may be said to have to deal with maybes. Not a victory is gained, not a deed of faithfulness or courage is done, except upon a maybe; not a service, not a sally of generosity, not a scientific exploration or experiment or textbook, that may not be a mistake. It is only by risking our persons from one hour to another that we live at all. And often enough our faith beforehand in an uncertified result *is the only thing that makes the result come true*. Suppose, for instance, that you are climbing a mountain, and have worked yourself into a position from which the only escape is by a terrible leap. Have faith that you can successfully make it, and your feet are nerved to its accomplishment. But mistrust yourself, and think of all the sweet things you have heard the scientists say of *maybes*, and you will hesitate so long that, at last, all unstrung and trembling, and launching yourself in a moment of despair, you roll in the abyss. In such a case (and it belongs to an enormous class), the part of wisdom as well as of courage is to *believe what is in the line of your needs*, for only by such belief is the need fulfilled. Refuse to believe, and you shall indeed be right, for you shall irretrievably perish. But believe, and again you shall be right, for you shall save yourself. You make one or the other of two possible universes true by your trust or mistrust—both universes having been only *maybes*, in this particular, before you contributed your act.

Now, it appears to me that the question whether life is worth living is subject to conditions logically much like these. It does, indeed, depend on you *the liver*. If you surrender to the nightmare view and crown the evil edifice by your own suicide, you have indeed made a picture totally black. Pessimism, completed by your act, is true beyond a doubt, so far as your world goes. Your mistrust of life has removed whatever worth your own enduring existence might have given to it; and now, throughout the whole sphere of possible influence of that existence, the mistrust has proved itself to have had divining power. But suppose, on the other hand, that instead of giving way to the nightmare view you cling to it that this world is not the *ultimatum*. Suppose you find yourself a very well-spring, as Wordsworth says, of—

> Zeal, and the virtue to exist by faith
> As soldiers live by courage; as, by strength
> Of heart, the sailor fights with roaring seas.

Suppose, however thickly evils crowd upon you, that your unconquerable subjectivity proves to be their match, and that you find a more wonderful joy than any passive pleasure can bring in trusting ever in the larger whole. Have you not now made life worth living on these terms? What sort of a thing would life really be, with your qualities ready for a tussle with it, if it only brought fair weather and gave these higher faculties of yours no scope? Please remember that optimism and pessimism are definitions of the world, and that our own reactions on the world, small as they are in bulk, are integral parts of the whole thing, and necessarily help to determine the definition. They may even be the decisive elements in determining the definition. A large mass can have its unstable equilibrium overturned by the addition of a feather's weight; a long phrase may have its sense reversed by the addition of the three letters *n-o-t*. This life *is* worth living, we can say, *since it is what we make it, from the moral point of view;* and we are determined to make it from that point of view, so far as we have anything to do with it, a success.

Now, in this description of faiths that verify themselves I have assumed that   10 our faith in an invisible order is what inspires those efforts and that patience which make this visible order good for moral men. Our faith in the seen world's goodness (goodness now meaning fitness for successful moral and religious life) has verified itself by leaning on our faith in the unseen world. But will our faith in the unseen world similarly verify itself? Who knows?

Once more it is a case of *maybe;* and once more *maybes* are the essence of the situation. I confess that I do not see why the very existence of an invisible world may not in part depend on the personal response which any one of us may make to the religious appeal. God himself, in short, may draw vital strength and increase of very being from our fidelity. For my own part, I do not know what the sweat and blood and tragedy of this life mean, if they mean anything short of this. If this life be not a real fight, in which something is eternally gained for the universe by success, it is no better than a game of private theatricals from which one may withdraw at will. But it *feels* like a real fight—as if there were something really wild in the universe which we, with all our idealities and faithfulnesses, are needed to redeem; and first of all to redeem our own hearts from atheisms and fears. For such a half-wild, half-saved universe our nature is adapted. The deepest thing in our nature is this *Binnenleben* (as a German doctor lately has called it), this dumb region of the heart in which we dwell alone with our willingnesses and unwillingnesses, our faiths and fears. As through the cracks and crannies of caverns those waters exude from the earth's bosom which then form the fountainheads of springs, so in these crepuscular depths of personality the sources of all our outer deeds and decisions take their rise. Here is our deepest organ of communication with the nature of things; and compared with these concrete movements of our soul all abstract statements and scientific arguments—the veto, for example, which the strict positivist pronounces upon our faith—sound to us like mere chatterings of the teeth. For here possibilities, not finished facts, are the realities with which we have actively to deal; and to quote my friend William Salter, of the Philadelphia Ethical Society, "as the essence of courage is to stake one's life on a possibility, so the essence of faith is to believe that the possibility exists."

These, then, are my last words to you: Be not afraid of life. Believe that life *is* worth living, and your belief will help create the fact. The "scientific proof" that you are right may not be clear before the day of judgment (or some stage of being which that expression may serve to symbolize) is reached. But the faithful fighters of this hour, or the beings that then and there will represent them, may then turn to the faint-hearted, who here decline to go on, with words like those with which Henry IV[3] greeted the tardy Crillon after a great victory had been

---

[3] At the Battle of Arques, 1589, Henry IV of France put down a rebellion. —ED.

gained: "Hang yourself, brave Crillon! We fought at Arques, and you were not there."

QUESTIONS AND SUGGESTIONS FOR WRITING

1. James says (paragraph 6) that, believing only in "the bare assurance that this natural order is not ultimate but a mere sign or vision . . . of a many-storied universe, in which spiritual forces have the last word," people can live and die by the help of a sort of faith that goes without a single dogma or definition. But what principles *would* guide such a believer? For instance, would such a believer necessarily have only one spouse? Or be charitable? Explain.
2. In 250 to 500 words, define what a "Christian" is and then discuss whether James can reasonably be called a Christian.

Will Herberg (American. 1909–1977)

RELIGIOSITY AND RELIGION

Religion is taken very seriously in present-day America, in a way that would have amazed and chagrined the "advanced" thinkers of half a century ago, who were so sure that the ancient superstition was bound to disappear very shortly in the face of the steady advance of science and reason. Religion has not disappeared; it is probably more pervasive today, and in many ways more influential, than it has been for generations. The only question is: What kind of religion is it? What is its content? What is it that Americans *believe in* when they are religious?

"The 'unknown God' of Americans seems to be faith itself."[1] What Americans believe in when they are religious is . . . religion itself. Of course, religious Americans speak of God and Christ, but what they seem to regard as really redemptive is primarily religion, the "positive" attitude of *believing*. It is this faith in faith, this religion that makes religion its own object, that is the outstanding characteristic of contemporary American religiosity. Daniel Poling's formula: "I began saying in the morning two words, 'I believe'—those two words *with nothing added* . . ."[2] (emphasis not in original) may be taken as the classic expression of this aspect of American faith.

On the social level, this faith in religion involves the conviction, quite universal among Americans today, that every decent and virtuous nation is religious, that religion is the true basis of national existence and therefore presumably the one

---

[1] Reinhold Niebuhr, "Religiosity and the Christian Faith," *Christianity and Crisis*, Vol. XIV, No. 24, January 24, 1955.

[2] Daniel A. Poling, "A Running Start to Every Day," *Parade: The Sunday Picture Magazine*, September 19, 1954.

sure resource for the solution of all national problems.[3] On the level of personal life, the American faith in religion implies not only that every right-minded citizen is religious, but also that religion (or faith) is a most efficacious device for getting what one wants in life.[4] "Jesus," the Rev. Irving E. Howard assures us, "recommended faith as a technique for getting results. . . . Jesus recommended faith as a way to heal the body and to remove any of the practical problems that loom up as mountains in a man's path."[5]

As one surveys the contemporary scene, it appears that the "results" Americans want to get out of faith are primarily "peace of mind," happiness, and success in worldly achievement. Religion is valued too as a means of cultural enrichment.

Prosperity, success, and advancement in business are the obvious ends for which religion, or rather the religious attitude of "believing," is held to be useful.[6] There is ordinarily no criticism of the ends themselves in terms of the ultimate loyalties of a God-centered faith, nor is there much concern about what the religion or the faith is all about, since it is not the content of the belief but the attitude of believing that is felt to be operative.

Almost as much as worldly success, religion is expected to produce a kind of spiritual euphoria, the comfortable feeling that one is all right with God. Roy Eckardt calls this the cult of "divine-human chumminess" in which God is envisioned as the "Man Upstairs," a "Friendly Neighbor," Who is always ready to give

---

[3] At the Conference on the Spiritual Foundations of Our Democracy, held in Washington, D.C., in November 1954, Monsignor George G. Higgins, director of the social action department of the National Catholic Welfare Conference, issued a sharp warning against the widespread notion that a "return to God" on the part of the American people was in itself sufficient to solve all national problems, without the necessity of resorting to responsible and informed thinking on the "secular" level, on the level of institutions and social strategies. His warning was echoed by others at the conference.

[4] For a critique of this conception of religion, see H. Richard Niebuhr, "Utilitarian Christianity," *Christianity and Crisis,* Vol. VI, No. 12, July 8, 1946.

[5] Howard, "Random Reflections," *Christian Economics,* March 8, 1955.

[6] This is the burden of the philosophy of "positive thinking" so effectively expounded by Norman Vincent Peale, and may be documented in any of Dr. Peale's many writings. For example: "How do you practice faith? First thing every morning, before you arise, say out loud, 'I believe,' three times" *(The Power of Positive Thinking* [Prentice-Hall, 1952], p. 154). For a sharp criticism of this philosophy, see Miller, "Some Negative Thinking about Norman Vincent Peale," *The Reporter,* January 13, 1955; see also Paul Hutchinson, "Have We a 'New Religion?" *Life,* April 11, 1955, pp. 148–157. A penetrating critique of the Peale gospel of "positive thinking" by a Catholic theologian will be found in Gustave Weigel, "Protestantism as a Catholic Concern," *Theological Studies,* Vol. XVI, No. 2, June 1955. A Jewish version of the same cult of "faith in faith" may be found in Louis Binstock, *The Power of Faith* (Prentice-Hall, 1952). Declares Rabbi Binstock: "You, like everyone else, have access to a great storehouse of dynamic power on which you can draw. . . . That storehouse is *Faith.* Not religion. Not your immortal soul. Not this House of Worship. Not God. But—FAITH" (p. 4). For a critical review of this book, see Herberg, "Faith and Idolatry," *The Pastor,* Vol. XVI, No. 3, November 1952. One of the oldest and most respectable of Protestant denominations recently ran a newspaper advertisement in which the readers were told that "there are times in life when faith alone protects" and were urged to attend church because "regular church attendance helps you build your own personal reserve of faith." Neither God nor Christ was anywhere mentioned.

you the pat on the back you need when you happen to feel blue. "Fellowship with the Lord is, so to say, an extra emotional jag that keeps [us] happy. The 'gospel' makes [us] 'feel real good.'"[7] Again, all sense of the ambiguity and precariousness of human life, all sense of awe before the divine majesty, all sense of judgment before the divine holiness, is shut out; God is, in Jane Russell's inimitable phrase, a "livin' Doll." What relation has this kind of god to the biblical God Who confronts sinful man as an enemy before He comes out to meet repentant man as a Savior? Is this He of Whom we are told, "It is a fearful thing to fall into the hands of the living God" (Heb. 10:31)? The measure of how far contemporary American religiosity falls short of the authentic tradition of Jewish-Christian faith is to be found in the chasm that separates Jane Russell's "livin' Doll" from the living God of Scripture.

The cultural enrichment that is looked for in religion varies greatly with the community, the denomination, and the outlook and status of the church members. Liturgy is valued as aesthetically and emotionally "rewarding," sermons are praised as "interesting" and "enjoyable," discussions of the world relations of the church are welcomed as "educational," even theology is approved of as "thought provoking." On another level, the "old-time religion" is cherished by certain segments of the population because it so obviously enriches their cultural life.

But, in the last analysis, it is "peace of mind" that most Americans expect of religion. "Peace of mind" is today easily the most popular gospel that goes under the name of religion; in one way or another it invades and permeates all other forms of contemporary religiosity. It works in well with the drift toward other-direction characteristic of large sections of American society, since both see in adjustment the supreme good in life. What is desired, and what is promised, is the conquest of insecurity and anxiety, the overcoming of inner conflict, the shedding of guilt and fear, the translation of the self to the painless paradise of "normality" and "adjustment"! Religion, in short, is a spiritual anodyne designed to allay the pains and vexations of existence.

---

[7] "The cult of the 'Man Upstairs.' A rhapsodic inquiry greets us from the TV screen and the radio: 'Have you talked to the Man Upstairs?' God is a friendly neighbor who dwells in the apartment just above. Call on him any time, especially if you are feeling a little blue. He does not get upset over your little faults. He understands. . . . Thus is the citizenry guided to divine-human chumminess. . . . Fellowship with the Lord is, so to say, an extra emotional jag that keeps him [the individual] happy. The 'gospel' makes him 'feel real good' " (Eckardt, "The New Look in American Piety," *The Christian Century,* November 17, 1954). A strong strain of this "divine-human chumminess" is to be found in certain aspects of American revivalistic religion; there, too, the gospel makes you "feel real good." "What today's cult of reassurance most lacks—and indeed disavows—is a sense of life's inevitable failures. Here is the point at which it stands in starkest contrast to the teaching of America's most searching contemporary theologian, Reinhold Niebuhr. . . . There is one central idea in his writing which . . . is validated by universal experience. This is his contention that all human effort, however noble, however achieving contains within it an element of failure. Perhaps one reason Americans say they cannot understand Niebuhr is because their minds simply will not harbor this fact that all success is dogged by failure" (Hutchinson, "Have We a 'New Religion? *Life,* April 11, 1955, p. 148).

It is this most popular phase of contemporary American religiosity that has aroused the sharpest criticism in more sophisticated theological circles. The Most Rev. Patrick A. O'Boyle, Catholic archbishop of Washington, has warned that although "at first glance piety seems to be everywhere . . ." many persons appear to be "turning to religion as they would to a benign sedative to soothe their minds and settle their nerves."[8] Liston Pope emphasizes that the approach of the "peace of mind" school is not only "very dubious on psychological grounds," but its "identification [with] the Christian religion . . . is of questionable validity."[9] Roy Eckardt describes it as "religious narcissism," in which "the individual and his psycho-spiritual state occupy the center of the religious stage" and piety is made to "concentrate on its own navel."[10] I have myself spoken of it as a philosophy that would "dehumanize man and reduce his life to the level of sub-human creation which knows neither sin nor guilt."[11] It encourages moral insensitivity and social irresponsibility, and cultivates an almost lascivious preoccupation with self. The church becomes a kind of emotional service station to relieve us of our worries: "Go to church—you'll feel better," "Bring your troubles to church and leave them there" (slogans on subway posters urging church attendance). On every ground, this type of religion is poles apart from authentic Jewish-Christian spirituality which, while it knows of the "peace that passeth understanding" as the gift of God, promotes a "divine discontent"[12] with things as they are and a "passionate thirst for the future,"[13] in which all things will be renewed and restored to their right relation to God.[14]

---

[8] Address at the forty-first annual meeting of the Association of American Colleges, held in Washington, January 1955, as reported in *New York Herald Tribune*, January 12, 1955.

[9] Address at the dinner meeting of the broadcasting and film commission of the National Council of Churches, New York City, March 1, 1955 (unpublished). See also Hutchinson, "Have We a 'New' Religion?" *Life*, April 11, 1955, pp. 147–148; Hutchinson calls it the "cult of reassurance."

[10] Eckardt, "The New Look in American Piety," *The Christian Century*, November 17, 1954.

[11] Herberg, *Judaism and Modern Man: An Interpretation of Jewish Religion* (Farrar, Straus, and Young, 1951), p. 29.

[12] "I most emphatically prefer a divine discontent to peace of mind. . . . Are you satisfied with the state of the world? Are you content with the behavior of modern man? Have you reached the point where soporific relaxation is the real goal, where more than anything else you want rest and quiet and protection from stimulation? . . . It that's what you want, count me out. . . . God pity me on the day when I have lost my restlessness! God forgive me on the day when I'm satisfied! God rouse me up if ever I am so dull, insensitive, lazy, complacent, phlegmatic, and apathetic as to be at peace!" (Warren Weaver, "Peace of Mind," *The Saturday Review*, December 11, 1954). Mr. Weaver is director of the division of natural sciences of the Rockefeller Foundation.

[13] Ernst Renan is reported to have described the "true Israelite" as a man "torn with discontent and possessed with a passionate thirst for the future."

[14] "We are undoubtedly in the midst of a widespread and powerful revival of religion. There is, however, a real danger of this spiritual current running up against a steep wall of compulsive escapism and becoming a giant pool of stagnation and futility, instead of a vital tide of constructive energy and new creative work" (Charles W. Lowry, co-chairman of the Foundation for Religious Action, Washington, D.C., in a press release of the Foundation, issued June 10, 1954).

The burden of this criticism of American religion from the point of view of   10
Jewish-Christian faith is that contemporary religion is so naively, so innocently
man-centered. Not God, but man—man in his individual and corporate being—is
the beginning and end of the spiritual system of much of present-day American
religiosity. In this kind of religion there is no sense of transcendence, no sense of
the nothingness of man and his works before a holy God; in this kind of religion
the values of life, and life itself, are not submitted to Almighty God to judge, to
shatter, and to reconstruct; on the contrary, life, and the values of life, are given
an ultimate sanction by being identified with the divine. In this kind of religion it is
not man who serves God, but God who is mobilized and made to serve man and
his purposes—whether these purposes be economic prosperity, free enterprise,
social reform, democracy, happiness, security, or "peace of mind." God is conceived as man's "omnipotent servant,"[15] faith as a sure-fire device to get what we
want. The American is a religious man, and in many cases personally humble and
conscientious. But religion as he understands it is not something that makes for
humility or the uneasy conscience: it is something that reassures him about the
essential rightness of everything American, his nation, his culture, and himself;
something that validates his goals and his ideals instead of calling them into question; something that enhances his self-regard instead of challenging it; something
that feeds his self-sufficiency instead of shattering it; something that offers him
salvation on easy terms instead of demanding repentance and a "broken heart."
Because it does all these things, his religion, however sincere and well-meant, is
ultimately vitiated by a strong and pervasive idolatrous element.

QUESTIONS AND SUGGESTIONS FOR WRITING

1. Herberg several times uses the word "religiosity." How does "religiosity" differ from
   "religion"? Summarize Herberg's objections to "religiosity," and then in a sentence or
   two set forth what you take Herberg to mean by true "religion."
2. In an essay of 500 to 750 words, confirm Herberg's thesis (drawing on what you see
   around you), or reject it (again, drawing on evidence around you). Be as specific as
   possible. For instance, you may want to discuss in some detail a particular sermon,
   magazine article, or church advertisement, suggesting that it is typical of many.
3. Herberg is unhappy that many Americans simply have "faith in faith" (paragraph 2).
   Does William James's essay (page 592), written long before Herberg's, provide an
   adequate answer to Herberg? Explain.

[15] The phrase is from Jules H. Masserman, "Faith and Delusion in Psychotherapy: The Ur-
Defenses of Man," *The American Journal of Psychiatry*, Vol. 110, No. 5, November 1953. For a
critique of the theological aspects of Masserman's thesis, see Herberg, "Biblical Faith and Natural
Religion," *Theology Today*, Vol. XI, No. 4, January 1955.

☐ FICTION

Luke (First century A.D.)

THE PARABLE OF THE PRODIGAL SON
Luke 15:11–32, King James Version

And he said, "A certain man had two sons: and the younger of them said to his father, 'Father, give me the portion of goods that falleth to me.' And he divided unto them his living. And not many days after, the younger son gathered all together, and took his journey into a far country, and there wasted his substance with riotous living. And when he had spent all, there arose a mighty famine in that land, and he began to be in want. And he went and joined himself to a citizen of that country, and he sent him into his fields to feed swine. And he would fain have filled his belly with the husks that the swine did eat: and no man gave unto him. And when he came to himself, he said, 'How many hired servants of my father's have bread enough and to spare, and I perish with hunger? I will arise and go to my father, and will say unto him, "Father, I have sinned against heaven, and before thee, and am no more worthy to be called thy son: make me as one of thy hired servants."' And he arose, and came to his father. But when he was yet a great way off, his father saw him, and had compassion, and ran, and fell on his neck, and kissed him. And the son said unto him, 'Father, I have sinned against heaven, and in thy sight, and am no more worthy to be called thy son.' But the father said to his servants, 'Bring forth the best robe, and put it on him, and put a ring on his hand, and shoes on his feet. And bring hither the fatted calf, and kill it, and let us eat, and be merry. For this my son was dead, and is alive again; he was lost, and is found.' And they began to be merry. Now his elder son was in the field, and as he came and drew nigh to the house, he heard music and dancing. And he called one of the servants, and asked what these things meant. And he said unto him, 'Thy brother is come, and thy father hath killed the fatted calf, because he hath received him safe and sound.' And he was angry, and would not go in: therefore came his father out, and entreated him. And he answering said to his father, 'Lo, these many years do I serve thee, neither transgressed I at any time thy commandment, and yet thou never gavest me a kid, that I might make merry with my friends: but as soon as this thy son was come, which hath devoured thy living with harlots, thou hast killed for him the fatted calf.' And he said unto him, 'Son, thou art ever with me, and all that I have is thine. It was meet that we should make merry, and be glad: for this thy brother was dead, and is alive again: and was lost, and is found.'"

QUESTIONS AND SUGGESTIONS FOR WRITING

1. What is the function of the older brother? Characterize him, and compare him with the younger brother.

2. Is the father foolish and sentimental? Do we approve or disapprove of his behavior at the end? Explain.

Nathaniel Hawthorne (American. 1804–1864)

YOUNG GOODMAN BROWN

Young Goodman Brown came forth at sunset into the street at Salem village; but put his head back, after crossing the threshold, to exchange a parting kiss with his young wife. And Faith, as the wife was aptly named, thrust her own pretty head into the street, letting the wind play with the pink ribbons of her cap while she called to Goodman Brown.

"Dearest heart," whispered she, softly and rather sadly, when her lips were close to his ear, "prithee put off your journey until sunrise and sleep in your own bed to-night. A lone woman is troubled with such dreams and such thoughts that she's afeared of herself sometimes. Pray tarry with me this night, dear husband, of all nights in the year."

"My love and my Faith," replied young Goodman Brown, "of all nights in the year, this one night must I tarry away from thee. My journey, as thou callest it, forth and back again, must needs be done 'twixt now and sunrise. What, my sweet, pretty wife, dost thou doubt me already, and we but three months married?"

"Then God bless you!" said Faith, with the pink ribbons; "and may you find all well when you come back."

"Amen!" cried Goodman Brown. "Say thy prayers, dear Faith, and go to bed at dusk, and no harm will come to thee." 5

So they parted; and the young man pursued his way until, being about to turn the corner by the meeting-house, he looked back and saw the head of Faith still peeping after him with a melancholy air, in spite of her pink ribbons.

"Poor little Faith!" thought he, for his heart smote him. "What a wretch am I to leave her on such an errand! She talks of dreams, too. Methought as she spoke there was trouble in her face, as if a dream had warned her what work is to be done to-night. But no, no; 'twould kill her to think it. Well, she's a blessed angel on earth; and after this one night I'll cling to her skirts and follow her to heaven."

With this excellent resolve for the future, Goodman Brown felt himself justified in making more haste on his present evil purpose. He had taken a dreary road, darkened by all the gloomiest trees of the forest, which barely stood aside to let the narrow path creep through, and closed immediately behind. It was all as lonely as could be; and there is this peculiarity in such a solitude, that the traveller knows not who may be concealed by the innumerable trunks and the thick boughs overhead; so that with lonely footsteps he may yet be passing through an unseen multitude.

"There may be a devilish Indian behind every tree," said Goodman Brown to himself; and he glanced fearfully behind him as he added, "What if the devil himself should be at my very elbow!"

His head being turned back, he passed a crook of the road, and, looking   10
forward again, beheld the figure of a man, in grave and decent attire, seated at the
foot of an old tree. He arose at Goodman Brown's approach and walked onward
side by side with him.

"You are late, Goodman Brown," said he. "The clock of the Old South was
striking as I came through Boston, and that is full fifteen minutes agone."

"Faith kept me back a while," replied the young man, with a tremor in his
voice, caused by the sudden appearance of his companion, though not wholly
unexpected.

It was now deep dusk in the forest, and deepest in that part of it where these
two were journeying. As nearly as could be discerned, the second traveller was
about fifty years old, apparently in the same rank of life as Goodman Brown, and
bearing a considerable resemblance to him, though perhaps more in expression
than features. Still they might have been taken for father and son. And yet,
though the elder person was as simply clad as the younger, and as simple in
manner too, he had an indescribable air of one who knew the world, and who
would not have felt abashed at the governor's dinner table or in King William's
court, were it possible that his affairs should call him thither. But the only thing
about him that could be fixed upon as remarkable was his staff, which bore the
likeness of a great black snake, so curiously wrought that it might almost be seen
to twist and wriggle itself like a living serpent. This, of course, must have been an
ocular deception, assisted by the uncertain light.

"Come, Goodman Brown," cried his fellow-traveller, "this is a dull pace for
the beginning of a journey. Take my staff, if you are so soon weary."

"Friend," said the other, exchanging his slow pace for a full stop, "Having   15
kept covenant by meeting thee here, it is my purpose now to return whence I
came. I have scruples touching the matter thou wot'st of."

"Sayest thou so?" replied he of the serpent, smiling apart. "Let us walk on,
nevertheless, reasoning as we go; and if I convince thee not thou shalt turn back.
We are but a little way in the forest yet."

"Too far! too far!" exclaimed the goodman, unconsciously resuming his walk.
"My father never went into the woods on such an errand, nor his father before
him. We have been a race of honest men and good Christians since the days of the
martyrs; and shall I be the first of the name of Brown that ever took this path and
kept—"

"Such company, thou wouldst say," observed the elder person, interpreting
his pause. "Well said, Goodman Brown! I have been as well acquainted with your
family as with ever a one among the Puritans; and that's no trifle to say. I helped
your grandfather, the constable, when he lashed the Quaker woman so smartly
through the streets of Salem; and it was I that brought your father a pitch-pine
knot, kindled at my own hearth, to set fire to an Indian village, in King Philip's
war. They were my good friends, both; and many a pleasant walk have we had
along this path, and returned merrily after midnight. I would fain be friends with
you for their sake."

"If it be as thou sayest," replied Goodman Brown, "I marvel they never
spoke of these matters; or, verily, I marvel not, seeing that the least rumor of the

sort would have driven them from New England. We are a people of prayer, and good works to boot, and abide no such wickedness."

"Wickedness or not," said the traveller with the twisted staff, "I have a very   20 general acquaintance here in New England. The deacons of many a church have drunk the communion wine with me; the selectmen of divers towns make me their chairman; and a majority of the Great and General Court are firm supporters of my interest. The governor and I, too—But these are state secrets."

"Can this be so?" cried Goodman Brown, with a stare of amazement at his undisturbed companion. "Howbeit, I have nothing to do with the governor and council; they have their own ways, and are no rule for a simple husbandman like me. But, were I to go on with thee, how should I meet the eye of that good old man, our minister, at Salem village? Oh, his voice would make me tremble both Sabbath day and lecture day."

Thus far the elder traveller had listened with due gravity; but now burst into a fit of irrepressible mirth, shaking himself so violently that his snakelike staff actually seemed to wriggle in sympathy.

"Ha! ha! ha!" shouted he again and again; then composing himself, "Well, go on, Goodman Brown, go on; but, prithee, don't kill me with laughing."

"Well, then, to end the matter at once," said Goodman Brown, considerably nettled, "there is my wife, Faith. It would break her dear little heart; and I'd rather break my own."

"Nay, if that be the case," answered the other, "e'en go thy ways, Goodman   25 Brown. I would not for twenty old women like the one hobbling before us that Faith should come to any harm."

As he spoke he pointed his staff at a female figure on the path, in whom Goodman Brown recognized a very pious and exemplary dame, who had taught him his catechism in youth, and was still his moral and spiritual adviser, jointly with the minister and Deacon Gookin.

"A marvel, truly, that Goody Cloyse should be so far in the wilderness at nightfall," said he. "But with your leave, friend, I shall take a cut through the woods until we have left this Christian woman behind. Being a stranger to you, she might ask whom I was consorting with and whither I was going."

"Be it so," said his fellow-traveller. "Betake you the woods, and let me keep the path."

Accordingly the young man turned aside, but took care to watch his companion, who advanced softly along the road until he had come within a staff's length of the old dame. She, meanwhile, was making the best of her way, with singular speed for so aged a woman, and mumbling some indistinct words—a prayer, doubtless—as she went. The traveller put forth his staff and touched her withered neck with what seemed the serpent's tail.

"The devil!" screamed the pious old lady.   30

"Then Goody Cloyse knows her old friend?" observed the traveller, confronting her and leaning on his writhing stick.

"Ah, forsooth, and is it your worship indeed?" cried the good dame. "Yea, truly is it, and in the very image of my old gossip, Goodman Brown, the grandfather of the silly fellow that now is. But—would your worship believe it?—my broomstick hath strangely disappeared, stolen, as I suspect, by that unhanged witch, Goody Cory, and that, too, when I was all anointed with the juice of smallage, and cinquefoil, and wolf's bane—"

"Mingled with fine wheat and the fat of a new-born babe," said the shape of old Goodman Brown.

"Ah, your worship knows the recipe," cried the old lady, cackling aloud. "So, as I was saying, being all ready for the meeting, and no horse to ride on, I made up my mind to foot it; for they tell me there is a nice young man to be taken into communion to-night. But now your good worship will lend me your arm, and we shall be there in a twinkling."

"That can hardly be," answered her friend. "I may not spare you my arm,   35 Goody Cloyse; but here is my staff, if you will."

So saying, he threw it down at her feet, where, perhaps, it assumed life, being one of the rods which its owner had formerly lent to the Egyptian magi. Of this fact, however, Goodman Brown could not take cognizance. He had cast up his eyes in astonishment, and, looking down again, beheld neither Goody Cloyse nor the serpentine staff, but his fellow-traveller alone, who waited for him as calmly as if nothing had happened.

"That old woman taught me my catechism," said the young man; and there was a world of meaning in this simple comment.

They continued to walk onward, while the elder traveller exhorted his companion to make good speed and persevere in the path, discoursing so aptly that his arguments seemed rather to spring up in the bosom of his auditor than to be suggested by himself. As they went, he plucked a branch of maple to serve for a walking stick, and began to strip it of the twigs and little boughs, which were wet with evening dew. The moment his fingers touched them they became strangely withered and dried up as with a week's sunshine. Thus the pair proceeded, at a good free pace, until suddenly, in a gloomy hollow of the road, Goodman Brown sat himself down on the stump of a tree and refused to go any farther.

"Friend," said he, stubbornly, "my mind is made up. Not another step will I budge on this errand. What if a wretched old woman do choose to go to the devil when I thought she was going to heaven: is that any reason why I should quit my dear Faith and go after her?"

"You will think better of this by and by," said his acquaintance, composedly.   40 "Sit here and rest yourself a while; and when you feel like moving again, there is my staff to help you along."

Without more words, he threw his companion the maple stick, and was as speedily out of sight as if he had vanished into the deepening gloom. The young man sat a few moments by the roadside, applauding himself greatly, and thinking with how clear a conscience he should meet the minister in his morning walk, nor shrink from the eye of good old Deacon Gookin. And what calm sleep would be his that very night, which was to have been spent so wickedly, but so purely and sweetly now, in the arms of Faith! Amidst these pleasant and praiseworthy meditations, Goodman Brown heard the tramp of horses along the road, and deemed it advisable to conceal himself within the verge of the forest, conscious of the guilty purpose that had brought him thither, though now so happily turned from it.

On came the hoof tramps and the voices of the riders, two grave old voices, conversing soberly as they drew near. These mingled sounds appeared to pass along the road, within a few yards of the young man's hiding-place; but, owing doubtless to the depth of the gloom at that particular spot, neither the travellers nor their steeds were visible. Though their figures brushed the small boughs by the wayside, it could not be seen that they intercepted, even for a moment, the faint gleam from the strip of bright sky athwart which they must have passed. Goodman Brown alternately crouched and stood on tiptoe, pulling aside the branches and thrusting forth his head as far as he durst without discerning so much as a shadow. It vexed him the more, because be could have sworn, were such a thing possible, that he recognized the voices of the minister and Deacon Gookin, jogging along quietly, as they were wont to do, when bound to some ordination or ecclesiastical council. While yet within hearing, one of the riders stopped to pluck a switch.

"Of the two, reverend sir," said the voice like the deacon's, "I had rather miss an ordination dinner than to-night's meeting. They tell me that some of our community are to be here from Falmouth and beyond, and others from Connecticut and Rhode Island, besides several of the Indian powwows, who, after their fashion, know almost as much deviltry as the best of us. Moreover, there is a goodly young woman to be taken into communion."

"Mighty well, Deacon Gookin!" replied the solemn old tones of the minister. "Spur up, or we shall be late. Nothing can be done, you know, until I get on the ground."

The hoofs clattered again; and the voices, talking so strangely in the empty air, passed on through the forest, where no church had ever been gathered or solitary Christian prayed. Whither, then, could these holy men be journeying so deep into the heathen wilderness? Young Goodman Brown caught hold of a tree for support, being ready to sink down on the ground, faint and overburdened with the heavy sickness of his heart. He looked up to the sky, doubting whether there really was a heaven above him. Yet there was the blue arch, and the stars brightening in it.   45

"With heaven above and Faith below, I will yet stand firm against the devil!" cried Goodman Brown.

While he still gazed upward into the deep arch of the firmament and had lifted his hands to pray, a cloud, though no wind was stirring, hurried across the zenith and hid the brightening stars. The blue sky was still visible, except directly overhead, where this black mass of cloud was sweeping swiftly northward. Aloft in the air, as if from the depths of the cloud, came a confused and doubtful sound of voices. Once the listener fancied that he could distinguish the accents of townspeople of his own, men and women, both pious and ungodly, many of whom he had met at the communion table, and had seen others rioting at the tavern. The next moment, so indistinct were the sounds, he doubted whether he had heard aught but the murmur of the old forest, whispering without a wind. Then came a stronger swell of those familiar tones, heard daily in the sunshine at Salem village, but never until now from a cloud of night. There was one voice, of a young woman, uttering lamentations, yet with an uncertain sorrow, and entreating for some favor, which, perhaps, it would grieve her to obtain; and all the unseen multitude, both saints and sinners, seemed to encourage her onward.

"Faith!" shouted Goodman Brown, in a voice of agony and desperation; and the echoes of the forest mocked him, crying, "Faith! Faith!" as if bewildered wretches were seeking her all through the wilderness.

The cry of grief, rage, and terror was yet piercing the night, when the unhappy husband held his breath for a response. There was a scream, drowned immediately in a louder murmur of voices, fading into far-off laughter, as the dark cloud swept away, leaving the clear and silent sky above Goodman Brown. But something fluttered lightly down through the air and caught on the branch of a tree. The young man seized it, and beheld a pink ribbon.

"My Faith is gone!" cried he, after one stupefied moment. "There is no good on earth; and sin is but a name. Come, devil; for to thee is this world given." 50

And, maddened with despair, so that he laughed loud and long, did Goodman Brown grasp his staff and set forth again, at such a rate that he seemed to fly along the forest path rather than to walk or run. The road grew wilder and drearier and more faintly traced, and vanished at length, leaving him in the heart of the dark wilderness, still rushing onward with the instinct that guides mortal man to evil. The whole forest was peopled with frightful sounds—the creaking of the trees, the howling of wild beasts, and the yell of Indians; while sometimes the wind tolled like a distant church bell, and sometimes gave a broad roar around the traveller, as if all Nature were laughing him to scorn. But he was himself the chief horror of the scene, and shrank not from its other horrors.

"Ha! ha! ha!" roared Goodman Brown when the wind laughed at him. "Let us hear which will laugh loudest. Think not to frighten me with your deviltry. Come witch, come wizard, come Indian powwow, come devil himself, and here comes Goodman Brown. You may as well fear him as he fear you."

In truth, all through the haunted forest there could be nothing more frightful than the figure of Goodman Brown. On he flew among the black pines, brandishing his staff with frenzied gestures, now giving vent to an inspiration of horrid blasphemy, and now shouting forth such laughter as set all the echoes of the forest laughing like demons around him. The fiend in his own shape is less hideous than when he rages in the breast of man. Thus sped the demoniac on his course, until, quivering among the trees, he saw a red light before him, as when the felled trunks and branches of a clearing have been set on fire, and throw up their lurid blaze against the sky, at the hour of midnight. He paused, in a lull of the tempest that had driven him onward, and heard the swell of what seemed a hymn, rolling solemnly from a distance with the weight of many voices. He knew the tune; it was a familiar one in the choir of the village meeting-house. The verse died heavily away, and was lengthened by a chorus, not of human voices, but of all the sounds of the benighted wilderness pealing in awful harmony together. Goodman Brown cried out, and his cry was lost to his own ear by its unison with the cry of the desert.

In the interval of silence he stole forward until the light glared full upon his

eyes. At one extremity of an open space, hemmed in by the dark wall of the
forest, arose a rock, bearing some rude, natural resemblance either to an altar or
a pulpit, and surrounded by four blazing pines, their tops aflame, their stems
untouched, like candles at an evening meeting. The mass of foliage that had
overgrown the summit of the rock was all on fire, blazing high into the night and
fitfully illuminating the whole field. Each pendent twig and leafy festoon was in a
blaze. As the red light arose and fell, a numerous congregation alternately shone
forth, then disappeared in shadow, and again grew, as it were, out of the darkness, peopling the heart of the solitary woods at once.

"A grave and dark-clad company," quoth Goodman Brown.   55

In truth they were such. Among them, quivering to and fro between gloom
and splendor, appeared faces that would be seen next day at the council board of
the province, and others which, Sabbath after Sabbath, looked devoutly heavenward, and benignantly over the crowded pews, from the holiest pulpits in the land.
Some affirm that the lady of the governor was there. At least there were high
dames well known to her, and wives of honored husbands, and widows, a great
multitude, and ancient maidens, all of excellent repute, and fair young girls, who
trembled lest their mothers should espy them. Either the sudden gleams of light
flashing over the obscure field bedazzled Goodman Brown, or he recognized a
score of the church members of Salem village famous for their especial sanctity.
Good old Deacon Gookin had arrived, and waited at the skirts of that venerable
saint, his revered pastor. But, irreverently consorting with these grave, reputable,
and pious people, these elders of the church, these chaste dames and dewy
virgins, there were men of dissolute lives and women of spotted fame, wretches
given over to all mean and filthy vice, and suspected even of horrid crimes. It was
strange to see that the good shrank not from the wicked, nor were the sinners
abashed by the saints. Scattered also among their pale-faced enemies were the
Indian priests, or powwows, who had often scared their native forest with more
hideous incantations than any known to English witchcraft.

"But where is Faith?" thought Goodman Brown; and, as hope came into his
heart, he trembled.

Another verse of the hymn arose, a slow and mournful strain, such as the
pious love, but joined to words which expressed all that our nature can conceive of
sin, and darkly hinted at far more. Unfathomable to mere mortals is the lore of
fiends. Verse after verse was sung; and still the chorus of the desert swelled
between like the deepest tone of a mighty organ; and with the final peal of that
dreadful anthem there came a sound, as if the roaring wind, the rushing streams,
the howling beasts, and every other voice of the unconcerted wilderness were
mingling and according with the voice of guilty man in homage to the prince of all.
The four blazing pines threw up a loftier flame, and obscurely discovered shapes
and visages of horror on the smoke wreaths above the impious assembly. At the
same moment the fire on the rock shot redly forth and formed a glowing arch
above its base, where now appeared a figure. With reverence be it spoken, the
figure bore no slight similitude, both in garb and manner, to some grave divine of
the New England churches.

"Bring forth the converts!" cried a voice that echoed through the field and rolled into the forest.

At the word, Goodman Brown stepped forth from the shadow of the trees   60 and approached the congregation, with whom he felt a loathful brotherhood by the sympathy of all that was wicked in his heart. He could have well-nigh sworn that the shape of his own dead father beckoned him to advance, looking downward from a smoke wreath, while a woman, with dim features of despair, threw out her hand to warn him back. Was it his mother? But he had no power to retreat one step, nor to resist, even in thought, when the minister and good old Deacon Gookin seized his arms and led him to the blazing rock. Thither came also the slender form of a veiled female, led between Goody Cloyse, that pious teacher of the catechism, and Martha Carrier, who had received the devil's promise to be queen of hell. A rampant hag was she. And there stood the proselytes beneath the canopy of fire.

"Welcome, my children," said the dark figure, "to the communion of your race. Ye have found thus young your nature and your destiny. My children, look behind you!"

They turned; and flashing forth, as it were, in a sheet of flame, the fiend worshippers were seen; the smile of welcome gleamed darkly on every visage.

"There," resumed the sable form, "are all whom ye have reverenced from youth. Ye deemed them holier than yourselves, and shrank from your own sin, contrasting it with their lives of righteousness and prayerful aspirations heavenward. Yet here are they all in my worshipping assembly. This night it shall be granted you to know their secret deeds: how hoary-bearded elders of the church have whispered wanton words to the young maids of their households; how many a woman, eager for widows' weeds, has given her husband a drink at bedtime and let him sleep his last sleep in her bosom; how beardless youths have made haste to inherit their fathers' wealth; and how fair damsels—blush not, sweet ones— have dug little graves in the garden, and bidden me, the sole guest, to an infant's funeral. By the sympathy of your human hearts for sin ye shall scent out all the places—whether in church, bed-chamber, street, field, or forest—where crime has been committed, and shall exult to behold the whole earth one stain of guilt, one mighty blood spot. Far more than this. It shall be yours to penetrate, in every bosom, the deep mystery of sin, the fountain of all wicked arts, and which inexhaustibly supplies more evil impulses than human power—than my power at its utmost—can make manifest in deeds. And now, my children, look upon each other."

They did so; and, by the blaze of the hell-kindled torches, the wretched man beheld his Faith, and the wife her husband, trembling before that unhallowed altar.

"Lo, there ye stand, my children," said the figure, in a deep and solemn tone,   65 almost sad with its despairing awfulness, as if his once angelic nature could yet mourn for our miserable race. "Depending upon one another's hearts, ye had still hoped that virtue were not all a dream. Now are ye undeceived. Evil is the nature of mankind. Evil must be your only happiness. Welcome again, my children, to the communion of your race."

"Welcome," repeated the fiend worshippers, in one cry of despair and triumph.

And there they stood, the only pair, as it seemed, who were yet hesitating on the verge of wickedness in this dark world. A basin was hollowed, naturally, in the rock. Did it contain water, reddened by the lurid light? or was it blood? or, perchance, a liquid flame? Herein did the shape of evil dip his hand and prepare to lay the mark of baptism upon their foreheads, that they might be partakers of the mystery of sin, more conscious of the secret guilt of others, both in deed and thought, than they could now be of their own. The husband cast one look at his pale wife, and Faith at him. What polluted wretches would the next glance show them to each other, shuddering alike at what they disclosed and what they saw!

"Faith! Faith!" cried the husband, "look up to heaven, and resist the wicked one."

Whether Faith obeyed he knew not. Hardly had he spoken when he found himself amid calm night and solitude, listening to a roar of the wind which died heavily away through the forest. He staggered against the rock, and felt it chill and damp; while a hanging twig, that had been all on fire, besprinkled his cheek with the coldest dew.

The next morning young Goodman Brown came slowly into the street of   70
Salem village, staring around him like a bewildered man. The good old minister was taking a walk along the graveyard to get an appetite for breakfast and meditate his sermon, and bestowed a blessing, as he passed, on Goodman Brown. He shrank from the venerable saint as if to avoid an anathema. Old Deacon Gookin was at domestic worship, and the holy words of his prayer were heard through the open window. "What God doth the wizard pray to?" quoth Goodman Brown. Goody Cloyse, that excellent old Christian, stood in the early sunshine at her own lattice, catechizing a little girl who had brought her a pint of morning's milk. Goodman Brown snatched away the child as from the grasp of the fiend himself. Turning the corner by the meeting-house, he spied the head of Faith, with the pink ribbons, gazing anxiously forth, and bursting into such joy at sight of him that she skipped along the street and almost kissed her husband before the whole village. But Goodman Brown looked sternly and sadly into her face, and passed on without a greeting.

Had Goodman Brown fallen asleep in the forest and only dreamed a wild dream of a witch-meeting?

Be it so if you will; but, alas! it was a dream of evil omen for young Goodman Brown. A stern, a sad, a darkly meditative, a distrustful, if not a desperate man did he become from the night of that fearful dream. On the Sabbath day, when the congregation were singing a holy psalm, he could not listen because an anthem of sin rushed loudly upon his ear and drowned all the blessed strain. When the minister spoke from the pulpit with power and fervid eloquence, and, with his hand on the open Bible, of the sacred truths of our religion, and of saint-like lives and triumphant deaths, and of future bliss or misery unutterable, then did Goodman Brown turn pale, dreading lest the roof should thunder down upon the gray blasphemer and his hearers. Often, awaking suddenly at midnight, he shrank from the bosom of Faith; and at morning or eventide, when the family knelt down at prayer, he scowled and muttered to himself, and gazed sternly at his wife, and turned away. And when he had lived long, and was borne to his grave a hoary corpse, followed by Faith, an aged woman, and children and grandchildren, a goodly procession, besides neighbors not a few, they carved no hopeful verse upon his tombstone, for his dying hour was gloom.

QUESTIONS AND SUGGESTIONS FOR WRITING

1. What do you think Hawthorne gains (or loses) by the last sentence?
2. Evaluate the view that when Young Goodman Brown enters the dark forest he is really entering his own evil mind. Why, by the way, does he go into the forest at night? (Hawthorne gives no explicit reason, but you may want to offer a conjecture.)
3. In a sentence or two summarize the plot, and then in another sentence or two state the theme of the story. (On theme, see page 716.)
4. If you have read the selection from Paul on page 591, write an essay of 500 words on the evidence, or lack of evidence, for Brown's "faith, hope, and charity." One way to approach this topic is to write a commentary on the story, from Paul's point of view.

Katherine Anne Porter (American. 1890–1980)
THE JILTING OF GRANNY WEATHERALL

She flicked her wrist neatly out of Doctor Harry's pudgy careful fingers and pulled the sheet up to her chin. The brat ought to be in knee breeches. Doctoring around the country with spectacles on his nose! "Get along now, take your schoolbooks and go. There's nothing wrong with me."

Doctor Harry spread a warm paw like a cushion on her forehead where the forked green vein danced and made her eyelids twitch. "Now, now, be a good girl, and we'll have you up in no time."

"That's no way to speak to a woman nearly eighty years old just because she's down. I'd have you respect your elders, young man."

"Well, Missy, excuse me." Doctor Harry patted her cheek. "But I've got to warn you, haven't I? You're a marvel, but you must be careful or you're going to be good and sorry."

"Don't tell me what I'm going to be. I'm on my feet now, morally speaking. It's Cornelia. I had to go to bed to get rid of her." 5

Her bones felt loose, and floated around in her skin, and Doctor Harry floated like a balloon around the foot of the bed. He floated and pulled down his waistcoat and swung his glasses on a cord. "Well, stay where you are, it certainly can't hurt you."

"Get along and doctor your sick," said Granny Weatherall. "Leave a well woman alone. I'll call for you when I want you. . . . Where were you forty years ago when I pulled through milk-leg and double pneumonia? You weren't even born. Don't let Cornelia lead you on," she shouted, because Doctor Harry appeared to float up to the ceiling and out. "I pay my own bills, and I don't throw my money away on nonsense!"

She meant to wave good-by, but it was too much trouble. Her eyes closed of themselves, it was like a dark curtain drawn around the bed. The pillow rose and floated under her, pleasant as a hammock in a light wind. She listened to the leaves rustling outside the window. No, somebody was swishing newspapers: no, Cornelia and Doctor Harry were whispering together. She leaped broad awake, thinking they whispered in her ear.

"She was never like this, *never* like this!" "Well, what can we expect?" "Yes, eighty years old. . . ."

Well, and what if she was? She still had ears. It was like Cornelia to whisper   10
around doors. She always kept things secret in such a public way. She was always being tactful and kind. Cornelia was dutiful; that was the trouble with her. Dutiful and good: "So good and dutiful," said Granny, "and I'd like to spank her." She saw herself spanking Cornelia and making a fine job of it.

"What'd you say, Mother?"

Granny felt her face tying up in hard knots.

"Can't a body think, I'd like to know?"

"I thought you might want something."

"I do. I want a lot of things. First off, go away and don't whisper."   15

She lay and drowsed, hoping in her sleep that the children would keep out and let her rest a minute. It had been a long day. Not that she was tired. It was always pleasant to snatch a minute now and then. There was always so much to be done, let me see: tomorrow.

Tomorrow was far away and there was nothing to trouble about. Things were finished somehow when the time came; thank God there was always a little margin over for peace: then a person could spread out the plan of life and tuck in the edges orderly. It was good to have everything clean and folded away, with the hair brushes and tonic bottles sitting straight on the white embroidered linen: the day started without fuss and the pantry shelves laid out with rows of jelly glasses and brown jugs and white stone-china jars with blue whirligigs and words painted on them: coffee, tea, sugar, ginger, cinnamon, allspice: and the bronze clock with the lion on top nicely dusted off. The dust that lion could collect in twenty-four hours! The box in the attic with all those letters tied up, she'd have to go through that tomorrow. All those letters—George's letters and John's letters and her letters to them both—lying around for the children to find afterwards made her uneasy. Yes, that would be tomorrow's business. No use to let them know how silly she had been once.

While she was rummaging around she found death in her mind and it felt clammy and unfamiliar. She had spent so much time preparing for death there was no need for bringing it up again. Let it take care of itself now. When she was sixty she had felt very old, finished, and went around making farewell trips to see her children and grandchildren, with a secret in her mind: This is the very last of your mother, children! Then she made her will and came down with a long fever. That was all just a notion like a lot of other things, but it was lucky too, for she had once for all got over the idea of dying for a long time. Now she couldn't be worried. She hoped she had better sense now. Her father had lived to be one hundred and two years old and had drunk a noggin of strong hot toddy on his last birthday. He told the reporters it was his daily habit, and he owed his long life to that. He had made quite a scandal and was very pleased about it. She believed she'd just plague Cornelia a little.

"Cornelia! Cornelia!" No footsteps, but a sudden hand on her cheek. "Bless you, where have you been?"

"Here, Mother." 20

"Well, Cornelia, I want a noggin of hot toddy."

"Are you cold, darling?"

"I'm chilly, Cornelia. Lying in bed stops the circulation. I must have told you that a thousand times."

Well, she could just hear Cornelia telling her husband that Mother was getting a little childish and they'd have to humor her. The thing that most annoyed her was that Cornelia thought she was deaf, dumb, and blind. Little hasty glances and tiny gestures tossed around her and over her head saying, "Don't cross her, let her have her way, she's eighty years old," and she sitting there as if she lived in a thin glass cage. Sometimes Granny almost made up her mind to pack up and move back to her own house where nobody could remind her every minute that she was old. Wait, wait, Cornelia, till your own children whisper behind your back!

In her day she had kept a better house and had got more work done. She 25 wasn't too old yet for Lydia to be driving eighty miles for advice when one of the children jumped the track, and Jimmy still dropped in and talked things over: "Now, Mammy, you've a good business head, I want to know what you think of this? . . ." Old. Cornelia couldn't change the furniture around without asking. Little things, little things! They had been so sweet when they were little. Granny wished the old days were back again with the children young and everything to be done over. It had been a hard pull, but not too much for her. When she thought of all the food she had cooked, and all the clothes she had cut and sewed, and all the gardens she had made—well, the children showed it. There they were, made out of her, and they couldn't get away from that. Sometimes she wanted to see John again and point to them and say, Well, I didn't do so badly, did I? But that would have to wait. That was for tomorrow. She used to think of him as a man, but now all the children were older than their father, and he would be a child beside her if she saw him now. It seemed strange and there was something wrong in the idea. Why, he couldn't possibly recognize her. She had fenced in a hundred acres once, digging the post holes herself and clamping the wires with just a negro boy to help. That changed a woman. John would be looking for a young woman with the peaked Spanish comb in her hair and the painted fan. Digging post holes changed a woman. Riding country roads in the winter when women had their babies was another thing: sitting up nights with sick horses and sick negroes and sick children and hardly ever losing one. John, I hardly ever lost one of them! John would see that in a minute, that would be something he could understand, she wouldn't have to explain anything!

It made her feel like rolling up her sleeves and putting the whole place to rights again. No matter if Cornelia was determined to be everywhere at once, there were a great many things left undone on this place. She would start tomorrow and do them. It was good to be strong enough for everything, even if all you made melted and changed and slipped under your hands, so that by the time you finished you almost forgot what you were working for. What was it I set out to do? she asked herself intently, but she could not remember. A fog rose over the valley, she saw it marching across the creek swallowing the trees and moving up the hill like an army of ghosts. Soon it would be at the near edge of the orchard, and then it was time to go in and light the lamps. Come in, children, don't stay out in the night air.

Lighting the lamps had been beautiful. The children huddled up to her and breathed like little calves waiting at the bars in the twilight. Their eyes followed the match and watched the flame rise and settle in a blue curve, then they moved away from her. The lamp was lit, they didn't have to be scared and hang on to mother any more. Never, never, never more. God, for all my life I thank Thee. Without Thee, my God, I could never have done it. Hail, Mary, full of grace.

I want you to pick all the fruit this year and see that nothing is wasted. There's always someone who can use it. Don't let good things rot for want of using. You waste life when you waste good food. Don't let things get lost. It's bitter to lose things. Now, don't let me get to thinking, not when I am tired and taking a little nap before supper. . . .

The pillow rose about her shoulders and pressed against her heart and the memory was being squeezed out of it: oh, push down the pillow, somebody: it would smother her if she tried to hold it. Such a fresh breeze blowing and such a green day with no threats in it. But he had not come, just the same. What does a woman do when she has put on the white veil and set out the white cake for a man and he doesn't come? She tried to remember. No, I swear he never harmed me but in that. He never harmed me but in that . . . and what if he did? There was the day, the day, but a whirl of dark smoke rose and covered it, crept up and over into the bright field where everything was planted so carefully in orderly rows. That was hell, she knew hell when she saw it. For sixty years she had prayed against remembering him and against losing her soul in the deep pit of hell, and now the two things were mingled in one and the thought of him was a smoky cloud from hell that moved and crept in her head when she had just got rid of Doctor Harry and was trying to rest a minute. Wounded vanity, Ellen, said a sharp voice in the top of her mind. Don't let your wounded vanity get the upper hand of you. Plenty of girls get jilted. You were jilted, weren't you? Then stand up to it. Her eyelids wavered and let in streamers of blue-gray light like tissue paper over her eyes. She must get up and pull the shades down or she'd never sleep. She was in bed again and the shades were not down. How could that happen? Better turn over, hide from the light, sleeping in the light gave you nightmares. "Mother, how do you feel now?" and a stinging wetness on her forehead. But I don't like having my face washed in cold water!

Hapsy? George? Lydia? Jimmy? No, Cornelia, and her features were swollen and full of little puddles. "They're coming, darling, they'll all be here soon." Go wash your face, child, you look funny.

Instead of obeying, Cornelia knelt down and put her head on the pillow. She

30

seemed to be talking but there was no sound. "Well, are you tongue-tied? Whose birthday is it? Are you going to give a party?"

Cornelia's mouth moved urgently in strange shapes. "Don't do that, you bother me, daughter."

"Oh, no, Mother. Oh, no. . . ."

Nonsense. It was strange about children. They disputed your every word. "No what, Cornelia?"

"Here's Doctor Harry."   35

"I won't see that boy again. He just left five minutes ago."

"That was this morning, Mother. It's night now. Here's the nurse."

"This is Doctor Harry, Mrs. Weatherall. I never saw you look so young and happy!"

"Ah, I'll never be young again—but I'd be happy if they'd let me lie in peace and get rested."

She thought she spoke up loudly, but no one answered. A warm weight on   40
her forehead, a warm bracelet on her wrist, and a breeze went on whispering, trying to tell her something. A shuffle of leaves in the everlasting hand of God. He blew on them and they danced and rattled. "Mother, don't mind, we're going to give you a little hypodermic." "Look here, daughter, how do ants get in this bed? I saw sugar ants yesterday." Did you send for Hapsy too?

It was Hapsy she really wanted. She had to go a long way back through a great many rooms to find Hapsy standing with a baby on her arm. She seemed to herself to be Hapsy also, and the baby on Hapsy's arm was Hapsy and himself and herself, all at once, and there was no surprise in the meeting. Then Hapsy melted from within and turned flimsy as gray gauze and the baby was a gauzy shadow, and Hapsy came up close and said, "I thought you'd never come," and looked at her very searchingly and said, "You haven't changed a bit!" They leaned forward to kiss, when Cornelia began whispering from a long way off, "Oh, is there anything you want to tell me? Is there anything I can do for you?"

Yes, she had changed her mind after sixty years and she would like to see George. I want you to find George. Find him and be sure to tell him I forgot him. I want him to know I had my husband just the same and my children and my house like any other woman. A good house too and a good husband that I loved and fine children out of him. Better than I hoped for even. Tell him I was given back everything he took away and more. Oh, no, oh, God, no, there was something else besides the house and the man and the children. Oh, surely they were not all? What was it? Something not given back. . . . Her breath crowded down under her ribs and grew into a monstrous frightening shape with cutting edges; it bored up into her head, and the agony was unbelievable: Yes, John, get the doctor now, no more talk, my time has come.

When this one was born it should be the last. The last. It should have been born first, for it was the one she had truly wanted. Everything came in good time. Nothing left out, left over. She was strong, in three days she would be as well as ever. Better. A woman needed milk in her to have her full health.

"Mother, do you hear me?"

"I've been telling you—"   45

"Mother, Father Connolly's here."

"I went to Holy Communion only last week. Tell him I'm not so sinful as all that."

"Father just wants to speak to you."

He could speak as much as he pleased. It was like him to drop in and inquire about her soul as if it were a teething baby, and then stay on for a cup of tea and a round of cards and gossip. He always had a funny story of some sort, usually about an Irishman who made his little mistakes and confessed them, and the point lay in some absurd thing he would blurt out in the confessional showing his struggles between native piety and original sin. Granny felt easy about her soul. Cornelia, where are your manners? Give Father Connolly a chair. She had her secret comfortable understanding with a few favorite saints who cleared a straight road to God for her. All as surely signed and sealed as the papers for the new Forty Acres. Forever . . . heirs and assigns forever. Since the day the wedding cake was not cut, but thrown out and wasted. The whole bottom dropped out of the world, and there she was blind and sweating with nothing under her feet and the walls falling away. His hand had caught her under the breast, she had not fallen, there was the freshly polished floor with the green rug on it, just as before. He had cursed like a sailor's parrot and said, "I'll kill him for you." Don't lay a hand on him, for my sake leave something to God. "Now, Ellen, you must believe what I tell you. . . ."

So there was nothing, nothing to worry about any more, except sometimes in   50
the night one of the children screamed in a nightmare, and they both hustled out shaking and hunting for the matches and calling, "There, wait a minute, here we are!" John, get the doctor now, Hapsy's time has come. But there was Hapsy standing by the bed in a white cap. "Cornelia, tell Hapsy to take off her cap. I can't see her plain."

Her eyes opened very wide and the room stood out like a picture she had seen somewhere. Dark colors with the shadows rising towards the ceiling in long angles. The tall black dresser gleamed with nothing on it but John's picture, enlarged from a little one, with John's eyes very black when they should have been blue. You never saw him, so how do you know how he looked? But the man insisted the copy was perfect, it was very rich and handsome. For a picture, yes, but it's not my husband. The table by the bed had a linen cover and a candle and a crucifix. The light was blue from Cornelia's silk lampshades. No sort of light at all, just frippery. You had to live forty years with kerosene lamps to appreciate honest electricity. She felt very strong and she saw Doctor Harry with a rosy nimbus around him.

"You look like a saint, Doctor Harry, and I vow that's as near as you'll ever come to it."

"She's saying something."

"I heard you, Cornelia. What's all this carrying on?"

"Father Connolly's saying—"   55

Cornelia's voice staggered and bumped like a cart in a bad road. It rounded corners and turned back again and arrived nowhere. Granny stepped up in the cart very lightly and reached for the reins, but a man sat beside her and she knew him by his hands, driving the cart. She did not look in his face, for she knew without seeing, but looked instead down the road where the trees leaned over and bowed to each other and a thousand birds were singing a Mass. She felt like singing too, but she put her hand in the bosom of her dress and pulled out a rosary, and Father Connolly murmured Latin in a very solemn voice and tickled her feet. My God, will you stop that nonsense? I'm a married woman. What if he did run away and leave me to face the priest by myself? I found another a whole world better. I wouldn't have exchanged my husband for anybody except St. Michael himself, and you may tell him that for me with a thank you in the bargain.

Light flashed on her closed eyelids, and a deep roaring shook her. Cornelia, is that lightning? I hear thunder. There's going to be a storm. Close all the windows. Call the children in. . . . "Mother, here we are, all of us." "Is that you, Hapsy?" "Oh, no, I'm Lydia. We drove as fast as we could." Their faces drifted above her, drifted away. The rosary fell out of her hands and Lydia put it back. Jimmy tried to help, their hands fumbled together, and Granny closed two fingers around Jimmy's thumb. Beads wouldn't do, it must be something alive. She was so amazed her thoughts ran round and round. So, my dear Lord, this is my death and I wasn't even thinking about it. My children have come to see me die. But I can't, it's not time. Oh, I always hated surprises. I wanted to give Cornelia the amethyst set— Cornelia, you're to have the amethyst set, but Hapsy's to wear it when she wants, and, Doctor Harry, do shut up. Nobody sent for you. Oh, my dear Lord, do wait a minute. I meant to do something about the Forty Acres, Jimmy doesn't need it and Lydia will later on, with that worthless husband of hers. I meant to finish the altar cloth and send six bottles of wine to Sister Borgia for her dyspepsia. I want to send six bottles of wine to Sister Borgia, Father Connolly, now don't let me forget.

Cornelia's voice made short turns and tilted over and crashed. "Oh, Mother, oh, Mother, oh, Mother. . . ."

"I'm not going, Cornelia. I'm taken by surprise. I can't go."

You'll see Hapsy again. What about her? "I thought you'd never come." 60 Granny made a long journey outward, looking for Hapsy. What if I don't find her? What then? Her heart sank down and down, there was no bottom to death, she couldn't come to the end of it. The blue light from Cornelia's lampshade drew into a tiny point in the center of her brain, it flickered and winked like an eye, quietly it fluttered and dwindled. Granny lay curled down within herself, amazed and watchful, staring at the point of light that was herself; her body was now only a deeper mass of shadow in an endless darkness and this darkness would curl around the light and swallow it up, God, give a sign!

For the second time there was no sign. Again no bridegroom and the priest in the house. She could not remember any other sorrow because this grief wiped them all away. Oh, no, there's nothing more cruel than this—I'll never forgive it. She stretched herself with a deep breath and blew out the light.

QUESTIONS AND SUGGESTIONS FOR WRITING

1. In a paragraph, characterize Granny Weatherall. In another paragraph, evaluate her claim that the anguish of the jilting has been compensated for by her subsequent life.
2. The final paragraph alludes to Christ's parable of the bridegroom (Matthew 25: 1–13). With this allusion in mind, write a paragraph explaining the title of the story.

Ernest Hemingway (1899–1961)

A CLEAN, WELL-LIGHTED PLACE[1]

It was late and every one had left the café except an old man who sat in the shadow the leaves of the tree made against the electric light. In the day time the street was dusty, but at night the dew settled the dust and the old man liked to sit late because he was deaf and now at night it was quiet and he felt the difference. The two waiters inside the café knew that the old man was a little drunk, and while he was a good client they knew that if he became too drunk he would leave without paying, so they kept watch on him.

"Last week he tried to commit suicide," one waiter said.

"Why?"

"He was in despair."

"What about?"

"Nothing." 5

"How do you know it was nothing?"

"He has plenty of money."

They sat together at a table that was close against the wall near the door of the café and looked at the terrace where the tables were all empty except where the old man sat in the shadow of the leaves of the tree that moved slightly in the wind. A girl and a soldier went by in the street. The street light shone on the brass number on his collar. The girl wore no head covering and hurried beside him.

"The guard will pick him up," one waiter said. 10

"What does it matter if he gets what he's after?"

"He had better get off the street now. The guard will get him. They went by five minutes ago."

The old man sitting in the shadow rapped on his saucer with his glass. The younger waiter went over to him.

"What do you want?"

The old man looked at him. "Another brandy," he said. 15

"You'll be drunk," the waiter said. The old man looked at him. The waiter went away.

"He'll stay all night," he said to his colleague. "I'm sleepy now. I never get into bed before three o'clock. He should have killed himself last week."

The waiter took the brandy bottle and another saucer from the counter inside the café and marched out to the old man's table. He put down the saucer and poured the glass full of brandy.

"You should have killed yourself last week," he said to the deaf man. The old man motioned with his finger. "A little more," he said. The waiter poured on into the glass so that the brandy slopped over and ran down the stem into the top

---

[1] The story uses a few Spanish words: *bodega* = wineshop; *nada* = nothing; *nada y pues nada* nothing and then nothing; *otro loco mas* = another madman; *copita* = little cup. —ED.

saucer of the pile. "Thank you," the old man said. The waiter took the bottle back inside the café. He sat down at the table with his colleague again.

"He's drunk now," he said.   20

"He's drunk every night."

"What did he want to kill himself for?"

"How should I know."

"How did he do it?"

"He hung himself with a rope."   25

"Who cut him down?"

"His niece."

"Why did they do it?"

"Fear for his soul."

"How much money has he got?"   30

"He's got plenty."

"He must be eighty years old."

"Anyway I should say he was eighty."

"I wish he would go home. I never get to bed before three o'clock. What kind of hour is that to go to bed?"

"He stays up because he likes it."   35

"He's lonely. I'm not lonely. I have a wife waiting in bed for me."

"He had a wife once too."

"A wife would be no good to him now."

"You can't tell. He might be better with a wife."

"His niece looks after him. You said she cut him down."   40

"I know."

"I wouldn't want to be that old. An old man is a nasty thing."

"Not always. This old man is clean. He drinks without spilling. Even now, drunk. Look at him."

"I don't want to look at him. I wish he would go home. He has no regard for those who must work."

The old man looked from his glass across the square, then over at the wait- 45
ers.

"Another brandy," he said, pointing to his glass. The waiter who was in a hurry came over.

"Finished," he said, speaking with that omission of syntax stupid people employ when talking to drunken people or foreigners. "No more tonight. Close now."

"Another," said the old man.

"No. Finished." The waiter wiped the edge of the table with a towel and shook his head.

The old man stood up, slowly counted the saucers, took a leather coin purse 50
from his pocket and paid for the drinks, leaving half a peseta tip.

The waiter watched him go down the street, a very old man walking unsteadily but with dignity.

"Why didn't you let him stay and drink?" the unhurried waiter asked. They were putting up the shutters. "It is not half-past two."

"I want to go home to bed."

"What is an hour?"

"More to me than to him."   55

"An hour is the same."

"You talk like an old man yourself. He can buy a bottle and drink at home."

"It's not the same."

"No, it is not," agreed the waiter with a wife. He did not wish to be unjust. He was only in a hurry.

"And you? You have no fear of going home before your usual hour?"   60

"Are you trying to insult me?"

"No, hombre, only to make a joke."

"No," the waiter who was in a hurry said, rising from pulling down the metal shutters. "I have confidence. I am all confidence."

"You have youth, confidence, and a job," the older waiter said. "You have everything."

"And what do you lack?"   65

"Everything but work."

"You have everything I have."

"No. I have never had confidence and I am not young."

"Come on. Stop talking nonsense and lock up."

"I am of those who like to stay late at the café," the older waiter said. "With   70 all those who do not want to go to bed. With all those who need a light for the night."

"I want to go home and into bed."

"We are of two different kinds," the older waiter said. He was now dressed to go home. "It is not only a question of youth and confidence although those things are very beautiful. Each night I am reluctant to close up because there may be some one who needs the café."

"Hombre, there are bodegas open all night long."

"You do not understand. This is a clean and pleasant café. It is well lighted. The light is very good and also, now, there are shadows of the leaves."

"Good night," said the younger waiter.   75

"Good night," the other said. Turning off the electric light he continued the conversation with himself. It is the light of course but it is necessary that the place be clean and pleasant. You do not want music. Certainly you do not want music. Nor can you stand before a bar with dignity although that is all that is provided for these hours. What did he fear? It was not fear or dread. It was a nothing that he knew too well. It was all a nothing and a man was nothing too. It was only that and light was all it needed and a certain cleanness and order. Some lived in it and never felt it but he knew it all was nada y pues nada y pues nada. Our nada who art in nada, nada be thy name thy kingdom nada thy will be nada in nada as it is in nada. Give us this nada our daily nada and nada us our nada as we nada our nadas and nada us not into nada but deliver us from nada; pues nada. Hail nothing full of nothing, nothing is with thee. He smiled and stood before a bar with a shining steam pressure coffee machine.

"What's yours?" asked the barman.

"Nada."

"Otro loco mas," said the barman and turned away.

"A little cup," said the waiter.   80

The barman poured it for him.

"The light is very bright and pleasant but the bar is unpolished," the waiter said.

The barman looked at him but did not answer. It was too late at night for conversation.

"You want another copita?" the barman asked.

"No, thank you," said the waiter and went out. He disliked bars and bodegas.   85
A clean, well-lighted café was a very different thing. Now, without thinking further, he would go home to his room. He would lie in the bed and finally, with daylight, he would go to sleep. After all, he said to himself, it is probably only insomnia. Many must have it.

QUESTIONS AND SUGGESTIONS FOR WRITING

1. In an essay of 500 words compare and contrast the two waiters. What does the young waiter believe in? Does the older waiter believe in anything? In your answer devote some space to each waiter's view of the café.

2. What is the point of the parody of the Lord's Prayer? In this context, note, too, the setting in which it is spoken: a bar in a *bodega* equipped with a steam-pressure coffee machine.

3. In 250 words explain why, if the older wiater is a nihilist (Latin *nihil*, like Spanish *nada* = nothing), he is concerned that there be a clean, well-lighted place?

Flannery O'Connor (American. 1925–1964)

A GOOD MAN IS HARD TO FIND

The grandmother didn't want to go to Florida. She wanted to visit some of her connections in east Tennessee and she was seizing at every chance to change Bailey's mind. Bailey was the son she lived with, her only boy. He was sitting on the edge of his chair at the table, bent over the orange sports section of the *Journal.* "Now look here, Bailey," she said, "see here, read this," and she stood with one hand on her thin hip and the other rattling the newspaper at his bald head. "Here this fellow that calls himself The Misfit is aloose from the Federal Pen and headed toward Florida and you read here what it says he did to these people. Just you read it. I wouldn't take my children in any direction with a criminal like that aloose in it. I couldn't answer to my conscience if I did."

Bailey didn't look up from his reading so she wheeled around then and faced the children's mother, a young woman in slacks, whose face was as broad and innocent as a cabbage and was tied round with a green head-kerchief that had two points on the top like rabbit's ears. She was sitting on the sofa, feeding the baby his apricots out of a jar. "The children have been to Florida before," the old lady said. "You all ought to take them somewhere else for a change so they would see different parts of the world and be broad. They never have been to east Tennessee."

The children's mother didn't seem to hear her but the eight-year-old boy, John Wesley, a stocky child with glasses, said, "If you don't want to go to Florida, why dontcha stay at home?" He and the little girl, June Star, were reading the funny papers on the floor.

"She wouldn't stay at home to be queen for a day," June Star said without raising her yellow head.

"Yes and what would you do if this fellow, The Misfit, caught you?" the   5
grandmother asked.

"I'd smack his face," John Wesley said.

"She wouldn't stay at home for a million bucks," June Star said. "Afraid she'd miss something. She has to go everywhere we go."

"All right, Miss," the grandmother said. "Just remember that the next time you want me to curl your hair."

June Star said her hair was naturally curly.

The next morning the grandmother was the first one in the car, ready to go.   10
She had her big black valise that looked like the head of a hippopotamus in one corner, and underneath it she was hiding a basket with Pitty Sing, the cat, in it. She didn't intend for the cat to be left alone in the house for three days because he would miss her too much and she was afraid he might brush against one of the gas burners and accidentally asphyxiate himself. Her son, Bailey, didn't like to arrive at a motel with a cat.

She sat in the middle of the back seat with John Wesley and June Star on either side of her. Bailey and the children's mother and the baby sat in the front and they left Atlanta at eight forty-five with the mileage on the car at 55890. The grandmother wrote this down because she thought it would be interesting to say how many miles they had been when they got back. It took them twenty minutes to reach the outskirts of the city.

The old lady settled herself comfortably, removing her white cotton gloves and putting them up with her purse on the shelf in front of the back window. The children's mother still had on slacks and still had her head tied up in a green kerchief, but the grandmother had on a navy blue straw sailor hat with a bunch of white violets on the brim and a navy blue dress with a small white dot in the print. Her collar and cuffs were white organdy trimmed with lace and at her neckline she had pinned a purple spray of cloth violets containing a sachet. In case of an accident, anyone seeing her dead on the highway would know at once that she was a lady.

She said she thought it was going to be a good day for driving, neither too hot nor too cold, and she cautioned Bailey that the speed limit was fifty-five miles an hour and that the patrolmen hid themselves behind billboards and small clumps of trees and sped out after you before you had a chance to slow down. She pointed out interesting details of the scenery: Stone Mountain; the blue granite that in some places came up to both sides of the highway; the brilliant red clay banks slightly streaked with purple; and the various crops that made rows of green lace-work on the ground. The trees were full of silver-white sunlight and the meanest of them sparkled. The children were reading comic magazines and their mother had gone back to sleep.

"Let's go through Georgia fast so we won't have to look at it much," John Wesley said.

"If I were a little boy," said the grandmother, "I wouldn't talk about my native state that way. Tennessee has the mountains and Georgia has the hills." 15

"Tennessee is just a hillbilly dumping ground," John Wesley said, "and Georgia is a lousy state too."

"You said it," June Star said.

"In my time," said the grandmother, folding her thin veined fingers, "children were more respectful of their native states and their parents and everything else. People did right then. Oh look at the cute little pickaninny!" she said and pointed to a Negro child standing in the door of a shack. "Wouldn't that make a picture, now?" she asked and they all turned and looked at the little Negro out of the back window. He waved.

"He didn't have any britches on," June Star said.

"He probably didn't have any," the grandmother explained. "Little niggers in the country don't have things like we do. If I could paint, I'd paint that picture," she said. 20

The children exchanged comic books.

The grandmother offered to hold the baby and the children's mother passed him over the front seat to her. She set him on her knee and bounced him and told him about the things they were passing. She rolled her eyes and screwed up her mouth and stuck her leathery thin face into his smooth bland one. Occasionally he gave her a faraway smile. They passed a large cotton field with five or six graves fenced in the middle of it, like a small island. "Look at the graveyard!" the grandmother said, pointing it out. "That was the old family burying ground. That belonged to the plantation."

"Where's the plantation?" John Wesley asked.

"Gone with the Wind," said the grandmother. "Ha. Ha."

When the children finished all the comic books they had brought, they opened the lunch and ate it. The grandmother ate a peanut butter sandwich and an olive and would not let the children throw the box and the paper napkins out the window. When there was nothing else to do they played a game by choosing a cloud and making the other two guess what shape it suggested. John Wesley took one the shape of a cow and June Star guessed a cow and John Wesley said, no, an automobile, and June Star said he didn't play fair, and they began to slap each other over the grandmother. 25

The grandmother said she would tell them a story if they would keep quiet. When she told a story, she rolled her eyes and waved her head and was very dramatic. She said once when she was a maiden lady she had been courted by a Mr. Edgar Atkins Teagarden from Jasper, Georgia. She said he was a very good-looking man and a gentleman and that he brought her a watermelon every Saturday afternoon with his initials cut in it, E. A. T. Well, one Saturday, she said, Mr. Teagarden brought the watermelon and there was nobody at home and he left it on the front porch and returned in his buggy to Jasper, but she never got the watermelon, she said, because a nigger boy ate it when he saw the initials, E. A. T.! This story tickled John Wesley's funny bone and he giggled and giggled but June Star didn't think it was any good. She said she wouldn't marry a man that just brought her a watermelon on Saturday. The grandmother said she would have done well to marry Mr. Teagarden because he was a gentleman and had bought Coca-Cola stock when it first came out and that he had died only a few years ago, a very wealthy man.

They stopped at The Tower for barbecued sandwiches. The Tower was a part stucco and part wood filling station and dance hall set in a clearing outside of Timothy. A fat man named Red Sammy Butts ran it and there were signs stuck here and there on the building and for miles up and down the highway saying, TRY RED SAMMY'S FAMOUS BARBECUE. NONE LIKE FAMOUS RED SAMMY'S! RED SAM! THE FAT BOY WITH THE HAPPY LAUGH. A VETERAN! RED SAMMY'S YOUR MAN!

Red Sammy was lying on the bare ground outside The Tower with his head under a truck while a gray monkey about a foot high, chained to a small chinaberry tree, chattered nearby. The monkey sprang back into the tree and got on the highest limb as soon as he saw the children jump out of the car and run toward him.

Inside, The Tower was a long dark room with a counter at one end and tables at the other and dancing space in the middle. They all sat down at a broad table next to the nickelodeon and Red Sam's wife, a tall burnt-brown woman with hair and eyes lighter than her skin, came and took their order. The children's mother put a dime in the machine and played "The Tennessee Waltz," and the grandmother said that tune always made her want to dance. She asked Bailey if he would like to dance but he only glared at her. He didn't have a naturally sunny disposition like she did and trips made him nervous. The grandmother's brown eyes were very bright. She swayed her head from side to side and pretended she was dancing in her chair. June Star said play something she could tap to so the children's mother put in another dime and played a fast number and June Star stepped out onto the dance floor and did her tap routine.

"Ain't she cute?" Red Sam's wife said, leaning over the counter. "Would you like to come be my little girl?"   30

"No I certainly wouldn't," June Star said. "I wouldn't live in a broken-down place like this for a million bucks!" and she ran back to the table.

"Ain't she cute?" the woman repeated, stretching her mouth politely.

"Aren't you ashamed?" hissed the grandmother.

Red Sam came in and told his wife to quit lounging on the counter and hurry with these people's order. His khaki trousers reached just to his hip bones and his stomach hung over them like a sack of meal swaying under his shirt. He came over and sat down at a table nearby and let out a combination sigh and yodel. "You can't win," he said. "You can't win," and he wiped his sweating red face off with a gray handkerchief. "These days you don't know who to trust," he said. "Ain't that the truth?"

"People are certainly not nice like they used to be," said the grandmother.   35

"Two fellers come in here last week," Red Sammy said, "driving a Chrysler. It was a old beat-up car but it was a good one and these boys looked all right to me. Said they worked at the mill and you know I let them fellers charge the gas they bought? Now why did I do that?"

"Because you're a good man!" the grandmother said at once.

"Yes'm, I suppose so," Red Sam said as if he were struck with the answer.

His wife brought the orders, carrying the five plates all at once without a tray, two in each hand and one balanced on her arm. "It isn't a soul in this green world of God's that you can trust," she said. "And I don't count anybody out of that, not nobody," she repeated, looking at Red Sammy.

"Did you read about that criminal, The Misfit, that's escaped?" asked the   40
grandmother.

"I wouldn't be a bit surprised if he didn't attact this place right here," said the woman. "If he hears about it being here, I wouldn't be none surprised to see him. If he hears it's two cent in the cash register, I wouldn't be a tall surprised if he . . ."

"That'll do," Red Sam said. "Go bring these people their Co'Colas," and the woman went off to get the rest of the order.

"A good man is hard to find," Red Sammy said. "Everything is getting terrible. I remember the day you could go off and leave your screen door unlatched. Not no more."

He and the grandmother discussed better times. The old lady said that in her opinion Europe was entirely to blame for the way things were now. She said the way Europe acted you would think we were made of money and Red Sam said it was no use talking about it, she was exactly right. The children ran outside into the white sunlight and looked at the monkey in the lacy chinaberry tree. He was busy catching fleas on himself and biting each one carefully between his teeth as if it were a delicacy.

They drove off again into the hot afternoon. The grandmother took cat naps   45
and woke up every few minutes with her own snoring. Outside of Toombsboro she woke up and recalled an old plantation that she had visited in this neighborhood once when she was a young lady. She said the house had six white columns across the front and that there was an avenue of oaks leading up to it and two little wooden trellis arbors on either side in front where you sat down with your suitor after a stroll in the garden. She recalled exactly which road to turn off to get to it. She knew that Bailey would not be willing to lose any time looking at an old house, but the more she talked about it, the more she wanted to see it once again and find out if the little twin arbors were still standing. "There was a secret panel in this house," she said craftily, not telling the truth but wishing that she were, "and the story went that all the family silver was hidden in it when Sherman came through but it was never found . . ."

"Hey!" John Wesley said. "Let's go see it! We'll find it! We'll poke all the woodwork and find it! Who lives there? Where do you turn off at? Hey, Pop, can't we turn off there?"

"We never have seen a house with a secret panel!" June Star shrieked.

"Let's go to the house with the secret panel! Hey, Pop, can't we go see the house with the secret panel!"

"It's not far from here, I know," the grandmother said. "It wouldn't take over twenty minutes."

Bailey was looking straight ahead. His jaw was as rigid as a horseshoe. "No," he said.

The children began to yell and scream that they wanted to see the house with   50
the secret panel. John Wesley kicked the back of the front seat and June Star hung over her mother's shoulder and whined desperately into her ear that they never had any fun even on their vacation, and that they could never do what THEY wanted to do. The baby began to scream and John Wesley kicked the back of the seat so hard that his father could feel the blows in his kidney.

"All right!" he shouted, and drew the car to a stop at the side of the road? "Will you all shut up? Will you all just shut up for one second? If you don't shut up, we won't go anywhere."

"It would be very educational for them," the grandmother murmured.

"All right," Bailey said, "but get this: this is the only time we're going to stop for anything like this. This is the one and only time."

"The dirt road that you have to turn down is about a mile back," the grand-mother directed. "I marked it when we passed."

"A dirt road," Bailey groaned.   55

After they had turned around and were headed toward the dirt road, the grandmother recalled other points about the house, the beautiful glass over the front doorway and the candle-lamp in the hall. John Wesley said that the secret panel was probably in the fireplace.

"You can't go inside this house," Bailey said. "You don't know who lives there."

"While you all talk to the people in front, I'll run around behind and get in a window," John Wesley suggested.

"We'll all stay in the car," his mother said.

They turned onto the dirt road and the car raced roughly along in a swirl of   60
pink dust. The grandmother recalled the times when there were no paved roads and thirty miles was a day's journey. The dirt road was hilly and there were sudden washes in it and sharp curves on dangerous embankments. All at once they would be on a hill, looking down over the blue tops of trees for miles around, then the next minute they would be in a red depression with the dust-coated trees looking down on them.

"This place had better turn up in a minute," Bailey said, "or I'm going to turn around."

The road looked as if no one had traveled on it in months.

"It's not much farther," the grandmother said and just as she said it, a horri-ble thought came to her. The thought was so embarrassing that she turned red in the face and her eyes dilated and her feet jumped up, upsetting her valise in the corner. The instant the valise moved, the newspaper top she had over the basket under it rose with a snarl and Pitty Sing, the cat, sprang onto Bailey's shoulder.

The children were thrown to the floor and their mother, clutching the baby, was thrown out of the door onto the ground, the old lady was thrown into the front seat. The car turned over once and landed rightside up in a gulch on the side of the road. Bailey remained in the driver's seat with the cat—gray-striped with a broad white face and an orange nose—clinging to his neck like a caterpillar.

As soon as the children saw they could move their arms and legs, they scrambled out of the car, shouting, "We've had an ACCIDENT!" The grandmother was curled up under the dashboard, hoping she was injured so that Bailey's wrath would not come down on her all at once. The horrible thought she had had before the accident was that the house she had remembered so vividly was not in Georgia but in Tennessee. 65

Bailey removed the cat from his neck with both hands and flung it out the window against the side of a pine tree. Then he got out of the car and started looking for the children's mother. She was sitting against the side of the red gutted ditch, holding the screaming baby, but she only had a cut down her face and a broken shoulder. "We've had an ACCIDENT!" the children screamed in a frenzy of delight.

"But nobody's killed," June Star said with disappointment as the grandmother limped out of the car, her hat still pinned to her head but the broken front brim standing up at a jaunty angle and the violet spray hanging off the side. They all sat down in the ditch, except the children, to recover from the shock. They were all shaking.

"Maybe a car will come along," said the children's mother hoarsely.

"I believe I have injured an organ," said the grandmother, pressing her side, but no one answered her. Bailey's teeth were clattering. He had on a yellow sport shirt with bright blue parrots designed in it and his face was as yellow as the shirt. The grandmother decided that she would not mention that the house was in Tennessee.

The road was about ten feet above and they could see only the tops of the trees on the other side of it. Behind the ditch they were setting in there were more woods, tall and dark and deep. In a few minutes they saw a car some distance away on top of a hill, coming slowly as if the occupants were watching them. The grandmother stood up and waved both arms dramatically to attract their attention. The car continued to come on slowly, disappeared around a bend and appeared again, moving even slower, on top of the hill they had gone over. It was a big black battered hearselike automobile. There were three men in it. 70

It came to a stop just over them and for some minutes, the driver looked down with a steady expressionless gaze to where they were sitting, and didn't speak. Then he turned his head and muttered something to the other two and they got out. One was a fat boy in black trousers and a red sweat shirt with a silver stallion embossed on the front of it. He moved around on the right side of them and stood staring, his mouth partly open in a kind of loose grin. The other had on khaki pants and a blue striped coat and a gray hat pulled down very low, hiding most of his face. He came around slowly on the left side. Neither spoke.

The driver got out of the car and stood by the side of it, looking down at them. He was an older man than the other two. His hair was just beginning to gray and he wore silver-rimmed spectacles that gave him a scholarly look. He had a long creased face and didn't have on any shirt or undershirt. He had on blue jeans that were too tight for him and was holding a black hat and a gun. The two boys also had guns.

"We've had an ACCIDENT!" the children screamed.

The grandmother had the peculiar feeling that the bespectacled man was someone she knew. His face was as familiar to her as if she had known him all her life, but she could not recall who he was. He moved away from the car and began to come down the embankment, placing his feet carefully so that he wouldn't slip. He had on tan and white shoes and no socks, and his ankles were red and thin. "Good afternoon," he said. "I see you all had you a little spill."

"We turned over twice!" said the grandmother.   75

"Oncet," he corrected. "We seen it happen. Try their car and see will it run, Hiram," he said quietly to the boy with the gray hat.

"What you got that gun for?" John Wesley asked. "Watcha gonna do with that gun?"

"Lady," the man said to the children's mother, "would you mind calling them children to set down by you? Children make me nervous. I want all you all to sit down right together there where you're at."

"What are you telling us what to do for?" June Star asked.

Behind them the line of woods gaped like a dark open mouth. "Come here,"   80
said their mother.

"Look here now," Bailey began suddenly, "we're in a predicament! We're in . . ."

The grandmother shrieked. She scrambled to her feet and stood staring. "You're The Misfit!" she said. "I recognized you at once."

"Yes'm," the man said, smiling slightly as if he were pleased in spite of himself to be known, "but it would have been better for all of you, lady, if you hadn't of recognized me."

Bailey turned his head sharply and said something to his mother that shocked even the children. The old lady began to cry and The Misfit reddened.

"Lady," he said, "don't you get upset. Sometimes a man says things he don't   85
mean. I don't reckon he meant to talk to you thataway."

"You wouldn't shoot a lady, would you?" the grandmother said and removed a clean handkerchief from her cuff and began to slap at her eyes with it.

The Misfit pointed the toe of his shoe into the ground and made a little hole and then covered it up again. "I would hate to have to," he said.

"Listen," the grandmother almost screamed, "I know you're a good man. You don't look a bit like you have common blood. I know you must come from nice people!"

"Yes ma'm," he said, "finest people in the world." When he smiled he showed a row of strong white teeth. "God never made a finer woman than my mother and my daddy's heart was pure gold," he said. The boy with the red sweat shirt had come around behind them and was standing with his gun at his hip. The Misfit squatted down on the ground. "Watch them children, Bobby Lee," he said. "You know they make me nervous." He looked at the six of them huddled together in front of him and he seemed to be embarrassed as if he couldn't think of anything to say. "Ain't a cloud in the sky," he remarked, looking up at it. "Don't see no sun but don't see no cloud neither."

"Yes, it's a beautiful day," said the grandmother. "Listen," she said, "you   90
shouldn't call yourself The Misfit because I know you're a good man at heart. I
can just look at you and tell."

"Hush!" Bailey yelled. "Hush! Everybody shut up and let me handle this!"
He was squatting in the position of a runner about to sprint forward but he didn't
move.

"I pre-chate that, lady," The Misfit said and drew a little circle in the ground
with the butt of his gun.

"It'll take a half a hour to fix this here car," Hiram called, looking over the
raised hood of it.

"Well, first you and Bobby Lee get him and that little boy to step over yonder
with you," The Misfit said, pointing to Bailey and John Wesley. "The boys want to
ask you something," he said to Bailey. "Would you mind stepping back in them
woods there with them?"

"Listen," Bailey began, "we're in a terrible predicament. Nobody realizes   95
what this is," and his voice cracked. His eyes were as blue and intense as the
parrots in his shirt and he remained perfectly still.

The grandmother reached up to adjust her hat brim as if she were going to
the woods with him but it came off in her hand. She stood staring at it and after a
second she let it fall on the ground. Hiram pulled Bailey up by the arm as if he
were assisting an old man. John Wesley caught hold of his father's hand and Bobby
Lee followed. They went off toward the woods and just as they reached the dark
edge, Bailey turned and supporting himself against a gray naked pine trunk, he
shouted, "I'll be back in a minute, Mamma, wait on me!"

"Come back this instant!" his mother shrilled but they all disappeared into
the woods.

"Bailey Boy!" the grandmother called in a tragic voice but she found she was
looking at The Misfit squatting on the ground in front of her. "I just know you're a
good man," she said desperately. "You're not a bit common!"

"Nome, I ain't a good man," The Misfit said after a second as if he had
considered her statement carefully, "but I ain't the worst in the world neither. My
daddy said I was a different breed of dog from my brothers and sisters. 'You
know,' Daddy said, 'it's some that can live their whole life out without asking
about it and it's others has to know why it is, and this boy is one of the latters.
He's going to be into everything!' " He put on his black hat and looked up suddenly and then away deep into the woods as if he were embarrassed again. "I'm
sorry I don't have on a shirt before you ladies," he said, hunching his shoulders
slightly. "We buried our clothes that we had on when we escaped and we're just
making do until we can get better. We borrowed these from some folks we met,"
he explained.

"That's perfectly all right," the grandmother said. "Maybe Bailey has an   100
extra shirt in his suitcase."

"I'll look and see terreckly," The Misfit said.

"Where are they taking him?" the children's mother screamed.

"Daddy was a card himself," The Misfit said. "You couldn't put anything over
on him. He never got in trouble with the Authorities though. Just had the knack of
handling them."

"You could be honest too if you'd only try," said the grandmother. "Think how wonderful it would be to settle down and live a comfortable life and not have to think about somebody chasing you all the time."

The Misfit kept scratching in the ground with the butt of his gun as if he were   105
thinking about it. "Yes'm, somebody is always after you," he murmured.

The grandmother noticed how thin his shoulder blades were just behind his hat because she was standing up looking down on him. "Do you ever pray?" she asked.

He shook his head. All she saw was the black hat wiggle between shoulder blades. "Nome," he said.

There was a pistol shot from the woods, followed closely by another. Then silence. The old lady's head jerked around. She could hear the wind move through the tree tops like a long satisfied insuck of breath. "Bailey Boy!" she called.

"I was a gospel singer for a while," The Misfit said. "I been most everything. Been in the arm service, both land and sea, at home and abroad, been twict married, been an undertaker, been with the railroads, plowed Mother Earth, been in a tornado, seen a man burnt alive oncet," and he looked up at the children's mother and the little girl who were sitting close together, their faces white and their eyes glassy; "I even seen a woman flogged," he said.

"Pray, pray," the grandmother began, "pray, pray . . ."   110

"I never was a bad boy that I remember of," The Misfit said in an almost dreamy voice, "but somewheres along the line I done something wrong and got sent to the penitentiary. I was buried alive," and he looked up and held her attention to him by a steady stare.

"That's when you should have started to pray," she said. "What did you do to get sent to the penitentiary that first time?"

"Turn to the right, it was a wall," The Misfit said, looking up again at the cloudless sky. "Turn to the left, it was a wall. Look up it was a ceiling, look down it was a floor. I forget what I done, lady. I set there and set there, trying to remember what it was I done and I ain't recalled it to this day. Oncet in a while, I would think it was coming to me, but it never come."

"Maybe they put you in by mistake," the old lady said vaguely.

"Nome," he said. "It wasn't no mistake. They had the papers on me."   115
"You must have stolen something," she said.

The Misfit sneered slightly. "Nobody had nothing I wanted," he said. "It was a head-doctor at the penitentiary said what I had done was kill my daddy but I know that for a lie. My daddy died in nineteen ought nineteen of the epidemic flu and I never had a thing to do with it. He was buried in the Mount Hopewell Baptist churchyard and you can go there and see for yourself."

"If you would pray," the old lady said, "Jesus would help you."

"That's right," The Misfit said.

"Well then, why don't you pray?" she asked trembling with delight suddenly.   120
"I don't want no hep," he said. "I'm doing all right by myself."

Bobby Lee and Hiram came ambling back from the woods. Bobby Lee was dragging a yellow shirt with bright blue parrots in it.

"Throw me that shirt, Bobby Lee," The Misfit said. The shirt came flying at him and landed on his shoulder and he put it on. The grandmother couldn't name what the shirt reminded her of. "No, lady," The Misfit said while he was buttoning it up. "I found out the crime don't matter. You can do one thing or you can do another, kill a man or take a tire off his car, because sooner or later you're going to forget what it was you done and just be punished for it."

The children's mother had begun to make heaving noises as if she couldn't get her breath. "Lady," he asked, "would you and that little girl like to step off yonder with Bobby Lee and Hiram and join your husband?"

"Yes, thank you," the mother said faintly. Her left arm dangled helplessly and she was holding the baby, who had gone to sleep, in the other. "Hep that lady up, Hiram," The Misfit said as she struggled to climb out of the ditch, "and Bobby Lee, you hold onto that little girl's hand."

"I don't want to hold hands with him," June Star said. "He reminds me of a pig."

The fat boy blushed and laughed and caught her by the arm and pulled her off into the woods after Hiram and her mother.

Alone with The Misfit, the grandmother found that she had lost her voice. There was not a cloud in the sky nor any sun. There was nothing around her but woods. She wanted to tell him that he must pray. She opened and closed her mouth several times before anything came out. Finally she found herself saying, "Jesus, Jesus," meaning Jesus will help you, but the way she was saying it, it sounded as if she might be cursing.

"Yes'm," The Misfit said as if he agreed. "Jesus thown everything off balance. It was the same case with Him as with me except He hadn't committed any crime and they could prove I had committed one because they had the papers on me. Of course," he said, "they never shown me my papers. That's why I sign myself now. I said long ago, you get you a signature and sign everything you do and keep a copy of it. Then you'll know what you done and you can hold up the crime to the punishment and see do they match and in the end you'll have something to prove you ain't been treated right. I call myself The Misfit," he said, "because I can't make what all I done wrong fit what all I gone through in punishment."

There was a piercing scream from the woods, followed closely by a pistol report. "Does it seem right to you, lady, that one is punished a heap and another ain't punished at all?"

"Jesus!" the old lady cried. "You've got good blood! I know you wouldn't shoot a lady! I know you come from nice people! Pray! Jesus, you ought not to shoot a lady. I'll give you all the money I've got!"

"Lady," The Misfit said, looking beyond her far into the woods, "there never was a body that give the undertaker a tip."

There were two more pistol reports and the grandmother raised her head like a parched old turkey hen crying for water and called, "Bailey Boy, Bailey Boy!" as if her heart would break.

"Jesus was the only One that ever raised the dead," The Misfit continued, "and He shouldn't have done it. He thown everything off balance. If He did what He said, then it's nothing for you to do but thow away everything and follow Him, and if He didn't, then it's nothing for you to do but enjoy the few minutes you got left the best way you can—by killing somebody or burning down his house or doing some other meanness to him. No pleasure but meanness," he said and his voice had become almost a snarl.

"Maybe He didn't raise the dead," the old lady mumbled, not knowing what   135
she was saying and feeling so dizzy that she sank down in the ditch with her legs twisted under her.

"I wasn't there so I can't say He didn't," The Misfit said. "I wisht I had of been there," he said, hitting the ground with his fist. "It ain't right I wasn't there because if I had of been there I would of known. Listen lady," he said in a high voice, "if I had of been there I would of known and I wouldn't be like I am now." His voice seemed about to crack and the grandmother's head cleared for an instant. She saw the man's face twisted close to her own as if he were going to cry and she murmured, "Why you're one of my babies. You're one of my own children!" She reached out and touched him on the shoulder. The Misfit sprang back as if a snake had bitten him and shot her three times through the chest. Then he put his gun down on the ground and took off his glasses and began to clean them.

Hiram and Bobby Lee returned from the woods and stood over the ditch, looking down at the grandmother who half sat and half lay in a puddle of blood with her legs crossed under her like a child's and her face smiling up at the cloudless sky.

Without his glasses, The Misfit's eyes were red-rimmed and pale and defenseless-looking. "Take her off and thow her where you thown the others," he said, picking up the cat that was rubbing itself against his leg.

"She was a talker, wasn't she?" Bobby Lee said, sliding down the ditch with a yodel.

"She would of been a good woman," The Misfit said, "if it had been some-   140
body there to shoot her every minute of her life."

"Some fun!" Bobby Lee said.

"Shut up, Bobby Lee," The Misfit said. "It's no real pleasure in life."

QUESTIONS AND SUGGESTIONS FOR WRITING

1. What are the associations of the names June Star, John Wesley, and Bobby Lee?
2. What are the values of the members of the family?
3. Flannery O'Connor, a Roman Catholic, wrote, "I see from the standpoint of Christian orthodoxy. This means that for me the meaning of life is centered in our Redemption by Christ and what I see in the world I see in its relation to that." In the light of this statement, and drawing on "A Good Man Is Hard to Find," explain what O'Connor saw in the world.
4. Let's assume that a reader, unlike O'Connor, does *not* "see from the standpoint of Christian orthodoxy." In an essay of 500 words, explain what interest "A Good Man Is Hard to Find" can have for such a reader.
5. The Misfit says, "I can't make what all I done wrong fit what all I gone through in punishment." What would O'Connor's explanation (i.e., the orthodox Christian explanation) be? In 250 to 500 words, explain what the Misfit means by saying that Jesus has "thown everything off balance."

Flannery O'Connor (American. 1925–1964)

REVELATION

The doctor's waiting room, which was very small, was almost full when the Turpins entered and Mrs. Turpin, who was very large, made it look even smaller by her presence. She stood looming at the head of the magazine table set in the center of it, a living demonstration that the room was inadequate and ridiculous. Her little bright black eyes took in all the patients as she sized up the seating situation. There was one vacant chair and a place on the sofa occupied by a blond child in a dirty blue romper who should have been told to move over and make room for the lady. He was five or six, but Mrs. Turpin saw at once that no one was going to tell him to move over. He was slumped down in the seat, his arms idle at his sides and his eyes idle in his head; his nose ran unchecked.

Mrs. Turpin put a firm hand on Claud's shoulder and said in a voice that included everyone that wanted to listen, "Claud, you sit in that chair there," and gave him a push down into the vacant one. Claud was florid and bald and sturdy, somewhat shorter than Mrs. Turpin, but he sat down as if he were accustomed to doing what she told him to.

Mrs. Turpin remained standing. The only man in the room besides Claud was a lean stringy old fellow with a rusty hand spread out on each knee, whose eyes were closed as if he were asleep or dead or pretending to be so as not to get up and offer her his seat. Her gaze settled agreeably on a well-dressed gray-haired lady whose eyes met hers and whose expression said: If that child belonged to me, he would have some manners and move over—there's plenty of room there for you and him too.

Claud looked up with a sigh and made as if to rise.

"Sit down," Mrs. Turpin said. "You know you're not supposed to stand on   5
that leg. He has an ulcer on his leg," she explained.

Claud lifted his foot onto the magazine table and rolled his trouser leg up to reveal a purple swelling on a plump marble-white calf.

"My!" the pleasant lady said. "How did you do that?"

"A cow kicked him," Mrs. Turpin said.

"Goodness!" said the lady.

Claud rolled his trouser leg down.   10

"Maybe the little boy would move over," the lady suggested, but the child did not stir.

"Somebody will be leaving in a minute," Mrs. Turpin said. She could not understand why a doctor—with as much money as they made charging five dollars a day just to stick their head in the hospital door and look at you—couldn't afford a decent-sized waiting room. This one was hardly bigger than a garage. The table was cluttered with limp-looking magazines and at one end of it there was a big green glass ash tray full of cigaret butts and cotton wads with little blood spots on them. If she had had anything to do with the running of the place, that would have been emptied every so often. There were no chairs against the wall at the head of the room. It had a rectangular-shaped panel in it that permitted a view of the office where the nurse came and went and the secretary listened to the radio. A plastic fern in a gold pot sat in the opening and trailed its fronds down almost to the floor. The radio was softly playing gospel music.

Just then the inner door opened and a nurse with the highest stack of yellow hair Mrs. Turpin had ever seen put her face in the crack and called for the next patient. The woman sitting beside Claud grasped the two arms of her chair and hoisted herself up; she pulled her dress free from her legs and lumbered through the door where the nurse had disappeared.

Mrs. Turpin eased into the vacant chair, which held her tight as a corset. "I wish I could reduce," she said, and rolled her eyes and gave a comic sigh.

"Oh, *you* aren't fat," the stylish lady said.   15

"Ooooo I am too," Mrs. Turpin said. "Claud he eats all he wants to and never weighs over one hundred and seventy-five pounds, but me I just look at something good to eat and I gain some weight," and her stomach and shoulders shook with laughter. "You can eat all you want to, can't you, Claud?" she asked turning to him.

Claud only grinned.

"Well, as long as you have such a good disposition," the stylish lady said, "I don't think it makes a bit of difference what size you are. You just can't beat a good disposition."

Next to her was a fat girl of eighteen or nineteen, scowling into a thick blue book which Mrs. Turpin saw was entitled *Human Development*. The girl raised her head and directed her scowl at Mrs. Turpin as if she did not like her looks. She appeared annoyed that anyone should speak while she tried to read. The poor girl's face was blue with acne and Mrs. Turpin thought how pitiful it was to have a face like that at that age. She gave the girl a friendly smile but the girl only scowled the harder. Mrs. Turpin herself was fat but she always had good skin, and, though she was forty-seven years old, there was not a wrinkle in her face except around her eyes from laughing too much.

Next to the ugly girl was the child, still in exactly the same position, and next   20
to him was a thin leathery old woman in a cotton print dress. She and Claud had three sacks of chicken feed in their pump house that was in the same print. She had seen from the first that the child belonged with the old woman. She could tell by the way they sat—kind of vacant and white-trashy, as if they would sit there until Doomsday if nobody called and told them to get up. And at right angles but next to the well-dressed pleasant lady was a lank-faced woman who was certainly the child's mother. She had on a yellow sweat shirt and wine-colored slacks, both gritty-looking, and the rims of her lips were stained with snuff. Her dirty yellow hair was tied behind with a little piece of red paper ribbon. Worse than niggers any day, Mrs. Turpin thought.

The gospel hymn playing was, "When I looked up and He looked down," and Mrs. Turpin, who knew it, supplied the last line mentally, "And wona these days I know I'll we-eara crown."

Without appearing to, Mrs. Turpin always noticed people's feet. The well-dressed lady had on red and grey suede shoes to match her dress. Mrs. Turpin had on her good black patent leather pumps. The ugly girl had on Girl Scout shoes and heavy socks. The old woman had on tennis shoes and the white-trashy mother had on what appeared to be bedroom slippers, black straw with gold braid threaded through them—exactly what you would have expected her to have on.

Sometimes at night when she couldn't go to sleep, Mrs. Turpin would occupy herself with the question of who she would have chosen to be if she couldn't have been herself. If Jesus had said to her before he made her, "There's only two places available for you. You can either be a nigger or white-trash," what would she have said? "Please, Jesus, please," she would have said, "just let me wait until there's another place available," and he would have said, "No, you have to go right now and I have only those two places so make up your mind." She would have wiggled and squirmed and begged and pleaded but it would have been no use and finally she would have said, "All right, make me a nigger then—but that don't mean a trashy one." And he would have made her a neat clean respectable Negro woman, herself but black.

Next to the child's mother was a red-headed youngish woman, reading one of the magazines and working a piece of chewing gum, hell for leather, as Claud would say. Mrs. Turpin could not see the woman's feet. She was not white-trash, just common. Sometimes Mrs. Turpin occupied herself at night naming the classes of people. On the bottom of the heap were most colored people, not the kind she would have been if she had been one, but most of them; then next to them—not above, just away from—were the white-trash; then above them were the homeowners, and above them the home-and-land owners, to which she and Claud belonged. Above she and Claud were people with a lot of money and much bigger houses and much more land. But here the complexity of it would begin to bear in on her, for some of the people with a lot of money were common and ought to be below she and Claud and some of the people who had good blood had lost their money and had to rent and then there were colored people who owned their homes and land as well. There was a colored dentist in town who had two red Lincolns and a swimming pool and a farm with registered white-face cattle on it. Usually by the time she had fallen asleep all the classes of people were moiling and roiling around in her head, and she would dream they were all crammed in together in a box car, being ridden off to be put in a gas oven.

"That's a beautiful clock," she said and nodded to her right. It was a big wall   25
clock, the face encased in a brass sunburst.

"Yes, it's very pretty," the stylish lady said agreeably. "And right on the dot too," she added, glancing at her watch.

The ugly girl beside her cast an eye upward at the clock, smirked, then looked directly at Mrs. Turpin and smirked again. Then she returned her eyes to her book. She was obviously the lady's daughter because, although they didn't look anything alike as to disposition, they both had the same shape of face and the same blue eyes. On the lady they sparkled pleasantly but in the girl's seared face they appeared alternately to smolder and to blaze.

What if Jesus had said, "All right, you can be white-trash or a nigger or ugly"!

Mrs. Turpin felt an awful pity for the girl, though she thought it was one thing to be ugly and another to act ugly.

The woman with the snuff-stained lips turned around in her chair and looked   30 up at the clock. Then she turned back and appeared to look a little to the side of Mrs. Turpin. There was a cast in one of her eyes. "You want to know wher you can get one of themther clocks?" she asked in a loud voice.

"No, I already have a nice clock," Mrs. Turpin said. Once somebody like her got a leg in the conversation, she would be all over it.

"You can get you one with green stamps," the woman said. "That's most likely wher he got hisn. Save you up enough, you can get you most anythang. I got me some joo'ry."

Ought to have got you a wash rag and some soap, Mrs. Turpin thought.

"I get contour sheets with mine," the pleasant lady said.

The daughter slammed her book shut. She looked straight in front of her, 35 directly through Mrs. Turpin and on through the yellow curtain and the plate glass window which made the wall behind her. The girl's eyes seemed lit all of a sudden with a peculiar light, an unnatural light like night road signs give. Mrs. Turpin turned her head to see if there was anything going on outside that she should see, but she could not see anything. Figures passing cast only a pale shadow through the curtain. There was no reason the girl should single her out for her ugly looks.

"Miss Finley," the nurse said, cracking the door. The gum-chewing woman got up and passed in front of her and Claud and went into the office. She had on red high-heeled shoes.

Directly across the table, the ugly girl's eyes were fixed on Mrs. Turpin as if she had some very special reason for disliking her.

"This is wonderful weather, isn't it?" the girl's mother said.

"It's good weather for cotton if you can get the niggers to pick it," Mrs. Turpin said, "but niggers don't want to pick cotton any more. You can't get the white folks to pick it and now you can't get the niggers—because they got to be right up there with the white folks."

"They gonna *try* anyways," the white-trash woman said, leaning forward. 40

"Do you have one of those cotton-picking machines?" the pleasant lady asked.

"No," Mrs. Turpin said, "they leave half the cotton in the field. We don't have much cotton anyway. If you want to make it farming now, you have to have a little of everything. We got a couple of acres of cotton and a few hogs and chickens and just enough white-face that Claud can look after them himself."

"One thang I don't want," the white-trash woman said, wiping her mouth with the back of her hand. "Hogs. Nasty stinking things, a-gruntin and a-rootin all over the place."

Mrs. Turpin gave her the merest edge of attention. "Our hogs are not dirty and they don't stink," she said. "They're cleaner than some children I've seen. Their feet never touch the ground. We have a pig-parlor—that's where you raise them on concrete," she explained to the pleasant lady, "and Claud scoots them down with the hose every afternoon and washes off the floor." Cleaner by far than that child right there, she thought. Poor nasty little thing. He had not moved except to put the thumb of his dirty hand into his mouth.

The woman turned her face away from Mrs. Turpin. "I know I wouldn't scoot   45
down no hog with no hose," she said to the wall.

You wouldn't have no hog to scoot down, Mrs. Turpin said to herself.

"A-gruntin and a-rootin and a-groanin," the woman muttered.

"We got a little of everything," Mrs. Turpin said to the pleasant lady. "It's no
use in having more than you can handle yourself with help like it is. We found
enough niggers to pick our cotton this year but Claud he has to go after them and
take them home again in the evening. They can't walk that half a mile. No they
can't. I tell you," she said and laughed merrily, "I sure am tired of buttering up
niggers, but you got to love em if you want em to work for you. When they come
in the morning, I run out and I say, 'Hi yawl this morning?' and when Claud drives
them off to the field I just wave to beat the band and they just wave back." And
she waved her hand rapidly to illustrate.

"Like you read out of the same book," the lady said, showing she understood
pefectly.

"Child, yes," Mrs. Turpin said. "And when they come in from the field, I run   50
out with a bucket of icewater. That's the way it's going to be from now on," she
said. "You may as well face it."

"One thang I know," the white-trash woman said. "Two thangs I ain't going to
do: love no niggers or scoot down no hog with no hose." And she let out a bark of
contempt.

The look that Mrs. Turpin and the pleasant lady exchanged indicated they
both understood that you had to *have* certain things before you could *know* certain
things. But every time Mrs. Turpin exchanged a look with the lady, she was aware
that the ugly girl's peculiar eyes were still on her, and she had trouble bringing her
attention back to the conversation.

"When you got something," she said, "you got to look after it." And when
you ain't got a thing but breath and britches, she added to herself, you can afford
to come to town every morning and just sit on the Court House coping and spit.

A grotesque revolving shadow passed across the curtain behind her and was
thrown palely on the opposite wall. Then a bicycle clattered down against the
outside of the building. The door opened and a colored boy glided in with a tray
from the drug store. It had two large red and white paper cups on it with tops on
them. He was a tall, very black boy in discolored white pants and a green nylon
shirt. He was chewing gum slowly, as if to music. He set the tray down in the
office opening next to the fern and stuck his head through to look for the secretary. She was not in there. He rested his arms on the ledge and waited, his
narrow bottom stuck out, swaying slowly to the left and right. He raised a hand
over his head and scratched the base of his skull.

"You see that button there, boy?" Mrs. Turpin said. "You can punch that and   55
she'll come. She's probably in the back somewhere."

"Is that right?" the boy said agreeably, as if he had never seen the button
before. He leaned to the right and put his finger on it. "She sometime out," he
said and twisted around to face his audience, his elbows behind him on the
counter. The nurse appeared and he twisted back again. She handed him a dollar

and he rooted in his pocket and made the change and counted it out to her. She gave him fifteen cents for a tip and he went out with the empty tray. The heavy door swung to slowly and closed at length with the sound of suction. For a moment no one spoke.

"They ought to send all them niggers back to Africa," the white-trash woman said. "That's wher they come from in the first place."

"Oh, I couldn't do without my good colored friends," the pleasant lady said.

"There's a heap of things worse than a nigger," Mrs. Turpin agreed. "It's all kinds of them just like it's all kinds of us."

"Yes, and it takes all kinds to make the world go round," the lady said in her   60
musical voice.

As she said it, the raw-complexioned girl snapped her teeth together. Her lower lip turned downwards and inside out, revealing the pale pink inside of her mouth. After a second it rolled back up. It was the ugliest face Mrs. Turpin had ever seen anyone make and for a moment she was certain that the girl had made it at her. She was looking at her as if she had known and disliked her all her life—all of Mrs. Turpin's life, it seemed too, not just all the girl's life. Why, girl, I don't even know you, Mrs. Turpin said silently.

She forced her attention back to the discussion. "It wouldn't be practical to send them back to Africa," she said. "They wouldn't want to go. They got it too good here."

"Wouldn't be what they wanted—if I had anythang to do with it," the woman said.

"It wouldn't be a way in the world you could get all the niggers back over there," Mrs. Turpin said. "They'd be hiding out and lying down and turning sick on you and wailing and hollering and raring and pitching. It wouldn't be a way in the world to get them over there."

"They got over here," the trashy woman said. "Get back like they got over."   65

"It wasn't so many of them then," Mrs. Turpin explained.

The woman looked at Mrs. Turpin as if here was an idiot indeed but Mrs. Turpin was not bothered by the look, considering where it came from.

"Nooo," she said, "they're going to stay here where they can go to New York and marry white folks and improve their color. That's what they all want to do, every one of them, improve their color."

"You know what comes of that, don't you?" Claud asked.

"No, Claud, what?" Mrs. Turpin said.   70

Claud's eyes twinkled. "White-faced niggers," he said with never a smile.

Everybody in the office laughed except the white-trash and the ugly girl. The girl gripped the book in her lap with white fingers. The trashy woman looked around her from face to face as if she thought they were all idiots. The old woman in the feed sack dress continued to gaze expressionless across the floor at the high-top shoes of the man opposite her, the one who had been pretending to be asleep when the Turpins came in. He was laughing heartily, his hands still spread out on his knees. The child had fallen to the side and was lying now almost face down in the old woman's lap.

While they recovered from their laughter, the nasal chorus on the radio kept the room from silence.

> *You go to blank blank*
> *And I'll go to mine*
> *But we'll all blank along*
> *To-geth-ther*
> *And all along the blank*
> *We'll hep each other out*
> *Smile-ling in any kind of*
> *Weath-ther!*

Mrs. Turpin didn't catch every word but she caught enough to agree with the spirit of the song and it turned her thoughts sober. To help anybody out that needed it was her philosophy of life. She never spared herself when she found somebody in need, whether they were white or black, trash or decent. And of all she had to be thankful for, she was most thankful that this was so. If Jesus had said, "You can be high society and have all the money you want and be thin and svelte-like, but you can't be a good woman with it," she would have had to say, "Well don't make me that then. Make me a good woman and it don't matter what else, how fat or how ugly or how poor!" Her heart rose. He had not made her a nigger or white-trash or ugly! He had made her herself and given her a little of everything. Jesus, thank you! she said. Thank you thank you thank you! Whenever she counted her blessings she felt as buoyant as if she weighed one hundred and twenty-five pounds instead of one hundred and eighty.

"What's wrong with your little boy?" the pleasant lady asked the white-trashy woman.   75

"He has a ulcer," the woman said proudly. "He ain't give me a minute's peace since he was born. Him and her are just alike," she said, nodding at the old woman, who was running her leathery fingers through the child's pale hair. "Look like I can't get nothing down them two but Co'Cola and candy."

That's all you try to get down em, Mrs. Turpin said to herself. Too lazy to light the fire. There was nothing you could tell her about people like them that she didn't know already. And it was not just that they didn't have anything. Because if you gave them everything, in two weeks it would all be broken or filthy or they would have chopped it up for lightwood. She knew all this from her own experience. Help them you must, but help them you couldn't.

All at once the ugly girl turned her lips inside out again. Her eyes were fixed like two drills on Mrs. Turpin. This time there was no mistaking that there was something urgent behind them.

Girl, Mrs. Turpin exclaimed silently, I haven't done a thing to you! The girl might be confusing her with somebody else. There was no need to sit by and let herself be intimidated. "You must be in college," she said boldly, looking directly at the girl. "I see you reading a book there."

The girl continued to stare and pointedly did not answer.   80

Her mother blushed at this rudeness. "The lady asked you a question, Mary Grace," she said under her breath.

"I have ears," Mary Grace said.

The poor mother blushed again. "Mary Grace goes to Wellesley College," she explained. She twisted one of the buttons on her dress. "In Massachusetts," she added with a grimace. "And in the summer she just keeps right on studying. Just reads all the time, a real book worm. She's done real well at Wellesley; she's taking English and Math and History and Psychology and Social Studies," she rattled on, "and I think it's too much. I think she ought to get out and have fun."

The girl looked as if she would like to hurl them all through the plate glass window.

"Way up north," Mrs. Turpin murmured and thought, well, it hasn't done   85
much for her manners.

"I'd almost rather to have him sick," the white-trash woman said, wrenching the attention back to herself. "He's so mean when he ain't. Look like some children just take natural to meanness. It's some gets bad when they get sick but he was the opposite. Took sick and turned good. He don't give me no trouble now. It's me waitin to see the doctor," she said.

If I was going to send anybody back to Africa, Mrs. Turpin thought, it would be your kind, woman. "Yes, indeed," she said aloud, but looking up at the ceiling, "it's a heap of things worse than a nigger." And dirtier than a hog, she added to herself.

"I think people with bad dispositions are more to be pitied than anyone on earth," the pleasant lady said in a voice that was decidedly thin.

"I thank the Lord he has blessed me with a good one," Mrs. Turpin said. "The day has never dawned that I couldn't find something to laugh at."

"Not since she married me anyways," Claud said with a comical straight face.   90
Everybody laughed except the girl and the white-trash.

Mrs. Turpin's stomach shook. "He's such a caution," she said, "that I can't help but laugh at him."

The girl made a loud ugly noise through her teeth.

Her mother's mouth grew thin and tight. "I think the worst thing in the world," she said, "is an ungrateful person. To have everything and not appreciate it. I know a girl," she said, "who has parents who would give her anything, a little brother who loves her dearly, who is getting a good education, who wears the best clothes, but who can never say a kind word to anyone, who never smiles, who just criticizes and complains all day long."

"Is she too old to paddle?" Claud asked.   95

The girl's face was almost purple.

"Yes," the lady said, "I'm afraid there's nothing to do but leave her to her folly. Some day she'll wake up and it'll be too late."

"It never hurt anyone to smile," Mrs. Turpin said. "It just makes you feel better all over."

"Of course," the lady said sadly, "but there are just some people you can't tell anything to. They can't take criticism."

"If it's one thing I am," Mrs. Turpin said with feeling, "it's grateful. When I   100
think who all I could have been besides myself and what all I got, a little of everything, and a good disposition besides, I just feel like shouting, 'Thank you,

Jesus, for making everything the way it is!' It could have been different!" For one thing, somebody else could have got Claud. At the thought of this, she was flooded with gratitude and a terrible pang of joy ran through her. "Oh thank you, Jesus, Jesus, thank you!" she cried aloud.

The book struck her directly over her left eye. It struck almost at the same instant that she realized the girl was about to hurl it. Before she could utter a sound, the raw face came crashing across the table toward her, howling. The girl's fingers sank like clamps into the soft flesh of her neck. She heard the mother cry out and Claud shout, "Whoa!" There was an instant when she was certain that she was about to be in an earthquake.

All at once her vision narrowed and she saw everything as if it were happening in a small room far away, or as if she were looking at it through the wrong end of a telescope. Claud's face crumpled and fell out of sight. The nurse ran in, then out, then in again. Then the gangling figure of the doctor rushed out of the inner door. Magazines flew this way and that as the table turned over. The girl fell with a thud and Mrs. Turpin's vision suddenly reversed itself and she saw everything large instead of small. The eyes of the white-trashy woman were staring hugely at the floor. There the girl, held down on one side by the nurse and on the other by her mother, was wrenching and turning in their grasp. The doctor was kneeling astride her, trying to hold her arm down. He managed after a second to sink a long needle into it.

Mrs. Turpin felt entirely hollow except for her heart which swung from side to side as if it were agitated in a great empty drum of flesh.

"Somebody that's not busy call for the ambulance," the doctor said in the offhand voice young doctors adopt for terrible occasions.

Mrs. Turpin could not have moved a finger. The old man who had been sitting next to her skipped nimbly into the office and made the call, for the secretary still seemed to be gone.   105

"Claud!" Mrs. Turpin called.

He was not in his chair. She knew she must jump up and find him but she felt like some one trying to catch a train in a dream, when everything moves in slow motion and the faster you try to run the slower you go.

"Here I am," a suffocated voice, very unlike Claud's, said.

He was doubled up in the corner on the floor, pale as paper, holding his leg. She wanted to get up and go to him but she could not move. Instead, her gaze was drawn slowly downward to the churning face on the floor, which she could see over the doctor's shoulder.

The girl's eyes stopped rolling and focused on her. They seemed a much   110 lighter blue than before, as if a door that had been tightly closed behind them was now open to admit light and air.

Mrs. Turpin's head cleared and her power of motion returned. She leaned forward until she was looking directly into the fierce brilliant eyes. There was no doubt in her mind that the girl did know her, knew her in some intense and personal way, beyond time and place and condition. "What you got to say to me?" she asked hoarsely and held her breath, waiting, as for a relevation.

The girl raised her head. Her gaze locked with Mrs. Turpin's. "Go back to hell where you came from, you old wart hog," she whispered. Her voice was low but clear. Her eyes burned for a moment as if she saw with pleasure that her message had struck its target.

Mrs. Turpin sank back in her chair.

After a moment the girl's eyes closed and she turned her head wearily to the side.

The doctor rose and handed the nurse the empty syringe. He leaned over   115
and put both hands for a moment on the mother's shoulders, which were shaking. She was sitting on the floor, her lips pressed together, holding Mary Grace's hand in her lap. The girl's fingers were gripped like a baby's around her thumb. "Go on to the hospital," he said. "I'll call and make the arrangements."

"Now let's see that neck," he said in a jovial voice to Mrs. Turpin. He began to inspect her neck with his first two fingers. Two little moon-shaped lines like pink fish bones were indented over her windpipe. There was the beginning of an angry red swelling above her eye. His fingers passed over this also.

"Lea' me be," she said thickly and shook him off. "See about Claud. She kicked him."

"I'll see about him in a minute," he said and felt her pulse. He was a thin grey-haired man, given to pleasantries. "Go home and have yourself a vacation the rest of the day," he said and patted her on the shoulder.

Quit your pattin me, Mrs. Turpin growled to herself.

"And put an ice pack over that eye," he said. Then he went and squatted   120
down beside Claud and looked at his leg. After a moment he pulled him up and Claud limped after him into the office.

Until the ambulance came, the only sounds in the room were the tremulous moans of the girl's mother, who continued to sit on the floor. The white-trash woman did not take her eyes off the girl. Mrs. Turpin looked straight ahead at nothing. Presently the ambulance drew up, a long dark shadow, behind the curtain. The attendants came in and set the stretcher down beside the girl and lifted her expertly onto it and carried her out. The nurse helped the mother gather up her things. The shadow of the ambulance moved silently away and the nurse came back in the office.

"That ther girl is going to be a lunatic, ain't she?" the white-trash woman asked the nurse, but the nurse kept on to the back and never answered her.

"Yes, she's going to be a lunatic," the white-trash woman said to the rest of them.

"Po' critter," the old woman murmured. The child's face was still in her lap. His eyes looked idly out over her knees. He had not moved during the disturbance except to draw one leg up under him.

"I thank Gawd," the white-trash woman said fervently, "I ain't a lunatic."   125

Claud came limping out and the Turpins went home.

As their pick-up truck turned into their own dirt road and made the crest of the hill, Mrs. Turpin gripped the window ledge and looked out suspiciously. The land sloped gracefully down through a field dotted with lavender weeds and at the start of the rise their small yellow frame house, with its little flower beds spread out around it like a fancy apron, sat primly in its accustomed place between two giant hickory trees. She would not have been startled to see a burnt wound between two blackened chimneys.

Neither of them felt like eating so they put on their house clothes and lowered the shade in the bedroom and lay down, Claud with his leg on a pillow and herself with a damp washcloth over her eye. The instant she was flat on her back, the image of a razor-backed hog with warts on its face and horns coming out behind its ears snorted into her head. She moaned, a low quiet moan.

"I am not," she said tearfully, "a wart hog. From hell." But the denial had no force. The girl's eyes and her words, even the tone of her voice, low but clear, directed only to her, brooked no repudiation. She had been singled out for the message, though there was trash in the room to whom it might justly have been applied. The full force of this fact struck her only now. There was a woman there who was neglecting her own child but she had been overlooked. The message had been given to Ruby Turpin, a respectable, hard-working, church-going woman. The tears dried. Her eyes began to burn instead with wrath.

She rose on her elbow and the washcloth fell into her hand. Claud was lying   130
on his back, snoring. She wanted to tell him what the girl had said. At the same time, she did not wish to put the image of herself as a wart hog from hell into his mind.

"Hey, Claud," she muttered and pushed his shoulder.

Claud opened one pale baby blue eye.

She looked into it warily. He did not think about anything. He just went his way.

"Wha, whasit?" he said and closed the eye again.

"Nothing," she said. "Does your leg pain you?"   135

"Hurts like hell," Claud said.

"It'll quit terreckly," she said and lay back down. In a moment Claud was snoring again. For the rest of the afternoon they lay there. Claud slept. She scowled at the ceiling. Occasionally she raised her fist and made a small stabbing motion over her chest as if she was defending her innocence to invisible guests who were like the comforters of Job, reasonable-seeming but wrong.

About five-thirty Claud stirred. "Got to go after those niggers," he sighed, not moving.

She was looking straight up as if there were unintelligible handwriting on the ceiling. The protuberance over her eye had turned a greenish-blue. "Listen here," she said.   140

"What?"

"Kiss me."

Claud leaned over and kissed her loudly on the mouth. He pinched her side and their hands interlocked. Her expression of ferocious concentration did not change. Claud got up, groaning and growling, and limped off. She continued to study the ceiling.

She did not get up until she heard the pick-up truck coming back with the Negroes. Then she rose and thrust her feet in her brown oxfords, which she did not bother to lace, and stumped out onto the back porch and got her red plastic bucket. She emptied a tray of ice cubes into it and filled it half full of water and went out into the back yard. Every afternoon after Claud brought the hands in, one of the boys helped him put out hay and the rest waited in the back of the truck until he was ready to take them home. The truck was parked in the shade under one of the hickory trees.

"Hi yawl this evening?" Mrs. Turpin asked grimly, appearing with the bucket and the dipper. There were three women and a boy in the truck.

"Us doing nicely," the oldest woman said. "Hi you doin?" and her gaze stuck immediately on the dark lump on Mrs. Turpin's forehead. "You done fell down, ain't you?" she asked in a solicitous voice. The old woman was dark and almost toothless. She had on an old felt hat of Claud's set back on her head. The other two women were younger and lighter and they both had new bright green sun hats. One of them had hers on her head; the other had taken hers off and the boy was grinning beneath it.

Mrs. Turpin set the bucket down on the floor of the truck. "Yawl hep yourselves," she said. She looked around to make sure Claud had gone. "No. I didn't fall down," she said, folding her arms. "It was something worse than that."

"Ain't nothing bad happen to you!" the old woman said. She said it as if they all knew that Mrs. Turpin was protected in some special way by Divine Providence. "You just had you a little fall."

"We were in town at the doctor's office for where the cow kicked Mr. Turpin," Mrs. Turpin said in a flat tone that indicated they could leave off their foolishness. "And there was this girl there. A big fat girl with her face all broke out. I could look at that girl and tell she was peculiar but I couldn't tell how. And me and her mama were just talking and going along and all of a sudden WHAM! She throws this big book she was reading at me and . . ."

"Naw!" the old woman cried out.

"And then she jumps over the table and commences to choke me."

"Naw!" they all exclaimed, "naw!"

"Hi come she do that?" the old woman asked. "What ail her?"

Mrs. Turpin only glared in front of her.

"Somethin ail her," the old woman said.

"They carried her off in an ambulance," Mrs. Turpin continued, "but before she went she was rolling on the floor and they were trying to hold her down to give her a shot and she said something to me." She paused. "You know what she said to me?"

"What she say?" they asked.

"She said," Mrs. Turpin began, and stopped, her face very dark and heavy. The sun was getting whiter and whiter, blanching the sky overhead so that the leaves of the hickory tree were black in the face of it. She could not bring forth the words. "Something real ugly," she muttered.

"She sho shouldn't said nothing ugly to you," the old woman said. "You so sweet. You the sweetest lady I know."

"She pretty too," the one with the hat on said.

"And stout," the other one said. "I never knowed no sweeter white lady."

"That's the truth befo' Jesus," the old woman said. "Amen! You des as sweet and pretty as you can be."

Mrs. Turpin knew just exactly how much Negro flattery was worth and it added to her rage. "She said," she began again and finished this time with a fierce rush of breath, "that I was an old wart hog from hell."

There was an astounded silence.

"Where she at?" the youngest woman cried in a piercing voice.

"Lemme see her. I'll kill her!"   165

"I'll kill her with you!" the other one cried.

"She b'long in the sylum," the old woman said emphatically. "You the sweetest white lady I know."

"She pretty too," the other two said. "Stout as she can be and sweet. Jesus satisfied with her!"

"Deed he is," the old woman declared.

Idiots! Mrs. Turpin growled to herself. You could never say anything intelli-   170
gent to a nigger. You could talk at them but not with them. "Yawl ain't drunk your water," she said shortly. "Leave the bucket in the truck when you're finished with it. I got more to do than just stand around and pass the time of day," and she moved off and into the house.

She stood for a moment in the middle of the kitchen. The dark protuberance over her eye looked like a miniature tornado cloud which might any moment sweep across the horizon of her brow. Her lower lip protruded dangerously. She squared her massive shoulders. Then she marched into the front of the house and out the side door and started down the road to the pig parlor. She had the look of a woman going single-handed, weaponless, into battle.

The sun was a deep yellow now like a harvest moon and was riding westward very fast over the far tree line as if it meant to reach the hogs before she did. The road was rutted and she kicked several good-sized stones out of her path as she strode along. The pig parlor was on a little knoll at the end of a lane that ran off from the side of the barn. It was a square of concrete as large as a small room, with a board fence about four feet high around it. The concrete floor sloped slightly so that the hog wash could drain off into a trench where it was carried to the field for fertilizer. Claud was standing on the outside, on the edge of the concrete, hanging onto the top board, hosing down the floor inside. The hose was connected to the faucet of a water trough nearby.

Mrs. Turpin climbed up beside him and glowered down at the hogs inside. There were seven long-snouted bristly shoats in it—tan with liver-colored spots— and an old sow a few weeks off from farrowing. She was lying on her side grunting. The shoats were running about shaking themselves like idiot children, their little slit pig eyes searching the floor for anything left. She had read that pigs were the most intelligent animal. She doubted it. They were supposed to be smarter than dogs. There had even been a pig astronaut. He had performed his assignment perfectly but died of a heart attack afterwards because they left him in his electric suit, sitting upright throughout his examination when naturally a hog should be on all fours.

A-gruntin and a-rootin and a-groanin.

"Gimme that hose," she said, yanking it away from Claud. "Go on and carry   175
them niggers home and then get off that leg."

"You look like you might have swallowed a mad dog," Claud observed, but he got down and limped off. He paid no attention to her humors.

Until he was out of earshot, Mrs. Turpin stood on the side of the pen, holding the hose and pointing the stream of water at the hind quarter of any shoat that looked as if it might try to lie down. When he had had time to get over the hill, she turned her head slightly and her wrathful eyes scanned the path. He was nowhere in sight. She turned back again and seemed to gather herself up. Her shoulders rose and she drew in her breath.

"What do you send me a message like that for?" she said in a low fierce voice, barely above a whisper but with the force of a shout in its concentrated fury. "How am I a hog and me both? How am I saved and from hell too?" Her free fist was knotted and with the other she gripped the hose, blindly pointing the stream of water in and out of the eye of the old sow whose outraged squeal she did not hear.

The pig parlor commanded a view of the back pasture where their twenty beef cows were gathered around the hay-bales Claud and the boy had put out. The freshly cut pasture sloped down to the highway. Across it was their cotton field and beyond that a dark green dusty wood which they owned as well. The sun was behind the wood, very red, looking over the paling of trees like a farmer inspecting his own hogs.

"Why me?" she rumbled. "It's no trash around here, black or white, that I   180
haven't given to. And break my back to the bone every day working. And do for the church."

She appeared to be the right size woman to command the arena before her. "How am I a hog?" she demanded. "Exactly how am I like them?" and she jabbed the stream of water at the shoats. "There was plenty of trash there. It didn't have to be me."

"If you like trash better, go get yourself some trash then," she railed. "You could have made me trash. Or a nigger. If trash is what you wanted why didn't you make me trash?" She shook her fist with the hose in it and a watery snake appeared momentarily in the air. "I could quit working and take it easy and be filthy," she growled. "Lounge about the sidewalks all day drinking root beer. Dip snuff and spit in every puddle and have it all over my face. I could be nasty."

"Or you could have made me a nigger. It's too late for me to be a nigger," she said with deep sarcasm, "but I could act like one. Lay down in the middle of the road and stop traffic. Roll on the ground."

In the deepening light everything was taking on a mysterious hue. The pasture was growing a peculiar glassy green and the streak of highway had turned lavender. She braced herself for a final assault and this time her voice rolled out over the pasture. "Go on," she yelled, "call me a hog! Call me a hog again. From hell. Call me a wart hog from hell. Put that bottom rail on top. There'll still be a top and bottom!"

A garbled echo returned to her.   185

A final surge of fury shook her and she roared, "Who do you think you are?"

The color of everything, field and crimson sky, burned for a moment with a transparent intensity. The question carried over the pasture and across the highway and the cotton field and returned to her clearly like an answer from beyond the wood.

She opened her mouth but no sound came out of it.

A tiny truck, Claud's, appeared on the highway, heading rapidly out of sight. Its gears scraped thinly. It looked like a child's toy. At any moment a bigger truck might smash into it and scatter Claud's and the niggers' brains all over the road.

Mrs. Turpin stood there, her gaze fixed on the highway, all her muscles rigid, until in five or six minutes the truck reappeared, returning. She waited until it had had time to turn into their own road. Then like a monumental statue coming to life, she bent her head slowly and gazed, as if through the very heart of the mystery, down into the pig parlor at the hogs. They had settled all in one corner around the old sow who was grunting softly. A red glow suffused them. They appeared to pant with a secret life. 190

Until the sun slipped finally behind the tree line, Mrs. Turpin remained there with her gaze bent to them as if she were absorbing some abysmal life-giving knowledge. At last she lifted her head. There was only a purple streak in the sky, cutting through a field of crimson and leading, like an extension of the highway, into the descending dusk. She raised her hands from the side of the pen in a gesture hieratic and profound. A visionary light settled in her eyes. She saw the streak as a vast swinging bridge extending upward from the earth through a field of living fire. Upon it a vast horde of souls were rumbling toward heaven. There were whole companies of white-trash, clean for the first time in their lives, and bands of black niggers in white robes, and battalions of freaks and lunatics shouting and clapping and leaping like frogs. And bringing up the end of the procession was a tribe of people whom she recognized at once as those who, like herself and Claud, had always had a little of everything and the God-given wit to use it right. She leaned forward to observe them closer. They were marching behind the others with great dignity, accountable as they had always been for good order and common sense and respectable behavior. They alone were on key. Yet she could see by their shocked and altered faces that even their virtues were being burned away. She lowered her hands and gripped the rail of the hog pen, her eyes small but fixed unblinkingly on what lay ahead. In a moment the vision faded but she remained where she was, immobile.

At length she got down and turned off the faucet and made her slow way on the darkening path to the house. In the woods around her the invisible cricket choruses had struck up, but what she heard were the voices of the souls climbing upward into the starry field and shouting hallelujah.

QUESTIONS AND SUGGESTIONS FOR WRITING

1. When Mrs. Turpin goes toward the pig parlor, she has "the look of a woman going single-handed, weaponless, into battle" (paragraph 171). Once there, she dismisses Claud, uses the hose as a weapon against the pigs, and talks to herself "in a low fierce voice." What is she battling, besides the pigs?
2. In 500 words, characterize Mrs. Turpin before her revelation.

□ POETRY

John Donne (English. 1572–1631)

HOLY SONNET IV

At the round earth's imagined corners, blow
Your trumpets, angels, and arise, arise
From death, you numberless infinities
Of souls, and to your scattered bodies go,   4
All whom the flood did, and fire shall o'erthrow,
All whom war, dearth, age, agues, tyrannies,
Despair, law, chance, hath slain, and you whose eyes,
Shall behold God, and never taste death's woe.   8
But let them sleep, Lord, and me mourn a space,
For, if above all these, my sins abound,
'Tis late to ask abundance of thy grace,
When we are there; here on this lowly ground,   12
Teach me how to repent; for that's as good
As if thou hadst sealed° my pardon, with thy blood.   *Confirmed, with a seal*

QUESTIONS AND SUGGESTIONS FOR WRITING

1. What is the speaker envisioning in the first four lines? Put into your own words the meaning of line 5.
2. What is the effect of piling up nouns in lines 6–7?
3. In which line is there the most marked change of tone? Why does the change occur?

John Donne (English. 1572–1631)

HOLY SONNET XIV

Batter my heart, three-personed God; for you
As yet but knock, breathe, shine, and seek to mend;
That I may rise and stand, o'erthrow me, and bend
Your force, to break, blow, burn, and make me new.   4
I, like an usurped town, to another due,
Labor to admit you, but oh, to no end,
Reason, your viceroy in me, me should defend,
But is captived, and proves weak or untrue.   8
Yet dearly I love you, and would be loved fain,
But am betrothed unto your enemy:
Divorce me, untie, or break that knot again,
Take me to you, imprison me, for I   12
Except you enthrall me, never shall be free,
Nor ever chaste, except you ravish me.

QUESTIONS AND SUGGESTIONS FOR WRITING

1. Explain the paradoxes (apparent contradictions) in lines 1, 3, 13, and 14. Explain the double meanings of "enthrall" (line 13) and "ravish" (line 14).
2. In lines 1-4, what is God implicitly compared to (considering especially lines 2 and 4)? How does this comparison lead into the comparison that dominates lines 5-8? What words in lines 9-12 are especially related to the earlier lines?
3. What is gained by piling up verbs in lines 2-4?
4. Are sexual references necessarily irreverent in a religious poem? (Donne, incidentally, was an Anglican priest.)

Emily Dickinson (American. 1830–1886)
APPARENTLY WITH NO SURPRISE

Apparently with no surprise
To any happy Flower
The Frost beheads it at its play—
In accidental power—
The blonde Assassin passes on—   5
The Sun proceeds unmoved
To measure off another Day
For an Approving God.

QUESTIONS AND SUGGESTIONS FOR WRITING

1. What is the implication of the action described in lines 1-3?
2. Why is the frost's power called "accidental"?
3. Why is the assassin called "blonde"? What does this word contribute to the poem?
4. Is the last line shocking? Explain.

Emily Dickinson (American. 1830–1886)
THOSE—DYING, THEN

Those—dying, then
Knew where they went
They went to God's Right Hand—
The Hand is amputated now
And God cannot be found—   5

The abdication of Belief
Makes the Behavior small—
Better an ignis fatuus
Than no illume at all—

QUESTIONS AND SUGGESTIONS FOR WRITING

1. In a sentence or two, state the point of the poem.
2. Is the image in line 4 in poor taste? Explain.
3. What is an *ignis fatuus?* In what ways does it connect visually with traditional images of hell and heaven?
4. If you have read William James's "Religious Faith" (page 592), in an essay of 500 words consider the degree to which these two writers agree.

Christina Rossetti (English. 1830–1894)

AMOR MUNDI[1]

"Oh where are you going with your love-locks flowing,
  On the west wind blowing along this valley track?"
"The downhill path is easy, come with me an it please ye,
  We shall escape the uphill by never turning back."   4
So they two went together in glowing August weather,
  The honey-breathing heather lay to their left and right;
And dear she was to doat on, her swift feet seemed to float on
  The air like soft twin pigeons too sportive to alight.   8

"Oh what is that in heaven where grey cloud-flakes are seven,
  Where blackest clouds hang riven just at the rainy skirt?"
"Oh that's a meteor sent us, a message dumb, portentous,
  An undeciphered solemn signal of help or hurt."   12

"Oh what is that glides quickly where velvet flowers grow thickly,
  Their scent comes rich and sickly?" "A scaled and hooded worm."
"Oh what's that in the hollow, so pale I quake to follow?"
  "Oh that's a thin dead body which waits the eternal term."   16

"Turn again, O my sweetest,—turn again, false and fleetest:
  This beaten way thou beatest, I fear, is hell's own track."
"Nay, too steep for hill mounting; nay, too late for cost counting:
  This downhill path is easy, but there's no turning back."   20

QUESTIONS AND SUGGESTIONS FOR WRITING

1. Taking into account "she" in line 7, try to assign all of the quoted passages, giving some to this "she" and the others to (presumably) a "he." Is it clear whether the seducer is male or female?

---

[1] *amor mundi*: Latin for "love of the world." "World" here has the sense, common in the New Testament, of an arena of sin, or of human alienation from God.

2. The speaker of the last line of the poem says, "There's no turning back." Do you assume that the reader is to believe this assertion? Why, or why not? Christina Rossetti was a devout Anglo Catholic, but could one use this poem as evidence that she sometimes had moments of doubt about the possibility of free will and of salvation?

3. The poem uses anapests, feminine rhymes, and internal rhymes (on these terms, see the Glossary at the rear of this book). What is their cumulative effect here?

Christina Rossetti (English. 1830–1894)

UPHILL

Does the road wind uphill all the way?
  Yes, to the very end.
Will the day's journey take the whole long day?
  From morn to night, my friend.   4

But is there for the night a resting-place?
  A roof for when the slow dark hours begin.
May not the darkness hide it from my face?
  You cannot miss that inn.   8

Shall I meet other wayfarers at night?
  Those who have gone before.
Then must I knock, or call when just in sight?
  They will not keep you standing at that door.   12

Shall I find comfort, travel-sore and weak?
  Of labor you shall find the sum.
Will there be beds for me and all who seek?
  Yea, beds for all who come.   16

QUESTIONS AND SUGGESTIONS FOR WRITING

1. Suppose that someone told you this poem is about a person preparing to go on a hike. The person is supposedly making inquiries about the road and the possible hotel arrangements. What would you reply?

2. Who is the questioner? A woman? A man? All human beings collectively? "Uphill," unlike Rossetti's "Amor Mundi" (see the next poem), does not use quotation marks to distinguish between two speakers. Can one say that in "Uphill" the questioner and the answerer are the same person?

3. Are the answers unambiguously comforting? Or can it, for instance, be argued that the "roof" is (perhaps among other things) the lid of a coffin—hence the questioner will certainly not be kept "standing at that door"? If the poem can be read along these lines, is it chilling rather than comforting?

Gerard Manley Hopkins (English. 1844–1889)

GOD'S GRANDEUR

The world is charged with the grandeur of God.
    It will flame out, like shining from shook foil;
    It gathers to a greatness, like the ooze of oil
Crushed. Why do men then now not reck his rod?   4
Generations have trod, have trod, have trod;
    And all is seared with trade; bleared, smeared with toil;
    And wears man's smudge and shares man's smell: the soil
Is bare now, nor can foot feel, being shod.   8

And for all this, nature is never spent;
    There lives the dearest freshness deep down things;
And though the last lights off the black West went
    Oh, morning, at the brown brink eastward, springs—   12
Because the Holy Ghost over the bent
    World broods with warm breast and with ah! bright wings.

QUESTIONS AND SUGGESTIONS FOR WRITING

1. Hopkins, a Roman Catholic priest, lived in England during the last decades of the nineteenth century—that is, in an industrialized society. Where in the poem do you find him commenting on his setting? Circle the words in the poem that can refer both to England's physical appearance and to the sinful condition of human beings.

2. What is the speaker's tone in the first three and a half lines (through "Crushed")? In the rest of line 4? In lines 5–8? Is the second part of the sonnet (the next six lines) more unified in *tone* or less? In an essay of 500 words describe the shifting tones of the speaker's voice. Probably after writing a first draft you will be able to form a thesis that describes an overall pattern. As you revise your drafts, make sure that: (1) the thesis is clear to the reader, and that (2) it is adequately supported by brief quotations.

Robert Frost (American. 1874–1963)

DESIGN

I found a dimpled spider, fat and white,
On a white heal-all,° holding up a moth   *A flower, usually blue*
Like a white piece of rigid satin cloth—
Assorted characters of death and blight   4
Mixed ready to begin the morning right,
Like the ingredients of a witches' broth—
A snow-drop spider, a flower like froth,
And dead wings carried like a paper kite.   8

What had that flower to do with being white,
The wayside blue and innocent heal-all?
What brought the kindred spider to that height,
Then steered the white moth thither in the night?   12
What but design of darkness to appall?—
If design govern in a thing so small.

QUESTIONS AND SUGGESTIONS FOR WRITING

1. Do you find the spider, as described in line 1, cute or disgusting? Why?
2. What is the effect of "If" in the last line?
3. The word "design" can mean "pattern" (as in "a pretty design"), or it can mean "intention," especially an evil intention (as in "He had designs on her"). Does Frost use the word in one sense or in both? Explain.

Kristine Batey (American. b. 1951)

LOT'S WIFE

While Lot, the conscience of a nation,
struggles with the Lord,
she struggles with the housework.
The City of Sin is where
she raises the children.   5
Ba'al or Adonai—
Whoever is God—
the bread must still be made
and the doorsill swept.
The Lord may kill the children tomorrow,   10
but today they must be bathed and fed.
Well and good to condemn your neighbors' religion;
but weren't they there
when the baby was born,
and when the well collapsed?   15
While her husband communes with God
she tucks the children into bed.
In the morning, when he tells her of the judgment,
she puts down the lamp she is cleaning
and calmly begins to pack.   20
In between bundling up the children
and deciding what will go,
she runs for a moment
to say goodbye to the herd,
gently patting each soft head   25
with tears in her eyes for the animals that will not understand.

⅄ She smiles blindly to the woman
who held her hand at childbed.
It is easy for eyes that have always turned to heaven
not to look back;   30
those that have been—by necessity—drawn to earth
cannot forget that life is lived from day to day.
Good, to a God, and good in human terms
are two different things.
On the breast of the hill, she chooses to be human,   35
and turns, in farewell—
and never regrets
the sacrifice.

QUESTIONS AND SUGGESTIONS FOR WRITING

1. Paraphrase lines 6–9.
2. The story of the pious Lot, his wife, and the destruction of the wicked city of Sodom is told in the Old Testament, in Genesis 19: 1–28. Briefly, Lot sheltered two angels who, in the form of men, visited him in Sodom. The townspeople sought to rape the angels, and the city was marked for destruction, but the angels warned Lot's family and urged them to flee and not to look back. Lot's wife, however, looked back and was turned into a pillar of salt. What was the message of the biblical tale? What does Batey see in the original tale? Do you find her interpretation compelling? Why?
3. In line 35, why "breast" instead of, say, "crest" or "foot"?
4. Exactly what is "the sacrifice" Lot's wife makes in the last line?
5. If you have read Will Herberg's essay "Religiosity and Religion" (page 598), write a 500-word essay setting forth what you think Herberg's response to the poem would be. You may want to begin your essay by quoting lines 33–34 of the poem.

□ DRAMA

A Note on Greek Tragedy

Little or nothing is known for certain of the origin of Greek tragedy. The most common hypothesis holds that it developed from improvised speeches during choral dances honoring Dionysos, a Greek nature god associated with spring, fertility, and wine. Thespis (who perhaps never existed) is said to have introduced an actor into these choral performances in the sixth century B.C. Aeschylus (525–456 B.C.), Greece's first great writer of tragedies, added the second actor, and Sophocles (496?–406 B.C.) added the third actor and fixed the size of the chorus at fifteen. (Because the chorus leader often functioned as an additional actor, and because the actors sometimes doubled in their parts, a Greek tragedy could have more characters than might at first be thought.)

All of the extant great Greek tragedy is of the fifth century B.C. It was performed at religious festivals in the winter and early spring, in large outdoor

Greek theater of Epidaurus on the Peloponnesus east of Nauplia.
(Photograph: Frederick Ayer, Photo Researchers, Inc.)

amphitheaters built on hillsides. Some of these theaters were enormous; the one at Epidaurus held about fifteen thousand people. The audience sat in tiers, looking down on the *orchestra* (a dancing place), with the acting area behind it and the *skene* (the scene building) yet farther back. The scene building served as dressing room, background (suggesting a palace or temple), and place for occasional entrances and exits. Furthermore, this building helped to provide good acoustics, for speech travels well if there is a solid barrier behind the speaker and a hard, smooth surface in front of him, and if the audience sits in tiers. The wall of the scene building provided the barrier; the orchestra provided the surface in front of the actors; and the seats on the hillside fulfilled the third requirement. Moreover, the acoustics were somewhat improved by slightly elevating the actors above the orchestra, but it is not known exactly when this platform was first constructed in front of the scene building.

A tragedy commonly begins with a *prologos* (prologue), during which the exposition is given. Next comes the *parados,* the chorus's ode of entrance, sung while the chorus marches into the theater, through the side aisles and onto the orchestra. The *epeisodion* (episode) is the ensuing scene; it is followed by a *stasimon* (choral song, ode). Usually there are four or five *epeisodia,* alternating with *stasima.* Each of these choral odes has a *strophe* (lines presumably sung while the chorus dances in one direction) and an *antistrophe* (lines presumably sung while the chorus retraces its steps). Sometimes a third part, an *epode,* concludes an ode. (In addition to odes that are *stasima,* there can be odes within episodes; the fourth episode of *Antigonê* (here called Scene IV) contains an ode complete with *epode.*) After the last part of the last ode comes the *exodos,* the epilogue or final scene.

The actors (all male) wore masks, and seem to have chanted much of the play. Perhaps the total result of combining speech with music and dancing was a sort of music-drama roughly akin to opera with some spoken dialogue, like Mozart's *Magic Flute.*

Sophocles (Greek. 496?–406 B.C.)

OEDIPUS REX

An English Version by Dudley Fitts and Robert Fitzgerald

List of Characters

OEDIPUS
A PRIEST
CREON
TEIRESIAS
IOCASTÊ
MESSENGER
SHEPHERD OF LAÏOS
SECOND MESSENGER
CHORUS OF THEBAN ELDERS

Scene: Before the palace of OEDIPUS, *King of Thebes. A central door and two lateral doors open onto a platform which runs the length of the façade. On the platform, right and left, are altars; and three steps lead down into the "orchestra," or chorus-ground. At the beginning of the action these steps are crowded by* SUPPLIANTS *who have brought branches and chaplets of olive leaves and who lie in various attitudes of despair.* OEDIPUS *enters.*

PROLOGUE

OEDIPUS. My children, generations of the
 living
In the line of Kadmos,° nursed at his
 ancient hearth:
Why have you strewn yourselves before
 these altars
In supplication, with your boughs and
 garlands?
5 The breath of incense rises from the city
With a sound of prayer and lamentation.
        Children,
I would not have you speak through mes-
 sengers,
And therefore I have come myself to hear
 you—
I, Oedipus, who bear the famous name.
(*To a* PRIEST.) You, there, since you are
10   eldest in the company,
Speak for them all, tell me what preys
 upon you,
Whether you come in dread, or crave
 some blessing:
Tell me, and never doubt that I will help
 you
In every way I can; I should be heartless
Were I not moved to find you suppliant
15   here.
PRIEST. Great Oedipus, O powerful King of
 Thebes!
You see how all the ages of our people
Cling to your altar steps: here are boys
Who can barely stand alone, and here are
 priests

² **Kadmos** mythical founder of Thebes

By weight of age, as I am a priest of God,   20
And young men chosen from those yet
 unmarried;
As for the others, all that multitude,
They wait with olive chaplets in the
 squares,
At the two shrines of Pallas,° and where
 Apollo°
Speaks in the glowing embers.
       Your own eyes   25
Must tell you: Thebes is in her extremity
And cannot lift her head from the surge of
 death.
A rust consumes the buds and fruits of
 the earth;
The herds are sick; children die unborn,
And labor is vain. The god of plague and
 pyre   30
Raids like detestable lightning through the
 city,
And all the house of Kadmos is laid waste,
All emptied, and all darkened: Death alone
Battens upon the misery of Thebes.
You are not one of the immortal gods, we
 know;   35
Yet we have come to you to make our
 prayer
As to the man of all men best in adversity
And wisest in the ways of God. You saved
 us
From the Sphinx,° that flinty singer, and
 the tribute
We paid to her so long; yet you were
 never   40
Better informed than we, nor could we
 teach you:
It was some god breathed in you to set us
 free.

²⁴ **Pallas** Athena, goddess of wisdom, protectress of Athens ²⁴ **Apollo** god of light and healing ³⁹ **Sphinx** a monster (body of a lion, wings of a bird, face of a woman) who asked the riddle, "What goes on four legs in the morning, two at noon, and three in the evening?" and who killed those who could not answer. When Oedipus responded correctly that man crawls on all fours in infancy, walks upright in maturity, and uses a staff in old age, the Sphinx destroyed herself.

Therefore, O mighty King, we turn to
      you:
Find us our safety, find us a remedy,
Whether by counsel of the gods or the
45   men.
A king of wisdom tested in the past
Can act in a time of troubles, and act well.
Noblest of men, restore
Life to your city! Think how all men call
      you
50 Liberator for your triumph long ago;
Ah, when your years of kingship are re-
      membered,
Let them not say *We rose, but later fell*—
Keep the State from going down in the
      storm!
Once, years ago, with happy augury,
You brought us fortune; be the same
55   again!
No man questions your power to rule the
      land:
But rule over men, not over a dead city!
Ships are only hulls, citadels are nothing,
When no life moves in the empty passage-
      ways.
OEDIPUS. Poor children! You may be sure I
60   know
All that you longed for in your coming
      here.
I know that you are deathly sick; and yet,
Sick as you are, not one is as sick as I.
Each of you suffers in himself alone
65 His anguish, not another's; but my spirit
Groans for the city, for myself, for you.

I was not sleeping, you are not waking
      me.
No, I have been in tears for a long while
And in my restless thought walked many
      ways.
In all my search, I found one helpful
70   course,
And that I have taken: I have sent Creon,
Son of Menoikeus, brother of the Queen,
To Delphi, Apollo's place of revelation,
To learn there, if he can,
What act or pledge of mine may save the
75   city.
I have counted the days, and now, this
      very day,

I am troubled, for he has overstayed his
      time.
What is he doing? He has been gone too
      long.
Yet whenever he comes back, I should do
      ill
To scant whatever hint the god may give.   80
PRIEST. It is a timely promise. At this
      instant
They tell me Creon is here.
OEDIPUS.   O Lord Apollo!
May his news be fair as his face is radiant!
PRIEST. It could not be otherwise: he is
      crowned with bay,
The chaplet is thick with berries.
OEDIPUS.   We shall soon know;   85
He is near enough to hear us now.

Enter CREON.

                              O Prince:
Brother: son of Menoikeus:
What answer do you bring us from the
      god?
CREON. It is favorable. I can tell you, great
      afflictions
Will turn out well, if they are taken well.   90
OEDIPUS. What was the oracle? These
      vague words
Leave me still hanging between hope and
      fear.
CREON. Is it your pleasure to hear me
      with all these
Gathered around us? I am prepared to
      speak,
But should we not go in?
OEDIPUS.   Let them all hear it.   95
It is for them I suffer, more than myself.
CREON. Then I will tell you what I heard
      at Delphi.

In plain words
The god commands us to expel from the
      land of Thebes
An old defilement that it seems we shel-
      ter.   100
It is a deathly thing, beyond expiation.
We must not let it feed upon us longer.
OEDIPUS. What defilement? How shall we
      rid ourselves of it?
CREON. By exile or death, blood for blood.

It was

Murder that brought the plague-wind on

105   the city.

OEDIPUS. Murder of whom? Surely the

god has named him?

CREON. My lord: long ago Laïos was our

king,

Before you came to govern us.

OEDIPUS.   I know;

I learned of him from others; I never saw

him.

CREON. He was murdered; and Apollo

110   commands us now

To take revenge upon whoever killed him.

OEDIPUS. Upon whom? Where are they?

Where shall we find a clue

To solve that crime, after so many years?

CREON. Here in this land, he said.

                    If we make enquiry,

We may touch things that otherwise es-

115   cape us.

OEDIPUS. Tell me: Was Laïos murdered in

his house,

Or in the fields, or in some foreign coun-

try?

CREON. He said he planned to make a

pilgrimage.

He did not come home again.

OEDIPUS.   And was there no one,

No witness, no companion, to tell what

120   happened?

CREON. They were all killed but one, and

he got away

So frightened that he could remember one

thing only.

OEDIPUS. What was that one thing? One

may be the key

To everything, if we resolve to use it.

CREON. He said that a band of highway-

125   men attacked them,

Outnumbered them, and overwhelmed the

King.

OEDIPUS. Strange, that a highwayman

should be so daring—

Unless some faction here bribed him to do

it.

CREON. We thought of that. But after

Laïos' death

New troubles arose and we had no

130   avenger.

OEDIPUS. What troubles could prevent

your hunting down the killers?

CREON. The riddling Sphinx's song

Made us deaf to all mysteries but her

own.

OEDIPUS. Then once more I must bring

what is dark to light.

It is most fitting that Apollo shows,   135

As you do, this compunction for the dead.

You shall see how I stand by you, as I

should,

To avenge the city and the city's god,

And not as though it were from some

distant friend,

But for my own sake, to be rid of evil.   140

Whoever killed King Laïos might—who

knows?—

Decide at any moment to kill me as well.

By avenging the murdered king I protect

myself.

Come, then, my children: leave the altar

steps,

Lift up your olive boughs!

                    One of you go   145

And summon the people of Kadmos to

gather here.

I will do all that I can; you may tell them

that.   (*Exit a* PAGE.)

So, with the help of God,

We shall be saved—or else indeed we are

lost.

PRIEST. Let us rise, children. It was for

this we came,   150

And now the King has promised it himself.

Phoibos° has sent us an oracle; may he

descend

Himself to save us and drive out the

plague.

Exeunt OEDIPUS *and* CREON *into the palace by the central door. The* PRIEST *and the* SUP-PLIANTS *disperse right and left. After a short pause the* CHORUS *enters the orchestra.*

PÁRODOS

CHORUS. What is God singing in his pro-

found   *Strophe 1*

---

[152] **Phoibos** Phoebus Apollo, the sun god

Delphi of gold and shadow?
What oracle for Thebes, the sunwhipped
    city?
Fear unjoints me, the roots of my heart
    tremble.
Now I remember, O Healer, your power,
5   and wonder;
Will you send doom like a sudden cloud,
    or weave it
Like nightfall of the past?
Speak, speak to us, issue of holy sound:
Dearest to our expectancy: be tender!
Let me pray to Athenê, the immortal
10   daughter of Zeus,   *Antistrophe 1*
And to Artemis her sister
Who keeps her famous throne in the
    market ring,
And to Apollo, bowman at the far butts of
    heaven—

O gods, descend! Like three streams leap
    against
The fires of our grief, the fires of dark-
15   ness;
Be swift to bring us rest!

As in the old time from the brilliant house
Of air you stepped to save us, come again!
Now our afflictions have no end, *Strophe 2*
20 Now all our stricken host lies down
And no man fights off death with his mind;

The noble plowland bears no grain,
And groaning mothers cannot bear—
See, how our lives like birds take wing,
25 Like sparks that fly when a fire soars,
To the shore of the god of evening.

The plague burns on, it is pitiless,
    Antistrophe 2
Though pallid children laden with death
Lie unwept in the stony ways,
30 And old gray women by every path
Flock to the strand about the altars

There to strike their breasts and cry
Worship of Phoibos in wailing prayers:
Be kind, God's golden child!

There are no swords in this attack by
35   fire,   *Strophe 3*
No shields, but we are ringed with cries.

Send the besieger plunging from our
    homes
Into the vast sea-room of the Atlantic
Or into the waves that foam eastward of
    Thrace—
For the day ravages what the night
    spares—   40

Destroy our enemy, lord of the thunder!
Let him be riven by lightning from heaven!

Phoibos Apollo, stretch the sun's bow-
    string,   *Antistrophe 3*
That golden cord, until it sing for us,
Flashing arrows in heaven!
                 Artemis, Huntress,   45
Race with flaring lights upon our moun-
    tains!
O scarlet god, O golden-banded brow,
O Theban Bacchos° in a storm of Mae-
    nads,°

Enter OEDIPUS, *center.*

Whirl upon Death, that all the Undying
    hate!
Come with blinding cressets, come in joy!   50

SCENE I

OEDIPUS. Is this your prayer? It may be
    answered. Come,
Listen to me, act as the crisis demands,
And you shall have relief from all these
    evils.

Until now I was a stranger to this tale,
As I had been a stranger to the crime.   5
Could I track down the murderer without
    a clue?
But now, friends,
As one who became a citizen after the
    murder,
I make this proclamation to all Thebans:
If any man knows by whose hand Laïos,
    son of Labdakos,   10
Met his death, I direct that man to tell me
    everything,

---

48 **Bacchos** Dionysos, god of wine, thus scarlet-
faced 48 **Maenads** Dionysos's female attendants

No matter what he fears for having so long
    withheld it.
Let it stand as promised that no further
    trouble
Will come to him, but he may leave the
    land in safety.

Moreover: If anyone knows the murderer
15   to be foreign,
Let him not keep silent: he shall have his
    reward from me.
However, if he does conceal it; if any man
Fearing for his friend or for himself dis-
    obeys this edict,
Hear what I propose to do:

I solemnly forbid the people of this coun-
20   try,
Where power and throne are mine, ever to
    receive that man
Or speak to him, no matter who he is, or
    let him
Join in sacrifice, lustration, or in prayer.
I decree that he be driven from every
    house,

Being, as he is, corruption itself to us: the
25   Delphic
Voice of Zeus has pronounced this releva-
    tion.
Thus I associate myself with the oracle
And take the side of the murdered king.

As for the criminal, I pray to God—
Whether it be a lurking thief, or one of a
30   number—
I pray that that man's life be consumed in
    evil and wretchedness.
And as for me, this curse applies no less
If it should turn out that the culprit is my
    guest here,
Sharing my hearth.
              You have heard the penalty.
35 I lay it on you now to attend to this
For my sake, for Apollo's, for the sick
Sterile city that heaven has abandoned.
Suppose the oracle had given you no
    command:
Should this defilement go uncleansed for
    ever?

You should have found the murderer: your
    king,   40
A noble king, had been destroyed!
                       Now I,
Having the power that he held before me,
Having his bed, begetting children there
Upon his wife, as he would have, had he
    lived—
Their son would have been my children's
    brother,   45
If Laïos had had luck in fatherhood!
(But surely ill luck rushed upon his
    reign)—
I say I take the son's part, just as though
I were his son, to press the fight for him
And see it won! I'll find the hand that
    brought   50
Death to Labdakos' and Polydoros' child,
Heir of Kadmos' and Agenor's line.
And as for those who fail me,
May the gods deny them the fruit of the
    earth,
Fruit of the womb, and may they rot ut-
    terly!   55
Let them be wretched as we are
    wretched, and worse!

For you, for loyal Thebans, and for all
Who find my actions right, I pray the favor
Of justice, and of all the immortal gods.
CHORAGOS. Since I am under oath, my
    lord, I swear   60
I did not do the murder, I cannot name
The murderer. Might not the oracle
That has ordained the search tell where to
    find him?
OEDIPUS. An honest question. But no man
    in the world
Can make the gods do more than the gods
    will.   65
CHORAGOS. There is one last expedient—
OEDIPUS.   Tell me what it is.
Though it seem slight, you must not hold
    it back.
CHORAGOS. A lord clairvoyant to the lord
    Apollo,
As we all know, is the skilled Teiresias.
One might learn much about this from
    him, Oedipus.   70
OEDIPUS. I am not wasting time:

Creon spoke of this, and I have sent for
    him—
Twice, in fact; it is strange that he is not
    here.
CHORAGOS. The other matter—that old
    report—seems useless.
OEDIPUS. Tell me. I am interested in all
75   reports.
CHORAGOS. The King was said to have
    been killed by highwaymen.
OEDIPUS. I know. But we have no wit-
    nesses to that.
CHORAGOS. If the killer can feel a particle
    of dread,
Your curse will bring him out of hiding!
OEDIPUS.   No.
The man who dared that act will fear no
80   curse.

Enter the blind seer TEIRESIAS, *led by a*
PAGE.

CHORAGOS. But there is one man who may
    detect the criminal.
This is Teiresias, this is the holy prophet
In whom, alone of all men, truth was
    born.
OEDIPUS. Teiresias: seer: student of mys-
    teries,
Of all that's taught and all that no man
85   tells,
Secrets of Heaven and secrets of the
    earth:
Blind though you are, you know the city
    lies
Sick with plague; and from this plague, my
    lord,
We find that you alone can guard or save
    us.

90 Possibly you did not hear the messengers?
Apollo, when we sent to him,
Sent us back word that this great pesti-
    lence
Would lift, but only if we established
    clearly
The identity of those who murdered Laïos.
They must be killed or exiled.
95   Can you use
Birdflight or any art of divination
To purify yourself, and Thebes, and me

From this contagion? We are in your
    hands.
There is no fairer duty
Than that of helping others in distress.   100
TEIRESIAS. How dreadful knowledge of the
    truth can be
When there's no help in truth! I knew this
    well,
But did not act on it: else I should not
    have come.
OEDIPUS. What is troubling you? Why are
    your eyes so cold?
TEIRESIAS. Let me go home. Bear your
    own fate, and I'll   105
Bear mine. It is better so: trust what I
    say.
OEDIPUS. What you say is ungracious and
    unhelpful
To your native country. Do not refuse to
    speak.
TEIRESIAS. When it comes to speech, your
    own is neither temperate
Nor opportune. I wish to be more pru-
    dent.   110
OEDIPUS. In God's name, we all beg you—
TEIRESIAS.   You are all ignorant.
No; I will never tell you what I know.
Now it is my misery; then, it would be
    yours.
OEDIPUS. What! You do know something,
    and will not tell us?
You would betray us all and wreck the
    State?   115
TEIRESIAS. I do not intend to torture my-
    self, or you.
Why persist in asking? You will not per-
    suade me.
OEDIPUS. What a wicked old man you are!
    You'd try a stone's
Patience! Out with it! Have you no feeling
    at all?
TEIRESIAS. You call me unfeeling. If you
    could only see   120
The nature of your own feelings . . .
OEDIPUS.   Why,
Who would not feel as I do? Who could
    endure
Your arrogance toward the city?
TEIRESIAS.   What does it matter!

Whether I speak or not, it is bound to
   come.

OEDIPUS. Then, if "it" is bound to come,
125   you are bound to tell me.

TEIRESIAS. No, I will not go on. Rage as
   you please.

OEDIPUS. Rage? Why not!
           And I'll tell you what I think:
You planned it, you had it done, you all but
Killed him with your own hands: if you had
   eyes,
I'd say the crime was yours, and yours
130   alone.

TEIRESIAS. So? I charge you, then,
Abide by the proclamation you have made:
From this day forth
Never speak again to these men or to me;
You yourself are the pollution of this coun-
135   try.

OEDIPUS. You dare say that! Can you
   possibly think you have
Some way of going free, after such insolence?

TEIRESIAS. I have gone free. It is the truth
   sustains me.

OEDIPUS. Who taught you shamelessness?
   It was not your craft.

TEIRESIAS. You did. You made me speak. I
140   did not want to.

OEDIPUS. Speak what? Let me hear it
   again more clearly.

TEIRESIAS. Was it not clear before? Are
   you tempting me?

OEDIPUS. I did not understand it. Say it
   again.

TEIRESIAS. I say that you are the murderer
   whom you seek.

OEDIPUS. Now twice you have spat out
145   infamy. You'll pay for it!

TEIRESIAS. Would you care for more? Do
   you wish to be really angry?

OEDIPUS. Say what you will. Whatever you
   say is worthless.

TEIRESIAS. I say you live in hideous shame
   with those
Most dear to you. You cannot see the evil.

OEDIPUS. It seems you can go on mouth-
150   ing like this for ever.

TEIRESIAS. I can, if there is power in
   truth.

OEDIPUS.   There is:
But not for you, not for you,
You sightless, witless, senseless, mad old
   man!

TEIRESIAS. You are the madman. There is
   no one here
Who will not curse you soon, as you curse
   me.   155

OEDIPUS. You child of endless night! You
   cannot hurt me
Or any other man who sees the sun.

TEIRESIAS. True: it is not from me your
   fate will come.
That lies within Apollo's competence,
As it is his concern.

OEDIPUS.   Tell me: 160
Are you speaking for Creon, or for yourself?

TEIRESIAS. Creon is no threat. You weave
   your own doom.

OEDIPUS. Wealth, power, craft of states-
   manship!
Kingly position, everywhere admired!
What savage envy is stored up against
   these,   165
If Creon, whom I trusted, Creon my
   friend,
For this great office which the city once
Put in my hands unsought—if for this
   power
Creon desires in secret to destroy me!

He has brought this decrepit fortune-teller, 170
   this
Collector of dirty pennies, this prophet
   fraud—
Why, he is no more clairvoyant than I am!
                          Tell us:
Has your mystic mummery ever ap-
   proached the truth?
When that hellcat the Sphinx was perform-
   ing here,
What help were you to these people?   175
Her magic was not for the first man who
   came along:
It demanded a real exorcist. Your birds—
What good were they? or the gods, for
   the matter of that?

But I came by,
Oedipus, the simple man, who knows
180   nothing—
I thought it out for myself no birds helped
        me!
And this is the man you think you can
        destroy,
That you may be close to Creon when he's
        king!
Well, you and your friend Creon, it seems
        to me,
Will suffer most. If you were not an old
185   man,
You would have paid already for your plot.
CHORAGOS. We cannot see that his words
        or yours
Have been spoken except in anger, Oedi-
        pus,
And of anger we have no need. How can
        God's will
Be accomplished best? That is what most
190   concerns us.
TEIRESIAS. You are a king. But where
        argument's concerned
I am your man, as much a king as you.
I am not your servant, but Apollo's.
I have no need of Creon to speak for me.

Listen to me. You mock my blindness, do
195   you?
But I say that you, with both your eyes,
        are blind:
You cannot see the wretchedness of your
        life,
Nor in whose house you live, no, nor with
        whom.
Who are your father and mother? Can you
        tell me?
200 You do not even know the blind wrongs
That you have done them, on earth and in
        the world below.
But the double lash of your parents' curse
        will whip you
Out of this land some day, with only night
Upon your precious eyes.
Your cries then—where will they not be
205   heard?
What fastness of Kithairon° will not echo
        them?

²⁰⁶ **fastness of Kithairon** stronghold in a mountain near Thebes

And that bridal-descant of yours—you'll
        know it then,
The song they sang when you came here
        to Thebes
And found your misguided berthing.
All this, and more, that you cannot guess
        at now,   210
Will bring you to yourself among your
        children.
Be angry then. Curse Creon. Curse my
        words.
I tell you, no man that walks upon the
        earth
Shall be rooted out more horribly than
        you.
OEDIPUS. Am I to bear this from him?—
        Damnation   215
Take you! Out of this place! Out of my
        sight!
TEIRESIAS. I would not have come at all if
        you had not asked me.
OEDIPUS. Could I have told that you'd talk
        nonsense, that
You'd come here to make a fool of your-
        self, and of me?
TEIRESIAS. A fool? Your parents thought
        me sane enough.   220
OEDIPUS. My parents again!—Wait: who
        were my parents?
TEIRESIAS. This day will give you a father,
        and break your heart.
OEDIPUS. Your infantile riddles! Your
        damned abracadabra!
TEIRESIAS. You were a great man once at
        solving riddles.
OEDIPUS. Mock me with that if you like;
        you will find it true.   225
TEIRESIAS. It was true enough. It brought
        about your ruin.
OEDIPUS. But if it saved this town?
TEIRESIAS (*to the* PAGE.). Boy, give me your
        hand.
OEDIPUS. Yes, boy; lead him away.
                    —While you are here
We can do nothing. Go; leave us in peace.   230
TEIRESIAS. I will go when I have said what
        I have to say.
How can you hurt me? And I tell you
        again:
The man you have been looking for all this
        time,

The damned man, the murderer of Laïos,
That man is in Thebes. To your mind he is
235   foreignborn,
But it will soon be shown that he is a
    Theban,
A revelation that will fail to please.
                            A blind man,
Who has his eyes now; a penniless man,
    who is rich now;
And he will go tapping the strange earth
    with his staff;
To the children with whom he lives now
240   he will be
Brother and father—the very same; to her
Who bore him, son and husband—the
    very same
Who came to his father's bed, wet with
    his father's blood.

Enough. Go think that over.
245   If later you find error in what I have said,
You may say that I have no skill in proph-
    ecy.

Exit TEIRESIAS, *led by his* PAGE. OEDIPUS
goes into the palace.

ODE I

CHORUS. The Delphic stone of prophecies
                            Strophe 1
Remembers ancient regicide
And a still bloody hand.
That killer's hour of flight has come.
5   He must be stronger than riderless
Coursers of untiring wind,
For the son of Zeus° armed with his fa-
    ther's thunder
Leaps in lightning after him;
And the Furies° follow him, the sad Fu-
    ries.

10   Holy Parnossos' peak of snow
                            Antistrophe 1
Flashes and blinds that secret man,
That all shall hunt him down:
Though he may roam the forest shade
Like a bull gone wild from pasture

To rage through glooms of stone.   15
Doom comes down on him; flight will not
    avail him;
For the world's heart calls him desolate,
And the immortal Furies follow, for ever
    follow.
But now a wilder thing is heard   *Strophe 2*
From the old man skilled at hearing Fate
    in the wingbeat of a bird.   20
Bewildered as a blown bird, my soul hov-
    ers and cannot find
Foothold in this debate, or any reason or
    rest of mind.
But no man ever brought—none can bring
Proof of strife between Thebes' royal
    house,
Labdakos' line,° and the son of Polybos;°   25
And never until now has any man brought
    word
Of Laïos' dark death staining Oedipus the
    King.

Divine Zeus and Apollo hold   *Antistrophe 2*
Perfect intelligence alone of all tales ever
    told;
And well though this diviner works, he
    works in his own night;   30
No man can judge that rough unknown or
    trust in second sight,
For wisdom changes hands among the
    wise.
Shall I believe my great lord criminal
At a raging word that a blind old man let
    fall?
I saw him, when the carrion woman faced
    him of old,   35
Prove his heroic mind! These evil words
    are lies.

SCENE II

CREON. Men of Thebes:
I am told that heavy accusations
Have been brought against me by King
    Oedipus.
I am not the kind of man to bear this
    tamely.

---

²⁵ **Labdakos' line** family of Laïos ²⁵ **son of Polybos** Oedipus (so the Chorus believes)

⁷ **son of Zeus** Apollo ⁹ **Furies** avenging deities

5   If in these present difficulties
He holds me accountable for any harm to
    him
Through anything I have said or done—
    why, then,
I do not value life in this dishonor.
It is not as though this rumor touched
    upon
Some private indiscretion. The matter is
10   grave.
The fact is that I am being called disloyal
To the State, to my fellow citizens, to my
    friends.
CHORAGOS. He may have spoken in anger,
    not from his mind.
CREON. But did you not hear him say I
    was the one
15 Who seduced the old prophet into lying?
CHORAGOS. The thing was said; I do not
    know how seriously.
CREON. But you were watching him! Were
    his eyes steady?
Did he look like a man in his right mind?
CHORAGOS.   I do not know.
I cannot judge the behavior of great men.
But here is the King himself.

    Enter OEDIPUS.

20 OEDIPUS.   So you dared come back.
Why? How brazen of you to come to my
    house,
You murderer!
                    Do you think I do not know
That you plotted to kill me, plotted to
    steal my throne?
Tell me, in God's name: am I coward, a
    fool,
That you should dream you could accom-
25   plish this?
A fool who could not see your slippery
    game?
A coward, not to fight back when I saw it?
You are the fool, Creon, are you not?
    hoping
Without support or friends to get a
    throne?
Thrones may be won or bought: you could
30   do neither.
CREON. Now listen to me. You have
    talked; let me talk, too.

You cannot judge unless you know the
    facts.
OEDIPUS. You speak well: there is one
    fact; but I find it hard
To learn from the deadliest enemy I have.
CREON. That above all I must dispute with
    you.   35
OEDIPUS. That above all I will not hear you
    deny.
CREON. If you think there is anything good
    in being stubborn
Against all reason, then I say you are
    wrong.
OEDIPUS. If you think a man can sin
    against his own kind
And not be punished for it, I say you are
    mad.   40
CREON. I agree. But tell me: what have I
    done to you?
OEDIPUS. You advised me to send for that
    wizard, did you not?
CREON. I did. I should do it again.
OEDIPUS.   Very well. Now tell me:
How long has it been since Laïos—
CREON.   What of Laïos?
OEDIPUS. Since he vanished in that onset
    by the road?   45
CREON. It was long ago, a long time.
OEDIPUS.   And this prophet,
Was he practicing here then?
CREON.   He was; and with honor, as now.
OEDIPUS. Did he speak of me at that
    time?
CREON.   He never did;
At least, not when I was present.
OEDIPUS.   But . . . the enquiry?
I suppose you held one?
CREON.   We did, but we learned nothing.   50
OEDIPUS. Why did the prophet not speak
    against me then?
CREON. I do not know; and I am the kind
    of man
Who holds his tongue when he has no
    facts to go on.
OEDIPUS. There's one fact that you know,
    and you could tell it.
CREON. What fact is that? If I know it, you
    shall have it.   55
OEDIPUS. If he were not involved with you,
    he could not say

That it was I who murdered Laïos.
CREON. If he says that, you are the one
    that knows it!—
But now it is my turn to question you.
OEDIPUS. Put your questions. I am no
60   murderer.
CREON. First, then: You married my sis-
    ter?
OEDIPUS.   I married your sister.
CREON. And you rule the kingdom equally
    with her?
OEDIPUS. Everything that she wants she
    has from me.
CREON. And I am the third, equal to both
    of you?
OEDIPUS. That is why I call you a bad
65   friend.
CREON. No. Reason it out, as I have done.
Think of this first. Would any sane man
    prefer
Power, with all a king's anxieties,
To that same power and the grace of
    sleep?
70 Certainly not I.
I have never longed for the king's power—
    only his rights.
Would any wise man differ from me in
    this?
As matters stand, I have my way in every-
    thing
With your consent, and no responsibilities.
If I were king, I should be a slave to pol-
75   icy.
How could I desire a scepter more
Than what is now mine—untroubled influ-
    ence?
No, I have not gone mad; I need no hon-
    ors,
Except those with the perquisites I have
    now.
I am welcome everywhere; every man
80   salutes me,
And those who want your favor seek my
    ear,
Since I know how to manage what they
    ask.
Should I exchange this ease for that anxi-
    ety?
Besides, no sober mind is treasonable.
85 I hate anarchy

And never would deal with any man who
    likes it.

Test what I have said. Go to the priestess
At Delphi, ask if I quoted her correctly.
And as for this other thing: if I am found
Guilty of treason with Teiresias,   90
Then sentence me to death! You have my
    word
It is a sentence I should cast my vote
    for—
But not without evidence!
                              You do wrong
When you take good men for bad, bad
    men for good.
A true friend thrown aside—why, life itself   95
Is not more precious!
                        In time you will know this well:
For time, and time alone, will show the
    just man,
Though scoundrels are discovered in a day.
CHORAGOS. This is well said, and a pru-
    dent man would ponder it.
Judgments too quickly formed are danger-
    ous.   100
OEDIPUS. But is he not quick in his duplic-
    ity?
And shall I not be quick to parry him?
Would you have me stand still, hold my
    peace, and let
This man win everything, through my
    inaction?
CREON. And you want—what is it, then?
    To banish me?   105
OEDIPUS. No, not exile. It is your death I
    want,
So that all the world may see what treason
    means.
CREON. You will persist, then? You will not
    believe me?
OEDIPUS. How can I believe you?
CREON.   Then you are a fool.
OEDIPUS. To save myself?
CREON.   In justice, think of me.   110
OEDIPUS. You are evil incarnate.
CREON.   But suppose that you are wrong?
OEDIPUS. Still I must rule.
CREON.   But not if you rule badly.
OEDIPUS. O city, city!
CREON.   It is my city, too!

CHORAGOS. Now, my lords, be still. I see the Queen,

Iocastê, coming from her palace cham-
115   bers;

And it is time she came, for the sake of you both.

This dreadful quarrel can be resolved through her.

Enter IOCASTÊ.

IOCASTÊ. Poor foolish men, what wicked din is this?

With Thebes sick to death, is it not shameful

That you should rake some private quarrel
120   up?

(*To* OEDIPUS.) Come into the house.

—And you, Creon, go now:

Let us have no more of this tumult over nothing.

CREON. Nothing? No, sister: what your husband plans for me

Is one of two great evils: exile or death.

OEDIPUS. He is right.

Why, woman, I have
125   caught him squarely

Plotting against my life.

CREON.   No! Let me die

Accurst if ever I have wished you harm!

IOCASTÊ. Ah, believe it, Oedipus!

In the name of the gods, respect this oath of his

For my sake, for the sake of these people
130   here!

CHORAGOS. Open your mind to her, my lord. Be ruled by her, I beg you!

                              Strophe 1

OEDIPUS. What would you have me do?

CHORAGOS. Respect Creon's word. He has never spoken like a fool,

And now he has sworn an oath.

OEDIPUS. You know what you ask?

CHORAGOS.   I do.

OEDIPUS.   Speak on, then.

CHORAGOS. A friend so sworn should not
135   be baited so,

In blind malice, and without final proof.

OEDIPUS. You are aware, I hope, that what you say

Means death for me, or exile at the least.

CHORAGOS. No, I swear by Helios,° first in Heaven!   *Strophe 2*

May I die friendless and accurst,

The worst of deaths, if ever I meant that!   140

It is the withering fields

That hurt my sick heart:

Must we bear all these ills,

And now your bad blood as well?

OEDIPUS. Then let him go. And let me   145
die, if I must,

Or be driven by him in shame from the land of Thebes.

It is your unhappiness, and not his talk,

That touches me.

                As for him—

Wherever he is, I will hate him as long as I live.   150

CREON. Ugly in yielding, as you were ugly in rage!

Natures like yours chiefly torment them-selves.

OEDIPUS. Can you not go? Can you not leave me?

CREON.   I can.

You do not know me; but the city knows me,

And in its eyes I am just, if not in yours.

                    (*Exit* CREON.)   155

CHORAGOS. Lady Iocastê, did you not ask the King   *Antistrophe 1*
                to go to his chambers?

IOCASTÊ. First tell me what has happened.

CHORAGOS. There was suspicion without evidence; yet it rankled

As even false charges will.

IOCASTÊ.   On both sides?

CHORAGOS.   On both.

IOCASTÊ.   But what was said?

CHORAGOS. Oh let it rest, let it be done with!   160

Have we not suffered enough?

OEDIPUS. You see to what your decency has brought you:

You have made difficulties where my heart saw none.

---

¹³⁹ **Helios** sun god

CHORAGOS. Oedipus, it is not once only I
　　have told you—　　　　　*Antistrophe 2*
You must know I should count myself
165　　unwise
To the point of madness, should I now
　　forsake you—
　　You, under whose hand,
　　　In the storm of another time,
　　Our dear land sailed out free.
170　　　But now stand fast at the helm!
IOCASTÊ. In God's name, Oedipus, inform
　　your wife as well:
Why are you so set in this hard anger?
OEDIPUS. I will tell you, for none of these
　　men deserves
My confidence as you do. It is Creon's
　　work,
175　His treachery, his plotting against me.
IOCASTÊ. Go on, if you can make this clear
　　to me.
OEDIPUS. He charges me with the murder
　　of Laïos.
IOCASTÊ. Has he some knowledge? Or
　　does he speak from hearsay?
OEDIPUS. He would not commit himself to
　　such a charge,
But he has brought in that damnable
180　　soothsayer
To tell his story.
IOCASTÊ.　　　　　Set your mind at rest.
If it is a question of soothsayers, I tell you
That you will find no man whose craft
　　gives knowledge
Of the unknowable.
　　　　　　　Here is my proof:

185　An oracle was reported to Laïos once
(I will not say from Phoibos himself, but
　　from
His appointed ministers, at any rate)
That his doom would be death at the
　　hands of his own son—
His son, born of his flesh and of mine!

Now, you remember the story: Laïos was
190　　killed
By marauding strangers where three
　　highways meet;
But his child had not been three days in
　　this world

Before the King had pierced the baby's
　　ankles
And left him to die on a lonely mountain-
　　side.

Thus, Apollo never caused that child　　195
To kill his father, and it was not Laïos' fate
To die at the hands of his son, as he had
　　feared.
This is what prophets and prophecies are
　　worth!
Have no dread of them.
　　　　　　　　　It is God himself
Who can show us what he wills, in his
　　own way.　　　　　　　　　　　200
OEDIPUS. How strange a shadowy memory
　　crossed my mind,
Just now while you were speaking; it
　　chilled my heart.
IOCASTÊ. What do you mean? What mem-
　　ory do you speak of?
OEDIPUS. If I understand you, Laïos was
　　killed
At a place where three roads meet.
IOCASTÊ.　　　　　　So it was said;　205
We have no later story.
OEDIPUS.　　　　　Where did it happen?
IOCASTÊ. Phokis, it is called: at a place
　　where the Theban Way
Divides into the roads towards Delphi and
　　Daulia.
OEDIPUS. When?
IOCASTÊ. We had the news not long before
　　you came
And proved the right to your succession
　　here.
OEDIPUS. Ah, what net has God been　　210
　　weaving for me?
IOCASTÊ. Oedipus! Why does this trouble
　　you?
OEDIPUS.　　　　　Do not ask me yet.
First, tell me how Laïos looked, and tell
　　me
How old he was.
IOCASTÊ. He was tall, his hair just touched
With white; his form was not unlike your
　　own.　　　　　　　　　　　　　215
OEDIPUS. I think that I myself may be
　　accurst

By my own ignorant edict.

IOCASTÊ.   You speak strangely.
It makes me tremble to look at you, my
    King.
OEDIPUS. I am not sure that the blind man
    cannot see.
But I should know better if you were to
220   tell me—
IOCASTÊ. Anything—though I dread to
    hear you ask it.
OEDIPUS. Was the King lightly escorted,
    or did he ride
With a large company, as a ruler should?
IOCASTÊ. There were five men with him in
    all: one was a herald;
And a single chariot, which he was driv-
225   ing.
OEDIPUS. Alas, that makes it plain enough!
                    But who—
Who told you how it happened?
IOCASTÊ.   A household servant,
The only one to escape.
OEDIPUS.   And is he still
A servant of ours?
IOCASTÊ.   No; for when he came back at
    last
And found you enthroned in the place of
230   the dead king,
He came to me, touched my hand with
    his, and begged
That I would send him away to the frontier
    district
Where only the shepherds go—
As far away from the city as I could send
    him.
I granted his prayer; for although the man
235   was a slave,
He had earned more than this favor at my
    hands.
OEDIPUS. Can he be called back quickly?
IOCASTÊ.   Easily.
But why?
OEDIPUS.   I have taken too much upon
    myself
Without enquiry; therefore I wish to con-
    sult him.
IOCASTÊ. Then he shall come.
240   But am I not one also
To whom you might confide these fears of
    yours!

OEDIPUS. That is your right; it will not be
    denied you,
Now least of all; for I have reached a pitch
Of wild foreboding. Is there anyone
To whom I should sooner speak?   245
Polybos of Corinth is my father.
My mother is a Dorian: Meropê.
I grew up chief among the men of Corinth
Until a strange thing happened—
Not worth my passion, it may be, but
    strange.   250

At a feast, a drunken man maundering in
    his cups
Cries out that I am not my father's son!

I contained myself that night, though I felt
    anger
And a sinking heart. The next day I vis-
    ited
My father and mother, and questioned
    them. They stormed,   255
Calling it all the slanderous rant of a fool;
And this relieved me. Yet the suspicion
Remained always aching in my mind;
I knew there was talk; I could not rest;
And finally, saying nothing to my parents,   260
I went to the shrine at Delphi.
The god dismissed my question without
    reply;
He spoke of other things.
                    Some were clear,
Full of wretchedness, dreadful, unbear-
    able:
As, that I should lie with my own mother,
    breed   265
Children from whom all men would turn
    their eyes;
And that I should be my father's murderer.
I heard all this, and fled. And from that
    day
Corinth to me was only in the stars
Descending in that quarter of the sky,   270
As I wandered farther and farther on my
    way
To a land where I should never see the
    evil
Sung by the oracle. And I came to this
    country
Where, so you say, King Laïos was killed.

275 I will tell you all that happened there, my
       lady.

There were three highways
Coming together at a place I passed;
And there a herald came towards me, and
       a chariot
Drawn by horses, with a man such as you
       describe
280 Seated in it. The groom leading the
       horses
Forced me off the road at his lord's com-
       mand;
But as this charioteer lurched over to-
       wards me
I struck him in my rage. The old man saw
       me
And brought his double goad down upon
       my head
285 As I came abreast.
                    He was paid back, and more!
Swinging my club in this right hand I
       knocked him
Out of his car, and he rolled on the
       ground.
                                    I killed him.
I killed them all.
Now if that stranger and Laïos were—kin,
Where is a man more miserable than I?
290 More hated by the gods? Citizen and alien
       alike
Must never shelter me or speak to me—
I must be shunned by all.
                         And I myself
Pronounced this malediction upon myself!

Think of it: I have touched you with these
       hands,
295 These hands that killed your husband.
       What defilement!

Am I all evil, then? It must be so,
Since I must flee from Thebes, yet never
       again
See my own countrymen, my own country,
300 For fear of joining my mother in marriage
And killing Polybos, my father.
                                    Ah,

If I was created so, born to this fate,
Who could deny the savagery of God?

O holy majesty of heavenly powers!
305 May I never see that day! Never!
Rather let me vanish from the race of men
Than know the abomination destined me!
CHORAGOS. We too, my lord, have felt
       dismay at this.
But there is hope: you have yet to hear
       the shepherd.
OEDIPUS. Indeed, I fear no other hope is
310 left me.
IOCASTÊ. What do you hope from him
       when he comes?
OEDIPUS.   This much:
If his account of the murder tallies with
       yours,
Then I am cleared.
IOCASTÊ.   What was it that I said
Of such importance?
OEDIPUS.   Why, "marauders," you said,
Killed the King, according to this man's
315 story.
If he maintains that still, if there were
       several,
Clearly the guilt is not mine: I was alone.
But if he says one man, singlehanded, did
       it,
Then the evidence all points to me.
IOCASTÊ. You may be sure that he said
320 there were several;
And can he call back that story now? He
       cannot.
The whole city heard it as plainly as I.
But suppose he alters some detail of it:
He cannot ever show that Laïos' death
325 Fulfilled the oracle: for Apollo said
My child was doomed to kill him; and my
       child—
Poor baby!—it was my child that died
       first.

No. From now on, where oracles are
       concerned,
I would not waste a second thought on
       any.
OEDIPUS. You may be right.
                         But come: let someone go
330 For the shepherd at once. This matter
       must be settled.
IOCASTÊ. I will send for him.
I would not wish to cross you in anything,

And surely not in this.—Let us go in.
Exeunt into the palace.

ODE II

CHORUS. Let me be reverent in the ways
    of right,   *Strophe 1*
Lowly the paths I journey on;
Let all my words and actions keep
The laws of the pure universe
5 From highest Heaven handed down.
For Heaven is their bright nurse,
Those generations of the realms of light;
Ah, never of mortal kind were they begot,
Nor are they slaves of memory, lost in
    sleep:
Their Father is greater than Time, and
10   ages not.

The tyrant is a child of Pride *Antistrophe 1*
Who drinks from his great sickening cup
Recklessness and vanity,
Until from his high crest headlong
15 He plummets to the dust of hope.
That strong man is not strong.
But let no fair ambition be denied;
May God protect the wrestler for the
    State
In government, in comely policy,
Who will fear God, and on His ordinance
20   wait.

Haughtiness and the high hand of disdain
                        Strophe 2
Tempt and outrage God's holy law;
And any mortal who dares hold
No immortal Power in awe
25 Will be caught up in a net of pain:
The price for which his levity is sold.
Let each man take due earnings, then,
And keep his hands from holy things,
And from blasphemy stand apart—
30 Else the crackling blast of heaven
Blows on his head, and on his desperate
    heart;
Though fools will honor impious men,
In their cities no tragic poet sings.

Shall we lose faith in Delphi's obscuri-
    ties.   *Antistrophe 2*
35 We who have heard the world's core

Discredited, and the sacred wood
Of Zeus at Elis praised no more?
The deeds and the strange prophecies
Must make a pattern yet to be under-
    stood.
Zeus, if indeed you are lord of all,   40
Throned in light over night and day,
Mirror this in your endless mind:
Our masters call the oracle
Words on the wind, and the Delphic vision
    blind!
Their hearts no longer know Apollo,   45
And reverence for the gods has died away.

SCENE III

Enter IOCASTÊ.

IOCASTÊ. Prince of Thebes, it has oc-
    curred to me
To visit the altars of the gods, bearing
These branches as a suppliant, and this
    incense.
Our King is not himself: his noble soul
Is overwrought with fantasies of dread,   5
Else he would consider
The new prophecies in the light of the old.
He will listen to any voice that speaks
    disaster,
And my advice goes for nothing.

She approaches the altar, right.

                To you, then, Apollo,
Lycean lord, since you are nearest, I turn
    in prayer.   10
Receive these offerings, and grant us deliv-
    erance
From defilement. Our hearts are heavy
    with fear
When we see our leader distracted, as
    helpless sailors
Are terrified by the confusion of their
    helmsman.

Enter MESSENGER.

MESSENGER. Friends, no doubt you can
    direct me: 15
Where shall I find the house of Oedipus,
Or, better still, where is the King himself?
CHORAGOS. It is this very place, stranger;
    he is inside.

This is his wife and mother of his children.

MESSENGER. I wish her happiness in a
20   happy house,
Blest in all the fulfillment of her marriage.

IOCASTÊ. I wish as much for you: your
        courtesy
Deserves a like good fortune. But now,
        tell me:
Why have you come? What have you to
        say to us?

MESSENGER. Good news, my lady, for
25   your house and your husband.

IOCASTÊ. What news? Who sent you here?

MESSENGER.   I am from Corinth.
The news I bring ought to mean joy for
        you,
Though it may be you will find some grief
        in it.

IOCASTÊ. What is it? How can it touch us
        in both ways?

MESSENGER. The people of Corinth, they
30   say,
Intend to call Oedipus to be their king.

IOCASTÊ. But old Polybos—is he not
        reigning still?

MESSENGER. No. Death holds him in his
        sepulchre.

IOCASTÊ. What are you saying? Polybos is
        dead?

MESSENGER. If I am not telling the truth,
35   may I die myself.

IOCASTÊ (*to a* MAIDSERVANT). Go in, go
        quickly; tell this to your master.
O riddlers of God's will, where are you
        now!
This was the man whom Oedipus, long
        ago,
Feared so, fled so, in dread of destroying
        him—
40 But it was another fate by which he died.

Enter OEDIPUS, *center.*

OEDIPUS. Dearest Iocastê, why have you
        sent for me?

IOCASTÊ. Listen to what this man says,
        and then tell me
What has become of the solemn prophe-
        cies.

OEDIPUS. Who is this man? What is his
        news for me?

IOCASTÊ. He has come from Corinth to
        announce your father's death!   45

OEDIPUS. Is it true, stranger? Tell me in
        your own words.

MESSENGER. I cannot say it more clearly:
        the King is dead.

OEDIPUS. Was it by treason? Or by an
        attack of illness?

MESSENGER. A little thing brings old men
        to their rest.

OEDIPUS. It was sickness, then?

MESSENGER.   Yes, and his many years.   50

OEDIPUS. Ah!
Why should a man respect the Pythian
        hearth,° or
Give heed to the birds that jangle above
        his head?
They prophesied that I should kill Polybos,
Kill my own father; but he is dead and
        buried,   55
And I am here—I never touched him,
        never,
Unless he died in grief for my departure,
And thus, in a sense, through me. No.
        Polybos
Has packed the oracles off with him un-
        derground.
They are empty words.

IOCASTÊ.   Had I not told you so?   60

OEDIPUS. You had; it was my faint heart
        that betrayed me.

IOCASTÊ. From now on never think of
        those things again.

OEDIPUS. And yet—must I not fear my
        mother's bed?

IOCASTÊ. Why should anyone in this world
        be afraid,
Since Fate rules us and nothing can be
        foreseen?   65
A man should live only for the present
        day.
Have no more fear of sleeping with your
        mother:
How many men, in dreams, have lain with
        their mothers!

---

⁵² **Pythian hearth** Delphi (also called Pytho because a great snake had lived there), where
Apollo spoke through a priestess

No reasonable man is troubled by such
things.
70 OEDIPUS. That is true; only—
If only my mother were not still alive!
But she is alive. I cannot help my dread.
IOCASTÊ. Yet this news of your father's
death is wonderful.
OEDIPUS. Wonderful. But I fear the living
woman.
MESSENGER. Tell me, who is this woman
75   that you fear?
OEDIPUS. It is Meropê, man; the wife of
King Polybos.
MESSENGER. Meropê? Why should you be
afraid of her?
OEDIPUS. An oracle of the gods, a dreadful
saying.
MESSENGER. Can you tell me about it or
are you sworn to silence?
80 OEDIPUS. I can tell you, and I will.
Apollo said through his prophet that I was
the man
Who should marry his own mother, shed
his father's blood
With his own hands. And so, for all these
years
I have kept clear of Corinth, and no harm
has come—
Though it would have been sweet to see
85   my parents again.
MESSENGER. And is this the fear that
drove you out of Corinth?
OEDIPUS. Would you have me kill my fa-
ther?
MESSENGER.   As for that
You must be reassured by the news I gave
you.
OEDIPUS. If you could reassure me, I
would reward you.
MESSENGER. I had that in mind, I will
90   confess: I thought
I could count on you when you returned to
Corinth.
OEDIPUS. No: I will never go near my
parents again.
MESSENGER. Ah, son, you still do not
know what you are doing—
OEDIPUS. What do you mean? In the name
of God tell me!

MESSENGER. —If these are your reasons
for not going home.   95
OEDIPUS. I tell you, I fear the oracle may
come true.
MESSENGER. And guilt may come upon
you through your parents?
OEDIPUS. That is the dread that is always
in my heart.
MESSENGER. Can you not see that all your
fears are groundless?
OEDIPUS. How can you say that? They are
my parents, surely?   100
MESSENGER. Polybos was not your father.
OEDIPUS.   Not my father?
MESSENGER. No more your father than the
man speaking to you.
OEDIPUS. But you are nothing to me!
MESSENGER.   Neither was he.
OEDIPUS. Then why did he call me son?
MESSENGER.   I will tell you:
Long ago he had you from my hands, as a
gift.   105
OEDIPUS. Then how could he love me so,
if I was not his?
MESSENGER. He had no children, and his
heart turned to you.
OEDIPUS. What of you? Did you buy me?
Did you find me by chance?
MESSENGER. I came upon you in the
crooked pass of Kithairon.
OEDIPUS. And what were you doing there?
MESSENGER.   Tending my flocks.   110
OEDIPUS. A wandering shepherd?
MESSENGER.   But your savior, son, that
day.
OEDIPUS. From what did you save me?
MESSENGER.   Your ankles should tell you
that.
OEDIPUS. Ah, stranger, why do you speak
of that childhood pain?
MESSENGER. I cut the bonds that tied your
ankles together.
OEDIPUS. I have had the mark as long as I
can remember.   115
MESSENGER. That was why you were
given the name you bear.°

---

¹¹⁶ **name you bear** "Oedipus" means "swollen-
foot"

OEDIPUS. God! Was it my father or my
    mother who did it?
Tell me!
MESSENGER. I do not know. The man who
    gave you to me
120 Can tell you better than I.
OEDIPUS. It was not you that found me,
    but another?
MESSENGER. It was another shepherd gave
    you to me.
OEDIPUS. Who was he? Can you tell me
    who he was?
MESSENGER. I think he was said to be one
    of Laïos' people.
OEDIPUS. You mean the Laïos who was
125   king here years ago?
MESSENGER. Yes; King Laïos; and the man
    was one of his herdsmen.
OEDIPUS. Is he still alive? Can I see him?
MESSENGER.   These men here
Know best about such things.
OEDIPUS.   Does anyone here
Know this shepherd that he is talking
    about?
Have you seen him in the fields, or in the
130   town?
If you have, tell me. It is time things were
    made plain.
CHORAGOS. I think the man he means is
    that same shepherd
You have already asked to see. Iocastê
    perhaps
Could tell you something.
OEDIPUS.   Do you know anything
About him, Lady? Is he the man we have
135   summoned?
Is that the man this shepherd means?
IOCASTÊ.   Why think of him?
Forget this herdsman. Forget it all.
This talk is a waste of time.
OEDIPUS.   How can you say that,
When the clues to my true birth are in my
    hands?
IOCASTÊ. For God's love, let us have no
140   more questioning!
Is your life nothing to you?
My own is pain enough for me to bear.
OEDIPUS. You need not worry. Suppose
    my mother a slave,

And born of slaves: no baseness can touch
    you.
IOCASTÊ. Listen to me, I beg you: do not
    do this thing!   145
OEDIPUS. I will not listen; the truth must
    be made known.
IOCASTÊ. Everything that I say is for your
    own good!
OEDIPUS.   My own good
Snaps my patience, then: I want none of
    it.
IOCASTÊ. You are fatally wrong! May you
    never learn who you are!
OEDIPUS. Go, one of you, and bring the
    shepherd here.   150
Let us leave this woman to brag of her
    royal name.
IOCASTÊ. Ah, miserable!
That is the only word I have for you now.
That is the only word I can ever have.

                    Exit into the palace.

CHORAGOS. Why has she left us, Oedipus?
    Why has she gone   155
In such a passion of sorrow? I fear this
    silence:
Something dreadful may come of it.
OEDIPUS.   Let it come!
However base my birth, I must know
    about it.
The Queen, like a woman, is perhaps
    ashamed   160
To think of my low origin. But I
Am a child of luck; I cannot be dishon-
    ored.
Luck is my mother; the passing months,
    my brothers,
Have seen me rich and poor.
                    If this is so,
How could I wish that I were someone
    else?   165
How could I not be glad to know my birth?

ODE III

CHORUS. If ever the coming time were
    known   *Strophe*
To my heart's pondering,

Kithairon, now by Heaven I see the
  torches
At the festival of the next full moon,
And see the dance, and hear the choir
5   sing
A grace to your gentle shade:
Mountain where Oedipus was found,
O mountain guard of a noble race!
May the god who heals us lend his aid,
10   And let that glory come to pass
For our king's cradling-ground.

Of the nymphs that flower beyond the
  years,   *Antistrophe*
Who bore you, royal child,
To Pan of the hills or the timberline
  Apollo,
15   Cold in delight where the upland clears,
Or Hermês for whom Kyllenê's° heights
  are piled?
Or flushed as evening cloud,
Great Dionysos, roamer of mountains,
He—was it he who found you there,
20   And caught you up in his own proud
Arms from the sweet god-ravisher
Who laughed by the Muses' fountains?

SCENE IV

OEDIPUS. Sirs: though I do not know the
  man,
I think I see him coming, this shepherd
  we want:
He is old, like our friend here, and the
  men
Bringing him seem to be servants of my
  house.
But you can tell, if you have ever seen
5   him.

Enter SHEPHERD *escorted by servants.*

CHORAGOS. I know him, he was Laïos'
  man. You can trust him.
OEDIPUS. Tell me first, you from Corinth:
  is this the shepherd
We were discussing?

MESSENGER.   This is the very man.
OEDIPUS (*to* SHEPHERD). Come here. No,
  look at me. You must answer
Everything I ask.—You belonged to Laïos?   10
SHEPHERD. Yes: born his slave, brought up
  in his house.
OEDIPUS. Tell me: what kind of work did
  you do for him?
SHEPHERD. I was a shepherd of his, most
  of my life.
OEDIPUS. Where mainly did you go for
  pasturage?
SHEPHERD. Sometimes Kithairon, some-
  times the hills near-by.   15
OEDIPUS. Do you remember ever seeing
  this man out there?
SHEPHERD. What would he be doing
  there? This man?
OEDIPUS. This man standing here. Have
  you ever seen him before?
SHEPHERD. No. At least, not to my recol-
  lection.
MESSENGER. And that is not strange, my
  lord. But I'll refresh   20
His memory: he must remember when we
  two
Spent three whole seasons together,
  March to September,
On Kithairon or thereabouts. He had two
  flocks;
I had one. Each autumn I'd drive mine
  home
And he would go back with his to Laïos'
  sheepfold.—   25
Is this not true, just as I have described
  it?
SHEPHERD. True, yes; but it was all so
  long ago.
MESSENGER. Well, then: do you remem-
  ber, back in those days
That you gave me a baby boy to bring up
  as my own?
SHEPHERD. What if I did? What are you
  trying to say?   30
MESSENGER. King Oedipus was once that
  little child.
SHEPHERD. Damn you, hold your tongue!
OEDIPUS.   No more of that!
It is your tongue needs watching, not this
  man's.

---

¹⁶ **Hermês . . . Kyllenê's** Hermês, messenger
of the gods, was said to have been born on Mt.
Kyllenê.

SHEPHERD. My King, my Master, what is it I have done wrong?

OEDIPUS. You have not answered his question about the boy.

SHEPHERD. He does not know . . . He is only making trouble. . . .

OEDIPUS. Come, speak plainly, or it will go hard with you.

SHEPHERD. In God's name, do not torture an old man!

OEDIPUS. Come here, one of you; bind his arms behind him.

SHEPHERD. Unhappy king! What more do you wish to learn?

OEDIPUS. Did you give this man the child he speaks of?

SHEPHERD.   I did.
And I would to God I had died that very day.

OEDIPUS. You will die now unless you speak the truth.

SHEPHERD. Yet if I speak the truth, I am worse than dead.

OEDIPUS. Very well; since you insist upon delaying—

SHEPHERD. No! I have told you already that I gave him the boy.

OEDIPUS. Where did you get him? From your house? From somewhere else?

SHEPHERD. Not from mine, no. A man gave him to me.

OEDIPUS. Is that man here? Do you know whose slave he was?

SHEPHERD. For God's love, my King, do not ask me any more!

OEDIPUS. You are a dead man if I have to ask you again.

SHEPHERD. Then . . . Then the child was from the palace of Laïos.

OEDIPUS. A slave child? or a child of his own line?

SHEPHERD. Ah, I am on the brink of dreadful speech!

OEDIPUS. And I of dreadful hearing. Yet I must hear.

SHEPHERD. If you must be told, then . . .
               They said it was Laïos' child,
But it is your wife who can tell you about that.

OEDIPUS. My wife!—Did she give it to you?

SHEPHERD.   My lord, she did.

OEDIPUS. Do you know why?

SHEPHERD.   I was told to get rid of it.

OEDIPUS. An unspeakable mother!

SHEPHERD.   There had been prophecies . . .

OEDIPUS. Tell me.

SHEPHERD.   It was said that the boy would kill his own father.

OEDIPUS. Then why did you give him over to this old man?

SHEPHERD. I pitied the baby, my King,
And I thought that this man would take him far away
To his own country.
          He saved him—but for what a fate!
For if you are what this man says you are,
No man living is more wretched than Oedipus.

OEDIPUS. Ah God!
It was true!
              All the prophecies!
                        —Now,
O Light, may I look on you for the last time!
I, Oedipus,
Oedipus, damned in his birth, in his marriage damned,
Damned in the blood he shed with his own hand!

He rushes into the palace.

ODE IV

CHORUS. Alas for the seed of men.
                              Strophe 1
What measure shall I give these generations
That breathe on the void and are void
And exist and do not exist?

Who bears more weight of joy
Than mass of sunlight shifting in images,
Or who shall make his thought stay on
That down time drifts away?

Your splendor is all fallen.

10   O naked brow of wrath and tears,
      O change of Oedipus!
      I who saw your days call no man blest—
      Your great days like ghósts góne.

      That mind was a strong bow. *Antistrophe 1*
      Deep, how deep you drew it then, hard
15   archer,
      At a dim fearful range,
      And brought dear glory down!

      You overcame the stranger—
      The virgin with her hooking lion claws—
20   And though death sang, stood like a tower
      To make pale Thebes take heart.

      Fortress against our sorrow!

      Divine king, giver of laws,
      Majestic Oedipus!
      No prince in Thebes had ever such re-
25   nown,
      No prince won such grace of power.

      And now of all men ever known   *Strophe 2*
      Most pitiful is this man's story:
      His fortunes are most changed, his state
30   Fallen to a low slave's
      Ground under bitter fate.

      O Oedipus, most royal one!
      The great door that expelled you to the
          light
      Gave at night—ah, gave night to your
          glory:
35   As to the father, to the fathering son.

      All understood too late.

      How could that queen whom Laïos won,
      The garden that he harrowed at his height,
      Be silent when that act was done?

      But all eyes fail before time's eye,
40   *Antistrophe 2*
      All actions come to justice there.
      Though never willed, though far down the
          deep past,
      Your bed, your dread sirings,
      Are brought to book at last.
45   Child by Laïos doomed to die,
      Then doomed to lose that fortunate little
          death,

Would God you never took breath in this
          air
That with my wailing lips I take to cry:

For I weep the world's outcast.

I was blind, and now I can tell why: 50
Asleep, for you had given ease of breath
To Thebes, while the false years went by.

EXODOS

Enter, from the palace, SECOND MESSENGER.

SECOND MESSENGER. Elders of Thebes,
          most honored in this land,
What horrors are yours to see and hear,
          what weight
Of sorrow to be endured, if, true to your
          birth,
You venerate the line of Labdakos!
I think neither Istros nor Phasis, those
          great rivers,   5
Could purify this place of the corruption
It shelters now, or soon must bring to
          light—
Evil not done unconsciously, but willed.

The greatest griefs are those we cause
          ourselves.
CHORAGOS. Surely, friend, we have grief
          enough already;   10
What new sorrow do you mean?
SECOND MESSENGER.   The Queen is dead.
CHORAGOS. Iocastê? Dead? But at whose
          hand?
SECOND MESSENGER.   Her own.
The full horror of what happened you
          cannot know,
For you did not see it; but I, who did, will
          tell you
As clearly as I can how she met her
          death.   15

When she had left us,
In passionate silence, passing through the
          court,
She ran to her apartment in the house,
Her hair clutched by the fingers of both
          hands.
She closed the doors behind her; then, by
          that bed   20

Where long ago the fatal son was
  conceived—
That son who should bring about his father's death—
We heard her call upon Laïos, dead so
  many years,
And heard her wail for the double fruit of
  her marriage,
A husband by her husband, children by
25   her child.

Exactly how she died I do not know:
For Oedipus burst in moaning and would
  not let us
Keep vigil to the end: it was by him
As he stormed about the room that our
  eyes were caught.
From one to another of us he went, beg-
30   ging a sword,
Cursing the wife who was not his wife,
  the mother
Whose womb had carried his own children
  and himself.
I do not know: it was none of us aided
  him,
But surely one of the gods was in control!
35 For with a dreadful cry
He hurled his weight, as though wrenched
  out of himself,
At the twin doors: the bolts gave, and he
  rushed in.
And there we saw her hanging, her body
  swaying
From the cruel cord she had noosed about
  her neck.
A great sob broke from him heartbreaking
40   to hear,
As he loosed the rope and lowered her to
  the ground.

I would blot out from my mind what happened next!
For the King ripped from her gown the
  golden brooches
That were her ornament, and raised them,
  and plunged them down
Straight into his own eyeballs, crying, "No
45   more,
No more shall you look on the misery
  about me,

The horrors of my own doing! Too long
  you have known
The faces of those whom I should never
  have seen,
Too long been blind to those for whom I
  was searching!
From this hour, go in darkness!" And as
  he spoke,   50
He struck at his eyes—not once, but
  many times;
And the blood spattered his beard,
Bursting from his ruined sockets like red
  hail.
So from the unhappiness of two this evil
  has sprung,
A curse on the man and woman alike. The
  old   55
Happiness of the house of Labdakos
Was happiness enough: where is it today?
It is all wailing and ruin, disgrace, death—
  all
The misery of mankind that has a name—
And it is wholly and for ever theirs.   60
CHORAGOS. Is he in agony still? Is there
  no rest for him?
SECOND MESSENGER. He is calling for
  someone to lead him to the gates
So that all the children of Kadmos may
  look upon
His father's murderer, his mother's—no,
I cannot say it!
              And then he will leave Thebes,   65
Self-exiled, in order that the curse
Which he himself pronounced may depart
  from the house.
He is weak, and there is none to lead him,
So terrible is his suffering.
              But you will see:
Look, the doors are opening; in a moment   70
You will see a thing that would crush a
  heart of stone.
The central door is opened; OEDIPUS,
blinded, is led in.
CHORAGOS. Dreadful indeed for men to
  see.
Never have my own eyes
Looked on a sight so full of fear.

Oedipus!   75

What madness came upon you, what
    daemon°
Leaped on your life with heavier
Punishment than a mortal man can bear?
No: I cannot even
80 Look at you, poor ruined one.
And I would speak, question, ponder,
If I were able. No.
You make me shudder.
OEDIPUS. God. God.
85 Is there a sorrow greater?
Where shall I find harbor in this world?
My voice is hurled far on a dark wind.
What has God done to me?
CHORAGOS. Too terrible to think of, or to
    see.

90 OEDIPUS. O cloud of night,   *Strophe 1*
Never to be turned away: night coming on,
I cannot tell how: night like a shroud!
My fair winds brought me here.
                   Oh God. Again
The pain of the spikes where I had sight,
95 The flooding pain
Of memory, never to be gouged out.
CHORAGOS. This is not strange.
You suffer it all twice over, remorse in
    pain,
Pain in remorse.

100 OEDIPUS. Ah dear friend   *Antistrophe 1*
Are you faithful even yet, you alone?
Are you still standing near me, will you
    stay here,
Patient, to care for the blind?
                 The blind man!
Yet even blind I know who it is attends
    me,
105 By the voice's tone—
Though my new darkness hide the com-
    forter.
CHORAGOS. Oh fearful act!
What god was it drove you to rake black
Night across your eyes?
110 OEDIPUS. Apollo. Apollo. Dear *Strophe 2*
Children, the god was Apollo.
He brought my sick, sick fate upon me.
But the blinding hand was my own!

⁷⁶ **daemon** a spirit, not necessarily evil

How could I bear to see
When all my sight was horror everywhere? 115
CHORAGOS. Everywhere; that is true.
OEDIPUS. And now what is left?
Images? Love? A greeting even,
Sweet to the senses? Is there anything?
Ah, no, friends: lead me away.   120
Lead me away from Thebes.
                Lead the great wreck
And hell of Oedipus, whom the gods hate.
CHORAGOS. Your fate is clear, you are not
    blind to that.
Would God you had never found it out!

OEDIPUS. Death take the man who un-
    bound   *Antistrophe 2* 125
My feet on that hillside
And delivered me from death to life! What
    life?
If only I had died,
This weight of monstrous doom
Could not have dragged me and my dar-
    lings down.   130
CHORAGOS. I would have wished the same.
OEDIPUS. Oh never to have come here
With my father's blood upon me! Never
To have been the man they call his moth-
    er's husband!
Oh accurst! Oh child of evil,   135
To have entered that wretched bed—
              the selfsame one!
More primal than sin itself, this fell to me.
CHORAGOS. I do not know how I can an-
    swer you.
You were better dead than alive and blind.
OEDIPUS. Do not counsel me any more.
    This punishment   140
That I have laid upon myself is just.
If I had eyes,
I do not know how I could bear the sight
Of my father, when I came to the house of
    Death,
Or my mother: for I have sinned against
    them both   145
So vilely that I could not make my peace
By strangling my own life.
           Or do you think my children,
Born as they were born, would be sweet
    to my eyes?

Ah never, never! Nor this town with its
    high walls,
Nor the holy images of the gods.

150   For I,

Thrice miserable—Oedipus, noblest of all
    the line
Of Kadmos, have condemned myself to
    enjoy
These things no more, by my own male-
    diction
Expelling that man whom the gods de-
    clared
155 To be a defilement in the house of Laïos.
After exposing the rankness of my own
    guilt,
How could I look men frankly in the eyes?
No, I swear it,
If I could have stifled my hearing at its
    source,
I would have done it and made all this
160   body
A tight cell of misery, blank to light and
    sound:
So I should have been safe in a dark agony
Beyond all recollection.
                       Ah Kithairon!

Why did you shelter me? When I was cast
    upon you,
165 Why did I not die? Then I should never
Have shown the world my execrable birth.

Ah Polybos! Corinth, city that I believed
The ancient seat of my ancestors: how fair
I seemed, your child! And all the while
    this evil
Was cancerous within me!
170   For I am sick
In my daily life, sick in my origin.

O three roads, dark ravine, woodland and
    way
Where three roads met: you, drinking my
    father's blood,
My own blood, spilled by my own hand:
    can you remember
The unspeakable things I did there, and
175   the things
I went on from there to do?
                  O marriage, marriage!

The act that engendered me, and again
    the act
Performed by the son in the same bed—
                  Ah, the net
Of incest, mingling fathers, brothers,
    sons,
With brides, wives, mothers: the last evil   180
That can be known by men: no tongue can
    say
How evil!
     No. For the love of God, conceal me
Somewhere far from Thebes; or kill me;
    or hurl me
Into the sea, away from men's eyes for
    ever.
Come, lead me. You need not fear to
    touch me.   185
Of all men, I alone can bear this guilt.

Enter CREON.

CHORAGOS. We are not the ones to decide;
    but Creon here
May fitly judge of what you ask. He only
Is left to protect the city in your place.
OEDIPUS. Alas, how can I speak to him?
    What right have I   190
To beg his courtesy whom I have deeply
    wronged?
CREON. I have not come to mock you,
    Oedipus,
Or to reproach you, either.
(*To* ATTENDANTS.)   —You, standing there:
If you have lost all respect for man's dig-
    nity,
At least respect the flame of Lord Helios: 195
Do not allow this pollution to show itself
Openly here, an affront to the earth
And Heaven's rain and the light of day. No,
    take him
Into the house as quickly as you can.
For it is proper   200
That only the close kindred see his grief.
OEDIPUS. I pray you in God's name, since
    your courtesy
Ignores my dark expectation, visiting
With mercy this man of all men most
    execrable:

205 Give me what I ask—for your good, not
    for mine.
CREON. And what is it that you would have
    me do?
OEDIPUS. Drive me out of this country as
    quickly as may be
To a place where no human voice can ever
    greet me.
CREON. I should have done that before
    now—only,
God's will had not been wholly revealed to
210   me.
OEDIPUS. But his command is plain: the
    parricide
Must be destroyed. I am that evil man.
CREON. That is the sense of it, yes; but
    as things are,
We had best discover clearly what is to be
    done.
OEDIPUS. You would learn more about a
215   man like me?
CREON. You are ready now to listen to the
    god.
OEDIPUS. I will listen. But it is to you
That I must turn for help. I beg you, hear
    me.

The woman in there—
Give her whatever funeral you think
220   proper:
She is your sister.
                    —But let me go, Creon!
Let me purge my father's Thebes of the
    pollution
Of my living here, and go out to the wild
    hills,
To Kithairon, that has won such fame with
    me,
The tomb my mother and father appointed
225   for me,
And let me die there, as they willed I
    should.
And yet I know
Death will not ever come to me through
    sickness
Or in any natural way: I have been pre-
    served
230 For some unthinkable fate. But let that be.
As for my sons, you need not care for
    them.

They are men, they will find some way to
    live.
But my poor daughters, who have shared
    my table,
Who never before have been parted from
    their father—
Take care of them, Creon; do this for me.   235
And will you let me touch them with my
    hands
A last time, and let us weep together?
Be kind, my lord,
Great prince, be kind!
                    Could I but touch them,
They would be mine again, as when I had
    my eyes.   240

Enter ANTIGONÊ *and* ISMENÊ, *attended.*

Ah, God!
It is my dearest children I hear weeping?
Has Creon pitied me and sent my daugh-
    ters?
CREON. Yes, Oedipus: I knew that they
    were dear to you
In the old days, and know you must love
    them still.   245
OEDIPUS. May God bless you for this—
    and be a friendlier
Guardian to you than he has been to me!

Children, where are you?
Come quickly to my hands: they are your
    brother's—
Hands that have brought your father's
    once clear eyes   250
To this way of seeing—
                    Ah dearest ones,
I had neither sight nor knowledge then,
    your father
By the woman who was the source of his
    own life!
And I weep for you—having no strength to
    see you—,

I weep for you when I think of the bitter-
    ness   255
That men will visit upon you all your lives.
What homes, what festivals can you attend
Without being forced to depart again in
    tears?
And when you come to marriageable age,

Where is the man, my daughters, who
260   would dare
Risk the bane that lies on all my children?
Is there any evil wanting? Your father
      killed
His father; sowed the womb of her who
      bore him;
Engendered you at the fount of his own
      existence!
That is what they will say of you.
265   Then, whom
Can you ever marry? There are no bride-
      grooms for you,
And your lives must wither away in sterile
      dreaming.
O Creon, son of Menoikeus!
You are the only father my daughters have,
Since we, their parents, are both of us
270   gone for ever.
They are your own blood: you will not let
      them
Fall into beggary and loneliness;
You will keep them from the miseries that
      are mine!
Take pity on them; see, they are only
      children,
Friendless except for you. Promise me
275   this,
Great Prince, and give me your hand in
      token of it.

CREON *clasps his right hand.*

Children:
I could say much, if you could understand
      me,
But as it is, I have only this prayer for
      you:
Live where you can, be as happy as you
280   can—

Happier, please God, than God has made
      your father!
CREON. Enough. You have wept enough.
      Now go within.
OEDIPUS. I must; but it is hard.
CREON.   Time eases all things.
OEDIPUS. But you must promise—
CREON.   Say what you desire.
OEDIPUS. Send me from Thebes!
CREON.   God grant that I may!   285
OEDIPUS. But since God hates me . . .
CREON.   No, he will grant your wish.
OEDIPUS. You promise?
CREON.   I cannot speak beyond my knowl-
      edge.
OEDIPUS. Then lead me in.
CREON.   Come now, and leave your chil-
      dren.
OEDIPUS. No! Do not take them from me!
CREON.   Think no longer
That you are in command here, but rather
      think   290
How, when you were, you served your
      own destruction.

Exeunt into the house all but the CHORUS;
the CHORAGOS *chants directly to the audience.*

CHORAGOS. Men of Thebes; look upon
      Oedipus.
This is the king who solved the famous
      riddle
And towered up, most powerful of men.
No mortal eyes but looked on him with
      envy,   295
Yet in the end ruin swept over him.
Let every man in mankind's frailty
Consider his last day; and let none
Presume on his good fortune until he find
Life, at his death, a memory without pain.   300

QUESTIONS AND SUGGESTIONS FOR WRITING

1. On the basis of the Prologue, characterize Oedipus. What additional traits are revealed in Scene I and Ode I?
2. How fair is it to say that Oedipus is morally guilty? Does he argue that he is morally
   innocent because he did not intend to do immoral deeds? Can it be said that he is
   guilty of *hubris* (see pages 741–742) but that *hubris* has nothing to to with his fall?
   Explain.

3. Oedipus says that he blinds himself in order not to look upon people he should not. What further reasons can be given? Why does he not (like his mother) commit suicide?

4. How fair is it to say that the play shows the contemptibleness of man's efforts to act intelligently?

5. How fair is it to say that in *Oedipus* the gods are evil?

6. Are the choral odes lyrical interludes that serve to separate the scenes, or do they advance the dramatic action?

7. Matthew Arnold said that Sophocles saw life steadily and saw it whole. But in this play, is Sophocles facing the facts of life or is he, on the contrary, avoiding life as it usually is and presenting a series of unnatural and outrageous coincidences?

8. Can you describe your emotions at the end of the play? Do they include pity for Oedipus? Pity for all human beings, including yourself? Fear that you might be punished for some unintended transgression? Awe, engendered by a perception of the interrelatedness of things? Relief that the story is only a story? Exhilaration?

Sophocles (Greek. 496?–406 B.C.)

ANTIGONÊ

An English Version by Dudley Fitts and Robert Fitzgerald

List of Characters

ANTIGONÊ
ISMENÊ
EURYDICÊ
CREON
HAIMON
TEIRESIAS
A SENTRY
A MESSENGER
CHORUS

Scene: *Before the palace of* CREON, *king of Thebes. A central double door, and two lateral doors. A platform extends the length of the façade, and from this platform three steps lead down into the "orchestra," or chorus-ground.*

Time: *Dawn of the day after the repulse of the Argive army from the assault on Thebes.*

PROLOGUE

ANTIGONÊ *and* ISMENÊ *enter from the central door of the palace.*

ANTIGONÊ. Ismenê, dear sister,

You would think that we had already suffered enough
For the curse on Oedipus.°

° **Oedipus,** once King of Thebes, was the father of Antigonê and Ismenê, and of their brothers Polyneicês and Eteoclês. Oedipus unwittingly killed his father, Laïos, and married his own mother, Iocastê. When he learned what he had done, he blinded himself and left Thebes. Eteoclês and Polyneicês quarreled. Polyneicês was driven out but returned to assault Thebes. In the battle each brother killed the other; Creon became king and ordered that Polyneicês be left to rot unburied on the battlefield as a traitor.

I cannot imagine any grief
That you and I have not gone through.
5   And now—
Have they told you of the new decree of
   our King Creon?
ISMENÊ. I have heard nothing: I know
That two sisters lost two brothers, a
   double death
In a single hour; and I know that the
   Argive army
10   Fled in the night; but beyond this, nothing.
ANTIGONÊ. I thought so. And that is why I
   wanted you
To come out here with me. There is
   something we must do.
ISMENÊ. Why do you speak so strangely?
ANTIGONÊ. Listen, Ismenê:
15   Creon buried our brother Eteoclês
With military honors, gave him a soldier's
   funeral,
And it was right that he should; but Poly-
   neicês,
Who fought as bravely and died as
   miserably,—
They say that Creon has sworn
No one shall bury him, no one mourn for
20   him,
But his body must lie in the fields, a
   sweet treasure
For carrion birds to find as they search for
   food.
That is what they say, and our good Creon
   is coming here
To announce it publicly; and the penalty—
Stoning to death in the public square!
25   There it is,
And now you can prove what you are:
A true sister, or a traitor to your family.
ISMENÊ. Antigonê, you are mad! What
   could I possibly do?
ANTIGONÊ. You must decide whether you
   will help me or not.
ISMENÊ. I do not understand you. Help
30   you in what?
ANTIGONÊ. Ismenê, I am going to bury
   him. Will you come?
ISMENÊ. Bury him! You have just said the
   new law forbids it.
ANTIGONÊ. He is my brother. And he is
   your brother, too.

ISMENÊ. But think of the danger! Think
   what Creon will do!
ANTIGONÊ. Creon is not strong enough to
   stand in my way.   35
ISMENÊ. Ah sister!
Oedipus died, everyone hating him
For what his own search brought to light,
   his eyes
Ripped out by his own hand; and Iocastê
   died,
His mother and wife at once: she twisted
   the cords   40
That strangled her life; and our two broth-
   ers died,
Each killed by the other's sword. And we
   are left:
But oh, Antigonê,
Think how much more terrible than these
Our own death would be if we should go
   against Creon   45
And do what he has forbidden! We are
   only women,
We cannot fight with men, Antigonê!
The law is strong, we must give in to the
   law
In this thing, and in worse. I beg the
   Dead
To forgive me, but I am helpless: I must
   yield   50
To those in authority. And I think it is
   dangerous business
To be always meddling.
ANTIGONÊ.   If that is what you think,
I should not want you, even if you asked
   to come.
You have made your choice, you can be
   what you want to be.
But I will bury him; and if I must die,   55
I say that this crime is holy: I shall lie
   down
With him in death, and I shall be as dear
To him as he to me.
                              It is the dead,
Not the living, who make the longest
   demands:
We die for ever . . .
                              You may do as you like,   60
Since apparently the laws of the gods
   mean nothing to you.
ISMENÊ. They mean a great deal to me;

but I have no strength
To break laws that were made for the
    public good.
ANTIGONÊ. That must be your excuse, I
    suppose. But as for me,
I will bury the brother I love.
65 ISMENÊ.   Antigonê,
I am so afraid for you!
ANTIGONÊ.   You need not be:
You have yourself to consider, after all.
ISMENÊ. But no one must hear of this,
    you must tell no one!
I will keep it a secret, I promise!
ANTIGONÊ.   O tell it! Tell everyone!
Think how they'll hate you when it all
70   comes out
If they learn that you knew about it all the
    time!
ISMENÊ. So fiery! You should be cold with
    fear.
ANTIGONÊ. Perhaps. But I am doing only
    what I must.
ISMENÊ. But can you do it? I say that you
    cannot.
ANTIGONÊ. Very well: when my strength
    gives out,
75 I shall do no more.
ISMENÊ. Impossible things should not be
    tried at all.
ANTIGONÊ. Go away, Ismenê:
I shall be hating you soon, and the dead
    will too,
For your words are hateful. Leave me my
    foolish plan:
I am not afraid of the danger; if it means
80   death,
It will not be the worst of deaths—death
    without honor.
ISMENÊ. Go then, if you feel that you
    must.
You are unwise,
But a loyal friend indeed to those who love
    you.

Exit into the palace. ANTIGONÊ *goes off, left.*
Enter the CHORUS.

PÁRODOS

CHORUS. Now the long blade of the sun,
    lying   *Strophe 1*

Level east to west, touches with glory
Thebes of the Seven Gates. Open, un-
    lidded
Eye of golden day! O marching light
Across the eddy and rush of Dircê's
    stream,°   5
Striking the white shields of the enemy
Thrown headlong backward from the blaze
    of morning!
CHORAGOS.° Polyneicês their commander
Roused them with windy phrases,
He the wild eagle screaming   10
Insults above our land,
His wings their shields of snow,
His crest their marshalled helms.

CHORUS. Against our seven gates in a
    yawning ring   *Antistrophe 1*
The famished spears came onward in the
    night;   15
But before his jaws were sated with our
    blood,
Or pine fire took the garland of our tow-
    ers,
He was thrown back; and as he turned,
    great Thebes—
No tender victim for his noisy power—
Rose like a dragon behind him, shouting
    war.   20
CHORAGOS. For God hates utterly
The bray of bragging tongues;
And when he beheld their smiling,
Their swagger of golden helms,
The frown of his thunder blasted   25
Their first man from our walls.

CHORUS. We heard his shout of triumph
    high in the air   *Strophe 2*
Turn to a scream; far out in a flaming arc
He fell with his windy torch, and the earth
    struck him.
And others storming in fury no less than
    his   30
Found shock of death in the dusty joy of
    battle.
CHORAGOS. Seven captains at seven gates
Yielded their clanging arms to the god
That bends the battle-line and breaks it.
These two only, brothers in blood,   35

---

⁵ **Dircê's stream** a stream west of Thebes
⁸ **Choragos** leader of the Chorus

Face to face in matchless rage,
Mirroring each the other's death,
Clashed in long combat.

CHORUS. But now in the beautiful morning
    of victory   *Antistrophe 2*
Let Thebes of the many chariots sing for
40   joy!
With hearts for dancing we'll take leave of
        war:
Our temples shall be sweet with hymns of
        praise,
And the long nights shall echo with our
        chorus.

SCENE I

CHORAGOS. But now at last our new King
        is coming:
Creon of Thebes, Menoikeus' son.
In this auspicious dawn of his reign
What are the new complexities
5   That shifting Fate has woven for him?
What is his counsel? Why has he sum-
        moned
The old men to hear him?

Enter CREON *from the palace, center. He addresses the* CHORUS *from the top step.*

CREON. Gentlemen: I have the honor to inform you that our Ship of State, which re-
10   cent storms have threatened to destroy, has
come safely to harbor at last, guided by the
merciful wisdom of Heaven. I have summoned you here this morning because I
know that I can depend upon you: your de-
15   votion to King Laïos was absolute; you
never hesitated in your duty to our late
ruler Oedipus; and when Oedipus died,
your loyalty was transferred to his children.
Unfortunately, as you know, his two sons,
20   the princes Eteoclês and Polyneicês, have
killed each other in battle; and I, as the
next in blood, have succeeded to the full
power of the throne.
    I am aware, of course, that no Ruler can
25   expect complete loyalty from his subjects
until he has been tested in office. Nevertheless, I say to you at the very outset that I
have nothing but contempt for the kind of
Governor who is afraid, for whatever rea-

son, to follow the course that he knows is   30
best for the State; and as for the man who
sets private friendship above the public
welfare,—I have no use for him, either. I
call God to witness that if I saw my country
headed for ruin, I should not be afraid to   35
speak out plainly; and I need hardly remind
you that I would never have any dealings
with an enemy of the people. No one values
friendship more highly than I; but we must
remember that friends made at the risk of   40
wrecking our Ship are not real friends at all.
    These are my principles, at any rate, and
that is why I have made the following decision concerning the sons of Oedipus: Eteoclês, who died as a man should die, fighting   45
for his country, is to be buried with full military honors, with all the ceremony that is
usual when the greatest heroes die; but his
brother Polyneicês, who broke his exile to
come back with fire and sword against his   50
native city and the shrines of his fathers'
gods, whose one idea was to spill the blood
of his blood and sell his own people into
slavery—Polyneicês, I say, is to have no
burial: no man is to touch him or say the   55
least prayer for him; he shall lie on the
plain, unburied; and the birds and the scav-
enging dogs can do with him whatever they
like.
    This is my command, and you can see   60
the wisdom behind it. As long as I am King,
no traitor is going to be honored with the
loyal man. But whoever shows by word and
deed that he is on the side of the State,—
he shall have my respect while he is living   65
and my reverence when he is dead.

CHORAGOS. If that is your will, Creon son of
        Menoikeus,
You have the right to enforce it: we are
    yours.

CREON. That is my will. Take care that you
    do your part.

CHORAGOS. We are old men: let the youn-
    ger ones carry it out.   70

CREON. I do not mean that: the sentries
    have been appointed.

CHORAGOS. Then what is it that you would
    have us do?

CREON. You will give no support to who-
    ever breaks this law.

CHORAGOS. Only a crazy man is in love with
    death!

75 CREON. And death it is; yet money talks,
    and the wisest
Have sometimes been known to count a few
    coins too many.

Enter SENTRY *from left.*

SENTRY. I'll not say that I'm out of breath
from running, King, because every time I
stopped to think about what I have to tell
80 you, I felt like going back. And all the time
a voice kept saying, "You fool, don't you
know you're walking straight into trouble?";
and then another voice: "Yes, but if you let
somebody else get the news to Creon first,
85 it will be even worse than that for you!"
But good sense won out, at least I hope it
was good sense, and here I am with a story
that makes no sense at all; but I'll tell it
anyhow, because, as they say, what's going
90 to happen's going to happen and—
CREON. Come to the point. What have you
    to say?
SENTRY. I did not do it. I did not see who
did it. You must not punish me for what
someone else has done.
CREON. A comprehensive defense! More
95   effective, perhaps,
If I knew its purpose. Come: what is it?
SENTRY. A dreadful thing . . . I don't know
    how to put it—
CREON. Out with it!
SENTRY.   Well, then;
The dead man—
         Polyneicês—

Pause. The SENTRY *is overcome, fumbles for
words.* CREON *waits impassively.*

              out there—
              someone,—
New dust on the slimy flesh!

Pause. No sign from CREON.

100 Someone has given it burial that way, and
Gone . . .

Long pause. CREON *finally speaks with
deadly control.*

CREON. And the man who dared do this?

SENTRY.   I swear I
Do not know! You must believe me!
                Listen:
The ground was dry, not a sign of digging,
    no,
Not a wheeltrack in the dust, no trace of
    anyone.   105
It was when they relieved us this morning:
    and one of them,
The corporal, pointed to it.
              There it was,
The strangest—
              Look:
The body, just mounded over with light
    dust: you see?
Not buried really, but as if they'd covered
    it   110
Just enough for the ghost's peace. And no
    sign
Of dogs or any wild animal that had been
    there.

And then what a scene there was! Every
    man of us
Accusing the other: we all proved the
    other man did it,
We all had proof that we could not have
    done it.   115
We were ready to take hot iron in our
    hands,
Walk through fire, swear by all the gods,
It was not I!
I do not know who it was, but it was not I!

CREON'S *rage has been mounting steadily,
but the* SENTRY *is too intent upon his story to
notice it.*

And then, when this came to nothing,
    someone said   120
A thing that silenced us and made us stare
Down at the ground: you had to be told
    the news,
And one of us had to do it! We threw the
    dice,
And the bad luck fell to me. So here I am,
No happier to be here than you are to
    have me: 125
Nobody likes the man who brings bad
    news.

CHORAGOS. I have been wondering, King:
　　can it be that the gods have done
　　this?

CREON. *(furiously).* Stop!
Must you doddering wrecks
Go out of your heads entirely? "The
130　　gods"!
Intolerable!
The gods favor this corpse? Why? How
　　had he served them?
Tried to loot their temples, burn their
　　images,
Yes, and the whole State, and its laws
　　with it!
Is it your senile opinion that the gods love
135　　to honor bad men?
A pious thought!—
　　　　　　No, from the very beginning
There have been those who have whis-
　　pered together,
Stiff-necked anarchists, putting their heads
　　together,
Scheming against me in alleys. These are
　　the men,
And they have bribed my own guard to do
140　　this thing.
(Sententiously.) Money!
There's nothing in the world so demoraliz-
　　ing as money.
Down go your cities,
Homes gone, men gone, honest hearts
　　corrupted,
Crookedness of all kinds, and all for
　　money!
145　*(To* SENTRY.*) But you—!*
I swear by God and by the throne of God,
The man who has done this thing shall pay
　　for it!
Find that man, bring him here to me, or
　　your death
Will be the least of your problems: I'll
　　string you up
Alive, and there will be certain ways to
150　　make you
Discover your employer before you die;
And the process may teach you a lesson
　　you seem to have missed:
The dearest profit is sometimes all too
　　dear:

That depends on the source. Do you
　　understand me?
A fortune won is often misfortune.　　155
SENTRY. King, may I speak?
CREON.　　Your very voice distresses me.
SENTRY. Are you sure that it is my voice,
　　and not your conscience?
CREON. By God, he wants to analyze me
　　now!
SENTRY. It is not what I say, but what has
　　been done, that hurts you.
CREON. You talk too much.
SENTRY.　　Maybe; but I've done nothing.　160
CREON. Sold your soul for some silver:
　　that's all you've done.
SENTRY. How dreadful it is when the right
　　judge judges wrong!
CREON. Your figures of speech
May entertain you now; but unless you
　　bring me the man,
You will get little profit from them in the
　　end.　　165

Exit CREON *into the palace.*

SENTRY. "Bring me the man"—!
I'd like nothing better than bringing him
　　the man!
But bring him or not, you have seen the
　　last of me here.
At any rate, I am safe!　　*(Exit* SENTRY.*)*

ODE I

CHORUS. Numberless are the world's
　　wonders, but none　　*Strophe 1*
More wonderful than man; the stormgray
　　sea
Yields to his prows, the huge crests bear
　　him high;
Earth, holy and inexhaustible, is graven
With shining furrows where his plows have
　　gone　　　　　　　　　　　　　　　5
Year after year, the timeless labor of stal-
　　lions.

The lightboned birds and beasts that cling
　　to cover,　　*Antistrophe 1*
The lithe fish lighting their reaches of dim
　　water,

All are taken, tamed in the net of his
    mind;
10   The lion on the hill, the wild horse windy-
    maned,
Resign to him; and his blunt yoke has
    broken
The sultry shoulders of the mountain bull.

Words also, and thought as rapid as air,
                      Strophe 2
He fashions to his good use; statecraft is
    his,
And his the skill that deflects the arrows
15   of snow,
The spears of winter rain: from every
    wind
He has made himself secure—from all but
    one:
In the late wind of death he cannot stand.

O clear intelligence, force beyond all
    measure!   *Antistrophe 2*
20   O fate of man, working both good and evil!
When the laws are kept, how proudly his
    city stands!
When the laws are broken, what of his
    city then?
Never may the anárchic man find rest at
    my hearth,
Never be it said that my thoughts are his
    thoughts.

SCENE II

Reenter SENTRY *leading* ANTIGONÊ.

CHORAGOS. What does this mean? Surely
    this captive woman
Is the Princess, Antigonê. Why should she
    be taken?
SENTRY. Here is the one who did it! We
    caught her
In the very act of burying him.—Where is
    Creon?
CHORAGOS. Just coming from the house.

Enter CREON, *center.*

5   CREON.   What has happened?
Why have you come back so soon?
SENTRY (*expansively*).   O King,

A man should never be too sure of any-
    thing:
I would have sworn
That you'd not see me here again: your
    anger
Frightened me so, and the things you
    threatened me with;   10
But how could I tell then
That I'd be able to solve the case so
    soon?
No dice-throwing this time: I was only too
    glad to come!
Here is this woman. She is the guilty one:
We found her trying to bury him.   15
Take her, then; question her; judge her as
    you will.
I am through with the whole thing now,
    and glad of it.
CREON. But this is Antigonê! Why have
    you brought her here?
SENTRY. She was burying him, I tell you!
CREON (*severely*).   Is this the truth?
SENTRY. I saw her with my own eyes. Can
    I say more?   20
CREON. The details: come, tell me
    quickly!
SENTRY.   It was like this:
After those terrible threats of yours, King,
We went back and brushed the dust away
    from the body.
The flesh was soft by now, and stinking,
So we sat on a hill to windward and kept
    guard.   25
No napping this time! We kept each other
    awake.
But nothing happened until the white
    round sun
Whirled in the center of the round sky
    over us:
Then, suddenly,
A storm of dust roared up from the earth,
    and the sky   30
Went out, the plain vanished with all its
    trees
In the stinging dark. We closed our eyes
    and endured it.
The whirlwind lasted a long time, but it
    passed;
And then we looked, and there was Antig-
    onê!

35 I have seen
A mother bird come back to a stripped
    nest, heard
Her crying bitterly a broken note or two
For the young ones stolen. Just so, when
    this girl
Found the bare corpse, and all her love's
    work wasted,
She wept, and cried on heaven to damn
40   the hands
That had done this thing.
                And then she brought more dust
And sprinkled wine three times for her
    brother's ghost.

We ran and took her at once. She was not
    afraid,
Not even when we charged her with what
    she had done.
She denied nothing.
45   And this was a comfort to me,
And some uneasiness: for it is a good
    thing
To escape from death, but it is no great
    pleasure
To bring death to a friend.
                      Yet I always say
There is nothing so comfortable as your
    own safe skin!
CREON *(slowly, dangerously)*. And you,
50   Antigonê,
You with your head hanging,—do you
    confess this thing?
ANTIGONÊ. I do. I deny nothing.
CREON *(to* SENTRY*)*.   You may go.
                    (Exit SENTRY.*)*
(To ANTIGONÊ.*)* Tell me, tell me briefly:
Had you heard my proclamation touching
    this matter?
ANTIGONÊ. It was public. Could I help
55   hearing it?
CREON. And yet you dared defy the law.
ANTIGONÊ.   I dared.
It was not God's proclamation. That final
    Justice
That rules the world below makes no such
    laws.

Your edict, King, was strong,

But all your strength is weakness itself
    against   60
The immortal unrecorded laws of God.
They are not merely now: they were, and
    shall be,
Operative for ever, beyond man utterly.

I knew I must die, even without your
    decree:
I am only mortal. And if I must die   65
Now, before it is my time to die,
Surely this is no hardship: can anyone
Living, as I live, with evil all about me,
Think Death less than a friend? This death
    of mine
Is of no importance; but if I had left my   70
    brother
Lying in death unburied, I should have
    suffered.
Now I do not.
              You smile at me. Ah Creon,
Think me a fool, if you like; but it may
    well be
That a fool convicts me of folly.
CHORAGOS. Like father, like daughter: both
    headstrong, deaf to reason!   75
She has never learned to yield:
CREON.   She has much to learn.
The inflexible heart breaks first, the
    toughest iron
Cracks first, and the wildest horses bend
    their necks
At the pull of the smallest curb.
                        Pride? In a slave?
This girl is guilty of a double insolence,   80
Breaking the given laws and boasting of it.
Who is the man here,
She or I, if this crime goes unpunished?
Sister's child, or more than sister's child,
Or closer yet in blood—she and her sister   85
Win bitter death for this!
(To SERVANTS.*)*   Go, some of you,
Arrest Ismenê. I accuse her equally.
Bring her: you will find her sniffling in the
    house there.

Her mind's a traitor: crimes kept in the
    dark
Cry for light, and the guardian brain shud-
    ders;   90

But how much worse than this
Is brazen boasting of barefaced anarchy!
ANTIGONÊ. Creon, what more do you want
   than my death?
CREON.   Nothing.
That gives me everything.
ANTIGONÊ.   Then I beg you: kill me.
This talking is a great weariness: your

95   words
Are distasteful to me, and I am sure that
   mine
Seem so to you. And yet they should not
   seem so:
I should have praise and honor for what I
   have done.
All these men here would praise me
Were their lips not frozen shut with fear of

100   you.
(Bitterly.) Ah the good fortune of kings,
Licensed to say and do whatever they
   please!
CREON. You are alone here in that opinion.
ANTIGONÊ. No, they are with me. But
   they keep their tongues in leash.
CREON. Maybe. But you are guilty, and

105   they are not.
ANTIGONÊ. There is no guilt in reverence
   for the dead.
CREON. But Eteoclês—was he not your
   brother too?
ANTIGONÊ. My brother too.
CREON.   And you insult his memory?
ANTIGONÊ *(softly).* The dead man would
   not say that I insult it.

110 CREON. He would: for you honor a traitor
   as much as him.
ANTIGONÊ. His own brother, traitor or not,
   and equal in blood.
CREON. He made war on his country.
   Eteoclês defended it.
ANTIGONÊ. Nevertheless, there are honors
   due all the dead.
CREON. But not the same for the wicked
   as for the just.

115 ANTIGONÊ. Ah Creon, Creon,
Which of us can say what the gods hold
   wicked?
CREON. An enemy is an enemy, even
   dead.

ANTIGONÊ. It is my nature to join in love,
   not hate.
CREON *(finally losing patience).* Go join
   them then; if you must have your
   love,
Find it in hell!
CHORAGOS. But see, Ismenê comes: 120

Enter ISMENÊ, *guarded.*

Those tears are sisterly, the cloud
That shadows her eyes rains down gentle
   sorrow.
CREON. You too, Ismenê,
Snake in my ordered house, sucking my
   blood   125
Stealthily—and all the time I never knew
That these two sisters were aiming at my
   throne!
                           Ismenê,
Do you confess your share in this crime,
   or deny it?
Answer me.
ISMENÊ. Yes, if she will let me say so. I
   am guilty.   130
ANTIGONÊ *(coldly).* No, Ismenê. You have
   no right to say so.
You would not help me, and I will not have
   you help me.
ISMENÊ. But now I know what you meant;
   and I am here
To join you, to take my share of punish-
   ment.
ANTIGONÊ. The dead man and the gods
   who rule the dead   135
Know whose act this was. Words are not
   friends.
ISMENÊ. Do you refuse me, Antigonê? I
   want to die with you:
I too have a duty that I must discharge to
   the dead.
ANTIGONÊ. You shall not lessen my death
   by sharing it.
ISMENÊ. What do I care for life when you
   are dead?   140
ANTIGONÊ. Ask Creon. You're always
   hanging on his opinions.
ISMENÊ. You are laughing at me. Why,
   Antigonê?
ANTIGONÊ. It's a joyless laughter, Ismenê.

ISMENÊ.   But can I do nothing?

ANTIGONÊ. Yes. Save yourself. I shall not
    envy you.

145 There are those who will praise you; I
    shall have honor, too.

ISMENÊ. But we are equally guilty!

ANTIGONÊ.   No more, Ismenê.
You are alive, but I belong to Death.

CREON *(to the* CHORUS*)*. Gentlemen, I beg
    you to observe these girls:
One has just now lost her mind; the other,

150 It seems, has never had a mind at all.

ISMENÊ. Grief teaches the steadiest minds
    to waver, King.

CREON. Yours certainly did, when you
    assumed guilt with the guilty!

ISMENÊ. But how could I go on living
    without her?

CREON.   You are.
She is already dead.

ISMENÊ.   But your own son's bride!

CREON. There are places enough for him

155   to push his plow.
I want no wicked women for my sons!

ISMENÊ. O dearest Haimon, how your
    father wrongs you!

CREON. I've had enough of your childish
    talk of marriage!

CHORAGOS. Do you really intend to steal
    this girl from your son?

CREON. No; Death will do that for me.

160 CHORAGOS.   Then she must die?

CREON *(ironically)*. You dazzle me.
            —But enough of this talk!
(To GUARDS.*)* You, there, take them away
    and guard them well:
For they are but women, and even brave
    men run
When they see Death coming.
    Exeunt ISMENÊ, ANTIGONÊ, *and* GUARDS.

ODE II

CHORUS. Fortunate is the man who has
    never tasted God's vengeance!
                    Strophe 1
Where once the anger of heaven has
    struck, that house is shaken

For ever: damnation rises behind each
    child
Like a wave cresting out of the black
    northeast,
When the long darkness under sea roars
    up   5
And bursts drumming death upon the
    windwhipped sand.

I have seen this gathering sorrow from
    time long past   *Antistrophe 1*
Loom upon Oedipus' children: generation
    from generation
Takes the compulsive rage of the enemy
    god.
So lately this last flower of Oedipus' line   10
Drank the sunlight! but now a passionate
    word
And a handful of dust have closed up all its
    beauty.

What mortal arrogance   *Strophe 2*
Transcends the wrath of Zeus?
Sleep cannot lull him nor the effortless
    long months   15
Of the timeless gods: but he is young for
    ever,
And his house is the shining day of high
    Olympos.
    All that is and shall be,
    And all the past, is his.
No pride on earth is free of the curse of
    heaven.   20

The straying dreams of men *Antistrophe 2*
    May bring them ghosts of joy:
But as they drowse, the waking embers
    burn them;
Or they walk with fixed eyes, as blind men
    walk.
But the ancient wisdom speaks for our
    own time: 25
    Fate works most for woe
    With Folly's fairest show.
Man's little pleasure is the spring of sor-
    row.

SCENE III

CHORAGOS. But here is Haimon, King, the
    last of all your sons.

Is it grief for Antigonê that brings him
    here,
And bitterness at being robbed of his
    bride?

Enter HAIMON.

CREON. We shall soon see, and no need of
    diviners.
              —Son,
You have heard my final judgment on that
5   girl:
Have you come here hating me, or have
    you come
With deference and with love, whatever I
    do?
HAIMON. I am your son, father. You are
    my guide.
You make things clear for me, and I obey
    you.
No marriage means more to me than your
10   continuing wisdom.
CREON. Good. That is the way to behave:
    subordinate
Everything else, my son, to your father's
    will.
This is what a man prays for, that he may
    get
Sons attentive and dutiful in his house,
15 Each one hating his father's enemies,
Honoring his father's friends. But if his
    sons
Fail him, if they turn out unprofitably,
What has he fathered but trouble for him-
    self
And amusement for the malicious?
                    So you are right
20 Not to lose your head over this woman.
Your pleasure with her would soon grow
    cold, Haimon,
And then you'd have a hellcat in bed and
    elsewhere.
Let her find her husband in Hell!
Of all the people in this city, only she
Has had contempt for my law and broken
25   it.

Do you want me to show myself weak
    before the people?
Or to break my sworn word? No, and I
    will not.

The woman dies.
I suppose she'll plead "family ties." Well,
    let her.
If I permit my own family to rebel,   30
How shall I earn the world's obedience?
Show me the man who keeps his house in
    hand,
He's fit for public authority.
                   I'll have no dealings
With lawbreakers, critics of the govern-
    ment:
Whoever is chosen to govern should be
    obeyed—   35
Must be obeyed, in all things, great and
    small,
Just and unjust! O Haimon,
The man who knows how to obey, and
    that man only,
Knows how to give commands when the
    time comes.
You can depend on him, no matter how
    fast   40
The spears come: he's a good soldier, he'll
    stick it out.

Anarchy, anarchy! Show me a greater evil!
This is why cities tumble and the great
    houses rain down,
This is what scatters armies!
No, no: good lives are made so by disci-
    pline.   45
We keep the laws then, and the law-
    makers,
And no woman shall seduce us. If we
    must lose,
Let's lose to a man, at least! Is a woman
    stronger than we?
CHORAGOS. Unless time has rusted my
    wits,
What you say, King, is said with point and
    dignity.   50
HAIMON *(boyishly earnest)*. Father:
Reason is God's crowning gift to man, and
    you are right
To warn me against losing mine. I cannot
    say—
I hope that I shall never want to say!—
    that you
Have reasoned badly. Yet there are other
    men   55

Who can reason, too; and their opinions
    might be helpful.
You are not in a position to know every-
    thing
That people say or do, or what they feel:
Your temper terrifies—everyone
60 Will tell you only what you like to hear.
But I, at any rate, can listen; and I have
    heard them
Muttering and whispering in the dark
    about this girl.
They say no woman has ever, so unrea-
    sonably,
Died so shameful a death for a generous
    act:
"She covered her brother's body. Is this
65   indecent?
She kept him from dogs and vultures. Is
    this a crime?
Death?—She should have all the honor
    that we can give her!"

This is the way they talk out there in the
    city.

You must believe me:
Nothing is closer to me than your happi-
70   ness.
What could be closer? Must not any son
Value his father's fortune as his father
    does his?
I beg you, do not be unchangeable:
Do not believe that you alone can be right.
75 The man who thinks that,
The man who maintains that only he has
    the power
To reason correctly, the gift to speak, the
    soul—
A man like that, when you know him,
    turns out empty.

It is not reason never to yield to reason!

In flood time you can see how some trees
80   bend,
And because they bend, even their twigs
    are safe,
While stubborn trees are torn up, roots
    and all.
And the same thing happens in sailing:

Make your sheet fast, never slacken,—
    and over you go,
Head over heels and under: and there's
    your voyage.   85
Forget you are angry! Let yourself be
    moved!
I know I am young; but please let me say
    this:
The ideal condition
Would be, I admit, that men should be
    right by instinct;
But since we are all too likely to go astray,   90
The reasonable thing is to learn from
    those who can teach.
CHORAGOS. You will do well to listen to
    him, King,
If what he says is sensible. And you,
    Haimon,
Must listen to your father.—Both speak
    well.
CREON. You consider it right for a man of
    my years and experience   95
To go to school to a boy?
HAIMON.   It is not right
If I am wrong. But if I am young, and
    right,
What does my age matter?
CREON. You think it right to stand up for
    an anarchist?
HAIMON. Not at all. I pay no respect to
    criminals.   100
CREON. Then she is not a criminal?
HAIMON. The City would deny it, to a
    man.
CREON. And the City proposes to teach
    me how to rule?
HAIMON. Ah. Who is it that's talking like a
    boy now?
CREON. My voice is the one voice giving
    orders in this City!   105
HAIMON. It is no City if it takes orders
    from one voice.
CREON. The State is the King!
HAIMON.   Yes, if the State is a desert.

Pause.

CREON. This boy, it seems, has sold out
    to a woman.
HAIMON. If you are a woman: my concern
    is only for you.

CREON. So? Your "concern"! In a public
110   brawl with your father!
HAIMON. How about you, in a public brawl
with justice?
CREON. With justice, when all that I do is
within my rights?
HAIMON. You have no right to trample on
God's right.
CREON *(completely out of control).* Fool,
adolescent fool! Taken in by a woman!
HAIMON. You'll never see me taken in by
115   anything vile.
CREON. Every word you say is for her!
HAIMON *(quietly, darkly).*   And for you.
And for me. And for the gods under the
earth.
CREON. You'll never marry her while she
lives.
HAIMON. Then she must die.—But her
death will cause another.
120   CREON. Another?
Have you lost your senses? Is this an open
threat?
HAIMON. There is no threat in speaking to
emptiness.
CREON. I swear you'll regret this superior
tone of yours!
You are the empty one!
HAIMON.   If you were not my father,
125   I'd say you were perverse.
CREON. You girlstruck fool, don't play at
words with me!
HAIMON. I am sorry. You prefer silence.
CREON.   Now, by God—!
I swear, by all the gods in heaven above
us,
You'll watch it, I swear you shall!
(To the SERVANTS*)*   Bring her out!
Bring the woman out! Let her die before
130   his eyes!
Here, this instant, with her bridegroom
beside her!
HAIMON. Not here, no; she will not die
here, King.
And you will never see my face again.
Go on raving as long as you've a friend to
endure you.   *(Exit* HAIMON.*)*
135   CHORAGOS. Gone, gone.
Creon, a young man in a rage is danger-
ous!

CREON. Let him do, or dream to do, more
than a man can.
He shall not save these girls from death.
CHORAGOS.   These girls?
You have sentenced them both?
CREON.   No, you are right.
I will not kill the one whose hands are
clean.   140
CHORAGOS. But Antigone?
CREON *(somberly).* I will carry her far away
Out there in the wilderness, and lock her
Living in a vault of stone. She shall have
food,
As the custom is, to absolve the State of
her death.
And there let her pray to the gods of hell: 145
They are her only gods:
Perhaps they will show her an escape
from death,
Or she may learn,
                                        though late,
That piety shown the dead is pity in
vain.   *(Exit* CREON.*)*

ODE III

CHORUS. Love, unconquerable   *Strophe*
Waster of rich men, keeper
Of warm lights and all-night vigil
In the soft face of a girl:
Sea-wanderer, forest-visitor!   5
Even the pure Immortals cannot escape
you,
And mortal man, in his one day's dusk,
Trembles before your glory.

Surely you swerve upon ruin   *Antistrophe*
The just man's consenting heart,   10
As here you have made bright anger
Strike between father and son—
And none has conquered but Love!
A girl's glánce wórking the will of heaven:
Pleasure to her alone who mocks us,   15
Merciless Aphroditê.°

Ode III. ¹⁶ **Aphroditê** goddess of love

SCENE IV

CHORAGOS (*as* ANTIGONÊ *enters guarded*).
   But I can no longer stand in awe of
     this,
Nor, seeing what I see, keep back my
     tears.
Here is Antigonê, passing to that chamber
Where all find sleep at last.

ANTIGONÊ. Look upon me, friends, and
5   pity me   *Strophe 1*
Turning back at the night's edge to say
Good-by to the sun that shines for me no
     longer;
Now sleepy Death
Summons me down to Acheron,° that cold
     shore:
There is no bridesong there, nor any
10   music.
CHORUS. Yet not unpraised, not without a
     kind of honor,
You walk at last into the underworld;
Untouched by sickness, broken by no
     sword.
What woman has ever found your way to
     death?

ANTIGONÊ. How often I have heard the
15   story of Niobê,°   *Antistrophe 1*
Tantalos' wretched daughter, how the
     stone
Clung fast about her, ivy-close: and they
     say
The rain falls endlessly
And sifting soft snow; her tears are never
     done.
20   I feel the loneliness of her death in mine.
CHORUS. But she was born of heaven, and
     you
Are woman, woman-born. If her death is
     yours,

Scene IV. ° **Acheron** a river of the underworld,
which was ruled by Hades ¹⁵ **Niobê** Niobê
boasted of her numerous children, provoking
Leto, the mother of Apollo, to destroy them.
Niobê wept profusely, and finally was turned into
a stone on Mount Sipylus, whose streams are
her tears.

A mortal woman's, is this not for you
Glory in our world and in the world be-
     yond?

ANTIGONÊ. You laugh at me. Ah, friends,
     friends,   *Strophe 2*   25
Can you not wait until I am dead? O
     Thebes,
O men many-charioted, in love with For-
     tune,
Dear springs of Dircê, sacred Theban
     grove,
Be witnesses for me, denied all pity,
Unjustly judged! and think a word of love   30
For her whose path turns
Under dark earth, where there are no
     more tears.
CHORUS. You have passed beyond human
     daring and come at last
Into a place of stone where Justice sits.
I cannot tell   35
What shape of your father's guilt appears
     in this.

ANTIGONÊ. You have touched it at last:
     that bridal bed   *Antistrophe 2*
Unspeakable, horror of son and mother
     mingling:
Their crime, infection of all our family!
O Oedipus, father and brother!   40
Your marriage strikes from the grave to
     murder mine.
I have been a stranger here in my own
     land:
All my life
The blasphemy of my birth has followed
     me.
CHORUS. Reverence is a virtue, but
     strength   45
Lives in established law: that must prevail.
You have made your choice,
Your death is the doing of your conscious
     hand.
ANTIGONÊ. Then let me go, since all your
     words are bitter,   *Epode*
And the very light of the sun is cold to
     me.   50
Lead me to my vigil, where I must have
Neither love nor lamentation; no song, but
     silence.

CREON *interrupts impatiently.*

CREON. If dirges and planned lamentations
    could put off death,
Men would be singing for ever.
(To the SERVANTS.*)*   Take her, go!
You know your orders: take her to the
55   vault
And leave her alone there. And if she lives
    or dies,
That's her affair, not ours: our hands are
    clean.

ANTIGONÊ. O tomb, vaulted bride-bed in
    eternal rock,
Soon I shall be with my own again
Where Persephonê° welcomes the thin
60   ghosts underground:
And I shall see my father again, and you,
    mother,
And dearest Polyneicês—
                    dearest indeed
To me, since it was my hand
That washed him clean and poured the
    ritual wine:
65   And my reward is death before my time!

And yet, as men's hearts know, I have
    done no wrong,
I have not sinned before God. Or if I have,
I shall know the truth in death. But if the
    guilt
Lies upon Creon who judged me, then, I
    pray,
May his punishment equal my own.
70   CHORAGOS. O passionate heart,
Unyielding, tormented still by the same
    winds!
CREON. Her guards shall have good cause
    to regret their delaying.
ANTIGONÊ. Ah! That voice is like the voice
    of death!
CREON. I can give you no reason to think
    you are mistaken.
ANTIGONÊ. Thebes, and you my fathers'
75   gods,
And rulers of Thebes, you see me now,
    the last
Unhappy daughter of a line of kings,

Your kings, led away to death. You will
    remember
What things I suffer, and at what men's
    hands,
Because I would not transgress the laws
    of heaven.   80
(To the GUARDS, *simply.)* Come: let us wait
    no longer.

            (Exit ANTIGONÊ, *left, guarded.)*

ODE IV

CHORUS. All Danaê's beauty was locked
    away   *Strophe 1*
In a brazen cell where the sunlight could
    not come:
A small room still as any grave, enclosed
    her.
Yet she was a princess too,
And Zeus in a rain of gold poured love
    upon her.   5
O child, child,
No power in wealth or war
Or tough sea-blackened ships
Can prevail against untiring Destiny!

And Dryas' son° also, that furious
    king,   *Antistrophe 1*   10
Bore the god's prisoning anger for his
    pride:
Sealed up by Dionysos in deaf stone,
His madness died among echoes.
So at the last he learned what dreadful
    power
His tongue had mocked: 15
For he had profaned the revels,
And fired the wrath of the nine
Implacable Sisters° that love the sound of
    the flute.

And old men tell a half-remembered tale
                    Strophe 2
Of horror where a dark ledge splits the
    sea   20
And a double surf beats on the gray
    shóres:

---

⁶⁰ **Persephonê** queen of the underworld

¹⁰ **Dryas' son** Lycurgus, King of Thrace ¹⁸ **sisters** the Muses

How a king's new woman,° sick
With hatred for the queen he had impris-
    oned,
Ripped out his two sons' eyes with her
    bloody hands
While grinning Arês° watched the shuttle
    plunge
Four times: four blind wounds crying for
25   revenge,

Crying, tears and blood mingled.—
    Piteously born,   *Antistrophe 2*
Those sons whose mother was of heav-
    enly birth!
Her father was the god of the North Wind
And she was cradled by gales,
She raced with young colts on the glitter-
30   ing hills
And walked untrammeled in the open
    light:
But in her marriage deathless Fate found
    means
To build a tomb like yours for all her joy.

SCENE V

Enter blind TEIRESIAS, *led by a boy. The
opening speeches of* TEIRESIAS *should be in
singsong contrast to the realistic lines of*
CREON.

TEIRESIAS. This is the way the blind man
    comes, Princes, Princes,
Lock-step, two heads lit by the eyes of
    one.
CREON. What new thing have you to tell
    us, old Teiresias?
TEIRESIAS. I have much to tell you: listen
    to the prophet, Creon.
CREON. I am not aware that I have ever
    failed to listen.
TEIRESIAS. Then you have done wisely,
5   King, and ruled well.

CREON. I admit my debt to you. But what
    have you to say?
TEIRESIAS. This, Creon: you stand once
    more on the edge of fate.
CREON. What do you mean? Your words   10
    are a kind of dread.
TEIRESIAS. Listen, Creon:
I was sitting in my chair of augury, at the
    place
Where the birds gather about me. They
    were all a-chatter,
As is their habit, when suddenly I heard
A strange note in their jangling, a
    scream, a   15
Whirring fury; I knew that they were
    fighting,
Tearing each other, dying
In a whirlwind of wings clashing. And I
    was afraid.
I began the rites of burnt-offering at the
    altar,
But Hephaistos° failed me: instead of
    bright flame,   20
There was only the sputtering slime of the
    fat thigh-flesh
Melting: the entrails dissolved in gray
    smoke,
The bare bone burst from the welter. And
    no blaze!

This was a sign from heaven. My boy
    described it,
Seeing for me as I see for others.

I tell you, Creon, you yourself have   25
    brought
This new calamity upon us. Our hearths
    and altars
Are stained with the corruption of dogs
    and carrion birds
That glut themselves on the corpse of
    Oedipus' son.
The gods are deaf when we pray to them,
    their fire
Recoils from our offering, their birds of   30
    omen
Have no cry of comfort, for they are
    gorged
With the thick blood of the dead.

---

²² **king's new woman** Eidothea, second wife of
King Phineus, blinded her stepsons. Their
mother, Cleopatra, had been imprisoned in a
cave. Phineus was the son of a king, and Cleopatra, his first wife, was the daughter of Boreas,
the North wind, but this illustrious ancestry
could not protect his sons from violence and
darkness. ²⁵ **Arês** god of war

¹⁹ **Hephaistos** god of fire

O my son,
These are no trifles! Think: all men make
    mistakes,
But a good man yields when he knows his
    course is wrong,
And repairs the evil. The only crime is
35   pride.
Give in to the dead man, then: do not
    fight with a corpse—
What glory is it to kill a man who is dead?
Think, I beg you:
It is for your own good that I speak as I
    do.
You should be able to yield for your own
40   good.
CREON. It seems that prophets have made
    me their especial province.
All my life long
I have been a kind of butt for the dull
    arrows
Of doddering fortune-tellers!
                              No, Teiresias:
If your birds—if the great eagles of God
45   himself
Should carry him stinking bit by bit to
    heaven,
I would not yield. I am not afraid of pollu-
    tion:
No man can defile the gods.
                              Do what you will,
Go into business, make money, speculate
In India gold or that synthetic gold from
50   Sardis,
Get rich otherwise than by my consent to
    bury him.
Teiresias, it is a sorry thing when a wise
    man
Sells his wisdom, lets out his words for
    hire!
TEIRESIAS. Ah Creon! Is there no man left
    in the world—
CREON. To do what?—Come, let's have
55   the aphorism!
TEIRESIAS. No man who knows that wis-
    dom outweighs any wealth?
CREON. As surely as bribes are baser than
    any baseness.
TEIRESIAS. You are sick, Creon! You are
    deathly sick!

CREON. As you say: it is not my place to
    challenge a prophet.
TEIRESIAS. Yet you have said my prophecy
    is for sale.   60
CREON. The generation of prophets has
    always loved gold.
TEIRESIAS. The generation of kings has
    always loved brass.
CREON. You forget yourself! You are
    speaking to your King.
TEIRESIAS. I know it. You are a king be-
    cause of me.
CREON. You have a certain skill; but you
    have sold out.   65
TEIRESIAS. King, you will drive me to
    words that—
CREON.   Say them, say them!
Only remember: I will not pay you for
    them.
TEIRESIAS. No, you will find them too
    costly.
CREON.   No doubt. Speak:
Whatever you say, you will not change my
    will.
TEIRESIAS. Then take this, and take it to
    heart!   70
The time is not far off when you shall pay
    back
Corpse for corpse, flesh of your own
    flesh.
You have thrust the child of this world into
    living night,
You have kept from the gods below the
    child that is theirs:
The one in a grave before her death, the
    other,   75
Dead, denied the grave. This is your
    crime:
And the Furies and the dark gods of Hell
Are swift with terrible punishment for
    you.

Do you want to buy me now, Creon?
                              Not many days,
And your house will be full of men and
    women weeping,   80
And curses will be hurled at you from far
Cities grieving for sons unburied, left to
    rot

Before the walls of Thebes.

These are my arrows, Creon: they are all
  for you.

85 *(To* BOY.*)* But come, child: lead me home.
Let him waste his fine anger upon younger
  men.
Maybe he will learn at last
To control a wiser tongue in a better
  head.   *(Exit* TEIRESIAS.*)*
CHORAGOS. The old man has gone, King,
  but his words
90 Remain to plague us. I am old, too,
But I cannot remember that he was ever
  false.
CREON. That is true. . . . It troubles me.
Oh it is hard to give in! but it is worse
To risk everything for stubborn pride.
CHORAGOS. Creon: take my advice.
95 CREON.   What shall I do?
CHORAGOS. Go quickly: free Antigonê
  from her vault
And build a tomb for the body of Polynei-
  cês.
CREON. You would have me do this!
CHORAGOS.   Creon, yes!
And it must be done at once: God moves
Swiftly to cancel the folly of stubborn
100   men.
CREON. It is hard to deny the heart! But I
Will do it: I will not fight with destiny.
CHORAGOS. You must go yourself, you
  cannot leave it to others.
CREON. I will go.
  —Bring axes, servants: Come with me to
105   the tomb. I buried her, I
Will set her free.
          Oh quickly! My mind misgives—
The laws of the gods are mighty, and a
  man must serve them
To the last day of his life!   *(Exit* CREON.*)*

PAEAN°

CHORAGOS. God of many names *Strophe 1*

Paean a hymn (here dedicated to Iacchos, also
called Dionysos. His father was Zeus, his mother
was Sémelê, daughter of Kadmos. Iacchos' wor-
shipers were the Maenads, whose cry was
"Evohé evohé."

CHORUS.   O Iacchos
                    son
of Kadmeian Sémelê
                    O born of the Thunder!
Guardian of the West
                    Regent
of Eleusis' plain
                    O Prince of maenad Thebes
and the Dragon Field by rippling Ismenós:°   5
CHORAGOS. God of many names
                    Antistrophe 1
CHORUS.   the flame of torches
flares on our hills
              the nymphs of Iacchos
dance at the spring of Castalia:°
from the vine-close mountain
                    come ah come in ivy:
Evohé evohé! sings through the streets of
    Thebes   10
CHORAGOS. God of many names *Strophe 2*
CHORUS.   Iacchos of Thebes
heavenly Child
      of Sémelê bride of the Thunderer!
The shadow of plague is upon us:
                        come
with clement feet
              oh come from Parnassos
down the long slopes
              across the lamenting water   15

CHORAGOS. Iô Fire! Chorister of the
    throbbing stars!   *Antistrophe 2*
O purest among the voices of the night!
Thou son of God, blaze for us!
CHORUS. Come with choric rapture of
    circling Maenads
Who cry *Iô Iacche!*
                    God of many names!   20

EXODOS

Enter MESSENGER *from left.*

MESSENGER. Men of the line of Kadmos,°
    you who live

⁵ **Ismenós** a river east of Thebes. From a dragon's teeth, sown near the river, there sprang
men who became the ancestors of the Theban
nobility. ⁸ **Castalia** a spring on Mount Parnassos
¹ **Kadmos,** who sowed the dragon's teeth, was
founder of Thebes.

Near Amphion's citadel,°
                I cannot say
Of any condition of human life "This is
    fixed,
This is clearly good, or bad." Fate raises
    up,
And Fate casts down the happy and un-
5   happy alike:
No man can foretell his Fate.
                Take the case of Creon:
Creon was happy once, as I count happi-
    ness:
Victorious in battle, sole governor of the
    land,
Fortunate father of children nobly born.
And now it has all gone from him! Who
10   can say
That a man is still alive when his life's joy
    fails?
He is a walking dead man. Grant him rich,
Let him live like a king in his great house:
If his pleasure is gone, I would not give
So much as the shadow of smoke for all
15   he owns.
CHORAGOS. Your words hint at sorrow:
    what is your news for us?
MESSENGER. They are dead. The living
    are guilty of their death.
CHORAGOS. Who is guilty? Who is dead?
    Speak!
MESSENGER.   Haimon.
Haimon is dead; and the hand that killed
    him
Is his own hand.
20 CHORAGOS. His father's? or his own?
MESSENGER. His own, driven mad by the
    murder his father had done.
CHORAGOS. Teiresias, Teiresias, how
    clearly you saw it all!
MESSENGER. This is my news: you must
    draw what conclusions you can from
    it.
CHORAGOS. But look: Eurydicê, our
    Queen:

Has she overheard us?   25

Enter EURYDICÊ *from the palace, center.*

EURYDICÊ. I have heard something,
    friends:
As I was unlocking the gate of Pallas'°
    shrine,
For I needed her help today, I heard a
    voice
Telling of some new sorrow. And I fainted
There at the temple with all my maidens
    about me.   30
But speak again: whatever it is, I can bear
    it:
Grief and I are no strangers.
MESSENGER.   Dearest Lady,
I will tell you plainly all that I have seen.
I shall not try to comfort you: what is the
    use,
Since comfort could lie only in what is not
    true?   35
The truth is always best.
                  I went with Creon
To the outer plain where Polyneicês was
    lying,
No friend to pity him, his body shredded
    by dogs.
We made our prayers in that place to
    Hecatê
And Pluto,° that they would be merciful.
    And we bathed   40
The corpse with holy water, and we
    brought
Fresh-broken branches to burn what was
    left of it,
And upon the urn we heaped up a tower-
    ing barrow
Of the earth of his own land.
                When we were done, we ran
To the vault where Antigonê lay on her
    couch of stone.   45
One of the servants had gone ahead,
And while he was yet far off he heard a
    voice

---

² **Amphion's citadel** Amphion played so
sweetly on his lyre that he charmed stones to
form a wall around Thebes. ²⁷ **Pallas,** Pallas
Athene, goddess of wisdom

⁴⁰ **Hecatê / And Pluto** Hecatê and Pluto (also
known as Hades) were deities of the underworld.

50 Grieving within the chamber, and he came
   back
And told Creon. And as the King went
   closer,
The air was full of wailing, the words lost,
And he begged us to make all haste. "Am
   I a prophet?"
He said, weeping, "And must I walk this
   road,
The saddest of all that I have gone before?
My son's voice calls me on. Oh quickly,
   quickly!
55 Look through the crevice there, and tell
   me
If it is Haimon, or some deception of the
   gods!"

We obeyed; and in the cavern's farthest
   corner
We saw her lying:
She had made a noose of her fine linen
   veil
60 And hanged herself. Haimon lay beside
   her,
His arms about her waist, lamenting her,
His love lost under ground, crying out
That his father had stolen her away from
   him.

When Creon saw him the tears rushed to
   his eyes
65 And he called to him: "What have you
   done, child? Speak to me.
What are you thinking that makes your
   eyes so strange?
O my son, my son, I come to you on my
   knees!"
But Haimon spat in his face. He said not a
   word,
Staring—
                And suddenly drew his sword
70 And lunged. Creon shrank back, the blade
   missed; and the boy,
Desperate against himself, drove it half its
   length
Into his own side, and fell. And as he died
He gathered Antigonê close in his arms
   again,
Choking, his blood bright red on her white
   cheek.
75 And now he lies dead with the dead, and
   she is his

At last, his bride in the house of the dead.
                Exit EURYDICÊ *into the palace.*

CHORAGOS. She has left us without a
   word. What can this mean?
MESSENGER. It troubles me, too; yet she
   knows what is best,
Her grief is too great for public lamentation,
80 And doubtless she has gone to her chamber to weep
For her dead son, leading her maidens in
   his dirge.

Pause.

CHORAGOS. It may be so: but I fear this
   deep silence.
MESSENGER. I will see what she is doing.
   I will go in.
                Exit MESSENGER *into the palace.*

Enter CREON *with attendants, bearing*
HAIMON*'s body.*

CHORAGOS. But here is the king himself:
   oh look at him,
85 Bearing his own damnation in his arms.
CREON. Nothing you say can touch me any
   more.
My own blind heart has brought me
From darkness to final darkness. Here you
   see
The father murdering, the murdered son—

90 And all my civic wisdom!

Haimon my son, so young, so young to
   die,
I was the fool, not you; and you died for
   me.
CHORAGOS. That is the truth; but you
   were late in learning it.
CREON. This truth is hard to bear. Surely
   a god
95 Has crushed me beneath the hugest
   weight of heaven,
And driven me headlong a barbaric way
To trample out the thing I held most dear.

The pains that men will take to come to
   pain!

Enter MESSENGER *from the palace.*

MESSENGER. The burden you carry in your
    hands is heavy,
But it is not all: you will find more in your
100   house.
CREON. What burden worse than this shall
    I find there?
MESSENGER. The Queen is dead.
CREON. O port of death, deaf world,
Is there no pity for me? And you, Angel of
    evil,
I was dead, and your words are death
105   again.
Is it true, boy? Can it be true?
Is my wife dead? Has death bred death?
MESSENGER. You can see for yourself.

The doors are opened and the body of EURY-
DICÊ *is disclosed within.*

CREON. Oh pity!
All true, all true, and more than I can
110   bear!
O my wife, my son!
MESSENGER. She stood before the altar,
    and her heart
Welcomed the knife her own hand guided,
And a great cry burst from her lips for
    Megareus° dead,
And for Haimon dead, her sons; and her
115   last breath
Was a curse for their father, the murderer
    of her sons.
And she fell, and the dark flowed in
    through her closing eyes.
CREON. O God, I am sick with fear.
Are there no swords here? Has no one a
    blow for me?
MESSENGER. Her curse is upon you for
120   the deaths of both.

CREON. It is right that it should be. I
    alone am guilty.
I know it, and I say it. Lead me in,
Quickly, friends.
I have neither life nor substance. Lead me
    in.
CHORAGOS. You are right, if there can be
    right in so much wrong.   125
The briefest way is best in a world of
    sorrow.
CREON. Let it come,
Let death come quickly, and be kind to
    me.
I would not ever see the sun again.
CHORAGOS. All that will come when it will;
    but we, meanwhile,   130
Have much to do. Leave the future to
    itself.
CREON. All my heart was in that prayer!
CHORAGOS. Then do not pray any more:
    the sky is deaf.
CREON. Lead me away. I have been rash
    and foolish.
I have killed my son and my wife.   135
I look for comfort; my comfort lies here
    dead.
Whatever my hands have touched has
    come to nothing.
Fate has brought all my pride to a thought
    of dust.

As CREON *is being led into the house, the*
CHORAGOS *advances and speaks directly to
the audience.*

CHORAGOS. There is no happiness where
    there is no wisdom;
No wisdom but in submission to the gods.   140
Big words are always punished,
And proud men in old age learn to be
    wise.

---

114 **Megareus** Megareus, brother of Haimon, had died in the assault on Thebes.

QUESTIONS AND SUGGESTIONS FOR WRITING

1. Although Sophocles called his play *Antigonê*, many critics say that Creon is the real
   tragic hero, pointing out that Antigonê is absent from the last third of the play. Evaluate this view.
2. In some Greek tragedies, fate plays a great role in bringing about the downfall of the
   tragic hero. Though there are references to the curse on the House of Oedipus in
   Antigonê, do we feel that Antigonê goes to her death as a result of the workings of

fate? Do we feel that fate is responsible for Creon's fall? Is the Messenger right to introduce the notion of "fate" *(Exodos,* line 4)? Or are both Antigonê and Creon the creators of their own tragedy? Explain.

3. Are the words *hamartia* and *hubris* (pages 741–742) relevant to Antigonê? To Creon? Explain.

4. Why does Creon, contrary to the Chorus's advice (Scene V, lines 96–97), bury the body of Polyneicês before he releases Antigonê? Does his action show a zeal for piety as shortsighted as his earlier zeal for law? Is his action plausible, in view of the facts that Teiresias has dwelt on the wrong done to Polyneicês, and that Antigonê has ritual food to sustain her? Or are we not to worry about Creon's motive?

5. A *foil* is a character who, by contrast, sets off or helps to define another character. To what extent is Ismenê a foil to Antigonê? Is she entirely without courage? Explain.

6. What function does Eurydicê serve? How deeply do we feel about her fate?

PART III

Reading and Writing about Literature

Writing About Fiction

12

The World of the Story

Plot and Character

It is customary to say that a narrative—a story, whether a short story or a novel—has an introduction, a complication, and a resolution; that is, it gets under way, some difficulty or problem or complexity (usually a conflict of opposed wills or forces) arises, and there is some sort of untying or settling down.[1] The term **plot** is perhaps a little more difficult to grasp, but fortunately E. M. Forster offers an admirably concise comment, distinguishing plot from story. A story, he says, is something alleged to have happened; a plot is a story containing a strong sense of causality.

Forster illustrates his distinction thus:

> A plot is also a narrative of events, the emphasis falling on causality. "The king died and then the queen died," is a story. "The king died, and then the queen died of grief" is a plot. The time-sequence is preserved, but the sense of causality overshadows it.[2]

Some fiction has a good deal of physical action—wanderings, strange encounters, births, and deaths. But there is also fiction in which little seems to happen. These apparently plotless stories, however, usually involve a mental action—a significant perception, a decision, a failure of the will—and the process of this mental action is the plot.

The sense of causality, valued so highly by Forster, is in part rooted in **char-**

---

[1] A short story, of course, is not a novel summarized. Most often a *short story* reveals only a single character at a moment of crisis, whereas a *novel* usually traces the development of an individual or a group through cumulative experiences. If the short story is very short, an essayist has a fairly good chance of elucidating the whole, or writing about all the aspects that seem important. But an essayist who writes about a longer story or a novel will have to be content with treating either a few pages or one thread that runs through the work.

[2] *Aspects of the Novel* (New York: Harcourt, Brace, 1927) 86.

acter. Things happen, in most good fiction, at least partly because the people have certain personalities or character traits (moral, intellectual, and emotional qualities) and, given their natures, because they respond plausibly to other personalities. What their names are and what they look like may help you to understand them, but probably the best guide to characters is what they do and what they say. As we get to know more about their drives and goals—and especially about the choices they make—we enjoy seeing the writer complete the portraits, finally presenting us with a coherent and credible picture of people in action. In this view, plot and character are inseparable. Plot is not simply a series of happenings, but happenings that come out of character, that reveal character, and that influence character. Henry James puts it thus: "What is character but the determination of incident? What is incident but the illustration of character?" James goes on: "It is an incident for a woman to stand up with her hand resting on a table and look out at you in a certain way."

But, of course, characters are not defined only by what they do. The narrator often describes them, and the characters' words and dress reveal aspects of them.

You may want to set forth a character sketch, describing some person in the story or novel. In preparing such a sketch, take these points into consideration:

1. What the character says (but remember that what he or she says need not be taken at face value; the character may be hypocritical, or self-deceived, or biased—you will have to detect this from the context).
2. What the character does.
3. What other characters say about the character.
4. What others *do* (their actions may help to indicate what the character could do but does not do).

A character sketch—such as "Holden Caulfield: Adolescent Snob or Suffering Saint?"—can be complex and demanding (see pp. 74–75 for an example), but usually you will want to do more than sketch a character. You will probably discuss his function, or contrast him with other characters, or trace the development of his personality. (One of the most difficult topics, the character of the narrator, will be discussed later in this chapter, under the heading "Narrative Point of View.") You will probably still want to keep in mind the four suggestions for getting at a character, but you will also want to go further, relating your findings to additional matters of the sort we will now examine.

Foreshadowing

The writer of fiction provides a coherent world in which the details work together. The **foreshadowing** that would eliminate surprise, or at least greatly reduce it, and thus destroy a story that has nothing else to offer, is a powerful tool in the hands of a writer of serious fiction. Even in such a story as Faulkner's "A Rose for Emily," where we are surprised to learn near the end that Miss Emily has slept beside the decaying corpse of her dead lover, from the outset we expect something strange; that is, we are not surprised by the surprise, only by its precise nature. The first sentence of the story tells us that after Miss Emily's funeral (the narrator begins at the end) the townspeople cross her threshold "out of curiosity to see the inside of her house, which no one save an old manservant . . . had seen in at least ten years." As the story progresses, we see Miss Emily prohibiting people from entering the house, we hear that after a certain point no one ever sees Homer Barron again, that "the front door remained closed," and (a few paragraphs before the end of the story) that the townspeople "knew that there was one room in that region above the stairs which no one had seen in forty years." The paragraph preceding the revelation that "the man himself lay in the bed" is devoted to a description of Homer's dust-covered clothing and toilet articles. In short, however much we are unprepared for the precise revelation, we are prepared for some strange thing in the house; and, given Miss Emily's purchase of poison and Homer's disappearance, we have some idea of what will be revealed. (The story is printed beginning on p. 340.)

Joyce's "Araby" (p. 206) is another example of a story in which the beginning is a preparation for all that follows. Consider the first two paragraphs.

> North Richmond Street, being blind, was a quiet street except at the hour when the Christian Brothers' school set the boys free. An uninhabited house of two storeys stood at the blind end, detached from its neighbours in a square ground. The other houses of the street, conscious of decent lives within them, gazed at one another with brown imperturbable faces.
>
> The former tenant of our house, a priest, had died in the back drawing-room. Air, musty from having been long enclosed, hung in all the rooms, and the waste room behind the kitchen was littered with old useless papers. Among these I found a few paper-covered books, the pages of which were curled and damp: *The Abbot,* by Walter Scott, *The Devout Communicant* and *The Memoirs of Vidocq.* I liked the last best because its leaves were yellow. The wild garden behind the house contained a central apple-tree and a few straggling bushes under one of which I found the late tenant's rusty bicycle pump. He had been a very charitable priest; in his will he had left all his money to institutions and the furniture of his house to his sister.

A dead-end ("blind") street contains "imperturbable" houses, including an uninhabited one. The former tenant of the house that the narrator lived in was a priest who died in the back drawing-room, leaving, among other things, musty air, yellowing books, and a rusty bicycle pump. If we have read and reread with care and sympathy, we find that Joyce gives us in these paragraphs a vision of the paralysis of Ireland that he elsewhere speaks of.

Setting and Atmosphere

Foreshadowing normally makes use of **setting.** The setting or environment in the first two paragraphs of Joyce's "Araby" is not mere geography, not mere locale: it provides an **atmosphere,** an air that the characters breathe, a world in which they move. Narrowly speaking, the setting is the physical surroundings—the furniture, the architecture, the landscape, the climate—and these often are highly appropriate to the characters who are associated with them. Thus, in Emily Brontë's *Wuthering Heights* the passionate Earnshaw family is associated with Wuthering Heights, the storm-exposed moorland, whereas the mild Linton family is associated with Thrushcross Grange in the sheltered valley below.

Broadly speaking, setting includes not only the physical surroundings but also a point (or several points) in time. The background against which we see the characters and the happenings may be specified as morning or evening, spring or fall. In a good story, this temporal setting will probably be highly relevant; it will probably be part of the story's meaning, perhaps providing an ironic contrast to or exerting an influence on the characters.

Symbolism

Writers draw on experience, but an experience is not a happening through which the author necessarily passed; rather, it is a thought, an emotion, or a vision that is meaningful and is embodied in the piece of fiction for all to read. Inevitably the writer uses **symbols.** Symbols are neither puzzles nor colorful details but are among the concrete embodiments that give the story whatever accuracy and meaning it has. Joyce's dead-end street, dead priest, apple tree (suggestive of the Garden of Eden, and thus of the fallen state of humanity?), and rusty bicycle pump all help to define very precisely the condition of a thoroughly believable Dublin. In Hemingway's *A Farewell to Arms* the river in which Frederic Henry swims when he deserts the army is not only symbolic of his cleansing himself from war; it is also a river, as material as the guns he flees from.

Narrative Point of View

An author must choose a **point of view** (or sometimes, several points of view) from which he or she will narrate the story. The choice will contribute to the total effect that the story will have.

Narrative points of view can be divided into two sorts: **participant** (or **first-person**) and **nonparticipant** (or **third-person**). That is, the narrator may or may not be a character who participates in the story. Each of these two divisions can be subdivided:

I. Participant (first-person)
   A. Narrator as a major character
   B. Narrator as a minor character
II. Nonparticipant (third-person)
   A. Omniscient
   B. Selective omniscient
   C. Objective

Participant Points of View

In Frank O'Connor's "Guests of the Nation" (p. 213), the narrator is a major character. He, and not O'Connor, tells the story, and the story is chiefly about him; hence one can say that O'Connor uses a first-person (or participant) point of view. O'Connor has invented an Irishman who has fought against the English, and this narrator tells of the impact a happening had on him: "And anything that happened to me afterwards, I never felt the same about again."

But sometimes a first-person narrator tells a story that focuses on someone other than himself; he is a minor character, a peripheral witness, for example, to a story about Jones, and we get the story of Jones filtered through, say, the eyes of Jones's friend or brother or cat.

Nonparticipant Points of View

In a nonparticipant (third-person) point of view, the teller of the tale does not introduce himself as a character. If the point of view is **omniscient,** the narrator relates what he wants to relate about the thoughts as well as the deeds of his characters. When he chooses, the omniscient teller enters the mind of any or all of his characters; whereas the first-person narrator can only say, "I was angry," or "Jones seemed angry to me," the omniscient narrator can say, "Jones was inwardly angry but gave no sign; Smith continued chatting, but he sensed Jones's anger." Furthermore, a distinction can be made between **neutral omniscience** (the narrator recounts deeds and thoughts but does not judge) and **editorial omniscience** (the narrator not only recounts but also judges). An editorially omniscient narrator knows what goes on in the minds of all the characters and might comment approvingly or disapprovingly: "He closed the book, having finished the story, but, poor fellow, he had missed the meaning."

Because a short story can scarcely hope to develop a picture of several minds effectively, authors may prefer to limit their omniscience to the minds of a few of their characters, or even to that of only one of the characters; that is, they may use **selective omniscience** as the point of view. Selective omniscience provides a focus, especially if it is limited to a single character. When thus limited, the author sees one character from outside and from inside and sees the other characters only from the outside, and from the impact they have on the mind of this selected receptor. When selective omniscience attempts to record mental activity ranging from consciousness to the unconscious, from clear perceptions to confused longings, it is sometimes labeled the **stream-of-consciousness** point of view. The following example is from Katherine Anne Porter's "The Jilting of Granny Weatherall" (p. 613):

> Her eyelids wavered and let in streamers of blue-gray light like tissue paper over her eyes. She must get up and pull the shades down or she'd never sleep. She was in bed again and the shades were not down. How could that happen? Better turn over, hide from the light, sleeping in the light gave you nightmares. "Mother, how do you feel now?" and a stinging wetness on her forehead. But I don't like having my face washed in cold water!

Finally, sometimes a third-person narrator does not enter even a single mind, but records only what crosses an apparently dispassionate eye and ear. Such a point of view is **objective** (sometimes called the **camera** or **fly-on-the-wall** point of view). The absence of editorializing and of dissection of the mind often produces the effect of a play; we see and hear the characters in action. Much of

Hemingway's "A Clean, Well-Lighted Place" (p. 620) is objective, consisting of bits of dialogue that make the story look like a play:

> "Last week he tried to commit suicide," one waiter said.
> "Why?"
> "He was in despair."
> "What about?"
> "Nothing."
> "How do you know it was nothing?"
> "He has plenty of money."
> They sat together at a table that was close against the wall near the door of the café and looked at the terrace where the tables were all empty except where the old man sat in the shadow of the leaves of the tree that moved slightly in the wind. A girl and a soldier went by in the street. The street light shone on the brass number on his collar. The girl wore no head covering and hurried beside him.
> "The guard will pick him up," one waiter said.
> "What does it matter if he gets what he's after?"

But the word *objective* is almost a misnomer, for to describe happenings is—by one's choice of words—to comment on them, too, however unobtrusively. How objective is the point of view if a man is described as "fat" instead of "stout" or "stout" instead of "heavy" or "heavy" instead of "two hundred and fifty pounds in weight"? The objective point of view, even though it expressly enters no mind, is often a camouflaged version of the selective omniscient point of view.

Determining and Discussing the Theme

First, we can distinguish between story and theme in fiction. *Story* is concerned with "How does it turn out? What happens?" But **theme** is concerned with "What is it about? What does it add up to? What motif holds the happenings together? What does it make of life, and, perhaps, what wisdom does it offer?"[3] In a good work of fiction, the details add up, or, to use Flannery O'Connor's words, they are "controlled by some overall purpose." In F. Scott Fitzgerald's *The Great Gatsby,* for example, there are many references to popular music, especially to Negro jazz. These references contribute to our sense of the reality of Fitzgerald's depiction of America in the 1920s, but they do more: They help to comment on the shallowness of the white middle-class characters and they sometimes (very gently) remind us of an alternative culture. One might study Fitzgerald's references to music with an eye toward getting a deeper understanding of what the novel is about.

---

[3] A theme in a literary work is sometimes distinguished from a *thesis,* an arguable message such as "Men ought not to struggle against fate." The theme, it might be said, is something like "Man's Struggle against Fate" or "The Process of Growing Up" or "The Quest for Knowledge." In any case, the formulation of a theme normally includes an abstract noun or a phrase, but it must be remembered that such formulations as those in the previous sentence are, finally, only shorthand expressions for highly complex statements.

Another method of talking about the theme is to focus on a single speech. A work, especially if it is told from an editorially omniscient point of view, may include an explicit statement of the theme, but it need not; think twice before you detach any passage and say that it states the theme. Be especially wary of assuming that the words of any character state the theme—though, of course, this is not to say that no character in any work of fiction ever says anything that can serve as a statement of the theme. The difficulty is that a character has a personality, and what he or she says is usually colored by this personality and the momentary situation. The statement, apt in the immediate context, may not adequately cover the entire work.

Take, for example, Phoebe's comment to her brother Holden Caulfield in *The Catcher in the Rye:* "You don't like *any*thing that's happening." Many readers believe that Phoebe has put her finger on the matter: Holden doesn't like anything. But with a little work one can find a number of things Holden likes. He likes, for example, the kettle drummer at Radio City, he likes *The Return of the Native,* he likes the music of carousels, he likes his brother Allie, and he likes talking to Phoebe. She mentions that Allie is dead and so he "really" doesn't count, but Holden replies:

> "I know he's dead! Don't you think I know that? I can still like him, though, can't I?"

And when Phoebe says that talking to her "isn't anything *real*ly," he insists it is:

> "It is something *real*ly! Certainly it is! Why the hell isn't it? People never think anything is anything *real*ly. I'm getting goddam sick of it."

Phoebe may have touched on an important point. An essay suggesting that *The Catcher* is about a boy whose perception of corruption is so keen that it overwhelms him, and in turn corrupts his vision, will make use of Phoebe's statement, but it will also establish the limitations of that statement. The essay may, for instance, go on to argue that Holden's perception of "phoniness"—for example, Ossenburger's speech in the chapel at Pencey Prep—is thoroughly warranted. One might, in fact, write an interesting essay on exactly what sorts of things Holden finds "phony."

Questions to Help Generate Essays on Fiction

Plot. What is the conflict, or what are the conflicts? Does the plot grow out of the characters, or does it depend on chance or coincidence? Are there irrelevant episodes, or do episodes that at first seem irrelevant have a function? If the development is not strictly chronological, what is gained by the arrangement? Does surprise or foreshadowing play an important role?

Character. Is a particular character highly individualized, or is that character highly typical (for example, representative of a social class or age)? Are we chiefly interested in the character's unique psychology, or does the character seem to be a representation of a type? Are there characters who by their similarities and differences define each other—for instance, two boys who react differently to the same stimulus? How else is a particular character defined? How do words, actions (including thoughts and emotions), dress, setting, narrative, and point of view contribute to the character? To what extent does a character change, and what causes the change? Remember, unless you are simply writing a character sketch, your essay should advance a thesis. Suppose, for example, you feel that by the end of the story or novel a character has changed. You may want to propose one of several theses: The character is inconsistent and therefore unsatisfying; or the character is inconsistent but acceptable because (for example) the change is for the better and we approve of it even though we don't believe it; or the overall structure of the work requires this inconsistency; or the change is well-motivated and psychologically plausible.

Point of View. Who is the narrator? Does the point of view change in the story? If so, to what effect? How does the point of view help to shape the theme? After all, the basic story of "Little Red Riding Hood" remains unchanged whether told from the wolf's point of view or from the girl's, but (to simplify grossly) if we hear the story from the wolf's point of view we may feel that the story is about terrifying yet pathetic compulsive neurotic behavior; if from the girl's point of view, about terrified innocence.

Setting. What is the relation of the setting to the plot and the characters? To what degree does the landscape play a role? How does it illustrate Henry James's assertion that in fiction, "landscape is character"? What would be lost if the setting were changed? As the novelist Elizabeth Bowen has said, "Nothing can happen nowhere. The locale of the happening always colors the happening, and often, to a degree, shapes it." A rocky New England farm may be an illustration of the farmer who cultivates it, and the story may be as much about the farm as about the farmer. An obvious example is the setting of Thomas Hardy's *The Return of the Native*. Oppressive Egdon Heath is so much a part of the novel that it almost takes on the role of a major character and it is made largely responsible for the tragic fate of the novel's characters.

Style. What role is played by the author's style? Is the style (not only the words, but the sentence structure and paragraphing) colloquial, formal, understated, figurative, or what? And why? A brief example: In William Carlos Williams's "The Use of Force" (page 210) the sentences tend to be colloquial. For instance, the story begins, "They were new patients to me, all I had was the name, Olsen." This is the language of ordinary talk. Strictly speaking, the sentence includes a grammatical error called a comma splice, for grammar requires a semicolon rather than a comma after "me": "They were new patients to me; all I had was the name, Olsen." But even when thus revised, the sentence is informal. A more formal version would be, "They were new patients to me. I knew only their name, Olsen." Williams's language throughout the story is simple, the most unusual words being "profusion," "photogravure," "diphtheria," "mouth cavity" (a doctor is speaking), and "spatula," but none of these words is notably difficult.

A brief comparison with Bierce's "An Occurrence at Owl Creek Bridge" (p. 81) is useful to establish this point. In the first two paragraphs of "An Occurrence" we encounter such expressions as *closely encircled, at a short remove, a formal and unnatural position, a gentle declivity, a single embrasure through which protruded, Death is a dignitary who when he comes is to be received with formal manifestations of respect*. Such diction, including the rather solemn reflection on death, is unthinkable in Williams's story—not because the plot is dissimilar but because Williams's view of life is very different from that of Bierce, and he has a very different meaning to convey.

Theme. Does the story imply a meaning (or meanings), a relation to the outside world? The title may be especially significant, and so too may certain passages that offer explicit ideas, but remember that these may be offered by an unreliable narrator or by a particular character whose views are probably shaped by his or her personality. Is the author imposing a theme that the rest of the story does not support?

The least fruitful way to study a novel is to seek to extract whatever overt philosophizing it seems to contain and to discuss it as philosophy; the most fruitful way is to pay close attention to all the words. In writing an essay on a very short piece of fiction, for example a short short story, one can perhaps study in some detail all aspects of it—or all that one sees. But most fiction is too big for such analysis. Normally one decides either to examine a particular passage or to examine some significant thread that runs through the work.

Writing Fiction about Fiction

Your instructor may ask you to write a short story, perhaps even a story in the style of one of the authors you have studied, or a story that is in some way a variation of—perhaps a modernization of, or a response to—one of the stories you have studied. If you have read Poe's "The Cask of Amontillado," for instance, you might rewrite the story, setting it in the present and telling it from the point of view of the victim instead of the point of view of the murderer. And you might vary the plot, so that the would-be murderer is outwitted by the man who (he thinks) is so stupid.

Such an exercise, which requires you to read and re-read a model, will teach you a good deal about the ways in which your author uses language, and about the ways in which he or she uses the conventions of fiction. In short, you will learn much about the art of the short story. One thing you will surely learn is that writing a story is difficult; another is that it can be fun.

Here is an example, written by Lola Lee Loveall for a course taught by Diana Muir at Solano Community College. Ms. Loveall's story is a response to Kate Chopin's "The Story of an Hour" (p. 63). Notice that Loveall's first sentence is close to her source—a good way to get started, but by no means the only way; notice, too, that elsewhere in her story she occasionally echoes Chopin—for instance, in the references to the treetops, the sparrows, and the latchkey. A reader enjoys detecting these echoes. What is especially interesting, however, is that before she conceived her story Loveall presumably said to herself something like, "Well, Chopin's story is superb, but suppose we shift the focus a bit. Suppose we think about what it would be like, *from the husband's point of view*, to live with a woman who suffered from 'heart trouble,' a person whom one had to treat with 'great care' " (Chopin's words, in the first sentence of "The Story of an Hour"). "And what about Mrs. Mallard's sister, Josephine—so considerate of Mrs. Mallard? What, exactly, would *Mr.* Mallard think of her? Wouldn't he see her as a pain in the neck? And what might he be prompted to do? That is, how might this character in this situation respond?" And so Loveall's characters and her plot began to take shape. As part of the game, she committed herself to writing a plot that, in its broad outline, resembled Chopin's by being highly ironic. But read it for yourself.

Lola Lee Loveall
English 6

The Ticket
(A Different View of "The Story of an Hour")

Knowing full well his wife was afflicted with heart trouble, Brently Mallard wondered how he was going to break the news about the jacket. As he strode along his boots broke through the shallow crust from the recent rain, and dust kicked up from the well-worn wagon road came up to flavor his breathing. At least, the gentle spring rain had settled the dusty powder even as it had sprinkled his stiffly starched shirt which was already dampened from the exertion of stamping along. The strenuous pace he set himself to cover the intervening miles home helped him regain his composure. Mr. Brently Mallard was always calm, cool, and confident.

However, he hadn't been this morning when he stepped aboard the train, took off his jacket and folded it neatly beside him, and settled in his seat on the westbound train. He had been wildly excited. Freedom was his. He was Free! He was off for California, devil take the consequences! He would be his old self again, let the chips fall where they may. And he would have been well on his way, too, if that accursed ticket agent hadn't come bawling out, "Mr. Mallard, you left your ticket on the counter!"

just when Mallard himself had spied that nosy Jan Ardan
bidding her sister goodbye several car lengths down the depot.
How could he be so unfortunate to run into them both twice this
morning? Earlier, they had come into the bank just as the banker
had extended the thick envelope.

"You understand, this is just an advance against the estate
for a while?"

Only Mallard's persuasiveness could have extracted that
amount from the cagey old moneybags.

Mallard had carefully tucked it into his inside pocket.

This was the kind of spring day to fall in love—or lure an
adventurer to the top of the next hill. Sparrows hovered about
making happy sounds. Something about their movements
reminded Mallard of his wife—quick, fluttering, then darting
away.

He had loved her at first for her delicate ways. They had
made a dashing pair—he so dark and worldly, she so fragile and
fair—but her delicacy was a trap, for it disguised the heart
trouble, bane of his life. Oh, he still took her a sip of brandy in
bed in the morning as the doctor had suggested, although, of
course, it wasn't his bed anymore. He had moved farther down
the hall not long after her sister, Josephine, came to help, quick
to come when Mrs. Mallard called, even in the middle of the
night. After one such sudden appearance one night—"I thought
I heard you call"—he had given up even sharing the same bed
with his wife, although there had been little real sharing there
for some time.

"No children!" the doctor had cautioned.

Mallard concentrated harder on the problem of the missing
jacket. What to say? She would notice. Maybe not right away, but
she would be aware. Oh, he knew Louise's reaction. She would
apparently take the news calmly, then make a sudden stab
toward her side with her delicate hands, then straighten and
walk away—but not before he observed. A new jacket would cost
money. Discussing money made the little drama happen more
often, so now Mr. Mallard handled all the financial affairs,
protecting her the best he could. After all, it was her inheritance,

and he took great care with it, but there were the added costs: doctors, Josephine living with them, the medications, even his wife's brandy. Why, he checked it daily to be sure it was the proper strength. Of course, a man had to have a few pleasures, even if the cards did seem to fall against him more often than not. He manfully kept trying.

Everyone has a limit, though, and Mr. Mallard had reached his several days ago when the doctor had cautioned him again.

"She may go on like she is for years, or she may just keel over any time. However, the chances are she will gradually go downhill and need continual care. It is impossible to tell."

Mallard could not face "gradually go downhill." His manhood revolted against it. He was young, full of life. Let Josephine carry the chamber pot! After Louise's demise (whenever that occurred!) the simple estate which she had inherited reverted to Josephine. Let her earn it. Also, good old friend Richards was always about with a suggestion here or a word of comfort there for Louise. They'd really not care too much if Mallard were a long time absent.

As he drew nearer his home, Mallard continued to try to calm his composure, which was difficult for he kept hearing the sound of the train wheels as it pulled away, jacket, envelope, and all, right before his panic-stricken eyes: CALIFORNIA; California; california; california.

DUTY! It was his duty not to excite Louise. As he thought of duty he unconsciously squared his drooping shoulders, and the image of Sir Galahad flitted across his mind.

The treetops were aglow in the strange afterlight of the storm. A shaft of sunlight shot through the leaves and fell upon his face. He had come home.

He opened the front door with the latchkey. Fortunately, it had been in his pants pocket.

Later, the doctors did not think Mr. Mallard's reaction unusual, even when a slight smile appeared on the bereaved husband's face. Grief causes strange reactions.

"He took it like a man," they said.

Only later, when the full significance of his loss reached him, did he weep.

Writing **13** *About Poetry*

The Speaker of the Poem

The **lyric poem** commonly presents a speaker expressing an emotion. The name suggests that such a poem was once a song to be accompanied by a lyre. The genre now includes much that cannot possibly be sung, but let us begin with the singable.

> Oh mistress mine! where are you roaming?
> Oh! stay and hear; your true love's coming,
>   That can sing both high and low.
> Trip no further, pretty sweeting;
> Journeys end in lovers meeting,
>   Every wise man's son doth know.
>
> What is love? 'tis not hereafter;
> Present mirth hath present laughter;
>   What's to come is still unsure:
> In delay there lies no plenty;
> Then come kiss me, sweet and twenty,
>   Youth's a stuff will not endure.
>
> —William Shakespeare (1564–1616), *Oh Mistress Mine*

It is not stretching a point to say that Shakespeare's song imitates, or re-creates, a state that we all know in some degree. There are moments when we feel that journeys end in lovers meeting—that is, moments when we feel that love is the only proper reward for our labor (compare the Beatles' "All You Need Is Love"); and these moments are fused with awareness of the brevity of life ("Youth's a stuff will not endure"). This last sentence of ours is an inept summary of the poem, but it affords a prologue to a simple question that may clarify the point: Do we not feel that "Oh Mistress Mine" has perfectly caught, or imitated, an attitude or emotion, a state of mind? Is it not an embodiment or imitation of a human experience? We value its sound, and we also value its sense, the representation of a moment of human feeling. We hear a voice that is not at all literally like any voice we have ever heard (no one talks in rhymes) but that nevertheless makes us say, "Yes, I understand that experience. I see what that state of mind is."

Almost any good blues song—maybe "St. Louis Woman," or "St. James Infirmary"—can similarly illustrate the point that a lyric is a highly artificial (and artful) expression that precisely communicates to us a particular state of mind. It is valuable not only to the singer, who may gain some relief from sorrow by singing about it, but to the hearer, who at least for the moment feels that a state of mind is being revealed with a clarity almost never encountered in ordinary talk.

Now here is another voice, very far from a singing one; but this voice, too, was created by Shakespeare:

> Let me not to the marriage of true minds
> Admit impediments. Love is not love
> Which alters when it alteration finds,
> Or bends with the remover to remove.

Admit has at least two senses: the speaker says he will not allow impediments to enter into the marriage of true minds, and he also says he will not grant *(admit)* that impediments can exist when there is a marriage of true minds. In these four lines (the beginning of a sonnet that is printed in full on page 370), we hear a somewhat authoritative or commanding note ("Let me not to the marriage of true minds / Admit impediments") rather than the note of longing in *"Oh mistress mine! where are you roaming?"* Now, *"Oh Mistress Mine"* also includes lines that seem to be imperative (for instance, "stay and hear"), but in their context we see that they do not convey the assurance of "Let me not"; rather, they can almost be said to convey a sense of the speaker's awareness that without his beloved he is lost. "Oh! stay and hear" is more a plea than a command. Indeed, the person to whom it is addressed cannot take it as an imperious command, since she is not even present: "Oh mistress mine! where are you roaming?" Our point: The reader of a poem must understand who the speaker is and what the dramatic situation is.

The Speaker and the Poet

The **voice**, or **mask**, or **persona** (Latin for "mask") that speaks the poem is usually not identical with the poet who writes it. The author counterfeits the speech of a person in a particular situation. Shakespeare, we have just seen, invented a lover longing for his absent beloved, and he invented another lover, rather assured, who gives a little lecture on the nature of true love. Robert Browning invented a Renaissance duke who speaks of his first wife and his art collection in "My Last Duchess"; Robert Frost in "Stopping by Woods on a Snowy Evening" invented the speech of a man who, sitting in a horse-drawn sleigh, is surveying woods that are "lovely, dark and deep."

The speaker's voice does often have the ring of the author's own voice, and to make a distinction between speaker and author may at times seem perverse, because some poetry (especially contemporary American poetry) is highly autobiographical. Still, even in autobiographical poems it may be convenient to distinguish between author and speaker: The speaker is Frost the meditative man, or Frost the compassionate man, not simply Frost the poet.

The Language of Poetry

Diction and Tone

How is a voice or mask or persona created? From the whole of language, one consciously or unconsciously selects certain words and grammatical constructions; this selection constitutes one's **diction.** It is partly by the diction that we come to know the speaker of a poem. *Auld* and *lang* and *syne* tell us that the speaker of "Auld Lang Syne" is a Scot; an American or an Englishman would say "long ago." In the four lines quoted above from one of Shakespeare's sonnets, "impediments" tells us that the speaker is educated. Of course, some words are used in virtually all poems: *I, see, and,* and the like. The fact remains, however, that although a large part of language is shared by all speakers, some parts of language are used only by certain speakers.

Like some words, some grammatical constructions are used only by certain kinds of speakers. Consider these two passages:

In Adam's fall
We sinnèd all.
    —from *The New England Primer*

Of Man's first disobedience, and the fruit
Of that forbidden tree whose mortal taste
Brought death into the World, and all our woe,
With loss of Eden, till one greater Man
Restore us, and regain the blissful seat,   5
Sing, Heavenly Muse, that, on the secret top
Of Oreb, or of Sinai, didst inspire
That shepherd who first taught the chosen seed
In the beginning how the heavens and earth
Rose out of Chaos. . . .   10
    —John Milton, *Paradise Lost* (Book I, lines 1–10)

There is an enormous difference in the diction of these two passages. Milton, speaking as an inspired poet who regards his theme as "a great argument," appropriately uses words and grammatical constructions somewhat removed from common life. Hence, while the anonymous author of the primer speaks directly of "Adam's fall," Milton speaks allusively of the fall, calling it "Man's first disobedience." Milton's sentence is nothing that any Englishman ever said in conversation; its genitive or possessive beginning ("Of Man's"), its length (the sentence continues for six lines beyond the quoted passage), and its postponement of the main verb until the sixth line mark it as the utterance of a poet working in the tradition of Latin epic poetry. The primer's statement, by its choice of words as well as by its brevity, suggests a far less sophisticated speaker.

The voice in a poem is established not only by broad strokes but also by such details as **alliteration** (the repetition of initial consonants), **assonance** (the repetition of vowel sounds), and rhyme. (More will be said about rhyme later.) F. W. Bateson, in *English Poetry*,[1] aptly notes the role that alliteration plays in reinforcing the contemptuous tone we hear in "Die and endow a college or a cat," a line from Pope's "Epistle to Bathurst." Bateson points out that "the *d*'s hint that there is a subtle identity in the dying and the endowing (the only interest that the world takes in this particular death is in the testamentary endowments), and the *c*'s point the contrast between founding colleges and financing cats' homes."

Speakers (or voices, to use the previous terminology) have attitudes toward themselves, their subjects, and their audiences, and, consciously or unconsciously, they choose their words, pitch, and modulation accordingly; all these add up to their **tone.** In written literature, tone must be detected without the aid of the ear, although it's a good idea to read poetry aloud, trying to find the appropriate tone of voice. That is, the reader must understand by the selection and sequence of words the way they are meant to be heard—playfully, angrily, confidentially, ironically, or whatever. The reader must catch what Frost calls "the speaking tone of voice somehow entangled in the words and fastened to the page for the ear of the imagination."[2]

Paraphrase

Our interest in the shifting tones of the voice that speaks the words should not, of course, cause us to neglect the words themselves, the gist of the idea expressed. Take the first two lines of a passage from Pope's *Essay on Man*, addressed to Pope's friend Henry St. John:

> Awake, my St. John! leave all meaner things
> To low ambition, and the pride of kings.

If we *paraphrase* (reword) these two lines, we get something like this: "Wake up, my friend St. John [*my* implies intimacy], leave low things to such lowly people as are ambitious and (equally low) to arrogant monarchs." A paraphrase at least has the virtue of making us look hard at all of the words. We have just seen, for example, that in paraphrasing these lines of Pope, we become aware that *my* in the first line reveals the intimacy Pope feels toward St. John. The point of a paraphrase is to help you understand at least the surface meaning, and it will usually help you to understand at least some of the implicit meaning. Furthermore, a paraphrase makes you see that the poet's words—if the poem is a good one—are exactly right, better than the words you might substitute. It becomes clear that the thing said in the poem—not only the "idea" expressed but the precise tone with which it is expressed—is a sharply defined experience.

Figurative Language

Robert Frost has said, "Poetry provides the one permissible way of saying one thing and meaning another." This, of course, is an exaggeration, but it

---

[1] (New York: Longmans, 1950), pp. 31–32.
[2] This discussion concentrates on the speaker's tone. But sometimes one can also talk of the author's tone, that is, of the author's attitude toward the invented speaker. The speaker's tone might, for example, be angry, but the author's tone (as detected by the reader) might be humorous.

shrewdly suggests the importance of **figurative language**—saying one thing in terms of something else. Words have their literal meanings, but they can also be used so that something other than the literal meaning is implied. "My love is a rose" is, literally, nonsense, for she is not a five-petaled, many-stamened plant with a spiny stem. But the suggestions of *rose* include "delicate beauty," "soft," and "perfumed," and thus the word *rose* can be meaningfully applied—figuratively rather than literally—to "my love." The girl is fragrant; her skin is perhaps like a rose in texture and (in some measure) color; she will not keep her beauty long. The poet, that is, has communicated a perception very precisely.

People who write about poetry have found it convenient to name the various kinds of figurative language. Just as the student of geology employs such special terms as *kames* and *eskers,* the student of literature employs special terms to name things as accurately as possible. The following paragraphs discuss the most common terms.

In a **simile,** items from different classes are explicitly compared by a connective such as *like, as,* or *than,* or by a verb such as *appears* or *seems.* (If the objects compared are from the same class, for example, "New York is like London," no simile is present.)

> Float like a butterfly, sting like a bee.
> —Muhammad Ali

> It is a beauteous evening, calm and free.
> The holy time is quiet as a Nun,
> Breathless with adoration.
> —William Wordsworth

> How sharper than a serpent's tooth it is
> To have a thankless child.
> —Shakespeare

> Seems he a dove? His feathers are but borrowed.
> —Shakespeare

A **metaphor** asserts the identity, without a connective such as *like* or a verb such as *appears*, of terms that are literally incompatible.

> She is the rose, the glory of the day.
> —Edmund Spenser

> Yes! It's true all my visions
> have come home to roost at last.
> —Richard Brautigan

Notice how in the last example only one of the terms *(visions)* is stated; the other *(chickens)* is implied in "have come home to roost."

Two common types of metaphor have Greek names. In **synecdoche** the whole is replaced by the part, or the part by the whole. For example, *bread* in "Give us this day our daily bread" replaces all sorts of food. In **metonymy** something is named that replaces something closely related to it. For example,

James Shirley names certain objects, using them to replace social classes to which they are related:

> Scepter and crown must tumble down
> And in the dust be equal made
> With the poor crooked scythe and spade.

The attribution of human feelings or characteristics to abstractions or to inanimate objects is called **personification.**

> The fixed bells rang, their voices
> came like boats over the oil-slicks.
>   —Charles Olson

> There's Wrath who has learnt every trick of guerilla wafare,
> The shamming dead, the night-raid, the feinted retreat.
>   —W. H. Auden

> Hope, thou bold taster of delight.
>   —Richard Crashaw

Crashaw's personification, "Hope, thou bold taster of delight," is also an example of the figure called **apostrophe,** an address to a person or thing not literally listening. Wordsworth begins a sonnet by apostrophizing Milton:

> Milton, thou shouldst be living at this hour.

What conclusions can we draw about figurative language? First, figurative language, with its literally incompatible terms, forces the reader to attend to the *connotations* (suggestions, associations) rather than to the *denotations* (dictionary definitions) of one of the terms. Second, although figurative language is said to differ from ordinary discourse, it is found in ordinary discourse as well as in poetry and other literary forms. "It rained cats and dogs," "War is hell," "Don't be a pig," "Mr. Know-it-all," and other tired figures are part of our daily utterances. But through repeated use, these, and most of the figures we use, have lost whatever impact they once had and are only a shade removed from expressions which, though once figurative, have become literal: the *eye* of a needle, a *branch* office, the *face* of a clock. Third, good figurative language is usually concrete, condensed, and interesting.

We should mention, too, that figurative language is not limited to literary writers; it is used by scientists and social scientists—by almost everyone who is concerned with effective expression. Take, for instance, R. H. Tawney's *Religion and the Rise of Capitalism* (1926), a classic of economics. Among the titles of Tawney's chapters are "The Economic Revolution," "The Puritan Movement," and "The New Medicine for Poverty," all of which include metaphors. (To take only the last: Poverty is seen as a sick person or a disease.) Or take this sentence from Tawney (almost any sentence will serve equally well to reveal his bent for metaphor): "By the end of the sixteenth century the divorce between religious theory and economic realities had long been evident." Figures are not a fancy way of speaking. Quite the opposite: Writers use figures because they are forceful and exact. Literal language would not only be less interesting, it would also be less precise.

Imagery and Symbolism

When we read *rose* we may more or less call to mind a picture of a rose, or perhaps we are reminded of the odor or texture of a rose. Whatever in a poem appeals to any of our senses (including sensations of heat as well as of sight, smell, taste, touch, sound) is an image. In short, images are the sensory content of a work, whether literal or figurative. When a poet says "My rose" and is speaking about a rose, we have no figure of speech—though we still have an image. If, however, "My rose" is a shortened form of "My love is a rose," some would say that he is using a metaphor; but others would say that because the first term is omitted ("My love is"), the rose is a **symbol**. A poem about the transience of a rose might compel the reader to feel that the transience of female beauty is the larger theme even though it is never explicitly stated.

Some symbols are **conventional symbols**—people have agreed to accept them as standing for something other than their literal meanings: A poem about the cross would probably be about Christianity; similarly, the rose has long been a symbol for love. In Virginia Woolf's novel *Mrs. Dalloway,* the husband communicates his love by proffering this conventional symbol: "He was holding out flowers—roses, red and white roses. (But he could not bring himself to say he loved her; not in so many words.)" Objects that are not conventional symbols, however, may also give rise to rich, multiple, indefinable associations. The following poem uses the traditional symbol of the rose, but uses it in a nontraditional way:

O rose, thou art sick!
The invisible worm
That flies in the night,
In the howling storm,

Has found out thy bed
Of crimson joy,
And his dark secret love
Does thy life destroy.
　　　—William Blake, "The Sick Rose"

A reader might perhaps argue that the worm is invisible (line 2) merely because it is hidden within the rose, but an "invisible worm / That flies in the night" is more than a long, slender, soft-bodied, creeping animal; and a rose that has, or is, a "bed / Of crimson joy" is more than a gardener's rose. Blake's worm and rose suggest things beyond themselves—a stranger, more vibrant world than the world we are usually aware of. They are, in short, symbolic. We find ourselves half thinking, for example, that the worm is male, the rose female, and that the poem is about the violation of virginity. Or that the poem is about the destruction of beauty: Woman's beauty, rooted in joy, is destroyed by a power that feeds on her. But these interpretations are not fully satisfying: The poem presents a worm and a rose, and yet it is not merely about a worm and a rose. These objects resonate, stimulating our thoughts toward something else, but the something else is elusive. This is not to say, however, that symbols mean whatever a reader says they mean. A reader could scarcely support, we imagine, an interpretation arguing that the poem is about the need to love all aspects of nature. All interpretations are not equally valid; it's the reader's job to offer a reasonably persuasive interpretation.

A symbol, then, is an image so loaded with significance that it is not simply literal, and it does not simply stand for something else; it is both itself *and* something else that it richly suggests, a kind of manifestation of something too complex or too elusive to be otherwise revealed. Blake's poem is about a blighted rose and at the same time about much more. In a symbol, as Thomas Carlyle wrote, "the Infinite is made to blend with the Finite, to stand visible, and as it were, attainable there."

Verbal Irony and Paradox

Among the most common devices in poems is **verbal irony.** The speaker's words mean more or less the opposite of what they seem to say. Sometimes verbal irony takes the form of **overstatement,** or **hyperbole,** as when Shakespeare's John of Gaunt says "Not all the waters in the rude rough sea / Can wash the balm from an anointed king." Sometimes it takes the form of **understatement,** as when Andrew Marvell's speaker in "To His Coy Mistress" (page 372) remarks with cautious wryness, "The grave's a fine and private place, / But none, I think, do there embrace," or when Sylvia Plath sees an intended suicide as "the big strip tease." Speaking broadly, intensely emotional contemporary poems like those of Plath often use irony to undercut—and thus make acceptable—the emotion presented.

Another common device in poems is **paradox:** the assertion of an apparent contradiction, as in Marvell's "am'rous birds of prey" in "To His Coy Mistress." Normally we think of amorous birds as gentle—doves, for example—and not as birds of prey, such as hawks. Another example of an apparent contradiction: In "Auld Lang Syne" there is the paradox that the remembrance of joy evokes a kind of sadness. The student who wishes to see irony and paradox examined at length should consult Cleanth Brooks's *The Well-Wrought Urn*.

Explication

A line-by-line or episode-by-episode commentary on what is going on in a text is an **explication** (literally, unfolding or spreading out). It takes some skill to work one's way along without saying, "In line . . ., in the second line . . ., in the third line. . . ." One must sometimes say boldly something like, "The next stanza begins with . . . and then introduces. . . ." And, of course, one can discuss the second line before the first line if that seems to be the best way of handling the passage.

An explication is not concerned with the writer's life or times, and it is not a paraphrase, a rewording—though it may include paraphrase; it is but a commentary revealing your sense of the meaning of the work. To this end it calls attention, as it proceeds, to the implications of words, the function of rhymes, the shifts in point of view, the development of contrasts, and any other contributions to the meaning.

A Sample Explication

Take, for example, this short poem.

Hands, do what you're bid:
Bring the balloon of the mind
That bellies and drags in the wind
Into its narrow shed.
        —William Butler Yeats, "The Balloon of the Mind"

W. B. Yeats's "The Balloon of the Mind"

Yeats's "Balloon of the Mind" is about the difficulty of getting one's floating thoughts ("the balloon of the mind") down to earth, that is, into lines on the page. The first line, a short, stern, heavily stressed command to the speaker's hands, perhaps implies by its severe or impatient tone that these hands will be disobedient or inept or careless if not watched closely: The poor bumbling body so often fails to achieve the goals of the mind. The bluntness of the command in the first line is emphasized by the fact that all of the subsequent lines have more syllables. Furthermore, the first line is a grammatically complete sentence, whereas the thought of line 2 spills over into the subsequent lines, implying the difficulty of fitting ideas into confining spaces, that is, of getting one's thoughts into order, especially into a coherent poem. Lines 2 and 3 amplify the metaphor already stated in the title (the product of the mind is an airy but unwieldy balloon), and they also contain a second command, "Bring." Alliteration ties this command, "Bring," to the earlier "bid"; it also ties both of these verbs to their object, "balloon," and to the verb that most effectively describes the balloon, "bellies." In comparison with the peremptory first line of the poem, lines 2 and 3 themselves seem almost swollen, bellying and dragging, an effect aided by using adjacent unstressed syllables

("of the," "[bell]ies and," "in the") and by using an eye-rhyme
("mind" and "wind") rather than an exact rhyme. And then
comes the short last line: Almost before we could expect it, the
cumbersome balloon—here, the idea that is to be packed into the
stanza—is successfully lodged in its "narrow shed." Aside from
the relatively colorless "into," the only words of more than one
syllable in the poem are "narrow," "balloon," and "bellies," and
all three emphasize the difficulty of the task. But after
"narrow"—the word itself almost looks long and narrow, in this
context like a hangar—we get the simplicity of the monosyllable
"shed"; and the difficult job is done, the thought is safely packed
away, the poem is completed—but again with an off-rhyme ("bid"
and "shed"), for neatness can go only so far when hands and
mind and a balloon are involved.

As we can see from this excellent discussion of Yeats's poem, the language of
a literary work is denser (richer in associations or connotations) than the language
of such discursive prose as this paragraph. Explication of a literary work is, therefore, much concerned with bringing to the surface the meanings that are in the
words but that may not be immediately apparent. Explication, in short, seeks to
make explicit the implicit.

Note: The reader of an explication needs to see the text, and because the
explicated text is usually short, it is advisable to quote it all, and to number the
lines. (Remember, your imagined audience consists of your classmates; even if
they have already read the work you are explicating, they have not memorized it,
and so you helpfully remind them of the work by quoting it.) You can quote the
entire text at the outset, or you can quote the first unit (for example, a stanza),
then explicate that unit, and then quote the next unit, and so on. And if the poem
or passage of prose is longer than, say, five lines, it is advisable to number each
line at the right for easy reference.

Questions to Help Generate Essays on Poetry

If you are going to write about a fairly short poem (say, under thirty lines),
it's not a bad idea to copy out the poem, double-spaced. By writing it out you will
be forced to notice details, down to the punctuation. After you have copied the
poem, proofread it carefully against the original. Catching an error—even the
addition or omission of a comma—may help you to notice a detail in the original
that you might otherwise have overlooked. And of course, now that you have the
poem with ample space between the lines, you have a worksheet with room for
jottings.

A good essay is based on a genuine response to a poem; a response may be stimulated in part by first reading the poem aloud, and then considering the following questions.

Speaker. Who is the speaker? (Consider age, sex, personality, frame of mind.) Is the speaker fully aware of what he or she is saying, or does the speaker reveal himself or herself unconsciously? In short, what is the speaker's personality? What are his or her moral and intellectual values?

Audience. To whom is the speaker speaking? What is the situation (including the time and place)?

Structure. Does the poem proceed in a straightforward way, or at some points does the speaker reverse course, altering his or her tone or perception? Does the poem proceed by sections? If so, what are these sections, and how does each section (characterized, perhaps, by a certain tone of voice) grow out of what precedes it?

Center of Interest. Is the interest chiefly in character or in meditation— that is, is the poem chiefly psychological or is it chiefly philosophical?

Diction. Do certain words have rich and relevant associations that relate to other words to help define the theme? What is the role of the figurative language, if any? Does it help to define the speaker or the theme? What is to be taken symbolically, and what literally?

Sound Effects, Metrics. What is the role of sound effects, including repetitions of sound and of entire words, and shifts in versification? If there are off-rhymes, what function do they serve? If there are unexpected stresses or pauses, what functions do they serve?

Form. What is the effect of the form—say, quatrains (stanzas of four lines), or blank verse (unrhymed lines of ten syllables), or couplets (pairs of rhyming lines)? If the sense overflows the form, running without pause from (for example) one quatrain into the next, what explanation can be offered?

By the way, most of these questions can be adapted easily to any piece of writing—prose or poetry. If you ask these questions of whatever you are reading (and of your own writing, when you are rereading it with a view toward revising), they will probably assist you to see the strength—or weakness—of the material you are reading.

Rhythm and Versification: A Glossary

Rhythm (most simply, in English poetry, stresses at regular intervals) has a power of its own. A highly pronounced rhythm is common in such forms of poetry as charms, college yells, and lullabies; all of them are aimed at inducing a special effect magically. It is not surprising that *carmen,* the Latin word for poem or song, is also the Latin word for charm and the word from which our word *charm* is derived.

In much poetry, rhythm is only half heard, but its omnipresence is suggested by the fact that when poetry is printed it is customary (though it is less frequent today) to begin each line with a capital letter. Prose (from Latin *prorsus,* "forward," "straight on") keeps running across the paper until the right-hand margin is reached; then, merely because the paper has given out, the writer or printer starts again at the left, with a small letter. But verse (Latin *versus,* "a turning") often ends well short of the right-hand margin, and the next line begins at the left—usually with a capital—not because paper has run out but because the rhythmic pattern begins again. Lines of poetry are continually reminding us that they have a pattern.

Note that a mechanical, unvarying rhythm may be good to put the baby to sleep, but it can be deadly to readers who want to stay awake. Poets vary their rhythm according to their purpose; they ought not to be so regular that they are (in W. H. Auden's words) "accentual pests." In competent hands, rhythm contributes to meaning; it says something. Ezra Pound has a relevant comment: "Rhythm *must* have meaning. It can't be merely a careless dash off, with no grip and no real hold to the words and sense, a tumty tum tumty tum tum ta."

Consider this description of Hell from *Paradise Lost* (stressed syllables are marked by ´; unstressed syllables by ˘):

    Rocks, cave, lakes, fens, bogs, dens, and shades of death.

The normal line in *Paradise Lost* is written in iambic feet—alternate unstressed and stressed syllables—but in this line Milton immediately follows one heavy stress with another, helping to communicate the "meaning"—the oppressive monotony of Hell. As a second example, consider the function of the rhythm in two lines by Alexander Pope:

    When Ajax strives some rock's vast weight to throw,
    The line too labors, and the words move slow.

The stressed syllables do not merely alternate with the unstressed ones; rather, the great weight of the rock is suggested by three consecutive stressed words, "rock's vast weight," and the great effort involved in moving it is suggested by another three consecutive stresses, "line too labors," and by yet another three, "words move slow." Note, also, the abundant pauses within the lines. In the first line, for example, unless one's speech is slovenly, one must pause at least slightly after "Ajax," "strives," "rock's," "vast," "weight," and "throw." The grating sounds in "Ajax" and "rock's" do their work, too, and so do the explosive *t*'s. When Pope wishes to suggest lightness, he reverses his procedure, and he groups *un*stressed syllables:

    Not so, when swift Camilla scours the plain,

    Flies o'er th' unbending corn, and skims along the main.

This last line has twelve syllables and is thus longer than the line about Ajax, but the addition of *along* helps to communicate lightness and swiftness because in this line (it can be argued) neither syllable of *along* is strongly stressed. If *along* is omitted, the line still makes grammatical sense and becomes more "regular," but it also becomes less imitative of lightness.

The very regularity of a line may be meaningful too. Shakespeare begins a sonnet thus:

> ˘ ′ ˘ ′ ˘ ˘ ′ ˘ ′ ˘ ′
> When I do count the clock that tells the time.

This line about a mechanism runs with appropriate regularity. (It is worth noting, too, that "*c*ount the *c*lock" and "*t*ells the *t*ime" emphasize the regularity by the repetition of sounds and syntax.) But notice what Shakespeare does in the middle of the next line:

> ˘ ′ ˘ ′ ′ ′ ˘ ′ ˘ ′
> And see the brave day sunk in hideous night.

The technical vocabulary of **prosody** (the study of the principles of verse structure, including meter, rhyme and other sound effects, and stanzaic patterns) is large. An understanding of these terms will not turn anyone into a poet, but it will enable you to discuss some aspects of poetry more efficiently. The following are the chief terms of prosody.

Meter

Most English poetry has a pattern of stressed (accented) sounds, and this pattern is the **meter** (from the Greek word for "measure"). Strictly speaking, we really should not talk of "unstressed" or "unaccented" syllables, since to utter a syllable—however lightly—is to give it some stress. It is really a matter of *relative* stress, but the fact is that "unstressed" or "unaccented" are parts of the established terminology of versification.

In a line of poetry, the **foot** is the basic unit of measurement. It is on rare occasions a single stressed syllable; but generally a foot consists of two or three syllables, one of which is stressed. The repetition of feet, then, produces a pattern of stresses throughout the poem.

Two cautions:

1. A poem will seldom contain only one kind of foot throughout; significant variations usually occur, but one kind of foot is dominant.
2. In reading a poem, one chiefly pays attention to the sense, not to a presupposed metrical pattern. By paying attention to the sense, one often finds (reading aloud is a great help) that the stress falls on a word that according to the metrical pattern would be unstressed. Or a word that according to the pattern would be stressed may be seen to be unstressed. Furthermore, by reading for sense one finds that not all stresses are equally heavy; some are almost as light as unstressed syllables, and sometimes there is a **hovering stress**—that is, the stress is equally distributed over two adjacent syllables. To repeat: One reads for sense, allowing the syntax to help indicate the stresses.

Metrical Feet. The most common feet in English poetry are the six listed below.

Iamb (adjective: **iambic**): one unstressed syllable followed by one stressed syllable. The iamb, said to be the most common pattern in English speech, is surely the most common in English poetry. The following example has five iambic feet:

```
  ˘  /    ˘   /   ˘     /    ˘     /    ˘     /
I saw  the sky  descend - ing black  and white.
```
—Robert Lowell

Trochee (trochaic): one stressed syllable followed by one unstressed.

```
  /   ˘    /   ˘    /    ˘     /˘
Let her  live to  earn her  dinners.
```
—J. M. Synge

Anapest (anapestic): two unstressed syllables followed by one stressed.

```
  ˘    ˘   /    ˘   ˘    /    ˘  ˘   /    ˘  ˘   /
There are man - y who say  that a dog  has his day.
```
—Dylan Thomas

Dactyl (dactylic): one stressed syllable followed by two unstressed. This trisyllabic foot, like the anapest, is common in light verse or verse suggesting joy, but its use is not limited to such material, as Longfellow's *Evangeline* shows. Thomas Hood's sentimental "The Bridge of Sighs" begins:

```
  /    ˘   ˘    /   ˘  ˘
Take her up  tenderly.
```

Spondee (spondaic): two stressed syllables; most often used as a substitute for an iamb or trochee.

```
  /    /    ˘   /   ˘    /    ˘  /
Smart lad,  to slip  betimes  away.
```
—A. E. Housman

Pyrrhic: two unstressed syllables; it is often not considered a legitimate foot in English.

Metrical Lines. A metrical line consists of one or more feet and is named for the number of feet in it. The following names are used:

monometer: one foot   **pentameter:** five feet
dimeter: two feet   **hexameter:** six feet
trimeter: three feet   **heptameter:** seven feet
tetrameter: four feet

A line is scanned for the kind and number of feet in it, and the **scansion** tells you if it is, say, anapestic trimeter (three anapests):

```
  ˘  ˘   /   ˘  ˘    /    ˘  ˘    /
As I came  to the edge  of the woods.
```
—Robert Frost

Or, in another example, iambic pentameter:

$\breve{\ }\ \prime\ \breve{\ }\ \prime\ \breve{\ }\ \prime\ \breve{\ }\ \prime\ \breve{\ }\ \prime$

Since brass, nor stone, nor earth, nor boundless sea.
>   —Shakespeare

A line ending with a stress has a **masculine ending;** a line ending with an extra unstressed syllable has a **feminine ending.** The **caesura** (usually indicated by the symbol / /) is a slight pause within the line. It need not be indicated by punctuation (notice the fourth and fifth lines in the following quotation), and it does not affect the metrical count:

> Awake, my St. John! / / leave all meaner things
> To low ambition, / / and the pride of kings.
> Let us / / (since Life can little more supply
> Than just to look about us / / and to die)
> Expatiate free / / o'er all this scene of Man;
> A mighty maze! / / but not without a plan;
> A wild, / / where weeds and flowers promiscuous shoot;
> Or garden, / / tempting with forbidden fruit.
>   —Alexander Pope

The varying position of the caesura helps to give Pope's lines an informality that plays against the formality of the pairs of rhyming lines.

An **end-stopped line** concludes with a distinct syntactical pause, but a **run-on line** has its sense carried over into the next line without syntactical pause. (The running-on of a line is called **enjambment.**) In the following passage, only the first is a run-on line:

> Yet if we look more closely we shall find
> Most have the seeds of judgment in their mind:
> Nature affords at least a glimmering light;
> The lines, though touched but faintly, are drawn right.
>   —Alexander Pope

Meter produces **rhythm,** recurrences at equal intervals, but rhythm (from a Greek word meaning "flow") is usually applied to larger units than feet. Often it depends most obviously on pauses. Thus, a poem with run-on lines will have a different rhythm from a poem with end-stopped lines, even though both are in the same meter. And prose, though it is unmetrical, can have rhythm, too. In addition to being affected by syntactical pause, rhythm is affected by pauses attributable to consonant clusters and to the length of words. Polysyllabic words establish a different rhythm from monosyllabic words, even in metrically identical lines. One can say, then, that rhythm is altered by shifts in meter, syntax, and the length and ease of pronunciation. But even with no such shift, even if a line is repeated verbatim, a reader may sense a change in rhythm. The rhythm of the final line of a poem, for example, may well differ from that of the line before, even though in all other respects the lines are identical, as in Frost's "Stopping by Woods on a Snowy Evening" (p. 529), which concludes by repeating "And miles to go before I sleep." One may simply sense that this final line ought to be spoken, say, more slowly and with more stress on "miles."

Patterns of Sounds

Though rhythm is basic to poetry, **rhyme**—the repetition of the identical or similar stressed sound or sounds—is not. It is, presumably, pleasant in itself; it suggests order; and it also may be related to meaning, for it brings two words sharply together, often implying a relationship, as in the now trite *dove* and *love,* or in the more imaginative *throne* and *alone.* **Perfect** or **exact rhymes** occur when differing consonant sounds are followed by identical stressed vowel sounds, and the following sounds, if any, are identical *(foe—toe; meet—fleet; buffer—rougher).* Note that perfect rhyme involves identity of sound, not of spelling. *Fix* and *sticks,* like *buffer* and *rougher,* are perfect rhymes.

In **half-rhyme** (or **off-rhyme**), only the final consonant sounds of the rhyming words are identical; the stressed vowel sounds as well as the initial consonant sounds, if any, differ *(soul—oil; mirth—forth; trolley—bully).* **Eye-rhyme** is not really rhyme; it merely looks like rhyme *(cough—bough).* In **masculine rhyme,** the final syllables are stressed and, after their differing initial consonant sounds, are identical in sound *(stark—mark; support—retort).* In **feminine rhyme** (or **double-rhyme**) stressed rhyming syllables are followed by identical unstressed syllables *(revival—arrival; flatter—batter).* **Triple-rhyme** is a kind of feminine rhyme in which identical stressed vowel-sounds are followed by two identical unstressed syllables *(machinery—scenery; tenderly—slenderly).* **End-rhyme** (or **terminal-rhyme**) has the rhyming word at the end of the line. **Internal rhyme** has at least one of the rhyming words within the line (Oscar Wilde's "Each narrow *cell* in which we *dwell").*

Alliteration is sometimes defined as the repetition of initial sounds ("*All* the *aw*ful *au*guries" or "*B*ring me my *b*ow of *b*urning gold"), sometimes as the prominent repetition of a consonant ("a*f*ter li*f*e's *f*it*f*ul *f*ever"). **Assonance** is the repetition, in words in proximity, of identical vowel sounds preceded and followed by differing consonant sounds. Whereas *tide* and *hide* are rhymes, *tide* and *mine* are assonantal. **Consonance** is the repetition of identical consonant sounds and differing vowel sounds in words in proximity *(fail—feel; rough—roof; pitter—patter).* Sometimes consonance is more loosely defined merely as the repetition of a consonant *(fail—peel).* **Onomatopoeia** is said to occur when the sound of a word echoes or suggests the meaning of a word. *Hiss* and *buzz* are onomatopoetic. There is a mistaken tendency to see onomatopoeia everywhere—for example, in *thunder* and *horror.* Many words sometimes thought to be onomatopoeic are not clearly imitative of the thing they denote; they merely contain some sounds which—when we know what the word means—seem to have some resemblance to the thing they denote. Tennyson's lines from "Come down, 0 maid" are usually cited as an example of onomatopoeia:

> The moan of doves in immemorial elms
> And murmuring of innumerable bees.

Stanzaic Patterns

Lines of poetry are commonly arranged in a rhythmical unit called a **stanza** (from an Italian word meaning "room" or "stopping-place"). Usually all the stanzas in a poem have the same rhyme pattern. A stanza is sometimes called a **verse,** though *verse* may also mean a single line of poetry. (In discussing stanzas, rhymes are indicated by identical letters. Thus, *abab* indicates that the first and third lines rhyme with each other, while the second and fourth lines are linked by a different rhyme. An unrhymed line is denoted by *x*.) Common stanzaic forms in English poetry are the following:

Couplet: a stanza of two lines, usually, but not necessarily, with end-rhymes. *Couplet* is also used for a pair of rhyming lines. The **octosyllabic couplet** is iambic or trochaic tetrameter:

> Had we but world enough and time,
> This coyness, lady, were no crime.
> > —Andrew Marvell

Heroic couplet: a rhyming couplet of iambic pentameter, often "closed," that is, containing a complete thought, with a fairly heavy pause at the end of the first line and a still heavier one at the end of the second. Commonly, there is a parallel or an *antithesis* (contrast) within a line, or between the two lines. It is called heroic because in England, especially in the eighteenth century, it was much used for heroic (epic) poems.

> Some foreign writers, some our own despise;
> The ancients only, or the moderns, prize.
> > —Alexander Pope

Triplet (or **tercet**): a three-line stanza, usually with one rhyme.

> Whenas in silks my Julia goes
> Then, then (methinks) how sweetly flows
> That liquefaction of her clothes.
> > —Robert Herrick

Quatrain: a four-line stanza, rhymed or unrhymed. The **heroic (or elegiac) quatrain** is iambic pentameter, rhyming *abab*. That is, the first and third lines rhyme (so they are designated *a*), and the second and fourth lines rhyme (so they are designated *b*).

Sonnet: a fourteen-line poem, predominantly in iambic pentameter. The rhyme is usually according to one of two schemes. The **Italian** (or **Petrarchan**[3]) **sonnet** has two divisions: The first eight lines (rhyming *abba abba)* are the **octave,** the last six (rhyming *cd cd cd,* or a variant) are the **sestet.** Gerard Manley Hopkins's "God's Grandeur" (page 654) is an Italian sonnet. The second kind of sonnet, the **English** (or **Shakespearean**) **sonnet,** is usually arranged into three quatrains and a couplet, rhyming *abab cdcd efef gg.* (For examples see pages 369–370.) In many sonnets there is a marked correspondence between the rhyme scheme and the development of the thought. Thus an Italian sonnet may

---

[3] So called after Francesco Petrarch (1304–1374), the Italian poet who perfected and popularized the form.

state a generalization in the octave and a specific example in the sestet. Or an English sonnet may give three examples—one in each quatrain—and draw a conclusion in the couplet.

Blank Verse and Free Verse

A good deal of English poetry is unrhymed, much of it in **blank verse,** that is, unrhymed iambic pentameter. Introduced into English poetry by Henry Howard, Earl of Surrey, in the middle of the sixteenth century, late in the century it became the standard medium (especially in the hands of Christopher Marlowe and Shakespeare) of English drama. In the seventeenth century, Milton used it for *Paradise Lost,* and it has continued to be used in both dramatic and nondramatic literature. For an example see the first scene of *Hamlet* (page 229), until the Ghost appears.

The second kind of unrhymed poetry fairly common in English, especially in the twentieth century, is **free verse** (or **vers libre**): rhythmical lines varying in length, adhering to no fixed metrical pattern and usually unrhymed. The pattern is often largely based on repetition and parallel grammatical structure. For an example, see T. S. Eliot's "The Love Song of J. Alfred Prufrock" (page 533).

Writing 14 *About Drama*

Types of Plays

Most of the world's great plays written before the twentieth century may be regarded as one of two kinds: **tragedy** or **comedy.** Roughly speaking, tragedy dramatizes the conflict between the vitality of the single life and the laws or limits of life (the tragic hero reaches his heights, going beyond the experiences of other men, at the cost of his life), and comedy dramatizes the vitality of the laws of social life (the good life is seen to reside in the shedding of an individualism that isolates, in favor of a union with a genial and enlightened society). A third kind of drama, somewhat desperately called **tragicomedy,** is harder to epitomize, but most of the tragicomedies of our century use extravagant comic scenes to depict an absurd, senseless world. These points must be amplified a bit before we go on to the further point that, of course, any important play does much more than can be put into such crude formulas.

Tragedy

Most tragic heroes are males. There are a few splendid exceptions, such as Antigonê, Medea, Juliet, Cleopatra, and Phèdre, but for the most part women in tragic plays are pathetic rather than tragic; that is, they are relatively passive, chiefly being images of vulnerability rather than of exceptional strength at its breaking point. The following remarks, then, will speak of the tragic "hero" and of "his" actions, partly because repetition of "hero or heroine" and "his or her" is tiresome, but chiefly because tragic heroines are relatively few.

The tragic hero usually goes beyond the standards to which reasonable people adhere; he does some fearful deed which ultimately destroys him. This deed is often said to be an act of *hubris,* a Greek word meaning something like "overweening pride." It may involve, for instance, violating a taboo, such as that against taking life. But if the hubristic act ultimately destroys the person who performs it, it also shows him (paradoxically) to be in some way more fully a living being—a person who has experienced life more fully, whether by heroic action or by capacity for enduring suffering—than the people around him. (If the hero does not die, he usually is left in some deathlike state, as is the blind Oedipus in *Oedipus Rex.)* In tragedy, we see humanity pushed to an extreme; in his agony and grief the hero enters a world unknown to most and reveals magnificence. After his departure from the stage, we are left in a world of littler people.

Tragedy commonly involves **irony** of two sorts: unconsciously ironic deeds and unconsciously ironic speeches. **Ironic deeds** have some consequence more or less the reverse of what the doer intends. Macbeth thinks that by killing Duncan he will gain happiness, but he finds that his deed brings him sleepless nights. Brutus thinks that by killing Caesar he will bring liberty to Rome, but he brings tyranny. In an **unconsciously ironic speech**, the speaker's words mean one thing to him but something more significant to the audience, as when King Duncan, baffled by Cawdor's treason, says:

> There's no art
> To find the mind's construction in the face:
> He was a gentleman on whom I build
> An absolute trust.

At this moment Macbeth, whom we have already heard meditating the murder of Duncan, enters. Duncan's words are true, but he does not apply them to Macbeth, as the audience does. A few moments later Duncan praises Macbeth as "a peerless kinsman." Soon Macbeth will indeed become peerless, when he kills Duncan and ascends to the throne.[1] Sophocles' use of ironic deeds and speeches is so pervasive, especially in *Oedipus Rex,* that **Sophoclean irony** has become a critical term.

When the deed backfires or has a reverse effect, such as Macbeth's effort to gain happiness has, we have what Aristotle (the first—and still the greatest—drama critic) called a **peripeteia,** or a **reversal.** When a character comes to perceive what has happened (Macbeth's "I have lived long enough: my way of life / Is fall'n into the sere, the yellow leaf"), he experiences (in Aristotle's language) an **anagnorisis,** or **recognition.** Strictly speaking, for Aristotle the recognition was a matter of literal identification—for example, the recognition that Oedipus was the son of a man he killed. In *Macbeth,* the recognition in this sense is that Macduff, "from his mother's womb / Untimely ripped," is the man who fits the prophecy that Macbeth can be conquered only by someone not "of woman born." In his analysis of drama, Aristotle says that the tragic hero comes to grief through his **hamartia,** a term sometimes translated as **tragic flaw** but perhaps better translated as **tragic error,** since *flaw* implies a moral fault. Thus it is a

---

[1] *Dramatic irony* (ironic deeds, or happenings, and unconsciously ironic speeches) must be distinguished from *verbal irony*, which is produced when the speaker is conscious that his words mean something different from what they say. In *Macbeth* Lennox says: "The Gracious Duncan / Was pitied of Macbeth. Marry, he was dead! / And the right valiant Banquo walked too late. / . . . / Men must not walk too late." He *says* nothing about Macbeth having killed Duncan and Banquo, but he *means* that Macbeth has killed them.

great error for Oedipus (however apparently justifiable his action) to kill a man old enough to be his father, and to marry a woman old enough to be his mother. If we hold to the translation *flaw,* we begin to hunt for a fault in the tragic hero's character; and we say, for instance, that Oedipus is rash, or some such thing. In doing this, we may diminish or even overlook the hero's grandeur.

Comedy

In comedy, the fullest life is seen to reside within enlightened social norms: At the beginning of a comedy we find banished dukes, unhappy lovers, crabby parents, jealous husbands, and harsh laws; but at the end we usually have a unified and genial society, often symbolized by a marriage feast to which everyone, or almost everyone, is invited. Early in *A Midsummer Night's Dream,* for instance, we meet quarreling young lovers and a father who demands that his daughter either marry a man she does not love or enter a convent. Such is the Athenian law. At the end of the play the lovers are properly matched, to everyone's satisfaction.

Speaking broadly, most comedies fall into one of two classes: **satiric comedy** or **romantic comedy.** In the former, the emphasis is on the obstructionists—the irate fathers, hardheaded businessmen, and other members of the Establishment who at the beginning of the play seem to hold all of the cards, preventing joy from reigning. They are held up to ridicule because they are repressive monomaniacs enslaved to themselves, acting mechanistically (always irate, always hardheaded) instead of responding genially to the ups and downs of life. The outwitting of these obstructionists, usually by the younger generation, often provides the resolution of the plot. Ben Jonson, Molière, and George Bernard Shaw are in this tradition; their comedy, according to an ancient Roman formula, "chastens morals with ridicule"—that is, it reforms folly or vice by laughing at it. On the other hand, in romantic comedy (one thinks of Shakespeare's *A Midsummer Night's Dream, As You Like It,* and *Twelfth Night*) the emphasis is on a pair or pairs of delightful people who engage our sympathies as they run their obstacle race to the altar. There are obstructionists here too, but the emphasis is elsewhere.

Aspects of Drama

Theme

If we have read or seen a drama thoughtfully, we ought to be able to formulate its **theme,** its underlying idea, and perhaps we can even go so far as to say its moral attitudes, its view of life, its wisdom. Some critics, it is true, have argued that the concept of theme is meaningless. They hold that *Macbeth,* for example, gives us only an extremely detailed history of one imaginary man. In this view, *Macbeth* says nothing to you or me; it only says what happened to some imaginary man. Even *Julius Caesar* says nothing about the historical Julius Caesar or about the nature of Roman politics. Here we can agree; no one would offer Shakespeare's play as evidence of what the historical Caesar said or did. But surely the view that the concept of theme is meaningless, and that a work tells us only about imaginary creatures, is a desperate one. We *can* say that we see in *Julius Caesar* the fall of power, or (if we are thinking of Brutus) the vulnerability of idealism, or some such thing.

To the reply that these are mere truisms, we can counter: Yes, but the truisms are presented in such a way that they take on life and become a part of us rather than remaining things of which we say, "I've heard it said, and I guess it's so." The play offers instruction, in a pleasant and persuasive way. And surely we are in no danger of equating the play with the theme that we sense underlies it. We recognize that the play presents the theme with such detail that our statement is only a wedge to help us enter into the play, so we can appropriate it more fully.

Some critics (influenced by Aristotle's statement that a drama is an imitation of an action) use **action** in a sense equivalent to theme. In this sense, the action is the underlying happening—the inner happening—for example, "the enlightenment of a character," or "the coming of unhappiness to a character," or "the finding of the self by self-surrender." One might say that the theme of *Macbeth*, for example, is embodied in some words that Macbeth himself utters: "Blood will have blood." Of course this is not to say that these words and no other words embody the theme or the action; it is only to say that these words seem to the writer (and, if the essay is effective, to the reader) to bring us close to the center of the play.

Plot

Plot is variously defined, sometimes as equivalent to *story* (in this sense a synopsis of *Julius Caesar* has the same plot as *Julius Caesar*), but more often, and more usefully, as the dramatist's particular *arrangement of the story*. Thus, because Shakespeare's *Julius Caesar* begins with a scene dramatizing an encounter between plebeians and tribunes, its plot is different from that of a play on Julius Caesar in which such a scene (not necessary to the story) is omitted.

Handbooks on drama often suggest that a plot (arrangement of happenings) should have a **rising action,** a **climax,** and a **falling action.** This sort of plot can be diagramed as a pyramid: the tension rises through complications or **crises** to a climax, at which point the climax is the apex, and the tension allegedly slackens as we witness the **dénouement** (literally, *unknotting*). Shakespeare sometimes used a pyramidal structure, placing his climax neatly in the middle of what seems to us to be the third of five acts. In *Hamlet,* the protagonist proves to his own satisfaction Claudius's guilt in III.ii, with the play within the play; but almost immediately he begins to worsen his position, by failing to kill Claudius when he is an easy target (III.iii) and by contaminating himself with the murder of Polonius (III.iv).

Of course, no law demands such a structure, and a hunt for the pyramid usually causes the hunter to overlook all the crises but the middle one. William Butler Yeats once suggestively diagramed a good plot not as a pyramid but as a line moving diagonally upward, punctuated by several crises. Perhaps it is sufficient to say that a good plot has its moments of tension, but that the location of these will vary with the play. They are the product of **conflict,** but it should be noted that not all conflict produces tension; there is conflict but little tension in a ball game when the home team is ahead 10–0 and the visiting pitcher comes to bat in the ninth inning with two out and none on base.

Regardless of how a plot is diagramed, the **exposition** is that part which tells the audience what it has to know about the past, the **antecedent action.** Two gossiping servants who tell each other that after a year away in Paris the young master is coming home tomorrow with a new wife are giving the audience the exposition. But the exposition may also extend far into the play, being given in small, explosive revelations.

Exposition has been discussed as though it consists simply of informing the audience about events, but exposition can do much more. It can give us an understanding of the characters who themselves are talking about other characters, it can evoke a mood, and it can generate tension. When we summarize the opening act, and treat it as "mere exposition," we are probably losing what is in fact dramatic in it.

Gestures

The language of a play, broadly conceived, includes the **gestures** that the characters make and the **settings** in which they make them. As Ezra Pound says, "The medium of drama is not words, but persons moving about on a stage using words." When Ibsen's Nora "walks cautiously over to the door to the study and listens," the gesture and silent action are as important as the words that precede and follow them. Gesture can be interpreted even more broadly: The mere fact that a character enters, leaves, or does not enter may be highly significant. John Russell Brown comments on the actions and the absence of certain words that in *Hamlet* convey the growing separation between King Claudius and his wife, Gertrude:

> Their first appearance together with a public celebration of marriage is a large and simple visual effect, and Gertrude's close concern for her son suggests a simple, and perhaps unremarkable modification. . . . But Claudius enters without Gertrude for his "Prayer Scene" (III.iii) and, for the first time, Gertrude enters without him for the Closet Scene (III.iv) and is left alone, again for the first time, when Polonius hides behind the arras. Thereafter earlier accord is revalued by an increasing separation, often poignantly silent, and unexpected. When Claudius calls Gertrude to leave with him after Hamlet has dragged off Polonius' body, she makes no reply; twice more he urges her and she is still silent. But he does not remonstrate or question; rather he speaks of his own immediate concerns and, far from supporting her with assurances, becomes more aware of his own fears:
>
> >   O, come away!
> > My soul is full of discord and dismay.   (IV.i.44–45)
>
> Emotion has been so heightened that it is remarkable that they leave together without further words. The audience has been aware of a new distance between

Gertrude and Claudius, of her immobility and silence, and of his self-concern, haste, and insistence.[2]

Setting

Drama of the nineteenth and early twentieth centuries (for example, the plays of Henrik Ibsen, Anton Chekhov, and George Bernard Shaw) is often thought to be "realistic," but even a realistic playwright or stage designer selects from among many available materials. A **realistic setting** (indication of the **locale**), then, can say a great deal, and can even serve as a symbol. Over and over again in Ibsen we find the realistic setting of a nineteenth-century drawing room, with its heavy draperies and its bulky furniture, helping to convey his vision of a bourgeois world that oppresses the individual who struggles to affirm other values.

Twentieth-century dramatists are often explicit about the symbolic qualities of the setting. Here is an example from Eugene O'Neill's *Desire under the Elms:* Only a part of the initial stage direction is given.

> The house is in good condition but in need of paint. Its walls are a sickly grayish, the green of the shutters faded. Two enormous elms are on each side of the house. They bend their trailing branches down over the roof. They appear to protect and at the same time subdue. There is a sinister maternity in their aspect, a crushing, jealous absorption. . . . They are like exhausted women resting their sagging breasts and hands and hair on its roof. . . .

Characterization and Motivation

Characterization, or personality, is defined, as in fiction (see p. 712), by what the characters do (a stage direction tells us that "Nora dances more and more wildly"), by what they say (she asks her husband to play the piano), by what others say about them, and by the setting in which they move. The characters are also defined in part by other characters whom they in some degree resemble or from whom they in some degree differ. Hamlet, Laertes, and Fortinbras have each lost their fathers, but Hamlet spares the praying King Claudius, whereas Laertes, seeking vengeance on Hamlet for murdering Laertes's father, says he would cut Hamlet's throat in church; Hamlet meditates about the nature of action, but Fortinbras leads the Norwegians in a military campaign and ultimately acquires Denmark.

Other plays, of course, also provide examples of such **foils**, or characters who set one another off. Macbeth and Banquo both hear prophecies, but they act and react differently; Brutus is one kind of assassin, Cassius another, and Casca still another. Any analysis of a character, then, will probably have to take into account, in some degree, the other characters who help to show what he or she is, and who thus help to set forth his or her **motivation** (grounds for action, inner drives, goals). For an example of an essay on a character, see page 74.

---

[2] *Shakespeare's Plays in Performance* (New York: St. Martin's, 1967), p. 139.

Questions to Help Generate Essays on Plays

Character. What sort of character is so-and-so? How is he or she defined? If the figure is tragic, does the tragedy proceed from a moral flaw, from an intellectual error, from the malice of others, from sheer chance, or from some combination of these? If the figure is comic, do we laugh *with* or *at* him or her? Whether tragic or comic, how do his or her values compare to the values of other characters, characters who for better or worse may be taken to represent society? Are the characters adequately motivated—that is, are their actions believable, rooted in their personalities? What are their functions?

Plot. Does the plot depend on chance? If there is a subplot, is it related in theme to the main plot? Are there irrelevant scenes? What is the function of a particular scene? Is the resolution satisfactory?

Setting. Is the setting functional? Does it help to reveal character? Or to provide atmosphere? Does it have symbolic overtones?

Conflict. What kinds of conflict are there? One character against another, one group against another, one part of a personality against another part in the same character? How is the conflict resolved? By an unambiguous triumph of one side, or by a triumph that is also in some degree a loss for the triumphant side?

In writing about drama, most of us are likely to pay attention chiefly to the dialogue, the words on the page—an understandable procedure if we regard drama as literature. Probably the great majority of essays are about the characterization of so-and-so. These essays usually look at a character's words, actions, and the setting in which he or she moves, as well as at what others say about him and do to him. With a play of great complexity—for example, one of Shakespeare's major plays—a short essay may do well to take an even smaller topic, such as Hamlet's bawdy talk (Why does this prince sometimes make dirty remarks?). Even here we will not be able merely to hunt through the play looking at Hamlet's bawdry; we will have to pay some attention to other jesting in *Hamlet,* if we are to see the exact nature of the problem we have chosen to isolate.

But as we said above, words are not the only language of drama, and a student will sometimes want to explore matters of staging. What is especially difficult for most of us, confronted with only a printed page, is to catch the full dramatic quality of a play—to read the words and also to have a sense of how they will sound in the context of gestures and a setting. If you can see a production of the play you are writing about, you can recall at least some of the physical presentation when you reread the play, but if a production is not available, you will have to try to read the play with an actor's or a director's imagination. Otherwise you will be reading the play as literature rather than as dramatic literature, or theater. Try to read, then, with an actor's imagination, seeing the characters standing or moving within a setting, and trying to understand *why*.

Appendix A:
Research Papers

What Research Is

Because a research paper requires its writer to collect and interpret evidence—usually including the opinions of earlier investigators—one sometimes hears that a research paper, unlike a critical essay, is not the expression of personal opinion. But such a view is unjust both to criticism and to research. A critical essay is not a mere expression of personal opinions; if it is any good, it offers evidence that supports the opinions and thus persuades the reader of their objective rightness. And a research paper is in the final analysis largely personal, because the author continuously uses his or her own judgment to evaluate the evidence, deciding what is relevant and convincing. A research paper is not the mere presentation of what a dozen scholars have already said about a topic; it is a thoughtful evaluation of the available evidence, and so it is, finally, an expression of what the author thinks the evidence adds up to.

Research can be a tedious and frustrating business; there are hours spent reading books and articles that prove to be irrelevant, there are contradictory pieces of evidence, and there is never enough time.

Still, even though research is time-consuming, those who engage in it feel (at least sometimes) an exhilaration, a sense of triumph at having studied a problem thoroughly and arrived at conclusions that—for the moment, anyway—seem objective and irrefutable. Later, new evidence may turn up and require a new conclusion, but until that time one has built something that will endure wind and weather.

Primary and Secondary Materials

The materials of literary research can be conveniently divided into two sorts, primary and secondary. The *primary materials* or sources are the real subject of study; the *secondary materials* are critical and historical accounts already written about these primary materials. For example, if you want to know whether Shakepeare's attitude toward Julius Caesar was highly traditional or highly original (or a

748

little of each), you read the primary materials (*Julius Caesar,* and other Elizabethan writings about Caesar); and, since research requires that you be informed about the present state of thought on your topic, you also read the secondary materials (post-Elizabethan essays, books on Shakespeare, and books on Elizabethan attitudes toward Caesar, or, more generally, on Elizabethan attitudes toward Rome and toward monarchs).

The line between these two kinds of sources is not always clear. For example, if you are concerned with the degree to which Joyce's *A Portrait of the Artist as a Young Man* is autobiographical, primary materials include not only *Portrait* and Joyce's letters, but perhaps also his brother Stanislaus's diary and autobiography. The diary and autobiography might be considered secondary sources (certainly a scholarly biography about Joyce or about his brother would be a secondary source), but because Stanislaus's books are more or less contemporary with your subject and are more or less Joycean, they can reasonably be called primary sources.

From Topic to Thesis

Almost every literary work lends itself to research. We have already mentioned that a study of Shakespeare's attitude toward Julius Caesar would lead to a study of other Elizabethan works and of modern critical works. Similarly, a study of the ghost of Caesar—does it have a real, objective existence or is it merely a figment of Brutus's imagination?—could lead to a study of Shakespeare's other ghosts (for instance, those in *Hamlet* and *Macbeth*), and a study of Elizabethan attitudes toward ghosts. Or, to take an example from our own century, a reader of Edward Albee's *The Sandbox* might want to study the early, critical reception of the play. Did the reviewers like it? More precisely, did the reviewers in academic journals evaluate it differently from those in popular magazines and newspapers? Or, what has Albee himself said about the play in the decades that have passed since he wrote it? Do his comments in essays and interviews indicate that he now sees the play as something different from what he saw when he wrote it? Or, to take yet another example of a work from the middle of our century, a reader might similarly study George Orwell's *1984*, looking at its critical reception, or Orwell's own view of it, or, say, at the sources of Orwell's inspiration. Let's look, for a few minutes, at this last topic.

Assume that you have read George Orwell's *1984* and that, in preparing to do some research on it, browsing through *The Collected Essays, Journalism, and Letters,* you come across a letter (17 February 1944) in which Orwell says that he has been reading Evgenii Zamyatin's *We* and that he himself had been keeping notes for "that kind of book." And in *The Collected Essays, Journalism, and Letters* you also come across a review (4 January 1946) Orwell wrote of *We,* from which it is apparent that *We* resembles *1984*. Or perhaps you learned in a preface to an edition of *1984* that Orwell was influenced by *We,* and you have decided to look into the matter. You want to know exactly how great the influence is. You borrow *We* from the library, read it, and perceive resemblances in plot, character, and theme. But it's not simply a question of listing resemblances between the two books. Your topic is: What do the resemblances add up to? After all, Orwell in the letter said he had already been working in Zamyatin's direction without even knowing Zamyatin's book, so your investigation may find, for example, that the closest resemblances are in relatively trivial details and that there is really nothing important in *1984* that was not already implicit in Orwell's earlier books; or your investigation may find that Zamyatin gave a new depth to Orwell's thought; or it may find that though Orwell borrowed heavily from Zamyatin, he missed the depth of *We*. In the earliest stage of your research, then, you don't know what you will find, so you cannot yet formulate a thesis (or, at best, you can formulate only a tentative thesis). But you know that there is a topic, that it interests you, and that you are ready to begin the necessary legwork.

Locating Material: First Steps

First, prepare a working bibliography, that is, a list of books and articles that must be looked at. The catalog of your library is an excellent place to begin. If your topic is Orwell and Zamyatin, you'll want at least to glance at whatever books by and about these two authors are available. When you have looked over the most promising portions of this material (in secondary sources, chapter headings and indexes will often guide you), you will have found some interesting things. But you want to get a good idea of the state of current scholarship on your topic, and you realize that you must go beyond the card catalog's listings under *Orwell*, *Zamyatin*, and such obviously related topics as *utopian literature*. Doubtless there are pertinent articles in journals, but you cannot start thumbing through them at random. The easiest way to locate articles and books on your topic is to consult the *MLA International Bibliography*, which until 1969 was published as part of *PMLA (Publications of the Modern Language Association)* and since 1969 has been published separately. This bibliography, published annually, lists scholarly studies published in a given year; you look, therefore, in the most recent issue under *Orwell* (in the section on *English Literature*, the subsection on *Twentieth Century)* to see if anything is listed that sounds relevant. A look at *Zamyatin* may also turn up material. (Note that in the past few years the number of entries in the *MLA International Bibliography* has so increased that for each year from 1969 the annual bibliography consists of more than one volume. Writings on literature in English are in one volume, writings on European literature in another; so the volume that gives you information about Orwell will not be the one that gives you information about Zamyatin.)

If, by the way, you are indeed working on Orwell, when you consult the *MLA International Bibliography* for 1975 you'll find you are lucky; it lists an article, in an issue of a periodical entitled *Modern Fiction Studies,* that is itself a bibliography of writings on Orwell. If you consult this article, you'll see that it is a supplement to an earlier bibliography of writings on Orwell, published in *Bulletin of Bibliography* in 1974. This last item, of course, could also have been located by looking at the *MLA International Bibliography* for 1974.

Because your time is severely limited, you probably cannot read everything published on your two authors. At least for the moment, therefore, you will use only the last ten years of this bibliography. Presumably any important earlier material will have been incorporated into some of the recent studies listed, and if when you come to read these recent studies you find references to an article of, say, 1958 that sounds essential, of course you will read that article too.

Other Bibliographic Aids

The *MLA International Bibliography* is not the only valuable guide to scholarship. The *Year's Work in English Studies,* though concerned only with English authors (hence it will have nothing on Zamyatin, a Russian, unless an article links Zamyatin with an English author), and though not nearly so comprehensive even on English authors as the *MLA International Bibliography,* is useful partly because it is selective—presumably listing only the more significant items—and partly because it includes some evaluative comments on the books and articles it lists.

For topics in American literature, there is a similar annual publication, *American Literary Scholarship,* edited by J. Albert Robbins (earlier volumes were edited by James Woodress), valuable for its broad coverage of articles and books on major and minor writers and for its evaluative comments. There are two useful guides to scholarly and critical studies of some chief American figures: James Woodress et al., eds., *Eight American Authors: A Review of Research and Criticism,* rev. ed. (New York: Norton, 1972), covering Poe, Emerson, Hawthorne, Thoreau, Melville, Whitman, Mark Twain, and Henry James; and Jackson R. Bryer, ed., *Sixteen Modern American Authors: A Survey of Research and Criticism* (Durham, N.C: Duke University Press, 1974), covering such figures as Sherwood Anderson, Eugene O'Neill, William Carlos Williams, and Ezra Pound (living authors are excluded). Also useful is Robert E. Spiller et al., *Literary History of the United States,* 4th ed. revised (New York: Macmillan, 1974). In this revised edition, volume II is a *Bibliography* listing significant books and articles on American literature through 1970.

None of the bibliographic aids mentioned thus far covers ancient writers; there is no point, then, in looking at these aids if you are writing about the Book of Job, or Greek conceptions of the tragic hero, or Roman conceptions of comedy. For articles on ancient literature as well as on literature in modern languages, consult the annual volumes of *Humanities Index,* issued since 1974; for the period from 1965 to 1974 it was entitled *Social Sciences and Humanities Index,* and before that (1907–1964) it was *International Index.* In *Humanities Index* (to use the current title) you can find listings of articles in periodicals on a wide range of topics. This breadth is bought at the cost of depth, for *Humanities Index,* though it includes the chief scholarly journals, includes neither the less well known scholarly journals nor the more popular magazines, nor does it include books. For the more popular magazines, consult the *Readers' Guide to Periodical Literature.* If, for example, you want to do a research paper on the reception given to Laurence

Olivier's films of Shakespeare, the *Readers' Guide* can quickly lead you to reviews in such magazines as *Time, Newsweek,* and *The Atlantic Monthly.*

Bibliographies of the sort mentioned are guides, and there are so many of them that there are guides to these guides. Three useful guides to reference works (that is, to bibliographies and also to such helpful compilations as handbooks of mythology, quotations, dates, place names, and critical terms) are Richard D. Altick and Andrew Wright, *Selective Bibliography for the Study of English and American Literature,* 6th ed. (New York: Macmillan, 1979); Donald F. Bond, *A Reference Guide to English Studies,* 2nd ed. (Chicago: University of Chicago Press, 1971); and Arthur G. Kennedy and Donald B. Sands, *A Concise Bibliography for Students of English,* 5th ed., revised by William E. Colburn (Stanford, Calif: Stanford University Press, 1972).

And there are guides to these guides to guides: reference librarians. If you don't know where to turn to find something, turn to the librarian.

Taking Notes

Let's assume now that you have checked some bibliographies, and that you have a fair number of references to things you feel you must read to have a substantial knowledge of the evidence and the common interpretations of the evidence. Most researchers find it convenient, when examining bibliographies and the card catalog, to write down each reference on a 3 × 5 index card—one title per card. On the card put the author's full name (last name first), the exact title of the book or of the article, and the name of the journal (with dates and pages). Titles of books and periodicals (publications issued periodically—for example, monthly or four times a year) are underlined; titles of articles and of essays in books are put within quotation marks. It's also a good idea to put the library catalog number on the card, to save time if you need to get the item for a second look.

Next, you have to start reading or scanning the materials whose titles you have collected. Some of these items will prove irrelevant or silly; others will prove valuable in themselves and also in the leads they give you to further references, which you should duly record on 3 × 5 cards. Notes—aside from these bibliographic notes—are best taken on 4 × 6 cards. Smaller cards do not provide enough space for summaries of useful materials, but 4 × 6 cards— rather than larger cards—will serve to remind you that you should not take notes on everything. Be selective in taking notes.

1. In taking notes, write brief *summaries* rather than paraphrases. There is rarely any point to paraphrasing; generally speaking, either quote exactly (and put the passage in quotation marks, with a notation of the source, including the page numbers), or summarize, reducing a page or even an entire article or chapter of a book to a single 4 × 6 card. Even when you summarize, indicate your source on the card, so you can give appropriate credit in your paper. (On plagiarism, see pages 754–756.)

2. Of course, in your summary you will sometimes quote a phrase or a

sentence—putting it in quotation marks—but quote sparingly. You are not doing stenography, but rather, thinking and assimilating knowledge; for the most part, then, you should digest your source rather than engorge it whole. Thinking now, while taking notes, will also help you avoid plagiarism later. If, on the other hand, you mindlessly copy material at length when taking notes, when you are writing the paper later you may be tempted to copy it yet again, perhaps without giving credit. Similarly, if you photocopy pages from articles or books, and then merely underline some passages, you will probably not be thinking; you will just be underlining. But if you make a terse summary on a note card, you will be forced to think and to find your own words for the idea. Most of the direct quotations you copy should be effectively stated passages or especially crucial passages, or both. In your finished paper some of these quotations will provide authority and emphasis.

3. If you quote but omit some irrelevant material within the quotation, be sure to indicate the omission by three spaced periods, as explained on page 771.

4. *Never* copy a passage changing an occasional word under the impression that you are thereby putting it into your own words. Notes of this sort will find their way into your paper, your reader will sense a style other than your own, and suspicions of plagiarism may follow.

5. In the upper corner of each note card, write a brief key—for example, "Orwell's first reading of *We*," or "Characterization," or "Thought control"—so that later you can tell at a glance what is on the card.

As you work, you'll find yourself returning again and again to your primary materials—and you'll probably find to your surprise that a good deal of the secondary material is unconvincing or even wrong, despite the fact that it is printed in a handsome book or a scholarly journal. There are times when, under the weight of evidence, you will have to abandon some of your earlier views, but there are also times when you will have your own opinions reinforced, or even times when you will feel that your ideas have more validity than those you are reading. One of the things we learn from research is that not everything in print is true; this discovery is one of the pleasures we get from research.

Writing the Paper

There remains the difficult job of writing up your findings, but if you have taken good notes and have put useful headings on each card, you are well on your way. Read through the cards and sort them into packets of related material. Discard all notes, however interesting, that you now see are irrelevant to your paper. Go through the cards again and again, sorting and resorting, putting together what belongs together. Probably you will find that you have to do a little additional research—somehow you aren't quite clear about this or that—but after you have done this additional research, you should be able to arrange the packets in a reasonable and consistent sequence. You now have a kind of first draft, or at least a tentative organization for your paper. Two further pieces of advice:

1. Beware of the compulsion to include every note card in your essay; that is, beware of telling the reader, "*A* says . . . ; *B* says . . . ; *C* says . . ."
2. You must have a point, a thesis.

Remember: As you studied the evidence, you increasingly developed or documented or corrected a thesis. You may, for example, have become convinced that the influence of Zamyatin was limited to a few details of plot and character, and that Orwell had already developed the framework and the chief attitudes that are implicit in *1984*. Similarly, now, as you write and revise your paper, you will probably still be modifying your thesis to some extent, discovering what in fact the evidence implies. But the final version of the paper should be a finished piece of work, without the inconsistencies, detours, and occasional dead ends of an early draft. Your readers should feel that they are moving toward a conclusion (by means of your thoughtful evaluation of the evidence) rather than merely reading an anthology of commentary on the topic. And so we should get some such structure as: "There are three common views on . . . The first two are represented by *A* and *B*; the third, and by far the most reasonable, is *C*'s view that . . . *A* argues . . . but . . . The second view, *B's*, is based on . . . but . . . Although the third view, *C's*, is not conclusive, still . . . Moreover, *C*'s point can be strengthened when we consider a piece of evidence which he does not make use of . . ." All of this, of course, is fleshed out with careful summaries, effective quotations (documented as explained on pages 754–766), and judicious analyses of your own, so that by the end of the paper your readers not only have read a neatly typed paper (see page 767) but also are persuaded that under your guidance they have seen the evidence, heard the arguments justly summarized, and reached a sound conclusion.

A bibliography or list of works consulted (see pages 758–766) is usually appended to a research paper, so readers may easily look further into the primary and secondary material if they wish; but if you have done your job well, readers will be content to leave the subject where you left it, grateful that you have set matters straight.

Documentation

What to Document: Avoiding Plagiarism

Honesty requires that you acknowledge your indebtedness for material, not only when you quote directly from a work, but also when you appropriate an idea that is not common knowledge. Not to acknowledge such borrowing is plagiarism. If in doubt as to whether or not to give credit, give credit. But you ought to develop a sense of what is considered common knowledge. Definitions in a dictionary can be considered common knowledge, so there is no need to say, "According to Webster, a novel is . . ." (This is weak in three ways: It's unnecessary, it's uninteresting, and it's unclear, since "Webster" appears in the titles of several dictionaries, some good and some bad.) Similarly, the date of first publication of *The Scarlet Letter* can be considered common knowledge. Few can give it when asked, but it can be found out from innumerable sources, and no one need get the credit for providing you with the date. The idea that Hamlet delays is also a matter of common knowledge. But if you are impressed by so-and-so's argument that Claudius has been much maligned, you should give credit to so-and-so.

Suppose that you happen to come across Frederick R. Karl's statement, in the revised edition of *A Reader's Guide to the Contemporary English Novel* (New York: Farrar, Straus & Giroux, 1972), that George Orwell was "better as a man than as a novelist." This is an interesting and an effectively worded idea. You cannot use these words without giving credit to Karl. Nor can you retain the idea but alter the words, for example, to "Orwell was a better human being than he was a writer of fiction," presenting the idea as your own, for here you are simply lifting Karl's idea—and putting it less effectively. If you want to use Karl's point, give him credit and—since you can hardly summarize so brief a statement—use his exact words and put them within quotation marks.

But what about a longer passage that strikes you favorably? Let's assume that in reading Alex Zwerdling's *Orwell and the Left* (New Haven: Yale, 1974) you find the following passage from page 105 interesting:

> *1984* might be said to have a predominantly negative goal, since it is much more concerned to fight *against* a possible future society than *for* one. Its tactics are primarily defensive. Winston Smith is much less concerned with the future than with the past—which is of course the reader's present.

You certainly *cannot* say:

> The goal of 1984 can be said to be chiefly negative, because it is
> devoted more to opposing some future society than it is to
> fighting for a future society. Smith is more concerned with the
> past (our present) than he is with the future.

This passage is simply a theft of Zwerdling's property: The writer has stolen Zwerdling's automobile and put a different color paint on it. How, then, can a writer use Zwerdling's idea? (1) Give Zwerdling credit and quote directly, or (2) give Zwerdling credit and summarize his point in perhaps a third of the length, or (3) give Zwerdling credit and summarize the point but include—within quotation marks—some phrase you think is especially quotable. Thus:

1. *Direct quotation.* In a study of Orwell's politics, Alex Zwerdling says, "*1984* might be said to have a predominantly negative goal, since it is much more concerned to fight *against* a possible future society than *for* one" (105).
2. *Summary.* The goal of *1984*, Zwerdling points out (105), is chiefly opposition to, rather than advocacy of, a certain kind of future society.
3. *Summary with selected quotation.* Zwerdling points out (105) that the goal of 1984 is "predominantly negative," opposition to, rather than advocacy of, a certain kind of future society.

If for some reason you do not wish to name Zwerdling in your lead-in, you will have to give his name with the parenthetical citation so that a reader can identify the source:

> The goal of <u>1984</u>, one critic points out, is "predominantly
> negative" (Zwerdling, 105), opposition to, rather than advocacy of,
> a certain kind of future society.

But it is hard to imagine why the writer preferred to say "one critic," rather than to name Zwerdling immediately, since Zwerdling sooner or later must be identified.

How to Document: Footnotes and Internal Parenthetical Citations

Documentation tells your reader exactly what your sources are. Until recently, the standard form was the footnote, which, for example, told the reader that the source of such-and-such a quotation was a book by so-and-so. But in 1984 the Modern Language Association, which had established the footnote form used in hundreds of journals, university presses, and classrooms, substituted a new form. It is this new form—parenthetical citations *within* the text (rather than at the foot of the page or the end of the essay)—that we will discuss at length. Keep in mind, though, that footnotes still have their uses.

Footnotes. If you are using only one source your instructor may advise you to give the source in a footnote. (Check with your instructors to find out their preferred forms of documentation.)

Let's say that your only source is this textbook. Let's say, too, that all of your quotations will be from a single story—Kate Chopin's "The Story of an Hour"—printed in this book on pages 63–64. The simplest way to cite your source is to type the digit 1 (elevated, and *without* a period after it) after your first reference to (or quotation from) the story, and then to put a footnote at the bottom of the page, explaining where the story can be found. After the last line of type on the page, triple-space, indent five spaces from the left-hand margin, raise the typewriter carriage half a line, and type the arabic number 1. Do *not* put a period after it. Then lower the carriage half a line, hit the space bar once, and type a statement (double-spaced) to the effect that all references are to this book. Notice that although the footnote begins by being indented five spaces, if the note runs to more than one line the subsequent lines are given flush left.

[1] Chopin's story appears in Sylvan Barnet, Morton Berman, and William Burto, eds., <u>Literature for Composition</u>, 2nd ed. (Glenview, Ill.: Scott, Foresman, 1988), 63–64. All page references are to this book.

(If a book has more than three authors or editors, give only the name of the first author or editor, and follow it with a comma and et al., the Latin abbreviation for "and others.")

Even if you are writing a comparison of, say, two stories in this book, you can use a note of this sort. It might run thus:

> [1] All page references, given parenthetically within the essay,
> refer to stories in Sylvan Barnet, Morton Berman, and
> William Burto, eds., Literature for Composition, 2nd ed.
> (Glenview, Ill.: Scott, Foresman, 1988).

If you use such a note, you do not need to use a footnote after each quotation that follows. You can give the citations right in the body of the paper, by putting the page references in parentheses after the quotations.

Internal Parenthetical Citations. On page 770 we distinguish between embedded quotations (which are short, are run right into your own sentence, and are enclosed within quotation marks) and quotations that are set off on the page (for example, three or more lines of poetry, five or more lines of typed prose that are not enclosed within quotation marks).

For an embedded quotation, put the page reference in parentheses immediately after the closing quotation mark, *without* any intervening punctuation. Then, after the parenthesis that follows the number, put the necessary punctuation (for instance, a comma or a period).

> Orwell says that until he shot the elephant his experience in
> Burma was "perplexing and upsetting" (6). He goes on to ex-
> plain . . .

Notice that the period comes *after* the parenthetical citation. Notice, similarly, that in the next example *no* punctuation comes after the first citation—because none is needed—and a comma comes *after* (not before or within) the second citation, because a comma is needed in the sentence.

> This is ironic because almost at the start of the story, in the
> second paragraph, Richards with the best of motives "hastened"
> (63) to bring his sad message; if he had at the start been "too
> late" (64), Mallard would have arrived at home first.

For a quotation that is not embedded within the text but is set off (by being indented ten spaces), put the parenthetical citation on the last line of the quotation, flush with the right margin *after* the period that ends the quoted sentence.

> Orwell is a master at varying the lengths of his sentences in
> order to convey meaning. For instance, in describing the death of
> the elephant, he uses longish sentences to convey the slow death

of the great animal, and short sentences to convey the brevity of the act of shooting him:

> At the second shot he did not collapse but climbed with
> desperate slowness to his feet and stood weakly upright,
> with legs sagging and head drooping. I fired a third time.
> That was the shot that did for him. You could see the agony
> of it jolt his whole body and knock the last remnant of
> strength from his legs.   (10)

Notice that the quotation ends with the period, and that the parenthetical citation is flush with the right-hand margin.

Four additional points:

1. "p.," "pg.," and "pp." are *not* used in citing pages.
2. If a story is very short—perhaps running for only a page or two—your instructor may tell you there is no need to keep citing the page reference for each quotation. Simply mention in the footnote that the story appears on, say, pages 200–202.
3. If you are referring to a poem, your instructor may tell you to use parenthetical citations of line numbers rather than of page numbers. But, again, your footnote will tell the reader that the poem can be found in this book, and on what page.
4. If you are referring to a play with numbered lines, your instructor may prefer that in your parenthetical citations you give act, scene, and line, rather than page numbers. Use arabic (not roman) numerals, separating the act from the scene, and the scene from the line, by periods. Here, then, is how a reference to act three, scene two, line 118 would be given:

(3.2.118)

Parenthetical Citations and List of Works Cited. Footnotes have fallen into disfavor. Parenthetical citations are now usually clarified not by means of a footnote but by means of a list, headed Works Cited, given at the end of the essay. In this list you give, alphabetically (last name first), the authors and titles that you have quoted or referred to in the essay.

Briefly, the idea is that the reader of your paper encounters an author's name and a parenthetical citation of pages. By checking the author's name in Works Cited, the reader can find the passage in the book. Suppose the writer is writing about Kate Chopin's "The Story of an Hour." Let's assume that the writer has already mentioned the author and title of the story—that is, has let the reader know what the subject of the essay is—and now uses a quotation from the story, in a sentence such as this. (Notice the parenthetical citation of page numbers immediately after the quotation.)

True, Mrs. Mallard at first expresses grief when she hears the
news, but soon (unknown to her friends) she finds joy in it. So,
Richards's "sad message" (63), though sad in Richards's eyes, is
in fact a happy message.

Turning to Works Cited, the reader, knowing the quoted words are by Chopin,
looks for Chopin and finds the following:

Works Cited

Chopin, Kate. "The Story of an Hour." <u>Literature for Composition,</u>
2nd ed. Ed. Sylvan Barnet, Morton Berman, and William
Burto. Glenview, Ill.: Scott, Foresman, 1988. 63–64.

Thus the essayist is informing the reader that the quoted words ("sad message")
are to be found on page 63 of this anthology.

If the writer had not mentioned Chopin's name in some sort of lead-in, the
name would have to be given within the parentheses so that the reader would
know the author of the quoted words:

What are we to make out of a story that ends by telling us that
the leading character has died "of joy that kills" (Chopin 64)?

(Notice, by the way, that the closing quotation marks come immediately after the
last word of the quotation; the citation and the final punctuation—in this case, the
essayist's question mark—come *after* the closing quotation marks.)

If you are comparing Chopin's story with Ambrose Bierce's "An Occurrence
at Owl Creek Bridge," in Works Cited you will give a similar entry for Bierce—his
name, the title of the story, the book in which it is reprinted, and the page
numbers that the story occupies.

If you are referring to several works reprinted within one volume, instead of
listing each item fully, it is acceptable in Works Cited to list each item simply by
giving the author's name, the title of the work, then a period, two spaces, and the
name of the anthologist followed by the page numbers that the selection spans.
Thus a reference to Chopin's "The Story of an Hour" would be followed only by:
Barnet, 63–64. This form, of course, requires that the anthology itself be cited
under the name of the first-listed editor, thus:

Barnet, Sylvan, Morton Berman, and William Burto, eds.,
<u>Literature for Composition.</u> 2nd ed. Glenview, Ill.: Scott,
Foresman, 1988.

If you are writing a research paper, you will of course use many sources.
Within the essay itself you will mention an author's name, and then will quote or
summarize from this author, and follow the quotation or summary with a paren-

thetical citation of the pages. In Works Cited, you will give the full title, place of publication, and other bibliographic material.

Forms of Citation in Works Cited.   In looking over the following samples of entries in Works Cited, remember:

1. The list of Works Cited is arranged alphabetically by author (last name first).
2. If a work is anonymous, list it under the first word of the title, unless the first word is *A, An,* or *The,* in which case list it under the second word.
3. If a work is by two authors, although the book is listed alphabetically under the first author's last name, the second author's name is given in the normal order, first name first.
4. If you list two or more works by the same author, the author's name is not repeated but is represented by three hyphens followed by a period and two spaces.
5. Each item begins flush left, but if an entry is longer than one line, subsequent lines in the entry are indented five spaces.

For details about almost every imaginable kind of citation, consult Joseph Gibaldi and Walter S. Achtert, *MLA Handbook for Writers of Research Papers,* 2nd ed. (New York: Modern Language Association, 1984). We give here, however, information concerning the most common kinds of citations.

Here are samples of the citations of the kinds of publications you are most likely to include in your list of Works Cited.

Entries (arranged alphabetically) begin flush with the left margin. If an entry runs more than one line, indent the subsequent line or lines five spaces from the left margin.

A book by one author

Douglas, Ann. The Feminization of American Culture. New York:
    Knopf, 1977.

Notice that the author's last name is given first, but otherwise the name is given as on the title page. Do not substitute initials for names written out on the title page. But you may shorten the publisher's name—for example, from Little, Brown and Company to Little.

Take the title from the title page, not from the cover or the spine. But disregard unusual typography—for instance, the use of only capital letters, or the use of *&* for *and*. Underline the title and subtitle with one continuous underline, but do not underline the period. The place of publication is indicated by the name of the city. But if the city is not well known, or if several cities have the same name (for instance, Cambridge, Massachusetts, and Cambridge, England) the name of the state is added. If the title page lists several cities, give only the first.

A book by more than one author

Gilbert, Sandra, and Susan Gubar, The Madwoman in the Attic:

<u>The Woman Writer and the Nineteenth-Century Literary</u>

<u>Imagination</u>. New Haven: Yale UP, 1979.

Notice that the book is listed under the last name of the first author (Gilbert) and that the second author's name is then given with first name (Susan) first. *If the book has more than three authors*, give the name of the first author only (last name first) and follow it with et al. (Latin for "and others.")

A book in several volumes

Abrams, M. H., et al., eds. <u>The Norton Anthology of English</u>

<u>Literature</u>. 5th ed. 2 vols. New York: Norton, 1986.

Pope, Alexander. <u>The Correspondence of Alexander Pope</u>. 5 vols.

Ed. George Sherburn. Oxford: Clarendon, 1956.

Trevor, Meriol. <u>Newman</u>. 2 vols. Garden City, New York:

Doubleday, 1963.

Notice that the total number of volumes is given after the title, regardless of the number that you have used.

If you have used more than one volume, within your essay you will parenthetically indicate a reference to, for instance, page 30 of volume 3 thus: (3:30). But if you have used only one volume of a multivolume work—let's say you used only volume 2 of Abrams's anthology—in your entry in Works Cited write, after the period following the date, Vol. 2. In your parenthetical citation within the essay you will therefore cite only the page reference (without the volume number), since the reader will (on consulting Works Cited) understand that in this example the reference is in volume 2.

If, instead of using the volumes as whole, you used only an independent work within one volume—say a poem in volume 2—in Works Cited omit the abbreviation "Vol." Instead give an arabic 2 (indicating volume 2) followed by a colon, a space, and the page numbers that encompass the selection you used.

Coleridge, Samuel Taylor. "Kubla Khan." <u>Norton Anthology of</u>

<u>English Literature</u>. 5th ed. 2 vols. New York: Norton, 1986.

2:353–355.

Notice that this entry for Coleridge specifies not only that the book consists of two volumes, but also that only one selection ("Kubla Khan," occupying pages 353–355 in volume 2) was used. If you use this sort of citation in Works Cited, in the body of your essay a documentary reference to this work will be only to the page; the volume number will *not* be added.

A book with a separate title in a set of volumes

Churchill, Winston. The Age of Revolution. Vol. 3 of A History of
 the English-speaking Peoples. New York: Dodd, 1957.

Jonson, Ben. The Complete Masques. Ed. Stephen Orgel. Vol. 4 of
 The Yale Ben Jonson. New Haven: Yale UP, 1969.

A revised edition of a book

Ellmann, Richard. James Joyce. Rev. ed. New York: Oxford UP,
 1982.

Chaucer, Geoffrey. The Works of Geoffrey Chaucer. Ed. F. N.
 Robinson. 2nd ed. Boston: Houghton, 1957.

A reprint, for instance, a paperback version of an older clothbound book

Rourke, Constance. American Humor. 1931. Garden City, New
 York: Doubleday, 1953.

Notice that the entry cites the original date (1931) but indicates that the writer is using the Doubleday reprint of 1953.

An edited book other than an anthology

Keats, John. The Letters of John Keats. Ed. Hyder Edward
 Rollins. 2 vols. Cambridge, Mass.: Harvard UP, 1958.

An anthology. You can list an anthology either under the editor's name or under the title.

A work in a volume of works by one author

Sontag, Susan. "The Aesthetics of Silence." In Styles of Radical
 Will. New York: Farrar, 1969. 3–34.

This entry indicates that Sontag's essay, called "The Aesthetics of Silence," appears in a book of hers entitled *Styles of Radical Will*. Notice that the page numbers of the short work are cited (not page numbers that you may happen to refer to, but the page numbers of the entire piece).

A work in an anthology, that is, in a collection of works by

several authors. Begin with the author and the title of the work you are citing, not with the name of the anthologist or the title of the anthology. The entry ends with the pages occupied by the selection you are citing.

> Bowen, Elizabeth. "Hand in Glove." The Oxford Book of English Ghost Stories. Ed. Michael Cox and R. A. Gilbert. Oxford: Oxford UP, 1986. 444–452.

> Porter, Katherine Anne. "The Jilting of Granny Weatherall." Literature for Composition. Ed. Sylvan Barnet, Morton Berman, and William Burto. 2nd ed. Glenview, Ill.: Scott, Foresman, 1988. 613–619.

Normally you will give the title of the work you are citing (probably an essay, short story or poem) in quotation marks. But if you are referring to a book-length work (for instance, a novel or a full-length play), underline it to indicate italics. If the work is translated, after the period that follows the title, write "Trans." and give the name of the translator, followed by a period and the name of the anthology.

If the collection is a multivolume work, and you are using only one volume, in Works Cited you will specify the volume, as in the example (page 761) of Coleridge's "Kubla Khan." Because the list of Works Cited specifies the volume, your parenthetical documentary reference within your essay will specify (as mentioned earlier) only the page numbers, not the volume. Thus, although Coleridge's "Kubla Khan" appears on pages 353–355 in the second volume of a two-volume work, a parenthetical citation will refer only to the page numbers because the citation in Works Cited specifies the volume.

Remember that the pages specified in the entry in your list of Works Cited are to the *entire selection*, not simply to pages you may happen to refer to within your paper.

If you are referring to a *reprint of a scholarly article*, give details of the original publication, as in the following example:

> Mack, Maynard. "The World of Hamlet." Yale Review 41 (1952): 502–523. Rpt. in Hamlet. By William Shakespeare. Ed. Edward Hubler. New York: New American Library, 1963. 234–256.

Two or more works in an anthology. If you are referring to more than one work in an anthology (for example, in this book), in order to avoid repeating all the information about the anthology in each entry in Works Cited, under each author's name (in the appropriate alphabetical place) you can give the author and title of the work, then a period, two spaces, and the name of the anthologist followed by the page numbers that the selection spans. Thus, a reference to Shakespeare's *Hamlet* would be followed only by

Barnet 229–299

rather than by a full citation of this book. But this form of course requires that the anthology itself also be listed, under Barnet.

Two or more works by the same author.   Notice that the works are given in alphabetical order (*Fables* precedes *Fools*) and that the author's name is not repeated but is represented by three hyphens followed by a period and two spaces. If the author is the translator or editor of a volume, the three hyphens are followed not by a period but by a comma, then a space, then the appropriate abbreviation (trans. or ed.), then (two spaces after the period) the title.

Frye, Northrop. Fables of Identity: Studies in Poetic Mythology.
    New York: Harcourt, 1963.

———. Fools of Time: Studies in Shakespearian Tragedy. Toronto: U
    of Toronto P, 1967.

A translated book

Gogol, Nikolai. Dead Souls. Trans. Andrew McAndrew. New York:
    New American Library, 1961.

If, however, you are discussing the translation itself, as opposed to the book, list the work under the translator's name. Then put a comma, a space, and "trans." After the period following "trans." skip two spaces, then give the title of the book, a period, two spaces, and then "by" and the author's name, first name first. Continue with information about the place of publication, publisher, and date, as in any entry to a book.

An introduction, foreword, or afterword, or other editorial apparatus

Fromm, Erich. Afterword. 1984. By George Orwell. New American
    Library, 1961.

Usually a book with an introduction or some such comparable material is listed under the name of the author of the book rather than the name of the author of the editorial material (see the citation to Pope on page 761). But if you are referring to the editor's apparatus rather than to the work itself, use the form just given.

Words such as preface, introduction, afterword, and conclusion are capitalized in the entry but are neither enclosed within quotation marks nor underlined.

A book review. First, an example of a review that does not have a title.

Vendler, Helen. Rev. of Essays on Style. Ed. Roger Fowler. Essays
    in Criticism 16 (1966): 457–463.

If the review has a title, give the title after the period following the reviewer's name, before the word "Rev." If the review is unsigned, list it under the first word of the title, or the second word if the first word is *A*, *An*, or *The*. If an unsigned review has no title, begin the entry with "Rev. of" and alphabetize it under the title of the work being reviewed.

An encyclopedia. The first example is for a signed article, the second for an unsigned article:

Lang, Andrew. "Ballads." Encyclopaedia Britannica. 1910 ed.

"Metaphor." The New Encyclopaedia Britannica: Micropaedia.
    1974 ed.

An article in a scholarly journal. Some journals are paginated consecutively—that is, the pagination of the second issue picks up where the first issue left off. Other journals begin each issue with a new page one. The forms of the citations in Works Cited differ slightly.
    First, the citation of *a journal that uses continuous pagination*:

Burbick, Joan. "Emily Dickinson and the Economics of Desire."
    American Literature 58 (1986): 361–378.

This article appeared in volume 58, which was published in 1986. (Notice that the volume number is followed by a space, then by the year, in parentheses, then by a colon, a space, and the page numbers of the entire article.) Although each volume consists of four issues, you do *not* specify the issue number when the journal is paginated continuously.
    For *a journal that paginates each issue separately* (if the journal is a quarterly, there will be four page 1's each year), give the issue number directly after the volume number and a period, with no spaces before or after the period.

Spillers, Hortense J. "Martin Luther King and the Style of the
    Black Sermon." The Black Scholar 3.1 (1971), 14–27.

An article in a weekly, biweekly, or monthly publication

McCabe, Bernard. "Taking Dickens Seriously." Commonweal 14
    May 1965.

Notice that the volume number and the issue number are omitted for popular weeklies or monthlies such as *Time* and *Atlantic*.

An article in a newspaper. Because newspapers usually consist of several sections, a section number may precede the page number. The example indicates that an article begins on page 1 of section 2 and is continued on a later page.

Wu, Jim. "Authors Praise New Forms." New York Times 8 March

1987, Sec. 2: 3 + .

Appendix B: Remarks about Manuscript Form

Basic Manuscript Form

Much of what follows is nothing more than common sense. Unless your instructor specifies something different, you can adopt these principles as a guide.

1. Use 8 1/2 × 11-inch paper of good weight. Keep as lightweight a carbon copy as you wish (or a photocopy), but hand in a sturdy original.
2. Write on one side of the page only. If you type, double-space, typing with a reasonably fresh ribbon. If you submit a handwritten copy, use lined paper and write, in ink—on every other line if the lines are closely spaced. Do not use pages that have been torn out of a spiral notebook.
3. Put your name and class or course number in the upper right-hand corner of the first page. It is a good idea to put your name in the upper left corner of each page so the instructor can easily reassemble your essay if somehow a page gets mixed in with other papers.
4. Center the title of your essay about two inches from the top of the first page. Capitalize the first letter of the first and last words of your title, and capitalize the first letter of all the other words except articles, conjunctions, and prepositions; thus:

The Diabolic and Celestial Images in The Scarlet Letter

Notice that your title is neither underlined (indicating italics) nor enclosed in quotation marks. (If, though—as here—it includes material that normally would be italicized or in quotation marks, that material continues to be so written.)

5. Begin the essay an inch or two below the title. If your instructor prefers a title page, begin the essay on the next page.
6. Leave an adequate margin—an inch or an inch and a half—at the top, bottom, and sides.
7. Number the pages consecutively, using arabic numerals in the upper right-

hand corner. If you give the title on a separate page, do not number the page; the page that follows it is page 1.

8. Fasten the pages of your paper with a paper clip in the upper left-hand corner. Stiff binders are unnecessary; indeed, they are a nuisance to the instructor, adding bulk and making it awkward to write annotations.

Corrections in the Final Copy

Your extensive revisions should have been made in your drafts, but minor last-minute revisions may be made on the finished copy. In proofreading, you may catch some typographical errors, and you may want to change a word here and there. You need not retype the page, or even erase. You can make corrections with the following proofreader's symbols:

Changes in wording may be made by crossing through words and rewriting just above them, either on the typewriter or by hand in pen:

                            toward
Orwell is sympathetic ~~for~~ most of the animals in <u>Animal Farm</u>,
but he seems to have special affection for the work-horse.

Additions should be made above the line, with a caret (∧) below the line at the appropriate place:

                                     of
Orwell is sympathetic toward most ∧ the animals in <u>Animal Farm</u>,
but he seems to have special affection for the work-horse.

Transpositions of letters may be made thus:

Orwell is sympathetic tow̺a̺rd most of the animals in <u>Animal</u>
<u>Farm</u>, but he seems to have special affection for the work-horse.

Deletions are indicated by a horizontal line through the word or words to be deleted. Delete a single letter by drawing a vertical or diagonal line through it.

Orwell is sympathetic toward most ~~most~~ of the animals in <u>Animal</u>
<u>Farm</u>, but he seems to have special afff̸ection for the work-horse.

Separation of words accidentally run together is indicated by a vertical line, *closure* by a curved line connecting the things to be closed up.

Orwell is sympathetic toward most|of the a∩nimals in <u>Animal</u>
<u>Farm</u>, but he seems to have special affection for the work-horse.

Paragraphing is indicated by the symbol ¶ before the word that is to begin a new paragraph.

Orwell is sympathetic toward most of the animals in <u>Animal</u>
<u>Farm</u>, but he seems to have special affection for the work-horse.
¶ Only the pigs seem to be pictured unsympathetically.

Quotations and Quotation Marks

Excerpts from the literature you are writing about are indispensable. Such quotations (not to be called *quotes—quote* is a verb, not a noun) not only let your readers know what you are talking about; they also give your readers the material you are responding to, thus letting them share your responses.

Our marginal comments on a student's essay (page 22) call your attention to some of the strengths as well as to some of the conventions of editing a final draft. Here we remind you of procedures for using quotations (covered in detail in most handbooks). These procedures are not noteworthy when handled properly, but they become noticeable and even ruinous to your essay when bungled. Read the following reminders over, check them against the student's essay, and consult them again the first few times you write about an essay.

1. Quote. Quotations from the work under discussion provide indispensable support for your thesis.
2. Don't overquote. Most of the essay should consist of your own words.
3. Quote briefly. Use quotations as evidence, not as padding.
4. Comment on what you quote, immediately before or immediately after the quotation. Make sure your reader understands why you find the quotation relevant. Don't count on the quotation to make your point for you.
5. Distinguish between short and long quotations, and treat each appropriately. Short quotations (usually defined as fewer than three lines of poetry or five lines of typed prose) are enclosed within quotation marks and are not otherwise set off. That is, they are embedded within your own writing. (In the first example, the digits refer to the line numbers of a poem; in the second example, quoting *Hamlet*, they refer to act, scene, and line.)

In "Song for a Dark Girl," Langston Hughes imagines a young
woman grieving for her lover, who has been hanged "On a
gnarled and naked tree" (12). Her prayers to "the white Lord
Jesus" (7) have been unavailing, and she is left only with the
memory of the hanging body.

Although King Claudius begins by saying, "Though yet of Hamlet
our dear brother's death / The memory be green" (1.2.1–2), fairly
early in the speech a reader or spectator gets the idea that
Claudius is insincere.

Notice that in the second example a slash (diagonal line, virgule) is used to indicate the end of a line of verse other than the last line quoted. The slash is, of course, not used if the poetry is set off, indented, and printed as verse. Thus:

> King Claudius is a master politician. When we first see him, he
> begins with a smooth speech, and not until fairly late in the
> speech do we realize he is manipulating us. His first lines are
>> Though yet of Hamlet our dear brother's death
>> The memory be green, and that it us befitted
>> To bear our hearts in grief, and our whole kingdom
>> To be contracted in one brow of woe,
>> Yet so far hath discretion fought with nature
>> That we with wisest sorrow think on him
>> Together with remembrance of ourselves.   (1.2.1–8)
>
> He continues for another thirty-one lines, making it clear that
> despite his grief for "dear brother's death" (19) he plans to run
> the kingdom efficiently.

Material that is set off (again, three or more lines of poetry, five or more lines of typed prose) is *not* enclosed within quotation marks. To set off poetry, center it. To set off prose, indent ten spaces from the left margin. (The right margin remains unchanged.) Be sparing in your use of long quotations. Use quotations as evidence, not as padding. Do not bore the reader with material that can be effectively reduced either by summarizing or by cutting. If you cut, indicate ellipses as explained below in number 7.

6. Take care with embedded quotations (quotations within a sentence of your own). A quotation must fit grammatically into the sentence of which it is a part. Suppose, for example, you wish to quote the following words from Orwell: "the only time in my life that I have been important enough for this to happen to me."

Incorrect:

> The first sentence does not sound egotistical because "the only
> time in my life that I have been important enough for this to
> happen to me."

Correct:

> The first sentence does not sound egotistical because Orwell
> adds that this was "the only time in my life that I have been
> important enough for this to happen to me."

Don't try to fit a long quotation into one of your own sentences. It is almost impossible for the reader to come out of the quotation and pick up the thread of your sentence. It is better to lead into the long quotation with something like "Orwell's language here is markedly colloquial:" or even "Orwell says:" (usually a colon introduces a long quotation) and then, after quoting, to begin a new sentence of your own.

7. Quote exactly. Any material that you add (to make the quotation coherent with your sentence) must be in square brackets. Thus:

Orwell says the torture of prisoners "oppressed [him] with an intolerable sense of guilt."

Any material that you omit from within a quotation must be indicated by an ellipsis, or three spaced periods:

He knew that "a sahib has got to . . . know his own mind and do definite things."

If a quotation ends before the end of the author's sentence, add a period and then three spaced periods to indicate the omission:

As Orwell claims, "It was a tiny incident in itself. . . ."

(Orwell's sentence followed the word "itself" with "but it gave me a better glimpse than I had had before of the real nature of imperialism—the real motives for which despotic governments act.")

8. Quote fairly. It would not be fair, for example, to say "Orwell claims he 'had done the right thing' " when in fact he says "legally I had done the right thing." His qualification "legally" is important, and it would be unfair to omit it.

9. Identify the quotation clearly for your reader, with such helpful expressions as "Orwell . . . adds," and "The next paragraph . . . represents."

10. Identify the source of quotations in a footnote or in a list of Works Cited.

11. Check your punctuation. Remember: Periods and commas go inside of quotation marks; semicolons and colons go outside. Question marks and exclamation points go inside if they are part of the quotation, outside if they are your own.

12. Use *single* quotation marks for material contained within a quotation that itself is within quotation marks; thus:

T. S. Eliot says, "Mr. Richards observes that 'poetry is capable of saving us' " (137).

13. Use quotation marks around titles of short works—that is, for titles of chapters in books, and for stories, essays, and poems that might not be published by themselves, songs, speeches, and lectures. Unpublished works, even book-length dissertations, are also enclosed in quotation marks.

　　When does one *not* use quotation marks around a title? (1) Use *italics* (indicated by underlining) for titles of books—for example, for novels, periodicals, pamphlets, collections of stories or essays, plays, and long poems like *Paradise Lost* and *The Rime of the Ancient Mariner*. (2) Titles of sacred works (for example, the Bible, the Old Testament, Genesis, the Gospel according to John, the Koran), and titles of political documents (the Declaration of Independence, the Magna Carta).

Appendix C:
Glossary of Literary Terms

The terms briefly defined here are for the most part more fully defined earlier in the text. Hence many of the entries below are followed by page references to the earlier discussions.

Absurd, Theater of the plays, especially written in the 1950s and 1960s, which call attention to the incoherence of character and of action, the inability of people to communicate, and the apparent purposelessness of existence (481)

accent stress given to a syllable (735)

act a major division of a play

action (1) the happenings in a narrative or drama, usually physical events (B marries C, D kills E), but also mental changes (F moves from innocence to experience); in short, the answer to the question, "What happens?" (2) less commonly, the theme or underlying idea of a work (744)

allegory a work in which concrete elements (for instance, a pilgrim, a road, a splendid city) stand for abstractions (humanity, life, salvation), usually in an unambiguous, one-to-one relationship. The literal items (the pilgrim, and so on) thus convey a meaning, which is usually moral, religious, or political. To take a nonliterary example: The Statue of Liberty holds a torch (enlightenment, showing the rest of the world the way to freedom), and at her feet are broken chains (tyranny overcome). A caution: Not all of the details in an allegorical work are meant to be interpreted. For example, the hollowness of the Statue of Liberty does not stand for the insubstantiality or emptiness of liberty.

alliteration repetition of consonant sounds, especially at the beginnings of words (*f*ree, *f*orm, *ph*antom) (725–726, 738)

allusion an indirect reference; thus when Lincoln spoke of "a nation dedicated to the proposition that all men are created equal," he was making an allusion to the Declaration of Independence.

ambiguity multiplicity of meaning, often deliberate, which leaves the reader uncertain about the intended significance

anagnorisis a recognition or discovery, especially in tragedy—for example, when the hero understands the reason for his or her fall (742)

analysis an examination, which usually proceeds by separating the object of study into parts (15–16, 60–79)

anapest a metrical foot consisting of two unaccented syllables followed by an accented one. Example, showing three anapests: "As I came / to the edge / of the wood" (736)

anecdote a short narrative, usually reporting an amusing event in the life of an important person

antagonist a character or force which opposes (literally, "wrestles") the main character

apostrophe address to an absent figure, or to a thing as if it were present and could listen. Example: "Oh rose, thou art sick!" (728)

archetype a theme, image, motive, or pattern that occurs so often in literary works it seems to be universal. Examples: a dark forest (for mental confusion), the sun (for illumination)

assonance repetition of similar vowel sounds in stressed syllables. Example: light/bride (725–726, 738)

atmosphere the emotional tone (for instance, joy, or horror) in a work, most often established by the setting (713–714)

ballad a short narrative poem, especially one that is sung or recited, often in a stanza of four lines, with 8, 6, 8, 6 syllables, with the second and fourth lines rhyming. A **popular ballad** is a narrative song that has been transmitted orally by what used to be called "the folk"; a **literary ballad** is a conscious imitation (without music) of such a work, often with complex symbolism. (156)

blank verse unrhymed iambic pentameter, that is, unrhymed lines of ten syllables, with every second syllable stressed (740)

cacophony an unpleasant combination of sounds

caesura a strong pause within a line of verse (737)

catastrophe the concluding action, especially in a tragedy

catharsis Aristotle's term for the purgation or purification of the pity and terror supposedly experienced while witnessing a tragedy

character (1) a person in a literary work (Romeo); (2) the personality of such a figure (sentimental lover, or whatever). Characters (in the first sense) are sometimes classified as either "flat" (one-dimensional) or "round" (fully realized, complex).

characterization the presentation of a character, whether by direct description, by showing the character in action, or by the presentation of other characters who help to define each other (71–75, 711–712, 717–718)

cliché an expression that, through overuse, has ceased to be effective. Examples: acid test, sigh of relief, the proud possessor

climax the culmination of a conflict; a turning point, often the point of greatest tension in a plot (744)

comedy a literary work, especially a play, characterized by humor and by a happy ending (741, 743)

comparison and contrast to compare is, strictly, to note similarities, whereas to contrast is to note differences. But "compare" is now often used for both activities. (80–89)

complication an entanglement in a narrative or dramatic work which causes a conflict

conflict a struggle between a character and some obstacle, for example, another character, fate, or between internal forces such as divided loyalties (747)

connotation the associations (suggestions, overtones) of a word or expression. Thus "seventy" and "three score and ten" both mean "one more than sixty-nine," but because "three score and ten" is a biblical expression it has an association of holiness; see *denotation*. (728)

consonance repetition of consonant sounds, especially in stressed syllables. Also called "half rhyme" or "slant rhyme." Example: arouse/doze (738)

convention a pattern (for instance the fourteen-line poem, or sonnet) or motif (for instance, the bumbling police officer in detective fiction) or other device occurring so often that it is taken for granted. Thus it is a convention that actors in a performance of *Julius Caesar* are understood to be speaking Latin, though in fact they are speaking English. Similarly, the soliloquy (a character alone on the stage speaks his or her thoughts aloud) is a convention, for in real life sane people do not talk aloud to themselves. (729)

couplet a pair of lines of verse, usually rhyming (739)

crisis a high point in the conflict, which leads to the turning point (744)

criticism the analysis or evaluation of a literary work

dactyl a metrical foot consisting of a stressed syllable followed by two unstressed syllables. Example: underwear (736)

denotation the dictionary meaning of a word. Thus "soap opera" and "daytime serial" have the same denotation, but the connotations (associations, emotional overtones) of "soap opera" are less favorable. (728)

dénouement the resolution or the outcome (literally, the "unknotting") of a plot (744)

deus ex machina literally, "a god out of a machine"; any unexpected and artificial way of resolving the plot—for example, by introducing a rich uncle, thought to be dead, who arrives on the scene and pays the debts that otherwise would overwhelm the young hero

dialogue exchange of words between characters; speech

diction the choice of vocabulary and of sentence structure. There is a difference in diction between "One never knows" and "You never can tell." (27, 725–726, 733)

didactic pertaining to teaching; having a moral purpose

dimeter a line of poetry containing two feet (737)

discovery see *anagnorisis* (747)

drama (1) a play; (2) conflict or tension, as in "The story lacks drama" (741–747)

dramatic monologue a poem spoken entirely by one character, but addressed to one or more other characters, whose presence is strongly felt

elegy a lyric poem, usually a meditation on a death

elision omission (usually of a vowel or unstressed syllable), as in "o'er" (for "over") and in "Th' inevitable hour"

end rhyme identical sounds at the ends of lines of poetry (738)

end-stopped line a line of poetry that ends with a pause because the grammatical structure and the sense reach (at least to some degree) completion (737)

English (or **Shakespearean**) **sonnet** a poem of fourteen lines (three quatrains and a couplet), rhyming *ababcdcdefefgg* (739)

enjambment a line of poetry in which the grammatical and logical sense run on, without pause, into the next line or lines (737)

epic a long narrative, especially in verse, which usually records heroic material in an elevated style

epigram a brief, witty poem or saying

epiphany a "showing forth," as when an action reveals a character with particular clarity

episode an incident or scene which has unity in itself but is also a part of a larger action

epistle a letter, in prose or verse

essay a work, usually in prose and usually fairly short, that purports to be true and that treats its subject tentatively. In most literary essays the reader's interest is as much in the speaker's personality as in any argument that is offered. (28–31)

euphony literally, "good sound," a pleasant combination of sounds

explication a line-by-line unfolding of the meaning of a text (731–732)

exposition a setting-forth of information. In fiction and drama, introductory material introducing characters and the situation; in an essay, the presentation of information, as opposed to the telling of a story or the setting forth of an argument (745)

eye rhyme words that look as though they rhyme, but do not rhyme when pronounced. Example: come/home (738)

fable a short story (often involving speaking animals) with an easily grasped moral

feminine rhyme a rhyme of two or more syllables, with the stress falling on a syllable other than the last. Examples: fatter/batter; tenderly/slenderly (738)

fiction an imaginative work, usually a prose narrative (novel, short story), that reports incidents that did not in fact occur. The word can include all works that invent a world, such as a lyric poem or a play. (711–719)

figurative language words intended to be understood in a way that is other than literal. Thus "lemon" used literally refers to a citrus fruit, but "lemon" used figuratively refers to a defective machine, especially a defective automobile. Other examples: "He's a beast," "She's a witch," "A sea of troubles." Literally such expressions are nonsense, but writers use them to express meanings inexpressible in literal speech. Among the commonest kinds of figures of speech are *apostrophe*, *metaphor*, and *simile* (see the discussions of these words in this glossary). (726–729)

flashback an interruption in a narrative, which presents an earlier episode

flat character a one-dimensional character (for instance, the figure who is only and always the jealous husband, or the flirtatious wife) as opposed to a round or many-sided character

foil a character who makes a contrast with another, especially a minor character who helps to set off a major character (746)

foot a metrical unit, consisting of two or three syllables, with a specified arrangement of the stressed syllable or syllables. Thus the iambic foot consists of an unstressed syllable followed by a stressed syllable. (735–737)

foreshadowing suggestions of what is to come (712–713)

free verse poetry in lines of irregular length, which is usually unrhymed (740)

genre kind or type, roughly analogous to the biological term "species." The four chief literary genres are nonfiction, fiction, poetry, and drama, but these can be subdivided into further genres. Thus "fiction" obviously can be divided into the short story and the novel, and "drama" obviously can be divided into tragedy and comedy. But these can be still further divided—for instance, tragedy into heroic tragedy and bourgeois tragedy, comedy into romantic comedy and satirical comedy.

gesture physical movement, especially in a play (745–746)

half rhyme repetition in accented syllables of the final consonant sound but without identity in the preceding vowel sound; words of similar but not identical sound. Also called near rhyme, slant rhyme, approximate rhyme, and off-rhyme. Examples: light/bet; affirm/perform (738)

hamartia a flaw in the tragic hero, or an error made by the tragic hero (742)

heptameter a metrical line of seven feet (736)

hero, heroine the main character (not necessarily heroic or even admirable) in a work; cf. *protagonist*

heroic couplet an end-stopped pair of rhyming lines of iambic pentameter (739)

hexameter a metrical line of six feet (736)

hubris, hybris a Greek word, usually translated as "overweening pride," "arrogance," "excessive ambition," and often said to be characteristic of tragic figures (741–742)

hyperbole figurative language using overstatement, as in "He died a thousand deaths" (730)

iamb, iambic a poetic foot consisting of an unaccented syllable followed by an accented one. Example: alone (736)

image, imagery imagery is established by language that appeals to the senses, especially sight ("deep blue sea") but also other senses ("tinkling bells," "perfumes of Arabia") (729–730)

internal rhyme rhyme within a line (738)

interpretation the exposition of meaning, chiefly by means of analysis

irony a contrast of some sort. For instance, in **verbal irony** or **Socratic irony** the contrast is between what is said and what is meant ("You're a great guy," meant bitterly). In **dramatic irony** the contrast is between what is intended and what is accomplished (Macbeth usurps the throne, thinking he will then be happy, but the action leads him to misery), or between what the audience knows (a murderer waits in the bedroom) and what a character says (the victim enters the bedroom, innocently saying "I think I'll have a long sleep") (730, 742–743)

Italian (or **Petrarchan**) **sonnet** a poem of fourteen lines, consisting of an octave (rhyming *abbaabba*) and a sestet (usually *cdecde* or *cdccdc*) (739)

litotes a form of understatement in which an affirmation is made by means of a negation; thus "He was not underweight," meaning "He was grossly overweight"

lyric poem a short poem, often songlike, with the emphasis not on narrative but on the speaker's emotion or reverie (723–724)

masculine rhyme rhyme of one-syllable words (lies/cries) or, if more than one syllable, words ending with accented syllables (behold/foretold) (737)

melodrama a narrative, usually in dramatic form, involving threatening situations but ending happily. The characters are usually stock figures (virtuous heroine, villainous landlord).

metaphor a kind of figurative language equating one thing with another: "This novel is garbage" (a book is equated with discarded and probably inedible food), "a piercing cry" (a cry is equated with a spear or other sharp instrument) (727)

meter a pattern of stressed and unstressed syllables (733–740)

metonymy a kind of figurative language in which a word or phrase stands not for itself but for something closely related to it: "saber-rattling" means "militaristic talk or action" (727–729)

monologue a relatively long, uninterrupted speech by a character

monometer a metrical line consisting of only one foot (736)

mood the atmosphere, usually created by descriptions of the settings and characters

motif a recurrent theme within a work, or a theme common to many works

motivation grounds for a character's action (746)

myth (1) a traditional story reflecting primitive beliefs, especially explaining the mysteries of the natural world (why it rains, or the origin of mountains); (2) a body of belief, not necessarily false, especially as set forth by a writer. Thus one can speak of Yeats or Hardy as myth-makers, referring to the visions of reality that they set forth in their works.

narrative, narrator a narrative is a story (an anecdote, a novel); a narrator is one who tells a story (not the author, but the invented speaker of the story). On kinds of narrators, see *point of view.* (714–716, 718)

novel a long work of prose fiction, especially one that is relatively realistic

novella a work of prose fiction longer than a short story but shorter than a novel, say about forty to eighty pages

octave, octet an eight-line stanza, or the first eight lines of a sonnet, especially of an Italian sonnet (739)

octosyllabic couplet a pair of rhyming lines, each line with four iambic feet

ode a lyric exalting someone (for instance, a hero) or something (for instance, a season)

omniscient narrator a speaker who knows the thoughts of all of the characters in the narrative (780)

onomatopoeia words (or the use of words) that sound like what they mean. Examples: buzz, whirr (738)

oxymoron a compact paradox, as in "a mute cry," "a pleasing pain," "proud humility"

parable a short narrative that is at least in part allegorical, and which illustrates a moral or spiritual lesson

paradox an apparent contradiction, as in Christ's words: "Whoever will save his life shall lose it; but whosoever will lose his life for my sake, the same shall save it" (730–732)

paraphrase a restatement, which sets forth an idea in diction other than that of the original (4, 726)

parody a humorous imitation of a literary work, especially of its style

pathos pity, sadness

pentameter a line of verse containing five feet (736)

peripeteia a reversal in the action (742)

persona literally, a mask; the "I" or speaker of a work, sometimes identified with the author but usually better regarded as the voice or mouthpiece created by the author (4, 15, 31, 724–725)

personification a kind of figurative language in which an inanimate object, animal, or other nonhuman is given human traits. Examples: "the creeping tide" (the tide is imagined as having feet), "the cruel sea" (the sea is imagined as having moral qualities) (728)

plot the episodes in a narrative or dramatic work—that is, what happens—or the particular arrangement (sequence) of these episodes (711–713, 717, 744–745, 747)

poem an imaginative work in meter or in free verse, usually employing figurative language

point of view the perspective from which a story is told—for example by a major character, or a minor character, or a fly on the wall; see also *narrative, narrator* (714–716, 718)

prosody the principles of versification (735–740)

protagonist the chief actor in any literary work. The term is usually preferable to "hero" and "heroine" because it can include characters—for example, villainous or weak ones—who are not aptly called heroes or heroines.

quatrain a stanza of four lines (739)

realism presentation of plausible characters (usually middle-class) in plausible (usually everyday) circumstances, as opposed, for example, to heroic characters engaged in improbable adventures. Realism in literature seeks to give the illusion of reality.

recognition see *anagnorisis* (742)

refrain a repeated phrase, line, or group of lines in a poem, especially in a ballad

resolution the dénouement or untying of the complication of the plot (744)

reversal a change in fortune, often an ironic twist (742)

rhetorical question a question to which no answer is expected, or to which only one answer is plausible. Example: Do you think I am unaware of your goings-on?"

rhyme similarity or identity of accented sounds in corresponding positions, as, for example, at the ends of lines: love/dove; tender/slender (738–740)

rhythm in poetry, a pattern of stressed and unstressed sounds; in prose, some sort of recurrence (for example, of a motif) at approximately identical intervals (733–740)

rising action in a story or play, the events that lead up to the climax (744)

rising meter a foot (for example, iambic or anapestic) ending with a stressed syllable

romance narrative fiction, usually characterized by improbable adventures and love

round character a many-sided character, one who does not always act predictably, as opposed to a "flat" or one-dimensional, unchanging character

run-on line a line of verse whose syntax and meaning require the reader to go on, without a pause, to the next line; an enjambed line (737)

sarcasm crudely mocking or contemptuous language; heavy verbal irony

satire literature that entertainingly attacks folly or vice; amusingly abusive writing (89)

scansion description of rhythm in poetry; metrical analysis (735–737)

scene (1) a unit of a play, in which the setting is unchanged and the time continuous; (2) the setting (locale, and time of the action); (3) in fiction, a dramatic passage, as opposed to a passage of description or of summary

sentimentality excessive emotion, especially excessive pity, treated as appropriate rather than as disproportionate

sestet a six-line stanza, or the last six lines of an Italian sonnet (739)

sestina a poem with six stanzas of six lines each, and a concluding stanza of three lines. The last word of each line in the first stanza appears as the last word of a line in each of the next five stanzas, but in a different order. In the final (three-line) stanza, each line ends with one of these six words, and each line includes in the middle of the line one of the other three words.

setting the time and place of a story, play, or poem (for instance, a Texas town in winter, about 1900) (713–714, 718, 740, 747)

short story a fictional narrative, usually in prose, rarely longer than thirty pages and often much briefer (711–719)

simile a kind of figurative language explicitly making a comparison, for example by using *as, like*, or a verb such as *seems* (727)

soliloquy a speech in a play, in which a character, alone on the stage, speaks his or her thoughts aloud

sonnet a lyric poem of fourteen lines; see *English sonnet, Italian sonnet* (739–740)

speaker see *persona* (723–725, 733)

spondee a metrical foot consisting of two stressed syllables (736)

stage direction a playwright's indication to the actors or readers—for example, offering information about how an actor is to speak a line

stanza a group of lines forming a unit that is repeated in a poem (714–716)

stereotype a simplified conception, especially an oversimplification—for example, a stock character such as the heartless landlord, the kindly old teacher, the prostitute with a heart of gold. Such a character usually has only one personality trait, and this is boldly exaggerated.

stream of consciousness the presentation of a character's unrestricted flow of thought, often with free associations, and often without punctuation (715)

stress relative emphasis on one syllable as compared to another (735)

structure the organization of a work, the relationship between the chief parts, the large-scale pattern—for instance, a rising action or complication followed by a crisis and then a resolution

style the manner of expression, evident not only in the choice of certain words (for instance, colloquial language) but in the choice of certain kinds of sentence structure, characters, settings, and themes (718–719)

subplot a sequence of events often paralleling or in some way resembling the main story

summary a synopsis or condensation (6, 13, 69–70, 752–753)

symbol a person, object, action, or situation that, charged with meaning, suggests another thing (for example, a dark forest may suggest confusion, or perhaps evil), though usually with less specificity and more ambiguity than an allegory. A symbol usually differs from a metaphor in that a symbol is expanded, or repeated, and works by accumulating associations. (714, 729–730)

synecdoche a kind of figurative language in which the whole stands for a part ("the law," for a police officer), or a part ("all hands on deck," for all persons) stands for the whole (727–728)

tale a short narrative, usually less realistic and more romantic than a short story; a yarn

tercet a unit of three lines of verse (739)

tetrameter a verse line of four feet (736)

theme what the work is about; an underlying idea of a work; a conception of human experience suggested by the concrete details. Thus the theme of *Macbeth* is often said to be that "Vaulting ambition o'erleaps itself." (716–717, 719, 743–744)

thesis the point or argument that a writer announces and develops. A thesis differs from a *topic* by making an assertion. "The fall of Oedipus" is a topic, but "Oedipus falls because he is impetuous" is a thesis, as is "Oedipus is impetuous, but his impetuosity has nothing to do with his fall." (5, 25, 61–62, 716–717, 749–750)

third-person narrator the teller of a story who does not participate in the happenings (714–716)

tone the prevailing attitude (for instance, ironic, genial, objective) as perceived by the reader. Notice that a reader may feel the tone of the persona of the work is genial while the tone of the author of the same work is ironic. (4–5, 725–726)

topic a subject, such as "Hamlet's relation to Horatio." A topic becomes a *thesis* when a predicate is added to this subject, thus: "Hamlet's relation to Horatio helps to define Hamlet." (5, 17, 61–62, 749–750)

tragedy a serious play showing the protagonist moving from good fortune to bad, and ending in death or a deathlike state (740–743)

tragic flaw a supposed weakness (for example, arrogance) in the tragic protagonist (299, 742–743)

tragicomedy a mixture of tragedy and comedy, usually a play with serious happenings which expose the characters to the threat of death, but which ends happily (741)

transition a connection between one passage and the next (21)

trimeter a verse line with three feet (736)

triplet a group of three lines of verse, usually rhyming (739)

trochee a metrical foot consisting of a stressed syllable followed by an unstressed syllable. Example: garden (736)

understatement a figure of speech in which the speaker says less than what he or she means; an ironic minimizing, as in "You've done fairly well for yourself" said to the winner of a multimillion-dollar lottery (730)

unity harmony and coherence of parts, absence of irrelevance

verse (1) a line of poetry; (2) a stanza of a poem

vers libre free verse, unrhymed poetry (740)

villanelle a poem with five stanzas of three lines rhyming *aba*, and a concluding stanza of four lines, rhyming *abaa*. The first and third lines of the first stanza rhyme. The entire first line is repeated as the third line of the second and fourth stanzas; the entire third line is repeated as the third line of the third and fifth stanzas. These two lines form the final two lines of the last (four-line) stanza.

voice see *persona, style,* and *tone* (724–725)

Doubleday, 1950. Reprinted by permission of Don Congdon Associates, Inc. Copyright © 1950 by Ray Bradbury; renewed 1978 by Ray Bradbury.

Walter de la Mare, "The Listeners" from *The Collected Poems of Walter de la Mare*. Reprinted by permission of The Literary Trustees of Walter de la Mare and The Society of Authors as their representative.

Emily Dickinson, "Apparently with no surprise" and "Those—dying, then." Reprinted by permission of the publishers and the Trustees of Amherst College from *The Poems of Emily Dickinson*, edited by Thomas H. Johnson, Cambridge, Mass.: The Belknap Press of Harvard University Press, Copyright 1951, © 1955, 1979 by the President and Fellows of Harvard College.

T. S. Eliot, "The Love Song of J. Alfred Prufrock" from *Collected Poems 1909–1962* by T. S. Eliot, copyright 1936 by Harcourt Brace Jovanovich, Inc.; copyright © 1963, 1964 by T. S. Eliot. Reprinted by permission of Harcourt Brace Jovanovich and Faber and Faber Ltd.

Henry Fairlie, "Lust or Luxuria" from *The New Republic*, October 8, 1977. Reprinted by permission of *The New Republic*. © 1977 The New Republic, Inc.

William Faulkner, "A Rose for Emily." Copyright 1930 and renewed 1958 by William Faulkner. Reprinted from *Collected Stories of William Faulkner*, by William Faulkner, by permission of Random House, Inc.

William Faulkner, "Spotted Horses." Copyright 1931 and renewed 1959 by William Faulkner. Copyright 1940 and renewed 1968 by Estelle Faulkner and Jill Faulkner Summers. Reprinted from *Collected Stories of William Faulkner*, by William Faulkner, by permission of Random House, Inc.

William Faulkner, "Letter to the New York Times" December 26, 1954. Copyright 1954 by the Estate of William Faulkner. Reprinted from *Essays, Speeches and Public Letters*, by William Faulkner, by permission of Random House, Inc. Copyright © 1954 by The New York Times Company. Reprinted by permission.

E. M. Forster, "My Wood" from *Abinger Harvest*, copyright 1936, 1964 by Edward Morgan Forster. Reprinted by permission of Harcourt Brace Jovanovich, Inc. and Edward Arnold (Publishers) Ltd.

Mary E. Wilkins Freeman, "The Revolt of 'Mother'" from *A New England Nun and Other Stories*, 1891.

Erich Fromm, "Erotic Love" (pp. 52–57) in *The Art of Loving* by Erich Fromm. Vol. Nine of World Perspectives, Planned and Edited by Ruth Nanda Anshen. Copyright © 1956 by Erich Fromm. Reprinted by permission of Harper & Row, Publishers, Inc.

Robert Frost, "The Silken Tent," "Stopping by Woods on a Snowy Evening," "The Wood-Pile," "Design," "The Gift Outright," "Mending Wall," and "The Road Not Taken" from *The Poems of Robert Frost*, edited by Edward Connery Lathem. Copyright © 1969 by Holt, Rinehart and Winston. Copyright © 1958 by Robert Frost. Copyright © 1970 by Lesley Frost Ballantine. Reprinted by permission of Henry Holt and Company, Inc.

Susan Glaspell, "Trifles." Reprinted by permission of Dodd, Mead & Company, Inc. from *Plays* by Susan Glaspell. Copyright 1920 by Dodd, Mead & Company, Inc. Copyright renewed 1948 by Susan Glaspell.

Louise Glück, "Gretel in Darkness" from *The House on Marshland*, © 1971, 1972, 1973, 1974, 1975 by Louise Glück, published by The Ecco Press in 1975. Reprinted by permission.

Robert Hayden, "Those Winter Sundays" is reprinted from *Angle of Ascent: New and Selected Poems* by Robert Hayden, by permission of Liveright Publishing Corporation. Copyright © 1975, 1972, 1970, 1966 by Robert Hayden.

Ernest Hemingway, "A Clean, Well-Lighted Place," from *Winner Takes Nothing*. Copyright 1933 Charles Scribner's Sons; renewed © 1961 Mary Hemingway. Reprinted with the permission of Charles Scribner's Sons, a division of Macmillan, Inc.

Will Herberg, "Religiosity and Religion." Excerpt from *Protestant, Catholic, Jew* by Will Herberg. Copyright © 1955, 1960 by Will Herberg. Reprinted by permission of Doubleday Publishing, a division of Bantam, Doubleday, Dell Publishing Group.

Gerard Manley Hopkins, "Spring and Fall: To a Young Child," "God's Grandeur," and "Thou Art Indeed Just, Lord" from *The Poems of Gerard Manley Hopkins*, fourth edition (1967), edited by W. H. Gardner and N. H. MacKenzie, published by Oxford University Press for the Society of Jesus.

A. E. Housman, "When I Was One-and-Twenty" and "Loveliest of trees, the cherry now" from "A Shropshire Lad," from *The*

Index of Terms

Index of Authors, Titles, and First Lines of Poems

Questionnaire

To the Student

Please help us make *Literature for Composition*, Second Edition, an even better book. When we revise our textbooks, we take into account the experiences of both instructors and students with the previous edition. At some time, your instructor will be asked to comment extensively on *Literature for Composition*, Second Edition. Now we would like to hear from you.

Please complete this questionnaire and return it to:

College English
Scott, Foresman/Little, Brown College Division
34 Beacon St.
Boston, Massachusetts 02108

SCHOOL _____

COURSE TITLE _____

OTHER TEXTS REQUIRED _____

INSTRUCTOR'S FULL NAME _____

1. Did you like the book overall? Why or why not?

2. Did you find Part I, "Getting Started," useful preparation for the work you did later in the course? Why or why not?

3. Were the "Questions and Suggestions for Writing" helpful? Why or why not?

4. Please rate the selections you were assigned in Part II, "A Thematic Anthology."

Chapter 6: Strange Worlds

	Liked best				Liked least	Didn't read
☐ **ESSAYS**						
Juanita Miranda IN DEFENSE OF FANTASY	5	4	3	2	1	___
Bruno Bettelheim THE THREE LITTLE PIGS: PLEASURE PRINCIPLE VERSUS REALITY PRINCIPLE	5	4	3	2	1	___
☐ **FICTION**						
Nathaniel Hawthorne DR. HEIDEGGER'S EXPERIMENT	5	4	3	2	1	___
Edgar Allan Poe THE MASQUE OF THE RED DEATH	5	4	3	2	1	___
Leo Tolstoy HOW MUCH LAND DOES A MAN NEED?	5	4	3	2	1	___
Jean Rhys I USED TO LIVE HERE ONCE	5	4	3	2	1	___
Elizabeth Bowen THE DEMON LOVER	5	4	3	2	1	___
Ray Bradbury OCTOBER 2060: THE MILLION-YEAR PICNIC	5	4	3	2	1	___
Gabriel García Márquez A VERY OLD MAN WITH ENORMOUS WINGS	5	4	3	2	1	___
Joyce Carol Oates WHERE ARE YOU GOING, WHERE HAVE YOU BEEN?	5	4	3	2	1	___
☐ **POETRY**						
Anonymous THE WIFE OF USHER'S WELL	5	4	3	2	1	___
Anonymous THE DEMON LOVER	5	4	3	2	1	___
John Keats LA BELLE DAME SANS MERCI	5	4	3	2	1	___
Thomas Hardy CHANNEL FIRING	5	4	3	2	1	___
Walter de la Mare THE LISTENERS	5	4	3	2	1	___
☐ **DRAMA**						
W. W. Jacobs and Louis N. Parker THE MONKEY'S PAW	5	4	3	2	1	___

Chapter 7: Innocence and Experience

	Liked best				Liked least	Didn't read
☐ **ESSAYS**						
Maya Angelou GRADUATION	5	4	3	2	1	___
☐ **FICTION**						
Nathaniel Hawthorne MY KINSMAN, MAJOR MOLINEUX	5	4	3	2	1	___
Sherwood Anderson I WANT TO KNOW WHY	5	4	3	2	1	___
James Joyce ARABY	5	4	3	2	1	___
William Carlos Williams THE USE OF FORCE	5	4	3	2	1	___
Frank O'Connor GUESTS OF THE NA-TION	5	4	3	2	1	___
☐ **POETRY**						
William Blake THE LAMB	5	4	3	2	1	___
William Blake THE TYGER	5	4	3	2	1	___
John Keats ODE ON A GRECIAN URN	5	4	3	2	1	___
Gerard Manley Hopkins SPRING AND FALL: TO A YOUNG CHILD	5	4	3	2	1	___
A. E. Housman WHEN I WAS ONE-AND-TWENTY	5	4	3	2	1	___
Robert Hayden THOSE WINTER SUN-DAYS	5	4	3	2	1	___
Louise Glück GRETEL IN DARKNESS	5	4	3	2	1	___
☐ **DRAMA**						
William Shakespeare THE TRAGEDY OF HAMLET, PRINCE OF DENMARK	5	4	3	2	1	___

Chapter 8: Love and Hate

	Liked best				Liked least	Didn't read
☐ **ESSAYS**						
James Thurber COURTSHIP THROUGH THE AGES	5	4	3	2	1	___
Erich Fromm EROTIC LOVE	5	4	3	2	1	___
Henry Fairlie LUST OR LUXURIA	5	4	3	2	1	___
☐ **FICTION**						
Edgar Allan Poe THE CASK OF AMON-TILLADO	5	4	3	2	1	___
Edith Wharton ROMAN FEVER	5	4	3	2	1	___
D. H. Lawrence THE HORSE DEALER'S DAUGHTER	5	4	3	2	1	___
William Faulkner A ROSE FOR EMILY	5	4	3	2	1	___
John Steinbeck THE CHRYSANTHE-MUMS	5	4	3	2	1	___
Frank O'Connor MY OEDIPUS COM-PLEX	5	4	3	2	1	___
Eudora Welty A WORN PATH	5	4	3	2	1	___
☐ **POETRY**						
William Shakespeare WHEN, IN DIS-GRACE WITH FORTUNE AND MEN'S EYES (SONNET 29)	5	4	3	2	1	___

	Liked best				Liked least	Didn't read

	Liked best			Liked least	Didn't read
William Shakespeare LET ME NOT TO THE MARRIAGE OF TRUE MINDS (SONNET 116)	5 4	3	2	1	___
John Donne A VALEDICTION: FORBIDDING MOURNING	5 4	3	2	1	___
Robert Herrick TO THE VIRGINS, TO MAKE MUCH OF TIME	5 4	3	2	1	___
Andrew Marvell TO HIS COY MISTRESS	5 4	3	2	1	___
Robert Browning PORPHYRIA'S LOVER	5 4	3	2	1	___
Robert Browning MY LAST DUCHESS	5 4	3	2	1	___
Matthew Arnold DOVER BEACH	5 4	3	2	1	___
Robert Frost THE SILKEN TENT	5 4	3	2	1	___
Sylvia Plath DADDY	5 4	3	2	1	___
Margaret Atwood SIREN SONG	5 4	3	2	1	___

Chapter 9: American Dreams and Nightmares

☐ ESSAYS

Thomas Jefferson THE DECLARATION OF INDEPENDENCE	5 4	3	2	1	___
Chief Seattle MY PEOPLE	5 4	3	2	1	___
Martin Luther King, Jr. I HAVE A DREAM	5 4	3	2	1	___
Studs Terkel ARNOLD SCHWARZENEGGER'S DREAM	5 4	3	2	1	___

☐ FICTION

Sherwood Anderson THE EGG	5 4	3	2	1	___
James Thurber THE SECRET LIFE OF WALTER MITTY	5 4	3	2	1	___
E. B. White THE SECOND TREE FROM THE CORNER	5 4	3	2	1	___
Shirley Jackson THE LOTTERY	5 4	3	2	1	___
Toni Cade Bambara THE LESSON	5 4	3	2	1	___

☐ POETRY

Edwin Arlington Robinson RICHARD CORY	5 4	3	2	1	___
Robert Frost THE GIFT OUTRIGHT	5 4	3	2	1	___
Langston Hughes HARLEM (A DREAM DEFERRED)	5 4	3	2	1	___

☐ DRAMA

Edward Albee THE SANDBOX	5 4	3	2	1	___

Chapter 10: The Individual and Society

☐ ESSAYS

May Sarton THE REWARDS OF LIVING A SOLITARY LIFE	5 4	3	2	1	___
Andy Rooney IN AND OF OURSELVES WE TRUST	5 4	3	2	1	___

	Liked best				Liked least	Didn't read
Judy Syfers I WANT A WIFE	5	4	3	2	1	—

☐ FICTION

Nathaniel Hawthorne THE MAYPOLE OF MERRY MOUNT	5	4	3	2	1	—
Mary E. Wilkins Freeman THE REVOLT OF "MOTHER"	5	4	3	2	1	—
William Faulkner SPOTTED HORSES	5	4	3	2	1	—
Alice Munro BOYS AND GIRLS	5	4	3	2	1	—

☐ POETRY

Robert Frost STOPPING BY WOODS ON A SNOWY EVENING	5	4	3	2	1	—
Robert Frost MENDING WALL	5	4	3	2	1	—
Robert Frost THE ROAD NOT TAKEN	5	4	3	2	1	—
Robert Frost THE WOOD-PILE	5	4	3	2	1	—
T. S. Eliot THE LOVE SONG OF J. ALFRED PRUFROCK	5	4	3	2	1	—
W. H. Auden MUSÉE DES BEAUX ARTS	5	4	3	2	1	—
W. H. Auden THE UNKNOWN CITIZEN	5	4	3	2	1	—
Marge Piercy BARBIE DOLL	5	4	3	2	1	—
Marge Piercy WHAT'S THAT SMELL IN THE KITCHEN?	5	4	3	2	1	—

☐ DRAMA

Henrik Ibsen A DOLL'S HOUSE	5	4	3	2	1	—
Susan Glaspell TRIFLES	5	4	3	2	1	—

Chapter 11: Men, Women, God, and Gods

☐ ESSAYS

Paul I CORINTHIANS 13	5	4	3	2	1	—
William James RELIGIOUS FAITH	5	4	3	2	1	—
Will Herberg RELIGIOSITY AND RELIGION	5	4	3	2	1	—

☐ FICTION

Luke THE PARABLE OF THE PRODIGAL SON	5	4	3	2	1	—
Nathaniel Hawthorne YOUNG GOODMAN BROWN	5	4	3	2	1	—
Katherine Anne Porter THE JILTING OF GRANNY WEATHERALL	5	4	3	2	1	—
Ernest Hemingway A CLEAN, WELL-LIGHTED PLACE	5	4	3	2	1	—
Flannery O'Connor A GOOD MAN IS HARD TO FIND	5	4	3	2	1	—
Flannery O'Connor REVELATION	5	4	3	2	1	—

☐ POETRY

John Donne HOLY SONNET IV (AT THE ROUND EARTH'S IMAGINED CORNERS)	5	4	3	2	1	—

	Liked best			Liked least	Didn't read
John Donne HOLY SONNET XIV (BATTER MY HEART, THREE-PERSONED GOD)	5	4	3	2	1	___
Emily Dickinson APPARENTLY WITH NO SURPRISE	5	4	3	2	1	___
Emily Dickinson THOSE—DYING, THEN	5	4	3	2	1	___
Christina Rossetti AMOR MUNDI	5	4	3	2	1	___
Christina Rossetti UPHILL	5	4	3	2	1	___
Gerard Manley Hopkins GOD'S GRANDEUR	5	4	3	2	1	___
Robert Frost DESIGN	5	4	3	2	1	___
Kristine Batey LOT'S WIFE	5	4	3	2	1	___

☐ DRAMA

Sophocles OEDIPUS REX	5	4	3	2	1	___
Sophocles ANTIGONÊ	5	4	3	2	1	___

5. Are there other authors or topics you would like to see added?

6. Were you assigned Part III, "Reading and Writing about Literature"?

7. If not, did you use Part III as a reference source in completing your writing assignments? _____ Did you find the material useful? Why or why not?

8. Were Appendixes A and B assigned? _____ Were they useful in completing your writing assignments?

9. Please add any comments or suggestions on how we might improve this book.

YOUR NAME _____ DATE _____

MAILING ADDRESS _____

May we quote you either in promotion for this book or in future publishing ventures?

YES _____ NO _____

Thank you.